READINGS IN AFRICAN LAW

READINGS IN AFRICAN LAW

Edited by

E. COTRAN

LL.B., LL.M., DIP.I.L.

of Lincoln's Inn, Barrister at Law,
Lecturer in African Law, School of Oriental and African Studies,
University of London

and

N. N. RUBIN

B.A., LL.B.

Advocate of the Supreme Court of South Africa and the
High Court of Swaziland
Lecturer in African Law, School of Oriental and African Studies,
and Hayter Lecturer in African Law, Institute of Advanced Legal Studies,
University of London

IN TWO VOLUMES

VOLUME II

APC

AFRICANA PUBLISHING CORPORATION · NEW YORK

First Published in 1970 by
FRANK CASS & COMPANY LIMITED
Published in the United States of America in 1970
by Africana Publishing Corporation
101 Fifth Avenue, New York N.Y. 10003

Library of Congress Catalog Card No. 74-115047
SBN 8419 0043 4

Printed in Great Britain

CONTENTS

Part I: THE LAW OF PERSONS AND THE FAMILY

Part II: THE LAW OF MARRIAGE

Part III: THE LAW OF SUCCESSION

EXPLANATION OF FOOTNOTES

The footnotes that appear on the same page of extracts (marked *, †, ‡, §, ‖ etc.) are inserted by the Editors where some explanation is required, e.g. where a vernacular term is defined by the author in a place other than the extract reproduced, or where some abbreviation used by the author requires explanation.

The numbered footnotes which appear at the end of each extract are those of the author and page references therein are to the pages of the book or article and not to these Readings.

Editors

Part I

THE LAW OF PERSONS AND THE FAMILY

In many ways, the Law of Persons is the most difficult part of African customary law to describe. It has seldom been treated comprehensively by writers on customary law: most have chosen one or other aspect of the subject, such as the family or the clan, and have dealt with that alone to the exclusion of the large number of other topics which constitute this branch of the law. The subject is one which is everywhere concerned with conceptual problems involving semantic and philosophical questions. Frequently, in the material that follows, two characteristics—vagueness on the one hand and over-precision on the other—will be noticed; it is necessary, therefore, to guard against the assumption of universal applicability in this instance perhaps more than in any other.

The vast variety of different social structures (and *a fortiori* of legal structures) in Africa makes this warning all the more significant. Yet it is in this section that one encounters several unique features of customary law in Africa, all of them related to the greater emphasis on the legal role of groups—principally, but not only, groups of persons who share some form of family or descent relationship. It is this aspect of the subject which gives it its importance, though it is equally necessary as a background to a proper understanding of several other branches of customary law. Thus, there is a close connection between matters of status and capacity, parental responsibility and guardianship on the one hand and the law of contract and tort on the other: the attribution of liability in both branches of law may depend very largely on the underlying family or clan structure and the web of mutual obligations that arise between members of these groups as a result.

Chapter I

STATUS OF SOCIAL AND FAMILY GROUPS

As already indicated, the emphasis in traditional African society on family and larger kin groups is one of its outstanding features. The traditional legal systems of Africa reflect this clearly and the extracts which follow are designed to point to the ways in which the social structure has created situations and problems which are unique in any contemporary legal system. Given the immense number of different (and differently-organised) societies, it was possible only to select a few representative discussions of the issues which are involved in this subject. *Elias*' contribution is useful, both for its analytical qualities and for its broad scope in geographical terms; it will also serve as an introduction to the subject as a whole. *Schapera* describes the family and kindred groups among the Tswana, as does *Kuper* among the Swazi. *Rattray* provides an account of the clan among the Ashanti, and *Colson* deals with family and clan groups among the matrilineal Plateau Tonga of Zambia.

T. O. Elias: Nature of African Customary Law*

General Introduction

The role of the individual in a given society depends in the last resort upon his place in it. How he fits into that place is largely conditioned by the nature of the particular society. As a matter of legal theory the reason why it is important to determine the exact position of the individual in the social structure is that only by it can we assess the extent of his rights and duties, the range of social activities in which he may or must participate, and his opportunities for personal differentiation within his community.

Our concern here is mainly with those legal aspects of his social relations which affect his acts or omissions with regard to all others within his universe of daily activity. On what the exact criteria should be for determining whether or not an individual belongs to a group or class with limited rights and duties within a given community, jurists are still in dispute. Various attempts have been made by writers on jurisprudence to define the term 'status' for legal purposes, but a satisfactory formula has yet to be devised. The trouble is that 'status' is a word which has no very precise connotation.

Thus, with respect to English law, John Austin argues[1] that the term cannot be used with exactness, but says that 'where a set of rights and duties, capacities and incapacities, specially affecting a narrow class of persons, is detached from the bulk of the legal system, and placed under a separate head for the convenience of exposition, that set of rights and duties, capacities and incapacities, is called a status'. This implies that the grouping together of those persons who are said to have a status is a mere classificatory device of the law—which is true enough as a generalisation but which does not define how narrow the class must be, or in what the rights and duties, capacities and incapacities must really consist.

Salmond, finding Austin's formula too vague, proposes[2] the following four alternative meanings of status:

(*a*) legal condition of any kind, whether personal or proprietary;
(*b*) personal legal condition, excluding proprietary relations;
(*c*) personal capacities and incapacities, as opposed to other elements of personal status;
(*d*) compulsory as opposed to conventional legal position.

Because all this is hardly an improvement on Austin's definition, Allen suggests that status should be taken to mean 'the condition of belonging to a particular class of persons to whom the law assigns certain peculiar legal capacities or incapacities or both'.[3] Status may arise from a variety of conditions such as sex, minority, and marriage, all of which are bound up with the problem of the family. Mental or bodily defect such as insanity or congenital idiocy may occasion legal incapacities or privileges, as may membership of a caste, profession or official rank. Criminality may curtail or destroy personal liberty, and bankruptcy may divest of property. Also, foreign nationality, race, or colour (where these exist) may cause the law to distinguish a group. It is therefore clear, says Allen, that status is not merely a basis for legal classification, but a matter of great political, legal and social importance.

Paton has recently offered[4] the following commentary on Allen's analysis: Firstly, status arises from membership of a class whose powers are determined extrinsically by law, rather than by agreement between the members. No member can vary the conditions thus imposed by the law: for instance, the status of marriage is conclusively fixed beforehand by the law and cannot be varied by either party to the marriage.

Secondly, although an infant cannot choose whether or not to enter the status of

* T. O. Elias, *The Nature of African Customary Law*, Manchester University Press, 1956, pp. 76–95.

infancy, it is nevertheless not always true that the membership of a status class is necessarily forced upon the individual affected. Thus a mortgager defines for himself his own rights and duties *vis-à-vis* the mortgagee and other persons interested in the mortgaged property. He may and often does understand those rights imperfectly, but he must be presumed to know and to choose the legal consequences which flow from his act of agreement. Also, a girl cannot be forced into the status of matrimony against her will; but if she does marry, certain legal incidents attach to the marital status which do not depend upon the will of either party. Thus, she becomes immune from actions in tort brought against her by her husband: she has a claim to support from her husband, and in cases of necessity a power to pledge his credit. The status of marriage cannot be ended merely by the wish of the parties. Graveson suggests[5] that the will of the party may affect the beginning or the end of status, but never both. Marriage illustrates freedom at the beginning, and the control of law at the dissolution, of the status. An ambassador can be made such only by act of the State, but presumably he can destroy his status by resignation.

Thirdly, Maine's argument that status normally arises nowadays because of a defect in judgment of the members of a status class is, however, not universally true. It is not the desire to protect certain classes against their own weaknesses that determines their being given special treatment in modern legal systems. Thus, the law of every sovereign State gives a special status to ambassadors, not because they suffer from occasional defects of judgment, but for the better promotion of international comity.

Fourthly, membership of a status does not always result in restricted power. Thus, while in the case of an infant or a lunatic, legal power is restricted, in that of an ambassador (for example) additional privileges are normally conferred. It is, therefore, incorrect to imagine that only incapacities attach to status.

Fifthly, not all group membership gives rise to a status. Status arising from membership of a group inevitably affects a member's legal relations, or at least his power to enter into legal relations. There is no status of the blue-eyed or of bridge-players, for although both of these groups may be regarded as forming a class, that class has no precise legal significance. Paton suggests that the test is that status is a condition which affects generally, although in varying degrees, a person's claims, liberties, powers and immunities; e.g. in the case of a trustee, certain powers relating to the trust property are granted to him while duties are owed by him to the beneficiaries of the trust. We cannot, however, infer any special status from this fact of trusteeship, since it does not at all affect the trustee's general legal relations.

On the other hand, when we speak of the status of infancy, we at once imply an absence of legal capacity which is not limited to one act in the law but extends to all his legal relationships with others generally.

Holland therefore asks:[6] 'Does the peculiarity of the personality arise from anything unconnected with the nature of the act itself which the person of inherence can enforce against the person of incidence?' If I am an mortgagee or a trustee of one particular transaction my other legal relations are unaffected. But if I am a lunatic so found, my power is gone and I cannot for the duration of the lunacy exercise any legal powers.

A very useful point made by Allen in his analysis of status, is his insistence that 'there is a clear distinction between capacity to acquire and exercise rights, and the rights which are exercised'.[7] Status is a *condition*, while capacity is a *power*. Allen accordingly emphasises: 'We must, then, distinguish three quite different things: *Status*, the condition which gives rise to certain capacities or incapacities or both; *Capacity*, the power to acquire and exercise rights; and the *Rights* themselves which are acquired by the exercise of capacity.'[8] Paton's own conclusion is: 'Using the terminology of Hohfeld, we would say that status is the condition of being a member of a particular group, which membership affects generally claims, liberties, powers and immunities.' But even this does not solve our problem.

One of Sir Henry Maine's famous generalisations is: 'If then we employ status, agreeably with the usage of the best writers, to signify these personal conditions only, and avoid applying them to such conditions as are the immediate or remote result of agreement, we may say that the movement of the progressive societies has hitherto been a movement *from Status to Contract*.'[9] The four words in this statement that call for special comment are 'progressive', 'hitherto', 'status' and 'contract'.

The application of the epithet 'progressive' to societies in this context implies that there are those that are static, either because they lack the intrinsic quality essential for change or because they have generally remained unaffected by any extrinsic factors. Now, African societies, to the extent to which modern research has revealed their known character, are anything but static. It is true that the tempo of social change is slower in some African societies than in others, and that most of them have managed somehow to preserve the outward mechanisms of their social structure all through the ages. But this does not mean that *within* the societies themselves there has not always been a good deal of dynamism, making for change in interpersonal relationships no less than in inter-group contacts. We may therefore say that, if it were really the case that a human society could be regarded as eternally the same and unchanging, at least African societies exhibit all the marks of 'progressive' societies as conceived by Maine.

When the great jurist framed his formula about the social progression from status to contract, he was careful to insert as a limiting factor the word 'hitherto', although his followers have tended to assume that the statement without any such qualification has a universal validity. Basing himself on his study of Indian village communities and his researches into Roman and Greek societies, Maine saw[10] the gradual unfolding of the human spirit from the thraldom of tribe or group into the condition of a free-willing individual uninhibited by ties of kinship or group. The evolution of the law concerning the rights of the married woman shows a movement from status to contract, as does the comparative freedom of modern man in contrast with the bondage of early man.

But it must have been apparent to Maine even in his own day that, because it became necessary to restrict freedom of contract in order to give real freedom to economically weaker classes, dialectical developments from contract back to status had set in in various departments of life: new relationships were already forming between landlords and tenants, mortgagors and mortgagees, employers and employees, and similar opposing groups members of each one of which look upon those of the other as belonging to new classes based upon status.[11] These are in essence the old medieval relationships between lords of the manor and their villeins, lenders and borrowers, owners of industries and their workers—all in new guises. The Industrial Revolution, while breaking down still further what Renaissance humanism left of the feudal organisation of society, created in its turn new but parallel social classes grouped around the opposing interests brought into being by this industrial civilisation.

It would, therefore, seem that status will always be with us. There is no doubt that the various communities of miners, factory workers and industrialists are not watertight and that the individual members of any of them are in theory free to move from one community to another, but we also know that in practice the prospects for such movement are often dim. For a variety of reasons a miner's son, for example, who would become a lawyer without external aid must be prepared to face an uphill task indeed. The stratification of society into more or less organised classes seems to have been an inevitable feature of human existence throughout the ages, although the basis of the division has neither been constant nor the same at all times and in all places.

Maine also contends that 'ancient' law is a jurisprudence of personal inequalities. In early societies, a man's whole legal position depends on whether he is bound or free, native or foreign, child or parent, male or female: and these tests of legal standing are clearly matters which the individual does not decide for himself—they are accidents of birth and circumstance. The law has abolished many of the lower grades of society, and the tendency is to confine the creation of status to those cases where there is special justification. What were once the lower ranks begin to enjoy many of the privileges of their 'betters'. Nevertheless, as we have shown above, age, sex, and alienage are still indicia of status in ancient as in modern societies.

Status in African Law

1. *Group status.* When we come to consider the African situation, what do we find? We are at once confronted with the popular fallacy that all members of a given African society, without exception, belong to one status only—the one generic status of the clan or tribe. Thus Hartland wrote: 'The unit is not the individual, but the kin. The individual is but part of the kin.' While this may be the broad social picture presented to the observer by the interplay of co-ordinate groups within the tribe or State, it fails as a theory of the legal unity of the clan. The trouble is that the myth of kinship communism,

while making such great play of the 'pervading group-sentiment, if not group-instinct', does not pierce the veil of clan corporateness in order to discover the tensions, the personal jealousies and rivalries, as well as the individual self-assertions that go on *within* the group itself. Anyone who cares to look into the actual social relations between the individuals who make up the group—whether this is family, clan or tribe—will realise soon enough that disputes do take place in all manner of situations.[12] For instance, the clothes of one individual are sometimes unlawfully worn or torn by another of the group; hoes and cutlasses, bows and arrows, spears and traps, fishing rods and fishing baskets are freely borrowed by one individual from another and are sometimes returned damaged or never returned at all; A may grab a portion or the whole of B's allotment in the family or clan holding: in all these constant inter-actions of social and economic forces within the group, the headman performs the function of 'guide, philosopher and friend', and compensations and penalties are exacted and paid just as much as the Chief or council of elders deal with inter-group disputes, or even those intra-group ones in which the headman's decision is impugned by a member on the ground of partiality, or again those involving any two or more important personalities in the community.

This internal judicial administration accounts for the apparent placidity of clan organisation and the seeming solidarity of its members in relation to other groups. It is probably true to say that the ascription of unity to a clan is only valid as a fiction adopted by its members as a defence mechanism in the external relations of the clan to others in the community. It is rather like the unity often claimed nowadays by a political party or even a State *vis-à-vis* other parties or States, though these are naturally on a much larger scale and with a more impersonal dependence.

2. *Primitive communism.* The individual certainly has fairly well-defined rights and duties within his group. It is true that land is held, not by the individual as in Western societies, but by a group, the family being almost invariably the unit of land-holding. But a close study of the actual arrangement within the family shows that there are specific assignments of plots to all the individual members of it who are old and able enough usefully to exploit the resources of the soil, or who have reached an age to claim a portion of the family house to live in, or of family land on which to build their house or hut. Such a portion of the house or land once allocated is always transmissible to the descendants of the original allottee *ad infinitum* and can be put to any kind of use which is compatible with the requirements of good house management or good husbandry. The only serious restriction is that land is inalienable by any individual member of the owing family unless (1) the prior consent of the family has been obtained thereto, or (2) the land has been partitioned among all the members thereto and the individual is merely disposing of his own portion. With these two provisos, then, the individual is quite free to do what he likes with his own.

Similarly, careful analysis of the rights of the individual in the products of the soil cultivated by the family group or the catch from co-operative fishing discloses that his is not the case of someone without definite claims upon or mutual obligations towards the other members of the group. In most cases the proceeds of the common effort are shared among the participants according to individual deserts or by mutual agreement and, even when the necessity arises for garnering a fixed surplus as provision against a rainy day, the respective rights and obligations of members attach to it until ultimate distribution. If the products are sold all those who have contributed labour towards their provenance are entitled to share in the sale price.

The head *as head*, whether of the family or of the co-operative group, may be allowed an extra portion for his additional responsibilities towards the younger members of the family, or on account of capital or labour contributed by him over and above that contributed by the others. But in no case is the individual treated as an unknown quantity who merely gives his labour to the group and thereafter remains entirely at its mercy in the matter of subsequent disposal.

The bargaining powers of the individual naturally increase as the co-operative unit moves away from a kinship basis towards a territorial alliance based on purely social and economic, non-kinship association. The rights and duties of the individuals within the family or clan are, by the inevitable economic and kinship ties, naturally more circumscribed than are those of party members or State nationals considered as individuals. Even in African societies these individual rights and duties vary with the type of social organisation and the degree of cohesion already achieved. Thus, kinship as a bond of social cohesion is more powerful in any society that lacks a developed political organisation than it is in one less heterogeneous or atomistic. Family and, to a greater extent, clan ties weaken as the blood span spreads out and group solidarity becomes of less account in the normal life of the members. The degree of interdependence of members depends, after all, upon the intensity of social relations, and these obviously vary in different societies no less than in the diverse organisations of the family, clan, or tribe. This is where Durkheim falls into serious error when he dogmatises[13] that intensity of social relations grows more and more as the group expands. He fails to appreciate the sociological fact that with the increasing social integration of the disparate clans or other kinship groups, there gradually develops a wide tribal loyalty or even national solidarity in place of the narrow one of the clan. In the end, tribal or national unity triumphs over the erstwhile unity of the clan. The family becomes absorbed into the clan which itself forms one of the aggregates making up the community; the community finally turns into a society, which is just the name we give to the group of individuals with the least intensity of personal relations, that is, in which kinship ties are weakest and social and political solidarities are strongest.

Thus it is that in African societies which have achieved strong centralised political organisations, kinship affiliations are generally limited more or less to autonomous families made up of very close blood members. These acknowledge the usual economic and social obligations towards only the restricted few within their own immediate families and, often towards only their full brothers and sisters and their parents. In other types of African society with no highly organised social groupings, kinship plays an important, though not the only, part in human relations. The individual's behaviour is largely affected by his place in the kin-group, more so than in other forms of human association. But the group is not an independent self-contained unit; rather it is made up of individuals who often re-act upon it and even sometimes change its character. Besides, there does not seem to exist in any known human society simply 'the' group, but always a multiplicity of groups, the individual being a member whose rights and duties within such groups naturally differ according to the type of group.

In any group, however, psychological differences are sure to lead to inevitable differences in social valuations so that the group becomes an aggregate of individuals and not, as the doctrine of group solidarity would have us believe, a mere agglomeration of undifferentiated automata. As Marrett points out,[14] Morgan's discovery of the classificatory system of relationships, though useful in providing a clue to the study of the more rudimentary types of social organisation, yet tends to 'bring all those to whom the same relational term applies into one unwavering line as regards their rights and duties in regard to the remaining categories. As a matter of fact, however, a man not only knows his own mother apart from his merely tribal mothers, but treats her quite differently.' The admission by a clan member of the *sociological* paternity or fraternity of certain of his fellow-members does not mean that he equates either of these with the *physiological*, to which alone he feels immediately bound socially and economically.

In conclusion, we may note that the theory of unity of the clan is further vitiated by such important factors as the following:

(1) It is necessary to bear in mind that there are few African communities that can claim tribal purity or homogeneity. Most tribes are in varying degrees heterogeneous: for example, war captives are being continually absorbed into the conquering tribe, and exogamous marriages usually imply the admixture with indigenous stock of foreign strains through women married from other clans or tribes.

(2) Inter-tribal economic co-operation in the form of trade or a joint enterprise like hunting may involve the individual in a new type of economic dependence which cuts across not only family or clan autonomy but also tribal exclusiveness.

(3) Again, puberty initiation rites tend almost invariably to aggregate the individual to wider groupings than those based purely on kinship ties of family or clan. This often results in stronger bonds of loyalty and therefore of disposition to help an associate at need. Age-grade associations, warrior classes, social clubs, secret societies—all these and more play their by no means insignificant part in increasing the range and widening the boundaries of the social and economic interests of the individual beyond the restricted ones of the family or the clan.

It is not unknown for secret societies and other large associations to operate over a number of unrelated neighbouring tribes, with the mutual adoption of one another's customs and the consequent forging of strong links of social and economic inter-dependence and of inter-tribal solidarity. According to Beaufaict, formerly hostile tribes like the Ababua, Abarambo, Mangbettu and the Azande formed associations known as the Nebeli and Ngobo Societies which, by bringing them into frequent contact with one another, succeeded in welding them together.

(4) Since the compelling reason for the normal closeness of kinship groups is the economic dependence of the individual upon his family—joint exploitation of the family land until partition, joint rearing of the family herds of cattle, etc.—it follows that the marriage of a member and the new responsibilities of raising his own family all too often effect a loosening of the former blood bonds, and consequently of the claims of his relatives upon him for the usual economic help. It is also at this stage in his development that his orientation to wider social alignments impels his estrangement from the blood group.

Perhaps it should be emphasised here, if any emphasis were needed, that there is no legal restriction on the absolute liberty of the individual member of a family to set up house on his own as soon as he is old enough for it, or to join any association he likes so long as he complies with the relevant formalities.

Before we go on to examine the status of the individual, we may here touch briefly on another important aspect of the conception that only the group has status in African society, that clan unity is everywhere triumphant.

3. *Collective responsibility*. Arising out of the idea that the individual is merged in his group is the theory that the latter is collectively responsible for his offences against outsiders. The group pays all compensations for his private wrongs and answers for all his public offences. Such is the principle of group solidarity, according to this view, that a crime committed by one member of the group against another is no concern of anyone else but the group. Some say that in such a case the offender goes unpunished since it is hardly to be expected that the group would fine itself in order to appease itself. Others believe that the group would itself punish the offending member by expulsion from the group, which would mean that he thereby might be treated as an outlaw, as outside the pale of group protection and therefore anybody's meat. If killed thereafter by someone else his group would take no action either of revenge or of composition of a possible feud between his own group and that of his killer by the payment of *wergild*. It is said that in certain cases, the group itself gets rid of a persistently criminal member by expulsion or otherwise, as he is then considered a liability rather than an asset to the clan or family inheritance.

Durkheim is certain that all legal reactions like group responsibility or revenge are founded in the psychology of the group and not in that of the individual, who is a mere unit of the group whole.[15] From this has been deduced the further idea that when, for example, a member X of group A is killed by a member Y of group B, the whole of group A troop out to avenge X's death by killing in reprisal any member Z of group B if Y cannot be got hold of. Sometimes, group A may accept compensation in the nature of cattle or other forms of tribal currency; at other times, member Y or another member Z is merely seized into group A as a substitute for the unfortunate victim X. Since social equilibrium is restored by such mechanical adjustment of the loss of one economic unit by its replacement by another or, in the case where the murderer or his group-member is killed in revenge, by the mutual diminution of both groups, there is nothing more to be done. If we may so express it, it is all a question of Group A—X = Group B—(Y or Z), or Group A + (Y or Z) = Group B—(Y or Z). But either equation would be false as an explanation of the process of restoring the social equilibrium of the given community, not only because Group A is not necessarily always equivalent in quantity to Group B but also because even if cattle are substituted for X, Y or Z, the punishment does not fit the crime and this is bound to disturb the social equilibrium.

Apparently, this theory of group collectivity implies also that the process of redressing the balance is the same whether it is private wrongs (i.e. purely civil offences) or public wrongs (i.e. criminal offences) that are in question. So that if Y in the above illustration breaks X's borrowed hoe or fishing rod instead of killing X, the whole of Group A must at once engage in a free vendetta to secure just reparation from Group B or any of its available members. Of course, we know that this is not so. We need not go into all the other interesting ramifications often claimed for the doctrine of group responsibility. But what are the facts?

Now, the so-called 'unity of the clan' is an inaccurate description when used to explain why the clan pays for the wrong-doing of one of its members. As we have shown earlier, the paying group, where the group pays at all, is rarely larger than the family or occasionally the extended family of the offender; it never embraces all the hundreds or thousands with more or less tenuous blood relationships to the wrong-doer. It is true that a distant member, perhaps a wealthy cousin 'to the fortieth remove' of the offender, may sometimes offer to pay part or all of the latter's fine imposed by the court; but so may any unrelated but sympathetic neighbour of the offender's group. In most, if not all, African societies, playing the role of 'a good neighbour'—the good Samaritan—is a virtue highly valued and generally expected of the more fortunate members of the community, in times of stress or emergency, towards the less fortunate. Blood relations of the offender obviously feel a higher moral obligation to help their kin.

In all these cases of so-called group responsibility, the *legal liability* is without question that of the offending individual alone, but the discharge of that liability is very often the concern of all those close relatives of his whom local opinion regards as *morally* bound to succour him. To this there are at least two exceptions, when there is a legal duty on the relatives to come to an offender's rescue: (1) The first is where the relative is father of or is otherwise *in loco parentis* to the offender who is yet a minor or a weakling for whose good behaviour the former is ordinarily responsible; (2) The second exception occurs if the offender has rendered services to the relative or the group of relatives now called upon to answer for his misdeeds, or if he has a recognised claim of right to contribution from or indemnity by the relative or the other members of the group. The basis of such a right is economic, and is usually the result of joint enterprise or co-operative labour activities carried on by the family or other social group as a scheme of social insurance. While parental obligation to answer for the 'debts, defaults or miscarriage' of a dependent is generally unlimited, the amount of contribution or indemnity to which the offender is entitled under the second head of exception tends to be proportional to the amount of his own just share of the common pool, unless indeed the others loyally concede to him more than his deserts. With regard to these two heads of exceptions, then, the foregoing analysis shows that the *primary* liability is that of the offender while the *secondary* liability is that of the parent or the group. This secondary liability is of course a *vicarious* one. In all other cases, the *legal* liability is that of the wrong-doer, although the *moral* responsibility to see that liability discharged is almost invariably that of the group.

What we have so far been considering concerns all private wrongs as well as such public wrongs as are susceptible of reparation in cash or in kind. Where the penalty for an offender's public wrong is death, mutilation or any other corporal punishment, even the protagonists of the theory of group responsibility agree that the first and only person subject to the particular punishment is the criminal himself. Only if he is unavailable either because his kin are hiding him and will not surrender him on demand, or because they have helped him to escape or again because the offender is party to a conspiracy for the commission of the crime alleged, is someone else, believed to be actively associated with the criminal or the crime, seized and punished instead. Anyone who has reason to fear his being seized for another's offence has the legal right to seek asylum in one of the public sanctuaries or in a chief's palace until the proper determination of the issue.[16] The choice of who is to pay for a crime in default of the actual criminal is thus seen to be not as arbitrary as is commonly alleged by lay observers. It is precisely because those exacting the particular form of penalty follow some clearly accepted channels that vendettas are so comparatively rare on such occasions.[17] And when the offender's group take the punishment appropriately inflicted by the other side without any retaliation, this is instantly acclaimed by the advocates of group solidarity as an illustration of the automatic operation of custom.

Both the civil and the criminal aspects of collective responsibility may be paralleled by analogous concepts of English law. Thus, to take random illustrations in English civil law, it is clear law that a master or employer is vicariously liable for all the wrongs committed by his servant or employee in the course of the latter's employment; an employer of an independent contractor is vicariously liable for the latter's wrongs to third parties while carrying out very hazardous activities; while only the father or legal guardian of a child under 21 can be sued for the latter's torts and contracts for 'necessaries'. In all these instances, the offender is also liable, of course. As for crimes one naturally recalls the medieval English law of *frankpledge* which, because of the lack of any organised police, was 'a system by which all free men of a tithing were responsible for the general good behaviour of its members'. But a closer parallel is afforded by the modern English rules governing the liability of 'parties to a crime'. These are four in number: (1) Accessories before the fact; (2) Accessories after the fact; (3) Principal in the first degree; and (4) Principal in the second degree. The first category means all those who counsel, procure or instigate the commission of the crime; the second, all those knowing that a crime has been committed, help the criminal to escape or aid and succour him—this class is to be distinguished, by the way, from another class of ancillary offenders who are liable to quite often heavy penalties for what is technically known as 'misprision of felony', i.e. knowing of the commission of a crime by another and omitting to report it;[18] the third category describes the actual perpetrators of the crime and they are of course liable as such; the fourth category comprises those who aid and abet the criminal in the act of committing the offence alleged. In heinous crimes called 'felonies', all four types are punishable equally with the criminal: paradoxically enough, only the one considered most guilty among the escaping criminal's relations is normally punished in the African situation. In misdemeanours, i.e. lesser criminal offences, the punishment varies according to the category under which the participants come.

Enough has now been said to disprove the fallacy of unity of the clan, primitive communism or group responsibility, at least so far as African societies are concerned. Status does not attach only to the group and the latter is not the unit-bearer of rights and duties. The individual member of the group is, in the final analysis, the prime actor although, as we have pointed out, he is not as independent of his fellows as is his opposite number in a non-collectivist Western society. To appreciate fully the actual role of the individual in an African community, two further misconceptions must be briefly examined:

4. *The 'sheep' theory*. An extreme view is reflected in the saying 'custom is king'. While this may express the authority of customary law, it certainly cannot be taken to imply that the individual is a slave of custom, that he is bogged down inexorably by kinship ties of family, clan or tribe, or that he just follows the line of least resistance—a blind worshipper of tradition, a gregarious member of the tribal flock. Hartland, for example, was emphatic that 'he never seeks to break forth'.[19] To this classic expression of a widely-held view, Marrett retorts: 'But, as Freud points out, such tyrannous prohibitions (i.e. taboos) would be unnecessary, were there not rebellious feelings to be crushed into submission. On the contrary, let us pay due attention to the spiritual effort needed on the part of each and all to maintain the social energy at the required pitch. Thus, on the one hand, the gerontocracy, or whatever other government is responsible for keeping order, must be equal to the constant strain. To deny individuality to the successful functionary would be to overlook the fact that the good workman finds himself in the competent execution of his job.'[20]

Culwick, in his usually forthright way, also warns: 'We find the tribal code is the code of a closely-knit group. No one in that group is in an economic position which renders him wholly independent of the goodwill of his fellows: none can therefore afford to forego his privileges by ignoring his obligations. At the same time, the fact that he is economically and socially bound to his fellows does not rob him of his individuality, his desire to evade irksome and unpleasant duties if he can, his natural preoccupation with the needs and desires of himself and his immediate family, let what will happen to others.'[21]

It is therefore clear that the theory of automatic submission to custom cannot hold simply because the African rates the immemorial rules of his society probably no higher than Edmund Burke rated the traditions of the English people and the sacrosanctity of immemorial usage.[22] The regularity and apparent passivity with which he observes the norms of social and political life must not be taken as an indication that he cannot or will not do otherwise.

5. *The 'peacock' theory*. At the other extreme are those who from their practical know-

ledge of the real nature of African society are anxious to show that, far from being the docile, sheepish creature of popular imagination, the African individual is a real peacock. He is nothing if not boastful, arrogant and self-assertive. His aggressive, equalitarian attitude makes him impatient of authority, truculent and insubordinate. Let us hear Malinowski speak:

'Take the real savage, keen on evading his duties, swaggering and boastful when he has fulfilled them, and compare him with the anthropologist's dummy who slavishly follows custom and automatically obeys every regulation. There is not the remotest resemblance between the teachings of anthropology on this subject and the reality of native life.'[23]

Other writers have been even more trenchant in their language, citing instances of some individualist African communities as evidence of the peacock theory. If that were so, there should be perpetual conflict between such rugged individualists,[24] and any African community would be a veritable Bedlam. The evil, selfish nature of man so specially remarked upon by Hobbes in his epigram: *homo homini lupus* (i.e. man is a wolf to man) would be a perfect description of African societies. The leviathan would jostle his fellow tribesmen out of existence every time he felt the impulse to assert his prerogatives. But alas for the prospect of peace among the protagonists of the peacock theory, such a pessimistic view of human nature stands contradicted by the realities of African society.[25]

In sum, the truth is that the African individual is neither a robot nor a peacock. He is, like any other of the human species, a social animal. In that respect he has his life to live among his immediate kith and kin no less than among the other members of his community. The range of his relationships, as of his obligations, will of course depend upon the social set-up, particularly on the degree of intensity obtaining within the group or community to which he happens to belong. Whatever the character of a given society may be, however, close and informed analysis will disclose that the several members retain their individualities to a greater extent than is usually realised.

Nor is it accurate to argue, as does a *third* school of thought, that only the eccentric in an African group can claim any individuality. We have seen that there is more scope for self-realisation for the individual than one is led to believe possible in a normal African society. But, seeing that the member's margin of safety is too narrow for abnormal egotism to be fashionable, it behoves the individual aspiring to high office or craving the esteem of his fellows to curb his personal idiosyncrasies if he is to have any chance of success. No doubt, as will be shown later, intellectual endowments and character and courage are highly prized in African society, since lack of these in persons normally entitled to offices like those of war-leaders, chiefs, and family-heads, is often a legitimate ground for passing them over in favour of others endowed with these qualities. But this is far from saying that the revered intellectual or warrior is erratic, any more than is the wealthy member who defies the usual norm of generosity to his fellows in their hour of need. Yet, the possession of brains, brawn or wealth is an index of individuality. The eccentric has no place in the ordinary scheme of things in an African, as in any other, society.

Notes

[1] In his 'Lectures on Jurisprudence' (ed. Campbell), Lects. XL–XLIV, particularly at pp. 699–700 and 710.

[2] *Jurisprudence* (9th edn.), pp. 323–8.

[3] *Legal Duties*, p. 42; see also pp. 32–3, where Salmond's views are also criticised. Allen's admirable discussion of the whole subject will be found at pp. 28–47.

[4] See his *A Textbook of Jurisprudence*, pp. 256–7.

[5] See his article 'The Movement from Status to Contract' in *Modern Law Review* (1941), p. 261; also *Status in the Common Law*, pp. 128–36. The learned author's definition of status, at p. 2, is:

'A special condition of a continuous and institutional nature, differing from the legal position of the normal person, which is conferred by law and not purely by the act of the parties, whenever a person occupies a position of which the creation, continuance or relinquishment, and the incidents are a matter of sufficient social or public concern.'

Most of the difficulties about this definition are, however, implied in the explanation of the expression 'the normal person' which the author himself immediately proceeds to give (pp. 2–3).

But one serious point of weakness in it is the failure to indicate the sufficiency or otherwise of the 'social or public concern' that should mark off a status condition from other conditions. This weakness, it may be pointed out with respect, is of the same order as Austin's failure to define the narrowness of the class or indicate in what the 'rights and duties, capacities and incapacities' must consist (see p. 2, *supra*).

[6] *Jurisprudence* (13th edn.), p. 143.

[7] *Legal Duties*, p. 46.

[8] *Ibid.*, p. 47.

[9] *Ancient Law*, p. 174.

[10] *Ancient Law*, pp. 172 ff.

[11] But this use of the word 'status' is true only in a loose sense, since membership of each of the opposing classes still leaves the individuals free in other respects.

[12] Malinowski also made this point at p. 48 of his *Crime and Custom in Savage Society*

[13] See E. Durkheim, *De la Division du Travail Social.*

[14] R. R. Marrett, 'The Individual in Primitive Society', an essay in a book entitled *The Individual in East and West*, (ed. E. R. Hughes).

[15] E. Durkheim, *L'Année Sociologique*, I, pp. 353 ff.

[16] Thus, C. Dundas wrote of certain East African peoples that blood revenge was usually 'directed against the murderer or some near relative', and that sanctuary was provided for the murderer who sought refuge with the chief to avoid blood revenge. Blood revenge was restricted to the slaying of one person, but it naturally tends to further reprisals, and so to feuds or open warfare, which was not to the interest of the chief, sultan, or king, who thereby lost subjects, and consequently intervened. And the degree to which such intervention was effectual was according to the power of these supreme authorities. (See p. 236 of the *Jnl. Roy. Afr. Inst.*, Vol. 51 (1921), pp. 217–78, an article entitled 'Native laws of Some Bantu Tribes of East Africa').

[17] This is not to deny the incidence of feuds between some clans or tribes, or of the attempts often made to pay off old scores, sometimes after a long distance of time from that of the original offence. It is only to emphasise that the incidence of feuds is strictly outside the sphere of law.

[18] This is now an obsolete offence: see *R. v. Aberg* (1948), 1 A.E.R. 601.

[19] *Primitive Law*, p. 138. Cf. 'A primitive people, virtuous by rote rather than by reason, followed unthinkingly that principle of "mutual service" which Aristotle held to be the natural bond of a well-ordered community'—K. J. Spalding in his article, 'A Chinese Aristotle' in *The Individual in East and West*, p. 65.

[20] *Op. cit.*, p. 22.

[21] *Op. cit.*, p. 30.

[22] Notably in his *Thoughts on the Cause of the Present Discontents* and *Reflections on the Revolution in France.*

[23] *Op. cit.*, p. 30. But Seagle (in his article 'Primitive Law and Professor Malinowski' in *The American Anthropologist*, Vol. 39, Pt. II, pp. 275–90, 1937), complained that Malinowski 'completely misunderstands' the dogma of the automatic submission to custom: 'All that the remarks as to the *automatic* force of custom imply is that somehow, marvellous to relate, the savage recognises the obligatory character of his customs although they are backed by no specific judicial sanctions of a repressive character as in civilised society. In this sense the custom of the savage is certainly automatic, and while he may behave as if he were its slave, he is not a slave who never revolts.'

[24] Well might the unbridled individualist, like Edmund in Shakespeare's *King Lear*, question—

Wherefore should I
Stand in the plague of custom?

[25] 'The extreme individualism often found in primitive communities does not favour universal anarchy'—Lowie, *op. cit.*, p. 384.

I. Schapera: A Handbook of Tswana Law and Custom*

The family and household. In addition to the territorial units formed by the districts and villages, the people of each tribe are divided into several different groups all derived ultimately from the relationships established by blood and by marriage. The smallest of these groups is the *family*, consisting of a man, his wife or wives, and their unmarried children, own or adopted. One or more families make up a *household*, the group of people living in the same collection of huts. Several closely related households, living together in the same part of the village, make up the *family-group*. One or more family-groups, organized together into a well-defined local administrative unit of the tribe, make up the *ward*. Cutting across the grouping into family-groups and wards is the

* I. Schapera, *A Handbook of Tswana Law and Custom*, Oxford University Press, 1938, pp. 12–19.

ill-defined body of *kindred*, embracing all the people genealogically connected by consanguinity or by marriage. Among the Kgatla and the Ngwato, finally, the wards are grouped together into the major divisions of the tribe here termed *sections*.

The two units most clearly defined in all the tribes are the household and the ward. The family, the family-group, and the kindred are less conspicuously demarcated. The family is merged in the household, and the family-group in the ward: while the kindred is a body widely scattered through the tribe. For convenience in exposition, we shall commence our description with the household, the smallest well-defined social unit in the tribe. . . .

Typically, the household consists of a man with his wife or wives and dependent children, together with any other relatives or unrelated dependants who may be attached to him. Its actual size and composition depend largely upon the rank, wealth, and age of the household-head. It may consist simply of husband and wife, with their dependent children, own or adopted; or of a widower with his second wife, and his children by one wife or both; or of a polygamist, with two or more wives, and his children by each. Often it may also contain unmarried dependants, such as the husband's younger brothers or sisters; or married dependants, such as sons, brothers, and possibly even sisters or daughters, with their respective spouses and children. Occasionally, too, there may be servants or other unrelated strangers living in the group.[1]

Except in the case of polygamous households, the members of a household all live together in the same homestead or dwelling-enclosure (*lolwapa*, *lapa*). This consists of a number of huts and granaries, enclosed within a courtyard by a low rectangular wall of dried mud, a wooden palisade, or a reed fence. Chiefs and the wealthier or more 'civilized' people nowadays frequently have rectangular dwellings after the European style. Normally, however, the huts are of the traditional Tswana type, consisting essentially of a circular wall of dried mud surmounted by a conical roof of thatch with protruding eaves. They are used principally as bedrooms and stores, most activities taking place in the open courtyard, except in wet weather. Each married couple in the household has its own hut, which it generally shares with its infant children. Young children of both sexes may share another hut, or live together with an older female relative, either unmarried, divorced, or widowed; while adolescent children or young unmarried people have separate huts according to their sex.

It is seldom nowadays that the household is based upon a polygamous family. Probably even in the olden days most of the men had only one wife; and few commoners had more than two or, in exceptional instances, three. Large polygamous households, of four wives or more, were met with only among the Chiefs, their relatives, important headmen, and other prominent or wealthy people. Under modern conditions, polygamy is obviously declining. This is due in the main to the spread of Christianity. All mission societies operating in the Protectorate forbid their converts to have more than one wife, nor will they allow a woman belonging to the Church to become the wife of a polygamist. The Administration, by imposing additional taxation upon polygamists, has made it even more difficult for them to exist in large numbers, at least openly. Educational progress, and contact with Western civilization generally, have also contributed to the widespread abandonment of the practice. Accurate statistics are not available, but it is doubtful if at the present time more than five per cent of Tswana men have more than one wife, while the number with three or more is very small indeed. Nevertheless, polygamy is still a recognized institution and, except among the Ngwaketse, has nowhere been explicitly forbidden.[2] Kgama strongly discouraged it among the Ngwato proper, and often intervened to prevent men from taking additional wives; but, even in his tribe, polygamy is still practised by such affiliated communities as the Birwa, Kalaka, Tswapong, and Sarwa.

The wives in a polygamous household are normally ranked in order of priority of marriage. The first wife married is the 'great wife' (*mosadi o mogolo*). The next wife is spoken of simply as the 'second wife' (*mosadi wa bobedi*); then comes the 'third wife' (*mosadi wa boraro*); and so on.[3] Any junior wife, irrespective of her ranking, may also be spoken of as *mogadingwana* or *mosadi o mmôtlana* (the 'small wife'), in contrast with the 'great wife'. In the bigger polygamous households formerly found, junior wives were occasionally affiliated to those of senior rank. A wife thus affiliated to another was spoken of by the Ngwato as her 'younger sister' (*monnawé*), and by the Kgatla as her 'daughter-in-law' (*ngwetsi*). There does not seem to have been any regular number of senior wives; nor, apparently, was it essential that every senior wife should have an affiliated wife. The arrangement depended solely upon the wishes of the husband. Any wife who had no sons of her own might also, by arrangement with her husband and parents, formally bring in a *seantlo* (lit., 'one who enters the hut') to bear a son in her 'house'. The husband could similarly take a *seantlo* for any wife who had died without male issue. The *seantlo* was generally the younger sister or some other close relative of the woman concerned. She was socially identified with the latter, to whose 'house' any children she might bear were regarded as belonging.

Each wife in a polygamous household has her own establishment or 'house' (*ntlo, lolwapa*). By this is meant the social group comprising the wife herself, her children, and any other people directly attached to her. Each house is distinct from and independent of the rest, and has its own property in the form of cattle, fields, and household utensils, which are inherited within that house. An affiliated wife, however, is linked to the house of the wife to whom she is affiliated. Failing a direct heir by any senior wife, the eldest son of her affiliated wife succeeds to the property of her house, in preference to a son by the senior wife in another house. But every wife, whether senior or affiliated, generally has her own dwelling. The dwelling-enclosures of the various wives are as a rule built on to one another, but are not arranged in any specified order. The husband sometimes ranges them according to the ranking of the wives; he may, however, also place them as he likes.

The family-group. Several different households, whose members are all closely related to one another, and which occupy the same part of the village or ward settlement, make up a family-group. This term is used here for the group sometimes but not exclusively referred to as *bana ba mpa* or *bana ba motho*, 'children of the same man'; or, in a wider sense, as *lesika*, 'people descended from a common ancestor'. More generally it is spoken of, from the administrative aspect, as *lekgotlana* (the diminutive form of *lekgotla*, 'ward').

The family-group varies considerably in size and composition. Basically it consists of several families, whose menfolk are all descended in the male line from the same grandfather or great-grandfather. There may, however, also be a few married female relatives (aunts, sisters, or daughters of these men), with their husbands and children; possibly also one or more nephews (sisters' sons), who have come from their own fathers' homes to live permanently with their mothers' people; and in rare instances also one or more relatives (brothers or sisters) of a woman married into the group. Finally there may be one or more household servants or other unrelated strangers accepted into the group with their respective families. The family-group, therefore, is fundamentally, but not exclusively, a group of families closely united by blood or by marriage.

The family-group is essentially a local unit, its members living side by side in adjacent homesteads. This fact needs to be stressed. The grandsons and great-grandsons of a man need not necessarily all live together. Some may have gone to live in other parts of the village, or even in other villages, generally with their wife's or mother's people. They are still connected by ties of kinship to their relatives remaining behind in the paternal home; but the latter are also specially linked together by ties of common residence. The same special ties bind to them people marrying into their midst or coming for some other reason to live with them. It is this community of residence that gives the family-group its distinctive character as a unit in the social and administrative system of the tribe.

The family-group is the setting for the more important domestic events and activities of its constituent families. It deals as a unit with such purely domestic affairs as betrothal and marriage negotiations, the organization of feasts, and the division of an estate—matters regarded as concerning, not only one particular family, but the group as a whole. Its members co-operate in such major tasks as building and thatching huts, clearing new fields, weeding, and reaping; and they help one another with gifts of food, livestock, and other commodities. If big enough, the group may have its own little *kgotla*, presided over by its hereditary elder (*mogolwane*), the senior male descendant of the common ancestor whose name it bears. This man, in conjunction with the other adult members of the group, arbitrates over any disputes occurring between any of its people; while, should any member be involved in a lawsuit with an outsider, he is assisted by the rest in the preliminary discussions and in the actual hearings at the tribal courts. In all these activities, negotiations, and discussions, the members of the family-group may also be assisted by other relatives, or by other members of their ward. But the members of the group are in any case bound to take part, whether these other people do so or not.

The kindred. The family-group embraces only a small portion of a man's kindred, i.e. the people related to him by ties of blood or of marriage. Among the Tswana, as among other Bantu peoples, recognition of relationship is carried much further than is common in European society. Close relatives are distinguished from one another according to sex, relative age, and line of descent or marriage. A special kinship term is applied to each class of relative. These distinctive terms are then fairly consistently extended, along similar lines, to the more remote relatives. In this way everybody with whom genealogical connexion can be traced, no matter in how remote a degree, is brought within the circle of kindred. Associated with each kinship term is a special pattern of behaviour, involving reciprocal rights and duties. In theory a man should observe the prescribed pattern of behaviour towards all the relatives whom he calls by one term. In practice it is usually only towards his closer relatives that he carries it out fully. Some of these patterns of behaviour will be described in detail in a later chapter. Here we shall merely outline the more general rights and duties prevailing within each major category of relationship.

Unlike the household and the family-group, which are definitely localized bodies, the kindred is widely scattered through the tribe. Normally, it is true, a man's paternal relatives (*ba ga etsho*) will belong to the same family-group and ward as himself; and this community of residence undoubtedly tends to strengthen the solidarity both of these groups and of the paternal kin. But his maternal relatives (*ba ga etsho mogolo*) more often than not belong to some other family-group or ward, as do also his relatives-in-law (*bagwê* or *bagwagwadi*). These particular categories of kin therefore cut across the local groupings, bind people together by a new series of relationships, and ensure a wider diffusion through the tribe of reciprocal obligations of service and protection.[4]

Ga etsho is applied primarily to a man's home, the place of his father, which is therefore also the place where most of his paternal relatives live. In effect these are the people belonging to his family-group, although the latter, as we have indicated, may also include both maternal relatives and relatives-in-law, as well as unrelated dependants. On the other hand, some paternal relatives are generally also found living outside the family-group. But all paternal relatives, whether belonging to the same or to different family-groups, must carry out towards one another certain special obligations, the nature of which varies with the nature and closeness of the relationship. These obligations will be specified in a later chapter. Paternal relatives as a body also have certain more general obligations towards one another. These obligations are in effect those already described in connexion with the family-group, and need not therefore be repeated here. The only point that needs stressing is that as a rule it is only the relatives within the family-group who carry out their obligations most fully and conscientiously.

Ga etsho mogolo is the place from which a man's mother comes, the home of her parents and brothers. Occasionally a man's maternal relatives will belong to his own family-group, for marriage within the group is not forbidden. More generally they belong to some other family-group and even to some other ward. In such cases children during their early years may be sent to live for a while with their mother's people; and they should always, even when grown-up, visit it frequently. A child is greatly honoured at its mother's home. *Setlogolo se segolo kwa gabo-mogolo*, says the proverb: 'A uterine nephew is an important person at the home of his mother's people.' He takes precedence there over his cousins at the eating of the firstfruits and in other ceremonies where precedence is involved; his word carries great weight in their family councils; and generally speaking he is treated there with utmost respect and has many privileges. Between him and his maternal uncle there exists a specially intimate relationship, reflected more particularly in exchanges of property and services, which plays a very important part in the whole social life of the people. A man should, if possible, marry the daughter of his maternal uncle; but whether he does so or not, he associates on terms of the greatest intimacy with her and her brothers. His maternal relatives, further, help him in all his domestic undertakings and troubles; and he can always, if necessary, find a welcome home among them.

Bogwé, the home of a man's wife, is likewise a place where he is greatly honoured.

In some tribes (Ngwaketes, Rolong, Malete), the first few years of his married life are spent there. During this time he co-operates actively with his wife's people at work. After setting up his own home, he must still visit his parents-in-law frequently, help them at work, and make them occasional presents of food and other commodities. They reciprocate in the same way. A woman's lot at the home of her husband's parents (*bo-matsalê*) is, on the other hand, at first rather difficult, especially in those tribes where immediately after marriage she goes to live with him in his mother's homestead. Here she must be humble and respectful, work hard, and in general serve the whole household. But when her husband sets up his own household, and she becomes its mistress, she obtains much greater freedom. She should, however, spend much of her time with his people and assist them, as they assist her, in the various major domestic and agricultural tasks and undertakings.

Notes

[1] Detailed analyses of the composition of sixteen Kgatla and eighteen Ngwato households are given in Schapera's 'The Social Structure of the Tswana Ward', *Bantu Studies*, ix (1935), pp. 208–12, 215–18. In the Kgatla series the average number of persons (men, women, and children) per household was 6.6; in the Ngwato series, 5.3.

[2] Among the Ngwaketse, Chief Seepapitso forbade young men to marry more than one wife, except with his permission. This law, after being allowed to lapse, was revived in 1936 by Chief Bathweng II. Any man breaking it is punished, and his second marriage annulled.

[3] The only exceptions to this rule of ranking occur when a man, after marrying one or more wives, either marries the girl to whom he was first betrothed, as in cases of infant betrothal, or marries the daughter of his maternal uncle (*malome*). This new wife then takes precedence over the rest, and acquires the corresponding privileges, just as if she had been married first. Among the Ngwato, where infant betrothal was formerly practised on a large scale, the first wife married was known as *mmamoleta*, because she 'waited for' (*go leta*) the great wife; and she ranked as the second wife in the household. The great wife when married was known as *mmadikgomo* (mother of cattle), because the cattle due to her parents as *bogadi* (bride-wealth) had to be given out before those for any other wife.

[4] Nowadays, as marriage between members of different tribes is becoming more common, a man's maternal relatives or relatives-in-law may even belong to a different tribe from his own. The customary kinship obligations prevail in such cases also, although there is generally far less opportunity or occasion for their exercise.

R. S. Rattray: Ashanti Law and Constitution*

The Clan

The society, the composition of one of whose units has now been sketched, was regarded not as being composed of so many persons, but as consisting of an aggregation of units, each of which was a family group. These families possibly lived in close proximity to one another, but each was an *imperium in imperio*, having its own head, whose utterances were the only law binding his group. Each family was possibly at first insulated from its neighbours, save only on special occasions when temporary contact was effected to allow the settlement of some inter-family dispute or to permit of some inter-family amenity or ceremonial. The tie of a common blood alone conferred the privilege to command obedience and alone imposed an obligation to obey commands. The incidence of casual, or even permanent, residence in an alien household seemed to be ignored, for free persons resident in such a habitation appeared to enjoy a certain claim to extra-territoriality.

The family was a corporation; action and even thought were corporate affairs. It is not easy to grasp what must have been the effect on West African psychology of untold generations of acting and thinking, not in terms of oneself, but in relation to one's group. The Ashanti's ideas of what we should term 'moral responsibility for his actions' must surely have been more developed than with peoples where individualism is the order of the day.

All the germs of the more advanced system of government, the development of which

* R. S. Rattray, *Ashanti Law and Constitution*, Oxford University Press, 1929, pp. 62–71.

will presently be followed, already existed in the little family democracy.[1] For example, the methods by which disputes were brought before the family head for settlement were the exact procedure of later days, when a higher central authority came to supersede the more or less irresponsible commands of the house-father. The routine, the half-formulated rules binding the individuals in the family, rules relating to property, inheritance, ownership of land, collection of family contributions, became the customary laws governing the larger group. The *lares et penates* of the house-father became the sacred *agyapadie* (heirlooms) of the Stool; the various duties assigned to the different members of the family gave rise, as these duties became more onerous, to the appointment of individuals whose business it became to supervise and to be responsible for their performance. Various family groups, in course of time, came under the head of one particular family, to whom, in all important matters, appeals were made. This process of amalgamation went on in independent localities, and in this manner numerous Territorial Divisions grew up under different heads, independent and often rivals of each other. The lesser of these again tended to be merged into the greater, and, at the period when Ashanti history begins, we find this people grouped into the five or six great Divisions whose history and growth will be dealt with in these pages. To use a metaphor upon which I shall later enlarge in more detail, the family was like a circle. Later, lines of contact—at first weak and undefined—stretched from the centres of many such circles, and converged upon a point which was the centre of another, but greater, *eccentric* circle, the house-father of which now came, at least nominally, to control the heads of all the lesser circles. These latter now assumed very much the nature of satellites grouped around a greater body. This central body was itself ever expanding and throwing out greater and yet greater *concentric* circles, each new ring embracing fresh systems, until, finally, the circumference of the largest circle of all formed the boundary of a kingdom. Its centre remained our original family group—now the royal house—its head was still a house-father, but now also a King (*Asante Hene*). He governed a nation, but on lines exactly analogous to those on which, as a 'father', he still ruled his family.

The family had expanded into the Clan, the Clan into the Tribe.

'A clan is an exogamous division of a tribe, all the *clansmen* or members of which are held to be related to one another and bound together by the common tie of *clanship*.' This tie in Ashanti is, for all ordinary purposes, belief in a common descent from some ancestress; reaching back still farther, it was belief in a common descent from an ancestress who was descended from some animal. I was many years in Ashanti before I discovered that clans had ultimately this totemic origin.

The family, as we have seen, is *bi-* or *multilateral* the clan is unilateral. 'A number of families do not make up a clan or a number of clans a community, i.e. members of any particular clan may belong to many communities, but the community is composed of various families and clans.'[2] The Ashanti appear to be grouped in eight clans. Reindorf give their numbers as seven and their names as follows:

(1) *Asekyiri*, (2) *Asena*, (3) *Agona*, (4) *Oyoko*, (5) *Aduena*, (6) *Asokore*, (7) *Abrade* (Asenee).
Sarbah gives them as:
(1) *Nsonna*, in some localities known as *Dwimina*.
(2) *Annona*, Yoko, Aguna, Eguana.
(3) *Twidan*, Eburotow.
(4) *Kwonna*, Ebiradzi, or Odumna.
(5) *Aburadzi*, Eduana, Ofurna, Egyira.
(6) *Ntwa*, Abadzi.
(7) *Adwinadzi*, Aowin.

In *Ashanti* (see pedigree chart) I gave the Ashanti clans as follows:

(1) *Aduana*, (2) *Agona*, (3) *Asinie*, (4) *Asokore*, (5) *Asona*, (6) *Beretuo*, (7) *Ekuana*, and (8) *Oyoko*.

Sarbah's list of clans is given for the Fanti, and, accounting for the differences in dialect, contain several names which are recognizable in the Ashanti. This is not surprising, as they (the Fanti) are considered as belonging to the same stock as the Ashanti.

Both Ashanti and Fanti are generally considered to have migrated from a common centre in Northern Ashanti near Tekiman, where the Brong, who are generally thought to be of the same stock, still reside. I was surprised therefore to discover that the pure

Brong are apparently wholly ignorant of these Ashanti and Fanti clan names, and that their exogamous divisions seem based upon an entirely different model. In Tekiman one does not ask, 'To what *abusua* (totemic clan) do you belong?' but 'In what street (*abrono*) do you reside?' There, such exogamous divisions as appear to exist apparently take their names from streets or quarters in the towns. If my information be correct, we have here a problem of considerable interest to students of Gold Coast history. It is one which I have so far been unable satisfactorily to solve. I can only hazard two tentative suggestions. One is that, in accordance with the common belief, Brong, Fanti, and Ashanti had a single origin, and that all originally had this local or 'street' organization (in place of the totemic groups); that Fanti and Ashanti moved south, separating from the parent stock, and at a much later date, possibly due to some contact with another culture, adopted their present totemic clan organization. The traditional evidence of the survival of street names, mentioned in the last chapter, seems to be some proof of this supposition, unless of course these were the relics of another civilization. My second suggestion is that the Brong and Ashanti were not from the same original stock; that the Ashanti were an alien race who overran the Brong, bringing with them their own clan organization and passing southward, and settled down, ousting, or exterminating, or absorbing the local Brong inhabitants, and later, to strengthen their position, which was that of mere usurpers in the land, they encouraged the fiction of a common descent from the real proprietors, or alternatively, and again ignoring their own origin, declared that they had sprung from the ground which they had in reality appropriated. I commend this problem to other students of Gold Coast history.[3]

I have stated that clans in Ashanti had a totemic origin, but that I was formerly unaware of this fact. I was, of course, aware of a truth which every European knows, namely, that many chiefs use emblems on the top of State umbrellas, and elsewhere, which are generally accepted as being the clan totems. Careful inquiry, however, elicited the information that these anthropomorphic, zoomorphic, phytomorphic, or hylomorphic representations do not necessarily exhibit the clan eponym. In none of my inquiries have I encountered greater reluctance to discuss any subject than the question relating to clan origins. *Obi nkyere obi ase* ('One does not disclose the origin of another') is the usual reply to all such inquiries. First-hand information has, however, been obtained from certain clansmen themselves, and I now, with all reverence for the feelings and susceptibilities of my venerable informants, record what I have been told.

'We really believe (as do members of all other clans) that we were descended from some animal.[4] This is one of the greatest mysteries of the clan, and it is told in secret to the Chief on the occasion on which he is for the first time permitted to enter the room containing the blackened Stools.[5] The *Okyeame* (Spokesman) will say, *Ma me biribi ma me nka nkyere wo biribi* ("Give me something that I may tell you something"). It would be impossible for a member of a clan to kill its *tweneboa* (totem animal). Young children of the clan are admonished at a very early age to respect the particular animal from whom their race sprang, but they are not told the reason.'

A Queen Mother stated: 'If I ever ate an——, which would be impossible, I should be destooled, and the whole nation would come to harm. We are proud to be called the——people' (mentioning the sobriquet of her clan), 'but if any one in olden times called us the——' (mentioning the real totem) 'people he would have been killed, and even to-day it would be a very great offence. No one looks back whence he came. No one ventures to ask another, *Wo tweneboa*[6] *ben?* ("What is your totem animal?"), but will put the question, *Wo bo abusua ben?* ("To what clan do you belong?"). No one would have dared to make a crest representing his real *atweneboa*; in olden days any one doing so would have been killed.'

Again: 'I would not kill an——; he is my brother, my blood; if I were hunting with another man and he wished to kill it, I would ask him not to.' I asked this informant if he would bury an——if he saw it dead. He replied, 'I would not even look at it; I would run home, drink a little, and not eat until evening'.

The following are the totems given me as being those of the various clans:

Aduana, atwere (the Frog).
Agona (?).
Asenie, Asenewa (the Bat); also a bead (*bodom*).
Asokore (?)

Asona, *Anene* (the Crow).
Beretuo, *Afwea* (the Mole).
Ekuana, *Eko* (the Buffalo).
Oyoko, *Ako* (the Parrot), who dipped his tail in the red *oyoko* pot; or just possibly *sansa* (the hawk), but I am inclined to believe the former is the correct one.

During my last 'tour' in Ashanti, traces came to light that what anthropogists term 'the dual organization' (i.e. the division of an entire tribe into two endogamous clans) once existed in Ashanti. This discovery, which I ventured to think is of some interest,[7] was made possible owing to the chance survival of certain proverbs (*abubesem*). These particular sayings were to the effect that 'Persons of such and such clans are filthy or depraved people, for they used to marry each other'.[8] Of the two *moieties* mentioned, the first is one or other of the commonly known clans, but the second is some name which is seldom or never heard, and is that of a clan to which few now appear to belong. On making further inquiries, I was informed that most of the present-day clans once upon a time had a twin clan (moiety) with which it was always coupled, and that persons of one of these *moieties* always married into the other half. Later on, they state that *Komfo Anotche* made a law that such marriages were to be discontinued, as an individual belonging to one of these *moieties* was the 'brother' or 'sister' of a person belonging to the other. The result apparently was that these 'halves' became merged into each other, under a name formerly applied to one or other of the *moieties*, one thus tending to become extinct, or, where it survived, instead of, as originally, being the only clan into which a member of the tribe could marry, became the only clan with which that person might not legally mate.

These moieties, so far as I have been able to ascertain, were as follows:

Aduana	and	*Atwea* (*Abrade* ?).
Agona	,,	*Toa* (*Adome* ?).
Asenie[9]	,,	—?
Asokore	,,	*Ekuana*?
Asona	,,	*Dwum*. (*Dwumana* or *Dwumina*).
Beretuo	,,	*Tana*.
Ekuana	,,	*Asokore*?
Oyoko	,,	*Dako*.[10]

While clans in Ashanti thus appear to bear the stamp of typical totemic institutions found elsewhere, there would still appear to be one important exception. The child in Ashanti, though thought to inherit its mother's clan, i.e. blood, apparently also inherits the *ntoro* totemic spirit of its father. All the numerous food taboos that every Ashanti observes (with the exception only of the clan totem avoidance) are regulated not by the clan, but by the *ntoro* relationship.[11] I have dealt fully with these patrilineal exogamous divisions in a previous volume.[12] In this place I will only again refer to them in connexion with what appears to be a parallel in these institutions with the old dual organizations in the tribe. As soon as I became aware of the fact of the previous existence of these moieties, it appeared to me to be a logical conclusion to expect that a similar dual organization might once have existed in connexion with the *ntoro*. Direct inquiries revealed the fact that such was the case. In *Ashanti* I gave a list of nine *ntoro* exogamous divisions. It has since been discovered that many of these had a subdivision or branch division entailing the same food restrictions, but apparently having a different totem.

(1) *Bosommuru* (which is also known as *Bosummuru pa*[13]) or *Busummuru Adufodie*, i.e. the real (*pa*) *Bosommuru*, with its other moiety *Bosommuru Asafodie*.
(2) *Bosompra* and *Bosompra Awiri*.
(3) *Bosomtwe* and *Bosomtwe Atwedie*.
(4) *Bosommaram* and *Bosommaram Nnuamoa*.
(5) *Abankwadie* and *Abankwadie Asankadie*.

The tendency here seems again, as in the case of the dual clans, for one moiety to become merged into the other, for unless one inquires very particularly, e.g., to which *Bosommuru ntoro* a person belongs, that person will not make any distinction, but will merely reply '*Bosommuru*', and in many cases will not even have heard of the other moiety.

The result of the merging of the two clans or two *ntoro* has been, as Mr. Dudley

Buxton pointed out, to enlarge the inbreeding group.[14] We have seen that in theory all persons bearing the same clan name were considered as being descended from a common ancestress. In practice, however, as members of a kindred group became more and more widely dispersed, they established new family groups which in time came to boast a more limited and localized descent from the female whose descendant had founded the new offshoot. This more modern ancestress now headed a new genealogical tree, and, as the process was ever continuing, it soon became impossible to link up all these females with the ancestress originally common to all.

For administrative purposes on a wide scale, the clan organization would appear always to have been breaking down, leaving the kindred group again all-powerful; for, although theoretically the head of a particular kindred group (or his successor) might have been expected to remain head of all the offshoots of his kindred, i.e. of his clan, however numerous and widely scattered they became, in practice this did not apparently occur.

Beyond an implied recognition of the original tie which bound them all—practical evidence of the existence of which remained in the prohibition to marry a person bearing the clan name, however remote her residence, or impossible the tracing of any blood affinity—the claim of any single clansman to rule an entire group of persons because all bore his clan name appears never to have been raised. Later, when amalgamations of household groups took place, and a common head had to be chosen for this new community, these amalgamations were based on territorial groupings and considerations and were not carried out with any idea of arranging groups according to clan descent, each under a chief of their own clan. The germs that gave rise to expansion and amalgamation on these lines were already planted in the *bi-* or *multilateral* family group, the ambition of whose head it seemed ever to have been to bring the 'conventional' members of his household more and more under his direct control. If there ever was a time in Ashanti when entire clans were united *qua* clans for political or administrative purposes, I cannot now find any trace of such organizations, and it would appear, as I have suggested, that, as kindred groups threw off new branches and spread out in ever-widening circles to form a clan, the authority of the head of the original kindred group over his more remote clansmen ceased altogether, unless he happened also to have become Chief in the territorial sense.

The main characteristics of the clan system in Ashanti appear, then, to be:

(1) All persons bearing a common clan name, resident however widely apart, are held to be related by blood. In consequence, they are considered to stand to each other in a prohibited degree of relationship with regard to marriage, and to be bound together by a sentimental tie of brotherhood.

(2) The heads of the various household groups exercise complete control only over these members of their clan who are directly related by a blood-tie that is practically, not theoretically, capable of demonstration, as being traceable to a common female ancestress who founded that particular family group; in other words, their authority extends only to the nearer kinsmen.

(3) Clan descent alone confers the right (*a*) to inherit property; (*b*) to perform the *sacra* for ancestral spirits; (*c*) to succeed to certain offices; (*d*) to be buried in a particular cemetery; (*e*) to unite in the performance of certain funeral rites.

(4) The clan tie cannot be lost or broken save by expulsion from the clan.

(5) By a legal fiction, clan relationship might sometimes be acquired otherwise than by birth.

Some of these points may now be examined in more detail; others, e.g. rights in relation to property and succession, will be investigated later.

Clan exogamy has been discussed in *Ashanti*,[15] to which I would refer my readers. With regard to the sentimental tie existing between all persons of the same clan, the following is taken from statements in the vernacular: 'When a man goes on a journey and arrives in a town, he will find out in course of conversation where persons of his clan reside. He will go to them and be received as a brother; he will be introduced to the wife of his host as her "husband".' Again: 'My brother once went trading and came to Akyim Taffo, where he put up at the house of one Kwesi Abokyi. On hearing that my brother belonged to the Beretuo clan, his host told him he was also Beretuo. He made my brother his *wofase* (nephew), and gave him his daughter in marriage. My brother settled there and died: we went to fetch his skeleton, but Kwesi Abokyi told us the Government would not allow skeletons to be removed.'

Clan burial-grounds: 'If there are only two clans represented in a village, one would have the *samanpow* (thicket of the ghosts) on the right, the other on the left. If there were a larger number of clans, there would be a larger *samanpow* marked out in plots, one for each clan, the plots being separated by fences of *nkrandudua, ntome,* or *nsomasa* sticks.'

'A head of a family, with special permission from the Chief, and after presenting him with sheep and wine,[16] may receive permission that when he dies, he may be buried under the floor of his sleeping-room. His successor will then be able to place a sleeping-mat over the grave, and will be comforted by the knowledge that his predecessor is sleeping beneath him.'

Expulsion from, and adoption into the clan: When the head of a kindred group decides to repudiate the debts or offences of one of its members or to sell one of the clan, a public declaration was made to the effect that this person was no longer one of their clansmen. The ceremony was called *pae abusua* (to split off from the clan). Such action in olden days would generally amount to sentence of slavery or death. *Adoption* into a clan was achieved by the slow and almost imperceptible process of time rather than by any public ceremony. It applied almost wholly to the descendants of slave women and to their descendants, who grew up to consider themselves members of the clan which had originally purchased their ancestress. Such persons, though nominally free members of the kindred group to which they now belonged, never entirely lost their original status, which would always be known, at least to the head of their family.[17]

Such is briefly the history of the Ashanti family and clan, and their extension into the tribe, which is a unit consisting of many families belonging to many different clans; the central authority which has now made its appearance attempts, so far as lies in its power, to regard them all, not in terms of such, but as one territorial entity.[18]

Notes

[1] A democracy, however, in a sense different from that with which we are now familiar.

[2] *The Ila-speaking Peoples of N.W. Rhodesia*, p. 283.

[3] There was a well-authenticated record of a migration, in comparatively modern times, of Brong from Tekiman to the Gold Coast, where they became Fanti. One old Ashanti once told me that the Fanti and Brong were one, but not the Ashanti. The Tekiman Fanti might possibly in the course of a few hundred years have adopted their present clan organization from the neighbouring tribes.

[4] Ashanti folk-lore contain many stories of persons changing into animals and vice versa.

[5] A 'royal' (*odehye*) is never permitted to enter the Stool house until he becomes a Chief.

[6] The word *ahoboa* (beast that is oneself) is also sometimes used.

[7] I believe I am correct in stating that the dual organization was not known to have existed in Africa.

[8] *Oyoko ne Dako nnipa dapafo* (or *kwabusufo busua*) *na ye de aware.*

[9] *Asenie*, I was informed, had never any moiety. 'This clan sprang from a *bodom* bead, which later gave birth to bats.'

[10] *Osai Kwame*, an *Oyoko*, son of Kantanka, is alleged to have married a *Dako* woman from Kuntenase and to have been destooled in consequence.

[11] See *Ashanti*, p. 47.

[12] *Ibid.*, Chapter II.

[13] Sometimes also *Bosummuru aninie.*

[14] See *Religion and Art in Ashanti*, pp. 380 et seq.

[15] See Chapters I–II.

[16] These gifts are for the '*samanfo* (spirit ancestors) of the Chief, and ensure that the promise will not later be repudiated.

[17] Adoption of a child already belonging to the adopter's clan, but not to his particular kindred-group, should not be confused with the above.

[18] Since this chapter was writen, I returned to the Gold Coast and was stationed at Kwahu. On investigating the local traditions, I discovered that the Kwahu tribe had emigrated from Ashanti some centuries ago *as two compact endogamous clans*, i.e. *Beretuo and Tana*—a most valuable confirmation of what was already written.

H. Kuper: Kinship among the Swazi*

The Family Unit

The starting-point of the Swazi kinship system—the 'elementary family' of father, mother, and child—depends as in all societies on a recognition of a social relationship which may or may not coincide with a physical tie. The Swazi say 'A child is one blood with its father and its mother', but if a man has refused to perform the recognized marriage ceremony the children will belong to the mother's kin. The indisputable, but by no means sole, evidence of legal marriage is the acceptance by the bride's people of a number of cattle known as *emabeka* under the custom of *ukuloɓola*.[1]† *Ukuloɓola* is specifically connected with the woman's fertility and with rights over children. In cases where the woman is sterile and cattle have already been paid, a substitute must be sent 'to bear for her'. The rights conferred over the children appear when a subject obtains marriage-cattle from his chief; the first daughter of the union is then spoken of as the chief's child, and cattle received on her marriage go to his heir. If the king contributes even one beast, he receives the full *emabeka* of the first daughter. In both cases the woman is recognized as the legal wife of the subject and the payment of the cattle gives the other men no sexual rights. All children other than the first daughter are regarded as the husband's, even though he may not be the genitor. A man may *loɓola* a woman long after she has borne him children, and thereby establish them as his legitimate offspring, but—and in this the Swazi differ markedly from neighbouring Bantu tribes—he may simply *loɓola* the children, leaving the woman to marry elsewhere.

The sociological relationship of father and child may conflict with the physiological bond, for while the genitor may be denied the right of social paternity, a child is said to be impelled by the 'call of blood' to seek him out in later life. Here we have one of the many instances in which a social norm is challenged by individual emotions; viewed from the other angle, the emotional interests of a man and woman for legitimate 'blood' offspring is a major sanction behind family stability. The importance which children attach to the respectability of their mother, and to their own rights in the paternal family, appears from the cases where sons, after the death of the father and sometimes even after the death of the mother, give *emabeka* for her to her people.

Swazi consider the production of legitimate children a social obligation of adult men and women. For a few years after puberty, boys and girls are expected to have *tingani* (sweethearts), but the girls may not fall pregnant without losing value on the marriage market and the boys are fined anything up to ten head of cattle depending on the rank of the girl and the ruling of the court. After marriage the emphasis is on child-bearing. 'The marriage-cattle are closed by the carrying sling' (in which the baby is tied on the mother's back) is a common saying. Should a grown man die without children, but leaving behind a lover, it is the duty of his father or his father's heir to give cattle for her and provide a 'thigh' from the kinship group to raise children for the deceased. This is an instance of what Evans-Pritchard has styled 'ghost marriage'. Should a woman be childless, her husband is entitled to a co-wife from her family to produce children, and they are spoken of as the children of the older woman as well as of the younger. The extension of maternity through kinship of co-wives is described as 'to put into the womb of another'. A husband may even take the child of any junior wife and 'put it into the womb' of a senior unrelated co-wife as heir. This type of adoption is most frequently practised in the case of main wives who have no sons, and it is then always best to choose boys whose own mothers are dead or whose mothers are deeply attached to the senior woman. Adoption of non-related children is unknown, the nearest thing to this being the ancient custom of taking over orphans whose parents had been killed in war or for witchcraft. In many respects these children were identified with those of the family head, but they were described—in their absence—as *tigcili* (domestic serfs), and were not included in the full kinship circle.

Wives and children are regarded as a man's greatest assets and polygyny is the ambition of the tribesmen, an ambition most frequently achieved by aristocrats and

* H. Kuper, 'Kinship among the Swazi', in A. R. Radcliffe-Brown and D. Forde (eds.), *African Systems of Kinship and Marriage*, Oxford University Press, pp. 88–91.

† Marriage consideration.

wealthy elderly commoners. The king is expected to take more wives than any of his subjects, and the present king, who was born in 1902, has more than forty wives. Not only do the queens enhance his prestige and provide him with labour, but they are diplomatically selected from a wide range of clans which are thereby drawn into in-law relationship with the royal family. Swazi say, 'polygamy (*isithembu*) is the nature of man, while the nature of woman is satisfied through children'.

The Homestead

On marriage a Swazi girl leaves her family and goes to live in her husband's homestead (*umuti*). If his parents are alive he may attach his huts to the paternal circle or build in the vicinity. Should a patriarch have a number of wives, there is a strong tendency, especially when the sons marry, for his homestead to subdivide into smaller units of mothers and sons. Women always move with their own sons, but as long as the patriarch is alive he is the main authority in all legal and economic issues. Full brothers are more likely to continue to share a homestead after marriage than sons by different mothers, but when they have many wives, full brothers often build separately, the mother staying with the older son and visiting the younger. The section of the homestead in which the mother lives is known as the capital (*umpakatsi*), and in relation to it any other section is merely the barracks (*lilau*).

The homesteads, scattered irregularly over the country-side, vary considerably in size, with the wealth and status of the headman. In a sample area of 66 homesteads, the average number of occupants was 7·2 for commoners' families and 22.5 in the homesteads of aristocrats. The largest *umuti* in the whole county is owned by the ruling family; the smallest that I came across belonged to a Christian widow living with two unmarried sons several miles from their nearest kin. The small isolated group without even a single complete family unit is a modern development and is still most unusual, though for various reasons—economic, religious, and political—homesteads are undoubtedly dwindling in size. The diminishing of the local kinship group is an indication of certain changes taking place in the traditional structure, but space does not permit an analysis of these changes.

A conservative homestead is shaped in a semicircle facing a central circular cattle byre. Each married woman has her own quarters consisting of living- and store-huts and kitchen enclosed by a high reed fence. An enclosure is spoken of as 'the hut of so-and-so' and relationship is counted through the different 'huts'. There is no rigid placing of 'huts' in order of rank as amongst some southern Bantu, but the 'great hut' (*indlunkulu*) is usually in the middle of the semicircle. It is occupied by the mother of the headman, or, if she is dead, by a classificatory mother or a special wife raised to the status of 'mother'. The *indlunkulu*, associated with the elders of the headman's lineage, is the shrine of the homestead. Wives are grouped on either side of it in an order largely determined by the wishes of the headman, though he frequently places the enclosure of the first wife on the right of the 'mother' and the second on her left, the third on the right, and so on. Subdivision of a homestead does not, however, follow any defined grouping of huts, and it breaks up the original order. In the harem of the king and leading princes the arrangement of the wives is somewhat different: there are a number of 'big queens', each with a number of 'little queens' attached to their huts.

In every homestead the headman's line is dominant. All his children have the paternal *isiɓongo*,[2] which is the same as that of his brothers and their children and any sisters living in his home. Wives always keep their own clan names and this distinguishes them as the 'strangers', the out-group. Unrelated people may attach themselves to the headman and live in his *umuti*, but a sharp distinction following the difference in *isiɓongo*[2] is drawn between 'our folk' and 'cold people'.

Like all southern Bantu, the Swazi live by cultivating crops and by animal husbandry, and the homestead is the main unit of tribal economy, with the division of labour regulated by sex and age. The women are primarily responsible for the routine work, which carries lower prestige value than the activities monopolized by men.

In the homestead Swazi religion, like Swazi economics, gives greater power to the males than to the females. While both men and women become ancestral spirits after death, it is the men who officiate as family priest for the entire homestead.

The group living in the homestead is always impermanent and fluctuating, affected by marriages, births, deaths, migration, and immigration. At the same time, initial behaviour is shaped in the elementary family with its local basis in the homestead. Here the individual acquires the stereotyped norms reflecting the economic, legal, and religious values of the society, essential for the stability and perpetuation of the total social structure.

Notes

[1] Only the king need not give *emabeka* for his queens.
[2] Clan name.

E. Colson: Marriage and the Family among the Plateau Tonga of Northern Rhodesia*

Groups Based on Kinship

Every Tonga is a member of some clan, and the clans are the most enduring units in the society. Though specific clan origin myths seem to be absent, the clans are thought to have come into existence with mankind and to have continued without change to the present day. In the north-western portion of the District. the clan system seems to resemble that of the Ila and the Sala. Throughout the rest of the District representatives of the same 12 to 14 clans are found. The clans are named, dispersed, exogamous units in which membership is derived through matrilineal descent. Each clan is linked or paired with several others individually in what is known as *bujwanyina*, a relationship of which joking is only one aspect of a wider range of duties and rights. But clans are not corporate bodies. They own no property, have no ritual centres or leaders, and never on any occasion assemble as a group. Furthemore, the tie of clanship does not create joint responsibility for one another's actions.

The corporate kinship groups are much smaller bodies of kinsmen which I refer to as 'matrilineal groups'. The Tonga word for such a group is *mukowa*. The same term is used for clan and has the wider meaning of species, kind, sort, or type. In some areas older people recognize the words *citiba* or *cilongo* as referring specifically to a matrilineal group, but in practice most apply these words also to the clan. Other words which seem to be used as synonyms for clan and matrilineal group are *cibuwa*, *mukwaasi cikoto*, *cikombo*, *iciinga*, *luzubo*, and *cipani*. Specific kinship terms, however, are commonly used only within the matrilineal group, while fellow-clansmen are addressed by the generic term *mukwesu*, which Tonga translate as 'brother' though it would not be used between siblings.

A matrilineal group is a corporate body since it has a common legal personality *vis-à-vis* all other similarly organized bodies. Inheritance, succession, provision and sharing of bridewealth, vengeance—though to a very attenuated degree today—and a common ritual responsibility, are functions of the group. Groups range in size from those composed of only a few adults to some which have around a hundred adult members.

Matrilineal groups are dispersed, though not to the same degree as clans. They are unnamed. Theoretically membership rests on actual descent through females from a common ancestress, but exact genealogical ties are usually irrelevant either for ensuring membership or for assignment of position within the group. No one bothers to remember the name of the founding ancestress, or the links between her and the living members of the group. In the past slaves were incorporated into the matrilineal groups of their owners, and thus also into their clans, and female slaves passed the right of full membership to their descendants.

Matrilineal groups of the same clan are not linked together in any fashion save by their common clan membership. Thus there are no perpetual kinship relationships within the clan or between clans to give a rigid structure phrased in kinship terms to Tonga society, and there is no segmentary lineage system.[1] Matrilineal groups are bound together, however, by ties which are purely temporal and tied to the life-span of particular individuals.

* E. Colson, *Marriage and the Family among the Plateau Tonga of Northern Rhodesia*, Manchester University Press, 1958, pp. 15–23.

Each person is an 'honorary member' of his father's matrilineal group, and also of his father's clan. Indeed, if asked to identify himself, a Tonga is more likely to reply with the name of his father's clan than with that of his own clan, and it is courteous to address him in the same fashion. In this way his ties with his father's kin and clan are stressed.

In all matters which concern an individual, there should be co-operation between his matrilineal kinsmen (his *basimukowa*) and his father's matrilineal kinsmen (his *basyanausi*). This continues throughout his lifetime, but on his death the tie which binds them together vanishes. Each matrilineal group is thus bound to a number of similar groups in other clans as it co-operates with the *basyanausi* of its members and with the *basimukowa* of the children of its male members. But these ties are not stable and impervious to time. They change with each death and with each marriage.

The Cohesion of the Matrilineal Group. It is Tonga dogma that the matrilineal group is not internally differentiated into segments based on a common descent from one woman. They admit that uterine siblings may feel themselves a unit in contrast to other members of the group, that the own mother is likely to be more important to a person than a classificatory mother, that a man is more likely to take an interest in his own sister's children than he is in his classificatory sister's children. But these are unpleasant facts, and not values enshrined in the social structure. The dogma was clearly stated by a man when I asked him whether he felt more attached to Reuben, his own sister's son, or to Nathan, a classificatory sister's son with whom he cannot trace his relationship. All three men live in the same village. The man answered: 'I make no difference between them. They are equally close because they are both of my matrilineal group. Nathan mourns that he was born alone because he has no brothers or sisters born of his mother, but we think he is foolish. No man is born alone even if he is the only one from his womb, for all have *mukowa* and they are as close as those of one womb.'

Rights and obligations therefore vest in the matrilineal group as such and not in particular segments. I have suggested elsewhere that this may be due to the dispersed nature of the group. 'Members of a matrilineal group who do live close together are also in constant association with people who belong to other groups—indeed, the majority of their associates will be outsiders. . . . Since people are surrounded by outsiders, amongst whom they live and with whom they co-operate in ordinary activities, membership within the matrilineal group as a whole is the overwhelming fact that they stress. The relationships which they have with outsiders are different in kind from those which they have with each other, and the differences in degree that may mark their own relationships sink into unimportance and are barely recognized in the dogma of the group. This is the more true since members of a matrilineal group act alone on very few occasions. Their corporate activity takes place within situations where outsiders are also present. At a funeral, and in subsequent mourning ceremonies, all those living in one neighbourhood should participate. All attend, but the members of the matrilineal group concerned have special roles in the ceremony. Girls' puberty ceremonies are occasions for general neighbourhood gatherings, but again the matrilineal group involved has a special role to play. Formerly when they gathered to protect a member, or to seek vengeance for some offence against him, they were posed as a united group against a similarly mobilized unit. People see themselves therefore in general as members of an undifferentiated body of matrilineal kinsmen, in contrast to the outsiders who are also present.'

The customary rules governing inheritance and the rights to seek asylum and protection are in conformity with the dogma of common unity. When a man or woman dies all members of his or her group have a right to share in the inheritance. Uterine siblings and their descendants have no greater rights than any other. Indeed uterine brothers, though they may inherit property from one another, should not inherit each other's wives. The bridewealth of a woman is not necessarily taken by her own mother's brother to the exclusion of classificatory mothers' brothers, though today there is some tendency for this to happen. Men accumulate property for their bridewealth by approaching any matrilineal relative whom they think likely to help them. In the past if one member killed another, no vengeance could be taken or compensation exacted, save by the *basyanausi* of the dead, for all members of the *basimukowa* were bound equally to the murderer and his victim.

The dogma of unity is also reflected in ritual. Each matrilineal group is thought to have a single body of ancestral spirits which may affect any member of the line and to which all members of the line have equal right of appeal. Any fully adult person may approach the ancestors on his own behalf. There are no ancestral shrines or localized foci for the cult. Instead the ancestors follow each person in his wanderings.

Matrilineal groups are thus in their nature undifferentiated. They are also usually small, which is probably a reflection of the first condition. An undifferentiated body quickly grows unwieldy as it increases in size. To maintain any hope of common action, it must somehow shed a portion of its members. The fact that the group is also expected as a body to co-operate with various other matrilineal groups which have either begotten its children or which contain the children of its male members is also relevant. Small groups can co-operate in this manner without undue strain: large ones would find it either difficult or impossible to maintain such relationships unless a rigid system of preferential mating kept the number of other groups at a minimum. This, however, is not the Tonga solution. Their marriage rules force them to disperse their marriages and build up a diffuse network of kinship ties which in the past had its utility in maintaining peaceful relations over a local area.

To maintain this system, it is necessary for matrilineal groups to lose members from time to time. Mobility provides for this. Those who wander too far away to be able to maintain common rights and duties are automatically eliminated. Mobility is an individual matter as a rule, rather than the migration of a closely related segment of the group.

Quarrels or personal difficulties also lead people to disregard their common membership within a kinship group, even though they remain within the same locality, but this again is a matter of persons rather than of sections. Two brothers in a Mujika village seemed to have no matrilineal group. The daughter of one said that formerly they had been members of a group but that they were so cantankerous that their relatives ceased to seek them: they were no longer summoned for funerals, no one sought assistance from them, no one visited them. The daughter ended philosophically, 'So now my father has no *mukowa*, but since he has wealth he has a *mukowa* for wealth helps in the same way as do kinsmen.'

John, another Mujika man, complained that his classificatory brother David 'is not my own relative. He is only of my clan'. A bystander asked how this could be and John replied, 'I say this because he does not help me in the field or with any other work. He wanders from village to village. He has no wife, but when he comes to live with me he does not help with the work. Therefore I say he is not my relative. He who does not help me is not my relative. If he is sued, I will not help him because he does not help me.' The bystander commented, 'You say this because David is poor. If he were rich, you would not say it. If he were a good man, you would not say it.' John agreed, 'Yes, if he were a good man, I would not talk like this.' Then his son spoke up, 'My father cannot say that David is not his own kinsman. Why, when one of David's brothers died my father was the one who did the purification!'

Here we find what is probably the basic Tonga formulation: those who help one another in a particular fashion are relatives, and those who do not so help one another are to be considered unrelated. Matrilineal groups may therefore break apart either on the score of distance or on the score of personal differences. So long as the memory of the former alliance persists, it is possible for people to re-establish their common membership within a single group. Where two bodies of kindred have evolved, the split is likely to remain permanent. Then people say, 'Once we were one. Now it looks as though we are different.'

To maintain the ties of kinship, it is not necessary for all, or even the major portion of a group, to remain in close proximity with one another. The Tonga have never believed that kinsmen should live together in a single village, or even within a single neighbourhood. There are geographical limits beyond which co-operation becomes impossible but within these limits kinsmen are free to disperse without detriment to their common solidarity. Indeed, the frequency of localized droughts accompanied by local crop failures turns the dispersal of kindred into an asset rather than a liability, for each person is provided with a claim on food produced in other localities. When a hunger year strikes, those with money or goods for exchange can buy food if they can find people with a surplus. Those without resources can depend only upon their personal claims upon others. They can beg from kinsmen with the expectation that they will be fed so long as there is food to be divided. In the past, they could approach fellow clansmen or clan joking-partners, though with less assurance of support. Failing these, their only resource once lay in selling themselves or some child into slavery in return for grain. Today the Administration arranges for the importation and subsidized sale of grain in times of general famine, but in a hunger year people still walk many miles to beg from kinsmen living in villages where there is some hope of finding food. These may grumble, but so long as anything remains in their granaries or they have funds with which to purchase grain, they are likely to divide with their indigent relatives, knowing that another year may reduce them to the same straits.

Prior to the 1920s, when the Tonga began to sell grain, they did not plant to obtain large surpluses of food. In a normal year, a neighbourhood or local area produced enough to be self-sufficient and had some slight excess above its urgent needs. This was not enough to cater for all from a near-by area who might be reduced to seeking food. If these scattered out through the surrounding country, they could be maintained. Moreover, it was impossible to predict that certain localities would have a surplus if another was short of food. For sheer survival over the years, it was best to have claims on residents in many different neighbourhoods. In these circumstances, a dispersed kindred was less vulnerable than a highly concentrated one, and in a better position to weather local periods of dearth. When real famine struck, of course, many died. Only those tough enough to survive on what could be grubbed from the bush were left, and they might have wandered far from their original homes in the frantic search for food. The history of a local section of a matrilineal group quite frequently begins, 'So-and-so came here to escape the famine in such-and-such a place. He liked it here and decided to stay. Then others followed him.'

Men depended upon their kinsmen rather than their neighbours to protect their interests against attack and to help to press their claims against other men, but so long as they stayed within the general area in which people were bound together by various ties of consanguineal and affinal relationship, they were usually safe enough. Disputes had to be settled peaceably by arbitration, for too many people including the disputants were affected by the resulting disruption of ordinary life if violence broke out. Only those living far apart could afford to attack one another. Older people constantly stress the necessity of staying within the area within which general amity prevailed. They stressed that marriages ought to take place with people belonging to kinship groups with which previous marriages had been contracted as this offered protection to the spouse who otherwise settled among strangers.

Men and women who drifted beyond the effective range of their kinship ties were lost to their matrilineal groups, as their kinsmen were not prepared to venture into strange territory to avenge the misfortunes of those who would have been wiser to remain near at hand. The obligation of mutual protection disappeared when intervening miles made it unlikely that the principle of mutual responsibility would be applied. Those who settled in remote areas had the task of building up around them a new network of ties to secure their position within the set of neighbourhoods with which they were now associated. At first they might place themselves under the protection of a local leader as semi-dependants, then develop a set of affinal ties, and in the next generation find themselves again with a matrilineal group related to others in the community through claims upon paternal groups.

Once this was done, they were again secure and could offer protection and hospitality to kinsmen who might follow them into the area. If all contact ceased, then within a generation or so, memory of their common origin was forgotten, kinship faded into clanship, and the area from which they originally sprang became alien territory where they ventured at their own risk unless protected by a brotherhood pact.

Clan and Matrilineal Groups. Clans and matrilineal groups have lost some of their functions in the new conditions of life, but no Tonga is likely to deny their importance even at the present time. Every Tonga past the age of early childhood knows his clan. Even the most emancipated Tonga maintain that it is wrong to marry within the clan. It is also felt to be necessary for every person to belong to a clan; for, in the event that no kinsmen are available, clansmen can be co-opted to perform kinship roles. Most foreign Africans who settle in the District come from tribes which also have clans, and they are able to equate their clans with those already represented in the area. They thus create quasi-kinship links with their neighbours and are fitted more readily into the society. When a Tonga marries a foreign woman, she and her children are thus fitted into the local system and find clansmen to fill the necessary kinship roles. Tonga who wander outside the District or who move into a portion of the District where they have no kinsmen, again turn to members of their clan who not only help to fill the roles of kinsmen on ceremonial occasions but also provide a focus from which to set about learning the intricacies of the new community.

On the other hand, though the Tonga still stress the importance of having matrilineal kinsmen, the average size of the matrilineal group is decreasing. It is no longer necessary to have large bodies of kinsmen united for protection and assistance. At the same time. the increase in personal wealth has given an incentive towards narrowing the size of the group with a claim upon it to a few immediate kinsmen; and even their claims are regarded with considerable dissatisfaction by some of the more progressive Tonga who would like to shift to a system of familial inheritance in the interests of their own children. Nevertheless, wealth and power attract kinsmen. The largest matrilineal groups today are those which centre on one of the new class of wealthy farmers or on a chief where the prospect of inheritance holds the members together.

Note

[1] The term 'perpetual kinship' was first used by Cunnison, 1950, with reference to the organization of the inhabitants of the Luapula region where titles of village headmen and certain other hereditary titles are related to one another through a set genealogy. See also Mitchell, 1956, for a similar situation among the Yao of Nyasaland.

Chapter 2

INDIVIDUAL STATUS (WOMEN, MINORS, ALIENS, ETC.)

It is not possible to distinguish absolutely in customary law between the status of individuals and the status of groups: the overlap between the matter contained in this section and that which was included in the last one is unavoidable. The material contained here, however, has a different stress: it looks at the various social relationships existing within the community from the point of view of the individual member thereof. As such, it deals not only with those attributes which establish the status of each individual (capacity, age, sex, marital condition, social or ethnic origin) but also with the hierarchy of different statuses which exist within a particular community. (It is worth bearing in mind in this regard that, although some attention has been paid in the extracts quoted to several categories of inferior status, e.g. castes and slaves, there are of little or no significance within the context of contemporary African society).

The two authors whose works have provided the extracts contained in this section deal respectively with the categories of persons who have enhanced (e.g. chiefs) or defective capacity (e.g. women, minors, aliens, etc.). All these topics are, of course, encountered elsewhere in relation to the powers of individuals in other branches of the law (e.g. contract, torts, property, etc.).

T. O. Elias: The Nature of African Customary Law*

Status of the Individual

Having disposed of the fallacy that status attaches only to the clan or tribe, we may now examine the nature of the status which we claim for the individual.

Driberg's conception of status is that of a layman to whom everything pertaining to an African individual in his relation to society is a mark of status. Thus, he says:

'Every individual is born into a certain status relative to all other members of his community. It is not a personal status, as it might be in an individualistic society, and does not imply rank, but reciprocal obligations and benefits which he incurs as a member of the community. All his conduct is conditioned by his status, which is not a permanent one but changes with his age and experience and may be affected by the decrease of relatives and the inheritance of new responsibilities. (The principle of substitution is a correlative to status, since all of the same status in the community may at any time be called upon to act as a substitute for another member, a principle which, as we shall see, is of considerable importance in African legal theory).'[1]

Four aspects of this statement deserve comment:

(*a*) That every African is born into a status: In saying this Driberg is being better than his own argument; indeed, he is expressing a truism with even wider validity than he knew. In an African, as in the European or any other society that we know of, birth always determines status—for example, the status of being a British subject or a Bemba, a Yoruba or an Ashanti. In short, birth as a determinant of national status is a universal factor and is accordingly not a peculiar feature of African society.

(*b*) That this status 'does not imply rank, but reciprocal obligations and benefits

* T. O. Elias, *The Nature of African Customary Law*, Manchester University Press, 1956, pp. 95–109.

which he incurs as a member of the community': The difficulty here is to know what meaning to give to 'rank' in the present context. Rank as a result of social differentiation may in its literal sense be a mark of status, as showing the stratification of society into distinct groups with special rights and duties. But mere membership of a community considered as a community cannot, as Driberg implies here, confer a status upon the individual, unless indeed one accepts the otiose theory of group status implicit in the so-called unity of the clan.

Of course, the status of being 'a citizen of the British Empire and Commonwealth' comprehends the one hundred and twenty million odd souls who live in Great Britain and the colonial territories. But when we employ the word status in talking about the individuals in each country we usually refer to a special legal condition implying peculiar capacities and incapacities. Austin, it will be remembered, would ascribe status only to 'a narrow class of persons' detached from the bulk of the community and endowed with special 'rights and duties, capacities and incapacities'.

Perhaps the most workmanlike view is that of Allen who suggests that status is 'the condition of belonging to a particular class of persons to whom the law assigns certain peculiar legal capacities or incapacities or both'. Thus, to be said to have a status in the legal sense, an individual must belong to a special class within the community; he may but need not be placed in the group by the law, although he must not be able both to 'contract in' and to 'contract out' at his own free will; again, while a special status may be conferred on mental defectives or other incapacitated groups, it is not every group that enjoys a status in law.

(*c*) That it is not a personal status but that it is nevertheless not permanent in that it changes with the individual's age, experience and personal condition: This, to say the least of it, implies a contradiction in terms—the status is not personal but it changes with the change in personal conditions. Moreover, Driberg seems here to be confusing status with prestige.

In all African societies with no strong centralised political systems as well as in some with such systems, the institution of age-grades has important juridical functions. The puberty initiation rites, for example, may be the means in some societies of determining the legal capacity of the individual to marry, to become a warrior or to take part in certain other public activities of a social or legal character. Sometimes these rites are merely preparatory to some later public ceremony or display of certain personal attributes as among the Masai and the Zulu, on the successful performance or display of which alone may depend the conferment of a status requisite to prescribed forms of social participation.

Similarly, membership of such public institutions as the Ogboni (Secret) Societies among the Yorubas or the Poro (Secret) Societies among the Mende can and does confer authority upon its members to act as State police in certain circumstances and as courts of trial in others. On the other hand, there are innumerable other social groups which have no institutionalised legal functions of any kind which either confer mere prestige upon their members or exist only for their mutual benefit. These cannot confer any legal status on their members, although the courts will protect their ordinary rights if otherwise infringed.

(*d*) That 'the principle of substitution is a correlative to status, since all of the same status in the community may at any time be called upon to act as a substitution for another member': It does not seem quite clear what Driberg means by 'the principle of substitution'.

Firstly, it may mean the same thing as one aspect of the theory of the unity of the clan, whereby one member may be seized to answer for the default of another in relation to other clans. We have seen, however, that this is not a case of the simple substitution of one member for another.[2]

Secondly, it may mean the limited practice among some tribes, notably the Masai, by which a married member of an age-grade association may have sexual relations with an unrelated wife of another member of the same age-grade group.

Thirdly, it may mean the widely-prevalant practice in African societies according to which a member of a family or extended family who shows special aptitude in that capacity is deputed to act in law-suits in which other family members may happen to be involved from time to time. This champion-at-law, concerning whom we shall hear more in the chapter on the judicial process, is the African version of the modern British barrister-at-law or advocate. But, surely, one does not ordinarily conceive of such legal representation as 'a correlative to status'? And yet it seems that this is the real sense in which Driberg employs his principle of substitution, for he goes on a little later to give instances of this practice amongst the Mangbettu and the Chagga.[3]

We now see that neither the group nor just any individual of a community *ipso facto* enjoys a status in the strictly legal sense. In an African society, just as much as in an English one, the law makes certain arrangements for treating some groups differently from the rest of the community in the matter of rights and duties, capacities or incapacities or both, though the forms and rules of the particular arrangements are not the same in both societies. Thus English law gives a special status to the Sovereign, ambassadors, infants, lunatics, married women, aliens, convicts and others. In African law, the main categories we have to consider are kings and chiefs, women, infants, aliens, slaves, and castes.

1. *The king or chief.* It may at first seem that in societies with a hierarchical system of chieftaincy and particularly those in which there are kings at their heads, the rulers must necessarily be despots. The institution of kingship or chiefship is, except among certain tribes,[4] generally regarded as sacred in African society;[5] but no holder of either office is in the political thinking of the people above the law on that account. He has no divine right to dispense and suspend the law of the tribe, although there have been tyrants who have sometimes set the law at naught. But, by and large, an African king or chief is in theory at least a constitutional ruler. Thus Dr. Mair wrote:

'In most indigenous African societies, in the specific case of obedience to political authority, there were on the one hand recognised limitations to the exercise of authority—for the "absolute powers" of an African chief extended only to his personal relationships, not to interference with what was traditionally established as the normal conduct of life among his subjects and on the other recognised ways of expressing dissatisfaction. Thus, situations in which authority could become so oppressive that the advantages which it gave in the organisation of security, offensive warfare, justice, provision against famine, and the like, did not compensate for the toll demanded of the subject in tribute or services, were rare.'[6]

Certain well-defined prerogatives often attach to the kingly or chiefly office, since the proper and effective exercise of authority would be impossible without them in any human society with a system of monarchical rule. But the council of elders and notables acting as a kind of cabinet ensures that the king's doings do not run counter to accepted standards of propriety; and a king or chief, who exceeds his legitimate powers and proves unamenable to such discipline, may be deposed, or is sometimes asked to commit voluntary suicide, or is put to death by the unanimous verdict of public opinion. In these cases, the council of elders or some powerful secret society made up of the chief's coevals often acts as a court of trial before his execution.

It may be added that any individual in the realm can aspire to the highest office that is not strictly hereditary. Members of the established ruling 'houses' are normally entitled to become chiefs, local or paramount; and also, war-chieftaincies are often created for those deserving of public distinction but who are not of the ruling houses. Even slaves are known to have become war-chiefs in many communities.

2. *Women.* It is a notorious fact that women in African, as in even many a modern, society play little if any part in public life. Their place is in the home, looking after their husbands and children. This somewhat restricted sphere of a woman's social functions is not as is often supposed, due to the fact that so-called 'bride-price' is paid on them by their prospective husbands before marriage. Such a payment is not a purchase money for the woman, any more than the now obsolescent[7] English system of a prospective wife's father's dowry payment to the husband at marriage can be described as the purchase of a husband for her. Hilde Thurnwald, herself a European woman who had studied East African peoples, wrote:

'Considering these circumstances, it becomes obvious that the paying of the bride-price cannot be regarded in the same way as the rationalistic purchase of a commodity or be compared with the acquisition of a slave. The idea of such a "purchase" has been absent even in the previous epochs; it is lacking in the modern times, too, when money is more often given for payments in kind.'[8]

The position of women can, therefore, only be the result of the particular mode of ordering social, economic and even military affairs in a given African society. Thus, the Amazons of Dahomey, redoubtable women warriors, left the care of the household chores to their effeminate husbands whilst they waged their formidable wars of conquest against tribal enemies.[9] Even where women did not occupy such a dominating position, we find that their lot has never been other than reasonably wholesome. 'Woman's life is passed differently from that of the men and has its own sphere, but the woman's position among most tribes cannot be regarded as depressed or slavish. Indeed, the mothers, who possess a moral force as guardians of the tribal traditions, often wield considerable influence over the fate of their people.'[10]

In Uganda, for example, we notice the pre-eminence of the queen dowager of the Baganda who often reigns in her own court. The king of the Bakuba, although commonly regarded by his people as the incarnation of the supreme diety, yields precedence to his mother whose prerogative it is to address him first—a local etiquette denoting her temporal superiority.[11] In many African households the woman is usually, though not always, the mistress of the family.[12] Her predominance is unquestionable in those social organisations which have the matrilineal and matrilocal systems of kinship arrangement, since the husband is then generally in a position of dependence upon the wife's family. The man's position is, however, often better where the kinship system is matrilineal but marriage is patrilocal (as among the Ashanti, for instance), although even here the woman retains and often embarrassingly asserts her independence of her husband.[13] The children of such marriages look upon, or until recently used to look upon, their maternal uncles as more important than their fathers.[14]

But, as Lowie pertinently remarks, we must guard against the tendency to confuse the multilateral forms of a woman's social and legal relations within a given African community. 'First of all, it should be noted that the treatment of woman is one thing, her legal status another, her opportunities for public activity still another, while the character and extent of her labours belong again to a distinct category.'[15] In the matter of status, then, a married woman can among the majority of African peoples hold a portion of the family land, particularly in such agricultural communities as favour farmwork for women. In urban areas, she is entitled to have a portion of the family house allotted to her so that she can reside there and otherwise deal with it as her brothers can.

Among trading communities, women are normally liable for their personal debts and other defaults to others; and they may themselves sue others for these. But, for household or other family requirements, it seems that on the whole the husbands are usually held liable in their position as the breadwinners of the family. The husbands will, however, often deny liability for debts incurred by their wives for ordinary personal effects and may often suspect the suppliers (if these be men) of adultery with such wives: no man who is not a blood relation ought to furnish a married woman with such chattels without the knowledge and concurrence of the husband.

It appears, also, that except in matrimonial causes, such as divorce on the grounds of cruelty, adultery or impotence, husband and wife can hardly sue each other for the usual subjects of dispute between ordinary, independent individuals. Even in the matter of the repayment of the so-called 'bride-price', it is usually the wife's parents or her lover who are or is sued by the husband. In any case, it seems extremely doubtful whether the traditional African courts will entertain ordinary suits brought by one spouse against another during the subsistence of the marriage.

3. *Infants*. Infancy is a concept that has universal legal validity among all African societies, though the age at which it terminates naturally varies from one community to another. Particular ages entitle the individual to particular types of social participation in the various affairs of life, and legal capacity or incapacity accompanies certain ages. But almost everywhere one finds among the different societies the requirement that the attainment of puberty by the infant is the minimum condition for recognition as a member of his community. Thus, one sees that until the infant has performed the prescribed puberty rites, he or she is not legally entitled to get married; also, only passage through the puberty school can initiate one into the various age-grades proper.

Now, puberty is normally attained at between the ages of 14 and 16 for girls, and 16 and 18 for boys.[16] But in point of fact most communities insist on their girls waiting at least a little longer; while the compulsion to acquire the often high 'bride-price' or to participate in some military expedition or, in some communities, to organise raids for the boys, generally requires that marriage must take place at still more advanced ages. Sometimes, the puberty initiation ceremony is only a prelude to yet more ceremonies which alone fix the legal and social status of the growing infant. For instance, among the Masai,[17] every infant is expected to advance from boyhood to bachelorhood and from bachelorhood to the elder's estate. But there is no implication of superior and inferior caste as the basis of differentiation of the age-grades among the elders. Initiation makes him a warrior; two years later, he becomes an apprentice (a shaved one); at between the ages of 28 and 30 years[18] he figures as a full-fledged brave, gets married on leaving the bachelor's kraal, and so assumes the dignity of an elder. Similarly, the girls become known as 'novices' after the appearance of their first menses; a little thereafter, they are generally regarded as fully-grown women ready for marriage; they however continue to enjoy a distinct rank until they attain their menopause.

Among the Chagga,[19] initiation of girls takes place usually when they are 16 or older, and they marry as late as 20 or even later. At any rate, in 1935, the average marriage age was between 18 and 26 years.[20] We learn from our source also the interesting fact that before the Lindi dynasty Chagga girls used to get married at between 18 and 20 years of age but, when the Lindi family imposed their domination after the middle of the last century, they began to drag as many girls as they liked into marriage. The only way of discouraging this habit was for parents to betroth their girls very early, about the age of 9 or 10. After the fall of the Lindi dynasty, however, the marriage age went up again until it stood at 16 for 'pagan' girls. Early betrothal seems to have taken place also among the wa-Shambala and the wa-Gogo; and we are assured by Hilde Thurnwald: 'The girl's wish is more frequently taken into account than generally conceded as true. . . . The girl is expressly consulted and her wish respected. . . . If not, the girl considers her self-respect impaired and may even commit suicide from loss of prestige.'[21]

Further instances[22] could be given of the practices among other African communities but probably little useful purpose would be served thereby. What stands out from the preceding analysis is that for capacity to marry and perhaps to do certain other legal acts, the attainment of puberty is a necessary minimum condition. Infants often have to wait, however, before they are fully received into adulthood. It may not be far wide of the mark to add that, so long as they remain unmarried and attached to the parents' home, they are for all practical purposes regarded as infants. The parents are still responsible to others for their good behaviour as well as for liabilities to others, though exceptional circumstances may warrant a different inference. Where, however, they get married but remain with the parents, the new status of matrimony will usually mean the assumption of full legal capacity by the infants.

It will have become clear by now that age plays at least as important a part in African society as it does in the English or any other human society. The means employed for social differentiation by age varies, however, in different societies. The absence of official records in traditional African societies has led to the formality of public initiation rites for groups of approximate coevals at various levels of the social strata. The public has always been the best witness to these age ceremonies on which the individual's social and legal standing in the community so largely depends. Without such symbolic acts of public testimony it would often have been difficult to ascertain when or whether an individual had reached the legal age to marry, to become a warrior, or to stand for election into such important public bodies as the so-called secret societies with definite political and juridical functions.

Although age-classes play such an important part in social life, it would nevertheless be wrong to imagine that membership of every such group necessarily confers a legal status upon the individual.[23] The various coming-of-age ceremonies must, therefore, be carefully distinguished from those that are merely designed to celebrate the formal inauguration of cultural, religious or social clubs—all being forms of the social instinct for masculine gregariousness.

4. *Aliens.* It has been frequently asserted with some truth that the African customary law of a tribe applies only to its members. Thus, Driberg emphasises: 'Law is the possession and privilege of a restricted group.' He goes on to insist that the scope and

protection of this law extend only to members of the group. But he concedes that strangers are often assimilated with the group by the rules of hospitality, the protection of friends, inter-marriage, and inter-tribal associations, all of which generally make it possible for members of the group to plead the strangers' cause in a vicarious capacity. But, instead of going on to argue that African law is, nevertheless, different from 'European' law in this respect, what Driberg might usefully have added is that most if not all customary legal systems, as the English legal system, for example, make their own legal arrangements for the formal incorporation of aliens with the indigenous community.

The requirement in the African situation is that the stranger must have been previously introduced to the chief or elders of the district, must have resided with his host for such period as would enable the elders to judge of his general suitability for membership of the group, and should then be formally adopted by the chief and his council of elders at a small public ceremony witnessed by as many people as care to be present. Thereafter, he becomes a full member of the community, subject alike to its law and custom and to the normal privileges and responsibilities of its membership. This is, of course, the procedure for permanent naturalisation of stranger immigrants into the tribe.[24]

It does not mean that aliens on casual visits among the members of a tribe are without legal protection. Indeed, so meticulously observed are the rules of hospitality that persons from the king down to the merest peasant in the community will go out of their way to protect the life and property of all friendly aliens during the sojourn of the latter in their midst. If they err at all, it is in their over-anxious tendency to favour the foreigner in many disputes with members of the host community. But he will be given no quarter if he wantonly commits a flagrant breach of the laws of hospitality or of tribal rules of a solemn character. The ultimate fate which awaits him depends on the circumstances of his temporary visit to the group, his opportunities of knowing the enormity of his crime and his general disposition before and at the trial.

5. *Slaves.*[25] In discussing the status of slavery in African society, a necessary distinction must be made between slaves who were captured in inter-tribal wars and those who gave themselves into the bondage[26] of creditors for unpaid debts either incurred by themselves or by a relative. In the latter case but not in the former, the bondsman or bondswoman retained the normal attributes of a member of the community except in matters likely to prejudice the creditor's rights to the recovery of his debt. In some societies the personal services of the bonded person were reckoned towards the eventual liquidation of the debt; in others, they were not. But the creditor was ever under a duty to treat the bonded as he would a member of his own family, and the instances were numberless in which the bondage ended abruptly in marriage between a male creditor and a bondswoman or between a female creditor and a bondsman. Where marriage did not supervene the bonded person either worked off his redemption or was ransomed by a relative or friend paying his debt.

In the case of war captives practice differs in the various African communities. Some bluntly refused to make slaves of fellow human beings merely as a result of the accident of war, and the captives were either immediately absorbed into the conquering community or immediately released to go where they listed. But many communities in East, Central and West Africa took war slaves whom they usually treated rather less favourably than bondsmen, at least at the beginning. The relationship between master and slave was not one of abject degradation but one of keeping each other at arm's length until the slave's character and ability, or lack of these, should decide whether his future lay in assimilation into the master's household or whether he should, if still young and virile, be sold off. In nearly all cases they were on first acquistion given portions of their masters' family land for their personal exploitation, while they served the masters by assisting in the cultivation of the latters' farms on a certain number of days per week.

The master's powers seem limited to reasonable chastisement of young slaves or sale of old ones if they could still fetch any money. Nowhere was there a legal right in a master to kill his innocent slave, although masters sometimes abused their powers. On the other hand, it was very frequent that slaves were adopted into their masters' families and, by dint of hard work and honest solicitude for the welfare of their masters and of the latter's families, they often became heads of such families in course of time.[27] It was not unusual for slaves or their descendants to become chiefs in communities with a non-hereditary chieftaincy system. The position subsequently attained in society accordingly depended very often on his own innate resourcefulness, character and ability.

It may be remarked in passing that these two forms of customary slavery are now as dead as the Dodo in all the British territories in Africa, with which we are immediately concerned. They were formally abrogated, wherever they still existed, by means of several Abolition of Slavery Ordinances and Proclamations.

6. *Caste.* It remains for us briefly to note the existence of a rare institution which had all the hall-marks of caste. Certain communities, usually of the non-centralised and atomistic type, regarded sections of their members as unclean pariahs with whom it was considered degrading to associate in the normal intercourse of daily life Of course, marriage with them was completely forbidden. Among the Ibos of Nigeria they were known as 'Osu',[28] and it is certainly strange that so democratic and equalitarian a people should have abandoned certain of their number to such an abject status. Among the Masai, where they formed guilds or sibs of blacksmiths, these were segregated from the rest of the community though such a martial community was to a great extent dependent on these untouchables for their weapons.[29]

By a strange coincidence, and this is as much as one can say in the absence of positive evidence as to a possible common origin, both the Ibo and the Masai social and political organisations have no strong centralised political authorities in the persons of kings or chiefs, but both have only spiritual functionaries who are more of tribal saints than rulers, and who rarely wield any judicial or other temporal power. Both place a premium on the dignity of the individual to a remarkable degree. But, strange to relate, both suffer in their democratic arrangements the existence of this curious phenomenon of caste.

It does not seem, however, that members of the caste in either type of social organisation are really prejudiced in many ways. They are quite free to pursue their trade, to acquire land and other forms of property, to get married among themselves and rear their own children, and generally to be left unmolested by their more fortunate but contemptuous fellow tribesmen. The one serious disability is the stigma of social inferiority which operates legally to forbid intermarriage between them and the rest of the community. The only opportunity for intercourse with the rest is the economic one forced upon the 'superior' majority by the need for trade or purchase of the goods in the making of which members of the caste excel.

It should be interesting to know how disputes between the full citizens and these esser breeds, which are bound to arise out of even this limited intercourse, are settled.[30] It is not difficult to imagine that the democratic instinct of the leaders of the community would dispose them to accord members of the caste in such disputes at least a modicum of their economic rights.

Notes

[1] P. 232 of his article entitled 'African Conception of Law' in the *Journal of Comparative Legislation and International Law*, Nov., 1934.

[2] See also p. 8, *supra*.

[3] *Journal of Comparative Legislation and International Law*, Nov., 1934, p. 232.

[4] E.g. the Olubadans among the Yorubas of Ibadan, have never been regarded as sacred; also, the chiefly office among the Mendes of Sierra Leone has no sacred character.

[5] K. A. Busia, *The Role of the Chief in the Modern Political System of Ashanti.*

[6] L. P. Mair, *Native Policies in Africa*, p. 271; also her 'Chieftainship in Modern Africa' in *Africa*, 1937, Vol. X.

Sjoerd Hofstra, in his 'Personality and Differentiation in the Political Life of the Mende' in *Africa*, Vol. X, pp. 436–57, stressed that the chief's authority depended upon a genuine respect for and a sense of loyalty on the part of the subjects, which varied according to the personal qualities of the particular chief.

Malinowski, in *Crime and Custom in Savage Society*, p. 46: 'Even the chief . . . has to conform to strict norms and is bound by legal fetters. When he wants to declare war, organise an expedition, or celebrate a festivity, he must issue formal summons, publicly announce his will, deliberate with the notables, receive the tribute, services and assistance of his subjects in a ceremonial manner, and finally repay them according to a definite scale.'

[7] Though it is still the case that Personalty Settlement under a Trust for Sale (ss. 23–33 L.P.A., 1925) often secures the same end in English law.

[8] R. C. Thurnwald, *Black and White in East Africa*, p. 147.

'The Africans rightly defend themselves against the assertion of superficial European observers that women are bought and sold by them. If it were so, the woman would be the slave of the man, which is true neither in law nor in fact'—D. Westermann, *The African Today*, p. 125. See also Pts. I and II of *African Marriage Survey*, ed. by A. Phillips.

'The position of women in African society has often been misunderstood. It has often been assumed that a woman was merely a chattel with no rights and no authority of her own, and that *lobola* was, in the well-known words of Sir Harry Smith, "the sin of buying wives". The matter is not quite so simple as that and the effective status of some women in certain tribes and of all women at certain times in all tribes is considerable'—Prof. A. V. Murray in 'Education under Indirect Rule', pp. 227–68 of *Jnl. Roy. Afr. Soc.*, Vol. 34, 1935, p. 247.

[9] Be it remembered, too, that the monarchs of Dahomey were notorious tyrants in many ways.

[10] Thurnwald, *op. cit.*, p. 172.

[11] Lowie, *Primitive Society*, pp. 335–6.

[12] For a recent account of the role of women in the Bamenda agricultural communities of the Cameroons under United Kingdom Trust, see P. Kaberry, *Women of the Grassfields*, particularly Chs. 5 and 6.

[13] Perhaps we may be permitted to draw here the analogy of the husband–wife relationship between Portia and Bassanio in *The Merchant of Venice*. The same Portia that knelt so meekly at Bassanio's feet declaring her love and accepting his overlordship—

> *Happiest of all is that her gentle spirit*
> *Commits itself to yours to be directed*
> *As from her lord, her governor, her king.*

could, on the proper occasion, round so superbly on Shylock in the trial scene or even on Bassanio himself for parting with her keepsake ring.

[14] Rattray, *Ashanti Law and Constitution*, p. 41; Danquah, *Akan Laws and Customs*, pp. 153, 183 ff.

[15] Lowie, *Primitive Society*, p. 178.

[16] In Eire, Northern Ireland, Great Britain (until the 1929 Age of Marriage Act), and practically all European countries, the ages of marriage *are* 12 for a girl and 14 for a boy. Marriageable age in Great Britain is now 16 years (since 1929) for both boy and girl.

[17] Lowie, *ibid*, pp. 259, 265. Initiation involves circumcision for boys and clitoridectomy for girls.

[18] Among the Yorubas the age of marriage used to be 30: see Johnson, *History of the Yorubas*, pp. 100 ff.

[19] Thurnwald, *Black and White in East Africa* (1935), pp. 144–7.

[20] Among the Hottentots, the marriageable age was 18: see A. W. Hoernle, 'Certain Rites of Transition and the Conception of Nau Among the Hottentots' in *Harvard African Studies*, Cambridge, Vol. II (1918), pp. 67–8.

[21] Thurnwald, *ibid.*, pp. 146–7.

[22] E.g. among the Basuto most men marry at about the age of 23 to 26. The rich might marry earlier and the poor later. Women usually marry at between 18 and 24. (H. Ashton, *The Basuto*, p. 62.)

[23] One does not often realise how important age is in English law, for example, until one looks at some such facts as these:

(*a*) 3-year-olds must be paid for on public transport.

(*b*) 5-year-olds must go to school.

(*c*) 8-year-olds may now be prosecuted for crimes (below this age they are *doli incapax*).

(*d*) 14-year-olds may enter a 'public house' but may not drink; they now enter the category of 'Young Persons'. (For (*c*) and (*d*) see *Children and Young Persons Act*, 1938.)

(*e*) 15-year olds may now leave school.

(*f*) 16-year-olds may get married, subject to parental consent; they may also smoke in public, drive a motor-bicycle but not a motor-car, and be sent to Borstal.

(*g*) 17-year-olds cease to be 'Young Persons', may drive a motor-car, and be charged and tried for offences in courts for adults.

(*h*) 18-year-olds may drink in public, may be conscripted into the army, navy and air force; and may be hanged for treason or murder.

(*i*) 21-year-olds have full legal capacity—may marry without parents' consent, are responsible for own debts, and may vote at elections.

[24] Not entirely dissimilar in essence from the requirements of the British Nationality Act, 1948, in the matter of application by foreigners in the United Kingdom for Certificate of Naturalisation.

[25] This is an example of a word which has quite reversed its meaning, for the Russian 'slava' means glory or fame and was applied to the peoples we now know as Slavs. But when captured

by the Huns they became bondsmen, and so the word 'slave' came into being to describe a servant without privilege.

[26] This is sometimes referred to as the Pawn System, and the bonded person is said to be 'pawned'.

[27] Lowie, *ibid*, p. 336: 'In Uganda a slave girl who bore children to a freeman became free together with her progeny, and sometimes, though not generally, her sons were permitted to inherit property.'

[28] Green, *Ibo Village Affairs*, pp. 23–4; Meek, *Law and Authority in a Nigerian Tribe*, pp. 31, 203–4. Also, W. R. G. Horton, 'The Ohu System of Slavery in a Northern Ibo Village-Group', an article in *Africa*, Vol. XXIV, No. 4, Oct., 1954, pp. 311–35, particularly pp. 316–17, 326-8, 334–5.

[29] Lowie, *op. cit.*, at pp. 336, 368.

[30] We are told that, among the Ibos, the 'Osu' are or may be a part of the mechanism whereby law and order are preserved' and that 'a big strong *osu* of Umueke sometimes assumed, or was given, mild police functions'—Green, *op. cit.*, pp. 50–1, 123.

J. van Tromp: Xhosa Law of Persons*

General Remarks

A. *Persons.* A human being is in SiXhosa termed *umntu.* This term is applied to any human being surviving its birth, and has no juridical significance. If still-born or deceased before its umbilical cord (imfesane) has been cut off, a child is not considered to have been an umntu.

An umntu is sometimes referred to as an *inja*, a dog, to show the relationship of legal dependency existing between Chief and subject, or between father and child. The word inja is used to denote both the responsibility of the father for the torts or misdemeanours of his child, and the lack of capacity of the child to acquire and maintain rights for itself: Inja yakho, i bambela wena (inja i bambela umniniwe): the dog catches for its master. When used of the relations between chief and subject, it denotes the power of the Chief over his subject.

A human being, umntu, only gradually acquires the full legal status, according to his development in life.

According to Xhosa Law there are two stages in the life of a person which mark off his legal status. These stages are:

(i) When he has reached the age of puberty, and undergoes the *initiation ceremony* (ukwaluka kwa makwenkwe),

(ii) Marriage.

These two stages cover three periods: from birth to initiation; from initiation to marriage; from marriage onwards, as will be described below.

B. *Differentiation of legal status according to age.* Before we describe how the legal status of a human being increases according to his development it is necessary to note that under Proclamation 112 of 1879, Section 39, 'All persons, male or female, when they shall attain, or who have attained, the full age of twenty-one years, shall be deemed to have attained the legal age of majority.' This is not so in Xhosa Law. The idea of majority and minority as being dependent on the attainment of a certain number of years is foreign to the Xhosa mind. Where I, nevertheless, use the terms minority and majority, I do so in the sense in which the ideas are understood in Xhosa Law and not in Roman Dutch Law.

1. The first period, from birth to initiation, may be divided into two stages:

(*a*) from birth to the time when he is capable of herding the cattle, and

(*b*) from the cattle-herding stage to initiation.

(a) *The male:* From birth to about six or seven years, that is when he begins to herd, a boy is not considered to have 'eyes to see', *that is, to do anything wrong:* 'A yi ka tungululi'[1] he has not had his eyes opened. He cannot distinguish between right and wrong nor can he see his danger. If he should commit a wrong, e.g. allowing cattle to stray into the lands, or burning the veld, he is punished by the injured party or his parents and the matter is over. Where the mischief results in damage, the father or lawful guardian of the

* J. van Tromp, *Xhosa Law of Persons*, Juta & Co. Ltd., 1947, pp. 1–16.

child is not responsible: 'A yi ka tungululi.' But the father or lawful guardian may, in order to preserve friendship and good relations, help to restore what has been damaged by his inja, child.

(b) The boy has an enhanced social status from the cattle-herding stage to initiation. He is now considered to have more experience and better judgment, and is allowed to herd cattle and milk the cows. He has to do light jobs at the kraal (umzi), and help with the cultivation of the lands. His legal status, however, has not increased. From birth to the cattle-herding stage, and from this stage to initiation, the boy remains an *inkwenke,* a boy, and is in no way legally responsible for his actions though he may be punished by anyone who finds him committing a wrong. He has no hearing in any court, he cannot enter into a contract. If he receives anything, by labour or otherwise, it falls to the household property of the hut, indlu (house), of which he is an inmate. He cannot be betrothed or married for, as a rule, only persons who have undergone the initiation ceremony are considered ripe for marriage. The initiation is the ritual transition from boyhood (ubukwenkwe) to manhood (ubudoda).

During the seclusion period the initiates, *abakhwetha,* are treated like iinyamezane, wild animals. They are not considered to be abantu, human beings, with a status or a say. Corporal punishment is common but they have no redress. They are guarded by one or more amakankatha (a kind of male nurse), representing the fathers of the initiates. The fathers and not the amakankatha accept responsibility for the actions of the initiates. The amakankatha nurse the wounds of the boys.

2. On initiation the boy acquires the status of a man. His eyes are opened and now that he has undergone the initiation ceremony he is accepted as an *indoda,* man. He can accept presents which belong to him though these may be controlled by his father. He is ripe for marriage, can be betrothed and can enter into a valid marriage.

The day he comes out of the isutu (itonto, ipempe) or seclusion hut, while at the umzi of the umnin'umzi (owner of the seclusion hut) the act or ceremony of *ukusoka* (presenting gifts), also takes place. This is the final ceremony in which his father, family and friends[2] give him presents indicating his status, for these now become his own. Participation in the final ceremony is an essential for attaining the status of an indoda. For only then will he be an indoda in the true sense of the word. This became clear to me in a case where an umkhwetha was charged with theft. He was imprisoned[3] and felt much distressed about the matter, because he would not be able to attend the ceremonies on the final day, and this would, I was assured, affect his status. He could not rightly be considered an indoda although he had undergone all the previous ceremonies in connection with the initiation.

The short period from the time the abakwetha leave the isutu to the time they enter marriage, is an important one. They are called *amarwala;* sometimes abafana, meaning adolescents or young men. They can mix freely with the opposite sex, have sexual intercourse with amadikazi, loose women. In fact, in this irwala-period plans for a marriage are being started. Marriage is mainly a family affair and though the adolescent is allowed freedom in his choice, his father has a great say, especially with regard to the first wife he marries. Though he has the status of a man he is still under the control of his father as long as he is considered an inmate of his father's umzi.

Through initiation he attains greater rights and privileges. He takes part in his family court or inkundla[4] where he can, discreetly, question the parties. When needful he may act for his father. He can now be selected by the Chief for work, perhaps as an umsengi, one who milks and provides milk for the calabashes of the Chief. He may go to the Great Place (Komkulu) and attend the Chief's Court.

In social life he has a higher status. He can attend beer-drinks and feasts with other young men of more or less his own age. He will not be pushed aside at these feasts and be branded a 'kwedini' or child.

I met a middle-aged native undergoing this rite. He was married and had children.[5] The reason why he underwent the ceremony, he told me, was because he was treated like a kwedini by other amadoda. At beer-drinks or feasts he was pushed aside and told to go and enjoy himself with the amakwedini, boys. And for all this treatment, treatment amounting to insult, Xhosa Law affords no remedy. Not only men look down upon an uninitiated male and treat him with contempt, but also women.

Once he is circumcised and has undergone the initiation ceremony, he can also sacrifice to the ancestral spirits, *izinyanya.* For only men can sacrifice and speak to the ancestral spirits. He is now a potential kraalhead and may one day sacrifice for his children.

The amaXhosa even hold that an uncircumcised male—being a kwedini—cannot inherit. He must be treated as a minor. He cannot therefore succeed his father. The Courts probably would not uphold this view, for they accept all persons of 21 years or more as majors, and will allow an uninitiated son to succeed his father, if he has reached the age of 21 years—or even before.

3. Marriage gives an initiated male the full status of a member of his umzi and tribe. He has a say in the family court as well as in the Chief's Court. His word now carries more weight. His first wife having been sanctioned and lobolaed by his father, he may hereafter marry freely as many wives as he can afford to lobola. With the consent of his father he can build his own separate umzi, and thus become a kraalhead, umnin'-umzi. The father is then no longer legally responsible, according to Xhosa Law, for the deeds of his son, but public opinion urges him to help his son in case of difficulty, and because he is his son's father he sometimes pays the fine for his son. While the son remained in the umzi of his father, the latter was responsible. Now that the son has his own umzi he can acquire anything and what he acquires he acquires for his umzi. He can enter into any contractual obligation and is responsible for his own acts and for those of his wife and children.

From birth to marriage a female is under the guardianship of her father or his lawful heir and successor. Because she is a minor and a female, she cannot inherit. No female can in Xhosa Law become heir (indlamafa) or succeed her father or husband in his estate.

Puberty, marked off by the *intonjane* ceremony, brings a change in the female's social status. After the age of puberty the girl is taken more notice of, has a higher social status, can do more work, can take part in feasts where women are concerned and can now be betrothed and married.

The intonjane ceremony is a kind of initiation similar in object to that of males. It is customary for girls to undergo this ceremony before marriage, but a female may marry even if she has not undergone it, and no stigma will cling to her or to any of her children for neglecting it. When she reaches puberty she enters the domain of womanhood (ubufazi) and is now marriageable and ready to bear children.

Xhosa Law sanctions the intonjane ceremony and in certain cases insists that it shall be performed, for it is believed that upon its proper performance will depend successful maternity and the health of the children. Should the girl not have undergone this ceremony before marriage and certain mishaps, e.g. miscarriage (ukuphuma kwesisu) or the ill-health of the woman be ascribed to its non-performance, the father or lawful guardian of the woman is forced to take her back and put her through this ceremony at his own expense. In these circumstances the husband may also send his wife back to her people to put her through the ceremony and they may not refuse. Her family must support and maintain her and her baby, should she have one, while she is with them.[6]

It is well to note here that under Act No. 16 of 1891, Intonjane Dances are prohibited. The screening of the girl (woman), however, is not mentioned in this act and it may be taken that the legislature intended to abolish the accompanying dances only. To abolish the intonjane ceremony itself would be bad policy and in direct conflict with Xhosa Law.

Marriage changes the status of a woman, both socially and legally. She is now more respected and has greater authority and say among women in the affairs of the family. She has certain definite domestic rights and privileges. She is given and holds a piece of land to cultivate and to produce crops for her indlu. Until marriage she has no proprietary capacity and could not acquire anything for herself. After marriage, though she is under the guardianship of her husband, she has a proprietary capacity which, though limited makes it possible for her, among others, to own the *ubulunga* beast (inkomo yobulunga) and those cattle given to her by her family at the time of her marriage, though she must consult her husband if she wishes to alienate them. She can also acquire household property.

When a woman has reached the menopause she is considered in many respects like a man. This change affects mainly her social status. She can now sit in the inkundla of her husband. This she could previously not have done. She may freely speak to older men.

She has a say in the affairs of the umzi and her word is taken into consideration. She may now also go into and sweep that side of the indlu which is reserved for men. Because of all this a woman at this age is sometimes referred to as an indoda.

Widows seem to enjoy an even greater freedom. A widow has more say in the affairs of the umzi than she had during the life of her husband. The older she is, the greater her say. She may express her opinion, which is sometimes sought by the new umnin' umzi who has succeeded her husband, but her word cannot override his. Should a widow wish to return to her own people, she is at liberty to do so, but for dissolution of the marriage part of the lobola cattle must be returned to the deceased husband's umzi. When this is done she is free and again reverts to the guardianship of her father or his lawful heir and successor. She then is an *inkazana ya se khaya apha*, a woman of her father's umzi.

If she remains at the umzi of her deceased husband, the new umnin' umzi must care for her and maintain her.

C. *Differentiation of the legal status according to sex.* In no sense are men and women of the same status in Xhosa Law. A male becomes a major but a female remains a minor and remains under perpetual guardianship. Because she is a female she cannot inherit or become heir or successor to her father, husband or any other male. Females in general take no part in the political or administrative life of the tribe. They cannot become councillors or have a seat in any court. But Sarili, Paramount Chief of the amaXhosa, created a precedent to the contrary between 1858 and 1865, by appointing his hunch-backed daughter, Nogqoloza, chieftainess and ruler over a portion of the tribe. He furnished her with councillors (amaphakathi) and said she could be looked upon as an indoda. The tribe accepted Sarili's ruling.

Because of her sex the female has to observe certain rules and restrictions. She may not go into the ubuhlanti, cattle kraal, of her husband. While an umtshakazi, newly married wife, she must not walk through the inkundla but must keep close to the izindlu (huts). If she commits a breach of this custom she will be termed a bad woman and the public will turn against her. She must *hlonipha*, pay reverence to, her father-in-law and all male members related to her husband in the patrilineal line.[7] If she disobeys this rule she may be sent home and the dissolution of the marriage may result. It is true the husband also hloniphaes his mother-in-law, but the rule in his case is not strictly observed.

Certain work is done by women only, other work, again, is reserved for men. The division between the work of men and of women is a social affair and has no legal sanction. The female members of the umzi must gather the firewood; they must draw water and prepare the food for the men and the children. They must see that the huts are kept in order. Cutting grass for thatching and thatching itself are the work of the female sex. But at present men may be seen helping the women thatch. Women have to cultivate the lands, but this, too, is largely done by men, except the hoeing (ukuhlagula).

Men, on the other hand, are the warriors and hunters. They herd the cattle and milk the cows for no woman is allowed to do this. If women work with the cows they believe that some evil will befall them. Men slaughter the animals and also sacrifice to the izinyanya or ancestral spirits, though women may take part in the feasts—when not menstruating or pregnant.

Though a Xhosa female, on account of her sex, cannot in Xhosa Law, sue or be sued unassisted, she has a right of action, as was decided in the case of Noseki *vs.* Fubesi (1900) Henkel, 36, and quoted by Whitfield.[8] In this case it was decided: 'According to Native custom a woman has a right of action against her husband unassisted when the husband is alleged to be making an improper disposition of property belonging to her house.'

However, the 'right of action' does not mean that a woman may, in accordance with Xhosa Law, sue unassisted. She may have a right of action, but can exercise this right only with assistance in accordance with rules of Xhosa Law. Usually she is assisted by her eldest son or some male relative should her husband or lawful guardian not be in a position to do so.[9]

In Xhosa Law a *widow*, if she remains at the umzi of her deceased husband, is under the guardianship of the lawful heir and successor of the deceased husband. But here, too, our Courts have created a peculiar position. The Court has decided that every widow has the *right* to sue unassisted the guardian of her deceased husband's estate in order to protect herself and the rights of her children.[10] The principle relied on that a widow has a right of redress in her own name against the guardian as above, is not altogether contrary to Xhosa Law, for she may complain to the members of the deceased husband's family, or even to the headman. But she cannot sue the guardian in Court unassisted; she is a female, and a male, either one of the deceased husband's relatives or the headman, will have to appear on her behalf.

A widow may, according to the Native Appeal Court, sue the heir of her deceased husband for maintenance and support in cases where he neglects his duty. In Nosentyi *vs.* Makonza (1900) Henkel 37, it was said that every widow 'has a right of action, unassisted, against the guardian of her late husband's estate to protect herself, her children and property from improper administration by the heir.'[11] What is probably meant here is that a widow may sue unassisted. But even in this case a woman would be protected in Xhosa Law. Here, too, the principle as laid down in this case is not contrary to the spirit of Xhosa Law, which allows the woman to complain to the guardian, or to her husband's brothers who will take up the case, and finally the headman or the Chief, who will see that justice prevails. Therefore, that a woman has no remedy against the guardian if she is not afforded the right to sue unassisted, does not hold good in Xhosa Law.

The Courts have gone further and have given the female sex the same status and rights under certain conditions as an indoda. The Court has, for instance, accepted and established the right of a woman to sue for the return of her husband's property which has been spoliated, and also to interplead for her husband's property attached under a writ when the husband is absent 'and the wife has been left in charge of the kraal.'[12]

This is contrary to Xhosa Law, according to which a woman can never be in the position of an umnin' umzi, not even temporarily.

The husband always makes provision in case he goes away. If he has not done so then his nearest male relative or the headman is the person who will sue for any property belonging to her husband.

The passage quoted from the above case goes on: '. . . but the right of a woman to sue for the property belonging to her husband and which has never been in his possession has never been recognised by this Court.' This case seems to be self-contradictory. Surely this also is the property of the husband, and, if so, why in the light of what has been said in this case may the woman not sue?

D. *Differentiation of the legal status according to rank*. Rank is acquired by birth, appointment or wealth and affects the social status of a Xhosa, but it is only the rank by birth or appointment that plays an important part in the legal life of the amaXhosa.

There are roughly three classes distinguishable among the amaXhosa. They are formed by the Paramount Chief and his family; the minor (petty) chiefs, and lastly the common people (abantu abamnyama). The Paramount Chief, and the minor chiefs to a lesser degree, have certain rights and privileges which commoners do not possess.

It may be stated that slaves and other aboriginal inhabitants or subjected tribes generally, no longer form a separated class among the amaXhosa.

The Paramount Chief represents the whole tribe. 'All blood belongs to the Chief', and because of this he receives the *izizi* or blood money: a fine payable by a person who has physically injured or killed another. 'Under Native Law the right to claim damages for assault vested in the Chief—not in the individual concerned.'[13] The injured party, or his family in the case of manslaughter, has no claim to compensation, but the Chief (Kumkani, inkosi enkulu) may, and usually does, give the injured party or his family a portion of the fine.

This view was expressed and accepted by the Native Appeal Courts: 'Now according to Native Custom the person of each individual was the property of the Chief and any injury to the person or character of such individual was an offence against the Chief, punishable as a crime by fine. The Chief might, as an act of grace, award a portion of the fine to the injured person, who, however, had no right of action for damages.'[14]

Now the word or term 'property' used by the Court in this case is incorrect for it is not applicable to human beings in Xhosa Law. A human being, male or female, can never be a piece of property.

So also is the term 'character' wrongly inserted in '. . . and injury to the person or character of such individual. . . .' A person, if he is the umnin' umzi, or if he is the guardian of a female, can always institute an action when his own character or reputation, or the character or reputation of his daughter or wife has been injured. The fine goes to him and not to the Chief. The Chief has no legal rights to such a fine. But if the case is heard by the Chief's Court the injured party will always give the Chief a beast or two out of the fine he has received. It is only in cases of physical injury, or manslaughter, where blood has been spilt, that the Chief has a claim.

(a) *Is the Chief above law and order?* The Chief, in spite of his status, does not possess arbitrary power of life and death over his subjects. He cannot order the death of a person unless that person has been tried, or he has consulted his councillors (amaphakathi) and given them some proof of the person's dangerous character. The Chief will then insist that he would be acting in the interest of the tribe to have this person removed. The Chief respects the person and property of his subjects. He is bound by Xhosa customary law, and in maintaining this, he follows the advice of his Councillors and he is checked by his Councillors and public opinion.

The fear that he may lose some of his followers has a great effect on the actions of a Chief. If he should commit a crime or a breach resented by his people, his punishment may be tribal disintegration. His dissatisfied subjects may leave him and join the ranks of another Chief. This actually is what happened, I was told by old men both from among the Amandlambe and Amangqika, to a portion of Ngqika's tribe when Ngqika took Tutula, the wife of his uncle Ndlambe, as his wife. For, being the wife of his uncle, she was considered to be his 'mother', because an uncle is considered also to be a 'father'. The subjects of a Chief may even resort to civil war. If the sons of the Chief commit a crime, they will be rebuked by the Chief and the older Councillors. The sons may be found guilty but the imposing of punishment in their case is difficult. Should they not be *rehabilitated*, the people would refuse, when the time came, to acknowledge them as Chiefs and rulers.

(b) *Offences against the Chief.* Because of his rank an offence against the Chief is relatively greater and more serious than a similar offence against a commoner, umntu umnyama. If the Chief or one of his family is assaulted or insulted the guilty party is liable to have his property confiscated or he may even be killed.

(c) *Marriage of the Chief.* The Chief may marry any woman, and as many as he can afford to lobola, but the Great Wife must be of royal blood (u ne gazi) and sanctioned by the people. His people will contribute towards the ikhazi to lobola the Great Wife. He marries her in his capacity as representative of his tribe. She is *umfazi wesizwe*, the woman of the land; sometimes she is called 'the mother of the tribe'. The Chief gives more lobola for a woman than a commoner does.

A commoner may marry a girl of royal blood but has to give a greater ikhazi. It sometimes happens that a Chief sends one of his daughters by a minor wife to be married to a rich commoner who may not refuse and thereby slight the Chief, for he may take revenge and—eat up the rich commoner.

E. *Termination of a person's legal Status:* A person's legal status is terminated according to Xhosa Law:

(i) by death, and
(ii) by excommunication; but not by
(iii) long absence.

(i) Death terminates the existence of a person. He may be considered to continue to exist for religious purposes if he was the head of a family, because he will then be an inyanya, spirit, that forms a link between the living and the Great Power and other izinyanya, but this does not interest us at present. The question whether a deceased man is considered to exist for certain matrimonial customs like *ukungena*[15], does not arise here, for this is not a Xhosa custom and is not practised by the amaXhosa, who consider it to be incest, umbula, therefore a disgrace and punishable by fine.

When a person dies, especially in the case of a male, it must be reported by his family to the nearest isibonda (headman) or inkosi (petty or minor Chief) who in turn will report the matter to the Chief at the Great Place. The Chief must know when he loses a member of his tribe. There is as yet no registration of deaths among the amaXhosa.

(ii) A person ceases to exist for his own family and tribe when he is excommunicated, *ukucithwa*, by his father or his lawful guardian. If a son, after repeated warnings and chastisement from his father or lawful guardian, insists upon committing torts, misbehaving himself, disobeying the authority of his father or lawful guardian, publicly degrading his family after repeated remonstrations, and becoming a public danger, causing heavy loss to his family as a whole and to his father in particular, he may be excommunicated by adopting the proper and recognised procedure and thus be placed in the same position as if he were dead or had never existed at all.

It is also asserted that if a son goes away, never works for his parents, neglects them and refuses to come back, his father may also 'wash off' (ukuhlamba) his son.

The procedure for the father or lawful guardian to adopt is to discuss the whole question with his own family and in the family court. If the family court decides that the son has had opportunity enough to reform and that he is evidently becoming too heavy a burden and a dangerous subject the father will report the decision to the Chief, who has the final say.[16] Should the Chief think the son unworthy of any further care and protection and confirm the decision of the family court, the son is told to leave the tribal boundaries, or, if he refuses, he is driven away by force over the boundaries of the tribe. He is considered non-existent for his family and tribe, and forfeits everything he may have possessed.

It sometimes happens that an excommunicated son comes back and begs for pardon from his father or lawful guardian. If he is sincere and truly wishes to reform, he is again taken into the family circle by the consent of his father and the Chief. If he was the eldest son and general heir and successor to his father before he was excommunicated he will, now that he has come back and been accepted, still be the heir and successor to his father. Should he come back only after the death of his father, he will, some say, succeed his deceased father in spite of the fact that he was excommunicated. This hardly seems possible. The usual procedure for him is to apply to the Chief and to his father during the lifetime of the latter to rescind the order of excommunication. Whether he will, after the death of his father, be again taken into the family circle and become successor to his father, will depend upon circumstances and upon the decision of the Chief's Court.

(iii) The fact that a person has disappeared and is not heard of for a long period does not raise the presumption of death. If he is unmarried there is little to worry about. If, on the other hand, he is married and has a family, whether he lives within the precincts of his father's umzi or has established an umzi for himself with the consent of his father, and he disappears for a long period, his rights and obligations are temporarily transferred according to Xhosa Law to his lawful heir and successor until such time as he comes back or his family hears of his death and has proof thereof.

Should the man who has disappeared have no heir or next of kin in the male line, the Chief will appoint a fit and proper person to act in the absence of the person who has so disappeared.

Unless the man is proved to be dead his property may not be disposed of except in the case of necessity, as, for example, to maintain and support his family. But such cases are very uncommon among the amaXhosa, because if a person disappears his whereabouts are soon found out.

It is unusual for a man to go away for many years in order to work, leaving everything and everyone behind, and then unexpectedly to return after the lapse of many years. As soon as he returns he automatically takes charge of his property and effects and should there be a dispute, the Chief decides.

Notes

[1] 'Ukutungulula' is a word indicating a pup when it begins to open its eyes.

[2] At the ukusoka ceremony, everyone who wishes to give him a present gets up, congratulates him on becoming an indoda, and then presents him with a beast, a pig, a fowl, a blanket or the like.

[3] European Criminal Law is applicable to all persons in the Union, also to the Bantu.

[4] This word implies both the courtyard and the court itself.

[5] It is not uncommon for an uncircumcised man to marry and such males are not welcome sons-in-law. It is considered a disgrace.

[6] On one occasion I attended an intonjane ceremony of two married women. One had had two miscarriages and the other was continuously ailing. On the evidence of the igqira, doctor, the court of the women's family decided that these women should come back to undergo the ceremony. The one had a baby whom she took with her to her people's umzi where it was also cared for.

[7] See Soga: *The amaXhosa: Life and Customs*, p. 208.

[8] *South African Native Law*, p. 195.

[9] See also Whitfield: *South African Native Law*, p. 195.

[10] *Noveliti* vs. *Ntwayi* 1911 Henkel 170.

[11] See also: *Noseyi* vs. *S. Gobozana* (1908 Henkel) 124, where it is said that a widow has the right to maintain the interests of her children in the property of her late husband and she is therefore entitled to be heard.

[12] *Gxwalintloko Mpahlwa* vs. *Nolam Mcwaba* 1919 Dickinson & Meaker's Rep. 302, and a later decision *M. Toleni* vs. *Makamba* 1 P.H. 1940 R. 38, where it was emphatically stated that a woman does not control the stock in an estate.

[13] *H. Nkatali* vs. *M. Mjwacu and others*, 2 P.H. 1939 R. 46.

[14] *Richard Mbambo* vs. *Jack Swaai* 1931 N.C.A. 19.

[15] This custom is practised by the amaZulu, amaMpondo and cognate tribes, and means 'to go in unto'. Should a man die, his widow will be ngenaed (*gone in unto*) by the eldest brother, and the children born will be the children of the deceased husband of the widow. This custom is anathema to the amaXhosa. See: Soga: *The amaXhosa: Life and Customs*, p. 139, and *Tembani* vs. *Malindi and Another*, 2 P.H. 1944 R. 42.

[16] See: *Z. Mnengelwa* vs. *Mnengelwa* 1 P.H. 1942 R. 20. This is a case decided upon Basuto Custom, but holds good also for Xhosa Law.

Chapter 3

LEGITIMACY

Legitimacy is a controversial topic among writers on customary law. There is considerable debate as to whether there is any place in African law for the notion at all. It has frequently been argued that, strictly speaking, no child is considered illegitimate since its birth in or out of wedlock is irrelevant to its status in the community or its legal rights and duties. Such matters are determined by the acceptance of a child as a member of a family—and the only question which arises in customary law is *which* family it adheres to, that of its father or its maternal grandfather. This view seems to be widely accepted today, and it underlies the detailed examination of the subject which follows in the extracts given here, particularly those by *Cory* and *Holleman*. Both of these writers stress the connection between the payment of marriage consideration and 'legitimacy'. An interesting aspect of the African law of legitimacy is the concept of acknowledgement prevalent in Nigeria and referred to by *Nwogugu* in his more recent article on the contemporary law of Nigeria, an extract from which concludes this discussion.

H. Cory: Sukuma Law and Custom*

Legitimate Children

Children born in wedlock belong to their father.

NOTE: As a rule all the children living in a house receive the same treatment from the grown-up persons, whatever may be the reason for their membership in the family. For instance, a grandfather will pay school fees for the illegitimate child of his daughter as he would for one of his own sons. No discrimination is made between an illegitimate and a legitimate child, and this attitude is understandable if one considers that a legitimate child may become illegitimate and an illegitimate child may be legitimized by its father.

Should a father neglect his child, his kinsmen or the child's maternal relatives would strongly object. Very likely the child would run away to them and remain with them. If a father remarries after he has been divorced from his first wife and sees that her children are unhappy in the house, he will send them to his parents or to one of his married siblings.

Step-Children

A. If a child remains with its mother in the house of its step-father, it can never become an heir to the latter's property.

B. If the father remarries after a divorce from his first wife, in which he kept the children, these children retain their position as *nkuruwabo*,† etc., even if their step-mother gives birth to children.

Illegitimate Children

(*Ng'wana wa nda ya bu* or *ng'wana wa butende*)

1. *General rules.* Children not born in wedlock belong to the maternal family.

A. If the illegitimate child is a boy, he is entitled to a share in his maternal grandfather's estate.

* H. Cory, *Sukama Law and Custom*, Oxford University Press, 1953, pp. 89–93.

† First born son.

B. If the maternal grandfather has sons, the illegitimate child follows his maternal uncles in the sequence of heirs.

C. If the maternal grandfather has no sons, the illegitimate child becomes the *nkuruwabo* of his grandfather.

NOTE: If a father has only daughters, one of whom becomes pregnant without being married, he may not insist on finding the man who caused the pregnancy; he may wait and see whether the child is a boy, in which case he has obtained his *nkuruwabo*.

D. If the illegitimate child is a girl, the bridewealth for her is received by her maternal grandfather or his heirs.

D.C.'s Appeal 1/47. Ibadakuli (Shinyanga). *Wande d/o Nhola* v. *Nhola*.

Wande was the illegitimate daughter of Nhola who had never paid bridewealth for her mother. When Wande married, her bridewealth was received by her grandmother. Nhola took the cattle away from the old woman. At her grandmother's death, Wande, as her heir, claimed the cattle. The court held that the father had no right to keep the cattle and that he must hand them over to his illegitimate daughter.

2. *Legitimization* (*kikindikamata or kukwang'wana*). A father has the right to legitimize his illegitimate children at any time:

A. by paying bridewealth and marrying their mother;
B. by the payment of cattle for each child and compensation for rearing the child;
C. by paying bridewealth on behalf of an illegitimate son.

A. The lover may start negotiations about marriage and payment of bridewealth as soon as he is informed of the pregnancy. It is the custom everywhere for the father of the woman to accept the bridewealth and agree to the marriage, but he is not bound to do so.

B. The father can legitimize his children after he has broken off relations with their mother by making payments for each child as follows:

where the father or grandfather is a commoner	5 cattle
where the father or maternal grandfather is a village headman, regent, *munang'oma*,* direct descendant of a chief, or a deposed chief . .	6 ,,
where the father or the maternal grandfather of the child is a chief .	10 ,,

Only the man who has been named as father by the mother of the child and who has paid *misango*† has the right to legitimize the child.

It is within the discretion of the maternal family to accept or refuse the offer of the child's natural father.

The maternal family is entitled to compensation for the upbringing of the child. The amount of the compensation varies from two to ten head of cattle according to the sex of the child and its age when the father makes his offer of legitimization.

C. A special kind of legitimization, sometimes but not always recognized by the courts, may be effected by the father's payment of bridewealth on behalf of his illegitimate son. The son belongs to his maternal family, but if the latter agrees to the father paying bridewealth for him, the son becomes a member and heir of the paternal family.

D.C.'s Appeal 4/45. Ibadakuli (Shinyanga). *Shilinde* v. *Kibonela*.

Since his father (Gindo) had not paid bridewealth for his mother, Kibonela was illegitimate and belonged to his mother's family. When he wished to marry, his father, with the consent of the maternal family, paid bridewealth for him and thereby legitimized him. On Gindo's death the children of Kibonela inherited the property. Their right to do so was contested by Shilinde, a distant relative of Gindo; the court decided in favour of the children of Kibonela.

3. *Illegitimate child of an unmarried woman.* The man whom a woman names as father of her child must admit paternity, unless he can prove that he had no sexual intercourse with the woman.

* Hereditary councillor.

† Compensation payable for illegitimate pregnancy.

NOTE: Sexual intercourse with unmarried girls is considered natural and desirable, consequently the pregnancy does not cause embarrassment to the man or to the girl or her parents; the girl is not disgraced, and the birth of her child does not prejudice her chances of an early marriage. Every child is an asset and not a liability to the family to which it belongs.

If she has had many lovers, the one whom the woman names is the father of her child.

If the man insists that he has never had sexual intercourse with her and produces some sort of proof, the woman may be required to prove her assertion by giving details regarding place, hour, physical characteristics of the man, &c.

If the man named had intercourse with the woman within the period during which conception could have taken place, which is considered to be about two months, no argument about paternity can be admitted.

NOTE: A refusal to admit paternity was rare, even when proof of paternity was not beyond reasonable doubt. Although the man took upon him certain obligations, pride outweighed material considerations. To be chosen as the father of her child, especially by a young girl, was looked upon by the man himself and by the world as a proof of her feelings for him. Therefore, the man would not refuse to admit paternity if he had ever had sexual intercourse with the girl.

In recent times more cases of disputed paternity have come before the courts, possibly because girls now have more opportunities for taking lovers who are not Sukuma men. Investigation in such cases is becoming more thorough, especially if the suspected father is a stranger or has left the country.

If the woman names as father of her child a man who can prove the falsity of her statement, the question of paternity would be closed; the woman would not be allowed to name another man.

If an unmarried woman becomes pregnant, her father or, failing him, her nearest paternal relative, sends two relatives to the lover or his father who announce that the woman has named the lover as the father of her child. This procedure is called *kutwalilwa nda*, and takes place when the pregnancy becomes obvious. If the lover agrees he hands over an arrow or some tobacco as token of his consent.

NOTE: In some areas the pregnant woman is sent to her lover, accompanied by two friends. Thus the whole village becomes witness to the *kutwalilwa nda*. Sometimes the lover comes to live with the woman's family during her pregnancy (*kulela nda*). He helps in all kinds of work, but he gains nothing except that he lives as the husband of the pregnant woman. As soon as the woman gives birth to a child, he has to leave the house.

If the woman is living in her lover's house, no *kutwalilwa nda* takes place, but this does not affect the legal liability of the lover. It is considered obvious in this case which man is responsible for the pregnancy. If the lover wishes to deny paternity, it is up to him to prove his case. . . .

4. *Illegitimate child of a married woman*. If a wife has conceived a child during the absence of her husband, the latter can, after his return, either acknowledge the child as his own or refuse to do so, in which case the child is considered illegitimate and belongs to the wife's family.

NOTE: Nowadays the younger generation shows a tendency to be more strict in questions of paternity, and absent husbands after their return now make a lot of 'fuss' which the older generation considers excessive. The conservative element argues that the majority of absent husbands do not worry about providing for the maintenance of their wives at home. Absent husbands, moreover, do not keep their promises, made before departure, about the length of their absence from home. In view of these signs of negligence, the 'fuss' made on their return is disproportionate.

If the pregancy has been caused by a relative of the absent husband, it is the general custom to acknowledge the child as legitimate.

If a husband, after a lengthy absence from home, returns and finds that his wife is pregnant or has borne a child during his absence of which he cannot be the father, he must decide at once whether to acknowledge paternity of the child or not. If he has once acknowledged paternity and resumed married life, he cannot later disown the child.

NOTE: Cases have occurred—especially if the illegitimate child happens to be the only son and therefore the *nkuruwabo*—of a subsequent change of mind on the part of the husband. If the husband takes a second wife who has a child, or if his first wife later has a child, he may wish to have a son of his own as *nkuruwabo* and try to disown the son of another man.

If the husband after his return makes no decision and resumes married life, it is understood that he acknowledges paternity. If he disowns an unborn child or a child already born, he must do so before witnesses.

J. F. Holleman: Shona Customary Law*

Legitimacy and Paternal Responsibility

Introduction. Legitimacy in Shona Law has two aspects. The first concerns the question of paternal rights and duties, amongst which are the right to have custody of the child, the duty to sustain and protect it, the right to receive marriage compensation for a daughter and the duty to provide a wife for a son, and the duty to accept responsibility for the child's actions. The second aspect concerns the child's membership of the patrilineage and his right to succeed to the name and dignity of his father and other paternal ascendants.

Normally, when lawful marital relations exist between the child's parents, the child is fully legitimate: it suffers no legal disabilities, and legitimacy is, so to speak, a single indivisible concept. But when the child is born under irregular circumstances the two aspects become separate issues which need not necessarily coincide. Parental rights and duties will be determined by the question whether the child has been covered by the payment of cattle to its mother's family or its legal guardian. Lineage membership is determined by the question whether it has the same blood (*ropa*) as its legal father.

The discussion on legitimacy therefore falls into two parts. I shall first deal with the acquisition of parental rights. After that the position of various classes of children will be examined in order to ascertain whether they fail in either of the two aspects of legitimacy mentioned above.

Acquisition of Parental Rights. Parental rights to a child born of a lawfully married or betrothed woman are vested in its mother's husband or affianced groom by virtue of the affinition agreement between the two families; but if the child is an adulterine child of such a betrothed or married woman, the natural father may sometimes be allowed to obtain parental rights upon payment of a compensation (*maputiro, butiro*) to the legal guardian of the child.

Parental rights to a child born of an unmarried or not-betrothed woman are vested in its mother's family, but may be transferred to the natural father, either when the latter subsequently marries the mother, or upon his payment of *maputiro*.

The position regarding parental rights of a father to the children he has raised with his lawfully wedded or affianced wife needs little discussion. When the child is born, the professional midwife (*vanyamukuta*) and one or two elderly female relatives of the wife or husband who have assisted during the confinement, announce its birth by cheering (*kupururudza*), once when it is a boy, twice when it is a girl. It is the duty of the midwife to notify the husband[1] who is normally not present at the confinement.

There is no specific act or token by which a father recognizes his child, but when he comes to see his newly-born baby he has to give a token present (*cioneso*, from *kuona*, to see) to the midwife. Such a present is, however, also given by any relative or friend who wishes to see the baby. On the other hand, the refusal of a father to give *cioneso* is an indication that he denies his paternity and is not interested in the child. In one case which I witnessed this omission became a major issue. The defendant had refused to give the token and had not wanted to see the child he had raised by his affianced bride because he did not want to marry her. When the child (a girl) grew up and was about to be married, he suddenly claimed parental rights in order to collect her marriage cattle. He only succeeded in getting the child after he had confirmed his paternity by offering a concrete token (a half-crown piece) to the maternal relatives.

* J. F. Holleman, *Shona Customary Law*, Oxford University Press, Cape Town, 1952, pp. 242–259.

No name is given to a child until the umbilical cord has fallen off. Before this time it is referred to as *cirume* (little male) when a boy, or *majika* when a girl. Some people consider it the prerogative of the child's mother's mother (*mbuya*) to name the child, but in practice any close relative such as the mother, father or even father's sister may give it a name and it will depend on the circumstances which name will actually stick to the child. There is no particular ceremony or ritual connected with name-giving, but the birth of a child—especially when it is the first-born—may be the occasion for a common celebration amongst members of its mother's and father's family.

A child born in wedlock is under full control of its father and paternal family. It should be mentioned, however, that the father may have to relinquish his rights in favour of the maternal family if the marriage is subsequently dissolved and he has failed to meet his *rovoro* obligations.

I shall now deal with the acquisition of parental rights by a natural father to children he has raised by women other than his lawfully married wife or affianced bride.

(i) *Pre-marital children.* The person who has unlawfully impregnated an unmarried woman may obtain parental rights to his child either by marrying the woman or, if he refuses to marry her, by paying adequate compensation to her family. The first alternative is in every respect regarded as the most satisfactory. If the seducer is prepared to marry the woman there is seldom if ever any question of an additional compensation for unlawful impregnation, except that the woman's family may sustain their demand for a *mackorwa* or *mavunwa* (purification) animal. If an agreement regarding a marriage is reached before the child is born, the father's rights are covered by the normal marriage compensation payable to the woman's family. Owing to the particular conception of the affinition agreement the child is considered to have been born to lawfully 'married' parents even if it is born before the marriage has actually been contracted.

If the child is born before the affinition agreement has been reached, the parental rights are vested in the mother's family and are, in principle at least, only transferable to the natural father upon payment of *maputiro*. In practice, however, this time limit is not always strictly adhered to. When for some reasons or other the action against the seducer has not been settled by the time the child is born, the defendant may, if he subsequently agrees to marry the woman against a normal marriage compensation, be allowed to assume his right to the child without an additional payment of *maputiro*. On the other hand, when a defendant in the Wedza Reserve had first refused to marry the girl he had impregnated and had actually paid due compensation for unlawful impregnation and parental rights, he was required to pay full marriage compensation when he later—after he had impregnated her for the second time—decided to marry the girl.

Maputiro, the compensation covering parental rights to an unlawfully begotten child, should be distinguished from the damages (*muripo*) payable for unlawful impregnation—and also from the purification (*mackorwa*) animal which is not, strictly speaking, a legal issue—although these may in practice often seem to form a single issue. The position can be briefly outlined as follows: The offender who unlawfully impregnates an unmarried woman whom he refuses to marry, is legally obliged to pay *muripo* for the delict—and in cases of first pregnancy he has no choice but to pay the purification animal as well, so that the woman can be re-accepted in her parents' home. The payment of *muripo* is not in itself sufficient to establish the defendant's right to the child, but it confirms his natural paternity and enables him to claim parental rights by tendering *maputiro* to the woman's family. Once the woman's family have accepted compensation for the delict they cannot deny the defendant's right to claim the child if he offers *maputiro*, unless he is deemed to have forfeited his claim; neither can they force the defendant to press his claim if he does not want the child.

Normally when an action on account of pre-marital impregnation is brought against a seducer who is unwilling to marry the woman, it is taken for granted that he intends to press his claim to the child when he agrees to pay damages. Often no specific term is given to the compensation payable to the woman's family. The defendant merely promises to pay two or three head of cattle, and, unless specifically stated to be otherwise, this amount covers both damages for the delict and parental rights to the child. Assessors of the Rozwi court in the Narira Reserve stated, in fact, that in such cases the complainants were awarded a standard compensation of 'two head of cattle, whether or not the offender wants to take the child'.

If the defendant assumes custody of the child shortly after it is born, nothing more is payable. But if he leaves it in the care of its maternal grandparents for a considerable number of years he may be required to pay one (at the most two) head of cattle as compensation for its maintenance[2] before they allow him to take custody.

Under certain circumstances a natural father may forfeit his right to tender *maputiro*. The parents of a pre-maritally pregnant girl are obviously anxious to see her married before the child is born, and if the seducer is unwilling to marry her they may try to find another suitor who is prepared to give marriage compensation for her. The party who then marries the girl before her child is born, acquires parental rights to the child by virtue of the marriage agreement. It is a case of *ngombe ya vuya nouswa pa muromo*—'the cow comes with grass (wealth) in its mouth'. It is on the one hand an emergency measure to protect the name and interests of the woman, her family and the child, but on the other hand a perfectly honourable marriage which in no way affects the dignity of the husband. Indeed, most informants subscribed to the view expressed in the above phrase and were of the opinion that marrying such a woman was something of a windfall. The woman's husband may, if he wishes, transfer his parental rights to the natural father against payment of *maputiro*, but this is said to be very uncommon. The natural father has lost his right to claim the child, and it would be regarded as a serious affront if he were to offer *maputiro* to the woman's husband after the child had been born in wedlock.

The natural father may also forfeit his claim to the child if he fails to give *maputiro* before the child is married. Amongst the Hera probably more than elsewhere, it may happen that the defendant provides the purification animal and pays some compensation as *muripo* for unlawful impregnation, but delays paying *maputiro*, thus leaving the child after it is born with its maternal grandparents. The common excuse advanced for this delay is his inability to find the necessary cattle, but more often than not the real reason is that he wants to be certain of making a profitable transaction. It is generally admitted that a natural father 'is more interested in the child when it is a girl, than in a boy. For a daughter he can get marriage cattle but for a son he has to provide a wife.' And even when the child is born and proves to be a girl, he may hesitate to claim it until it has reached a marriageable age. Then he will claim his daughter by tendering *maputiro* in order to collect her marriage cattle. The maternal family apparently have no right to dispute his belated claim for parental control but are entitled to demand (apart from *maputiro*) adequate compensation (*uredzwa*, *marero*) for all the years they have looked after the child.

Amongst the Hera it is definitely stated that once the maternal family have concluded a valid affinition agreement in connexion with the child, her natural father can no longer claim custody by tendering *maputiro* (and *marero*). He is then debarred from receiving her marriage cattle. These go to her maternal family who will argue: 'She no longer belongs to us but to her husband.' On the other hand it is said that the maternal family cannot, without notifying the natural father, betroth the girl before she has reached a marriageable age (*kuputsira*, *kuzwarira*) because this is considered to be unfair to him. If, in such a case, they have failed to notify him he still has the right to claim her marriage cattle because he could not have foreseen such an early marriage agreement.

Generally speaking, however, a man is expected to assume parental control of his natural offspring as soon as possible, and public opinion takes a poor view of a father who, for obviously mercenary consideration, postpones pressing his claims until the last moment. The child's maternal family will therefore urge an early settlement of *maputiro*. In the southern Sabi Reserve, Hera informants stated that the maternal family of the child, having failed for many years to effect a final settlement, might try to force the issue by appealing to a tribal court. They would explain that the defendant had, despite their efforts, failed to make the necessary compensation, that his failure should be interpreted as evidence that he was no longer interested in the child he had unlawfully begotten, and that they (its maternal family) now wished to be free to arrange a marriage without running the risk that the father at the eleventh hour would come to offer *maputiro* and take charge of his daughter and marriage cattle. The court would then call upon the defendant to produce *maputiro* and *marero* immediately, and his failure to do so would debar him from any further action regarding his daughter or her marriage cattle. I could find no case in which this procedure had actually been adopted.

In the Wedza and Narira Reserves informants agree in principle that 'once the daughter belongs to another (that is, when she is formally engaged or married) her father cannot get her cattle if he has failed to give *maputiro*'. But it is doubtful if this rule is often rigidly enforced in practice. Instead of denying the father all further rights to his child, the court may decide to grant him the child, but require him to pay an exceptionally high compensation to the maternal family to punish him for his belated claim. This flexible attitude is clearly revealed in the following case (Wedza Reserve) which is reported extensively because of its characteristic treatment of the various issues involved.

Defendant Mudakwa, son of Cizengwe, had privately courted the daughter of Mashandure. When she became pregnant she fled (alone) to her lover's village. Mudakwa himself denied 'that the womb belonged to him', but when the girl threatened to strike him with her front skirt (*kupuma neshashiko*) his family accepted his responsibility and sent an intermediary to her family with five shillings as notification (and proposal) token (*rushewedzero, kudaidzira, kuridza mhere*). Mashandure accepted the token, believing that a marriage was about to be negotiated. He sent his *muzukuru* (sister's son) as his representative to collect the goats for the *masunggiro* purification ritual. The ritual was performed in the presence of members of both families. But when the marriage negotiations progressed Mudakwa again denied that he was responsible for the girl's condition and refused to marry her. Negotiations were then suspended. The girl gave birth to a daughter in due time at her parents' village and Mudakwa's family was notified by Mashandure that 'your wife has given birth to a child'.

When it became clear that there was no hope of a marriage, Mashandure demanded three head of cattle as compensation (*muripo*, and *maputiro*). Cizengwe, father of Mudakwa, agreed to pay them and actually pointed out the animals to be given for this purpose. There was some delay in collecting the cattle and when Mashandure later sent for them, his representative was told that 'Mudakwa had used the cattle to marry another wife'. When Cizengwe was told that he would have no right to the child unless he produced the cattle as he had promised, he offered one pound in cash as *rumiriro* ('wait for me'). Mashandure accepted the money and decided to wait. A year late Cizengwe was again pressed for payment of the cattle, and again he gave *rumiriro* (ten shillings). Then the girl eloped with another lover, Denere, who offered her parents full *rovoro* and married her. As there was no suitable nurse for the baby at her parents' home the young wife took her baby with her when she followed her husband to his village in the Sabi Reserve. Her parents no longer pursued their action against the family of her previous lover.

When the child was a full-grown girl (*mhandara*), Mudakwa, hearing that she was about to be married, hastened to Mashandure (the old man had died in the meantime but his eldest son had taken his name and position in the family) and offered nine pounds cash as *maputiro*, claiming custody of the daughter, who was still staying with her mother and step-father in the Sabi Reserve. Mashandure declined, telling Mudakwa that if he had any serious offer to make he should follow the customary procedure of employing an intermediary (*munyai*). Mudakwa left him and went straight to the Sabi Reserve, where he abducted his daughter. When the husband of the child's mother notified Mashandure, the latter brought a formal action against Mudakwa in the court of the Rozwi Chief, in whose territory the defendant lived.

Amongst those present at the hearing were: complainant Mashandure (the child's mother's brother), the child, her mother and step-father (Denere), defendant Mudakwa and senior members of his family.

The complainants' charge was to the effect that: defendant not only had failed to produce three head of cattle as *maputiro* as his family had promised, but had actually denied being the father of the child; now the child was about to be married, he had 'stolen' her in order to collect her marriage cattle.

Before the court, defendant denied that he had ever denounced his natural parentage of the child; he alleged that, apart from *masunggiro*, he had given four pounds as part-payment of *maputiro*; he stated that complainant had prevented him from paying the balance and had sent the child away to her mother in order to marry her off and collect marriage cattle himself. Defendant also maintained that he had not abducted the child but that she had on her own account and unescorted, made the long journey to her father's village after she had heard from her mother who her real father was.

The process was remarkable in more than one respect. After it had been proved that defendant had indeed abducted his daughter, the court (and members of the public) devoted a considerable time to the piling up of evidence that the defendant had on more than one occasion denied that he had fathered the child, in spite of the fact that his natural parentage was never seriously challenged by the complainants. When the child's mother was called to give evidence on this point she refused to do so 'because defendant had rejected her (some seventeen years ago) and had never compensated her for breach of promise' (*kuputira nhumbi*—to cover her love token). The court summarily ordered the defendant to pay her thirty shillings as *butiro*. The woman then stated that, although she had always maintained that the defendant was the 'owner of her womb', she did not now want him to take the child 'because he had never bought her any clothes'.

The court formally recognized the defendant as the father of the child by making him produce a half-crown piece to substantiate his statement that 'with this half-crown I declare that I am the father of this child'. The money was first handed to the child, who touched it, and then to the complainant, who pocketed it.

When the complainant queried the statement of the defendant that he had given four pounds as part-payment of the *maputiro* for the child, the court adjourned for a week in order to get evidence from the original intermediary (living some ninety miles away near Umtali) who was supposed to have transmitted the money to the complainant some twelve years ago. It took the court messenger a week's journey (costing the defendant thirty shillings) to bring back a written statement (written by the messenger himself and signed by the witness with a cross) saying that no such money had been given to him by the defendant. Only then did the court ask the complainant to state the amount of compensation he wanted.

Right through the hearing it was evident that neither the court nor the complainants ever seriously thought of disputing the defendant's claim to the child, but that they regarded his attitude and belated action as obviously opportunistic. But instead of arguing along these lines they piled up evidence to prove that the defendant was a liar and a person of disreputable character. Having thus paved the way for a stiff judgment the Chief declared: 'According to the law of my people you should now have paid three head of cattle for (*muripo* and) *maputiro*, and one head of cattle for *uredzwa* (maintenance). But because you have been so "proud" (i.e., cocky, troublesome) you must pay Mashandure six head of cattle'

Complainant then demanded another two pounds because 'I had to walk a long distance when I heard that my sister's child had been stolen'. And the child's mother obstinately said: 'I do not want to give my child (to the defendant) because I have brought her up. I want another thirty shillings because Mudakwa has never given any clothes to her.'

The Chief, to the defendant: 'Have you heard?'

The defendant said he had 'heard' and agreed to pay everything before taking the child to his village.

(ii) *Extra-marital children.* Parental rights to all children born during the subsistence of a valid affinition agreement are vested in the *vakuwasha*, whether or not such children have been raised by the affianced groom or husband. The basic principle regarding children born as the result of the woman's adultery, is expressed in the popular maxim *gomba hari nomwana*—'a lover has no child', or more precisely, the lover of a formally betrothed or wedded woman has no right to the child he has raised by her.

Paternity of a child is rarely queried when a woman has committed adultery while living with her husband, but inevitably becomes an issue when she conceives either before normal conjugal relations have been established, or during her husband's absence.

The *mukuwasha* whose affianced bride has been unlawfully impregnated by another, can rightfully claim the child if he actually marries the woman—in which case he is also entitled to receive damages for unlawful impregnation from the offender. Generally speaking he should not object to marrying the woman if she has repented and promised to remain faithful to him, because such a marriage in no way impairs his dignity. If the woman is handed over to her husband before the child is born, the previously mentioned phrase *ngombe ya vuya nouswa pa muromo* ('the cow comes with grass in its mouth') is applicable and expresses approval instead of ridicule.

If the *mukuwasha* refuses to marry his affianced bride on account of her adultery he can claim his *rovoro* back from the *tezwara*, but he is then usually considered to have relinquished both his right to the child and his right of action against the guilty third party. These rights have now passed into the hands of the *tezwara* who can either claim damages from the offender (*gomba*) or allow him to marry his daughter. If the *gomba*[3] marries the woman without undue delay he will normally be given the child without having to pay additional compensation. If he does not marry the woman but wants to have control of his natural offspring, he must pay the *tezwara* full compensation for unlawful sexual intercourse and a few head of cattle as *maputiro* (*kuputira mwana*, to cover the child), a total of about four or five head.[4]

Some Mbire informants stated that the *mukuwasha* does not necessarily lose his claim to the child even if he refuses to marry his adulterous bride. But in such cases the *tezwara* has the right to retain a few head of cattle when he returns the *rovoro*. I have found no case material to support this view.[5]

Sometimes the *mukuwasha* decides to marry his bride but refuses to take the child. Under such circumstances he may allow the lover to take the child against a few head of cattle. The compensation payable by the lover then comprises: two or three head of cattle as *muripo* for adultery, and two or three head as *maputiro* for the child. The total number seldom exceeds five head of cattle and is commonly referred to as *maputiro*.

Informants expressed the opinion that the mother of the child, perhaps more than anyone else, will in practice determine to whom the child will go in case of dispute. Knowing that the child, although legitimate because it is covered by the *rovoro* paid by the *vakuwasha*, may nevertheless suffer certain disabilities in the family of its legal father because it is of different blood, she may urge her husband to leave the child to its natural father where she hopes it will meet with less prejudice. If the husband fears that he may lose his wife altogether if he does not heed her wishes, he may allow the natural father to take the child 'so that he can keep his wife and raise his own children by her'.

> The same realistic view was expressed by the Rozwi court in connexion with a case in the Wedza Reserve. The court had granted the complainant three head of cattle when his affianced bride (at the time of hearing she had become his wedded wife) had been impregnated by the defendant. The woman promised to be faithful to her husband but insisted that the child be given to its natural father because her *murume* (husband) had told her that he did not care about a "*mwana wegomba* (lover's child)" '. The court assessors said they 'could not say anything because the rule was "*gomba hari nomwana*—a lover has no child" ', but discreetly suggested to the complainant that 'if he did not listen to his wife he might well expect trouble in the future'. The defendant said that he was prepared to give *maputiro* for the child. The final arrangement was that the defendant agreed to pay a total of four head of cattle to the complainant and that the child should be placed in the care of its maternal grandmother until it was big enough to follow its natural father.

Other exceptions to the rule that 'a lover has no child' may be found when a married woman conceives during the absence of her husband and when there can be no doubt about the paternity of the child. In such cases the husband's family may occasionally agree to grant the child to its natural father against *maputiro*. The court has, however, no power to make such an order and will act only as an arbitrator and public witness to any arrangement reached by the parties. For example:

> H, the wife of F, committed adultery with and was impregnated by M. She was staying at the time in her parents' village while her husband was away at his work. Her father reported the matter to C (husband's elder brother and head of the *vakuwasha*) and sued M before the court of the Rozani Chief (Wedza Reserve). Defendant M was told to pay four head of cattle to the husband's family, which he agreed to do on the condition that he could have the child when it was born, 'because the husband could not have been the father of the child'. The court said that it could not grant the child to him because it had to abide by the rule that 'a lover has no child'.

C, representing the husband's family, first refused to relinquish his right to the child, but the wife herself insisted that M and no one else had 'caused her womb', and threatened that she would become *nggozi* (malevolent spirit) if the child were not given to him. C then agreed to leave the child to M.

One peculiar aspect of this case is that the original amount of damages granted to the husband's family was not increased. As informants put it: 'It was first regarded as *muripo* but then became *maputiro*.'

The rights of children. We must now examine the rights of children with regard to the two aspects of legitimacy mentioned above, that is, first as members of a patrilineage, and then as dependants of their legal guardian and as claimants to his estate. Since females do not occupy a hereditary position in their patrilineage and normally cannot claim a share in the estate of their father (regardless of any other property rights which they may hold) the discussion will mainly be concerned with the rights of male children.

For the purposes of this section four classes of children are distinguished:

(*a*) children of lawfully married parents;
(*b*) children legitimized by their natural father by the customary *maputiro* compensation;
(*c*) adulterine children of a married woman under parental control of their mother's husband;
(*d*) children who are neither legitimized by their natural father nor recognized by their mother's husband.

(*a*) The first class of children comprises not only children conceived and born at a time when their parents were lawfully married, but also those born before the actual conclusion of their parents' marriage. Even when no formal affinition agreement has existed between the father's and mother's families at the time of birth, a satisfactory marriage agreement reached soon after the child is born, will normally transfer parental rights and control to the father's family, and the child is then considered to be fully legitimate as a matter of course. In Shona law the correct and logical sequence of legal events is of relatively minor importance in comparison with the ultimate, satisfactory result of the transaction.

The children belonging to this class are fully legitimate. They are members of their father's patrilineage and the sons are therefore entitled to succeed to the name and genealogical position of their father and other paternal ancestors. The father and paternal family exercise full control over the children, who owe them obedience and filial support. Inversely, the father is legally responsible for their actions and he must feed, clothe and shelter his children to the best of his ability as long as they are dependent upon him. When they are ill the father must search for a remedy or consult a diviner or herbalist. Both sons and daughters belong to the unity of their father's family and estate, which means that the daughters are regarded as providers of cattle in which the sons have the right to share. To a Shona man, full legitimacy primarily means that he is a potential successor to his father's name and genealogical position, and that he can claim marriage cattle from the paternal estate.

(*b*) The second class of children result from the illicit pre-marital or extra-marital relations of their mother. If the mother, at the time the child is born, is neither married nor formally betrothed, parental rights to the child are vested in the maternal family. But the child is nevertheless assumed to be a member of the lineage of its natural father because it has the latter's blood and—if a boy—has a potential right of succession in such a lineage. If the father pays the customary compensation (*maputiro*) to the maternal family (with or without additional compensation for maintenance) he can assume full parental control over the child.

If the child is born when the mother is legally betrothed or married to another than the natural father, parental rights are in principle vested in the family of the affianced groom or husband of the mother. In these cases the natural father has no rightful claim to the child but the legal guardian may sometimes agree to transfer parental rights to the natural father against the payment of *maputiro*.

Whenever the legal guardian has accepted *maputiro*, the child becomes the fully legitimate child of its natural father and, as far as the latter's patrilineage and estate are concerned, suffers no legal disabilities. When it is a boy he has the right to claim *rovoro* from his father's estate, and when he happens to be the first-born son (*danggwe, nevanje*) of his father, he has the right to succeed to his father's name after the latter's death. For example:

T 'gave a womb' to the wife of another man. During the action for adultery against T it appeared that the woman's husband did not want the child and was prepared to relinquish his rights in favour of T, who paid three head of cattle as *maputiro*. After the child was born (a boy, named Mondiwa) T assumed custody. In due time T provided Mondiwa with a wife, and when T died Mondiwa, being the first-born son, duly succeeded to his name and position.

In practice, however, there may be difficulties because the other children of the father may regard such an extra-marital son as an intruder, a *mwana wefambi* (child of a loose woman), and therefore resent his succession to their father's name. In one or two cases it appeared that the half-brothers successfully sustained their objections, but the general opinion amongst informants was that by withholding such a legitimized son his right of succession, his paternal relatives were risking the mystical sanctions of their enraged father's spirit. The result is that more often than not such a son indeed succeeds to his father's name after the latter's death.

Another difficulty confronting an extra-marital son is due to the fact that he is not associated with any of the established 'houses' of his father's wives, and that his step-mothers and half-brothers oppose the idea that marriage cattle received for any of the father's daughters should be used to provide a wife for him. When the father is alive their opposition may be overruled, but when he is dead the step-mothers and half-brothers may sometimes succeed in denying the extra-marital son his rightful share in the common estate of the deceased father. For example:

Tanjanyiwa was the natural son of Mayesorewa (a Rozwi in the Wedza Reserve), who had given *maputiro* for him. During the lifetime of the father, T was regarded as his heir because he was the first-born. Mayesorewa died before any of his children were married. His family was opposed to T's candidacy for succession because 'he was the child of a loose woman'—*mwana wefambi*. T's younger half-brother Matsungguma (eldest son of the first wife) was installed as the heir and the deceased's younger full-brother was given control of the family estate. When T asked his *baba munini* (father's younger brother) for *rovoro* cattle he was refused. The result was that T broke with his father's family, provided his own marriage cattle and went to live in the village of his father-in-law.

When I asked the informants why T had not brought an action against his father's family to vindicate his rights, they said that T 'expected that the spirit of his father would cause trouble (*kupfukira*) amongst his children to show his anger'. In that event the half-brothers would be forced to make amends to T.

(*c*) Regarding the third class of children—those resulting from the adultery of a formally betrothed or married woman, various terms are used. The term *mubvandiripo* refers to a child 'that was there when the mother came' (i.e. was born by the time the mother went to live with her husband). The phrase *ngombe ya vuya nouswa pa muromo*—the cow comes with grass in its mouth—refers to a woman marrying her husband while pregnant by another man. *Mwana wa pa itundu*[6] likewise refers to an unlawfully conceived child that was not yet born when the mother married her husband, but usually implies that the natural father is unknown. *Mhamba muceka*[7] is used in the same sense as *ngombe ya vuya nouswa pa muromo*. The term that would be most useful for general purposes, *mwana wegomba* (lover's child), is unfortunately used mostly with reference to an unlawfully conceived child that is brought up by its maternal grandparents because its natural father is either unknown or reluctant to legitimize it (see next class). *Mwana womukadzi* (wife's child) is fairly often employed as a general term for a pre-marital or extra-marital child of a married woman. This term implicitly stresses the fact that the child does not belong to the patrilineage of the mother's husband.

Unlike the natural children of the husband, whose main practical obstacle lies in the fact that they are not associated with the house of any particular father's wife, the extra-marital child of a wife suffers no disability in this respect. Since the blood of a common mother establishes a closer unity amongst children than the blood of a common father, an extra-marital wife's son will meet no prejudice amongst the other children in his mother's house. He will have no difficulty in obtaining his rightful share in the estate of such a house. But since this child does not have the blood of the mother's husband it does not really belong to the latter's patrilineage. Even when the child is *pro forma* accorded the clan and sub-clans of his legal father—which would normally establish his membership in his *rudzi* (lineage)—the fact that he has the 'blood of another' (*ropa romumwe*) may disqualify him from succeeding to the name and dignity of his legal father or any other ancestor in the latter's lineage. In this respect informants in the Wedza Reserve were generally outspoken in their opinion that such a son 'cannot inherit the name of his father', and they were able to quote cases in support of their view. For example:

K had married his wife when she was pregnant, but took it for granted that he himself had impregnated her. No confession to the contrary was made by the woman during her confinement when she gave birth to a son, M. Many years later, after M had married with cattle given to him by K, he quarrelled with K. K's wife sided with her son and told him that 'he need not listen to K because K was not his real father'. Thereupon M broke with K and went to his natural father, C, who received him cordially. In his anger and disappointment K proceeded to claim back from M the *rovoro* he had given to him, stating that the latter had no right to these cattle. M failed to pay back and K managed to have the marriage dissolved and to get a refund of cattle from the *tezwara*. C now promised his son to provide a wife for him, but before he could fulfil his promise M had a violent quarrel with C's other sons and went back to K, whom he asked to forgive him. K agreed to a reconciliation ('How can I refuse him after I have regarded him as my first-born during all these years? It was not his fault that this happened, but the fault of his mother.'). But in spite of the fact that M was apparently forgiven by K (who again provided him with a wife), he was no longer regarded as K's successor. K's second son was now considered to be the heir presumptive. Explained K: 'How can M get my name when I am dead, now it is known that he is *mwana womukadzi*, a person without my blood?' (When the informants were asked if M could succeed to the name and genealogical dignity of his natural father C, they unanimously agreed that, legally speaking, M had the right to succeed because he was C's first-born son. But they expressed doubt if he would be able or even willing to press his claim in view of the opposition he had encountered at C's village.)

In the Narira Reserve, however, most informants were not prepared to accept as a fixed principle that such a 'wife's child' cannot succeed to the genealogical position of his legal father on account of his different blood. Some were even inclined to take the view that since the legal father had given *rovoro* for the mother, the child was legitimate in every respect, and therefore not only entitled to share in his father's estate but was also eligible to succeed to his name and position in the lineage. They admitted, however, that 'the other children would probably object to his getting the father's name and refuse to obey him (*kunzwa*, literally, to 'listen'). The position in this area may have been influenced by a classic case upon which the informants relied heavily because it concerned one of the houses of the Chief's lineage (Rozwi):

When Watambgha married his fourth wife it was a matter of *ngombe ya vuya nouswa pa muromo*, the woman being pregnant by a man other than her husband. This child, Matibe, later became a candidate for the name and genealogical position of his legal father Watambgha. His candidacy was seriously opposed by his collaterals in the house of Watambgha and there was a move to bestow the name and dignity upon Matibe's younger half-brother (same mother). But Matibe successfully defended his candidacy. 'Watambgha gave *rovoro* for my mother and I became his child. I have treated him as my father. I have obeyed him and worked for him and done everything a good son does for his father. How can you say that I cannot get his name?' Matibe also threatened that he would become *nggozi* (malevolent spirit) after his death if he was not allowed to succeed. He then got the name Watambgha and was recognized as the head of his father's house.

In contrast with this case an instance from the Wedza Reserve should be reported:

Cikumbirike was the founder of one of the old houses of the Mbire clan (Mbiranunggi branch). His name first devolved upon his eldest son Gumira, then upon the latter's younger brother Manjeke. Manjeke had parental control over the children of his deceased half-brother Matakanure, the pre-marital son (*mubvandiripo*) of one of Cikumbirike's wives. Manjeke left no surviving children of his own when he died, and Matakanure's eldest son, Zwaodza, remained in charge of his uncle's village, although this hereditary name and dignity was duly bestowed after Manjeke's death upon Manjeke's younger brother Cikwepa, who had his own village.

Zwaodza posed as 'Cikumbirike' and after pulling some strings with the then Mbire Chieftain, managed to get an annuity from the Administration as a recognized headman. Informants, amongst whom were high-ranking members of the Mbire clan, found the position anomalous, said that Zwaodza was only a *sabuku* (village headman) and not a *mucinda* (member of the ruling lineage) because he did not really belong to the Mbire lineage.[8] He actually had no authority except in his own village. 'No other people bring their cases to him because they know that he is not a *mucinda*.' In short, they regarded him as a usurper who had no right to occupy the position and enjoy the privileges which should have belonged to Cikwepa as the rightful heir to the house of Cikumbirike.

No disabilities whatsoever seem to exist in connexion with children raised by an approved seed-raiser with the wife of a sterile husband. Although such children do not have the blood of their legal father, the nature and secrecy of the *kupindira* arrangement are an effective guarantee that they will in practice be regarded as having been raised by their mother's husband. I have found no record of any difficulties arising from this particular issue.

The question arose whether a son could succeed to the name and genealogical position of his natural father when the latter had not given *maputiro* for him. Informants argued that the question of *rudzi* (patrilineage) is determined by the blood of the father rather than by the payment of cattle. If there is no doubt about the paternity of the son he will be regarded as a member of the lineage of his natural father and as such be entitled to succeed to his father's name also if no *maputiro* has been given for him. Informants found an analogy in the case of a husband who has raised children by his wife but loses control over his children when he fails to fulfil his *rovoro* obligation. In such a case, when the marriage is dissolved, the son will nevertheless be eligible to succeed to his father's name. But it was also pointed out that failure to pay *maputiro* practically always implies that the natural father is not interested in the child, which is then brought up either by its maternal grandparents or mother's husband, away from its natural father. Only in exceptional circumstances will the latter's family consider such a child as the most eligible candidate for succession when his father dies.

(*d*) We must now consider the fourth-mentioned class of children, those neither legitimized nor recognized by their natural father or mother's husband. The majority of these children are born to unmarried or divorced women, and left in the care of their maternal grandparents because the father is either unknown (rare) or refuses to accept them. A few of them are born to married women but rejected by the legal father who denies paternity. They are usually boys, because girls represent a potential value in marriage cattle and are therefore as a rule either duly claimed by their natural father or retained by their mother's husband.

The common term usually employed with reference to such children is *mwana wegomba*, 'lover's child'.[9] Amongst the Hera the term *mbaratume* ('born to be sent about on errands') is sometimes used. Since both terms carry a social stigma they are seldom used in the presence of the child or its relatives, and the ordinary kinship terms—such as *muzukuru*, by its maternal relatives—are used in everyday speech.

Such a child falls under the control of, and is almost invariably brought up by, its maternal grandparents, who assume full responsibility, rights and duties in connexion with it. When it is a girl they can negotiate her marriage and accept her marriage cattle. When it is a boy they are expected to provide a wife for him, and are in return entitled to receive his full filial support. When the natural father is unknown or cannot be traced the child may be given the clan and sub-clan names of the mother, but he is never regarded as a full member of his mother's patrilineage and cannot therefore succeed to the name of his *sekuru* (mother's father). As one Rozwi explained: 'How can my daughter's child ever get my name? It would mean that I myself had raised the child with my daughter!'

Notes

[1] When the child is born at the village of the maternal family, as is often the case with a woman's first confinement, the midwife formally notifies the wife's father, who then notifies the husband's family.

[2] *Ciredzwa, uredzwa, marero, ngombe yokurera* (from *kurera*, to bring up) sometimes also: *ngombe yokunyarura mwana*, beast for fetching the child.

[3] Rozwi informants in the Wedza Reserve stated that, if the relations with the *vakuwasha* have been broken off by a return of *rovoro*, the term *gomba* no longer applies to the lover of the woman because she can no longer be regarded as *tswinggudzi*. The implication of this peculiar twist seems to be that the lover—now *cikomba*—has the *right* to claim the child payment of *maputiro*, even if he does not marry the woman.

[4] If the child is left in the care of its maternal grandparents for a number of years, another head of cattle may be payable as *uredzwa* (maintenance) before the father can assume custody.

[5] What usually happens is that the *mukurwasha* first claims both the woman and damages from her lover. The marriage is then duly contracted. When the woman subsequently deserts her husband there can be no doubt that the latter can keep the child, often without losing a single head of cattle when the *rovoro* is returned to him.

[6] Probably correct free translation: 'child picked up in the forest'.

[7] Said to be derived from *kubamba*, to take or accept something that is not yours, and *muceka*, a strip of cloth or the 'white stripe along the belly of a goat'; the meaning of the phrase is not clear.

[8] His father Matakanure was reported to have had the sub-clan name Mrewa, instead of the local Mbire sub-clan name Mondizo.

[9] The distinction between *gomba*—lover of a betrothed or married woman—and *cikomba*—lover of an unmarried girl—is apparently disregarded in this term.

E. I. Nwogugu: Legitimacy in Nigerian Law*

Legitimacy under Customary Law

Here we shall examine the position where a father had two sets of children under customary law. The first are children of customary law marriages, while the others are natural children born during the subsistence of the native marriages. The latter may be legitimated in accordance with the applicable customary law. For instance, P married R, F and O under customary law. During the subsistence of those marriages he had natural children by other women whom he legitimated according to his customary law. Are all the children of P legitimate and equally entitled to partake in the distribution of his estate?

The problems raised here came up for decision in *In the Estate of Herbert Macaulay*.[1] As we saw in an earlier consideration of this case, the West African Court of Appeal held that the legitimacy of the children in relation to succession is to be determined by the law of their country of domicile. The court therefore remitted the question of deciding which of the children were legitimate under the relevant customary law in Nigeria to the lower court.

This reference was decided by the late Jibowu, J., in the old Supreme Court of Nigeria, Lagos Judiciary Division. His judgment of 15th December, 1952, is unreported.[2] The learned judge found that four of the women were married to the deceased by customary law and so their children were legitimate as issues of lawful wedlock. The other women were the concubines of the deceased, but their children were acknowledged by the deceased. Evidence of the Yoruba customary law that a natural child can be legitimated by acknowledgment by the father and will thus enjoy the same status as a child born in native wedlock was given and accepted.[3]

But Jibowu, J., refused to accord legal validity to the proved law in the case before him because to rank legitimated natural children with children of a native marriage

* E. I. Nwogugu, 'Legitimacy in Nigerian Law', in *Journal of African Law*, Vol. 8, No. 1, pp. 96–98.

would offend the Marriage Act, and encourage loose and immoral living which is contrary to public policy. In his opinion,

> 'The position is then that we have two conflicting systems of law: one which does not recognize a child as legitimate unless the parents are lawfully married, and the other, a crude rule obviously intended to meet the requirements of primitive society, which says that marriage is not necessary and that the issue of concubinage or adulterous connection is legitimate as long as he is acknowledged by his father. Such a customary law is repugnant to the Marriage Ordinance and the Legitimacy Ordinance and offends against common sense, decency and public policy.'

He came to the conclusion that the customary law rule that legitimated natural children could share in the distribution of their father's estate may be applied only when there is no marriage recognized by the law or no children of such marriage.

It is submitted that this decision should not be followed as binding authority. While it may be said that the courts lean towards preserving the institution of marriage under the Marriage Act, the same cannot be said where there are two sets of children legitimate under customary law. As they are accorded equal status by the same legal system, it will be unjust to discriminate between them in the enjoyment of legal benefits.

An important factor in the determination of this question should be whether the natural children are legitimated under the customary law of their domicile or not. If they are so legitimated there are no good grounds for denying them the same rights as the children of the native marriages. It may be argued that to do so would be contrary to public policy as encouraging promiscuous associations. But promiscuity is an essential ingredient of customary law marriages where there are several wives or the husband has the right to take more than one wife. The moral reprobation, if any, does not seem to be greater in one case than in the other.

On the other hand, if the natural children are not legitimated under customary law, it is submitted that they are not entitled to the status of legitimacy or the right to share in the estate of their putative father. A child born out of wedlock is illegitimate at birth. He can only acquire a new status through the act of legitimation by customary law or under the Legitimacy Act.

JIBOWU, J.'s view was not followed in the later case of *Jirigho* v. *Chief Anamali*[4] which arose in connexion with a claim by dependants of the deceased under the Fatal Accidents Acts. The deceased died as a result of a collision between two vehicles one of which was being driven by the defendant. The plaintiff, who was the mother of the deceased, claimed under the Fatal Accidents Act, 1846 and 1864 (being statutes of general application) on behalf of herself, the widow of the deceased who had been married under native law and custom, and his six infant children, one of whom was the child of that marriage and the others the children of lovers of the deceased. Under s. 2 of the 1846 Act, action may be brought for the benefit of the wife, husband, parent and child of the deceased. By s. 5 of the same Act, the word 'child' includes son and daughter, grandson, granddaughter, stepson and stepdaughter.[5] The term 'child', under the Fatal Accidents Act, 1846 and 1864, does not include illegitimate children.[6]

DUFFUS, J., held that the widow of the deceased and her child came within the meaning of 'wife' and 'child' in the Fatal Accidents Acts, being the wife of a valid marriage and the child thereof respectively. With regard to the other five children of the deceased by lovers, the learned judge held as follows. They were acknowledged by the deceased as his children during his lifetime. By the native law and custom of the Kwale tribe of the Mid-Western Region (where the deceased lived and was married and to which he belonged) an acknowledged natural child enjoys the same status and rights in every respect as a child of a native law marriage. Consequently, he concluded that the 'five children of the deceased's lovers are according to Kwale native law and custom, of equal status with a child born in lawful wedlock and within the meaning of a "child" in s. 2 of the Fatal Accidents Acts, 1846 . . .'[7]

This decision is consistent with the rules of legitimacy in Nigeria as shown above. In determining the children who come within the term 'child' in the English Acts (statutes of general application), the test is not that of English internal law but the conflict of law rule as laid down in *Bamgbose* v. *Daniel.*[8] By the personal law of the deceased's children they are all entitled to the status of legitimacy. No distinction was made between the two customary law methods of acquiring that status.

Notes

[1] 13 W.A.C.A. 304.
[2] Suit No. AG. 68.
[3] See also *Savage* v. *Macfoy* (1909), Ren. 504, at p. 508 (Gold Coast).
[4] (1958), W.R. N.L.R. 195.
[5] The same definition is contained in the Fatal Accidents Acts, 1864.
[6] *Dickinson* v. *N.E. Railway Company* (1863), 9 L.T. 299. In England, illegitimate children were included in the class of dependants by the Law Reform (Miscellaneous Provisions) Act, 1934, s. 2 (1). The same position was achieved in Lagos by the Fatal Accidents Act, 1961, s. 2 (2) and Western Region by the Torts Law, 1958, s. 5.
[7] (1958), W.R.N.L.R. 195, at p. 197.
[8] (1955) A.C. 107: see p. 94, above.

Chapter 4

ADOPTION

In view of the importance of adoption in relation to family law it has received surprisingly little attention among writers on African law. The exposition by *Simmance* of the rules governing adoption among the Kikuyu is, therefore, particularly valuable, while the shorter extracts from works by *van Tromp*, *Schapera* and *Cory and Hartnoll* provide useful comparative material.

A. J. F. Simmance: Adoption of Children among the Kikuyu of the Kiambu District*

The Adoption of Children among the Kikuyu of Kiambu District

This article is not concerned with the substantive law of adoption in Kenya, which is contained in the Adoption Ordinance, 1958. Section 36 of the Ordinance recognises the impossibility or inexpediency of applying the general law to all races in the Colony, and adoption among Africans continues to be regulated almost entirely by the provisions of tribal custom.

In indigenous Kikuyu society, genuine adoption was rare and took place only in particular and carefully-defined circumstances where the principle of collective responsibility by the natural father's clan or *muhiriga* could not be invoked. The usual case in which an outsider could adopt and legally take as his own an orphaned child was on the death in child-birth of an unmarried mother. Either the surviving infant was killed and buried with its mother or claimed by a foster-parent who needed to have no kinship affinity with the mother or father (if known). Similarly, although first-born twins and adulterine children were habitually destroyed, a foster-parent could intervene and claim them. They would then be recognised as his as completely as if he were their father by blood. On him would fall the duty of ensuring that his adopted children participated in the appropriate initiation ceremonies before reaching maturity. To him would be paid the bride-price on the marriage of an adopted daughter, and he would be expected to provide the bride-price for the marriage of his adopted son. An adopted child would take the family name of the foster-father, i.e. that of the paternal grandparent and an adopted son would assume the full rights and duties of membership of his foster-father's family and clan.

Finally, on the death of the foster-father, an adopted son would bury him and conduct the funeral ceremonies if there were no senior natural son to do so. In short, the rights and status of an adopted child became identical to those of the natural issue, provided that the adoption had taken place in the restricted circumstances described above.

A form of semi-adoption also existed in tribal law (and still exists) to provide for the rearing of a child whose natural married mother had died in child-birth or shortly after. The father would seek out the services of a woman who was prepared to rear the child. Such a woman would *not* assume the status of a natural parent but would act for the child on behalf of the father, and would be entitled to a set recompense (normally ten goats and one ram) for her services. This she could sue for in default of payment. On reaching maturity a male child who had been brought up in this way would choose whether to return to his father or to stay with his mother. Normally, and principally because of his prospective inheritance rights he would elect to do the former, but would none the less be bound to assist the woman who had cared for him if she needed his support. There is no easy term with which to describe her position; she was and is

* A. J. F. Simmance, 'Adoption of Children among the Kikuyu of the Kiambu District', in *Journal of African Law*, Vol. 3, No. 1, pp. 33–38.

something more than a children's nurse and something less than a true foster-mother.

Despite these cases, however, it must be stressed that the over-riding principle in Kikuyu society has always been to stress the predominance of the proprietary interest of a child's family or clan.

A natural father cannot, however, establish his interest without legally marrying the mother of his children. If he does not do this, they are regarded by tribal law not as his but as the offspring of the mother's father, or if the father is dead, of her senior male relative.

If the mother is already married to someone else, then the children belong to him—the true husband—and the natural father can never establish a claim to then. Thus, although the children of an unmarried mother can be 'adopted' by their own father '*per subsequens matrimonium*', it would be incorrect to describe this as legitimation since no Kikuyu child whose antecedents are known is ever illegitimate in the sense of having no legal parent who can, if he wishes, assert authority over him. Within the context of customary law, ties of kinship carry overwhelming weight in determining the custody of a child, and little recognition has been given until recently to the interplay of parental rights and duties.

In the higher Courts of the Commonwealth, it is now held that the exercise of parental rights necessarily imports the correlative of parental duties and that in so far as these duties are not properly carried out, proportionately less emphasis should be placed on the proprietary rights of the parents.[1]

Pure Kikuyu law, in contrast, is clear that parental and clan rights are not extinguished or indeed affected by indifference or neglect, although because of the harshness of the strict application of the principle, its force has been somewhat modified in recent years. However, except under such statutory provisions as the Prevention of Cruelty to and Neglect of Children Ordinance, 1955, a parent is never deprived of the custody of his child by reason of his treatment of it, nor is the absence of parental responsibility a ground for permitting adoption. The type of case, therefore, which causes the greatest difficulty in the African Court is that in which a natural parent claims custody of a child after many years of indifference and tacit acceptance of another's guardianship. This occurs usually for pecuniary motives, such as the recovery of bride-price for a daughter reaching maturity after being in the care of an outsider since early infancy. For example, in the Provincial Commissioner, Central Province's Civil Appeal Case No. 3 of 1951 the facts were briefly as follows:

1. The mother of a female and legitimate child, Gacheri, died (many years before the case) in child-birth.

2. The father of the child, Muraya, wished to bury her with her mother, but was prevented from doing so by the mother's sister Ruth, who took the child, nurtured her and brought her up. The father, by occasional visits and small gifts, acknowledged the existence of the child but made no effort to recover custody.

3. The father died and the child remained with Ruth until she reached maturity. She was then married and Ruth received the full bride-price from the husband's family.

4. This finally stirred Muraya's eldest son, Warima, into litigation. He claimed in the Chura African Court in 1950 for the recovery of the child (his sister) and the bride-price in full. The action to recover the child was, of course, merely a formal preliminary to demanding the bride-price for her.

5. The Chura elders recognised that in strict Kikuyu law, Muraya, and on his death his son, was entitled to custody. However, conscious of the inequity which would result from a rigid adherence to the law, they dismissed the suit on the grounds that there had been unreasonable delay in bringing the matter to Court, and that if Muraya had had his way in the first place, the child would never have survived. In short, finding the law burdensome and outdated they looked for and found a way to avoid it.

6. The case was taken on appeal by Warima to the African Court of Appeal at Kiambu, which reversed the decision of Chura elders and allowed the appeal, reserving, however, 20 goats, 1 ram, and 200/- for Ruth as *ureri* or customary payment for the maintenance of the child.

7. Naturally enough, the appeal was taken further to the District Officer. In his judgment he found cautiously that 'there is much to be said for the decisions of both courts in this case'. After remarking that the 'child' whose custody was claimed was then a mother with three children he decided against the African Court of Appeal which had 'disregarded the just and humane aspect of the case', and restored the judgment of the Chura African Court by dimissing Warima's claim in full.

8. The Provincial Commissioner, who heard the final appeal in the case in 1952 adopted a compromise solution, awarding a token payment in recognition of the custom to Warima, dividing costs between the parties, and leaving the remainder of the bride-price with Ruth. He did not dispute, or attempt to vary, the law.

There have been no significant African Court cases on the subject since, and an anomalous situation persists in which the elders of the tribe are reluctant to take steps to modify the general law, yet have recognised as for example in connection with the Kenya Emergency, the empirical necessity for reducing its burden in particular circumstances. Their reluctance to act generally has led to illogicality and to at least one judgment which is narrowly indefensible, although equitable and just. There are seldom, of course, any absolute objective standards in tribal law, as Professor Phillips has remarked,[2] but the application of the law has at present an undesirable air of uncertainty about it.

The whole traditional fabric of family law is threatened by the transition to modern life and this uncertainty will persist until the society commits itself to far-reaching decisions on the status of parents, the rights of women, and the upbringing of children which it is not at present ready to concede. Meanwhile formal decisions on a part of the law are bound to affect the whole, and as a result have been largely postponed through a mixture of caution and distaste.

At the beginning of this article, it was made clear that adoption was a rare occurrence in the normal pattern of Kikuyu life. This pattern was sharply disrupted by the declaration of an Emergency in October, 1952. Large-scale repatriations from other parts of the Colony to the Kikuyu Reserves and the arrest and detention of 77,000 Mau Mau adherents inevitably brought about separations of parent and child, and Mau Mau killings resulted in many children becoming orphans and destitute. Action by the Administrative authorities, Community Development workers in the field, the Red Cross, and unofficial organisations such as the Child Welfare Society of Kenya has resulted in nearly all divided families being reunited, but a few problem cases have remained in the care of Missions or in institutions such as the Dagoretti Children's Centre. Mau Mau orphans have also become the responsibility of these organisations, and their desire to restore the children in their care from an institutional background to a normal family life has been coupled with a desire on the part of many decent Kikuyu folk to adopt unclaimed children into their homes.

The stumbling-block to this kind of adoption has always been the fear of the prospective foster-parent that he may be deprived of the custody of the child he wishes to adopt by the appearance at any time of even a remote natural relative, who by Kikuyu law would have a prior claim.

Specifically in order to avoid this, the Kiambu Law Panel—the body concerned with the clarification, definition and change of customary law—met on the 22nd June, 1956 and approved the following rules. I quote from their Minute:

'1. When any question of the adoption of a child is raised efforts will first be made to trace the Muhiriga of the child. If the Muhiriga can be found, the Muhiriga are responsible for providing for the child. This is a continuation of traditional custom.

'2. If the child's Muhiriga is not known, the proposed foster-parents and the orphan will be placed before a Divisional Baraza where a Chief will explain in public that the foster-parents will be given custody of the child if no one at the baraza raises an objection.

'3. If no objection is raised by anyone claiming to be the parent of the child or member of the same Muhiriga the foster-parents will then be given custody.

'4. At any time during the five years immediately after the date of the baraza at which the child is handed over to the foster-parents, the real parents of the child may claim it back again on payment of all costs incurred by the foster-parents.

No other member of the child's Muhiriga except the real parents may claim the child during this period if they remained silent at the original baraza. The reason for this five year period of grace is that the Panel feels that present circumstances in Kiambu are abnormal and that many families have been disrupted and broken up by the Emergency. The proposed rule allows the child to be cared for until the Emergency is over but at the same time gives the real parents an adequate period in which to establish their claim.

'5. If a parent of the child is alive but has abandoned the child, that parent will be called before the African Court with two elders of his or her own Muhiriga, two Councillors of the African District Council from the Division in which the parent is living, and two Councillors of the African District Council from the Division in which the foster-parents live. In front of these witnesses and the elders of the African Court the parent who has abandoned the child will make a written declaration that he or she renounces all claim to the child.

'6. The above rules are intended to apply to children who at age of adoption are aged 10 years or less, but may apply to any child in need of care.'

These rules are, again, a compromise solution, and are related to circumstances arising out of the Emergency—they do not affect the traditional methods for ensuring the care of a motherless child. There is, however, one notable advance in the provision that a parent who has abandoned a child may voluntarily relinquish his or her claim to it, and another in the restriction of claims during the five-year period following the original baraza to the parents only.

As a method of dealing with the 'war orphan' or child abandoned during the Emergency, this procedure has had a moderate success only. It is restricted pratically speaking to children under ten years of age, on the entirely reasonable grounds that a child over that age will seldom adjust itself to a new home environment and will resist control and discipline by its new guardians. Moreover, the reponsibility for many children has been assumed by the *muhiriga* either before or at the baraza stage and the need for formal adoption has not arisen.

Finally, even in the comparatively few cases where no tribal relations whatsoever have been established, suspicion on the part of the prospective foster-parent that a natural parent may purposely be keeping silent and delaying the presentation of his claim, has been difficult to overcome. However, there have been some successful and happy adoptions—to force the pace would be unwise, particularly since even the limited success which the scheme has achieved is likely to encourage its assimilation into the general law.

Furthermore—and this should be stressed—nothing must be done which would tend to divest the Kikuyu tribe of its customary responsibilities for its members. We have no effective substitute to offer for the sense of collective guardianship and duty which still persists and should be encouraged to persist—at least until the advent of the Welfare State.

Notes

[1] See L. J. Blom-Cooper, 'Adoption Applications and Parental Responsibility', (1957) 20 M.L.R. 485.

[2] *Report on Native Tribunals*, Government Printer, Nairobi, 1945; esp. paras. 826–832.

J. van Tromp: Xhosa Law of Persons*

Adoption. Adoption is the taking of the child of another as one's own. The amaXhosa usually adopt only heirs when a man has no heir in general, or when there is no heir in one or other of his houses. A man may, however, also adopt a child to enlarge his own family.

As a rule children are adopted from among the family of the adopting father; but adopting of a stranger's child is not excluded. The adoption of a child from among the family of the wife is unknown.

* J. van Tromp, *Xhosa Law of Persons*, Juta & Co. Ltd., 1947, pp. 147–149.

Where a man adopts a child, especially with regard to boys, certain lines of procedure must be followed: The parent who allows his son to be adopted by another man must publicly declare in his family court that this or that man is adopting this particular son. Hereafter he must notify the Chief of the intended adoption of the son by another man.[1]

If the father whose son is thus to be adopted does not follow this procedure, such adopted son has the right to claim the inheritance of his father after the latter's death, if he is the eldest son. Or, if he is the eldest son of a particular indlu, he retains the rights and privileges of such a son.

The adopting father, on the other hand, must also make a declaration in his own family court to the effect that he adopts this particular son. The position and status of this adopted child is then fixed by the family court. Whether this adopted son will inherit or become general heir and successor of his adopted father will depend upon his status fixed by the family court. After this the adopting father will inform the Chief and then everything will be in order.[2]

Adoption takes place after the child is weaned, when it is able to obey orders, and before it is to undergo the rite of circumcision. This is so especially where a son is adopted as heir; for it is incumbent upon the adopting father that such son shall be circumcised from the former's umzi; this is to show that the son now is his own son.

If a man adopts a child he will put that child in one or other indlu, but such a child will not oust the son in that house. He will be treated as any other child of the umzi, with the same rights and obligations as other children, except that he cannot inherit before other sons who are the legitimate children of the adopting father.

The adopting father or his lawful heir and successor will also have to care and maintain this child and, if a son, will have to help him to lobola a wife. 'Where a man has adopted another, and has paid lobola on his behalf, he has a claim on the children of his adopted son, he having the right under Native Law to a portion of the lobola received for a girl born to the adopted son, or, if more than one daughter is born of the marriage, he might claim the eldest daughter.'[3]

It is doubtful whether this is good Xhosa Law or whether it is good Native Law in general. For a man who adopts a child takes that child as his own. The only possible basis for accepting the view expressed above is that this child is not the blood (igazi lakhe) of the adopting parent.

Where a man adopts a child as heir to one or other of his houses, that son will be recognised as the eldest son of that house and have all the rights and duties of a son of that house. But if the wife of this house gives birth to a son, being the child of her lawful husband, such a son will oust the adopted son, who will then be recognised as the minor brother of that son.

Another form of adoption found among the amaXhosa, especially in former times as a result of wars and famine, is in connection with the *umcholwa*, a picked-up child.

The man who finds such a child, umcholwa, will formally adopt the umcholwa and it will enjoy the same privileges as any other child of the umzi.

If she is a girl she will undergo the intonjane ceremony here and be married from this umzi, her adopting father or his lawful heir and successor receiving her ikhazi.

Should it be a boy, he will be circumcised at this umzi, as a son of the umzi, and he will be helped to lobola a wife. Where there is no heir in one or other of the houses, the adopting father may place this son so adopted in that heirless indlu as heir. In case of lack of all male issue, this adopted son has a right to heirship. If there are other legitimate sons the adopted son will enjoy the same rights and privileges as the former, except that he cannot inherit.

Notes

[1] See: *J. Kamani* vs. *Q. Sigongo*, 1 P.H. 1941 R. 6, where it was said: "The adoption of children among Natives is a matter of some formality. The adoption of a child must be publicly performed, otherwise it is not valid". Also: *S. Nongqayi* vs. *M. and T. Mdose*, 2 P.H. 1942 R. 25.

[2] *Zondani* vs. *Dayman* 1911 *Henkel*, p. 132. This holds good for Xhosa Law also.

[3] Whitfield: *South African Native Law*, pp. 39 and 40. Also *Kokwe* vs. *Gubela* 1902 Henkel, p. 48, and *Ladodana* vs. *Ntlanganiso* 1911 Henkel, p. 135.

I. Schapera: A Handbook of Tswana Law and Custom*

It is very common for a child to be sent to live for a while with some paternal or maternal relative, particularly with its mother's father or brother. It is generally taken to their home soon after weaning and may live there for a number of years, helping in the domestic work. This is sometimes done simply as a sign of the attachment between the two families, and so that the child may enjoy the use of the *bogadi* cattle given for its mother. Occasionally, however, a child is also sent to a relative for some special reason, e.g. because it is sickly or unhappy at its own home, and its parents believe that a change of environment will do it good. The parents of the child are its natural guardians, and they have the sole right to decide whether it should stay with them or go to a relative. The relatives cannot claim as a right that children should come to stay with them. It is a privilege about which the parents have the main say, and depends upon the intimacy and friendliness of the relations between the two families.

These instances of temporary adoption do not make any difference to the child's status at its own home or to its parents' claim over it. But in some cases a child may be permanently adopted, either by a relative or by a friend. This generally takes place when the people to whom it is sent have no children of their own, in which case they may be given either a boy or a girl. Or their children may all be of the same sex, in which case they are given a child of the opposite sex—a girl to help in the home, or a boy to look after the cattle, according to their need. Sometimes people will ask relatives or friends to give them such a child. But often enough the parents themselves may decide beforehand to hand over their nextborn child to some special relative or friend. It is then said: *Ngwana o mo tsaletswe*, 'The child has been born for him.'

The child is handed over when still young, sometimes soon after weaning, and grows up with its foster-parents. They look after it, feed and clothe it, provide for its other needs, and punish it when necessary. It is considered in every way their own, and not subject to the control of its true parents. The latter will visit it from time to time, and if it is ill-treated may even take it back, or it may flee to them. But normally it remains with its foster-parents until fully grown up. It is treated on the same footing as any children they may have themselves: it is consulted in all household affairs, and may be given property of its own. If it is staying with relatives, they may subsequently arrange its marriage, and, if a boy, pay *bogadi* for his wife, while, if a girl, they will receive the *bogadi* given for her. An adopted son may even inherit the property of the foster-father, if the latter has no sons of his own. But, if he has, preference is given to them, although the adopted son can keep anything specially given to him.

If a child has been adopted by friends, they do not exercise equal control over it, being expected to inform and consult its parents about any important matters affecting its welfare. An adopted daughter, e.g., will in such cases have her marriage arranged by her true parents, who will, however, give her foster-parents part of the *bogadi*; while an adopted son may, after marriage, go back to his own home, taking with him any property given to him. He will not as a rule inherit from his foster-father, even in the absence of a direct heir; the estate in such cases is claimed by the man's own near relatives.

H. Cory and M. M. Hartnoll: Customary Law of the Haya†

Adopted son. A man can adopt a child as his son.

NOTE: If a man wants to adopt a child who is not his heir presumptive he must call witnesses and explain to them the reasons why he has changed the customary sequence. If the witnesses do not consider his reasons sufficient they refuse to act, as in the case of a will. The heir presumptive can take the initiative and call elders to examine the reasons for the man's choice. If the elders definitely decide that the man's reasons are insufficient and he refuses to give up his adopted son, they will delare that

* I. Schapera, *A Handbook of Tswana Law and Custom.* Oxford University Press, 1938, pp. 173–175.

† H. Cory and M. M. Hartnoll, *Customary Law of the Haya,* Lund Humphries for International African Institute, 1945, p. 35.

he can do what he likes during his lifetime, but when he dies the adopted son will not be allowed to be Musika to his land.

He is bound in his choice by the same rules as those regulating his choice of heirs by will.

An adopted son has no rights if a natural son is born later.

He must also leave his adopted father's property, if he has inherited it, when a real son who has been absent, returns and claims his rights to inherit, unless the father has by will disinherited his true son.

Chapter 5

RELATIONS BETWEEN PARENTS AND CHILDREN: GUARDIANSHIP

The last of the topics dealt with in the Law of Persons concerns one aspect of the law of guardianship—that of the relations between parents and children. It is probably unnecessary to point out at this stage that this is not by any means the only relationship which gives rise to guardianship: African law contains rather more of these than most other systems, since it acknowledges the existence of a wider range of persons (e.g. wives, unmarried women, and in some cases unmarried men) who require assistance in order to perform acts, and assume rights or duties in law. Most of these have, however, been dealt with elsewhere in these Readings. The special emphasis given here to the powers of parents and the reciprocal or unilateral obligations of parents and children arises from their importance to an understanding of the manner in which the family functions. Both *Schapera* and *Cory* deal at length with the duties and responsibilities of guardians and the latter also contributes a description of the manner in which guardians are appointed and dismissed. *Fortes*, on the matrilineal Ashanti, also emphasises the manner in which a guardian comes to assume his duties. In passing, he deals with the question of legitimacy as well as with the specific powers and obligations which the guardian possesses, or, in some cases, lacks.

I. Schapera: A Handbook of Tswana Law and Custom*

Parental Control

The nature and extent of parental control varies considerably according to the personal characteristics of the people concerned. Some parents are notoriously strict with their children, others indulge them considerably; and the children themselves differ equally in the respect and obedience they show to their parents. There is nevertheless some uniformity of opinion regarding the general pattern of behaviour that should exist between parents and children, and which in practice is not infrequently found.

In their early years children are more directly under the control of their mother. They are always at home with her; she gives them their food, helps them in their little troubles, and in general keeps a close watch over them. On the other hand, most scoldings and whippings inevitably come from her at this stage. The father is frequently away, whether at the cattlepost or abroad, so that his authority is less continuously felt. Girls as they grow older remain in close contact with their mother. They work with her, and most of their domestic education comes from her. They must therefore behave principally so as to please her. There is a better understanding between mother and daughter than between father and daughter, and the mother is often the girl's guide and confidante in matters of love. Boys, after they go to the cattlepost, are freed to a considerable extent from the control of the mother. Their work now brings them into much closer association with the father. They learn from him the behaviour expected of men, and must always be ready to please him. They are sometimes apt at this stage to be rather scornful of the mother, and when at home seldom show her due respect or obedience except when the father is about. On the other hand, relations between mother

* I. Schapera, *A Handbook of Tswana Law and Custom*, Oxford University Press, 1938, pp. 175-184.

and son are normally less formal and more intimate than between father and son. The boy finds his mother more sympathetic as a rule than his father, and she often enough is the medium through whom he conveys requests to the latter. But she seldom inspires the same respect as the father, especially as she too is obviously in a position of dependence upon him.

Duties of the father. The father is the founder and legal head of his family. He must formally recognize his children as his own at the time of birth, by giving them a name and providing for the mother during her confinement. He must see to it also that all necessary ceremonies and 'doctorings' are performed over them during their infancy. He must see to it that their mother is in a position to rear and feed them, by providing her with a hut in which to stay, land to cultivate, and meat and milk from his cattle and the game he hunts to supplement the crops she raises. He must further see that they are properly clothed. He must pair off the children according to their sex and age, allocating a sister to a brother, and a younger brother to an elder, and must teach them their duties in regard to one another. He must also make them known to their relatives, and teach them the appropriate forms of behaviour towards the latter. He must further protect his children, get doctors for them when they are sick, and in general take cognizance of all matters affecting them and their welfare. *Motsadi ke ênê thêbê ya me le momphemedi*, says the proverb: 'My parent is my shield and my defender.' He is also expected to inform his children of everything he does in connexion with household affairs, and to consult with his older sons, although he is not bound to follow their advice. He may further, in consultation with his wife, hand over a child to be adopted by some relative or friend, or may hire out his son to herd some one else's cattle.

He must see to it also that the children are promptly initiated into tribal life and, nowadays, that they go to school. At the pre-puberty stage he is supposed to instruct his sons in cattle-herding and veld lore, and to see to it that his daughters have a proper opportunity of learning women's work. At puberty, he had in former times to provide the necessary fees for them to enter the initiation camps. Subsequent to initiation, he must see to it that his children are properly married off. In the case of girls, this consists in ensuring that they get husbands reasonably early, and in not too varied an order of seniority, i.e. the eldest daughter first, and so on. In the case of sons, it involves getting together the *bogadi* for their respective wives, and seeing to the conduct of the customary marriage negotiations. Formerly, as has been shown, marriages were arranged with little reference to the two persons most closely concerned, but nowadays the latter have the initiative and are much more consulted.

All the property acquired by the father is held to be destined for his children. He should, during his lifetime, formally and publicly set aside for each of his sons one or more heifers and other livestock. This usage is known as *go tshwaisa*, and the animals themselves as *tshwaisô* or *setshwaêlô*. The animals thus set aside for any particular son are together with their offspring, regarded as his personal property; but he does not obtain full control over them until he marries. Daughters when they marry must be given domestic utensils to take with them to their new home; and the father, if wealthy enough, may also give them goats or cows for milking, and, as among the Kgatla, a plot of land for cultivation. Their gifts are known as *ketêêtsô* (Ngwato) or *serotwana* (Kgatla). When sons marry, the father must see to it that they eventually obtain a building site and land to cultivate. He must also, if he has not yet done so, provide them with one or more heifers to start their own herds of cattle. He must finally see to it that at his death each house is provided with cattle so that it can acquire wives for its unmarried sons.

As head of the family, the father must keep order and maintain discipline over his children. In this direction he exercises considerable authority, and has the right to punish the children for any offences they commit. He acts also as their legal representative at the tribal courts, and they cannot sue or be sued except with his assistance and through him. He is, in matters affecting outsiders, responsible for their conduct, and can be held liable for their misdeeds. If, e.g. a son allows livestock to enter a field and damage crops, or seduces a girl, the father must pay the necessary damages. His position in such cases is not that of a wrongdoer, but of a surety responsible for the good conduct of members of his family.

All complaints of any importance against a child must be formally lodged with its father. He will then call together the male members of his family group, including the maternal uncles, and discuss the matter with the complainant and his people. If they cannot arrive at a satisfactory agreement, the complainant can take the case to court. There, if the accused son is found guilty, the court will order him to pay for the damage he has done; or, if he has nothing at all, will call upon his father to pay. Among the Kgatla and Kwena the father can, if necessary, be compelled to pay. This does not appear to be the case among the Tlôkwa and Malete, although it is said that the issue has very seldom risen, for no tribesman has ever been known to refuse to pay for his son. But the father is not held responsible for a son who has left him and set up a household of his own, or whom he has publicly disowned. He may further, if he has previously been called upon to pay for other delinquencies of a son still living with him, excuse himself or disclaim responsibility, and request the court to impose a thrashing instead upon the son. But this is also exceptional.

Duties of the mother. The mother must during pregnancy and at birth observe all the ceremonies and taboos held to be necessary for the well-being of her child. She must further see to it that the child is 'doctored' according to custom. She must tend it during its infancy, suckling it as long as possible, and keeping it clean. She must see to it that her children are properly fed, by cultivating the ground assigned to her, and by cooking for them the produce of her labour, and any food that may be provided in addition. *Ngwana wa mosadi ga a ke a wêla mo isong*, says the proverb: 'A woman's child does not fall into the fire' (from exhaustion due to starvation); and again: *Bana ba mosadi ga ba ke ba bopama kampo be e swa*, 'A woman's children do not get lean or die' (from starvation). She must see to it that they are decently clothed, assisting where necessary in making up, washing, and repairing the clothes. She must instruct her daughters in women's work and the prevailing conceptions of sexual physiology, and supervise their general health and behaviour, e.g. at the time of menstruation. She should also prevent them from having illicit lovers.

She takes her part in the family councils at the time of the marrige of her sons and more particularly of her daughters; and if she objects to a proposed marriage it should not be carried any further, although she may be overruled by the wishes of her husband. She proves and trains her daughters-in-law while they live at her home, and acts as perpetual confidante of her own daughters after they have been married, visiting them frequently, nursing them when sick, assisting them in their household tasks, looking after their corn, and inviting them to all feasts. She also assists when her daughters and daughters-in-law are confined, and subsequently helps them to bring up the babies. Upon the death of her husband she assists her eldest son in regulating the affairs of her house.

Duties of children. Children are expected from a fairly early age to assist in the routine occupations of the household, their elders acting as their mentors. The girls are made to help their mothers by fetching water and wood, stamping corn and cooking, cleaning and repairing the homestead, and acting as nursemaids of the babies. These and the many other household duties pertaining to their sex they carry on until they reach womanhood, when on marriage they assume for themselves the responsibilities of housewives. Young boys must help their mother by going messages for her and performing any small menial tasks she sets them to do. Older boys must work for their father by herding and milking his cattle, going out hunting with him, helping him to build huts, plough and protect the family property, running errands, and so on. In all these activities the child too contributes towards the maintenance of the household. It is a duty he owes towards his parents or guardians, and failure to comply with it is punished.

When a child is grown up and able to earn a living by work, he must also support his parents, 'because they are old and have no more strength'. *O busa dikotlô*, it is said: 'He repays them for his maintenance.' Sons must give their fathers everything they obtain by hunting, gift, or purchase, and nowadays also by work among the Europeans. This is known to the Ngwato as *go šôma*. The father can take it all for himself, or may otherwise dispose of it as he thinks fit. But he is expected to consider the son, and see that he gets something out of what he has acquired.

The children must further be at all times subservient to their elders. *Motsala-motho ke modimo wa gagwê*, it is said: 'A child's parent is its god.' They are expected to fear and honour their parents, to address and speak to them politely and with the use of the appropriate relationship terms, to behave towards them and in their presence with considerable respect, and to seek their permission before going anywhere. Above all, unquestioning obedience is demanded from them, particularly towards the father, and they must willingly do whatever they are told. The saying goes: *Ngwana yo o sa utlweng molao wa ga rraagwê o tla utlwa wa manong*, 'The child who does not listen to the law of his father will hear that of the vultures.' (The word *manong* in this context may also refer to the young men in charge of the initiation camps, who would severely thrash any boy known to have been disobedient towards his parents.) Older children are expected to consult and live on friendly terms with their mother. Sons must consult their father in all their business dealings, and are dependent upon his consent for their marriages to be arranged. Daughters' marriages are also arranged through the father, who receives and retains a portion of the *bogadi* given for them.

Children are further taught numerous rules of etiquette and correct behaviour in regard to social life generally, including particularly the payment of respect towards all their seniors, whether related to them or not. They are taught habits of bodily cleanliness and hygiene, and are warned to refrain from such vices as swearing, stealing, and telling lies. The older children receive some instruction in matters of sex and in the prevailing moral code. Here again the child is duty-bound to his parents. Obedience and respect are their due, while conformity to the general code of behaviour is a means of gaining them esteem or at least of saving them from shame and disgrace. Children are finally responsible for the ritual burial of their parents. Elder sons are expected to care for their mother after the death of their father. The eldest son of the great house must also see that provision is made for the younger wives of his father to have lawful opportunities of continuing to bear children.

The authority of the parents is weakened when a child marries and leaves the household. A daughter then comes under the control of her husband, and is primarily responsible to him. But she is still expected to visit her parents frequently and to obey them, to help her mother at work, to keep some if not all her corn at their home, to give her parents occasional gifts of food and clothes, to bear her first child at their home, and to inform them whenever she is to be doctored or is involved in any trouble. A son, when he marries and sets up his own household, becomes for all practical purposes his own master. But he should still render his father a good deal of obedience and service, and consult him in all his business undertakings, help him plough and look after the family cattle, send him occasional gifts of food and other things, including a portion of the earnings he brings back from work among the Europeans, show his parents every respect, and support them in their old age.

Enforcement of discipline. Parents have the right to punish any of their dependent children for disobedience of orders, insolence, the use of bad language, leaving the homestead without permission, letting the cattle go astray, failing to stamp corn or fetch water, and similar breaches of duty. The punishments administered sometimes take the form of stinting the child in food or clothes, but generally consist in a scolding or whipping. Small children are slapped with the bare hands or lightly beaten, mainly on the buttocks, with a small wooden switch or broom. Bigger girls are generally beaten with switches on the body or shoulders. Bigger boys are made to *kgwatha*, lie face downwards at full length, and are whipped on the bare back with a cane. The standard punishment among the Kgatla for letting cattle go astray is four cuts (*mabêlê a kgomo*, the teats of a cow), and for letting goats go astray two cuts (*mabêlê a podi*, the teats of a goat). For other offences the punishment given is according to the will of the parents. Both parents have a right to punish undutiful children, although women seldom venture to thrash their adolescent sons.

The right to punish children formerly extended also to the community in general. Any man or woman insulted or otherwise injured by a child was entitled to thrash it on the spot. Nowadays, parents are growing apt to resent this, and it is more usual for the offended adult to complain to them, so that they may themselves punish the child. But if a boy is caught sleeping with a girl, or stealing food from a field, or allowing his cattle to damage standing crops, the girl's father or the owner still has the right to thrash him at once, and the boy's parents should not complain.

The authority of the father was in the olden days greatly strengthened by the belief in *thogô* or *go hutsa*, the power of the curse. If a child shamefully and persistently neglected his father, or indeed any senior relative, the latter would deliberately invoke some evil upon him, and it was firmly believed that the curse would take effect. Even the mere anger of the offended person was thought to be supernaturally potent. If a child fell ill soon after a family quarrel, the diviner would often attribute the illness to the anger of the father or some other senior relative. This illness, known as *dikgaba*, could not be cured until the anger of the offended person had been appeased. The latter would then wash the child with certain medicines, saying at the same time: *Fa e le nna, a ngwana a fôlê*, 'If it was I (who caused the illness) [or 'For my part'], may the child recover.' Even at the present time the belief in *dikgaba* is still very strong; and a child refusing to go when sent on an errand is often warned: *Fa O gana batho bagolo ba Go roma ba tla Go tsenya dikgaba*, 'If you refuse to obey when old people send you, they will afflict you with *dikgaba*.'

It is generally admitted nowadays that parental discipline has suffered decay. Children no longer do willingly what they are ordered, and the parents instead of commanding them have to request. In particular the younger unmarried men still under the authority of their father soon become impatient of the traditional forms of family control, object to interference with their freedom of movement, keep back most of their earnings, and are openly insolent towards their elders. The young people no longer look to their parents for guidance, but are tending to act more and more upon their own responsibility.

It is alleged that one powerful cause of this change in discipline has been the modifications produced in the initiation ceremonies preceding the formation of a regiment. In the olden days, children known to be disobedient or insolent towards their elders were treated with special severity in the initiation camps, which accordingly served as a powerful disciplinary force. Parents would exercise every possible control over the behaviour of their children, and the latter themselves acted with restraint, for fear of the additional hardships and tortures they would otherwise have to suffer when being initiated. With the abolition of the old usages, excessive punishment was no longer to be dreaded. As a result, parental vigilance has gradually slackened, while among the children there has been a growth of irresponsibility and even licence, manifesting itself more particularly in regard to sex. Labour migration, by drawing men away for long periods of time and so freeing their children from direct paternal supervision, has contributed to the same result, and so have education and the general infiltration of European ideas of individual responsibility. But the Natives themselves most frequently stress, as the main cause of the modern lack of respect for parental control, the abandonment of the old initiation ceremonies.

Treatment of disputes. Disputes often arise between parents and children. A father may consistently favour one son by allocating him more cattle than the rest, or he may allow a second wife to use property belonging to the first; he may ill-treat or neglect his children, punishing them excessively or failing to provide them with clothes and other necessities; he may ignore the right of his eldest son to be actively consulted in family affairs; he may attempt to force his daughter into a marriage she does not like, or will refuse to let his son marry the girl the latter wants. The children, on the other hand, may deliberately and persistently disobey their parents, or abuse and dissipate the family property, selling cattle without permission or authority; they may refuse to work with their parents, or fail to support them in their old age, or in some other way openly commit a breach of duty.

If the matter cannot be settled within the household, it is dealt with at a general family gathering (*phuthêgô ya bana ba mpa, puô ya lolwapa*). The injured child will complain to a senior paternal relative, or more frequently to his maternal uncle, who then calls the meeting; or the injured father may summon it. If no reconciliation can be effected here, the matter is referred to the headman of their ward, and if sufficiently serious may ultimately even come before the Chief. If it is shown that the parents do not treat their child properly, and that they are unable to live together harmoniously, they may be ordered to separate. The son may then build his own home in another part of the village, or go to live with some other relative, or, nowadays, go out to work among the Europeans. The father may also be ordered in case of a separation to give his son the share due to him of the family estate. The son will then be debarred from inheriting in future.

If the son is in the wrong, he will be severely reprimanded and ordered to obey his father. Sometimes he is also thrashed. The father may further be given the right, if the offence is sufficiently serious, to take back any property he may have given his son. This will not debar the latter from subsequently receiving a share of his father's estate, but he can no longer claim the cattle originally allocated to him. In extreme cases a father may completely disown his son. The son must be brought before the Chief at the *kgotla*. The father will there publicly declare that he no longer acknowledges the boy as his son. He will then be ordered to give the son whatever is due to him of the inheritance. Henceforth the latter has no further claim upon his father's estate, nor is the father liable for his misdeeds and debts. If the eldest son is disowned in this way, his next brother will become the main heir to the estate. But a father cannot disown a son without first taking him before the Chief at the *kgotla* and there publicly announcing his intention.

H. Cory: Sukuma Law and Custom*

Guardianship

Introduction. Cases concerning questions of guardianship are seldom brought to court. Complaints by widows against their co-guardians, or vice versa, and consequent changes, demands for the dissolution of a leviratic marriage in order to contract another, are customarily decided by the family council, and considerations of equity have much weight with members of the family when arbitrating between guardians, co-guardians, and wards. The law is often so vague that different courts belonging to the same local federation are inclined to differ in their interpretation of similar cases. There seems to be no clear conception of the extent of the responsibility of a guardian for the property of his ward. Apart from fundamental laws which are generally observed, each case is judged according to its merits.

It would have been contrary to the principles adopted in this recording of the customary law, as well as injurious to the efforts to achieve a much needed unification, to interfere with the existing situation to the extent of creating rules where there are none.

Especially in the matter of guardianship, any undue pressure or interference might endanger the existence of highly beneficial native institutions. No good purpose would be served by trying to formulate strict rules regarding responsibility of guardians for the property of their wards. In the majority of cases the guardians are next-of-kin who willingly incur financial sacrifices for their wards by helping them, when they are grown up, with the payment of bridewealth if the father has left no property. There are more poor than rich men in Sukumaland. Also it may be assumed that a father who leaves minor children has died a young man and has had little opportunity to acquire property.

If guardianship were to be regularized on a more business-like footing, with a clear definition of the responsibility of the guardian for the property of his ward, entailing an obligation to render an account when the ward became of age, and a limitation of rewards accruing to the guardian, the probable result would be that relatives of rich wards would be reluctant to act as guardians on account of the financial responsibilities involved, while relatives of poor wards would refuse because they could derive no advantage from it.

I. *Guardian of Minors*

A. *Choice of co-guardian by widow.* If a father leaves minor children, the widow becomes their guardian in conjunction with a male co-guardian (*nang'hani*).

a. If a widow chooses to be inherited and to become the wife of a kinsman of her deceased husband, this relative becomes the co-guardian of her minor children.

NOTE: The mother is so obviously the natural guardian of her children, whether they are small or grown up, that she is never called guardian. If a man dies and leaves a widow and children there will then be a 'mother' and a guardian. In order to make the situation clear, the mother is considered in this chapter the 'guardian' and the appointed relative the 'co-guardian'.

If a widow refuses to be inherited but agrees to remain within her deceased husband's family, she is entitled to choose the co-guardian from among the close kinsmen.

* H. Cory, *Sukuma Law and Custom*, Oxford University Press, 1953, pp. 100–108.

NOTE: No case is known in which a mother of small children remained within her deceased husband's family and refused to choose a leviratic husband.

It depends entirely on the widow whether she remains in the holding of her deceased husband or moves into the house of her leviratic husband and the co-guardian of her children.

In a polygynous household each widow can choose her husband and therefore each 'house' can have its separate co-guardian.

In case of a *numba ya bugongo* the *nkima wa bugongo* must choose her husband and co-guardian from the nearest relatives of her deceased husband's maternal family, preferably one of the sons of the maternal uncle.

NOTE: The question arises why a maternal uncle is never the guardian of his minor great-nephews. Usually the maternal uncle (*mami*) leaves the office of guardianship and the inheritance of *nkima wa bugongo* to one of his sons. In the Sukuma language no distinction is made between paternal and maternal cousins. The word in use is actually the same as that used for brother. This usage leads to a wrong conception of the relationship between the guardian and the deceased father of the wards.

If a widow and her leviratic husband decide to terminate their marriage and the widow chooses another member of the family as her husband, no change is made in the guardianship of the children. The relative who was chosen by the widow as her husband and the co-guardian of her children after the *isabingula* remains co-guardian.

If a co-guardian dies, the mother may choose another leviratic husband and co-guardian from among the near relatives of the deceased or a co-guardian may be chosen by the family council.

If the mother dies, the co-guardian becomes the sole guardian of the children.

B. *Appointment of co-guardian by the family*. If a widow refuses to be inherited or to remain with her deceased husband's family, the guardian of her minor children is selected and appointed by the family council. Usually the relative who would have been the *nkuruwabo* of the deceased had there been no children is appointed.

If in a polygynous household all the widows refuse to be inherited one male guardian for all the houses is appointed.

C. *Deprivation of guardianship*. If a widow thinks that her co-guardian is neglecting his duties, she has the right to bring her complaint before the family council.

The family council has the right to deprive a co-guardian of his office and appoint another member of the family instead.

NOTE: No court cases of this kind are known; such complaints are always settled in private.

If a widow neglects the house and her children the family council can decide to return her to her paternal family and to hand over the children to the co-guardian.

NOTE: Not a single case is known in which a widow neglected her children or squandered their property.

D. *Authority and responsibility of guardians*

General rules. Mother and co-guardian jointly take over the position of the deceased father within the family until the eldest son (*nkuruwabo*) is grown up and himself occupies the father's position.

NOTE: The functions of the guardian (mother) and the co-guardian are not clearly defined. The relationship of the two guardians must be one of friendship, otherwise a change would be considered necessary by all persons concerned. In practice the influence of the two guardians will depend on their respective characters and intelligence.

Generally speaking the authority of the mother is greater in the south than in the north, just as the property of wards in the south is more often considered their personal property than in the north. The difference between north and south may be illustrated by the following example. In Buduhe, if the sister of a ward is granted a divorce, and bridewealth has to be returned, it must be claimed from the full brother (minor or adult), and if there is no property it becomes his debt. In a similar situation in Nunghu, the guardian is responsible for repayment of bridewealth. Normally the relationship between mother and co-guardian is that of man and wife, and therefore both make their decisions as do parents about matters concerning their children. But it must be remembered that such a relationship is not obligatory and, if it does not exist, the co-guardian is supposed to interfere only as representative of the family interests in questions relating to property.

The mother runs the house and decides the number of fields to be cultivated during the current year. She has the right to dispose of all crops except bulrush millet and sorghum and can use the proceeds of their sale as she likes; she also has rights of disposal of all cattle products (ghee, meat, and hides).

Any transactions in corn and in cattle must be undertaken after mutual consultation between mother and co-guardian.

NOTE: In all chiefdoms of the Sukuma Federation corn and cattle are treated alike in law. Corn is the true cash-crop of the Sukuma; cotton, ground-nuts, rice, beans, and all other minor crops may bring money to the cultivator which he uses for paying tax and for buying clothing and implements, but little of this constitutes permanent material gain. With corn the Sukuma peasant acquires cattle. It is the traditional currency with which he is thoroughly familiar. The demand for corn seldom falls owing to the fact that there is a semi-famine nearly every year somewhere in Sukumaland or in neighbouring areas. The peasant possessing a good quantity of corn does not sell it for money but barters it for cattle. But even if a man does not barter his corn in one season, he has no loss because he can keep it for two, or even three years. Native traders, not the cultivators themselves, buy the corn with cattle and bring it to the areas of scarcity where they barter it for cattle, obtaining more cattle for it than they paid originally. The corn sold on the markets comes from peasants who have only a small surplus or who need quick cash and have nothing else to sell at the moment.

The conventions of barter have no relation to the market prices of commodities, and there is a considerable difference between the market value of corn and cattle and that taken as a basis for barter. A heifer is obtainable for two bags of corn, a young bull for one bag. A bag of sorghum would fetch on the market Shs. 6/- to Shs. 7/- while the price for a heifer may go up to Shs. 50/- and more. A family needing corn cannot buy it for money because peasants do not sell it for money. The Sukuma prefers the barter system; firstly, it is traditional; secondly, the handling of money, still a problem for many peasants, is avoided; and thirdly, the owner of corn sells his commodity on his own doorstep. An elder explained: If one sells a heifer at the auction, one is paid in money, but whatever may have been the price, one never contrives to buy two bags of corn for it. A part of the money disappears on the way home and the other part is lost while arrangements for buying corn are in progress.

It now becomes clear why corn is treated by law in the same manner as cattle. If a widow gave away too much corn—perhaps to her relatives—it would mean that stock would have to be bartered to replace it. On the other hand, if there is a surplus of corn, cattle can be acquired with it and cattle guarantee the prosperity of the whole family.

A mother has no right to betroth her daughter without the consent of her co-guardian who undertakes all duties regarding the arrangements for the marriage just as the bride's father would have done were he still alive.

The co-guardian has to handle all public business for the deceased's family which the widow, according to custom, cannot attend to (representation in court or at a cattle-market, etc.).

The authority of the co-guardian varies according to his relationship to the deceased father and according to the age of the wards.

If the co-guardian is a close kinsman

1. *If the wards are small children.* The co-guardian becomes in every respect the complete substitute for the deceased father. The wards become his children. The position of the mother as guardian is bound up with her position as the co-guardian's wife.

The children of the deceased occupy a special position in the sequence of heirs of the co-guardian, depending on their father's position in the sequence of heirs of his own father, i.e. the paternal grandfather of the wards. If the ward's father was the eldest among his brothers, the ward becomes the *nkuruwabo* of the co-guardian's family even if the latter has children of his own who are older. If the ward's father was the younger brother of the co-guardian, the eldest of the wards becomes *nzuna* in the co-guardian's house, irrespective of his age compared with that of the co-guardian's own children.

If a childless brother inherits the wife and children of his elder brother, the *nkuruwabo* of the deceased becomes *nkuruwabo* of the co-guardian and retains this position even if the co-guardian should afterwards marry another wife and have sons by her. But if an elder brother (childless) inherits the wife and children of his younger brother, the eldest of the wards remains *nkuruwabo* of the co-guardian only so long as the co-guardian has no male children of his own. The first-born child of the co-guardian would become *nkuruwabo* of his father and the eldest of the wards would follow him as *nzuna.*

The property of the deceased is taken over by the co-guardian and merged with his own. The wards cannot ask for an account when they come of age.

NOTE: No case is known in which a co-guardian has given an account of the estate to the wards when they come of age.

Whether the widow decides to remain with her children in the homestead of her husband or to follow her leviratic husband into his house, these provisions remain unaltered.

2. *If the wards are grown children.* If the *nkuruwabo* at the time of his father's death has attained an age of approximately thirteen years, the co-guardian must keep the property of the wards separate from his own, because they then have no position within the sequence of his own heirs. The wards will inherit the property left them by their father in due course.

NOTE: Obviously, the rules given below are very vague. The underlying idea is probably either that a guardian can adopt the wards as his own children and merge their property with his, or that the wards should remain wards, in which case the guardian should keep their property separate from his own. But there is no rule permitting a guardian to follow the first course, or binding him to follow the second. In any case the guardian is the '*baba*' and as such can do no wrong.

In this case the widow usually remains in the homestead of her deceased husband and does not move into the house of the co-guardian; she continues to live in the holding in order to keep it for the day when the *nkuruwabo* will be able to take it over.

The mother as well as the *nkuruwabo* will exercise control over the co-guardian and any transaction affecting the wards' property can only be carried out with their full consent. They can always appeal for help to the family council if the co-guardian should neglect their property or use it to his own advantage. The mother can also file a suit against the co-guardian.

NOTE: There would be no objection to a mother filing a suit against a dishonest co-guardian if the relatives should fail to assist her. In such a case proof of bad guardianship would probably not be difficult to produce. If the mother does not take action in the interests of her children, and they themselves after several years go to court, proof of misuse is almost impossible to obtain. Then the usual solution is to award to the children the same number of cattle as the co-guardian actually received when taking over the guardianship. This is not a rule in itself. If exact numbers of losses in and additions to the herd can be given by the wards, they are entitled to receive the exact number of beasts.

If such control has not been exercised a ward cannot, after many years under guardianship, ask for an exact account including all details about the death of beasts and the birth of calves. Equally, the co-guardian cannot withold cattle which are clearly the offspring of the ward's herd.

NOTE: If the co-guardian voluntarily hands over the number of cattle which he originally took over, the general opinion is that he is acting fairly and in accordance with tradition. He is not expected to keep a detailed account and is not considered dishonest if he does not do so. A truculent attitude on the part of a ward is deemed to be out of place.

A ward who thinks he has been wronged has the right to file a suit against his guardian.

NOTE: This rule was decided upon by the chiefs of the Sukuma Federation and their people in 1949. Formerly the relevant rules differed in the various chiefdoms.

In UF, NF, BD, KF* a ward could not file a suit in court against his guardian; the courts refused to hear such cases and referred the complaint to the family council.

In SS, BS, KS, SBS, KM* the court accepted such cases.

In BSN neither a full brother nor any other relative as guardian could use property of the wards to his own advantage. A co-guardian had to keep his own property and that of his wards strictly separated.

The mother of the wards, helped by the other relatives, exercised strict control. On the other hand the wards when they came of age could not file a suit in court if a co-guardian had misappropriated part of their property; they had to bring their case before the family council.

NOTE: Quarrels between guardians and wards are usually settled through arbitration by senior members of the family or by village elders. When such a quarrel reaches the court, two assumptions can be made with fair certainty: it will be almost impossible for anyone outside the family to determine the true facts of the case; the dispute has become so bitter that the parties and their witnesses will have a more than usual disregard for the truth. Reconciliation of accounts or interests will therefore be difficult to achieve. The provisions of this para. can only be taken at present as an attempt by the chiefs and their people to initiate more specific rules of guardianship and, ultimately, unification of these rules.

If the co-guardian is a distant relative. The co-guardian has to keep the property of the wards separate from his own.

NOTE: Nearly every Sukuma cattle-owner has in his herd cattle which he has acquired in different ways or which belong to different people. He is required in law to keep them and their offspring separate, not physically, but in his mind. Frequently there are cattle inherited from his father or from paternal relatives, or received as bridewealth for daughters, or received in trusteeship, or acquired by his own efforts, or cattle of *kuyinza*, or cattle which he holds as guardian of minors.

The wards, when they come of age, have the right to ask the co-guardian for an account of the property, especially if their mother died while they were minors.

NOTE: As long as the mother is alive she is expected to exercise strict control over the actions of the co-guardian regarding her children's property. If the mother is found to be weak or too compliant with the wishes of the co-guardian, the rest of the maternal relatives have the right to intervene. They feel themselves to be the true blood relatives in a case where the guardian is a distant paternal relative; although they have no legal rights, they exercise great influence over the children and their up-bringing, because the children when they grow up will tend to look upon their maternal uncles as their next senior relatives, and follow their advice.

The co-guardian cannot be asked to give an account of the products of the herd which are his due. The guardian is also entitled to dispose of beasts of a ward's herd in the latter's interest.

NOTE: In practice, the courts refuse to investigate deaths and births which have occurred in the ward's herd if the guardian asserts that disease, &c., has caused considerable loss. The court may ask for witnesses to such incidents. Generally and customarily the court considers the guardian only responsible for the original number of beasts which he received when he took over the estate. The cost of bringing up the children is roughly accounted for by this means.

While the authority of the co-guardian depends on factors already mentioned the situation between the two guardians—mother and co-guardian—is not legally altered by the degree of the co-guardian's relationship to the deceased husband.

NOTE: If the co-guardian is a near relative the question of whether the mother marries him or not does not affect his position as co-guardian; but if he is a distant relative his marriage to the mother does alter the situation to some extent. In these circumstances the authority of the co-guardian is obviously greater and control by

* These letters refer to districts of Sukumaland.

outsiders is more difficult. Therefore, a mother may refuse to be inherited and to become the wife of a co-guardian who is a distant relative for fear that the property of her children may not be safe in his care and that, as wife, she will be less able to forbid transactions involving her children's property.

E. *Distribution of property by the co-guardian between the heirs.* (The following rules refer only to cases where property has to be kept separate from that of the co-guardian.)

Children of the same mother who is still alive when they come of age. It is Sukuma custom that the property is not distributed between the children so long as the mother is alive and living on her deceased husband's estate.

A different custom prevails in the chiefdoms of SS, KS, and BSN,* where the property is nominally distributed after the father's death between his minor children, i.e. each child receives his share but the herd is kept together. No redistribution takes place if the cattle of a certain child's share should die.

NOTE: The distribution of the estate does not necessarily take place when the *nkuruwabo* has attained a certain age or when he wishes to marry or when a sister marries. The herd is kept together as long as all the heirs live in amity with each other and as long as an heir has no special reason for demanding his share. This was considered a custom and not a rule, and therefore no unification of the above rules has been attempted.

Any one of the heirs when grown up is entitled to demand the distribution of the estate and the handing-over of his share.

When the *nkuruwabo* grows up, he takes over the guardianship of his minor siblings from the co-guardian, but the handing-over is not performed on any special day or with special ceremonies. The *nkuruwabo* grows into the guardianship. If ever he fails in his duties, the mother will check him, or if her efforts are unsuccessful she will call for the help of the former co-guardian or even of the family council.

A. The *nkuruwabo* is entitled to take cattle from his father's herd for paying bridewealth and, if the herd consists of no more than the number of beasts required for the bridewealth, he can take them all. Younger brothers have no claim against the elder brother for a share in the estate if the cattle have been used for payment of bridewealth.

B. If the father has left many cattle, one son after the other, as he comes of age and wishes to marry, receives cattle for payment of bridewealth from the estate. The remaining cattle may be distributed only after the death of the mother.

C. Payment of *misango*, *njigu*, repayment of bridewealth in case of divorce of a sister, and payment of compensation for adultery committed by a brother can be met by using cattle of the estate. In the final distribution of the estate, no such payment would be regarded as a debt of the brother for whom it had been made.

D. If a brother needs one beast for paying a practitioner's fee for himself or a member of his family, he receives it from the estate if he has no property of his own.

E. If a brother wishes for a few beasts for trading, he must obtain the consent of the *nkuruwabo*, the mother, and a few senior members of the family, preferably the former co-guardian. In any case it would be understood that the profit of the transaction had to be put back into the estate.

NOTE: Generally it may be said that the estate is considered as capital which can be used for the purpose of perpetuating the family and for meeting necessary demands in connexion with this purpose.

If one of the brothers demands and receives his share, the other heirs can decide that the remainder of the estate, i.e. their shares, shall remain undivided.

2. *Children of the same mother who dies before they come of age.* If the mother dies, the co-guardian becomes sole guardian and is entitled to take the children and property into his house.

As soon as the *nkuruwabo* is grown up, he will take over the guardianship of his minor siblings, but he will not be able to do this before he gets married as he must give them a home.

* These letters refer to districts of Sukumaland.

If the *nkuruwabo* should fail in his guardianship of his younger siblings, the family council can decide that the property shall be distributed and the minors, together with their shares in the estate, be put once more under the guardianship of the original guardian, while the *nkuruwabo* is given his own share.

3. *Children of different mothers.* If the widows choose different co-guardians the property is usually distributed between the houses shortly after the father's death.

NOTE: If several widows choose the same co-guardian the estate need not be distributed.

The distribution of the estate within each house follows the rules contained in first two sections of E.

M. Fortes: Kinship and Marriage among the Ashanti*

Father and child. The crux of this aspect of Ashanti kinship lies in the great affective as well as jural weight attached to the recognition of paternity. The general rule that a child is considered by law to be the offspring of its pater prevails in Ashanti,[1] but the ideal is that pater and genitor should be the same person. It is a sin and a crime, for which both parties are nowadays liable to a heavy fine and to public obloquy,[2] for a girl to conceive before her puberty ceremony. But after this ceremony no disgrace follows premarital pregnancy, if the girl has not been promiscuous. What is, however, reprobated and considered shameful, to the man as well as to the girl and her maternal kin, is refusal on his part to acknowledge paternity of the child. The latter is fully legitimate, as far as his status in his matrilineal lineage is concerned, but he carries a stigma which may be thrown at his head in later life in a quarrel. Paternity is acknowledged by the man's accepting the responsibility of maintaining his lover during her pregnancy and by his giving her and her child a number of customary gifts immediately after delivery.[3] On the eighth day after its birth (or nowadays, very soon after the eighth day), the child is named by its acknowledged father; and this is the critcal assertion of fatherhood. If an unmarried girl's child and its physical parents suffer disgrace it is because the child was not named by its father.[4]

A man generally chooses a name for his child from among those of his forebears on either side of his parentage, but he is not bound to do so. Ashanti say that a man wants children so that he can pass on the names of his forebears. It is a very important filial duty as well as a source of pride. Hence the children of brothers and the children of a polygynist by different wives often bear the same names. The modern custom of using one's father's or one's own personal name as a surname (and not a name indicating one's lineage affiliation) goes back to the father's right of naming.

Ashanti connect this with the father's *sunsum* (his personality conceptualized as a personal soul) or his *kra* (his spirit, the source of his life and destiny), or if they are versed in traditional religion, his *ntoro*. The ideas connecting the three ritual concepts thus associated with fatherhood cannot be discussed here.[5] It is enough to say that Ashanti believe that a child cannot thrive if its father's *sunsum* is alienated from it;[6] that its destiny and disposition are fixed by the *kra* which is transmitted by the father; and that this puts every person into one of a limited number of named quasi-ritual categories, the *ntoro* divisions. Each *ntoro* appears to be under the aegis of a god (*obosom*), from whom it takes its name, and whose abode is a river or lake.[7] The number of *ntoro* groupings recognized varies from seven to twelve in different areas, as the major nation-wide groupings have split up in adaptation to local circumstances. Each local *ntoro* division has its sacred day for the ritual purification of the *kra* of its adherents, specific totemic taboos, a distinctive form of response to a greeting from any of its members, and a number of names which are commonly though not exclusively found among its members. It is also believed that each *ntoro* goes with a particular type of character which its adherents are prone to have. The *ntoro* concept thus gives expression through ritual beliefs and sanctions, through etiquette and through names, to the value attached to paternity. Women as well as men are bound to honour paternity. A woman does so by observing her husband's

* M. Fortes, 'Kinship and Marriage among the Ashanti', in A. R. Radcliffe-Brown and D. Forde (eds.), *African Systems of Kinship and Marriage*, Oxford University Press, pp. 265–270.

ntoro taboos during pregnancy and nursing. If she does not, the child suffers injury through the anger and hostility of the father's *ntoro*. The *ntoro* concept emphasizes, in particular, the bonds of father and son which give continuity to the male side of family and kinship relations. Adherents of the same *ntoro* in any locality do not meet for ritual or social purposes and do not constitute an organised group analogous to the lineage. Nor, according to my information,[8] is membership of the same *ntoro* division a bar to marriage, as Rattray asserts. What is prohibited is marriage between patrilateral kin connected through males only not farther back than a common great-grandfather. As Ashanti put it, marriage is prohibited between the descendants of a man in the male line up to the fourth generation. The possession of a common *ntoro* is incidental in this connexion. It is the kinship thus symbolized which is the bar to marriage, not the ritual bond. This rule is asserted not by a count of generations but by a reference to known ancestry; and paternal ascendants farther back than the great-grandfather (or descendants of a man beyond the fourth generation) are rarely remembered. One of the main reasons for this is that there is no corporate organization based on the father's line, nor are jural or political rights (such as rights of inheritance) or duties derived from paternal descent.[9] The relations of father and child[10] are rooted wholly and solely in the fact of paternity. The bond is as unique as that of mother and child, though with very different emphasis. One's father's brother (i.e. any man whom one's father calls brother (*nua barima*) is addressed and spoken of as 'father' (*agya, papa, &c.*) and his sister (any woman whom he calls sister (*nua baa*) is one's 'female father' (*sewa*); but the respect and the frequent affection and goodwill shown to them are said bluntly to be because of one's father. It arises from their mutual identification as siblings.

An Ashanti father has no legal authority over his children. He cannot even compel them to live with him or, if he has divorced their mother, claim their custody as a right. Ashanti say that children should grow up in their father's house[11] but investigation shows that not more than 50 per cent. of pre-adolescent children are found living with their fathers at a given time. Nevertheless it is regarded as the duty and the pride of a father to bring up his children, that is, to feed, clothe, and educate them, and, later, to set them up in life. Even after the divorce or the death of the mother, a conscientious father discharges these duties. This applies especially to sons. Their moral and civic training, in particular, is his responsibility and this gives him the right to punish them if necessary. If anything, Ashanti fathers (unlike mothers) tend to be over-strict in exacting obedience, deference, and good behaviour from their children. Nowadays it is strongly felt that a child's schooling, which is widely regarded as the most important preparation for gaining a living in the modern world, is his father's responsibility. Formerly he took his sons to farm with him or taught them his craft. Investigation shows that in practice approximately half of all children attending school are kept there by their fathers. Of the rest, half (25 per cent. of the total) are supported at school by their maternal uncles, and between 10 and 15 per cent. by their mothers.[12] An uncle, a mother, or other kinsman will only take on this responsibility if the father fails to do so.

The spiritual tie believed to unite father and child is a ritual symbol of the moral aspect of their relationship. Ashanti say that a man has no hold over his children except through their love for him and their conscience. A father wins his children's affection by caring for them. They cannot inherit his property, but he can and often does provide for them by making them gifts of property, land, or money during his lifetime or on his death-bed[13] (by written will nowadays). To insult, abuse, or assault one's father is an irreparable wrong, one which is bound to bring ill luck (*mmusuo*). While there is no legal obligation on a son or daughter to support a father in old age, it would be regarded as a shame and an evil act if he or she did not do so. And, as with all kinship ties, the bond with the father is given tangible expression in funeral rites. It is the sons and daughters (*mmaa mma*), own and classificatory,[14] of a man and the brother's sons and daughters of a woman who provide the coffin.

Parents have a very important part in the marriage of their children, for it is by marriage that a child is established as a socially responsible person. The consent of both parents, though not legally compulsory, is by usage deemed indispensable for any marriage to take place. A father should provide his son with a wife; and even if he seeks out a bride for himself, no respectable young man would marry without his father's approval. Nor would a respectable girl marry without her parents' approval. In recognition of the parents' labours in nurturing her and of their concern for her well-being, special gifts are due to them from the bridegroom on her marriage. In this respect the father receives as much honour and consideration as the girl's legal guardian, her mother's brother. Indeed the former carries greater weight than the latter, as can be seen from statistics collected in 1945. It was found that in a sample of 525 women of all ages, about 33 per cent. had been given in marriage by their fathers, as compared with 28 per cent. given in marriage by their mothers' brothers; and though success in courtship depends to a very great extent on winning the girl's mother's favour, yet without the father's approval (if he is alive) the match would not be allowed. For it is the father's duty to make sure that the suitor is able to support his daughter. This appears from the sample just mentioned. Only 13 per cent. of the women interviewed claimed that their mothers gave them in marriage to their husbands.

The idea that a father is primarily responsible for his son's moral behaviour is seen in the rule that if a man commits adultery with another man's wife, the responsibility for paying the adultery damages falls on the father, not the mother's brother. Ashanti say that is why fathers take pains to get their sons married as soon as the boys are old enough. A girl's moral conduct is chiefly her mother's concern.

Ashanti say that no man loves his sisters' children as much as his own children. They say that sons are the support of their fathers. Chiefs, in particular, stress this. The more sons and son's sons a chief has, the more secure does he feel. As their social standing depends on him and as they have no rights to his office, they will support him in all circumstances. They are his most trusted followers, and important chiefs appoint their own and their brothers' sons and sons' sons (*ohenemma* and *ohenenana*) as titled councillors to attend closely on them. In the old days, men say, a youth preferred to follow his father to war rather than his mother's brother.

Ashanti kinship, both from the point of view of the individual and from that of the system as a whole, is an arrangement of polar relationships. Where kinship is involved, a person is always looking two ways. The division between the sexes is a first consideration. Men have greater political power than women; but political status comes from lineage affiliation which is conferred by women, and this redresses the balance. The result, in practice, is that there is a high degree of equality between the sexes.[15] In terms of personal behaviour and attitudes, there is often no apparent difference between the relations of mother and children and those of father and children. The warmth, trust, and affection frequently found uniting parents and offspring go harmoniously with the respect shown to both. In terms of jural and moral relations, however, Ashanti contrast the parents who, as we have seen, very often live apart. Through one's father one is given access to social relationships in which voluntary choice can play a part. These affect one's personal life, not one's public character and roles. Men and women are usually very fond of their half-siblings by the same father; but there is no sense of inescapable obligation about this, as there is about all social ties through one's mother. And this is what Ashanti emphasize in regard to everything that concerns matrilineal kinship.

Notes

[1] Thus an adulterine child belongs to its mother's legal husband, in accordance with the maxim *Okromfo nni ba*, a thief has no child.

[2] Part of the fine is used to procure sheep for a purification sacrifice to the community's ancestral stools. Formerly (cf. Rattray, 1927, p. 74; 1929, p. 306) both culprits were put to death or driven out of the village.

[3] Rattray, 1927, p. 6. Nowadays the gifts consist of imported toilet articles, clothes, soap, trinkets, &c., which may cost two or three pounds.

[4] *Ibid.* This rule applies as strictly to Christian as to pagan Ashanti. If the father refuses to name a love-child its mother's brother will do so and will accept paternal responsibility for it.

[5] Cf. Rattray, 1923, pp. 77 ff.; 1927, pp. 51 ff., 154. Cf. also Herskovits, *loc. cit.*

[6] Cf. Rattray, 1929, p. 8.

[7] This is seen from the names of the most widespread *ntoro*, e.g. Bosommuru—the god of the river Buru, Bosomtwe—the god of the sacred lake of the same name, etc. See Rattray, 1923, chap. xi.

[8] I have records of cases of men marrying women of their own *ntoro*, and Dr. Busia has given me instances of this as well. Elders assured me that this is not due to modern changes.

[9] The exceptions are certain high palace functionaries serving the king whose titles are transmitted from father to son. This is explained either on the assumption that the original

holder of a title was a slave or captive, or on the grounds that the duties involved can only be learnt by growing up with them, as a son grows up under his father's care and instruction.

[10] Rattray, 1929, chap. xi, discusses this subject with profound insight.

[11] The proverb says, 'A child grows up in its father's house but does not remain there'.

[12] Unpublished data based on a sample of nearly 700 children of all ages.

[13] Cf. Rattray, 1929, chap. xi.

[14] Generally those descendants of the deceased's father's father whom he called sons and daughters.

[15] Rattray showed this in many places in his books.

Part II

THE LAW OF MARRIAGE

The law of marriage is probably the most important subject in the field of customary law and has naturally attracted the attention of many writers. The length of this Part is a clear indication of this fact. Because of the voluminous literature on the subject and the different approach of the various writers, we had particular difficulty in selecting the extracts for this Part. The final product gives, we hope, a balanced picture of the customary law of marriage paying particular regard to geographical distribution and the various approaches and views of the commentators on the subject.

The law of marriage is of particular importance because unlike other branches of customary law such as contract and tort which are gradually dying out, it still plays a very important role in the everyday lives of the people of Africa and remains as probably the most widely observed branch of customary law in African countries. It has for this reason attracted the attention not only of writers, but also of African governments. In Ghana, for example, there was an attempt in 1961[1] to enact legislation intended to bring in a uniform system of marriage, but this was unsuccessful. Tanzania has tackled the problem by a unification of the different customary marriage laws,[2] whilst in Uganda a Marriage Commission was appointed which made recommendations as to the unification of the customary and statutory systems of marriage.[3] Finally, in Kenya, a start was made with a restatement of the customary laws of marriage, followed recently by the appointment of a Marriage Commission.[4]

In presenting the material, we have sought to maintain a chronological sequence of marriage, commencing with capacity and consents, then preliminaries and betrothal, formalities and so on until the marriage is finally dissolved. Needless to say there is a close relationship and sometimes an overlap between this Part and other Parts and in particular Part I of this volume dealing with the law of persons.

Notes

1 See Ghana Marriage, Divorce and Inheritance Bill.

2 See Schedule to the Local Customary Law Declaration (Order) 1963.

3 Report of the Commission on Marriage, Divorce and the Status of Women, 1965, Government Printer, Entebbe.

4 See *Kenya Gazette*, Vol. LXVIX, No. 18, Gazette Notice No. 1261. Since writing, the Commission has published its report (see *Report of the Commission on the Law of Marriage and Divorce*, Government Printer, Nairobi 1968).

CHAPTER 6

DEFINITIONS AND GENERAL CHARACTERISTICS

Although we have, as mentioned earlier, sought to maintain a chronological sequence of marriage, we have thought it helpful, by way of introduction, to include certain extracts about the nature of marriage in African customary law and its general characteristics. In the first extract, *Phillips* argues, quite rightly it is submitted, that 'African customary marriage has sufficient in common with marriage in other parts of the world (including "European" marriage) to warrant the usage of describing it . . . by the same generic term "marriage".' He then goes on to describe the distinctive features of African customary marriage.

The second extract from *Radcliffe-Brown* stresses the social aspects of the marriage relationship and has an interesting comparison between an African customary marriage and a wedding in early England. Like Professor Phillips, he then describes the characteristics of customary marriages laying more stress on the social rather than the legal aspects.

A. Phillips: Survey of African Marriage and Family Life*

Marriage as an Indigenous African Institution†

In studying 'African marriage' and comparing it with 'European marriage' we are liable to be confronted at the outset with the question whether these are simply different forms of varieties of the same institution or, on the other hand, fundamentally different institutions. In other words, does the relationship of husband and wife which in European society constitutes 'marriage' exist, in its essentials, in the indigenous African social system? It has sometimes been doubted whether there is a sufficient basic identity between the two types of relationship to justify the use of a common term of description. In the South African case of *Guma* v. *Guma*,[1] for example, the following view was expressed:

> 'It is necessary to guard against the assumption that, because the single term "marriage" is used to describe the conjugal relationships established under both the common law of the country and Native law, they are one and the same thing. They have, indeed, so much in common, that each form regularises sexual union and the status of offspring, but in other respects the two institutions are fundamentally different in nature and the law governing them.'[2]

The fact that such views have been held, and have had a certain amount of influence —even to the extent that in the Union of South Africa a statutory distinction has been made between 'marriages' and 'customary unions'—is in itself a matter of importance. For the present purpose it does not seem to be necessary to examine in detail the arguments on both sides; but in order to make clear the presuppositions and implications of the discussion which follows, attention may be drawn to a few salient points:

(*a*) In the words of Vinogradoff,[4] 'it can hardly be doubted that there are certain fundamental ideas which assert themselves in all forms of human marriage'; and

* A. Phillips (ed.), *Survey of African Marriage and Family Life*, Oxford University Press, 1953, pp. xi–xvii.

† References to Parts I and II in the ensuing extract are to *A Survey of African Marriage and Family Life*, ed. A. Phillips.

these fundamental ideas, as generally understood by both jurists and anthropologists, appear to be inherent in the typical African conception of marriage.

(*b*) The institution of 'bride-price',[5] which in one form or another is characteristic of marriage in the great majority of African tribes, is not a peculiarly African institution; it was indeed a feature of the social systems of European peoples in earlier times.

(*c*) While the case of polygamy is different—for it cannot, historically speaking, be ranked among the antecedents of European marriage[6]—the idea of it has long been familiar to the European mind through the Old Testament scriptures, and this has perhaps tended to produce a more tolerant attitude towards African custom in this matter.

(*d*) Although it seems that in Africa (as in ancient Rome) the dividing line between marriage and concubinage is not always precisely marked, the broad distinction is usually plain and well recognized. Not only is the 'validity' of a marriage important in African eyes in relation to parental rights and claims for damages for adultery, but it is probably true to say that the 'sanctity' of marriage is a conception by no means foreign to African thought.[7]

(*e*) Recognition in fact, if not in name, is almost universally accorded by European authorities, administrative and judicial, to the distinction between a 'marriage' by native custom and other, irregular, forms of sexual relationship, and to the effect of the former as regards the legal status of spouses and children.[8]

(*f*) It may be added that Church authorities have commonly been disposed to regard an African customary marriage—provided it is in fact monogamous—as a valid 'natural' marriage.[9]

It seems legitimate to conclude, therefore, that African customary marriage has sufficient in common with marriage in other parts of the world (including 'European' marriage) to warrant the usage of describing it, in a context such as the present one, by the same generic term 'marriage'.

If we may take it for granted, then, that there is an indigenous African institution which can rightly be called 'marriage', what (it may be asked) are its main characteristics and distinguishing features?

Distinctive Features of African Customary Marriage

Any attempt to sketch in a few pages the outlines of African customary marriage must inevitably illustrate the dangers of generalization on a subject so great in its range and variety. Not only is there a vast diversity in matters of detail between the customs of different tribes and localities; but it is not even possible, save to a very limited extent, to trace any broad uniformity of basic principles. As warrant for this statement, it is sufficient to refer to the contrast between patrilineal and matrilineal societies, or to Dr. Mair's exposition of the differing implications of 'cattle bride-price' and of that type of custom in which the transfer of property is essentially of a token character.[10] The fact that Dr. Mair has found it necessary to deal separately with each of four different regions of Africa is itself an indication of the difficulty of a completely unified treatment.

If, subject to this caution, we seek to identify the main distinguishing features of African customary marriage, as compared with 'European marriage', there will no doubt be general agreement that the most obvious of such features is the toleration, and even approval, accorded to polygamy.[11] Almost universally, a marriage according to native law and custom is potentially polygamous in the sense that there is during its subsistence no legal impediment to the contracting of another marriage (or of an unlimited number of other marriages) by the husband. Any suggestion of compulsory monogamy as an indigenous institution must be interpreted as having reference only to exceptional cases—e.g. to the restriction imposed on the husband of a female chief—or to quite unrepresentative tribes (such as possibly the Galla).[12] In general, monogamy is either a self-denying ordinance, in the sense that a man voluntarily renounces or abstains from polygamy, or it is dictated by inability to afford more than one wife. Where the traditional outlook still prevails, the possession of a number of wives is normally a mark of importance and success in life, and—for this among other reasons—is something which the average African man would gladly achieve if he could: in other words, monogamy is, for the majority who are in fact monogamists, a matter of necessity rather than of choice.

It is this polygamous element which most radically differentiates African marriage (though not African marriage alone) from European marriage.[13] It constitutes, moreover, the point of greatest resistance to the teaching of Christian missions concerning marriage. It may be added that it reflects, and at the same time intensifies, the fundamental inequality between the sexes which appears to be typical of African social systems, even in matrilineal societies. Whatever may be said as to the material advantages accruing to a wife as a result of having co-wives to share her duties, it can hardly be denied that the institution of polygamy is normally associated with a social system in which there is unchallenged male dominance.

Another outstanding feature of African customary marriage is the institution commonly called 'bride-price'.[14] There are few African tribes in which it is not found in one form or another. To quote Professor Radcliffe-Brown:

> 'In most African marriages . . . the making of a payment of goods or services by the bridegroom to the bride's kin is an essential part of the establishment of "legality".'[15]

Within the wide limits of the institution as so defined there is a great diversity of custom. The payment may be in livestock, in other chattels (e.g. hoes, brass rods, or lengths of cloth), or in money. Its value may be great or small. The total amount may be required on the handing-over of the bride, or it may be payable by deferred instalments. Differing (and sometimes elaborate) rules govern the repayment of bride-price in the event of death or divorce. Correlated with these differences are characteristic differences in the legal effects of the transaction (e.g. in regard to the attachment of children to the father's or the mother's lineage). There is, moreover, considerable difference of opinion as to the essential significance of the institution. Thus bride-price is variously interpreted as being primarily in the nature of compensation to the woman's family for the loss of one of its members (and that member a potential childbearer); as 'part of a transaction in which the dominant emphasis is on the formation of an alliance between two kinship groups; as a species of 'marriage insurance', designed to stabilize the marriage and/or to give protection to the wife; as a symbol, or as a 'seal' marking the formal conclusion of the marriage contract; and in accordance with other theories as to the nature and significance—or even the historical origin—of the custom.

It is sometimes implied, if not stated expressly, that the possibility of easy dissolution is characteristic of African customary marriage. But as a generalization this appears to be too sweeping. It is true that in very many tribes (probably in the great majority) a marriage can be dissolved by inter-family arrangement, without the necessity for any judicial pronouncement. But it does not follow that a divorce can be easily obtained at the mere wish of husband or wife (or even of both of them) in the absence of substantial grounds. Native law frequently requires that the wife's relatives should refund the bride-price (in part, at least) as an essential condition of the validity of the divorce; and this requirement tends to have an obstructive effect. Another possible deterrent is the prospect of losing the right to the children.[16] Attention may be drawn, on the other hand, to the fact that in some tribes a union does not acquire the strictly binding quality of marriage until it has been in existence for a number of years; and doubtless other examples could be cited in support of the view that African marriage is easily dissoluble. On the whole, however, it would seem that no very definite conclusions can be drawn from a comparison between African and European marriage in the matter of dissolubility. It must be remembered that divorce by mutual consent is not unknown in European secular law; and that while in some African tribes (e.g. the Yakō as described by Professor Daryll Forde)[17] divorce is exceedingly common, there are others in which (to quote Professor Gluckman's account of the position in Zululand) it is 'almost unknown'[18]—in practice, at any rate, and occasionally, it seems, even in law.

In seeking to identify the outstanding characteristics of African customary marriage, we may justifiably include a reference to the collective aspect of the marriage transaction and relationship. There is a considerable weight of authority for the statement that, from the point of view of indigenous law and custom, a marriage is to be regarded primarily as an alliance between two kinship groups and only in a secondary aspect as a union between two individual persons. Such a formula can easily be pressed too far; nevertheless, it does appear to embody a principle of great importance—viz. that the indigenous institution of marriage can only be understood if it is viewed as an integral part of the kinship system as a whole. It is here, for example, that we find the key to certain customs which obviously presuppose a conception of marriage as a transaction giving rise to reciprocal rights and obligations between two groups of kinsmen and binding those groups together in a relationship which remains effective beyond the lifetime of the original individual spouses. This principle of a continuing relationship is closely connected with the institution of bride-price; and it finds expression in, for example, the levirate (or the somewhat different custom of 'widow-inheritance'),[19] under which a widow is expected to co-habit with one of her deceased husband's kinsmen; and in the sororate, which imposes on the kinsmen of a barren or deceased wife an obligation to provide another woman to make good the deficiency or loss. Among the consequences of the operation of these and similar customs is inevitably a curtailment of the woman's freedom of choice. The interests of the group are in such cases regarded by traditional law and opinion as overriding the personal wishes of the individual.

We are thus brought back to the question of the African woman's inferiority of status. There is no doubt that, according to modern European standards, she is subject to serious legal disabilities, not only in relation to specific situations such as those mentioned above, but also, more generally, by reason of her condition of perpetual minority. On the other hand, apart from the fact that legal status is merely one—and perhaps not the most important—among the factors which determine the actual position and influence of women in a particular society, there are certain considerations which seem to make a hasty judgement in this matter inadvisable. First, it must be remembered that African girls were (and still are) almost invariably married at an age at which they would in any case (i.e. even according to European ideas) have to be regarded as minors. Secondly, the problem of the African spinster was, under the indigenous régime, unknown, and has indeed not yet seriously arisen. Thirdly, the granting to married women of legal independence in such matters as property rights is a comparatively recent development in western Europe; and it represents the kind of reform which, however strongly it may be favoured in principle, demands a realistic approach, taking full account of the social and economic background. There remains the question of African widows and divorced women; and this again is a question which needs to be viewed in relation to the whole social structure. While such customs as that of the levirate are manifestly open to abuse, and even apart from the possibility of abuse are unacceptable to the European mind, they seem to form an integral part of the traditional system of 'social security': from which it follows that their disappearance would necessitate some alternative provision for 'unattached' women.

It is, no doubt, only in relation to possible alternatives that value judgements can profitably be made on African marriage customs. Where no such alternative presented itself, there would be comparatively little tendency towards revolt: and much that now seems objectionable, not only to the foreign observer but also to many Africans, was probably in the past, within the closed circle of the traditional environment, a matter of unquestioning acceptance. It is probably that even at the present day the actual 'victims' of customs which shock the outside world are often oblivious of their own grievances. Hence in connexion with attacks on *la grande polygamie* as practised by high-ranking Africans such as the Fon of Bikom,[20] the question may arise whether the condemnation is based on principles of morality and public policy or on 'fundamental human rights'; and (if on the latter) whether the wishes of the woman concerned are to be treated as relevant. There are, of course, some practices, tolerated (if not approved) by custom, which call for unequivocal condemnation and suppression—e.g. the sale and purchase of young girls (not yet, it seems, entirely eradicated) in the Cross River area of Nigeria.[21] Nevertheless, the majority of cases in which African traditional practice offends European principles and sentiments seem, on examination, to involve issues which—from the secular point of view at any rate—are neither so plain nor so simple as might at first sight appear.

Before concluding this brief sketch of the main distinctive features of African customary marriage, we must not omit to mention the emphasis laid on procreation as the chief end of marriage. Dr. Mair points out that 'the importance of securing legitimate descendants accounts for the most characteristic features of African marriage law'. This tendency to concentrate attention on the procreative aspect of marriage seems to be the key to the understanding of much that would otherwise be puzzling to a European observer and it is illustrated by the fact that in a very large proportion of the disputes involving customary marriage law the crucial issue concerns the determination of the question, To which kinship group shall the children belong? Although there are great differences between patrilineal and matrilineal descent systems, the importance attached to the procreation and 'ownership' of children seems to be common to both.

Notes

[1] (1919), 4 N.A.C., 220, *per* C. J. Warner C.M., at p. 222.

[2] Cf. also *Rex* v. *Amkeyo*, 7 E.A.L.R. (1917) 14, where Sir Robert Hamilton C.J. said: 'In my opinion the use of the word "marriage" to describe the relationship entered into by an African native with a woman of his tribe according to tribal custom is a misnomer which has led in the past to a considerable confusion of ideas. . . . The elements of a so-called marriage by native custom differ so materially from the ordinarily accepted idea of what constitutes a civilized form of marriage that it is difficult to compare the two.'

[3] Cf. Part II, p. 178, *post.*

[4] Sir Paul Vinogradoff, *Outlines of Historical Jurisprudence* (1920), vol. i, p. 167.

[5] Much consideration was given to the question of the term or terms to be used in this Survey to denote that transfer of property by or on behalf of the bridegroom to the bride's kin which is generally an essential part of the procedure for the formation of an African customary marriage. After a good deal of discussion it was decided that it would not be practicable to maintain uniformity of usage in all parts of this work.

Dr. Mair has preferred to avoid the use of the term 'bride-price'; and her view accords with that of many (though by no means all) modern anthropologists. (Among the numerous exceptions are Fortes, Nadel, Meek and Piddington.) The Rev. Lyndon Harries and Mr. Phillips, on the other hand, have not thought it necessary to discard a term which is well known and has been widely used in the literature dealing with human marriage generally—i.e. in relation not only to 'bride-price' in Africa but also to corresponding institutions which exist or have existed in other parts of the world, including Europe. It must, of course, be admitted that the objections to the term are not without weight; and its retention would be less easy to justify if a really satisfactory substitute were available. Unfortunately none of the alternative expressions so far suggested seems so entirely suitable as to be likely to gain universal acceptance. In many instances, where a writer has been concerned only with a single tribe or group of related tribes the difficulty has been avoided by the use of a native term, e.g. *lobolo*, *bogadi*, *mahari*, &c. But this expedient is of no avail in dealing with Africa as a whole. Similarly, the expression 'marriage cattle' is inapplicable to tribes whose custom provides for payment in other forms of property than cattle.

The term adopted by Dr. Mair is 'marriage payment' (see Part I p. 5); it may be argued, however, that it is preferable to reserve this term for use in a generic sense, to cover not only 'bride-price' proper but reciprocal payments (e.g. dowry) and also such conventional payments, gifts, etc., as may be made by or on behalf of the bridegroom in addition to what is strictly required by native law. (Radcliffe-Brown appears to favour the use of the term 'prestations' in this generic sense: cf. Introduction to *African Systems of Kinship and Marriage*, p. 47). The English 'dowry' and the French *dot* are widely used as equivalent to 'bride-price', but with little regard for their proper meaning. The English term most favoured by anthropologists at the present day appears to be 'bride-wealth'; but it can hardly be regarded as an apt term of description, as it tends to suggest that wealth is brought by (or possibly given to) the bride, and in any case the word 'wealth' seems inappropriate where the property concerned consists of (for example) a few hoes of negligible value. A better substitute for 'bride-price' (if a substitute is really necessary) might be 'marriage consideration' (which has received statutory recognition in Southern Rhodesia) or possibly 'marriage dues'.

The conclusion here drawn is that any term which may be used will be a mere label rather than an accurate description and that, on the whole, it is best to adhere to the old-established term 'bride-price', with a caution to the effect that it is to be interpreted in a neutral sense—i.e. as conveying no suggestion that a mercenary element of sale and purchase is necessarily inherent in the transaction. It seems unlikely that any serious reader of these pages will be under any misapprehension on this point.

[6] Cf. Part II p. 241, note 2, *post.*

[7] Cf. Dr. Mair's remarks in Part I at pp. 2 and 4, *post.*

[8] In the English courts, moreover, there have in recent years been signs of a more liberal attitude towards marriages contracted under a system of law which admits of polygamy. See the references given in Part II, pp. 178–9, note 6, *post.*

[9] Cf. pp. xxx–xxxi *post.*

[10] Cf. Part I, pp. 5–6, 14–16, 73 seq., *post.*

[11] For the present purpose it seems unnecessary to distinguish between the two possible forms

of polygamy—viz. polygyny and polyandry—since the latter is almost, though perhaps not quite, unknown in Africa. Cf. Part II, p. 194, *post*; also Part I, pp. 90–91, *post*.

[12] Cf. C. G. Seligman, *Races of Africa* (revised ed., 1939), p. 123. But, though it is stated that 'monogamy is general, except among the Borana', it is not clear that it is obligatory.

[13] Cf. the observations of Lord Brougham in *Warrender* v. *Warrender*, 2 Cl. & F. 531: '. . . Marriage is one and the same thing substantially all the world over. Our whole law of marriage assumes this: and it is important to observe that we regard it as a wholly different thing, a different status from Turkish or other marriages among infidel nations, because we clearly should never recognise the plurality of wives, and consequent validity of second marriages, standing the first, which second marriages the laws of those countries authorise and validate.' Cf. also Part II, pp. 178–9, 191, *post*.

[14] As to the use of this term, see *ante* note 7.

[15] Radcliffe-Brown, A. R., and Forde, D. (ed.), *African Systems of Kinship and Marriage* (1950) p. 46.

[16] Cf. Schapera, I., *Handbook of Tswana Law and Custom*, p. 159.

[17] Cf. Forde, C. D., *Marriage and the Family among the Yakö of South-Eastern Nigeria* (1941), p. 75, where it is estimated that in Umor not less than 30 per cent. of the women are divorced at least once in their marital history.

[18] Gluckman, M., 'Kinship and Marriage among the Lozi of Northern Rhodesia and the Zulu of Natal', *African Systems of Kinship and Marriage*, p. 180. For other examples see Peristiany, J. G., *The Social Institutions of the Kipsigis*, pp. 87–89; and East, R. M., *Akiga's Story*, p. 172. Cf. also Ashton, H., *The Basuto*, pp. 85–86.

[19] Cf. Radcliffe-Brown, *op. cit.*, p. 64.

[20] Cf. Part II, p. 190, note 2, *post*. See also p. xx, note 4, *post*.

[21] Cf. Forde, Daryll: 'Double Descent among the Yakö', *African Systems of Kinship and Marriage* (1950), p. 291: 'It is . . . likely that the general practice of polygynous marriage has been made possible only through the purchase of foreign children, mainly from Ibo country, west of the Cross river, who are known as *yafoli*, and are adopted into the household and kin groups of the purchaser, and the great majority of whom have been girls. There has recently been increasing governmental check on this trafficking in children, but it has for a considerable period made available a surplus of girls especially for marriages to older men as later wives.' (See also *ibid.*, p. 305).

A. R. Radcliffe-Brown and D. Forde: African Systems of Kinship and Marriage*

In order to understand the African customs relating to marriage we have to bear in mind that a marriage is essentially a rearrangement of social structure. What is meant by social structure is any arrangement of persons in institutionalized relationships. By a marriage certain existing relationships, particularly, in most societies, those of the bride to her family, are changed. New social relations are created, not only between the husband and the wife, and between the husband and the wife's relatives on the one side and between the wife and the husband's relatives on the other, but also, in a great many societies, between the relatives of the husband and those of the wife, who, on the two sides, are interested in the marriage and in the children that are expected to result from it. Marriages, like births, deaths, or initiations at puberty, are rearrangements of structure that are constantly recurring in any society; they are moments of the continuing social process regulated by custom; there are institutionalized ways of dealing with such events.

We tend, unless we are anthropologists, to judge other people's customs by reference to our own. To understand African marriage we must remember that the modern English idea of marriage is recent and decidedly unusual; the product of a particular social development. We think of a marriage as an event that concerns primarily the man and woman who are forming a union and the State, which gives that union its legality and alone can dissolve it by divorce. The consent of parents is, strictly, only required for minors. Religion still plays some part, but a religious ceremony is not essential.

We may compare English marriage with the following account of a 'wedding' in early England.[1]

> 'If people want to wed a maid or a wife and this is agreeable to her and to her kinsmen, then it is right that the bridegroom should first swear according to God's right and secular law and should wage (pledge himself) to those who are her for-

* A. R. Radcliffe-Brown and D. Forde, *African Systems of Kinship and Marriage*, Oxford University Press, 1950, pp. 43–54.

speakers, that he wishes to have her in such a way as he should hold her by God's right as his wife—and his kinsmen will stand pledge for him.

'Then it is to be settled to whom the price for upfostering her belongs, and for this the kinsmen should pledge themselves.

'Then let the bridegroom declare what present he will make her for granting his desire, and what he will give if she lives longer than he does.

'If it is settled in this way, then it is right that she should enjoy half the property, and all if they have a child, unless she marries another man.

'All this the bridegroom must corroborate by giving a gage, and his kinsmen stand to pledge for him.

'If they are agreed in all this, then let the kinsmen of the bride accept and wed their kinswoman to wife and to right life to him who desires her, and let him take the pledge who rules over the wedding.

'If she is taken out of the land into another lord's land, then it is advisable that her kinsmen get a promise that no violence will be done to her and that if she has to pay a fine they ought to be next to help her to pay, if she has not enought to pay herself.'

The marriage here is not any concern of the State or political authorities; it is a compact between two bodies of persons, the kin of the woman who agree to wed their daughter to the man, and his kinsmen who pledge themselves that the terms of the agreement will be carried out. The bridegroom and his kinsmen must promise to make a payment (the 'marriage payment') to her father or other legal guardian. He must also state what present he will give to his bride for permitting the physical consummation of the marriage; this was the so-called 'morning-gift' to be paid after the bridal night. There was further an agreement as to the amount of the dowry, the portion of the husband's wealth of which the wife should have the use during her lifetime if her husband died before her. The agreement is concluded by the giving of the *wed*, the symbolic payment made by the bridegroom and his kin to the woman's kinsmen.

In modern England the pledge or gage, in the form of a 'wedding' ring, is given, not to the bride's kinsmen when the marriage arrangement is made, but to the bride herself at the wedding ceremony. The change in custom is highly significant. The 'giving away' of the bride is a survival of something which at one time was the most important feature of the ceremonial of marriage.

Thus in Anglo-Saxon England a marriage, the legal union of man and wife, was a compact entered into by two bodies of kin. As the Church steadily increased in power and in control of social life, marriage became the concern of the Church and was regulated by canon law. There was a new conception that in marriage the man and woman entered into a compact with God (or with His Church) that they would remain united till parted by death. The marriage was under the control of the Church; matrimonial cases were dealt with in the ecclesiastical courts.

At the end of the Middle Ages there came the struggle for power between Church and State in which the State was, in Protestant countries, victorious. Marriage then came under State control. At the present day to legalize a union of man and wife the marriage, whether there is or is not a religious ceremony, must be registered by someone licensed by the State and a fee must be paid. It is the State that decides on what conditions the marriage may be brought to an end by a divorce granted by a court which is an organ of the State.

A most important factor in the development of the modern English (and American) conception of marriage was the idea of romantic love, a theme that was elaborated in the nineteenth century in novel and drama and has now become the mainstay of the cinema industry. In its early development romantic love was conceived as not within but outside marriage, witness the troubadours and their courts of love and Dante and Petrarch. In the eighteenth century Adam Smith could write: 'Love, which was formerly a ridiculous passion, became more grave and respectable. As a proof of this it is worth our observation that no ancient tragedy turned on love, whereas it is now more respectable and influences all the public entertainments.' The idea that marriage should be a union based on romantic love leads logically to the view that if the husband and wife find they do not love one another they should be permitted to dissolve the marriage. This is the Hollywood practice, but conflicts with the control of marriage by the Church or by the State.

Another very important factor has been the change in the social and economic position of women during the nineteenth and twentieth centuries. A married woman may now hold property in her own right; she may take employment that has no connexion with her family life but takes her away from it. In the marriage ceremony many women now refuse to promise that they will obey their husbands.

Not only are marriage and ideas about marriage in England and America the product of a recent, special, and complex development, but there is good evidence that they are still changing. The demand for greater freedom of divorce is one indication of this. Yet it is clear that despite all this some people take twentieth-century English marriage as a standard of 'civilized' marriage with which to compare African marriage.

The African does not think of marriage as a union based on romantic love although beauty as well as character and health are sought in the choice of a wife. The strong affection that normally exists after some years of successful marriage is the product of the marriage itself conceived as a process, resulting from living together and co-operating in many activities and particularly in the rearing of children.

An African marriage is in certain respects similar to the early English marriage described above. The dowry or dower does not exist in Africa, though writers who do not know, or do not care about, the meanings of words use the term 'dowry' quite inappropriately to refer to the 'marriage payment'.[2] There is also in Africa nothing exactly corresponding to the English 'morning-gift' regarded as a payment for accepting sexual embraces, though it is usual for the bridegroom to give gifts to his bride. The two other features of the early English marriage are normally found in African marriages. Firstly, the marriage is not the concern of the political authorities but is established by a compact between two bodies of persons, the kin of the man and the kin of the woman. The marriage is an alliance between the two bodies of kin based on their common interest in the marriage itself and its continuance, and in the offspring of the union, who will be, of course, kin of both the two kin-groups. The understanding of the nature of this alliance is essential to any understanding of African kinship systems. Secondly, in Africa generally, as in early England, and in a great number of societies in ancient and modern times in all parts of the world, a marriage involves the making of a payment by the bridegroom of his kin to the father or guardian of the bride. Africans distinguish, as we do, between a 'legal' marriage and an irregular union. In modern England a marriage is legal if it is registered by a person licensed by the State. Only children born of such a union are legitimate. But in Africa the State or political authority is not concerned with a marriage. How, then, are we to distinguish a legal marriage? The answer is that a legal marriage, by which the children who will be born are given definite 'legitimate' status in the society, requires a series of transactions and formalities in which the two bodies of kin, those of the husband and those of the wife, are involved. In most African marriages, as in the early English marriage, the making of a payment of goods or services by the bridegroom to the bride's kin is an essential part of the establishment of 'legality'.

Some people regard payments of this kind as being a 'purchase' of a wife in the sense in which in England to-day a man may purchase a horse or a motor-car. In South Africa it was at one time held officially that a marriage by native custom with the payment of cattle (*lobala*) was 'an immoral transaction' and not a valid marriage. The Supreme Court of Kenya in 1917 decided that 'a so-called marriage by the native custom of wife-purchase is not a marriage'. The idea that an African buys a wife in the way that an English farmer buys cattle is the result of ignorance, which may once have been excusable but is so no longer, or of blind prejudice, which is never excusable in those responsible for governing an African people.

A marriage in many, perhaps most, African societies involves a whole series of prestations[3] (payments, gifts, or services), and while the most important of these are from the husband and his kin to the wife's kin, there are frequently, one might say usually, some in the other direction. One of the best accounts of the whole procedure is that given by Father Hulstaert for the Nkundo of the Belgian Congo.[4] The procedure begins with the presentation, on the part of the future husband, of the *ikula*, at one time an arrow, now two copper rings. The acceptance of this by the woman and her kin constitutes a formal betrothal. The marriage, i.e. the 'tradition' of the bride, may take place before any further payment. At the marriage, gifts are made to the bride by the parents of the bridegroom, by other of his relatives, and by the bridegroom himself. The next step is the formal prestation of the *ndanga*, formerly a knife, to the bride's father. It signifies that the husband thereafter becomes responsible for accidents that might befall his wife. In return there is a prestation from the bride's family to the husband and his family. This is part of the *nkomi*, the payment that is made to the bridegroom by the wife's family. The marriage is not fully established until the husband pays his father-in-law the *walo*, a substantial payment consisting chiefly of objects of metal. After this the woman becomes fully the man's wife. When the *walo* is handed over the woman's family make a return payment (*nkomi*) and give a present of food to the husband's family. The husband must also make a special payment to his wife's mother and must give a considerable number of presents to the father, mother, brothers, and other relatives of the bride. The relatives of the husband then demand and receive presents from the wife's family. The final payment to be made by the husband is the *bosongo*, formerly a slave, now a quantity of copper rings.

There is, of course, an immense diversity in the particulars of prestations connected with betrothal and marriage in different societies and in each case they have to be studied, with regard to their meanings and functions, in relation to the society in which they are found. For general theory, however, we have to look for general similarities. In the first place it is necessary to recognize that whatever economic importance some of these transactions may have, it is their symbolic aspect that we chiefly have to consider. This may be made clear by the English customs of the engagement ring, the wedding ring, and the wedding presents. Though an engagement ring may have considerable value (more than many Africans 'pay' for their wives), the giving of it is not regarded as an economic or at least not as a business transaction. It is symbolic.

In what follows the term 'marriage payment' will be used for the major payment or payments made by the bridegroom to the wife's kin. Where there is a payment from the wife's kin to the husband (as in the Nkundo) this will be called the 'counter-payment'. The rule in many African societies is that if there is a divorce the marriage payment and the counter-payment must be returned. There are qualifications of this; for example, in some tribes where on divorce there are children and they belong to the father the marriage payment may be not returnable, or returnable only in part. Also, there are tribes in Africa in which, instead of a payment in goods, the bridegroom must serve for his wife by working for her kin, just as Jacob served his mother's brother Laban seven years for each of the two sisters, Leah and Rachel, his cousins, whom he married (Genesis xxix). This service, the equivalent of the marriage payment or of part thereof, is of course not returnable if there is divorce.

Let us return to the early English marriage. In the formulary quoted above the marriage payment was called 'the price of upfostering' and was thus interpreted as a return to the father or guardian of the expense of rearing a daughter. But in somewhat earlier times the payment was differently interpreted. It was a payment for the transfer of the woman's *mund* from the father or guardian to the husband, whereby the latter gained and the former lost certain rights. The term for a legitimately married wife in Old Norse law was *mundi kjöbt*, meaning one whose *mund* has been purchased. In Sweden the transfer of *mund* was not by purchase but by gift, and the expression for marriage was *giftarmal*. In Roman law the marriage by *coemptio*, sometimes called 'marriage by purchase', was not the sale of a woman but the legal transfer of *manus* to her husband, and *mund* and *manus* are roughly equivalent terms. In these Roman and Teutonic marriages the important point is that to legalize the union of a man and a woman, so that it is really a marriage, legal power over his daughter must be surrendered by the father and acquired by the husband, whether the transfer be by gift or by payment. The early English marriage was of this type.

In Africa an unmarried woman is in a position of dependence. She lives under the control and authority of her kin, and it is they who afford her protection. Commonly, if she is killed or injured her guardian or her kinsfolk can claim an indemnity. At marriage she passes to a greater or less extent, which is often very considerable, under the control of her husband (and his kin), and it is he (and they) who undertake to afford her protection. (Note the *ndanga* payment amongst the Nkundo, by which the bridegroom accepts responsibility for accidents that may befall the bride.) The woman's kin, however, retain the right to protect her against ill treatment by her husband. If she is killed or injured by third parties it is now the husband and his kin who can claim an indemnity. It is this transfer of *mund*, to use the Old English term, that is the central feature of the marriage transaction.

To understand African marriage we must think of it not as an event or a condition but as a developing process. The first step is usually a formal betrothal, though this may have been preceded by a period of courtship or, in some instances in some regions, by an elopement. The betrothal is the contract or agreement between the two families. The marriage may proceed by stages, as in the instance of the Nkundo mentioned above. A most important stage in the development of the marriage is the birth of the first child. It is through the children that the husband and wife are united and the two families are also united by having descendants in common.

We may consider African marriage in three of its most important aspects. First, the marriage involves some modification or partial rupture of the relations between the bride and her immediate kin. This is least marked when the future husband comes to live with and work for his future parents-in-law while his betrothed is still a girl not old enough for marriage. It is most marked when, as in most African societies, the woman when she marries leaves her family and goes to live with her husband and his family. Her own family suffers a loss. It would be a gross error to think of this as an economic loss.[5] It is the loss of a person who has been a member of a group, a breach of the family solidarity. This aspect of marriage is very frequently given symbolic expression in the simulated hostility between the two bodies of kin at the marriage ceremony, or by the pretence of taking the bride by force (the so-called 'capture' of the bride). Either the bride herself or her kin, or both, are expected to make a show of resistance at her removal.

Customs of this kind are extremely widespread not only in Africa but all over the world, and the only explanation that fits the various instances is that they are the ritual or symbolic expression of the recognition that marriage entails the breaking of the solidarity that unites a woman to the family in which she has been born and grown up. Ethnographical literature affords innumerable instances. One example may be given here. In Basutoland, or at least in some parts of it, on the day fixed for the marriage the young men of the bridegroom's group drive the cattle that are to constitute the marriage payment to the home of the bride. When they draw near, the women of the bride's party gather in front of the entrance to the cattle kraal. As the bridegroom's party try to drive the cattle into the kraal the women, with sticks and shouts, drive them away so that they scatter over the veld and have to be collected together again and a new attempt made to drive them into the kraal. This goes on for some time until at last the cattle are successfully driven into the kraal. The women of the group make a show of resistance at the delivery of the cattle which will have as its consequence the loss of the bride. The proper interpretation of these customs is that they are symbolic expressions of the recognition of the structural change that is brought about by the marriage.

When this aspect of marriage is considered the marriage payment can be regarded as an indemnity or compensation given by the bridegroom to the bride's kin for the loss of their daughter. This is, however, only one side of a many sided institution and in some kinship systems is of minor importance. In societies in which the marriage payment is of considerable value it is commonly used to replace the daughter by obtaining a wife for some other member of the family, usually a brother of the woman who has been lost. A daughter is replaced by a daughter-in-law, a sister by a wife or sister-in-law. The family is compensated for its loss.

A second important aspect of legal marriage is that it gives the husband and his kin certain rights in relation to his wife and the children she bears. The rights so acquired are different systems. Some of these are rights of the husband to the performance of duties by the wife (rights *in personam*) and he accepts corresponding duties towards her. He has, for example, rights to the services of his wife in his household. But the husband usually also acquires rights *in rem* over his wife. If anyone kills or injures her, or commits adultery with her, he may claim to be indemnified for the injury to his rights.

The husband acquires his rights through an action by the wife's kin in which they surrender certain of the rights they have previously had. The marriage payment may be regarded in this aspect as a kind of 'consideration' by means of which the transfer is formally and 'legally' made. It is the objective instrument of the 'legal' transaction of the transfer of rights. Once the payment, or some specific portion of it, has been made the bride's family have no right to fetch their daughter back, and in most tribes, if the union is broken by divorce at the instance of the husband, the payment has to be returned and the woman's family recover the rights they surrendered.

The rights obtained by a husband and his kin are different in some respects in different systems. The most important difference is in the matter of rights over the children the wife bears. An African marries because he wants children—*liberorum quaerendorum gratia*. The most important part of the 'value' of a woman is her child-bearing capacity. Therefore, if the woman proves to be barren, in many tribes her kin either return the marriage payment or provide another woman to bear children.

In a system of father-right, such as the Roman *patria potestas*, the rights of the father and his kin over the children of a marriage are so preponderant as to be nearly absolute and exclude any rights on the part of the mother's kin. On the other hand, in a system of mother-right such as that formerly existing amongst the Nayars of southern India, the father has no legal rights at all: the children belong to the mother and her kin. This does not, of course, exclude a relationship of affection between father and child. Both father-right and mother-right are exceptional conditions; most societies have systems which come between these extremes and might be called systems of joint right or divided right. The system of division varies and there may be an approximation either to father-right or to mother-right.

Some societies in Sumatra and other parts of the Malay Archipelago have two kinds of marriage. If a full marriage payment is made the children belong to the father; we may call this a father-right marriage. But if no payment is made the children belong to the mother and her kin, the marriage being one of mother-right.

The same sort of thing is reported from some parts of Africa, for example from Brass in Southern Nigeria.[6] The father-right marriage, with a substantial marriage payment, is the usual form, but if only a small payment is made the children belong to the mother's kin. The most definite example is from the Nyamwezi. In the *kukwa* form of marriage there is a payment (*nsabo*) made by the bridegroom to the father or guardian of the bride; children of such a marriage fall into the possession of the husband and his agnatic kin. In the *butende* form of marriage there is no payment and the children belong to the mother and her kin.

There is another aspect of marriage that must be taken into account. In Africa a marriage is not simply a union of a man and a woman; it is an alliance between two families or bodies of kin. We must consider the marriage payments in this connexion also.

In so-called primitive societies the exchange of valuables is a common method of establishing or maintaining a friendly relation between separate groups or between individuals belonging to separate groups. Where material goods are exchanged it is common to speak of gift-exchange. But the exchange may be of services, particularly those of a ritual character. There are societies in which there is an exchange of women, each group (family, lineage, or clan) providing a wife for a man of the other. The rule governing transactions of this kind is that for whatever is received a return must be made. By such exchanges, even by a single act of exchange, two persons or two groups are linked together in a more or less lasting relation of alliance.[7]

There are societies in some part of the world in which the marriage payment and the counter-payment are equal or approximately equal in value. We may regard this as an exchange of gifts to establish friendship between two families, of which the son of one is to marry a daughter of the other. The kind, and to some extent the amount of the gifts is fixed by custom. But where the marriage payment is considerable in amount and there is a much smaller counter-payment, or none at all, we must interpret this as meaning that the bride's family is conferring a specific benefit on the bridegroom by giving him their daughter in marriage, a benefit that is shared by his kin, and that the marriage payment is a return for this. The transaction can still be regarded as a form of 'gift-exchange' and as such establishes a relation (or alliance) between the parties.

It is characteristic of a transaction of purchase and sale that once it has been completed it leaves behind no obligations on either the buyer or the seller. (This does not, of course, exclude claims based on warranty.) In an African marriage the position is very different. For one thing the marriage payment may in certain circumstances have to be repaid. In some tribes where the payment consists of cattle it is the same cattle with all their increase that should be returned. Further, in some African societies the family that has made the marriage payment continues to have an interest in the cattle or other goods of which it consists. The payment received for a woman's marriage may be used to obtain a wife for a member of her family, usually her brother. This sets up a number of important relations between the persons involved.

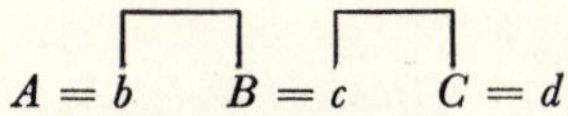

B and *b* are brother and sister, and so are *C* and *c*. *A* marries *b* and makes a marriage payment which is used to obtain a wife (*c*) for *B*. In various tribes the marriage payment establishes a series of special personal relations between *b* and *B*, between *A* and *B*, between *b* and *c*, and between *A* and *c*. These are defined differently in different tribes. we may briefly consider three varieties.

It is usual to speak of *B* and *b* as 'linked' brother and sister, and *B* is the 'linked' mother's brother of the children of *A* and *b*, while *b* is the 'linked' father's sister of *B*'s children. In the Shangana-Tonga tribes there is a very special relation between *A* and his 'great *mukonwana*' *c*, the wife that *B* married with the payment provided by *A*. *A* can claim in marriage a daughter of *c*, particularly if his wife *b* dies and there is no younger sister to take her place.[8]

In the Lovedu the relations between the families of *A*, *B*, and *C* ought to be continued in the next and succeeding generations. A son of *A* should marry a daughter of *B* and a son of *B* should marry a daughter of *C*. There is thus established a chain of connected families. The *B* family (or lineage) gives brides to and receives cattle from the *A* family and gives cattle to and receives brides from *C*. The linked sister *b* is said to have 'built the house for her brother' *B*, and she 'has a gate' by which she may enter the house. She has the right to demand a daughter of the house to come as her daughter-in-law, to marry her son and be her helper. Thus, in this tribe, cross-cousin marriage is systematized in terms of marriage payments, and a complex set of relations between persons and between families is created.[9] In the Shangana-Tonga tribes *b* can demand a daughter of *c* as her co-wife or 'helper', the wife of her husband, not as her daughter-in-law.[10]

Amongst the Nkundo the relationships are given a different form. There is a special relation of *b* to *c*, the wife of her linked brother whose marriage was provided for by her marriage payment. The sister *b* is the *nkolo* of *c*, who is her *nkita*. The *nkolo* (*b*) stands in a position of superiority to the *nkita* (*c*). This relation is continued in the succeeding generations; the children of *b* (the *nkolo*) are in a position of superiority to the children of *c*. This is connected with a peculiar ordering of relations amongst the Nkundo by which the relation between cross-cousins is an asymmetrical one in which they are treated as if they belonged to different generations. The children of the father's sister are 'fathers', male and female (*baise*), to their cousins, the children of the mother's brother who are their 'children' (*bana*). The 'children' must show respect to their 'fathers' and help them. As a consequence a man regards the son of his father's sister's son as his 'brother' and uses that term for him.[11]

It should now be evident that the marriage payment is a complex institution having many varieties in form and function. In any given society it has to be interpreted by reference to the whole system of which it is a part. Nevertheless, there are certain general statements that seem to be well grounded. In Africa the marriage payment, whether it be small or large, is the objective instrument by which a 'legal' marriage is established. In some instances it is a compensation or indemnity to the woman's family for the loss of a member. This is particularly so where the marriage payment is considerable and is used to obtain a wife for the woman's brother. The payment may in some instances be regarded as part of an exchange of a kind that is used in many parts of the world to establish a friendly alliance between two groups. In some societies of South Africa and the Nilotic region it is the derivation of the cattle used in the marriage payment that fixes the social position of the children born of the union. Where the same cattle or other goods are used in two or more successive marriages this is in some tribes held to establish a special relation between the families thus formed. Where cattle are sacred in the sense that the cattle of a lineage are the material link between the living and their ancestors (having been received from those ancestors and being used for sacrifices to them), the use of cattle in marriage payments has a significance which a transfer of other goods would not have. This is not intended as a complete survey, which would be impossible within the limits of this essay. It is only an indication of how this institution, which is the procedure by which a husband acquires those rights which characterize a legal marriage (rights that vary in different societies), may be elaborated in different ways.

Notes

[1] Quoted by Vinogradoff, *Outlines of Historical Jurisprudence*, i, p. 252, from Liebermann, *Gesetze der Angelsachsen*, i, p. 442. The 'wedding' was the agreement or contract entered into by the kinsfolk of bride and bridegroom, equivalent to the Roman *sponsalia*, not the ceremony of handing over the bride (the Roman *traditio puellae*).

[2] Belgian and some French writers make a similar misuse of the term 'dot', which is a woman's marriage portion of which the annual income is under her husband's control.

[3] 'Prestation' is defined in the *Oxford Dictionary* as 'the act of paying, in money or service, what is due by law or custom'. The prestations with which we are here concerned are all those gifts and payments of goods or services which are required by custom in the process of establishing a valid marriage.

[4] R. P. G. Hulstaert, *Le Mariage des Nkundo*, Inst. roy. colon. belge, Mémoires, tome viii, 1938, chap. ii.

[5] This is the view of modern English law. If an unmarried woman is seduced her father can recover damages for the loss of her 'services'; as though the only value attached to a daughter is as a servant.

[6] P. Amaury Talbot, *Southern Nigeria*, 1926, vol. iii, pp. 437—40.

[7] See Marcel Mauss, *Essai sur le Don*.

[8] H. Junod, *op. cit.*, pp. 231 *et seq.*

[9] E. J. and J. D. Krige, *The Realm of a Rain Queen*, 1943; J. D. Krige, 'The Significance of Cattle Exchanges in Lovedu Social Structure', *Africa*, xii. 4 Oct. 1939, pp. 393–424.

[10] E. Dora Earthy, *Valenge Women*.

[11] Hulstaert, *Le Mariage des Nkundo*, p. 164, et seq.

Chapter 7

CAPACITY AND CONSENTS

This chapter covers certain preliminary aspects of the marriage relationship by dealing with the question whether persons are capable of marrying (age and personal status), or inter-marrying (impediments to marriage) and what consents are necessary before a marriage can be contracted.

(a) Age and Personal Status

The question as to what age persons become legally capable of marrying in customary law is not free from difficulty. This is hardly surprising since traditionally African societies did not calculate age by calendar years, but rather by events. The tests that may be applied as constituting marriageable age in African customary law include (*a*) circumcision or initiation of boys and girls (see *Snell* on Nandi and cf. *Wagner* on the Kavirondo Bantu; (*b*) membership of a regiment (*Schapera* on Tswana); (*c*) puberty (*Roberts* on Malawi); (*d*) ability to engage in tribal warfare (for males) and to carry out household duties (for females) (*Wagner*).

Another difficulty in regard to the question of age is that many writers, as the extracts show, rely on the prevailing practice or norm (e.g. 'a man was *usually* in his middle twenties when he married', *Snell*) rather than a prescribed age as a legal minimum.

Bars based on personal status other than age, include those on (*a*) imbeciles and sexually malformed females (*Snell* on Nandi); (*b*) lepers (*Roberts* on Malawi); and (*c*) persons with contagious diseases, e.g. epilepsy (*Wagner* on Kavirondo Bantu). But here too, it is not often made clear whether these bars are legal or merely social.

G. S. Snell: Nandi Customary Law*

A man was usually in his middle twenties when he married. As males were circumcised only at twelve to fifteen-year intervals, some bridegrooms would have been recently circumcised while others would have been circumcised some years previously, the youngest age for the circumcision of boys being about thirteen years. Occasionally a boy was married in his 'teens where his father was wealthy or old and had no other sons who could inherit his property. In such an instance the bride might be several years older than her husband; her correct behaviour towards him being ensured by the authority of his parents. Bachelordom was not unknown among the Nandi, especially in the southernmost part of Aldai in cases where a man's father could not raise enough animals to provide the bride-price, and the prospective bride-groom was unsuccessful in finding a bride whose father was prepared to allow payment to be deferred.

Similarly, a girl was never married until she had been circumcised. Female initiation ceremonies took place every year from about a month after the beginning of the rains (Iwot Kot, i.e. March) until Kipsunde (September) 'so that there will be plenty of good food for them'. A bride would usually be in her middle or later 'teens and would

* G. S. Snell, *Nandi Customary Law*, Macmillan & Co. Ltd., 1954, pp. 19–20.

have been circumcised within the previous two or three years, having spent the intervening period in strict seclusion. Spinsterhood was unthinkable except in the case of imbeciles or the sexually malformed, who were cared for by their parents or by some member of their tiliet. The girls in a family were normally married in order of age, but this was not necessarily so. Where, for instance, a girl had been circumcised without her parents' consent or had become pregnant she would be married off quickly, irrespective of her seniority in relation to her sisters.

I. Schapera: A Handbook of Tswana Law and Custom*

Conditions of Marriage

Various conditions must be fulfilled by people before they are able to marry. Boys and girls in the olden days could not get married until they had passed through initiation ceremonies conferring upon them the status of adults, i.e. until they had become members of a regiment. Nowadays this restriction no longer prevails in the case of girls, except among tribes still practising the *bojale*. Boys, however, are still generally expected to wait until they have been admitted into a regiment, and cannot marry sooner without the special permission of the Chief. This restriction, however, is also tending to fall away. Formerly, even after they had been initiated, boys could not marry until the leader of their regiment had done so; but this also is no longer the case, at least among the Kgatla and Ngwato.

S. Roberts: Matrilineal Family Law and Custom in Malawi: A Comparison of Two Systems†

Capacity to Marry

Among the Tonga a form of betrothal is possible before the age of puberty, but no marriage can take place before this age is reached. A girl is looked upon as of marriageable age as soon as she has had her first menstrual period.[1] Marriage between the ages of 15 and 17 is common, but may well take place much later than this. Marriage is theoretically possible for Lomwe men and women as soon as puberty is reached, but especially for men it is very rare to marry as early as this.[2] A woman usually marries at about the age of 18 whereas a man does not usually marry until he is 25 or 28, and may possibly not do so until he is even older than this. The reason that men marry relatively late appears to be that marriage entails strenuous duties, the thought of which deters them from a hurried choice. A man spends his youth practising for these duties. The chief of these is to build a house for his wife. This task will be completed under the critical scrutiny of the wife's family. He will suffer considerable ridicule if the house is improperly constructed or, even worse, collapses. He also has to prepare a garden out of a piece of virgin bush. These are tests of his manhood, which he will hesitate to undertake until he is well able to perform them.

In both tribes certain defects are regarded as making a person unfit for marriage.[3] Lepers are not permitted to marry, but epilepsy and insanity are not bars to marriage, unless they show themselves in a very advanced form. Among the Tonga a man's refusal to disclose the village he comes from is also a bar to his marriage.

Notes

[1] When a girl experiences her first menstrual period she will report the fact to older women in the village, and she will immediately receive instruction as to its nature and explanations of her approaching womanhood. The initiation among the Tonga is not a celebration or ceremony. When she tells the elders of her condition she will be confined for about a week and receive private instructions and advice from older women. After the girl's second menstrual period she will be given a shorter course of instruction, following which she will be regarded as ready for marriage.

* I. Schapera, *A Handbook of Tswana Law and Custom*, Oxford University Press, 1938, pp. 127.

† S. Roberts, 'Matrilineal Family Law and Custom in Malawi: a Comparison of Two Systems' in *Journal of African Law*, Vol. 8, No. 2, p. 78.

[2] According to strict Lomwe custom no one may marry until he has been initiated. Males can undergo initiation at any time between the ages of ten and twenty. Each year in the cold season an elderly male (*namuku*) takes a group of young men from each village into the bush for instruction. The initiation formerly took up up to six months, but now is usually completed in a few weeks. The boys remain in the bush strictly separate from the rest of the community. The instruction is not only related to sexual matters and includes teaching on social behaviour in general. During the initiation the youths are encouraged to eat little food and to bathe in cold streams to toughen them.

The female initiation is carried out by elderly women in a similar manner. The young women remain away from the village for about a month, and are not permitted any social contact for a short period after they return to the village.

[3] The exact status of the albino in the two tribes is an interesting question. They appear to be treated normally and live with the other members of the community. However, none of my informants could recall an instance of an albino marrying. At the same time, there does not appear to be any strict customary rule against this being permitted.

G. Wagner: The Bantu of North Kavirondo*

Whereas a boy must always be circumcised before he is permitted to carry and use the weapons of a real warrior and before he can take an active part in fighting, circumcision is not necessarily a prerequisite of marriage. Although the majority of men marry only after they have been circumcised, there is no direct connexion between the two events, and a girl would not refuse to marry an uncircumcised man, provided he was still young. A man, however, who is past the proper age when he should have been circumcised obviously has shirked the operation and would, therefore, find it difficult to get a wife. He would, as a rule, have to be satisfied with a widow or with a girl who for some reason or other did not find a more desirable suitor. . . . .

Certain diseases are likewise a bar against marriage, especially if they are contagious or thought to be so. Thus persons afflicted with epilepsy, leprosy, serious ulcers, and similar diseases generally remain unmarried and often have to live by themselves in the bush at a safe distance from other homesteads. . . .

The *age* of the bridegroom and, to a lesser extent, that of the bride also enter into the considerations which determine the choice or rather the approval of the marriage partner by the parents of either of them. Apart from a grudge that is often felt by the young men against the wealthy elders of their clan when they see them snatching away the young girls as 'junior wives', there is no general feeling that marriages ought to be concluded between persons of approximately equal age. I have attended pagan weddings where a girl of seventeen or less was married to an old, decrepit man, without noticing any signs of disapproval among the adult men and women present. Conversely, a man may marry a widow who is much his senior, although such cases are far less frequent. Among the Vugusu, some young men complained to me that most fathers preferred to marry their daughters to middle-aged men, not only because the older men can pay more marriage cattle but also 'because they know how to look after women' and because they prefer a son-in-law who is socially and economically well established to a youngster of whom they do not yet know how he will turn out. This preference given by the fathers of many girls to middle-aged suitors appears to be one of the chief causes for elopement marriages, as the girls themselves naturally prefer to be married to a youngish man. Among the Vugusu, a lad whose sweetheart had been betrothed against her will to an elderly man collects some friends and secretly goes with them to where the girl is working in the field. In the presence of the bride and her girl friends they sing songs of ridicule and shout derogatory remarks (*xusekeya*) about the bridegroom. The idea is to incite the girl to such a pitch of contempt for the man to whom she is betrothed that she will run home and drive the marriage cattle back to the bridegroom's place as a sign of her refusal to marry him. Once married, however, many women seem to reconcile themselves to the fate of being the wife of a man who is twenty-five or thirty years their senior. Provided that they are treated well they often prefer the life of a junior wife to that of a 'great wife', as it means less work and less control of their activities by their husband.

* G. Wagner, *The Bantu of North Kavirondo*, Oxford University Press, 1949, pp. 340, 392, and pp. 394–395.

Finally, personal qualities of character count as weighty factors in the competitive efforts of finding a husband or of being accepted as a suitor. I have repeatedly heard of cases where a man, although he had cattle enough to pay the bride-wealth, had for a long time tried in vain to find a wife because he had a reputation for cruelty or stinginess. Most of the standardized considerations, however, refer to the qualities which make a desirable wife. Young men are taught by their mothers and their maternal uncles not to choose a wife for her looks but to court a girl who is industrious, modest, and physically strong, so that she can stand up under the strain of the heavy work that is expected of a wife. The various emissaries who are sent to the girl's place to negotiate the betrothal and, later on, to hand over the marriage cattle, take these opportunities to inquire into the girl's character and achievements. Moreover, the work which both the bridegroom and the bride perform for their respective parents-in-law during the period of betrothal serves *inter alia* to test their willingness and ability to work. Among the Vugusu, a father whose daughter has industriously cultivated a large garden of her own and filled a granary or two with the fruits of her own labour usually asks for an extra cow to be added to the bride-wealth when he negotiates the amount with the suitor's father. I was told that formerly the bridegroom used to go with his friends to the girl's garden where, standing at one end of the strip of cultivation, he would shoot off an arrow with all his strength to measure the length of her garden. If the arrow fell down at the end of the garden or even beyond it, the girl would be considered lazy and this fact would be used as an argument when settling the amount of the bride-wealth. . . .

(b) Impediments to marriage

The most important impediment to marriage is that the two parties are within the prohibited degrees of relationship. In most customary laws, these prohibited degrees are very wide, extending to persons descended from a common patrilineal ancestor, in the case of patrilineal people (see *Cory* on Sukuma, *van Tromp* on Xhosa, *Howell* on Nuer), and to persons of the same matrilineage among matrilineal people (*Fortes* on Ashanti). The details of the prohibitions vary from tribe to tribe as demonstrated by the extracts that follow. It is to be noted that marriage or intercourse within the prohibited degrees is regarded as a very serious offence. (See Vol. I, Part 2, pp. 119, 125, 133.)

Apart from blood-relationship or consanguinity, marriage between two persons may be prohibited on other grounds, viz. (*a*) affinity, (*b*) blood-brotherhood, (*c*) curse, (*d*) professional restrictions (see *Cory*).

Another aspect to note under this section are the complexities arising from the system of classificatory relationships, an example of which is provided by *Gluckman* on the Lozi.

S. Roberts: Matrilineal Family Law and Custom in Malawi: A Comparison of Two Systems*

The Prohibited Degrees

There is now no rule among the Tonga prohibiting marriage between two people of the same clan name, but such a rule almost certainly existed in the past. In both tribes a father may not marry his daughter nor a son his mother. Uncles cannot marry their nieces and nephews cannot marry their aunts. A man may not marry his paternal uncle's daughter or his maternal aunt's daughter, but cross-cousins may marry in both tribes.

The two tribes differ strongly in their attitude towards levirate and sororate unions.

* S. Roberts, 'Matrilineal Family Law and Custom in Malawi: a Comparison of Two Systems', in *Journal of African Law*, Vol. 8, No. 2, pp. 78–79.

Among the Tonga these marriages are quite common. Frequently a man will marry his wife's sister when the wife dies, or even during the subsistence of the marriage. Occasionally a woman will marry her deceased husband's brother. The possibility of a second marriage of this kind will depend upon relations between the two families. If the wife's parents like the husband, and the first marriage is a success, they will be willing to offer him another of their daughters. Where relations between the two families are bad a second marriage is unlikely. These second marriages usually take place either when there are very young children to be looked after, or when the first wife fails to bear children.

The Lomwe have a strict rule against levirate and sororate marriages. Once a man's wife has died all connection with her family is broken.

H. Cory: Sukuma Law and Custom*

Restrictions on Marriage

1. *Consanguinity* Persons who can trace their descent from a common ancestor (agnatic or uterine) are prohibited from marrying.

NOTE: Rules restricting marriages are no longer so strictly observed as in the past. Public opinion enforces them only in cases where transgressions are denounced by a diviner as the cause of some ill fortune which may have befallen the community.

Two persons belonging to the same clan are allowed to marry if they cannot discover a common ancestor.

NOTE: It is the custom for *babuja bas hikalile*† to investigate this point, but with regard to consanguinity their research is very superficial. (Their main concern is with leprosy and epilepsy.) If the families are not aware of any relationship it is assumed that they are unrelated. If a common ancestor should be discovered, the man or his father has to give to the girl's father one head of cattle (*ng'ombe ya budugu*) which the receiver may keep or kill for a feast to which he may invite the relatives of both sides. This beast has also to be paid if it is discovered after the wedding that the newly married couple are related. Thus people observing the same taboos are allowed to marry. In any case taboos (*migilo*) inherited from the father are obligatory for the offspring, those from the mother are voluntary. In a family often the taboos of both father and mother are observed. Cases are known in which the matrimonial peace has been disturbed by a husband who refused to acknowledge the wife's taboo. If a wife wishes to adopt the taboo of her husband and to relinquish her own, a simple rite is performed the main feature of which is that she eats—with special magical precautions—the food forbidden to her.

If two persons, who are regarded as belonging to the circle of relatives for whom intermarriage is prohibited, should have sexual intercourse resulting in the pregnancy of the girl, the man has to pay the *ng'ombe ya budugu*. The child belongs to the maternal family.

NOTE: No exact definitions of the expressions 'near relative' and 'distant relative' exist. It is sometimes stated that near relatives are not allowed to marry but distant relatives are. The term 'near relative' is in this case interpreted as a person who has remained in close contact with the family. For instance, if a grandfather's brother has emigrated and nothing has been heard of him, so that his name has fallen into oblivion, cousins of the second generation could marry perhaps after payment of the *ng'ombe ya budugu*. The relatives would not have agreed to the union if the grandfather's brother had not emigrated and if his descendants were still living in the same village.

2. *Affinity*. A man is not allowed to marry his wife's sister so long as his wife is alive, nor is he allowed to marry his step-daughter so long as her mother is alive. A man cannot marry the persons whom he customarily has to avoid, e.g. his mother-in-law or his daughter-in-law.

* H. Cory, *Sukuma Law and Custom*, Oxford University Press, 1953, pp. 55–57.
† Delegates for the investigation of family circumstances.

3. *Blood brotherhood* (*lusalago*). A blood-brother is treated as a natural brother; he can therefore marry the widow of his blood-brother, but not the sister.

NOTE: These rules are not always strictly observed.

4. *A curse* (*kizumo*). *Kizumo* is the name given to a relationship of enmity between two persons belonging to two different clans, originating in an event in the past; a member of one such clan cannot marry a member of the other.

NOTE: Hindi and Lenge are two clans in the Mwanza chiefdom (NF). One of two brothers belonging to the Hindi clan was in the habit of questioning his wife whether she had been faithful to him during his absence. Once when he returned home unexpectedly he saw his brother leaving his house. He followed him and killed him with a spear in a fury of jealousy. Their father cursed the murderer exclaiming: 'Whosoever of the Hindi clan shall talk to the murderer or to his descendants will die.' The son left the village and settled in another area, where he was called Nlenge, and became the founder of the Lenge sub-clan. On account of that curse members of the two clans are afraid to intermarry.

Members of the Hindi and Bayungu clans are also exogamous. When Lemi, the ancestor of the Hindi clan (which is the clan of the ruling chiefs), left Buha and arrived on the shores of Lake Victoria, he and his followers continued their journey by boat. His brother Muyungu was in another boat and, when the moon rose over the lake, he saw the moonlight reflected in the water. He had never before seen such a phenomenon and he ordered one of his sons to fetch the light. The young man jumped overboard and was never seen again. When Lemi heard of this foolishness he was very offensive to his brother, who became angry, left him, and returned to the shore and settled in an area nearby. When he heard later that Lemi also had returned to the shore he declared solemnly: 'Lemi is not my brother any more; he laughed and cursed me when my son disappeared. Any descendant of my family who marries a descendant of Lemi's family shall die.'

5. *Profession* In former times a number of clans were forbidden to intermarry with families of blacksmiths and potters. This rule was never general and is now obsolete.

NOTE: The blacksmiths of the area belonged to the Longo tribe which had immigrated from alien countries (Ruanda). They settled down where ironstone (*mbale*) was to be found and it is said (but this tradition may be only a local version) that they had their own chief in SM. The Tuta (Ngoni) raided the area but the Longo chief was so engrossed with his smithies that when the drums of war sounded he was unprepared and many Longo were killed. The survivors fled in all directions without leaders, but in course of time groups of them settled again where they found *mbale;* others made themselves independent of the mineral and collected old hoes, smelted them and made new ones from the material. The trade in hoes was very important in Sukumaland and hoes were in many parts the common currency of the people. The smiths were neither cattle-breeders not agriculturists; they bartered hoes for corn and cattle but consumed the latter and did not keep them. The blacksmith's way of life was fundamentally different from that of the rest of the population and depended on different factors. They therefore developed different rites. For instance, the agriculturist makes sacrifices and prayers to ensure rain in times of drought, while the blacksmith can work better in the dry than in the wet season. The Sukuma themselves give this as a reason for the earlier prohibition of marriage with smiths.

J. van Tromp: Xhosa Law of Persons*

(a) *Consanguinity of blood-relationship.* People with the same *isiduko* or patrilineal clan name (sometimes also called the isibiso), are not allowed to marry because they are blood-relatives descended from a common ancestor. It is said that people of the same isiduko may not even metsha.

But it has happened that people who originally had the same isiduko have inter-

* J. van Tromp, *Xhosa Law of Persons*, Juta & Co. Ltd., 1947, pp. 36–39.

married. Because people of the same isiduko do not always remain together, the clans become sub-divided; some of these subdivisions even adopt different isiduko, and the blood-relationship is forgotten.

Should the existing consanguinity, however, be discovered, the proposed marriage will not be concluded. If previous investigation has not revealed blood-relationship and the marriage has been concluded in good faith, it stands and is not considered to be null and void. Hence it seems that the fact that people belong to the same isiduko is a more serious impediment to marriage than the underlying principle of blood-relationship.

On account of blood-relationship, however, a marriage is also prohibited between *ascendants and descendants* ad infinitum, both patrilineal and matrilineal.[1]

All these marriages are considered *incestuous* (umbulo). Incestuous marriages deliberately concluded are null and void and the guilty parties heavily punished; in some instances the culprits are branded as sorcerers and are driven away; formerly the men were killed.

So strong is the general abhorrence of incestuous intercourse that people are prohibited even to metsha with each other if they can trace relationship back to a common ancestor. Children born of such incestuous intercourse are called *abantwana bombulo*, incestuous children. A father may reject and cast out, *uku m citha*, his son should he commit incest. His daughter would be in no better position. The idea of consanguinity, and consequently of sexual intercourse amounting to incest, is not limited to patrilineal or matrilineal ascendants and descendants; it is also extended to *classificatory relations*. Thus, according to Xhosa Law, a man may not marry two sisters, the first one being alive while he marries the second. The second sister is considered to be his own 'sister'. But a man may marry a wife's sister after the death of the wife, though this is rare.

According to Thembu Law (Ntlangwene vs. Mkwabane, 1920, Dickinson and Meaker's Reports, p. 381) and also Pondo Law (P. Yoywana *vs*. T. Yoywana, 1917, Meaker's Reports, p. 301) a man may marry a 'seed-bearer' (better called a womb) from the same family as his wife for whom he married this womb.[2] This is not the case in Xhosa Law. A man may in Xhosa Law under no circumstances marry a second sister (or girl from the same family) while the first one is still living. In Xhosa Law a stranger is married as a womb.

The following illustrations may serve to indicate how serious the amaXhosa consider incest: Ngqika managed secretly to take Tutula, the wife of his uncle Ndlambe, as wife for himself. All the amaXhosa considered this as incest (umbolo). For, Ndlambe being the uncle of Ngqika, was considered to be also a 'father' according to the amaXhosa rules of relationship. It follows therefore that the wife of Ndlambe would be considered as a 'mother' to Ngqika. Thus Ngqika could not marry or cohabit with Tutula, who was considered to be one of his 'mothers'. This act of Ngqika's was the direct cause of the War of Amalinda (indabi la malinda).

Again, a brother may not marry or cohabit with his brother's widow.[3] This custom of ukungena, though allowed by the amaZulu, is not practised among the amaXhosa; intercourse or marriage of this kind being considered incestuous.

Also '*cousins*' (usually called aba za), may not marry; both paternal and maternal cousins are deemed to be related by blood. It is rightly said that no marriage is allowed with a blood relative less than at least four generations removed, be it on father's or on mother's side.[4] In this respect no distinction is made between 'parallel' and 'cross cousins'. All sexual intercourse between cousins is invariably considered as incest.

(b) *Impotent Persons*. Persons suffering from a permanent incurable incapacity to procreate children are, according to our Native Appeal Court, deemed to be incompetent to marry.[5]

(c) *Existing Marriage*. In Xhosa Law a woman may not contract a second marriage nor her family contract one for her while the previous marriage subsists. A marriage is considered to subsist while the lobola cattle handed to her family by her husband, or part thereof, have not been returned to mark the dissolution of the marriage. Should another man marry her before dissolution, such a marriage cannot be countenanced by Xhosa Law, and the man is treated as an adulterer.[6] Moreover, as a result of this, a father can never, according to Xhosa Law, hold two amakhazi at the same time for the same woman.

Before the passing of the Union Act No. 38 of 1927 in the Transkeian Territories by Section 3 of Proclamation No. 142 of 1910, a *male* Native could not validly contract a marriage according to Xhosa Law (Native Law) while his marriage by Christian or Civil rites still subsisted. 'If a Native is married by Christian rites, the law can acknowledge no rights to another woman based upon the payment of dowry, seeing that the taking of this other and the payment of dowry for her are a clear breach of the solemn contract already entered into.'[7] And also, 'The plaintiff having married under Colonial Law, cannot contract any other marriage during its subsistence. The arrangement he entered into is an immoral contract. The woman is not his wife, nor can he recover the cattle (lobola) paid.'[8]

The second marriage may be an immoral contract from the point of view of Colonial Law; but according to Xhosa Law it is not. The man does not get the woman and there is no marriage. In Xhosa Law, if there is no marriage, the person who handed over the ikhazi has a claim to get it back. The contrary ruling of the Court is felt by the Xhosa as an enrichment at the expense of the other man and as an injustice.

Under Act 38 of 1927, which is applicable to all Bantu people in the Union, 'polygamous relationships are recognised under the Native Administration Act only in so far as they are contracted by persons neither of whom is a party to a marriage according to civil or Christian rites. A native may contract a marriage during the subsistence of a customary union between himself and another woman but may not contract a customary union during the subsistence of his marriage.'[9]

Notes

1 See also: Whitfield: *South African Native Law*, p. 133.
2 See: Whitfield: *South African Native Law*, pp. 34 and 179.
3 This, however, acording to the amaMfengu, is allowed among them.
4 See: Mrs. Hoernle in: *The Bantu-speaking Tribes of South Africa*. Edited by I. Schapera, p. 73.
5 Whitfield: *South Africa Native Law*, p. 127; and: *Yapi* vs. *Ngayi* 1903 Henkel, p. 61.
6 *Feliti* vs. *Mkumbeni* 1910 Henkel 11. This is good Xhosa Law.
7 *Mnduze* vs. *Mdlimbi* 1898 Henkel, p. 27.
8 *Matee* vs. *Njongwana* 1909 Henkel, p. 272.
9 H. Rogers: *Native Administration in the Union of South Africa* 1933, p. 238.

P. P. Howell: Manual of Nuer Law*

Note on the Rules of Exogamy and Incest

An account of Nuer marriage laws would not be complete without mention of the laws of exogamy. It must be stated at once, however, that breaches of the rules of exogamy and incestuous extra-marital intercourse are not generally the subject of dispute or of litigation in the courts. Both parties are equally guilty, there is no question of compensation, and the spiritual contamination which is considered to follow incest (*rual*) and which is manifested in physical disorders (*nueer*), sometimes resulting in death, falls equally on both parties and even upon their relatives. There are therefore strong social and ritual sanctions. For the purposes of this Manual I shall do no more than summarize the laws of exogamy, and refer the reader to published literature on the subject.

Nuer clans and lineages are exogamous. The patrilineal descendants of a common ancestor may not intermarry. The laws of exogamy extend farther than this and include persons who are closely related by marriage; persons related by blood but not legal kinship; and, finally, persons standing in a particular social relationship to each other. The prohibited degrees of relationship and other circumstances may be summarized as follows:

* P. P. Howell, *Manual of Nuer Law*, Oxford University Press, 1954, pp. 82–86.

(i) A man may not marry or have sexual intercourse with a clanswoman, and therefore with a woman of his lineage. The limits of clan exogamy are not, however, so rigid as to be unalterable. If the ancestral link is remote (beyond ten generations or so) the prohibition may be ignored or effectively removed by appropriate sacrifice and prescribed ritual.

(ii) A man may not marry or have sexual intercourse with a woman who is a clanswoman of his mother. This prohibition is not, however, carried back beyond six or seven generations.

(iii) As we have seen, a Nuer may be the legal son of one man and the physiological son of another. The prohibited degrees recorded above would apply to the Nuer through his legal father, but the relationship of the *genitor* to his natural child has a degree of social recognition, and it is also not permissible to marry a close kinswoman of the *genitor*. The extent of this prohibition is not as wide as that created by legal kinship.

(iv) Adoption, especially of Dinka children, is a common occurrence[1] among the Nuer, and the links created between father and adopted child receive social recognition and ultimately legal recognition amounting to true kinship. A man would not be allowed to marry or have sexual intercourse with a kinswoman of his adopted father, though in the initial stages this prohibition would be less extensive. In the next generation it would probably be identical, for a man who is fully adopted into a Nuer lineage assumes all the characteristics of that lineage, and in the future his origin may be forgotten. Similarly, an adopted girl would not marry into the lineage of her adoption, and would be bound by the same prohibitions. The reason here is clearer. Members of the lineage of her adoption would be the recipients of her bridewealth cattle and could not also be her relatives-in-law.

(v) A man may not marry again into his wife's lineage. Nuer say that a man may not have intercourse with two closely related women at the same period of time. The link is really through the children; a man may not marry his wife's sister because she will also be the maternal aunt of his children and entitled to a portion of the bridewealth of his daughters. A confusion of status of this kind must be avoided.

(vi) A man may not marry the daughter of an age-mate. Common initiation brings about an association similar to kinship. This is symbolized in the giving of the 'cow of the age-mate' (*yang ric* or *ruath ric*). To marry the daughter of any age-mate is to bring him into the category of father-in-law; the avoidance due to the latter is incompatible with the conventional familiarity which exists between age-mates.

Professor Evans-Pritchard summarizes these rules in an article on the subject.[2] He says:

> The exogamous rules . . . can be generalized by saying, as the Nuer do, that a man may not marry a woman who is *mar*, kin, to him. In defining exogamy kinship is traced farther in some directions than in others and is of different kinds: the clan kinship of the *mut*, the common spear; the kinship of *buth*, of collateral lineage and of adoption; uterine kinship; kinship through the *genitor*; the kinship of cognation, *mar* in the usual sense of the word; kinship which the birth of a child creates between husband and wife; the kinship acknowledged by acceptance of bridewealth; the kinship of analogy by the *ric*, the age-set, and the *twac*, the leopard-skin.[3]

We shall see that the greatest care is taken during the social processes of marriage to avoid any possible breach of these rules and it is unlikely that a bar to marriage would be discovered subsequently, at any rate one which involves a prohibition sufficiently strong to be unavoidable. Unless the relationship is singularly remote, however, the union would be dissolved without further delay and the appropriate ritual of appeasement and decontamination performed. This is usually performed by a Leopard-Skin Chief, who neutralizes the effects of the breach of taboo. A cow is sacrificed to the ancestral spirits, and the whole carcase divided into halves,[4] one half being consumed by the relatives of the man, the other half by the relatives of the woman. The presence of the Leopard-Skin Chief and the fact that a cow (possibly only a barren one) is sacrificed would indicate that the breach is a serious one and likely to bring great misfortune to the people concerned. As Professor Evans-Pritchard points out, the value of the sacrifice is usually an indication of the seriousness of the breach. For less serious offences of this sort, a smaller animal would be sacrificed, a bull-calf or a ram, and the ritual performed by the kinsmen of the parties concerned would be less elaborate. In some cases it is sufficient to cut in two a wild fruit known in Nuer as *kwol.* I think that the Leopard-Skin Chief is called in more usually when a legal union between persons within the prohibited degrees has taken place, and not in cases of extra-marital intercourse which will not continue. These ceremonies may also be performed before the union takes place, but clearly only in borderline cases where the relationship of the parties is so remote as to be almost fictitious. Similarly, as already mentioned, it would be performed if the impediment were discovered subsequent to legal marriage, but again the union would be unlikely to continue unless the relationship was exceptionally remote, especially, as is so often the case, if disasters (infant mortality or sickness in the family and other misfortunes) have occured and have been attributed to this cause after searching investigation. As a ground for divorce, should both parties demand it, a breach of the exogamy rules would be indisputable, and I think that a Nuer court would nowadays grant a divorce without much argument. This is, however, a matter of conjecture only, as I have only known one case of divorce brought before the courts for this reason, and then there were circumstances unconnected with exogamy which would have made the dissolution of marriage inevitable. Such matters are strictly limited to the families, or at most to the lineages, of the parties concerned, and are not usually brought to light in a public manner.

We have so far been principally concerned with the laws of exogamy and the prohibition of legal union between persons who fall within the forbidden degrees. We have seen also that these laws are relative to the position in the social and kinship structure of the persons concerned, and if their relationship is sufficiently distant, the prohibition may be permanently cancelled by the performance of sacrifice and ritual. In any case the consequences (*nueer*) may be thus avoided, even if the ritual is not sufficiently effective to ensure a safe continuance of the union. These rules also apply to extra-marital and illicit sexual intercourse, though not necessarily with the same force, and the consequences of infringement may be less serious. There is also an obvious difference between a casual act of sexual intercourse which is not repeated, and intercourse which results in the pregnancy of the woman. The birth of a child in such circumstances is a permanent reminder of the offence, and because the child is a link between the mother and the physiological father the situation is more dangerous. There is a confusion of legal and social status which at all costs must be avoided. Among the Nuer such difficulties can still be overcome by suitable sacrifice, but the implications are clearly more serious.[5]

Incestuous intercourse may sometimes be relevant to disputes which arise in the courts. Examples of this will be seen later. I do not propose to digress further on the subject of exogamy and incest, because the laws of exogamy are not in themselves a subject for dispute. There is now adequate published literature on the subject,[6] of which I have no criticisms to make and little except detailed information to add.

Notes

[1] Obviously more common in the past.

[2] *Social Structure: Studies presented to A. R. Radcliffe-Brown,* Oxford, 1949.

[3] Evans-Pritchard points out that 'a leopard-skin chief may not marry into the family of another leopard-skin chief, even though they are unrelated'. This contention may be true of Lou and eastern Nuer, where Leopard-Skin families are few, but I doubt whether it is applied in the western parts of Nuerland, where they are more common.

[4] *Yang me bak ke rual,* 'the cow of dividing for incest'.

[5] Among some African tribes children born in incest would be destroyed. It is reported of the eastern Dinka that children born in such circumstances are sold to the Murle. There is, however, no published evidence to substantiate this statement. The idea of infanticide, except perhaps in the case of deformities, is, so far as I know, alien to Nuer ideas.

[6] Evans-Pritchard, *The Nuer,* Oxford, 1940, pp. 6, 17, 192, 202, 225–8, 235, 257; in *Social Structure: Essays presented to A. R. Radcliffe-Brown,* Oxford, 1949. Further information will be found in various articles by the same author: 'Nuer bridewealth', *Africa,* XVI, 4, 1946; 'Nuer Marriage Ceremonies', ibid,. XVIII, 1, 1948; 'Some aspects of Marriage and the family among the Nuer', *Rhodes-Livingstone Paper,* No. 11, 1945; and more recently in *Kinship and Marriage among the Nuer,* Oxford, 1951.

M. Fortes: Kinship and Marriage among the Ashanti*

Ashanti marriage is restricted in accordance with the Ashanti concept of incest. Marriage is prohibited between individuals who would be committing the sin of incest if they had sexual relations. Thus marriage is forbidden between members of the same matrilineage, and this includes accessory lineages which have been attached to the authentic lineage for four or more generations. This taboo extends to the clan throughout Ashanti.[1] Marriage is also prohibited with any 'patrilineal' descendant of one's father's father's father—i.e. of one's father's paternal *nanâ* up to the fourth generation. This taboo is an extension of the taboo on sex relations with a father's brother's child (a sibling (*nua*) in Ashanti kinship terminology), which is regarded as a sin almost as heinous as incest with a full sibling. The basis of this is the identification of brothers. Thus the taboo applies to the children and sons' children of half-brothers by the same mother but different fathers. Lastly marriage with a lineal descendant to the fourth generation, or with a lineal ascendant (or the sibling of such an ascendant) to the fourth generation, is prohibited.[2] The ideal match is with a cross-cousin on either side, though there is a preference, for men, for marriage with a mother's brother's daughter (*wofa ba*)[3]—i.e. the daughter of a man of his mother's generation belonging to the lineage segment descended from her great-grandmother. Again, marriage with a member of one's own village or chiefdom is preferred to marriage with an 'outsider' (*ahoho*). The reasons given are that the character and family background of the parties are known to their respective parents and this enables them to make a careful choice. It is also said that such a marriage enables the parents and other kin of both spouses to take a personal interest in and help in the care of their children. But undoubtedly the most important factor is the strength of matrilineal ties in domestic organization. Intra-village marriage enables husband and wife to reside with their maternal kin if they wish to or have to. My investigations in 1945 showed that 75 per cent and upwards of married people have spouses from the same village or adjacent villages. Chiefs still have two matrimonial prerogatives recorded by Rattray. Twin girls (*ntaa*) who are not kin to the chief of their place of birth within forbidden degrees are regarded from birth as his future wives and cannot marry anyone else unless he relinquishes his prior rights. Secondly, every ranking chief has a number of stool wives (*ayete*). These wives are obligatorily provided by various lineages of the chief's subjects; and if a stool wife dies she must be replaced by another girl of her lineage.[4]

Notes

[1] And, where clan affiliation is known, throughout the Akan-speaking peoples.

[2] The prohibited marriages listed by Rattray, 1923, p. 37 all fall under these rules. As has been pointed out, a common *ntoro* is not by itself a bar to marriage. Any attempt to defy these rules is nowadays treated as a crime subject to a fine. It should be noted that the count of four generations is always *exclusive* of the generation of *Ego*.

[3] Cf. Rattray, 1927, chap. xxix.

[4] This is the only form of 'sororate' practised in Ashanti. Cf. Rattray, 1929, p. 27.

M. Gluckman: Order and Rebellion in Tribal Africa†

A Lozi may marry a woman with the same descent-name as himself. He should not marry a woman with whom he can trace genealogical relationship in any way, and we have seen that Lozi fail to trace genealogical relationships beyond four generations. In fact intermarriages occur earlier, while relationship can still be traced. The Lozi say, *sikowa sakukwata okusatunda kasapula*, 'a kindred gets so big that relationship is broken with time'. They apply this saying when a young man wants to marry a girl whom his elders consider is related to him. The elders protest, the young man counters with the

* M. Fortes, 'Kinship and Marriage among the Ashanti', in A. R. Radcliffe-Brown and D. Forde, *African Systems of Kinship and Marriage*, Oxford University Press, 1950, pp. 278–279.

† M. Gluckman, *Order and Rebellion in Tribal Africa*, Routledge & Kegan Paul, 1963, pp. 173–176.

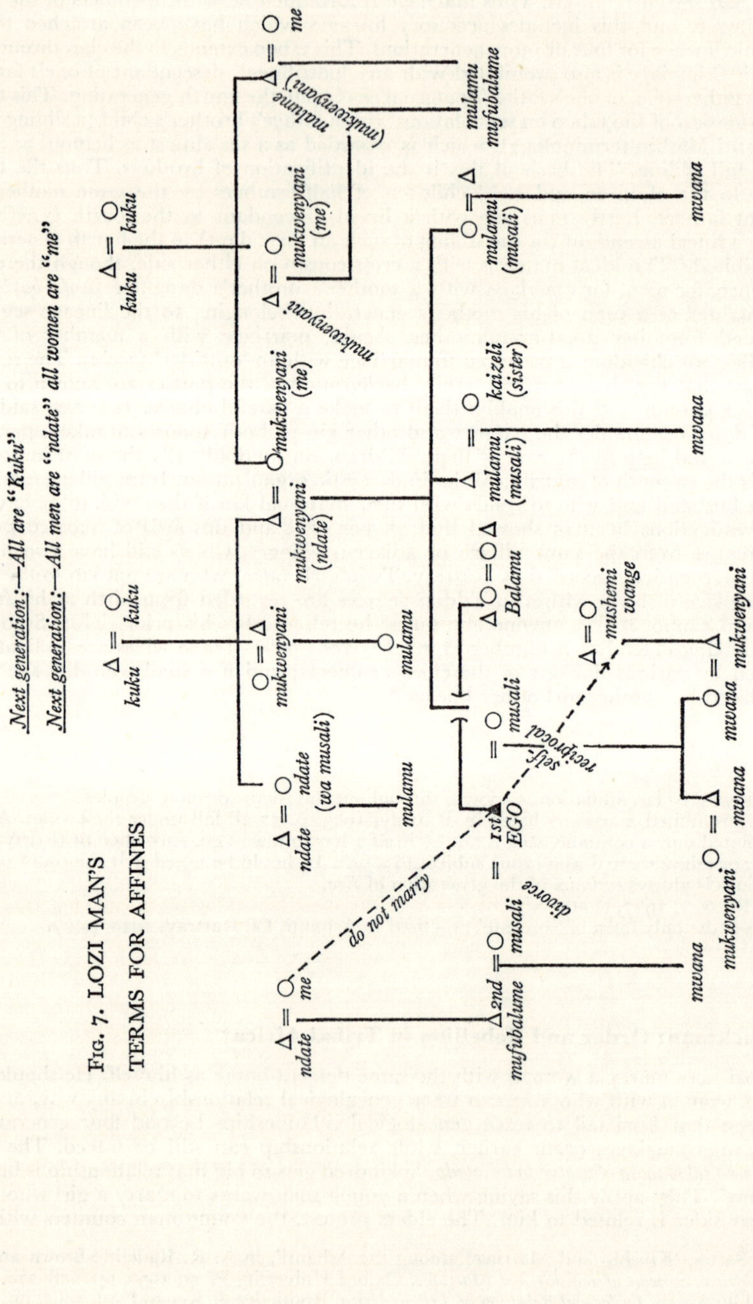

FIG. 7. LOZI MAN'S
TERMS FOR AFFINES

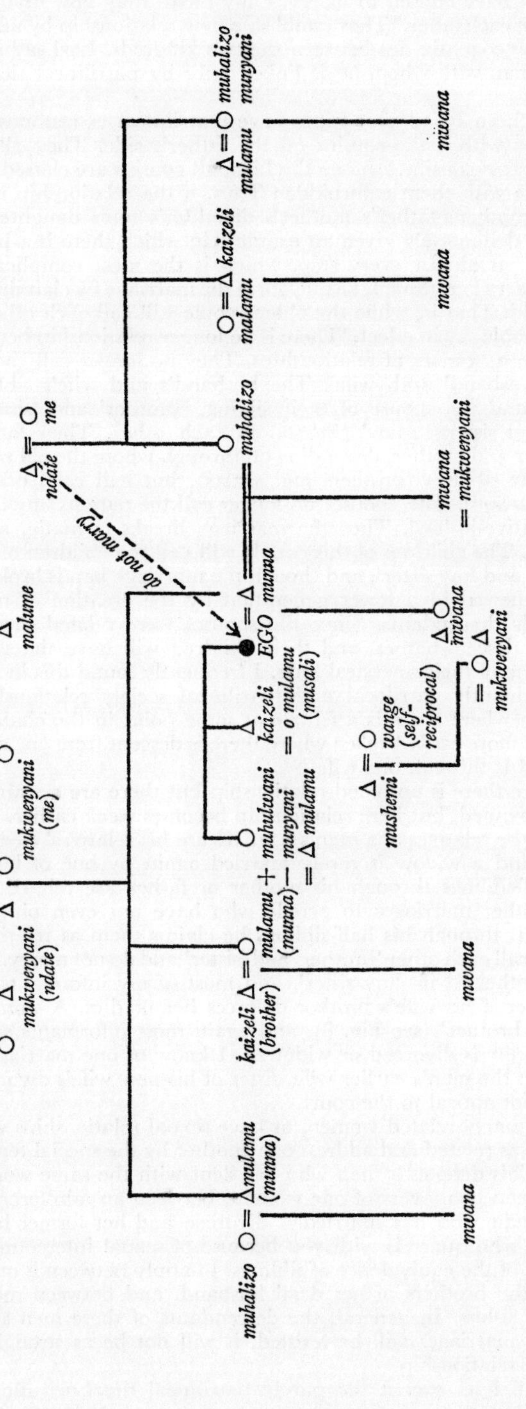

FIG. 8. LOZI WOMAN'S TERMS FOR AFFINES

maxim and marries her. It is significant for my later analysis that the couple will be cursed: 'You have chosen to marry. Only death may now divorce you: you may not separate from each other.' They establish a new relationship by affinity which ultimately produces new cognatic ties between the two kindreds. Lozi say that a man should not marry a woman with whom he is linked only by patrilineal ties, but such marriages occur.

Most Northern Rhodesian tribes have matrilineal exogamous clans but also forbid intermarriage with ortho-cousins on the father's side. They allow, and often prefer, marriage of cross-cousins. Among the Lozi, all cousins are classed as brothers and sisters and marriage with them is forbidden Thus, if the relationship is remembered, a man will call his mother's father's mother's daughter's son's daughter 'my sister' (*kaizeli*). Here I have deliberately given an example in which there is a jump from maternal to paternal line at almost every step, which is the most complicated combination. He should not marry her, though he may force the marriage by claiming that the relationship has grown old. That is, while the older people still call each other 'brother' and 'sister' the young people say in effect, 'There is no longer relationship between us'. By marrying they establish a new set of relationships. They no longer call each other 'brother' and 'sister' but 'husband' and 'wife'. The husband's and wife's siblings also stop calling each other, and the spouse of their sibling, 'brother' and 'sister', and they become 'brothers- and sisters-in-law' (*balamu*) to each other. Their fathers or their mothers or their father and mother, depending on through whom the old relationship was traced, are no longer siblings (brothers and sisters), but call each other 'the other parent' (*mukwange muchemi*). The spouses no longer call the parents 'my father' or 'my mother', but 'my relative-in-law'. Thus the marriage breaks cognatic, and establishes affinal, relationships. The children of this couple will call the children of their parents' siblings 'my brother' and 'my sister', and though the marriage ban is broken for the one generation, it is renewed in a lower generation by the creation of new cognatic relations between their descendants. Since the spouses were related they will probably share at least two descent-names, and their children will have the same descent-names in more than one of their ancestral lines. I frequently found this in recording genealogies. In this dominantly patrilocal and patrilineal society relationship is obviously more easily broken where there is a female at some point in the chain of genealogical connexions; and more easily broken where there is descent from one man through two wives than where it is through one wife.

Even where there is no blood-relationship but there are certain marriage connexions marriage is banned, but here relationship becomes weak earlier. The Lozi say *mwaboyu ta mwaboyu*, 'the relatives of a man's relatives are his relatives' (see Fig. 7). Since divorce is frequent and a widow is rarely married again by one of her husband's kinsmen, a man's half-siblings through his mother or father are related through his mother's or father's other marriages to people who have not even pirative blood-connexions with him, but through his half-siblings he claims them as relatives. Men and women related thus call each other 'brother' and 'sister' and do not marry. Similarly, a man calls his wife's brother's wife 'my sister', and most of my informants agree that he should not marry her if his wife's brother divorces her or dies. A woman calls her co-wife's brother 'my brother' (see Fig. 8), and again most informants say that he should not marry her if she is divorced or widowed. I know of one marriage in the former set of relationships; the man's earlier wife, sister of his new wife's divorced husband, left him and he did not appeal to the court.

Men who marry related women, or have sexual relationships with the same woman, are regarded as related and address one another by the special term *mufubalume* ('fellow-husband'). This denotes a man who has slept with the same woman as oneself, and it applies between two lovers of one woman, between an adulterer and his cuckold, and between a man who has married a divorcee and her former husband. Lozi explain it as 'a man who quarrels with you because of sexual intercourse'. It is extended, on the principle of the equivalence of siblings, to apply between a man who has married a widow and the brothers of her dead husband, and between men who have married classificatory sisters. In general, the descendants of these men should not marry, but though their marriages will be resisted, it will not be as strongly as where there is a real cognatic relationship.

Thus in all lines except the purely patrilineal the Lozi allow marriages where a distant genealogical connexion can be traced, and ultimately welcome them, to renew the relationship. Perhaps, therefore, these marriages are cursed with a ban on divorce. This process also occurs in some Zulu lines; it is approved for a man to renew relationships by marrying a woman of his father's mother's or mother's mother's clan with whom he cannot trace links. He cannot marry a known cognate. Nor can he marry a woman of his father's or mother's clan, even though she belongs to a different lineage with which genealogical links are no longer remembered.

(c) Consents

It has often been stated that African customary marriage is not so much a union between two individuals but an alliance between two family groups (see chapter 6). It is therefore natural that when it comes to the question of consents, it is the consent of the spouses' families, rather than the spouses themselves (at least traditionally) that was all important. But as *Seymour* and *Duncan* show in the following pages, the consent of the parties themselves is now becoming an essential ingredient.

S. M. Seymour: Native Law in South Africa*

(i) *The Consent of the Bride's Guardian*

The consent of the bride's guardian is essential to the validity of a union.[1] When in dispute, his consent is ascertainable from his acceptance of dowry, or, perhaps, from his receipt of earnest cattle or a fine for seduction only, if he allows his daughter to go to, or remain with, as the case may be, the bridegroom or suitor, on the understanding that dowry will be paid in due course.[2]

Where, however, a girl's guardian has suffered or allowed her to stay at another kraal, the head thereof (call him her custodian) is competent to give her away in a valid customary union, without reference to her guardian.[3]

Should a girl's guardian withhold his consent to her union, however unreasonably, there is no means of compelling him to give it; if she should go to live with her lover without his consent, no union can possibly result—only an illicit cohabitation rendering the latter liable for damages for seduction. But in this connexion, Native law indirectly tends to force a girl's guardian's hands or adjusts the matter. In most tribes the law permits him to claim damages for illicit intercourse with his daughter in respect of her first two pregnancies only; after that he can claim no further damages because his daughter is regarded as immoral. While the total of these damages or fines is comparatively substantial, it normally amounts to less than one-half of the customary dowry; he might be considered wise, therefore, to give way to the force of circumstances and accept dowry. In *Pondo* law he is allowed to claim a fine for each and every pregnancy of his daughter.[4]

(ii) *The Consent of the Bride*

Section 29 of Cape Proclamation 140 of 1885 (and the similar provisions of contemporary proclamations dealing with the various parts of the Transkei) lays down that 'it shall not be lawful for any person to compel any woman to marry against her wish'. Under original Native law her consent was probably forthcoming, as a rule, even if sometimes reluctantly, but it is doubtful if it was strictly necessary.[5] But it is today; so much so, that, without it, there is no valid union. This rule is applied in the interests of public policy, even in areas where no express legislation exists.[6]

(ii) *The Consent of the Bridegroom*

That the consent of the bridegroom is necessary is so obvious that it hardly needs mentioning. His consent need not necessarily be given at the same time as his father

* S. M. Seymour, *Native Law in South Africa*, Juta & Co. Ltd., 1960, pp. 72–74.

enters into the negotiations for the union, but until it is gven no customary union can come into being.[7]

Among the *Thembu*, it is not competent for an uncircumcised youth to contract a customary union.[8]

Children under the age of puberty are legally incapable of giving consent to a customary union. The former practice whereby parents arranged customary unions for their young children has been abolished by the courts on the ground of public policy. If a union is so arranged, it only comes into being if and when both the boy and the girl become capable of consenting and give their consent. The former agreement by the parents is null and void *ab initio*, but a subsequent 'ratification' by the boy and girl would validate the union from the time of ratification.[9]

Notes

[1] *Goina* v. *Ntengo*, 1935 N.A.C. (C. & O) 21, Port St. Johns; *Dlomo* v. *Mahodi*, 1946 N.A.C. (C & O) 61, Tsolo; *Sila* v. *Masuku*, 1937 N.A.C. (T & N) 121.

[2] *Stimela* v. *Madolo*, 5 N.A.C. 102, Umtata; *Gijana* v. *Mangali*, 1946 N.A.C. (C & O) 60 Engcobo; *Dlomo* v. *Mahodi*, 1946 N.A.C. (C & O) 61, Tsolo; *Mothombeni* v. *Matlou*, 1945 N.A.C (T & N) 123, Pietersburg; *Memani* v. *Makaba*, 1950 N.C.A. (S.D.) 178, Nqamakwe; *Ngcongolo* v. *Parkies*, 1953 N.A.C. (S.D.) 103, Dordrecht.

[3] See chapter VI, 7, where this matter is dealt with fully.

[4] See chapter XIV, 2A.

[5] *Nbono* v. *Manoxoweni*, 6 E.D.C. 62, General; *Nomatusi* v. *Nompetu*, 3 N.A.C. 165, Lusikisiki; *Gebeleiseni* v. *Sakumani*, 1947 N.A.C. (C & O) 105, Qumbu.

[6] *Sila* v. *Masuku*, 1937 N.A.C. (T & N) 121.

[7] *Sofika* v. *Gova*, 1 N.A.C. 7, Engcobo; *Neku* v. *Moni*, 1938 N.A.C. (C & O) 61, Kentani; *Sila* v. *Masuku*, 1937 N.A.C. (T & N) 121.

[8] *Gebeleiseni* v. *Sakumani*, 1947 N.A.C. (C & O) 105, Qumbu.

[9] Van Warmelo, pp. 53, 57; *Gempeza* v. *Ntsizi*, 5 N.A.C. 103, Tabankulu; *Butelezi* v. *Ndhlela*, 1938 N.A.C. (T & N) 175, Mahlabantini. In some tribes, immature girls were married to old men; these unions were probably entered into to maintain a policy of mutual friendship and respect between two families; although the husband would occupy the same bed as his girl wife for a night or two as a symbol of their nuptial relation, the girl was not brutalized; when she attained maturity, however, her husband would appoint one of his young male relatives to *ngena* her, in order to raise seed for the House created by her union. These unions are, however, contrary to public policy, and null and void *ab initio* (*Sibeka* v. *Malaza*, 1938 N.A.C. (T & N) 117, Carolina).

P. Duncan: Sotho Laws and Customs*

Parents' Consent

Marriage partners' consent essential. Traditionally parents had the choice of marriage partners for their children. Now, however, the young people are taking more and more responsibility for this choice. It occasionally happens that parents withhold their consent from a match which the young people wish, and in certain circumstances courts will order parents to give their consent, and, in the case of the boy's parents, to give dowry. In 1932, one, John, abducted a girl named 'Ma-Junia, and paid six head of cattle as abduction-compensation for her. He wished to marry her, but her mother, Lydesia Mosiuoa, withheld her consent on the ground that she, a Roman Catholic, did not want her daughter to marry a polygamist. The matter went to court, and the Boqate court made an order that Lydesia should permit the marriage. This was reversed on appeal by the Paramount Chief's Court, relying on section 1 of the Basutoland Marriage Rule (LL.† II:34) which does not seem to have any bearing on this case. The appeal noted to the judicial commissioner was not prosecuted, but if it had been it is probable that it would have succeeded—*Mosiuoa* v. *Mosiuoa*, J.C. 271/48. It is doubtful whether on grounds of public policy a parent should have a complete veto, and it would seem desirable that where the necessary permission was refused, a court should have discretion in the matter, and power to give permission.

* P. Duncan, *Sotho Laws and Customs*, Oxford University Press, Capetown, 1960, pp. 21–22.

† Laws of Lerotholi.

2. In this connexion see also LL.* II:4(2), which reads:

> If the man abducts the same unmarried girl a second time against the wishes of either his or her parents, the amount of compensation to be awarded the parents of such girl shall be at the discretion of the court, and the court may order the dissenting parents to arrange the marriage.

This gives wide discretion to courts. It would of course be unthinkable for a court to make such an order if the young people did not wish it.

* Laws of Lerotholi.

Chapter 8

THE FORMATION OF MARRIAGE

In this chapter, there is a chronological account of the formalities of entering into a marriage from the preliminary meetings to the wedding. Of particular significance is the involvement of the spouses' families at almost every stage of the formalities. In this connection, the overlap with the preceding section on consents should be borne in mind.

The marriage described here is a normal type marriage to be distinguished from marriages with special formalities described in the next chapter.

(a) Preliminaries and Betrothal

The extracts here are descriptive of the preliminaries to marriage and the negotiations between the families up to the stage of betrothal. Of special importance is the property (whether cattle or otherwise), that passes between the two parties and their families and the connection with the marriage-consideration. In addition to describing the ceremonies, *Schapera* deals with the 'usages' of the betrothal period and the dissolution of the engagement.

I. Schapera: A Handbook of Tswana Law and Custom*

Marriages in the olden days were always arranged by the parents of the young people concerned. The latter were not consulted at all, and only after the necessary arrangements had been made would they be informed. The boy was called home from the cattlepost and told that a wife had been found for him, whom he might never even have seen; and a girl was often betrothed while still a child, or even before she was born! The children had no right to choose their own mates. They were bound to comply with the wishes of their parents, and if they refused to do so could be forced, if necessary, by punishment and (in the case of a boy) by the threat of disinheritance. Only the girl's father had the power to enforce her marriage, even against her own wish and that of her mother. If he were dead, her guardian could not force the marriage if her mother objected; but, if the mother also agreed, the girl could be compelled to take the boy chosen. The selection of a wife applied only in the case of a man's first marriage. Any additional wives he might marry were chosen by himself.

Nowadays, parents may still on occasion choose wives for their sons. But it is far more usual for the young people to make their own choice. The boy informs his father that he would like to marry a certain girl. Should his parents approve of her, they will then undertake the necessary betrothal negotiations. If they do not approve, they will try to dissuade him from his choice. Sometimes their efforts are successful. But if he insists on marrying her, and her family also is willing to accept him, little can be done, for he will deliberately oppose his parents and may even go to live altogether at the girl's home. Similarly, if a girl's parents refuse to let her marry the boy she prefers, she may attempt to force their consent by allowing him to seduce her. It is still not uncommon for parents to force their daughters into unwelcome marriages, but with the growing independence of the younger generation such marriages are becoming less frequent. The control of parents over the marriage of their children has been greatly weakened, the actual choice

* I. Schapera, *A Handbook of Tswana Law and Custom*, Oxford University Press, 1938, pp. 128–134.

being made by the people most directly concerned. But if there is sufficient reason the Chief will still uphold the rights of parents to dispose of their children in marriage.

Occasionally, if the girl's parents refuse to let her marry the boy of her choice (or vice versa), the young couple may elope. The parents report the matter to the *kgotla*, where the Chief inquires if the boy intends to marry the girl, and if the relatives on both sides consent. If the girl's parents still refuse to accept the boy as a son-in-law, she is ordered to return to them; while the boy—and sometimes the girl also—is publicly thrashed for having taken her away without the consent of her parents. It is said that in the olden days the girl's parents had the right to kill him if they caught him eloping with their daughter; or, if the matter was brought to the *kgotla*, the young couple were severely beaten and even tortured by order of the Chief. Nowadays, however, it is possible for them to get married according to European civil rites, even if their parents refuse to give them permission; and it is possibly to some extent for this reason that permission is not often withheld if it is evident that the young couple are determined to marry.

Betrothal Ceremonies

Once the boy's people have selected a suitable bride for him, they must formally seek the consent of her parents to the marriage. It often happened in the olden days that a man would bespeak as his son's future wife a girl who was still very young or who might even not yet have been born. This form of betrothal (variously known as *go tlhoma letlhôkwa*, 'to plant a stalk of grass'; *go baya monwana*, 'to put down a finger'; or, in the case of an unborn girl, *go ôpa mpa*, 'to strike the womb') was practised especially between close relatives. If the girl's parents agreed to the match, the boy's father would send them a beast (*kgomo ya potsa* or *kgomo ya perepetsha*). It was slaughtered, and the peritoneum (*lomipi*) hung round the neck of the girl, or round the neck of the woman whose unborn daughter was being bespoken. This ceremony marked the formal ratification of the betrothal. The boy's people would now from time to time send various gifts to the girl and her people, such as clothing, milk, and meat; and the boy would be taken to their home in the usual way to be introduced. If, while the girl was growing up, the boy's people thought that he was already old enough to marry, they would select another wife for him, whom he would marry first. But this wife would always be regarded as junior in status to the one originally engaged. The latter when she was married to the boy became his great wife, and the *bogadi* for her had to be given before that of any of his other wives.

Infant betrothal is still practised to some extent at the present time, but is tending to die out fairly rapidly, especially in the more civilized parts. It does not appear that the girl can be forced into the marriage if she obstinately refuses to have the boy, although her parents must then restore his betrothal gifts.

Where the girl selected is already eligible for marriage, there is still a long series of formal negotiations to be gone through before the betrothal (*patlô*, *pêêlêlô*) is complete. There appears to be only a slight difference between the ceremonies now observed and those of former times. The usages outlined below refer more particularly to the present day. Many differences of detail exist from tribe to tribe, and even within the same tribe; but the general procedure is fundamentally the same.

The first step is for the boy's father to consult informally with the father of the girl selected, if the two are related or friendly. If they agree, they will then discuss the proposed marriage with their close relatives, especially the maternal uncles (*bomalome*) of the children concerned. Should these relatives raise any convincing objections, the matter may be allowed to drop. But, if they approve, the boy's father next sends one of his near relatives, accompanied by some other man as witness, to 'seek' the girl from her parents (*go batla*). They are received in the local *kgotla*, and at a suitable opportunity privately inform the girl's father of their mission. In doing so they conventionally use the formula: *Re tsile go kopa segô sa metse*, 'We have come to beg for a calabash of water'. The girl's father makes some non-committal reply, indicating that he has no authority to agree to or reject the proposal. But if he is himself favourably inclined, he may give the messengers some food or beer as a sign of encouragement. They depart to report upon the result of their mission. The girl's people now discuss the proposal thoroughly with their relatives, and may decide to accept or reject it. When the messengers come again and ask for the girl in the same way, the girl's father, if agreement has been reached, will ask them to send the women.

After a few days, one of the boy's senior female relatives comes with another woman to the girl's mother *go tlhatswa puô ya banna*, 'to wash the words of the men', i.e. to confirm their proposal. They are told to come back on a stipulated day, when they will receive their answer. At this meeting, known as *katlholô* (the judgement), all the girl's relatives are usually present. Many of the boy's relatives, including his parents, also come, together with the original messengers. Then, if the decision is favourable, as it is almost certain to be if negotiations have been allowed to reach this stage, the boy's people are formally told: *Ngwana ke o, le ka mo tsaya, tsayang go thenyathenya, le be le busê go thenyathenya*, 'Here is the child, you can take her, take her living, and if you return her, return her while she is still alive', i.e. if you become tired of her in future, send her back unharmed. To this they reply: *Re nesa pula*, 'We cause it to rain (for you)', i.e. we thank you.

This completes the first stage of the negotiations, known as *patlô* or *go batla* (to seek, request), without which no marriage is regarded as proper. Sometimes a number of such visits have to be made, spread over a fairly considerable time; for it is regarded as good etiquette not to consent too readily to the proposed marriage. But there is no essential difference in procedure.

The next step is to confirm the betrothal. This is done by the boy's people sending to the girl's people an animal for slaughter, or some such things as dress material, blankets, and shawls for the girl herself. These objects are variously known as *mokwele* (Rolong), *perepetsha* (Ngwato), or *maisiwa* (Kgatla). Once they are accepted, the betrothal is regarded as complete. The girl's people make a small feast to celebrate the occasion. About the same time, or soon afterwards, the boy is taken to the girl's home one evening by a senior male relative (generally the original messenger), and is formally presented to the girl's parents and to the girl herself as her future husband. He is now free to visit their home whenever he likes, which he could not do openly while the negotiations were being conducted.

Usages of the Betrothal Period

Once the betrothal has been confirmed, a considerable time generally elapses before the wedding takes place. Few engagements last less than a year, and the majority last at least two. But from the moment the final pledge has been given, the boy and girl are referred to as 'husband' and 'wife', while their two families speak of each other as 'relatives-in-law'. The boy's people refer to the girl's people as *bagwagwadi*, and are themselves called *bagwê* by the latter. They visit and entertain each other frequently, help each other at work, and send each other occasional presents of slaughter animals, meat, thick milk, and other things. The boy's people will also from time to time send the girl herself gifts of food or clothes, or household utensils such as pots and baskets; they may plough a field for her, and generally also take her to their cattlepost to drink fresh milk and grow fat. All such gifts made by the boy's people to the girl and her family are known by the same name as the final betrothal pledge, viz. as *mokwele*, *perepetsha*, or *maisiwa*.

During all this time the girl must behave with great circumspection whenever she meets the boy in public, and must be even more reserved and dignified in the presence of his older relatives, and especially of his parents. Her general conduct is under observation, and if she misbehaves they may break the engagement. Among the Kgatla she should refrain from visiting the boy's home until she is actually married to him. Among the Ngwato, however, she is expected to go there occasionally to help in such work as fetching water or wood, cooking, or stamping corn. She must always be accompanied by a senior female relative and by some of her own companions. They are entertained, not by the boy himself, but by his parents.

The boy, on the other hand, may visit the girl's home at any time, and is expected to do so frequently. He is treated there with great respect and special hospitality. He may be asked or may volunteer to perform various services for her parents, such as bringing them loads of firewood or earth, building fences at their fields or round their homesteads, helping them plough, and so on. Among the Kgatla he is also expected, once he is engaged, to go to work for some time in European centres of employment, in order to earn money with which to buy the girl's wedding garments. He should also, while away, send her occasional small gifts of money or clothes.

Dissolution of Engagement

An engagement, once confirmed, may subsequently be broken by one of the parties concerned if there is any good and sufficient reason. The boy's people may break it if they find the girl associating too freely with other young men, or taking little notice of the boy when he visits her. Her own parents, similarly, may break it if the boy neglects to visit them and spends most of his time with other girls. In both instances the two family-groups first come together to discuss the situation. If they cannot come to a satisfactory arrangement the matter will be referred to the courts. The headman or Chief, as the case may be, will sometimes order the marriage to take place, especially if it is only the boy or the girl who is anxious to break the engagement, and not the whole of the family. But if the families themselves agree with their respective children, he will usually order them to separate.

If the girl and her parents are found in the wrong, they must return everything given to them as *perepetsha*, or its equivalent. If the boy and his people are in the wrong, they not only forfeit all that they have given, but may also be made to pay compensation, according to the circumstances of the case, for having wasted the girl's opportunities of making a good marriage in the meantime. If the boy has himself impregnated the girl, and then refuses to marry her, he is almost always ordered to do so, as her chances of marrying any one else have been greatly diminished. Or, if it is found better to separate the couple, his people will be made to pay heavy compensation.

The boy's people have the right to break the engagement if the girl has become pregnant by someone else. In that event they are entitled to the restoration of all that they have given as *perepetsha*. But they may agree to go on with the marriage, in which case the gifts remain with the girl's parents. The cattle paid as damages by the girl's seducer belong in both cases to the girl's people, the boy having no claim to them.

Should a betrothed girl die before marriage, her parents were formerly expected to replace her by a younger sister. This is still generally practised. The boy if he likes this girl will then marry her; but if he does not wish to do so he cannot recover his betrothal gifts. Nor can he claim them if there is no other girl in the family to take the place of his dead fiancée. Similarly, if a betrothed boy dies before marriage, his fiancée was formerly taken over by one of his younger brothers. Any children she bore to this man would be regarded as those of deceased, and entitled to his estate. Nowadays this custom is still occasionally practised, but the girl can refuse to marry the man if she does not like him. In that case her people will not be held liable for the return of the gifts they have received.

H. Cory and M. M. Hartnoll: Customary Law of the Haya*

Courtship

It is stated that it was originally the custom in Buhaya for a father, or his son or his brother, during a meeting with friends, to offer a girl to one of them as a wife. The man who accepted threw himself on the ground and embraced the legs of the father as a sign of his gratitude. The girl's consent was never asked and no brideprice was paid.

Later the custom altered and the suitor took the initiative, he sent an arbitrator (*musigire*†) to the chosen girl's father to ask for her hand in marriage. The father and mother discussed the acceptability of the suitor. Usually the father delayed his consent by convention. The girl was not asked for her consent either by her parents or her suitor, but the latter was unlikely to be a stranger to her as wives were usually chosen from the man's home district.

If the answer of the father was in the affirmative the young man then went to his own father, whose consent had already been obtained before the girl's father was approached, and asked for a goat. This goat was called *kiteme ilembo* (to see the way). This goat was sent to the girl's parents, and the day of its delivery was considered the real day of betrothal. Relatives of bride and bridegroom, and the *musigire*, assembled but not the bridegroom himself as it was a strict rule that the couple should never meet during their betrothal time.

* H. Cory and M. M. Hartnoll, *Customary Law of the Haya*, Lund Humphries for International African Institute, 1945, pp. 242–243.

† The more usual name is *musheiezi*.

At the end of the meeting the *musigire* received the *rutwa rw'cmwani*, a small basket filled with coffee beans. This he kept until the wedding day as a sign of the consent of the bride's parents. All those present at the meeting had sexual intercourse on the night following it to bring good luck to the wedding. From the day of his betrothal the young man carefully avoided meeting his mother-in-law to be. No day was fixed for the marriage. The time of betrothal lasted several months.

Betrothal

During his betrothal a man had to make certain ritual gifts to the girl's family, which were counted part of the brideprice. He had to send another goat to his future father-in-law called *katanga* in Kiamtwara or *mberere mpugura* (shining fate) in Karagwe. To his future mother-in-law he had to send a hoe, called *nfuka*. The goat was eaten by the girl's family after a piece had been consecrated to the spirits of their clan. The hoe was made by a native blacksmith and used only by the girl's mother. When it eventually became worn out she took it to her son-in-law who replaced it with a new hoe.

It was also the duty of the betrothed man to send regular presents of beer to his future father-in-law.

When several months had elapsed the man sent word to the girl's father that he wished to arrange a day for his wedding. If the father agreed to the proposed date arrangements were made for the payment of brideprice which was always paid in full before marriage.

P. P. Howell: Manual of Nuer Law*

Courting and Betrothal

When a Nuer youth has been accepted by a girl she will hasten to inform her family, provided she knows that her lover has sufficient cattle to legalize the union. It may be that her legal representatives in the family—that is, her more important male kinsmen—will ban the marriage from the start for some reason or other. Relations with the prospective bridegroom's family may already be strained, and they may have no desire to associate with it; there may even be blood between them (*teke riem kamdien*), or the memory of a blood feud. They may know at once that a marriage is precluded by the rules of exogamy. In such circumstances the girl will be discreetly told to avoid her lover in future. If, however, there is no objection she will be encouraged to continue and will receive their permission, though this is not made public. The first ceremony may then take place. This does not concern the older members of either family, and is confined to the prospective bride and bridegroom and their friends and coevals. It is in fact no more than a formal recognition among the younger people that the couple are courting, and it does not involve any legal negotiation. It is known in Nuer as *luom nyal*.

Luom nyal: 'Courting the girl'. The meeting is held at the home of some person who is related neither to the girl nor to the young man, often the home of the latter's best friend (*math*). A few friends of both parties are present, and among them is the prospective bridegroom's official spokesman, who is known as the *gwan twac* and performs the duties of a 'Best Man'. The girl also has a personal friend, a girl who is known as *ngi nyal*, and who takes her part in the ceremony, and leads the conversation and the friendly chaff which are characteristic of these occasions.[1] The meeting usually takes place at night, sometimes all night, inside a hut. No elderly people are present, and the time is spent in the exchange of elaborate compliments which sometimes go on for half an hour or more without break.[2] The verb *lum* in Nuer, from which *luom* is derived, is used to describe any form of courting, even casual flirtation at dances, but its use here implies a degree of formality not previously recognized, the recognition of the engagement being restricted to the young people who take part in dances together, and not including the adult members of the communities concerned.

Thiec nyal: 'Asking for the girl'. After the *luom nyal*, which is not a serious engagement and

* P. P. Howell, *Manual of Nuer Law*, Oxford University Press, 1954, pp. 87–90.

more often than not comes to nothing, a meeting takes place known as *thiec nyal*, 'asking for the girl'. This again may lead to nothing, but it is a more formal affair than any preceding it, and for the first time the girl's parents or guardian are approached by the prospective bridegroom and possibly by some of his senior kinsmen. It amounts to an opening of negotiations between the two families, but is not binding. If the members of the girl's family are satisfied by this time that the young man is in earnest and has cattle in support of his suit—for they have probably made discreet enquiries long before this—they will ask that the first tokens of formal betrothal be paid. They hope to receive at least four head of cattle (though they may be satisfied with less) known as the *yang gwan nyal*, a cow and calf which are intended to supply the girl's father with milk, *thak deman nyal*, a bull or bull-calf for the bride's brother,[3] and a *yang kwoth*, a cow which will be dedicated to the spirits of their lineage. The distribution of these cattle is significant. In the first place the girl's father or, if he is dead, her eldest brother or paternal uncle, must receive a guarantee in material form that the prospective bridegroom is in earnest. The ancestral spirits must be called in to bless and assure the future union, and the *yang kwoth* is dedicated to them. Finally, the bride's eldest brother, often a coeval of the bridegroom, must be placated, for it is he who expects to benefit most by her marriage, which will bring in bridewealth which he himself will use for his own marriage. If the girl's family are in agreement, a day is then fixed for the formal betrothal, in the form of a meeting when the cattle of engagement will be paid over. This is known as *cuei*, and the *Nuer* will say *ce cuei-de cuei*, 'he has engaged himself'.

Cuei: Betrothal. The *cuei* is part of the betrothal negotiations, and amounts to a more public acknowledgement by the bridegroom's family in paying, and by the bride's family in accepting, the cattle which are considered necessary for that purpose. The cattle are driven straight to the homestead of the girl's father, and there remain shut in the cattle-byre while the meeting takes place. The prospective bridegroom and his *gwan twac* are expected to observe rigidly the special restrictions on their movements in the bride's home, the signs of respect and other observances which characterize behaviour towards relatives-in-law. They are not allowed to enter any of the houses, and they must cover their nakedness with a special cat-skin known as *twac thoan*. It is for this reason that the principal assistant of the bridegroom is known as *gwan twac*, 'owner of the skin', and a husband is usually expected to wear it in the presence of his wife's mother.[4] Beer has been brewed beforehand, and is handed round among the senior guests; dancing takes place, and a bull-calf known as *yang kwen* or *yang lum* (the 'cow of marriage' or 'of courting') is sacrificed and eaten.[5]

The adult males of the two families (with the exception of the bridegroom himself) have therefore drunk together and the kinsmen of the bridegroom have partaken of meat provided by the girl's father. The bridegroom's kinsmen have accepted hospitality and provided the cattle of betrothal to give legal stability to the pledge. This preliminary betrothal feast does not concern the rest of the local community, though many of them will turn up uninvited because of the beer and meat which are available. The formal gathering really concerns only the kinsmen of the girl and the kinsmen of the bridegroom. As in the case of negotiations for the composition of homicide, Nuer have a concise terminology for both parties. The bride's family are throughout known as the *ji nyal* while those of the bridegroom are known as *ji wuta*. These terms mean no more than the 'girl's people' and the 'man's people', but they are used expressly in connexion with marriage negotiations,[6] and stress the distinction between the two parties.

Sometimes girls are betrothed at a very early age, and quite often when they are ten to fifteen years old. This does not mean that they are pledged by their families without their knowledge or consent, for they are usually approached first by the man concerned and are proud to accept, for girls thus engaged appear to have an enhanced attraction for other Nuer youths. Two cows are paid, which are known as the *dau cieh*, the 'cow-calf of the ring or bracelet' (*cieh*), and a larger cow-calf called *nac pieth*, the 'heifer of up-bringing' (referring to the fact that her family will have to continue to care for her and provide her with food for a long time to come). These cattle are not included in the bridewealth, and are not usually returned if, after the marriage has gone through, there is a divorce. Early betrothals of this sort are not common and, even if made, often come to nothing. If this is the case, the *dau cieh* and the *nac pieth* will be quietly returned; they are rarely a subject for dispute in the courts because, until they are returned, it would not be seemly to start the negotiations for another engagement.

Professor Evans-Pritchard speaks of the betrothal as *larcieng* or *bul luom*.[7] It is clear that this is the same ceremony as that described above, which is sometimes known as *dour* in Lou country, and although his description gives the impression of greater formality and more elaborate ceremonial than I have encountered myself, I do not think that there is any difference in principle. The *cuei* ceremony is usually performed in the rainy season when grain is plentiful, but sometimes takes place in the dry season, in which case it is likely to be less elaborate for there will be little or no beer, and the final wedding ceremonies will have to wait until the people return to the cultivations.

Notes

[1] *Gwan twac* and *ngi nyal* might be translated as 'Best Man' and 'Bridesmaid' respectively, but although the part they play in this and subsequent ceremonies is similar to our conception of the functions of the Best Man and Bridesmaid, I prefer to use Nuer terms hereafter.

[2] Complimentary speeches of this sort, often full of subtle and suggestive phrases with a good deal of badinage, are spoken in a language which is almost poetic in form and not easy to understand.

[3] The *thak deman nyal*, by bringing in the interest of the brother who expects to benefit most by his sister's marriage, is in the nature of a personal guarantee, and is important. The prospective bridegroom expects this brother to further his cause with the girl's family and to keep other lovers away from her. These cattle which are really the father's portion, are sometimes included in the bridewealth payments, sometimes not; i.e. a man will sometimes have to pay a further four as *ghok gwan nyal* (see p. 102, n. 1). It is, on the whole, unusual for a man to pay as many as four head of cattle on betrothal, especially if there is likely to be delay in the actual marriage ceremonies. If any of those cattle died while in the possession of the betrothed girl's family, the prospective bridegroom would be expected to replace them.

[4] The *thoan* or serval cat-skin is to the Nuer a mark of respect shown to a wife's relatives by any of her husband's kin, and in a sense is a symbol of marriage.

[5] The word *yang*, cow, is used here in a figurative sense, for the animal should more correctly be referred to as *ruath* (bull-calf). Nuer say that in older and better times a cow would be sacrificed, though doubtless a barren one. *Yang* means cow, and it might be supposed that a cow would be slaughtered. It may refer to a past custom when cattle were more plentiful, but nowadays the use of these terms in connexion with sacrificial animals is often elastic, and *yang*, which is certainly cow, is often used to refer to cattle of either sex.

[6] It is useful to know these terms for they are sufficiently concise to avoid obvious confusion in cases of litigation over marriage payments.

[7] Evans-Pritchard, 'Nuer Marriage Ceremonies', *Africa*, 1948, and *Kinship and Marriage among the Nuer*, pp. 58–74.

(b) Marriage Ceremonies and Formalities

For the sake of continuity and to give the reader a complete picture of the marriage formalities, we have continued in this section the extracts started in the preceding one from *Schapera* and *Howell.*

The customary marriage formalities vary extensively from tribe to tribe. From the legal point of view, the principal difficulties, which are by no means resolved by the writers, are (*a*) to distinguish between those formalities that have legal significance from those that are purely social occasions, and (*b*) to discover at what stage of the formalities the parties become husband and wife legally.

A further difficulty stems from the fact that the customary formalities (as *Schapera* shows for the Tswana) have been considerably modified through the influence of Western civilization and Christianity.

Interesting distinctions to note from the extracts that follow are:

(*a*) those people who have several ceremonies connected with marriage (Tswana as described by *Schapera* and Nuer as described by *Howell*),

(*b*) people who appear to have one ceremony that creates the marriage bond (*Snell* on the Nandi),

(*c*) people amongst whom no special ceremony is necessary (*Roberts* on Malawi).

I. Schapera: A Handbook of Tswana Law and Custom*

Wedding Ceremonies

Formerly when the boy's people thought it was time for the wedding (*lenyalô, tsêô*) to take place, they would send messengers to obtain the consent of the girl's people. The procedure followed was similar to that in arranging a betrothal: first men, then women, would go formally to ask for *segô sa metse*. The girl's people having agreed, preparations were taken in hand for the wedding feast.

Among the Rolong and Ngwaketse, the boy's people went to the girl's home on the appointed day, driving with them the *bogadi* cattle. The girl's people would slaughter one or more animals of their own, according to the number of *bogadi* cattle. The *lomipi* (peritoneum) of one of the oxen killed was hung round the necks of the bride and her intimate companions of the same sex. Feasting was continued the whole day, meat and beer forming the principal foods; and there was much singing and dancing. A similar feast was held the next day at the boy's home.

From this time on, the boy would sleep with the girl at the home of her parents, in a small hut set aside for them at the back of her mother's homestead. But by day he would return to his own home to attend to his duties there. This form of cohabitation, known as *go ralala*, would be kept up for several years, or at least until the girl had given birth to a child. The boy's people would then send to ask that she be allowed *go gorosa*, i.e. to come and live with them. A final feast would be held, where oxen would be slain *go jesa bogadi* or *go tlhabisa bogadi*, to acknowledge the *bogadi*; and the *lomipi* of one of these animals would be hung round the necks of the bride and her children. After this the young couple would go to live in the hut built by the boy at the home of his parents.

The ceremonies just outlined were those found among tribes where the *bogadi* had to be paid before the marriage could be consummated.[1] In other tribes, such as the Kgatla, Hurutshe, and Malete, the *bogadi* was not given out until after children had been born of the marriage. But in the main the general procedure was the same. After the girl's people had agreed to the marriage taking place, the boy's people would go to them with an ox or a goat. This animal was termed *serufô* by the Hurutshe and *podi ya go bôna mênô* by the Kgatla. It was slaughtered, and a small feast made, attended by the people of both family-groups. After this the boy could *ralala*, i.e. sleep regularly with the girl at the home of her parents.

After some time, generally when the girl had already given birth to a child, the boy's people would send to ask for her to come home. The usual formal negotiations and discussions followed, after which a day was fixed for the wedding, and preparations taken in hand for the customary festivities. The girl was kept in seclusion for several days or even weeks before the date of the ceremony, 'in order to grow fat and beautiful'. On the appointed day, the boy's people would drive the *bogadi* cattle to her home. Her relatives would slaughter some animals for the feast. Her maternal uncle in particular was expected to slaughter an ox *go jesa bogadi* ('to feed the *bogadi*'). The peritoneum was hung round her neck. Feasting continued the whole day, until towards sunset. The boy's people then once again formally asked for permission to take the girl to their home. Her older female relatives would first lecture her on the behaviour expected of her in her new home, and also warn the boy's people to look after her carefully. The bridal party then went to the boy's home, where another feast had been prepared, which was con-

* I. Schapera, *A Handbook of Tswana Law and Custom*, Oxford University Press, 1938, pp. 134–138.

tinued the whole of the following day. These feasts, together known as *marallô*, constituted the final stage of the marriage ceremonies. Once they were over, the young couple resided at the boy's home in a hut specially set aside for them.

Since the introduction of Western civilization, and especially of Christianity, these ceremonies have in most tribes been considerably modified. Among the Rolong they appear to be conducted along the same lines as formerly with the addition in some cases of a Church marriage, held at the time that the *bogadi* is given out. The custom of *go ralala* is still observed. The Ngwato proper, on the other hand, have completely abandoned the payment of *bogadi*; but the marriage feasts formerly held at the time of its delivery are still observed, whether the marriage takes place in Church or not. The date of the marriage is fixed by consultation between the two families, the boy's people as usual taking the initiative. On the appointed day a feast is first held at the girl's home, the food being provided by her people. In the afternoon the boy's people formally request permission to take her to their home. Before being allowed to do so, they are warned to look after her carefully, and not to ill-treat or abuse her. The bridal party then goes to the boy's home, where another feast has been prepared. The girl now remains there; but a few days later she is taken by one of the boy's senior female relatives back to her own home for a brief visit. This gives her the right to visit her own people afterwards whenever she wishes to. There is no period of preliminary residence at the girl's home, such as is still found among the Rolong and Ngwaketse; nor is it regarded as right for the boy to cohabit with her before she is brought to his own home. If he does so and makes her pregnant, he will, when he marries her, have to pay her parents an ox, termed *kgomo ya go tlhagêla*, as compensation for having 'broken through their fence'.

Among the Kgatla many instances are still found where the boy, after the betrothal has been confirmed, visits the girl at her home and cohabits with her until one or more children have been born, when he brings her to his own home. A small feast may be held on the latter occasion, but it is seldom that *bogadi* is paid until long afterwards. This form of marriage, nowadays known as *mohuhumêlô* (from *go huhumêla*, 'to creep in'), is regarded with some contempt by the more 'civilized' members of the tribe. Among the latter the boy never lives openly at the girl's home, but brings her straight to his own home after the wedding festivities. It does happen often enough that he cohabits with her before this is done; and although his behaviour is not regarded as correct, no great objection is raised by her parents. If she becomes pregnant, he is not penalised in any way; but the wedding ceremonies are then less elaborate than where she is still 'unspoiled'.

Normally, after the usual negotiations have taken place between the two families, a day is appointed some time ahead, to enable preparations to be made for the feasts. The girl herself goes into seclusion from this time until the wedding itself takes place. The wedding feast is an elaborate affair, extending over three days, during which meat, beer, porridge, tea, and other foods are provided in abundance, specially rehearsed choirs of girls sing at both homes, and there is much general rejoicing. The guests are fed in small groups according to their sex and relationship. On the first day the boy's people are entertained at the girl's home; on the second a feast is held at the boy's home; and on the third the young couple and their own companions go again to the girl's home for a small feast, the purpose of which is to give the girl the right to revisit her parents whenever she wishes to in future. With such marriages the *bogadi* is generally, but not always, delivered to the girl's people the day before the festivities commence. Many people nowadays get married in church on the morning of the first feast; and where this is the case the *bogadi* must be delivered to the girl's people before the missionary will allow the service to be held. The girl's maternal uncle, as in former times, must kill a beast *go jesa bogadi*, but the ceremony of *go apesa lomipi* is no longer carried out. It is also expected that some meat and pots of beer (collectively termed *thupa*, 'ribs') should be sent to the Chief's *kgotla* for the people who are there. This is regarded as a formal notification to them of the marriage that is taking place.

Note

[1] Commenting upon this passage, Mr. Matthews writes: 'I am inclined to disagree with the view that, among the Rolong, *bogadi* had to be paid before the marriage was consummated. I made repeated inquiries on that point, and the answer was invariably that the *bogadi* payment

was not insisted upon before the consummation unless it appeared that the boy's parents did not intend at all to pay. Otherwise it was left to them to take the steps necessary to give them power over the children of the union. Again, the *go ralala* may follow the *mokwele* and does not necessarily depend upon the *bogadi* except among Christians, who in any case object to the *go ralala* even after *bogadi*.'

P. P. Howell: Manual of Nuer Law*

Twoc ghok: 'Invocation of the cattle'. The betrothal ceremonies . . . are followed by the first marriage ceremony, the *twoc ghok*, 'invocation of the cattle'. The length of time which is allowed to elapse between them is variable, and depends largely on the agreement reached at the *cuei* ceremony. It is not usually in the interests of either of the parties to delay matters, though this sometimes happens if the bridegroom finds difficulty in collecting sufficient cattle and yet retains the goodwill of the girl's family who wish the union to take place.

The *twoc* is the crucial ceremony of all the processes of marriage and is public in the widest sense, although the actual negotiations over cattle and the more intimate ritual are restricted to the closer kinsmen of the bride and bridegroom. Most of the bride's kinsmen who expect to receive a portion of the bridewealth are actually present, and if they are not they will usually send someone to represent their interests. We see therefore that, as the processes of betrothal and marriage proceed, increasingly large numbers of persons from both kinship groups are concerned. This emphasizes the collective nature of a union and the extent of the social ties and obligations which are involved.

Dancing begins early in the morning and the bridegroom, his father, and the *gwan twac*, as well as the senior legal representative of the bridegroom's lineage, appear dressed in cat-skins (*twac thoan*) as a conventional sign of respect to the bride's mother and her kinsmen and those of her husband. It should be noted that the bridegroom and the bride really have two representatives. At the bridegroom's side is the *gwan twac*, who is his personal aide. At the *twoc* ceremony he is represented also by the *gwan buthni*, an agnatic kinsman of a collateral branch of the lineage, whose activities are not so much personal as concerned with the interests of the bridegroom's lineage as a whole. His duties are both legal and ritual. He is expected to take the lead in the arguments which arise about the bridewealth cattle and to see that the claims of all those connected with the marriage are noted. It is also his duty to invoke the ancestral spirits of the lineage and to seek their blessing, to call out the honorific (*paak*) and spear-names (*mut*) of the clan and state any further distinctions so that all possibility of a breach of the rules of exogamy is avoided. Similarly, the bride has her personal attendant in the *ngi nyal*, who is a girl of her own age, usually from another and unconnected lineage, while the *gwan buthni* of her lineage represents them in ritual and legal procedures. The *gwan twac* and the *ngi nyal* are usually age-mates of the bridegroom and bride respectively, they are unrelated to either, and their duties are essentially personal, while the *gwan buthni*, usually much older men, represent the kinship interests of their respective sides.

After preliminary dancing and singing, which go on more or less continuously throughout the day, the people most nearly concerned in the negotiations take up their positions in the cattle-byre. The bride's family seat themselves on the left of the entrance facing the bridegroom's party, and her *gwan buthni* sits in the central hearth (*gorei*) of the byre. On the right side mats are laid (*yih*), and on these sit the bridegroom's party with their *gwan buthni* nearest the door. The bride herself and her *ngi nyal* do not appear during the negotiations. They are usually closeted inside the mother's hut (*dwil* or *ghot*) nearby. When all are seated the *gwan buthni* of the bride breaks up some tobacco and hands it to the father, paternal uncles, and other senior relatives of the bridegroom as a symbol of friendship and hospitality.[1] It is also calculated to ease the tension, for Nuer regard the whole procedure as a nerve-racking ordeal, and like to smoke when they are nervous. He then rises to his feet and calls out the honorific and spear-names of the bride's lineage, and calls upon their ancestors to take note of the proceedings. The *gwan buthni* of the bridegroom's family then rises and scatters tobacco at the entrance of and

* P. P. Howell, *Manual of Nuer Law*, Oxford University Press, 1954, pp. 91–96.

inside the cattle-byre as an offering to the ancestral spirits of the bride. He then calls upon his own ancestral spirits, which are those of the bridegroom's lineage, to witness the negotiations, and calls out their honorific and spear-names. If the honorific or spear-names of the bridegroom coincide with those called out by the bride's *gwan buthni*, it will be obvious that the rules of exogamy preclude all possibility of the union, but the invocation is largely a formality, because it is unlikely that negotiations for the marriage would be allowed to go so far if there were any possibility of incest.

Negotiations about the cattle then begin. The number of cattle subsequently handed over, as well as those actually transferred during the final marriage ceremonies, will vary considerably, but there are a number of persons standing in certain relationships to the bride who expect to receive their share. They are the *ji cuongni*—the 'people of rights'. In theory, the bridegroom must produce cattle to meet the claims of all these kinsmen of the bride, but in fact negotiations usually deteriorate into a heated argument, not always in keeping with the supposed solemnity of the occasion, and the main object of the bride's party is to get as many good cattle as possible, and of the bridegroom's family to avoid payment. It is, however, noticeable that negotiations of this sort are less clamorous than other Nuer affairs. The *gwan buthni* are expected to speak for the parties they represent, but most of those present will have their say. The colours, sex, and qualities of the cattle are fully discussed, and it is probable that the recipients will have a clear idea of what those qualities are. As soon as negotiations have started the immediate kinsmen of the bride will have set to work to find out as much as they can about these cattle. In the initial stages of the discussion, however, a certain formality is observed; it is opened by the *gwan buthni* of the bride, who will speak the names of those persons in the bride's family who have a claim on the cattle and, as the argument continues in connexion with each animal quoted by the bridegroom's family, will state to which relative they should go. No cattle are handed over on this day, though a cow called *yang gorei*, the 'cow of the hearth', which is part of the bride's father's portion, is sometimes handed over on the spot. This is a convention which is not often followed nowadays.

When the negotiations over the cattle are finished, the parties go outside for the feasting which follows. There is no prohibition on the two families eating together,[2] but the bridegroom himself and his *gwan twac* are not expected to eat of the meat or drink of the beer provided by the bride's people. They are allowed to join in the dancing, and the bride and her *ngi nyal* appear for the first time on the scene and enter the dance. The bride wears a black skin known as *twac cara*, usually the skin of a black calf.

After the dancing is over, those who are not closely related to either party go home, but the legal representatives of the bridegroom and the bride's family and some of their close kinsmen, both male and female, go into a hut specially prepared for them which is known as the *dwil koam* for the occasion. There they sit all night joking and conversing with their hosts until dawn. Another hut, known as the *dwil twacni* or *dwil kwen*, is set aside for the young people of both parties, and the bride and bridegroom, their *gwan twac* and *ngi nyal*, sit there with their friends and coevals singing and exchanging courting badinage all night through. This completes the ceremony known as *twoc*.[3] The marriage is not supposed to have been consummated, but has acquired by this time a degree of legality. Some Nuer say that the marriage is now legal in the sense that, were another man to have intercourse with the bride, full compensation for adultery could be claimed by the bridegroom. Lak and Thiang Nuer at any rate say that the significant act which confirms the status of the bride as a wife and which subsequently will be recognized in law, is the ceremony known as *yier nyal*, which takes place on the evening immediately after the conclusion of the negotiations for the cattle, when the bride, and also her brothers and sisters present, are rubbed with butter by the *gwan buthni* of the bridegroom. The legal status of the bride in relation to the bridegroom and his family at this point in the social and ritual processes of marriage (and it must be remembered that the bridewealth has not necessarily yet been transferred in full to the bride's family) is a controversial subject and one which is sometimes disputed in legal arguments. . . .

The *twoc* ceremony, at which negotiations over the cattle are completed and the blessing of the ancestral spirits is publicly invoked, does not usually take place before the girl has not only reached puberty but is ready for marriage. When talking of a girl who has reached marriageable age the Nuer will say that she is ready for the *muot* ('shaving') which is the next ceremony to take place. *Muot* amounts to a public recognition of physical consummation, although this does not necessarily mean that the girl has not had sexual relations with her bridegroom before. In fact, previous to the *muot*, he has no legal right to physical consummation and must visit his wife in secret, though her family will usually allow him to do so. *Muot nyal* therefore follows the *twoc* ceremony almost immediately.

Muot nyal: 'The shaving of the bride'. The ceremonies which are known collectively under this heading are of distinct legal significance, as will be seen later, and include three important stages.

Loiny deb: 'Loosing the rope'. First, the bridegroom with his *gwan twac*, again suitably dressed in cat-skins for the occasion, accompanied by other youths of his own age, goes to the bride's home to ask for her people's official consent to consummation. There they enter a hut specially set aside for them and are joined by the bride, her *ngi nyal*, and other girls of her lineage and neighbourhood. They spend the day and the whole of the night in conversation and singing. There is as usual a good deal of sexual badinage, but no physical consummation. Next morning, the bridegroom approaches his mother-in-law on the subject of the *muot* which is to follow. Before giving her consent she will expect to receive, or at any rate obtain the promise of, special presents, which are known as the *nyin daba*.[4] These include a goat or two, a spear, a fish-spear, a ring and other offerings, and if she has any co-wives who stand in the relationship of mother to the bride they will expect to benefit too. There follows the ritual performance known as *loiny deb*, 'loosing the rope', which symbolizes the bride's release from her father's homestead.[5] The bridegroom and his representatives stand on one side of the cattle-byre, the bride and her friends on the other, while her father casts a cattle rope between them. The bride is then ceremonially dressed in the clothes which distinguish a married woman from unmarried girls: a leather apron or a skirt of plaited cotton.

Noong nyal: 'The bringing of the bride'. The same evening, representatives of the bridegroom go to inform the bride's relatives that all is ready for them. The bride is then conducted to the bridegroom's home by a party of her girl friends (who are called *nong*, 'bringers'). On her arrival she sits down on a special mat provided for her outside the bridegroom's house by his *gwan buthni*. A bull is brought out and sacrificed, while the *gwan buthni* again calls out the honorific and spear-names of the lineage and calls upon the ancestral spirits to bless the union, to accept the bride, and to give her male children to uphold the spear-name in posterity and girl children to bring cattle to the kinship group. The bride then lies on the mat and is covered with a skin (*twac cara*). Meanwhile the bridegroom presents his mother-in-law with a goat or sheep in order to release her, temporarily at any rate, from the taboo on eating in his home.[6] The bride is then assisted into the hut and the bridegroom, whip in hand, goes after her. After he has given her a thorough beating inside the hut (*woc dhouri nyal*), the couple spend the night together and the marriage is said to be officially consummated. The beating is said to symbolize the bridegroom's authority over his bride who is now his wife, emphasizing the rights he now has in her.[7]

Muot nyal: 'Shaving the bride'. The next day the *muot nyal*, the actual 'shaving of the bride', takes place. In the morning the bride is usually taken away to the home of some unrelated person nearby, but is brought back to the bridegroom's home towards evening. Her head is then ceremonially shaved by one of the senior female relatives of the bridegroom, usually his elder sister, a co-wife of his mother, or sometimes the wife of his *gwan buthni*. At any rate the shaving should be performed by a married woman of the bridegroom's family, and signifies the bride's reception into the status of married woman in that family. She is then taken once more to her own home.

After these ceremonies are over the bride rarely takes up residence in her husband's home, but lives for a period in her own home, where her husband has the right to visit her. Often a special hut is set aside for her there. There is no general rule in this matter, but it is regarded by the Nuer as proper that she should remain in her own home until her first child is born and weaned, for until then, although the marriage has a legal basis, it is not considered to be confirmed. Sometimes, however, the husband has no one to assist him in his home and to cook for him, in which case he may receive permission from his wife's people for her to live with him permanently as soon as the *muot* has been performed. When the first child is weaned, the wife's mother can claim the *yang doth gata*, the 'cow of bearing a child', a cow which is considered a fee for assisting the girl to give birth to a child. This is usually followed by a formal change of residence. The *yang doth gata* is the last cow which need be paid by the husband, although his wife's family may beg him to give them other cattle when further children are born and weaned; but he is not bound to do so and claims of this sort, if they ever arise, would not nowadays be upheld in a Nuer court.[8]

Notes

[1] For this service he can demand payment of a bull-calf. It is not, however, always paid, and it is not considered good manners to argue about the matter or press for payment.

[2] An ox is sacrificed and the meat divided between the bride's people and those of the bridegroom in a formal manner. The bulk of the meat is given to the bridegroom's family, and much of it is taken back to their home to share with the old people who have not been able to attend the ceremony.

[3] The account of the *twoc* ceremony given by Professor Evans-Pritchard does not differ in any substantial way from my own, but he mentions certain rites which take place on the same day which I have not myself witnessed but which I have heard Nuer mention when describing the ceremonial. One is the ceremony in which the bridegroom and his followers rush the homestead of the bride and he tries to spear the *buor* or mud hearth of his future mother-in-law, while the bride's brothers and the young men of her group try to stop him and to wrest from him his special wedding stick or *dang*. This and other rites symbolize the potential opposition between the two parties and the resistance of the bride's people to the demands of the bridegroom, and the final removal of their resistance by the payment of cattle. All such rites, although not always performed and often substantially different in one part of Nuer-land from those performed in another, are part of the enactment of marriage and are highly symbolic of the conventional attitude which both parties are expected to display. From the legal point of view they are significant in emphasizing these attitudes and explaining the rules and conventions which govern the social relations subsisting between relatives-in-law. They are not, of course, the subject of subsequent litigation.

[4] *Nyin daba*, 'the things of bearing'. In other words the mother's due for bearing the bride and bringing her up.

[5] *Deb* means a cattle rope, and the phrase signifies her release from her father's herd.

[6] She does not, of course, eat with the bridegroom himself, or with any of the male members of his lineage, for women do not eat in the company of men on any occasion, but she is thereby allowed to partake of the food of the house with the other women.

[7] In the case of opposite twins this performance is inflicted on the bride's twin brother as well.

[8] It may be noted here that among some Nuer tribes the husband may claim a cow from his wife's family, the *yang jokni*, 'cow of the spirits'. I do not think this is normally paid unless the first child dies, and it is then given in the form of a dedication to ancestral spirits to ensure that the next child will live.

G. S. Snell: Nandi Customary Law*

The Marriage Bond

The marriage ceremony was presided over by the 'boiyotab katunisiet' or wedding elder, a respected senior member of the kokwet who was usually the same person who presided over male initiation rites in the capacity of 'boiyotab tum'. The ceremonial centred around a beer drink provided by the bridegroom's father and lasted several days, according to the host's resources. Much of the significance of the social celebrations served the purpose of stressing the essentially family nature, in the wider sense, of the union and of giving it public affirmation.

One of the most important parts of the rite—greater in significance, it is said, than the transference of bridewealth itself from the point of view of the validity of the marriage

* G. S. Snell, *Nandi Customary Law*, Macmillan & Co. Ltd., 1954, pp. 25–26.

—consisted in the placing on the ground of a piece of the 'segutiet' grass (sp. *vernonia*) The pair stood on it, the bridegroom then tied a piece on the bride's wrist and the latter performed the same act on her husband's. This was done in the back room of the hut and the act created the legal bond of betrothal or marriage.[1] The marriage was nevertheless to some extent uncertain and could be annulled or terminated by divorce at any time before a child was born.

Nandi marriage was patrilocal and after the wedding the newly married couple were allowed the use to themselves of the bridegroom's father's hut for a few nights. Thereafter, if their new home was incomplete, the bridegroom returned to the sigroina while his wife lived with her mother-in-law until their new house was ready for occupation. It was the duty of the bridegroom to erect the wooden framework; his mother super vised and assisted his sisters and wife in the mud plastering.

Note

[1] These were not clearly differentiated. Whether the tying of the segutiet was bethrothal or marriage depended on the time at which it was done. If it preceded the marriage it was in fact betrothal; if it took place during the ceremony it was a significant part of the act of marriage.

S. Roberts: Matrilineal Family Law and Custom in Malawi: A Comparison of Two Systems*

The Marriage Ceremony of the Tonga

When half the *chimaro*† has been paid the marriage may take place. No special ceremony is necessary, and the complete absence of one does not affect the validity of the marriage. The ceremony usually takes place in the chief's court at the man's village. The wife's relatives come over and presents are exchanged between the two families as tokens of goodwill. The ceremony itself consists of parties and dances which may well go on for 24 hours. The following evening the parties are given joint instruction in their marital duties. The procreation of children is explained and the husband warned of certain occasions when he may not have intercourse with the wife. From that evening onwards intercourse between the parties is permitted.[1] Intercourse may well have taken place before this, but such connexion before the ceremony would certainly be regarded unfavourably if it came to the notice of the elders. At the same time as the parties are instructed about their marital rights and duties, they will be reminded of any wrongs that they have done in the past and solemnly warned to behave well in the future.

The last act of the ceremony takes place the next morning when the wife and her relatives are expected to prepare food for the members of the husband's village. The initial favour with which the wife is regarded by the husband's relatives and neighbours will depend upon the quality of this first breakfast.

What is the status of a union between a man and a woman where no *mtenga*‡ has been sent, no *chimaro* given, and no ceremony arranged? None of these formalities is regarded as a vital constituent of a marriage. The course of events which I have described is the usual but not the necessary prelude to a marriage. Many unfavourable results may flow from the absence of one or other of the formalities, but such absence will not invalidate the marriage. If the marital status of a man and a woman is questioned, they can point to the *mtenga*, the *chimaro*, or the ceremony, but they would also regard other factors as equally good evidence of a marriage. In the absence of any formality, the following three factors combined would certainly be regarded as constituting a valid marriage: (i) that the parties have lived together with the knowledge and acquiescence of the wife's family; (ii) that this union had persisted for some time, at least a year or more; (iii) that the parties have healthy children resulting from their union. The situation can be briefly summarized. A marriage will be taken to exist as a valid union whenever a

* S. Roberts, 'Matrilineal Family Law and Custom in Malawi: a Comparison of Two Systems', in *Journal of African Law*, Vol. 8, No. 2, pp. 83–84.

† Marriage payment.

‡ Marriage messenger.

man and woman live together openly and without censure. It is the fact of consortium rather than anything else that constitutes a valid marriage. The formalities which I have described will be regarded as evidence that this situation exists or has existed at some time in the past.

The Lomwe marriage is not marked by any ceremony. The man decides when he wishes cohabitation to begin and informs his *namunkhoswe*.* On the appointed evening, the *namunkhoswe* takes the bridegroom to the girl's village with his personal belongings, and leaves him at the house of the girl's family. The parties thereafter live together and are from that evening man and wife. There are two essentials to the Lomwe marriage. First, a *namunkhoswe* must be appointed; and, secondly, the parties must cohabit. Given these circumstances, and provided the parties have the necessary capacity to marry each other, a valid marriage exists.

Note

[1] After the marital rights and duties have been explained by the old women of the village, and before she grants him sexual intercourse, the wife demands a small sum of money from the husband. Five shillings is the usual amount. If the husband refuses to pay, it is regarded as a sign that he is impotent or that he does not love his wife. If, when the money has been paid and intercourse takes place, the husband penetrates the wife freely, and finds the hymen already broken, he will report the matter to the wife's old women. The five shillings is then returned and the woman scolded for having shamed her parents by having sexual intercourse with other men.

* Senior maternal uncle or other relative with the duty to arrange the marriage.

CHAPTER 9

MARRIAGE WITH SPECIAL FORMALITIES

In the preceding chapter we pointed out that the extracts described marriages contracted with the regular formalities. The extracts in this chapter differ in that they deal with marriages with special formalities. These marriages, in the words of *Wilson* on the Luo 'contain certain elements which distinguish [them] from the usual'.

In section (*a*) the institution of 'child betrothal' is described for the Ashanti by *Danquah*, the Sukuma by *Cory* and the Luo by *Wilson.*

Section (*b*) describes elopement or abduction which, as *Hunter* shows, may be regular, i.e. part of the custom, or irregular in the sense that it is a method of overcoming lack of consent by the parties' families.

(a) CHILD BETROTHAL

J. D. Danquah: Akan Laws and Custom*

Asiwa (*Infant Betrothal*)

Another form of courtship—if I may so call it—is 'Asiwa' or Infant betrothal. This had almost become the principal form of getting married until it was abolished, in 1918, by the Okyeman Council. It was simply a form of marriage in which a girl might upon, or some days after, her birth—whilst she was still a minor—be lawfully given in marriage by her father to his nephew, i.e., his sister's son, or to such relative or any person who may have done some service to the father or mother of the infant girl. But such person cannot be a member of the girl's clan. In this case, besides the usual 'Aseda' ('Thanks-money'), the husband of the infant girl had to pay certain extra fees and to perform certain peculiar customs, such as tying a small nugget of gold on the infant girl's hand. The young man was to care for the girl in many ways, and was at least once every year to give her a present until the infant girl reached the age of puberty. The manner of celebration of the day on which the girl attains puberty largely depends upon the means of the husband. Consequently, if such a wife was, prior to her being properly wedded, committed into adultery, the adulterer had to pay an extra half amount of the lawful Ayefare ordinarily due to the injured husband. This money is called '*Twebon*'.[1] This was a procedure which brought many innocent young men into the unpleasant experience of being arraigned on trivial grounds as adulterers, and the Okyeman Council thought it wise to abolish the system. In its working order it clashed with certain modern ideas of social life. It also led to very ill-matched unions, which in many cases resulted in unhappiness in the married life.

Another form of '*Asiwa*' is called '*Abaso Kyekyere*' usually followed by a Chief or a rich man by laying hand on an infant girl as his future wife. The same rules apply in both cases.

[1] That is, for having made her cease to be *virgo intacta*.

* J. D. Danquah, *Akan Laws and Custom*, Routledge & Kegan Paul, 1928, p. 147.

H. Cory: Sukuma Law and Custom*

Kukindikila (SS, KS)† or *Dimeli* (BSN)†

This custom is known only in the areas mentioned above, and even there it rarely occurs. Two fathers make a mutual agreement regarding the future marriage of their minor children.

NOTE: The reason for such a contract may be poverty but is sometimes friendship.

The total bridewealth is agreed upon and a few cattle, often only a cow and a bull, are paid immediately after the conclusion of the contract between the parties.

The children remain with their parents and, when they come of age, the remainder of the bridewealth becomes payable and the young couple marry. The offspring of the beasts which were handed over as the first instalment are not counted as part of the bridewealth.

If one of the couple dies before the marriage takes place or refuses to marry, the instalments of bridewealth already paid have to be returned. If the father of the girl has no property the debt has to be paid at the latest if and when the girl marries another man.

G. Wilson: Luo Customary Law and Marriage Laws and Customs‡

We have been discussing what the JOLUO call MEKO, the blessed form of marriage, KENY MOGWEDHI, and these form the largest percentage of Luo marriages even today. There are other forms, some of which are also regarded as blessed but each contains certain elements which distinguish it from the usual.

Child Marriage: Nyar Osiep

The first of these is 'child marriage' or 'child betrothal' called NYAR OSIEP. These marriages are arranged by the father of the bride and the father of the groom while the boy and girl are still very young. This is done for a variety of reasons, the most common of which is to seal a friendship between two persons. For example, when animals are loaned for safe keeping, RIEMBO DHIANE, the person who is caring for the animals may wish to ensure that some day these will come into his possession and therefore he will press his benefactor to consider a marriage between his daughter and the other's son. This happens more particularly when the person who is caring for the animals has success with the herd, that means he is honest and the herd increases. These contracts are most frequently arranged at beer parties and the two men may exchange their drinking reeds, KISEKE, to seal the bargain. Brides of this type are called NYAR KISEKE in some parts of Luo land.

In other circumstances, a man may have cattle belonging to somebody else and may be in a position where he is in dire need of an animal to repay a debt or to contract a marriage. He may under these circumstances betroth a young girl to the owner of the animals or to his son, in order to receive the first animal of the bride wealth immediately.

In unions of these types it is believed that the ceremonies and exchanges described above *must* be completed in detail or the ancestors will invoke CHIRA on the lineage of the party which breaks the contract. The effect of this type of CHIRA is to make the lineage of such a person, RAM, that is to die out or fade away completely. While in normal marriages a girl may be left at any time before RISO and, providing that the bride wealth is repaid, there are no drastic supernatural consequences. Because of these beliefs connected with marriages which are contracted while the parties to the marriage are still children, it is the custom that if one of the parties to the contract dies before the wedding has been consummated, that a relative must take that person's place and raise seed to him or her. If, for example, a boy dies, whose father has contracted to marry a girl to him, perhaps while the children were only a few years old, she is regarded as a widow, CHI LIEL. She will be taken in levirate by a relative of the dead man to raise

* H. Cory, *Sukuma Law and Custom*, Oxford University Press, 1953, p. 50.

† These letters refer to districts in Sukumaland.

‡ G. Wilson, *Luo Customary Law and Marriage Laws and Customs*, Government Printer, Nairobi, 1961, pp. 117–118.

seed to his name as soon as she reaches puberty. On the other hand, if a girl dies, who has contracted such a union, another will be nominated in her place, but the house built for her will be regarded as the house of the dead girl and the replacement will be regarded as her co-wife, NYAR OT.

The ceremonies which take place to marry a person of this type are the same as for ordinary unions. Even if one of the parties has died, the replacement will go through the ceremonies in that person's name. There is one exception. In the case of a girl dying, her replacement will go to the house of the groom voluntarily, without being 'pulled', as does any girl who fills the place of a sister who died before producing a male child.

(b) ELOPEMENT AND ABDUCTION

M. Hunter: Reaction to Conquest*

Sometimes, instead of approaching her father, a young man may carry off (*ukuthwala*), or cause to be carried off by some of his young men friends, the girl he wishes to marry. She is seized when walking abroad, hustled along with much shouting and some blows, and taken to the groom's kraal. It is seemly that she should make a great show of resistance, even though she is pleased to marry the man who has taken her, and sometimes girls lie down and are dragged along the ground, getting their limbs grazed, before they will submit to going with their captors. Some boy from the groom's kraal is sent to the girl's people to tell them where she is. The father consults his kinsmen, and if he and they agree that it is a suitable match, men are sent to the groom's home to arrange about *ikhazi*, the ritual killing marking a marriage is performed, and the marriage consummated.

Sometimes the girl's father is privy to the plot to carry off his daughter, and even may let the groom know privately that he is sending his daughter to such and such a place on such and such a day, and that he may take her. The reasons given for the girl being carried off when her father had already been consulted are that 'her parents do not like to hear their daughter cry'. When a girl leaves her home to be married she is obliged by custom to weep and make a fuss about going. Or 'Her father may want her to marry that man, and her mother disagree'. A case was cited in which the groom and some friends had come three times to fetch his bride. She had wept and struggled, and each time her mother and sisters and the other women of the *umzi*† had rescued her. Eventually her father told the groom to take her when he found her going to the shop on Monday. He did so.

Sometimes a man persuades a girl to elope (*ukugcagca*) with him. He takes her to his home, a message is sent to her people, and matters proceed as in a case where the girl is carried off. Sometimes he arranges for her to come to his home at dusk. She sits down outside the *umzi*. When asked what she wants, she replies that she wants shelter for the night, but 'every one knows why she has come'.

If the father and kinsmen of a girl who has been carried off or eloped disapproves of an alliance with the family to which the young man belongs, they may demand the return of the girl, together with a fine of one beast, called *ibopha* (from *ukubopha*, to bind up). Or if the relatives of the man who has brought the girl disapprove of her or her family, and forbid him to marry her, or refuse to help him with cattle for *ikhazi*, a beast must be sent back with the girl.

To carry off a girl to marry her is considered quite respectable. There is no shame in such a marriage to either bride or groom. For a girl to elope, however, is rather shameful, for a girl should never admit that she goes willingly to any man. Always when she is married she should weep and protest; not to do so is immodest. Hence elopement is considered improper, but there are many who do it.

All informants are agreed that both carrying a girl off and elopement were usual before contact with Europeans.

* M. Hunter, *Reaction to Conquest*, Oxford University Press, 1961, pp. 187–188.

† House or hut.

G. Wilson: Luo Customary Law and Marriage Laws and Customs*

Elopement, Por.

Traditional marriage is called MEKO, meaning the girl was taken by force or 'pulled'. POR is the opposite of MEKO. It must be made clear that there are two forms; the traditional and the modern. This form of marriage, which can only be directly translated as elopement, is becoming increasingly popular among the young educated JALUO, and the preliminary ceremonies are omitted and the bride wealth begins with the payment of DHER KETE. It often happens, however, when escape to the towns is easily accomplished that bride wealth is not paid at all and these unions end in separation and the women frequently turn to other forms of marriage or concubinage which are outside the customary law of the LUO. The LUO describe all these unions as POR. Traditionally, however, POR took place in pre-European times when the couple sincerely believed they would, in fact, pay the bride wealth but poverty or some other circumstance prevented them, temporarily, from doing so. Today, however, these unions take place without this sincerity.

The LUO rationalize the traditional need for such marriages within the cultural structure as follows: the most commonly stated reason is that the parents of the boy refuse to grant him permission to hunt for a wife on the grounds of poverty or that the time is not auspicious; the second reason given is that the parents of the girl may have, for personal reasons, not the realistic ones based on incest or the laws of exogamy, refused to allow her to marry a boy she wishes to marry. Thirdly, that of a man who has been forced into a NYAR OSIEP contract who refuses to honour it because he has another girl in mind who is determined to become the senior wife, MIKAYI. In the latter case the runaway wife will be regarded as MIKAYI, but the union will be thought in some way to be CHIRA and will not therefore be a fruitful one because, by custom, NYAR OSIEP must be married first and be MIKAYI for the union to be fruitful.

* G. Wilson, *Luo Customary Law and Marriage Laws and Customs*, Government Printer, Nairobi, 1961, p. 118.

Chapter 10

SPECIAL TYPES OF MARRIAGE

This chapter must be distinguished from the previous one on the ground that the latter dealt with special *formalities* whereas this one deals with marriages which are of a completely different *type* or nature from the normal type described in chapter 8. In a sense, they are altogether different institutions.

The most important of these institutions, dealt with in section (*a*), is the levirate or widow-inheritance under which a brother or other relative of a deceased husband cohabits with the latter's widow in order to raise children.

Section (*b*) contains extracts describing sororate or substitute unions, which are really the converse of levirate unions, in that they consist of the substitution of a wife by a sister or other relative, e.g. in case of death or barrenness.

In section (*c*) both *Howell* and *Evans-Pritchard* describe the institution of 'ghost-marriage' prevalent amongst the Nuer.

The final section (*d*) entitled 'others' contains descriptions of slave marriage by *Rattray* for the Ashanti and concubinage by *Howell* for the Nuer.

(a) Levirate and Widow Inheritance

I. Schapera: A Handbook of Tswana Law and Custom*

Fate of Widows

A woman's dependence upon her husband and his family is not severed when she becomes a widow. It is her duty to remain with her late husband's family, and normally she does so. If she is an old woman or has adult children, she continues to live in her own homestead under the guardianship of her husband's heir, who must provide for her. If she is still capable of bearing children, her subsequent fate may be settled in various ways.

In the olden days, she could not as a rule remarry unless, having no children, she returned to her parental home and her *bogadi* was sent back. It was very seldom that a widow left her husband's family in this way. In the vast majority of instances she remained with them, and passed, by the custom of *go tsêna mo tlung* ('to enter the hut'), into the care of some close male relative of her late husband. Some time after the period of mourning was over, a small feast was made at her homestead, where all the late husband's relatives assembled. She was then expected to choose, or was allotted, one from among the men eligible to look after her. Among the Kgatla, a large covered pot of beer was placed in the centre of the courtyard, and the widow sat next to it. The men eligible to claim her then came forward in order of precedence. Each went in turn to the pot of beer, and uncovered it. If the widow replaced the lid, it showed that she rejected him. But if she left the lid lying where he placed it, and began to serve out the beer, it was known that she accepted that particular man. She was, however, entitled to refuse them all if she had a son old enough to look after her and take care of his father's estate.

The men from whom the choice of a 'seed-raiser' was made were in the first place the younger brothers of the dead husband, preferably the next in order of seniority.

* I. Schapera, *A Handbook of Tswana Law and Custom*, Oxford University Press, 1938, pp. 164–166.

An older brother could not as a rule enter the hut of his junior, being regarded as his father. Sometimes the eldest son of a polygamist by his great wife was allowed to take over the junior widows, but not his own mother. Hence the saying: *Molala le mmaagwê ga a bolawe, o itsala monnawê*, 'The man who lies with his mother is not killed, he is begetting his own younger brother.' Occasionally, too, a widow might be taken over by the *setlogolo* (sister's son) of her late husband. But if any unauthorized person entered her hut, and particularly if he belonged to some other ward, he was regarded as an adulterer, and could be dealt with accordingly.

The man selected had henceforth the acknowledged right and duty to cohabit with the widow, even if he himself was already married. He was also obliged to take care of her and her children, to clothe them, and in all other ways act as the guardian of their household. The widow, however, was not regarded as his wife, but still as that of her late husband; and her consort was not regarded as her husband, nor was he expected to pay additional *bogadi* for her. The children he begot by her were legally those of the dead man, and entitled to share in the inheritance of his estate. *Ke bana ba ditlhomesô*, it was said: 'They are the children of the rafters' (of the hut); or *Ke bana ba marapô a moswi*, 'They are the children of the dead man's bones'; or simply *Ke bana ba dikgomo*, 'They are the children of cattle', by virtue of the *bogadi* paid on behalf of their reputed father for their mother.

Most widows nowadays continue to live at their late husband's home. His close relatives, especially his brothers, are expected while her children are still young to help her plough, look after the family cattle, assist her if she is involved in lawsuits, and generally watch over the welfare and interests of her household. She must, however, be informed and consulted regarding the disposal of the household cattle and all other forms of property.

The inheritance of widows is still met with occasionally. In such cases the accompanying rights and obligations are accepted as binding. Widows, however, are no longer ceremonially allotted to the younger brothers of their deceased husbands. But a younger brother will of his own accord, and with the woman's consent, visit her from time to time at night, and public opinion tends to condemn a man who fails to do so. Or the widow may accept any other man of the same family-group as paramour, without arousing any unfavourable comment. Children born of these men are still considered those of the late husband. But, if the woman accepts an outsider as lover, the people of her husband's family generally object, and may make life difficult for her. Her children by her late husband will regard with contempt those she bears to such an unauthorized lover, and treat them as servants, even going so far as to debar them from sharing in the family estate. The real father of the children has no claim over them.

R. S. Rattray: Ashanti Law and Constitution*

Kune awadie:[1] This term, which means literally 'marriage with a widow', generally implies the inheritance of a widow or widows by the heir of the late husband. It is the levirate and is the natural converse of *Ayete*. Strangely enough, the former practice has survived generally among all classes, whereas, as we have seen, *Ayete* is now almost entirely confined to chiefs.

When a man dies and leaves a wife and children, it is considered proper for his heir, *fa ne kunafo*, to take his widow (or widows); not to do so is *musuo* (an evil or unlucky thing), and the *saman* (ghost) of the late husband would be expected to take revenge. Public opinion, indeed, would be quick to condemn the man who shirked this responsibility. A year must elapse before the heir has sexual intercourse with such a woman. Even when the widow be a very old woman, the heir may go through the required ceremony, although he does not intend to cohabit with her. A younger, wifeless brother—not the heir—may sometimes take or be given the widow in preference to his elder relative. Should a woman refuse to marry her late husband's surviving brother or other heir, she will not be compelled to do so (the *saman* (ghost) is left to deal with her), but the *Aseda* and all presents have to be returned to him unless there are children, in which case 'you may give these things to them'.[2] The widow and children remain in the house

* R. S. Rattray, *Ashanti Law and Constitution*, Oxford University Press, 1929, pp. 28–30.

which they always occupied, and are maintained by the late husband's heir. 'The one who takes the gun of the deceased also takes his widow', is an Ashanti proverb. The following are the words addressed to the ghost of the late husband before the heir begins cohabitation with his widow. Pouring wine upon the ground, he says:

Asumasi, ye se adere bu a, ye bo bi poma m;? nne na wo ye', ye de no ama me, me sere wo fwe me ne no so fwe pa. Ma nkoda yi nye yiye ne tna yen som me; ma menwo 'ba, bi nka wodie yi ho.

('So-and-so, they say that when a cutlass breaks, they put a new shaft to it; to-day they have taken your wife and given her to me, I beg you to look well after me and her. Let these children prosper and serve me, and let me beget others to add to your own.')

It would appear that the rights of the contracting parties are tending to some inequality. The husband of a woman who dies (unless he be a Chief) can apparently no longer claim her replacement by a sister, yet, in the event of the husband's death, the support of his widow and children remains, at least as a moral obligation, upon the heir. What follows is mainly a translation of what an Ashanti laid down as being the law on this custom. 'The heir says, *Ma fa me nua anase me wofa akunafo;* or *Me ko kyekyere me nua anase me wofa yere abaso* (i.e. "I have taken my brother's or uncle's widows; or I went and bound beads on their writsts").' It will be noted that the word 'marry' is not used, as the widows in a sense are still considered as married, the original contract not having been dissolved by the death of the husband. 'It is a man's heir who succeeds to his late kinsman's wives, i.e. his brother, or nephew, or grandson.' If such a one does not take them, people say, *W'afa n'akyiri adie, na wa ka ne yere ne ne mma* ('He has taken that which he left behind, but has abandoned his wife and children'). The *saman* (ghost) of the deceased husband is expected in this case to kill the heir.[3] The widows, in fact, consider such conduct in the nature of defamation of character, for they may demand a public declaration on the part of the heir to the effect that they had not caused the death of their late husband. In case a man refuses 'to take' the wives of his late kinsman, these wives have a right to take all the children away with them. If the widow, on the other hand, refuses 'to be taken', the heir can claim all the customary expenses that the deceased had incurred in connexion with the marriage. If the widow is very old she has every right to remain in her late husband's house, and will possibly insist on doing so, declaring, *Me ware me kunu saman* ('I shall mate with the ghost of my (late) husband'). If a man had married his *wofa 'ba*, i.e. his cross-cousin, and on the death of his uncle became the latter's heir, unless he be a chief, he may not marry his uncle's wife, for he has already married her daughter.[4] In old days the heir did not claim the widow for a year; at the end of that time he would send a *domma* (7*s*.) and *gyanie* beads, and if the widow bound the beads on her right wrist, that was a sign she would marry the heir. This was all the marriage ceremony required. The heir's '*samanfo* (spirit ancestors) were then informed and asked to bless the union. Until a year had expired, any one having sexual intercourse with a widow was said to have had sexual intercourse with the wife of a ghost, and he would be fined. If the heir, who has the legal right to inherit widows, does not himself wish to take them all, he may pass them on to his younger brothers or nephews, or *nana* (grandchildren), but not to any one else.[5]

Where the heir to widows is a woman, she will address them as her 'wives', and before she allows them to return home (i.e. to their *abusua*) she will make them 'swear an oath' that they have never been unfaithful to their late husband.

Notes

[1] The taking of a widow as part of the *ayibuadie* on the death of Kings or Chiefs is possibly an adaptation of this custom.

[2] Possibly for fear of the *saman* (ghost).

[3] The following is a concrete example which came under my notice. A certain man of the Beretuo clan, resident at Beposo, neglected to take his kinsman's widow, but instead gave five sheep to his brother's *saman*. Later it was ascertained through an *obosom* (lesser god) that the dead man would not accept this, but insisted on the woman 'coming back into his house'. By this time, however, the woman was already married elsewhere, and the heir soon after dying, his death was ascribed to his neglect to take his brother's widow.

[4] There are however, many alleged cases of chiefs having done so, e.g. Safo Kantanka, who married Aberefi Ya and also her daughter Kwadu Yadom; Kobina Dwumo, who is alleged to

have married Nyantakyi and her daughter Afua Pokua; Owusu Sekyere, who married Denta and Afrakuma.

[5] The present *Omanhene* of—, when he came to the Stool, is alleged to have called all his predecessors' wives before him and said, 'You see I am already an old man; if you do not wish to remain, you may go'. All save one elected to stay.

D. J. Penwill: Kamba Customary Law*

Custody of Widows

When a man has died and his funeral ceremonies are over, his near relations go to his widow (or widows) and tell her that she cannot live by herself, but must choose from amongst the dead man's brothers one who will protect her. The widow ('ndiwa') normally chooses one of her dead husband's full brothers, but the choice of a half-brother by another wife of her father-in-law is acceptable. The man who lives with and protects a widow is called 'musina'.

This man is then told by the clan elders that it is his duty to look after the woman and protect her; to live with her and to eat the food and drink the beer prepared by her; to manage the property she has been left with, but not to use it for his own ends. The widow is told that she must not annoy her 'musina' or cause trouble with his own wives. Normally, the two will have intercourse together; if the woman has not previously borne male children, it is obligatory. However, if the woman has already had many children she can refuse, saying that she no longer needs a man. Children born after the death of her husband, although the 'musina' is actually their father, are treated as being the children of the dead man and bear his name. If his name was Musau, the widow's children are all called 'wa Musau'. They call the 'musina', their father, 'mwenda asa'—'my paternal uncle'. In this connection, if a man dies after being 'affianced', his father having paid half the bride price but not all and the woman having stayed at her father's house, a brother of the dead man can, by agreement of all concerned, take his place in the bargain. Even in this case, the children will not be regarded as his but will be looked upon as belonging to his dead brother and named after him. The Kamba elders say that this is because of the payment of the two 'mubui sya ntheo' and the 'nthenge' that followed; these are the binding part of the marriage agreement, and until they are returned all the woman's children belong to the man who paid them.

If the dead man had no full or half-brothers (comparatively rare, the Kamba birth-rate being what it is), a close male relative takes the responsibility of protecting the widow. It is not the undisputed right of the eldest surviving brother to take her (*contra* Lindblom,† p. 84); the clan elders will ensure that if there are other brothers the widow is allowed a choice. Nor does he become in any sense her 'owner'—he cannot make her over to another man and receive payment for her. Nor can he lend her. If the woman annoys him and he does not wish to continue in his role, he should call the clan elders and suggest that someone else take over the task. Similarly, if the woman objects to her 'musina' and causes difficulties, she will probably be allowed a second choice.

If none of the brothers or close relatives will protect the woman—which would be a very rare happening—an unrelated man can be called in to live in her house and look after her, provided that the woman agrees to the choice. It would probably be a poor man who could not afford a wife of his own. He does not pay for the woman, and the dead man's eldest brother will be responsible for all formal obligations and take part in all ceremonies, e.g. the payment of the bride price for one of the widow's children. This brother, therefore, takes the dead man's place in all important matters, but the woman will live with and work for her new and probably poor 'protector'. Any children are regarded as being the children of the dead husband. (Much of the above is *contra* Lindblom, p. 84.)

If a widow behaves very badly, her dead husband's relative can send her back to her father and recover her bride price, as her husband could have done. This almost never happens, for the relatives will want the woman to stay if she has had a few or no children in order to bear them to carry on the name; and if she has had several male children they will refuse the bride price in order to retain them. If the woman, having

* D. J. Penwill, *Kamba Customary Law*, Government Printer, Nairobi, 1951, pp. 23–26. o

† *The Akamba*.

had children, insisted on returning to her father, she would probably be allowed to go if she were obstinate, but no bride price will be returned. What it comes to is that women usually do what they want in the long run, and custom has to provide for their whims.

A young widow may be given to one of the dead man's sons by an older wife, who will be her 'musina'. It does not matter that she has had intercourse with her dead husband, since purification ceremonies remove this difficulty (*contra* Lindblom, p. 85). A man cannot give his wife to a son by another wife in his lifetime, even if they have never had intercourse, because they are 'of different beds'; a man's brothers are a different matter—they are 'of one bed' with him. As before, the children of this young widow are regarded as children of the dead man, and eventually as half-brothers of their true father.

A fully grown son can look after his own mother himself if he has married, had children, and has his own homestead, always provided that he has permission from the appropriate uncle. This is only if his mother has no need or further inclination to bear children. He can also take his uncle's place, with permission, at appropriate ceremonies concerning his brothers and sisters. To do this, a son would have to be passed as suitable not only in age and family but in wisdom and dignity. The President of the Iveti Native Tribunal, Jese Kitabi, is at present looking after two of his father's widows, his mother and another; but if there is some important matter at issue, he calls upon the two uncles who are formally responsible for them.

No man normally becomes responsible for more than one widow.

(b) Sororate and Substitute

R. S. Rattray: Ashanti Law and Constitution*

Ayete (*Sororate*)

This form of marriage at the present day appears to be almost obsolete,[1] except among Chiefs. *Ayete* means the substitution by the wife's family of another woman to take the place of a wife who has died (or, sometimes, the exchange of a young for an old wife), the substitute being generally the sister of the deceased wife. New *Aseda* is not paid; the husband nevertheless continues to enjoy all the rights (no less than obligations) which the original payment conferred. This procedure clearly indicates that the original contract into which the parties entered is not considered as being terminated by the death of the wife (nor in fact by that of the husband, for the levirate, which will be described presently, appears only to be the converse of the *Ayete* custom). If the deceased wife's sister is already married, she is (in the case of a Stool subject) expected to divorce her husband. The marriage of two or more sisters contemporaneously to the same man is not called *Ayete*, but is termed *Ahen' awadie* (Chief's marriage). At the present day a commoner may not enter upon such a union.[2] We may perhaps infer in both such cases, from the fact that they are now the recognized prerogatives of Chiefs, that the house-father once upon a time possessed similar privileges. A man still calls his wife's sister 'my wife', but a Chief may not do so unless he be actually married to her, 'as no one would then ever dare to marry her'.

Notes

[1] It survives, however, in certain cases where the man has 'bought his wife', and may even be practised, I am informed, in cases 'where the *abusua* of your late wife love you very much'. The derivation of the word *ayete* is said to be *ye*', 'wife', and *te*, 'to patch', 'to mend'.

[2] Sororate, among commoners, is in fact considered a crime, the offence being known as *atwebenefie*.

* R. S. Rattray, *Ashanti Law and Constitution*, Oxford University Press, 1929, pp. 27–28.

G. Wilson: Luo Customary Law and Marriage Laws and Customs*

Bride of Replacement: Nyar Hidho

In the case of NYAR HIDHO, a girl who replaces her dead sister or a close agnatic kinswoman who died without male issue, several of the customs described for MEKO† are not followed. Firstly, she goes to the village of her own volition accompanied only by an elderly woman of her village. She is the bride of replacement and will take the status position of the woman she replaces after she has given birth to a male child. Until that time, she is much in the position of a bride prior to RISO.‡ If the woman she replaced has died before RISO, then the stage in the ceremonies which was left off when the woman died is continued for NYAR HIDHO, as if she was the same woman. Secondly, she is not deflowered publicly. However, in the case of a separation, her parents will retain a cow for virginity. The husband will be expected to pay the status animals and DHO MILUHINI, however, he will only pay half of the usual bride wealth animals, DHO I KENY'. If the NYAR HIDHO is particularly fertile, the man may pay full bride wealth for her. This depends entirely upon the relationship of the two groups. In any case, however, the series of ceremonies for the first woman should be fulfilled first. In the case where a NYAR OSIEP elopes with a young man prior to going to her betrothed, it will be the duty of her father to supply a NYAR HIDHO.

Nyar hidho may not occupy the actual house of the dead woman which is left to fall down but when a new village is built, her house will be built in the status position normally occupied by the woman who she replaces. If she replaces MIKAYI, for example, her house will be built facing the gate, PANGACH, of the new village. Brides who are NYAR HIDHO are sometimes called OGO KUOM NGET, a typical circumlocution, meaning the cut of meat which includes two ribs and the heart, that is two ribs instead of the usual one allocated to a wife.

To Marry a Relative of Wife: Siweho

Another form of marriage is SIWEHO, that is a marriage with a sister or close agnatic relative of a wife. It is customary for most Luo women to bring a girl from their own village to act as a nurse for their children. The nurse, JAPITI, lives with the family as a sister-in-law and gradually, over time, begins to perform the functions of a wife. The wife who brought her is then regarded as JAGAM and frequently this relationship ends in marriage of the MEKO type. If a woman is barren, she will try to bring SIWEHO from her village to marry her husband as her NYAR OT in order to raise seed, not only to him, but also to her house. SIWEHO is often brought to a village when a woman has reached the menopause, OSEA E RIA, because of the Luo custom which forbids a man to cohabit with a wife who has reached this stage. In this way the newcomer becomes the NYAR OT of the house of her sister and the man cohabits with her. In all cases of SIWEHO, the ceremonies are as for MEKO.

Siweho is usually the sister of the wife or someone who stands to her in this relationship. The woman may bring her brother's daughter or someone who stands in this relationship, if she has reached the menopause and is PIM. Women who are PIM endeavour to contract such marriages. A niece may not come to the village as SIWEHO, if her aunt is till able to produce, for this would be CHIRA.

E. J. Krige: Individual Development§

No marriage is complete without children. Should the wife be barren or die childless, a sister or other younger relative would have to take her place.[1] Any children born will be considered children of the barren sister, and the seed-raiser has no hut or status of her own. No *lobola* is due for her,[2] though a gift of from one to three head of cattle is

* G. Wilson, *Luo Customary Law and Marriage Laws and Customs*, Government Printer, Nairobi, 1961, pp. 118–119.

† Marriage ceremony. ‡ Final wedding ceremony.

§ E. J. Krige, 'Individual Development', in I. Schapera (ed.) *The Bantu Speaking Tribes of South Africa*, Routledge & Kegan Paul, 1947, pp. 116–117.

usually given to thank the parents. If, however, the deceased has borne children; her husband would have to pay *lobola* in the usual way on marrying her sister. Among some tribes, e.g. Shangana-Tonga,[3] Ndebele,[4] Swazi,[5] marriage with the wife's sister is at all times, not only on the death or sterility of the first wife, considered very appropriate, and it is usual for a Swazi man when visiting his wife's people to engage one of her sisters to spend the night with him. If a child is born he would either give *lobola* for the girl or, if on friendly terms with her people, he might be allowed to give a beast and take the child, leaving the girl to be married to someone else.

A form of marriage related to the sororate is that with the wife's brother's daughter. Among the Venda, a man may, failing his wife's sister, be given one of her brother's children.[6] This brother, having used his sister's *lobola,* is responsible for satisfying the just claims of her husband. Among the Swazi, too, a man is entitled to his wife's brother's daughter,[7] while Shangana-Tonga and Lobedu consider this kind of marriage appropriate at any time. The Lobedu kinship term for a girl's father's sister's husband is 'husband'.

Notes

[1] The Huruthse go so far as to send a woman who has already been married, if necessary; while Zulu often send a younger sister of the bride as her *inhlanzi* to remain with her in her new home and take her place, if need be.

[2] This is mentioned for the Southern Sotho (Whitfield, 1929, 175), Swazi (Engelbrecht, 1930, 6), Venda (Lestrade, 1930, 202), Huruthse (Lestrade, 1926, 941–2), and is common all over the union. Among Pedi a 'nominal charge' never exceeding three head of cattle is always made (Whitfield, 1929, 208).

[3] Junod, 1927, i, 247.

[4] Eiselen, 1928*c*, 417.

[5] Engelbrecht, 1930, 6.

[6] Stayt, 1931, 152.

[7] Engelbrecht, 1930, 2.

H. Ashton: The Basuto*

These obligations differ according to circumstances. If the marriage has subsisted for many years, and especially if the woman has borne children, the wife's family are considered to have fulfilled their side of the contract. On her death, therefore, they are under no further obligation to her husband's people, apart from their 'maternal uncle' relationship to her children. If, however, she dies childless soon after marriage, they should provide another wife to take her place. If they do so, they should be given a reduced number of *bohali*† cattle (usually half) as well as any outstanding from the first marriage. If they refuse, they forfeit their right to the latter, but they do not have to return any if the full number have already been given—hence the precaution mentioned earlier of withholding a few. If the wife dies leaving young children, it is desirable that her younger sister should take her place because the latter's 'blood will cry out for the children' and she can be expected to take better care of them than a stranger would. Full *bohali* is payable for her. Both these are *seantlo*‡ marriages. Such marriages are only agreed to in the case of the senior wives of important people, and even then not always.[1] In both these *seantlo* marriages and in the '*mala* marriages described below, the substitute wife should be the other's younger sister, and failing that, her father's younger brother's daughter, her father's elder brother's daughter or her brother's daughter. Examples of all four relationships were found among the Tlokoa. Although the second type of *seantlo* marriage is contracted to provide a sympathetic stepmother for the children, the latter are actually often cared for by other relations, such as the paternal or maternal grandmother.

If the senior wife proves barren, she should encourage her husband to marry another to be her womb (*ho mo etsetsa mala*). The husband should then approach her people and ask for her younger sister or other close relative and they should accede to this request on the same conditions as with the first type of *seantlo*. The new wife will form part of the senior wife's household and, although she will have her own separate hut, she will work and cook for the senior wife, who will be regarded as the mother of her children.

* H. Ashton, *The Basuto*, Oxford University Press, 1952, pp. 82–83.

† Marriage consideration. ‡ Substitute.

Note

[1] Chief Matlere Lerotholi's mother was a junior wife of Lerotholi, her position being somewhere in the tens. In 1949 he told me that she was married *seanto* for her paternal aunt (*rakhali*) Taeli who was Lerotholi's fifth wife and died childless. If this is so, her children should rank as the latter's children and therefore be regarded as fairly senior. Unfortunately, I was unable to check this, but I feel this claim cannot be substantiated and is an interesting attempt to bolster up his genealogical status. He is a man of considerable political importance as the Paramount Chief's representative in Mokhotlong, but is regarded by many as rather an upstart owing to his comparatively lowly birth.

(c) Ghost-Marriage

P. P. Howell: Manual of Nuer Law*

The main characteristics of 'ghost-marriage' are as follows:

(1) It is the dead man, to whose name the wife is married, who is considered the legal father of the children. The ritual processes of marriage are performed in his name, and the bridewealth is paid on his behalf. Therefore, while he is not the physiological father of the children, he is their legal father, and it is from his name that they trace their descent.

(2) The man who marries a wife to the name of his dead kinsman is father in all roles and is in every respect the husband of the woman except in the strictly legal sense.

(3) The physiological father fulfils all the domestic duties of husband and father. In this respect the characteristics are the same as in a normal legal union, and it is only by enquiry that his true legal status can be discovered.

(4) On enquiry, though not in normal circumstances, the wife will be called *ciek jooka*, 'ghost-wife', and the children will be called *gaat jooka*, 'children of a ghost'.

(5) Since the husband is a substitute for his dead kinsman and performs all ritual and domestic obligations on his behalf, the features of a simple legal marriage are found in the structure of this form of union.

(6) The behaviour and obligations of the pro-husband are indistinguishable from those of a man who is both legal and physiological husband and father.

E. E. Evans-Pritchard: Kinship and Marriage among the Nuer†

A very common feature of Nuer social life is a union I have called ghost-marriage. If a man dies without legal male heirs, a kinsman of his or the succeeding generation—brother, natural son, paternal nephew, or, where a man has, in the absence of lineal heirs, inherited cattle from his mother's brother, sister's son—ought to take a wife to his name.

Except in the case of a barren woman and in the special circumstances and manner mentioned on page 16, where it might be said that in a sense she does so, a daughter does not carry on the lineage of her father. She becomes one of her husband's people and her children belong to his lineage. Hence Nuer say: '*Nyal, mo ram me gwagh*', 'A daughter, that is an unrelated person.' As the Roman lawyers put it, she is *finis familiae*, the terminus of the family. But a man's name must continue in his lineage, and Nuer consider it very wrong if a man who dies without male heirs is not married a wife by a kinsman who will raise up seed to him by her so that he will be remembered in his sons. This is a most elementary obligation of kinship, and if it is neglected the dead man's ghost may haunt his kin.

In speaking of these ghost-marriages Nuer say, for example, that '*ce deman kwen cick*', 'he-his brother-married-wife' ('he married his brother a wife'). This is a clumsy and ambiguous expression in English, so I shall speak of a man marrying a wife to the name of a dead kinsman, it being understood that it is not her, but the dead man, who is the legal husband. Nuer also speak of a man 'kindling the fire' of his dead kinsman, a euphemism for raising up seed to him.

* P. P. Howell, *Manual of Nuer Law*, Oxford University Press, 1954, p. 74.

† E. E. Evans-Pritchard, *Kinship and Marriage among the Nuer*, Clarendon Press, Oxford, 1951, pp. 109–112.

This is a vicarious marriage, the vicarious husband acting as though he were the true husband in the marriage ceremonies and afterwards in cohabitation and domestic life. In all but the strict legal sense he counts as husband and father in the family. He has the same legal rights over the wife as her husband would have were he alive, and he exercises the same authority over the children when they are minors as their pater would do. While the children are small, at any rate, one cannot observe any difference in sentiment and behaviour between a ghost-family and a simple legal family. It is only when the sons grow up that their connexion with their pater becomes significant. In everyday usage people speak of the living man as though he were the true husband and father, so that it is only by inquiring that one discovers the name of the true husband. The name of the pater looms larger when the children grow up, and Nuer told me that it is his name which finally survives in the genealogy of the lineage; but when the pater and the genitor are agnatic kin it is by reference to the name of the genitor that the children will be addressed, except in certain legal and ceremonial situations when it is desired to indicate their correct genealogical position. A child always knows the name of his pater.

Nevertheless, the legal partners to the union are not the man and woman living together. The legal husband is the ghost in whose name the bridewealth was paid and the ritual of matrimony was performed. The woman is *ciekjooka,* the wife of a ghost, and her children are *gaatjooka,* children of a ghost. The family that develops out of a ghost-marriage may be called a ghost-family in acknowledgement of the ghostly status of the pater of the children. It consists of a ghost, his wife, his children born in the union of marriage, and the kinsman who begat these children and acts as father to them. It is a variety of the simple legal family, which is contained in its structure. This is why, Nuer say, a man may not marry a wife to the name of a kinsman of a younger generation, for such a marriage would mean that the wife would cohabit with a man who was her father-in-law.

These ghost-marriages must be almost as numerous as simple legal marriages. Not only do many youths die before marriage but for one reason or another married men do not always have male heirs. A man's wife may bear him only daughters or her sons may die before marriage. In this last eventuality, his kinsmen must raise up seed not only to him but to his sons also, unless they died in childhood. A very common circumstance is that a man takes a wife to the name of a dead kinsman and is unable later to marry a wife in his own right, for, seeing that he enjoys the material benefits of marriage, his younger brothers must be allowed to marry from the family herd before he can contract a second, and legal, marriage. If he is ever rich enough to marry again he may feel that he must forgo the privilege in the interests of the sons he has raised up to his dead kinsman. He thus dies legally childless and it will be the duty of one of these sons to marry a wife to his name. In a case of this kind, it is more than ever incumbent on his sons to marry a wife to his name because he has died in possession of cattle. These cattle, *ghok jookni,* cattle of the ghosts, are sacred and in the special circumstances ought not to be used for any purpose other than marrying a wife to the name of their dead owner. When Nuer raid a herd to seize cattle in compensation for some injury they will not take cattle reserved for the marriage of a ghost.

Except in the circumstances I have just related, it is usually a younger brother who marries a wife to the dead. As brothers marry in order of seniority, it is fitting that when it comes to the turn of the dead man to take a wife the brother next junior to him should marry in his name. However, if the next brother is only a paternal half-brother they are likely to leave the pious obligation to a full brother who is yet younger.

The custom of marrying a wife to the name of a dead man makes obvious complications in the kinship system of the Nuer, for a child of the union is both a son of the man who is in the place of his pater and, in virtue of his attachment to his pater, stands also to him in a different relationship: father's brother's son, brother, brother's son, or maternal uncle's son.

A further complication arises when as occasionally happens, a woman marries a wife to the name of a dead kinsman, usually of a dead uterine brother. It is said: '*Ce rode kwen ciek, ciek thok dwiel man*', 'She has taken a wife to herself, a wife for the hut of her mother', that is to say, for her uterine brother. The persons involved in a marriage of this kind are the dead man, his kinswoman who marries a wife to his name, the wife, and the man who is brought in to cohabit with the wife. A woman may instead marry a wife herself and instruct the son of this marriage to marry a wife, when he grows up, for her brother (his paternal uncle, since the sister is his pater).

Yet more rarely a man marries a wife to the name of a dead sister or other kinswoman who was barren in her life, 'for she then counts as a man'. This is perhaps only done when the dead woman's ghost causes sickness to draw attention to her unhappy condition. The children are called after their female pater, and her brother, who has married their mother to her name, counts as their paternal uncle, 'for his sister has become his brother'. On the marriage of the daughters he gets the cattle due to a paternal uncle. It seems that he must not cohabit with the wife himself, because in these circumstances 'your wife is like your sister' (she stands in the place of your sister), but must arrange for a stranger, perhaps a Dinka, to cohabit with her in the hut he builds for her in his homestead.

(d) Others

R. S. Rattray: Ashanti Law and Constitution*

Marriage

A male slave (i.e. an *ondonko* or *akoa pa*) might enter into a contract of marriage. The union might be with:

(*a*) A female slave owned by his own master.
(*b*) A female slave owned by another master.
(*c*) A free woman (but possibly only in case of an Ashanti slave, *akoa pa*).

In case (*a*) the master, in case (*b*) the master of the slave-girl, and in case (*c*) the father of the woman, would receive the *aseda*, which would enable the slave to claim adultery damages from any person, free man or slave, who 'took his wife'. Not only so, but the Ashanti law further decreed that the 'adulterer', if the master, should pay double the customary 'satisfaction',[1] and the adulterer, if a Chief, was liable to be destooled. In the case of a slave's master committing adultery with the wife of his own slave, the following additional ceremony sometimes took place. The master was ordered by the Chief to find a sheep and place it across his shoulders. He then knelt down in front of his slave, who was seated, brought the sheep over his head, and as soon as it touched the ground in front of him, said, *Di bim apeafo* ('Yours is the just cause' *apeafo*). The slave would then reply, *Ma gyae, me ka ntam se me som wo se me som wo da da* ('I leave it, and I "swear the oath" that I will serve you as I served you before this happened'). 'Every one would then hoot at the master.' Should a slave fear revenge on the part of his master after such an event, he might swear the following oath: *Me ka ntam se fa me ko ma Ohene na gye wo sika, na wa di me ye' mensom wo bio* ('I "swear the oath" that you must take me to the Chief, and he will hand you the money you paid for me, for you have, "eaten" my wife, and I will not serve you any more'). A slave, it will be seen, might 'swear an oath'. A master would demand the damages for his slave from the person who had wronged him. A slave ultimately sued and was sued through his master. The offspring from unions (*a*) and (*b*) were slaves, and were in theory known as *nnonkofo mienu mma* or *afona mma*, i.e. the children of a man and woman both of whom were alien slaves, or Ashanti slaves. Their position, however, was very different. The children of union (*a*) belonged to their master as absolutely as did their parents; the children of union (*b*) belonged to the master of the slave's wife. The children of union (*c*) were free and did not come under the *potestas* of their slave father's master.

The owner of a slave was ultimately responsible for all the acts of his slave, and in consequence he became responsible for the debts and torts of his slave's wife, but always, in case of a slave incurring any liability which he was himself unable to meet, his master might sell him in liquidation of the debt.

A female slave (*odonko 'ba* or *afona*) might marry:

(*a*) A male slave owned by her master.
(*b*) A male slave owned by another master.
(*c*) A free man, possibly her master, or master's nephew, or his son (*odonko awadie*).

Unions (*a*) and (*b*) have already been discussed. In the case of (*c*) all the children

* R. S. Rattray, *Ashanti Law and Constitution*, Oxford University Press, 1929, pp. 38–40.

of the marriage belonged to the master of the female slave, and were of course slaves; they were known as *Kanifa*, i.e. half Akan, but grew up to consider themselves Ashanti and were adopted, by a kind of legal fiction, into some clan. When a master married his own *afona*, and had children by her, the offspring of such a union were the only children over whom he had any real authority. The degraded status of a mother alone gave an Ashanti father the privilege of claiming rights over his children which we might consider as a man's natural prerogative. Where a female slave married a free man, other than her master, any children of the union belonged to her master. 'When a master married his own slave-girl, he would pay *Aseda* to the Chief, if he wished to be able to claim adultery fees; if she did any wrong, he could sell her to the Chief and she would possibly be selected as a sacrifice at some funeral custom. All the children of such a marriage were the father's slaves, whom he could sell without consulting anyone. The children of these children in the female line were considered slaves for ever.'

Again: 'If I married my slave-girl and had children, I would not give them my own clan name, for if I did so, and gave them to my nephews and nieces to marry, there would be trouble.' Slave children, the descendants of bought slaves, are already adopted into the family. They take their master's clan name in many cases, although persons who are aware of their descent may laugh and in private refer to their clan as a 'left-hand clan' (*abusua benkum*), or make a kind of pun out of the real name, e.g. *Beretuo* may be called *Bereto* ('I am weary of having bought you'), or *Oyoko* become *Oyoko sasa*.[2] ('So long as the descendants of your slaves served you, you would never disclose their origin; you only did so when they would wish to cease to serve you, when you were at liberty to disclose their real status'). *Obi nkyere obi ase* ('No one must disclose the origin of another') is a legal maxim of tremendous import in Ashanti, as we shall see again and again. A man's children by a slave-wife are treated just as well as his free children. The father has now more authority over the former than their uncle over the latter. 'If I had bought the mother myself, then I could pawn or sell her children without consulting my uncle; he would have to consult with his *abusua* before doing the like to his nephews and nieces. I would not openly say so, but I preferred my slave children to my children by an *odehye awadie*.'

Notes

[1] On the analogy that a Chief's subjects are his *nkoa*, a Chief who commits adultery with the wife of such is at the present day called upon to pay double adultery damages.

[2] *Sasa*, the rag in a red clay pot.

P. P. Howell: Manual of Nuer Law*

'*Widow-Concubines*'

The main points are as follows:

(i) The man who performs the duties of husband to the widow is in no sense the legal father of her children, nor is he heir to the legal husband.

(ii) He cannot compel her to live with him or claim compensation if she commits adultery. The compensation for adultery would concern her late husband as represented by his living brothers or legal heirs.

(iii) He cannot divorce her or demand back her bridewealth for there is no legal marriage between him and the widow, only between the widow and her late husband.

(iv) He is not even the legal representative of the dead man and therefore, unlike the levirate or 'ghost-marriage', the characteristics of the simple legal family are not contained in the structure of this union.

The man's position is therefore, in theory, a precarious one. In fact, most of these unions are arranged with the agreement of the dead man's legal representative and thereby receive social recognition not only from the world at large, but also from the dead man's family.[1] If no such agreement exists the control over the children and the widow may be a source of legal dispute. Such disputes are not uncommon.

* P. P. Howell, *Manual of Nuer Law*, Oxford University Press, 1954, pp. 81–82.

Unmarried Concubines

All these forms of domestic and procreative union have one principal common factor: the children of the woman, whether she be wife, 'ghost-wife', widow or widow-concubine, belong to the man on whose behalf the bridewealth cattle were transferred to her family, and they trace their descent through his name to his more remote ancestors. There are, however, forms of union which are in no sense legal because no cattle have been paid as bridewealth for the woman. Children born of such unions will be attached in name to their mother's lineage unless their father chooses to legalize their status and attach them to his lineage by payment of a special fee, or unless the mother is legally married later to some other man who assumes the status of legal father to the children.

The status of women among Nilotic peoples is high. In the question of marriage they usually have a fairly free choice, though there are undoubtedly many occasions when father or brothers will use persistent persuasion or even force to compel a girl to marry a man she dislikes simply because they are avaricious for the many cattle he possesses or wish to link themselves to some important family. More often control is exercised in the form of a prohibition rather than positive compulsion. In other words, although they will not use force to compel her to marry a man she detests, they will not allow her to marry the man she loves if he has not sufficient cattle to provide the bridewealth. Whether or not they will take this attitude depends on a variety of circumstances. Some Nuer girls are headstrong and of independent spirit and will not allow their wills to be thwarted by the conventions of the bridewealth system. They therefore live as they please with lovers of their own choice and without either the sanction of bridewealth or the ritual processes of marriage which go with it.[2] A woman of this sort is known in Nuer as *ciek me keagh*. The circumstances in which a woman becomes a *ciek me keagh* are many. Any woman who lives with a man without payment of bridewealth (either on his own behalf or on behalf of the man who is considered her legal husband) is called *keagh*, but she may not be of the restless independent spirit which characterizes most of these women. She may be a young girl who has borne a child to a man who refuses to marry her, though this is rare, or a woman who simply cannot stand life with the husband of her family's choice and has therefore run away and provoked a divorce.

Women who are *keagh* are not regarded as immoral in our sense of the word in these circumstances, but their families are naturally often exasperated by their behaviour and disappointed that no bridewealth cattle have been paid for them. Their social position as unmarried concubines is not generally so high as that of married women, but no distinction is made in the every-day behaviour of their neighbours towards them. The basic difference between widow-concubines and unmarried concubines is that in the former case bridewealth has been paid, even though it has not been paid by the man with whom they live and by whom they produce children. In the latter case bridewealth has not been paid at all or has been returned in divorce.

Notes

[1] A widow living in this form of union with a man is known as *ciek me lak* and her children as *gaat cana*.

[2] For this reason Nuer do not go to extreme lengths of compulsion for, if the girl runs away, they will lose the chance of getting any cattle at all.

Chapter 11

MARRIAGE PAYMENTS

African customary marriage is associated with many payments made by the bridegroom and his family to the bride's family and vice-versa. The most important of these payments is the marriage consideration, dealt with in section (*a*). Other payments are described in section (*b*).

(a) Marriage Consideration

As has been pointed out in chapter 6, one of the most important characteristics of African customary marriages is the provision for the payment of goods or services by the bridegroom or his family to the wife's family before or at the time of or after the marriage.

In the past, this payment was commonly referred to as 'brideprice', but this term has been severely criticised in that it connotes the element of wife purchase which is not the case. Other terms that have been used include 'dowry', 'marriage cattle', 'bridewealth', 'childprice' and 'marriage consideration'. Criticism can in fact be levelled against the use of each of these terms. 'Dowry' could be confused with the 'dowry' as understood in the Western sense; 'marriage cattle' can only apply to societies where the payment is in the form of cattle; 'bridewealth' is misleading when the payment is a token one consisting for example of a hoe; 'childprice' may be correct for societies where the payment is for the sole purpose of affiliating the children to the husband's control, but not for societies where this is not so.

As will be seen from the title, we have opted for 'marriage consideration', a term suggested by Professor Allott. We do not pretend that the term is ideal, for it can be said against it that 'consideration' is no more than a sophisticated lawyer-like word for 'price'. However, we feel that of all the words that have been employed by the various writers on African law and in African legislation, it is the least inappropriate.

In selecting the extracts which follow, we have tried to include all facets of the payment, including its significance, its character, who supplies it, to whom it is paid, the method of its payment, the effect of non-payment, and its return. The chapter starts with *Schapera* on Tswana and concludes with *Seymour* on South Africa, both of whom deal with all these aspects. In the second extract, *Rattray* deals specifically with the significance of the payment and the legal rights and liabilities which a husband acquires or incurs through the payment. Then follows a long extract from *Mayer*'s *Gusii Bridewealth Law and Custom* in which he deals in some considerable detail with the composition of marriage consideration, the rules for its allotment, and its legal implications.

I. Schapera: A Handbook of Tswana Law and Custom*

Significance

According to Tswana law, no marriage is regarded as complete unless *bogadi* has been given by the husband's people to the wife's people. This transfer has often been looked upon by missionaries and others as constituting a purchase of the woman, and as involving her in many humiliating consequences. As will appear from the information given below, this conception of *bogadi* is altogether wrong. There is no bargaining over the number of cattle to be given: the husband's parents give as many as they like and can, which fact alone should dispel the idea of a purchase. It is certainly true that a woman married with *bogadi* is under the control of her husband to a greater extent than a woman who has not; and that if she leaves him her parents will usually send her back, unless there is very good reason for her action. It is also true that in old Tswana law, when such a woman's husband dies, his younger brother or some other close male relative has the right to cohabit with her. On the other hand, a woman married with *bogadi* holds a far more honoured position in the tribe generally than a woman who has not been thus married. If she is ill-treated, or has any justifiable complaint against her husband she can appeal to his parents and senior male relatives, who will protect her; whereas a woman for whom *bogadi* has not been given has no legal remedy against the actions of her 'husband'.

The Tswana themselves speak of *bogadi* as being a thanksgiving (*tebogô*) to the wife's parents for the care they have spent on her upbringing, and as a sign of gratitude for their kindness in now allowing her husband to marry her. Some say also that it is compensation to the wife's parents for the loss of her services, and others that it is a sort of register of the marriage, showing that the cohabitation of the man and woman meets with the full approval of their respective families. Others stress the fact that *bogadi* creates a special bond between the two family-groups, just as the transfer of cattle in other situations creates special relationships between Chief and subject, or owner and herdsman. The payment of *bogadi* is further said to give the children of the union certain privileges at the home of their mother's people to which they are not otherwise entitled. They have the right, e.g. to go or be sent to their mother's home to grow up there, and to be supported from the cattle given out as her *bogadi*.

But the main function of *bogadi* is to transfer the reproductive power of a woman from her own family into that of her husband. This fact is of considerable importance, for upon it rests the whole Tswana conception of legitimacy. Summarizing this briefly, it may be said that no form of cohabitation between a man and a woman is held to be a proper marriage unless it is accompanied by the transfer of, or understanding to transfer, *bogadi*. No man can claim, for any purpose, the children he has by any woman, until he and his family have agreed to transfer, and under certain circumstances until they have actually transferred, *bogadi*. On the other hand, all children borne by a married woman, no matter who their actual father may be, are held to be the legal offspring of the man on whose behalf *bogadi* for that woman was given out.[1] '*Bogadi*', in the words of one informant, 'is given out because the woman is coming *go agêla motse* (to raise up the village)'. All the incidents flowing out of the *bogadi* transfer are directly derived from this conception.

Nature, Amount, Contributors

Bogadi almost invariably consists in cattle. It is said that a man possessing no cattle at all may give sheep instead, or that sheep may be given as well as cattle; but such payments appear to be very rare. Goats are apparently never given as *bogadi*, owing, it is said, to their destructive tendencies. Some informants state that long ago poor people would even give out brayed skins as *bogadi*, or the bast of certain trees, and that such objects were gladly received. But at present it is the universal Tswana practice to pay *bogadi* in livestock, and especially cattle. Money payments do not appear as yet to have been substituted, as in some other parts of South Africa.

The cattle given may be heifers, oxen, or cows, and should normally be fairly young animals. At least one of them must be a female, to provide for the possibility of natural

* I. Schapera, *A Handbook of Tswana Law and Custom*, Oxford University Press, 1938, pp. 138–147.

increase. If a cow is given which still has a sucking calf, the calf must also be given, and will count as an additional beast. Male animals which have not yet been castrated must never form part of the *bogadi*. They are regarded as 'warriors' (*batlhabani*), and so to portend a disastrous marriage lacking peace. It is in fact highly insulting to include them among *bogadi* cattle.

There is no fixed number of cattle which must be given as *bogadi*. Every family gives as much as it can afford or wishes. Nor is there any discussion beforehand between the two families as to the number to be given. There is none of that preliminary bargaining found among the Nguni tribes of South-East Africa, which has given rise to the conception of *bogadi* as a mercenary transaction. The husband's people give out as many cattle as they think fit or can get together, the number being determined to some extent by the standing of thir own or the wife's family, and the wife's people are bound to accept them. They may protest if they think that the husband's people are sufficiently wealthy to give more than is actually done, but they do not appear to have the right to reject the *bogadi* as insufficient or to claim more at the *kgotla*. The husband's people may in such cases add more if they wish, but are not bound to do so. The only recognized limitation is that the number given should be even, 'each with its mate, to show that two people are being bound to each other'. An odd number is occasionally accepted, but the *bogadi* must in any case never consist of seven animals, for this number is held to be extremely unlucky. Actually, the number of cattle given among the Kgatla is seldom more than six, and generally less; but in other tribes the usual number is said to be about ten.

The *bogadi*, in the case of a man's first wife, is given by his father or guardian and various other relatives. The father himself, e.g., may give two; and the other relatives, who are all informed that *bogadi* is being collected, contribute as much as they can or wish. The man's principal maternal uncle is expected to contribute at least one animal, which must be a female. The paternal uncle and the paternal aunt are also looked to for special assistance, if they can afford it; while any other relatives, such as the man's mother or brothers, are welcome to contribute if they wish. There is, however, no compulsion in the matter, and such relatives as do not assist will not be blamed if they are unable to do so. The bridegroom himself, if he has any cattle, may add from his own resources to the number collected. For any additional wives he must in any case provide the *bogadi* from out of his own stock. He may be helped by other relatives, but not necessarily, and his father is not held responsible for collecting the *bogadi* together.

Delivery

The *bogadi* must all be paid at once. There is no system of payment by instalments, save to the extent that when one or two of the promised cattle are far away the husband's people inform the wife's people about them when the rest of the *bogadi* is being paid, and will deliver them as soon afterwards as possible.

There is no generally accepted time for the payment of *bogadi*. In some tribes e.g., Rolong, Ngwaketse, and formerly Ngwato), the *bogadi* should in theory be handed over at the time of the marriage, i.e. when the man receives the right to start living with the woman. Nowadays this is also obligatory among the Kgatla in the case of Church weddings, for it is the policy of the Church to refuse to marry a couple if *bogadi* has not yet been paid. But in other tribes (e.g. Hurutshe and Malete), and in all other forms of marriage among the Kgatla also, *bogadi* is hardly ever paid until children have been born of the marriage. It may then be paid at any time afterwards. It is even maintained that no *bogadi* is due if the marriage proves barren, or if either party to the marriage dies childless, unless arrangements are made for the procreation of children by the customs of *seantlo* (substitute wife) or *go tsêna mo tlung* (raising 'seed') respectively.

The delivery and acceptance of *bogadi* are conducted with ceremony. When the necessary cattle have been collected together, the wife's people are informed that they will be sent on a certain day. In some tribes, as just mentioned, this will be the wedding day; in others, it may be years after the marriage has taken place. On the appointed day the cattle are driven to the wife's home by the husband's male relatives, led by a senior uncle. They stop at the *kgotla* of her ward, where, after the usual formal greetings, the man in charge of the cattle says something to the following effect: *Re tlisitse lemaô la rona ke leo, ke lôna le re tsileng go kopa metse ka lôna* ('We have brought our needle, there it is, it is this with which we have come to beg for water'). The wife's people, who have assembled in great numbers to inspect the cattle, receive them with acclamation and rejoicing, and formally thank the messengers. The cattle are then driven into the adjoining kraal.

The wife's people after receiving the *bogadi* must provide a feast for the husband's people. This feast, known variously as *go jesa bogadi* (to feed the *bogadi*), *go tlhabisa bogadi* (to stab the *bogadi*), or *go apêêla bogadi* (to cook for the *bogadi*), was among the Ngwato held on the day that the *bogadi* was delivered; but in other tribes it generally takes place a considerable time afterwards. The husband's people, especially those who have contributed towards the *bogadi*, go the wife's home, where they are given beer to drink and cattle to slaughter. The number of animals offered depends upon the size of the *bogadi*. Generally one is given if the *bogadi* is four cattle or less, and another for every additional two head given. When two or more beasts are offered for slaughter, at least one must come from the wife's maternal uncle. One of the animals, termed *tlhwaiwa*, is taken by the husband's people to their own home, where it will be slaughtered at a later date for those who had contributed towards the *bogadi*. The rest are killed and eaten at the wife's home. Formerly the peritoneum (*lomipi*) from one of these animals was taken, after being doctored, and hung around the necks of the wife and her children, if she already had any, as a sign that the marriage was now complete. The day is spent in eating and drinking, singing and dancing, and in the evening the husband's people return home.

Allocation

The *bogadi* cattle after being handed over may be distributed at once among the wife's relatives. But generally they are kept together by her father for several years, so as to breed sufficiently to allow everybody entitled to it to receive his share. He then makes a feast (which may be the same *tlhabisô ya bogadi* described above), at which he divides the animals among those concerned. The following people are held to have preferential claims (in the order mentioned): the wife's principal maternal uncle, who must receive at least one animal; her principal paternal uncle; and her principal paternal aunt.[2] Her mother is usually also given one beast (termed *kgomo ya phatê*, 'the ox of the sleeping-mat', or *kgomo ya pitsa*, 'the ox of the pot'). Each of these relatives must be satisfied, if there are sufficient cattle to go round. The remainder are kept by the father, or he may allocate one or more to additional relatives.

The wife's special 'linked' brother also has a recognized claim. He may be given one beast, if his father is still alive; and it is maintained by some that on his father's death all the cattle retained by the latter from the *bogadi* of the boy's sister are taken by the boy. Others go so far as to say that these cattle do not really belong to the father, but are merely held by him in trust for his son, who takes them as his own property after the father's death. If the father is dead at the time when *bogadi* is paid, the wife's linked brother receives them and keeps the balance of the cattle after the claims of the various other relatives have been satisfied. If he is still young, they will be received and held in trust for him by his guardian.

Consequences of Non-payment

There does not appear to be any right on the part of the wife's people to sue the husband's people for the payment of *bogadi*; and in fact there is very little litigation of any sort concerning *bogadi* cattle. As already shown, it may be many years before the *bogadi* is paid; but in the meantime the wife's people must patiently wait. But as long as *bogadi* is not paid, the union between a man and a woman, although considered regular if based upon the approval and consent of both their families, is nevertheless not yet held to be a complete marriage. The children of the union are in consequence not legally the children of the man. They belong to their maternal uncle, who can claim them at any time, this being the only means by which he can enforce the payment of *bogadi*; they go with their mother in case of separation; and their father, generally speaking, has no rights over them at all. They are spoken of as *dilebeledi*, 'forgotten things', and formerly were not admitted into the initiation ceremonies until *bogadi* had been paid, or until their maternal uncle had killed an animal and hung its *lomipi* round their necks.

Normally, where the marriage has taken place with the approval of both families, the father's claim to his children is not disturbed, even if he has not yet paid *bogadi*, and he can ultimately obtain full legal rights over them when his first daughter is married. The *bogadi* given for her cannot be taken by him, but goes to her mother's relatives. It is regarded as replacing the *bogadi* which should have been given in the first instance for her mother. *Kgomo tse di nyadisa mmaagwê*, it is said: 'These cattle cause her mother to be married.' The girl's father occasionally ventures to claim the cattle as his own, refusing to hand them over when he receives them from his daughter's husband. But whenever a case of this sort is brought to the *kgotla*, the cattle are invariably adjudged to the wife's people. Until they have received *bogadi* for their sister or daughter, all rights over her reproductive power remain in their family, and accordingly the *bogadi* paid for her first daughter goes to them. Thereafter the girl's father is held to have full rights over his offspring, and the *bogadi* paid for any of his other daughters goes to him.

Should a man die before having paid *bogadi* for his wife, the obligation to do so falls upon his eldest son, if old enough, or upon his own brother failing this. The boy brings cattle to his mother's people, with the words: *Ke nyadisa mmê*, 'I am causing my mother to be married.' Should he fail to do so, he must hand over the *bogadi* he receives when his first sister is married. If he has no sister, he must find the cattle elsewhere, as otherwise he himself with his brothers are held to belong to his mother's family. In such cases his father's relatives will generally come to his assistance.

Should a married woman die before *bogadi* has been paid for her, her children can be claimed by her parents or her linked brother, unless her husband prevents this by now handing over some cattle. The children, if they do go to their maternal relatives, can when grown up return to the home of their father if they wish, although strictly they have no legal rights there. Should the woman not have any children, and *bogadi* have not been paid, there is no obligation on the part of her husband to pay it after her death.

Ih all these instances, it is evident, a marriage is not regarded as complete until *bogadi* has been paid; and, although the children may remain with their father, their mother's people have a claim upon them as long as this payment has not been made. It must also be noted, however, that in the instances just described the status of the children is more regular than is that of children born to a woman whose union with a man has not been formally approved through the betrothal ceremonies. It is only the latter children who are stigmatized as 'bastards' (*bana ba dikgora*). If the woman's people have formally agreed to the union, then even although *bogadi* has not been paid and she is, in consequence, not completely married, her children do not suffer from the same stigma of being fatherless. It is the offspring of casual and unrecognized liaisons who are despised, not those of standing unions which meet with the approval and consent of the girl's family.

Recovery

Cases involving the return of *bogadi* cattle to the husband's people are apparently very infrequent. Theoretically, *bogadi* can be taken or claimed back only: (*a*) if the wife dies childless, and (*b*) in case of divorce, if she is barren. It is sometimes said that the husband can recover his *bogadi*, even when there are children, if he is willing to forfeit his rights to these children. But this is very exceptional and occurs only in cases where he denies the paternity of the children. It may be taken as a general rule that *bogadi* is not recoverable where the marriage has resulted in offspring. The position is different when the woman is barren, or dies childless, for here she has, as it were, failed to carry out her contract. In such cases matters are usually remedied through the practice of *seantlo*, by which one of her sisters or some other female relative is given to the husband as 'substitute wife', to bear children in the house of the barren wife. This practice will be described below in more detail. If no such arrangement is arrived at, the *bogadi* can be taken back.

Where *bogadi* is taken back, the same number of cattle, although not necessarily the same animals, must be returned. But if any of the original cattle given as *bogadi* are still alive and can be traced, they must be restored together with their progeny. The cattle must be replaced by the people to whom they were allocated, and must then be restored by the husband to the people by whom they were contributed.

Abandonment of the 'Bogadi' Practice

The usages described above in connexion with *bogadi* are still practised by most Tswana tribes. The only one which appears to have abandoned them completely is the Ngwato, where Kgama deliberately abolished them. His main reason for doing so, apart from the pressure put upon him by the London Missionary Society, appears to have been the fact that when a woman's husband died, she could not, under the old law, leave his home, and any children she subsequently bore were still regarded as those of her late husband. Even if she had been divorced and then gave birth to any children, these were also regarded as those of her former husband. Kgama now said: *Mongwe le mongwe a a itsalêlê*, 'Every man should be the father of his own children', i.e. if a woman is divorced or widowed, and then marries again, any children she bears should belong to her new husband. At the present time, the payment of *bogadi* among the Ngwato is said to be a punishable offence, and the practice is no longer openly carried out, although there are still said to be people who practise it secretly.

Among the Kgatla the payment of *bogadi* was also suspended for a time during the reign of Lentswe. This seems to have been due in the first instance to missionary influence. The early missionaries regarded *bogadi* payments as a form of wife-purchase and forbade their converts to make them. Lentswe's brothers, Ramono and Segale, the commanders of the maKoba regiment,were both leading members of the Church and consequently refused to pay *bogadi* for their wives. Their example was followed by the rest of their regiment. Lentswe himself soon after this became a Christian, and his acceptance of the missionary view regarding *bogadi* was probably facilitated by the great rinderpest epidemic of 1896, which decimated the herds of his people. For the next decade or so *bogadi* payments were completely abandoned. By that time, however, Lentswe had found that the abandonment of these payments was leading to confusion and dissatisfaction, and tending to make marriages unstable, in that wives separated more readily from their husbands. Since the tribe had again become rich in cattle, he ordered the people to revert to the custom, after having successfully persuaded the Church authorities that *bogadi* was a registration of marriage rather than a form of wife-purchase. Those men who had married while *bogadi* payments were still suspended were likewise required now to make them.

Isang when he became regent revived the custom more strongly, and even enforced it. He used to insist that *bogadi* should be paid before the marriage, and that it should be brought and shown at the tribal *kgotla* the day before the wedding, so that people should know what marriage was taking place and what *bogadi* had been given. At the present time, then, the payment of *bogadi* is once again an essential element of Kgatla marriage; and when matrimonial disputes come to court the two facts first inquired into are whether the marriage took place with the consent of the families concerned and whether *bogadi* was paid. No special importance is attached to any ceremonies that may have taken place. Moreover, as already mentioned, no marriage can take place in church until *bogadi* has been paid.

Notes

[1] Cf. G. P. Lestrade, 'Some Notes on the *Bogadi* System of the BaHurutshe', *S. Afr. J. Sci.*, vol. xxiii (1926), p. 938, from whom I have borrowed some passages in this paragraph.

[2] These 'principal' uncles and aunts are those specially 'linked' with the man's father or mother respectively.

R. S. Rattray: Ashanti Law and Constitution*

Aseda is a thank-offering given to the person or persons from whom some gift or benefit has been received, not so much with the basic idea of showing politeness by

* R. S. Rattray, *Ashanti Law and Constitution*, Oxford University Press, 1929, pp. 24–26.

tendering thanks, as to serve as a record for all concerned that such a gift or benefit has been conferred and accepted. Its presentation and acceptance make it difficult or impossible for either the donor or donee later to repudiate the transaction. Briefly, it is to ensure having witnesses. In marriage ceremonies the *Aseda* may perhaps loosely be termed 'the bride-price', although this term may easily create a somewhat erroneous impression, for in no way is the wife 'purchased' in the literal sense. All that is bought and sold is a sexual prerogative, coupled with the benefit of her services and later those of her children, the last two within strictly defined limits. The 'bride-price' does not even enrich the parents of the bride, for it is distributed among many individuals who thus become the witness to the contract.

The following are some of the definitions of this term given by various Ashanti whom I have questioned concerning *Aseda* in marriage:

Ya Amponsa, a Queen Mother, stated that *Aseda* is given to the parents on the marriage of their daughter. 'For myself', she continued, 'I prefer sometimes not to take it, for then I can get my daughter back without any trouble or expense should the husband not treat her properly.' A trifling gift, such as a pot of palm wine, may constitute legal *Aseda*. When *Aseda* is either not paid or accepted, the husband has not any right to claim damages for adultery, but on the other hand he does not become liable for his 'wife's' debts or torts.

Again: *Aseda* is paid by the father of the man to the father of the girl. The latter gives part of it to the *abusua* of the bride, including her uncle, who takes a half. It is shared among the males of the *abusua*. *Aseda* may never be paid directly to the bride's mother; it must be given to her father, or if he is dead, to his heir. *Oba ngye aseda* (Women do not receive *Aseda*) is a legal maxim.[1]

'Even the *sewa*', i.e. the bride's paternal aunt (lit. female father), my informer remarked, 'does not receive *Aseda*'. A portion of the *Aseda* wine is given to the '*samanfo* (spirit ancestors), who thus become witnesses along with the living to the contract.

The payment and acceptance of *Aseda* is all that is necessary to constitute a strictly legal marriage. Its non-payment or non-acceptance, however, as we may note from the statement of Ya Amponsa (and many others whom I have questioned), while rendering a union in a sense irregular, did not, in olden times, necessarily seem to brand a couple who lived together openly as man and wife with the same stigma which in civilized countries would attach to a couple living together out of wedlock. The cause for this is twofold: first, that considerations of immorality simply do not enter into the question at all, any more than they will be seen to do in cases of what we term 'adultery'; secondly, that owing to the incident of clan descent being traced through the female, the children by a union which with us confers no legal status are, in Ashanti, not penalized or deemed illegitimate.[2]. . .

Before proceeding any further let us summarize the preceding paragraphs. By the payment of *Aseda* for a wife, the husband acquires the following legally enforceable rights:

(1) To claim damages, in event of his wife's infidelity, from the correspondent, who might be sold by his *abusua* to pay the debt; this is another way of saying that by the payment of *Aseda* he acquired the exclusive right to the woman's body, a right in which customary law would now support him.

(2) The right to profit by the fruits of her labour and later that of her children.[3] Such a right does not by any means entitle the husband to order about either wife or children like slaves, and in reality amounts only to the mutual assistance that persons living together and sharing a common *ménage* would naturally accord to each other.

The husband incurs the following liabilities:

(1) He becomes liable for his wife's debts and torts and for her maintenance and that of her children.

(2) He takes into his house someone over whom neither he nor his clan ultimately have control, and one whose acceptance of her position seems largely to depend upon the kind of treatment she meets with in her new surroundings.

Notes

[1] The bride's mother may be given a special gift (called *afayie*), by the bridegroom to recompense her for 'having taken her daughter from her side'.

[2] See however Sarbah, *Fanti Customary Laws*, p. 44. He is, I think, confusing the right of a son to the house of his father with rights of succession on the mother's side.

[3] See also Miss Kingsley's *West African Studies*. In the case of the wife, the Ashanti look upon this right as the natural corollary of being responsible for her debts.

P. Mayer: Gusii Bridewealth Law and Custom*

The Composition of the Bridewealth Proper

The bridewealth proper consists nowadays of a number of cows and heifers, one bull, and a number of goats (including at least one he-goat). If both parties agree, the goats may be commuted for an extra heifer, which has a fixed value in terms of goats according to the prevailing rate of exchange.[1] The cows and goats are called animals of substitution (*nyaika*) i.e. replacement for the girl.

The rules concerning these animals of 'substitution' are as follows:

1. Nine cows cannot make a bridewealth, since this number is considered magically dangerous. Any other number is possible.

2. The position of the goats in the bridewealth payment has to be specially noted. They are definitely reckoned as an essential part of the transaction, yet they are little esteemed in comparison with the cattle, and the rules about their return and replacement differ accordingly. Thus the return of identical animals has never been claimed for goats as it has for cows; in the same way, a claimant may willingly accept a he-goat in place of a she-goat, though nobody would agree to accept a bull instead of a cow.

This equivocal attitude towards the bridewealth goats has a historical explanation. Elders maintain that before the great cattle shortage of the 1890's the bridewealth proper consisted of cows only. Goats and bulls when given at all were given as customary presents, or for sacrifices connected with the marriage, and not as an integral part of the bridewealth. The traditional practice of bartering goats for cattle at a fixed rate made the goats the obvious substitute when cows for bridewealth were hard to come by. Goats, then as now, could play the part of small change: various numbers of them could be included in the bridewealth to represent various 'fractions' of a cow at the defined rate of exchange. It may be because the practice of including goats in the bridewealth has outlived the real *raison d'être* it had during the cattle shortage that we find certain incongruities and inconsistencies in connection with it.

3. The number both of cows and of goats will depend partly on individual bargaining, but still more on the current rate or standard which at any time prevails all over Gusii country, with only minor variations from tribe to tribe. The Gusii themselves say simply, 'we see that all the other fathers are asking so much for their daughters, so we also demand the same'. Except for those occasions when conscious policy has intervened to fix the rate, they can only explain the fluctuations in terms of what the European might call the price mechanism that governs the price of a commodity in a more or less perfect market. The vicissitudes of the bridewealth rate—it has been known to number anything from one heifer or less to 20 cows or more—as well as the various forces which seem to govern them, cannot be fully discussed in this paper.[2]

4. Each animal, cow or she-goat, must be accompanied by its offspring if the latter are still suckling. But these calves and kids are not now usually reckoned in the amount of the dowry proper. Whereas the full-grown animals are *nyaika*, 'replacement', the calves and kids—together with any born after the transfer—are merely *emebiara*, 'offspring', or *amabere*, 'milk'. If to-day a Gusii states that the cattle paid in bridewealth on a certain occasion were 'ten', he will probably mean eleven head of full-grown cattle (ten cows and one bull), together with perhaps three or four calves; the stated number of goats must be interpreted similarly. The fact that the offspring are not reckoned in the bridewealth proper means of course that their number is less significant and less

* P. Mayer, *Gusii Bridewealth Law and Custom*, Oxford University Press for the Rhodes-Livingstone Institute, 1950, pp. 15–16, 26–37, 57–64.

memorable, and hence the fittest subject for haggling or evasion in the event that the bridewealth has to be returned. The distinction between *nyaika* and *emebiara* also concerns the laws about replacing bridewealth animals which died after transfer.

Like the inclusion of goats in the bridewealth, the non-counting of calves and kids seems to be a fairly recent development, though probably older than European influence. Elders ascribe its origin to a time just before or perhaps just after the coming of the Europeans; they say that it developed as a means of evasion provoked by a native attempt to reduce the bridewealth rate. Up till that time (about the first decade of the twentieth century), it is said, all female animals had been reckoned as *nyaika*, but now fathers began to demand the extra 'milk' (i.e. offspring) in order to make up for the reduction in the number of cows without an overt breach of the law. In some of the more remote of the conservative districts, calves are even now counted as *nyaika* and not as *emebiara*.

5. The bull included with the bridewealth, too, serves a rather equivocal function. No bridewealth payment would be considered complete without it, but it seems to constitute a compulsory 'gift' to the bride's father, not a part of the *nyaika* herd given to 'replace' the bride herself. It is known as the 'apron bull' (*eeriy'egesicho*). Traditionally the bride's father would slaughter it to make himself a new *egesicho*, the apron of hide that formed part of the dress of elders in pre-contact days. In modern times, as we shall see, it is sometimes supplemented by the gift of a greatcoat for the father to wear.

Rules of Allotment of Bridewealth within the Family

The allotment of bridewealth within the individual family is normally the function of the father. But the father, though he directs and co-ordinates all matters connected with bridewealth, is not free to act at his own discretion. He is bound by well-known rules, which may be broken only in very exceptional cases—for instance, if a son behaves so that the father punishes him by withholding what would otherwise be his due (even then, the son is expected to be reinstated in due course as the reward of submission). The father has free scope only in arranging for his sons to help each other with loans. Here his legal right of dictating may be rendered invalid in practice by the play of personalities within the homestead.

If the father, the natural head of the family, dies too early to complete his task of allocating the bridewealth among its members, the responsibility for enforcing the known rules passes to his brothers or other related elders, until the eldest son is old enough to take it over.

The father's discretionary right of enforcing loans between his sons, however, is evidently an attribute of his kinship status, for it does not pass on to anyone else. Whoever takes his place after his death applies only the known law. The Gusii law of inheritance—which deals mainly with cattle, the chief form of heritable wealth—therefore consists of little more than these same rules of allotment of bridewealth among the family, in the rigid form into which they crystallize upon the father's death.

From the nature of the conception of *egesaku*—the lineage that can be founded only by paying bridewealth for a wife—arises the chief sanction for the father's just allotment of bridewealth between the various male members of his family (including himself). The temptation to engross an undue proportion for himself or for one favourite son is not so strong as it might appear because the conception of *egesaku* extends to all those generations claiming legitimate descent from the founder. A man's interest in his sons' marriages is scarcely less direct than that of the sons themselves, since in raising their own *ebisaku* they will also be increasing that of their father's, whereas if none of them can raise an *egesaku*, the father's likewise will soon die out. Hence it rests with the father to see that his own 'name is not lost' by securing to as many sons as possible the cattle without which no *egesaku* can be carried on. Moreover, should he fail to do so, he and his may suffer under the vengeance of the spirits of any sons who happened to die unmarried through his fault.[3]

It is a corollary of the importance attached to *egesaku* that the Gusii believe that 'cattle should not die for nothing'. The precious asset which alone can secure the lawful continuation and increase of the lineage ought not to be left idle, particularly since it is felt that a herd is more likely to die out than to multiply with the passage of years—a feeling that still persists to-day in spite of the decrease of risks from epidemics and raids.

Hence if the person rightfully entitled to certain bridewealth cattle is not in a position to use them (e.g. by reason of youth or of absence) the animals should not be kept waiting for him but should be 'borrowed' meanwhile by another member of the family. In considering the following rules of priority, particular care must be taken to distinguish between the ultimate right to bridewealth on the one hand, and the temporary right of user on the other. The right to 'borrow' bridewealth is itself a legal right, governed by its own set of legal rules; it is in fact almost as firm a right as the ultimate right; but it can never extinguish the latter. All Gusii are quite clear in their minds about the difference between 'borrowing' bridewealth and using it in one's own ultimate right, even though they may not always make the distinction explicit when discussing bridewealth law or cases.

1. *The rules of priority.* (a) *Priority of bachelors.* A bachelor's demand for cattle to marry his first wife takes precedence over a married man's demand for cattle for a junior wife. This is of course an expression of the principle of securing to every man his own *egesaku.*

(b) *Seniority.* Both sons and daughters should marry in order of age. Unless there are exceptional circumstances, e.g. chronic illness, a man is never entitled to marry before his elder full-brother. Only to a lesser extent is he debarred also from marrying before his elder half-brother: this restriction, being bound to conflict with the principle next to be stated—the independence of 'houses'—can be upheld only through the making of loans.

The marrying of daughters as well as sons in order of birth means that the bridewealth received for the eldest daughter is well known to be reserved for the eldest son, that of the second daughter for the second son, and so on. Where the father exercises his privilege of marrying with the eldest daughter's bridewealth, this will of course mean that the eldest son has to use the second daughter's, and so on. The son for whom a particular daughter's bridewealth is reserved is acknowledged to have a special interest in the marriage of that daughter; he may be asked to give his consent in case she wishes to divorce her husband, and it is he who will later have to meet her son's claim for an *emesuto* heifer.

(c) *Inalienability of bridewealth from the 'house': independence of 'houses'.* In no circumstances can bridewealth animals be permanently alienated from the 'house' which produced them. A 'house' in this context means the group consisting of one wife together with her sons and daughters. To it belongs of right all the bridewealth received for those daughters, as well as any cattle added through the labour of the mother and unmarried daughters. Any transfer of cattle or goats from one house to another is in the nature of a repayable loan. The claim to repayment can never die out, so long as there exists an actual or potential male representative or heir in the creditor house. 'A bridewealth debt is a piece of dried meat (*ekemoro*), say Gusii: it keeps for any length of time and never goes bad.' The claim can lapse only if the creditor house becomes extinct; i.e. if no sons of that wife are alive, nor any descendants of theirs in the direct male line. Even then it may be recovered if a male heir is born to the widow of any male member of the house, no matter how many years have elapsed. When a house becomes extinct its claims and its obligations are transferred to the house which inherits from it under the recognized rules of the law of inheritance.

The principle that bridewealth cannot be alienated from the house results in the independence of houses as property-holding units. In the polygynous family assets and liabilities cannot be simply pooled; a deficit of bridewealth in one house cannot be made good by a surplus in another, except through the expedient of a loan. Hence, if the loan is impracticable (see below No. 5) it may not be possible to follow out the principle of seniority, according to which it is preferable for sons to marry in order of age regardless of the house to which they belong.

Furthermore, it should always be remembered that debtors and creditors, where bridewealth loans are concerned, are not individuals but houses. The individual borrower or lender will naturally be the person expected to act when the debt comes to be settled, but his death or absence makes no difference to the indebtedness.

(d) *Linking of houses.* The successive pairs of houses 'belong together'—the first with the second, the third with the fourth, and so on—in a way which gives each a preferential right for assistance from its partner, and makes it the heir in case the other becomes extinct. For instance, if there are sons in both the first and the third houses who are in need of a bridewealth loan, and if the second houses is able to lend, the loan must be made to the first house (which is linked with the lending second house) and not to the third. If there is an uneven number of houses the last three are considered to be linked together, but the middle one of the three ought to act as intermediary in any bridewealth transaction between the other two.

(e) *Enforcement of loans: the father's powers.* The temporary transfer of bridewealth from one house to another by way of loan is made at the instance of the father, and is theoretically enforceable by him so long as it does not conflict with known principles such as the linkage of houses. Here, however, the legal theory—which would allow nobody to contest the father's right—is more stringent than actual Gusii practice. It is by no means certain that a husband will actually be able to force one house to lend to another if the wife in question resists, although her resistance might be severely condemned by general opinion.

(f) *Respective claims of the father and his sons.* The father is theoretically entitled to use the bridewealth of the eldest daughter of each or any house in order to obtain a new wife for himself. He is not allowed to use in this way the bridewealth of more than one daughter in any one house; nor does the right apply in the case of a girl who is the only daughter of her house, unless she has no full-brothers.

In accordance with the principle that bridewealth cannot be permanently alienated from the house which produced it, the remarriage of a father with his daughter's bridewealth establishes a debt. The house of the new wife is indebted to the house by which her bridewealth was provided (or, if that becomes extinct, to the house next in order of succession). In practical terms this may mean that a son of the lending-house marries with bridewealth received for his young half-sister; but if this simple solution does not fit the circumstances, the claim will persist into the second or third generation and may give rise to prolonged litigation.

The exercise of this right of the father's is deemed to be subject to consideration of equity. If the father's own wife is no longer capable of bearing children he 'ought to' re-marry, even if this means keeping a son waiting. Perhaps the commonest type of Gusii polygynous family comprises two wives one of whom is a whole generation older than the other. If the father is a widower, especially a comparatively young one, he has a strong prior claim, and may even be considered justified in using for re-marriage the bridewealth of a younger daughter, to which he is not strictly entitled. In other cases the claim of a still unmarried son is likely to be held superior to that of the father. If surplus bridewealth became available after all sons were married, the question of priority between father and sons would depend on their relative ages, the number of times each had already married, and similar personal considerations.

(g) *Special rules applying to 'cattle of saving'.* Cattle acquired in other ways than through the marriage of a female member of the family—acquired, for instance, by means of purchase, exchange or raiding—fall into a special category, that of *chiombe chia'nibo*, cattle of *enibo* or 'saving', and their disposal is governed by rules different from those applied to *chiombe chia' basubati*, cattle of girls or daughters.

(i) If the father acquires cattle or goats through his own personal effort, e.g. if he grew in his own private garden (*emonga*) the grain which was subsequently exchanged for these animals, he is free to dispose of them as he will. If he marries with them, or gives them to any son for marriage no debt is established.

It is however considered that the children of a man's youngest wife are those best entitled to be helped out by the father with gifts of cattle of saving; for 'the elder sons married and had wives to help them, while the younger ones were still children with their mother'. Hence there is a presumption that such personal cattle of the father should be reserved for his youngest wife's children; and if he gives them to members of any other house, the recipients may later be faced with a claim for repayment on behalf of the youngest house. The nature of this 'debt' seems to be on the very borderline between a legal right and an ethical claim.

The father may, and often does, allot some or all of his own cattle of saving to the house of a certain wife. By letting it be known that he wishes them to belong to that wife, he is said to have 'tied the cattle for so-and-so' (*ogosibera chiombe omokungu*, to tie cattle for a woman). Once this is done, the animals are attached to that house as firmly as those produced through its daughters' marriages, and cannot be shifted from it without establishing a debt.

(ii) If a wife acquires cattle or goats through her own effort—e.g. by exchanging grain grown by herself—these animals belong to her house and cannot be shifted without establishing a debt.

If, as often happens, cattle of saving are acquired through a joint effort—e.g. of husband and wife, or of two co-wives—an attempt is made to apportion them according to the extent of the contribution estimated to have been made by each partner; for instance the first heifer calf of a cow so acquired may be allotted to the house of the wife who produced less of the purchasing grain, the cow itself remaining with the other.

(iii) Cattle of daughters cannot be (as it were) released to become personal cattle of the father. There is however one beast given in bridewealth which is deemed to belong to the father personally. This is the 'bull of apron' given together with the herd of bridewealth cows, which is expressly allotted to the father for the making of a new hide-apron.

Cattle of saving become subject to all the restrictions governing cattle of daughters as soon as they have been once used for marriage or have been 'tied' to a house.

2. *Restrictions on the exercise of bridewealth rights.* The above principles indicate in which order male members of a family group have the right to marry with cattle obtained through marriage of its female members. There are however certain restrictions on the exercise of this right. Two have already been indicated: the obligation of lending in cases where the ultimate right cannot be exercised immediately, and the obligation of the father to consider the equitable claims of his sons before re-marrying with bridewealth of his eldest daughter. Apart from these, the elders regard it as a general principle that the elder brothers should try to exercise their rights in such a way as to protect the interests of the younger also.

If it appears that the incoming bridewealth will not be enough to go round, and that the younger members of the house or the family run the risk of being left portionless, the cattle which are to be used by the elder ones should be kept at home until they have increased sufficiently to provide the nucleus of bridewealth for the younger brothers. The right of the eldest sons to the first available bridewealth is in no way impaired, but they are expected to delay its exercise in the interests of the family as a whole. The fact that this principle is rapidly becoming obsolescent, besides diminishing the marriage prospects of the younger sons, has meant that in case of divorce the return of the identical beasts that had been handed over is becoming increasingly difficult to enforce. It has thus dealt a blow to the method which was formerly recognized as the most correct one for return of bridewealth.

A somewhat different situation is which an elder brother may be expected to waive his right of prior marriage is when the younger brother, having already acquired a 'chooser', is threatened with the loss of her and all her children unless they can be legitimized forthwith. It may be felt that the immediate gain to the family as a whole outweighs the desirability of strict observance of the rule of seniority.

Remaining Aspects of Assembly and Distribution

I. *Assembly.* Apart from the bridewealth of his sisters or daughters allotted to him under the fixed rules just described, a Gusii has few sources for assembling his marriage cattle. No person besides his own father[4] is obliged to help him.

The only bridewealth animal which a man is likely to receive from outside the immediate family circle is the heifer of *emesuto*, which an eldest son obtains directly from his maternal kin. The custom of giving *emesuto* is not specifically connected with bridewealth assembly. The heifer may be claimed and given at any time during the life of the claimant, either before or after marriage. Besides, it is not a kinship due owed by the maternal uncle to his sister's sons as such but a reciprocal due from the man who had the benefit of the mother's bridewealth. It will therefore be dealt with more fully where it belongs, under the heading of a distribution.

'Cattle of saving' produced by a young man's own effort are, naturally, considered as his own to marry with. This category has increased enormously in importance since the days when a bachelor's principal hope of acquiring cattle for himself lay in raiding. The Gusii themselves are aware of a difference that European rule has brought about in the relative 'earning capacity' of the sexes. They say that formerly it was daughters who produced cattle, but now sons too acquire them since money can be earned in employment. Gusii law has not been specifically adapted to this change. A younger brother who earns his own cattle may marry before his elder brother, in contravention of the traditional rule of seniority; or he may be forced to wait by a father who insists on the old forms being preserved. It is mainly a matter of personal relations between the parties.

II. *Distribution.* We have described the rules that govern the allotment of a woman's bridewealth as between her brothers or other members of the receiving family. We now have to deal with the remaining aspects of the distribution. Although it was the main part of a bridewealth herd which normally remained to be handed on intact to the rightful user—at any rate before Europeans came, when there was less likelihood of dissipation by sale or slaughter—a few animals would have to be set aside from the herd or its offspring in order to meet customary obligations.

The more complex features of the once customary distribution are now forgotten by all but the most conservative elders. What remains in fullest force is the principle that at least one animal at some time will have to be returned to the donor's group. This obligation, however, is usually discharged out of the increase of the bridewealth, not from the original herd itself. It usually takes the form of payment of the *emesuto* heifer, which the Gusii people regard as one of their most distinctive customs, and which is still as vigorously alive as the giving of bridewealth itself.

The distribution can be discussed under three headings:

1. Portion of bridewealth to be kept 'at home', i.e. in the house of the bride's mother.
2. Portion of bridewealth or its increase to be returned to donor's group.
3. Portion to be distributed among paternal and maternal kin of bride.

1. *Portion of bridewealth to be kept 'at home'*. (a) *Cow of seeing the daughter.* Conservative elders agree that when a daughter marries, one of her bridewealth cows ought to be kept at home in her mother's house, separated from the rest of the herd which may be immediately handed on in marriage by a male member of the family. This cow is known by various names, of which the commonest are 'cow of seeing the daughter', 'of greeting the daughter', or 'of feeding the daughter'. When the beast dies one of its heifers should be kept in its place. The purposes served are twofold:

(i) To meet such further obligations as may arise in connection with the daughter's marriage. Chief of these will be the claim for a heifer of *emesuto* of of *egesango*, which should be met out of the progeny of this cow. Further, if the woman dies and a claim arises for a 'cow of shaving' (*eng'ombe ye ritati*) or of 'feeding the children' (*eng'ombe y'okogonkia abana*), this cow can be used to meet the obligation. Another demand that may arise, and that cannot be refused, is a request by the daughter for milk to help her children. She may take away as much as she likes from her 'cow of feeding the daughter', either for food or to make butter for ceremonial and everyday anointing; and when the mother visits her she should carry a gift of milk produced by this cow. 'The daughter will complain if none of her cows is left with mother. She will ask: "Who is going to help with milk for my children?" She likes to see the cow there when she visits her mother. It makes her proud to say: "That is *my* cow".'

(ii) '*Nursing up*' (*Okogoyerera*). The retention of one cow can also serve the quite distinct purpose of providing bridewealth for younger sons of the family. If several daughters have married and one cow is kept at home for each, the increase may ultimately amount to quite a respectable bridewealth herd for a younger brother.

The custom of retaining a cow 'at home' is by no means obsolete, but is definitely losing ground. It seems never to have been considered as an obligation of overriding importance. That is to say, if a brother very urgently needed the one cow for his marriage it would always be conceded to him. In that case he might find himself the person liable to meet the woman's demands for milk.

(iii) *Goat or cow of heat.* The goat or heifer 'of heat' may be claimed by the mother out of her daughter's bridewealth and kept behind by her when her son uses the rest of the bridewealth for his marriage.

Alternatively she can make the claim at the time of *enyangi*. She may then either claim for herself the '*enyangi* cow' which is given as a last instalment of the bridewealth or, if this is not agreed, demand an extra heifer or bullock or goat from the bridegroom himself. Thus the custom is vague where details are concerned; like that of marriage gifts in general, it lays down definitely who has to be the recipient, but leaves the exact form to be decided according to circumstances.

2. *Return of animal to donor's group.* (a) *Heifer of emesuto.* In pre-contact days the heifer of *emesuto* was claimed by the woman herself from the brother or other relative who had married with her bridewealth. 'She went and asked her brother for a heifer that one of the cows had borne, and he gave it to her because he loved her. In those days the sister was respected and feared by her brother.' If the heifer was persistently withheld, the woman could go and tie her belt round the animal of her choice: it would then be taboo (*omogiro*) for the brother to touch it for any other purpose.

In historical times the custom has changed its form a little, in that the heifer is now claimed by the woman's eldest son and not by herself. The present-day Gusii will define *emesuto* as 'the heifer we get from our *mame* (maternal uncle)'. The *emesuto* heifer can be claimed at any time. In practice it is often demanded when the eldest son is beginning to assemble cattle for his own marriage. It must be claimed from the man (if he is alive) who actually married with the mother's bridewealth, so that if her cattle were used by her own father, the claim for the *emesuto* animal will be made against him—the grandfather, not the uncle, of the claimant. In any case, the claim lies against the house which the grandfather or maternal uncle in question founded by means of the claimant's mother's bridewealth; it can be pressed against members of this house even if the original debtor is dead.

In the highland districts a heifer of *emesuto* can be claimed by a woman's stepson if she has no sons of her own, i.e. by a son of the house which is linked with hers. In the lowland, it will nowadays be refused to any but the real son of the woman herself.

The son who received the *emesuto* heifer has to give its first heifer-calf to his next younger brother. This brother in turn should give the female progeny of his heifer to his own younger brother, and so until every brother in the house has received a heifer. Claims for replacement of an *emesuto* heifer which dies without progeny are not recognized nowadays, 'unless the parties are on good terms and like to arrange it between them'.

According to tradition the *emesuto* animal has to be a physical descendant of one of the actual bridewealth cows paid for the mother; but practice is now laxer in this respect, since the 'cow of feeding the daughter' is not always kept at home as security for it.

The conception of *emesuto* is clearly reciprocal: the mother's brother does not owe a heifer to his *omoigwa* (sister's son) simply as *omoigwa*, but because he—the uncle—benefited by the mother's bridewealth. The relationship is outwardly symbolized during the *enyangi* ceremony. On the solemn second night the officiating priest puts down eight sticks in a certain corner of the bride's mother's hut, of which six are taken away next morning by the married couple when they set out for home; the other two which remain behind are known as *emesuto*, and the elders explain their meaning as a symbolic pledge left with the wife's parents to remind them that 'one day somebody must come back to claim the heifer of *emesuto*'.[5]

(b) *Heifer of helping* (*egesango*). A simple form of discharging the same obligation was the payment of the 'heifer of helping' (*egesango*, cf. *ogosanga*, to help). The first heifer-calf produced by the bridewealth cattle after the transfer could be immediately reclaimed by the bride and brought back to her husband.

This custom may well be associated (as Gusii elders themselves think) with the period of extreme cattle shortage caused by the great plague of the 1890's when the whole bridewealth might consist of one cow. Though now practically obsolete, it still crops up in litigation from time to time as the basis of some inherited claim. It has been almost completely discarded in favour of payment of *emesuto*. In the days of the cattle shortage the claimant was supposed to have the right of choice between receiving the heifer of *egesango* at once or that of *emesuto* at a later date—the two being mutually exclusive—but later the bride's father recovered the right to insist that his son-in-law wait for the *emesuto*.

(c) *Other alternatives to emesuto heifer*. In certain cases the return of bridewealth made in case of a woman's death will consist of a 'cow of shaving' (*eng'ombe ye ritati*) and/or a 'cow of feeding the children' (*eng'ombe y'okogonkia abana*). Some elders say that *emesuto* cannot necessarily be claimed, if one of these other animals had been returned to the widower. For instance, (they say) if a widower with four children recovered his cow of feeding the children the eldest son would have no further claim for an *emesuto* heifer; if more then four children survived, not a cow but a heifer would be due which the eldest son would be able to claim as his heifer of *emesuto* later. These are not cut-and-dried rules that can be applied without variation; they are rather illustrations of the underlying principles as conceived by the Gusii—the principle that the recipient of a woman's bridewealth owes a sort of return: this is not bound to take place in any single way or at any single time, but must be of such a kind that her house receives the benefit.

(d) *Cow of chewing millet*. The legal obligation is fully discharged by returning out of the increase of the bridewealth either the *emesuto* heifer or the 'heifer of helping', or (in certain cases) by returning the 'cow of feeding the children'. The amount returned, however, might be increased by the optional gift of a 'cow of chewing millet' (*eng'ombe y'ogotakuna obori*). When the bride first visited her parents after the *enyangi* ceremony they might give her this cow to take home to her husband. 'After this she is permitted to chew millet in her husband's presence. A wife who has not brought the cow could not do this—it would be mocking her husband.' This custom, which is now obsolete, seems to have aimed at raising the status of the young wife in her husband's household by a display of the parents' generosity. It was rather a freewill gift than an obligation in law. Its sanctions were not legal but social, and no replacement could be enforced if the animal died.

(e) *Goat of the sister*. We have mentioned, in connection with customary gifts, that at the time of *enyangi* the parents of the bride may be expected to send one of the bridewealth goats to that sister of the bridegroom who provided the animals he has now paid them for their daughter. This is not now considered as a binding obligation unless the sister attends the *enyangi* and puts forward her claim in person. It may be included here in connection with bridewealth returned to the husband's group, although the sister in question will have ceased to belong to that group because of her marriage to a member of another clan.

3. *Distribution among paternal and maternal kin*. (a) *Paternal kin: cow of paternal uncle*. The only known custom involving distribution among the bride's paternal kin has now entirely died out, and can be reconstructed only from the reminiscences of old men. It consisted in a reciprocal exchange: a father would give one cow from his daughter's bridewealth to his brother, on the understanding that this brother undertook to return one from the bridewealth of his own daughter. It would be rash to speculate at this stage about the functions of this dimly-remembered practice, but possibly it was no more than a manifestation of normal brotherly helpfulness, the loan of a cow to one's needy brother against a mortgage on the latter's daughter's bridewealth.

(b) *Maternal kin: cow of honey*. Better remembered is the process by which a maternal uncle of the bride may secure one cow out of her bridewealth by following out an elaborate series of exchanges and counter-gifts. The beast thus obtained is called 'cow of honey' (*eng'ombe y'oboke*), the usual interpretation being that 'the man gets this cow because of the love between him and his sister, which is sweet like honey'. Whether or not this is good etymology, what is certainly true is that the giving of the 'cow of honey' does not nowadays take place unless the parties are on friendly terms: it is not a universal legal obligation.

The mother's brother in question is the one who married with the bridewealth of the bride's mother. His right to a 'honey cow' is explained by Gusii elders as being linked in some way with his obligation to provide a heifer of *emesuto* for the son of the same sister. The cow of honey, like the *emesuto* heifer, can only be demanded once.

The bride herself takes the initiative in the complex procedure by going to her mother's brother's place on the day before the first night of *enyangi* and spending the night there. She brings him a present of two pots of beer; when she goes home next morning she takes with her his return gift of three or five pots of beer, which are to be used that same evening at the *egetaorio* celebration. In the evening the mother's brother follows her and demands first of all a goat, the 'goat of honey'. Next day, the solemn day of *echorwa*, he asks his sister (the bride's mother) for the cow of honey itself. This is met by a counter-demand for a bull. He must then go home and fetch a bull; if it is not a big one he will have to provide in addition a 'goat for the neck-muscle' (*embori y' esuti*). Only after slaughtering the bull—and the goat if required—at the home of the bride is the mother's brother entitled to his cow: he can enforce his right if necessary by placing his hand on the sacrificial *enyangi* goat and thus holding up the proceedings until his demand is met.

This is not the end of the transaction. After receiving the cow the mother's brother has to send to his sister the 'goat of belt' (*embori y' orokini*)[6] which she in turn has to pass on to the bride. 'When the bride receives the goat she knows that her mother's brother has had his cow of honey. If she does not get it the bridegroom will complain, and even refuse her food, because her mother's brother ought to acknowledge the cow he received out of the bridewealth.'

Thus the maternal uncle will have given three or five pots of beer, one or two goats and one bull, and he will have received two pots of beer, one goat and one cow. According to the Gusii scale of values he comes out of it with a slight but definite profit.

The custom is now almost obsolete, but is clearly remembered by most elders. Emphasis lies on the fact that the whole transaction depends on friendly relations. If bridewealth had to be returned because of divorce, the wife's father could reclaim the cow from her mother's brother only by friendly persuasion. The mother's brother on his part could not demand replacement as of right if the cow died without progeny.

(c) *Goat of the grandmother*. The maternal grandmother of the bride (or the grandmother' son) may also receive from the bridegroom one goat at the time of *enyangi*. This gift, which is not strictly part of the distribution of the bridewealth, has already been dealt with in connection with the customary marriage gifts.

The Bridewealth Principle in Family Law

1. *Bridewealth and man's status*. The man on whose behalf bridewealth has been paid for a woman acquires rights connected with her capacities for child-bearing and for working: but whereas the right to her labour may be lost without compensation (e.g. if she deserts) the right to her children is enduring and incontrovertible. As has already been indicated, bridewealth payment serves to give the husband a permanent status as father of the woman's children,—that is, unless the bridewealth is returned to him or his heirs. It does not matter if the woman is living with another man, either during the husband's lifetime or after his death. The living together of man and wife, and their sharing of the daily routine of the homestead, is regarded as a desirable and natural consequence of marriage, but the bridewealth system as such does nothing to secure it. It is the subsequent *enyangi* ceremony—not the bridewealth mechanism—that provides the specific overt sanctions against desertion or adultery on the wife's part. What the bridewealth mechanism as such is mainly designed to protect is not exclusive right to that woman's society nor even to her sexual enjoyment, but the exclusive right over her offspring.

In short we may say that bridewealth serves primarily to make men fathers—*enyangi* makes them husbands. The primary function of bridewealth payment is to secure a woman's house for a man's *egesaku*. We have now to consider what this implies in practical terms.

(a) *Children over whom rights can be claimed*. The first time a woman is married for bridewealth, any children she may already have are thereby legitimized and belong to the husband's *egesaku*. Subsequently all her children by whomever begotten belong to that *egesaku* until such time as he or his heirs may recover bridewealth by way of divorce. As mentioned before, traditional and modern practice differ regarding the legal right to children in case of divorce. Nowadays a father may retain his children even after divorcing their mother, on condition that some cows are offset from the return of bridewealth.

Under the old divorce law it was possible for children to have at successive times more than one jural father and impossible for a woman to have legitimate children by more than one man at a time. This is reversed under the present law, which makes it practically impossible for children to change their legal filiation, but allows a woman to have legitimate children in two places at one time. If *A*'s wife goes to live with *B*, *A* will normally recover his bridewealth at the same time as *B* pays new bridewealth; if the condition of offsetting has been observed, *A* will then have the right to all children born before this transaction, and *B* to those born after it. There is not usually any interregnum, because both *A* and his father-in-law are interested in postponing the return of *A*'s bridewealth until *B* is absolutely ready to pay (*A* because he wants to prolong his paternal rights, and the father-in-law because he does not want to be left without cattle). If by any chance there is such an interregnum the children born during it are on the same footing as those born to an unmarried girl: they can be legitimized by whoever pays bridewealth for her.

A difficulty might seem to arise in the case of children conceived during one marriage and born during another. This is obviated by Gusii observance of the convention that no bridewealth transactions can be conducted in connection with a woman who is pregnant. Gusii say that, as she is 'in danger', her fate must be known for certain before cattle can be moved on her account. Thus if a woman conceives a child by her husband *A* and then leaves him for *B*, the birth of the child has to be awaited before either *A* can recover cattle or *B* pay cattle. 'The woman has your spear, and the spear may kill her.'

It will be convenient to summarize the status of children under the terms used by the Gusii themselves:

(i) *The 'born child'* (*omobiare*, cf. *okobiara*, to give birth): this describes a child born in the ordinary way at the homestead of the husband after the payment of bridewealth. The category includes the great majority of legitimate children, but also those conceived in adultery, whose legal status in no way differs from that of the former.

(ii) *The 'adopted child'* (*omogore*) artificially acquired for the house of an otherwise sonless or childless mother. Such children are practically always of alien origin, being kidnapped, captured or bought from non-Gusii neighbours, or at most from another Gusii tribe. This enables them to be completely absorbed into the adoptive family since there are no competing ties of descent to bind them mystically to a different lineage. Hence the adopted child is legally and ritually on exactly the same footing as a 'born' child of the mother, though personal discrimination is always a latent possibility and tends to flare up at times of disagreement.

(iii) *'Belly (i.e. pregnancy) of the house'* (*enda ye nyomba*): this refers to children borne by an unmarried girl who is still at home in her mother's house. When a subsequent bridewealth payment has legitimized them their origin should gradually be forgotten, and they can grow up with 'father' and mother on exactly the same footing as the real 'born children'.

(iv) *'Swallowed thing'* (*ekemerwa*) *or 'brought thing'* (*ekerentane*). This refers to a child which has been brought into the home by its mother but is still legally the child of another man. The unfortunate 'swallowed' child is often reminded in moments of friction that 'you don't belong to us'. As soon as it is old enough to act independently of its mother, it will probably run back to the house of its 'proper' father where it has full legal and ritual status. To taunt anyone with the epithet *ekemerwa* or *ekerentane* is considered a fairly serious insult.

(v) *'Lineage of a girl'* (*egesaku kia omoiseke*). There is a small residue of children for whom no legal paternity is ever established outside the mother's own family group; e.g. those born to a girl who died before anybody could marry her. These go by default (as it were) to the *egesaku* of the mother's father, but are distinguished from the rest of the lineage by the name 'lineage of a girl'. No slur seems to attach to *egesaku kia omoiseke* of the second generation and onwards. In fact it appears that such links are sometimes fabricated in order to justify genealogically the presence of a strange group among a host lineage. The 'lineage of a girl' must of course, be distinguished from the ordinary 'sister's child' (*omoigwa*) who has his allegiance elsewhere.

(b) *Specific rights of the legal father.* In traditional times the first right of a father was the custody of his legitimate children. As a rule it was considered better not to separate an infant from its mother before the age of weaning (up to two years), but this scruple would not interfere with the pressing of the father's claims if they were likely to be endangered by it. In modern times both the Administration and the Missions have preferred on humanitarian grounds to leave custody in case of divorce with the mother, without necessarily affecting the ultimate legal rights of the father. This humaner compromise would scarcely have been practicable in days when the boundaries of the clan were also those of regular legal procedure.

Even to-day, the Tribunal elders of the old school like to use the new resources of the Administration in support of the father's claim to custody. If a woman has left her husband and no bridewealth has been recovered, they may order that every child she afterwards bears must be seized by askaris and brought home to its jural father. Elders of more modern outlook will take into account the character of the father, especially his ability to have the children properly looked after, before awarding the custody to him.

One of the main advantages of custody from the father's point of view is that it gives him a pull on the mother too, by drawing her back to the place where her children live. If the father is particularly 'cruel' she may stay away until her eldest son is old enough to defend her when necessary; in such cases she usually returns not to her former hut but to another which her son will build for her next to his own and at a little distance from the father's cattle pen.

Apart from its use in drawing back the mother, this right of custody was formerly the only effective guarantee of the father's other rights over his children. Chief among these is still right to the bridewealth received for daughters, involving a corresponding obligation to provide bridewealth for the sons. A related right is that of receiving compensation if any of the children are killed. Apart from this the legal father is entitled to all the natural advantages of being head of an *egesaku.* Its members should work with him, fight with him, promote the fame of his lineage by their numbers and good conduct, tend him in sickness, bury him when he dies, and thereafter make the proper sacrifices to his spirit. Besides, to the Gusii, a numerous *egesaku* is after all an end in itself; it is at a natural political advantage, and at the same time holds possibilities of immortalizing its founder by developing into a structural lineage group such as a clan.

(c) *Attitude to jural and physical children.* Even young and educated men insist that legal paternity means more to them than physical paternity. A man may be on excellent terms with his own children by another man's widow or wife, but if any choice has to be made he is far more likely to side with his own legal children even if they are not physically his.

The 'swallowed child' can be fairly sure his jural father will receive him as kindly as or more kindly than his physical father, in spite of the fact that he may have spent his whole life with the latter and never set eyes on the former. A typical Gusii comment is: 'Why should I set store by my (physical) son? After all, he has his own father' (i.e. his jural father). The difference of attitude is sometimes strikingly illustrated in a case where a widow has lived for years with a 'bachelor', to all intents and purposes like his wife, bearing all her children by him, working for him and sharing his life; as soon as he can get a wife of his own who bears him children that are legally his, the children of the widow become relatively uninteresting to him. A Gusii wants *egesaku,* not merely offspring.

(d) *Posthumous rights of the bridewealth donor*

(i) *The position of the 'warmer of the house'* (*omosoi nyomba*). When a husband dies his widow has the possibility of 'divorcing' him, i.e. returning to her own family and persuading them to pay back bridewealth to the dead man's heirs. She could then be remarried to anyone outside her late husband's clan, on payment of bridewealth in the regular way.

In practice it is very rare for any but a young childless widow to divorce her dead husband. By far the greater number of widows themselves elect—or are (sometimes rather forcibly) persuaded—to stay where they are, so as to be with their children and carry on their duties as a member of the dead husband's lineage. Indeed, as we shall see, widowhood often marks a woman's entry into the enjoyment of more freedom and influence than she has ever known before.

If she stays, a widow still capable of bearing children is obliged to take an *omosoi nyomba*, 'warmer of the house'; that is, a 'husband' who will continue to exploit her childbearing potentialities for the benefit of his dead forerunner. It has already been mentioned how a sexually impotent husband can select a 'warmer' to raise children for his wife. The position of the man who takes over a widow is exactly the same. The woman is not his wife, the children are not his children, the property of the 'house' is not under his control; he acts solely in the interests of the (dead) legal husband. The status of the 'warmer of the house' throws particularly clear light on the fact that the fundamental meaning of the bridewealth transaction is to secure the permanent right to the woman's children.

The man in question may be selected by the widow herself, who usually indicates her choice by beginning to send him cooked food as soon as she is ritually cleansed after the husband's death. (This means an interval of about six months to a year, terminated by the ceremony of 'turning over the things'.) It is open to a man to decline such an invitation if he wishes. The man selected must be somebody within the permitted kinship grades; i.e. he must be a real or classificatory[7] 'brother' of the husband (and therefore of the widow) not a real or classificatory 'son' or 'father'; he must not be the youngest full-brother if the dead husband was the eldest, nor vice versa, because he would then be 'like a son' or 'like a father'. Within these limits the choice is wide. For preference a widow should select a man descended from the same father or grandfather as her dead husband, but if she has strong views she is at liberty to pass over all the close relatives and choose any other man of the clan. She could even choose someone of a different clan altogether, but in that case the relatives would insist on his coming to live among them where they can keep an eye on him. Clearly, the point is not so much to choose a man related by real or supposed ties of kinship, but to choose one whose residence within the politically effective group will prevent his usurping any rights that belong to the husband's heirs.

The 'warmer of the house', if he is already married, will be expected to do no more than visit the widow from time to time at her late husband's home, and to help her with the 'man's work' such as building and bush clearing. But if the widow has no grown children and is afraid of living alone she is justified in moving over to live at his homestead; alternatively, if he is a bachelor and wants home comforts, he can move over to her place. It is in these cases, where the couple to all appearances live together as husband and wife, that the gap between legal and social realities is most marked. Old men warn their juniors of the fallacy of finding happiness with a widow. The bachelor 'warmer' of a widow's house may enjoy her society, live on her grain and her cattle, and watch his offspring by her growing up in the joint home; but in the end he will have to hand over everything to her dead husband's heirs, and the very sons whom she bore by him can strip him of everything.

The man who occupies such a position may reasonably expect that the widow will lend him cattle of her house for purposes of his own marriage, but he has no redress if she refuses, and in any case he cannot escape repayment to her sons. His chief hope lies in acquiring 'cattle of saving' (*chiombe chia'nibo*) with her help. He can then marry without establishing any debt; or if he lends them to the widow's sons, he or his heirs can claim them back later (which would not have been the case had the lender been the jural father).

Naturally, if the deceased has left no sons and the 'warmer of the house' happens to be the nearest heir (e.g. full-brother), his begetting sons by the widow will amount to deliberately cutting himself out of the inheritance. But the heir has no choice in the matter. The widow can on no account be denied the chance to raise sons for the deceased: if the heir himself does not help her, somebody else will. The fundamental right of the deceased to raise his posthumous *egesaku* is something that no Gusii would dare to call in question.

(ii) *The fictitious second-generation egesaku.* The process of founding an *egesaku* entails more than the right to all children begotten by the founder's widow. Even a childless man whose widows are all past childbearing can eventually achieve the satisfaction of a posthumous *egesaku* provided that the essential bridewealth is available.

A sonless widow can acquire by payment of bridewealth a marriageable girl whom she brings home with her. A suitable young man—often an impoverished nephew—is then chosen to live with the girl as husband. The couple may indeed be made husband and wife by the solemnization of *enyangi* but the children of the union are nevertheless members of the *egesaku* of the widow—i.e. of the deceased: they do not belong to the *egesaku* of their physical father. Such children are jural grandchildren of the deceased, legitimized by the bridewealth which 'he' (i.e. his widow) provided to bring their mother into the family. The girl herself has the status of a wife of some imagined son of the widow. If her young 'husband' dies then she ranks as any other widow of the family and if she herself dies or deserts, it is the old woman who will reclaim the bridewealth on behalf of the house.[8]

2. *Bridewealth and woman's status.* The effect of bridewealth payment on a woman's status is that it shifts the emphasis from her membership of a house in her father's *egesaku*, to her new position as foundress of a house in her husband's *egesaku.* But though from this time onwards all her children will belong unequivocally to the husband's *egesaku*, not until the *enyangi* ceremony is the woman herself ceremonially and finally cut off from her paternal *egesaku.* Until then her position within the husband's *egesaku* remains somewhat equivocal. We may parallel what has already been said of the man and say that bridewealth primarily makes women mothers whereas *enyangi* makes them wives.

The legal position of a woman for whom bridewealth has been paid is definable rather in terms of duties and restrictions than in terms of rights. She is indeed entitled to ask for divorce if persistently ill-treated or insulted but she has little personal liberty, no right of property, traditionally no claim against the husband for the custody of her own children (even if they are not physically his), and no power to restrain him from cruelty towards herself or from adultery.

Yet this does not give a true picture of the legal position of a Gusii wife and mother, still less of the social reality of her status. In herself she may be legally a 'minor', but in her capacity as head and focus of a house she holds a position of considerable importance. Just as the person of the husband unites the whole *egesaku* of which he is the head—including all the houses of his various wives—so does the person of each wife unite the house founded by her. The fundamental significance of the house in Gusii law, and the extent to which it functions as an independent unit, has already been indicated. It is the unit which acquires and holds property in cattle, which lends and inherits, which can never forfeit a claim or repudiate a debt. When the death of the husband snaps the personal bond and emphasizes the autonomy of the houses, the wife correspondingly finds her status enhanced; she now becomes representative and trustee for her house.

Every house is said to comprise or to possess its own 'live property', its *etugo* (cf. *ogotuga*, to feed or rear), that is, its wealth in terms of living creatures—human progeny, cattle, goats and other domestic creatures. Even while the husband is alive the property is loosely said to 'belong' to the wife. They are in some sense her children, her cattle, her goats, though of course the overriding right in all of them rests with the husband who has given bridewealth for the acquisition of the woman and everything she may produce. Even when the husband is alive, a wife may resist, in the interests of her house, attempts that he may make to 'lend' some of its property to another house. After the husband's death, the property (and in recent times the land) of each house is finally secured to it, and there is nobody with a right of forcing a transfer. The widow's control over the property of her house becomes at once more extensive and better defined. It approximates, in fact, to the rights formerly enjoyed by the husband. She cannot deny any son his proper share of bridewealth when he is ready to make use of it; but within these limits, and as long as she safeguards the interest of the direct heirs, she can do to some extent as she pleases, making or refusing loans to any man of the family. Often a widow with no warmer of the house and no grown son to help her will specially patronize some young man of the husband's near paternal kin who 'comes to work for her like a son'; she can lend him as many cattle as she likes, but (unless she has no sons and he is the next heir) cannot make them over to him for good.

It is significant of the woman's position as head of her house that neither the land nor the cattle of that house may be formally divided out between heirs while she is alive. Thus until a sonless widow dies the brothers of her husband who are going to inherit from him cannot make permanent boundaries between their fields; they will say 'all the land belongs to her, she only lends us portions to cultivate'. The same applies to cattle. If there are no sons and the dead man's property is to be divided between brothers or other heirs, no division can take place till the widow dies.

As trustee for her late husband's rights in her house, the widow has the first duty of seeing to the increase of his *egesaku*. It is up to her to choose—within certain limits—her own warmer of the house if she is still capable of bearing children; otherwise, and if she has no sons, it is she who takes the necessary steps to acquire fictitious 'grandchildren' for the deceased. Secondly, the widow is a sort of trustee over the property of her house, until such time as a son can take over her duties. Besides supervising the lending and borrowing of both cattle and land she may act as litigant in any cause affecting the interests of the house. If any of these functions are discharged by the warmer of the house or by someone of the kin of the deceased, he may be acting in the capacity of adviser and support to the widow but not, usually, as full legal representative of the deceased.

3. *Bridewealth and child's status.* We have seen how bridewealth payment determines legitimate filiation, i.e. the child's membership of its father's *egesaku* and its mother's house. It remains to be shown what this actually means, in concrete terms, for the status of the child.

In Gusii society, organized as it is into a hierarchy of patrilineal descent groups, legal filiation to the father constitutes perhaps the most important single determinant of social position. To begin with, it binds son to father by a network of legal and economic ties, it alone can confer the right to a marriage portion and to a share in the heritable patrimony, since neither of them can be claimed anywhere outside the rightful *egesaku*. Furthermore, it creates an inescapable mystical nexus that binds man to the spirits of his legal (not necessarily his physical) ancestors in the male line. Associated with this cardinal importance of the *egesaku* in the spirit cult is the fact that succession to most ritual or magical powers and offices passes in the same line.

Notes

1 At present (December 1947) ten or twelve goats are reckoned equal to one heifer.

2 More material on the bridewealth rate is included in a paper on 'Bridewealth Limitation among the Gusii' which I hope to publish (in *Two Studies in Applied Anthropology in Kenya*).

3 It is as an apology for failure to provide the marriage-portion that some elders explain the special rite observed at the funeral of a bachelor, that of throwing onto the grave a stick from the 'woman's side' of his bed, with the words, 'This is your wife'.

4 Or whoever stands in the father's place, e.g. the eldest brother if the father is dead.

5 The derivation of the word *emesuto* is unknown and is used only in this specific meaning of the sticks put down during *enyangi*.

6 Cf. the sister's use of her *orokini* to enforce her claim against the same brother for a heifer of *emesuto*.

7 The classificatory kinship terms are used throughout the exogamous clan: with few exceptions a wife follows the terminology used by her husband.

8 In rare cases, the procedure I have just outlined for old women is followed by an old man—a widower who feels himself past remarrying and raising children for himself.

S. M. Seymour: Native Law in South Africa*

The Dowry

1. *The origin, purpose and importance of dowry.* Although this view is based on speculation after a consideration of ancient law, it seems probable that the payment of dowry originated as a species of sale or exchange; in primitive patriarchal societies, the head of a family had the *jus vitae necisque* over his children, the power to sell them in bondage, or to give them in marriage.[1]

Native law discloses a considerable advance on those times, but much of the ancient *patria potestas* is retained by a kraalhead. The question whether the dowry contract was purely and simply a sale, or whether it was a payment in trust to ensure the proper treatment of the bride in her new home, was a subject of controversy among students of Native law.[1]

By intention of the Natives themselves, it is neither, although it may have some of the effects of the latter. Except for some coarse individuals, Natives repudiate the idea that the contract is a sale, which is a good reason for doubting the contrary opinions of too casual or unanalytical observers. It is fairer, as some writers state, to view the contract in all its aspects, before condemning it as a sale.[2] No matter what motives exist in a father's mind when he gives his daughter in exchange for a price, they carry no weight against the legal effect of the dowry contract.

The main effect of the contract is to transfer the reproductive capacity of the woman, and her ability to perform domestic services, from her guardian to her husband,[3] if the matter stopped there, the contract would be a sale, for the plight of the woman would be no better than that of an animal, which ceases to have any relationship with the seller after delivery, and is entirely subject to the will of its new owner.

But this is not the case, for the wife's guardian retains the role of her protector for the remainder of her life; should she be ill-treated or neglected by her husband, she has the right to return to her guardian, who is obliged to support her until a reconciliation has been effected.[4] This right to claim protection arises out of the dowry contract, for if, as quite often happens, the dowry is paid to a person (other than her guardian) at whose kraal she is staying at the time of her marriage, she can claim protection from him; he stands *in loco parentis* to her until he has accounted to her guardian for the dowry, whereupon the responsibility passes to the latter.

Whenever a wife deserts her husband and refuses to return, or is guilty of conduct giving him the right to reject her, he is entitled to the restoration of the dowry; a husband may reject his wife without cause, but he thereby forfeits the dowry he has paid. On the other hand, a wife's guardian, at her instance, may, without cause, dissolve the union by restoring the dowry to the husband, and, for good cause, may obtain an order of court for dissolution of the union and forfeiture of the dowry by the husband. These considerations may not be very significant to a European, but they operate with considerable force on a Native male. A husband will not lightly abandon or ill-treat his wife, and her guardian will not easily be persuaded to restore the dowry, or aid her in dissolving the union, when her husband is without blame, but will endeavour to persuade her to return to him if she has deserted him.[5]

Dowry is therefore the rock on which the customary union is founded; there is considerable justification for the view that a dowry contract has a greater binding force than a marriage at common law. In the latter, if a spouse is ordered to restore conjugal rights after desertion, there is no incentive, besides the influence of public opinion, religion, or conscience on a sensitive soul, for him to comply with the order; whereas the considerable value which Natives place on the possession of cattle may and does often prolong a union which has become tiresome to both spouses. Moreover, adultery, in itself, is not a good cause for either spouse to reject the other; consequently, a union is seldom dissolved for this reason, for the party dissolving it loses the dowry.[6]

The dowry contract is intended by all parties to create a lifelong conjugal association. A scrupulous man will feel a sense of shame if he has not properly *loboloed* his wife. The woman, too, realizes the insecurity of herself and her children if her guardian has not received a substantial dowry, and in most cases she will co-operate with him to see that she is sufficiently *loboloed*, for the fewer cattle a husband has paid, the more easily he

* S. M. Seymour, *Native Law in South Africa*, Juta & Co. Ltd., 1960, pp. 101–117.

will be able to persuade himself to forfeit them, should he wish to reject a wife of whom he has tired.[7]

In Natal, the payment of dowry is not essential to a customary union, but the consent of the bride's guardian is; he is unlikely to give it unless dowry has been paid or promised to him. Although, in this Province, the customary union is dissoluble by order of court only, if the bride's guardian's consent were not essential, the binding force of the union would, in practice, be weakened considerably.

2. *The nature and amount of dowry.* For a considerable time past most tribes have used cattle for dowry; when horses and small-stock were introduced into the country, Natives began to use these in a small way, not as the basis of dowry, but to supplement it. For instance, in some tribes a horse is payable in addition to cattle; the horse will have a special significance, for example, the *Sotho* and *Ntlangwini* call it the 'herdboy' in the theoretical contemplation that the herdboy will use it in tending the dowry cattle. The *Sotho* add ten sheep to their dowry; these are called the 'loincloth' of the bride's father, the theory being that he will use the skins to clothe himself. When money was introduced into Native life as a means of exchange, they began to use it in paying dowry; it happens frequently that dowry is paid in both livestock and money, sometimes in money only.[8]

But livestock, especially cattle, have remained the basis of dowry, so that even when paying in money, or both in money and livestock, the Native still thinks in terms of livestock; almost invariably, in tribal areas at any rate, it will be agreed how many cattle or other livestock a certain sum of money is to represent.[9]

In the absence of an express agreement to the contrary, therefore, a claim for dowry is made in livestock, but the plaintiff is obliged to add an alternative claim for their value in money. The alternative money values of the various types of livestock have been standardized by the court in the Cape, with minor variations in some districts, at £5 a head for cattle and horses, and 10s. a head for small-stock. These standards values are really supposed to represent the average market value of livestock, and are arrived at as follows: In satisfying a claim for dowry, in the absence of an express agreement to the contrary, a debtor is entitled to tender mixed cattle of the quality found in the Native reserves, including old cattle, full-grown cattle, and calves; it would, of course, be deemed inequitable if old cattle and calves predominated. Thus the standard value of a dowry beast is the market value of the average of a group of mixed cattle of the quality aforesaid.[10]

The standard values of livestock should, of course, vary from time to time, to reflect fluctuations in the market price, but they have remained static (in the Cape) since rinderpest (1896); this is because the court has never been pressed to alter them, though it would do so if Natives generally expressed a desire for a change. It must be noted, however that the plaintiff in an action concerning dowry is entitled to claim and prove that the average value of livestock in his area is higher than the standard value, and, presumably, the defendant is entitled to plead and show that it is less.[11]

In the Transvaal the alternative standard value of large stock is £3 a head.[12]

Native law does not compel the parties to a dowry agreement to contract for the payment of livestock or its equivalent in money; they may agree to the payment of any other article or thing and will be bound by their agreement.[13] What constitutes 'current legal tender' is therefore a matter of common usage; if any other article or property is used, it is a matter for agreement. For instance, one Transvaal tribe used to pay dowry in hoes—they now use livestock; one can visualize the gradual change from hoes to livestock as the current means of paying dowry—first by isolated but increasingly numerous agreements to pay in cattle, until, finally, by common consent, livestock took the place of hoes.[14]

When the husband is entitled to restoration of dowry on dissolution of the union, in most tribes he usually claims generically the number paid, less allowable deductions. If any of the original livestock are still with the payee, the husband is entitled, but not obliged, to claim them specifically, and the rest are claimed generically. As an alternative to delivery of specific stock, he may claim their present market value; as an alternative to delivery of generic stock, their present standard value is claimable.[15]

The amount of dowry payable varies with different tribes. In some it is fixed by custom, in others, by agreement; in still others, no definite amount is normally fixed, for in theory the dowry is without limit.

The *Sotho* have a dowry fixed at twenty, sometimes twenty-five, head of cattle, one horse and ten small stock.[16] The *Hlubi* have a dowry fixed at either twenty head of cattle and one horse or twenty-five head of cattle and one horse, according to the custom obtaining in various districts.[17] The *Ntlangwini* have fixed their dowry at twenty-four head of cattle and two horses.[18]

Among the *Tsonga*, the amount of dowry is regulated by agreement, usually at about eleven head of cattle, but it may range from nine to thirteen head.[19]

The *Venda*, too, have no fixed dowry; it is regulated by agreement. The dowry usually paid for a commoner's daughter is eight head of cattle, and for a chief's daughter about ten head. But if a chief should marry a commoner's daughter, the dowry is much reduced and ranges from four to six head of cattle.[20]

In some parts of the Transvaal, the customary dowry among the *Ndebele* is seven head of cattle, all of which are paid, apparently, before the consummation of the union. On the day the bride is handed to her husband, one more beast is paid making a total of eight head. No further dowry is claimable.[21] In other parts, where original *Ndebele* practice obtains, the dowry is fixed by agreement, and normally ranges between ten and twenty head of cattle.[22]

In tribes in which the amount of dowry is fixed by their custom, there would be nothing to prevent the parties from expressly agreeing to a greater or less amount; these cases are rare and, being contrary to normal, must be convincingly proved.[23]

In other tribes, where the dowry is fixed by agreement the amount may range considerably, being regulated, subject to the bargaining abilities of the parties, by the social standing or the charm of the bride.[24] If there is no agreement regarding the full dowry payable, then, of course, nothing more can be claimed until an agreement is arrived at.

In some tribes, notably the *Pondo*, *Thembu* and *Xhosa*, it is not usual to limit the amount by agreement; the theory is that the wife's guardian can continue indefinitely to claim further small payments from time to time, but in practice he is allowed to claim, in all, a reasonable amount fixed at the discretion of the court. In deciding what is a reasonable dowry, the court takes cognizance of the amount normally received in the tribe concerned for the daughter of a kraalhead of the same social standing as the wife's guardian; this amount, in turn, is usually regulated by the paucity or abundance, as the case may be, of cattle in the tribe.[25]

Among the *Tswana*, the dowry is not fixed by agreement: the bridegroom or his father, as the case may be, pays what he can. However, as in those *Nguni* tribes in which the dowry is unlimited, the amount usually paid is ascertainable by reference to statistical evidence: among the *Bakgatla* branch, the amount is seldom more than six head of cattle, and is generally less; in other branches the usual number is thought to be about ten head.[26]

When a union has been dissolved through the fault of the wife, and a seed-raiser, being her sister, is given by her guardian to replace her, in all tribes no dowry is claimable in excess of that due for the original wife.[27] Where the sister has been given to replace the original wife because the latter died shortly after the consummation of her union without bearing issue, then in those tribes in which the whole dowry for the original wife would otherwise have been refundable, the full dowry payable for the original wife covers the union of the seed-raiser as well.[28] Among the *Sotho*, when a deceased wife is replaced by her sister as *sehantlo*, the full dowry for the original wife, plus ten head of cattle for the *sehantlo*, is customarily payable,[29] among the *Pedi*, in these circumstances, a nominal amount of up to three head of cattle is usually asked for, in addition to the dowry payable for the deceased wife, and the same applies when the *sehantlo* wife has been furnished because the original wife is barren.[30] *Tsonga* and *Swazi* custom is similar to this.[31] Among the *Tswana*, no additional dowry is payable for the *sehantlo* wife, but if the dowry for the deceased wife has not been paid in full, payment of the balance due must be made forthwith.[32] The same applies when a *sehantlo* wife is taken to raise seed for a barren wife.[32]

In many tribes, when a bride is not a virgin, the amount of her dowry is reduced. In tribes having a fixed dowry, the amount of the reduction is the amount of the fine payable for her seduction; but when the woman is a *dikazi*, that is to say, a widow, divorcee, or a girl who has had more than one child, her dowry is regulated by agreement.[33] In tribes where the amount is normally regulated by agreement, the dowry for a woman who is not a virgin is obviously fixed by agreement.

Generally, the fine paid for the seduction or pregnancy of a spinster merges with, and is counted as part of the dowry, if and when she subsequently marries the man who paid the fine,[34] but the merger only takes place upon the consummation of the union, because until that time fines and dowry are separate—the former belong to the girl's guardian, while any earnest cattle remain the property of the payer.[35]

But in some tribes, where the seducer (who subsequently marries the girl) did not offer marriage *at the time* he seduced her and paid the fine, or to put it in another way, if his offer of marriage did not follow upon the seduction as a consequence of it, then the fine, although it may be taken into account by the girl's guardian in assessing the amount of dowry he requires, does not merge into it; the two transactions are regarded as separate.[36]

The whole dowry is not usually paid at the time of the consummation of the union; on the contrary, the general rule is that the girl's guardian will then require payment of a portion thereof only, leaving a balance to be paid later. The balance may be claimed by him at any time, unless there is an express agreement when it is to be paid.[37]

Sometimes it is agreed that a balance of dowry is to be paid out of the dowry to be received for the eldest daughter of the union; or it may be agreed that the balance of dowry is to be paid out of the dowry to be received for a specified female ward of the debtor; in such cases, of course, the creditor is bound to await the event before he can claim the balance due to him.[38] The debtor does not, of course, cease to be liable if the particular daughter or ward, whose dowry has been pledged, does not marry at the usual age when women marry, or dies before marriage; some other reasonable arrangement must then be made, and if the debtor should refuse to do this, the creditor could demand the balance there and then.

In tribes which practise *ukuteleka*, no agreement is ever made fixing a time for payment of the balance, for the balance is paid according to that practice.

Normally, of course, the girl's guardian has the final say in fixing the initial amount he will require before giving his daughter in a customary union. But where earnest cattle have been paid before the completion of the dowry agreement, if the girl's guardian does not then stipulate what initial amount is to be paid he cannot, at the final dowry discussion, make an exorbitant demand, unless the bridegroom or his representatives agree thereto; he is obliged to accept tender of a reasonable amount, and if, upon such a tender or payment, he refuses to proceed with the union, the bridegroom is entitled to cancel the engagement and reclaim the earnest cattle paid.[39] In *Sotho* law, in the absence of such a stipulation at the time of the engagement, the payment or tender of a total of ten head of cattle entitles the bridegroom to demand a slaughter and the consummation of the union. The *Hlubi* (in East Griqualand) have the same practice.[40] Among the Cape *Nguni* tribes, the payment or tender of about eight or ten head of cattle seems to be regarded as reasonable.[41]

Where there has been no engagement prior to the dowry negotiations, or where the girl's guardian, in agreeing to the engagement, stipulated the initial amount he would require before giving her in the customary union, then in the first case the suitor must either satisfy the demands of the girl's guardian or abandon his desire to marry the girl, and in the latter, he is obviously bound by the condition imposed by the girl's guardian in agreeing to the engagement.

In most tribes a beast is slaughtered upon completion of the dowry contract, that is, at that stage when the initial requirements of the bride's guardian have been satisfied, and arrangements, if any, regarding the balance of dowry have been concluded. Among the *Sotho* and tribes who follow their practices, this slaughter actually marks the consummation of the union, unless, after a payment on account of dowry, the girl had previously been allowed to live with the bridegroom, when the start of cohabitation will have marked the consummation. These tribes also slaughter a beast after the dowry has been paid in full, to mark this event.

3. *The ownership in Dowry.* As has already been noted, earnest cattle vest in the payer until the union has been consummated, whereupon they vest in the guardian of the bride and form part of the dowry; this applies to all payments made to the latter before consummation, whether delivery has been physical, or by 'description' or 'word of mouth'.

Sometimes prospective dowry rights are transferred to a third person before the girl marries. The allotment by a kraalhead of a daughter to a son, or from one House to another, has already been dealt with, and the effect thereof need not be repeated here.

Not infrequently, a kraalhead may promise payment of a debt out of the dowry of a daughter; if he retains the custody of the girl, the dowry paid for her vests in him, but he must, of course, settle the debt.[42] If, however, he gives the girl into the custody of his creditor, it is intended that the latter shall be entitled to keep the whole dowry in settlement of the debt; the creditor gives the girl away in her customary union, and the dowry becomes his property.[43]

On the question whether such a transaction may amount to trafficking in children and thus be contrary to public policy, the court distinguishes between a case where the intention is that the girl shall belong to the creditor as if he were her guardian, and one where the intention is that the guardianship of the girl is to remain with her guardian; the former is regarded as an attempted trading in children and the whole transaction is void *ab initio*, while in the latter it is contended that, since the only rights which are intended to pass are the rights in the dowry, the transaction is unobjectionable.[44]

4. *The Persons liable for Payment of Dowry*. The question of who is liable for the payment of dowry usually arises when the dowry holder requires payment of a balance which may be due.

In tribes which practise *ukuteleka* this question is of little importance in practice, because the payment of dowry is enforced by the wife's guardian's obtaining custody of, and holding, her until her husband pays further cattle, upon which she is returned to the latter.[45]

In other tribes, payment of dowry is enforced by legal action; therefore the question of liability for its payment is a matter of first importance to the wife's guardian.[46]

Liability for dowry is based wholly upon contract, and is never incurred by the operation of Native law.

The husband himself is liable for the dowries for all his wives, because the fact that he is a principle party to the union implies his acceptance of the terms of the dowry contract.[47]

A father (or his heir) is under a strong customary obligation, usually respected by him, to supply the dowry for his son's first wife. From this normal incidence in Native society, there may be said to have arisen in Native law a presumption that, in respect of a man's first wife, his father or guardian was a party to the dowry agreement; if he wishes to avoid liability, the onus is on him to rebut this presumption.[48]

This onus may be discharged as follows: Either he may show that at the time of the consummation of the union he expressly disassociated himself from, and repudiated liability for, his son's customary union and drowry contract. It is necessary for him openly to disavow connexion with the union, so that the girl's guardian may know how matters stand.[48] Or, he may show that neither he nor his lawful representative took any part in the marriage.[48]

Both of these methods of disowning liability require explanation.

Usually a son is living at his father's kraal when he marries his first wife; his father or guardian usually makes all the arrangements in regard to the union and dowry through spokesmen, and also contributes a greater portion of the dowry then paid on account. In such cases the father or guardian of the husband is clearly liable in respect of the whole of the dowry contract.[48]

Even though the bridegroom's father may take no active part in the dowry talks, or, perhaps, may not contribute towards the initial payment of dowry, his residence at his kraal, without expressly disassociating himself from the matter, warrants the inference that what is taking place has his approval, and he is bound by implication.[48]

The matter may be taken further. Suppose that the bridegroom's father was away from his kraal during the dowry negotiations, and never came to know of the union until after its consummation. As explained elsewhere, during his absence, the management of the kraal is lawfully either in the hands of a duly appointed 'keeper' or is the responsibility of his nearest major male relative. It is submitted that, should this person have associated himself with the matter on behalf of the kraalhead, the latter is estopped, as against the girl's guardian, from denying the authority of his representative to bind him, unless, of course, the girl's guardian was a party to a fraud perpetrated against him.[49]

Thus, whenever, a son's first marriage has taken place from his father's kraal, it is submitted that his father is liable under the dowry contract unless he or his lawful representative expressly repudiated liability.[49]

Where a father shows that his son was not living at his kraal on the occasion of his first marriage, it is submitted that the onus is then transferred to the wife's guardian to show that he consulted the father, and that the latter either expressly bound himself or did so impliedly by actively associating himself with the marriage, for example, by contributing to the dowry.[50]

It is not unusual for a man to have been brought up at a kraal other than his father's. He is usually regarded there as a 'son', and the head of the kraal will pay and make himself responsible for his first wife's dowry; clearly in such a case, the man's own guardian cannot be held liable under the dowry contract.

Whenever a man has married his first wife while living away from his guardian's kraal, it is submitted that the head of the kraal where he was staying when he married is liable under the dowry contract by implied agreement, unless he expressly repudiated liability. The principle involved has been expressed above in dealing with a father's liability: a kraalhead allowing a man's first union to take place at his kraal, without informing the girl's guardian that he is not the guardian of the bridegroom and expressly disassociating himself from the matter, would be estopped from denying the inferences arising from this conduct.

It is competent for a bridegroom's father or kraalhead, while taking part in the dowry discussions and subscribing towards the initial payment, to repudiate liability for the balance of the dowry; to be effective, this stipulation must be express, and, being unusual, would have to be convincingly proved by him at any dispute which may arise later.[51]

In the case of a man's secondary wives, since it is unusual for his father or erstwhile guardian to take part in, or associate himself with, these unions, Native law presumes that he has not agreed to be responsible for the payment of dowry; the onus is on the wife's guardian, if he seeks to hold him liable, to prove that he expressly agreed to be liable.[52] And so it has been held that even though a father contributed towards the dowry of his son's secondary wife, and even though he actually acted as his son's representative at the dowry discussions, his liability in respect of the dowry contract could not be implied from this conduct alone.[53]

A son has no right of action to compel his father or guardian to pay the dowry for his first wife; it is entirely the father's or guardian's affair whether he will assume liability or not.[54]

5. *The Manner of enforcing payment of Dowry*. For the purpose of considering the means whereby payment of a balance of dowry may be enforced, native tribes may be divided into two groups, those practising *ukuteleka* and those not.

A. *Tribes practising ukuteleka*. In most tribes practising *ukuteleka*, the amount of dowry payable is as a rule not limited, and constitutes a bond of good will between the families of the bride and bridegroom; during the whole of the wife's life, and even after her death, more dowry may be asked for from time to time (normally from one to three head of cattle at a time), and if the request is reasonable the husband should comply with it. There is no legal action for enforcing payment of dowry; if the husband has property and does not comply with a reasonable demand, the wife's guardian may *teleka* her until the demand is complied with. The husband has no valid complaint; if he wants his wife back, he must comply with the demand.[55] This is the theory of the dowry contract among the *Xhosa*, the *Thembu*, and the *Pondo*, at any rate, but the court has not given full effect to it.

The court will not allow the wife's guardian to *teleka* her any more once he has received in all a reasonable amount of dowry; what constitutes a reasonable total is in the court's discretion, having regard to what is an average received in the tribe concerned for a woman of her social standing.[56] The wife's guardian *telekas* her when he requires more, but if the husband feels that he has already paid enough, he will sue the former for the return of his wife or, failing this, the restoration of the dowry paid, alleging that she has deserted him; the wife's guardian may then plead that he is *telekaing* her, but that he is willing to release her on receiving a further reasonable payment:

If the court feels that the husband has already paid sufficient it will order the return of the wife or, failing this, the restoration of the dowry already paid; if the court considers that the wife's guardian's claim for a further payment is reasonable, it may either dismiss the summons, or may order the return of the wife subject to the tender to her guardian of a reasonable number of cattle, or, failing such return, that the dowry already paid be restored to her husband.[57]

In other tribes, such as the *Fengu*, the theory of unlimited dowry does not obtain. The parties usually agree what the total dowry is to be; if this is not paid in full at the consummation of the union, then from time to time the wife's guardian may *teleka* her for further payments of from one to three head of cattle at a time until the whole is paid.[58] Thereafter he may not *teleka* her save when she has been ill-treated by her husband in which case he may hold her until her husband has paid a beast.[59] In the tribes in which the dowry is limitless, a wife may also always be *telekaed* pending payment of a beast, when she has been ill-treated.[60]

Although the wife's guardian is entitled to *teleka* her on any occasion when she returns to his kraal, he will not usually do so, out of courtesy apparently, upon her first visit home after marriage.[61]

A child of the union may also be held under *ukuteleka* for an instalment of dowry.[62]

When the husband resists his wife's guardian's right to *teleka* her or a child of the union the court may order that the wife's guardian be given the custody of a child until the husband has paid a reasonable instalment of dowry.[63]

Subject to the two exceptions given hereinafter, the wife's guardian has no other means of enforcing payment of dowry.[64] If, despite the fact that his wife is being held, the husband, while having the means to do so, does not pay cattle to release her, this is regarded as neglect on his part; the wife and her guardian can then force the issue by claiming an order for the dissolution of the union, and, if granted, the husband will be ordered to forfeit the dowry he has paid up to that time.[65] If the husband has no cattle, dissolution will not be granted, and so stalemate may ensue.

In two exceptional instances an action to compel payment of dowry is tenable: Firstly, when a girl has been *thwalaed* and an *mvulamlomo* beast paid to her guardian while she is retained at the suitor's kraal, her guardian may sue for a reasonable amount of dowry. This beast is paid by the suitor or his guardian to induce the girl's guardian to talk dowry (to open his mouth, literally); consequently, if the girl is not returned and the suitor or his guardian makes no attempt, or refuses to pay dowry, the girl's guardian may sue him for a reasonable number of cattle, because he would have insisted on this initial payment before handing over the girl. Further payments must, however, be recovered by *ukuteleka*.[66] Secondly, in the singular circumstances of the case quoted in the reference hereunder, an action was allowed. The circumstances were so unusual that the transaction on which the action was based was without precedent in Native law; the court relied on a written agreement.[67]

If a wife's guardian holds a girl child of the union under *ukuteleka*, he is entitled to give her away in marriage, receive the dowry and withhold from it the balance of dowry due to him, or a reasonable instalment if the full dowry was not limited, as well as the normal allowances due to him for bringing up the child and supplying her wedding outfit.[68] The balance should be handed to the husband.

A claim for payment of further dowry must not, however, be confused with a claim for delivery of livestock already paid 'by word of mouth' or 'description'; the ownership of livestock so paid vests in the wife's guardian when the union is consummated, and they may be vindicated by him.[69]

B. *Other tribes*. In some tribes not practising *ukuteleka* there is no right of action to enforce the payment of dowry. The *Tswana* fall into this class: the amount of dowry is not fixed; the husband or his father, as the case may be, usually pays what he can and normally the whole dowry is paid at the same time. In some cases the dowry is paid at the time when the spouses begin cohabitation; in other cases payment may be deferred, although the spouses may live together as man and wife with the consent of all interested parties. There is a very good reason why dowry is almost invariably paid in due course, sometimes by the eldest son of the husband after the latter's death, namely, that the union is regarded as inchoate until dowry is paid, up to which time the children belong to, and can be claimed by, the wife's guardian.[70]

Tsonga law permits an action for the payment of the balance of dowry due, but, having obtained judgment, the wife's guardian is then permitted to impound her until her husband has made a payment on account of the balance due; this may happen from time to time until the matter is settled.[71]

In other tribes the wife's guardian has a right of action to compel payment of a balance of dowry outstanding. If the dowry agreement embodies a stipulation when such balance shall be paid, the parties are bound by the agreement, and the husband may only be sued when he is *in mora*. If there is no agreement, then the balance may be claimed at any time; it is not usual, however, to demand payment soon after the marriage, though sometimes it is done, especially where the husband has in some way displeased the wife's guardian.[72]

No action for recovery of further dowry is tenable while the wife is living away from her husband's kraal without his consent, except in these circumstances, viz., should she be staying at her guardian's kraal having left her husband because he has ejected, unreasonably ill-treated, or substantially insulted her, her guardian may claim payment of the balance of dowry; he does so, however, on the understanding that she will be returned to her husband when *putumaed*.[73] Of course, if the husband's treatment of his wife was of such a nature as to entitle her never to return to him, she and her guardian should claim dissolution of the union as well, and the claim for further dowry would not then imply the understanding that she would return to her husband.[74]

Where the husband's father or guardian is also liable under the dowry contract, it is usual to sue both of them together,[75] but since their liability is joint and several and is based on contract, it is submitted that they may be sued separately.

6. A. *The effect of the death of a spouse upon a claim for dowry.* In tribes practising *ukuteleka*, when the wife has died within a few years of the consummation of the union, having borne no children or one or two children only, her guardian has no claim for further dowry.[76] But if she had substantially fulfilled the purpose of the union, that is, if the union had subsisted for several years and she had borne one or more children, further dowry may be claimed; the claim is enforced by her guardian's holding a child of the union under *ukuteleka*.[77]

In Cape tribes in which the dowry is fixed by custom, the death of the wife does not bar her guardian from claiming the balance due, and he may sue for it.[78] But the *Sotho*, at any rate, distinguish a case where the wife has died within two or three years of marriage, even if she has borne a child; her guardian can claim no more than the number of cattle he had stipulated for the 'head' of the wife, that is to say, on receipt of which he had agreed to give a slaughter to complete the dowry contract; if this number was not stipulated, custom fixed it at ten head of cattle; where therefore, before the wife's death, there had already been a slaughter, or where her guardian had already received the stipulated number, or, in the event of no number having been stipulated, ten head of cattle, he can claim no more.[79]

In *Zulu*, *Pedi* and *Venda* law, there is no further claim for dowry, where the wife has died shortly after consummation of the union, having borne no children.[80]

Where the husband was responsible for the death of his wife shortly after marriage, her guardian was held entitled to claim a total of ten head of cattle only out of a full dowry fixed by *Ntlangwini* custom at twenty-four head of cattle and two horses.[81]

In all tribes, the death of the husband does not dissolve the union, and so the widow's guardian may claim payment of any balance of dowry due to him. In tribes practising *ukuteleka*, he must, of course, enforce payment in accordance therewith.[82]

B. *The effect of dissolution of the union upon a claim for dowry.* In tribes which practise *ukuteleka*, by the very nature of this practice, there can be no claim by the wife's guardian, after dissolution of her union, for further dowry, irrespective of which party was to blame for it.[83]

In other tribes, if the wife was at fault in bringing about dissolution of the union, her guardian loses his claim for any outstanding balance of dowry, but if the husband was at fault the wife's guardian may claim the whole amount outstanding.[84]

7. *The payment of dowry to a Kraalhead other than the bride's guardian.* Owing, no doubt, to the peculiarities of the Native social system, under which it is not unusual for a child to stay

for long periods, or even grow up, at a kraal other than his own guardian's Native law has evolved to ensure the validity of a customary union contracted in respect of a girl by the head of the kraal where she is living at the time.

When a man meets a girl he wishes to marry, he does not have to concern himself with her relationship to the head of the kraal where he finds her; even if he is aware that the kraalhead is not her guardian, he can enter into negotiations with him without a qualm. In fact, the matter of the relationship between a kraalhead and a girl staying at his kraal may not even be discussed; the suitor usually accepts that they are father and daughter, or guardian and ward.[85]

The dowry contract, and the resultant union, made between the suitor and the head of the kraal, are inviolable.[86]

It is, however, the duty of the head of the kraal (usually referred to in the decisions as her custodian, or the receiver of dowry, or her guardian's agent, and who will be referred to hereafter as the custodian) to report the proposed union to the girl's guardian; but since this is a matter between himself and her guardian his failure to make the report does not affect the validity of the union.[87]

Even where there is a dispute between two kraalheads regarding which of them is the guardian of a girl, it is not for the suitor to inquire into the merits of the dispute; he may enter into a valid agreement with and pay dowry to the kraalhead who has the custody of the girl, and it is left to the disputants to settle which of them is entitled to it.[88]

It is the duty of the custodian, when called upon to do so by the girl's guardian, to account to the latter and to deliver to him the dowry received and the progeny thereof.[89]

Where the girl's guardian has ceded or allotted his rights in the dowry to the custodian, then the question of the latter's rendering an account does not arise.[90]

In accounting to the girl's guardian, the custodian is not liable to replace cattle which have died or been lost without negligence on his part; he is entitled to deduct and keep one beast for *isondhlo* (if he is entitled to *isondhlo*) and a reasonable allowance, usually one beast for each item, for his expenses, if he incurred these, in regard to the girl's initiation ceremony and for supplying her wedding outfit;[91] he is not entitled to this allowance if, although able to obtain it, he incurred these expenses without the prior approval of the girl's guardian.[92] Furthermore, should the custodian have failed to report the receipt of the dowry to the girl's guardian, or, having reported, have failed to notify him forthwith of any death or loss among the dowry stock which may occur from time to time, he is liable, when making his account and delivery, to replace any beast he may subsequently allege to have died or been lost.[93]

When the girl's guardian demands an account from the custodian, it is no defence for the latter to say that another inmate of his kraal has used it up, or that he handed it to some other person, even the girl's mother; his duty is to account to the girl's guardian, or the latter's lawful representative.[94]

Until the custodian has accounted to her guardian, he stands, in so far as the wife and her husband are concerned, *in loco parentis* of the former. She may therefore look to him, as dowry holder, for the protection which the dowry contract affords her against ill-treatment or neglect by her husband, and the latter is entitled to enforce against the custodian every right to which the dowry contract entitles him. And so the husband may sue the custodian for the return of his deserting wife, or, failing this, the restoration of the dowry;[95] similarly any other action involving the restoration of the dowry may be taken against the custodian.

Where there is a dowry debt due by the girl's guardian to the custodian, in rendering his account the latter is entitled to *compensatio* for the debt due to him, and need only hand the excess to the girl's guardian.[96]

Once the custodian has accounted to the girl's guardian, the responsibility under the dowry contract is transferred to the latter; if the custodian is thereafter sued in respect of a liability pertaining to a dowry holder, he must succeed if he pleads and establishes the fact that he has so accounted.[97]

A judgment in favour of a husband against his wife's guardian for her return or, failing this, the restoration of the dowry, bars by estoppel a subsequent action by the husband against the custodian for the same cause, and vice versa.[98] The liability of the custodian and the wife's guardian is not joint and several, for they are not co-debtors, but in a sense, principal and agent; the husband should enforce his rights under the dowry contract against the one who holds the dowry.[99]

Where a girl's guardian has transferred his rights in her dowry to the custodian, the action for recovery of an outstanding balance may be brought by the latter; otherwise the custodian may only bring the action if he has obtained the permission of the guardian or his lawful representative in his absence, or without such permission if the guardian is an absconder having no known male relatives.[100] A custodian instituting an action for payment of dowry against the husband must allege in his summons the premises upon which he claims the right to sue.[101]

Generally speaking, a wife or widow is not competent to enter into a dowry agreement in respect of her daughter, nor to receive payment of the dowry; when she is living at her husband's kraal, then in his absence or that of his heir, as the case may be, his lawful representative (usually his nearest male relative) is the proper person to enter into the dowry agreement and take control of the dowry, and it is he who is responsible to the husband or his heir.[102] If there are no relatives of the absent or deceased husband available, then she is entitled to enter into the dowry agreement and receive payment of the dowry.[103] In this case, however, she is not personally liable to her daughter's husband under the dowry agreement, and in the event of an action at law arising out of the agreement, her husband or his heir is the proper person to sue or be sued.[104]

The head of the kraal where a wife or widow is staying at the time her daughter is given in a customary union is responsible to her husband or his heir for the dowry, even if it can be shown that she herself entered into the dowry contract, and took possession of the dowry.[105] In *Sotho* law, however, no liability attaches to the kraalhead in this case.[106]

Under exceptional circumstances a custodian may account to a wife or widow. Where the guardian of a girl has absconded or died, and there are no male relatives of his to whom an account can properly be made, the custodian is obliged, at the instance of the girl's mother, to deliver to her the dowry he has received, for in these circumstances she is entitled to claim it for the maintenance of herself and her House; thereafter the liability of the custodian, both to the girl's guardian for an accounting, and to her husband in respect of the dowry contract, is extinguished.[107]

Notes

1 Ellenberger and McGregor, pp. 272–4; *Maclean's Compendium*, pp. 55–6, 70–2; *Nbono* v. *Manoxoweni*, 6 E.D.C. 62.

2 Schapera, p. 138; Ashton, pp. 72–3; *Maclean's Compendium*, pp. 55–6; Ellenberger and McGregor, p. 273; Junod, pp. 262, 263; Harries, p. 3.

3 Schapera, p. 139; Ashton, pp. 72–3.

4 *Mashapo* v. *Sisane*, 1945 N.A.C. (T & N) 57, Pretoria.

5 Schapera, pp. 138–9; Ashton, pp. 72–3; *Nqambi* v. *Nqambi*, 1939 N.A.C. (C & O) 57.

6 See Soga, p. 263 et seq.; Schapera, pp. 138–9; Ashton, pp. 72–3.

7 Schapera, pp. 138–9; Ashton, pp. 72–3; Soga, p. 275.

8 Ashton, p. 71; *Maclean's Compendium*, pp. 55, 70, 71, 118; *Dana* v. *Nqiwa*, 2 N.A.C. 179, Qumbu; *Ngovuza* v. *Xelo*, 3 N.A.C. 9, Umtata.

9 See cases under note 8, *supra*; *Majongile* v. *Mpikeleli*, 1950 N.A.C. (S.D.) 260, Tsolo. For a discussion of the origin of the practice of claiming an alternative monetary value for livestock, see *Sigidi* v. *Mfamana*, 1954 N.A.C. (S.D.) 50, Lady Frere.

10 *Mapango* v. *Zuma*, 1 N.A.C. 207, Cofimvaba; *Ntlekwini* v. *Maqokolo*, 4 N.A.C. 345, Flagstaff; *Mahleza* v. *Ndandana*, 1945 N.A.C. (C & O) 31, Butterworth; *Sigidi* v. *Mfamana*, 1954 N.A.C. (S.D.) 50, Lady Frere; *Nkosi* v. *Mlota*, 1939 N.A.C. (T. & N.) 60.

11 *Ntlekwini* v. *Maqokolo*, 4 N.A.C. 345, Flagstaff; *Matolengwe* v. *Pateni*, 1949 N.A.C. (S.D.) 106; *Kodisang* v. *Seakgela*, 1945 N.A.C. (C & O) 51; *Majongile* v. *Mpikeleli*, 1950 N.A.C. (S.D.) 260.

12 *Mofokeng* v. *Vilikazi*, 1943 N.A.C. (T & N) 23, Krugersdorp; *Tombeel* v. *Nakani*, 1947 N.A.C. (T & N) 118, Potchefstroom.

13 *Dana* v. *Nqiwa*, 2 N.A.C. 179, Qumbu; *Tikolo* v. *Simanga*, 1 N.A.C. 51, Engcobo; *Majongile* v. *Mpikeleli*, 1950 N.A.C. (S.D.) 260, Tsolo; van Warmelo, pp. 99–101.

14 Schapera, p. 139; van Warmelo, pp. 99–101; *Shabangu* v. *Mkonto*, 1945 N.A.C. (T & N) 15, Bushbuckridge.

15 *Tshotsheibika* v. *Sapuka*, 4 N.A.C. 58, Bizana; *Mdingi* v. *Kotshini*, 1951 N.A.C. (S.D.) 270, Bizana. For *Ndebele* and *Pedi* law, see Chapter VII, 7, p. 138.

16 Ashton, pp. 71–2; *Mgogo* v. *Jan*, 1 N.A.C. 278, Tabankulu; *Makoro* v. *Bolofo*, 1943 N.A.C. (C & O) 24, Mt. Fletcher; *Maqhekhana* v. *Lenata*, 1943 N.A.C. (C & O) 49, Mt. Fletcher.

[17] *Ramncwana* v. *Siyotula*, 1937 N.A.C. (C & O) 172, Qumbu; *Kesa* v. *Ndaba*, 1935 N.A.C. (C & O) 64, Matatiele; *Ndabeni* v. *Mlobeli*, 1949 N.A.C. (S.D.) 158, Matatiele.

[18] *Bungane* v. *Nongwadu*, 1931 N.A.C. (C & O) 43.

[19] *Shabangu* v. *Mkonto*, 1945 N.A.C. (T & N) 15, Bushbuckridge; Ramsay, pp. 7, 13.

[20] Van Warmelo, p. 103.

[21] *Mogidi* v. *Ngomo*, 1948 N.A.C. (T & N) 18, Pretoria.

[22] *M'Tumunje* v. *Mahlangu*, 1938 N.A.C. (T & N) 196, Belfast.

[23] *Mojakisane* v. *Khoapa*, 1938 N.A.C. (C & O) 28, Matatiele.

[24] Harries, p. 14; Krige, pp. 121, 128; *Manqana* v. *Ntintili*, 1 N.A.C. 218, Mt. Frere; *Zenzile* v. *Roto*, 1 N.A.C. 223, St. Marks; *Magi* v. *Sibizwe*, 2 N.A.C. 50, Engcobo; *Solani* v. *Manxiwa*, 4 N.A.C. 342, Cofimvaba.

[25] See chapter VI, 5A; *Maclean's Compendium*, pp. 70, 71, 117, 118; *Magi* v. *Sibizwe*, 2 N.A.C. 50, Engcobo; *Mzamduli* v. *Bukwana*, 1903 N.A.C., a Kokstad, unreported; *Beleni* v. *Sidlo*, 4 N.A.C. 344, Flagstaff; and see the authorities in note 55, *infra*.

[26] Schapera, p. 140.

[27] *Sidlayiya* v. *Mangali*, 4 N.A.C. 218, Mt. Fletcher.

[28] See case under note 27, *supra*.

[29] Ashton, p. 82; *Nthole* v. *Lebata*, 1942 N.A.C. (C & O) 125, Mt. Fletcher.

[30] Harries, p. 25.

[31] *Maganu* v. *Maganu*, 1938 N.A.C. (T & N) 14, Sibasa; Kuper, p. 19; Ramsay, p. 9.

[32] Schapera, pp. 155, 167–8.

[33] *Nyokana* v. *Nkwali*, 6 N.A.C. 13, Matatiele; *Mbuko* v. *Letaka*, 1945 N.A.C. (C & O) 61, Mt. Fletcher. This is not so among the *Tsonga* (Ramsay, p. 13).

[34] *Tole* v. *Ndumiso*, 1 N.A.C. 141, Willowvale; *Gxonono* v. *Skuni*, 1 N.A.C. 154, Bizana; *Pumlomo* v. *Mbusi*, 1 N.A.C. 179, Willowvale; *Mngengo* v. *Goniwe*, 3 N.A.C. 69, Willowvale; *Makutywa* v. *Mxanywa*, 4 N.A.C. 63, Mt. Ayliff; *Mayi* v. *Mgengwana*, 4 N.A.C. 67, Matatiele; *Mothombeni* v. *Matlou*, 1945 N.A.C. (T & N) 123, Pietersburg.

[35] *Dlangamandla* v. *Gali*, 1930 (2) N.A.C. (C & O) 74, Mt. Frere.

[36] *Ngxabalaza* v. *Njovane*, 1939 N.A.C. (C & O) 96; *Majeke* v. *Nzuzane*, 4 N.A.C. 64; *Totoyi* v. *Sitimele*, 4 N.A.C. 66; *Kwezi* v. *Rayi*, 4 N.A.C. 65. The above decisions apply to the districts of Idutywa, Nqamakwe, Kentani, Butterworth, Engcobo, Willowvale and Glen Grey.

[37] See Schapera, p. 141.

[38] *Vatsha* v. *Mfenenduna*, 1936 N.A.C. (C & O) 39, Mt. Frere; Krige, p. 121.

[39] *Moke* v. *Mpangwa*, 1906 N.A.C., at Kokstad, reported in Seymour, p. 180; *Zombova* v. *Nowalaza*, 5 N.A.C. 54, Umzimkulu; *Mapiliba* v. *Mkohliwe*, 1944 N.A.C. (C & O) 101, Engcobo.

[40] *Govuzela* v. *Ngavu*, 1949 N.A.C. (S.D.) 156, Mt. Frere; *Mapiliba* v. *Mkohliwe*, 1944 N.A.C. (C & O) 101, Engcobo.

[41] See cases under note 39, *supra*; also *Mbamba* v. *Kepuzayo*, 1948 N.A.C. (S.D.) 48, Bizana; *Ngxabalaza* v. *Njovane*, 1939 N.A.C. (C & O) 96, Lady Frere.

[42] *Mkatshwa* v. *Nduluka*, 4 N.A.C. 170, Bizana.

[43] *Diniso* v. *Msilo*, 1941 N.A.C. (C & O) 14, Umtata; *Pennington* v. *Mcitwa*, 1942 N.A.C. (C & O) 45, Flagstaff; *Vatsha* v. *Mfenenduna*, 1936 N.A.C. (C & O) 39, Mt. Frere; see also chapter VI, 7; chapter XIII, 1.

[44] See cases under note 43, *supra*; and *Sidubedube* v. *Rune*, 4 N.A.C. 169, Umtata; *Vatsha* v. *Mfenenduna*, 1936 N.A.C. (C & O) 39, Mt. Frere; *Mhlala* v. *Mohlala*, 1938 N.A.C. (T & N) 112, Lydenburg; *Ndhlovu* v. *Kanetse*, 1940 N.A.C. (T & N) 64, Nelspruit.

[45] See cases quoted under note 56, *infra*.

[46] See cases under note 56, *infra*.

[47] See cases under note 56, *infra*. A bridegroom seldom conducts his own dowry negotiations. In respect of his first wife, his father or his father's chosen speakers will do so; in respect of subsequent wives, the bridegroom will nominate his own speakers (*Zibonda* v. *Jamandhlini*, 1948 N.A.C. (S.D.) 57, Umzimkulu).

[48] *Tala* v. *Matobane*, 1 N.A.C. 149, Mt. Fletcher; *Mti* v. *Mvacane*, 3 N.A.C. 56, Matatiele; *Mboqoko* v. *Sibudu*, 1934 N.A.C. (C & O) 3, Kokstad; *Jeliza* v. *Nyamende*, 1945 N.A.C. (C & O) 34, Matatiele; *Khemane* v. *Ned*, 1948 N.A.C. (S.D.) 15, Mt. Fletcher; *Rubushe* v. *Jiyane*, 1952 N.A.C. (S.D.) 69 Umzimkulu.

[49] Read with the cases in note 48, *supra*.

[50] See cases under note 48, *supra*; *Twayi* v. *Sirayi*, 5 N.A.C. 100, Tsolo; *Macwili* v. *Dunjana*, 1940 N.A.C. (C & O) 3, Willowvale; *Makoro* v. *Seemane*, 1948 N.A.C. (S.D.) 60, Mt. Fletcher, is also instructive.

[51] *Khemane* v. *Ned*, 1948 N.A.C. (S.D.) 15, Mt. Fletcher.

[52] See cases under note 53, *infra*.

[53] *Bokwa* v. *Ntambo*, 1 N.A.C. 75, Mt. Fletcher; *Baduza* v. *Dlova*, 6 N.A.C. 8, Mt. Fletcher; *Hoho* v. *Mtwesi*, 1939 N.A.C. (C. & O) 6, Mt. Fletcher; *Jeliza* v. *Nyamende*, 1945 N.A.C. (C & O) 34, Matatiele.

[54] *Gungubele* v. *Xoliswe*, 2 N.A.C. 65, Matatiele; *Langa* v. *Langa*, 1931 N.A.C. (T & N) 39; *Fynn* v. *Fynn*, 1937 N.A.C. (T & N) 99.

[55] Soga, pp. 263 et seq.; *Kiva* v. *Sifuba*, 1940 N.A.C. (C & O) 161, Ngqeleni; *Skweyiya* v. *Sixakwe*, 1941 N.A.C. (C & O) 126, Port Elizabeth; *Ngxabalaza* v. *Njovane*, 1939 N.A.C. (C & O) 96, Lady Grey.

[56] Soga, p. 266; *Maclean's Compendium*, pp. 70, 71, 117, 118; *Mzamduli* v. *Bukwana*, 1903 N.A.C. at Kokstad, unreported; *Magi* v. *Sibizwe*, 2 N.A.C. 50, Engcobo; *Baleni* v. *Sidlo*, 4 N.A.C. 334, Flagstaff; *Ndabeni* v. *Tingatinga*, 1 N.A.C. 142 Willowvale.

[57] *Magi* v. *Sibizwe*, 2 N.A.C. 50, Engcobo; *Tyomfa* v. *Mbane*, 2 N.A.C. 129, Butterworth.

[58] *Zenzile* v. *Roto*, 1 N.A.C. 223, St. Marks; *Monghayelana* v. *Msongelwa*, 3 N.A.C. 292, Mt. Frere; *Nkontwana* v. *Mlata*, 3 N.A.C. 294, Qumbu; *Solani* v. *Manxiwa*, 4 N.A.C. 342, Cofimvaba; *Skweyiya* v. *Sixakwe*, 1941 N.A.C. (C & O) 126, Port Elizabeth; *Tyomfa* v. *Mbane*, 2 N.A.C. 129, Butterworth.

[59] *Mlingisi* v. *Ngqotso*, 1949 N.A.C. (S.D.) 141, Lady Frere.

[60] *Zenzile* v. *Roto*, 1 N.A.C. 223, St. Marks; *Mlingisi* v. *Ngqotso*, 1949 N.A.C. (S.D.) 141, Lady Frere.

[61] *Zenzile* v. *Roto*, 1 N.A.C. 223, St. Marks.

[62] Soga, p. 284, *Mkholwa* v. *Mangaliso*, 1 N.A.C. 202, Flagstaff; *Tiyeka* v. *Feja*, 4 N.A.C. 343, Flagstaff; *Baleni* v. *Sidlo*, 4 N.A.C. 344, Flagstaff; *Ntlekwini* v. *Mawokolo*, 4 N.A.C. 345, Flagstaff.

[63] *Baleni* v. *Sidlo*, 4 N.A.C. 334, Flagstaff.

[64] *Adonis* v. *Zazani*, 1 N.A.C. 46, Butterworth; *Monghayelana* v. *Msongelwa*, 3 N.A.C. 292, Mt. Frere; *Skweyiya* v. *Sixakwe*, 1941 N.A.C. (C & O) 126, Port Elizabeth; *Ngalimkulu* v. *Mndayi*, 1947, N.A.C. (C & O) 65, Tsolo; *Tonya* v. *Matomani*, 1949 N.A.C. (S.D.) 138, Umtata; *Mlingisi* v. *Ngqotso*, 1949 N.A.C. (S.D.) 141, Mt. Frere.

[65] *Zenzile* v. *Roto*, 1 N.A.C. 223, St. Marks; *Ndabeni* v. *Tingatinga*, 1 N.A.C. 142, Willowvale.

[66] *Mbamba* v. *Kepuzayo*, 1948 N.A.C. (S.D.) 48, Bizana.

[67] *Kiva* v. *Sifuba*, 1940 N.A.C. (C & O) 161, Ngqeleni.

[68] *Tiyeka* v. *Feja*, 4 N.A.C. 343, Flagstaff.

[69] *Sofe* v. *Cibi*, 1936, N.A.C. (C & O) 11, Komgha; *Ngqungiso* v. *Gobo*, 1946 N.A.C. (C & O) 10, Tsolo; *Ngalimkuku* v. *Mndayi*, 1947 N.A.C. (C & O) 65, Tsolo; *Tonya* v. *Matomani*, 1949 N.A.C. (S.D.) 138, Umtata; *Dlamini* v. *Kuboni*, 1953 N.A.C. (S.D.) 230, Umzimkulu.

[70] Schapera, pp. 143–4, 170. In these times, however, the court would probably regard the children as legitimate from the time when cohabitation first began, and if so, might possibly also allow the wife's guardian a right of action to recover a reasonable amount of dowry. (See chapter V, 2C; *Mocumi* v. *Mocumi*, 1944 N.A.C. (C & O) 107, Mafeking.)

[71] Ramsay, p. 16.

[72] *Mgogo* v. *Jan*, 1 N.A.C. 278, Tabankulu; *Bungane* v. *Nongwada*, 1931, N.A.C. (C & O) 43, Matatiele; *Makoro* v. *Bolofo*, 1943 N.A.C. (C & O) 24, Mt. Fletcher; *Maphela* v. *Seshea*, 1943 N.A.C. (C & O) 25, Matatiele; *Nkuna* v. *Kazamula*, 1941 N.A.C. (T & N) 128, Duivelskloof; *Khasi* v. *Tabana*, 1944 N.A.C. (T & N) 67, Johannesburg; see also cases under note 78, *infra*.

[73] *Jas* v. *Mpunga*, 1946 N.A.C. (C & O) 5, Mt. Fletcher.

[74] See chapter VII, 6, C, D and F.

[75] See cases under notes 48, 51 and 72, *supra*. Compare the procedure when a kraalhead is sued for damages for the delict of an inmate (chapter IV, 2D).

[76] See chapter VII, 1; see *Skweyiya* v. *Sixakwe*, 1941 N.A.C. (C & O) 126, Port Elizabeth, for a case bearing out this contention in principle; and *Sofe* v. *Cibi*, 1936 N.A.C. (C & O) 11, Komgha.

[77] *Kiva* v. *Sifuba*, 1940 N.A.C. (C & O) 161, Ngqeleni.

[78] *Soga* v. *Sibikubula*, 5 N.A.C. 45, Mt. Frere; *Tseka* v. *Sautsi*, 1929 N. A.C. (C & O) 6, Matatiele.

[79] See chapter VII, 1; *Hlwili* v. *Mohlabelwana*, 3 N.A.C. 299, Matatiele; *Nthole* v. *Lebata*, 1942 N.A.C. (C & O) 125, Mt. Fletcher. It is essential, of course, that the woman was validly married according to Native law before her death took place; a mere engagement is insufficient to found such a claim (*Moketusne* v. *Ramathole*, 1936 N.A.C. (C & O) 54, Matatiele).

[80] Krige, p. 156; Harries, p. 24; Stayt, p. 152. For *Venda* law see footnote 1, p. 118, chapter VII.

[81] *Fosi* v. *Sixolo*, 3 N.A.C. 58, Umzimkulu.

[82] See chapter VIII, 3; chapter XI, 6; chapter VII, 1; chapter VI, 5A.

[83] See chapter VI, 5A.

[84] See chapter VII, 3, 5 and 6. For *Venda* law see footnote 1, p. 118, chapter VII.

[85] *Gagilanga* v. *Booi*, 1939 N.A.C. (C & O) 39, Cofimvaba; *Zeeland* v. *Machaba*, 1944 N.A.C. (C & O) 24, Kroonstad; *Mahleza* v. *Ndandana*, 1945 N.A.C. (C & O) 31, Butterworth; *Bushula* v. *Madap*, 1945 N.A.C. (C & O) 32, Mt. Fletcher. This branch of Native law does not appear to have been ventilated in the Transvaal (*Tomo* v. *Msibi*, 1939 N.A.C. (T & N) 79, Carolina).

[86] See cases under note 85, *supra*.

[87] See cases under note 85, *supra*, and especially *Mahleza* v. *Ndandana*, 1945 N.A.C. (C & O) 31, Butterworth; *Bushula* v. *Madap*, 1945 N.A.C. (C & O) 32, Mt. Fletcher.

[88] *Ntabeni* v. *Mlobeli*, 1949 N.A.C. (S.D.) 158, Matatiele; *Moitheri* v. *Khehleu*, 4 N.A.C. 76, Matatiele.

[89] *Ramncwana* v. *Siyotula*, 1937 N.A.C. (C & O) 172, Qumbu; *Lugebu* v. *Mbondwana*, 1939 N.A.C. (C & O) 5, Tsomo.

[90] *Mbelingo* v. *Daniel*, 2 N.A.C. 122, see also chapter XIII, 1.

[91] *Mziza* v. *Japie*, 1945 N.A.C. (T & N) 80, Middelburg; *Tiyeka* v. *Fega*, 4 N.A.C. 343, Flagstaff; *Mpengula* v. *Mnhase*, 1950 N.A.C. (S.D.) 257, Umtata.

[92] *Xosana* v. *Dalisile*, 3 N.A.C. 189, Engcobo; *Manunga* v. *Yekiso*, 1936 N.A.C. (C & O) 87, Mqanduli; *Mpengula* v. *Mnhase*, 1950 N.A.C. (S.D.) 257, Umtata.

[93] *Manunga* v. *Yekiso*, 1936 N.A.C. (C & O) 87, Mqanduli; but see chapter XIV, 1, last paragraph.

[94] *Domoyi* v. *Matshiki*, 4 N.A.C. 158, Libode; *Ngcongolo* v. *Jaji*, 6 N.A.C. 39, Engcobo; *Lugebo* v. *Mbondwana*, 1939 N.A.C. (C & O) 5, Tsomo; *Ramncwana* v. *Siyotola*, 1937 N.A.C. (C & O) 172, Qumbu; but see the exceptional circumstances in *Dlumti* v. *Sikade*, 1947 N.A.C. (C & O) 47, Port St. Johns.

[95] *Mantshupu* v. *Kwebi*, 1938 N.A.C. (C & O) 37, Umtata; *Mayekiso* v. *Quwe*, 1942 N.A.C. (C & O) 38, Cape Town; *Mkekana* v. *Langasiki*, 1942 N.A.C. (C & O) 51, Bizana; *Mondli* v. *Zibi*, 1942 N.A.C. (C & O) 102, Mqanduli.

[96] *Mojakisane* v. *Khoapa*, 1938 N.A.C. (C & O) 28, Matatiele.

[97] See cases under note 4, *supra*; esp. *Mkekana* v. *Langasiki*, 1942 N.A.C. (C & O) 51, Bizana.

[98] *Mbombo* v. *Guga*, 4 N.A.C. 99, Tsolo.

[99] See generally the cases under note 95 *supra*, and *Jonas* v. *Vulangengqele*, 4 N.A.C. 96, St. Marks; *Mbombo* v. *Guga*, 4 N.A.C. 99, Tsolo; *Ngamani* v. *Sitsaka*, 5 N.A.C. 58, Ngqeleni.

[100] See chapter XIII, 1; see chapter IV, 4; *Nobeqwa* v. *Sinekile*, 1942 N.A.C. (C & O) 70, Mt. Fletcher; *Mbokojwana* v. *Gwagweni*, 1950 N.A.C. (S.D.) 183, Bizana; *Mzozyana* v. *Pienaar*, 5 N.A.C. 38, Mt. Fletcher.

[101] See cases under note 100, *supra.*

[102] See chapter IV, 3; *Mogidi* v. *Ngomo*, 1948 N.A.C. (T & N) 18, Pretoria.

[103] *Magadla* v. *Gewabe*, 1940 N.A.C. (C & O) 69, Matatiele; *Maphela* v. *Seshea*, 1943 N.A.C. (C & O) 25, Matatiele; *Mpantshwa* v. *Ngolonkulu*, 1952 N.A.C. (S.D.) 40, Bizana.

[104] *Ngcongolo* v. *Jaji*, 6 N.A.C. 39, Engcobo.

[105] *Mokoatle* v. *Mokoatle*, 4 N.A.C. 73, Matatiele.

[106] *Dlumti* v. *Sikade*, 1947 N.A.C. (C & O) 47, Port St. Johns.

(b) Other Payments

Apart from the marriage consideration proper, other payments are usually made in connection with a customary marriage. The payments mentioned in the first extract from *Cory* on the Sukuma are all made by the bridegroom or his family to the bride's family. In the second extract, on the other hand, *Wagner* on the Kavirondo Bantu deals with the reciprocal expenses and gifts made both by the bridegroom's kin and by the bride's kin.

H. Cory: Sukuma Law and Custom*

Customary Payments other than Bridewealth

During the negotiations concerned with the amount of bridewealth, other payments, some obligatory and some not necessarily so, are specifically mentioned.

Note: Considerable variations exist regarding payments of ceremonial beasts. As these payments are customary ones no co-ordination of rules has been attempted. . . .

Ng'ombe ya maji or *Ng'ombe ya itono.* The *ng'ombe ya maji* is an obligatory payment in all chiefdoms, except those mentioned (below).

The payment consists of one bull or ox and is made with the first instalment of the bridewealth.

The custom regarding the use of the beast varies:

(*a*) NF, UF.† The beast is slaughtered after the consummation of the marriage, therefore normally on the morning after the wedding, and is considered public proof that the parties are now married.

* H. Cory, *Sukuma Law and Custom*, Oxford University Press, 1953, pp. 19–21.

† These letters refer to districts in Sukumaland.

(*b*) SBS, KF, KS, KM.* The beast is killed at a feast arranged several weeks after the marriage, when the two families meet. It is considered the official confirmation of the bond which now exists between the two families.

(*c*) BD, BS, SS.* *A mbuli ya maji* (goat) instead of a *ng'ombe ya maji* (bull) is killed at any time after marriage, but only if the couple had no sexual intercourse prior to marriage.

(*d*) BSN, ZM, SM.* Neither *ng'ombe* nor *mbuli ya maji* payments exist.

If bridewealth is paid in money, a sum of Shs. 20/– specifically called *ng'ombe ya maji* is handed over in addition to the amount of the bridewealth.

The slaughter of the *ng'ombe ya maji* is nowhere obligatory and a father-in-law can keep the beast in his herd even in those areas where it is more usual to slaughter it.

Note: The slaughter of the *ng'ombe ya maji* is not legal proof of the consummation of marriage and therefore does not legalize the union.

Mbuli ya kilezu. The customary gift of one goat made by the son-in-law to the maternal grandfather of the wife. It is handed over to the wife's father who passes it on to the grandfather only if the latter demands it. Recently payments of Shs. 2/– to Shs. 5/– have been accepted instead.

The mbuli ya kilezu is a customary payment in all chiefdoms except BSN, SBS, KS,* where one head of cattle is given instead of a goat.

Ng'ombe ya bugabu or *Ng'ombe ya butigu.* The customary payment of one cow made by the son-in-law to his father-in-law in the event of his wishing to take his wife into the homestead of his own father before he has completed payment of the whole bridewealth. If the young couple wish to move into their own homestead, no *ng'ombe ya butigu* is payable.

Note: The significance of the payment of *ng'ombe ya butigu* and *ng'ombe ya kugila* is that with the entrance of the son's wife into his paternal home her work will benefit her husband's family.

Ng'ombe ya kugila. When a daughter-in-law arrives in the homestead of her husband's father, she customarily refuses to take food in the house and will eat with neighbours or will only eat food brought for her from her parent's house, until her father-in-law has given her a cow, the *ng'ombe ya kugila.* In some areas a goat is given instead of a cow. A little later the husband's sister or other relative goes to the wife's father and reports on the well-being of his daughter. He gives this relative a bull which is sent to the husband's father.

Mbuli ya luswagilo or *Mbuli ya mumagulu ga ng'ombe.* The gift of a goat made by the bridegroom to the delegates of the bride's father when they come to fetch the cattle of bridewealth.

Tumbati (*tobacco*). Formerly a quantity of tobacco was given as a present by the son-in-law to his father-in-law; nowadays instead of tobacco the son-in-law makes a present of Shs.2/–.

G. Wagner: The Bantu of North Kavirondo*

The Economic Aspect of the Conclusion of Marriage

The preceding narrative clearly shows the importance which, in connexion with marriage, is attached to the exchange of gifts, especially food, between the wife's parents and those of the husband. Beginning with a series of formally arranged exchanges of gifts during and immediately after the wedding festivities, the mutual gift-making between the two groups of affinal relatives continues in a more or less formal

* These letters signify districts of Sukumaland.

* G. Wagner, *The Bantu of North Kavirondo*, Oxford University Press, 1949, pp. 430–433.

manner for many years, although it gradually becomes less as the new family which results from the marriage establishes a homestead of its own and acquires full social and economic status.

The economic aspect thus plays an important part in the conclusion of a marriage. Although the bride-wealth proper appears as the most outstanding item in the list of economic transactions that take place in connexion with marriage, its economic value is almost equalled by the aggregate of numerous gifts exchanged between the two parties as well as the frequent display of reciprocal hospitality, both in the course of the wedding festivities and on a number of subsequent occasions which we shall describe in their respective contexts. The following compilation is a list of gifts and counter-gifts which appears to be typical as regards families of average means among the Vugusu:

(A) *Expenses incurred and gifts made by the bridegroom's kin*

1. At the betrothal: Four or six pots of beer brewed for the beer of *enganana;* two pots sent over to the bride's mother (*gamalua gexusuta*). Fowls and flour for the meal offered to the bride's father; new beer-pipe and tube for the bride's father (small value only).
2. When handing over the bride-wealth: A fowl and porridge for the first party which comes to inspect the marriage cattle. The same if a second inspection takes place.
3. At the *siselelo* (first visit by the bride to the bridegroom's place): Two bullocks; one killed for the relatives of the bridegroom, some of the meat (front leg) sent over to the bride's place. The other bullock (bullock of *naŋeso*) sent alive or slaughtered, either before or a few days after the *siselelo.* Two basketfuls of porridge for the guests and bridesmaids; about six large pots of beer, some for the bridesmaids and others sent over to the bride's place during or after the bride's first visit. Small presents for the bridesmaids.
4. At second visit of bride (*kámafura* or *sifóroro*): Porridge and meat for the bridesmaids as well as small presents. Goat of defloration.
5. At third visit of bride: Bullock 'to make the bride eat'. Hoes, fowls, &c., for making her perform other 'duties'.
6. At subsequent visits: Small gifts of food (porridge, meat, fish, fowls) whenever the wife pays a visit to her parents.

(B) *Expenses incurred and gifts made by the bride's kin*

1. When asking for 'handle of hoe': Food (fowl and porridge) offered to emissary from bridegroom.
2. Betrothal: Nothing.
3. Transfer of marriage cattle: Nothing, unless the bridegroom's people accompany the cattle all the way, in which case they are offered hospitality at the bride's place.
4. *Siselelo:* A small granary full of sorghum for brewing beer. One 'bullock of eating', the hide and foreleg sent to the bridegroom's father. About eight basketfuls of eleusine flour sent to the bridegroom's place together with the cow of *naŋeso.* About four basketfuls of eleusine flour for porridge to be served to visitors and bridesmaids before they start off to the bridegroom's place.
5. Second visit of bride: About four baskets of eleusine flour and slaughtered bullock or goat as present for the bridegroom's father. No feast at the bride's place.
6. Third visit of bride: Fowls and flour and flour taken by the bride as a present for her mother-in-law.
7. The bride's granary handed over to her father-in-law.
8. The bullock or heifer of *kumuoulo* paid to the husband.
9. The ox or bullock of *sítexo* killed by the wife's father. Also a goat which is eaten in the house of the wife's parents.
10. Small gifts of food given to the wife by her mother whenever she returns to her husband's place after a visit to her mother's place.

A comparison of these two lists of gifts and expenses incurred for hospitality shows that they are to a large extent reciprocal, the slight preponderance on the bride's side being mainly due to the bullock of *kumuoulo* which is a return gift expressing the satisfaction of the wife's kin with the marriage cattle. The reciprocity on some of these occasions is almost immediate. The bull of *naŋeso* has hardly been sent from the bride's place to that of the bridegroom when a return gift of the same nature and even of the same name passes from the bridegroom's father to the bride's father. It differs from an actual returning of the gift only in so far as the bull which is handed over as the counter-gift must be a different animal. Similarly, the baskets of food carried to and fro between the two parties at every visit exchanged between them are, both in quality and in quantity, as nearly alike as possible, although here again it would be considered a gross violation of good manners if the same instead of different grain were returned as a counter-gift.

Being strictly reciprocal, these gifts must have a different meaning from the handing over of the bride-wealth, for this is clearly a one-sided transfer of material objects in exchange for the acquisition of rights and privileges concerning a human being. The care with which the actual quantities exchanged are listed in narratives on the subject, and the ostentation with which the gifts are transferred and displayed in the yard of the other party are significant. Here are two groups of people, hitherto entirely unconnected by any specific social ties, even expressly devoid of any joint interests save their common tribal background who now, through the marriage of two of their members, enter into a particularly close relationship with one another. To make it a success this relationship must be balanced; each side must feel and be made to feel that the other side is its equal. Accordingly, as the two groups establish their mutual relations, each side tends to be suspicious and jealous of the other, lest it might try to assume a superior attitude and consider itself of higher standing. The dominant feeling in each group seems aptly expressed by the lines which we have already quoted: 'Then over there the people can worry when they sleep and think: what can we do for them, because now they will be calling us the poor ones?' Hence, as one group demonstrates its wealth by sending presents to the other, the other group answers the 'challenge' by returning a gift of the same nature, either immediately or on a subsequent occasion laid down by convention. Thus the primary significance of the exchange of gifts appears to be the demonstration by the two parties, both to each other and to outsiders, of their equality of economic status.

But there are other elements involved as well. The fact that both parties test each other's economic resources by challenging one another with presents implies that the conclusion of marriages according to the full tribal norms between persons of unequal wealth tends to be discouraged, as the economically weaker party in the long run could not maintain the reciprocity on the scale established by the stronger party. The fear of being put to shame by the generous gifts of the in-law relatives thus induces people to intermarry with their economic equals, and counteracts the temptation which a father might feel to marry his daughter off to the wealthiest suitor, as he can offer the largest amount of bride-wealth.

Moreover, the economic burden which the wedding festivities entail is generally distributed over the different 'fathers' of the bridegroom or the bride respectively, i.e. their real fathers and their various paternal uncles as well as their maternal uncles will each furnish a gift. Thus the real father will pay for the *liaxa* or *siselelo*, one of his brothers will bear the expenses connected with the *kamafura*-visit, still another will provide the ox *sitexo*, while both paternal and maternal uncles will contribute towards the bull of *kumuoulo*. This sharing of expenses among the various kinsmen on both sides clearly serves to extend the group of people who take an active part in the arrangement of the marriage, and thus to strengthen the bonds established between two groups of people by the marriage of two of their members. The exchange of gifts and hospitality—as we shall point out more fully in one of the subsequent chapters—is one of the chief means of establishing and maintaining a relationship. The variety of reciprocal gifts and the number of people participating in the exchange are thus an indication of the strength and the scope of the relationship that is being established.

Chapter 12

THE LEGAL CONSEQUENCES OF MARRIAGE

In the extracts which follow an attempt is made to present a series of descriptions of the other legal relationships which arise as a result of the marriage relationship. This section is, for this reason, principally concerned with the rights and duties of husband and wife *inter se*, and the legal obligations which each of them is made to undertake under customary law.

It emerges quite clearly from the material in this chapter that this subject is one which must be viewed against the social background of the particular society. The extract from *Holleman* bears this out.

It is as well to bear in mind that the polygynous (more accurately, the potentially polygynous) character of African customary marriage lends special significance to this topic. All of the extracts given here indicate the peculiar nature of the problems which arise within a family which may contain a plurality of wives, and children whose allegiance may be divided between the immediate 'house' to which they are attached through their mothers and the over-all authority which their common father exercises as head of the household.

The writers who have dealt with this topic have tended to emphasise the purely personal aspects of the marital relationship. It is as well to recall, however, that this subject involves—and overlaps—other aspects of the law: thus it impinges on status relationships, in regard to wives as well as children, which are more properly dealt with in this volume under the Law of Persons; and it affects such other branches of the law as the Law of Property and the Law of Contract and Tort (insofar as a husband is liable for the tortious conduct of his wives and other wards).

The extract from *van Tromp*, is particularly useful as a comprehensive and thorough treatment of nearly every aspect of the topic.

J. van Tromp: Xhosa Law of Persons*

Relations Between Husband and Wife

General

As has already been pointed out in Chapter 1, a female, according to Xhosa Law, is always considered to be under the 'guardianship'[1] of a male. Upon her marriage a wife falls under the guardianship of her husband. The domicile of the husband is the domicile of the wife.[2] Because she is under his guardianship her husband fixes her place of residence, which is in the indlu he builds for her. He usually builds this indlu when she has borne him children. It is customary for the newly-married wife to sleep with her mother-in-law (unina zala) for the first few nights so that the unina zala may initiate her into the rights and duties connected with the umzi.

The relationship between husband and wife is, of course, *sui generis*, but to a degree resembles that which exists between a 'major' and a 'minor', between father and

* J. van Tromp, *Xhosa Law of Persons*, Juta & Co. Ltd., 1947, pp. 81–109.

daughter. The wife has passed from the guardianship of her father to that of her husband.

But let it not be supposed that the relationship between husband and wife is that which exists between an owner and his chattel, as some people think. A wife can never be treated as a piece of property. She is not the property of her husband, he cannot sell or prostitute her. She cannot be punished without cause. Her husband cannot injure or kill her, for if he does he is liable to pay a fine to the Chief.[3]

She must conduct herself like a good and respectable wife under the guardianship of her husband. She must fulfil her marital, domestic and social duties in accordance with the control of her husband (see (b) below). In spite of all this, the wife is, however, in no servile position. She is regarded as the mistress of the home. 'Umzi u ngu mzi ngomfazi,' which means that a home is such by virtue of the wife.[4]

To a certain extent the influence and control of her own people are also felt, as is clearly seen under the ukuteleka custom.

A. *Status of Wives:*

Where a man marries only one wife there is no difficulty with regard to her status (see Chapter I). But where a man marries more than one wife the status of these successive wives is different and must be fixed. The status of these wives is fixed according to the indlu—that is, hut or house system.

In order to understand the indlu system and therefore the status of the different wives, a sketch and a description of a Xhosa umzi are essential.

1. *Description of the umzi.* Coming out of the *Great House* (indlu enkulu or ibotwe), the *Right Hand House* (indlu ya se kunene) is on one's right hand.[5] Each of these izindlu has one or more *amaqadi* or '*rafters*' attached to it. The amaqadi or supporting houses of each of these two principal houses are situated on the side of the house which they support. It may happen, however, that the qadi is situated at a different spot, away from this umzi it supports. Each indlu has its own vimba or store hut. Sometimes each of the principal houses has its own ubuhlanti or cattle kraal and its own isibaya or kraal for the calves. But nowadays there is usually one ubuhlanti and one isibaya to the whole umzi.

There are separate huts for relatives and boys and for girls when they grow older; also a hut for the old mother (Xegokazi) of the umnin' umzi. The boys very often sleep here with the Xegokazi. This hut is situated on the side of the Great House (see sketch). The boys have their own hut when they grow older, on the right-hand side.

The open space between the ubuhlanti and the izindlu (huts) is called the *inkundla*, meaning both courtyard and court. It is here that the men gather on festival occasions; here laws and customs are discussed and cases decided; it is an open court of justice; here male strangers are attended to; a girl about to be married must kneel here in order to receive the blessings of her father and relatives; the bride must first walk through the inkundla; on the day the abakhwetha are released from the isutu they have to gather in the inkundla to receive the devotions (iziyalo) and gifts from their fathers, relatives and friends.

The right-hand side as one enters an indlu is the side reserved for the husband, and the left-hand side belongs to the wife. The usual place for the children is just ahead of the fireplace. If there are many children the girls will sleep on the mother's side and the boys on the father's side. When the children grow older they have their own huts to sleep in (see sketch).

2. *Chief's umzi.* The umzi of the Chief is built on the same principle as that of a commoner described above. The only difference of note is that an *ixhiba house* is found only in a Chief's umzi; this is a house to look after the interests of the deceased father of this house (see below) and prevent them from dying out. The xhiba house, as will appear below, is, however, not in the same umzi as the other houses but at a separate place.

UMZI WOM XHOSA.
(XHOSA KRAAL)

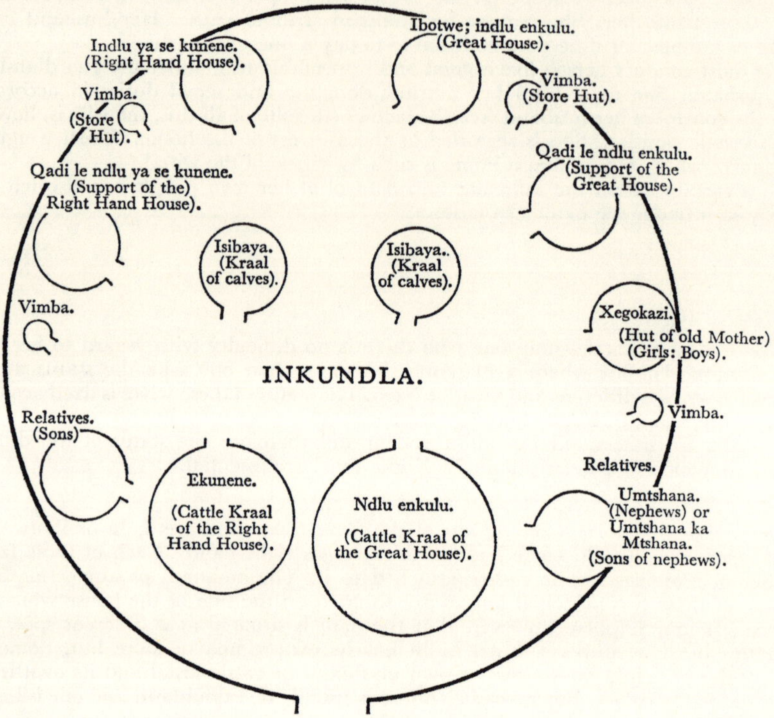

3. *Great Wife*

(a) *The Great Wife of a commoner*. The first wife a commoner marries is his Great Wife or umfazi omkhulu, who exercises great influence in the umzi. She has a good deal of authority over the other women, especially over the amaqadi. She is, as it were, the mother of the umzi and the other wives do most of the work in the umzi under her direction. But the Great Wife cannot force the other women to work, e.g. to hoe the gardens for her.

'Sometimes, when the Great Wife is a harsh woman and the minor wives do not care to submit to her, they appeal to the husband for protection, and in that way "rafters" are transferred from the Great Wife's section to that of the Right Hand Wife; more consequence would then be attached to the Right Hand section, but this practice is not usual.'[6]

The possibility exists for the commoner-husband, upon exceptionally good and sufficient cause, and for very strong reason, to change the order of the status of his wives. This happens, however, very seldom. He has to take the case before the family court, and the matter may even end before the Chief's Court.

Our Native Appeal Courts have decided that a commoner has no right to nominate the rank or status of his wives and that their rank or status follow the order of their priority of marriage.[7] This view holds good for Pondo Law but it is doubtful whether it is in conformity with Xhosa Law. Xhosa Law acknowledges the limited right of a husband to nominate upon very strong reason and good and sufficient cause.

The umnin' umzi divides his time between the Great House and the other houses. If he falls ill he must be taken to the Great House, for he must die there. Should he suddenly die elsewhere his body is taken there to be carried to the place of burial. This is to indicate, for the last time, that this is the Great House and to prevent any argument or strife as to which is the Great House.

It is customary for the husband to discuss with his umfazi omkhulu any intended or successive marriage. For she must preserve peace and harmony in the umzi and the dignity of the umzi largely depends upon her (see (b) below). Being the Great Wife she usually insists upon her husband's marrying more wives, for this means an increase in her authority and it also enhances her status in the eyes of the outside world.

The Great Wife gives birth to the *indlamafa*, or the heir and successor of the umnin' umzi. Because the first son born to the Great Wife is the successor to his father's status and property, he not only has a claim to all the property of his father not distributed to the specific houses, but he has also legal claim to the property of the *qadi le ndlu enkulu* (the support, rafter, of the Great House) if the heir and successor to this house dies. After the death of the umnin' umzi the indlamafa also succeeds to the control over the whole umzi in that he takes the place of the umnin' umzi.

If there be no heir at all to the Great Wife, the husband may marry a *womb* (isisu) for the Great Wife (see 7 below) or amaqadi (rafters) to the Great Wife (see 6 below).

Should the man (usually in the case of Chiefs), having two or more wives, die while it is uncertain which wife was married first and therefore who is the rightful heir of the deceased, the brothers of the latter and/or his nearest and closest relatives will bring the matter before the family court where the point at issue will be settled. If the court is divided and cannot decide, the case is taken to the Chief's Court where the Chief and his amaphakathi finally decide. In the case of a Chief the matter will be settled by the amaphakathi and minor chiefs.

(b) *The Great Wife of the Chief.* Unless she is the only wife he marries, the first wife married by a Chief is not his umfazi omkhulu (Great Wife) as is the case with abantu abamnyama (commoners); this is so even if she is of royal blood. The first wife married to a Xhosa Chief is called the *Umsul'udaka*, the wife that washes off the white clay (ifutha) of his initiation, and as such cannot be the Great Wife. As the name indicates, this umsul' udaka wife the Xhosa Chief marries not long after he has come out of the seclusion hut. She is not necessarily a woman of adequate rank and status, or one of royal blood. There are cases known where the first wife has been a woman of loose character, but because she was the one who cleansed the Chief of his boyhood, it did not matter, for her son would not become the heir and successor. The first wife of a Chief, however, is usually from amongst the daughters of his councillors or close friends.

According to Xhosa Law the Great Wife of a Chief may be married last, but there is no specified time when such marriage should take place. For this reason it is not uncommon for a Chief to marry his Great Wife not many years before his death. The method was, especially in olden days, resorted to as a means of protection, to prevent the eldest son of the Great Wife from usurping the power of his father and pushing his father aside. This method also prevented disputes with regard to succession during the life of the Chief.

The Chief has a right to nominate the status of his wives. Here Xhosa Law differs from the law in force in Western Pondoland, where the first wife married by the Paramount Chief is the Great Wife.[8] This has a historical origin but this rule differs also from the law in force in Eastern Pondoland where the custom of *ukubeka*, that is to nominate, like the amaXhosa Chiefs, prevails. This is usually done in collaboration with his amaphakathi or councillors, and a wife's status is sometimes proclaimed on the day the Chief marries her.

'In Gcalekaland it is held to be the custom that once a Chief's wife has had her precedence assigned to her she may not be deposed from it under any circumstances.'[9] This view is not, however, correct, as will appear below.

Should the Chief, during his lifetime, not have nominated a Great Wife with the help of his sub-chiefs and councillors, and hence, after his death it be known who the Great Wife is and who has to succeed the deceased, it will be the duty of the sub-chiefs, headmen and other councillors to nominate the Great Wife, whose son will then be the successor. In such cases, rare though they are, the wife nominated will be one who is of highest rank, of royal blood and one who has borne a son.

The status and rank of the Great Wife of a Xhosa Chief are determined by various factors which, if present, do away with any difficulty in respect of succession after the death of the Chief. These factors, I was told by the amaXhosa, are: (i) The woman must be of royal blood from some other Bantu tribe and not from among the amaXhosa tribes. Intimate research has revealed the fact that all Xhosa Chiefs took as Great Wives women from the Thembu tribe and other not Xhosa tribes. Should there be a dispute as to the status of wives of a Chief a wife from the Thembu royal house is sure to have priority. The fact that she is a *thembukazi*, is decisive, provided other factors are equal.

The only tribe in the Xhosa area whose Chiefs may marry a Great Wife from among the amaXhosa tribes is the amaGqunukwebe. This fact, however, and other facts and circumstances, tend to prove that the amaGqunukwebe are not a true Xhosa tribe though they have accepted Xhosa culture in full and consider themselves to be amaXhosa.

(ii) Furthermore, the Great Wife of a Chief is not lobolaed by himself, though he may also contribute towards the ikhazi. It is the tribe that contributes the lobola cattle and actually lobolaes the wife for the Chief. This Great Wife of the Chief is taken and spoken of as the woman or mother of the whole land, the nation. She is the *inkosikazi yesizwe*. Some amaXhosa express it by saying that not the Chief but the tribe marries the Great Wife and the Chief is there only as representative of the tribe to cohabit with this woman and to produce a successor to reign over the tribe. That is why the wish of the Chief to marry his Great Wife is discussed by his councillors (amaphakathi) who are the appropriate representatives of the tribe and are also instrumental in seeing to it that the marriage is so concluded.

(iii) Another factor which determines the status of the Great Wife is that she has to be accepted and formally declared such by the full court, *ibandla*, of the Chief. But this procedure is not strictly adhered to, for by contributing towards the ikhazi the tribe and sub-chiefs have accepted this woman as the Great Wife of their Chief, and the nature of the marriage and the fact that she inhabits the ibotwe or indlu enkulu are sufficient to convince anyone.

4. *The Right Hand Wife*. The second-married wife of a commoner is the *umfazi wa se kunene* (Right Hand Wife). This is not so among the Chiefs, as we have already seen.

The umfazi wa se kunene has a very important status. It is second only to that of the umfazi omkhulu (Great Wife) and she therefore exercises great authority in the umzi. She is not wholly subservient to the Great Wife, and has an independent status which is especially emphasised by the facts that (like the umfazi omkhulu to a certain degree): (i) she may have one or more amaqadi married for her, and amaqadi are only married for women of status; (ii) a womb, isisu (vulgo, 'seed-bearer') may be married for her; (iii) in case the lawful heir and successor is still a minor, her first son will function and act for him and in the case of a royal family he will act as regent for an heir and successor who is still a minor. A striking example is Ndlambe, the right hand brother of Mlawu, the son of Rharhabe. After his brother's death Ndlambe acted as regent for Ngqika, the lawful heir and successor of Mlawu. (iv) In case of both abantu abamnyama (commoners) and abantu negazi (Chiefs, royalty), the heir and successor of the husband does not become heir of the property of the indlu ya se kunene; the property of this house belongs to the eldest son born to this house. (v) In the case of Chiefs, as a result of his mother's status, he will be given a chieftainship over a portion of his father's tribe. An example of a very early date, as far back as one can trace it among the amaXhosa, is that of Gcaleka and Rharhabe, the sons of Chief Palo by his Great Wife and his Right Hand Wife respectively. Gcaleka, as a result of his mother's status, became Paramount Chief of *all* the amaXhosa tribes; Rharhabe became Paramount Chief of all the tribes descendant from the Right Hand House of Palo. That is why today the amaNgqika are superior in status to the amaNdlambe, but the amaGcaleka are superior to all other amaXhosa tribes. This position is known and acknowledged up to the present day among the amaXhosa.

5. *The origin of the Indlu Enkulu and the Indlu Ya Se Kunene*. In the case of commoners it

seems natural that the first wife a man marries should be his umfazi omkhulu (Great Wife); and the second one his umfazi wa se kunene (Right Hand Wife). But why is this not the case among the Chiefs? To this the amaXhosa give an explanation which, though it may seem feasible, cannot historically be correct, for the same principle is found among other and older Bantu tribes independent of the amaXhosa.

The amaXhosa say that the indlu enkulu and the indlu ya se kunene had their origin some time in the beginning of the eighteenth century, during the time of Palo, a younger son of Chief Tshiwo. Here, according to them, also lies the origin of the right of the Chief to nominate his wives.[10]

It was usual for a Chief to send one of his daughters as wife to a Chief of another tribe The Chief did this (*a*) to make an alliance with the other tribe; (*b*) to enhance his status; (*c*) to increase his own exchequer; (*d*) to prevent his daughter from becoming an old spinster, which was considered a disgrace; (*e*) because it was a great honour for a tribe if their princess was married to a prince, more especially if he was the future king.

During the reign of Palo two chiefs of other tribes each sent their daughters to be married to the young Chief. These daughters with their respective *ooduli* (bridal parties) arrived at the same time at the Great Place. Palo did not know what to do. He could not send the princesses back, for it meant insulting the other Chiefs and it might mean war.

Now there was a great adviser (iciko) or expert (ichule) on all matters of law and custom (some amaXhosa say this man was Majeke, the son of Kulile), and Palo sent for this adviser. Meanwhile the two princesses with their ooduli were staying at kraals near the Great Place.

On his arrival this expert was given all the details and shown the girls. He was to decide what each of the princesses would be called after they had undergone the *umdudo ozeleyo* or full-dress wedding ceremony which is concluded by the umdudo. The people were assembled in the inkundla. The expert requested King Palo to stand up, and he asked the King: '*Yi nto nina le i phakathi kweengalo zenkosi*,' what is this between the arms of the Chief? Palo said it was his head (intloko). Thereupon the expert took Palo's right arm and asked Palo what this was. Palo said: '*ingalo yokunene*,' the right arm. The expert then said, 'let it be so with these two women when you marry them; let one be the "head" and the other the "right hand".' This was to show, he said, that both women were of high status (nesibalo), for the 'head' was the thing with 'inqondo', brain, and the 'right hand' was the thing with strength. The 'head' came first and is greater; the 'right hand' is strong and can help the 'head'.

On the wedding day they therefore 'dalwaed' (created) these two women as the umfazi omkhulu (Great Wife) and the umfazi wa se kunene (Right Hand Wife). It was also then decided that each of these women should have power and authority,and the eldest son of the umfazi wa se kunene should also be a 'kumkani' or king; but the son of the umfazi omkhulu should be the greatest kumkani.

In the same year these two women each gave birth to a son. These sons are sometimes, incorrectly, said to have been twins. What the amaXhosa actually mean is that they were born in the same year by two women married at about the same time, each wife having a high status independently of the other.

In this way the umfazi wa se kunene (Right Hand Wife) became a woman of great status with authority and not totally subservient to the umfazi omkhulu (Great Wife). Because of her status her son also became a Chief with his own followers as distinct from the Great Wife's son.

6. *Amaqadi*. The amaqadi are women married and attached to the two principal houses; they give status to these principal houses and support the latter, hence they are often called 'supporting houses' or 'rafters'. Should there be no male issue in the house to which a qadi is attached, the eldest son of the senior qadi will become the lawful heir and successor of the house without male issue if the principal house has no male issue.

There is no limit in Xhosa Law to the number of wives a man may marry. In the case of a Chief, he nominates his wives; but in the case of a commoner, after the umfazi omkhulu and the umfazi wa se kunene comes the third wife a man marries. The third wife is, except in very extraordinary cases, according to the Native Appeal Courts (see below), the *qadi le ndlu enkulu* (the qadi of the Great House). She therefore supports the Great House.

It is sometimes asserted, though very rarely, that the third wife married by a Xhosa man is his 'left hand wife' (umfazi wa se khohlo) and her indlu or establishment is then spoken of as the indlu ya se khohlo (the left-hand house). This is confusing the Xhosa with the Zulu family system. Xhosa Family Law knows no left hand wife; the third wife of a commoner is the qadi wife of the indlu enkulu.

If, therefore, a man marries more than two wives, these subsequent wives will be attached to one or another of the two principal houses (see sketch), but each of these amaqadi or minor wives will have her own separate hut and establishment and cattle allocated to that establishment. It is here that a qadi and an isisu or womb (see 7 below) differ. The qadi is usually married after the first two wives and she has a separate indlu and also a vimba (store hut) of her own. She is not absorbed by the principal house. The children of the qadi belong to her own establishment and not the indlu to which she is a qadi. Because of her status the children of a qadi, if boys, may in future be able to establish separate and indpendent establishments, as, for example, when they marry.

The status of the amaqadi is inferior to those of the two principal houses, but they follow the rank and status of the principal house to which they are attached though they are subordinate. In the case of Chiefs, however, the amaqadi are accorded their status by the Chief in collaboration with his family and amaphakathi (councillors). Among commoners, the third wife is the qadi le ndlu enkulu; the fourth wife is the qadi le ndlu ya se kunene; the fifth wife again is the qadi le ndlu enkulu. As a rule the indlu enkulu has more amaqadi than the indlu ya se kunene, for, being the Great House, it is of higher status. Some say that the indlu ya se kunene can only have one qadi.

This is not according to Xhosa Law, and it has been correctly stated that 'the sixth is the qadi wife of the Right Hand House, and so on'.[11]

There can, however, never be a qadi to another qadi. Only the two principal wives have amaqadi. Nor is an isisu or womb married to a qadi.

The general principle is that the indlu enkulu will have a qadi before the indlu ya se kunene. But the Native Appeal Courts have accepted the statement and principle that a man may marry a qadi to the Right Hand House before marrying a qadi to the Great Wife when there is no stock in the latter house.[12]

This view clashes with the following case quoted by Whitfield, South African Native Law, p. 35, which holds good for Xhosa Law: 'That the wives of a commoner must take precedence in accordance with the custom applicable to common people (the custom, viz., that the Great House gets a qadi before the Right Hand House), and that where any variation of the custom is alleged, overwhelming proof of such variation must be adduced.'[13]

The principle accepted by our Native Appeal Courts that a man may under certain circumstances marry a qadi to the Right Hand House before marrying one to the Great Wife (*umfazi omkhulu*) clashes with the correct ruling in the case of Peko *vs.* Mantanzima (1903) Henkel p. 60, that a qadi wife could not be married in support of the Right Hand House before such a wife had been provided in connection with the Great House.[14]

The general principle is that the house which needs a qadi is expected to furnish lobola cattle for the ikhazi of such qadi wife. For every indlu or house has to produce the ikhazi for its own qadi. But this does not necessarily mean that the third wife, for instance, must be the qadi to the Right Hand House if the latter house paid the ikhazi, as it is stated in the case referred to above in connection with the question of stock in one of the houses (Mgudlwa *vs.* Paliso, above). If the ikhazi for the third wife comes from the indlu ya se kunene that does not in itself mean that this third wife is the qadi to the indlu ya se kunene. For the ikhazi of the qadi to the indlu ya se kunene may come from the indlu enkulu. Because of this the indlu ya se kunene is indebted to the indlu enkulu for the number of lobola cattle which lobolaed the wife of the indlu ya se kunene. Hence under normal conditions the indlu enkulu has a claim to the ikhazi of the eldest daughter of the indlu ya se kunene. Now, should the husband lobola a third wife with cattle from the indlu ya se kunene, he may take these cattle for the third wife and set them off against the debt owed by the indlu ya se kunene to the indlu enkulu for the ikhazi given to lobola the wife of the indlu ya se kunene. If he does this (he will as a rule publicly make this known to his family court) then the indlu enkulu has no claim to the ikhazi of the eldest daughter of the indlu ya se kunene.

It is, moreover, the custom that a wife of superior status should have an iqadi before a wife of inferior status.

Even if the Great House has taken the ikhazi given for the eldest daughter of the indlu ya se kunene, it seems as if the latter house has no claim to the third wife's being the qadi le ndlu ya se kunene.

Should the husband, in order to lobola a third wife, take cattle from both the indlu enkulu and the indlu ya se kunene, the position is clear: this wife will be the qadi le ndlu enkulu. This is the case even if the indlu ya se kunene has contributed the greater number of the lobola cattle.

Xhosa Law recognises no qadi wife to support another qadi wife; for this custom is practised only in connection with the indlu enkulu and the indlu ya se kunene. And, as has already been said, neither can an isisu (womb) be married for a qadi; it would be as if a qadi were married for another qadi. If a qadi bears no children it does not matter, and does not warrant the husband to marry another qadi for this childless qadi. If he wants an heir in case of total failure of male issue he will marry another qadi (or an isisu) to one of the principal houses.

Should there be no male issue in the indlu ya se kunene,the eldest son of the qadi le ndlu ya se kunene will, because of his mother's status, be heir to the indlu ya se kunene.

But where the husband decides to marry an isisu (womb) to the indlu enkulu and one to the indlu ya se kunene, the sons of these wombs will succeed to the respective houses with the exclusion of the eldest sons of the amaqadi (see 7 below).

7. *Isisu, Womb (Vulgo: Seed-Bearer)*.[15] Should either the umfazi omkhulu or the umfazi wa se kunene not give birth to any children and be proved to be barren, or should either die without male issue, her husband may marry an isisu or womb to that house.[16] The womb thus married will then give birth to and raise seed for the wife for whom she is married and, as it were, sit in the doorstep of the house: *ukuhlala emnyango*. Hence a husband cannot rightly marry a womb for a wife who has a son, and any additional woman married for this wife would rank as a qadi; he may marry this woman while the wife is living if she be past the child-bearing stage and has borne no male issue.

A husband might prefer to marry a womb rather than a qadi to a house where there is no male issue, because he need not give the womb a separate establishment, and she has no status in the umzi (see below).

It is customary for the husband not to marry a womb to the indlu enkulu before he has married the umfazi wa se kunene, unless the umfazi omkhulu is dead and has no male issue.

If the wife for whom a womb is married has only daughters, and cannot any longer give birth to children, the sons and daughters of the womb will be looked upon as the younger brothers and sisters of the daughters of the wife to whom their mother was married as womb.[17]

The womb that is married is not given the rank or status of the wife to whom she is married. Nor is she given the status of a qadi. The womb virtually loses her personality and becomes absorbed by the house to which she is married as a womb. She has no status 'but becomes the "body" of the woman for whom she has to raise up seed, and the children borne by her are regarded as being those of the woman to whom she is seed-bearer.'[18] This is true also for Xhosa Law, except that the amaXhosa do not view this woman as a 'seed-bearer' or the 'body' of the wife to whom he is married. They take this woman to be the womb, the isisu, of that woman who cannot give birth to an heir. For they believe that something is wrong with the latter's womb, since she cannot give birth to an heir. And because she is the womb of another wife and has to *vusa*, to awake, raise up, that house and hereby prevent it from dying out, the womb has no separate establishment.

8. *Xhiba House*. This is a house found among Chiefs only and not among abantu abamnyama (commoners); and the establishment of the xhiba wife is not the in same umzi or kraal as the establishment of other women may be. The status of this wife differs from that of any other house of the husband. It is not under the control of either the indlu enkulu or the indlu ya se kunene.

The xhiba house is sometimes spoken of as the *indlu ye ndlu enkulu*, meaning that it is the House of the Great House, thereby indicating that it is the house of the Chief's father. It must perform certain sacrificial ceremonies for the spirits of the forefathers who have occupied it.

'A xhiba wife may be married at any time after the marriage of the Great Wife.'[19] This was not the practice among the amaXhosa. The xhiba wife is married after the fourth wife, and usually is the fifth wife married by the Chief.

Though it is customary for the Chief to put a wife into this umzi of his father after the latter's death, this is not essential and a xhiba wife may be married and 'put in' even during the life of the father of the Chief if the former is very old. Should the father still be Chief, and wish it, he may take the fifth wife of his eldest son and heir, who is responsible for seeing that this house of his father's is kept alive, and place her in this umzi of his. She does not become the father's wife, but remains the fifth wife of his son.

If the Xhiba House is instituted during the life of the father, this wife must look after and care for the old people. She will then fall under the control of her father-in-law; her eldest son will succeed to the property which belongs to his grandfather and which has not yet been allocated to any of the other houses, and he will also become head of this umzi. In any case, adequate provision is made for him, for upon his shoulders rests the responsibility of keeping alive the umzi of his grandfather.

It is also customary for the husband who marries a woman who is to be the xhiba wife to give to her house certain cattle. These are inherited by the eldest son of the xhiba wife, for the xhiba house is not dependent upon any other house of the husband.

When the son of the xhiba wife marries, the ikhazi for his wife is provided from the stock of his grandfather.[20] This is natural, for he becomes the virtual heir and successor to all the property left at the umzi by his grandfather after the usual allocations to the different houses have been settled.

B. *The Rights and Duties of Husband and Wife*

1. *The duties of wife.* The duties of the wife or wives of a man may be classed as: (*a*) marital; (*b*) domestic; and (*c*) social duties.

Should a wife neglect any of the above group of duties, which will be enlarged on below, it may be a cause for the husband to repudiate her, and this may result in the dissolution of the marriage ties.

(*a*) The primary marital duty of a wife towards her husband is to be faithful to him and to cohabit and have carnal intercourse with him only. Should she commit adultery it will, as a rule, not lead to dissolution of the marriage though she may be beaten, but the adulterer (umrexezi) will be fined. She will have public opinion against her and will be called an irexezikazi, or an adulterous wife.

Though the wife is expected to be faithful to her husband, she is not always so. For, when the husband goes away, e.g. to work on the mines, his wife who remains behind soon finds a lover. There are instances where the husband's mother has selected from among friends a lover for her daughter-in-law. He metshaes with the woman and more often than not has sexual intercourse with her. This is contrary to the Xhosa Law of Marriage. If the husband should come back and find his wife commiting adultery or pregnant there would be no excuse.

The husband has an exclusive right to her body. She must be prepared to allow him the necessary conjugal rights. If she refuses these to her husband without valid reason it may lead the husband to repudiate her, which may lead to a dissolution of the marriage.

There are, however, instances where a woman may refuse her husband these conjugal rights:

(i) *When she is suckling a child.* It is an old Xhosa custom that no man shall force a woman to cohabit and have carnal connection with him while her breasts contain milk and she is suckling a child.[21]

It is also said that a man may not force his wife to cohabit with him when her child has just been weaned and is ill. But when the child is grown up and is ill it does not afford her an excuse to refuse carnal connection with her husband.

(ii) *If the woman is ill.* The husband will naturally not enjoy his marital rights when his wife is indisposed, and the law affords him no remedy under such conditions if she refuses him. When she menstruates she does not cohabit with her husband and is not expected to allow him even to try to cohabit with her.

(iii) *During pregnancy.* It is customary for a woman to refuse intercourse with her husband when she is pregnant. This refusal, however, is something personal and a local custom, and does not depend upon strict principles of law. But if the wife under such conditions refuses her husband he has no remedy. If the pregnant woman continues to cohabit with her husband he is expected to treat her with great consideration. Should he not, she may refuse him.

The next important marital duty of the wife is to care for her husband. He, as her husband, has primary right to her care, and her duty is in this respect first to her husband to the exclusion of all other people.

She must prepare the food for her husband and serve him. If he is thirsty there must be water for him to drink. When it is cold she must make a fire so that he may warm himself. If a feast is to be held she must prepare the beer for her husband and his friends. If he is ill it is her duty to look after him. She must mend his clothes and keep them in respectable order. Should he be in need of a sleeping mat she must see that he gets one. It is her duty to sweep his hut, smear it with cow-dung and keep it generally clean and in order.

Gross neglect of this duty may cause her husband to repudiate her, and may ultimately lead to the dissolution of the marriage.

(b) *The domestic duties* of the wife embrace primarily the care of the children: she must see that they get food to eat, doctor them when they are ill, clothe them and see to their welfare in general. It is customary for her for a few months after its birth to carry the child on her back during the day and sleep with it at night so that it will be in constant close proximity to her body and so be prevented from dying of exposure.

As their mother, she must teach them, especially the girls, how to do the various domestic duties and how to behave. When they grow older she is responsible for their general education in the work of a woman; she prepares them for the day when they marry.

But not only must she look after and care for her husband and children. Her domestic duties also extend to her parents-in-law. She must cook and draw water for them; she must make the fire and clean the huts. It is her duty to do this until a younger brother of her husband marries, when the latter's wife will take over this duty. It is generally accepted that her parents-in-law have a right to the services of their daughter-in-law.

A wife has to do her domestic work and also perform certain duties in the field.[22] She must keep her house clean and make it acceptable and as attractive as possible to her husband and his family. She must smear the huts, also that of her parents-in-law, but not the side allocated to men. If she refuses to perform these household duties the husband may repudiate his wife.

When a new indlu (hut, house) is built the wives must cut the grass to thatch it and also do the thatching. But nowadays, though the cutting of grass for the thatching is done exclusively by the women, the thatching itself has largely passed on to the shoulders of the men of the umzi. But in the case of the isutu or seclusion hut of the abakwetha, the thatching is still done by the women only; and they must be married women. The women must make the long grass ropes used in thatching; and when the indlu is finished they must make the clay and plaster the inside and the outside of the indlu. Plastering, whenever needed, is the work of women.

When it is time for sowing they must help one another to cultivate the lands given to them by their husband. The introduction of the plough has transferred much of this work to the man, but it is not uncommon to see a woman driving the oxen or leading them or even handling the plough. 'When Gcaleka first saw a plough about 100 years ago, he was greatly impressed and said it was worth ten wives.'

Hoeing is the work of women, though occasionally a man may help his wives and children. When the reaping starts the wives have to see that the crops are reaped and brought to the umzi. They are usually assisted by the young men and boys of the umzi.

Thrashing is done by the wives. But men nowadays also help with the thrashing in case of need. The wives must store away the mealies or take them out of the pit.

When some household utensil is needed and she has the consent of her husband, the wife must carry the mealies (she always does so on her head) to the trader where they are exchanged for the necessary tea, coffee, tobacco or piece of cloth or even medicine, or other household utensil.

Gross neglect of these duties may also cause repudiation of the wife, and the marriage ties may be dissolved.

(c) The *Social Duty* of the wife is to conduct herself with the utmost dignity. She must be an example to the children and take care that her deeds do not tend to cause trouble. She must preserve peace and harmony in the umzi and be friendly to the other umizi. A quarrelsome wife and one who disturbs the peaceful relations, not only between the different houses of the umzi, but between the umzi and the outside world, may be repudiated.

It is her duty to uphold the status of the umzi, to keep to the hlonipha rules (see Soga: *The amaXhosa: Life and Customs*, p. 208) and keep the peace between the children.

An umtshakazi, or newly married wife, dare not approach the huts of the umzi where she is now living from the inkundla. She must first go to the back of the hut and from there make her way into the indlu. She continues to observe this custom until she has one or more children. Should she be childless she still observes this custom but watches to see when women who were married at more or less the same time as she, but who have borne children, no longer observe this restriction.

A wife is not supposed to walk through the inkundla, especially when she is an umtshakazi. The following example may be related: While sitting in the inkundla at an umzi, I saw the wife of one of the inmates come in from the fields; she wore a necklace of herbs around her neck. This interested me. I asked her to come to me but she refused. I was then told that it was contrary to custom, and indeed looked upon as an offence for a woman to walk about in the inkundla or to go into the ubuhlanti. It is the duty of the wife to avoid the inkundla and ubuhlanti of her husband's people.[23]

In case the wife does not carry out these restrictions of magico religious importance she will soon be termed a bad and disobedient wife. The whole village will look down upon her. Her husband may punish her or even repudiate her.

There rests a solemn duty upon a wife to *hlonipha* or pay reverence to her husband's father and all his male relatives. She may not mention their names or any word that has the same root as the names of her father-in-law and his male progenitors. This duty is stringently laid upon the wives of a husband. The neglect of this duty, wilful or otherwise, is punishable. A wife who does not strictly adhere to this rule is very often not only beaten but immediately driven home to her people, and in many cases she will be fetched back only many years later, or not at all. She is a dangerous wife, may even be called an igqwirakazi or witch, and may cause damage to the umzi.

When I spoke to the old qadi le ndlu enkulu of a late Paramount Chief of the amaXhosa (she was a very old woman) she refused to mention the names of her father-in-law or any of his male progenitors. She told me it was strictly forbidden.

A wife who has committed a breach of the hlonipha custom will, even before her husband takes matters into hand, if she realises the offence, go to her own people, tell them what has happened and ask them for a goat, sheep or something to take back to her umzi to clear her of the guilt and prevent an evil from coming over the umzi. The gift is taken to her husband and she thereby 'washes off' the whole thing. If she does not do it her husband will send her to fetch something to settle the matter.

'Arising out of the hlonipha custom there is a peculiar custom observed. It is a prohibition placed upon the woman of a kraal by the paterfamilias against their use of some articles such as an axe or pipe or other object, into which he states has entered the spirit of an ancestor, or which may represent his father who may still be living.'[24]

No woman is allowed to consume milk in any form during the period of menstruation and while she is pregnant. If she does she is punished and perhaps driven away as a dangerous woman. A wife must avoid taking milk during these periods lest her deed have an ill effect on the cattle of the umzi and cause grave damage.

A pregnant woman must observe certain further restrictions, the breach of which will turn public opinion against her in the first place, and if she insists in spite of warnings from the people of the umzi, may lead to the breaking up of the marriage ties. For, if she insists upon doing the 'evil' thing and miscarriage results, she will be accused of witchcraft and sent home to her own people. This is tantamount to a repudiation and may result in the dissolution of the marriage.

Her movements are restricted in that she must not go to her own people when in an advanced state of pregnancy unless there is perfect agreement between the two families. The pregnant woman may only go to her own people if she has the consent of the umnin'ikhaya (umzi) or kraalhead. She first approaches her husband who in turn consults his father or the head of the kraal. This is the customary procedure and is especially rigidly observed in the case of a woman's first-born child. If the woman does not obey this rule it is believed that this will affect the child, because on her marriage day she was taken into the ubuhlanti (cattle kraal) which is a most sacred place and the 'home' of the izinyanya or ancestral spirits, and from that time all the children born of her while she is the wife of this man should be guarded by the izinyanya of the umzi of her husband. Should she therefore go to another umzi without consultation and consent, she is slighting the izinyanya, who are bound to take revenge and cause ill-fortune to befall the child.

Under normal conditions a pregnant woman is not allowed to give birth at her own family's umzi or at the umzi of any stranger, but only at that of her husband. If it happens that she is at her own people's umzi and her labour begins there, word is quickly sent to her husband's umzi to ask that she may be allowed to give birth at this umzi. After birth she will return home with the child and anything to be done to the child will be carried out at the umzi of her husband.

2. *Rights of wife.* Here the rights in general of a wife will be dealt with. . . .

The general idea that a Xhosa wife has no rights or rights so insignificant that they are not worth mentioning, that she herself is the property of her husband and is treated as a chattel by him, is incorrect (see 'General' above).

She has the right to come to him when her person or rights are assaulted and demand protection from him. He represents his wife in all actions and assists her in her rights against others. Should she have to institute an action against her husband, she will complain to his brothers or to the sub-chief, who will take the matter in hand.

If her husband assaults or injures her, she has the right to go home to her own people when she has an opportunity, and they will then resort to the *ukuteleka* custom. This is a right universally exercised by amaXhosa parents, in the first place to protect their married daughter against injury or cruel treatment by the husband, and it has the effect of a penalty to punish the husband for his deed. It is also resorted to in case her family wish to extract more lobola cattle.

When a wife feels unreasonably wronged by her husband she takes advantage of the first opportunity to go home to her family. Xhosa Law provides her with this right to return to her family so that her family may 'hold her back' and prevent her from returning to her husband, who is punished in that he has to pay a fine in order to get back his wife. Though the wife has no right to claim the fine or any portion of it from her husband or her people, who receive it, the uteleko safeguards her against ill-treatment by her husband.

It is the wife who takes the initial step, and whether this custom is resorted to or not, depends upon the wish of the wife to exercise the right she possesses.

The woman is kept at the umzi of her people until such time as the husband has paid the penalty for his acts. Usually one beast is imposed as fine and if he does not pay this fine his wife will remain at the umzi of her people.

She has the right to remain here for life if her husband refuses to redeem her, and conducts herself in this manner in order to place her family in a position to exercise the powers further afforded them under this custom.

The marriage ties are not broken, nor can the husband repudiate her for this conduct. This act of the woman in no way constitutes desertion, nor do the acts of her parents under such conditions afford her husband the right to repudiate her or lay an action against them. The husband and his family have no claim under such circumstances for the return of any part of the ikhazi.

When a woman is telekaed her husband usually goes to her people and discusses the situation with them. If he is willing and offers the fine imposed upon him, the wife's people have no right to refuse to give her up. They must deliver the wife to her husband upon the tendering of the fine by him. Should she refuse to go back to him, they will not have a right to keep the fine, and the dissolution of the marriage may result.

Where a husband exceeds his power of chastisement by severely harming or inflicting some permanent injury on his wife and drawing excessive blood, the case will go to the Great Place, and at the same time her people will (or may) hold her under the uteleko custom. Such acts, without exception, will be punished by the Chief, the penalty being in the form of izizi or blood money. In former times, if a wife in such a case was the daughter of a Chief, it might lead to war between the two tribes. A good example of this is the war between the amaXhosa and the abaThembu during the reign of Sarili in 1873, when his daughter was ill-treated by the Thembu Chief.

After marriage a wife has the right to a doctor when she is ill and her husband pays. He calls an igqira or doctor, and has to pay the doctor's fee. But should her illness be ascribed to the fact that she did not undergo the intonjane ceremony before her marriage she has the right to go back to her own people to be put through the ceremony, but she then has no right against her husband. Should her people refuse, she has the right, through her husband, to go to the Chief, who will force her people to put her through the intonjane ceremony.

Though her husband has the exclusive right to his wife's body, she has no such right against him. Even where the husband has more than one wife, his wives have no exclusive right to his body. It is their right that he should cohabit with them, but Xhosa Law does not demand conjugal fidelity from the husband. A man may and does therefore have extra-marital relations with other women, and his wife has to be satisfied. Of course, public opinion will turn against him if he commits adultery too often.

His wives have a right to demand that he should cohabit with them and not neglect them: he usually lives with one for a while and then proceeds to the next. The time he spends with each depends upon himself, as long as he does not seriously neglect any one of them, for neglect may mean a gross insult and cause the woman to return to her own people, to whom the husband will be answerable.

Once his wife has grandchildren she has the right to inform her husband that she now wishes to go and live with her eldest son. She exercises this right and her husband does not prevent her, for it is considered improper for a woman with grandchildren to be still cohabiting with her husband and bearing children. This act of the wife is not desertion and she undergoes no change of status or rank, though her husband may marry another woman.

A wife has the right to lead a normal social life; she may entertain her friends and, with the permission of her husband, make beer and hold beer-drinks. She may also attend beer-drinks and other social gatherings and feasts, but must not neglect her household duties.

3. *Duties of husband.* Being the head of a family, the husband must conduct himself with manly dignity. The future and welfare of his umzi depends largely upon the way he conducts himself and the affairs of his umzi.

Only the duties of the husband with regard to his household and not his social duties will be discussed here. To a certain extent the duties of a husband are the rights of his wife, as already described in sub (2) above. Apart from his great duty, amaXhosa say it is the husband's primary duty to 'go in unto' his wife and procreate children (see sub (2) above). The duties of a husband may be divided into:

(*a*) his duty towards his wife;
(*b*) his duty towards his children;
(*c*) his duty

- (i) in providing household necessities, and
- (ii) the preservation of law and order in his umzi.

(a) *Husband's duty towards his wife.* 'A Native husband is obliged under Native Law to maintain his wife in a manner commensurate with her rank and position, provided, she agrees to reside at his kraal or at any other where he decides to place her.'[25]

It is his duty to see that each of his wives obtains a plot of land which she may cultivate, but there is no obligation on him to cultivate it for her.

It has, however, become customary nowadays for the husband to do the ploughing and sowing. The wife and other females then do the hoeing and reaping. The husband must also provide his wife with the necessary seed to sow.

A wife must be provided with an indlu by her husband. He must build it and put the wooden structure on. After this it is the duty of the women to complete it. A man usually builds a house for his wife as soon as she has borne him one or more children.

Should the wife be in need of clothes her husband must provide her with these or give her permission to exchange mealies, kafir-corn or the like for clothes. The husband usually tacitly consents to the latter. If he likes his wife and if she is a good wife he may slaughter a beast and take the skin and prepare it as a dress (isikaka) for his wife. This dress is worn especially at feasts and other ceremonies of note.

If the husband shamefully neglects these duties, it may be a cause for the woman to go to her own people, who may hold her under the uteleko custom.

It is sometimes contended that the husband *must* provide his wife with an isikaka or skin-dress. However, it may safely be said that no enforceable obligation rests on the husband to do this. If he does, it is a voluntary, at most a dutiful act; if he does not, his wife cannot force him to do so.

Some people also contend that in Xhosa Law a husband has the right to call upon the father of the woman to take her to a doctor, igqira, and to pay the doctor when the woman falls ill within a year after marriage. This is not so. It may be that they are confusing general illness, where the igqira doctors the girl, with an illness which the igqira says can only be cured if the woman undergoes the intonjane ceremony because she has not undergone it before her marriage; in the latter case her father must bear the expense. The father of the woman may take her to a doctor when she is ill if he wishes to, and to prevent people from saying that he has married his daughter to a man while she is ill or that he has a sickly daughter. To repeat: it is the duty of the husband to take his wife to an igqira when she is ill, no matter how soon or how long after marriage she falls ill. And it is he who must pay the usual beast for the doctoring of his wife. Nowadays the equivalent is paid in money.

This is the case also when the woman gives birth to a child. He must provide the midwives (abafukamisi) and also the expert (ingcibi), if one is needed, and he must pay the costs.

Because he has become the husband of the daughter of another umzi, the hlonipha-rules also automatically apply to him, and he must pay reverence to his mother-in-law (umkwekazi) and her female progenitors by refraining from the use of their names or the roots of words containing the same syllable as their names in their presence or even before his wife.

The husband, however, no longer adheres strictly to these rules, and he has only public opinion against him if he neglects this 'duty'. His wife and family have no action against him if he does not observe the hlonipha custom.

(b) *Husband's duty towards his children.* As their father he is, as a general rule, responsible for their upkeep, protection and welfare. He is responsible for their education, especially that of the boys. He must see that they are well behaved and obedient. If they are ill he must get a doctor for them.

It is his duty to put his sons through the initiation ceremony and thereafter to give them advice where necessary. He must put his daughters through the intonjane ceremony and can be forced to do this, and he must bear all the costs (see 3 (*a*) above).

When his daughter marries he must provide her with certain household necessities and cattle. When his son marries he must help him to lobola a wife. He is compelled to do this in the case of his son's first wife.

(c) (i) On the day of her marriage his wife is usually provided with certain household necessities by her family. But after marriage she looks to her husband to supply her with these things if she is unable to replace them herself. It is his duty to see that his wife is provided with the minimum of household necessities; he does this by allowing her to buy the necessary utensils.

(ii) As head of the family he must see that law and order are preserved in his umzi. It is his duty to settle all family disputes which need not come before the family court.

He must warn his wives and children in case they commit misdeeds. The duty of chastisement rests upon him, though he must not exceed the limits of reasonable punishment.

4. *Rights of husband* (*a*) The husband has the exclusive right to enjoy all marital privileges with his wife without undue interference and to the exclusion of all other men. He has a right to the services of his wife and expects that she should be obedient and care for him (see 'Duties of Wife' above).

He has the right to choose the residence of his wife and can make her reside there, provided it does not adversely affect her and he makes the necessary provision for her welfare and maintenance.[26] Though his wives cultivate the lands, sow and reap the crops and do the thrashing, he, as head of the family, can 'utilise for the benefit of his whole estate proceeds of the produce of the various houses as he thinks best, provided the wife and family concerned are not impoverished'.[27]

(*b*) He has a right to the services of his children and to their obedience. Their names, especially in the case of boys, are given by the husband. It is a right jealously watched over by the father.

Notes

[1] This term is not a pure Xhosa legal term, but is used here to express the relationship spoken of.

[2] T. *Nodada* vs. *J. Nodada* 1921 Dickinson and Meaker's Reports, p. 304, expresses also Xhosa Law.

[3] There is an old maxim: 'induku a yi nomzi' which means there can be no peace or harmony where brute force (the stick) rules the home.

[4] See Soga: *The amaXhosa: Life and Customs*, p. 272.

[5] This is therefore different from the Zulu umzi.

[6] Report and Proceedings of the (Cape) Commission on Native Laws and Customs 1883, the Evidence of Toto C.S. Ques. 1958 p. 116.

[7] *Stena Ngcongolo* vs. *W. Ngcongolo* 1930 N.A.C. II. See also Whitfield, p. 34.

[8] This information I obtained from the Chiefs of Pondoland and many other informants.

[9] See Whitfield: *South African Native Law*, p. 34.

[10] See also Soga: *The South-Eastern Bantu*, p. 36.

[11] Whitfield: *South African Native Law*, p. 34.

[12] *Mgudlwa* vs. *Paliso* 1918 Dickinson and Meaker's Report, p. 378.

[13] *N. Tshemese* vs. *B. Tshemese and Another* (1921) Dickinson and Meaker's Reports, p. 143.

[14] Quoted by Whitfield: *South African Native Law*, p. 35.

[15] I prefer to use the word 'isisu', 'womb' for according to the amaXhosa this woman is considered to be the womb of the childless wife; she is the woman who brings life into the womb. 'Seed-bearer' is not well chosen.

[16] Wombs are not married to any but the two principal houses.

[17] *Mbangwa* vs. *Simungumungwana* 1913 Meaker's Reports, p. 271, case from Qumbu, the centre of the amaMpondomise tribe, but it expresses the same principle as that found in Xhosa Law.

[18] Whitfield: *South African Native Law*, p. 34.

[19] *Tshubuso* vs. *Nojaji* 1913 Meaker's Report, p. 303, per Native Assessors, quoted by Whitfield: *South African Native Law*, p. 35.

[20] *Jonginamba* vs. *Jonginamba* 1906 Henkel, p. 104.

[21] *B. Mlungwana* vs. *B. Tonyela* 1914 Meakers' Reports, p. 16.

[22] This is so even in the case of a pregnant woman, who does not abstain from carrying out her daily duties. But she is prohibited from carrying too heavy loads.

[23] Only women born at the umzi, that is, daughters of this umzi, may walk and sit in the inkundla and enter the ubuhlanti, though not when they menstruate.

[24] Soga: *The amaXhosa: Life and Customs*, p. 212.

[25] *Ngejana* vs. *Owane*: Seymour's *Native Law and Custom*, p. 166 quoted by Whitfield: *South African Native Law*, p. 194. This is true for Xhosa Law also.

[26] *N. Kopman* vs. *Nohakisa* 1917 Meaker's Reports, p. 228 explains also the position in Xhosa Law.

[27] *N. and N. Tshobo* vs. *S. Tshobo* 1920 *Dickinson and Meaker's* Reports, p. 142.

S. Roberts: Matrilineal Family Law and Custom in Malawi: A Comparison of Two Systems*

Marriage as a Going Concern

(a) *The Tonga.* Rights and duties upon both sides automatically accompany a marriage. First of all, the husband must maintain the wife. He must build her a house to live in and he must keep it in good repair. Secondly, he must provide her with land to cultivate and clothes according to his means. He must also provide the necessary household utensils, consisting of at least a sleeping mat and a few pots. It now often happens that the husband will be away from the village working or looking for work. He may go as far away as Southern Rhodesia or even South Africa. His duties are not suspended in his absence. While he is away he will be expected to provide money for his wife's support instead of his services. He may arrange with his family to support his wife while he is away or he may send money to her direct.

The husband, quite apart from the performance of these duties, owes a duty of respect to his wife's parents. This duty commences before the marriage and may well be more than formal. After the payment of the *cikole* he may be asked to perform various services for the wife's family to show respect and also to indicate that he is capable of supporting his wife. These duties continue for some time after the marriage ceremony. During the subsistence of the marriage and even after it has come to an end, a close tie should exist between the man and his wife's family. This tie is reciprocal; both parties regard it as their duty to help the other in time of hardship. Indeed, when the father-in-law dies, the husband may take on the responsibility of looking after his mother-in-law. If the man is poor, his wife's parents may help him to buy clothes for his wife or to educate the children. These factors go further to support the initial contention that the Tonga marriage is far more than the union of a man and woman for their exclusive benefit and pleasure. Finally, the husband owes a duty to his own village not to lower its reputation in the eyes of the wife's village by his unsatisfactory conduct towards the wife or her relatives.

Most of the husband's rights will appear when the wife's duties are discussed, but there are some that require separate treatment. First, the husband is allowed to beat his wife, but with moderation. The beating may be no more severe than is necessary for 'reasonable correction', and the permissible severity will depend upon the circumstances. A husband may certainly beat his wife for failure to perform her marital duties, for lack of respect, and for associating with other men. The beating should not be with a dangerous instrument, and if administered with the hand should be with the open palm and not with the clenched fist. Kicks are not favourably regarded. The husband should take great care how he administers correction, and should always refrain from it during the pregnancy of his wife. An obvious reason for this is that unreasonable treatment will incur the displeasure of the wife's family.

If the husband causes the death of his wife either by his positive acts or his neglect, the consequences as far as he is concerned may be extremely serious. If the wife dies, her father must be told by the *mtenga*, and she may not be buried without the father's consent. This will be refused if the death has been caused by the husband's ill treatment. There is no more serious disgrace than to have a body lying in your house without burial. The consent of the father may eventually be obtained upon payment of damages.

There is a reciprocal right of sexual intercourse between the parties, though the husband's right is certainly far stronger than the wife's. The husband may not demand sexual intercourse with the wife during a menstrual period, and during this time they should not sleep in the same bed. There is no absolute rule about intercourse during the wife's pregnancy, and it may even be practised for the first six months. But it is discouraged after that period apparently for two reasons. First, the semen of the man might suffocate the child; and, secondly, it would be unseemly if the midwives had to deliver the child with the semen of its father upon its head. The husband may not resume his sexual rights till the child has been weaned.[1]

The wife's duties towards the husband are regarded in a rather different light. They are regarded as duties towards the whole village, she is 'their wife', although her failure

* S. Roberts, 'Matrilineal Family Law and Custom in Malawi: a Comparison of Two Systems', in *Journal of African Law*, Vol. 8, No. 2, pp. 84–86.

to perform them may only affect the husband directly. Her three most important duties are: to cultivate the husband's garden, to cook food, and to bear children. The last is possibly the most important duty of the three, and she will certainly be judged by her success in this field to the same extent as in the others. The wife has only limited duties in bringing up the children because these are usually brought up by her mother from the moment they are weaned.

(b) *The Lomwe*. The main duties owed by the parties to each other do not differ substantially between the two tribes. The husband must support his wife, she must help him in the garden and cook for him, and there is a reciprocal right to sexual relations. However, certain Lomwe customs call for special discussion.

When the man is taken to his future wife's village by his *namunkhoswe*, he becomes part of the wife's family unit, and if her parents move he is obliged to move with them, if the marriage is to continue. He will live with the wife's parents for up to one year. During this time he is expected to accumulate the physical assets upon which the marriage is based. At first he eats food provided from the parent's store and uses the father's tools.

The husband's first duty is to build a house and prepare a plot of land. He will have spent the greater part of his protracted youth preparing for these tasks and should therefore be competent to undertake them. A hut can only be built between March and July, because the necessary grass is only available at this time of the year. His prestige in the new community will depend upon his ability to provide his wife with a well-constructed hut. If he fails to do this he will be an object of ridicule, and repeated failure will entitle the wife to divorce him. A reputation for ineptitude in hut-building will follow a man from village to village and is hard to lose. The hut is built in the immediate neighbourhood of the parent's house, and the parties go there as soon as it is finished.

When the husband arrives at his new village, he is lent tools by his father-in-law and will be allocated a patch of bush to make into a garden. As this will be new ground and it will be some months before it is productive, the husband and wife will still live off the wife's parents. To a certain extent this pattern continues throughout the marriage, as the family remains a single economic unit. The crops grown by the whole family are stored together and there is a communal kitchen.

As among the Tonga, the husband may go away as far as South Africa to find work. While he is away he is expected to send money to support his wife and it is the duty of his *namunkhoswe* to see that he does this. The wife may go back to live in her parents' house while he is away, or alternatively he will send for one of his young female relatives to come and live in the house to keep her company.

Note

[1] Because of the long period which elapses between the time when a woman is six months' pregnant and the time when the child is weaned, the husband may go away to work in Rhodesia or South Africa in order to avoid his desire to have intercourse with her. On the other hand, some husbands marry second or even third wives in order to have constant opportunities for sexual relations.

J. F. Holleman: Shona Customary Law*

Relations between Husband and Wife

(i) *Domestic authority*. The husband is the head of his family unit. He exercises authority over its members in internal domestic affairs, and represents the unit in its external relations with other units or individuals.

Except in the relatively rare cases of *kugarira* (service) marriage—when the husband is bound to stay with his wife's relatives—the wife must follow her husband where he decides to settle. In the first few years of their married life at least, they will almost

* J. F. Holleman, *Shona Customary Law*, Oxford University Press, Cape Town, 1952, pp. 206–222.

invariably live with the husband's relatives. Their domestic life will to a certain extent form part of the domestic life of the wider kin-group of the husband, and this means that the authority of the husband will inevitably be modified by the authority of the head (father or elder brother) of his family. Later the husband may decide to build his own village or village section (*mana*) apart from his family, with the result that, in practice at least, he will be more independent.

A woman owes her husband obedience and respect. She treats him with a good deal of etiquette which clearly reveals her subordinate position. When others are present she is meek and servile, and does not speak to her husband unless she is addressed by him. When answering his questions or offering him food or beer she has to kneel down, speak in a subdued voice and address him by his *cidawo* (sub-clan name). When he rebukes her or gives her an order she should whisper the traditional praise names of his lineage. Merely to disagree with her husband in public is regarded as a serious act of insubordination which he cannot tolerate because it impairs his dignity. There are few things a Shona relishes more than making fun of a hen-pecked husband.

Much of this etiquette also prevails in the privacy of their home life. Husband and wife will, for instance, never eat together. The wife will bring him his food—and water for washing his hands—in the prescribed manner and leave him to eat alone, having her own food later with her children.

Being alone with him, she may call him *baba* (father) 'because she needs his protection as do his children'. To arouse his pride and passion she will praise him often, repeating his lineage praise-names. During the day, except when they work in their own fields, husband and wife spend little time together. She has to fulfil her numerous domestic duties while he may decide to go about, visiting friends or relatives, cutting wood for necessary repairs, hunting, or instructing his sons in their duties. When he comes home he expects to be attended to whenever he commands, and watching his wife run her household, he shouts instructions from where he has comfortably seated himself.

The nights are spent together in the same hut and under the same blanket. To break this habit would mean that the woman had lost her husband's favour.

A man will boast of an efficient housewife but have little patience when he finds traces of negligence or slovenry. Women have to account for any prolonged absence from their home, may find their husband extremely short-tempered when his food is not prepared on time, or when the daily domestic routine has been interrupted.

When fieldwork is finished, the crops reaped and threshed, a woman may obtain her husband's permission to pay a few days' visit to her own relatives. Such permission is seldom refused when suitable arrangements can be made for running the household during her absence. And when there are grown-up daughters in the family some women may be given leave for a few weeks.

The husband need not account to his wife for his movements or an occasional absence from home when he chooses to visit distant friends or relatives, as long as he does not neglect his wife and children. But in practice a man will never leave his home without informing his wife and making arrangements for her protection. Few men who seek employment in towns or on European farms, will take their wives with them. The woman stays behind with the children, tending the gardens and raising food. Whenever possible the husband's relatives will assist her, protect her, watch her. Some women receive their husband's permission to go and stay instead with their own relatives for the time being, taking their children with them when they need personal care. But they must return when the husband comes back. In short, the movements and residence of a wife are determined by her husband or his legal representative.

A husband may beat his wife moderately when the occasion—neglect of household duties, disobedience or insubordination—warrants it. Such disciplinary measures are regarded as obvious manifestations of his marital authority and are therefore not seriously objected to by a woman. But on no account should it be imagined that a woman is expected to subject herself to the arbitrary whims and wishes of her husband. Women are never regarded as 'property' or 'chattel'; the very nature of the marriage agreement and the relations between the families-in-law sufficiently safeguard their personal dignity. A woman has the right to complain to her husband's relatives (especially his sister, father's sister or uterine cousin) or even her own family, when he ill-treats or neglects her or makes unreasonable demands upon her.

When a woman has proved her loyalty and efficiency as a wife and housekeeper she has considerable freedom of action. In matters of domestic routine she often acts without consulting her husband, turning to him only when important decisions have to be made. Inversely, a husband will seldom decide upon matters of any consequence without privately consulting his wife, realizing that her agreement and co-operation are essential elements of a successful domestic policy. In connexion with the cultivation of fields one may find illustrations both of the directive authority of the husband and of the relative independence of the wife. When husband and wife jointly cultivate a common field the wife is expected to follow the directions of her husband. Arrangements for collective and reciprocal aid with neighbours or relatives will be made by the husband, or at least have to be sanctioned by him. But in connexion with the subsidiary crops of vegetables or ground-nuts which a woman often raises on separate plots, she may make her own arrangements with other village women or neighbouring friends of hers without asking her husband's approval. But if the husband disapproves of certain of his wife's companions he may demand that she make other arrangements. In plural families each wife has her own field. She has the right to expect her husband to render her assistance, but she herself is primarily responsible for its cultivation. Like every other field-holder, she may occasionally require a large collective work-party of both men and women (*nhimbe*) for which she must brew beer from her own grain. She will consult her husband about the date on which such a party is to be held, but she is responsible for all the arrangements and for sending invitations around to nearby villages. But at the party her husband is the 'guest of honour'. The first beer (*shumo*, 'notification') is offered to him, and he will give the sign to start drinking. To pass him over would mean to deny his domestic authority.

The husband represents his family unit in its relations with other individuals or social units. His wife cannot bring an action against anyone (except her husband) without the assistance of her husband. Neither can she be sued alone. In such cases her husband formally acts as the complainant or defendant. Nowadays it sometimes happens that a married woman brings an action before a tribal court during the absence of her husband, and I have witnessed a number of clearcut cases[1] actually being entertained by the court without insisting that she be formally represented by a male party. But in more serious or complicated cases the court will usually postpone the hearing, telling the woman to bring a representative of her husband's family—or else one of her own male relatives—'to speak for her'. When her action is directed against another woman (for instance, in cases of slander, which are fairly common) the presence of her husband may be a mere formality (although an essential one). The women conduct their own cases, personally pay the required court fees, give evidence, cross-examine, and so on, without reference to or assistance from their husbands. The latter are, in fact, anxious not to get involved in such feminine squabbles.[2]

All invitations for communal or reciprocal aid which involve the husband or the family as a whole must be directed to the husband, because the wife has no power to bind her husband or any of her children to any such arrangement. Even the husband's father, who has the right to call the members of his family group together to work on his field (*zunde*) occasionally, will not give a direct order to his sons' wives but will ask his sons to transmit his wishes to their wives.

In a *plural family* one aspect of domestic authority concerns the status of the various co-wives and the relations between them. I must first emphasize that from a genealogical point of view there is no differentiation in rank between a man's various wives and their 'houses' (*dzimba*). In this respect the Shona differ from the south-eastern Nguni where a very definite rank position obtains amongst co-wives and their respective houses.

The Shona plural family consists of a number of component houses of equal rank, and succession to the position of head of the family is based on the order of birth of collateral sons or grandsons of a man, regardless of the particular house in which the heir is born.[3] From an *estate* point of view, however, each house constitutes an entity which is (potentially) distinct from the other houses, although they share a common family head. As domestic units these houses are mutually completely independent and—with the help of the common husband—self-supporting.

But from a *social* point of view there is a difference in personal status between co-wives, based upon the order in which they have been married to the husband. The first-married wife is the *vahosi*, the second *muronggo*, the third and subsequent wives are called *mukarangga* (plural *va-*). It there are only two wives, the second wife is usually referred to as either *mukarangga*[4] or *mukadzinyina* (younger wife) or *mukadzi muduku* (little wife). It should be noted that the order of marriage is not determined by the moment the women are handed over to their husband's family, but by the order in which the various affinition agreements have been made. It may happen, for instance, that the (*zwarira*) affinition agreement concerning wife A has been concluded before the agreement concerning wife B, but that A, on account of her youthful age, is handed over to her husband long after B has assumed her duties as a housewife. A will nevertheless be regarded as *vahosi*.

If a young girl becomes *cimutsamapfiwa* (substitute) of her deceased *vahosi* sister, she becomes *vahosi* in her husband's plural family, and thus takes precedence over his other wives, 'because she is married with the same cattle as her elder sister'. Similarly, the *ciberekeso* who raises issue to the house of her barren sister will become *vahosi* after her sister's death if the latter was the first-married wife of the husband.

On the other hand, the position of a widow who is inherited by her late husband's relative, is determined by the moment she becomes the wife of her second husband, regardless of her previous married status.

The *vahosi* is treated with respect by her co-wives. They call her *vakoma*,[5] and have to obey her when she gives general orders in connexion with domestic life in the village. The *vahosi* has some special responsibilities. The husband uses her as a mouthpiece when he gives orders to his wives. When he gives clothes and other presents, or food from his own granary, the *vahosi* will distribute them amongst the women. In cases of trouble between other co-wives the *vahosi* may act as an arbitrator.

The *vahosi* is also the custodian of her husband's weapons (Hera: *zombo*; Rozwi: *tswimbo*) which are stored in her hut.[6]

Amongst the other co-wives there is some difference in social rank which finds expression in the use of the terms *mukoma* or *mununguna* (elder or younger sister) when they address each other. Some informants say that the husband will make a careful distinction by slightly varying the length of cloth or size of blanket presented to each wife as a present. But the same informants also emphasize that such distinctions should never assume the character of undue favouritism because this would lead to jealousy (*shanje*) between the wives. The basic equality of co-wives is aptly expressed by the words of one Hera informant: 'They are all the same because all may get beaten by the same husband; and the child of any of them may one day be the "chief" (*ishe*) of the family.'

(ii) *Economic relations*. Broadly speaking the women are responsible for domestic work and the care of children, and the men attend to matters of public interest. In these two spheres the interests of men and women are sharply distinguished: no man will carry water,[7] nurse children, or prepare food for his family; and no woman will attend to public affairs.

But in the wide field covering the production of food, animal husbandry and the building and maintenance of dwellings, the responsibilities of men and women respectively are not so clearly divided. Regarding the cultivation of fields, no activities are considered to be exclusively man's work or woman's work. Members of both sexes may be found together in the same field, doing the same work—clearing, tilling, sowing, weeding, reaping. Clearing new ground of trees and heavy undergrowth is usually done by men, as is ploughing with animal-drawn ploughs. But in the absence of men, women may be seen swinging an axe or driving a team of oxen. In animal husbandry the women will raise chickens and small stock while the men are more interested in cattle. But there are no considerations of a mystical nature which prohibit the handling of cattle by women between puberty and menopause such as exists amongst the Nguni.

When homesteads have to be built the men usually cut the poles and rafters for huts and cattle enclosures and erect the bare structure. The women will provide the thatch and plaster the walls and floors with mud and manure. The digging of wells for water and the holes in which the mud for plastering is prepared, is as a rule done by men.

A few odd crafts, trades or pastimes are either habitually pursued by men or by women only. The men go out hunting—singly or collectively—do woodwork or metal work, prepare skins. Pottery and the plaiting of fibre bags or rugs (but these crafts have now largely fallen into disuse) are done by women. In areas near the big rivers both sexes may sometimes be busy catching fish; the men with traps and nets; the women by damming off and gradually narrowing a circular sandy patch of the river bed in shallow water until the few small fishes trapped in this manner can be scooped out by hand.

Any task of some magnitude in building or agriculture is invariably performed by the men and women of the village collectively, often with the assistance of neighbours, in which case the hosts have to provide ample quantities of beer. Depending on the type of work to be done various other arrangements for mutual or reciprocal assistance may be made amongst relatives and neighbours, involving women only, men only, or both sexes together. All these collective activities are organized for particular and limited purposes—helping to dig up a patch of ground-nuts, clearing each other's gardens, etc.,—and are therefore essentially temporary arrangements.

However considerable the proportion of necessary work thus performed collectively and on an inter-family or inter-village basis, every family and domestic unit must depend upon its own labour for the regular daily fieldwork, raising and tending the essential staple crops. In this task husband and wife work as a team. In a monogamous family they usually jointly cultivate a single big field (*munda*) in which the main crop or crops are planted. After reaping and threshing the product remains undivided. In addition to the main garden a woman will usually have a small plot (*bindu*) either near the village, or in a suitable corner of the main field, or near a spring, in which she raises vegetables or green mealies. A man may select the site of an abandoned cattle kraal to cultivate a tobacco patch (*dandare*). Ground-nuts, an important subsidiary crop, are often dispersed by women amongst the main crop of millet or maize.

In a *plural* family each wife has her own field in which she raises the food for herself, her children and her husband. Each wife keeps her produce apart in her own store-hut (*tsapi*) or granary (*dura*). The husband then also has his own field (*zunde*).

The wives are entitled to equal assistance from their husband with the cultivation of their gardens, and have to work in rotation—sometimes collectively—on their husband's field (*kukwira zunde*, literally to 'climb' the husband's field).

The husband's purpose of having his own field is twofold. It provides a supply of food in times of emergency when the granaries of the wives have been emptied. It enables him to entertain his friends and neighbours whenever he needs their assistance in connexion with some project (building a new village, making fresh gardens, etc.,) which benefits his family as a whole; or to make beer for ritual purposes.

It should be mentioned that when one wife runs out of food and has to be supplied by the husband, the other co-wives are entitled to receive the same quantity, even if their stocks are still adequate. Grain thus supplied by the husband to his wives is never expected to be returned because in connexion with food there is community of interest between the husband and each of his wives. In contrast, it should be mentioned that any assistance by one co-wife to another is given on a reciprocal and not on a communal basis. Should, for instance, one wife borrow seed from another, it has to be refunded.

In a plural family the wives are more independent in the cultivation of their fields than the wife of a monogamist, who works under the constant supervision of her husband. They can, for instance, decide for themselves whether to prepare beer for a collective work party, but will always consult their husband regarding a suitable date.

If a woman wants to raise more food than is needed for her household she can do so and it is not uncommon that by such efforts a woman acquires property (in livestock or otherwise) of considerable value. The husband has no right to such property which—together with property derived from other sources in her own name—forms part of her own estate, and devolves upon her heirs, independent of the rules of succession governing her husband's estate. The function and interrelation of the husband's (*patri-*) and wife's (*matri-*) estates will be discussed in a separate chapter, and I need here only briefly refer to the position of husband and wife as joint contributors to a *common* family estate.

As far as its economic subsistence is concerned each individual family unit (and this includes each component unit of a plural family) is considered to be completely independent of other like units of the husband's family. The combined efforts of both husband and wife and their children are needed to make their unit self-supporting. In the interest of the family unit a wife has as much right to demand that her husband help her cultivate her—or, their common—garden, as the husband has to demand his wife's assistance. In this respect the Shona woman is in a strong position. She can complain if her husband gives her insufficient support, and in some cases can even leave him as a sign of protest.

As long as the family unit remains intact, food stocks and other property *jointly acquired* by the spouses remain common property under the control of the husband. But when the wife dies or when the marriage is dissolved through the fault of the husband, her individual contribution is recognized. Her family may then claim a portion of the stock of grain in the granary,[8] and will also assume control over all the property which the woman has acquired in her own right.

A wife is entitled to receive clothing and blankets and various household necessities from her husband. Such property, too, is upon her death divided between her relatives and her husband (and children), and such division is again based on the idea that 'the wife has worked for these things'. But any outright non-essential gifts made by the husband to his wife will revert to the donor when she dies.

(iii) *Sexual relations.* Sexual gratification is recognized as a basic need in married life. A husband is expected to have frequent and regular intercourse with his wife, and in a manner which leaves her satisfied. Perhaps the most legitimate complaint a woman can bring against her husband is that he is neglecting her sexual needs. His failure to sleep with her is regarded as an indication that he no longer values her as a wife. The woman therefore has the right to report the matter to his family who, taking a serious view of it, will severely reprimand the husband. If necessary, the woman can even bring the matter before a tribal court with the assistance of her family. For example:

> A recent (1946) case of this kind came before the Rozwi Chief in the Wedza Reserve. It appeared that the husband's father had repeatedly ordered his son to have regular intercourse with his wife (the woman had first complained to her husband's sister who again had reported the matter to his father). But the son had refused. The wife now made a formal complaint against him, assisted by her brother.
>
> The court ordered the husband to pay ten shillings *muripo* (compensation) and told his father to 'take his son and his son's wife home and see to it that they slept in the same hut at night'.
>
> The husband obliged for a short time but then again refused to cohabit with his wife. He was then required to give a concrete rejection token (two shillings) to his wife in the presence of his father. The token was produced in court, and handed over by the Chief to the woman's father with the advice that he should take his daughter back and dissolve the marriage whenever it was convenient for him to do so—that is, when he could obtain marriage cattle from another suitor.

When a man has more than one wife he takes care to divide his attention equally between his wives. Some husbands may spend one night in the hut of one wife, sleeping with another wife the following night. Others make it a habit to change sleeping quarters every week or few days. Undue favouritism usually results in serious trouble between the various co-wives and in a disruption of normal domestic life.

There are certain periods when sexual intercourse between husband and wife is restricted, of which the following are the most common.

No intercourse takes place during menstruation (*kushamba*) lest the husband get *maswina*, stomach or back disease.

Until the seventh month of a pregnancy a husband should have regular intercourse with his wife because his semen (*urume*) is believed to be essential food for the foetus.[9] But after the seventh month cohabitation should stop because it may be detrimental to the foetus, and cause undue contraction of the uterus before and during the confinement. The *vernix caseosa* which sometimes covers a newly-born baby, is believed to be due to excessive intercourse after the seventh month of pregnancy, and is a case for ridicule amongst midwives. After child-birth there should be a total abstinence for a period up to six months. At any rate, before cohabitation can be resumed the professional midwife (*vanyamukuta*) who has attended to the confinement must be formally notified so that she can medically strengthen herself against the danger of 'breaking her back' (*kuckora musana*).[10]

Even after sexual intercourse can be resumed no conception should take place until the last-born child is weaned, that is, usually not until it is about two years old. *Coitus interruptus* is practised in the meantime.[11] If in spite of this precaution the woman does conceive, the child she is suckling is taken from the breast if it is old enough to be weaned. If it is too young, a Native doctor (*ngangga*) should treat the breasts of the mother so that the child can suckle without ill effect. Occasionally an abortion is procured (*kubvisa dumbu*, to 'extract' the womb).

No sexual intercourse may take place with a widow before the *kurovaguva* ceremony in connexion with her deceased husband has been performed. The consequences of this offence (*kupisa guva*, 'burning the grave') will be discussed later in this chapter. Generally speaking, however, death or illness amongst relatives does not seem to entail sexual prohibitions.

A woman is expected to be faithful to her husband, but a single act of adultery committed by her is seldom a cause for the dissolution of the marriage. If she repents she is usually forgiven. There is no formal action for adultery against a woman but disciplinary measures (e.g. thrashing by her husband or father) may be taken against her, and she may be required to make a formal promise not to sin again (see below). There is even a saying to illustrate the fact that a wife's adultery does not necessarily lead to a divorce: '*mukadzi nzenza ndi ma pfumise*—an adulterous wife makes me rich'. (Damages for adultery can be claimed from the guilty third party, but are not claimable if the husband decides to divorce his wife.)

The Shona believe that a woman cannot secretly commit adultery without threatening the well-being of her children or husband. During her first confinement a woman must confess (*kureva, kudura*) any act of infidelity committed by her after the conclusion of the affinition agreement. Failure to do this (*kunyararira mwana*, to keep a secret from the child) would imperil not only her own life—it would prolong the confinement—but especially that of her baby. The possibility that a confession may be forthcoming is said to be the main reason why a woman will have her first confinement at her parents' home whenever this can be arranged. The midwives attending to her must report any confession to her father. If everything goes normally and there is no difficulty in getting the baby to suckle, the confession may sometimes be kept secret from the husband's family—at the risk of having to report the matter later when something goes wrong with the child, in which case the *vakuwasha* may take a very serious view of it.

If the child starts crying the first time its father sees it, he has reason to believe that a confession has been made (or withheld) during the confinement. In such cases the midwives will have to tell the truth. Sometimes a suspicious husband will approach the hut in which his newly-born baby is sleeping, and drop a log of wood (*danda*) near by. If the baby starts crying he believes that his suspicions are warranted, and he will urge the midwife to tell the truth so as to safeguard the child.

Apart from a first confinement, any time when her husband or one of her children falls ill, a woman with a guilty conscience will confess her sins. Only by confessing can she hope to avert the mystical sanction which—as is the unshakable belief—will otherwise follow. If she fails to confess at such critical moments the woman runs the risk of being held responsible for the death of husband or child. She would be regarded as a witch (*muroyi*), and guilty of a heinous crime.[12]

A husband need not be faithful to his wife as long as he does not neglect her. Which does not mean that public opinion generally approves of a man's extra-marital affairs. Considerable damages are payable to the husband or legal guardian of a woman with whom a man has had illicit intercourse. But women will generally take a tolerant view of their husband's adultery as long as they do not keep their love affairs secret from them or become indifferent to their wives. A man has to confess his adultery to his wife for the same reasons which compel a woman to confess her own infidelity: to avert a mystical threat to their children's well-being. A Mbire informant said: 'Women know that a man may need more than one woman, and they do not mind much if he sleeps with another woman as long as he still loves his own wife. There are women, especially those who have married in Church, who will nag their husbands and say it is a wrong thing. But this is foolish because the next time the husband sleeps with another woman he will say nothing to his wife, and then her children may fall ill. And this is only because the husband was afraid to confess to his wife.'

A Shona woman cannot, therefore, instigate an action for dissolution of marriage on the grounds of her husband's adultery, unless she can prove that he has seriously neglected her personally.

(iv) *Sterility of husband.* Sterility of the husband (*nggomwa*) in the first place threatens the essential purpose of the marriage agreement—raising issue to his family—and in the second place, denies a married woman her natural right to have children. It does not, however, in itself constitute a ground for the dissolution of the marriage unless either the husband or the wife refuses to accept the customary remedy of seed-raising (*kupindira*, or *kusikira rudzi*[13]) which Shona law provides in these cases. The arrangement to invite another man (*munhu a no pindira*) to raise issue with the woman on behalf of her sterile husband must be based on a mutual agreement between husband and wife. On no account is a woman entitled to select a lover without her husband's approval—such an act would be regarded as common adultery. But the husband knows that under the circumstances he cannot expect his wife to submit to the arrangement unless she approves of the seed-raiser. The seed-raiser should preferably be a member of the husband's lineage ('so that the children will have the same blood as their legal father'), but if no such relative is acceptable to the woman, the husband will have to approve of any other man proposed by the woman and willing to perform the task. Owing to the extreme delicacy of the situation the matter is always conducted with the utmost discretion and secrecy. Informants maintain that even the husband's own father may be left ignorant of the arrangements.

The man who agrees to function as a seed-raiser will be given a concrete token (*mhiko*, 'promise'[14]) by the husband in the presence of the wife. The token is usually an arrow (*museve*) but may in fact be any other tangible object (a ring, hoe, shilling, fowl) and it contains the husband's assurance that no action for adultery will be taken against the seed-raiser, provided that the latter performs his function secretly and honourably.[15] Amongst the Hera there is information that the husband and seed-raiser may in addition go into the forest together, and cut a wedge (*shashi*, *sheshi*) in a big tree—'so deep that it remains a permanent mark'—as indelible proof of their bona fides. This practice is said to be unknown in the Wedza and Narira Reserves. Some informants say that the husband may demand a concrete token from the seed-raiser as an assurance 'that he will never lay claim to any of the children which he raises by the woman'.

The seed-raiser is not paid anything for his services but the woman will give him choice food and be pleasant to him. Informants say that no efforts are made to propitiate the ancestral spirits, but should any of the seed-raiser's own children—or his wife—become ill the agreement is called off. Some people say that the seed-raiser should notify his wife in order to forestall any possible misfortune. Others again maintain that this is not necessary (even inadvisable), but admit that the seed-raiser will be compelled to confess the matter to his wife, should any of his children fall ill.

The agreement may be called off by either party, in which case the token which had given the seed-raiser the right to cohabit with the woman, must be returned to the husband.

The difference between seed-raising on behalf of a sterile husband and seed-raising on behalf of a barren wife (*kuberekesa*) is that the provision of an additional wife is a legal obligation of the wife's family, arising from the marriage contract and the subject of formal negotiations between the respective families. *Kupindira*, on the other hand, is regarded as a strictly private matter between the individual spouses.

(v) *Quarrels and reconciliation*. The Shona husband has the right to apply disciplinary measures against his wife if she neglects her duties, and he may give her a light thrashing if the occasion warrants it. But a husband who unreasonably beats his wife is guilty of *rushusho* (maltreating), and an ill-treated wife is entitled to run away from her husband to find refuge with her own family. Repeated ill-treatment may be cause for divorce.

Occasional outbursts between husband and wife are regarded as natural incidents of married life and are no cause for worry or intervention on the part of either family. There is some truth in the remark of one old woman: 'A woman who is never beaten by her husband will think that he does not love her any longer.' But if there is serious trouble between the spouses, and the one bears a grudge (*daka*) against the other, it will be necessary for the family elders to intervene and try to restore normal relations. A woman who bears a grudge against her husband usually reveals this by denying him conjugal rights, or by dishing too little food into his plate, or by making his life unpleasant in any other manner. A husband most clearly shows his aversion to his wife by refusing to eat the food she has prepared for him (*kuramwa sadza*), or by refusing to sleep with her. The appropriate person to whom either spouse may turn to complain about the other is the husband's sister or father's sister (*samukadzi, vamwene*), who owes her influence to the assumption that her marriage cattle have been used to provide the wife for her family. The *samukadzi* may privately prevail upon her brother or her *murovora* to settle their differences. If she fails she may bring the matter before the family council. If the husband's father is alive he will usually guide the proceedings. But in all other cases the right person to act as arbitrator is the senior *muzukuru* (sister's son or father's sister's son) of the husband.[16]

The principal object of the proceedings is to reconcile the spouses. There may be a question of some petty compensation, *muripo* (from a chicken to ten shillings), payable to the aggrieved party, but the emphasis is placed upon some concrete act of reconciliation in which both spouses must participate. Most common is the custom of *kubata huku* (literally, to catch a chicken[17]). The woman has to prepare a chicken which is brought to the arbitrator (husband's father or *muzukuru*). The latter will call the spouses together and deliver a little sermon on good will and tolerance. He will then divide the chicken (keeping a bit for himself) and order them to eat.[18] When the chicken has been consumed the spouses are again called together. The arbitrator points out that the woman has prepared the food in the hope that her husband may think well of her again, while the husband has eaten her food as a sign that he has forgiven her.

In some cases when the wife has been sexually neglected by her husband, the husband's father may order his son to cohabit with her, telling him: 'Don't you know that she is *my* wife because I have given *rovoro* for her? If you don't treat her well I may build her another hut, and then you will stay alone without a wife.'

If the woman has committed adultery she may be required to make a solemn promise (*kupika*) in public that she will not sin again. She is told to scratch a little hole in the ground, utter the promise, spit into the hole (*kupfira mate*) and cover it up again.

In some cases, when the relations between the two families have suffered through the domestic quarrels between the spouses, both families may partake in a common meal for which a few chickens or a goat have been killed by the family of the spouse who is considered to have been the guilty party, and even beer may be served as an additional effort to re-establish good feelings between all concerned.

I mentioned in the previous chapter that a wife may be sent home to her parents for a period of correction. In these cases there is—as yet—no question of a repudiation of the woman by her husband. She will be returned after a short time, often after she has given proof of her good will by offering her husband a nicely-prepared chicken. After the acceptance of this gift normal conjugal relations will be resumed.

In some instances the husband, in an outburst of temper, may send his wife home with a *gupuro* token, the concrete message to her parents that he has repudiated her. Even this act need not necessarily lead to a dissolution of the marriage if the husband changes his mind before there is a question of return of cattle, or before a third party has negotiated a marriage agreement with the *tezwara*. But the husband who desires his wife back after he has returned her without sufficient cause, has to pay something, both to redeem his rejection token, and to compensate his wife for the humiliation she has suffered. For example:

> N had come home late from a beer party, and had found his wife asleep and no food prepared. He beat her and returned her to her parents with a head of cattle as *gupuro*. The *tezwara* said that he was surprised, but accepted daughter and beast. After two months N 'saw that he had been wrong and he went to his *tezwara*, telling him that he still loved his wife'. The *tezwara* said that he 'could not refuse his *mukuwasha* his wife', but supported his daughter's demand that N should first compensate her. 'How else can a wife who has been sent home with *gupuro* be sure that she is again loved by her husband?'
>
> N agreed to give her one beast. She had first asked for two beasts but her family thought this was too much 'considering the short time he has left you alone'. He then got his wife back and the beast he had given as *gupuro*.

The fact that the *mukuwasha* has thought it fit to make use of a formal rejection token may be a reason for the *tezwara* to bring the matter before a formal legal forum, if the husband subsequently changes his mind and wishes to be reconciled with his wife. The *tezwara* does not take this step because the matter cannot be settled between parties—

under the circumstances the decision whether to revoke the marriage contract lies entirely in the hands of the *tezwara*. His object is to teach his *mukuwasha* a lesson by requiring him to make public and formal amends for his frivolous behaviour towards his wife and family-in-law. For example:

D had sent his wife home with a hoe as *gupuro*. After about four months he told his *tezwara*, C, that he 'loved his wife again'. C said that he saw no reason why his daughter should not go back with her husband, seeing that she had not yet found another suitor. But since D had apparently sent her home without justification C thought it 'a good thing to talk the matter over before the *civara* (court) of the ward headman'.

D explained before the court that he had come home hungry one day and found his wife asleep without having prepared food for him. Being a bit drunk he had sent his wife home in a sudden rage. The court: 'But why didn't you ask your wife back sooner, seeing that you rejected (*kuramba*) her for such a small matter?'

D: 'It was a question of indignation (*shunggu*). I agree that I was wrong, but I want to pay for my foolishness (*ubenzi*)'.

Court: 'If your wife wants to go back to you, you should give her something.'

D produced one pound which he handed to the court. The court then asked the woman 'if she agreed (*kutenda*)'. She accepted the money and went back with her husband.

Questioned later about the hoe which had been given by D as *gupuro*, C told me that he had 'not bothered to give it back because D had never asked for it. It was no longer *gupuro* because D had given *muripo* (compensation) to his wife and this meant that all was well again.' C was therefore using the hoe in his garden.

Notes

1 For instance, damage done to her garden by trespassing cattle, in which case the damage could be assessed by an inspection *in loco*, and compensation awarded.

2 In one such case, when the court turned to the husband of the complainant to ask his opinion, he declined to commit himself, stating that 'this was his wife's case and not his, and that he had only come to listen'.

3 Slight modification of this collateral system may be found in some localities but these do not affect the general principle.

4 I have failed to find the meaning of these terms, but informants say that the term *mukarangga* expresses the husband's 'tender feeling' for his youngest wife.

5 *Mukoma*, elder sister, but with the honorific plural prefix *va-*.

6 At the *kurovaguva* ceremony after her husband's death these weapons are handed over to the *samukadzi*, who will give them to the heir.

7 Except in some cases when water has to be carried with drums and ox-drawn sledge from a river or distant well.

8 If she leaves small children who will remain with the father, the wife's family will leave the greater portion or food stock with the husband to provide for their subsistence.

9 If the husband is absent during the period the woman should eat liberal quantities of 'black jelly' (*derere*) to make up for the deficiency.

10 The belief that resumption of sexual intercourse before notification to the midwife will cause serious bodily harm to her, is so strong that even a Christian Native woman will invariably obtain the midwife's permission before allowing her husband to sleep with her. The midwife has the means of finding out whether the prohibition has been violated. When the mother visits her with the baby in order to obtain her permission to resume cohabitation, a little mother's milk mixed with medicine is dropped into the child's eyes, and has to be licked off by the mother. The child will get blind if intercourse has taken place. Hence the name of this custom, *kubata meso*, to catch—the child's—eyes.

The fear of maiming the child and the knowledge of a few actual cases in which a midwife was suddenly stricken with paralysis—believed to be due to a violation of the prohibition—for which the accused husband had to pay a beast to her as compensation, are a sufficient guarantee that a married couple will not treat the matter lightly.

11 The form of intercourse without actual penetration, known as *ukuhlobongga* or *ukumetsha* amongst the south-eastern Nguni tribes, and practised by these tribes as contraception, seems to be uncommon amongst the Shona.

12 I have observed an example of this at first hand. Shortly before I left the southern Sabi Reserve a young married woman whom I knew well, spent nearly three days in labour during

her first confinement. A few hours before the baby was delivered she confessed to a love affair shortly before her marriage. The child was still-born, and the general opinion was that it could have been saved had she confessed sooner. The woman was shunned by everyone, and her husband grimly confided to me that he was asking back his *rovoro* because his wife was a witch, a woman who had killed her own child.

[13] *Kupindira,* to go in on behalf of someone; *kusikira rudzi,* to raise issue (literally 'lineage') on behalf of someone.

[14] From *kupika,* to swear or take oath.

[15] The code of honour implies, according to one informant that 'the seed-raiser should not visit the woman when the husband is in or near the village, and on no account should he make use of the husband's sleeping mat. He should preferably perform his function out in the bush, at a time when the husband is away. If the seed-raiser breaks his promise of secrecy or acts indiscreetly, it is regarded as a deadly insult to the husband. If he starts boasting of his intimacy with the woman, any member of the husband's family is likely to kill him.'

[16] He owes his position of authority to the fact or assumption that 'the wife has been married with his mother's cattle'.

[17] In Hera also called *kubata maviri,* to 'hold the two'.

[18] Since husband and wife never eat together, the woman will eat her portion apart from her husband, who will eat with the *muzukuru.*

Chapter 13

DIVORCE

Many contemporary studies of customary law avoid using the term 'divorce' in their descriptions of marital law; the term 'dissolution of marriage' is preferred, because it decreases the likelihood of confusion between western legal notions of divorce and the African customary machinery for terminating marriage. We have chosen to retain the term here, not because we disagree with this view, but because 'Dissolution of Marriage' is too broad a term to embrace the limited aspects of the topic which are included in this section. In other words, this term should, if used correctly, encompass all the available modes of ending a marriage; here, we are only concerned to provide descriptions of those procedures which occur *inter partes*. To be properly comprehensive, extracts dealing with dissolution as a result of the death of either party should also have been included. (This aspect is, of course, dealt with elsewhere in these Readings, notably under Succession and in the foregoing sections on the Levirate, Sororate, Widow Inheritance and Ghost Marriage.

There is considerable controversy among writers on customary law as to whether divorce is difficult or easy to achieve in African society. It is not possible to deal with this question fully here, but it is worth noting that, in most traditional African societies, divorce was very rare. In some societies divorce was altogether unknown; in others it was recognised, but subject to procedural intricacies which involved not only the parties, but also their parents and other members of their immediate kin groups. It is certainly untrue to say of any customary law that divorce was obtainable at the will of either of the parties.

A notable feature of customary divorce procedure is its emphasis on machinery for conciliation and arbitration by the respective family groups of the disputant spouses. Indeed, the first step is almost invariably for the elders of each family group to meet and attempt a reconciliation of the spouses; only if this fails do the family groups—reconstituted frequently, by the addition of some outsiders—meet to exercise the judicial role of deciding whether or not a divorce is to be allowed. It should be noted, however, that this is still a family matter; and that divorce was not, in the traditional framework, a matter for the formally constituted courts or their equivalents.

It is not clear whether there are grounds for divorce in customary law. Many writers have inclined to this view, but there is good reason for doubting its validity—particularly if any analogy with the recognised grounds of divorce in English law is suggested. It is true that divorce may be refused because inadequate reasons are advanced by the parties, but there is no limitation on the number of reasons which are allowed; nor are they formalised into a set of watertight rules. Above all, the absence of specific grounds or reasons for divorce is not fatal to an attempt to end a marriage: their existence is but one of several factors which include, *inter alia*, the existence of children, the ability of the wife's father to return marriage consideration, and the existence of other possible remedies. Customary law has, in fact, long embodied the underlying notion of dissolving a marriage when it has broken down—a suggestion which has recently been proposed in Britain. (See '*Putting Asunder a Divorce Law for Contemporary Society*', The Report of a Group appointed by the Archbishop of Canterbury, London, 1966, S.P.C.K.; The Law Commission, *Report on Reform of the Grounds of Divorce*, 1966. Cmd. 3123; and the Divorce Reform Bill 1968.)

(a) INTRODUCTION

The extract given here, by *Schapera*, serves as a useful introduction to the whole topic of divorce in customary law. It touches on all the aspects of the topic, and enables the reader to obtain a synoptic view of it. In the sections which follow, each of the individual aspects is expanded through extracts taken from the writings of other authors.

I. Schapera: A Handbook of Tswana Law and Custom*

Despite the numerous domestic quarrels that occur, divorce (*tlhalanô*) is not very frequent among the Tswana. It means at the least that the husband deprives himself of a useful servant. Marrying an additional wife, or resorting to a concubine, is therefore the most common plan adopted to humble and annoy a wife inclined to be unruly. The wife on the other hand as a rule forfeits all claim to her children. This more than anything else makes her refrain from seeking a divorce, unless life is otherwise unbearable at her husband's home. The main grounds for divorce are flagrant ill-usage, excessive cruelty, or non-support on the part of the husband; and barrenness, the practice of sorcery, repeated adultery, wanton capriciousness, or non-performance of domestic duties on the part of the wife.

A husband seeking to divorce his wife will as a rule deliberately neglect her, e.g. by not ploughing for her, by not buying her clothes and other necessities, by not eating food at her house, and by not sleeping with her. The wife in these circumstances, or if the husband otherwise shows that he wants to get rid of her, will return to her parents' home and report what has happened. If she herself wishes to separate from her husband, she will similarly go back to her own home.

The parents and relatives on both sides then come together at the home of the wife's people to try and restore peace between husband and wife. If they do not succeed, the matter is referred to the court of her ward. Sometimes the court manages to bring about a reconciliation, and the couple resume life together. Or, if both they and their respective families insist on a separation, the court endorses their decision, and the couple are now regarded as divorced. In the olden days, it is said, domestic disputes were always finally settled in the court of the wife's people, and never taken to any higher court. But nowadays, if no reconciliation can be effected, the case is almost invariably sent on to the court of the Chief. Here it is dealt with anew, and a final attempt made to bring the couple together. Failing this, the Chief will order them to separate, and will also decide on the fate of the children, *bogadi*, and household property. He may further, if either husband or wife is flagrantly in the wrong, impose a special penalty upon the guilty party. He may, e.g. order the woman to be thrashed, or the husband to pay cattle as damages to her parents.[1]

When a couple are divorced, the household property is divided between them according to the circumstances of the case. Personal belongings, such as clothes, go to their respective owners. Household utensils, such as baskets, pots, and hoes, are usually taken by the wife, unless they have all been provided by the husband, who may then be allowed to keep some behind. The huts are generally left with the husband. But sometimes, as among the Ngwato, if there are two or more huts, and the husband is in the wrong, the Chief may order him to pull one up and help rebuild it at the wife's home, using the same rafters, doors, and thatch. The corn in the granaries is usually divided equally

* I. Schapera, *A Handbook of Tswana Law and Custom*, Oxford University Press, 1938, pp. 159–163.

between husband and wife. The cattle as a rule all remain with the husband, including any that he may have allotted to his wife. But if he is at fault, he may be ordered to give her a few animals to support her at her own home. Similarly, if he has deserted her, and she appeals to the Chief for maintenance, the latter may instruct her people to take some of her husband's cattle with which to support her, even if there is no divorce. If the wife is at fault, no such order will be made; but the husband may be asked to give her something according to his own inclinations. He is not, however, bound to do so. The wife is further entitled to any property she may have acquired in her own right, e.g. cattle and fields given to her by her parents as *serotwana* or *ketêêtsô* (marriage portion). But if she has any children, her cattle are generally kept back to be inherited by them.

If there are no children by the marriage, and *bogadi* has been paid, the husband can recover it, unless the wife's people provide a *seantlo*. It is said that normally, if this is not done, the *bogadi* is always recoverable, no matter who is in the wrong. But, among the Kgatla, Chief Lentswe introduced a distinction according to respective culpability. If the wife is at fault, the *bogadi* must be returned; whereas if the husband is at fault, he must forfeit it. The idea underlying this seems to have been that if the husband ever desires to take his wife back, he should be able to do so.

If there are children by the marriage, and no *bogadi* has been paid, the children in theory go with the mother. If the divorced wife afterwards marries some one else, who gives *bogadi* for her, he can claim these children by the first husband. It is stated, however, that a husband who has not yet paid *bogadi* for his wife will generally do so as soon as the trouble starts, so as not to forfeit his rights to the children.

If *bogadi* has already been paid, the children almost invariably belong to the father, while the cattle remain with the wife's people. The children, if small, may go with their mother; but the father is expected to send them occasional presents of food and clothing, and can reclaim them when they grow older. Even if there are no small children, the mother may be allowed to take one or more daughters to help her at home. The father must continue to support these children, conducts their marriages, and takes the *bogadi* given for them. But if he has altogether neglected both his wife and the children, the Chief may at times award the mother custody of the children. If the husband continues to neglect them, he will be held to have forfeited all his rights over them, although the children may, when grown up, return of their own accord to their father's people. Among the Ngwato, Kgama, on several occasions where the husband had gone away and taken no further interest in his wife and children, not only granted the mother custody of the children, but also ordered that the whole of the husband's property should be given to them. Nowadays, in case of divorce, the Chief may, if he thinks fit, divide the children between the parents.

Divorced women are free to marry again, but are not usually regarded with favour by the men. *Letsêlê go tshwarwa la moswêlwa, la motlhadiwa ke mogôfê*, says the proverb: 'Seize the breast of a widow, that of a divorced woman is unstable', i.e. she is regarded as a typical example of feminine frailty, a woman who may as readily leave her new husband as she did her former one. While living at home with her parents, she reverts to her status of unmarried daughter; but she is regarded as an adult woman capable of looking after herself, and it is said that among the Ngwato if she is seduced no case can be held against her lover.

Where the woman has no children, and her husband took back his *bogadi*, she can be married again in the ordinary way, her new husband paying *bogadi* as usual to her parents. But if the first husband did not take back his *bogadi*, and especially if there are also children by the marriage, it is much more difficult for her to remarry. *Mmapôô ga a tsewe*, says the proverb: 'A bull's mother is not married', i.e. a woman with sons by one man should not be married by any one else. If she is married again, and her second also gives *bogadi* for her, the children he has by her are regarded as his. But his wife is held still to be under the power of her children by her former husband, and is expected to return to them when no longer able to bear, or they may call her back. Her former husband, if still alive, cannot object to her return, as she will have come to her own children, who will feed and support her.

Moreover, as the saying goes: *Bogwê ga bo bole*, 'Relationship-in-law does not grow rotten', i.e. a man once married into a family is always regarded as its son-in-law, even in case of divorce. There is nothing to prevent a divorced couple from coming together again, if the *bogadi* has not been taken back. Among the Kgatla, if some one else wishes to marry a divorced woman, her parents must report the fact to her former husband, to give him the opportunity of taking her back, if he so wishes. Should he make no attempt to do so, she is free to get married again. The new husband must in any case pay *bogadi* to her people, otherwise any children he may beget by her will be regarded as those of the former husband. It is only by handing over *bogadi* that he obtains the right to claim the children as his own.

Similarly, if a divorced woman bears children to any other man without being married to him, these children can be claimed by her former husband's people, in virtue of the rights they acquired over her procreative power by the payment of *bogadi*. But among the Ngwato, where *bogadi* is no longer paid, the children of a divorced woman, if she has not been remarried, belong to her, and not to her lover or to her former husband.

Note

[1] Proclamation No. 75 of 1934 'following in this respect upon Proclamation No. 19 of 1926, as amended by Proclamation No. 6 of 1928) specially excludes from the jurisdiction of Native courts 'any cause or proceeding whereby in the case of persons married under the law of the Territory divorce is sought, or a declaration of nullity of marriage, or an order for judicial separation.' (Section 8 (2).)

(b) Procedure

While the procedural aspects of customary divorce are extremely important and are treated fully by the authors whose works are quoted in this section, it is not easy to distinguish these from several other facets of divorce law. Thus there is an almost inevitable overlap in the material which is presented here between procedure on the one hand and grounds and consequences of divorce on the other. Customary law did not distinguish its rules into neat and exclusive compartments; nor did the writers on the subject choose to do so.

The overriding feature of customary procedure which is amply demonstrated in what follows is its informality. Divorce occurred, for the most part, outside the framework of the traditional courts. It is, in fact, only since the advent of a modern judicial system that these matters have, for the most part, been considered by courts—something which is brought out in the latter part of *Holleman's* account of divorce procedure among the Shona.

J. D. Danquah: Akan Laws and Custom*

It cannot be exaggerated how easily and rapidly marriages may be dissolved with little trouble. Should a husband feel that he had been offended by the wife's conduct, he would summon her before friends for the settlement of differences. When her conduct continues to the inconvenience of the husband, a 'palaver' is generally held, either before both the sureties to the marriage or before other influential friends, notably the head of the wife's family. The saying is '*Awaree gu nkuro*', i.e. every divorce is preceded by 'palaver'. Therefore the aggrieved party will have to state his or her case before responsible men. The arbitrators deliver their finding after hearing each party, and then an attempt is made to reconcile the couple. At this juncture there is no law to bind either husband or wife to the other consort. He or she may or may not take the representations of the arbitrators. If it is the husband who is pressing for divorce because of his wife's misconduct, the odds are that he would rather divorce and get his money to marry a better girl, than retain an unserviceable wife. If it is the wife who has applied for divorce, because of ill-treatment, there is not the least probability of her submitting again to the wild habits of an imprudent husband. The argument on either side is strong and heated.

* J. D. Danquah, *Akan Laws and Custom*, Routledge & Kegan Paul, 1928, pp. 156–159.

The Arbitrators give in. The divorce is pronounced. They need not go to the Chief's Court, except for some special reason one of them wishes to do so. Any court of self-constituted arbitrators can witness a divorce. The fact is, it lies within nobody's power to declare married partners divorced. It rests with the will of the partners alone. A Chief's Court may, however, enforce a divorce when some special personal bodily harm is being done or had already been done by a husband who refuses to grant divorce to his wife. It is always easy for a husband to divorce his wife. There are minor difficulties in the way of a wife who applies for divorce, for she must satisfy her husband or her family, or the arbitrators, with at least one reason for her application. But on the whole it lies with the will of husband or of wife to say whether he or she will continue in the present married life. The saying is, '*Nea oda ne gya no onim senea ehyehye no*', i.e. 'He who is lying by the fire knows how much (or how little) the heat torments him'.

When divorce is once pronounced, its execution is left entirely in the hands of the husband. First he presents his Bill of Expenses. The wife may also present a bill stating any money due to her by her husband. These bills, or rather the husband's bills, will be subjected to the examination of the arbitration, and then all unlawful items are excluded from the bill. It shall not be lawful, for instance, for the husband to claim any amount to whatever value if it was presented to the wife prior to the payment of *Aseda*, i.e. during the period of courtship, but the cost of a cloth or kerchief presented to one's wife ten, fifteen or twenty years ago would be lawfully claimable if the divorce is on her application; if the divorce is being voluntarily given by the husband, then he shall only have payment for those cloths, etc., which are still new; he shall also have nothing more than the actual head-money paid; i.e. it need not be doubled, and no interest can be claimed. The Bill of Expenses, when properly settled, will then be added to the head-money plus the interest (if any), and together the surety to the wife's marriage will be called upon to pay. Laws passed recently make it lawful to double a wife's head-money when a divorce had been literally forced from the husband. The only exception to this rule is when the husband is known to be impotent. In such a case, the bare head-money, without interest, must be paid.

The surety may be given time for the repayment of the husband's bill; any length of time may be given, and when it is the wife who is applying for divorce the condition is that the customary 'white clay' which declares a woman as fully divorced shall not be sprinkled on her as a testimony of her having been so divorced, and although there would be a practical end to their married life, the wife would not be at liberty to contract another marriage or make love with another person, or she stands the risk of putting her new lover in jeopardy. The fact is, until the repayment of the head-money and other expenses is completed, the husband would have a right to claim satisfaction for adultery against the adulterer if the semi-divorced wife was so committed. This may properly be called a separation or suspensive divorce, not a final dissolution.

But as soon as the husband's bill is settled, the wife comes to him early in the morning before witnesses, ready to receive the chalking of white clay. It is a taboo to breakfast before going for the chalking, and the husband should not, when bedecking her with the white clay, sprinkle her feet with it, for that also is tabooed.

Hireguo or Ceremony of Divorce

Before the white clay is given as directed above, the wife must have taken the national or a family fetish, swearing as to her past fidelity towards her husband; and for fear of being adversely acted on by the fetish she should now mention the name of every person who had had carnal knowledge of her during her married life. This custom is termed '*Wiakyere*', or 'exposing' to the sun, i.e. bringing hidden facts to light. We may here state that it is in the interests of the husband giving divorce, to let his wife swear now, and it would also benefit the out-going wife to confess everything at this time. We are discussing the conclusions deducible from these statements under the heading 'Ayefare'.

The wife stands the further risk of losing any prospective lover she might privately have, for the husband, whether there is any known reason or no, is perfectly right to prohibit the out-going wife from getting married to any specific person, and she may even be prohibited to mention the name of, or have anything to do with, any particular person or persons. The wife is prohibited under pain of being adversely acted on by fetish and on penalty of the National Oath.

The expenses in connexion with the divorce, added to the original head-money, become another head-money which a new husband may be called upon to pay. This process is, however, adopted only in extreme circumstances, and however poor a family may be, care is always taken to see that a member of their family is left happy in her married life. So that in most cases the expenses are paid by the head of the divorced wife's family as ordinary debt, whilst the head-money remains the same. In several instances, it is not infrequent to see a family rallying to share for payment the expenses so incurred just to relieve them or their family from the consciousness of having among them a woman who is heavily loaded with head-money.

A careful reading of decided cases shows at once that this question of head-money is no trivial one. But the chief point to remember is that whilst the payment of 'Aseda' alone, in the absence of any named amount of head-money is sufficient to make a woman one's proper wife, the non-payment of the head-money, however small the amount, despite any larger sum one must have spent on one's wife at or before the wedding, disqualifies the marriage for full legal recognition.

With regard to expenses, it must be borne in mind that the wife is at liberty to deduct any debt owing to her by the husband from the husband's bill, and—but this is very rare—anything or its value which the wife may have given to the husband in the form of presents, etc., must also be claimed by the wife, for the saying is: '*Obi nnko obi abusua mu nnkobo dwetiri.*' 'One does not go into another's family to accumulate wealth.'

It is likewise a prevailing custom to claim from the wife as a part of the expense any amount that may have been spent by the husband at the funeral custom of any of the wife's relatives by way of condolence-money (Nsewabodee), etc. Sometimes there may be presents which had been given to the wife's relations on her behalf or by virtue of being married to a member of the family. These presents are often returnable to the husband.

We may add that not only does the law provide for deserted wives, but it explicitly limits the time for reasonable desertion. 'If', says the Law Record, 'a wife is deserted by her husband for a continued period of two years, she shall be at liberty to approach the relatives of her husband and demand a divorce.' The head-money is in this case not doubled, nor is the interest thereon payable. If there are any financial matters to go through, they would be reserved to await the husband's arrival. The husband's family may give her fetish to swear as to her fidelity, and may prohibit her, in the ordinary way, of any persons they wish. Whether the wife was or was not married on her husband's arrival, he would not be prejudiced to go into accounts with her.

J. F. Holleman: Shona Customary Law*

Procedure

In Common Law the dissolution of a marriage and the division of marital property are two separate legal issues. In Shona law the dissolution of marriage and the liquidation of the interests involved are a single issue: *the liquidation of the interests involved terminates the marriage relationship*. The principal question facing a European court in a divorce suit is *whether* sufficient legal cause exists to dissolve the marriage. In Shona practice the question is rather *on which terms* the marriage can be dissolved. This tends to make the problem a practical rather than a legal one.

It should further be remembered that in cases of dissolution the return of the wife (or her death) is an accepted fact. There is also the basic assumption that, whenever possible, the children are to be retained by the husband's family. The problem consequently ultimately hinges upon the question of the return of *rovoro* cattle (*kugura rovoro*, to 'cut' or divide the *rovoro*). For all practical purposes this becomes the vital issue, the crucial point upon which the attention of both parties (families) is focused. As a result the dominant feature of dissolution proceedings is usually an adroit manoeuvring of the opposing parties to gain the most favourable bargaining position with regard to the cattle involved: the *vatezwara* seek to retain possession of all or as many as possible of the

* J. F. Holleman, *Shona Customary Law*, Oxford University Press, Cape Town, 1952, pp. 280–297.

rovoro, the *vakuwasha* to recover the greatest possible number of cattle. In this connexion the *vatezwara* have the initial advantage of being the party 'in possession' of the disputed stakes, a fact which tends to place the onus on the *vakuwasha* to prove that they have a better claim, and to recover their due.

The ensuing process is a combination of legal considerations and practical tactics; the former are aimed mainly at determining the question of guilt (*mhoswa*), the latter are mainly employed to establish which party actually 'refuses' (*kuramba*) to continue the marriage relationship. Both factors—*mhoswa* and *kuramba*—influence the outcome of the process in their own particular manner. In this respect 'guilt' and 'refusal' are peculiar conceptions. Guilt broadly implies any action, failure or omission—not necessarily 'unlawful', e.g. death or barrenness of the wife—of one party which gives the other party a potential cause to seek a dissolution of the marriage. It determines the validity, and to some extent, the proportions, of the claim of the latter party. *Kuramba* (refusal) has a dual meaning: it may either be the action of one spouse repudiating or deserting the other without justification, in which case *kuramba* is merely an expression of guilt; it may also be the refusal of the innocent party to continue marriage relations when the guilty party makes a genuine effort to save the marriage—an attitude which tends to impair the innocent party's ability to recover their rightful claim. This being so, the innocent party will, whenever feasible, try to avoid an unequivocal 'refusal' (rejection) of the guilty party, because an (ostensibly) reconciliatory attitude will strengthen their case. For the same reason, however, the guilty party may try to provoke the innocent party to commit some act which, on the face of it, amounts to an outright repudiation. These tactics may often be observed between husband and wife. A woman who has lost affection for her husband may deliberately neglect him in order to provoke him to repudiate her, preferably with a rejection token. If she has a lover she may dish up her husband's food in a broken plate, so that he will lose his temper and give her a hiding, after which she will be able to show her bruises as a sign of 'maltreatment' (*rushusho*). The husband, again, when he wants to get rid of his wife but can find no justifiable reason for doing so, may try to provoke her to desert him or become unfaithful to him. By failing to give her sexual satisfaction he hopes to drive her into the arms of a paramour, so that he can accuse her of adultery or desertion. Sometimes he tries to frighten her by making her believe that she is being threatened by witchcraft. When cleverly executed such measures may have the desired result: the woman may flee because she is frightened, or even be induced to confess that, although unwittingly, she has committed acts of witchcraft.

All such tactics—often naïve and transparent to our way of thinking—reveal the character of Shona procedure and the presentation and evaluation of 'evidence'. The tendency is to judge the situation by its appearance rather than by its cause, and to be guided by facts that are self-evident rather than by motives that need to be explained. The mere fact that a woman leaves her husband apparently on her own account, raises the presumption that she is the 'refusing' as well as the guilty party. But if she is forcibly driven away or able to produce a rejection token, the husband is evidently the refusing party and the onus is on him to justify his action. In both cases the plainly observable acts of desertion or repudiation tend to prejudice the consideration that valid reasons may have prompted such acts.

For convenience' sake I shall therefore first describe the procedure followed in cases where (*a*) the wife is repudiated by her husband and (*b*) when she has deserted her husband.

Repudiation by the Husband

The husband[1] who, with or without just cause, wishes to repudiate his wife, should express his intentions in a concrete manner. A merely verbal communication to his wife that he does not want her any longer and that she should leave his village, does not amount to a formal repudiation. He must either notify her of his decision by handing her a concrete rejection token, or escort her back to her family, telling them that she does not satisfy him for particular reasons. Any tangible object such as a ring (*mhete*), hoe (*badza*), anklet (*rundarira*) or a coin may serve as a rejection token. But probably the clearest sign of repudiation is for the husband to hand his wife her cooking stones (*mapfiwa*) in a basket, or to throw them out of her kitchen.

A *mukuwasha* who acts in good faith and with just cause will escort his wife to her family, stating that he cannot keep her any longer (*jira renyu iguru, ndari konewa*—'your blanket is too big, it overpowers me') and giving them his reasons. Usually the *vatezwara* will try to persuade him to reconsider his decision, suggesting ways to improve marital conditions. Often the *mukuwasha* agrees to leave the matter in abeyance, giving his parents-in-law a chance to discipline their daughter in the hope of improving her attitude towards her husband or household duties. He then may re-accept the woman after some time. When the *mukuwasha* is not inclined to reconsider the matter the *vatezwara* may demand a concrete token[2] to confirm his decision. Acceptance of such a token indicates that both parties are in principle agreed that the marriage is to be dissolved. If the *vatezwara* have cattle available, a rejection token is usually not necessary because a final settlement can be made without undue delay, provided that the parties reach agreement on the terms of the liquidation. More often than not, however, the *vatezwara* do not have sufficient stock to satisfy the *vakuwasha* and therefore need time to 'look for' (*kutswaka*) cattle. The obvious solution for them is to find another suitor who is willing to marry the woman against payment of cattle. But unless the *vatezwara* have clear proof that the *vakuwasha* intend to terminate the marriage, they cannot encourage or negotiate a second marriage without committing a breach of the marriage contract. For this reason they ask the *mukuwasha* for a rejection token. But the latter may be reluctant to give such a token because this will place him in the relatively unfavourable position of the 'refusing' party. The result is often that the woman is left for the time being with her family without the *vakuwasha* having committed themselves to a final decision. The *vatezwara* may break this impasse by bringing the matter to a head before a formal court of law. Summoned before the court the husband must give a clear statement whether he still 'loves' his wife (i.e. is prepared to take her back), or 'refuses' her. If he repudiates her, the initiative passes into the hands of the *vatezwara*. They are now free to negotiate another marriage, and to use the cattle they receive from the second husband to liquidate the first marriage. But even if they fail to find cattle and their daughter stays at their home without finding another husband, they cannot, according to Shona ideas, be considered guilty of withholding the *vakuwasha* their due, for they remain willing and able to return the woman to her husband if he wants her. For example:

> C returned his last-married wife T to her parents because she 'always made trouble with his two other wives'. T's parents told C that they would 'teach T to behave better.' After about six months, when C had not fetched his wife back, *tezwara* M asked T whether 'he still loved his wife'. C said that he no longer loved her and that he wanted his cattle back. M demanded and received a rejection token 'to show that C really did not want his wife'. T stayed with her parents for another year during which no new suitor was found. C then sued M before the court of M's ward headman (Muzokomba, southern Sabi Reserve) for the return of cattle. M pleaded that he had no cattle in his kraal because 'T had not yet been taken (*kutorwa*) by another man'. T was asked by the court if she 'still loved her husband'. She said that she loved him. She was willing to go back to him and would try to live in peace with the other wives. C refused to take her back, claimed his cattle instead. The court held that since C was the one who 'refused the marriage', he would have to wait until T had found another husband before he could get his cattle back.

The position of a husband who has not taken the trouble to escort his wife back to her parents to account for his action, but who merely drives her from his village with a rejection token, is even weaker. In these cases there is a presumption that the husband is the guilty party. His action is deeply humiliating to the wife and an insult to her family. He has no choice but to wait until the woman has found another suitor, when he has the right to receive a refund of some of his *rovoro* cattle. The *tezwara* is entitled first to safeguard his own interests when he receives cattle from the second husband, that is, he may retain at least such portion as would, together with any cattle received from the first husband, amount to a full *rovoro* for his daughter. But he must hand the balance or a major portion of it to the first husband to liquidate the first marriage. The *tezwara* may, in view of the circumstances, make allowance for the humiliation he has suffered, but he should be careful not to exceed the limits of propriety. If the cattle he retains from the two husbands greatly outnumber a normal *rovoro*, he is guilty of having accepted 'two *matangga*' (literally, two cattle kraals), a double *rovoro* for the same daughter. He is then *nggarara* ('miser') and the inference is that he has prostituted his child. The basic tendency in Shona law is that, if through remarriage or other causes, the number of cattle transferred in respect of a woman exceeds the number of the original *rovoro* cattle, the first husband rather than her own family should have the benefit of such excess. But if the first marriage has been finally liquidated *before* a second marriage and transfer of cattle takes place, the *tezwara* can of course retain all cattle received from the second husband. For example:

> *Mukuwasha* D repudiated his wife because he believed she was malingering. *Tezwara* G refunded (from his own stock of cattle) four of the twelve head of cattle given as *rovoro*. G 'kept eight head because D would keep the three children the woman had given to him'. The marriage being formally dissolved, G subsequently married his daughter to another husband who gave a *rovoro* of ten head. When D sued G for a portion of these cattle, the court told him that he had no claim: 'when the woman was "taken" (*wa torwa*) by another, she was no longer your wife.'

Generally speaking the *tezwara* who has received his daughter back with a rejection token, can await her remarriage before settling the account with the first husband, as long as he acts in good faith and the existing circumstances do not materially change. Should the *tezwara*, for instance, receive a herd of cattle from the marriage of one of his other daughters, he cannot reasonably postpone the final settlement if the *mukuwasha* has repudiated his wife for a valid reason. But if the repudiation was not justified, the *tezwara* will even then often succeed in postponing the liquidation of the marriage until the repudiated woman herself has found another husband.

Since the marriage remains in force until cattle have been returned, the husband is entitled to change his mind and seek to resume marital relations with the wife he has previously repudiated, if she has not yet found another suitor. But the *tezwara* (or the woman herself) may require him to give some compensation to redeem his rejection token and to prove his sincerity. If the *tezwara* or the wife refuse to accept a genuine reconciliation offer, they become the 'refusing' party, and the *vakuwasha* can then sue them for an immediate settlement. Instead of being allowed to wait until a suitable husband turns up, the *vatezwara* are then obliged to find the necessary cattle by some means or other. If they cannot borrow from relatives or friends and there is no immediate prospect of receiving *rovoro* for an unmarried daughter, the obvious solution for them is to solicit another husband for the woman concerned in the dispute. If it is she rather than her family who has refused to be reconciled with her husband, she will be openly urged to find a suitable husband herself (e.g. by *kutizira*, flight marriage) in order to 'free' her parents.

As long as her marriage has not yet been finally liquidated, a woman who has been returned to her family—either to await the dissolution of her marriage or merely for a period of correction—cannot have sexual intercourse with another man without committing adultery. The offending male party (*gomba*) is in principle therefore liable to pay damages to the husband. But since the woman has returned to the immediate control of her family, the latter will be held primarily responsible by the husband if she commits adultery or elopes with a lover. In any action against the *gomba*, the *tezwara* is therefore inevitably involved as the intermediate party, and the course of the ensuing process is largely determined by his attitude regarding the conflict. If the *mukuwasha* has not, by word or by deed, made it absolutely clear that he has finally rejected his wife, the *tezwara* must act on the assumption that marital relations between husband and wife will be re-established, and he should support the *mukuwasha* in an action for damages against the *gomba*, at the same time trying to return the woman to her husband. But if there is clear evidence (such as a rejection token) that the *mukuwasha* has been seeking to dissolve the marriage and the *gomba* is prepared to give marriage cattle for her, the *tezwara* is entitled to negotiate a second marriage and liquidate the first marriage. Even under these circumstances the *tezwara* is expected to keep his *mukuwasha* informed of any developments. He must report that 'your wife has been taken by another man', show any tokens and hand over any payments which he receives from the *gomba*.

Quite often a dispute arises between the *tezwara* and the *mukuwasha* because the latter, after having repudiated the wife, decides at the eleventh hour that he 'still loves his wife' and therefore wants her back. This is a common—and if successful, profitable—manoeuvre to enable the *mukuwasha* first to claim compensation for adultery from the *gomba*, and later, when the woman again deserts him, a return of *rovoro* from the *tezwara*.

The possession of the rejection token or other irrebuttable evidence of repudiation, justifies the *tezwara's* decision to negotiate a new marriage and to insist upon the dissolution of the existing marriage. Under these circumstances it is impracticable for the *mukuwasha* to pursue an action for adultery against the *gomba*, because tribal courts will not support such an action if there is no prospect that conjugal relations will be resumed. The only course then left to the *mukuwasha* is to bring an action against his *tezwara*, claiming return of *rovoro* and, if possible, compensation for breach of the marriage agreement. If the matter cannot be settled between the parties, a tribal court may be asked to decide upon the total number of cattle to which the *mukuwasha* is entitled in the circumstances. If the *gomba* has agreed to marry the woman, the *tezwara* will expect him to foot the bill.

The death of a repudiated wife at her parents' village normally necessitates an early settlement of the cattle issue. The *vatezwara*, who have so far successfully deferred the liquidation of the marriage on the ground that the woman has 'not yet been taken by another man', are now faced with the bare fact that she has died a married woman with a considerable portion of her reproductive capacity unspent. If full marriage compensation has been given for her the *vakuwasha* are entitled to be compensated, even if she had been repudiated without a just cause. But while there is no doubt that in principle the *vakuwasha* are entitled to a division of the *rovoro*, regardless of guilt, the question whether they were guilty when sending the woman home, may affect their chances of recovering a compensation proportionate to their loss. In such cases, especially when the *vatezwara* are poor, a guilty *mukuwasha* may find it impossible to recover more than a nominal compensation. If he refuses to accept this as a final settlement and tries to recover his due by formal litigation, the court will not deny his rightful claim, but is usually disinclined to exert strong pressure upon the *vatezwara*. Under such circumstances the liquidation of the marriage relationship may be postponed indefinitely.

When a wife, after having been repudiated by her husband, goes to her family and remains there unmarried until she dies an old woman, the claim for a return of marriage cattle is considered to have lapsed. This principle is based upon the realistic consideration that a husband who has repudiated his wife without justification, has only himself to blame if he has failed to reap the full benefit of his marriage; and if he had a valid reason for repudiating her he should have insisted upon a liquidation of the marriage more vigorously at an earlier stage.

Desertion by the Wife

A woman who deserts her husband believing that she has a valid reason for running away, will usually seek refuge with her own family. Her action nevertheless places her family in the unfavourable position of the refusing party and raises a presumption of guilt on her part. She must therefore be able to justify her action. If she fails to convince her family, they will return her to her husband, often after having severely disciplined her. But if she is able to show visible evidence of maltreatment or neglect, or when she runs away after her repeated complaints about her husband's misconduct have left little doubt about his guilt, her family may decide to shelter her.

Various courses are now open to the *vatezwara*. They may take the initiative and immediately bring an action against the husband for maltreatment, before he sues them on account of his wife's desertion. But unless they can afford to liquidate the marriage forthwith, their action should be presented as a claim for compensation and subsequent reconciliation. In this way the *vatezwara* avoid creating the impression that they are actually the refusing party. When the husband, after his guilt has been sufficiently proved, refuses to give compensation, he is placed in virtually the same position as a man who has repudiated his wife without justification. On the other hand, if he agrees to make suitable amends, the woman or her family have no grounds for refusing a resumption of marital relations.

Another quite common course is for the *vatezwara* to await whatever action the husband chooses to take, in the meantime arousing popular sentiment by publicizing the fact that the woman has been maltreated by her husband. The husband may either claim his wife back, in which case there will first be a question of formal reconciliation; or he may demand a return of *rovoro*, in which case he may be required to give a rejection token which will label him as the refusing party.

Generally speaking, therefore, it is in the interest of either party first to suggest a reconciliation and resumption of marital relations, because the party who then fails to come to terms is virtually forced to accept a liquidation of the marriage when it suits the other party. For this reason the family of a woman who has deserted her husband even for justifiable reasons, will rarely actively seek to dissolve the marriage. Only in the relatively few cases when they are economically strong enough to lose a considerable portion of her *rovoro* cattle, or when they feel confident that they will soon find another husband for her and that his cattle will compensate this loss, will they take an uncompromising stand against the husband. As a rule, however, they will shelter the woman, but at the same time leave no doubt that, as far as they are concerned, the marriage should be continued, provided that the husband gives convincing proof of his intentions to treat his wife decently. Consequently, if the woman herself refuses to be reconciled when the husband is prepared to make amends, she will lose the support of her family and will be expected personally to solicit another husband in order to solve the problem of finding cattle.

From the above description it is clear that a woman who deserts her husband in bad faith cannot hope to find refuge with her own family, because they will severely take her to task and promptly return her to her husband. The obvious course for her under these circumstances is therefore to seek refuge with a third party who is willing to marry her and who is prepared to face a legal action in which he is inevitably placed in a most unfavourable position. When the woman has a lover (*gomba*) she may arrange to elope with him (*kutizisa*), in which case her action is almost certainly successful, provided he has sufficient cattle to satisfy thc demands that will be imposed on him. If she cannot make arrangements with a lover, she may decide to run away alone (*kutizira*) and present herself at the village of any person who she hopes will agree to marry her. This is almost invariably an act of desperation and for this reason seldom fails to arouse public sentiment in her favour. Women who run away like this are usually youthful wives married to elderly husbands under a *zwarira* (credit marriage) agreement.

The party (*gomba*) who *agrees to shelter and marry* a woman who has deserted her husband, can either notify her own family (*vatezwara*) with a concrete token, or merely await any action which her family and husband may take against him. The first alternative is probably the more honourable because it amounts to a marriage proposal. But it also renders the *gomba* solely responsible for the unlawful situation and thus deprives him of any defence or mitigation which the woman's flight might possibly have provided him. Many informants therefore expressed the opinion that, unless it was reasonably certain that the *tezwara* would be willing to compromise, the *gomba* would for tactical reasons prefer to wait until the husband brought his action against him. The *gomba* would at any rate follow the latter course when the family of the woman lived far away: he would be adding insult to injury if he were to notify the husband.

A husband whose wife has deserted him will as a rule immediately notify his *tezwara* (if the latter lives within reach), either because he hopes to find her there, or because he expects the *tezwara* to help him trace the woman. It is uncommon for a husband personally to recover his wife from the village of the third party who harbours her, because this may easily lead to bloodshed ('the husband must not meet the man who has taken his wife because the two will kill each other'). The regular procedure for the husband is either to seek the intervention of the chief or headman, or to establish contact with the *gomba* through an intermediary, preferably the *tezwara*.

The *tezwara*, in order to avoid the implication that he condones his daughter's action or has encouraged or assisted her, is obliged to give his *mukuwasha* full support, helping him to trace the woman and, if possible, bring her back. When the *tezwara* receives a notification token from the *gomba* he can either refuse to accept it or hand it over to the husband. By refusing to accept the token the *tezwara* summarily rejects the idea of liquidating the existing marriage. He will then immediately follow up his refusal by demanding his daughter back in order to return her to her husband. A *tezwara* who receives and transmits the token to the husband, still acts in good faith, but leaves it to the husband to decide whether to demand the return of the woman and compensation for unlawful cohabitation, or to seek to liquidate the marriage by claiming a refund of *rovoro* cattle. The first-mentioned action, which is clearly directed against the *gomba* as principal defendant, is under the circumstances the more appropriate, and potentially the most profitable for the husband. If the woman can be induced to go back to her husband, the *gomba* may be required to pay the husband three to five head of cattle as *muripo* (damages). If she later deserts him again and a continuation of the marriage proves to be impracticable, his claim for a return of marriage cattle is not impaired. But unless the woman can indeed be persuaded to resume marital relations with her husband, this course of action is impracticable, because a court will not support the husband's claim for damages (*muripo*: often carelessly called *maputiro*) against the *gomba* unless there is a reasonable prospect that marital relations will be resumed. In the past there was little doubt that a recalcitrant woman could be forced to return to her husband, and that her family would not shrink from using physical force if they believed that this would solve their problem. In such cases only her second or third desertion would convince the families-in-law that a continuation of the marriage was impossible. Nowadays, however, the parents will hesitate to use violent measures which they know may have serious repercussions in the Native Commissioner's Court. Consequently, when the woman shows enough determination in the face of threats or persuasion from her family and husband, she can usually successfully force a dissolution of her marriage after her first desertion, provided again that her lover is willing and able to pay. In this case the husband has no option but to claim a return of *rovoro* cattle in an action which is in principle directed against the woman's family.

Since the matter often remains undecided until the case and all the parties concerned are brought to a tribal court, the husband will, with the support of the *tezwara*, normally first demand his wife back and claim compensation for adultery from the *gomba*. If it then appears during the process that nothing will persuade the woman to return to her husband, the whole action for adultery may be dropped and summarily replaced by a claim for return of marriage cattle. Such cases reveal the extreme flexibility of Shona law and procedure. The new action implies the dissolution of the marriage, a matter which must be decided by the *vatezwara* and *vakuwasha*, and not by the court. Normally in actions for the return of marriage cattle, the *tezwara* is the defendant, while the guilty third party—if any—may be present during the process in the position of a 'co-respondent'. But if, during an action for adultery and desertion, the issue is summarily changed, it is taken for granted (unless either the *tezwara* or the *mukuwasha* sustain their objections) that there is a tacit agreement regarding the dissolution of the marriage. It is also assumed as a matter of course that the defendant (*gomba*) will have to supply the necessary cattle. The result is that, although technically the *tezwara* has become the principal defendant in the new case, the new action is actually directed against the *gomba*.

The process is different when the *tezwara* has acted in a manner inconsistent with good faith. If he enters into marriage negotiations with the *gomba* and commits himself to a new marriage agreement (usually by accepting cattle from the *gomba*), he is guilty of a breach of contract. The *mukuwasha*, realizing the futility of any attempt to recover his wife under such circumstances, has no choice but to bring an action against the *tezwara* for a liquidation of the marriage, while he is also entitled to additional damages for breach of contract. In such cases there is no longer a ground for action against the *gomba*. Although the latter may in practice, if the case is brought before a formal court, be summoned to attend the process, and be rebuked by the court for his unlawful behaviour, there is no doubt that the *tezwara* is the principal defendant against whom the action is directed. The court has no power to declare the second marriage invalid, or to demand a continuation of the first marriage, but will take such unlawful conduct into consideration when it determines the total amount of compensation due to the *mukuwasha*.

Procedure following Husband's failure to provide Rovoro

If the *mukuwasha* fails to provide *rovoro* as agreed upon, the *tezwara* is entitled to seek a dissolution of the marriage. It was found in practice that only in those cases when the relations between the families were strained because of lack of good faith, default of *rovoro* payment actually led to a liquidation of the marriage at the instance of the *vatezwara*. In Chapter IV,[3] I discussed the various remedies of which the parties, and especially the *vatezwara*, can avail themselves if they wish to save the marriage, and I made it clear that under such circumstances the decision whether to liquidate the marriage rests with the *tezwara*. If he decides that a continuation of the marriage is impracticable, he can follow one of the following procedures. When he chooses to keep the matter between the families he can fetch his daughter back from her husband (if he has not already done so in the hope of forcing his son-in-law to fulfil his *rovoro* commitments) and present him with an ultimatum: an immediate settlement of the outstanding *rovoro* debt, or a clear statement, usually supported by a concrete token, that the husband 'rejects' (*kuramba*) his wife and thus agrees to a liquidation of the marriage. Failing to satisfy the demand for *rovoro*, the husband is now forced into the position of the 'refusing' party, and this gives the *tezwara* a free hand to dissolve the marriage in the manner he thinks fit.

The *tezwara* may also bring a formal action against the *mukuwasha* for a settlement of the *rovoro* debt. This course is probably more common to-day, especially in the Wedza and Narira Reserves. In such cases, if the *tezwara* has proved the validity of his claim, the court will present the *mukuwasha* with a similar ultimatum: payment of the *rovoro*, or an agreement to dissolve the marriage. In this event there is usually no need for a concrete 'rejection' token because the public character of the proceedings would make a subsequent denial of the *mukuwasha's* consent to dissolve the marriage, impossible. Nevertheless, if the *tezwara* does not intend to liquidate the marriage immediately because he first wishes to seek another husband for his daughter, he may insist upon being given a token if he believes that this will facilitate his subsequent negotiations with any third party.

From a legal point of view informants generally regarded the second (formal) course of action as the more satisfactory. Both parties would have a fair opportunity of stating their case in public. The *tezwara* would be dissuaded from forcing the *mukuwasha* into a dissolution agreement if the court (and public) expressed the opinion that under the circumstances such an agreement would not be justified, or at least be premature. But if his demands were reasonable, he could rely on the invaluable support of the court and public opinion. It should be emphasized that in this process the marriage is *not* actually *dissolved* by the court; the court is asked to help decide the question *whether* the marriage should be dissolved and to be a public witness to any agreement which the parties may reach in this respect.

The informal procedure, which is fairly common especially in the more remote area of the Sabi Reserve, may lead to malpractice. The *tezwara*, having some measure of right on his side because of his *mukuwasha's* failure to discharge his *rovoro* obligations, may abuse his stronger position and force the issue before the latter has been given a fair chance to repair his omission. Chances of abuse are particularly great in those cases (a few of which have been reported to me) in which the *tezwara* is the social or political superior of his *mukuwasha*. If the wife then willingly obeys her family and agrees to remarry the suitor they have selected for her, the *mukuwasha* may find himself faced with a *fait accompli*. Not being in a position to challenge his *tezwara* on the legality of such an action, he can only demand a return of such cattle as circumstances may entitle him to.

Function and Powers of the Tribal Court

The jurisdiction of a tribal court in cases of dissolution of marriage is limited by the fact that the decision to dissolve a Shona marriage rests with the responsible parties, and that a marriage cannot be dissolved by a court order but only by the actual liquidation of the marriage by the parties themselves.[4] When the parties are able to reach a settlement amongst themselves the marriage can be liquidated for any reason which they consider valid, and no court or other extraneous agency can question the legality of their actions. But if the parties disagree, either on the question whether the marriage should be dissolved, or on the actual terms on which it should be liquidated, the court may be asked to express its opinion on these issues and lend its support to the party whose rightful interests are being threatened.

It has been shown that the court may often be used as a public platform upon which the parties seek to out-manoeuvre each other in order to attain the most favourable position regarding the cattle involved. They try to achieve their aim, not so much by a straight effort to terminate their relationship, but rather by suggesting apparently reasonable conditions under which they would be willing to continue the marriage. The party who fails to accept these conditions, has virtually no option but to await the time when it suits the other party to liquidate the marriage. It is the duty of the court to determine whether the terms proposed for such a reconciliation can be considered reasonable under the circumstances, and to suggest that they be modified if they are excessive. When a reconciliation is impracticable or obviously not sincerely meant, the court may advocate a dissolution of the marriage as the inevitable alternative. In all cases in which the question of *whether* the marriage should be dissolved is still undecided, the court is therefore actively engaged in seeking a reasonable basis for reconciliation. When necessary the court may make such a reconciliation conditional upon the fulfilment of certain obligations by the guilty party (e.g. compensation to an aggrieved spouse or payment of outstanding *rovoro* cattle). Non-fulfilment of the court's order then entitles the innocent party to a liquidation of the marriage.

In cases of marital trouble the court does not shrink from publicly censuring a guilty spouse and often advises the families to take certain steps to remedy the situation. In one or two cases which I witnessed, the wife refused to go back to her husband without apparent justification, but she denied that she had a lover. The court told her parents to take her back to her husband's village, by force if necessary. In other cases, when the husband had denied his wife conjugal rights but had given her no concrete rejection token, the court told his family to lock husband and wife up in one hut at night time. Such orders, however, do not mean that the court refuses to sanction a dissolution of the marriage; they are the crude but usually effective measures by which the court intends to break the impasse by forcing the issue one way or another. The unwilling spouses may submit to such pressure and resume normal marital relations, but if they refuse they are obliged to resort to some action which at least simplifies the dissolution of the marriage. The recalcitrant woman may for instance seek refuge with a third party who is willing to marry her, or the unwilling husband may repudiate his wife in an unambiguous manner, for instance by handing her a rejection token.

The significance of a formal litigation is that all facts and circumstances relevant to the conflict are exposed and analysed in public. The process is never confined to the one failure or wrongful act of the defendant which induced the complainant to seek the intervention of the court. What emerges during the process is a history of the marriage, a detailed record of human relations in which usually neither party is entirely blameless. The trouble often appears to have started with a comparatively trivial act of negligence or an insignificant wrong, which provoked resentment and ill-considered retaliations, which again gave rise to further provocation, finally culminating in a clear breach of marital obligations, serious enough to justify formal litigation and a dissolution of the marriage.

A common feature of such cases is that once it has been proved (or merely taken for granted) that a particular wrong has been committed by one party, the other party (or the court) will almost invariably ask *why* such a wrong has been committed.[5] A reasonable motive may shift the blame to the other party. While this need not actually exculpate the guilty party, it obliges the other party to justify his own behaviour or at least to show some leniency.

> This point was well illustrated in a recent case in the Wedza Reserve. Complainant charged his wife with adultery. The woman did not deny that she had slept with a lover but refused to be held guilty of adultery. She explained that her husband had blamed her for the fact that she had remained childless, while she believed him to be sterile. In order to 'prove' him wrong, she had solicited another man to have intercourse with her. Her explanation did not exculpate her and the court found reason to rebuke her severely. But the circumstances mitigated her act to such an extent that the case remained undecided: the court considered the husband's claim for damages (his condition for reconciliation) excessive, and did not agree with his alternative suggestion that the woman's family should be held responsible for an immediate return of *rovoro* cattle. The result was that the woman went home with her parents, pending further developments. (In the words of the court: 'The husband will now be able to find out whether she still loves him. If she does not love him, she will run away with another man.')

In cases when the *mukuwasha* has failed to meet his *rovoro* obligation he may be required to give an account of his efforts to get cattle, in order to prove his good faith. When he is able to allay the suspicion of bad faith the court will turn to the *tezwara* for an explanation why he is unable to grant his *mukuwasha* more time to find cattle. If the *tezwara* can neither disprove the *mukuwasha's* good faith nor furnish an acceptable explanation why he so urgently needs cattle, the court, though it has no power to prevent him from liquidating the marriage, may prevail upon him not to 'kill' his *mukuwasha* merely in order to 'seek riches' (*kupfumisa*).

The court is therefore not inclined to support an action for dissolution of marriage merely upon proof of guilt. Before lending its support to such an action it wants to be satisfied that, in view of any motives or circumstances revealed, the innocent party cannot reasonably be expected to condone the guilty action, and by condoning save the common interests of both families. The question of 'right' or 'wrong' in these cases is therefore not only interpreted in terms of legal principles but largely becomes a question of what appears to be reasonable and equitable under the circumstances.

When the question whether the marriage should be dissolved is no longer in doubt, but the parties fail to reach an agreement regarding the *terms* on which the marriage should be liquidated, the court may be asked to give a decision on this point. The nature of such a process is not essentially different from that which has just been described. In these cases, too, the court will need all possible information relevant to the marriage before it feels able to judge the conflict in its entirety and to decide what number of cattle should be awarded to the *vakuwasha*. The amount of marriage compensation originally promised and paid, the manner and time in which it was paid, the number of children born of the marriage, the marital and extra-marital relations of husband and wife, the economic position of the *vatezwara*, the possibility of a guilty third party being involved in the conflict and the latter's ability to provide cattle, all these factors are duly considered by the court and will influence its decision. Since the action concerns the refund of all or a portion of the marriage compensation, detailed information about all marriage payments made to the *vatezwara* are of special importance. The onus is on the *vakuwasha* to prove that such payments have been made. If their claims in this respect are disputed, the court will require the original intermediary (*munyai*, *samukuru*) between the families to give evidence. His statement is usually conclusive, and preferred to such documentary proof as a copy of the marriage certificate.

The time when such payments were made, may be important, especially in cases of credit marriage when the young wife or affianced bride has eloped with a lover before the *vakuwasha* have derived some benefit from the marriage transaction. If any *rovoro* have been in the possession of the *vatezwara* for a long time, there will be a question of *ceuka*, that is, allowance will be made for the fact that the *vakuwasha* have been denied the benefit of their cattle's offspring during these years and are therefore entitled to recover a greater number of cattle than they originally delivered.

As in other cases of Native litigation, judgment is pronounced by the chief or headman only after the court assessors (*vatonggi*, *makota*, *majuri*) have thrashed out the case, and usually not until there is some indication regarding the terms that may be acceptable to both complainant and defendant. It is not unusual, however, to find that the most strenuous bargaining takes place *after* the court has given judgment, and that the chief subsequently modifies his judgment when he finds that the defendant will otherwise remain in default. Occasionally, when it appears during the proceedings that little or no progress is being made towards an acceptable solution, the court or either of the parties (or even a member of the public) may suggest that the trial be interrupted for a while to enable the parties to withdraw and discuss the matter amongst themselves (*kusungga dumba*, lit., to make a watch-hut). The court is subsequently notified of the result of their private discussions, and if an agreement has been reached, judgment will be pronounced accordingly. If no agreement can be reached the court may either give such judgment as it thinks fit, or advise the parties to postpone the matter until they are in a better frame of mind.

Generally speaking a tribal court will hesitate to give judgment unless it is reasonably certain that its decision will be obeyed, and for this reason the chief will usually ask the parties if they 'agree' (*kutenda*) with his decision. This does not mean that their agreement is essential before the judgment can be considered valid, because the court has, at least in principle, the power to enforce its judgment upon an unwilling party, if necessary by attachment of his property. The practical effect of the parties' agreement is that they publicly bind themselves to liquidate the marriage in the manner suggested by the court. In the Wedza and Narira Reserves it is customary for the *tezwara* (or guilty third party) to bring the necessary cattle to the court at a later session, to be formally handed over to the *vakuwasha* by the court. In the Sabi Reserve the cattle are often delivered by the *vatezwara* direct to the *vakuwasha*, who then notify the court that the animals have been duly received and that the matter can be considered finished. But I must again emphasize that not the court's order for a return of a specified number of cattle, but the actual delivery of such cattle, terminates the relationship between the families.

Under Shona law a tribal court has the power to make an order regarding the custody of and parental rights to the children born of the marriage, but it will not do so unless this question is actually disputed by the parties. Normally it is taken for granted that all children remain under the control of their paternal family, unless they are very young, in which case the mother or maternal family may take care of them until they are big enough to return to the father. Since the latter arrangement, when it is expected to last for a number of years, may give rise to a claim for maintenance (*marero*, *uredzwa*) against the paternal family, the parties may ask the court to make a ruling on this point. The court may then lay down that the child or children concerned are to be returned to the custody of the father at a certain age, with or without compensation of maintenance. The question of maintenance is often influenced by the terms upon which the marriage is to be liquidated. If, for instance, the court considers these terms to be comparatively favourable to the *vatezwara*, it may deny them the right to claim maintenance.

Notes

[1] I may refer to the 'husband' or *mukuwasha* merely to simplify the description. It should be borne in mind that with regard to the conclusion as well as the dissolution of a marriage agreement, the families and not the individual spouses are the responsible parties. In any decisive or responsible action, 'husband' therefore means either the head of the husband's family or the husband acting in concurrence with his family.

[2] Amongst the southern Hera a distinction is made between a *duro* and *gupuro* token. The first token (from *kutura*, to put down a burden) implies that the husband is returning his wife in the hope that she can be corrected by her parents and then returned to him. The *gupuro* (from *kukupura*, to wipe off something) indicates a final rejection. In the Wedza and Narira Reserves only *gupuro* is known, but the manner and circumstances in which it is given will indicate whether a final rejection is meant.

[3] Means of enforcing *rovoro* obligation.'

[4] In *Takuleni* v. *Pedzisayi* (1942), S.R.N.A.C. 184, the President of the Court declared that 'it is most irregular (for the trial court) to grant return of *lobolo* without annulment of the marriage'. The omission of the lower court to make an order of annulment was, however, more in conformity with Shona law than the higher court's insistence that such an order should be made.

[5] It is common to hear a complainant-husband opening his case with the words: 'I want the court to find out why my wife has been sleeping with So-and-so.' To which the wife may reply with a counter-question, 'I want to know why my husband refuses to sleep with me.'

H. Cory: Sukuma Law and Custom*

Divorce (*Kulekana*)

The dissolution of a marriage did not and does not make any considerable change in the social and economic status of either of the two people concerned.

Formerly, if a man was tired of living with his wife he went with her to her father and claimed return of bridewealth; on the other side, if a father-in-law began to dislike his son-in-law he sent for his daughter and returned the bridewealth. If a divorce took place the children were always given to the father, and no concern was felt regarding the feelings of the mother. If a man was tired of living with the mother of his children, no provision of any kind existed within the law which would enable the mother to keep her children.

Adultery was seldom considered grounds for divorce, nor was it regarded as a reason for terminating conjugal life. An adulterer had to pay compensation to the husband.

Such was the conception of the law, and it has not changed much except in one important particular. Native courts and elders called as arbitrators do not immediately agree to dissolve a marriage. They grant a divorce only after many attempts to reconcile husband and wife. A decision or final judgment is delayed as long as possible, especially

* H. Cory, *Sukuma Law and Custom*, Oxford University Press, 1953, pp. 58–60.

in cases where one party demands divorce while the other is willing to continue married life, and in all cases where no acknowledged reason for divorce is forthcoming.

There are not many reasons why a man should divorce his wife. Sentiments are not complicated, life is simple, and economic extravagance on the part of the wife is impossible. Changes in the physical appearance of a woman in the course of years, or love for another woman, are never the hidden reason for domestic trouble started by the husband. The legal institution of polygyny, as well as the husband's legally and socially acknowledged right to extramarital liaisons, afford him opportunities for satisfying his aesthetic feelings. Men take great pride in possessing more than one wife; a polygynous household proves that the master is a man of means and authority. Further, a divorce is troublesome and the material gain for the husband, especially when there are children, may be small. It may also happen that the father-in-law has used the cattle of the bridewealth and is not in a position to return them. The most important factor which makes a husband reluctant to claim a divorce will be discussed later.

The situation of a wife is very different. There is no opportunity for her to meet other men without incurring censure; she readily exaggerates in her own mind any unpleasant quarrel at home, as this is the centre of nearly all her activities; and she may succumb too easily to temptation in the form of illusory promises of a life of more intense emotion with another man. Even the existence of children does not influence her decision if she has fallen in love with another man.

It would be wrong to assume that an African woman is a bad and heartless mother. It would appear rather that she remains all her life primarily a 'woman', reluctant to give up any natural rights in favour of motherhood, except during the infancy of her child, when it is completely helpless. Two factors may have influenced this attitude although it may be difficult to ascertain cause and effect in this matter. Firstly, a mother knows that she will keep her child only as long as she lives with her husband; she may lose her child at any time without being at fault; for instance, if her husband becomes so brutal or completely indifferent that she cannot endure life with him any longer. In all circumstances a father can claim possession of his children. Secondly, children themselves soon become independent of their mother. From their earliest days they are accustomed to have many 'mothers', i.e. female members of the family, as well as neighbours. Thus what a child may lack in individual care and love is often compensated for by the collective sentiment of the family and even of society. It may be said that a Sukuma child of three or four years old does not need its mother to the degree which is elsewhere considered essential for the child's well-being and for the building-up of its character.

Though a woman's legal status is inferior to that of her husband, in fact the value of her work, in the home and in the fields, secures for her an unassailable position in the household on account of which she enjoys considerably greater freedom than would appear to be the case. And in spite of the fact that the law allows extensive rights to the husband, most divorces are initiated by the wife.

Moreover, there is always a possibility that a divorced woman will remarry, even at an advanced age; in fact marriage, divorce, and remarriage are regarded as customary stages in a normal life-cycle. A woman's value is not diminished by sexual intercourse, and her right to a normal life (*bulambu*) is acknowledged.

General Procedure

A marriage contract can be dissolved:

(*a*) In BSN, UF, BS, KF* by mutual consent of the parties concerned without the intervention of a court but before a council of village elders. A case is only brought to court if there are quarrels and complications.

(*b*) In NF, BD, SBS, KS, KM* by a judicial decree at the suit of husband or wife.

The council of elders can only arbitrate, they cannot enforce their decision. Either party may refuse to accept it and may bring the matter before a Native Court.

NOTE: Wherever councils of elders deal with divorce cases there is a marked tendency to have the decision registered in the *ibanza*, i.e. to pay the fee and have the judgement issued by the *ibanza*, although the hearing takes place before the elders.

* These letters refer to districts of Sukumaland.

Should the decision of the elders be accepted by both parties and subsequently one of them fail to fulfil a condition of the judgement, an action can be filed against the delinquent before the Native Court. The decision of the elders would be recognized by the court as valid law.

Should a husband or wife fall sick during the negotiations and discussions about a divorce all procedure is stopped at once, and no judgement can be pronounced until the sick party has recovered.

(c) Grounds

In the prefatory remarks at the beginning of this section, reference was made to the controversy as to whether it is correct to refer to customary law as acknowledging 'grounds' for divorce. There is no need to traverse this ground again. There is ample evidence in what follows of the existence of reasons for granting a divorce, and *Cory* in particular has provided an extremely comprehensive list of those known among the Sukuma. Even if all of them are not found elsewhere in Africa, his very substantial catalogue of reasons gives the best available indication of the range of possibilities within this field and implications of each.

H. Cory: Sukuma Law and Custom*

RECOGNIZED GROUNDS FOR DIVORCE SUIT BROUGHT BY HUSBAND

I. *Adultery* (*Bushihya*)

General Rules

Adultery by a wife constitutes grounds for a divorce.[1]

A. A man cannot claim compensation on account of his wife's adultery more than twice during their married life.

B. If a wife lives in adultery with several men the husband can only sue the man with whom his wife is living when he finds her. He cannot sue more than one person in a single legal action.

C. The payment of damages for adultery confers no rights to any illegitimate child of the union.

No accusation of adultery or claim for damages can be supported unless there is direct or indirect evidence of sexual relationship between the man and the woman accused.

P.C.'s Appeal No. 48/44. Liwali's Court, Mwanza. *Saidi* v. *Maganga*.

Saidi claimed compensation for adultery from Maganga because his wife was seen by witnesses riding on the carrier of Maganga's bicycle. The claim was refused.

A charge of adultery can only be brought before the court:

A. by the husband, or

B. in the absence of the husband, by his nearest male relative.

D.C.'s Appeal No. 13/48. Ibadakuli (Shinyanga). *Kawili* v. *Ntwege*.

The court dismissed the appeal because it was ascertained that the plaintiff, Kawili, who claimed compensation for adultery from Ntwege, was neither husband nor brother-in-law of the woman with whom Ntwege had sexual intercourse.

D.C.'s Appeal No. 31/41. Fulo (Bukumbi). *Madadila* v. *Henry*.

Madadila accused Henry of committing adultery with his sister-in-law, whose husband, Mushimbe, Madadila's brother, had been away from home for about two years. The woman was four months gone with child. Compensation was awarded to the brother of the absentee.

* H. Cory, *Sukuma Law and Custom*, Oxford University Press, 1953, pp. 60–81.

NOTE: A brother is not entitled to bring his married sister and her lover to court. It is unknown for a father to lay a charge of adultery before a court citing his son or vice versa; further, no case is known in which a brother has cited a brother or half-brother. Customarily, relatives do not cite each other in court, but the adulterer must pay one head of cattle (*ibengwe*) to the relative whom he has wronged. The beast is killed and consumed by a gathering of members of the family.

The court is entitled to refuse to hear a charge of adultery which has been unreasonably delayed by the petitioner after he has obtained full knowledge of the matter. If the husband had no knowledge of the fact until he acquired it through the birth of a child, the claim for compensation cannot become time-barred by the delay.

D.C.'s Appeal No. 11/41. Fulo (Burima). *Leo* v. *Kazungu.*

Leo had divorced his wife and the bridewealth had been returned to him when he laid a charge for adultery against Kazungu and claimed damages, on hearing that his former wife had given birth to a child which must have been conceived before she was divorced. Kazungu, corroborated by the woman, admitted paternity. The court therefore ruled that Kazunga had to pay damages of five beasts although at the time of the hearing the divorce was legally valid.

A wife cannot be convicted of adultery if the identity of her partner is unknown; for instance, if he escaped unrecognized by his pursuers and the wife refused to disclose his identity.

Amount of compensation in case of adultery.

A man convicted of adultery has to pay compensation. The amount varies according to the social position of the superior in rank whether he is the husband or the adulterer.

NOTE: This rule was agreed by the chiefs of the Sukuma Federation and their people in 1949. Formerly the rule was one-sided: a tribal dignitary received from an adulterer more cattle than he himself would have to pay as adulterer. The damages to be paid varied in the different local federations and in different cases. For instance, in D.C.'s Appeal No. 19/48, the adulterer in a case brought by a village headman had to pay damages amounting to eight cattle, while in the same kind of case, Bukumbi No. 9/47, the adulterer paid five cattle.

Damages are payable to the husband as follows:

A. in case of a commoner: 5 head of cattle (4 cows and 1 bull).

NOTE: This rule was agreed by the chiefs of the Sukuma Federation and their people in 1949.

Formerly in all chiefdoms damages of 5 head of cattle were payable, except in BS, SBS, and KS,* where damages amounted to 3 cattle (2 cows and 1 bull).

B. in cases of *banangwa*, *banang'oma*, direct descendants of chiefs, and deposed chiefs: 10 cattle (8 cows and 2 bulls).

C. in the case of a regent (*neji*): 15 cattle (12 cows and 3 bulls).

D. in the case of chiefs: 25 cattle (20 cows and 5 bulls).

NOTE: These rules (B, C, D) were agreed by the chiefs of the Sukuma Federation and their people in 1949.

NOTE: The new rules mean that a man who commits adultery with a chief's wife has to pay damages of 25 cattle and a chief who commits adultery with a commoner's wife also has to pay damages of 25 cattle. Previously the tendency was for an officer of the Native Administration or a tribal dignitary to expect a special rate of compensation as an injured party (plaintiff) while paying the commoner's rate as an offender (defendant). This inequality of payment was applied in cases of 151, 176, 271, 300B, 313B. The commoners were not always satisfied and the NF and UF issued rules of reciprocity in 1939. These rules were not invariably applied as the following court cases show:

D.C.'s Appeal 3/47, Usega. *Makamelele* v. *Malangwa.*

Malangwa caused the pregnancy of Makamelele's daughter and, as Makamelele was a chief's son, the court awarded a *misango* (300B) of five head of cattle.

D.C.'s Appeal 2/44. Usega. *Petro* v. *Kamina s/o Ntemi Bahebe.*

* These letters refer to districts of Sukumaland.

Petro was not satisfied with the two head of cattle which the court awarded him as *misango*, because Kamina was a chief's son. The native appeal court stated that it had never been the custom for a commoner to demand five cattle from a commoner. (The court chose to ignore the fact that Kamina was a chief's son.) If in this case the defendant had been a headman, he would have had to pay five cattle in accordance with the rules promulgated in 10/11/39.

The bias in favour of a chief's family, shown in both these cases, although no longer legal in view of the rules issued in 1939, has a certain justification in that traditionally, as mentioned above, differing rates of payment according to whether a man was a commoner, a chief, or a tribal dignitary were recognized.

Cases in which a commoner disturbed the domestic life of a chief or other tribal dignitary were rare. For instance, no recent case is remembered in which a man was charged in court with adultery with a chief's wife. The fixing of compensation for adultery at twenty-five cattle is therefore arbitrary, but as the reciprocity had been accepted this high rate of compensation was not debated. There have, however, been a few cases of a man living in concubinage with a chief's unmarried daughter and causing her to become pregnant. For instance, a man of Ng'wagala (BD) had to pay twenty-five cattle as *ngwekwe* for living in concubinage with a daughter of *Ntemi* Masanja. This payment cannot be considered excessive when it is remembered that in earlier times a man causing the pregnancy of an unmarried daughter of a chief or committing adultery with a chief's wife was killed outright and all his property was sequestrated. If he had no property his family, and sometimes even the whole village, had to pay for the outrage; even cattle paid as bridewealth were liable to be seized. The daughters, sisters, and wives of a *ntemi* (and also those of *banangwa*) lived a very secluded life. They were never allowed to leave the residence (*ikuru*) without an escort of other women and courtiers. It was one of the duties of *banang'oma* to escort female members of the chief's family when they went visiting. The daughters of *banangwa* did not join the *maji* in the village. Not only were these women guarded by their own people, but the family of any man who showed signs of being interested in them would have him closely watched also, for fear he might do something to provoke the chief's displeasure. . . .

The following alternative proposal was put forward during the discussions: 'The right of chiefs and tribal dignitaries to a higher compensation is acknowledged; but if a court finds that a chief's or dignitary's daughter or sister has behaved in a manner calculated to lead to an illegal liaison, payments should not exceed those imposed in case of commoners.' This proposal takes account of the fact that the control of the female dependants of chiefs and dignitaries has now been generally and considerably relaxed, and there is therefore no reason for a man to be specially penalized for contracting a liaison with one of them, if she behaves in a provocative way. In a case of this kind the prestige of the chief's family is diminished whether a heavy penalty is imposed or not.

If the court comes to the conclusion that the wife in a case of adultery is to be considered guilty to an unusual degree, it can order that, of the five cattle payable by the adulterer as damages, the wife has to pay one cow.

NOTE: This rule was agreed by the chiefs of the Sukuma Federation and their people in 1949. Formerly rules regarding the punishment of the wife varied in the different chiefdoms, but nowhere was she liable to pay damages.

The scales of punishment in the different chiefdoms were as follows:

(*a*) KF* (Sima): Shs. 40/-;
(*b*) KF* (Nera): Shs. 40/-, but only if the woman was found to be chiefly responsible.
(*c*) NF,* KM: Shs. 20/-, but only if the wife ran away with a lover, not if she committed adultery while separated from her husband;
(*d*) UF, BSN, BD, SS, BS*: at one time a fine was imposed, but the penalty had been abolished.

The rule that a wife should share in the payment of damages, instead of paying a fine as formerly, was made because it was considered inequitable that the woman should pay a fine and the man damages; a situation might then arise in which, if neither the woman nor the man were able to pay the amount required the woman might be imprisoned while the man remained free. A wife may be considered liable to pay damages if, for

* These letters refer to districts in Sukumaland.

instance, it is proved that she has deluded her lover into believing that she is not married.

The following is an example of another case in which it may seem justifiable that the wife should participate in the payment of damages:

D.C.'s Appeal 3/43. Shinyanga (Mwanhini). *Magaji* v. *Magoge.*

Seven days after Magoge had been convicted and ordered to pay compensation for adultery to Magaji, Magaji's wife came to him again and was found there five days later by her husband. Although witnesses testified that Magoge had tried to expel her, he was ordered to pay compensation a second time, because his efforts to drive her away had not been successful.

Proof of Adultery

Two types of evidence are admissible in cases of adultery: (1) direct evidence; (2) circumstantial evidence.

1. *Direct evidence.* Any person assisted by at least two witnesses is entitled to catch a married woman *in flagrante delicto* and inform the husband about the act of adultery. If the husband is absent one of those persons who have the legal right to file a suit in his stead may be informed.

NOTE: The usual person is the husband and he needs witnesses as does anyone else. It is seldom that other people have any interest in this matter or will take the trouble to prove the fact to the husband. Such a case happens sometimes if the wife make a journey to visit relatives or friends, and is then caught *in flagrante delicto* by the wife of her paramour. The husband at home, when he hears of the fact and can obtain proof, has a good case for claiming compensation for adultery.

The witnesses must declare their presence to the guilty couple at the time. Their testimony is considered inadmissible if they watched the occurrence from a hiding-place without revealing themselves.

2. *Circumstantial evidence.* A. Whether a situation in itself is considered sufficient evidence of adultery or requires corroboration must be left to the discretion of the court.

B. Corroboration is not necessary if the available circumstantial evidence excludes any interpretation other than that of adultery.

C. Corroboration is necessary if the only available information is insufficient to prove adultery. In such an event the cumulative weight of a number of incidents indirectly suggesting adultery is admissible.

D.C.'s Appeal 28/47, NF. *Manoni* v. *Sumuni.*

Manoni accused Sumuni of adultery with his wife. After he had caught the couple *in flagrante delicto* in the open, the husband gave the following evidence in court:

1. he produced clothes belonging to the defendant;
2. he had brought the defendant naked to the house of a witness;
3. together with the witness he had reported the case at once to the village headman;
4. he had gone from there to the father of the defendant and had reported the case to him;
5. the village headman had dispatched people to the spot where the adultery was alleged to have taken place, and marks likely to be caused by the act were found.

The court awarded compensation to the husband.

NOTE: Examples where corroboration is not necessary:

I. A husband returns to his house at night earlier than was expected. He hears the voices of his wife and a man inside the house. He barricades the door from outside and calls witnesses, in whose company he enters the house. They find a man, fully dressed, who explains, when asked to give a reason for his presence, that he came to ask the husband for quarters for the night, or perhaps to borrow an axe. No man is supposed to enter a house in the husband's absence except a relative or a very intimate friend, and the court would therefore not accept the excuse and would consider the adultery to have been proved.

II. D.C.'s Appeal 1/44. Fulo, Mwanza. *Sumuni* v. *Lukugabilu.*

Sumuni searched for his wife who had left him in the morning and found her in

Lukugabilu's house. It was already night and neither Lukugabilu nor the wife could give any plausible explanation of the situation. Sumuni had four witnesses with him.

The court held that no proof of actual adultery was necessary and awarded damages to the husband.

III. A husband sees his wife and another man disappear in a field of sorghum. He calls witnesses and when he returns with them, finds the man already back on the path while the wife appears a moment later coming out of the field. The witnesses enter the field and find certain proofs of cohabitation. The court would find that adultery had been proved.

IV. A husband hears that his wife has entered a house with a man. He calls witnesses and with them forces an entrance into the house where they find the couple alone, but not *in flagrante delicto*. The court would consider it unnecessary to ascertain whether adultery had been committed or not. The situation, which cannot be explained otherwise, would be considered sufficient proof of adultery.

V. D.C.'s Appeal 63/44. Ngudu (Nera). *Sefu* v. *Sangija.*

Sangija stated in public that he had slept with Sefu's wife. The court held that this statement, made before several witnesses, did not require corroboration and awarded damages to the husband.

The most usual evidence requiring corroboration is the following:

1. if property of the alleged adulterer is produced;

2. if the wife confesses;

D.C.'s Appeal 20/44. Fulo (Ilemera). *Johanna* v. *Petro.*

Johanna's wife had confessed that she committed an act of adultery with Petro. No other evidence was forthcoming and the court refused to award damages to the husband.

D.C.'s Appeal 16/47. Ibadakuli (Shinyanga). *Kini* v. *Burchard.*

Kini's wife having admitted that sexual intercourse had taken place between her and Burchard, Kini claimed damages from Burchard who denied the charge; when it was shown that statements made by Kini's wife concerning Burchard's physical characteristics (circumcision) were incorrect, the court ruled that no damages were payable.

3. if the alleged adulterer has been injured;

4. if the alleged adulterer omitted to file a suit when publicly insulted or beaten by the husband.

D.C.'s Appeal 1/46. Ibadakuli (Mondo). *Madede* v. *Nyangindu.*

Madede claimed compensation for adultery from Nyangindu; he had no eye-witnesses, but he produced a bicycle and a broken bottle, the property of the defendant, and he had witnesses who had heard him chase the defendant down a path. The court held that this was sufficient corroboration and added that the defendant, who is a *ntwale*, would without doubt have arrested the plaintiff if he had not been guilty. As the *ntwale* had done nothing to defend his reputation the court awarded compensation to the husband.

Infection with Venereal Disease

Evidence of infection with venereal disease is counted among cases where corroboration is required.

D.C.'s Appeal No. 3/45. Ibadakuli (Lohumbo). *Luhende* v. *Luwayi.*

Luwayi was sued by Luhende for compensation for adultery, because his wife had been infected with syphilis and had named Luwayi as her lover. Luwayi suffered from syphilis, but as this was a known fact in the village, the statement of the wife without further corroboration was not held to be sufficient to warrant the award of compensation.

If husband and wife both have venereal disease and no adultery can be proved, no divorce can be granted on the grounds of infection alone.

NOTE: Additional evidence is required because the Sukuma is aware that venereal disease can be contracted without sexual intercourse. Infection of a wife by her husband (*kasogone, kashwende*) is no ground for divorce even if adultery by the husband can be proved; divorce may be granted on account of the wife's adultery, but not on account of adultery on the part of the husband.

If adultery is proved, the hearing is postponed until the infected person is cured, as in a case of injury.

If a wife should die of venereal disease the husband is not entitled to claim *njigu* from her lover, even if it can be proved that he infected her.

NOTE: This rule was agreed by the chiefs of the Sukuma Federation and their people in 1949. Formerly a husband could claim *njigu* in BSN and BS.*

NOTE: It is realized that only gross neglect of the disease by the infected person could cause his or her death in normal circumstances.

Damages payable in case of infection with venereal disease. A. A man who has infected a married woman must pay to the husband five cattle as compensation for adultery, two cows as damages for infection, and Shs.50/- fine.

B. A man who has infected an unmarried woman must pay to her father, her brother, or to the woman herself, two cows as damages and Shs.50/- fine.

NOTE: It must be left to the discretion of the court to decide whether or not the guilt of a person in all these cases is proved beyond reasonable doubt. As a matter of fact, such cases are frequently brought to court and a decision given, as the infecting person often admits the charge. In the D.C.'s appeal 13/42, Fulo, the lover declared: 'I agree that I have this disease. I thought I would not infect the girl. I do not know where I contracted the disease myself, perhaps from my concubine who has left me. These are my words, it is up to you to decide.'

This confession shows the kind of attribute on the part of a defendant which is frequently met with in such cases. As sexual intercourse is not considered immoral, and as the mechanism of infection, especially the incubation periods of the diseases, is not clearly understood, an infection is just 'bad luck'.

C. A woman who infects a man is liable to pay the same damages and fine as those described in B above.

NOTE: These rules were decided upon by the chiefs of the Sukuma Federation and their people in 1949. Formerly different rules existed in the various chiefdoms:

In KF, NF, BD, BS, SBS, KM, UF* the husband was not entitled to compensation for the infection of his wife, in addition to compensation for adultery. In BSN, KS, the adulterer had to pay a fine of Shs.50/-.

The man who infected the woman had to pay:

damages of 1 cow, no fine (BS, SBS, BD);*
" " 2 cows, fine of Shs.50/- (BSN);
" " 3 cows, no fine (KS, KF* (Nera));
" " 2 cows, no fine (NF, UF*);
" " Shs.60/-, fine of Shs.40/- (KM, KF* (Usmao, Sima)).

In BSN, UF, KM, KS* the same compensation was payable if a woman, married or unmarried, infected a man.

In BD, NF, BS, KF, SBS* a woman did not have to pay compensation.

NOTE: The rule imposing the same penalties on men and women was accepted unanimously. If few women are in a position to make a payment of two cows as damages, there are also men who possess nothing. Women can inherit property and the payment may be postponed indefinitely. The fact that a fine can now be imposed is important. It was considered advisable that if a woman were unable to pay the fine she should be imprisoned, since this would prevent an infected woman becoming a danger to the public, and furthermore while in prison she would be compelled to undergo medical treatment.

If a husband has been infected by his wife or vice versa, no damages are payable by either party.

Adultery during Husband's Prolonged Absence

If a husband, after an absence from his home, returns and finds his wife living with

* *Ibid.*

another man in concubinage, he can file a suit for divorce and can claim damages for adultery without producing any further proof.

If he returns to find his wife pregnant or having borne a child which cannot be his child because of the length of his absence, several courses are open to him:

1. he can claim damages for adultery, refuse to accept the child as his, and forgive his wife;
2. he can claim damages for adultery, acknowledge the child as his, and forgive his wife;
3. he can claim damages for adultery, divorce his wife, and claim return of bridewealth in full. The child then belongs to the maternal family;
4. he can acknowledge the child as his;
5. if the man who is named by the wife as responsible for the pregnancy refuses to accept responsibility, the provisions given in paragraphs 275–279 of Cory apply.

NOTE: The lover has to pay compensation for adultery only; he cannot be held liable for the payment of *misango* and *njigu*, except when the husband returns during his wife's pregnancy and is granted a divorce. In this case the lover may be liable for payment to the husband and of *misango* to the woman's father, or even of *njigu* if the case arises. If the husband only claims compensation for adultery and does not claim a divorce, he cannot demand return of bridewealth if the wife dies during pregnancy or in childbirth; by receiving damages and omitting to claim divorce he acknowledges wife and child as his.

If a husband, after his return, obtains proof that his wife has had sexual intercourse or has lived with another man during his absence, but had broken off the connexion before she knew of his return, he cannot claim compensation for adultery and the fact is not considered a ground for divorce.

NOTE: This rule was agreed by the chiefs of the Sukuma Federation and their people in 1949. Formerly this rule was applied in all chiefdoms except in BSN* and BD*, where the husband could claim damages and could obtain a divorce.

NOTE: The next-of-kin of the husband is entitled to claim damages from the adulterer at this time when the adultery was committed. The notion underlying this, and many similar rules and customary views, is that the law cannot be expected to correct nature and impose chastity on a healthy person. If the husband is absent for any length of time, he has no right to examine the conduct of his wife after his return; his next-of-kin has the right to object to the adultery of the wife, because he is the recognized substitute for the husband.

If the husband returns and hears that his wife has died in the house of her lover or during a pregnancy caused by a lover, he is entitled to claim compensation for adultery but he cannot claim return of bridewealth from his father-in-law. If the wife dies during childbirth, the child belongs to the husband.

Confirmed in D.C. Mwanza's Appeal No. 11/47—*Tungu* v. *Ngunya*.

Cohabitation with a Widow

If a widow, who has not been inherited but has remained in her deceased husband's family, cohabits with a man, he cannot be required to pay compensation for adultery, because she cannot be considered a married woman.

NOTE: This rule was agreed by the chiefs of the Sukuma Federation and their people in 1949. The rule has been generally accepted from 1927 onwards except in NF, UF,* where the lover of the widow had to pay damages for adultery.

D.C.'s Appeal No. 12/44. Ibadakuli. *Munyo* v. *Mwika*.

Munyo's son was married to Nyamuke and died after a few years. Munyo failed for two years to arrange a leviratic marriage for the widow. Nyamuke went to live with Mwika and Munyo claimed compensation for adultery. The court held that no compensation was payable, as Munyo had failed to arrange for Nyamuke to be remarried to a member of the family.

If a widow, having lived for a time as a leviratic wife with a relative of her deceased

* *Ibid.*

husband, leaves him and cohabits with another man, her lover is liable to pay compensation for adultery to the next-of-kin of the deceased husband.

NOTE: In the situation described in [the first paragraph of this section] the widow is no man's wife after her husband's death until she is inherited and remarried by a relative of the deceased husband. In the situation described [above] the widow has become the legal wife of the heir and, whether she lives with him or apart from him, her status as wife is unchanged.

Adultery in Ignorance of Wife's Status

It is the duty of a man to ascertain that a woman with whom he sleeps or whom he marries is eligible. Any statement which the woman may have made to the man has no legal value, and the man cannot use it in his defence if accused of adultery, even if such statement was made before witnesses.

D.C.'s Appeal No. 41/42. Fulo (Bukumbi). *Maliyabwana* v. *Abdullah.*

Maliyabwana's wife left him and was subsequently found by him living with Abdullah, whose defence was that he did not know that the woman was married; this was not accepted by the court, which ruled that a man is responsible for ascertaining whether a woman with whom he has intercourse is or is not married.

D.C.'s Appeal No. 11/47. Usega (Masanza I). *Tungu* v. *Ngunya.*

Tungu claimed from Ngunya damages for adultery. Ngunya stated: 'The woman came to my home at Masanza I, and I took her and lived with her. I questioned her as to whether she was married and where she had come from. She denied having been married, and stated that she had come from Kwimba and wished to find a home and a husband.' The court gave judgement in favour of the husband.

NOTE: The two cases are representative of many others. Whatever the circumstances, the law always supports the husband against the adulterer. A man who takes a woman as his concubine or invites her to follow him temporarily into his home, or who follows a woman temporarily into her home, must remember that he runs the risk of being charged with adultery.

The native courts consider only the injury to the husband and take no cognizance of the possibility of ignorance on the part of the adulterer.

If a man discovers that the woman with whom he lives is the wife of another man, he must sever the connexion at once, i.e. he must expel the woman. If he continues to live with the woman but goes to the headman and reports the situation, he is liable to pay damages when the husband claims them.

If the man who is found by the husband sleeping with his wife can prove that she has become a prostitute, the husband cannot claim damages.

NOTE: The man must be in the position to prove this fact; if he cannot do so and merely states that the woman has the reputation of being a prostitute, he is liable to pay damages. The fact that he proves that he gave a present to the woman in money or kind does not absolve him from responsibility. Other people as witnesses must prove that the woman lives by prostitution.

If circumstances prove that it was in fact impossible for the man to discover the truth about the woman's status, he cannot be charged with adultery.

Examples:

A. The husband is reported to have died on the coast, and the family performs the usual rites. The widow remarries and the second husband pays bridewealth. The first husband reappears later; the rumour of his death was false.

B. If a man marries a Sukuma woman abroad and pays bridewealth to a 'relative' he cannot be charged with adultery by her husband later. The court will have to ascertain whether the relative acted in good faith, but the man himself cannot be charged with adultery.

NOTE: It is for the court to decide whether or not the father of the wife should be held responsible in a case as described in A. If the husband dies, his brother is entitled to take the widow as his leviratic wife. If this solution is not accepted, the widow's father should return such portion of the bridewealth as is due to the family of the deceased husband before accepting a second bridewealth. Thus it may be contended that the father should be fined, and the second husband acquitted.

If neither of the two husbands agrees voluntarily to waive his claim to the wife, it is left to her to decide with whom she chooses to continue the marriage. The husband who is not chosen is given back his bridewealth. If the loser is the father of a child, he can take the child with him and the usual deduction is made from the bridewealth which has to be returned.

NOTE: As a matter of fact, the usual choice of the wife is her first husband.

II. *Desertion* (*Bupeji*)

Desertion by a wife is grounds for divorce. The husband is entitled to claim divorce and return of the bridewealth if he knows where the wife is living, or if he can prove by direct or indirect evidence that the wife ran away with intent not to return. When a divorce has been granted in the absence of the wife, the bridewealth should not be returned until six months have elapsed.

NOTE: This rule was agreed by the chiefs of the Sukuma Federation and their people in 1949. Formerly a man could claim divorce and return of the bridewealth only if he knew the new domicile of his wife.

NOTE: It was considered advisable to require a delay of six months for repayment of bridewealth, in case the wife should later decide to return to her husband. Sometimes special obstacles may have prevented her immediate return. For instance: A couple quarrels and the husband insults his wife; so she leaves the house and returns to her parents or goes to friends. The man follows her and asks her to return, but she refuses him exclaiming: 'I will not return; I shall never re-enter the door of our house. If ever you see me naked again, I shall die. Sleep with whom you like but never with me'. These words are spoken in the heat of the moment and as time passes, the wife, persuaded by mediators sent by her husband, feels inclined to return to him. She is, however, prevented by her oath, which she now regrets. A *nfumu* must be called to remove the spell. He asks for a goat and, after he has formed a figurine out of clay representing a couple having sexual intercourse, he invites the husband, the wife, and a few friends to follow him into the bush, where he digs a small hole, kills the goat, smears the blood on the figurine, and buries it in the hole saying: 'The bad words are buried here. This man and his wife may again sleep together without evil consequences.' The goat is roasted on the spot and consumed by those taking part in the ceremony.

In present conditions, especially in view of improved means of communication, the old law seems to be obsolete. Formerly the argument used by the father-in-law was that as long as the son-in-law could not show where the wife was living, it was possible that he had murdered her. In the olden days when an unhappy wife could go hardly anywhere except to one of her relatives, such an argument may have had some justification; today it seems to be far-fetched.

It is not considered to be desertion if the wife leaves her husband and goes to a relative.

If the wife goes first to a relative and, staying a short time with him, leaves and goes elsewhere, her husband can file a petition. In this case he is not obliged to make a statement about her whereabouts.

Any man who hides a married woman and denies her presence in his house when the husband comes in search of his wife is punishable, unless he is her father or brother. The fine would not be less than Shs.20/- (*Bugobya*).

A. Neither a relative nor any other man can be held responsible or incur penalties for giving shelter to a woman, or for not informing her husband (if he knows him) about the arrival of his wife.

B. But, if a man, especially a non-relative, is asked by a woman for shelter, he should bring her to the village headman, if he wishes to avoid the risk of being involved in an adultery case.

Although a husband very often follows a wife who has deserted him, it is not held to be his legal duty to do so.

NOTE: Sometimes courts applied a great measure of equity, sometimes they followed rigorously the letter of the law. An example of the first attitude:

Busule (Shinyanga) case 54/46. *Nholi* v. *Nyumbu.*

Nholi had lived apart from his wife for two years, during which time he neither looked after her nor cared for her. Nholi had inherited her after his brother's death, and had abandoned her completely after a few short visits. When he heard that his wife had settled down in Nyumbu's hut, he went there and claimed damages. The court held that Nholi 'has acted like a trapper who is out to catch game' and refused to award damages.

An example of the second attitude:

D.C.'s Appeal -/46. Ibadakuli (Busiha). *Nkinga* v. *Shinji.*

Ten years before the case Nkinga had separated from his wife Kulwa and handed her over to his brother Masele who took her as wife for some years and then in turn separated from her; she then returned to her parents' home. Masele came one day with the proposal that Kulwa should move to a third brother's house. Kulwa refused and when she was later found living with Shinji, Nkinga claimed damages from him. The lower court awarded damages on the ground that bridewealth had never been returned.

The appeal court held that the procedure adopted by the husband and his brothers was highly immoral and contrary to law and custom. The appeal court refused damages to the husband on the grounds that 'ex turpi causa non oritur actio'.

A husband whose wife runs away and later returns cannot claim damages if he hears that she has committed adultery. He can demand divorce and return of bridewealth if he does not wish to have her back.

Confirmed in D.C. Mwanza's Appeal No. 24/46.

Elopement

If a man persuades another man's wife to leave her husband and elope with him, the husband can claim a divorce. The case is treated as adultery, and no further proof of the fact of adultery is necessary in the following circumstances:

A. if the couple are caught in the act of elopement;

NOTE: If a husband meets his wife with another man and the wife has her personal belongings with her, it is an adultery case if the husband can prove that the man and his wife intended to elope together and that it was not a chance meeting. But if the husband hears from others or with his own ears that his wife intends to elope with another man, he cannot file a suit against this man.

B. if the couple are found in the new domicile either living in a common household or in separate quarters. Proof of sexual intercourse is not necessary in either case.

It is not accepted as an excuse if it can be proved that the wife followed the lover uninvited.

Confirmed in D.C. Shinyanga's appeal No. 3/43.

Any person who gives shelter to a couple whom he knows to have eloped is liable to a fine of Shs.20/- (*nalicha*).

NOTE: This rule was agreed by the chiefs of the Sukuma Federation and their people in 1949. Before that time this rule was in force in all chiefdoms except those of BS.*

If a wife elopes with a man who later leaves her, and then goes to live with another man, where her husband finds her, the man with whom she is then living has to pay the damages for adultery. If the wife is not living with another man, the man who eloped with her is liable to pay damages.

NOTE: This rule was decided upon by the chiefs of the Sukuma Federation and their people in 1949. Formerly some courts followed this rule, while others made the first man responsible for damages, even if he had left the woman and another man was living with her.

NOTE: It was held that the relative guilt of the two men is not in question. The only consideration is the wrong suffered by the husband, for which the law provides that he shall receive damages. The man who originally eloped with the wife may have gone away and it may, therefore, be difficult for the husband to claim damages from him.

* *Ibid.*

Refusal to Accompany Husband

A wife cannot be forced to accompany her husband to a new domicile inside or outside Sukumaland. But if the wife refuses to follow him, the husband can claim a divorce with return of the bridewealth and possession of his children.

If the bridewealth has not been fully paid and the wife agrees to follow her husband, the father-in-law is entitled to withhold the children until the remainder has been paid.

III. *Injuries Inflicted by Wife*

Any injury inflicted on her husband by a wife, or even the mere fact that she has struck him, is considered grounds for divorce.

IV. *Neglect of Domestic Duties*

Continual neglect of domestic duties, such as cooking, carrying water and fuel, and field-work, or habitual drunkenness of the wife, are acknowledged grounds for divorce. (A neglectful wife is called *ng'wolo.*)

V. *Irregularities with regard to Birth of Children*

A. *Abortion* (*Kufunda funda*)

1. If it can be proved that the wife has taken an abortifacient successfully, the husband is entitled to claim a divorce.
2. Should bridewealth be returned, no deduction may be made for a foetus deliberately aborted.
3. The husband is entitled to claim *njigu* from the practitioner who assisted in the abortion.

B. *Causing Death to a Child during Birth* (*Kukandikija ng'wana*)

1. If a mother by reason of her fear or pain disobeys the orders of the midwife and by so doing kills the child during labour, the husband can claim a divorce. But it is conceded that he can only do so after it has happened twice.
2. If the bridewealth has to be returned the usual number of cattle for a child are deducted.

VI. *Refusal of Conjugal Rights*

If the wife refuses to have sexual intercourse with her husband, her attitude is grounds for divorce.

VII. *Use of Magic Medicine*

If a wife, without having obtained the permission of her husband, consults a practi tioner and undergoes treatment, the husband is entitled to claim divorce.

NOTE: An exception is the use of love philtres or love amulets.

The practitioner is fined one head of cattle.

VIII. *Infertility of Wife*

This is a cause for divorce irrespective of the number of years of married life, but the court must consider in each case whether the husband is using the infertility of his wife as a pretext for claiming a divorce, or whether he considers it a genuine and decisive defect in his married life. Infertility of the wife is not held to be a cause for divorce if, after several years of childless married life, the husband decides that he wishes to divorce her because she is barren (*ngumba*). On the other hand, infertility of the wife must be considered a cause for divorce if the couple have tried all possible remedies of native or European science without result.

NOTE: The fact of a wife's infertility is taken very seriously by all concerned. It is the duty of the couple to ascertain the reason. The first step is to consult a diviner who is expected to indicate the cause of the defect. Here follow a few examples of alleged causes:

1. It is revealed by divination that husband and wife are related. A goat is killed and a strip cut from its skin. The husband is told to hold one end and the wife the other end of the strip, while an elder cuts through it, exclaiming that thereby all family connexion which may exist between the two is for ever severed.
2. A girl has been persuaded by her parents to marry a certain man, but she loves another one. Before the wedding she swears to herself 'I will marry this man but I shall never love him. I shall sleep with him but I shall not bear him any children.' The couple duly remain childless, but after she has been married for some time, the wife comes to like her husband and she wishes now to have children but is prevented by her oath. A *nfumu* is consulted to remove the spell.
3. Sometimes a husband chooses a more practical method of finding out the cause of sterility. He selects one of his nearest relatives and asks him to sleep with his wife, choosing a man who has had many children, preferably by several wives. If the experiment proves unsuccessful the husband knows that the failure is due to the wife. If the experiment is successful the husband pays one head of cattle to the relative.

It is possible for the husband to claim return of bridewealth and to continue married life. In this case the ceremonial beasts, and especially the *ng'ombe ya maji*, are regarded as bridewealth when the remainder of the bridewealth has been returned, so that the marriage shall remain legally intact.

D.C.'s Appeal No. 52/47. Fulo (Beda). *Jenu* v. *Mahyila.*

Jenu claimed return of bridewealth from Mahyila, his wife's father, because his wife was barren. The assessors of the case stated that it was good Sukuma customary law for the bridewealth to be returned to the husband of a barren wife, even though husband and wife remained living together. The headman should be informed that the bridewealth has been returned, but that the union continues by mutual consent.

NOTE: The return of bridewealth should enable a man to take a second wife and thus give him the chance of a family. At the same time the original couple may like each other and wish to remain together.

SUIT BROUGHT BY THE WIFE

I. *Adultery*

A. Adultery of the husband is no ground for divorce except if committed with his daughter or step-daughter.

NOTE: Adultery committed by the husband is not condemned by the family or by society and is not regarded as transgressing any moral convention. It does not normally endanger the domestic peace for any length of time, although the clamour at the time of the occurrence may be considerable. Many cases are known in which a husband brought a concubine into the house and, if she behaved herself with the expected degree of servility and respect towards the legitimate wife, the two women lived side by side in peace. Even if the husband were to bring home a woman for a few days, the family of the wife and the public would think such behaviour incorrect, but would not consider it sufficiently serious to warrant a divorce.

B. Adultery committed with the wife's sister is not considered grounds for divorce except in KS and SS.*

If a divorce is granted on account of incest, the court can order that the children be given into the guardianship of a paternal relative. If there is none, a maternal relative may be appointed as guardian. In every case the children remain the children of their father and he is entitled to receive the bridewealth for his daughters when they marry. If a reliable guardian can only be found in another district, the mother cannot refuse to allow the children to be handed over to him, even though it may be difficult for her to visit them frequently.

NOTE: The court might also try to persuade the father to accept repayment of the whole bridewealth, if no suitable paternal guardian can be found. If the father agrees

* *Ibid.*

the children would then belong to the maternal family; but the court has no right to order such procedure.

II. *Desertion*

If a man is absent from home for more than two years without special reasons, such as imprisonment, military service, sickness in hospital, the wife is entitled to claim a divorce.

NOTE: This rule was agreed by the chiefs of the Sukuma Federation and their people in 1949. Formerly no such rule existed but several chiefs had already made proposals for the introduction of this rule in the local federations. The chief of Buduhe (BS)* had adopted it already and judgements were given accordingly. Further, in one case (D.C.'s Appeal No. 29/46 Shinyanga) the Native Court of Busule acknowledged that after two years' absence of the husband a wife could consider herself divorced.

NOTE: It often happens, if the husband goes to work outside Sukumaland, that he never returns or not for many years, although his initial intention was to stay only a short period. The man becomes accustomed to and begins to like the life of a detribalized African; he may join an Islamic or Christian community; sometimes he marries and founds a family. In the beginning he may have provided for his wife at home, although even that is the exception rather than the rule, but soon he forgets his family at home altogether. It is rare for a man to ask his wife to follow him, after a time, into a foreign area, when he decides to settle there. All this time the wife at home is waiting for her husband's return. She often becomes a loose woman whom no one can control, and no one can blame her or produce arguments against her conduct, since her husband himself shows by his prolonged absence that he does not care; alternatively she may give birth to a few illegitimate children while living with another man in concubinage.

Although the husband's family has the legal right to interfere, it seldom uses the right which applies mainly to cases in which the absence of the husband is limited in time. Generally the courts were, and still are, reluctant to grant a divorce in the absence of the husband.

If the domicile of the husband is known, he must be contacted and warned that a divorce will be granted to the wife if he does not explain his intentions with regard to his matrimonial life and does not give a date for his return.

If a divorce is granted to the wife on the grounds of desertion the father has to return the bridewealth to the husband's nearest relative.

If a man, before his departure, left his wife in the care of his brother or a near relative and has not returned after two years, the wife is entitled to claim a divorce.

NOTE: A woman is not held to be the legal wife of such a trustee, as would be the case if her husband were dead. In the latter case she would have been invited, and have agreed, to be inherited by the heir in leviratic marriage.

III. *Injuries Inflicted by Husband*

The courts consider only severe injuries to be grounds for divorce. Generally the following injuries are considered sufficiently severe to warrant the granting of a divorce:

A. Any wounds inflicted by a spear, knife, bush-knife, or any sharp instrument; biting, fractures, permanent maiming, permanent disfigurement, for instance, by throwing a fire-brand into the face.

B. The following acts of violence and their consequences are not generally regarded as grounds for divorce: minor blows, beating with a stick (even when causing bruises or swellings), pushing, kicking, throwing household goods at the wife.

NOTE: The usual procedure in court is to call for the wife's father or brother and discuss the matter with him. If the father states that he objects to his daughter being beaten and that he wishes to return the bridewealth, divorce will be granted. But if the father does not regard the matter as serious or thinks the beating well deserved, the court will accept his point of view.

The court concerns itself primarily with the question of the injury. The case is adjourned until the wife is cured or at least until her health is restored so far as possible.

* *Ibid.*

A fine may be imposed and if the man has no property he may be imprisoned in default. Compensation for the injury is assessed and if the man has no property, it may remain a debt.

In both cases, where divorce is granted or not, a wife is entitled to compensation (*igwegwe*) for injuries. A wife can claim compensation without claiming a divorce and the court is entitled to impose a fine as well.

NOTE: It is the unanimous opinion that the payment of compensation and fine will not imperil the continuance of married life. There is no reason to presume that the wife after an action in court would be in danger of repeated and perhaps increased violence from her husband. In most cases the injury is inflicted in a state of drunkenness or rage, and the punishment is looked upon as a logical and merited consequence. All parties concerned consider the affair basically as a misfortune rather than the outcome of a bad disposition. If a husband should be of a dangerous disposition, the wife and her family will insist on a divorce.

The following is the scale of compensation:

A. One head of cattle to be paid as compensation by the husband to his wife: in case of fracture of finger, loss of tooth, minor wound inflicted with sharp instrument, injury to part of outer ear, any fracture which has completely healed.

B. Five head of cattle in case of any fracture which has not healed perfectly, any kind of permanent maiming, loss of eye, loss of ear, any permanent disfigurement of face.

NOTE: This rule was agreed by the chiefs of the Sukuma Federation and their people in 1949. Formerly scales of compensation varied slightly in the various chiefdoms.

NOTE: The scale is the same as that used generally in cases of injury.

The cursing of his wife by a husband, and vice versa, is not considered a ground for divorce; but if such a case is brought before elders they usually require a small payment to be made to the injured party.

NOTE: In some parts of the country the insulted wife invokes the help of the woman's organization of the village. The members may then decide to organize a procession to the house of the offender and claim from him the payment of *masumule*, for instance a big pot of beer.

IV. *Neglect of Conjugal Duties*

If a husband intentionally neglects his wife for more than six months, this fact is considered a cause for divorce.

NOTE: This rule was agreed by the chiefs of the Sukuma Federation and their people in 1949. Formerly no such rule existed, but various courts gave judgements in which neglect of conjugal duties by the husband was acknowledged as grounds for divorce. For this reason the chiefs of SS* proposed the above rule to the other chiefs who accepted it unanimously.

NOTE: The domestic life of the Sukuma is not conducted behind walls and closed doors. Therefore even in such difficult problems as proving intention in case of neglect, the court may find sufficient evidence to give judgement. For instance, the fact that a husband, without plausible reason, ceases to sleep in the same bed with his wife will assume great significance in such a case. This rule, however, was introduced mainly to provide for the frequent cases in which a leviratic wife is neglected by the heir of her deceased husband. As she often lives in a separate house, the visits of the heir are witnessed by many persons.

A wife will often accuse her husband in court of neglect of conjugal duties with no desire to obtain a divorce, but because she feels that it may lead to a reconciliation if both partners have an opportunity of airing their grievances in court, rather than continuing a series of fruitless quarrels at home.

Chief's court 52/44. Mondo (BS).* *Binti Malele* v. *Mnyankali*.

The two are wife and husband. The wife Malele explains: 'I file a suit against my husband because he does not want me, he wishes to drive me out of the house. He claims

* *Ibid.*

repayment of bridewealth from my relatives, but I still love him. Thus I consider it a good thing to accuse him before you. Here he may explain the cause of his attitude towards me.' The husband Mnyankali answers: 'It is true I asked for repayment of bridewealth, because my wife told me I was impotent. Thus I thought it right to ask for my property as she considers me impotent.'

After considerable discussion the parties agreed in court to continue their married life in peace. In a case of this kind the court is approached by the parties as though it were an assembly of village elders whose aim is to arbitrate and reconcile. Neither party desires a judgement to be given. The hearing gives the wife an opportunity to confess that her feelings for her husband are still strong, while the husband's refusal to go home with his wife would look like an avaricious desire on his part to obtain return of bridewealth.

V. *Impotence*
(*Atigwaga buthiku*) (*Ng'osha atimaja*)

A divorce may be granted to the wife if it can be proved:

A. that the husband was impotent at the time of marriage, i.e. during the wedding night and during the following days;

B. that the man, after years of married life, has become impotent;

NOTE: If the husband contradicts the statement of his wife, the court can order them to retire for a night to a house where a witness will be placed to ascertain the truth. If the statement of the wife proves to be true, a divorce is granted.

C. that the man has become impotent, although children were born before he became so.

NOTE: Cases of this kind are rare because an impotent husband usually closes his eyes to any irregular conduct of his wife as long as she does not neglect her household duties. As the wife has children, she is reluctant to break up the household.

VI. *Incapacity to Beget Children*

A husband's incapacity to beget children is grounds for divorce.

NOTE: A wife's legal position within the husband's family changes in her favour considerably as soon as she has given birth to a child, for the following reasons:

1. One possible ground for divorce is eliminated.
2. In the event of a divorce only part of the bridewealth has to be returned.
3. In the event of the husband's death the widow with children can choose her status within the husband's family.
4. A mother of children can consider her matrimonial life stable as long as she herself does not break it up.

For these reasons the wife is given an opportunity in law to dissolve a union in which she is prevented, through no fault of her own, from attaining the most advantageous status possible for her.

VII. *Irregularities of Sexual Intercourse*

A. Bestiality, sodomy, or the insistence on any abnormal form of sexual intercourse are held to be grounds for divorce.

NOTE: Such cases very seldom come into court; a divorce is arranged before a council of members of both families. Sexual irregularities, other than those mentioned [above], are looked upon as forms of insanity. They are not punished and, as long as they do not injure anyone, no damages have to be paid. In a case of bestiality the animal has to be killed and the evil-doer has to pay its price. Irregularities of any kind are very rare in Sukumaland.

B. Ejaculatio praecox (*mwangu giti ng'oko*) is considered grounds for divorce.

NOTE: Although the difficulty of obtaining reliable evidence is recognized, many cases are known to have been decided by councils of village elders or by councils of members of the families concerned.

VIII. *Neglect of Maintenance* (*Bugumanija*)

Intentional gross neglect of the family, accompanied by general misbehaviour, is considered grounds for divorce. Lesser signs of neglect such as failure to provide clothing, female accessories, or relishes are not considered grounds for divorce.

NOTE: The husband is often brought to court for the sole purpose of being taught a lesson. A divorce will be granted only if the husband is known to be a waster and provides neither clothing nor other necessities of life for his family.

In case of divorce on grounds of gross neglect of the family, the court has the right to make provision for the guardianship of minors. The father cannot be deprived of his children, but he can be deprived of their guardianship.

NOTE: This rule was agreed by the chiefs of the Sukuma Federation and their people in 1949. Formerly no rule existed.

IX. *Incompatibility*

If husband and wife both express a definite decision to terminate their marriage, a divorce is granted.

NOTE: If the wife's family declares its readiness to return the bridewealth, the procedure is simple and a divorce is granted forthwith. If the question of return of bridewealth cannot be settled at once, the court tends to prolong the procedure and to ascertain the true reasons for the incompatibility of the partners. Finally, if all efforts of the court to reconcile the parties fail to change their resolution, the court grants a divorce in order not to aggravate the situation. If the husband is the plaintiff a refusal to grant the divorce may drive him to improper actions, i.e. to create 'grounds for divorce' on purpose. If the wife is the plaintiff she may very likely run away if a divorce is refused. In either case the result would be divorce.

These provisions may seem to make the enumeration of acknowledged grounds for divorce irrelevant, since divorces can be granted without them. In practice, however, a divorce is only granted if the court ascertains the cause of the trouble and comes to the conclusion that it is irreparable. Incompatibility is acknowledged as a ground of divorce, but only after prolonged and critical deliberations.

The force which operates behind the letter of the law is public opinion, which supports the party who abides by the law, and will not favour the transgressor. Public opinion exercises the greatest influence in the close circle of the family and of the Sukuma village community. It derives its strength from knowledge; every incident has its witnesses and every loud conversation its uninvited listeners. No person who desires to remain within the circle can disregard public opinion. Everywhere the court is the forum where public opinion finds its most outspoken expression—not only within the canon of the law, but even more so in its interpretation. The procedure in native courts differs from that in others in that visitors intervene and put questions to witnesses, and the public does not hesitate to express agreement or displeasure with the attitude of the parties or the statements of witnesses. This atmosphere in court is more noticeable in divorce cases than in any others, because the human element and the general understanding of the implications of a case tend to make every spectator a judge. Thus, under the impact of public opinion, a court will hardly grant a divorce and a party will hardly insist on demanding one without stating adequate grounds.

If one partner to a marriage definitely, and after repeated attempts by the court to bring about a reconciliation, insists on a divorce, a divorce is granted.

Cases where No Divorce is Granted

If husband or wife is sentenced to imprisonment, this fact is not considered grounds for divorce. It is held that a wife cannot obtain a divorce without the consent of her imprisoned husband.

NOTE: Even if a person should be sentenced to a long term of imprisonment, it is not possible to know beforehand whether the term may not be considerably shortened.

Illness, chronic or acute, such as crippling, deformation, blindness, insanity, is not acknowledged as grounds for divorce.

Note

[1] The following is a description of the ancient procedure in cases of adultery:

In some chiefdoms, for instance in NF, UF,† adultery was a punishable offence and suspicion was sufficient for the filing of a suit. The ultimate aim of the procedure was to obtain a confession from the defendant. Testimony of the wife or of other persons, even if supported by indirect evidence, was not considered decisive for a conviction. For the satisfaction of the judges and of public opinion the accused had to admit his guilt. A persistent denial in the face of a threatened ordeal or curse could secure the acquittal of the defendant. The amount of the fine varied, but usually consisted of a bull and a cow or fifteen goats or sheep. The court knew the accused and his means, and did not hesitate to increase or reduce the fine accordingly.

If a man had no property, any one of his relatives could be held responsible for payment. The fine was sent to the chief. The plaintiff and defendant each had to pay two goats as court fees, which were received by the *ng'wanangwa* and shared with the assessors of the court.

If the defendant suffered injury when caught *in flagrante delicto*, he had to pay just the same. If he was killed, no blood-money (*njigu*) was payable. In other chiefdoms, for instance in BSN,* adultery was not acknowledged as grounds for filing a suit.

* *Ibid.*

Chapter 14

THE LEGAL CONSEQUENCES OF DIVORCE

It will already be evident that, since marriage and divorce are essentially matters of concern to a wider family group and not just the spouses, the breakdown of a marriage involves important personal and proprietary consequences. These occur particularly in regard to the custody of children and the question of the return or retention of marriage consideration, and both of these topics are dealt with in the first of the sections which follow. Doubtless because they are the most important aspects of the subject, many writers on customary law have dealt with these matters to the exclusion of any others. This approach is, however, incomplete—and we have therefore included a further section which deals with proprietary consequences of divorce *other than* those which relate to marriage consideration.

To illustrate both aspects of this subject, we have selected extracts from two works which deal with them extensively. *Van Warmelo and Phophi*, on the Venda, are notable for their inclusion of narrative material which indicates the actual course of events in a particular case; while *Cory* presents a comprehensive picture of the proprietary consequences of divorce among the Sukuma. Extracts from the same works are used in both sections, since the division was superimposed editorially while the authors deal with the two topics as part of a continuous description. Any overlap between the material in the respective sections is therefore the result of the structure of the chapter as a whole.

(a) On Children and Marriage Consideration

J. J. van Warmelo and W. M. D. Phophi: Venda Law*

Section 1: Custody of Children Inseparable from Question of thakha

As stated elsewhere, *thakha* is thought to be mainly or even exclusively given for the sake of children. In case of a divorce, the trouble is therefore usually about the custody of the children or the return of the cattle, in a sense two aspects of the same matter. As a general rule the one party keeps the children and the other party the cattle. But there are exceptions, to be dealt with hereunder, and adjustments in the repayment of cattle are also resorted to for the sake of justice to both sides. The important thing to bear in mind is that no arrangement can be made with regard to the children without reference to the question of *thakha* and vice versa.

Section 2: Guilt of spouse affects custody of children

The only case in which a man may be denied the right of keeping his children, when getting a divorce from their mother, is when he is a dangerous lunatic. [But even this is only done when the *makhulu* appeals to the court to get the children away from him. Otherwise no one may interfere.]

Only one type of crime of a wife affects the custody of the children, viz., witchcraft. A wife divorced for witchcraft always takes her children away, because the father will not have them. The reason is the belief that witchcraft is acquired from one's mother.

However, this applies mostly to witchcraft which has caused some person's death,

* J. J. van Warmelo and W. M. D. Phophi, *Venda Law*, Government Printer, Pretoria, South Africa, 1948, pp. 589–631.

not the mild form which merely made someone ill. In the latter case the mother might be divorced, but the children are kept by the father.

Apart from these clear-cut cases, the custody of the children is seldom considered anybody else's business. It is for the two parties to arrange between themselves. If a court adjudicates on the matter, it proceeds from the assumption that the father wants the children, which should always be the case (but see exceptions below). The fact that he habitually beats the children, for example, would not be a reason for giving them to the mother, because if he cannot be trusted with them, his relatives can take them.

Section 3: Children cannot be claimed unless thakha *was paid in full*

If a man is divorced from a wife for whom he did not pay *thakha* in full, it is too late for him to offer to pay the balance in order to gain a title to the children. These are now taken by the mother, and whatever was given as *thakha* is returned, together with the increase (calves).

Section 4: Different methods of arranging custody of children

The children of a divorced couple can be taken by either party. The natural course is for the husband to take them as he is supposed to have married for the sake of having children. If the *makhulu* resists this just claim, he is penalised by having to pay back not only the *thakha* cattle but also the increase thereof. If on the other hand the husband should refuse to take the children, and demand the *thakha* plus its increase, thinking to profit thereby, the court will consider this a most unnatural attitude, and refuse to allow the demand for the increase. This latter is a more hypothetical supposition to reveal the underlying conception, for in practice a man will not refuse to take his children, and even if he did, his relatives would elbow him aside, join the court in roundly declaring him to be a *mpengo* 'lunatic', and take charge of the children themselves. But [see above] the important exception relating to witchcraft.

If children are too young to be parted from their mother she is allowed to help them until they are old enough to return to their father.

Section 5: Husband may lose custody of children

According to former Venda custom the children of a woman, no matter whether begotten elsewhere by another man, were always welcome, because what held together the family was cattle [i.e., not actual blood relationship]. So if a man was deserted by his wife and he got all his cattle back, the children went with their mother. Her new husband would not mind her being old, as men do today. That is why he would be prepared to pay *thakha* plus its increase in order to secure the children, because sometimes the woman would be advanced in years. Men nowadays on the other hand have the new idea that, according to the proverb, 'of a club you cannot say: I picked it up, but only: I carved it myself', and furthermore they consider that the child of another cannot be kept like an animal. For these reasons they are less inclined to entice away the wife of another and her children and pay the increase of *thakha* for them.

Another important consideration with them is that if the woman's father does not really approve of the second husband and is not prepared to give him much support, it may happen that she goes back to her first husband, in which case the whole lot of cattle paid by the second husband is regarded as *beletshedzo* (amends for seduction) and completely lost to him. This rule acts as a deterrent against the luring away of other men's wives.

§ 1. Mukwasha's *spy*. A man when marrying may seek out a friend or relative, give him a goat in secret and tell him, 'Keep an eye on the cattle I have given as *thakha*. Take good note of the increase and of any that are sent elsewhere'. This appointed spy calls regularly at the *makhulu*'s place as a casual visitor and on the pasture enquires from the herd boys about the cows which have calved, and the colour and sex of the calves.

If the *makhulu* sells some or uses them to *mala*, the spy follows them now and then to see how many there are. He keeps their former owner informed of every new calf and of removals from kraal to kraal, keeping count for many years. A man who *mala*'d with two head only may find that in course of time they have increased in his *makhulu*'s kraal to ten or twenty.

§ 2. *Return of increase* (*calves*) *of* thakha. If there is a divorce and the *makhulu* refuses to let the husband take the children, there is a means of making things unpleasant for him, namely that of ordering him to repay not only the *thakha* animals, but also all their increase (calves). This may spell ruin for the *makhulu* and look like breaking up his village. [Actually the threat of demanding increase is usually effective in intimidating a *makhulu* and is not carried out.]

When a dispute over the children is taken to court because the *makhulu* refuses to hand them over, the jurors ask the *makwasha* whether he knows how many calves were born to the *thakha* cattle he gave. He may then call upon that spy of his to give evidence. [Actually this is not common, because the plaintiff has been kept fully informed about the progeny of his cattle and can enumerate them all without the assistance of his observer, whilst the latter will not be keen on appearing in public and giving evidence to the disadvantage of parties with whom he has hitherto been on good terms.] So they get all the information about the calves born at the *makhulu*'s, about the animals he sold and what calves they bore after that, how many were used to *mala* wives, and what calves they bore after that transaction.

A most important matter in this reckoning up of calves is to be able to say which wife the cattle *mala*'d [to claim her in settlement instead of the calves, cf. *-bva thovhoni*,] and the spy makes it his special business to watch them whilst they are still in the *makhulu*'s kraal.

Having heard the evidence about the calves, the court sends messengers to follow up the animals wherever they may be. If they were used to *mala* a wife, they are driven off and that marriage is broken up. They even threaten the *makhulu* that they will have those he sold followed up and taken back, leaving him to fight it out with the buyer. When all the animals have been recovered the *mukwasha* pays his spy one beast for having kept him informed of the increase and the whereabouts of the cattle he gave for his wife.

If the *makhulu* slaughtered some animals to barter for maize in times of famine, these are also claimed. He must return them all, because he wants his daughter to leave her husband together with her children. Therefore the *mukwasha* also wants all the issue of his cattle to return to him.

If goats or sheep were included with the *mala* cattle or were given as *misho* and not slaughtered, and if their whereabouts and increase are known, they are similarly followed up and fetched back to the last kid and lamb.

If animals were slaughtered, it is estimated how many calves they would have had. The *makhulu* cannot therefore escape the claim for increase by proving that there never was any.

Small stock are converted into cattle to assess the increase returnable.

If the plaintiffs had no spy and are unable to describe the increase of their cattle, the court assists them in another way, viz., by the ordinary arithmetic of assuming that every cow had a calf each year. Five cows in four years would make twenty calves; no allowance is made for deaths. Of course the defendant seeks to prove that there never were so many calves and calls in herdboys and other witnesses to prove it. In this fashion the truth is at length discovered and a decision made possible. But it must be stressed that all this is done more to frighten the *makhulu* into agreeing to part with the children, than actually to put it into effect.

Tshatshalikani married a daughter of Ramuima with eight beasts. When these had been delivered Tshatshalikani secretly gave a ram to Mugeri and asked him, 'Watch carefully what my *makhulu* does with my cattle lest later on, if his daughter should desert me, I lose my property'. Mugeri actually lived in Ramuima's village and was in an excellent position to spy on everything that happened there and keep a check on increase and deaths.

Ramuima's daughter was married and bore three daughters. The cattle paid for her also increased until there were fifteen head in her father's kraal, and Mugeri all this time went regularly, without the old man's knowledge, to Tshatshalikani to tell him how many cattle there were. Then six beasts were used to *mala* Mphingudzeni's daughter

Mudivhani and nine animals remained. Those that had gone increased to eight and of this also Mugeri kept their former owner informed.

One day Ramuima's daughter deserted her husband, and the case was taken to the court of Makonde. Tshatshalikani demanded the eight animals he had *mala*'d with, and also the children. [He had no right to make this claim, and he stood no chance of getting both the cattle and the children, but such extravagances are not uncommon and are even used as threats by the court itself to frighten the woman and her father if it thinks they are in the wrong and wants the wife to return to her husband. These methods may seem highly illegal; the aim however is, not to stick to rigid procedure for its own sake but to restore normality in the community.] Ramuima countered, 'We will give you all your *thakha* back', and offered him eight beasts. 'Take these,' said he, 'We shall not give you the children.' Tshatshalikani replied, 'Very well, if you won't give me my children I don't mind, but in that case I want the calves born to my cattle since they came into your hands.'

The *makhulu* replied, 'We shan't give you the calves, because we have been herding these cattle all the time'. Tshatshalikani objected, 'But the children were reared by me, I found their food. Their mother moreover did not immediately become pregnant, so I was continually running around to doctors and paid two beasts to have her treated, and besides I slaughtered goats for the medicine-men who came to give her treatment.'

The court supported Tshatshalikani and said, 'Let the calves be reckoned up'. Mugeri was called to give evidence about the cattle the plaintiff had *mala*'d with and their movements. He stated, 'The animals paid by Tshatshalikani were eight in number. After they had increased in the old man's kraal there were fifteen. He then used six to *mala* Mphingudzeni's daughter, and in the latter's kraal they increased to nine. That cow and that cow have got so many calves,' mentioning them by name, 'thus the total of those still at home and those yonder with his own *makhulu* makes eighteen.'

The court enquired whether Mugeri spoke the truth. Ramuima first tried to deny it so they called men who lived where he had *mala*'d and they corroborated Mugeri's statement. So messengers were sent to collect all the cattle, both at the place of Ramuima's *makhulu* (Mphingudzeni) and from his own kraal, to a total of eighteen head and these were given to Tshatshalikani. He gave two head to the court and one head to Mugeri to thank him for looking after his *thakha* that he would otherwise have been done out of.

Now that the cattle with which the Ramuimas had *mala*'d from the Mphingudzenis had been taken, trouble arose between them. The Mphingudzeni family decided to take their daughter back. She already had two daughters. They fetched her home and some time afterwards she married Maemu of Ṋevhutsila's. In this way the Ramuimas suffered considerable loss [viz., one wife and two daughters and nine beasts, getting back in return their daughter and her three daughters. On the whole the settlement therefore appears an equitable one].

In Sidogi's village Raswiswi's daughter Malokisa was married by Ṋetshifhefhe. She was *mala*'d with only five head. Subsequently she deserted him and returned home. She had two daughters. When accounts were being settled, Raswiswi refused to hand over the children, saying, 'We returned your cattle, thereby buying the children as it were'. Ṋetshifhefhe appealed to the court of Mbulu, which supported him. 'As the husband has agreed to take his *thakha* back,' said they, 'let him declare how many calves his cattle had, for he married a long time ago and the cattle must have increased in the mean time.'

Now Ṋetshifhefhe had appointed Mahlareni, a certain little Shangaan who lived near his *makhulu*'s place, to spy on the increase of his cattle. Mahlareni was asked and testified, 'I know of five head of *thakha* cattle. As four of them were cows and the fifth a bull, I saw that they had four calves each, which makes sixteen; adding their mothers and that bull, we get a total of twenty-one animals.'

Ṋetshifhefhe now abandoned his demand that he be given the children and asked for his cattle instead, whilst Raswiswi now also turned round and said, 'Take your children and go.' Ṋetshifhefhe retorted, 'As you first refused to give my children back, they are yours. Give me my cattle and let me go.' The court supported him, and sent a messenger to go with Raswiswi and find all the cattle. They were driven off and handed over to his *mukwasha*. Two animals were given to the court and the rest of the herd went off with the plaintiff.

Sometimes a wife who proves barren deserts her husband after a time. The latter's people come to their *makhulu* and demand all their cattle back. Knowing moreover that their cattle have increased and, though some were eaten, the rest *mala*'d a wife, they demand also the increase of their cattle. If the *makhulu* is not prepared to pay, that wife whom he *mala*'d is taken by them together with her children, as described elsewhere under *u bva thovhoni*.

§ 3. *Wife driven out for witchcraft takes children with her.* If a wife is driven out for witchcraft, her children go with her, because if they were to stay, their mother would continually be coming back to see them, there being no law to prevent this, and would cause misfortune by bewitching the people in revenge for having been driven away.

People are afraid of keeping the children of a woman they have driven away for witchcraft, because they fear the mother has already taught her children witchcraft, so that they will bewitch their father and others in the village and cause their death in order to be able to rejoin their mother. [Moreover public opinion and the local authorities usually compel a man who has chased away his wife for witchcraft to let the children go with her, because they fear their presence. If he wants to keep them they may compel him to keep the mother also. It is not possible to deal here with all the ramifications of witchcraft.]

Where a wife is thus driven out for witchcraft and takes her children with her, the cattle given for her must in the meantime have *mala*'d a hut at her father's place, and have increased besides, therefore not only the cattle but also their increase may be returnable.[1] In the case of all the women just mentioned their relatives repaid the cattle and also the calves of the calves of the cattle that had increased at their parents' place and of those already used to *mala* wives.

Despite the rule that a woman divorced for witchcraft should be accompanied by her children, it does happen that they stay with their father. In that case no *thakha* is repayable.

If the *makhulu* thus gets hold of both the children and the cattle he is obliged to furnish a substitute wife from another hut, because the other hut together with its issue has run to perversity. [There need be no enmity between *makhulu* and *mukwasha* over such an affair because the guilty woman's father holds her mother responsible, witchcraft being inherited or acquired from the mother only. But of course trouble and ill feeling are only too common.]

§ 4. *If children of divorced woman return to husband, he retains both them and his* thakha. 'To one's old dwelling site one may always go back,' so runs a proverb of the Venda. If a man is deserted by his wife and she takes her children with her to her new husband, these children sometimes find life with their stepfather disagreeable and run back to their father because they think, 'We are not going to be kept by a strange man whilst our father lives'.

If they sneak off like this, their step-father cannot fetch them back. If he appeals to a court, they tell him, 'The child of another cannot be kept like an animal. After all you seduced this woman, and moreover these children probably went back to their father because of some shortcomings in yourself'.

Ṋetshikweṱa married Musumeli, Ṋedzingahe's daughter, who bore him six children, but finally left him for another man named Ṋenguḓa. The cattle were returned to Tshikweṱa together with their increase and the children went with their mother. However, they found life at Ṋenguḓa's anything but pleasant because their mother was frequently beaten and they themselves sometimes got no food.

So one day the eldest five children took a stealthy departure and reached Tshikweṱa's village and said, 'We have come back. We did not want to herd cattle for another man and be kept by him whilst our father was alive.' The Tshikweṱa people took them in, and killed a sheep because of their return. Ṋetshikweṱa reported to the Tshaulu court that the children whose case that very court had decided had returned.

The men of the court replied, 'The children have returned to their actual father and there is none who can send them back. When they made this plan to return on their own, it was because they realised the other man was not their father. Therefore you, Ṋetshikweṱa, build a hut for them and keep them with you, they are your children. After all, Ṋenguḓa was merely an adulterer.'

Ṋenguḓa finding that the children had gone back to their father, appealed to the court but was told, 'It is difficult to rear the child of another like a pup. They left you because they knew you were not their father. You did not beget them, you only *mala*'d their mother. What you should do is to see that you get children of your own who will use your name to swear by because your are their father. We of this court have no power to fetch back children who have returned to their actual parent'. There the matter ended and the children remained at Tshikweṱa with their father. [Nor would the court allow the question of *thakha* to be brought up again.]

Masakona also *mala*'d a wife and was deserted by her when she had two children. He demanded the return of his *thakha*, and all the cattle were repaid together with the *misho* presents. The children were ordered by the court to go to their step-father, Munzhedzi, to whom their mother was now married. The children, a half-grown girl and a lad who was herding, went. Then a quarrel arose because Munzhedzi promised the girl in marriage to a man because he needed cattle to marry another wife himself. The girl was unwilling and her mother also disapproved.

Munzhedzi pressed the girl to marry the man to whom she had been promised, so one evening she stole away with her brother and returned to their father's village. 'We have come back to our father,' they told him, 'because we saw that fellow who went off with our mother troubling us, and then accepting cattle from people to bind me to a marriage. So we decided to come back. That other man provides no clothes for us, so we said to ourselves, as long as our father is alive, why should we bear this any longer? Our mother has unfortunately got this madness, but let her bear her troubles alone yonder.' So Masakona gladly took the children in.

The matter was reported to the headman who declared, 'The children have been brought back by the ancestor spirits of your family, therefore make offerings to them to keep them quiet'. A few days later Munzhedzi appealed to the chief's court at Tshidzini. 'The children whose mother I *mala*'d have run back to her first husband,' he explained. 'Let the court have them fetched back.' But the court replied, 'The children have come back to their father. We cannot fetch them back. Who are you to keep another's child as if it were an animal? When you got their mother to run away, your object was to give us an ache in our jaws from discussing your affairs.

'We would have fetched them back if their father had come to take them away from you. But now we have nothing to do with those children because you yourself were the thief that stole their mother. If you feel strongly about it, follow them up yourself; but remember that if the Masakonas injure you with an axe when you go there to try and lure their children away, it will be your own fault, you mustn't come and complain to us.' So the matter ended, and those children grew up in the village of their father.

When Nthangeni was deserted by Tshiḓaho, she took her five children with her to her new husband Lukhwareni of Vhuvumba. She lived with him a long time without any domestic trouble, and Lukhwareni promised two of the girls in marriage and accepted the *thakha* for them. But before they married trouble began. All the children, disliking the life they were leading, decided to return to their actual father.

So one day all five of them went out, as if to collect *nombelo* fruit on Tshamavhudzi mountain, but actually they went off and in the evening reached the *khoro* of Nthangeni's village. When the people saw them they sang a song containing a pun on Nthangeni's real name to the effect that, 'To one's former building site (*marubini*) one may return, the cattle have come home to their kraal, they had been swallowed by a crocodile, but now of what use is it? They are children of Mr. Vulture of the evil dream; a tree sat upon by owls, come and also behold this, see we have plucked out all the old parrot's feathers.'

That same night Nthangeni ran up to his chief's village to report that his children had returned. The chief told him, 'Let me hear that you have killed an ox for them; tomorrow I myself shall also come and greet them'. Nthangeni's relatives were summoned from all sides to rejoice over their return. Next morning a beast was killed and there was great rejoicing with all the relatives and friends invited to see them. The chieftain Rasiuba came himself; beer was obtained from another village nearby, and the chief partook of it there is Nthangeni's village.

Lukhwareni flew into a violent rage because he had already accepted *thakha* from people. He took a beast with him to lodge a complaint in the court of Tshamutulukwa, at Rasiuba's. 'The children of the woman I *mala*'d', said he, 'have left me to return to their father. What am I to do now as I have already accepted cattle for two of them?'

The court assembled and supported Nthangeni. 'The children are yours,' they said, 'they shall not leave again.' They told Lukhwareni, 'Even if you have already accepted cattle for those two girls, it is theft on your part. When you took that *thakha* didn't you know that these children were not yours, but had a father of their own? And don't you know what made them return home? Did you ever see one man's blood come out of his body and enter that of another and become one with his blood? Did you think one man could appropriate to himself what should be taken by another?

'We foresaw this the other day when you took the children belonging to another, thinking to keep them and we thought, very well, let us see what is going to come of this. Today, look! the cock has been caught in the trap. You thought you were clever, but your cleverness has got you into trouble. We cannot allow you to take the children back, because they returned to their father of their own free will. If he had come himself and taken them from you by force, then we would have said "No, this will not do. Take your children with you." But as they betook themselves home freely, go you and repay those people who gave you *thakha* from your own property. These children who have returned to their father are Nthangeni's own.'

Lukhwareni now appealed to the paramount chief's court Mukambani at Mbilwi. But there also he lost his case, for the councillors laughed at him, 'Who do you think you are, that you can seize persons belonging to another man? The children did well to come back to the man they knew for their father. Go you and be satisfied that you have got their mother at home, she will bear you other children whose *thakha* you can take for yourself.'

Lukhwareni, having failed in his appeal, returned home where he found his *vhakwasha* waiting for him, because they wanted to take their bride home. When he told them what had happened they demanded their cattle back. The other *vhakwasha*, learning that Lukhwareni's step-children had gone back to their father, also came to claim their *thakha*. Lukhwareni was in a daze and no longer knew what to do. He tried to borrow here and there from relatives and eventually found the amount he required to liquidate his debts.

Gatawa was deserted by his wife who went to live with Gupana. She took her son and daughter with her. The lad was already about six, whilst the girl was still an infant. The woman lived with Gupana until, after a number of years, the girl became nubile.

Then her step-father promised her in marriage and received eight beasts for her. A quarrel now arose because he wanted to use the cattle to get himself another wife, who would be a co-wife of the girl's mother. The son by this time was a young man. He refused to approve of this plan and threatened him, 'Let the sun go up and go down on our fighting. I am after all not your son; you stole my mother from my father.'

So one day, when the people were all away in the fields, he drove all those cattle away and took with him even the two little sisters of his who had been born to his step-father, sending them on in front with a little brother. The sister by this time was already married and gone. He drove the cattle towards the Nzhelele river, then they went through the bush and past Tshavhalovhedzi and by sunset arrived unexpectedly at Gatawa's village. The young man knew where his father lived because he had been accustomed to go there with others on their expeditions to gather *nombelo* berries and dig *mikwatule* roots for birdlime.

The Gatawas were surprised to see a herd of cattle suddenly entering their village, and everybody rushed out to look. Then they discovered it was Magombo himself, who told them, 'I have come with my sister's cattle and here are the two little sisters and a brother. I decided to come back to my father; I don't want to stay with a step-father as long as my father lives. And my sisters' *thakha* is not going to be taken by another whilst our father lives abandoned by us who followed our mother in her unfaithfulness'. This made all the Gatawa folk break out into wild rejoicing so that even old Gatawa himself picked up a sable antelope horn and pranced all round the *khoro* blowing it until even the neighbours came to see what was the matter, for they knew there was no beer.

Out of sheer joy Gatawa rushed into his cattle kraal and immediately slaughtered a huge ox without even bothering to consult his relatives first, intending it as savoury for his children who had come back. Their return was immediately reported at the *musanda* of Thononda where Ratshimphi, the paramount chief's son, was still in charge, and from there the news was passed to the capital Mukumbani. 'We are rejoicing with

Gatawa', they said, 'because his children have come home again, even bringing with them the cattle of a sister married yonder whilst with the seducer who married the mother.' The court sent a reply: 'Gatawa need not fear to take his children in. They belong to him; let us hear that he has put them in the hut of another wife of his who will be their mother. As for that young man who brought back the cattle of his sister, let there be found a hook for those cattle to be hung up, so that he can get a little woman [wife].'

Thus it was done. A few days later an appeal was lodged with the court of Mukumbani, the plaintiff being that Gupana whose children had left him. However, the court did not waste much time over him, but told him, 'After all, you were a thief the last time. Do you think you can seize another's ox and the bull of somebody else and think to put them inside your cattle kraal whilst its owner is alive? Do you imagine that when it grows up and starts bellowing it will not bellow at you too? Go away, we have nothing to say to you. The children came back to their father knowing full well what they were doing.' The matter ended there, and Gupana got nothing. The cattle he had given for the woman, he was told, were considered to be a fine for having seduced the woman.

§5. *Return of divorced wife to rejoin children.* It is not unusual, in cases where children forsake their step-father and return to their real father, for the mother to follow them when she realises that she has nothing to live for where she is. Her husband maybe gives her a beating because he thinks she was responsible for their running away. Or perhaps she is laughed at by other women when gathering firewood or at the river. They call her a fool and ask her, 'Why do you stay here longer now that your children are gone and are stamping for other women? And in any case how many children do you think you will get here?'

They urge on her. 'What your present husband has, that your former husband has also. As for your children, what is there more precious than that?' A woman hearing this argument often, will one day set out to her former husband. She doesn't care how she will get herself accepted, for after all she left because of a quarrel and moreover her *thakha* was returned to him. She does not enter the village but goes to one nearby and makes her presence known by sending perhaps an old woman with the message, 'Please go and tell them that I have come back altogether. I am tired of the country and I said to myself, let me go and just cook for my children.'

A proverb says, 'Old women keep people's villages in order'. This is also what the cock is supposed to say when it crows morning and evening, namely: '*Muhulwane ha shaiwi,* An elder is not lacking,' meaning that if there is no old person in a village, its troubles will not be settled. So the old woman goes to the man to tell him that his divorced wife has come back just to look after the children.

Perhaps he might feel like refusing, but the elders reason with him. 'Let her come,' they say, 'as she has come of her own accord and nobody is following her, and you already have the children! *You hate the old kraalsite but love the spinach growing on it* (a proverb), when you know the spinach only grows on such kraal sites?' So finally he agrees to allow her into his village, and allots a hut to her where she can live with the children. If his mother is still alive she may be lodged in her cooking hut. Her return is also reported at the chief's headquarters.

Where a wife has thus gone back to her former husband, much trouble results from the fact that her second husband reimbursed the first. Sometimes a part of the *thakha* paid by the second husband (not the full amount) is returned to him. [This requires some elucidation. The second husband never has direct dealings with the first, for fear of bloodshed. He pays to the *makhulu,* who repays the deserted party. If the woman now returns to her first husband, it makes no difference whether the second husband himself lured her away from her first husband or whether he found her already living with her parents and was therefore innocent even of intent to do anyone an injury. If the woman returns to her first husband, the second is deemed an adulterer either way. The first husband never pays anything back at all. If the second recovers anything of what he gave the *makhulu,* it has to come out of the latter's pocket. That is why he often resists. The court often supports him so that the second husband gets nothing, especially if he makes a fuss about his 'rights'. In other cases the court orders the *makhulu* to repay his whole *thakha,* then allows him to retain say half. Of this the *makhulu* then again gives say one beast out of four to the first husband. The latter, who has already got much more than he is entitled to, will not accept more than one beast in any case, for fear of being bewitched. The whole inequitable method of arranging things is defended by the argument that adulterers must be discouraged and ignores the fact that as a rule only bad husbands are deserted by their wives.]

Tshivhonammbi was deserted by his wife who had two sons. Her *thakha* was returned, but after five years the sons ran away to their first father as their step-father was disagreeable to them because he thought, 'They will challenge my right to the cattle I shall receive for the little daughters born after them'. [They would have no legal right to do so, but would cause trouble all the same.] So the sons ran away, and their mother, seeing no further reason for staying, took leave pretending she was going home on a visit. But from there she went straight on to her former husband Tshivhonammbi.

Arriving there she entered the village of an old man named Shuruma and after greeting him said, 'Please go and tell Tshivhonammbi that I am here, tell him Muyanaḽo sends this message: I have come back altogether, I have my other children with me. As my sons fled back to their father because they saw my doglike behaviour and my unfaithfulness, I thought to take the road also and follow them.' Shuruma went to Tshivhonammbi's leaving the woman behind, and delivered the message.

Tshivonammbi replied, 'Very well, a doctor does not treat himself (a proverb); I cannot settle this matter on my own. I shall first consult my elders and the headman of this area, because we discussed this matter at great length in court. Let her wait there.' As it was already late, Tshivhonammbi next day informed his relatives. They said, 'Very well, if the cow has come back to the kraal to follow her calves, we are glad of it. We thank our ancestors of Ratombo's who urged her on and made our wife come back with her children. For a woman is not driven away.'

The matter was also reported to the headman of Tshit̨ungulu, who replied, 'This is what we were waiting to hear. Let her come back. That other man, after all, was an adulterer the first time. As she has now brought back the children, let her stay. I am going to the chief's place, Khawela, tomorrow and shall let the chief and his councillors know what has happened.' So the woman was given quarters in the village in the kitchen of Tshilambavhunwa's mother, Nyamudzunga. The headman informed the court of the matter.

Ṋevhuḓane, the second husband of Muyanaḽo, hearing that she had returned to her former husband appealed to the court of Khawela. The council met, also the woman's former husband and her father. Evidence was taken from everybody and the decision was, 'Ṋevhuḓane must now be considered an adulterer. The cattle he paid to the woman's proper owner was really the equivalent of a fine for adultery because the woman has come back to her husband together with all her children. Tshivhonammbi didn't fetch her back, she came because she realised that you were not her proper husband, but simply an adulterer.' The court settled the affair in this way. Ṋevhuḓane took a beast to lodge an appeal with the supreme court of Mbilwi at chief Mphaphuli's. The matter was heard there also, but the court upheld the ruling of the court of Khawela that Ṋevhuḓane need not be indemnified as he was an adulterer. There it ended and the loss was Ṋevhuḓane's.

Muthungamat̨o caused Tshonyiwaho's wife to run away to him. He paid for her with thirteen head, and the court ordered that, as she had two children, they should go with their mother. This they did, and she lived with her new husband until she had borne him three further children, which made five in all. Then there was trouble because the two eldest sons were dissatisfied and refused to be sent on errands by their step-father because they said, 'We will not work for another's father whilst our own father is in distress'.

They continued to harp on this grievance and refused to herd the cattle because they would not work for a stranger whilst their own father was in trouble. Though their stepfather tried to scare them by beating them, it made no difference, but merely increased their hatred of him. Whenever he was away they urged their mother to return home to their father. She rebuked them so one day they started out and crossed over to Mat̨angari to their father.

There they told him, 'We have come back because we don't want to be kept like goats'. He took them in. When Muthungamat̨o thought to fetch them back, the people of Mat̨angari declared, 'These children do not go back to you, after all you have others that are your own'. He went to his own headman's court at Makonde to complain that the Maṱangari people would not hand over his children, but was roundly abused and told, 'Those children are not yours. If they went back to their father of their own free will, leave them alone. If you persist in going after them you are looking for trouble. Be satisfied that you have children of your own.' No sooner had this matter of the children been settled than their mother began to grieve at seeing her children gone.

So her things were packed into baskets, and one day when Muthungamaṱo had gone on a visit, she followed her children back to her former husband. There she came forward herself and told him, 'I have come back because I could not stay there any longer; I thought of our proverb, that one may return to former dwelling sites.' Tshonyiwaho took her in and told his relatives she had come back. The elders said this was very good, after all she had come to look after her children. They also sent a report to their headman Nyamande of Maṱangari.

A few days later Muthungamaṱo, who was seeking his wife everywhere and had even gone to her father without finding her, was told, 'Your wife has returned to her former husband.' At this he became greatly incensed, and, with his younger brother Musandiwa, lodged a complaint in the court of Maṱangari. The councillors assembled to hear the case and declared, 'Very well, the cow has come back to the cattle kraal. As the woman has returned with all her children, you Muthungamaṱo are now an adulterer. Your *thakha* cannot be returned to you. However, as you gave a great deal, the court will help you to regain part of it.'

§ 6. *No increase (calves) of thakha returnable if husband refuses children.* If the husband refuses to take the children and insists on getting back his *thakha* plus the increase, the *makhulu* may refuse to give the increase on the ground that he is not unwilling to hand over the children. The court supports the *makhulu* in this because as long as he does not withhold the children from their father he need not return any increase of *thakha.*

Section 6: Husband usually Retains Custody of Children

As we have seen it is painful to have to break up marriages by demanding the increase of *thakha* from a *makhulu* who refuses to render back the deserting wife's children, and it is therefore usual for them to stay with the father, except in cases of witchcraft. If they stay with the father the *thakha* returnable is reduced.

There is furthermore the fear that after all another man's children cannot be kept, and for this reason even if all the *thakha* has been repaid it is now common for the father to retain custody. For if you take them they will still run away to their father when they grow up or find life hard. In their stepfather's family they never cease causing trouble, and may even cause discord between the spouses when the husband wants to correct them and his wife reproaches him and says she sees they are obviously not his own. Hence the saying that only a club which one has carved can be called one's own, not one picked up. So that it comes down to this that when there is talk of having custody of stepchildren it is girls that are referred to, for to have a strange boy in one's family spells nothing but trouble.

Section 7: Runaway Wife left in Temporary Custody of Children

A wife sometimes deserts her husband to go and live with her parents with her children. Her husband may come to her father and tell him, 'Very well, I gave full *thakha* for your daughter at the time, and even if she has now left me, it must not worry you. Just look after my children, and I shall come now and then to see them. If food is scarce, let me know, so that I can buy what food you need for them.'

If the *makhulu* agrees to this [which he need not] the deserted husband does not make him pay anything back but looks forward to reimbursing himself from the *thakha* to be received for the daughters when they get married. Sometimes the woman runs to another man and both he and her father are equally unable to pay anything back. Then the husband may allow her to stay there but tells her, 'Very well, you can remain where you are but we shall come and take away the children born to you in the future'. This is usually done only with women who already have issue. Of the man who took such a woman in, though unable to *mala* her, they say, 'He managed to fell the tree but he can't chop off the branches', or 'he can climb into the branches of trees but he can't get down again'.

Cases like these do not come before the courts because there is nothing to be gained thereby.

If a woman deserts her husband and the *thakha* is not demanded back, all children born to her as a result of adultery, or from consorting with some other man, belong to her husband who *mala*'d her and was not repaid.

Section 8: Maintenance for Children of Divorced Wife

If a divorced woman has children too small to be taken from her, not all the *thakha* is returned. For every child that stays with the mother the *thakha* is reduced by one cow that is termed the 'beast' of the child [i.e. it is given to the child's mother to pay for her rearing of the child]. Any calves it may have belong to her. A cow is given irrespective of the age of the child, i.e. no matter whether the rearing period be long or short.

The father must also provide clothes for these children. If they fall ill, he must pay the doctor's fees. In a year of scarcity he gives the wherewithal to buy food for them.

If he provides no clothes and no food in scarce years and does not pay for medical treatment, he pays a beast to cover everything when he comes to take the child away.

If it is a girl, and *thakha* is accepted for her, the father gives his *makhulu* a female goat as *luphaso*, i.e. as fee to bribe him to pray to his ancestor spirits so that they will not molest the child after she is married. [The second husband is not given such a fee if the girl grew up at his place because his ancestor spirits will not trouble her. *Midzimu* do not bother themselves with adulterers, it is said.]

Note

[1] Even in cases of witchcraft, where the husband is always afraid of taking the children. the calves of the *thakha* animals are seldom paid back, because if repayment is demanded the *makhulu* will plead that he is not withholding the children. The court will usually take the view that since it is the husband who does not want the children, he cannot claim the increase of his *thakha*, but only the latter.

H. Cory: Sukuma Law and Custom*

Legal Effects of Divorce

Rules referring to children. The children always belong to the father, but the amount of bridewealth which has to be returned is reduced by five head of cattle for each living child and two head of cattle for each child which has died.

NOTE: This section contains some repetition of previous paragraphs but it has been considered useful for practical purposes to assemble them again under the above heading.

The father has the right to renounce possession of his children, in which case he can demand return of bridewealth in full.

NOTE: The usual motive in this case is not greed but the father's difficulty in finding a home for the children. If the father's parents are still alive this problem is easily solved, but if he has no suitable relatives, he may prefer to leave the children with their maternal family. It may also happen that, in the first bitterness of feeling, he wishes to break completely with the past. Frequently such a man leaves the locality for a time.

Neither the father-in-law nor any other member of the maternal family has a right to demand that the father should agree to receive the full amount of bridewealth and renounce his right to the children, even if it can be proved that the father is not a fit person to look after the children.

The father is permitted to demand his children at any subsequent date, and the maternal family cannot refuse to hand them back if the father is prepared to return the cattle which he received in respect of them when the bridewealth was returned. The maternal family then has the right to demand payment for the children's maintenance while under their care.

* H. Cory, *Sukuma Law and Custom*, Oxford University Press, 1953, pp. 81–85.

The amount claimed for maintenance must not exceed one cow, irrespective of the number of children maintained.

NOTE: This rule was agreed by the chiefs of the Sukuma Federation and their people in 1949. Formerly the amount payable for maintenance varied in different areas:

A. In UF, NF, KF, BSN, BD* a token payment of a blanket and perhaps Shs. 10/-.
B. In KM, KS* one head of cattle.
C. In BS, SS, SBS* the whole bridewealth, irrespective of the number of children.

NOTE: A number of chiefs proposed very high—almost prohibitive—amounts to be paid for maintenance by fathers. This was not generally accepted and finally the limit was set at one cow. It seems that the proposal for a high amount took into consideration the points of view of the father and maternal grandfather, but not the fate of the children. Such children are only minor heirs of the maternal family with whom they are living, while they would become their father's main heirs (*nkuruwabo* and *nzuna*).

The law distinguishes between the amounts payable by a father who claims his legitimate child and by a father trying to legitimize his illegitimate child. The payment of a large amount for the purpose of legitimization operates to prevent a father, who has not cared about his daughter for many years, attempting to enrich himself from her bridewealth.

A father is not allowed to take some of his children with him and leave the rest with the maternal family, taking in their stead a part of the bridewealth. He must either take all his children or leave them all.

A father-in-law cannot ask for more cattle for the children than the original amount of the bridewealth.

NOTE: For example: if the total bridewealth was ten head of cattle, and was returned in full, three children being left with the maternal grandfather, the father, if he later asks for the return of the children, will be required to pay only ten head of cattle plus maintenance.

An infant in arms remains with the mother until it is weaned and no maintenance can be demanded by the maternal family when the father comes to fetch his child.

D.C.'s Appeal No. 29/47. Msalala (KM)*. *Msuka* v. *Barabara*.

When Msuka obtained a divorce from Barabara's daughter, their child was not yet weaned and was therefore left with the mother, but the usual number of cattle was deducted when the bridewealth was returned. After five years Msuka demanded his child but Barabara wanted one head of cattle for the child's maintenance. The court held that no maintenance was payable and the child must be returned to his father. The elders held the view that Barabara could not claim for the child's maintenance, just as Msuka could not claim the produce and calves of the cattle he left with his father-in-law when the bridewealth was returned.

It is within the discretion of the husband to allow the mother and her children to visit each other; he cannot be coerced into giving such permission.

NOTE: The rules regarding the domicile of the children in case of divorce are usually treated very liberally by the father after his first rage at the time of the divorce case has given place to a cooler judgement of the whole affair. The children often spend months in the house of their maternal grandfather, uncle, or mother.

Rules referring to maintenance. The maintenance of a divorced wife (*nshimbe*) is a charge on her relatives and never upon her husband and his family.

Rules referring to property. A wife must be allowed to retain possession of her private property, i.e. property she brought with her from her father's house, inherited property, clothing, gifts from her husband, and gifts from members of her own and her husband's family.

The wife takes with her all kitchen utensils of native make. She is not entitled to implements which have been bought in a shop (aluminium pots, kettles, &c.). Mats made by her are her own property.

A. Property acquired by the wife through her skill as practitioner, midwife, potter,

* These letters refer to a district in Sukumaland.

beer-brewer, &c., is her property if the husband has not paid the practitioner's fee, which amounts to one heifer (*ng'ombe ya mhela*).

NOTE: The fees of practitioners vary according to the gravity of the disease and the duration of the cure. A doctor's fee (*mhela*) seldom exceeds one cow for a female patient and one bull for a male patient. The practitioner can only expect to be paid his or her fee if the patient recovers; but the payment of *simba nti* and *shilatu* is required from every patient; these fees usually amount to one or two shillings.

B. This heifer has to be paid by the husband, even if his wife's skill has been acquired during married life, if he wishes to obtain the right to the property acquired by the wife.

C. If husband and wife have jointly purchased cattle, house, or commodities, these possessions become the property of the husband, if no agreement before witnesses has been concluded.

The divorced wife has no claim to food in store or to crops in the field.

NOTE: This rule was agreed by the chiefs of the Sukuma Federation and their people in 1949. Formerly the divorced wife was entitled to the *shilandi* (wife's share in the harvest),[1] except in KS and SS* where she got nothing.

NOTE: It was the custom for the wife after her marriage to bring seed for the *shilandi* crops from her father's home. Nowadays many of the crops which comprised *shilandi* are planted for sale, the fields for them are prepared by ploughing, manuring, and by employing communal labour. Therefore the wife has lost her claim to *shilandi* because the crop is no longer brought from her home; moreover, *shilandi* has lost its meaning, because it originally consisted mainly of crops used for relishes and for consumption in the house and not of cash crops. During the last few years there has been a tendency to give the divorced wife less and less from the crops.

The village elders[2] were usually influenced in their decision regarding *shilandi* by consideration of the grounds of divorce. If the wife had deserted her husband or was guilty of adultery she got nothing; but if the divorce was granted because of the husband's neglect of maintenance, she was awarded a share of the *shilandi*, because she had probably done all the field-work.

If *shilandi* was awarded to the wife, the following rules were applied:

A. If some of the *shilandi* had been sold during the year of the divorce, the wife could not claim a share of the proceeds nor could she claim a share of anything brought with the proceeds.

B. The crops in the field were divided in the same way as the food in store.

C. If the *shilandi* crops and the husband's crops were interplanted, the cleaning of the field was the responsibility of both wife and husband even after divorce. If one of them neglected the work, the other was entitled to take the whole harvest. The court could award to the lazy party a share of the harvest in consideration of the work done before the divorce.

D. The division of crops into *shilandi* and husband's crops was not affected by the actual work done in the field. For instance, even if the wife looked after the cotton field by herself, the cotton remained the husband's crop.

Rules referring to return of bridewealth. It is the duty of the court to ascertain the degree of guilt of husband or wife, and to assess accordingly the amount of bridewealth which has to be returned, after the customary deduction for children has been made.

NOTE: Court judgements for many years past have given evidence of the careful consideration devoted to determining guilt in divorce cases.

Fulo Appeal Case 13/44. *Yamunda* v. *Kacheyeki.*

Yamunda claimed divorce and return of bridewealth from his wife's father Kacheyeki, without giving any grounds for his demand. The court decided that a divorce should be granted, but no bridewealth should be returned because the husband repudiated his wife without giving any reasons for his attitude.

Latterly the chiefs of KS and SS* agreed to introduce the question of guilt into divorce cases and to deduct two cows if bridewealth had to be returned and the court had found the husband to be the guilty party.

Opinion was unanimous in favour of the adoption of rules introducing the question of guilt into divorce cases. It was felt that the most frequent cases, in which the husband

* *Ibid.*

must leave cattle for maintenance, would be those of 'neglect of maintenance' and 'neglect of conjugal duties' concerning mainly levirate wives.

If the court finds that the wife is the guilty party, the whole bridewealth has to be returned. If the court finds that the husband is the guilty party, the maternal family is allowed to keep two cows.

A. Full bridewealth has to be returned if the court finds that any one of the following grounds for divorce has been established: adultery by wife; desertion by wife; injuries by wife; neglect by wife; irregularities by wife; refusal by wife; use of magic medicine by wife; infertility of wife; desertion by husband; impotence of husband; irregularities by husband; incapacity of husband (divorce claimed by wife); incompatibility (divorce claimed by wife).

B. Two cows can be retained by the wife's family in case of: adultery by husband; injuries by husband; neglect by husband; neglect of maintenance by husband; incompatibility (divorce claimed by husband).

NOTE: The payment of compensation, as in the case of injuries inflicted by the husband should not be confused with the payment of two cows in case of divorce. The court may impose both payments if it finds them justified.

C. The two cows do not have to be returned if the wife should remarry.

D. The two cows are reckoned as payment for the wife's maintenance and are handed over to that relative who received the original bridewealth, or his heir.

If, in consideration of the number of children, no bridewealth has to be returned and the court finds that the husband is the guilty party he has to pay two cows.

NOTE: The above Rules were decided upon by the chiefs of the Sukuma Federation and their people in 1949. Formerly the following rule existed everywhere: In any case of divorce, bridewealth, or a portion of it, depending on the number of children born to the couple, had to be returned to the husband irrespective of the grounds for divorce. If, in case of divorce, the amount to be deducted for children is greater than the amount of bridewealth which the husband has paid, he must either leave the children to the maternal family or, if he wishes to take his children, he must pay the balance of the bridewealth.

Notes

[1] The word *shilandi* is unknown in KS and SS.
[2] No lawsuit relating to the division of property after a divorce is recorded.

(b) PROPRIETARY CONSEQUENCES

J. J. van Warmelo and W. M. D. Phophi: Venda Law*

Property of Spouses Divided upon Divorce

Section 1: Categories of property. When a man and his wife are divorced, the property in their household is divided according to whether it is to stay or is to be taken away by its respective owner. Everything belonging to the husband is put into one category, no matter what class of goods or property it belongs to, because it remains his property in all circumstances. The wife has no claim to even the smallest part thereof. The wife's property (i.e. what is ordinarily considered to be hers when married) falls into four categories: (1) what she was given by her husband and his relatives, (2) what she acquired by her own efforts, but belongs to her husband nevertheless, (3) what she was given by her own relatives, and (4) what she acquired by her own efforts, and belongs to her entirely.

As the wife's property has been acquired in various ways, it follows that, upon divorce, she sometimes brings her relatives to prove that some of the property belongs to her. The only question the court wants evidence on is the origin of the property, that is, how it was acquired.

* J. J. van Warmelo and W. M. D. Phophi, *Venda Law*, Government Printer, Pretoria, South Africa, 1948, pp. 633–639 and pp. 643–647.

There rarely are court proceedings about old women past child-bearing because nothing is to be gained. But especially if such a woman owns property is it considered folly to start trouble with her. Her husband will build her a place of her own where she can live undisturbed. If such a woman has wives *mala*'d with her own property, no matter how acquired, and no matter whether given as *tshiozwi* to her son, or as concubines to her husband or others, these wives would leave with her if she were to be divorced. As to divorce such a woman would be the height of folly, it is never attempted. If she is found guilty of witchcraft by the divining dice the family elders will supress it or, if things get too bad, get rid of her by poisoning. The question of ownership of wives by women therefore does not come before the courts for reasons of self-interest on the part of *vhakwasha.*

Section 2: Property of husband. As stated above, a wife can claim no part of her husband's property upon her divorce, and it is therefore unnecessary to differentiate categories thereof.

Section 3: Property supplied to wife by husband and family. When a woman marries she is given a number of things by her husband and his relatives. These are usually household utensils, wooden platters, stirring sticks, winnows, baskets, shallow dishes, washing basins, mortars, pestles and other household odds and ends. Cooking pots, wash-basins and dishes are usually given by her husband's mother and sisters. From her husband she gets stirring sticks, spoons, platters, pestles and mortars, mats, blankets and clothing.

None of the goods a woman gets from her husband's people may be taken away by her when she is divorced because she did not bring any of these things from her home. She may however take away her blankets and clothes and the anklets and bangles she is wearing. A man who follows his wife when she has left him and deprives her of what she is wearing is a miscreant and will find the court prepared to punish him.

The rule is therefore that a woman's clothes and ornaments may not be taken from her. Only a woman who is chased away for witchcraft used to be deprived of all her garments, which were burnt to shame her for what she had done. This was customary in the olden days when people guilty of witchcraft were hurled from precipices together with all their relatives, their whole property being confiscated by the chief. Today a woman found guilty of witchcraft is allowed to take her clothes away with her.

Section 4: Property acquired by the wife's effort but belonging to husband. The maize that a wife has reaped she cannot take away with her. Sometimes she leaves a granary full of maize behind, but her family cannot come and take it away because the garden was not hers, and because he who bought the hoes, whittled the handles and put steel and handle together was not one of her family, but of her husband's.

A wife may buy a beast with the produce of her gardens and its increase may be numerous, or she may use her maize to buy goats which increase to quite a flock. This stock may, however, not be claimed by her family when she is divorced from her husband. It all belongs to her husband because it originated from her husband's property. He gave her the garden, he built the granary and grainbin.

Where profits made from medical knowledge are concerned it is the same. A woman ignorant of medicine, may be married by a doctor. Whenever he goes out to treat a patient, he takes her with him and shows her certain medicines, until she acquires some knowledge, so that sometimes when her husband is away she herself goes to doctor sick people. If the patient gets well, she may get a fee of a goat or a beast.

This beast belongs to her, though it remains under her husband's control, because the pouches from which the medicines came that cured the patient belonged to her husband. But where a woman has thus acquired a flock of goats or bought cattle, and she is divorced, this property may not be removed by her. It belongs to her husband, because she had no knowledge of medicine when she left home but learnt it from her husband, and because no fee was ever paid for this instruction.

Section 5: Property belonging to wife because obtained from her own family. Upon her marriage, a woman is given presents by her relatives. Rich people give their daughters a cow termed 'breast of the child', or a goat termed *muhungo* 'tied-up animal'. Others give fowls to take with her. Her female relatives give household vessels and utensils, such as mortars, pestles, winnowing baskets, stirring sticks, cooking pots and water jars.

Ṋevhuḓane was once ordered by the chief's court to pay a beast for knocking Kudzingana about the head in a fight over some fowls that had been scratching up the sprouting crops in the lands. As he had no beast to pay with, he borrowed one from his wife who owned five beasts earned in her medical practice. The fine was paid, and after many years he had still not repaid the debt, when a quarrel broke out between them and the wife took all her things and went home.

The husband took the matter to court at Vhusenga whilst Bababa was still the headman. The *makhulu* made no further objections but offered to give him all his *thakha* if he came with his relatives. But now the wife interposed, 'I lent him a beast to pay a fine for the bruises he gave to Kudzingana when he was unable to pay. He hasn't repaid it to this day'. Ṋevhuḓane admitted this, and when his *makhulu* gave his cattle back to him he selected a cow and offered it to the woman in settlement of the debt.

Bele also had a wife who owned many goats that came from her home. When he was fined for having stayed away from the *dzunde* of Dimani and he lacked the means to pay it he called his wife aside and asked her to help him out with a goat. She gave it to him, but before it had been repaid they fell out and the wife fled home to her people and refused to go back.

The court of Tshifuḓi was appealed to for return of *thakha*. The *makhulu* collected what he had to pay, but told the court, 'I want to remind you that I gave my daughter some goats when she was married, and these have increased to thirteen. They are still with my *mukwasha*. I want them back because they were not bought with my *mukwasha's* money, but given by us, her parents.'

The woman herself added, 'There is one goat also which he borrowed to pay his fine for staying away from the *dzunde*, because he had nothing. He promised to repay it later, but never did'. Bele at first denied this, but witnesses proved it, so he paid the thirteen goats and one more to repay the loan.

If the husband proves obstinate and refuses to let the wife remove her things, even if the court so directs, the method of dealing with him is to conduct an equivalent from the *thakha* returnable.

Section 6: Property belonging to wife because earned with knowledge belonging to her own family. There are many women who practice medicine. Most of them employ the skill they have been taught at home by their own relations. For this reason all the property a wife has earned with this knowledge is in the same class with the rest of the things she got from her own family. If she parts from her husband it is not left with him. Her relations come and take it away.

Section 7: Concealment of property by wife intending to desert. Since the law does not permit a wife to take away some of her things, it is common for a woman contemplating desertion to remove her small household utensils such as dishes, calabashes, pots, beer pots and winnows, and to conceal them with neighbours or in the bush where she can retrieve them later.

Grain that she wants to keep she hides with friendly neighbours who will not betray her. Finally when she decides to go, she takes a whole lot of things, unseen by her husband, and leaves by night. Unless a woman is formally sent home for witchcraft, she usually absconds at night when her husband suspects nothing or leaves when he is away on a journey so that he only finds out upon his return that she is gone.

H. Cory: Sukuma Law and Custom*

Rules referring to property.† A wife must be allowed to retain possession of her private property, i.e. property she brought with her from her father's house, inherited property, clothing, gifts from her husband, and gifts from members of her own and her husband's family.

* H. Cory, *Sukuma Law and Custom*, Oxford University Press, 1953, pp. 82–84.

† Parts of this section are a duplication of p. 254–255. This is done intentionally since it is difficult to separate the question of proprietary consequences and effects of dissomtion on the marriage consideration.

The wife takes with her all kitchen utensils of native make. She is not entitled to implements which have been bought in a shop (aluminium pots, kettles, &c.). Mats made by her are her own property.

A. Property acquired by the wife through her skill as practitioner, midwife, potter, beer-brewer, &c., is her property if the husband has not paid the practitioner's fee, which amounts to one heifer (*ng'ombe ya mhela*).

NOTE: The fees of practitioners vary according to the gravity of the disease and the duration of the cure. A doctor's fee (*mhela*) seldom exceeds one cow for a female patient and one bull for a male patient. The practitioner can only expect to be paid his or her fee if the patient recovers; but the payment of *simba nti* and *shilatu* is required from every patient; these fees usually amount to one or two shillings.

B. This heifer has to be paid by the husband, even if his wife's skill has been acquired during married life, if he wishes to obtain the right to the property acquired by the wife.

C. If husband and wife have jointly purchased cattle, house or commodities, these possessions become the property of the husband, if no agreement before witnesses has been concluded.

The divorced wife has no claim to food in store or to crops in the field.

NOTE: This rule was agreed by the chiefs of the Sukuma Federation and their people in 1949. Formerly the divorced wife was entitled to the *shilandi* (wife's share in the harvest),[1] except in KS and SS where she got nothing.

NOTE: It was the custom for the wife after her marriage to bring seed for the *shilandi* crops from her father's home. Nowadays many of the crops which comprised *shilandi* are planted for sale, the fields for them are prepared by ploughing, manuring, and by employing communal labour. Therefore the wife has lost her claim to *shilandi* because the crop is no longer brought from her home; moreover, *shilandi* has lost its meaning, because it originally consisted mainly of crops used for relishes and for consumption in the house and not for cash crops. During the last few years there has been a tendency to give the divorced wife less and less from the crops.

The village elders[2] were usually influenced in their decision regarding *shilandi* by consideration of the grounds of divorce. If the wife had deserted her husband or was guilty of adultery she got nothing; but if the divorce was granted because of the husband's neglect of maintenance, she was awarded a share of the *shilandi*, because she had probably done all the field-work.

If *shilandi* was awarded to the wife, the following rules were applied:

A. If some of the *shilandi* had been sold during the year of the divorce, the wife could not claim a share of the proceeds nor could she claim a share of anything bought with the proceeds.

B. The crops in the field were divided in the same way as the food in store.

C. If the *shilandi* crops and the husband's crops were interplanted, the cleaning of the field was the responsibility of both wife and husband even after divorce. If one of them neglected the work, the other was entitled to take the whole harvest. The court could award to the lazy party a share of the harvest in consideration for the work done before the divorce.

D. The division of crops into *shilandi* and husband's crop was not affected by the actual work done in the field. For instance, even if the wife looked after the cotton field by herself, the cotton remained the husband's crop.

The new rule, now accepted everywhere, seems to be hard on the wife, but since the great majority of divorce suits are initiated by the wife, the rule expresses public opinion.

Notes

[1] The word *shilandi* is unknown in KS and SS (Districts).

[2] No lawsuit relating to the division of property after a divorce is recorded.

Part III
THE LAW OF SUCCESSION

The treatment on the law of succession which follows contains chapters on the following topics:

1. The Estate and its administration.
2. Intestate Succession.
3. Dispositive and testamentary succession.

A discussion of the nature of the estate was chosen as the starting point of this part to enable the reader to appreciate that the subject matter of succession is not confined to property and the rights and duties inherited in relation to it, but also extends to rights and duties in relation to persons,[1] and also includes succession to headship of the family and other offices. This is brought out in the extracts from *Holleman* on the Shona and Allott on the Ashanti. There follows an account of the administration of estates in customary law, including, in particular, the method of selection of an administrator or successor, and a description of his rights and duties up to the point at which the estate passes to the heirs of the deceased. While the extract quoted from *Cory and Hartnoll* on the Haya concentrates on the technical rules which govern the collection of assets and liabilities as well as the powers and responsibilities of an administrator and executor, the passage taken from *van Warmelo and Phophi* on the Venda is a narrative account of the manner in which the administrator is appointed and the estate is disposed of. Of special interest is *Allott's* description of the manner in which the Ashanti provide for the deposition of a successor.

By far the largest chapter (chapter 16), is devoted to the customary laws of intestacy. The primary division which is maintained here is that between the patrilineal and the matrilineal systems. Within the patrilineal groups (who predominate) there are several categories, and an attempt has been made to illustrate all of these. Thus succession may be (i) elective (see *Rubin* on the Swazi) as opposed to (ii) automatic. Automatic succession may in turn be (iii) universal (*Seymour* on several South African tribes, *Lawrance* on the Iteso, and *Elias* on the Ibo and Yoruba) or (iv) joint, which, in turn may be (v) divisory (see *Cory* on the Sukuma) or (vi) communal (*Armstrong* on the Idoma). It would be wrong to assume, however, that these divisions may be maintained rigidly, since it is often possible to encounter both the universal and the divisory systems on the one hand, and the elective and automatic regimes on the other hand, within the same group. The reason for this overlap between two apparently opposed systems is, in many cases, polygyny, which requires provision to be made for each of the several 'houses' of the deceased polygynist. For example, *Seymour* in his description of the Cape Nguni shows how the heir of a monogamist is his eldest son (i.e. universal) whereas the estate of a polygynist is distributed

[1] I.e. guardianship over women and children. These topics are treated separately in this volume.

among the houses of his wives, each of whose oldest son is the heir to the property of that house (divisory).

In this chapter, we have included excerpts relating to the distribution of the property of deceased women as well as that of men (see, in particular, *Obi* on the Ibo, *Rubin* on the Swazi, *Cory* on the Sukuma, and *Ollenu* on Ghana).

Of special significance, too, is the distinction which is maintained (especially in West Africa) between family property and self-acquired property. This distinction is relevant not only to the rules of intestate succession (see *Elias* on the Ibo and the Yoruba, and *Sarbah* on the Fanti), but is also crucial to any consideration of dispositive and testamentary succession, which subject forms the final section of this chapter. It is evident from a reading of chapter 17 that, contrary to the once general belief that all customary succession was intestate, most customary laws do provide for the making of wills. It is, nevertheless, still true to say that although the *power* of disposition exists, its exercise is circumscribed by the requirement that the will must not depart substantially from the ordinary rules of succession. It is equally clear that a person may substantially affect the operation of the rules of intestate succession by *inter vivos* dispositions, although it should be observed that the distinction between wills and *inter vivos* dispositions is not maintained with any substantial degree of clarity.

Chapter 15

THE ESTATE AND ITS ADMINISTRATION

J. F. Holleman: Shona Customary Law*

The Estate

Introduction: Conception of estate. The traditional Shona conception of 'wealth' differs from ours. Material wants in pre-European times were very limited, and confined to the necessities of life: food, shelter, clothing, and the tools to help produce these. Little was needed to satisfy personal vanity or sense of beauty. It was a peasant population, and agriculture was the principal economic activity. Without exception, every able-bodied person was a farmer. Production was limited by the personal needs of the producers. Since every family unit was normally self-sufficient, there was no regular market for a surplus and hence little incentive to produce a surplus. In practically all other respects, too, the family was self-sufficient. Except for iron tools and weapons, produced by an exclusive guild of ironworkers, people provided their own utensils, as well as their clothing and housing. When necessary or expedient, the help of friends and neighbours was obtained on a reciprocal or communal basis. In some cases, however, individuals with a special skill in such lines as pottery, basketwork or woodcraft, produced more than they personally needed and exchanged their products for some consideration in kind. But such exchanges never amounted to a regular trade. Production along these lines remained essentially a spare-time occupation and was never meant to provide the producer with a regular income. Even those relatively few individuals who were recognized as 'professional' ironworkers, diviners or midwives, followed their professions as a side-line while devoting their main efforts to the production of food for their dependants. In short, the traditional economic pattern was on the whole aimed at self-maintenance and not at profit-making.

If we then find that, in spite of their very limited material needs, the people had a

* J. F. Holleman, *Shona Customary Law*, Oxford University Press, Cape Town, 1952, pp. 318–324.

well-defined idea of 'wealth' and strove to acquire wealth, it is clear that their conception of wealth must be interpreted in terms other than economic. It is no coincidence that the general term for livestock, *pfuma*, has the same root as the words for 'wealth' (*upfumi*) and 'to become rich' (*kupfuma*). Of all property, livestock and especially cattle were considered the most valuable. Whenever people found a demand for an occasional surplus of grain, or for the products of their manual skill, or for their 'professional' services, they would seek to obtain small or big stock in return. In the old Shona society, however, livestock could hardly be regarded as economic property in Western sense, since its economic use was strictly limited. Milk and meat formed no regular part of the daily diet, manure was not used as fertilizer, and until animal-drawn ploughs became popular about a generation ago, cattle had no function in the cultivation of crops. It is true that livestock always had a ready exchange value when a family had to replenish its exhausted stock of staple foods, but such exchanges (*kusunza*) were emergency transactions which formed no part of the normal pattern of family economy.[1] The primary use of livestock was for the purposes of marriages and the propitiation of ancestral spirits. Even stock acquired by women was used for these purposes for the benefit of her own blood-relatives. In these purposes the traditional idea of wealth in Shona society is revealed. Wealth meant the capacity to maintain and reproduce one's own kin-group as an organic unit and to safeguard its spiritual and material well-being by being able to propitiate the ancestral spirits. Prolific reproduction of the family was also the natural way to an enhanced social-status and political power. The acquisition of wealth for any other than these organic and primary needs was meaningless.

This particular conception of wealth established a very close correlation between livestock (especially cattle) and women. Cattle were thought of in terms of wives; wives meant children for one's kin-group; of these children the daughters represented a potential or actual value in cattle which provided wives for the sons and in this manner yet another generation of the family. In this sense cattle, wives and daughters, all having a procreative potentiality, were regarded as interchangeable values.

Nhaka, the Shona term for a deceased's estate, includes, besides livestock and other property, also a man's widows and daughters. This does not mean that women were ever regarded as 'property' in the ordinary sense.[2] But it does mean that the estate was primarily regarded as the capacity of the kin-group to reproduce itself, and that wives and children—that is, their reproductive value—were regarded as natural 'assets' of the estate. Since the reproductive assets of the estate were by far the most important—in fact, at the *kurovaguwa* ceremony of a deceased person the distribution of 'non-reproductive' property was of relatively small importance—the Shona conception of estate was 'organic' rather than 'economic' in Western sense.

Corresponding with these basic ideas, individual rights to property were largely limited to those goods which had a personal value rather than a reproductive value, such as clothing, weapons, tools, ornaments. In respect of such articles everybody, man, woman or child, could exercise a virtually unrestricted right of ownership.

As a rule a person was entitled to the fruits of his or her own labour, and would be able to exercise ownership over property so acquired. But rights to property tended to assume a communal element, either when it resulted from the common efforts of members of the family, or when its usefulness was not confined to the individual, as in the case of foodstuffs and livestock. When property was of such a nature that it served the common interests of the family, these interests had to be considered. Individual claims on the ground of personal production or acquisition would still be recognized, but these claims could be overruled when the wider interests of the family prevailed.

In principle a father could claim the earnings of his unmarried children and exercise control over any property acquired by them. Children capable of doing productive work had to help their parents with the production of food and with other duties. But both boys and girls were encouraged to make their own toys and tools in their spare-time, to cultivate their 'own' tiny plots allotted to them by their father and to use the produce to barter their 'own' fowls and small stock. The fruits of these special efforts were recognized as their own property, to be used for their own individual benefit, often with the idea of marriage in mind. The older boys and girls could thus contribute to their own *rovoro** or trousseau[3]. On this modest scale parents stimulated

* Marriage consideration.

the acquisition of personal property and duly respected their children's individual right to their possessions.

Sometimes a father gave his young son a goat or heifer in recognition of his services as a herd boy or farm hand or he would allot (*kugova*) such an animal to him to find out whether the child was 'lucky' (*a na ropa rakanhaka*, he has good blood), in the hope that the animal would prove unusually prolific under the child's care. Such property, too, was individual in the sense that it was meant primarily as a nest-egg for this particular child, the nucleus of his future *rovoro*, to which the child would be entitled in preference to all others.

A married woman could also acquire personal property by making a special effort *apart* from her duties and responsibilities regarding husband and children. When these activities did not interfere[4] with her normal obligations as a housewife, her husband had no right whatever to *any* property which she acquired by making pots, acting as a midwife, or by growing surplus crops.

It should be noted that property so acquired by a woman did not form part of the estate of her husband's family and the husband therefore had no control over it. This property was vested in the woman as a member of her own matrilineal kin-group. Neither her husband nor his paternal family had a claim to it after her death. Only her own kin-group (i.e. in the first place her children and her full-brothers and full-sisters) were entitled to claim.

Every person, however, would, even on the most modest scale, ultimately seek to invest in that kind of property which represented 'wealth', i.e. livestock, whether small or big. But the essential value of livestock as property was not based on personal usefulness but on its inherent capacity to help maintain and reproduce the kin-group, and in this respect the interests of the individual owners merged with those of his or her blood-relatives. By acquiring livestock a person increased the potential reproductive capacity of the family estate. Consequently, even when such vital assets were individually acquired, the family of the owner (in the case of a married woman: her children and the children of her mother) naturally assumed a legitimate interest in them, thus curbing individual ownership. The owner could not, for instance, dispose of such property without at least consulting the head of his family. The measure of this control varied with the personal status of the owner and the importance attached to the property. An unmarried person would certainly not be allowed to dispose of a goat or calf acquired by his own efforts without the permission of his father. The father could in principle even overrule his child's right and make use of such property against the child's will, but he would in practice never do so except in an emergency when the interests of the family demanded it. Married men or women would also be expected to seek the approval of the head of their respective families before disposing of their own livestock, but since they were no longer directly dependent upon the support of their family they could, if they insisted, act against the advice of their elders. But even a married person could hardly maintain his individual right if the common interests of his family claimed his property. Under such circumstances, to deny one's family the benefit of one's personal property, would amount to a denial of the organic unity of one's family and reveal a complete misconception of 'wealth' and estate.

In short, the nature of the property rather than the manner of its acquisition, determined the character of the rights pertaining to it. Individual rights could be freely exercised over property which had no value in connexion with the organic needs of the kin-group (such as personal clothing, tools, ornaments, weapons).[5] But property such as livestock or essential foodstuffs, which served organic or ritual needs, had communal value and was therefore regarded as part of the family estate. Individual acquisition would give a person a claim to such property in preference to all others. But if the common interests of the family demanded it, these individual rights could be overruled because the very nature of the property precluded a strictly individual conception of ownership.

In this connexion it should also be mentioned that land, whether cultivated or uncultivated, was never regarded as 'wealth' or even 'property' in the ordinary sense,[6] and therefore did not form part of a person's estate. The kind of shifting cultivation practised by the Shona was not conducive to permanent land rights. Informants explained: 'Land is not property (*cinhu*), it is something you use for a time and then abandon.' And although a son or daughter might be given the plot cultivated by the deceased father or mother in preference to other relatives, such arrangements did not form part of the distribution of a deceased person's estate.

Recent times have introduced new aspects in Shona life. Elements of a foreign, Western economic system have become part of everyday life. Taxes must be regularly paid in cash and European factory-made goods are available to people in the tribal reserves. Some of these goods have introduced new forms of economic activity or new ideas of luxury and comfort which are being accepted. The demand for such varied commodities as enamel ware, cotton clothing, woollen blankets, ploughs, bicycles, wagons, safety razors, soap, hurricane lamps and tinned food, is increasing. The traditional scope of economic and personal needs has thus been vastly enlarged. Wealth has acquired a new aspect, expressed in terms of money. Money has become accepted as a means of exchange, so far mainly to satisfy these new needs. People in the Reserves have not yet begun to think in terms of a regular money income, but in order to satisfy specific money needs they will either seek temporary paid employment outside the traditional scheme of economic activity, or (to a very much smaller extent) try to adapt the old forms of production in order to satisfy some of the new needs. They may produce a surplus crop and make use of the market offered to them by local traders to obtain some cash. Making money is still an adventure, an individual excursion away from the traditional sphere, and these efforts inevitably accentuate the individual character of the property so acquired.

Western economics have killed the old iron industry and have made Native pottery and wooden household utensils all but obsolete. But cattle have acquired a new value as draught animals in the cultivation of fields, as a means of obtaining cash to meet economic needs. Local butcher shops (their number is increasing) buy livestock and sell meat by the pound, thus making it possible for the people to consume meat more regularly without wrecking the family estate.

The new economy has gained a definite foothold in Shona society. It has created a sphere of its own, in a sense separate from and in addition to the traditional conceptions of wealth and property which, at least in the Reserves, have so far held their own. The need for cash, for instance, has added a mercenary element to the marriage transaction by introducing a cash *rutsambo*.[7] Christianity on the one hand and vastly increased material needs on the other are restricting polygyny and have thus curbed the organic needs of the family. But reproduction of the family has remained the primary and powerful urge in Shona life. There is no sign yet that the *rovoro* institution is weakening, and cattle, in spite of their enhanced economic value, are still primarily identified with *rovoro* purposes. Consequently, the reproductive potentialities of livestock as well as of wives and children are still regarded as prominent assets of the family estate.

As long as these traditional values are a living reality in Shona life the emphasis in a discussion of estate must necessarily fall upon its reproductive and communal aspects. The legal principles governing the estate are almost exclusively concerned with that portion which represents the reproductive capacity of the kin-group. *This portion of the estate is an integral and organic part of the kin-group, and the legal principles which govern it, are a natural corollary of the law of kinship.*

From the outset a sharp distinction must be made between *patri-estate* and *matri-estate*. The patri-estate comprises those assets which are considered to have originated from or been acquired by men or women as members of a patrilineal unit (patri-group), assets which are meant to serve their common and individual interests, and therefore devolve according to principles of patrilineal succession. The matri-estate, on the other hand, consists of such property (or the tangible assets derived from such property) as has been acquired by a woman (almost invariably married) as a consequence of the marriage of her daughter; and property which has been acquired by a woman in her own right and by her personal economic activities. In contrast with the patri-estate, the assets of the matri-estate are meant to serve the interests of members of the matrilineal blood-group, and therefore devolve upon such members according to matrilineal principles.

The distinction between the two estates is of the utmost importance because they form separate and in a sense opposing entities, in spite of the fact that practically every person is a member of both his or her patri-group and matri-group, and therefore has an interest in both estates.

Notes

[1] There is little evidence of an institution amongst the Shona corresponding to the *ukusisa* system amongst the south-east Nguni, whereby a wealthy cattle owner, by lending out cattle to others, could greatly enhance his social status and influence as a creditor. Amongst the Shona a cattle owner may leave his stock with a friend or relative when he has no one to look after his herd. But in such transactions (*kuronggedza*) it is the owner who becomes indebted to the receiver because the latter is entitled to a goat or heifer (depending upon the size of the herd) as herding fee (*upfuro*).

[2] For instance, the common terms for 'possession' or 'property' (*zwinhu, nhumbi*) do not apply to human beings. Although, generally speaking, women had no independent legal status, they had definite rights and privileges and were never regarded as chattels.

[3] Nowadays even very young children are encouraged to cultivate a vegetable plot, catch rock-rabbits or keep a few fowls, and so earn the means to buy a pocket-knife or pair of khaki-shorts, a length of cotton, a comb or mirror. Although a child is expected to consult its parents before making these transactions, the latter will look with pride and favour upon such youthful enterprise and fully respect the child's right to its own property.

[4] When a woman neglected her wifely duties her husband could curtail her activities but he would hesitate to lay claim to any property acquired by her for fear of her mystical retributions after her death.

[5] Except certain heirlooms.

[6] The common terms for property or possession do not apply to land.

[7] In the areas investigated there is no sign yet of a tendency to pay cash instead of cattle for *rovoro*, but near the towns and in urban areas a cash *rovoro* has become a common occurrence (see: H. Cripps, 'Should *lobolo* be restricted by Legislation?' *Nada* XXIV (1947) pp. 41–4).

A. N. Allott: The Ashanti Law of Property*

The Estate

The estate of a deceased will consist of self-acquired and inherited property held by deceased, excluding only any property of which he may have disposed *inter vivos* and any interests personal to him and lapsing at his death (e.g. a tenancy personal to him). The estate will include:

(*a*) Interests in land.
(*b*) Interests in movables.
(*c*) Rights and duties over persons: wives, children (and in former times slaves and pawns).
(*d*) Cash.
(*e*) Claims by deceased against third parties for debt.
(*f*) Debts left by deceased.

The estate in Ashanti law typically includes obligations as well as rights, debts as well as assets. In the past the successor succeeded to the debts, and was liable to pay them even where they exceeded the disposable assets; but in very recent times there has been a trend away from this principle.

Equally the successor succeeded to the obligations which deceased owed to his dependants. By the custom of widow-inheritance the successor succeeded to the wives left by deceased (though the family might decide to distribute them among the family), and the successor stepped into the shoes of deceased as regards the duty to maintain such wives and also the children of the deceased. Succession could therefore be onerous and unprofitable, and a sucessor might choose to decline the succession outright on that account.

Entry into Succession

The successor, or anyone else sharing in the estate, does not enter automatically upon his inheritance. It is at a family meeting called after the decease (very often it might be on the eighth day after) that the assets and debts of the deceased are ascertained, and it is decided who should succeed to them. The successor (and other participants)

* A. N. Allott, 'The Ashanti Law of Property', in *Zeitschrift fur vergleichende Rechtswissenschaft*, 1966, pp. 181–184.

are then placed in possession by the family. If the deceased has made an oral will (*samanseɛ*), it would be at this meeting that it would be decided whether to uphold it or not; if yes, then the beneficiary (often the child of the deceased) would be given the property bequeathed to him at this time.

The Choice of the Successor

Enough has already been said on the general principles of Ashanti succession to show that the circle of potential successors primarily coincides with the members of the deceased's *abusua* or matrilineal family, and secondarily that a member of the same segment or sub-lineage of the family as deceased has a prior claim to be selected. Within this broad framework, the ranking of the kin depends principally on the closeness of their relationship to deceased. Thus a brother by the same mother as deceased (two steps in the family tree) would take in preference to a sister's son (three steps). A classificatory brother (i.e. a cousin) would be preferred to a more remote lineally related kinsman.

Rattray* says that deceased's mother's brother (i.e. his maternal uncle) has an absolute and undisputed right to succeed in theory; I very much doubt if this is correct. Rattray adds that he would in practice waive his claim in favour of other potential claimants, notably elder and junior brother; mother's sister's son; sister's son, etc. Ashanti succession is often characterized as succession by nephews, but in fact brothers have priority over nephews, as will be seen. However, there is no point in pursuing the full table provided by Rattray any further, as it is most likely that a family will (once they find they have to go outside those who are fellow-members of deceased's minimal sub-lineage) have present in their minds an exact and lengthy table of heirs when deciding who is to succeed.

Failing the free-born, slaves and 'domestics' may come in to succeed.

Rattray stated in *Ashanti*† that a man succeeds to a man and a woman a woman. This statement is not completely correct; a woman only succeeds to a woman in respect of those articles which are peculiarly feminine.‡ In practice, there are instances where a woman succeeds to a man and vice versa, though these cases are rare.

The succession to certain special crafts and professions is peculiar; thus succession to the position of *okyeame* (chief's spokesman) and to the craft of goldsmith§ goes in the male line [cf. also Fortes||].

Deposition of Successor

A successor duly appointed by the family can be deposed by the family if they consider that he has grossly mismanaged the property or has been guilty of bad behaviour to the family. The family do not exercise a day-to-day supervision over the conduct of the successor in connexion with his inherited property, however. The sort of conduct likely to provoke each action would include:

(i) Wasting the property, i.e. permanently depreciating the value.

(ii) Attempting to alienate the property without the family's consent.

(iii) Refusing to assist other members of the family where possible (in other words, where there is unused land to spare, and the successor is approached by another member of the family for a loan of the land, he is under a moral obligation to accede to the request if he can).

(iv) Contumelious behaviour to the family, and especially to its senior members.

A successor is not required, on pain of forfeiture, to make profitable use of the property he inherits; nor are any specific dues payable out of the property to the family or its head.

* *Religion and Art in Ashanti*, pp. 41 *et seq.*

† *Ibid.*, p. 40.

‡ *Ashanti Law and Constitution*, p. 337.

§ *Religion and Art in Ashanti*, p. 301.

|| 'Kinship and Marriage among the Ashanti', in *African Systems of Kinship and Marriage*, ed. M. Fortes and E. E. Evans-Pritchard, p. 267 n 3.

H. Cory and M. M. Hartnoll: Customary Law of the Haya*

Assets and Liabilities

General rules. While a man's body is lying in his house awaiting burial his administrator (*ishento*) as far as possible claims assets outstanding and acknowledges debts outstanding.

The acknowledgment of these assets and liabilities by the persons concerned is considered binding.

There is no time limit for the presentation of their claims by creditors to the estate or *vice versa.*

Claims should be presented during the three months interim between the death of a man and the distribution of his estate, but a claim which comes in after this time cannot be disputed on the grounds that it is now too late (cf. proverb '*Eibanja tilyunda*' a debt cannot rot).

When the assets in hand are greater than the liabilities the latter are paid before the estate is distributed.

Both claims and debts are inheritable.

Collection of assets outstanding. Assets due to the estate after the distribution of property are distributed among the heirs in the customary manner, the Musika receiving the greater part, the Mainuka and lesser heirs receiving proportionately.

ILLUSTRATION: After the winding up of an estate there remained to be collected outstanding assets to the value of Shs. 150/-, which were divided among the three heirs. The Musika received the right to collect Shs. 75/-, The Mainuka received the right to collect Shs. 50/-, The Kyagati received the right to collect Shs. 25/-. Each was responsible for collecting his own debts.

Such assets may be divided among the heirs at the distribution of the property, in which case it is the duty of the heir to whom a credit has been alloted, himself to collect his dues from the debtor in question.

Repayment of Debts. Debts acknowledged before distribution are repaid from the assets, which are used in the following order:

1. Money in cash.
2. Coffee in store.
3. All claims either paid or outstanding.
4. Cattle.
5. Land.

Cloth, food stores and tools cannot be forcibly sold to repay debts.

If, after everything possible has been sold, debts still remain, the Musika, if he is a son, is responsible for them.

Debts which are acknowledged but not repaid before distribution are distributed among the heirs in the same way as are outstanding assets, provided that the total debts are less than the total assets.

Debts acknowledged after distribution of the estate are the liability of the Musika alone.

ILLUSTRATION: after the winding up of an estate there remained debts to be paid off to the value of Shs. 96/-.

Assets to be collected amounted to Shs. 150/-.

Debts and assets were divided among the heirs thus:

The Musika	inherited assets	Shs. 75/-,	and debts	Shs. 48/-
The Mainuka	,,	,, ,, 50/-,	,, ,,	,, 32/-
The Kyagati	,,	,, ,, 25/-,	,, ,,	,, 16/-

Each was responsible for the collection of his assets and the payment of his debts.

Creditors who first present their claims are paid first.

When several claims are presented together, debts first contracted take priority.

As many debts as possible are paid and every debt is paid in full. The estate cannot be distributed pro rata among the creditors.

Business obligations. If the deceased was part owner of a business, his heirs cannot

* H. Cory and M. M. Hartnoll, *Customary Law of the Haya*, Lund Humphries for International African Institute, 1945, pp. 26–28 and pp. 42–45.

claim from his partner the capital put into the business by the deceased, but they inherit his assets and liabilities in the firm at the time of his death.

Appointment of Administrator

When a man dies it is the duty of his nearest relatives to come to his house.

If a man dies suddenly and his relatives are not near at hand, the village headman will immediately appoint a blood-brother of the deceased to bury him and to look after his property until relatives arrive, or failing a blood-brother the Native Authority buries him and takes charge of his property.

It is the right of the eldest brother to act as administrator. If there is no brother, or he is for some reason incapacitated from acting, the assembled relatives will choose from among them the one most capable of carrying out these duties.

If no paternal relatives exist, a blood-brother may be appointed as administrator. Otherwise the Native Authority (Mwami) appoints a reliable elder as administrator; but the claims of a very distant paternal relative are preferred before an outsider is appointed.

Duties of Administrator

The administrator must immediately make an inventory of the property of the deceased in the presence of two relatives as witnesses.

The property of the deceased is vested in the administrator as soon as this inventory is made and his responsibility lasts until the property is distributed.

QUOTATION: D.O.'s appeal No. 27 of 1933.
Mugula *v.* Lyagoba.
Mugula was appointed administrator of the property of Ibrahim. When Ibrahim died he left a book which showed that two head of cattle were in the care of Lyagoba. Lyagoba refused to show these cattle to Mugula. 1 cow died and Lyagoba informed the son and father of Ibrahim, but not Mugula, who afterwards sued Lyagoba for two head of cattle. It was held that all property of the deceased is vested in the administrator, and that Lyagoba should have informed Mugula and not the son and father of the deceased.

The property is distributed after three months (In Ihangiro and Karagwe the period is usually shorter.) The lapse of three months is insisted upon so that heirs who live at a distance have time to arrive before the distribution of the inheritance and further so that all claims and debts can be presented. Nobody is entitled before this time to claim any payment of his share.

The distribution of the property by the administrator is not looked upon as final.

QUOTATION. D.O.'s appeal No. 10 of 1938.
Lauriani *v.* Lugeyamba.
These men were brothers. Their father's property was distributed by the clan elders. Lugeyamba, the Mainuka, was not satisfied and filed a suit for re-distribution, which was granted.

Any heir may ask for a redistribution within a reasonable time, if he is dissatisfied. He has two possible ways of procuring this:

(*a*) He can invoke the help of his Mkungu, Mwami or Omukama (village headman, sub-chief or chief), as private arbitrators, in which case two elders are usually sent to make the new distribution.

(*b*) He can take action in Court against the administrator, in which case if it is proved that the administrator failed in his duty he will be made to pay the Court fees and a redistribution will be ordered.

QUOTATION: D.O.'s appeal No. 1/P 1/15 of 1937.
Bibi Kokulamuka *v.* Lwilemera.
Kokulamuka filed a suit against Lwilemera, the Musika, in the interest of her son Theodor a minor, the Mainuka; the heirs were half-brothers. She stated that the Musika received too big a share in proportion to that of her son. The Musika inherited 22 tenants and the Mainuka only 3. It was held that a redistribution should be granted.

Rights of Administrator

The administrator has no claim to any compensation for his work except in Kiziba, Karagwe and Ihangiro.

Kiziba, Karagwe, Ihangiro. The administrator has the right to claim a share of the moveable property in payment of his service. His share is called obusikisa and the amount is not fixed, but is in proportion to the size of the property.

EXPLANATION: If there are 20 head of cattle for division the administrator may take one head. If there are several wives left, he may take one. If there are Shs. 70/- left he may take Shs. 10/- unless there are many children in which case he receives only Shs. 5/-. If there are only Shs. 20/- left he gets Shs. 1/-.

The administrator himself proposes the amount he may take on the day of distribution and the next of kin present consider his claims. He has no claim for any share of the real property.

In districts where the administrator is entitled to no reward for his service he is always an adult, but in Kiziba, Karagwe and Ihangiro where he receives payment, a minor may become administrator. He will be represented by an adult relative, but the fees are due to him.

The administrator has the right with the consent of the Musika to take some money or a goat or a head of cattle from the estate for the entertainment of guests during the period of mourning. He has to prove that anything he takes is spent for this purpose. He can spend whatever he thinks necessary provided that he can account for his expenditure.

Executor.

(*Musigire. Karagwe: Mulagwa.*)

The testator has the right to appoint by will any person he likes as executor. This person need not belong to his family.

The property of a testator is vested in the executor as soon as the testament is made known and the executor installed.

If an executor dies before he has wound up an estate either the Chief or the family appoints a new executor.

If the executor appointed in the will is not present in the district at the time of the death, some one will be appointed by the Native Authority to take over the administration under the control of the N.A. until the return of the executor.

NOTE: As it is clear from the fact that the testator has appointed an outsider executor that he did not wish his family to undertake this duty, no one of his relatives will be appointed by the N.A. to act for the absent executor.

If at the expiration of the usual time after the death of the testator and before distribution, the executor appointed in the will is still absent from the district, the person who has been put in temporarily under the N.A. will conclude the executor's duties.

For the rest the rules referring to administrators are to be applied with regard to the executor.

J. J. van Warmelo and W. M. D. Phophi: Venda Law*

Family Meetings to Appoint Heir and Arrange Estate.

1. *When meetings are held.* The two questions, who is to be heir and how the estate is to be divided, are commonly decided on the day of the *dzumo*,† or the next, because all the important relatives have to attend the latter to 'remove the shadow of death', as they say.

In other cases the *dzumo* is held but the appointment of the heir postponed because they say, 'We are still in mourning for our relative who has left us in sorrow and depri-

* J. J. van Warmelo and W. M. D. Phophi, *Venda Law*, Government Printer, Pretoria, South Africa, 1948, pp. 705–713 and 721–723.

† The day set aside for observance of rites associated with inheritance; it occurs approximately 3 months after the death of the deceased.

vation. We shall settle this matter another day.' So they perform the *dzumo* rites and then disperse.

The reason for thus postponing the appointment of a successor is that they fear there will be no proper mourning for the deceased. In other cases they fear scandal to the effect that they themselves killed the deceased to get hold of his property, or thirdly they postpone the day because of strife over the estate. If there is the feeling that a dispute is pending, they all agree to postpone the decision in order to gain time, for each party hopes to have manoeuvred into a stronger position when the clash becomes open.

The period allowed to elapse before appointing the heir is not uniform, but does not exceed a year. A common interval is around and up to six months.

Sometimes the reason for postponing the decision in cases of dispute is the intention of engaging a medicine-man to kill the person championed by the other party.

Another thing that often prevents the heir from being appointed at the *dzumo* is the absence of some of the relatives, especially the seniors, viz., the uncles and the principal *makhadzi*.*

2. *Non-attendance by important relatives*. It happens that the *makhadzi* or *khotsi-munene*† have been on bad terms with their bereaved relatives and in order to embarrass them stay away from the meeting for the appointment of the heir. Then the elders of the family send someone to mollify them, sometimes with a present of a sheep or goat, and persuade them to come and attend the installation of the heir. But other circumstances may prevent their coming, for example a death, sickness or other misfortunes of theirs or of the heir.

3. *Convener of meetings; by whom attended*. Whilst the actual decisions about the heir and the estate are taken by a small number of the most important members of the family, the subsequent installation is a public affair in which the heir is made known to all and sundry.

The family elders who meet to decide about the heir are the elder and younger brothers of the deceased's father, the *makhadzis*, the sisters and the elder and younger brothers of the deceased.

The most senior of these, seeing the mourning is over, says to his relatives, 'The family should not be left without a master any longer. Let us meet on such and such a day to put the deceased's children in their places, so that the creditors who want to have their debts paid can find someone to settle with them, and debtors have someone to follow them up and make them pay.'

Having thus informed his relations, he goes on his own to the grainbins of the deceased and takes out grain to give the widows for beer making, so that the relatives who will attend the proceedings to confirm the appointment may slake their thirst and not have to drink water when food is available.

The local headman is also invited to the public installation. If it is the headman himself that has died, the *nduna*‡ of the county who is his immediate superior has to be invited.

Before the discussion as to who should be made heir takes place there are secret eye-to-eye talks in private. This is where the disputes about the estate start.

The disputes are always between the *makhadzi* and the uncles, the elder or younger brothers of the deceased, or between his sons who cannot agree as to who should succeed or who claim the succession for themselves.

The *makhadzi* referred to here, who has such a great say in these matters, is the eldest full sister of the deceased; if she is a half-sister her position and influence are due to her being the eldest. The *khotsi-munene* who plays the largest part is the nearest full brother of the deceased. However, if there is another brother who takes precedence to him by virtue of his greater age, even though of another hut, then the latter has the greatest say in appointing the heir.

If there is a dispute between the brothers the eldest may simply announce, 'I appoint so-and-so as heir. Let whoever disputes this start the quarrel'. Even though there are

* The oldest full sister of the deceased.

† Deceased's younger brother(s)—actual or classificatory. In this case it is the full brother of the deceased who is nearest to him in age. But see infra.

‡ Ward-head.

no signs of a difference, he may still do so [i.e. appoint the heir without consulting the others. He would be ill advised to do this however, unless he were pretty sure of his ground].

Relatives who were on bad terms with the deceased, especially those suspected of having caused his death [by witchcraft] are seldom allowed to attend these private meetings because of the ill feeling that exists between them. They are not even invited, for an heir is chosen by the relatives who were friendly with the deceased. However, when he is formally installed by putting him on the mat, anyone who likes can come and those relations can also attend if they want to.

When they sit in conclave about the heir, the elder and younger brothers of the deceased attend, besides the *makhadzi*, the father and mother of the deceased, but they seldom total ten persons. Usually there are only three to five. In these private meetings the *khotsi-munene* and *makhadzi* determine most of what shall be done. Anyone they don't like they keep at a distance. If that person should be in the right, he lets them do what they like, and stays away. Or he pretends to make trouble in order that the matter may go to court, if they chose the wrong person.

The reason they give for not allowing an elder of the family to attend this meeting is always some imputation against his character or that he wrongfully disputes their choice of an heir, even though this is not the case.

If an action follows, that person who is found to have wrongfully disputed the succession may be fined for having begun strife, and be made to pay a beast or goat, which is eaten by the court, or he may be expelled from the village. [In practice the majority of relatives nearest to the deceased, if they stand together, will always have their own way. There would be little point in the court's deciding otherwise. The senior relatives have a beautifully simple way of disposing of a son's claim, be it never so valid. They tell the court: *Ro vhuya nae* 'We came back with him', which means 'The divining dice pointed him out as having caused the deceased's death'. There is no disputing this statement, as there were no neutral witnesses at the séance with the diviner. The son cannot ask the court to send a messenger to the diviner to ask him what he actually said. That is quite unthinkable. His only remedy would be to challenge them to go with him to another diviner. But the court's attitude is always that it is much more important to uphold family or group solidarity than to mete out mere justice.]

4. *Ceremony of appointing the heir*. Just as they slaughter for the *dzumo* an animal called *ṭhovhosa* (mourning beast), so for the heir's appointment another one is killed which is termed *phaladza-maanga* (vulture-scatterer). Its meat is cut up and put into pots to cook, and is eaten with a great quantity of porridge cooked from the maize supplies left by the deceased. Whilst the meat and porridge are being cooked, the beer is drunk nearby and the heir is installed. All the people assemble in the enclosure of the principal hut. The heir is put on a mat in the centre of the open place, amongst his younger brothers, his sisters and other relatives. The *khotsi-munene* speaking first, points out the heir to the people, and is followed by the *makhadzi* who says more or less the same thing.

The *khotsi-munene* addresses all those present in a loud voice and says, 'Our relative So-and-so whom we have buried, is dead. He will not return but before he died he left us this egg of his. This is now the kraal head. Whoever has troubles must come and tell him. Whoever is an unpaid creditor of the deceased must speak to him. Whoever borrowed something from the deceased, before his death, let him repay it to this one here. He is the kraal head left behind.' When he has spoken thus, they utter ululations of joy because their deceased So-and-so has come to life again.

5. *Refusal to Accept Inheritance*. Sometimes the proper heir refuses to accept the position, though no one challenges his right and there is no trouble whatever. His reason may be unmotivated fear of being killed by envious people, or having been scared by threats or hints, 'If you take the inheritance, you will be killed'. If younger than his half-brothers, an heir may refuse for fear of trouble and suggest that the heirship be given to an elder brother from a hut earned by the deceased himself [the proper heir being from the *dzekiso** hut].

* The hut of the wife whose brideprice is paid by her husband's mother.

But sometimes the heir refuses the position though there is no sign of a dispute. This may be because the father died a pauper or with many debts. Sometimes again it is the heir's mother who fears for his life or sees there is nothing in the estate except liabilities and says, 'There is nothing in the inheritance, let my son be passed over'. In that case her whole hut is passed over in favour of the next son, if her sons agree with what she says. Sometimes again the heir thinks his health is not good enough to allow him to discharge the duties of a family head and so he refuses the honour.

If the reluctant one cannot be persuaded, they appoint the next in order of precedence. If the mother refused on behalf of her children, the heirship passes to the next hut.

6. *Who disposes of estate.* After the semi-public meeting at which the heir is made known to the countryside and the family at large, there is another private family gathering, or several if need be, at which questions relating to the estate are settled, goods divided, gifts made, and the future of the widows arranged. There is no fixed procedure, much depending on the few senior members of the family who have most say, whether they agree or tend to be grasping, whether they come from far away or can come back next day, and so forth.

When handing over the estate to the heir, the elders admonish him, 'You must not waste this property, because it is there to provide for the whole village, and you are the administrator. If we see you squandering it we will take it away from you, and give it to another'. For this reason he consults these elders before taking any step of importance, or else first does what is necessary and tells them about it afterwards. It is rare, however, for a man to be deprived of an estate once it is given him, because of mismanagement or any other reason whatever.

Chapter 16

INTESTATE SUCCESSION

(a) Patrilineal

T. O. Elias: The Groundwork of Nigerian Law*

A. *The Yoruba Rules of Inheritance*

We may conveniently begin our examination of the evidence here with our old friend, *Lewis* v. *Bankole*,[1] in which, it will be remembered, the following propositions relevant to succession among the Lagos Yorubas were laid down by the Full Court:

(i) When the founder of a family dies, the eldest surviving son called the 'Dawodu', succeeds to the headship of the family with all that implies, including residence and the giving of orders in his father's house or compound;

(ii) On the death of the eldest surviving son, the next eldest surviving child of the founder, whether male of female, is the proper person to succeed as head of the family;

(iii) If there is going to be any important dealing with family property all branches of the family must be consulted, and representation on the family council is also *per stirpes* according as there are wives with children.

(iv) The division is into equal shares between the respective branches, regard being had to any property already received by any of the founder's children during his lifetime.

(v) The founder's grandchildren only succeed to such rights as their immediate parents had in the family property.

(vi) The founder's compound or house is usually regarded as the 'family house' which must be preserved for posterity.

In thus upholding the existing rules of inheritance with the help of Lagos chiefs and other witnesses from outside Lagos, Osborne, C.J., remarked:[2] 'That the present Lagos customs are modifications of the original Yoruba customs there is little reason to doubt; and the evidence as to those Yoruba customs is of undoubted value, as showing how far the general principles remain intact in Lagos, and how far they have been modified to meet present requirements.'[3] After observing that the eldest surviving son is the proper person to succeed the deceased founder of a family, the learned Chief Justice continued: 'This seems to be *a well-established rule both in Lagos and in other parts of Yorubaland.* It is after the death of the Dawodu that we begin to find variations; according to the plaintiff's witnesses, *by Yoruba custom the other sons of the founder of the family are taken in turn, and then the sons of the Dawodu and other son's sons, the headship being ever kept in the male line.* One explanation of this rule is that the women on marriage go and live with their husbands; another is that a woman is only "part of a man". . . . On the other hand the view of the Lagos chiefs is that it is the eldest child, whether male or female, who becomes head after the Dawodu.' And in the case before him His Honour saw no reason why the female plaintiff should not become the family head since the chiefs appointed by the Court to go into the matter described her as appearing to them 'gentle and intelligent and capable, in fact, she should be the mother and the guiding head of this family'.[4] This requirement of mental and cultural competence as a pre-requisite to the family headship, like the patriarchal principle itself, will be met with again when we come to deal with rules obtaining in the Eastern as well as the Northern regions of the country.

As a complement to the foregoing principles it is necessary to examine a few more cases in which other aspects of the customary rules of inheritance have been considered by the Courts.

We should next consider the rights, if any, of surviving parents in their child's property,

* T. O. Elias, *The Groundwork of Nigerian Law*, Routledge & Kegan Paul, 1954, pp. 216–231.

as against brothers and sisters of the whole or half-blood. In *Adedoyin* v. *Simeon and ors.*,[5] the plaintiff was the mother of a woman who died intestate (i.e. under customary law) and without issue. The defendants were the deceased's surviving three half-sisters, all four of them having inherited from their common father an estate the subject of this action. The three defendants claimed the whole estate on the ground that their deceased sister's share had lapsed into the residue for their benefit. This plea also amounted to the claim of a right of survivorship as if all four sisters had held the estate on an English joint tenancy. The plaintiff, the deceased sister's mother, disputed the three sister's contention and claimed to be entitled to her daughter's share of the property. *Held*: that, under Yoruba law and custom of inheritance, the mother must take her deceased daughter's share to the exclusion of the deceased sisters of the half-blood. The judgment is, however, of more general interest on account of the recorded evidence of certain important witnesses to the Yoruba customary rules of inheritance which will therefore be reproduced here:

'I have had the advantage of having the opinion of Chief Obanikoro, Chief Ojora, and Mr. Wilson the Interpreter in this Court, and I find that they are all agreed that under native law and custom in Lagos, and throughout Yorubaland, the personal property of Comfort Ajayi would on her death pass to her mother and to her mother alone. In reply to questions put by the Court, Chief Obanikoro stated:

"(1) If a child dies leaving personal property, *her father being dead but her mother alive*, the property will pass to the mother, *provided the child has no brother or sister being children of her mother*.

"(2) If the *father is alive as well as the mother* the property would be shared between the father and the mother, although the father would generally invite the mother to take the whole.

"(3) If the *father had been alive as well as the mother and also a brother and sister of the child by the same mother* the property would be divided between the brother and sister and *the parents would take nothing*. Half-brothers and half-sisters being the children of a different mother would not take any share. It makes no difference if the personal property was given to or left to the child by her father."

'These answers both Chief Ojora and Mr. Wilson agreed were correct statements of native law and custom *throughout* Yorubaland.'[6]

But it should not be inferred as a general rule that a mother can always inherit the share of her child who has died intestate and without issue. Thus, in *George & anor.* v. *Fajore*,[7] the defendant was the widow of a testator whose surviving executors were the plaintiffs. It appeared that the testator had left real property in Lagos to twelve named persons, one of whom was the widow's son who had been allotted a portion of the premises by the executors. This son died in 1931, leaving a widow and a son who also died in 1936. After her grandson's death, the defendant took possession of her son's allotment, to recover which the plaintiffs then sued this action. It was held (1) that succession to the testator's devised property was in the circumstances of the case governed by local customary law under which a mother could not acquire any interest upon the death of her son and failure of his issue: (2) that, in any case, the defendant could not succeed in the absence of proof of the death of her grandson's mother (i.e. her son's widow) who would be preferred to the defendant grandmother. Two important results of this case seem to be: (*a*) a mother cannot inherit her deceased child's allotted but not yet partitioned share of the family property; (*b*) there is here a tacit recognition of a widow's claim to her deceased husband's allotted portion; at least, to such of his rights thereto as are recognised under local law and custom. One short reason for this exclusion of the testator's widow in such a case is probably that she already has her own apartments in her husband's house which she can retain for her life; another is that succession to a deceased member's portion of the family land is by customary law given to that member's child or children, if any. On this analysis, the implied recognition in the above case of the deceased son's widow's right to his share of the family property would appear to be doubtful, for she would have had her own rooms during her husband's life-time and from these no one could have lawfully ejected her for her life—unless, of course, she merely intended to continue living in the common apartments previously occupied together with her husband. If she should decide to leave her husband's house after his death, the apartments would no doubt revert to the head of the family for necessary re-allocation or otherwise.

Under customary law, a husband cannot ordinarily inherit his deceased wife's share of her family property. This follows logically from the well-known principle that no one member of the family has any separate and alienable estate in the family property to which a stranger to the family can succeed on that member's death. Rules of inheritance apart, local sentiments would frown upon the idea of a scape-grace husband aspiring to a share in his deceased wife's family's property. Thus, in *Caulcrick* v. *Harding*,[8] property was left by a man to his three daughters, one of whom was the plaintiff's deceased wife. The plaintiff husband claimed a one-third share of the property in virtue of his deceased wife's right to such one-third share. Tew, J., held that the plaintiff had no such right as the family property was, under local law and custom, inalienable. It was not an English tenancy in common.

Another aspect of the customary law of inheritance is illustrated by *Andre* v. *Agbedi*[9] in which the question arose as to the succession to the property of a deceased intestate who had left him surviving two minors, one of whom was an uterine brother while the other was a half-sister born to his father in lawful wedlock with another woman. The issue to be decided then was whether the deceased's half-brother by the same mother or the deceased's half-sister by the same father was the proper person to inherit his estate. Webber, J., observed:[10] 'I am inclined to the opinion that the trend of the decisions is in favour of the uterine brother succeeding to some share of the inheritance. On other hand I cannot disregard the evidence of a chief who lays it down that the deceased's father's family is entitled to inherit.' The learned Judge, therefore, held that both the uterine brother and the half-sister must succeed to the inheritance in equal shares. In the present case the evidence of Chief Amodu Tijani as to succession was that 'if a child leaves property the family on his father's side will inherit'. But the case is different where the child has inherited the property from his or her mother who has herself inherited it from her own family. This point will become clear from a consideration of the next case.

Thus, in *Idewu* v. *Hausa & ors.*,[11] a man, Idewu, died in 1895, leaving three daughters, one of whom died intestate before the allocation of the land to the three branches, but the deceased daughter's third part was given to her surviving son, Belo, who through his father collected rents therefrom until his death in 1923. Belo's father thereupon claimed to succeed to his son's share, alleging a previous partition of Idewu's land in virtue of which his son had acquired a separate estate in his own portion capable of devolving upon him (the father) as next-of-kin. The plaintiff, on behalf of herself and other members of the Idewu family, invoked local law and custom whereby on the death of a man intestate without issue, family property inherited from his mother reverts to the mother's family. It was decided by Carey, J., that, in the absence of partition to Belo, the onus of proving which was on Belo's father who alleged it, Belo's allotment should revert on his death without issue to Belo's mother's family and not to Belo's father.

On the question of partition of the family property we have observed in *Sule & ors.* v. *Ajisegiri*[12] that the tendency is to hold that the children now take equal shares regardless of sex, thus in effect disregarding *dicta* in *Lopez* v. *Lopez*[13] that female rights in family property might be different from those of males. When *Lopez* v. *Lopez* came up on appeal to the Supreme Court, Combe, C.J., after stating that in the olden days the rights of daughters differed from those of sons and that the position had not changed up to the date of his judgment, continued:[14] 'However that may be, females undoubtedly have rights and the Court must have jurisdiction to make such order as may be necessary to protect a female in the enjoyment of her rights. . . . A case might arise in which an order of partition would be the only effective means of ensuring that a female and her issue shall live on her father's lands without being disturbed by other members of the family, and I can see no reason for holding that the Court could not order partition in such a case.' The occasion here envisaged arose in *Sule & ors.* v. *Ajisegiri* where the plaintiffs claimed partition and sale of six properties which had been left to their mother and the defendant, their mother's brother, as part of the undistributed estate of their grandfather. The defendant asserted that as a male child he was entitled to a larger share than the plaintiffs' mother, but Butler Lloyd in the Divisional Court held that the plaintiffs were entitled to demand partition in right of their mother and that the division of the property or its proceeds must be equally between their mother and the defendant, without regard to sex.

So inexorable in their operation are the rules of customary inheritance that land acquired by an individual as absolute private property, whether purchased with his own money or obtained as such in consequence of partition of family land, devolves upon his children as family property under the customary law of succession. Thus, in *Ogunmefun* v. *Ogunmefun*,[15] the plaintiff's grandfather died intestate, leaving a fee simple estate to his children only two of whom, however, survived him with issue. The plaintiff's mother was the sole surviving child of her father when she purported to devise by will her share of the estate. It was held that the purported devise was invalid, as until partition plaintiff's mother's succession rights were inalienable by her under the customary rules of inheritance which must be taken as governing the form of land tenure left by the intestate grandfather. The plaintiff, therefore, succeeded to his mother's share to the exclusion of the intended devisees.

Enough has now been noticed of the judicial findings as to the customary rules of inheritance and succession. Let us see next the extent to which these may be qualified or supplemented by evidence from other available sources. And, for this, one naturally turns in the first place to A. K. Ajisafe's little book on *The Laws and Customs of the Yoruba People*.[16] There the writer asserts the patrilineal principle of succession, but believes that goods and land of a deceased person are shared and distributed according to rank, title or age, the eldest taking the largest share and the other children's shares follow in a descending order of magnitude. While adopted children cannot inherit from their adoptive parents, slaves of good behaviour who had also spent much money on behalf of the family on certain ceremonial occasions formerly could inherit, probably because as the writer has observed elsewhere[17] a slave who had lived for some time in his master's compound and behaved well was considered a member of the family; but in modern times only blood relations can inherit. One other important observation made by the writer is that bequests of both movable and immovable property might be made or promised by the deceased before his death and these would normally be respected and carried out afterwards. This would seem to be a kind of *donatio mortis causa* of the deceased's goods or an *ante mortem* oral declaration calculated to institute or disinherit a particular person in the matter of succession to land.

Something similar to this last point has been recorded[18] by W. Price in his *Land Tenure in the Yoruba Provinces* to which we must now turn for a more extended treatment of the subject of succession rights. On the whole the general pattern of the rules of inheritance as outlined above is much the same as that described by Mr. Price in this his Report,[19] prepared by him in 1933 as an Administrative Officer, to the Government of Nigeria. It is, however, useful to make a note of certain peculiar features there recorded.

Firstly, the successor to the family-headship was usually the next younger brother of the deceased head, so chosen because he was the eldest male of the senior branch of the family. It was only when there was no such younger brother of the deceased that the deceased's eldest surviving son succeeded to the family headship; and it was a short step from this to hold that the eldest son should generally become head whenever his uncle was younger than he. A younger brother might supersede his senior eldest brother as the family head on the ground of ability or intelligence, 'the choice being confined to those descended from a common father through males'. If there were no males, the eldest female member would succeed. All these seem so reminiscent of the canons of descent which we have seen laid down above in *Lewis* v. *Bankole*, with the exception of the deceased's younger brother's priority of succession over the eldest surviving son. That this was also the ancient customary rule in Lagos is clear from these interesting passages which occurred in the judgments of Smalman Smith, C.J., first *In re Hotonu* (*deceased*) (1892)[20]: 'Under the native custom as applicable to this case, the eldest brother of the deceased succeeds to the whole of the property of the deceased including his wives and his personal property and is not in any way called upon to account for the personal property so received, but may distribute it or dispose of it much as he pleases, controlled only by the moral obligation of doing right in the eyes of his relatives and friends'; and, again, in *Omoniregun* v. *Sadatu* (1888):[21] the eldest son succeeds to the land in the place of his father for his own benefit and for that of the family. The children and wives have the right to live in the house. The widow who takes another husband loses her right. The son has no right to sell the land or house for he holds it in trust for the family. In order to sell he must consult the elders of the family (his father's brothers) and his own brothers who must give their consent. If there be no son or male issue the elder brother succeeds and if he be dead then the younger brother and so on. If all the brothers be dead, the land descends to the elder brother's male children; if they be dead, not to their issue (if any), but to the issue of the younger brother. Females cannot inherit land, they can only have the right to stay in the house. A female has no right to bring her husband to live in the family house, but she does not lose her right to return to it by marriage. Her children have the right.

In case of personal property—the eldest son takes charge of the house and the personalty is divided among collaterals (uncles and aunts). Among the Mohammedans, the male takes two parts and the female one part. Among the Yoruba heathen male and female share according to age, except the eldest son who comes first. The personal property follows no special or particular rule of distribution, all the relatives or collateral branches sharing with children, although not of right. It has become the custom to share some portion of the personal property with them.

Secondly, the potential head of the family might be displaced in the inheritance for shirking the responsibilities of headship or because the late head had requested, on pain of incurring his everlasting wrath even in death, that he be expressly excluded therefrom. If the nature of the victim's offence to the departed head be heinous enough to warrant the carrying out of such an injuction, the family would execute it.[22]

Thirdly, to land individually owned by a deceased, in ancient times as now, the eldest son always succeeds his father as the head of the family. On a division of the land and the permanent crops thereon, the deceased's brothers, whether of the whole blood or of the half-blood, are entitled to a share, as are his sisters, if willing. The children of the deceased will then divide the remainder of the farm-land or house among themselves, the eldest taking the largest share and each of the other children having more than each of his uncles. This last point is in substantial agreement with Mr. A. K. Ajisafe's statement above. The deceased's daughters are entitled to their shares which are heritable by their own children. But, although widows are given living apartments for their lives, they cannot as a rule inherit their deceased husband's land. Young children usually wait till puberty before being given their shares. If the deceased dies without issue, the nearest relative inherits his land and, if a woman, her husband's family can in no circumstances inherit the land.

Fourthly, in order to meet local or domestic requirements some families at Ibadan arrange that, if the eldest son dies in his father's life-time and the next eldest son happens to be of the same mother with him, such next eldest is (to avoid unnecessary jealousy) passed over in favour of the next eldest son by another mother. Another Ibadan practice of a more general nature occurs where the deceased was a title holder, when only a younger half-brother (i.e. of the same father but of a different mother) of the deceased succeeded to the titled head of the family in preference to the deceased full brother.[23] But, even at Ibadan, the old laws of inheritance have been undergoing some recent modifications, whereby sons claim to inherit their father's property to the exclusion of their father's younger brothers. The eldest son now steps into his father's shoes. This is as it should be.[24]

Fifthly, there is a general rule at Abeokuta that the eldest son cannot succeed his father as head of the family so long as an uncle, who may be much younger or less capable than he, is alive.[25] But if this be taken with the growing practice of children acquiring relatively absolute and individual ownership of their portions of family-land, which the writer has described in the preceding paragraph and again the duty postulated of a man to pass on to his children what he has himself inherited, which the writer has described in the following paragraph, it would seem that the alleged rule cannot be an unmitigated canon of descent.

There are no important modifications of the normal pattern of the laws of inheritance recorded for Ondo, Ijebu and Oyo Provinces.[26]

Sixthly, in Benin there exists the doctrine of primogeniture according to which the right of succession to property, town-land as well as country-land, belongs exclusively to the eldest son of a deceased person. The rights of the younger children to their father's house are very precarious and, if their eldest brother refuses to let any of them stay on, they must ask the Oba for fresh lands for themselves. The eldest son may lose his enviable prerogative by neglecting properly to perform his father's funeral obsequies.

If there is no son or if the eldest son dies without issue during his father's life-time, a daughter will succeed as head of the family until she can have a son, through the now largely discredited practice of entertaining in her father's house suitors who can inherit the property.[27]

But, thanks to the recent researches of Mr. C. W. Rowling in his *Notes on Land Tenure in the Benin Province*,[28] the following qualifications to Mr. Ward Price's statement must be made: (1) the strict rule of primogeniture would seem to be limited in Benin to (*a*) the house in which the deceased father had himself lived and (*b*) title-houses which must necessarily go to the eldest son; (2) of all other houses, apart from these, the younger children may claim their shares, nor can they be lightly excluded even from their father's house of residence over which the eldest son holds complete sway; (3) although it would seem that this Benin doctrine of primogeniture apparently rules out the question of a 'family house' which the Yoruba system[29] of joint inheritance by all the deceased's children makes possible, yet sufficient sanctity and inviolability are secured to the father's house to make it impossible for the eldest son to sell the house over the heads of the other children or, in effect, to treat it as if it were his own privately-acquired, absolute property: an appeal case (Oba. A 340/1946) in the Oba's Court, for example, upset a sale by the family head on the ground that other members with the right to live there had not been consulted.[30] There were two other appeal cases before the Chief Commissioner in which a partition of house property with the consent of the eldest son had been regarded as an accepted modification of Bini custom, though it is not clear whether if the eldest son objects to partition it can nevertheless be ordered on the precedent of these cases.[31]

No serious exception can be taken to this doctrine which seems hard on the younger children of the family, seeing that an exact parallel existed among English landed families until abolished[32] in 1925 by the Administration of Estates Act 1925, section 45. With the influx into Binin of Yoruba elements and their system of equality of succession rights, a better acquaintance with English property ideas and, above all, increased social and economic activities of the people themselves, it is to be hoped that the rule of primogeniture will be in increasingly bad odour with the rising generation and so hasten the dawn of the day of its abolition. It is significant that while the Ishan and Asaba Divisions of the Benin Province follow the main Benin rule of primogeniture, there exists in the Kukuruku Division of the same Province a dual system of matrilineal and patrilineal inheritance operating at the same time. The wife remains a member of her own family and, on the husband's death, the children take his estate with them to their mother's family.[33]

One more point to note in connexion with the Benin rules of inheritance is the one which has to do with the custom, by no means universal but nevertheless seriously asserted in some places, of limiting or attempting to limit succession to the house property of strangers (i.e. non-Binin Nigerians) to only the children of such strangers as are born to them by Bini women. This inequitable practice has met with Government opposition and is not likely to be persisted in.[34]

B. *The Ibo Rules of Inheritance*

In describing the Ibo customary laws of inheritance we may very well start with Onitsha, if only because of its historical and ethnic link with Benin with which Onitsha shares the rule of primogeniture. Succession is by the eldest surviving son of the deceased, to the exclusion of all others; and much of what we have said about the Benin law of inheritance applies with equal force to Onitsha the people of which are said to have migrated originally from Benin.

Perhaps the only High Court decision on Onitsha law of succession was that in *Nwugege* v. *Adigwe & anor.*[35] where the plaintiff claimed that, as the Okpala of the family of Ngbo Ogbuefi (deceased), a woman, he was the proper person under local law and custom to administer the deceased woman's estate. The defendant, on the other hand, asserted that he had a better right by virtue of the fact that his late father had married the deceased woman according to local law and custom. Each party had three chiefs ready to give evidence as to the local rules applicable to the case. At the close of the plaintiff's case both counsel agreed that the six chiefs should at that stage sit in Court together and give their respective answers to questions of customary law to be put by counsel. From the unanimous answers of the chiefs to the questions put to them the following propositions of Onitsha law emerged:[36]

(1) On the death of a married woman property which she had acquired before her marriage goes to her own family and not to her husband or his family, but movable properties acquired by the wife before marriage, if taken by the wife to her husband's house, go to the husband or his family on her death.

(2) Property acquired by a married woman after her marriage goes to her husband on her death.

(3) Where a man marries a woman who has a house and lives with her as man and wife in that house, it goes to the wife's family on her death.

'This last proposition,' said Graham Paul, J., 'I cannot accept as a proposition of native custom as in laying it down the chiefs explained that under their custom it was unheard-of that a man marrying a woman should live with her in her house. It is obvious that the native custom could not provide for a set of facts unknown to native law.' The learned Judge accordingly held that the defendant was the proper person to administer the deceased woman's estate in right of his father.

Now, if the principle underlying the above propositions of Onitsha rules of succession be compared with that behind the rules already stated above for the Yorubas in the three cases of *Caulcrick* v. *Harding*, *Andre* v. *Agbebi* and *Idewu* v. *Hausa & ors.*[37], it would be found that there is not much difference between the two. It may be that later judgments might reveal divergencies, but in the present state of our knowledge it would be wise not to speculate.

As to the succession rules among the Ibos generally, we may state the following available evidence:

According to Mr. G. T. Basden, 'personal property descended to the eldest son as heir or, failing a son, to the eldest brother or male relative'.[38] This looks like the pure patriarchal principle of the Yorubas which we have observed.

The same patrilineal system has been described for the Yako by Professor Daryll Forde[39] and for the Ozuitem Ibos by Dr. J. S. Harris.[40] Both state also that the deceased's sons inherit their father's lands as well as any other land that might have been pledged to him before his death. And land rights acquired by a woman either by purchase or on pledge, both through a male proxy, are inherited by her sons to whose male descendants the succession is restricted. If the woman's sons are too young at her death, her husband holds the land as trustee until they are old enough to take it up. As a rule, land cleared or otherwise acquired by one person is inherited jointly by the descendants who usually have particular areas allotted to them at the general distribution following the man's death. Dr. Meek's findings in the Owerri district agree generally with these principles, and he also says that, after a co-operative clearing of the bush by a patrilineal kin group, the land is shared out according to seniority and each member's plot becomes his permanent family property inheritable by his sons.[41]

Miss M.M. Green says that in Umueke Agbaja the inheritance of land is by a man's sons and, if the man dies without issue, his younger brother of the same mother, if there is one, will inherit him: 'In the first place a man holds his land in common with the other members of his land-owning group. At the time of his death it will not pass definitely to his sons or other heirs but will continue as the common property of the group of which they form a part. It is only when the children of the group increase and grow up and marry that the need of dividing up the land will make itself felt. In the second place when the division is agreed upon it will be done publicly and ceremonially by the elders of the village according to the rules of inheritance.'[42] In another place[43] she writes: 'Clearly, matriliny plays a considerable part in Ibo society. Descent and succession are patrilineal, marriage is patrilocal and a man inherits from his father. But the matrilineal principle is there asserting itself both legally and emotionally.' The writer warns that the fact that people will often refer to themselves or others as children of a particular mother may lead one to suppose that descent is matrilineal, whereas the society itself is patrilineal in spite of the horizontal alignments involved in the practice of exogamy.[44]

The principles of succession to titled family headship follow more or less the pattern noticed in the case of the Yorubas at Ibadan,[45] while the regard paid to mental and physical qualities in a family head, also already observed among the Yorubas, has been discovered among the Ibos of Umueke.[46] The value of this rather extended treatment of the rules of inheritance of a comparatively small village lies in the fact, admitted by the writer herself, that the main rules apply to other Ibos as well: 'Here the situation will be described chiefly with reference to the village of Umueke Agbaja. But in the main it seems to hold good over much of Ibo country.'[47]

Calabar. This area of Eastern Nigeria is important and distinct enough to deserve a separate, though brief, treatment.

The local customary rules of inheritance would seem to be substantially the same among the people of Calabar as those we have so far noted among the Yorubas and the majority of the Ibos. The eldest surviving male member of the family succeeds as head, and the succession may be automatic or subject to election at a family conclave after the death of the previous family head. So much was decided in *Inyang* v. *Ita & ors.*[48] by Berkeley, J., who, however, incidentally observed that 'the succession to the vacancy devolved on the next senior male, if he chose to take it up. . . . Thus we see, even under a system of *strict primogeniture*, the will of the family functioning as an important factor in placing a man in the headship, and in maintaining him there or ejecting him therefrom.'[49] There is here, it is submitted, an obvious difficulty: either the system is one of 'strict primogeniture'—in which case the eldest surviving son of the deceased takes to the exclusion of all the others—or, it is not. To say that the succession of the head depends on the consenting will of the family, even if that will is expressed 'by democratic suffrage, not by autocratic decree', is in terms to contradict the very principle of primogeniture as it is commonly understood in property law.

Indeed, the learned Judge's reference to primogeniture is, if we may say so, particularly unfortunate as it is unnecessary to the actual decision which he rightly reached in the case itself as it is most likely to mislead one into thinking that such a system as we have attributed to Benin and Onitsha in fact exists in Calabar. Fortunately, when we recall the express disavowal of any power in the family head arbitrarily to eject a member of the family in *Manuel* v. *Manuel*[50] and again the findings that a family head in Calabar as elsewhere is a mere trustee and that all the members are beneficiaries of the family property in *Bassey* v. *Cobham & ors.*,[51] we can dismiss Berkeley's, J., incautious reference to primogeniture as an inaccurate *obiter*.

It is, therefore, safe to say that the Calabar law and custom of inheritance follow the patrilineal principle which is not, however, of the primogeniture type.

Notes

1 (1909), 1 N.L.R. 82.
2 (1909), 1 N.L.R. 82, at p. 102.
3 Compare W. Price, *op. cit.*, para. 5: 'Whatever their degree of advancement now, however, it seems highly probable that there was only one ancient system of land tenure for all the sections of Yoruba-land and that any variations which may have occurred locally established themselves later than 'ancient' times.
4 (1909), 1 N.L.R. 82, at p. 103.
5 (1928), 9 N.L.R. 76.
6 (1928), 9 N.L.R. 76.
7 (1939), 15 N.L.R. 1.
8 (1926), 7 N.L.R. 48.
9 (1931), 10 N.L.R. 79.
10 At p. 80.
11 (1936), 13 N.L.R. 96.
12 (1937), 13 N.L.R. 146.
13 (1924), 5 N.L.R. 47.
14 *Ibid.*, at p. 51.
15 (1931), 10 N.L.R. 82.
16 Published in 1924 by George Routledge and Sons Ltd., London; see Chap. IV, paras. 5, 11, 23–7 on Yoruba rules of inheritance.
17 *Op. cit.*, Chap. I, para. 3.
18 Cf. W. Price, *op. cit.*, para. 46.
19 See, on the whole subject, paras. 44–52.
20 At p. 18 of 'Lagos: Reports of Certain Judgments of the Supreme Court. etc. (1884–1892), —Law Reports (Colonial), Nigeria A. Colonial Office Library, London.
21 At p. 15 of the same Report.
22 W. Price, *op. cit.*, paras. 46 and 47.

[23] See, *op. cit.*, paras. 51 and 65.
[24] Para. 182.
[25] Para. 272.
[26] *Op. cit.*, see paras. 235, 326–7, 339.
[27] Paras. 374 and 375.
[28] Govt. Printer, Lagos (1948)—paras. 18, 22—4, 36, 49, 65 and 99.
[29] W. Price, *op. cit.*, para. 60.
[30] C. W. Rowling, *op. cit.*, para. 18.
[31] C. W. Rowling, *op. cit.*, 23.
[32] See Cheshire, *Modern Real Property*, (5th edition), pp. 808 and 812.
[33] See C. W. Rowling, *op. cit.*, paras. 49, 65 and 99.
[34] *Ibid.*, paras. 23 and 36.
[35] (1934), 11 N.L.R. 134.
[36] *Ibid.*, at pp. 134–5.
[37] See p. 276, *supra.*
[38] *Niger Ibos*, Chap. XIX: 'Land Tenure and Inheritance', at p. 268.
[39] 'Land and Labour in a Cross River Village', *Geographical Journal*, Vol. XC (1937), pp. 24–51.
[40] 'Papers on the Economic Aspects of Life Among the Ozuitem Ibos'. *Africa*, Vol. V, No. 14, pp. 12–23; 302–334 (1943–4).
[41] *Law and Authority in a Nigerian Tribe* (1937), pp. 102–4.
[42] *Land Tenure in an Ibo Village* (1941), pp. 13 and 14.
[43] *Ibo Village Affairs* (1947), p. 161.
[44] *Ibid.*, at p. 16.
[45] Cf. *Ibo Village Affairs*, pp. 69–70 with pp. 225–6 herein.
[46] See *Ibo Village Affairs*, pp. 72–7.
[47] *Ibid.*, p. 153.
[48] (1929), 9 N.L.R. 84.
[49] (1929), 9 N.L.R. 84, at p. 85.
[50] (1926), 7 N.L.R. 101.
[51] (1924), 5 N.L.R. 90.

S. M. Seymour: Native Law in South Africa*

The Native law of succession is fundamentally a system of primogeniture, but in a polygamous household the rule of primogeniture is modified by the fact that the senior or general heir is the eldest son of the Great wife, even if he is not the first-born son of the kraalhead. The law of succession is also affected by the concept that 'the cattle, not the men, beget the children'; by cattle is meant the dowry cattle paid for a wife. The effect of this maxim is that a woman for whom dowry has been paid is not capable of bearing a child which does not belong to her husband. Although this maxim applies in all tribes, its strength varies in different tribe-groups; with regard to succession, in some tribes the position of promiscuous children of a wife or widow is very much stronger than in others.

The general rule is that a Native male belongs to the family to which his mother belonged at the time of his birth; a family belongs to the group of families known to be related through the male line. Every male member of a family has a potential right to succeed to his kraalhead, and, through the latter, to any other kraalhead in the group. Descendants of a kraalhead are given precedence over his ascendant and collateral relatives; under no circumstances does a woman inherit as heir.[1]

In each kraal, there are as many inheritances as there are Houses. Each inheritance can have no more than one heir at a time, but one heir is capable of succeeding to more than one inheritance; this happens, of course, when a House lacks a natural heir, that is, a son of the wife.

Subject to the position that a minor heir is under guardianship during his minority, no heir has any rights in the inheritance of another, which is under the latter's sole possession and control.

Finally, the Native law of succession should be viewed against the background, or perhaps it is better said that it is set up on the foundation, of two ideas: these are the desire for the perpetuation of a kraalhead's name, and the concept of collective right and responsibility within a family and family group. In sympathy with these ideas, not only

* S. M. Seymour, *Native Law in South Africa*, Juta & Co. Ltd., 1960, pp. 175–180.

is it right and proper for a kraalhead's relatives to endeavour to raise seed for him, when necessary, by all legitimate means, but the heir succeeds to a position entailing rights and liabilities in respect of which he was potentially interested and responsible before the death of his predecessor.

Thus the kraalhead lives on in his heir, and while the latter has the benefit of the claims, present possessions, and potential rights, due or belonging to his inheritance, he is unable to avoid the past, present and future debts and obligations attaching to his position.

In the forthcoming analysis, a table of simple succession, applying to a family comprising one wife and her legitimate children, will be followed by the rules of succession to a polygamous kraalhead; thereafter such matters as seed-raising, institution of heirs, and the rights of posthumous and promiscuous children will be dealt with.

1.—*The Rules of Succession*

A. *Table of simple succession.* The following table of succession,[2] which lays down the rules applying in the case of a deceased kraalhead leaving *one* wife and only *legitimate* children, forms the basis of succession in Native law:

(i) The heir of the kraalhead is his eldest son.

(ii) When the eldest son has predeceased the kraalhead leaving no male issue, the second son is the heir; and if he, too, has predeceased the kraalhead without leaving male issue, the third son is the heir; and so on through all the sons of the kraalhead.

(iii) If any son, who, had he lived, would have been the heir under paragraph (ii), predeceases the kraalhead leaving male issue, the eldest living of such issue is the heir; provided that if any such grandson predeceases the kraalhead leaving male issue, such issue take precedence over a younger grandson and his issue. This simple rule of primogeniture may possibly be expressed more intelligently by saying that if any male, who but for his death would have succeeded to the kraalhead, leaves male issue or their descendants, then such issue or their descendants, in order of primogeniture, are preferred to any other male relative of the kraalhead.

(iv) When the kraalhead has died without male issue, or has outlived all his sons and their male descendants, then his father succeeds.

(v) When the krallhead's father has predeceased him, then the eldest brother of the kraalhead, or one of his descendants, succeeds upon the principle stated in paragraph (iii).

(vi) Upon failure of the eldest brother or his descendants, the next brother and his descendants are then exhausted, and so on through all the brothers of the kraalhead and their descendants.

(vii) In default of any of the above, the kraalhead's grandfather is the heir.

(viii) If the kraalhead's grandfather has predeceased him, then one of the kraalhead's father's brothers (that is, one of the kraalhead's paternal uncles) or one of the male descendants of one of them, taken in order of priority as shown in paragraphs (iii), (v), and (vi) is the heir.

(ix) Failing the paternal grandfather or his sons or their descendants, then the great-grandfather and his sons and their descendants must be looked to in the same order of preference.

(x) And so on until all the known male relatives of the kraalhead have been exhausted, in which case the inheritance devolves upon the Paramount Chief of the kraalhead's tribe, who assumes the office of guardian of the female wards of the deceased.

(xi) If there is no Paramount Chief of the kraalhead's tribe, the inheritance devolves upon the Governor-General in his capacity as the Supreme Chief.

B. *Succession to a polygamous kraalhead.* In tribes which practise the simple system of polygamy, notably those parts of the *Tsonga* tribe which have not come under *Zulu* influence, succession presents no difficulties; the eldest son of the first married wife, or one of his descendants, is the sole heir of the deceased kraalhead. A wife does not create a House, and so the inheritance is undivided. If there are no sons born to the first married wife, the sons of the second-married wife and their descendants are looked to for the heir; and so on, through the sons of all the kraalhead's wives in order of their marriage.[3]

In the Cape *Nguni* tribes, all of which practise the complex system of polygamy, the property of the kraalhead is distributed among the Houses of his wives. Each House has its own identity and estate and, upon the death of the kraalhead, the eldest son of each House, whether he be a major or a minor, is the heir of the House, to the exclusion of the sons of the other Houses.[4]

Where there are two Houses only, that is, the Great and Right Hand Houses, and one of them has no sons, the eldest son of the other is heir of both.[5]

Where there are more than two Houses (suppose there are six of them), each main House will have two *Qadi** Houses in its section; the Great House will have the third and fifth Houses as *Qadis*, the Right Hand House, the fourth and sixth. A son of one section is preferred in his section to any son in the other.[6]

Thus the heir of a *Qadi* House which has no sons is the eldest son of the main House to which the *Qadi* is attached; where the main House is without sons, its heir is the highest-ranking son in its *Qadi* Houses.[6] To clarify this further, where there are no sons in the Great House, but each of its *Qadis* has sons, the Great House heir is the eldest son of its senior *Qadi*, being the third House; should there be no sons in this latter House too, the heir of both the Great and third Houses is the eldest son of the fifth House. Where, however, the Great and third Houses have sons, but the fifth has none, the fifth House is inherited by the eldest son of the Great House. The reciprocity between the Right Hand House and its *Qadis* is the same.[6]

When neither the Great House nor any of its *Qadis* has a son, the heir of the Great House section is the heir of the Right Hand House. Conversely, the heir of the Great House inherits the Right Hand section, when there is no son in any of the Houses of the latter.[7]

The above is generally the manner of succession in the majority of the Cape *Nguni* tribes, but there are some which have differences.

A *Xhosa* kraalhead may have three sections, namely, the Great, Right Hand and Left Hand sections. The Left Hand section is subordinate to the Great House section in matters of succession. When there are no sons in the Great House section, this section is inherited by the heir of the Left Hand House; the converse applies when there are no sons in the Left Hand section. The heir of the Great House also inherits the Right Hand section, when the latter section is without sons; the heir of the Right Hand House only inherits either and both of the other two sections, when neither of them has sons. The creation of a Left Hand section is not common; if there is none, the *Xhosa* law of succession is the same as in the other Cape *Nguni* tribes.[8] A *Xhosa* kraalhead may also have a House called the *Ixhiba*, which is dealt with elsewhere.[9]

Among the *Pondo*, who have two main House sections only, should there be no male issue in the Great House, its heir is the eldest son of the Right Hand House, to the exclusion of the sons of the Great House *Qadis*; the reverse holds good when the Right Hand House has no sons. It is only when both main Houses are without sons that the highest-ranking son of the *Qadi* Houses of a section is the heir of the main House of that section. Where a *Qadi's* House has no sons, the rule normal to other Cape *Nguni* tribes applies, namely, it is inherited by the eldest son of the main House to which it is attached.[10]

A *Zulu* kraalhead may also have three sections, of which the main Houses are the Great, the Left Hand and the Right Hand Houses, to each of which may have been affiliated one or more minor Houses. The result, in matters of succession, is more or less the same as in the Cape *Nguni* tribes, namely, each House has its own identity and estate, and is inherited by its eldest son; when a main House has no sons, its heir is the eldest son of its senior affiliated minor House; should an affiliated House be without sons, it is inherited by the heir of the main House to which it is attached.[11]

Where there are no sons in the Right Hand section, this section is inherited by their heir of the Great House, and vice versa; when the Left Hand section is without a son, it is inherited by the heir of the Great House. It is only where there are no sons in both the Great and Right Hand sections that the heir of the Left Hand House becomes heir of either and both of the former sections.[12]

An unaffiliated minor House which has no sons is inherited by the heir of the Great House.[12]

Other *Zulu* kraalheads may have more modest establishments consisting of the Great

* Qadi is the term for a co-wife, attached to one of the two major houses.

and Left Hand Houses only, with or without affiliated Houses; the result is exactly the same as has been set forth above except that there is no Right Hand section to precede the Left Hand section to the succession of the Great House section when there are no sons in the latter. Yet other kraalheads may have only a Great House, with or without minor Houses; until a Left Hand wife has been appointed, there is no affiliation of minor Houses, but the effect is the same as if the Houses of the minor wives were affiliated to the Great House in order of their marriage, viz. when there are no sons in the Great House, its heir is the eldest son of the House of first-married minor wife; when a minor House is without sons, it is inherited by the heir of the Great House.[12]

In the *Sotho-Tswana* group, and among the *Ntlangwini* and some *Hlubi* in East Griqualand, all of whom practise a different form of the complex system of polygamy, the Great wife is normally a kraalhead's first-married wife, but the true criterion is that she is the wife whose dowry was paid by his father; each other wife is a major or important wife, who creates a House having its own identity and estate, ranking in importance after the Great House in order of the wives' marriages. The heir of each House is its eldest son; if any House, other than the Great House, has no sons, it is inherited by the heir of the Great House; when there are no sons in the Great House, its heir is the eldest son of the next senior House, or, failing sons there too, of the next House, and so on. Among the *Tswana*, however, there is a difference: if the House ranking after the Great House is without an heir, the youngest son of the Great wife inherits it.[13]

Among the *Venda*, a kraalhead's Great wife is the one for whom his father paid the dowry: should a man marry his maternal uncle's daughter, she will be his Great wife, even if she was not the first-married wife. Next in rank after the Great wife is the wife, if any, whose dowry was paid with the cattle received as dowry from a daughter of the Great wife. After this come the wives, in order of marriage, whose dowries were paid with property earned by the kraalhead. Then come the wives, if any, whom the kraalhead took over from the household of his late father, not being those with whom he is cohabiting under the custom of *ukungena*,[14] but those whom he has actually taken over as his own wives; these rank *inter se* in the order of their importance in the deceased's father's household. Finally, should a kraalhead have a wife whose dowry was paid for by his mother out of her personal property, she is the least important of all his wives.[15]

Each of the above wives creates a House, and the heir of each House is the eldest son of the wife thereof. Should the Great House have no son, the eldest son of the next-ranking House is the heir of the Great House.

Among the *Pedi*, a kraalhead may regulate the rank of his wives, but if he has married the daughter of his father's younger brother or of another male relative, normally junior in position to his father, she automatically becomes his Great wife; the right of inheritance to a House which has no sons is, *mutatis mutandis*, the same as in *Sotho* law.[16]

In all tribes, if there are no sons in any of the kraalhead's Houses, his heir is his nearest male relative as shown in the above table and rules of succession.[17]

In the above rules, no account has been taken of seed-raiser wives or of servant wives; furthermore, it has been assumed that all the sons referred to are legitimate, that is, are sons of the kraalhead by his wife or wives; and lastly, a House can only be regarded as without an heir not only if there are no living sons there, but also if there is no male issue from any predeceasing son of the House; any such descendants are taken in the precedence set forth in the above table and rules.

Notes

1 *Madolo* v. *Nomawu*, 1 N.A.C. 12, Nqamakwe; *Myazi* v. *Mofenti*, 1 N.A.C. 74, Butterworth. But in some tribes of the *Sotho-Tswana* group she may inherit property. (See note 13, *infra*).

2 Krige, p. 180; *Madolo* v. *Nomawu*, 1 N.A.C. 12, Naamakwe; *Myazi* v. *Nofenti*, 1 N.A.C. 74, Butterworth; *Daniso* v. *Mzingeli*, 1 N.A.C. 67, Flagstaff; *Sonti* v. *Sonti*, 1929 N.A.C. (C & O) 23, Nqamakwe; *Nxelewe* v. *Mapunzi*, 1939 N.A.C. (C & O) 103, King William's Town; *Lehasa* v. *Cewane*, 1947 N.A.C. (T & N) 132, Johannesburg.

3 Ramsay, pp. 9, 26; *Sijila* v. *Masumba*, 1940 N.A.C. (C & O) 42, Umtata; *Maganu* v. *Maganu*, 1938 N.A.C. (T & N) 14, *Shangaan*, Sibasa.

4 Cook, pp. 155; *Mfenga* v. *Tshali*, 1 N.A.C. 31, Mt. Ayliff; *Sonti* v. *Sonti*, 1929 N.A.C. (C & O) 23, Nqamakwe; *Sijila* v. *Masumba*, 1940 N.A.C. (C & O) 42, Umtata.

5 Cook, p. 155; *Malinde* v. *Mpinda*, 4 N.A.C. 364, Tsomo; *Sonti* v. *Sonti*, 1929 N.A.C. (C & O) 23, Nqamakwe; *Magengelele* v. *Bam*, 1935 N.A.C. (C & O) 10, Tsomo.

[6] Cook, p. 155; *Zito* v. *Zito*, 4 N.A.C. 135, Xalanga; *Sonti* v. *Sonti*, 1929 N.A.C. (C & O) 23 Nqamakwe; *Nkumenge* v. *Nkumenge*, 1934 N.A.C. (C & O) 19; *Sinaku* v. *Sinaku*, 1937 N.A.C. (C & O) 152, Keiskammahoek; *Mahashi* v. *Mahashi*, 1938 N.A.C. (C & O) 17, Engcobo; *Salmini* v. *Salmini*, 1948 N.A.C. (S.D.) 33, Lady Frere.

[7] See cases under notes 1 and *supra*; *Salmani* v. *Salmani*, 1948 N.A.C. (S.D.) 33, Lady Frere.

[8] Soga, pp. 54–6; Cook, p. 15; and see the cases under notes 5, 6 and 7, *supra*.

[9] See Chapter V, 3A.

[10] *Mkwayi* v. *Kiloti*, 3 N.A.C. 193, Libode; *Matilose* v. *Matilose*, 1929 N.A.C. (C & O) 12, Ngqeleni; *Sonti* v. *Sonti*, 1929 N.A.C. (C & O) 23, Nqamakwe; *Vapi* v. *Vapi*, 1933 N.A.C. (C & O) 75; *Manjezi* v. *Manjezi*, 1942 N.A.C. (C & O) 49, Port St. Johns; *Sigcau* v. *Sigcau*, 1944 A.D. 67; *Mbulawa* v. *Mbulawa*, 1956 N.A.C. (S.D.) 104, Lusikisiki.

[11] See chapter V, 3A, for the manner in which the kraalhead orders the ranking of his Houses; Krige, pp. 177–82; *Maganu* v. *Maganu*, 1938 N.A.C. (T & N) 14, Sibasa; *Dhlamini* v. *Dhlamini*, 1939 N.A.C. (T & N) 95, Natal; *Nene* v. *Nene*, 1942 N.A.C. (T & N) 55, Natal; *Kekana* v. *Kekana*, 1945 N.A.C. (T & N) 39, Potgietersrus.

[12] See N. 11, *supra*.

[13] See chapter V, 3A; *Pureni* v. *Pureni*, 1932 N.A.C. (C & O) 35; *Hofman* v. *Hofman*, 1948 N.A.C. (C & O) 24, Mt. Fletcher; see the *Laws of Lerotholi*, sec. 11 (1); Ellenberger and McGregor pp. 271, 272; Schapera pp. 191, 232–3. It is submitted that there must have been some misunderstanding regarding *Sotho* law between the Court and the assessors in *Hofman's* case above; there is no such thing as a *Qadi* House among the *Sotho*; a supporting wife (*sehanthlo* or *ngoetsi*) is part and parcel of the House into which she has been placed. Among the *Tswana*, it is usual for the heir to divide a part of the estate among his brothers and sisters; how much he will give to each is in his discretion; but it would seem that their rights in this respect are enforceable at law, and so the appointment made by the heir must be reasonable having regard to the size of the estate and taking into account allotments which the deceased kraalhead may have made to the younger brothers. (See Schapera, pp. 231–2, 237.)

[14] I.e., the levirate.

[15] Stayt, pp. 167–8; chapter V, 3A; also van Warmelo, pp. 817–23.

[16] Harries, (176) pp. 15, 29–31, 40–2; see chapter V, 3A.

[17] See cases under note 1, *supra*.

J. C. D. Lawrance: The Iteso*

Inheritance

1. *General*. Inheritance is patrilineal.

Women can never inherit though they can act as co-guardians and receive and give property in that office.

QUOTATION: *(a) D.N.C. 138/51: D.C. Appeal 30/51: A. Adusa* v. *B. Osekeny:*
A. Adusa was sued by B. Osekeny for return of bride-price on divorce. The record shows that A. Adusa was the heir of deceased Opiri, whose daughter, Ilakut, was married to B. Osekeny's brother. Bride-price had been paid to Ilekata, mother of A. Adusa, as guardian Adusa was at the time a minor.

QUOTATION: *(b) D.N.C. 142/51: D.C. Appeal 29/51: Ojilong Isirete* v. *T. Ongwalu:*
This was a land dispute. The original owner, Ongenge, a relative of Ojilong's, died and left his wife, Amuron, on the land. She in turn gave a portion to Ongwalu. This gift was recognized as valid.

Women can also sue for debts to an estate.

QUOTATION: *Kaberamaido County Court 210/50: Alemo w/o Ocheny* v. *Esaru:*
Alemo sued successfully for a debt of nine head of cattle owed to her deceased husband. Ocheny had sons living.

Property of deceased persons is divided up by the head of the deceased's extended family, helped by the heir as defined below and clan leaders of the locality.

The heir inherits all property, though by custom some cattle are allowed to other relatives; the heir is responsible for all debts on the estate.

The heir must normally be a member of the deceased's extended family (*ekek*).

QUOTATION: *Kamuda Sub-County Court 155/53: Onyige* v. *I. Oniyo:*
Onyige sued his cousin Oniyo for nineteen head of cattle alleged to have been awarded

* J. C. D. Lawrance, *The Iteso*, Oxford University Press, 1957, pp. 228–231.

to him in the division of the estate at Elogu's death. The evidence was conflicting, some witnesses including one clan leader alleging that Onyige was awarded the cattle and others including a clan leader alleging that Oniyo was awarded the cattle. The Court dismissed the claim because it was clearly proved that 'Onyige was not of that clan; he was born in another clan' and had followed his mother when she married Oniyo's father.

2. *Sequence of heirs.* The sequence of heirs normally follows the rules below but the extended family head and clan leaders have discretion to depart from this sequence if the heir is unsuitable by reason of insanity or known profligate habits.

A man's heir is his eldest son; it is immaterial if the eldest son is the child of the first, second, or any other wife.

If a man dies without sons or if the sons predecease him, whether or not they leave issue, his heir is his eldest brother or half-brother.

If a man dies leaving no sons or brothers or half-brothers, his heir is his father.

If a man dies leaving neither sons, brothers, half-brothers, nor father, his father's brother's eldest son is his heir.

The subsequent sequence of heirs is:

(*a*) eldest son of eldest son;
(*b*) eldest son of eldest brother;
(*c*) eldest son of father's sister;
(*d*) eldest son of sister.

NOTE: It is of course extremely unlikely that an heir could not be found from the relatives listed above. It is very rare for any of the relations listed in this section to inherit.

The heir of an unmarried girl is her father; if her father is dead, her eldest brother or half-brother; if she has no father or brothers, her father's brother or his sons.

The heir of a childless married woman is her husband or if he is dead his heir as defined above. But the son of a married woman can inherit her property.

3. *Division of property.* The division of property takes place at the last day of mourning (*asuban*).

At the beginning of mourning (*aipuduno*) there is a gathering of all relatives of the deceased and of his neighbours at which debts on the estate are declared. This gathering is presided over by the head of the deceased's extended family and is held at the deceased's home.

The heir inherits all wives. Notwithstanding this, older wives are usually inherited by their deceased husband's brothers and only the younger wives are inherited by the eldest son. A widow can, if she wishes, remain in the family of her deceased husband without being inherited by an heir.

A widow has, however, absolute discretion to return to her parents, in which case bride-price is repayable to the heir of her deceased husband.

The status of an inherited wife does not differ from that of any other wife, nor is her status affected by the fact that she has or has not produced children.

NOTE: But there are many superstitions regarding wives of deceased husbands. One who has had several husbands all of whom have died is naturally shunned. A woman with hair on her chin is greatly feared. It is believed that if she shaves her chin her new husband will die.

If the deceased's wives stay within the extended family (*ekek*) their children stay with them.

If the deceased's wives return to their parents, their children belong to the heir and may be taken by him when old enough.

For inheritance of children. . . .

Claims are not frequent and are confined mainly to claims for female children.

QUOTATION: *D.C. 1/52: D.N.C. 172/51: Y. Semambo* v. *Kadhala:*
Semambo sued Kadhala for custody of a girl, the daughter of Ibulaim, deceased. He could not prove that he was Ibulaim's heir, whereas Ramadhani, Kadhala's brother, was undoubtedly Ibulaim's foster father and, in the absence of sons or brothers, his heir.

Semambo's claim was rejected by the D.C. and all three lower courts. The D.N.C. judgement states '. . . if Semambo had been a brother of the deceased he would have started suing for his brother's effects immediately after the burial ceremony . . .'.

Stock is the sole property of the heir, who is responsible for payment of the sons' or younger brothers' first bride-price from it. It is, however, usual to make allocations to younger brothers at the time of the division of estate.

Crops in the field or store are taken by the wives, who cultivated the fields or who filled the stores, when they go to their new husbands. But if the wife returns to her parents, the food or crops will remain with the heir.

Other property, including money which is not the personal property of one of the wives of the deceased, belongs to the heir.

Land and houses are the sole property of the heir. But a widow (*apuserut*) has the right to stay in her house and to use the land which she used in her husband's lifetime if she is not taken by the heir and does not return to her parents.

H. Cory: Sukuma Law and Custom*

The Heirs (*Bali*)

Inheritance is patrilineal.

NOTE: A few cases are known in which a sister's son inherited property when a man died leaving no other male relatives. Should a distant paternal relative of the deceased appear later, he would have the right to claim the inheritance. Such cases should not happen in future in view of the newly introduced rule that daughters may inherit, which extends the circle of rightful heirs.

Three grades of heirs are recognized:

A. *Nkuruwabo*, main heir.
B. *Nzuna kwandya*, second heir.
C. *Nzuna kabili, kadatu*, &c., minor heirs.

A. *Nkuruwabo*. 1. If there are sons the main heir is:

I. *in a monogamous household:*
the eldest son.

II. *in a polygynous household:* the eldest son of the first wife (*nkima ntale*) irrespective of his age;
the eldest son of the second wife, if the first wife has no sons;
if the first wife gives birth to a son after the death of her husband, this son is recognized as the *nkuruwabo* of the deceased father.

If there are daughters but no sons the first heir is:

I. *in a monogamous household:* the eldest daughter;

II. *in a polygynous household*: the eldest daughter of the first wife irrespective of her age; the eldest daughter of the second wife if the first wife has no children.

NOTE: The rule was decided upon by the chiefs of the Sukuma Federation and their people in 1949. Formerly the right of inheritance by women was acknowledged in BD, KF, BS, SS, SBS, KS.† Women had no right of inheritance in NF, UF, BSN, KM, ZM, SM.†

NOTE: Sukuma customary law, as it was applied before the advent of Europeans, did not recognize the right of women to inherit property. Subsequently, for unknown reasons, this right was recognized by the courts of several chiefdoms, first in special cases and later generally. It is said that Nung'hu and Ng'wagala applied it earlier than other chiefdoms. During the last few years, in all chiefdoms, including those which had never accepted a reform of the inheritance law regarding women, daughters have been given a few beasts voluntarily by the heirs; single cases are also known in which a court gave

* H. Cory, *Sukuma Law and Custom*, Oxford University Press, 1953, pp. 153–161 and pp. 122–124.

† There groups of letters refer to geographical districts of Sukumaland.

to daughters a share of the father's property. (Zinza Appeal case 42/44.) It may be said that family councils and even in those areas where they could not inherit by a generally acknowledged rule.

3. If there are no children, or if the children are minors, the first heir is the father of the deceased.

NOTE: It lies in the discretion of the father whether he takes over the inheritance or leaves it to the brothers of his deceased son. Widows are always left to the brothers of the deceased (levirate).

4. If there are neither children nor father the first heir is:
I. *in a monogamous household*: thc cldcst full brothcr;
II. *in a polygynous household*: the eldest full brother or, if there are no full brothers, the eldest half-brother.

NOTE: In a polygynous household the estate of one house is distributed between the full brothers to the exclusion of half-brothers, even if one of the half-brothers is the *nkuruwabo* of the whole family. Often in such a case the half-brother receives a token gift from the heirs.

5. If there are no near male relatives the first heir is the eldest sister.
D.C.'s Appeal No. 4/48. Ibadakuli. *Guga* v. *Bt. Mwandu.*
Bt. Mwandu's brother died and she was appointed his heir. Guga was the maternal uncle of the deceased and claimed the inheritance because he had paid bridewealth for Mwandu. The sister's right of inheritance was confirmed by the court.
6. If there are no close kinsmen the first heir is the eldest paternal uncle.
7. If there are no near relatives the first heir is the next paternal relative, however distant.

NOTE: The more distant the relationship between the deceased and the relative who may inherit the property, the more important becomes the function of the family council in appointing the heir. The number of heirs having equal rights increases in direct proportion to the remoteness of relationship. In choosing an heir among distant relatives of the same degree the family council will take into account the character and ability of the claimant as well as the nature of his personal contact with the deceased.

In every generation the descendants of senior brothers have the first right to inherit, but if it is necessary to go back a few generations it obviously becomes difficult to decide who is the rightful heir. Data referring to previous generations becomes unreliable in course of time. Thus the human element is taken into consideration. All those relatives who remain in contact with each other consider themselves the 'family'. The connexion is chiefly maintained at such important family events as births, deaths, marriage, payment of *njigu*,* and rites of the ancestor cult. This explains the importance which an African attaches to his presence in the family circle on such occasions. It is not always sentiment or love of adventure which induces him to undertake long journeys; it is the knowledge that contact with his family gives him rights and also entails duties.

8. If there are no relatives the first heir is the Native Treasury.

B. *Nzuna kwandya*. 1. If there are sons the second heir is:
I. *in a monogamous household*: the second son;
II. *in a polygynous household*: the second son of the first wife; if the first wife has only one son, the first son of the second wife.

NOTE: The order of seniority of heirs is: firstly all sons of the first wife; secondly all sons of the second wife.

2. If there are daughters but only one son the second heir is:
I. *in a monogamous household*: the eldest daughter;

NOTE: Neither in a monogamous nor in a polygynous household can the eldest daughter receive a larger share of the inheritance than her youngest full or half-brother.

II. *in a polygynous household*: the eldest daughter of the first wife; or the eldest daughter of the second wife, if the first wife has no daughter.

* Blood money.

3. If there are no children the second heir is:
I. *in a monogamous household*: the younger brother;
II. *in a polygynous household*: the younger full brother or the eldest half-brother if there is no full brother.
4. If there are no close kinsmen the second heir is the younger paternal uncle.

C. *Nzuna kabili, kadatu, etc.* With regard to the rights of minor heirs to a share in the estate the foregoing rules are similarly applied.

NOTE: In a case where the father or a remote relative is the heir, no minor heirs are recognized and the property is not divided.

Special Rules Determining the Sequence of Heirs

I. *Monogamous household.* If a son, who himself has children, dies before his father, these children do not receive that share of their grandfather's estate which would have been their father's. They receive shares as minor heirs after all their paternal uncles and aunts.

These children have to accept the position of minor heirs whether they are minors or adults when their grandfather dies.

The eldest son of the original heir, when he grows up, retains the title and exercises the privileges of his position in relation to his paternal cousins.

NOTE: The *nkuruwabo* would call his paternal uncles 'father', but their sons would call him 'father'.

The right of inheritance appertains to one collateral group of relatives. The estate is never distributed among family members of different degrees of relationship.

NOTE: For instance, if a man has no sons and only one brother, the brother becomes his sole heir and none of the paternal uncles has a right to a share.

II. *Polygynous household.* The status of *nkuruwabo* remains with the members of the house of the first wife so long as there is a younger brother alive who can take over. If there are no younger brothers the status of *nkuruwabo* is assumed by the eldest son of the second wife.

Heirs of Women

A. *Unmarried girls and wives without children.* The heir is the father; failing him, full brothers and sisters;
failing them, half-brothers and half-sisters;
,, ,, a paternal uncle;
,, him, the nearest paternal relative.

B. *Wives with children.* The heirs of property acquired by the wife are the children in sequence according to age and their shares are in descending scale of value. Inherited property passes to relatives as in [the preceding para.]. The husband is excluded from the inheritance of his wife's property in all circumstances.

Heirs of Chiefs

Chiefs own two kinds of property:

A. Private property (*sabo ya ntemi*).

This comprises all objects which a chief has bought with his own money as well as presents which he has received as chief. In this category are included his cattle, his houses other than official residences (*ikuru*), and his personal belongings.

B. Property which chiefs own *ex officio* (*sabo ya butemi*).

This comprises the royal insignia and the traditional cult objects of the chiefdom; the special cattle, identified by the bells they wear, and their offspring; the residence and the lands appertaining to it.

The son who succeeds to the chiefdom becomes the *nkuruwabo* of the family; as *nkuruwabo* he inherits a larger share of the father's estate than his brothers. He exercises the rights and duties attaching to this position in accordance with the customary law. It rests with him to distribute the estate of his father with the assistance of older members of the family.

The private property of a deceased chief is distributed between his children in accordance with the rules of inheritance.

There are no special rules with regard to succession, which nowadays is generally patrilineal.

If the successor to a chief is not his son, the sons of the successor, and not the sons of the former chief, are in the first line of succession to their father, but neither branch of the family can claim a legal right to succession.

Heirs of Village Headmen

The property of village headmen is their private property except for fields which they have allotted to themselves during their term of office or which have accrued to them by virtue of their office. If a deposed village headman, or the heir of a village headman who is not taking over the office of his father, wishes to keep such land, he must ask the authority which administers the land for the reallocation of it.

NOTE: The situation with regard to village headmen varies greatly in the different chiefdoms and is at the moment in a state of flux. Originally the position of headman (*ng'wanangwa*) was inheritable by one of his sons. If all the sons were still minors a brother of the deceased took over. When the latter died, the office was not inherited by one of his sons, but by a direct descendant of the original *ng'wanangwa*.

Usually when the father became old, he chose one of his sons as helper and this son became *ng'wanangwa* when the old man died. If this was not done the family of the deceased *ng'wanangwa* chose his successor. Commoners had no right to choose the *ng'wanangwa*. Daughters could inherit the office, if no sons were available. The new *ng'wanangwa* had to be confirmed by the chief. In course of time a custom has been established in many areas whereby the chief appoints the village headman.

DIVISION OF PROPERTY

Livestock

A. *In a monogamous household*

1. *If the heirs are minors.* The cattle are not distributed.

If the mother remains in the house of her deceased husband the cattle are left with her. If she moves into the house of her leviratic husband and the co-guardian of her children, she takes the cattle with her.

2. *If the heirs are adults.* The livestock is distributed among the heirs in unequal shares according to their positions in the sequence of heirs.

NOTE: A herd is considered small if it consists of less than ten beasts. If such a herd has to be divided between several sons, the youngest would receive not more than one or two beasts. If the small herd remains together, it is probable that after a few years each son will receive a number of cattle sufficient to become the parent stock of a future herd. Very often, therefore, adult heirs do not distribute the estate, but leave the herd in the father's homestead. If the mother is still alive she remains in the house and looks after the cattle in the interest of all the heirs.

The herd is given into the trusteeship of the *nkuruwabo*. If a younger brother has taken over the father's holding the cattle in the house come under his care, but the *nkuruwabo* retains the right of disposal.

When the cattle are distributed, not only is the number of beasts in each share fixed, but the individual beasts are specified. There is no exact rule about the proportion which each share bears to the total number of cattle left by the deceased.

The principle of distribution is that the shares, beginning with that of the *nkuruwabo* and ending with that of the youngest son or daughter, are graduated in a descending scale.

NOTE: Examples of distribution:

If there are three heirs and the estate consists of

		30 cattle	20 cattle
the *nkuruwabo*	receives	12 beasts	9 beasts
„ *nzuna* I	„	10 „	6 „
„ *nzuna* II	„	8 „	5 „

If there are four heirs and the estate consists of

		30 cattle	20 cattle
the *nkuruwabo*	receives	10 beasts	8 beasts
„ *nzuna* I	„	9 „	6 „
„ *nzuna* II	„	7 „	4 „
„ *nzuna* III	„	4 „	2 „

These empiric figures show that the difference between the shares received by the heirs is small and that the smaller the estate the larger proportionately is the share of the *nkuruwabo*.

If one of the heirs thinks that he has not received the share due to him, he can file a suit in court. He must accuse his coheirs, not the elders of the family and the *nkuruwabo* who divided the estate.

NOTE: Before an heir files a suit he should bring his complaint before a family council the members of which will probably be called as witnesses by the court.

B. *In a Polygynous Household*

1. *If the heirs are minors.* The cattle are usually distributed among the houses immediately after the death of the father.

The principle of distribution is that the shares, beginning with that of the house of the first wife (*nkima ntale*) and ending with that of the last wife, are in a descending scale.

The distribution of the estate is performed by the family council under the chairmanship of the *ntale wa ndugu*. There is no rule determining the size of the share of a certain house in proportion to the whole estate. The council takes many relevant points into consideration, for instance, the number of children in each house.

2. *If the heirs are adults.* A. It lies in the discretion of the heirs to leave the herd together or to distribute it. B. If the half-brothers decide that the estate of the deceased should be distributed, the individual shares of each heir are in a descending scale, beginning with the share of the *nkuruwabo* and ending with the share of the youngest son or daughter.

NOTE: Example of distribution:

A man leaves two wives, each with two children, and the estate amounts to fifteen head of cattle:

The *nkuruwabo*	receives	6 beasts
„ *nzuna* I	„	4 „
„ *nzuna* II	„	3 „
„ *nzuna* III	„	2 „

3. *Ng'ombe ya kuyinza.* The cattle acquired by any one house of the polygynous household are called *ng'ombe ya kuyinza*. The usual way of acquiring these cattle is by bartering for cattle corn which has been grown by one of the wives on her fields. As long as the husband is alive, he is the owner of the *ng'ombe ya kuyinza* and can dispose of his property as he likes. It is not customary for the husband to use a beast from one house to help another house without first asking the wife of the house, but the wife has no right to forbid her husband to do what he thinks best.

NOTE: Cattle belonging to the common estate, which the husband may have given into the care of particular houses, must after his death be distinguished from *ng'ombe ya kuyinza*.

After the father's death the *ng'ombe ya kuyinza* are considered part of the common estate and are distributed among all the children in the customary way.

NOTE: This rule was decided upon by the chiefs of the Sukuma Federation and their people in 1949. Formerly this rule was followed in SS, KS. In SBS, NF, UF, KM, KF,

BSN, BD, BS* the *ng'ombe ya kuyinza* became the property of the house which had acquired them and were inherited by the children of that house.

NOTE: The chiefs and their people had first agreed to accept the rule of the majority (north) but decided finally to accept the rules of SS and KS* (south). Arguments for and against were proffered by the protagonists of both opinions. The main argument of the south was that a wife, after ten years of married life, during which she had given birth to several children, would normally have less *ng'ombe ya kuyinza* than a wife with only one child who was considerably less impeded in field-work. But at the distribution of property after the father's death, the many children will have between them a small number of cattle as far as *ng'ombe ya kuyinza* are concerned, while the single child of the other house will have all the cattle belonging to that house for itself. Thus the *nkuruwabo* of the whole family, being one of many children of the *nkima ntale*, might inherit less cattle than a minor heir of another house of his father. Such a situation would not be in accordance with Sukuma ideas of inheritance. The argument of the north was that the rule accepted in the south would make the wives of a polygynous household lazy in field-work, to which the south answered that this did not happen in practice with their womenfolk and that husbands in the south are equally interested in big harvests as elsewhere. The rule of the south, which was finally accepted, tallies with the rule which follows.

The cattle of bridewealth which a father received for his daughters are counted as common property of the father and are distributed after his death among the sons of all houses.

NOTE: This rule was decided upon by the chiefs of the Sukuma Federation and their people in 1949. Formerly this rule was followed in BS, SBS, BD, SS, KS. In NF, UF, KF, BSN* the bridewealth received for a sister was not counted as common family property and was inherited by her full brother.

Money and Paraphernalia

Money left by the father is distributed between his children in a descending scale from the *nkuruwabo* to the youngest son or daughter.

NOTE: It was formerly the custom to give larger shares to daughters than to sons in all chiefdoms where daughters were excluded from inheritance.

If the children are minors the mother is given the money and with the help of the co-guardian will usually buy stock with it.

Money (like *ng'ombe ya kuyinza*) earned by one house in a polygynous household becomes the common property of the estate and is inherited by all the children.

NOTE: Rules regarding the inheritance of money are considered unimportant. It is explained that in most cases the money left by the deceased is spent on the entertainment of the mourners.

The paraphernalia of the ancestor cult are inherited by the *nkuruwabo*.

Land

A. A holding (*migunda ya ise*) is inherited undivided, i.e. one of the sons must take over the whole estate or leave it.

NOTE: The *nkuruwabo* has the first claim to the father's holding. If he already has his own home and refuses to leave it, one of his brothers may move into the father's holding. Very often the decision as to which of the sons shall enter into the father's holding is made long before his death. Probably one son after his marriage will remain with his wife in the parents' homestead. A son who has received a field from his father must return it to the estate after the father's death. If an elder brother after the father's death claims his right to inherit the father's house and estate, the decision as to whether the younger brother must give way to the demand of the elder lies with the family council.

B. He cannot choose certain plots and the house and leave the rest to another heir or to another applicant.

* These letters refer to districts in Sukumaland.

Note: This rule was agreed by the chiefs of the Sukuma Federation and their people in 1949. Formerly this rule was followed in NF, UF, KF, SS, BS.*

A son who did not wish to take over the father's holding and who lived in the same *gunguli*† as his father was allowed a first claim on single fields of his father's estate which were not situated in the vicinity of the house plot.

Note: Sometimes a man returns to a field which was once occupied by his father or grandfather or by another near relative; there is in fact a certain tendency to return to such fields. This reoccupation by a relative may look sometimes as if a single field has been inherited. It very seldom happens that all the sons refuse to take over the father's holding. Intensive pressure would be exercised by the relatives, even if it should mean that one of the sons had to give up his own homestead.

A. Only a son is entitled to take over the father's holding without asking permission of the authority. Any other relative, even though the family council may have agreed that he should take over the estate, must be allotted the estate by the authority.

B. If there are no sons, but a daughter and her husband have been living on the holding of the father, or a sister and her family on the holding of her brother, these near female relatives are entitled to inherit the holding.

The heir occupies the inherited holding under the same rules as his father did . . .

Note: In practice the degree of equity applied by the authority and reinforced by public opinion is even greater in the case of inherited land than in the case of allocated land. For instance, if the heir has three small sons and the estate of the father consists of a large piece of land, the heir can be certain of keeping the land, as it is expected that in course of time his sons will help him to occupy the estate effectively. No case is known in which an heir has lost part of his land in these circumstances; but it is also stated that there can be no doubt that an heir having no children, or perhaps only one child, would lose part of his land if it were needed; the authority would not take into account the number of possible grandchildren.

Trees and perennial crops, such as bananas, sisal, and sugar-cane, are divided among the heirs; except that trees planted in the immediate vicinity of the house are considered as belonging to the house and are therefore inherited by the heir to the house.

The small square rice plots (*majaruba*) are not divided between heirs, but are considered part of the indivisible holding. Customarily heirs are granted preferential rights to such plots when they apply for them to their headman or *basumba batale*.‡

Fields which have been improved by the owner by good cultivation and manuring belong to the indivisible holding. Heirs are not entitled to demand them separately if they do not wish to take over the complete holding.

Note: Such fields are not more fertile than a *litongo*§, but a *litongo* plot cannot be demanded by an heir who does not take over the complete holding. There is no danger that a man would refuse to improve the fertility of a field because it could not be inherited separately when he died.

It is the general custom in a polygynous household that each wife after her wedding or after the birth of her first child is given her individual house and fields within her husband's *kaya* (homestead). If the husband dies no question of the distribution of land arises because each section of the family knows the fields belonging to it. The death of the father does not change the original division.

A field which is the personal property of the husband and is cultivated by all his wives together is called *kilaba*; the *kilaba* may be divided among the houses.

Note: The division of a *kilaba* between houses does not affect the question of fragmentation of land; a single share is seldom a big field and the shares generally become united again after a short time. No dispute with regard to the distribution of a *kilaba* is remembered. Some men like to have a *kilaba*, others consider it unnecessary.

* *Ibid.*

† Parish.

‡ Leader of the younger village age-grade in a parish sub-division.

§ Field in the vicinity of a homestead.

R. G. Armstrong: Intestate Succession among the Idoma*

Intestate Succession

Intestate succession is the only form of succession, or inheritance, recognized by Idoma 'Native Law and Custom'. The idea of a person determining the distribution of his property after death by means of a will or testament was—and is—foreign to Idoma thinking. In principle the inheritance of property is governed strictly by legal rules. As in Europe and America it is the occasion of the most serious stock-taking the society does. As we shall see, below, certain conflicts are inherent in the system. These conflicts are settled by a legal—or at times an essentially personal—struggle between the various interested parties. Such struggles are not necessarily considered as undesirable, since the Idoma, like many other people, tend to see a fight or a struggle as a sort of oracle, in whose issue is expressed the will of God. Nevertheless, the Idoma law of succession is elaborate and highly systematized, and I am sure that the material presented here does no more than open the study of it. It is not easily amenable to case-study by outsiders, since most inheritance-matters are settled by the elders in the family. Only difficult cases, usually involving women, come before the court ordinarily.

The basic principle which governs the Idoma law of succession is that succession to property is from the father to his son or sons, and succession to the headship of the family, or compound, is to the oldest surviving brother. (This latter will very likely also be *ádōkwu*, 'executor'.†) Married daughters cannot inherit from their father, since this would result in family property passing into the hands of another family. The Idoma legal proverb which expresses this is, 'Smoke does not go from one house into another house' (*Oduduú gé nmíinu ẽe ginōháń*). That is to say, property does not pass from one patrilineal family to another through the marriage of its daughters. For various reasons neither the husband nor wife can inherit from each other. In certain situations and to a limited extent a woman's children can inherit from her. If a man's son has property and a wife and predeceases him, the father cannot inherit the property nor the wife. The legal proverb which expresses this limitation is, 'Water does not flow from the mouth of the river upstream; it flows downstream'. If a man dies without a son, his brothers, including his senior brother, may inherit from him without contravening the principle expressed in the proverb. (His full brothers have preference here over his half-brothers. If he has only two half-brothers, one with same father, different mother, the other different father, same mother, then the brother with the same father has full rights, to the total exclusion of the uterine brother. Thus the principle of patrilineal succession prevails over the far closer personal relationship of uterine brothers.) Apart from this, a man's brother or brothers do not, generally speaking, inherit from him. A man's surviving brother will be named *ádókwu* and trustee for the heir, if the son and heir is not old enough to manage for himself.

The biggest single exception to the above has to do with inheritance of the father's wives, for both the son and the father's brother may inherit these *by consent* of the woman involved. A son may inherit any of his father's wives except his own mother or her sisters. The father's brother is of course not limited by this rule. As Chief Ikongbe puts it:

> The . . . taking of wives can be done by any relative, without the consent of the son. What happens is that, if somebody dies, any member of the family [i.e. patrilineal family. *RGA*] can go secretly to any of the wives and find out if she could marry him. If the woman agrees, there is a customary present, which the relative gives to the woman. It could be tobacco or money, it could be firewood, if there is an agreement between the woman and the man. (Then) the man will go and inform the oldest person in the family.

The would-be new husband also gives a goat for sacrifice in order to sever the woman's connexion with her late husband. If a woman does not wish to marry any of her late

* R. G. Armstrong, 'Intestate Succession among the Idoma', in J. D. M. Derrett (ed.), *Studies in the Laws of Succession in Nigeria,* Nigerian Institute of Social and Economic Research, 1966, pp. 213–220.

† Literally, 'father of the corpse', perhaps 'father of the funeral', really, 'person in charge of the dead man's affairs'. The word 'executor' is not used in the technical sense of English or American law, but in the Idoma legal sense specified.

husband's relatives or sons, she may escape such obligations by refunding a token bride-price of £5 (or more recently £10) to her husband's family. If the heirs know exactly what the father or brother paid, they can demand the whole sum. (This is more apt to be the case with the younger wives.) In any case, she cannot be inherited against her will. Her consent *is* necessary. As has been noted, the father is precluded from marrying his deceased son's wife, by the 'Water does not flow upstream' rule. When a young married man dies, his brothers take his property, and failing them his cousins. They may all try to persuade the young widow. If she does not agree to marry any of them, she must refund the bride-price *to the brother or to the cousin*, not to the father who paid it in the first place. Children belong to the father's lineage, even if the bride-price is largely unpaid and even if the wife has been living with her father for years or is divorced from her children's father.

The main things that are inherited are personal effects of the deceased, his houses and rights in houses, his land-rights (including especially his rights to his farm-plots and their development and to the land on which his compound is located), his seed-capital, his plantations of economic trees, and his inherited rights in other economic trees. It is important to note that property which the wives of the deceased accumulated while they were married to him counts as his private property and will be inherited by his sons, or in appropriate cases by his brothers.

In Idoma, as in the rest of Northern Nigeria, all land is held by the Governor, and no land is bought or sold. Houses likewise are not bought or sold. The ordinary plot of land is seldom farmed for more than five years after being opened to cultivation. It then goes back to bush for a protracted and indefinite fallow period. After two or three years it may be claimed by any lineage-member who thinks that he can farm it successfully. A farm-plot which is being cultivated successfully is an important property in this sense, however; and the farmer will normally claim development rights over adjacent land in a well-recognized pattern. Idoma land-tenure is therefore a set of rights of use, development and enjoyment, and these rights in a particular farm area often have a prospective life of ten or fifteen years. Seed-capital is likewise a valuable property, and a young man who must begin by borrowing will need at least five hard-working, successful years in order to become independent in this respect. As Chief Ikongbe puts it:

> Now, if somebody dies, the first thing is that the father's brother will go to his farm with his son and check it. Then he will give some part of the farm, or the yams, to the wives; because if somebody dies, the first thing they do, is that the women do not leave the place immediately, so they give them part of the yams to feed themselves before they leave for their respective fathers' places. So it is the son who takes the seed-yams; because in Idoma, as you know, farming is one of the . . . principle occupations, and it is supposed that when somebody dies, his son will take charge of the seed-yams, so as to be able to stand on his own feet.

In answer to the observation that if the son is young the uncle will in fact control this capital for some years, Chief Ikongbe said: 'Yes . . . If the son is young, he has even got to work on the uncle's farm and then when he is grown up, his uncle will give him some seed-yam, whether he takes [has taken] his father's seed-yam or not.'

Economic trees, such as palm trees, banana trees, or citrus fruit trees, which a man has planted, are inherited by his children. They are not divided up amongst the individual children, however, '(They are) held together by the group and not divided. Any of the relatives too can go there and take either the palm (kernels), or oranges, whatever it might be.' After five or six generations there would obviously be hundreds of people with rights in the trees, including people who had migrated from that place years before. The trees pass, therefore, into something very like the public domain.

Houses are inherited by the whole group of sons of the deceased and they can all live in them, but the eldest son will take charge and will be compound-head. The same rule holds for large houses of the new type that are beginning to be used in Oturkpo Town. It needs the unanimous agreement of the sons who have inherited the house before it can be disposed of. Since sale of a house is impossible the procedure followed is for the owners to petition the Local Government in writing to transfer their rights to somebody else. This is done in connexion with a private financial arrangement with the other party. (I am uncertain whether such private arrangements would be construed as contracts enforceable at law.)

Titles in Idoma are not inherited, but are acquired individually in each generation, usually in return for a service of some kind to the Chief.

Payments due as compensation for adultery are inheritable in principle, but seldom collected. If the man to whom the money was due dies, his death may be attributed to the adultery of his wife; and his heir may be afraid that if he takes the money, he too will die. If the adulterer dies without paying, his family is not liable for the debt, since it is thought that he died as a result of his ill-doing and people will simply pass over the matter in silence.

Debt is likewise incumbent upon those who inherit the property generally. On the day of the burial, the creditor will come to the funeral. He will give ceremonial gifts of money to the relatives and sympathize with them. Then he will announce the debt, and this makes it a legal obligation on the heirs of the deceased. If he fails to do this, he loses his rights unless, in modern times, he can show documentary evidence of the debt. On being asked whether the debts of a bankrupt person are an obligation on those who would have been heirs had there been anything to inherit, Chief Ikongbe replied, 'Yes, even if the man has *no* penny, *nothing*, and he dies, well, the creditor will be a very lucky person if the person who is supposed to inherit the property is a wealthy man.' This is a situation that could arise with respect to a profligate young man or an unpopular old man. Debts which are not capable of being collected during the lifetime of the debtor may become so on his demise.

Chief Ikongbe tells of a case in which a man who owed him the refund of the bride-price died after paying only a little more than half. Chief Ikongbe had to sue the man's elder brother in court for the rest; he succeeded in his claim, and the man gave him clothes in court to the value of what was still due.

I understand from other Idoma that medicines (*ẹcí*) and important charms, such as the *ẹkocẹí*, are inherited in an entirely different way. They are essentially the property of individuals and may be owned by men or by women. The normal thing is for the owner to name his or her successor and to choose someone who shows talent for and interest in the charm. It is not necessary to keep the medicine or charm in the family. If the owner dies without naming a successor, the family may consider the matter. If they find a likely successor who knows what is necessary to use the medicine or charm successfully, he or she is chosen. If no likely person is found, the charm lapses. New charms can be brought into the district by women who marry in from other places or because a man has been given the charm by someone in another place. This is the closest approach to testamentary succession that I know of in the traditional culture.

When a dead man has been 'resurrected' in the form of an ancestral mask, the mask remains active as long as any of his children are alive. When his last child dies, the mask is cut up and certain of the most symbolically important parts of it are buried with him. The main part of the cloth that made up the body of the mask is given to 'a child of a woman' (*ọónyā*), that is to a man whose attachment to the lineage is through a woman —through his mother, perhaps, rather than through his father. (In other words, such a person is really a member of a different lineage, but has lived most or all of his life with the lineage to which the mask belongs). He may then wear this cloth, which becomes the visible sign of his acceptance into the lineage.

Although the wives of a man do not inherit from him, still inheritance is through them, for his estate is divided amongst his sons equally *by wife*. That is to say, if a man had three wives his property is divided into three equal parts and given to the sons of these three wives. If one wife has four sons and another has only one, then the latter gets four times as much as does one of the four sons by a different wife. It is not hard to see that certain tensions are inevitable in such a system. The senior wife has the best chance of having several sons. The junior wife (of whom she may well be jealous on other grounds) may very well have only one son. Still her son will have an inheritance equal to that of all the sons of the senior wife together. Under these circumstances the sons of the senior wife may well 'combine and cheat him'. Alternatively, one of the older brothers may marry the father's junior wife. He would not thereby come to own his half-brother's property, but he could probably exert considerable control over it, and may become *ádōkwū*.

The right of the sons to inherit equally from their father is not affected by the fact that the payment of bride-price was incomplete at the time of their father's death— or even by the fact that he had hardly started paying it. A legal marriage is constituted by the fact that one has given the customary present to the bride and by the fact that she has accepted it. As Chief Ikongbe puts it:

> According to (the) Idoma parable [*sc.* proverb], 'Two people do not owe themselves' (*Ācẹpa í ī bīīwā ulẽ́ń*). Once you have made the (marriage) present, the only thing you owe (her) father is money; so that if your . . . father-in-law takes (your) wife away, it's only a question of demanding his money . . . It does not mean that the wife is not yours, but (that) you have to pay him what you owe.

Even if the parents are divorced, the sons retain full rights of inheritance from their father. Even the offspring of adulterous unions have full rights of inheritance from their father, providing he has acknowledged them and has made the customary payment to the husband of the woman in question. (The payment is usually £5, which is the accepted equivalent of the bride-price in older marriages.)

On the other hand, the children which a man has by a concubine or prostitute have no right of inheritance. As Chief Ikongbe puts it: 'If the man paid no dowry on the woman, those other children have no right to his property. Because if the child is a woman, the son whose mother is lawfully married had a right in olden days to sell those of the concubine.'

I suspect that this 'right of sale' results from the fact that the concubine either had no family in the community, or else no family that would defend her interests. The other side of the matter is that the legitimate sons may well have felt cheated of their rights in the bride-price on their late father's illegitimate daughter, whom they would probably not dare to seize while their father was living. Since no bride-price had been paid on the mother, none was due on the daughter, and the only way they could realize on their 'rights' in inheritance was to seize and sell the daughter. On the other hand, if a girl from a strong family had a child before marriage, her father might well refuse to accept the proffered payment from her lover so as to keep his daughter's child as his own. If the child was a girl, he could keep the bride-price on her himself, when in due course she married. He thus acted as the girl's 'pater', and her *genitor* would receive only 10*s*. in recognition of the fact that she must go to him for certain sacrificial purposes.

N. N. Rubin: The Swazi Law of Succession: a Restatement*

Principles of Succession and the Distributable Estate

General principles. Inheritance in terms of Swazi customary law is patrilineal.[1] The pattern of inheritance in regard to both land and movables (as well as livestock) is based on the provision for a main heir and a number of lesser heirs. The system of inheritance is based on the principle that the eldest son of each house in a polygynous household, or the eldest son of a man who has only one wife, will receive the major portion of any estate left by his father; but that provision will also be made for younger sons (in each case) to a lesser extent. Widows though not normally entitled to inherit from their husbands[2] have a right of use over land and certain livestock which descend to the heirs of the particular house of which they were members, provided they continue to live with such heirs. Daughters receive no share of the estate. In the absence of sons in a particular minor house within a polygynous household, the inheritance of that house will descend to the main heir.[3]

Where there are no sons surviving a man who had only one wife[3,4] he is succeeded by the following persons (in the order in which they are given):

(*a*) *deceased's younger brother who was next after him in seniority*, or if such younger brother did not survive deceased,

(*b*) *by the eldest son of such younger brother*. Where such younger brother has died prior to deceased and leaves no male issue, deceased's heir will be –

(*c*) *a younger brother of deceased, next in seniority* after those brothers already deceased. In the case of each younger brother, if he has died before the deceased, his eldest

* N. N. Rubin, 'The Swazi Law of Succession: a Restatement', in *Journal of African Law*, Vol. 9, No. 2, pp. 97–98 and pp. 102–106.

son will become heir to the deceased. Only where such brother dies without male issue, does the inheritance pass to the next senior younger brother of deceased;

(*d*) where deceased is not survived by younger brothers or their sons, the inheritance passes to the *elder brothers of deceased in order of seniority*;

(*e*) where any such older brother fails to survive the deceased, his *oldest surviving son* will become the heir; only where the most senior brother is not survived by male issue does the inheritance pass to the next most senior brother;

(*f*) where the deceased is not survived by any of his brothers or their male issue, deceased's *senior male relative* will become his heir. Where none survives the deceased,

(*g*) the *senior male grandchild* of the deceased becomes the heir;[5] where there are no male grandchildren who survive the deceased,

(*h*) the heir will be the *oldest son of deceased's oldest married sister*; or, if he has died prior to the deceased,

(*i*) his eldest son. Where no persons in categories (*h*) and (*i*) are available to succeed, then,

(*j*) the heir will be the *oldest sons of deceased's other married sisters, in order of seniority of such sisters*. In each case, where such nephew has not survived deceased,

(*k*) the *oldest son of the deceased nephew will become the heir* (and, failing male issue of such nephew, the inheritance will then pass to the *oldest sons of the next most senior married sister of deceased*). In the absence of such persons, the heir will be –

(*l*) *the male children (in descending order of age) of the sisters of the deceased's father.*

Where no persons in categories (*a*)-(*l*) are available to succeed the deceased, his *wife may become his heir*. In such a case she will revert to the guardianship of her father (or his successor) and it is he who will control property inherited by her.

If, in the circumstances described above, the wife remarries, such property as she inherited will be taken with her to her new matrimonial home, and it will be controlled by her new husband.

Where there are no persons in categories (*a*)-(*l*) to succeed the deceased, *and* he is not survived by his wife, *the estate becomes the property of the King*.[6]

The institution of making a will is recognized by Swazi law,[7] although only livestock may be disposed of in this way. A will may in certain circumstances,[8] depart from the general pattern of intestate succession. In addition to disposition by will, property may be —and often is—distributed to persons who may inherit on intestacy during the lifetime of the deceased.[9]

Intestate Succession: Distribution of Property

1. *Estate of a married man with one wife.* (a) *Where he has no children who survive him.* The wife of such a man may be *ngena'd* (i.e. she may enter into a levirate union) where she has survived the deceased. In such a case, the first male child born of the levirate union will be the heir of deceased, and will inherit all the property of the deceased. The estate will remain in the charge of the male partner of the levirate union, who will also act as guardian of the minor heir and the deceased's wife until the *lusendvo*[10] determines that the heir is old enough to administer it himself.[11]

Where the deceased is not survived by his wife, cattle may be taken from the estate by the *umpatseli*[12] for the payment of marriage consideration in respect of a wife to be *ngena'd*, with the same effect as that described above.

Where this procedure is not followed, the rules given above[13] regarding the order of succession to the deceased's estate will be followed.

(b) *Where he has only daughters surviving him*,[14] one of them may arrange for the payment of marriage consideration in respect of a woman to be *ngena'd* by a person selected by the *lusendvo*. The first male child born of such a levirate union will be the heir; the estate will not be distributed until he is able to take charge of it himself. Until then, the male partner in the levirate will act as guardian of the heir and of deceased's daughters[15] and will also act as administrator of the estate.

Where this procedure is not followed, the heir will be determined according to the rules of intestate succession provided above.[13]

(c) *Where deceased is survived by sons and by daughters.* The oldest surviving son of deceased is his heir, and, as such he succeeds to the rights of guardianship over the widow and his sisters.

Subject to the rule given below regarding the *tinsulamnyembeti*,[16] and the rules governing distributions of the deceased during his lifetime (*iphakela*)[17] the heir receives all the property in the estate; this includes land, interests in land, livestock, traditional[18] and modern movable property, and crops.[19] The widow does, however, retain the right to the house which she occupied, and this is regarded as her property. The widow may also remain in undisturbed occupation of any land which she was given for cultivation prior to the death of her husband, though such land belongs to the heir. If he wishes to dispose of it, or to alter the way in which, or the persons by whom it may be used, he may not do so without the prior consent of the widow.

The widow also retains the *tinsulamnyembeti* received in respect of any daughters who are married (whether such marriage occurs before or after the deceased's death). She only acquires a right of use in them for the period of her lifetime. On her death, such cattle become the property of the youngest surviving son of deceased (where there is more than one who survives him).

2. *Estate of married man with two or more wives.* (a) *Where deceased is not survived by children*, one or more of his widows[20] may be *ngena'd*, with the results described above.

If this does not occur, the order of succession will be that outlined earlier.[21]

(b) *Where deceased is survived by daughters*, in addition to one or more of his widows (but there are no male descendants), one of the widows may be *ngena'd*,[22] or the procedure outlined under 1(b), *supra*, may be followed.[23]

Where there are no sons in a particular (minor) house—i.e. in a case in which there is a son who is heir to the major house—the main heir may place one of the junior sons[24] of his own, or any other house, in such a house, and he will then be regarded as the minor heir[25] of that house.

Similarly, where, in a polygynous household there are one (or more) houses without and one or more houses with only one son, such only son(s) may be placed by the heir in the house(s) which have only daughters. The houses concerned will then be regarded as having been merged, and the son(s) so placed will be the minor heir(s) to such merged houses.

(c) *Where deceased is survived by sons and daughters*, i.e. in each of the houses.

In such a case, deceased will have a main heir (*inkosana*),[26] and minor heirs (*bantfwana weyise*) in each of the minor houses.

(i) Selection of the *inkosana* (main heir). This takes place only after the death of the deceased. [27]The selection is made by the deceased's Council of Agnates (*lusendvo*), which does so by determining which of deceased's widows shall be regarded as his senior wife.[28]

(ii) Composition of the *lusendvo*. The Council of Agnates is composed of:

1. sisters (uterine or otherwise) of the deceased;
2. brothers (uterine or otherwise) of the deceased;
3. sons and daughters of deceased's mother's sisters (i.e. his maternal nieces and nephews);
4. deceased's father;
5. distinguished neighbours, the Chief, or other persons, invited to participate;
6. the widows of the deceased;
7. children of the deceased;

or such of these as may be available for the meeting[29] of the *lusendvo*.

(iii) Procedure for selection of the heir (*inkosana*).—The *lusendvo* is convened by the brother of the deceased, or such other person who is acting as administrator of the estate (*umpatseli*).

In deciding who is to be heir, the *lusendvo* designates the widow of deceased who is to be regarded as his main wife; the eldest son of such widow is the heir.

The decision as to who is/was the main wife/widow is determined by consideration of the following factors in relation to the wives or widows:

(1) that one of them is of royal blood,[30] in which case she will take precedence over any of the other widows;

(2) where no widow of the rank described in (1) *supra* was married by deceased[30] the next person in order of priority is a wife who has the same clan-name[31] as deceased's mother. Such a widow is known as deceased's *gogo*;

(3) next in order of priority is any widow of deceased who was married by *ukwendzisa*;[32] she is followed in the order by

(4) any wife who is the daughter of a chief (*sikulu*) or an *induna* (governor);[33]

(5) where deceased left no widow in any of the above categories, any of deceased's wives may be considered.[34]

In deciding which of the wives will be so designated, the *lusendvo* will regard a woman married as an *inhlanti*[35] in exactly the same way as if she had been married as a wife. (Where a son by an *inhlanti* to a wife has already been born, he will take precedence over any son born subsequently to a widow who has been *ngena'd*.)

Generally, when making the decision, the *lusendvo* may also have regard to the characters of their eldest sons, in addition to the fact that one or more do not have sons at all.

Where a wife who has no sons is selected as the main wife, the first-born of the deceased[36] may be placed in the house of such woman, and will become the *inkosana*.

(iv) Institution of the heir.—Once the *lusendvo* has designated the main wife, her oldest son becomes the heir. He is formally pointed out as such to the family of the deceased by the *umpatseli* at a ceremony which includes the ceremonial placing of a spear in his hand.[37]

(v) Distribution of the estate.—Subject to the rules regarding dispositive and testamentary succession, and to any allocations that may have been made by deceased during his lifetime to his wives or any of his children, the *inkosana* is entitled to the following on his succession:

(1) the rights of guardianship over widows, minor children and other dependants;
(2) such offices as deceased may have held;
(3) such land, or interests in land, as belonged to deceased: except such land as had been attached to other houses for cultivation and occupation by wives and their children;
(4) all cattle attached to the main house (*indlunkulu*);
(5) such cattle as are received for *lobolo* paid in respect of the oldest daughter in each minor house (and all the *lobolo* received for his uterine sisters);
(6) all other livestock, traditional and modern movables;[38]
(7) such crops as are not produced by minor houses.

The *inkosana* is not, however, entitled to the houses (*tindlu*) inhabited by the wives, which remain in the possession of the wives during their lifetime.

Each *umntfwana weyise* (minor heir) is entitled to any property allocated to his mother's house prior to the death of deceased, provided that the mother has a usufructuary right in respect of it during her lifetime. He is also entitled to receive any cattle paid as *lobolo* for the second and subsequent daughters in his house.

The youngest son in each house (including the *indlunkulu*) is entitled to receive the *tinsulamnyembeti* paid in respect of his uterine sisters: in the first instance, however, this is the property of the widow of deceased in each house, who has a lifetime right in respect of it.[39]

3. *Estate of an unmarried man.* Where an unmarried man dies, his father or the person appointed *umpatseli* in respect of his estate may use cattle from the estate for the payment of marriage consideration in respect of a woman who may cohabit in a levirate relationship with a person designated to do so by deceased's *lusendvo*.

If this procedure is not followed, deceased's intestate heir is his father; or, in the event of his not surviving deceased, the heir to the house of deceased's mother, i.e. his oldest uterine brother. If such a person is not available to be heir, the estate passes to the oldest son of deceased's father by another wife; and, if this is not possible, the order of succession outlined above is followed in relation to the latter.

4. *The estate of a woman.* (a) *An unmarried woman.*[40]—All property in her estate is transmitted on her death to her father, or his heir if he has predeceased her.[41]

(b) *A married woman,* who dies during the lifetime of her husband.

The property of any such woman, acquired by *iphakela,* will be inherited by the heir to her house, although it will remain in the custody of her husband during his lifetime. The same applies to any property she may have acquired as a result of her own efforts (e.g. by trading) and in respect of her personal possessions.

Any *tinsulamnyembeti*[42] which a woman may have received in respect of the marriage of her daughters will be similarly treated; except that, on the death of her husband they will be inherited by the youngest son in her house (unless she has indicated prior to her death that they should go to another of her sons).[43]

(c) *A widow.* Unless the deceased widow indicated otherwise during her lifetime, her estate will be distributed as follows:

(i) property allocated to her by *iphakela*, or obtained in any other way[44] will be inherited by the heir to her house, i.e. her first-born son;

(ii) cattle received as *tinsulamnyembeti*[45] on the marriage of her daughters will be inherited by the youngest son in her house.

It should be noted that where a woman has inherited property in the exceptional circumstances already described such property remains hers but it is in the custody of her father (or his heir) unless she remarries. If she dies without having remarried, her father or his heir succeeds to her estate, failing which it becomes the property of the King.

If such a widow remarries, her estate is transferred to the custody of her husband. The eldest son of such a marriage inherits her estate.[46]

In either of the two cases referred to above, the woman may dispose of such an estate *inter vivos*, provided she has obtained the prior consent of her guardian.

Notes

[1] Though descent is traced through women, *i.e.*, in a polygynous household the rank and status of a wife are the most important factors in determining the person who is to be the main heir of the deceased; "*Nkosi ngunina*" (a ruler [is ruler] by his mother).

[2] The exceptional instance in which they can do so appears below. See also under dispositions during lifetime, infra, pp. 313–314.

[3] This will only occur where the levirate is not resorted to. Clearly no levirate is possible where the surviving wife is beyond childbearing age; nor is it possible where she refuses her consent to the union. In all other circumstances, a levirate union may occur, and the male issue of such union may succeed to the deceased since they (and female children) are regarded as the children of deceased.

[4] The term monogamous has not been used because Swazi marriages are potentially polygynous.

[5] This presupposes that deceased left female children who have married and borne sons.

[6] I.e. the Ngwenyama or Paramount Chief.

[7] For details, see *post*, pp. 328–30.

[8] *Ibid.*

[9] See under *iphakela*.

[10] Family Council.

[11] The effect is to make the appointment of an administrator unnecessary, though the male member of the levirate will be subject to the same rules as would the administrator, *mutatis mutandis*. In practice, this makes little difference since the man who *ngena'd* the wife is normally the same person who would act as administrator.

[12] Administrator.

[13] See under pp. 298–99, *ante*.

[14] If his wife survives him, too, she may, of course, be *ngena'd*, in which case the rules given under 1(a) apply.

[15] Until they marry, when they pass into the guardianship of their husband(s).

[16] Sing, *insulamnyembeti*. This is one of the beasts paid to the father of the bride in respect of marriage. It is not part of the *lobolo*, and is provided specifically for the bride's mother (literally 'to wipe away the tears').

[17] See pp. 313–14.

[18] The generic term is *tibuga*. This includes furniture (*gwembe*); weapons (*tikali*); clothing (*tichoko*); agricultural implements (*emakhuba*); drinking pots (*tindziwo*).

[19] *Tilimo*.

[20] Normally only the main wife (as designated by the *lusendvo*).

[21] Pages 298–99, *ante*.

[22] Page 299, *ante*.

[23] If it is not followed, and the further rules referred to are not enforced, the intestate successor will be the person(s) already enumerated.

[24] I.e., his younger brother(s), uterine or otherwise.

[25] *Umntfwana weyise*, see under (c). This is the singular of *bantfwana weyise*.

[26] The term *indlalifa* is also used.

[27] The identity of the heir is not known until this time, although it may be surmised if one of the deceased's wives is obviously of such a rank as to make her selection as the main wife inevitable (*q.v.*).

[28] See pp. below, *post* for the basis on which the selection is made.

[29] Persons who must be present are widows, and at least one person from each of categories (2) and (3).

[30] *I.e.*, a member of the Dhlamini clan (the daughter of an *umntfwana benkosi*).

[31] *Tibongo.*

[32] I.e. an arranged marriage.

[33] These are rough translations.

[34] Informants claim that all wives are in any event considered simultaneously in relation to one another.

[35] *I.e.* a substitute or subordinate co-wife.

[36] Known as the *lisocankanti.*

[37] The form of words used is: 'In this homestead we are placing the burden on . . . (name of widow, with prefix *la*).' The heir is also given the wristlet of deceased.

[38] Unless, of course, some of these have been allocated prior to deceased's death: this will frequently be the case with such objects as jewellery, drinking pots, etc.

[39] The son may not dispose of such cattle without the consent of his mother.

[40] An unmarried woman would not normally own any property at all, since she is a minor. However the category is included here to embrace any estate which she might have acquired by *iphakela* (see *infra*) or in respect of minor personal possessions, clothing, etc.

[41] See *ante*, as to who such heir would be.

[42] See p. 301, note 16, *ante.*

[43] Such a disposition must have the consent of the *lusendvo.*

[44] Including *lobolo* received for daughters other than her oldest daughter (these are not, strictly speaking, hers; but she has custody over and a lifetime usufructuary interest in them).

[45] See p. 301, note 16, *ante.*

[46] I.e. whether or not he is his father's *inkosana.*

S. N. C. Obi: Women's Property and Succession thereto in Modern Ibo Law*

Succession to Women's Property

We define 'unmarried women' for the purposes of this section as women who have never been married and those who have been legally divorced in so far as concerns property which the latter acquired after the divorce. This definition excludes widows who choose to remain, unattached, in their late husband's place, for, as we have seen, they still retain the legal status of married women in some respects at least[1]. Women falling within this definition may perhaps better be designated as *femes soles*, as 'unmarried' seems to imply 'never married'. And the estate of a *feme sole* as thus understood may be defined as all her disposable property at death, including the ante-nuptial property of a divorcee which she never brought to her ex-husband's place. As we shall see later, property of this kind remains the woman's separate property even during coverture.

In the matter of succession, the estate of a *feme sole* may be said to consist of three parts: (a) articles of personal adornment such as trinkets and clothing; (b) land and economic trees; and (c) all movables other than (a).

(a) *Articles of personal adornment.*—These are inherited by the following persons and in the following order of priority:

(1) The eldest sister of the whole blood. She takes to the exclusion of all other sisters; but unlike a male heir, she assumes no corresponding obligations towards her junior sisters. Failing a sister, then:

(2) The mother. Her right to the articles is an absolute one. But if the deceased had died rather young, the mother would think of her inheritance as held in trust for her grand-daughters if any, as the items that constitute the subject-matter of inheritance under this head would naturally be a little too flashy for a middle-aged or old woman. However, there is nothing in law to stop her disposing of them at will and to anyone of her choice.

(3) Failing mother, the eldest brother of the whole blood succeeds. Naturally he will not have much use for these articles, and usually hands them over to his wife oı daughter. But here again, he has full legal rights to dispose of them at will.

(4) Failing brothers, the father may inherit, though in some societies half-sisters[2] have a higher priority than the father in this connexion.

* S. N. C. Obi, 'Women's Property and Succession thereto in Modern Ibo Law', in *Journal of African Law*, Vol. 6, No. 1, pp. 12–18.

(5) Failing fathers or half-sisters (according to the local rules), the nearest eldest female relative of the deceased on the father's line will succeed.

Children of a divorcee who were born before the divorce have no right of succession to their mother's post-divorce property.

(b) *Land and economic trees.*—These are inherited by men only, the order of priority being:

(1) The father. It is not surprising that the law gives him a higher priority than brothers in view of the fact that, after all, he was entitled to the deceased woman's 'bride-price' (i.e. marriage consideration) but never got it, or, having received it in the case of a divorcee, had to refund it.[3]

(2) Brothers of the whole blood come in next in order of seniority—the eldest taking to the exclusion of all others.

(3) Half-brothers[4] in order of seniority. Failing these—

(4) The nearest eldest male relative of the deceased's father.

(c) *Movables*[5] *other than articles of personal adornment.*—These are inherited in much the same order of priority as land and economic trees except that the mother comes in here. The order is therefore as follows:

1. The father
2. The eldest full-blood brother
3. The mother
4. The eldest half-brother
5. The eldest, nearest male relative on the male line.

Succession and illegitimate children of a feme sole. What, in terms of succession rights, is the legal position of any children the deceased woman might have had as a *feme sole*? To begin with, such children are illegitimate under Ibo law. Incidentally, this is the only case of illegitimacy known to Ibo customary law. A child is not illegitimate merely because he was born of a union between his mother and a man who is not her husband. Provided the woman concerned was, at the time the child was conceived, the lawful wife of anyone, or a widow whose marriage consideration (bride-price) has not been refunded, the child is a legitimate child of her husband whether living or dead. But a child born to a woman who is not married or had been legally divorced is an *odii*, *odanye* ('a fallen tree', 'a wild plant', the idea being that whereas legitimate children are sown by man, this one was self-sown). He is not a member of his mother's family into which he was born. He does not belong to the land. He cannot in strict legal theory inherit the land on anyone's intestacy. As far as the strict letter of the law is concerned, therefore, an illegitimate child has no rights of inheritance over property class (b) of his mother's estate.[6] But custom or sentiment may have other results.

As regards property of class (a) type, viz. articles of personal adornment, an illegitimate daughter ranks above any sisters of the deceased, for—father or no father—she is still her mother's daughter. An illegitimate son, too, has succession rights here, but he ranks below his illegitimate sister, though above everybody else.

The order of priority here is, therefore: daughters; son; full-sisters; mother; full brothers; father or half-brother; and the nearest male relative.

As to property class (c) viz. movables other than articles of personal adornment, an illegitimate son ranks highest in order of priority. Next comes an illegitimate daughter, followed by father, full-brother, mother, half-brother and nearest male relative, in that order. This means that, land apart, a *feme sole's* property is inherited by her illegitimate children, if any, irrespective of their sex.

Married woman's ante-nuptial property. We saw earlier on that though women as a rule do not inherit land, least of all in their place of birth, they can acquire exclusive rights and interests in land by purchase, pledge, gift, or lease.[7] This right to acquire is open to them both before and after marriage. And a woman can, of course, not only acquire but also inherit movables. What rules govern the right of succession to a woman's ante-nuptial property? Once more some classification of such property is necessary, this time into movables and land (including economic trees).

Movables.—She may have taken these to her husband's place on marriage. If she did, they thereby become integrated into his property *vis-à-vis* everybody but the wife,[8] and are inherited exclusively in *his* line of descent. Thus, at the wife's death, such movables (or what remains of them) will be inherited by her children born for him; articles of personal adornment by her daughters, the rest by her sons. If there are only daughters, they inherit the whole, so do sons where there are no daughters. In the absence of children, the husband succeeds, as he does to her post-nuptial property. If he is already deceased, *his* nearest relatives will inherit, in accordance with the rules already discussed. Where there are children but these are infants at the time of the woman's death, their father (or nearest male relative) takes over the property as caretaker for them.

Sometimes, however, a woman fails to take some of her movables to her husband's place following their marriage. This she may do for a variety of reasons. She may decide to give them away to friends or relatives. She may sell them or give them out on loan. In the case of livestock, she may farm them out to a third party under the traditional form of contract, whereby she is entitled to two of the progeny for every one of the caretaker's. What is the fate of property thus disposed of at the woman's death? In the case of sale or outright gift, there is nothing that her heir(s) could do. But in the other cases—pledge, conditional gifts and livestock contracts, a serious point of law could arise.

Does the fact of her retaining rights of ownership during her life-time and coverture constitute act of constructive 'bringing to her husband's place' so to to give him and his heirs a right of inheritance? Or is the fact of her thus keeping them away from her husband's place proof of her intention to take them off his line of succession? Where there are children of the marriage, this dilemma does not exist. They inherit the property, and may call on whoever has them for the time being to hand them over. This is because a woman's children inherit her movables whenever acquired. If, however, she left no surviving children, some extraneous evidence is required to tip the balance of claims in favour of either the husband or the woman's people. There must be evidence of her intention either to keep the property for her people or to pass it over to her husband. Any declarations of hers are admissible, whether as direct evidence by the person told, or as hearsay evidence by anyone. Ibo law does not reject hearsay evidence simply because it is hearsay. (The question of what weight is attached to it is a different matter.) Indeed it is good evidence of intention that she kept quiet about the property in her husband's place, while making no secret about them among her own people, and vice versa. Once this dilemma is solved, succession takes the same lines either as we have indicated above, or as will appear below ('Property acquired during coverture').

Land, including houses and economic trees.—In the nature of things, landed property acquired before marriage is not brought to the husband's place, and never comes under his control or ownership, however notional. Succession thereto is not by him or his heirs but by the woman's own people, if there are no children of the marriage. If there are such children, inheritance is confined to them and their issue, to the exclusion of their father's other children.[9] Sons inherit the property itself. Daughters succeed to their mother's exclusive right of user for life or until marriage (where there are no sons). If, there being no sons of the marriage, the daughters' rights of user ultimately determine, the property goes to the woman's brothers, etc., as if she were a *feme sole*. A husband does not succeed to the landed property acquired by his wife before marriage.[10] (This rule applies also to property received by a woman before marriage under the will of one of her relatives.)

A problem of growing importance is the husband's legal position with reference to his late wife's house acquired before their marriage and in which they lived at her death. Was such a house under the husband's control? Failing children of the marriage, can the husband succeed to this house à propos his wife's male relatives? The High Court has held with reference to Onitsha law that the woman's male relatives, not her husband, will succeed in these circumstances. This was in *Nwugege* v. *Adigwe*,[11] decided in 1934. There is every reason to believe that this principle is one of general application to all Ibo customary law. Our law is resolutely set against a non-member owning residential land within the confines of a given society, unless he intends to become absorbed into the social fabric.

Property acquired during coverture. This subject represents one of the most interesting aspects of Ibo customary law, cutting as it does right across the rules of inheritance to property. Here for the first time we are face to face with the principle of *ultimogeniture* (succession by the youngest child, which is incidentally found among the Marki of the Verre 'tribe' in Northern Nigeria),[12] running side by side with the normal Ibo principle of primogeniture.

Land.—A married woman can acquire rights and interests in land by purchase, loan, pledge or lease.[13] We saw, too, that so long as these rights and interests are acquired with the woman's own money or are given her for her own separate use, they are exclusive to her so that neither her husband nor his kinsmen could interfere with her use or disposition thereof during her life-time. At her death, these rights and interests pass to her sons. In some places, chiefly in Onitsha Division, there is joint inheritance by all the sons. Elsewhere, the eldest son succeeds to the exclusion of the others, on the familiar principle of primogeniture. If the sons are still infants, the husband (or his nearest relative, if he is dead) takes over control of the land as caretaker[14] for them.[15] Succession to a woman's rights and interests in land is restricted to her male issue on the patrilineal basis. Her own kinsmen have no right of succession to any property which she acquired during coverture. This includes property acquired after her husband's death but before her marriage-consideration (bride-price) was refunded.[16] Daughters have no right of inheritance over their mother's landed property. And so, failing sons,[17] the husband inherits. If he is already dead, his sons by other wives, or his brothers, or his nearest male relatives will succeed in that order. But in those cases where the deceased woman left daughters and no sons, her daughters have a right of user, for life or until marriage over their mother's land.

Movables.—While land and economic trees are inherited by sons exclusively, most movables are inherited by daughters. The chief heiress here is the *youngest* daughter, hence our remark about ultimogeniture above. The saying is; *odu nnwa na-eli aku nne ya* (lit. 'The youngest child eats the mother's property').[18] The eldest daughter is entitled to a few items. For instance, in parts of Onitsha Division all she gets is a right to select one article of clothing, one necklace and one or two cooking utensils. The rest of the mother's movable property other than money goes to her youngest daughter. Intermediate daughters get nothing. An only daughter gets the lot, of course. Money goes to the eldest *son*.

If there are no daughters, the youngest son inherits all the movables in some societies, and all but a few specific items in others. If the principal heir or heiress is already deceased, his/her children will succeed in their place irrespective of sex. We may point out here that so far as succession to a married woman's property is concerned, it is immaterial that her chief heiress or her eldest daughter, as the case may be, is already married at the time of her death. She retains her right of succession and may come over from her husband's place to claim her inheritance.[19] In the absence of sons or daughters or their issue, the husband inherits his wife's movables as he does her land. If he, too, is already dead, his sons by other wives, brothers or other male relatives inherit in that order.

To summarize: *Land* acquired by a married woman during coverture is inherited in the following order of priority: sons jointly or eldest son exclusively, husband, husband's sons by other wives,[20] husband's brothers or nearest male relatives. *Movables* are inherited in this order: youngest and eldest daughters,[21] youngest and eldest sons,[22] husband, husband's sons by other wives, husband's brothers, or his nearest male relatives. The husband takes control on behalf of infant heirs; so does his nearest male relative, if he is dead.

Notes

[1] E.g. any children born to them subsequent to their husband's death are legitimate children of those husbands; they retain their right of occupation and use over some, at least, of their late husband's landed property, etc.

[2] *I.e.* of the same father but different mothers. Half-sisters in the sense of daughters of the same mother by different fathers do not come in at all except perhaps where the second father was of the same family as the first so that there has been 'widow-inheritance'. Even here sentiment, not law, is at work.

[3] There could be no legal divorce under customary law till the marriage consideration ('bride-price') has been refunded.

[4] These have the same definition as half-sisters (f.n. 1) with the sexes changed.

[5] This class includes money and animals.

[6] Such a child has no legal relationship to his natural father and can never succeed to any of his property on intestacy. The position, would, however, be quite different if he were later legitimated by subsequent marriage between his 'parents'. But the question whether or not legitimation is recognized by Ibo law, fascinating as it is, falls outside the scope of this article and cannot be pursued here.

[7] Meek, *Land Tenure in Nigeria*, p. 186.
[8] E.g. it is his duty to defend them or sue for the appropriate remedy in case of detinue, conversion, or trespass.
[9] Cf. Harris, 'Papers on . . . Ozuitem Ibos' in (1943) *Africa*, at pp. 12 ff, 302 ff.
[10] Meek, *op. cit.*, p. 186.
[11] 11 N.L.R. 134.
[12] Elias, *Land Law*, (2nd ed.), p. 233, quoting Meek, *Tribal Studies in N. Nigeria*, Vol I, p. 415.
[13] Cf. Forde and Scott, *Native Economies of Nigeria*, pp. 66–7; Meek, *ibid.*, p. 186.
[14] Meek, and Forde and Scott use the term 'trustee'.
[15] Forde and Scott, *Native Economies of Nigeria*, pp. 66–7; Meek, *op. cit.*, p. 186.
[16] Marriage under customary law is not dissolved by the death of either spouse. To do this there must be either a formal dissolution and remarriage within the late husband's family, or a refund of the marriage-consideration (bride-price).
[17] Or grandsons (= sons' sons), for these succeed in their father's stead.
[18] *Aku* as 'property' does not include land and may be called 'personalty'.
[19] And to discharge her onerous and expensive duties in connexion with her mother's funeral and 'second-burial' rites.
[20] Or their male issue.
[21] The chief share going to the first-mentioned.
[22] *Ibid.*

(b) Matrilineal

J. M. Sarbah: Fanti Customary Law*

The first important rule which one has to learn and ever bear in mind when dealing with matters of succession is that the right of inheritance is only through the female, and pedigree is traced through the female line and *that* only.[1]

There is no such thing as succession, in the proper English meaning, in a family owning ancestral property. The whole family, consisting of males and females, constitutes a sort of corporation; some of the members being coparceners, i.e. persons entitled to a portion of the property on partition (cutting Ekar), and others who are dependants, and are entitled to reside in the dwelling-house for life, such as sons and daughters, subject to good conduct and not disputing right of the family. Partition being extremely rare, the idea of heirship scarcely presents itself to the mind of any member of the family. The members are entitled to reside in the ancestral house, and to enjoy that amount of affluence and consideration which springs from their belonging to a family possessed of greater or less wealth.

The head of a family holds his property either in severalty or in coparcenary, and this depends whether the property is self-acquired, family property, or ancestral property, and, if the last, whether it be attached to some political or public office.

The right of inheritance to ancestral property attached to a public or political office, varies as to whether such property is enjoyed with or without the immediate remote control of any person. For example, in the case of a captaincy (Tufuhin) or other commanding position in a fighting force, without election no one can fill the post left vacant by his father or uncle or brother.

Where the property is under or subject to another stool or head of a family, either by commendation or subjection, or by any other means, the superior lord or head of the family has an ultimate and absolute right of veto, whenever the person selected or elected by the retinue or members of the family is considered unfit or unsuitable by him.

E.g. Kudwo, brother or nephew of X deceased, is chosen by his family to sit on the stool under Y, whose chief he was. If the blood relatives and domestics and bondmen of the family concur, the proposal must be confirmed by king Y, before Kudwo can be placed in the room of X deceased. And on the failure of the blood relatives, domestics, and bondmen to present a suitable person, the king may himself choose one of the blood relatives; and this person will succeed if accepted by the major part of the family or people of the subordinate stool, otherwise one of the domestics or bondmen is to be

* J. M. Sarbah, *Fanti Customary Law*, Frank Cass & Co. Ltd., 1967, pp. 100–105.

appointed as the manager or trustee for life or for a specified period of the family possessions.[2]

The owner of self-acquired real property dying intestate, is not succeeded by his sons, they being outside the line of inheritance, but by his mother and her issue according to seniority.

Persons in the line of succession are:

Mother

Brothers, according to seniority.

Nephews, by seniority.

Sisters.

Sisters' daughters.

Failing these—

Mother's brothers, by seniority or election.

Mother's sisters.

Mother's sisters' children.

Failing these and their stock, the domestics in whose veins runs any of the heritable blood, take by seniority. Next, the head domestic; lastly, a member of the tribe. Provided always that a man is invariably preferred to a woman. Hence the saying, 'Obaa odan bayin' (a man is the mainstay of a woman).

There are therefore four kinds of successors, viz. Real, Proper, Ordinary, and Extraordinary.

The Real successor of a person is his mother.

We call those persons *Proper* successors who are the uterine brothers and sisters of the deceased, and the issue of such sisters; but never can the pedigree be traced out in the line of the male.

Ordinary successors are such persons as are descended from the maternal grandmother: E.g.: A person's uncle or aunts, and the issue of such aunts.

Extraordinary successors are:

(i) Issue by a house domestic with a male person of the heritable blood (Dihi).

(ii) Domestic.

(iii) Clan or tribal relative.

The rule of succession may be made plain perhaps by the following pedigree or table of descent:

In the pedigree below A, a male, is the owner of self-acquired property. On his death, his wife Abba does not succeed to his property, but his Real successor is his mother B; she waiving her right, his brothers C, D, and E take by seniority. Failing the brothers C, D, and E, his successor is found among his nephews, that is, children of his sisters F, G, and H.

The nephews are I, son of his sister F; and J, son of his sister G. These take by seniority; if, therefore, J, the nephew by his younger sister G, is older than I, J has a better right to the succession.

If the nephew I or J be older than the brothers C, D, E, such nephew can be preferred over the brothers C, D, E, and the sisters F, G, H, to succeed A, and although the brothers are capable to succeed, yet any of them can waive his right in favour of one of the nephews. On the death, however, of the nephew, the right of the brother passed over or who waived his right revives. Failing the brothers and nephews, the next persons in the succession are K and L; next to them are M, N, and O, then P, Q, and R. The persons so named are those who can be placed on the stool, if any, and can become head of the family. If any of them cannot succeed when it is his turn, and there is no proper person available, then S, a son of E, by a domestic of the house, or a suitable domestic is appointed manager of the property. It seems that where a house-born son as S is appointed guardian trustee, or manager, he holds his post for life, although he can resign in favour of any of the proper successors becoming fit to inherit.

The sisters F, G, and H are the natural and proper guardians of the property during the incapacity or minority of the proper successors, but their management of such property and their control goes by seniority, the eldest, F, taking before G and H. Where the nephews are capable to look after the property, they take by turns: e.g. if the three sisters had three sons each, after the death or disposition for misconduct of the eldest son of the eldest sister, one of the sons of the second sister will be entitled to succeed to the uncle's property, and on his death the eldest son of the youngest sister will be next

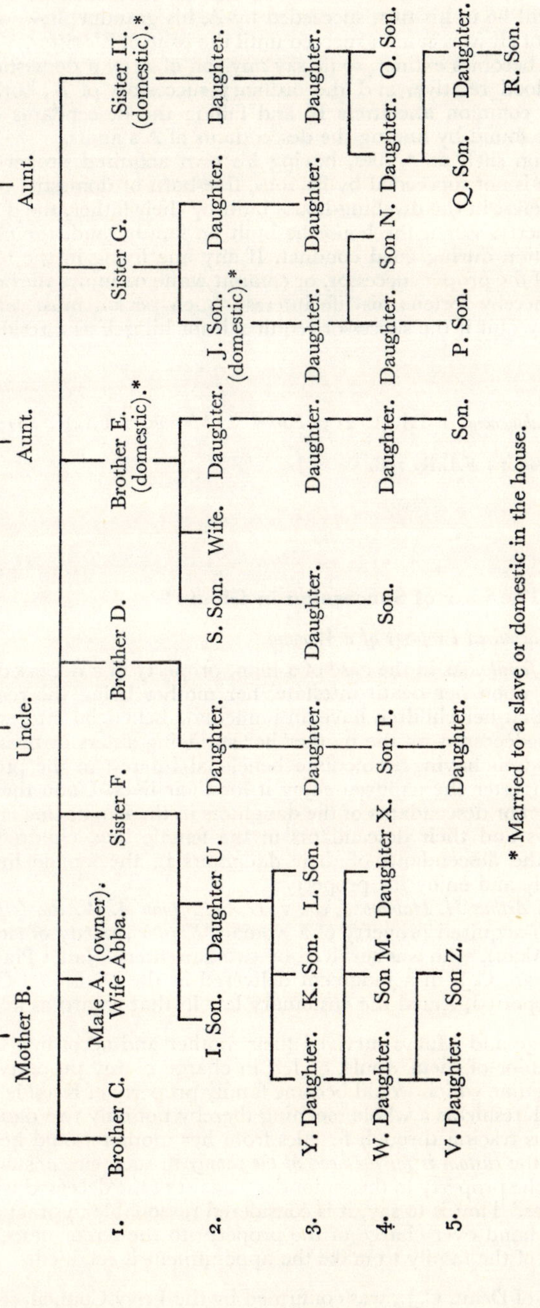
Mother B.
Uncle.
Aunt.
Aunt.
1. Brother C.
Male A. (owner). Wife Abba.
Sister F.
Brother D.
Brother E. (domestic).*
Sister G.
Sister H. (domestic).*
2. I. Son.
Daughter U.
Daughter.
S. Son.
Wife.
Daughter.
J. Son. (domestic).*
Daughter.
Daughter.
3. Y. Daughter.
K. Son.
L. Son.
Daughter.
Daughter.
Daughter.
Daughter.
Daughter.
4. W. Daughter.
Son M.
Daughter X.
Son T.
Son.
Daughter.
Daughter.
Son N.
Daughter.
O. Son.
5. V. Daughter.
Son Z.
Daughter.
Son.
P. Son.
Q. Son.
Daughter.
R. Son.
* Married to a slave or domestic in the house.

entitled, and one branch will not be exhausted before those of the other branch come in.

Suppose K, a son of U, the daughter of F, who is the sister of A, had died, leaving self-acquired property. After his mother he will be succeeded by L, then by M, his nephew, who will be in his turn succeeded by Z, his grandnephew, and not by O, the great grandson of H, who cannot succeed until the issue of Z's sister, V, becomes extinct. When that line becomes extinct, some say any son of Z by a domestic takes preference to O, who is blood relative, and the ordinary successors of K, both persons tracing descent from a common ancestress B, and failing the descendants of B, the persons entitled must be found by finding the descendants of A's aunts.

When a person such as A dies, having his own acquired property, moveable and immoveable, he is not succeeded by his sons, free-born or domestic, whose only right is that of a life interest in the dwelling-house built by their father, the deceased, on a land not family property. For if the house be built on family land, the children have only right of occupation during good conduct. If any one living in the house of his father deny the right of the proper successor, or commit waste or injure the house, or encumber or sell it, he thereby forfeits his life interest. Such person must make the necessary repairs, and may quit if the successor requires it for himself as a residence.

Notes

[1] *Abbacan* v. *Bubuwooni*, 1 F.L.R. 213; *Parker* v. *Mensah*, 1 F.L.R. 204; *Holdbrook* v, *Atta*, 1 F.L.R. 211.

[2] *Amfoo* v. *Yardonua* 1 F.L.R. 198.

N. A. Ollenu: The Law of Succession in Ghana*

Succession to Self-acquired Property of a Woman

In the matrilineal family. As in the case of a man, property of a deceased woman becomes family property upon her death intestate, her mother being the real successor; with this difference, that her children have an immediate beneficial interest in the property. Where she is predeceased by the mother her surviving sisters in turn become the successors, her children having immediate beneficial interest in the property. Upon the death of the last sister the children enjoy it for their lives. Upon the death of the last child the children or descendants of the daughters in the female line enjoy the property, failing daughters and their descendants in the female line, children of sisters of the deceased, and the descendants of their daughters in the female line, constitute the immediate family and enjoy the property:[1]

In the case of *Arthur H. Hammond, etc.* v. *U.A.C., John A. W. Randolph & anor.*, where succession to self-acquired property of a woman '*Kreshie*', partly of Accra and partly of Amanorkrom (Akan), who was survived by two daughters—Janet Plange and Momo—was in issue, Dean, C.J. in a judgment delivered in the Divisional Court on the 13th July, 1939, unreported, stated the customary law in that regard as follows:

> 'Janet Plange and Momo survived their mother and according to native law and custom the senior of them would be left in charge of any property acquired by her during her lifetime which would become family property of Kreshie. Strictly speaking the family of Kreshie as a whole meaning thereby not only two daughters but all her blood relations tracing through females from her mother would be interested in the property but the *custom is for the head of the family* in such circumstances to hand over the charge of the property to the senior descendant of the deceased whose self-acquired property it was.' That is to say, it is considered reasonable in practice for the head of the family to hand over charge of the property to the senior descendant. That is to say, the right of the family to make the appointment is retained.

That decision of Dean, C.J., was confirmed by the Privy Council, see 5 W.A.C.A. 42.

* N. A. Ollenu, *The Law of Succession in Ghana*, Presbyterian Press, Accra, 1960, pp. 35–37.

See also:

(1) *Mary Jones Nelson* v. *Ocansey & Margaret Tackie*, Judgment of W.A.C.A. unreported, dated 11th March, 1950.
(2) *Acquaye* v. *Naa Dedei & Crabbe*, Judgment of the Land Court, Accra, dated the 25th October, 1957, unreported.
(3) *Aki Mills* v. *F. L. Addy*, Judgment of the Land Court, Accra, dated 4th March, 1958, unreported.
(4) *Nana Juaben Serwah* v. *Nana Akyea Kesse*, Judgment of the Land Court, Accra, dated 10th April, 1959, unreported.

In the case of *Mary Jones Nelson* v. *Ocansey & Margaret Tackie*, the West African Court of Appeal held that although by custom children inherit the property of their deceased mother and are immediately entitled to enjoyment of beneficial interest in it, yet the sisters of the deceased are, in the absence of her mother, her successors by custom, having direct interest in her property, and are the proper persons to manage and control it for the benefit of themselves and the children; and that it is not until the death of the last of the sisters of the original owner, that the children can exercise that management and control which the head of the family or the successor exercises upon appointment.

Applying the principle in the case of, *Nelson* v. *Ocansey & Tackie*, the Land Court Accra held in the case of *Acquaye* v. *Naa Dedei & Crabbe* as follows:

> 'By native custom a woman's self-acquired property descends to her children upon her death........Upon the death of the last surviving child, that property becomes the property of the maternal family of that woman, children of her sons are not members of that family and have no interest in the grand-mother's said property.'

The deceased in that case died leaving no sister.

The custom was further explained in more detail in the case of *Aki Mills* v. *Addy* where the statement of the custom as set out in *Sarbah F.C.L.*, *Hammond* v. *U.A.C. and Randolph*, *Nunoo* v. *Cleland*, *Nelson* v. *Ocansey & Tackie*, and *Acquaye* v. *Naa Dedei & Crabbe* were fully considered. It was explained as follows:

> 'When a person, male or female, dies intestate his or her self-acquired property becomes family property to be administered by the head of his or her family. The head of the family by custom entrusts the property, as distinct from ancestral property to the "Real" or the "Proper" successor as the case may be. The question of who constitutes that family, and in the absence of the Real Successor—the mother—the question of who are the Proper Successors are questions to be decided in each particular case, upon well defined principles of native custom.
>
> 'In the case of a woman, the successors in the family are her children and her *children's "children"* in the female line. The word *children's children* should be construed to mean "*children's children who belong to the family and are by custom in the line of succession;* therefore where the family is the maternal family, the phrase *children's children*" can only mean the "children of daughters". Upon failure of "Proper" successor, succession is taken a step higher up the family tree to the trunk family of the "Real" successor, i.e. mother of the original owner of the property, and where necessary a step higher still to the trunk family of the grandmother of the original owner. It is only upon failure to trace any such maternal family trunk that recourse could be had to descendants of male members of the family. The interest which children take in the self-acquired property of their mother upon her death intestate is not an interest by purchase or of absolute ownership; it is only a life interest determinable upon the life of each of such child. The beneficial interest in such property is enjoyed by the direct descendants in the female line, but upon failure of such children and grandchildren in the female line, the property assumes the character of an ancestal property and must be under the direct control and management of the head of the immediate family or of the wider family as the case may be of the original owner.'

Note

[1] Sarbah, Fanti Customary Law, p. 256.

Chapter 17

DISPOSITIVE AND TESTAMENTARY SUCCESSION

(a) Dispositions During Lifetime

A. N. Allott: Ashanti Law of Property*

To what extent is a man able, by *inter vivos* act, to affect the course of succession to his estate? Can he, for instance, nominate his successor; or bequeath particular portions of his estate to family-members or strangers?

In the old law it is clear that a man had no legal power to affect succession to his estate; he could, by *inter vivos* gift or by *mortis causa* bequest, give away his property temporarily or permanently; but, in order for such a gift or bequest to be valid and have permanent effect, it was necessary that it should have been made with the knowledge and concurrence of his family, or at least should have been ratified by them. In practice, provided the property was given to those of whom the family approved or who had a definite connexion with or claim on deceased (e.g. his wife or child), and provided also that deceased left the bulk of his property to go according to the ordinary rules of intestate succession, it was probable that the wishes of deceased for the disposition of his property would be honoured by his family.

Today, whilst the family continue to control the disposition of inherited property left by deceased (which he cannot dispose of without the family's consent), it is probable that he can dispose as of right of his self-acquired property by an oral nuncupative will (*samansεε*—'what the ghost has arranged'), provided this is made in due form.

Whilst in earlier times it was likely that a bequest of this sort had to be made on his death-bed by the dying man, today a bequest in contemplation of death is probably valid. The bequest must be witnessed, preferably by independent witnesses as well as by the appropriate members of the family (especially the preferential successor, the head of family or section, etc), and the beneficiary must give *aseda* as soon as possible in order to stamp the bequest; this thank-offering is distributed among the witnesses, thus providing evidence of the will and at the same time estopping the family from disputing its validity.

Bequests of this nature are especially made by a father to his sons, who would otherwise be completely excluded from the succession. So a father might present one or more of his cocoa farms to a son who has served him well. Bequests to wives are much less frequent, though often they will be allowed to continue to reside in their late husband's house and also to work any land which he may have allowed them to farm.

Nomination of a successor appears much rarer; at least our sources tell us little about it.

C. K. Meek: Land Tenure and Land Administration in Nigeria and the Cameroons†

Normally, inheritance is governed by the rules of the customary law. But the customary law may be varied by gifts *inter vivos* (i.e., gifts made during life or between living persons).

It is hardly necessary to observe that gifts must be of property which can be legally given away and should therefore be made in front of disinterested witnesses. A member of a lineage or 'family' cannot legally give away a piece of his allotment of lineage land

* A. N. Allott, 'Ashanti Law of Property', in *Zeitschrift fur vergleichende Rechtswissenschaft*, 1966, pp. 184–185.

† C. K. Meek, *Land Tenure and Land Administration in Nigeria and the Cameroons*, H.M.S.O., 1957, p. 182.

since that would not be his to give. A lineage can, however, with the general consent of the lineage, give away a piece of its surplus land as a free gift. And a member of a lineage can give away a piece of land which he had acquired for himself by purchase or otherwise. He may give to a son, or daughter, or sister's child a gift of economic trees or of a plantation which he owned in his own right.

Gifts of land may be absolute gifts, carrying no conditions. But there may be an express or implied condition that the land given may not be alienated or re-given without the original donor's permission. In this connection it may be observed that gifts of virgin forest or of urban lands are unlikely to carry any conditions.

The necessity for witnesses to gifts is obvious, since many cases have come before the courts in which one of the parties has contended that the land in dispute had been an outright gift, while the other has maintained that it had been a conditional grant. For this reason gifts *inter vivos* are nowadays commonly supported by documentary evidence.

P. C. Lloyd: Yoruba Land Law*

Gifts inter vivos

A man's interests in property at his death may be classified into those which were self-acquired and those which he inherited, using this term loosely. In the case of the latter the interests either cannot be bequeathed outside the kin group of the original creator, as will be discussed later, or cannot be bequeathed at all since the deceased held the rights corporately with the remainder of the group—*omoiya*, *obakan* or kin group. His interests in self-acquired property he may use during his lifetime, or bequeath at his death as he pleases. No legal action can be taken to prevent him from alienating these interests and no consent is needed by other parties such as members of his family. In the case of a gift *inter vivos* he should make it plain that the donee is receiving the donor's total interests in the property and is not merely becoming a customary tenant or pawnee (pledgee) in either of which status his use of the property might not ostensibly be different from that of a true owner. The transaction should therefore be witnessed by the donor's *olori ebi*† as a certification that the donor does in fact possess the right to make the gift, and also by his children in order to forestall later claims by them that the grant was not outright. Gifts of property are so rare that the courts require strong evidence that a transfer of this nature has taken place.

N. N. Rubin: The Swazi Law of Succession: a Restatement‡

Dispositive and Testamentary Disposition

A. Distribution During Lifetime

1. *Power of distribution during lifetime.* Both men and women have the power to distribute property during their lifetime.

In the case of a woman's *inter vivos* disposition, this requires the consent of her husband or guardian, and the latter's *lusendvo*.[1] An *inter vivos* disposition by a woman may involve either actual distribution of her property to the persons indicated by her as entitled to receive it, or may merely operate as an indication of the manner in which her estate is to be distributed on her decease. In the latter case she retains her interest in the property.

In the case of a man, *inter vivos* disposition is known as *iphakela*.[2]

2. *Validity of inter vivos distribution: power to deviate from rules of intestacy.*

(a) *Alteration of shares of heirs.*—No man may *iphakela* land, and therefore he may not alter the rights of the heirs in this respect.[3]

* P. C. Lloyd, *Yoruba Land Law*, Nigerian Institute of Social and Economic Research, 1963, p. 17.

† Oldest male member of the kin group.

‡ N. N. Rubin, 'The Swazi Law of Succession: a Restatement', in *Journal of African Law*, Vol. 9, No. 2, pp. 106–107.

Only the property which belongs to the *indlunkulu* (main house) of the *umnumzana*[4] (*i.e.*, is attached to it) may be the subject of *inter vivos* distribution.

With the above exception, the *umnumzana* may *iphakela* any property: by doing so, he will thus automatically alter the inheritance to be received by heirs (both the *inkosana* and the *bantfwana weyise*).[5]

(b) *Manner of distribution.*—An *inter vivos* distribution may only be made to the wives[6] of a man, and may not be made to his children.[7]

A future interest in the property yet to be acquired may also be the subject of *liphakelo* (e.g. the right to acquire *lobolo* paid for a particular daughter who is not yet married may be given to someone who would not otherwise receive it).[8]

A *liphakelo* may be given subject to a condition as to the manner in which it is to be used (e.g. cattle may be provided for a wife to *lobolo* an *inhlanti* for herself).[9]

(c) *Formalities for valid iphakela.*—Any *inter vivos* distribution made by a man must be reported to his *lusendvo*. It is not necessary, however, that this body be convened specially for the purpose. The report may be made subsequently to the making of the actual *iphakela*, and may even be reported to the members of the *lusendvo* individually. The persons to whom a distribution must be reported include the wives of the person making the distribution; his senior paternal aunt; his oldest brother; and the *umnumzana* of the homestead adjacent to his; or to such of these persons (or their successors) as may be available.

3. *Disinheritance.* As a result of *iphakela* a man may disinherit a particular son: since the identity of his heir is not known[10] to him, the only manner in which this could occur in the case of a polygynist would be by giving all cattle and movables to sons other than the oldest son in each of the houses in the homestead. Even such action will not, however, deprive the son whose mother is selected as the main wife of all his inheritance. He is still entitled to succeed to his father's offices, to guardianship of minors, wives and dependants, and to rights in respect of land.

Thus, the only effective method of complete disinheritance is that described below in relation to wills.

4. *Alienation to strangers*

(a) Alienation of land is not permitted in Swazi law, though some interests may be transferred during the lifetime of a person.

(b) Alienation of livestock and other (movable) property is permissible, and can accordingly affect the nature of the estate left by deceased person.

An heir cannot question such alienation except where this was done in circumstances in which the person alienating it did not have complete authority to do so.[11]

Notes

[1] In practice, however, the consent of the guardian is sufficient, although the matter must be reported to the *lusendvo.*

[2] This is the verb form. An allocation in this way is known as a *liphakelo.*

[3] Note, however, that the rights of women in respect of land, land occupied and cultivated by them are preserved.

[4] Head of the household.

[5] The main heir and the minor heirs.

[6] In practice to the houses, not just the wives, *i.e.* it is intended for the use of the wife during her lifetime but will pass to the *inkosana* or *bantfwana weyise* when deceased dies.

[7] This can, however, be done in a will; see p. 329, *post.*

[8] See *ante,* for rules as to which sons receive *lobolo* cattle. In practice this would probably mean a son other than the senior son in each house. This apparently conflicts with the rules stated above that no allocation may be made other than to a wife and must be treated as an exception to it.

[9] *Tinhlanti* are subordinate co-wives.

[10] In theory.

[11] E.g. where the consent of some other person was required for the alienation and this had not been given. Such a case would be the cattle of which a wife has a lifetime usufructuary right as a result of *liphakelo.*

H. Cory and M. M. Hartnoll: Customary Law of the Haya*

Gifts

A gift of land made by a father to an heir at any time prior to his death is counted in with his real property and after his death it must be divided among his sons.

NOTE: Gifts of landed property which is under family tenure to persons who are not entitled to the inheritance of this real property are not legal. A father is therefore not allowed to make his wife or daughter or a friend etc. a gift of real property. Such a gift would not be acknowledged after his death, even if it should be confirmed in a last will or by witnesses.

At such time the Musika has the right to decide whether he will take over the father's plantation or the plot that was given him.

The decision of the Musika is irrevocable.

Other presents made during lifetime are not counted in with the estate.

An exception is made in the case when the Musika has received as a gift Shs. 100/- or a cow for brideprice from his father. If the father dies and leaves enough money or cattle and one or more unmarried sons, one hundred shillings each must be handed over to the guardians of the unmarried sons to be kept until they have to pay brideprice.

If a father makes gifts of land which is under family tenure or cattle to his sons, wives or daughters they are only considered the property of the recipients if presented formally before witnesses. If the gift is land the father must appoint a mutaya. If the gift is a cow see 'kuhela kimoi'.

H. Cory: Sukuma Law and Custom†

Distribution of Estate by the Father during his Lifetime

If a father distributes the estate during his lifetime, this distribution is valid, even if he does not follow the laws relating to inheritance. His decision cannot be impugned after his death by a disinherited son.

An heir who has been disinherited or who thinks that his share is not adequate can file a suit against the coheirs.

NOTE: This right is granted to the heir because he had no opportunity of trying to propitiate the father; but he has little chance of securing a redistribution of the estate if it can be proved that it was the express will of the father to disinherit his son, or to reduce his share.

(b) WILLS

J. Matson: Testate Succession in Ashanti‡

Testate Succession in Ashanti

Ashanti customary law, in common with the law of other branches of the Akan people, recognizes a form of oral will, or rather a form of inchoate gift that takes effect on death. This is called *saman-nse*, *saman* being an ancestral spirit and *nse* (or *nseɛ*) meaning a formal or solemn declaration;[1] *di nse*, for example, means to take an oath as a witness does in court. This is the derivation accepted in Ashanti and, with all respect to Rattray's great knowledge, he is in error if he suggests the root is *sie*, to put, preserve, take care of.[2] His contemptuous rejection of phonetic spelling makes it a little uncertain what

* H. Cory and M. M. Hartnoll, *Customary Law of the Haya*, Lund Humphries for International African Institute, 1945, p. 29.

† H. Cory, *Sukuma Law and Custom*, Oxford University Press, 1953, p. 169.

‡ J. Matson, 'Testate Succession in Ashanti', in *Africa*, Vol. 23, International African Institute, 1953, pp. 224–232.

sound he meant to record, but on linguistic grounds it is clear the word is not *sie*. The second *a* of *saman* is not modified; the use of a final *eɛ* instead of *e* in certain positions in a sentence is common in Ashanti; and the corresponding Fante forms are *saman-nsew*, *dzi nsew*, and *sie*.

When a man dies intestate his self-acquired property goes to a member of his own little sub-lineage, normally to a brother, or in default to a maternal nephew. In default of brothers and nephews the property is still retained within some branch of the lineage. But a man may not wish the normal successor (the elder brother, or the son of the elder sister, who has a prior right to be considered) to succeed to his property. He may also wish to leave something to his wife and children, who, the lineage being exogamous, cannot be of his own blood. It was probably reasons of this kind which gave rise to the oral will.

Sarbah,[3] writing sixty years ago of the coastal Akan, the Fante, considered the institution 'without doubt of modern growth', but Rattray[4] has described the Ashanti oral will as a long-established institution which existed before there was any question of outside influence. A father might give part (only) of the farms he had made to his son, provided always that the lineage consented. The modern Ashanti custom may be stated thus: a person may make a reasonable gift of part or all of his or her self-acquired property, to take effect on death, at the same time informing the lineage, though not necessarily obtaining their consent. The procedure is the same as that for making any other binding gift or agreement. The donor calls together witnesses and makes his declaration in their presence; the donee pays thanksgiving (*aseda*), of which the donor retains part and distributes the rest among the witnesses, who are thereafter obliged to testify to the transaction in future if necessary. Some of the *aseda* is normally given to the members of the lineage who are present. They accept it not simply as witnesses, however, but as persons who, like the donor, are giving up rights; for they would take the property in default of the gift. Their acceptance of *aseda* makes the gift binding upon them, and signifies their consent.

The controversy of today centres on the questions of whether lineage consent is necessary, and if not, what is a reasonable gift. It is generally agreed that consent was formerly necessary, but it is also clear that the lineage normally *did* consent, 'from feelings of respect, affection, or even superstition', as Sarbah[5] puts it; in other words, from fears of the ghost. One Ashanti, writing about 1946, has said that consent is necessary today,[6] and this is very likely so in the remoter rural areas. Actual cases in the courts, however, show that it is not always demanded, as may be seen from the case notes given hereafter. Fear of the ancestors, though still strong,[7] is no doubt weaker than it was, and the rule of 'reasonableness', even perhaps that of free disposition, seems to be taking the place of the rule requiring consent. There are two maxims (not confined to gifts within the lineage) which express the norm, and the overriding powers of the lineage. *Ade a saman akyɛ no, teasefo ngye* (what an ancestral ghost has given away, the living do not take); and *Sɛ saman kyɛ ade na ɔankyɛ no yiye a, teasefo kyɛ* (if the ghost has distributed his property and done it badly, the living will redistribute). The latter is said to be of more recent origin than the former.

What is reasonable depends very much on the circumstances. A man's prime duty is to increase the property and prestige of his lineage. If his gift (or even a death-bed wish without the formality of thanksgiving) does not mean that the property will be lost to the lineage, his wishes will normally be respected. Sarbah[8] goes so far as to say that among the Fante the lineage 'cannot ignore such dispositions'. While a man should support his lineage, there is also a reciprocal duty of the lineage to support and succour its members. A common cause of a gift outside the lineage is the failure of kinsmen to carry out this duty; and such a gift is reasonable in these circumstances. Parental affection, services rendered by donee, gifts made to the normal successor *inter vivos:* these are all circumstances which will be taken into account. A gift to a child or to a friend means that the property is lost to the lineage. The kinsmen will look on it with disfavour and may remind the donor that they are liable for his debts; the limits of the reasonable are much narrower in this case.

As to the procedural requirements, it seems that some disinterested witnesses are invariably at hand, and it is sometimes said that the presence of one such witness is essential to the validity of the gift. This seems to be confusing the legally necessary truth with the practically necessary, however—if the two can in this case be separated; for if there is no such witness, 'your father's kinsmen will run first to the place where the property is, and say you are a liar'.

The old desire to prevent the nephew taking all, leaving the son empty-handed, has become stronger with modern economic and religious changes. The question has been discussed by the Asanteman Council, but opinion in Ashanti is not ready for a statutory change in the customary law to make the nuncupative will revocable, not *mortis causa*, secret and independent of the lineage—attributes it does not appear now to possess. In 1946 the Asantehene persuaded the Asanteman Council to write into some notes on native custom a statement that 'when a person makes a gift of his own personal self-acquired property to his children or to any other person in the presence of accredited witnesses, whether the relatives of the donor approve of it or not it becomes valid'. This has no legislative effect and does not express the Council's settled opinion.

There has been a parallel move in the Colony. In 1949, following an exhibition of hard swearing by 'expert' witnesses before the Supreme Court, the Joint Provincial Council of Chiefs declared 'that for an oral death-bed disposition of self-acquired property to be valid the only requisite is the presence of some responsible and disinterested witnesses', and urged States to make declarations (which could be given the force of law) to this effect. Akyem Abuakwa alone did so, in the following words:[9]

1. No property other than personal property and real property which might have been disposed of by will or by gift may be disposed of by Samansew.

2. The disposition of property by Samansew is valid if it is made voluntarily and orally in the presence of two responsible and disinterested witnesses, by a person of sound mind in expectation of death from illness however caused.

3. Save where a person disposing of his property by Samansew recovers from the illness in the course of which the disposition was made, any disposition of property by Samansew is irrevocable.

It is clear that in Ashanti such gifts or wills are frequently made when there is no expectation of death from illness, though a man is reluctant to make testamentary dispositions until he feels that he is approaching the end of his days. If the Akyem declaration excludes such wills it probably marks a change in Akyem customary law. The same applies to revocability. Payment of *aseda* renders an ordinary gift *inter vivos* irrevocable, and the rule applies (at least in Ashanti) to a gift which takes effect on death. The Akyem Abuakwa State Council may have had in mind the mere expression of a wish by a sick man (who later recovers) without payment of thanksgiving by the donee. Here, as in the case of ordinary executory gifts, no right to the property is acquired by the donee.

These efforts made over the last decade to develop the customary will, both in Ashanti and the Colony, have not been either united or very vigorous. More attention has been paid to efforts to give the children of the deceased a fixed fraction of the estate on intestacy, instead of the whole going to the kindred. For various reasons this is probably a less satisfactory line of development, and in fact no change in the law has been made.

So far, the only system of law considered has been Ashanti custom. But there are two bodies of law operating concurrently in Ashanti, in their respective spheres: this customary law and English law—that is, 'common law, the doctrines of equity, and the statutes of general application which were in force in England on the 24th day of July 1874'. This English law was introduced into the Gold Coast Colony by the local legislature which was established on the date above mentioned, and was imported into Ashanti after that territory was annexed in 1901. Among the 'statutes of general application' was the Wills Act, 1837.

How are the spheres of operation of the two systems to be regulated? The rules laid down are unambiguous as far as they go.[10] Customary law 'shall be deemed applicable in causes and matters where the parties thereto are natives, and particularly . . . in causes and matters relating to . . . inheritance and testamentary dispositions'. Where the parties are mixed, customary law is also to apply if 'a strict adherence to the rules of English law, would result in substantial injustice. By implication, therefore, English law governs the disputes of non-natives, and prima facie also those where the parties are mixed.[11]

The method of resolving all conflicts of laws by reference to the personality of litigants is unscientific. The law applicable to a transaction may be uncertain until battle is joined in the courts; and where a single act in the law gives rise to more than one action, curious results may follow. If *A*, an Ashanti, makes an oral will leaving property to *S*, his son, and to *F*, his life-long friend, an immigrant from Freetown (a non-native for this purpose), and the heir refuses to honour either legacy, are the two suits that follow to be judged by different laws? However, these theoretical considerations do not seem to cause trouble in practice.

It might be thought from the foregoing rules that, on the one hand, the Supreme Court would not uphold statutory wills made by Africans, and on the other, the Judges would develop and enforce the oral will. In practice, however, neither of these things has happened. The neglect of the oral will has largely been caused by the ready application of the Wills Act, 1837, to all and sundry without consideration of whether it is part of the personal law applicable in any given case. This practice dates from the early days of the Supreme Court of the Colony, when the court was often curiously blind to the limits laid down for English law. The rule has been imported into Ashanti, and it is too well established now to be challenged.

It might also be said that statutory wills should be enforced so far as the testator has thereby done what customary law would allow him to do by other means; and perhaps some such synthesis could be achieved. Documentary evidence has great advantages over oral testimony, and a memorandum is frequently now made of an oral will. But it is clear that the two institutions are very different; in particular, the one recognizes no restrictions on the right to dispose of self-acquired property, and by fostering secrecy allows the claims of the lineage to be defeated.[12]

Once a succession dispute has been settled in a Native Court the Supreme Court will not reopen the matter.[13] But the Supreme Court will not grant probate, or letters of administration with the will annexed, in the case of an oral will. There is no provision for such a grant in the procedure rules, it is true, but this can hardly override the provisions of the Ordinance. In a case[14] heard in 1894 it was said *obiter* that 'there is no power conferred on this Court to grant probate with the will annexed, or probate of a will made according to native law'. Despite a contrary dictum[15] let fall by Michelin J. in 1927, this seems to have been tacitly accepted as correct, though Redwar[16] pointed out forty years ago that there is nothing in the Ordinance to prevent a grant, as the provision that probate jurisdiction may be exercised 'in conformity with the law and practice for the time being in force in England' is permissive only.

CASE NOTES

The following are notes of some cases on *saman-nse* decided by Native Courts in Ashanti.

(1) *Kwabena Brobbey* v. *Yaw Kyere*
(Kumasihene's Tribunal, 1934–35)

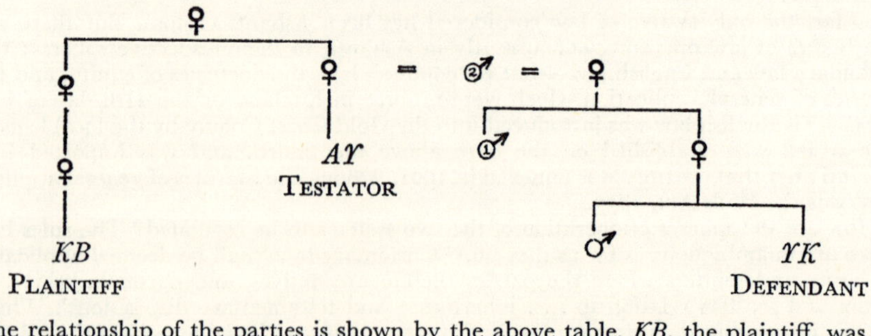

The relationship of the parties is shown by the above table. *KB*, the plaintiff, was the holder of the lineage stool, *AY* but not *YK*, the defendant, being of the same lineage. *KB* claimed the self-acquired property of *AY* on *AY*'s death, as head of the lineage. *YK* claimed under *AY*'s testament.

AY fell sick; his two wives, and his half-brother (No. 1 in the table) came to ask whether he had anything to say before he died. He called together eleven people, who included the village Headman and his linguist, *KD*, and others of the lineage (*KB* the stoolholder was not at hand), his two wives and *YK* the defendant. He then declared to the assembly that *YK* should succeed to his property when he died, even as he (*AY*) had inherited the property of Asamoa (No. 2 in the table), the father of himself (*AY*) and of *YK*'s mother. His shot-gun, however, should be given to *YK*'s brother.

The assembly wanted to call upon *YK* to pay £2.7*s*. *aseda*, but *AY* directed that they should demand only 16*s*. (i.e. a notional 'two bottles of gin'), saying he had left *YK* debts amounting to £65. So 16*s*. *aseda* was paid by *YK* and 16*s*. by his brother. *AY*'s daughter had offended him in some way so he took 3*s*. from her as amends. This 35*s*. was divided as follows:

7*s*. to be sent to the Asantehene (whose executioner *AY* was).
3*s*. to the Toasehene (on whose land the village was built).
4*s*. to the Adumhene (because he was *YK*'s 'father'—i.e. *YK* was one of the Adum people, descendants of the group brought back to Kumasi by Osei Tutu on his return from Akwamu).
3*s*. to his sons.
3*s*. to *KD* and the others of the lineage.
2*s*. to the village Headman.
2*s*. to some Ofuase people present.
5*s*. to others present, including 6*d*. to each of his wives.
6*s*. *AY* handed to his half-brother, saying it should be tied up in his cloth and buried with him. ('He showed me his share of the *aseda*, told me he was going to buy water with it in the other world'—evidence of the letter-writer who was called in later by *AY*).

After a moment *KD*, prompted by his nephew, returned the 3*s*. given to the lineage, saying he could not forgo the lineage's claim in the absence of some of the lineage elders. *AY*, annoyed, took the 3*s*. back, saying it was not the lineage who nursed him or helped him to make the two cocoa-farms he was leaving to *YK*. He then swore the Great Oath confirming his act, and dared anyone who objected to respond (which no one did). *KD* and some of the other lineage members left the meeting. *AY* then sent for a letter-writer and had the testament recorded. *AY* soon died, and *KB* sued *YK* for the property.

HELD: *YK* was entitled. The Court recited the material facts, that the gift had been made in the presence of witnesses including members of the lineage, that it had been confirmed by the Great Oath, and that 'in accordance with custom *YK* thanked *AY* with 16*s*., which he shared amongst himself . . . and the witnesses to the transaction'.

(*KB* had also claimed five executioner's knives, but the Court elicited from his witnesses that 'nephews' cannot succeed to the knife, 'because it is sons and grandsons who are entitled to hold the *sekan*' (the knife); that is, succession to the office of executioner is patrilineal, like succession to the office of all stool servants. As a witness put in another case, 'Any Ahenkoa who serves Otumfuo through any department used to offer his son to substitute for him when he grows old.') For the later history of the dispute see *Brobbey* v. *Kyere*, 3 W.A.C.A. 106.

(2) *Akosua Amankwa* v. *Yaw Berima*

(Kumasi Division Grade C Court, 1946, Asantehene's Court, 1947, on appeal)

EA's maternal great-grandmother and *E*'s maternal grandmother were the same person. *KA* had succeeded to *E*'s property on *E*'s death (as lineage property). In 1943 *KA* fell sick unto death. He sent for *E*'s daughter *AA* from her husband's village, and called together the Headman and elders of his village, the Catechist and elders of the Methodist Church, and the head and elders of his lineage (several individuals being members of more than one of these groups). *KA* said that when he died *KM*, AA's son, should have his shot-gun and *AA* should take the rest of his property and his debts. He died two weeks later; the lineage appointed or confirmed *AA* as his successor, taking £1. 3*s*. 6*d*. as *aseda* in acknowledgement.

People from another village (defendants) claimed to be the principal members of *E*'s and *KA*'s lineage and to have the right to dispose of property he left.

HELD: defendants had not proved blood relationships; testament upheld, *AA* to have all the property of which *KA* died possessed, except the gun.

HELD on appeal: blood relationship was proved, and *YB*, the defendant, was therefore entitled to any lineage property which *KA* had held (as he had no right to dispose of that by testament). *AA* admitted that some of the items which she claimed had been inherited by *KA* from *E*. *AA*'s list was as follows, items coming from *E* being marked with an asterisk:

*Three Silk cloths
*One Kente Cloth
*One S.B. Gun
Documents on debts totalling £174. 3*s*.
One compound house at Akodie
*One compound house at Domiabra
½ compound house at Goaso
*Two cocoa-farms at Domiabra
*One cocoa-farm at Kokobeng
One Gold Ring
*Two strings of Gyabum (gold nuggets)
*One Wooden Box
*One Cap Gun at Akodie
One big farm at Akodie
Petty amounts owed by people £3. 1*s*.
Petty amounts owed to people £8. 17*s*.

(3) *Dadzie* (*al. Asamoa*) v. *Poku*

(Kokofu Divisional Native Court, 1947; Asantehene's Court, 1948, on appeal)

Pea and Dadzie, the plaintiff, traced descent through women to a common great-great-grandmother. Pea and Dadzie were the only surviving males of their lineage. Pea made a testament described by a witness as follows:

'I visited Kwasi Pea, deceased, who was then seriously ill . . . (he) told me he was dying and that I should sit down as he was going to make his last dying declaration to me. (Others also were present.) He declared as follows:

(1) That his cocoa-farm situated and lying at Abesiwa should go to his son by name Abudulai.
(2) His house should go to his son, who had just passed his Elementary Education, as well as his cocoa-farm in which a cottage is situated. The farm proceeds should be used for the education of his children. He suggested that the son should also study or take a course in Arabic language. Two rings also should go to him. And thirdly Asamoa the Plaintiff should be responsible for his liabilities (debts). Again there is a cocoa-farm formerly belonging to Panin Kofi Agyekum also should go to Plaintiff. This should be used for paying off the liabilities. When that was done the farm should automatically go to him. Yaa Nimo should also take the farm which the Plaintiff fought for in a case against Akua Afriyie.

Late Kwasi Pea said that as the defendant had already had his share there was no need in giving him anything. That is all I know in the case.'

The defendant later claimed the farm left to Dadzie the plaintiff, on the ground that the alleged testamentary gift had not in fact been made, and that the defendant was the nearest blood relation, and so succeeded on intestacy The lower court found against defendant on both points.

'All that his claim amounts to is that late Kwasi Pea was his subject. [Defendant was a chief.] He could not prove that Kwasi Pea deceased was his relative. Defendant is of Agona Clan and late Kwasi Pea was also of Asona Clan. A very great and wide scope of distinction between the Asona and Agona Clans. Neither can inherit the estate of another who died intestate; excepting of course by a 'will' or dying declaration of the deceased person. The Plaintiff has been entrusted with the payment of £70, a debt left by late Kwasi Pea. This was one of late Kwasi Pea's declarations. It will be an injustice for one to be charged for liabilities of a deceased person and another to enjoy the assets.'

Questioned by the court as to the basis of his claim, the plaintiff said: 'I am claiming the cocoa-farm which Kwasi Pea gave me before his death because (1) that was his last declaration, (2) he was my relative.' That is to say, the testament provided for succession to a member of the lineage.

This dispute illustrates the unfortunate results which sometimes flow from the competing jurisdictions in succession matters of the Supreme Court and Native Courts. Certain Agona people purported to nominate Poku the defendant to succeed to Pea's brother who, they alleged, was of their lineage. This dispute between Pea and Poku was settled in arbitration before the Kokofuhene, the farm in dispute being awarded to Pea. Pea died. Poku was instigated to claim the farm again, this time as Pea's successor. Oaths were exchanged which led to the present case, which Poku again lost. The Agona people then purported to appoint another successor to Pea. The Kokofuhene called on the head of the lineage to explain his conduct. He apologized. Dadzie meanwhile sued the alleged successor, but the latter ran to Kumasi and applied for letters of administration in the Supreme Court and the case in the Native Court was suspended by the District Commissioner at the alleged successor's request. Dadzie entered a caveat. The Court referred the question of succession to the Asantehene's Divisional Native Court, because the Kokofu Court would not come to it with an open mind. The true succession had already been decided twice in Kokofu. How the Asantehene's Court could be considered the '*competent* native court' for the purpose of the reference under section 76 is not clear. However, it also reported in favour of Dadzie.

(4) *Toku* v. *Adae*

(Adansi Divisional Native Court, 1948; Asantehene's Court, on appeal, 1949)

A maximal lineage of the Asekyere clan, of a span of five generations, lives in Kusa, in Adansi. The Abontendomhene of Kusa is also head of the lineage. There are a number of sub-lineages ('Houses'), each of a two- or three-generation span. The self-acquired property of a member of a House descends on intestacy to another member of the House; other members of the maximal lineage have normally no claim on intestacy while there are House-members extant.

Kwame Ware's true nephew and presumptive successor, in default of legacies, was Adae. Toku was a classificatory nephew, having a common great-great-grandmother with Adae. Toku helped Ware make his farms; Adae went away and became a timber labourer.

In his old age Ware decided to give the cocoa-farms he had made to his nine (classificatory) 'nephews' and two 'nieces'. This was done at two or three separate meetings as the donees came back to Kusa. On one such occasion Ware took Toku the plaintiff (who was not of his House) and two other 'nephews' to a meeting of elders in the house of the Abontendomhene, whom he had told of his intention and who had approved. Before the elders he declared that he gave certain farms to the three nephews and to a fourth, Adae, the defendant, who was not present. Each nephew thanked Ware with 24*s*. and a bottle of 'rum'. Ware kept half, and half was divided among the witnessing elders. The Abontendomhene asked Ware who was to pay *aseda* on behalf of Adae, and Ware said he could pay it himself when he returned. 'Kwame Ware said, "Although I have dashed this farm to my nephew Toku I shall use the proceeds until my death. After my death Toku should take possession of it." '

Four months later Adae returned, and was told by the Abontendomhene of what had happened. As probable general successor to Ware he objected to the gifts to the other three, as his share was disproportionately small. He tried to make a 'case' with Ware before the Abontendomhene, but Ware ignored him, saying the farms were his own to do with as he liked.

A year or two later Ware died, and Adae was appointed by the House to succeed him. He paid 13*s*. *aseda* to those appointing him, to validate his appointment.

Adae took forcible possession of the farm left for Toku, saying the gift was too big and that he should have been consulted by Ware. The members of the lineage said he could not revoke this gift of the deceased, but he persisted and the dispute was taken before the Kusahene. At this point Toku, overborne by Adae's contumacy, said he did not want the farms and Adae could do what he liked with them. Adae promptly paid 16*s*. to the Kusahene and elders with the object of making this waiver binding. Toku later repented and brought the present suit.

HELD by the Adansi Divisional Native Court:

1. The farm was self-acquired property, and therefore Ware was competent to give to a nephew.
2. The gift was made in the presence of witnesses including responsible members of the lineage, and due formalities were observed.
3. The *aseda* of 24*s*. and one bottle of gin not having been repaid to Toku, his alleged renunciation was of no effect, and Adae's effort to pay 16*s*. as *aseda* did not cure the defect.
4. Furthermore, the renunciation had been made under duress, and was invalid for this reason.

HELD by the Asantehene's Court on appeal:

'We do not see how we can differ from the decision of the Court below. The property in question was self-acquired by the late Kwame Ware and we consider he had every right to dispose of it in any way he liked. If, as the Appellant contends, he assisted Kwame Ware in cultivating the farms, the Appellant has been compensated by Kwame Ware giving him his share. We are of the opinion that the Appellant has no right to oppose the wishes of Kwame Ware even if the Respondent had been a complete stranger and not a member of the lineage. The non-refund by the Appellant of the original *aseda* of 24*s*. and one bottle rum paid by the Respondent is an indication that the gift is still valid. In our opinion the alleged *aseda* of 16*s*. taken by the Kusahene from the Appellant is not right since the Kusahene is not the head of the parties' lineage. The *aseda* accepted by the owner of the property of Kwame Ware still stands.'

Notes

[1] The declaration is perhaps always backed by a threat: so Cristaller gives the meaning (under the Fante form *nsew*) as 'curse, malediction, imprecation, execration'.

[2] 'Samansie (lit. that which is left by the spirits)', *Ashanti*, p. 238; 'samansie (lit. that which is set aside by the ghost)', *Ashanti Law and Constitution*, p. 339.

[3] *Fanti Customary Law*, p. 97.

[4] *Ashanti*, p. 238.

[5] *Op. cit.*, p. 97.

[6] K. A. Busia, *The Position of the Chief in the Modern Political System of Ashanti*, pp. 43 and 125.

[7] Cf. Busia, *op. cit.*, p. 43.

[8] *Op. cit.*, p. 98.

[9] State of Akyem Abuakwa (Declaration of Native Customary Law) Proclamation, 1943. (*Gazette*, p. 377.)

[10] Courts Ordinance, sect. 74.

[11] See *Koney* v. *Union Trading Co.*, 2 W.A.C.A. 118, especially the judgment of Kingdon C.J.

[12] On this point and on the subject generally, see A. J. Loveridge, O.B.E., 'Wills and the Customary Law in the Gold Coast', *Journal of African Administration*, ii. 4. 24.

[13] *Brobbey* v. *Kyere*, 3 W.A.C.A. 106. This is the same dispute as that of which the earlier stage is noted below under the same name.

[14] *Re Anaman* (1894) F.C.L. 221.

[15] *Re Otoo*, 1926–29. Divisional Court 84, at 85.

[16] *Comments on Some Ordinances of the Gold Coast*, p. 19.

J. M. Sarbah: Fanti Customary Law*

Testamentary Dispositions

The Customary Law knows nothing of will in writing, and even in the matter of testamentary dispositions the members of the family exercise much influence.

Cruickshank describes the ceremony of will-making, as he calls it, which is still common among the people. 'In view of death, the head of the family summons around his death-bed his relations. He instructs them about the state of his affairs, and how his property was acquired, and how to be disposed of. He is most particular to furnish them with proofs respecting the acquisition of his pawns and slaves, mentions the names of the witnesses to the transactions, the circumstances under which they took place, and the sums paid for them, in order that his successor may be enabled to defend his rights,

* J. M. Sarbah, *Fanti Customary Law*, Frank Cass & Co. Ltd., 1967, pp. 95–100.

in the event of their attempting to obtain their liberty or redemption at the death of their master. He also recounts the names of his debtors with the sums which they owe to him, as well as the debts which he owes to others. His death-bed declarations, made in the presence of responsible witnesses, are always received as evidence in the event of litigation afterwards.' The curious inquirer may here be informed how suggestive are the death-bed scenes of the patriarch Jacob, as recorded in the sacred writ (Gen. xlix.), and that of King David.

Now, it has been affirmed as a general proposition by Sir Henry Maine, in his 'Ancient Law', that in all indigenous societies a condition of jurisprudence, in which testamentary privileges are not allowed, or rather not contemplated, has preceded the latter stage of legal development in which the mere will of the proprietor is permitted, with more or less restrictions, to override the claims of his kindred in blood. And even among the Romans, a will was never regarded by them as a means of disinheriting a family or of effecting the unequal distribution of a patrimony, and the rules of Law preventing its being turned to such a purpose increase in number and stringency as the jurisprudence unfolds itself. *Samansiw* is, in fact, not a word that accurately conveys the conception of a will as understood by an English lawyer, for the idea of making a disposition of property to take effect after the death of the giver, as has been noticed by observant European travellers on the Gold Coast, is really opposed to the fundamental principles of the ties binding the members of the family.

Without doubt, the custom of making wills with respect to self-acquired property is of modern growth, but no one can tell when the practice first began. Death-bed dispositions, known as *Samansiw*, seem to be recognized, not so much because of any assumed right to make such a disposition, as because, from feelings of affection, respect, or even superstition, the last wishes of the deceased are considered to be entitled to weight, among the members of his family. And this idea runs through the Customary Law relating to testamentary disposition of property. In fact, the only disposition of property known to the early Customary Law was a transfer followed by immediate possession. Contact with British rule in the old settlements gave rise to the practice of reducing into writing such transactions, and writing has in some localities become common, not so much because it is essential for the validity of transfer, but because it is a permanent record of such occurrence.

A stool-holder, or chief, or head of a family, or the manager of family property, has no power by testamentary disposition to alienate any part or portion of the family estate, moveable or immoveable, from the family. He may suggest some one to be his successor, but on his decree the people of the stool or members of the family may or may not act upon his suggestion or recommendation (*Coffie Yammoah* v. *Abban Cooma*).

The owner of self-acquired property can in his lifetime deal with it as he pleases, and where he intends to give the whole or a portion of it to his child by a freeborn wife, Adihiwa, or to any person not a member of his family, he does so before his death. As soon as he dies, his successor is entitled to all the property he died possessed as heritable and ancestral estate, subject to the usual rules of inheritance; of course the successor may give heed to the expressed desires of the deceased, who may have been so taken ill suddenly as to have been unable to accomplish his intention respecting the disposal of his property.

Where the owner of self-acquired property gives testamentary directions as to its disposal among the members of his family, who thereby take such property as heritable or ancestral property, the person, who would have succeeded to the deceased, cannot ignore such dispositions, and the persons benefited have a right to enforce such bequest.

E.g. Kwesi, owner of Addum and Donpim lands, four bendas, a house, and twelve pieces of salagha cloth, makes testamentary disposition, bequeathing Addum land to his son Kudwo, Donpin land to his youngest niece Araba, two bendas to Aduku, his younger brother, two pieces salagha cloth to Baidu, his friend. The said Kwesi had a mother, elder brother, and three sisters him surviving. By the Customary Law, his son Kudwo cannot take Addum land unless his father placed him in possession before his death; Araba is entitled to Donpin land, and can enforce her right to possess the land, she being of the heritable blood; and it is only on the failure of her issue to succeed that the other members of her family come in. Aduku also is entitled to take the two bendas, but Baidu cannot compel delivery of the two pieces of salagha cloth, if the mother, eldest brother, or the sisters refuse to deliver them to him. The owner of self-acquired property, after solemnly making his testamentary dispositions, may subsequently revoke a part or the whole of them.

Where a woman, having issue or descendants, possesses self-acquired property, her testamentary declarations as to the disposal of her property among her children and grandchildren are binding. When she fails to make such disposition her mother is her successor, then her children by seniority, failing whom, her sisters and brothers by seniority. So long as her children and their issue are alive, the right of the brothers, sister, and sisters' issue is subordinate to that of her own children.

The property of her son, which a mother succeeds to, is at her absolute disposal, and she can do whatever she pleases with it; but she has only a limited or at the most a life interest in property which comes to her from her deceased daughter leaving issue.

E.g. Amba has two daughters, Effua and Abba, both having issue, and sons Kwesi, Kobina, and Kwow. Effua, the possessor of four bendas, and Abba, the owner of a piece of land and some valuable beads, and Kobina, possessing a house, chattels, and some money, die, each leaving children, but without making any testamentary disposition: the mother takes the property of her son Kobina, and of this she has absolute control. She may appoint the youngest son Kwow to be Kobina's successor, or even give the estate of the deceased son to any of her grandchildren by her daughters Effua and Abba, and such person will hold the property as heritable or ancestral property. The said mother has only a limited interest, however, in the estate of her daughters, for the right of children to succeed to their mother is superior to that of the grandmother.

A stool-holder, who had kept his self-acquired property distinct from the stool property, to the knowledge of the senior and immediate member of the stool, can make a valid testamentary disposition of such self-acquired property to a member of the family. The Customary Law does not permit any person to bequeath to an outsider a greater portion of his property than is left for his family. Nor does the Customary Law permit any testamentary disposition, by a man weak in intellect, or imbecile, or insane, or under the influence of fraud or misrepresentation, to stand, or to be regarded at all.

It is not only on the death-bed that a man can make testamentary disposition. A person can make his testamentary disposition while enjoying perfect health; but at the time its is made, the witnesses must be distinctly told by him his words are his *Samansiw*, to take effect after his death. A subsequent *Samansiw* does not necessarily cancel or revoke a previous one, unless it is incompatible therewith.

Where a person, by testamentary declaration, releases his debtor from payment of any claim he may have against him, or directs that a person in possession of the testator's chattel shall retain it as his own, it is binding on his successor and other members of the family, who cannot claim from such debtor the amount of the debt, or from such legatee his legacy; for, says the Customary Law, what is given under solemn conditions cannot be recalled; the acts of gratitude should be cherished, and an act of restitution that calms a guilty conscience pricked with remorse should be respected.

H. Cory: Sukuma Law and Custom*

WILL

A. *Oral*

The institution of making verbal wills is an old one although not often practised. If a man wishes to make a verbal will, he must call at least six relatives as witnesses. If there are no relatives available, elders of the village are admissible as witnesses.

A man cannot transgress the rules of customary law by his will and he cannot appoint an heir outside the circle of those who are entitled to inherit.

NOTE: If a man in making his will does not follow the rules of customary law, it is not the duty of the witnesses to contradict him. But provisions of the testament which are contrary to the rules of customary law are not executed after the testator's death. For instance, if a testator stipulates that his brothers and heirs shall not claim return of bridewealth if the widow refuses to be inherited, the heirs could nevertheless claim it after his death.

Although everyone knows that the rules of customary law cannot be altered by a man's last will, many men express wishes regarding the disposal of their property.

* H. Cory, *Sukuma Law and Custom*, Oxford University Press, 1953, pp. 167–168.

They use the institution of the will to express their displeasure with an heir. Thus, for instance, a father may disinherit a son even though he knows that after his death the estate will be distributed among all his sons. The father simply makes the solemn declaration of disinheritance in order to effect an improvement in the relations between father and son. The most common reasons are adultery of a son with his step-mother, lavishness of a son at his father's expense, repeated theft in the house of the parents, refusal of a daughter to marry and to give up her various love affairs. The formulae used are of the following kind (said by the father before witnesses):

'Since you have always been only a loss to me, today I will pay for you, but remember it is for the last time. Do not come into my house again until I die. When I die I want other people to bury me.'

. . . . .

'I have borne you, I tell you, but I hope you will wander without rest. If you marry may your wife be barren. I have had a child whom now I have no more.'

. . . . .

'My fathers, look down upon your grandchild who insulted me! I pray that he will have no home, that he shall remain without peace and shall suffer, comfortless, until he dies.'

. . . . .

No son will disregard a ceremonial curse of this kind, which implies disinheritance. He will do his best to appease his father and to persuade him, with the help of relatives and elders, to revoke his words.

The testator has the right to change the sequence of heirs.

NOTE: This rule was decided upon by the chiefs of the Sukuma Federation and their people in 1949. Formerly various rules existed.

NOTE: Great importance is attached to the introduction of this rule, in the hope that it will restore their lost authority to fathers. Formerly sons were afraid to fall out with their fathers because they depended exclusively on them for payment of bridewealth as there were few ways in which a young man could obtain for himself the necessary amount of cattle. It is now not so difficult for a young man to acquire property, and therefore young people feel independent and have lost respect for the older generation. It is hoped that the fear of losing position within the family and some of the property in case of inheritance will have a wholesome effect.

A man cannot completely disinherit by will a person entitled to inherit

NOTE: This rule was decided upon by the chiefs of the Sukuma Federation and their people in 1949. Formerly a testator could disinherit an heir in SS, KS, BS, SBS*.

A father can disinherit a son by the procedure of *kujimula*. In this case the father returns his son to his wife's family and receives five head of cattle, thus giving his son the status of an illegitimate child.

NOTE: The procedure of *kujimula* is necessary for disinheritance; the fact that a son has left his father's house after a quarrel and is living with the maternal family is not considered in itself a proof of disinheritance.

Ibadakuli (Tinde) Appeal No. 15/45. *Guga* v. *Bt. Mwandu.*

Guga claimed from Bt. Mwandu the property of her brother which she had inherited. He stated that the deceased, who was his maternal nephew, had been expelled by his father and had lived in Guga's family for many years. Guga had even paid *misango* for him. The court held that Guga could not claim inheritance on these grounds, as it was not proved that the deceased had been disinherited by his father.

The maternal family of the child cannot refuse to accept him and must return the cattle.

NOTE: The custom of *kujimula* is known in BS, BD, SBS*, but is not practised in other chiefdoms.

The heirs of a disinherited son are not his natural brothers but his maternal relatives, if he dies childless.

D.C.'s Appeal 1/46. Bukwimba. *Filippo* v. *Nanayi.*

* These letters denote districts of Sukumaland.

Filippo was a maternal relative of Kaliyaya, deceased. Kaliyaya had been disowned by his father and went to Filippo who received him well. Kaliyaya looked upon Filippo as a father. When Kaliyaya died, Filippo inherited his property. Then one day Nanayi, a half-brother of Kaliyaya, appeared and claimed the inheritance. The court held that Nanayi had no claim to it, as their father had disowned Kaliyaya. When the father died, Kaliyaya had received no share of the estate because he no longer belonged to his paternal family; therefore, his maternal relative Filippo was his rightful heir.

Wishes and legacies of the testator are executed if they are not contrary to custom.

B. *In Writing*

The institution of making a written will is not yet widespread and no rules for the correct procedure have been issued.

J. C. D. Lawrance: The Iteso*

Wills

The custom of making wills is not general in Teso.

Verbal wills must be made before the heir and clan leaders as witnesses and would probably only be admitted if the terms conformed to customary procedure.

There are recognized grounds for disinheritance:

(*a*) If the heir offers violence to the testator or refuses all social contacts with the testator or commits adultery with the testator's wives.
(*b*) If the heir is guilty of witchcraft.
(*c*) If the heir is a known wastrel or by habitually committing adultery wastes property.
(*d*) If the heir is illegitimate (i.e. although the son of the deceased he was borne by a woman not married to the deceased and therefore belongs to the extended family (*ekek*) of his mother and not to the *ekek* of his father).

Whatever the contents of the will, debts against an estate must always be paid before wishes or legacies are met.

Written wills, though they exist, have not yet been widely tested and upheld in the courts. No clear rules exist regarding the witnessing or the form of written wills. It is given as the opinion of assessors that written wills would not be accepted if they departed in material matters from customary procedure.

QUOTATION: *D.C. Appeal 14/51: D.N.C. Appeal 34/51: Ekeru s/o Egulu* v. *E. Esingu:*

Ekeru's father on his deathbed made a will which included reference to a debt of thirty head of cattle owing from Esingu. The will was recorded by one, P. Emwochu. There were no other witnesses. It was stated by Ekeru that Esingu admitted the debt at the clan meeting but there was no evidence on this point. The evidence of the will was rejected by the Court.

NOTE: This example is quoted merely to show that oral evidence would probably be accepted in preference to a written testament. I have not seen any case in which disposition by written will has been disputed.

J. J. van Warmelo and W. M. D. Phophi: Venda Law†

Wills

Section 1: *Bequests are allowed to some extent.* Any person who possesses something may, upon seeing death approaching, direct that such and such a thing be left to a certain person. But he should not bequeath to a non-relative anything of value, such as a beast. An adult may bequeath a goat to a non-relative, and a youthful person not more than a fowl. The execution of such a bequest naturally rests with the family elders who con-

* J. C. D. Lawrance, *The Iteso*, Oxford University Press, 1957, pp. 232–233.

† J. J. van Warmelo and W. M. D. Phophi, *Venda Law*, Government Printer, Pretoria, South Africa, 1948, pp. 725–733.

sider the amount thereof in relation to what will be left over. Similarly with relatives, distant ones cannot be left as large bequests as close relatives.

A woman may leave to her children what she likes, provided it does not create jealousy and strife between them [this would seem to limit the testator very severely]. She may also leave to her friends certain household utensils.

A youth is seldom allowed to bequeath anything to a friend. Should he on his deathbed talk about leaving such articles as a bicycle, a sewing-machine or money, his relatives pretend to agree but never carry out his wish, because a 'child' cannot call anything his own. With a girl it is the same, she has nothing of her own.

As for small children, who are not legally owners of anything, they are not allowed to make bequests. Though a child may in his delirium say that a certain thing must be given to his comrade, his people merely pretend to agree but do not carry out his wish.

However, there is another aspect to such bequests, for a person to whom something is left often fears that acceptance will bring about his death. For the same reason the surviving relatives often refuse to execute the deceased's instructions that something be given to his friend, because they fear that if something befalls him, he will hold them responsible [he may suspect them of not having parted willingly with the gifts and having bewitched him through envy].

Section 2: *Nature of bequests.* A man's property during his lifetime falls into two categories, namely that which he has assigned to his wives' huts, and that termed *ndinda-muḓi* (village-provider) which he retains as a reserve under his sole control to use for the benefit of the whole family in emergencies such as lack of food or fines, because what he has allotted he cannot take back again. However, some men assign nothing to their sons for fear of causing jealousy and quarrelling, because to do this is said to amount to declaring the heir and creating a danger to oneself (by putting the future heir in a position where he would benefit from patricide).

Men who do not yield to these fears wait until they see their days are numbered, and then apportion their *thakha** and other property amongst their sons to render a division after their death unnecessary. Here also a part is left undivided. The reason for such division is usually that the old man distrusts his relatives, and fears that his sons may perhaps be set against one another by their uncles, or else he is afraid the eldest son might take everything and not give the younger brothers their rightful share to marry with.

When a father divides up his property and assigns part of it [usually cattle] to a son, then such portion is called *dzekiso* if the son has not yet been given *dzekiso,* but if he has, it is termed *muhungo* 'something to tie up'. [He will never be given the latter whilst there are other sons who have not yet been given *dzekiso.*] The reason for calling such a gift a *muhungo* is that it is intended to be kept to build up a herd [as it is always a female animal].

In bequeathing to his own children a man can do as he pleases. [Actually he can do nothing of the sort, as will be seen.] He may give much to the younger sons and be niggard with the seniors, provided he has given these latter their *dzekiso* [he may do this because his gifts to the juniors are their *dzekiso,* so the elders have no ground for complaint]. Where he oversteps the limits of fairness and favours some to the disadvantage of others, the elders will not carry out his wishes after his death but make a more equitable division. They say his last dispositions were the ravings of a dying man. [Actually, if all the sons have been given *dzekiso,* the bequests must follow seniority. In effect therefore, the testator has almost no liberty, and seniority overrides all other considerations. The patriarchal structure of the family makes this imperative. Only a crippled younger son might perhaps be given more than his due, say up to three animals.]

What a man bequeaths to his children is only cattle. If he is a carver or basket-maker he may leave his daughters the products of his craft. Money is not often shared out amongst children because it is scarce and because, as part of the estate, it may not be taken by anyone before his death. But where there is money, a son may be given some to buy himself a beast. This was done for example by Gurunngu, who gave money to his daughter Tshiwanḓalani who was married to Ṋephahwe. [The opposition to money as a form of wealth is still very strong, see later Part: Property, and is expressed, amongst

* Marriage consideration.

others, in the phrases *bonndo a i koni u itwa makhulu* 'A pound cannot be made to represent an ancestor' (as is done with goats and large stock) and *tshelede ndi muloi* 'money is a wizard, an evil-doer' and it has to be borne in mind that *muloi* implies the ultimate in perverse and murderous evil.]

A man may only share out his property to his children. What he gives to non-relatives or younger brothers are gifts but not *ifa* 'inheritance'.

The persons to whom a man usually bequeaths things of his are usually members of his household or family. It may be a favourite younger son or a younger brother to whom he leaves a beast with which he can in course of time acquire another wife, or it may be a brother-in-law or friend who cared for him in his illness when his own relations had abandoned him.

A man never says to another person, 'After my death you may have this or that of mine', for fear of having death sent to him by magic. Moreover they say this sort of thing sets people against one another. What he may do is to tell his *makhadzi* or *khotsi-munene*, 'When I am dead, give so-and-so this or that thing of mine'. But the thing so bequeathed must be of small value. A man would not get his relatives to agree to his leaving a beast for example, to a friend. He could leave him a goat or suchlike. If he were to bequeath things to non-relatives, his relations would pretend to agree but would not carry out his wish after his death.

The property allotted to sons does not, however, consist only of what is actually in the village. There is also another, that which is promised them by linking sisters to brothers. A son is told, 'So-and-so is your sister, who will draw water for you when you are thirsty, and will cook for you when you are hungry'. This means that the cattle received for her upon her marriage will be his *dzekiso* to get a wife with. Where a father has thus linked sisters to brothers, this arrangement may not be upset after his death. That would be quite contrary to the law. Immediately upon their being received, such animals are handed over to the hut to which they were assigned.

Another kind of will that a man may leave refers to his daughters. He may direct that a certain daughter must be married by a certain family. When the relatives meet after his death to appoint his heir, they will stress the fact that the girl must marry as the deceased has directed. Usually such a girl is desired to go to a *makhadzi* or an elder sister who is in ill-health or who has no children. A *mukwasha** who has served his *makhulu*† better than the others may also be so favoured. Such a will of a deceased should not be set aside by the surviving relatives, because as they say, 'the word of a deceased person is not disregarded'. Of course the girl is not given away. [The will merely refers to the place where she shall be married.]

A deceased may also have left still other directions. He may for example have told his family, 'After my death, my sons must not stay in this village any longer, lest they die of the disease that killed me, their father. They must go away to some other country or another sub-area'. Or they may be directed merely to remove from the kraal site and build nearby. In such cases the elders who meet for the *dzumo* immediately also decide how the sons may be moved to another place in accordance with the deceased's wishes.

Again the deceased may have said, 'After my death my sons must not go away from this village and leave me. They must stay here, the village may not be broken up. If they see the cattle are getting 'hot' [magically speaking] because of their numbers, they can move a little distance but not far from here.'

N. N. Rubin: The Swazi Law of Succession: a Restatement‡

WILLS (LUPHAWU)[1]

1. *Power to make wills.* Subject to the rules stated below in regard to capacity, any Swazi may make a will in respect of livestock. He may not do so in respect of land and other movable property.[2]

A will may be made at any time during the lifetime of the testator.

* A sister-in-law or brother-in-law (used by wife's people only).

† Wife's father or mother.

‡ N. N. Rubin, 'The Swazi Law of Succession: a Restatement', in *Journal of African Law*, Vol. 9. No. 2, pp. 108–109.

2. *Formalities for making wills.* The testator must convene his *lusendvo*, and must inform its members of his wishes with regard to the distribution of his estate. The persons to whom such a declaration must be made include the following:

(a) testator's oldest uterine brother (or his successor); or
(b) his wives, or all persons falling within both categories (a) and (b); or
(c) the testator's senior paternal aunt; or
(d) testator's children, or all persons falling within both categories (*c*) and (*d*); and
(e) the head of the homestead immediately adjacent to that of testator either side; or
(f) testator's first born son, or both the persons in categories (*e*) and (*f*).[3]

All of these persons do not have to be present simultaneously; the dispositions made under the will may be reported to them subsequently.

Apart from such reporting to the members of the *lusendvo*, no other formalities attend the making of a will, and no ceremony accompanies it.

Variation.—In the case of *bantfwana benkosi*[4] the same procedure is followed, but it is essential that a *luphawu* be reported to the testator's mother and his eldest uterine sister, as well as to the King.

3. *Capacity to make a will*

(a) any male or female who has property that may be disposed of by intestate succession may make a will;
(b) a valid will may not be made while the purported testator is drunk;
(c) a person may not make a valid will if he or she is incapable of understanding the nature of his act.[5]

4. *Revocation or alteration of a will.* A will may only be altered or revoked in certain, limited, circumstances; which include:

(*a*) violence by a beneficiary against the testator or his oldest son;[6]
(*b*) attempts by the beneficiary to sell or dispose of cattle to be inherited by him in terms of a will, prior to the death of the testator. [7, 8]

A will may be altered so as to benefit a person not originally included as a beneficiary at any time prior to the death of testator.

The revocation or alteration of a will must be done with the same formalities as are prescribed for the making of the original will.

5. *Coming into operation of wills.* The will becomes effective immediately on the death of the testator, although distribution in terms of it is left to the person who would be administrator if deceased had died intestate (the *umpatseli*).[9]

Prior to this, beneficiaries may only remove, or enjoy the use, fruits, etc. of property bequeathed to them with the consent of the testator.[10]

6. *Essential validity of a will: power to deviate from rules of intestacy.* (a) *Bequests to strangers.*—Bequests to strangers, *i.e.*, persons who are not members of testator's aganatic family or his descendants, may only be made where the bequest was made in return for some benefit received by testator. In all other circumstances, such bequests are invalid and may be set aside by the heir or the *umpatseli*.[11]

(b) Bequests may be made to *family or clan members* who would not be heirs on intestacy.

(c) *Alteration of the shares of heirs.* A person may in his will alter the shares of heirs so as to provide one of his sons who would otherwise not succeed to property with a share of the inheritance.[12, 13]

(d) In certain, limited, circumstances,[14] a person who may otherwise be an heir[15] may be completely disinherited. This must be done explicitly.

7. *Essential validity: power to deviate by will from* inter vivos *Distribution* (*Iphakela*). A will may not deviate from *liphakelo* unless it is explicitly intended to disinherit a person who would otherwise be entitled to property resulting from such lifetime distribution after the death of the wife to whom it was made.

Notes

[1] The literal translation of the term is 'earmarking'.

[2] All such property, unless it has been *iphakela'd*, becomes the property of the *inkosana* (main heir).

[3] In other words, the categories listed may be grouped in twos: so that (*a*) and (*b*) are alternatives; and so are (*c*) and (*d*) and (*e*) and (*f*).

[4] I.e. Princes. The singular is *umntfwana benkosi*.

[5] E.g. through insanity or senility.

[6] Known as *lisocankanti*.

[7] Such a purported disposition would be void; or, perhaps, validable by the testator.

[8] This, as well as the absence of the same limitation in regard to persons to be benefited, and the restriction as to the types of property which may be bequeathed, is a point of difference between *luphawu* and *ipkakela*.

[9] The *distribution* would be deferred until the *umpatseli* had been appointed.

[10] In such circumstances, the bequest operates in much the same way as a *liphakelo* except that persons other than wives may be benefited.

[11] It is more probable that they would not be confirmed by the *lusendvo* in the first place.

[12] E.g. by providing that a son other than the oldest son in each house may receive certain *lobolo* cattle, whether already received or yet to be received.

[13] Even if this was done in such a way as to provide cattle for the oldest sons of each house, it would not amount to disinheritance of the *inkosana* though it may result in the disinheritance of the *bantfwana woyise*.

[14] Only in extreme cases, e.g. treachery.

[15] I.e. of both kinds. This may not be necessary in the case of minor heirs.

Index

READINGS IN AFRICAN LAW

READINGS IN AFRICAN LAW

Edited by

E. COTRAN

LL.B., LL.M., DIP.I.L.

of Lincoln's Inn, Barrister at Law,
Lecturer in African Law, School of Oriental and African Studies,
University of London

and

N. N. RUBIN

B.A., LL.B.

Advocate of the Supreme Court of South Africa and the
High Court of Swaziland

Lecturer in African Law, School of Oriental and African Studies,
and Hayter Lecturer in African Law, Institute of Advanced
Legal Studies, University of London

IN TWO VOLUMES

VOLUME I

APC

AFRICANA PUBLISHING CORPORATION · NEW YORK

First Published in 1970 by
FRANK CASS & COMPANY LIMITED
Published in the United States of America in 1970
by Africana Publishing Corporation
101 Fifth Avenue, New York N.Y. 10003

Library of Congress Catalog Card No. 74-115047
SBN 8419 0043 4

Printed in Great Britain

CONTENTS

Part II: CRIMES AND CIVIL WRONGS

Part III: THE LAW OF CONTRACT

Part IV: LAND LAW

ACKNOWLEDGEMENTS

Permission to reprint excerpts from the following copyrighted works is gratefully acknowledged:

W. Allan, *Land Holding and Land Usage and the Plateau Tonga of Mazabuka District*, published by Oxford University Press for the Rhodes-Livingstone Institute; from the Institute for Social Research of the University of Zambia.

A. N. Allott, 'The Ashanti Law of Property', published in *Zeitschrift fur vergleichende Rechtswissenschaft;* from the author.

A. N. Allott, 'Evidence in African Customary Law', published in *Les Editions de la Librairie Encyclopedique*, Tome xviii; from the author.

A. N. Allott, 'Modern Changes in African Land Tenure', published in *Zeitschrift fur vergleichende Rechtswissenschaft;* from the author.

A. N. Allott, 'Towards a Definition of Absolute Ownership', published in *Journal of African Law*, Vol. 5, No. 2; from the author.

R. G. Armstrong, 'Intestate Succession among the Idoma', published in J. D. M. Derrett (ed.), *Studies in the Laws of Succession in Nigeria;* from the Nigerian Institute of Social and Economic Research.

H. Ashton, *The Basuto*; from the publishers, Oxford University Press.

J. H. M. Beattie, 'Informal Judicial Activity in Bunyoro', published in the *Journal of African Administration*, Vol. 9, No. 4; from the Ministry of Overseas Development.

J. H. M. Beattie, 'The Kibanja System of Land Tenure in Bunyoro, Uganda', published in the *Journal of African Administration*, Vol. 6, No. 1; from the Ministry of Overseas Development.

K. Bentsi-Enchill, 'Do African Systems of Land Tenure Require a Special Terminology?', published in *Journal of African Law*, Vol. 9, No. 2; from the author.

P. Bohannan, *Justice and Judgement among the Tiv*; from the publishers, Oxford University Press.

G. G. Browne and A. McD. B. Hutt, *Anthropology in Action*, published by Oxford University Press for the International African Institute; from Oxford University Press, and from the authors.

E. Colson, *Marriage and the Family among the Plateau Tonga of Northern Rhodesia;* from the publishers, Manchester University Press, and from the author.

E. Colson, *The Social Organisation of the Gwembe Tonga;* from the publishers, Manchester University Press, and from the author.

H. Cory, *Sukuma Law and Custom*; from the publishers, Oxford University Press.

H. Cory and M. M. Hartnoll, *Customary Law of the Haya*, published by Lund Humphries for the International African Institute; from the International African Institute.

E. Cotran, *Report on Customary Criminal Offences in Kenya*, published by the Government Printer of Kenya; from the Kenya Government.

J. D. Danquah, *Akan Laws and Custom*; from the publishers, Routledge & Kegan Paul Limited.

J. H. Driberg, 'The African Conception of Law', published in *The Journal of Comparative Legislation and International Law*, 1934; from the British Institute of International and Comparative Law.

P. Duncan, *Sotho Laws and Customs*; from the publishers, Oxford University Press, Cape Town.

T. O. Elias, *The Groundwork of Nigerian Law*; from the publishers, Routledge & Kegan Paul Limited.

T. O. Elias, *The Nature of African Customary Law*; from the publishers, Manchester University Press, and from the author.

T. O. Elias, *Nigerian Land Law and Custom*; from the publishers, Routledge & Kegan Paul Limited.

A. L. Epstein, *Juridical Techniques and the Judicial Process*, published by Manchester University Press for the Rhodes-Livingstone Institute; from the Institute for Social Research of the University of Zambia.

E. E. Evans-Pritchard, *Kinship and Marriage among the Nuer*; from the publishers, the Clarendon Press, Oxford.

M. Fortes and E. E. Evans-Pritchard, *African Political Systems*, published by Oxford University Press for the International African Institute; from Oxford University Press.

M. A. Gayer, *Report on Land Tenure in Bugisu*, from the publishers, the Government Printer of Uganda.

M. Gluckman, *The Ideas in Barotse Jurisprudence*; from the publishers, Yale University Press.

M. Gluckman, *The Judicial Process among the Barotse of Northern Rhodesia*; from the publishers, Manchester University Press.

M. Gluckman, *Order and Rebellion in Tribal Africa*; from the publishers, Routledge & Kegan Paul Limited.

P. H. Gulliver, *Social Control in an African Society*; from the publishers, Routledge & Kegan Paul Limited and Boston University Press.

J. F. Holleman, *Shona Customary Law*, published by Oxford University Press, Cape Town; from the Institute for Social Research of the University of Zambia.

P. P. Howell, *Manual of Nuer Law*; from the publishers, Oxford University Press.

M. Hunter, *Reaction to Conquest*; from the publishers, Oxford University Press.

E. J. Krige, 'Individual Development', in I. Schapera (ed.), *The Bantu Speaking Tribes of South Africa*; from the publishers, Routledge & Kegan Paul Limited.

H. E. Lambert, 'Land Tenure among the Akamba', published in *African Studies*, Vol. 6, 1947; from the publishers, Witwatersrand University Press.

J. C. D. Lawrance, *The Iteso*, published by Oxford University Press; from the author.

P. C. Lloyd, *Yoruba Land Law*; from the publishers, the Nigerian Institute of Social and Economic Research, and from the author.

J. Matson, 'Testate Succession in Ashanti' published in *Africa*, Vol. 23; from the International African Institute, and from the author.

P. Mayer, *Gusii Bridewealth Law and Custom*, published by Oxford University Press for the Rhodes-Livingstone Institute; from the Institute for Social Research of the University of Zambia.

C. K. Meek, *Land Law and Custom in the Colonies*; from the publishers, Oxford University Press.

C. K. Meek, *Land Tenure and Land Administration in Nigeria and the Cameroons*; from the publishers, Her Majesty's Stationery Office.

C. K. Meek, *Law and Authority in a Nigerian Tribe*; from the publishers, Oxford University Press.

N. Mugerwa, 'Land Tenure in East Africa: Some Contrasts', published in *East Africa Law Today*, 1966; from the British Institute of International and Comparative Law, and from the author.

Native Land Tenure in Kikuyu Province: Report of Committee, published by the Government Printer of Kenya; from the Kenya Government.

E. I. Nwogugu, 'Legitimacy in Nigerian Law', published in *Journal of African Law*, Vol. 8, No. 1; from the author.

S. N. C. Obi, 'Women's Property and Succession thereto in Modern Ibo Law', published in *Journal of African Law*, Vol. 6, No. 1; from the author.

N. A. Ollenu, *The Law of Succession in Ghana*; from the publishers, the Presbyterian Book Depot, Limited, and from the author.

D. J. Penwill, *Kamba Customary Law*, published by Macmillan & Co. Ltd. on behalf of the East African Literature Bureau; from the East African Literature Bureau, and from the author.

A. Phillips, *Survey of African Marriage and Family Life*; from the publishers, Oxford University Press.

R. J. H. Pogucki, *Gold Coast Land Tenure*, published by the Government Printer of Ghana; from the author.

A. R. Radcliffe-Brown and D. Forde (eds.), *African Systems of Kinship and Marriage*; from the publishers, Oxford University Press.

R. S. Rattray, *Ashanti Law and Constitution*, from the publishers, Oxford University Press.

S. Roberts, 'Matrilineal Family Law and Custom in Malawi; A Comparison of Two Systems', published in *Journal of African Law*, Vol. 8, No. 2; from the author.

N. N. Rubin, 'The Swazi Law of Succession: A Restatement', published in the *Journal of African Law*, Vol. 9, No. 2; from the author.

J. M. Sarbah, *Fanti Customary Laws*; from the publishers, Frank Cass & Co. Ltd.

I. Schapera, 'Contract in Tswana Law', published in *Journal of African Law*, Vol. 9, No. 3; from the author.

I. Schapera, *A Handbook of Tswana Law and Custom*; from the publishers, Oxford University Press.

I. Schapera, *Native Land Tenure in the Bechuanaland Protectorate*, published by The Lovedale Press; from the author.

S. M. Seymour, *Native Law in South Africa*; from the publishers, Juta & Company, Ltd., and from the author.

V. Sheddick, *Land Tenure in Basutoland*; from the publishers, Her Majesty's Stationery Office.

A. J. F. Simmance, 'Adoption of Children among the Kikuyu of the Kiambu District', published in the *Journal of African Law*, Vol. 3, No. 1; from the author.

S. R. Simpson, 'Towards a Definition of Absolute Ownership', published in *Journal of African Law*, Vol. 5, No. 3; from the author.

G. S. Snell, *Nandi Customary Law*, published by Macmillan & Co. Ltd., on behalf of the East African Literature Bureau; from the publishers, and from the author.

J. van Tromp, *Xhosa Law of Persons*; from the publishers, Juta & Company Ltd., and from the author.

G. Wagner, *The Bantu of North Kavirondo*; from the publishers, Oxford University Press.

J. J. van Warmelo and W. M. D. Phophi, *Venda Law*; from the publishers, the Government Printer of South Africa.

C. M. N. White, 'Terminological Confusion in Land Tenure', published in *Journal of African Administration*, Vol. X; from the publishers, Her Majesty's Stationery Office.

G. Wilson, *Luo Customary Law and Marriage and Customs*, published by the Government Printer of Kenya; from the Kenya Government.

R. Young and H. A. Fosbrooke, *Land and Politics among the Liguru of Tanganyika*; from the publishers, Routledge & Kegan Paul Limited and Northwestern University Press.

EXPLANATION OF FOOTNOTES

The footnotes that appear on the same page of extracts (marked *, †, ‡, §, ‖ etc.) are inserted by the Editors where some explanation is required, e.g. where a vernacular term is defined by the author in a place other than the extract reproduced, or where some abbreviation used by the author requires explanation.

The numbered footnotes which appear at the end of each extract are those of the author and page references therein are to the pages of the book or article and not to these Readings.

Editors

INTRODUCTION

THIS anthology of writings on African customary law is intended as a comprehensive introduction to the subject as a whole. It seeks to be comprehensive in several different ways. In the first place, it sets out to provide the contemporary student of African law with as wide a coverage as possible of the range of topics that is embraced by the customary systems of law. Secondly, it attempts to indicate the variety of different societies in which these systems operate. At the same time, it aims to give the reader some idea of the differences in approach which have been adopted, over the years, by the large (and growing) number of writers in this field, towards the legal institutions and the rules of customary law, as well as to the societies that have been described. In addition, it has sought, wherever practicable, to include material drawn from as many geographical regions in Africa as possible.

These objectives apply to the work generally. They have also determined the selection of the material for inclusion in each of the chapters which follows, although it has not always been possible to accomplish each object in relation to each of the topics that has been dealt with. The principal intention throughout has always been to provide a clear statement of the substantive rules of customary law under each heading. This has almost inevitably meant that some attention has had to be paid to the variations or different patterns of rules that exist in regard to a specific subject; and our object has been to try to illustrate these by selecting descriptions drawn from the work of writers on different parts of Africa. But this has not always been the case. Sometimes, an extract has been selected which has itself surveyed a number of different systems comparatively. On other occasions, the variations between one set of rules and another have been so slight or so insignificant that they did not warrant separate extracts dealing with them. And, often, it was felt that the inclusion of too many illustrations would give too fragmented a picture of a particular institution.

In general, the works which have been used in compiling these volumes are those which are not easily accessible to all students of African law[1]—particularly, if ironically, in Africa—or which, if they are available, are widely dispersed throughout a large number of books and journals not all of which are wholly relevant to the study of customary law. Nevertheless, a good deal of the material which has been included has been extracted from the well-known works of authors who have written classic studies of the customary law of

[1] We have, following this general policy, excluded many recent works that have appeared in London and which are widely available in Africa.

particular societies. Sometimes, it is true, these are also no longer in print: like Hans Cory's *Sukuma Law and Custom*, Rattray's *Ashanti Law and Constitution* or Holleman's *Shona Law*, to name but three examples; still others, such as Schapera's *A Handbook of Tswana Law and Custom*, Sarbah's *Fanti Customary Laws* or Danquah's works on the Akan have either been reprinted recently or are in the process of being re-issued. But all of these, like the writings of Professors Allott, Bohannan, Elias and Gluckman—to mention just a few of the better-known authors whose books and articles are more readily at hand—are utterly indispensable in any serious and all-embracing survey of this subject. If we have at times seemed to rely very heavily on these, and one or two others, this is hardly surprising: each has made an outstanding and unique contribution, either by describing in detail the laws and institutions of an African people, or in analysing and illuminating the legal systems with which we are concerned; or by doing both.

It will at once be apparent that many of the items selected for inclusion in this anthology are the work of non-lawyers. This, too, is only to be expected. It is a simple fact that the study of customary law in Africa was pioneered by those whose principal fields of endeavour lay elsewhere—either as administrators or, more frequently, as social anthropologists. And, until relatively recently, most of the active attempts to gather and interpret information on customary law were made by them. This is no longer true today. Over the last two decades in particular, the pattern has altered considerably. More and more, African law is being studied by lawyers, and they have therefore provided the other major source from which we have drawn material for these *Readings*.

Foremost among these writers are, of course, Professor A. N. Allott, the Professor of African Law at the School of Oriental and African Studies of the University of London, and Dr T. O. Elias, the Dean of the Faculty of law in the University of Lagos and now the Attorney General of Nigeria. Quite apart from their own outstanding contributions to the understanding of African law—which we have resorted to frequently—each has been responsible for stimulating a great deal of the other work by lawyers which appears in this collection. Professor Allott especially has worked indefatigably to encourage colleagues at his own and other universities, and countless students in Europe and in Africa, to add to the existing store of knowledge in an area which was previously much neglected by academic and professional lawyers alike. The establishment of the Restatement of African Law Project at the School of Oriental and African Studies has provided a major focus of activity for nearly a decade, and it is not untrue to say that it has engendered a very welcome and refreshing re-appraisal by lawyers of their entire approach to African law.

The greater interest shown by contemporary lawyers in the subject has, of course, raised the question of the relationship between them and the anthropologists who have worked, and are still working, in kindred fields. There can be no doubt of the great debt owed by the former to the latter. But it would be inaccurate, as well as unfortunate, to discuss their relationship as if it consisted of no more than the need of a new and different generation of scholars to pay tribute to the work of their precursors. New and different the lawyers certainly are—in their choice of topics for study, their methodology, their analysis of the customary law, and in the purposes for which they intend the results of their research to be used. The modern study of customary law is designed not only to add to (or, where necessary, to revise) the existing store of knowledge and information on the substance of the law. It also aims to pave the way for, and forms part of the process of achieving an altered attitude towards the legal relationships and legal disputes in customary law, on the part of the courts and the other authoritative bodies which are concerned with formulating policy towards it, or with administering it on a day-to-day basis.

This difference of approach has necessarily led to a change of emphasis in the nature of the work done on customary law and the writing about it. Lawyers have sought, on the one hand, to broaden the scope of the enquiry by relating their investigation of customary law and its rules to the other (mainly imported, or received) branches of law and legal study; and, on the other hand, they have narrowed the field of study by confining it to the statement and exposition of the purely normative rules which can be judged, applied and enforced in the manner in which other legal rules are. In other words, they have seen their task as that of re-casting and fashioning the rules of customary law into a form which will enable them to be used in the context of the modern Africa wherever this is possible; and of presenting those rules which cannot be treated in this way in a form which will enable lawyers, judges, civil servants, and, in the last resort, legislators, to determine the appropriate place which they are to enjoy in the African societies of today.

The demand for work of this kind has existed for a considerable time, and is growing. Conferences of lawyers, administrators and academics have discussed the role of customary law in Africa for nearly twenty years. (see the *Reports of the Judicial Advisers Conferences* of 1953 and 1957, as well as *The Future of Law in Africa*, edited by A. N. Allott in 1960, and the *Report of the African Conference on Local Courts and Customary Law*, edited by W. T. McClain in 1963, for example). Individual countries have, both before and since, established commissions of enquiry into these questions as well. In most cases, the initial concern was with the need to re-organise the court systems of African states, and often this was part of a more or less deliberate attempt to prepare for a measure of integration of customary law into the overall legal system. More recently, however, several African Governments have directed themselves towards reform of various branches of the law itself, with a view, *inter alia*, to redefining the place of customary law rules within the total legal framework which governs these sectors. Most prominent among the branches of law chosen for this kind of revision or re-appraisal have been marriage and divorce, succession and inheritance, but some attention has also been paid to aspects of the criminal law and civil wrongs, and matters such as adoption and legitimacy in the family law field, as well as land law.

All of this has meant that the special skills of lawyers have more and more been required to deal with customary law questions. And the recognition of a body of customary law—often, but not always, in written form—which is to be enforced by the ordinary (not specially created) courts, as well as a trend towards the increased use of professionally qualified magistrates to preside over them, have re-inforced the need to involve lawyers more fully with customary law.

This has, in one sense, led to a growing divorce between the work of anthropologists and that of lawyers on customary law. Lawyers, engaged in what is seen as an attempt to provide for the practical application of customary law in a viable relationship with other operating legal systems, have tended to eschew any preoccupation with the less pragmatic penumbra of juristic problems. And the almost natural disdain of the professional lawyer for any involvement with theoretical discussion—whether in the relatively discrete field of jurisprudence or in the wider context of the social foundations and implications of legal institutions—has been re-inforced by a number of criticisms levelled at anthropologists' work on these subjects in a more general way. This is almost certainly not the place to rehearse all the arguments on the question, but it will perhaps suffice to mention the more commonly made allegations that anthropologists have tended to: become infatuated with the customs of "primitive" communities, and have given undue stress to their exotic character; describe a single society—or sometimes only a sub-group within that society–and its institutions, while presenting generalised conclusions as to their nature as being applicable on a far more extensive basis than the evidence would allow; approach the social or jural affairs of a community with (often bold) preconceptions or hypotheses which pre-dispose the selection of material considered, and which result in description of that community's institutions by reference to a highly selective set of indices, to the total or partial exclusion of all others; depict societies and their customs for all time as they were when observed, thus locating social and legal relationships in a fixed position to one another and not allowing sufficiently for the alteration in one or other aspect, with the correlative effect this may have on the nexus between the two; and, as a rather more blunt variation of the last, that they preserve out-dated or outworn procedures, customs and the like.

We do not seek to support or justify these allegations. Some are grossly unfair, others apply to particular works alone, and frequently, much of the criticism can itself be directed with equal effect to lawyers and their efforts in the customary law field. What is important is that, irrespective of their validity either generally or in relation to specific studies, they should not be allowed to over-shadow the very real degree to which legal and anthropological work on customary law is interdependent. Quite apart from the need for lawyers to consult and rely upon a great deal of the work that ante-dated their own, there are important areas in which co-operation between the two disciplines is and will continue to be both valuable and necessary.

Both at a practical level and on the more remote plane of theoretical abstractions, there is a great deal of room for the mutual stimulus that derives from the interchange of ideas and active collaboration. It would be most unwise—if indeed it is still at all thinkable—for any government or body of lawyers which is concerned with intelligent reform of African legal systems to ignore the social context within which it is to operate; or to dismiss the vast fund of accumulated knowledge on the manner in which customary law once functioned when deliberating on the way in which it ought to work in the future. In order to arrive at a proper evaluation of any legal change that is being proposed, it is more than just highly desirable—it is crucial—that full account be taken of all that social anthropologists, and their sociologist colleagues, are uniquely qualified to describe and interpret regarding the interaction of social and legal phenomena.

To a certain extent, this is only part of a process whereby those in authority are coming to realise the significance of an inter-disciplinary approach to all major undertakings which take place in a modern, or a modernising, state. Recent efforts—whether at reform of the law of marriage or to build a dam, establish a new town or construct a railroad in or between African countries—have all demonstrated the need for joint planning in which the skills of lawyers and social scientists have been called upon in addition to those who have been purely concerned with the technical aspects of the project. And it would probably not be untrue to say that, to the extent that earlier experiments in all these fields have been defective, this has been caused by the ignoring of one or several of the possible contributions that might have been made on a multi-disciplinary basis.

Any suggested dichotomy between law and anthropology or sociology becomes even more illusory at the philosophical or jurisprudential level. The need for collaborative work in such fields, is, at any rate, at least equally apparent. This has in fact been recognised in the past. At the most theoretical limits of this area, there has been an almost overwhelming output of writing on the nature of law, by anthropologists as well as lawyers. It is no accident that this has occurred, to a very large extent, in relation to customary law. The main preoccupation has been to remove the obscurity and the ambiguities which have long been recognised as being inherent in the term "law" itself, but which are especially evident in the study of customary law. Both groups have been concerned to find a satisfactory way of describing the characteristics of law in such a way as to arrive at a definition which will embrace legal as well as social norms. Or, to put it another way, they have attempted to determine the precise point at which custom ends and law begins. If no solution has been found to this problem yet which commends itself universally—and there is an enormous number offered—the quest for one remains even more legitimate. But the answer is more likely to be found, in our view, if the search is undertaken jointly, and not by viewing law and anthropology as totally distinct from one another, or even as operating in parallel realms. They seem, indeed, to form part of a continuum which begins with the observable phenomenon of human society to establish for itself ordered patterns of conduct and ends with pragmatist lawyers view that law, in any one society, is what the courts will enforce. At both ends, and in the vast area between them, there is ample scope for lawyers and social scientists to work together.

This is equally true where we are faced with rather more immediate problems in the working of the law. Two examples should indicate areas where legal issues could be more easily understood and perhaps resolved on a theoretical level with the aid of a more intensive degree of collaboration between members of the two disciplines than has been attempted so far. In the first place, there is the whole series of questions that remain unanswered within the field of the Law of Persons. This involves, among other things a detailed consideration of the relation between status and capacity in African law; some attempt to arrive at a suitable definition of a human being at customary law; the translation of customary distinctions between persons on the basis of age, sex, marital condition etc. into useful legal categories; the accurate determination of the precise consequences in legal terms of defective capacity or status through age, infirmity, mental handicaps and the like. Above all, there is a crying need for some realistic consideration of the implications for law of the existence of groups and corporations, which require not only description but the precise delineation of the role of individual members as part of, and in relation to the totality as well as their co-members; and a clear indication of the procedures by which groups arrive at operable decisions, the sanctions which they are able to impose on recalcitrants, and the effects of their decisions *inter alios* as well as *inter partes*.

The other example of an aspect of customary law which requires consideration of this kind occurs in the field of land law. It is not necessary to go into this in great detail here, because we are fortunate in having available the views of a number of authors who have considered this matter at length, and we have been able to include some of their contributions in Part IV of these Readings. The nature of the dispute surrounding the terminology and the concepts which have hitherto been commonly employed in this sphere emerges clearly from the material by Allott, Bentsi-Eichill, Lloyd, Meek, Schapera, White and Wilson which we have incorporated in that Part. But equally it is clear that the problems are neither easily resolvable nor capable of treatment in isolation by lawyers and anthropologists. In so vital an area, for the future, there is an undeniable need for continued work in theory and *in situ* by both.

These are but some of the areas which need further exploration, within the study of African customary law as a whole. It is not difficult to name others. A good deal of useful work has been done, for instance, on questions of procedure in a traditional setting as well as within the changing framework of urban African social conditions. But a great deal more has yet to be done, and on court procedure in a rural as well as a town environment. It should aim not only at the purely descriptive treatment of the ways in which courts are managed, but also at the formulation of generalisations, and the statement of the rules (and the principles which underly them) that are applied in customary courts of all kinds in a host of different settings.

Much the same can be said of the law or the rules of evidence in customary law, which require far more detailed attention than they have hitherto been accorded. And there remains the need for a thorough-going look at the law of contract, in terms which do not accept all the limitations implied in Maine's classic—and, by now, very dated—*dictum* that ". . . the movement of the progressive societies has hitherto been a movement from Status to Contract." Some authors have already been able to redirect themselves towards this problem, notably Professors Gluckman and Schapera, and we have been able to present some of the conclusions they have reached in Chapters 10 and 11. But this continues to be a relatively unexplored aspect of customary law, and it remains a remarkable fact that very little has been done by others on this topic in recent years.

There is, then, no doubt that a great deal has yet to be discovered in and about African customary law. In the process of doing so, a great number of the shortcomings of the research done in the past will probably be avoided. But there are other dangers, arising from the present framework within which African law is studied, which we must guard against. One of these is the assumption that all customary law in Africa is the same.

Much has been written about the "unity" of customary law, and, in a sense, it is not difficult to understand why this has been so. The urgent demands of nation-building in post-colonial Africa have created a natural desire to stress unifying rather than discordant factors in the social structure, and law in Africa—as so often elsewhere—has been seen by governments all over the continent as an essential piece of the machinery that must be used for this purpose. At the same time, the growing body of knowledge about customary law has enabled those who are familiar with its manifold details and intricacies to stand back from their subject-matter and point to general trends and similarities between different systems of law. Professor Allott and Dr. Elias have both contributed greatly towards such a realisation of the areas in which a set of underlying concepts is found to be common to a number of greatly varying societies. They have also pointed to the possibilities that exist for grouping together several different legal phenomena under a relatively small collection of rubrics, and thus reducing once again the degree of diversity that exists between the various social and legal systems.

But the differences remain very great nonetheless. It would not be very fruitful to elaborate the extent of ethnic diversity in Africa; whatever the significance, now or in the future, of these ethnic groups, it must be acknowledged that very many of them maintain a discrete customary legal system. The number of differences between the customary laws of any given two or more such groups will obviously vary greatly, depending on a variety of factors (many of them non-legal, such as language, proximity origin, history, social structure, economy etc.) which cannot be discussed in detail here. But it is clear that the greater the number of branches of the law that are discussed in relation to them, the greater will be the differences that are observable; and this applies even more drastically as one increases the number of specific rules or customs that are used as indices of comparison. In the circumstances, it is not difficult to agree with Allott that the unity that emerges will be a "unity in diversity", which is to say, an acknowledgement of the differences that exist rather than their elimination. (Rather as an "agreement to differ" is an acknowledgement of disagreement more than the achievement of a consensus).

Also to be avoided is any temptation to think of the customary law as static; for it is anything but that, and never was. Even in its traditional setting, it was undergoing a continuous process of modification and development. Although the pace at which change occurred may at times and in places have been slow, change itself was endemic to customary law: the result of a subtle and intricate interplay between the respect for tradition, which gave to the law much of its legitimacy, and the dynamic capacity of any unwritten system of law to adapt itself to new and altered facts and circumstances as well as to changes in the economic, political and social environment.

This process continues today, and has done amid the additional stresses and impetus provided by contact with European and other foreign legal systems, not to mention such factors as the advent of a money economy, agricultural development and urbanisation during the colonial period; and the changes that have taken place since independence, in local as well as national political structures and institutions, as well as through the efforts made to promote economic development.

In both the colonial and the post-independence periods, there have been other important agents of change, including the superimposition of western legal systems during the former, and the many policy considerations which have resulted in legislative action by African governments in the latter. The effects can be seen not only in the altered framework within which the customary law operates, but also in the way it is applied, and, very often, in its substance as well. To appreciate more fully the extent of the changes that have been made, it is perhaps as well to review briefly the developments during the two periods.

With one or two exceptions, the whole of Africa was colonised by European powers in the 19th century. The basic policy of the colonising powers, whether English, French, Portuguese or Belgian was to introduce their own metropolitan law into the African country, and also their system of courts, but also to retain so much of customary law and the African judicial process which they did not deem contrary to basic justice or morality. There was, however, a slight difference in emphasis between the English on the one hand and the various Latin powers on the other, in their attitude towards civilising the native populations. Though much of what follows deals with African countries which were formerly British colonies or protectorates the Latin powers believed in a policy of assimilation whereby an African could renounce his own law of personal status in favour of a European status, whereas the English believed in a policy of indirect rule, whereby their ideas would be introduced more gradually.

The result of the imposition of colonial rule, therefore, was to produce a dual or parallel system of courts and laws. In the British colonies and protectorates, a completely novel system of courts and laws was introduced, while retaining existing tribal institutions.

The dualism in the courts system was particularly very marked. On the one hand, there were the British or General courts consisting usually of different grades of magistrates from which appeal lay to a High Court. The magistrates and judges were expatriate British officers, and their jurisdiction extended over all persons in criminal and civil matters. They applied the English common law and equity and local statutes based on English enactments. On the other hand, Native courts (otherwise called Native tribunals, African courts, Local courts etc.) were established. The British administration tried as far as possible to preserve the previous nature of these tribunals. Thus they were composed of either traditional local chiefs or local elders; they only had jurisdiction over Africans; and they applied, subject to a few exceptions, the customary law prevailing in the area of the jurisdiction of the court. The native courts were supervised by administrative officers, who also had control over the appointment and dismissal of the court members. Advocates were not allowed to appear before these courts or tribunals.

Thus the two systems of courts—British and African—developed separately and there was no link between them. It was only in the 1950's, towards the end of the colonial period, that an attempt was made to produce some sort of integration and this was done by giving the High Court an appellate or a revisionary jurisdiction over native court proceedings.

Another important development towards the end of the colonial period was the gradual change of personnel of the native courts from the traditional chiefs and elders to young lay magistrates with some basic training in law, and coupled with this a gradual process of anglicisation of the procedure in the native courts.

Dualism existed to the same extent in the substantive law. The British introduced their own laws, partly in the form of local codes or statutes and partly through a general reception clause which empowered the British type courts to apply the English common law, doctrines of equity and statutes of general application at a certain date. Although there were general provisos that such English law was to be administered "subject to local circumstances", and also that the British courts were to be "guided" by customary law where the parties were natives, these provisos were largely ignored and the British judges were solely guided by the law with which they were familiar, i.e. English law.

The African courts were enjoined to apply customary law "so far as it was not repugnant to natural justice or morality", but this proviso was also to a large extent ignored. Little use of it was made by the appellate or revising officers, and customary law was left to develop separately.

The result of this dualistic system was that there was an almost complete isolation of African courts and customary law in the colonial period. Further, there appears to have been a general lack of interest in the problems arising from the content and application of customary law, and generally speaking there were no serious attempts at studying the subject, no attempts at recording customary law, developing it, reforming it or unifying it with the other laws. Customary law remained to a large extent unwritten and was treated as a matter of fact rather than law in the courts. Lawyers were not in touch with customary law problems, and its study remained the domain of the social anthropologist or the administrative officer.

This is not to say, however, that the traditional African law remained static in the colonial period. There were certainly some radical changes, but what is significant is that whereas in the period of independence which followed there was an active attempt by the African Governments to tackle customary law problems, the changes that occurred in the colonial period were principally the result of indirect rule and natural evolution through culture contact generally.

Four important changes in the colonial period are worth stressing: (1) The departure from the traditional methods of settling disputes, i.e. the radical change which occurred gradually upon the introduction of a system of courts which, though originally based on existing tribal institutions, tended gradually to become more westernised. (2) The assimilation of English rules into the customary law by native court judges. An interesting example of this occurred in Buganda, where a glance at the customary law reports of Buganda will show how there has been a clear adoption of English legal principles in the Buganda customary law relating to contracts, torts and crimes.[2] (3) The introduction of

[2] Hone, H. R. "The Native of Uganda and the Criminal Law", Uganda Journal (1938–1939), Vol. 6.

English-type laws, which, though not specifically abolishing customary law, makes available to Africans the option of governing their legal relationships by the English-type law. For example in the laws of marriage, most British colonial territories had a Marriage Ordinance, which, while specifically recognising customary marriage, made available to Africans the choice of marrying monogamously under the Ordinance. (4) The direct abolition of certain customs considered barbarous such as slavery and mutilation.

The achievement of independence of the countries of British Africa in the late 1950's and early 1960's did not bring about a legal revolution, in the sense that none of the African countries decided to scrap the laws which they inherited from the colonial power, and replace them by completely new laws. They did, however, unlike the colonial Governments, take a very keen interest in the problems of law which arose out of the dualistic state of affairs bequeathed to them. Their reforms can be classed under three general heads; (1) Integration of courts; (2) Study of the customary laws; (3) Attempts at unification, harmonisation and codification.

First, the newly independent African Governments directed their attention at completing the process of integration or unification of the courts system, a process which had already begun in the later years of the colonial period.

The general tendency was to abolish the system of native or African courts, and to introduce a hierarchy of courts consisting of various grades of magistrates with a High Court at the top of the ladder. All courts now have jurisdiction over all persons irrespective of race, and all courts may apply English-type law or customary law. Some countries (e.g. Ghana and Tanzania) also introduced detailed rules in order to determine the conflicts that may arise between customary law and English law. The practice and procedure of all courts is uniform and is generally based on English law, and advocates may appear before all courts.

An outstanding characteristic of the independence period is the great interest shown by some African Governments in studying customary law, in recording it, and reforming it. Not content with researches previously undertaken by social anthropologists and administrators, many African Governments initiated projects for the detailed restatement of customary law. Such projects were, for example, initiated in Kenya, Tanzania, Malawi, Zambia, Botswana and Swaziland. One country, Tanzania, went even further, and has now virtually completed a project aimed at the unification of the customary laws of all the Tanganyika tribes.[3]

The final set of reforms introduced by independent African Governments consisted, not so much of studying and reforming customary law as an end in itself, but as a first step towards introducing codes of law that would tend to integrate or unify the different strands of law existing within the country, whether customary or English-based or religious. Whether this objective can ever be achieved will depend, inter alia, on precisely what kind of unity is aimed at. We would suggest that a distinction should be made between organic and structural unity. The former would indicate a notion closer in its meaning to "uniformity" or "identity". In this sense, it would seem that it is only

[3] For details, see Cotran E. "Integration of Courts and Application of Customary Law in Tanganyika," (1965) East African Law Journal, 1-15.

possible to achieve unity by the rather drastic means of eliminating one set of customary laws and replacing them with another.

This has indeed been done, for example, where the uniform rules of customary law have been issued for a region or a district within one country as in Tanzania. Its efficacy as a method must depend on the extent of the differences between the system which is abolished and its substitute, and this will vary according to the branches of the law that are being unified, and, of course, in relation to the significance of the particular rule or set of rules that is being lost to a community. It is difficult to believe, for instance, that the replacement of a matrilineal system of succession by a patrilineal one—which has been proposed in Tanzania and in Malawi—will be effective, all other things being equal. But then, all other things may not be equal; social, economic, and above all governmental pressure to accept the new system may outweigh adherence to tradition as the major operative social force at play. But this must remain doubtful, and, in the case of the example chosen, it is not really possible to judge the matter until there has been a reasonable opportunity to observe the actual pattern of succession and inheritance over the period of at least a generation.

Other methods of organic unification of customary laws which have been discussed are "rationalisation" and "assimilation". The former seems to us no more than a rather polite term for indicating that certain rules of the customary laws of one society are going to be eliminated in the process of aligning them to those of another. As such it is almost impossible to distinguish it from unification by abolition. Assimilation, on the other hand, suggests an altogether different process. Here, the customary law is seen as embodying the maximum number of rules which are observed in common by a given number of heteronomic units. It also envisages a dynamic process whereby, as extraneous forces such as a changing economy produce a greater degree of similarity in the laws of different units, individual rules of law which grow to be identical with one another are absorbed into the corpus of common customary law, by means of some clearly defined procedure. In many ways, this seems an admirable system. It has been written into the law of one African country (Ghana) but, unfortunately it has never been used extensively. It is therefore not yet possible to assert with any degree of assurance that it is anything more than a theoretically viable solution to the problem of unification.

In view of the unsatisfactory, or at least unproven, character of the proposals for organic unity, it is useful to take a closer look at the alternative of structural unification. This does not imply uniformity. Rather, it seeks to achieve a purely notional unity by being inclusive of as many distinct systems of customary law as possible within a single legal framework. At its most formal level, this can be accomplished merely by having a uniform court system, which superimposes an extraneous uniform procedure and machinery of enforcement, but leaves the substantive law of the different ethnic or other legal units basically unaltered. There is no precise term for this procedure, but it might be described as the co-existence of customary laws within a unitary framework.

The next method of attempting structural unity to be noted is one which is perhaps slightly less committed to accepting the irreconcilability of customary legal systems. This aims to make them mutually intelligible. The problem is, in part at least, a linguistic one, and for this reason it can be (and has been) dealt with through efforts at recording the relevant customary laws in a single language. Such a language should normally be common to all the groups involved, but in practice it is more likely to be that of the official who is charged with deciding disputes in terms of the different systems and vernacular languages have often been overlooked as a result. This is certainly so where English has been used as the language of transcription, though the decision by the Tanzanian authorities to issue the definitive text of the customary law statements in Swahili indicates that this difficulty can also be overcome. (Whether this is more or less satisfactory than having an official vernacular translation, which has been tried elsewhere, is a moot point). The system also has the merit of providing a useful way of resolving disputes between members of different ethnic groups. It may, in addition, create greater scope for the development of a coherent set of rules on inter-personal conflict of laws. There is a growing need for machinery to deal with intercustomary law conflicts, particularly where a single court has jurisdiction over people from groups whose customary law is not identical, as in the urban African courts of Zambia.

Another method of structural unification which has been proposed is that which is known as integration, by which is meant that the law would bring together under one enactment the different laws, with a view of laying down rules governing all of them. Where this has been proposed, it has normally been envisaged that a single enactment should be made for each branch of the law (for example, marriage or succession) on a national basis. It is also envisaged that uniform rules will only be established where this is possible, and that matters which cannot be unified will be left to the personal law of the parties. This technique is not greatly different from another, known as harmonisation, which seeks to eliminate points of friction between different systems of law but recognises the need to preserve certain aspects of each law separately.

Thus, integration and harmonisation embody a pragmatic approach to the question of unification, which is indeed common to all the proposals which aim at some sort of functional unity. They seek to achieve their object either gradually or by a cumulative process, dealing with one branch of the law at a time, and paving the way for a growth towards greater uniformity as actual differences between legal rules and institutions disappear under the impact of changing social conditions. They do, of course, imply the need for some sort of regular (if not continuous) procedure for reviewing and reforming the legal system, so that the law can be brought up to date regularly. But this is something which is needed in all countries. If the continuing drive to bring about unity in customary law culminates in the establishment of a permanent commission or other body charged with the task, this will represent an achievement every bit as significant for the future of African law as that involved in overcoming the differences which exit at present between the great number of customary laws.

In fact, none of the countries with a common law tradition has embarked on a full-scale project to unify every branch of the law (as was done, for example in Ethiopia); rather they have tended to choose particular branches of law as their target for harmonisation, with different goals in mind.

All ex-British African countries have, for example, taken the view that it was undesirable to have a unwritten criminal law. Indeed, many of the Constitutions of Commonwealth African countries (*e.g.* those of Kenya, Uganda, Nigeria) contain a provision to the effect that no person can be convicted of a criminal offence unless that offence was defined and the penalty therefore prescribed in a written law.

During the colonial period, all these countries (except Sierra Leone) had a Penal Code based on English law. This was applied side by side with certain customary criminal offences applied in the native courts. After independence, some of the African countries (*e.g.* Kenya and Uganda) initiated projects with a view to incorporating any surviving customary offences into the Penal Code but the majority of the others took the easy way out by simply abolishing customary criminal law and declaring the Penal Code to be the exhaustive penal law of the country. To this extent, customary criminal law in Commonwealth African countries is virtually no more.[4]

On the other hand the law of contract and tort has so far been neglected since none of the Commonwealth African countries have taken any steps aimed at integrating or unifying the customary laws with the English laws.[5]

Yet again, many African countries still adhere to the dualistic law in the fields of marriage, divorce and succession. But at least three African countries, namely Ghana, Uganda and Kenya, have taken bold steps aimed at unification of the different marriage, divorce and succession laws within their country.

Ghana led the field with the publication in May 1961 of a White Paper which was intended "to provoke discussion on the question of marriage and divorce" and the related problem of inheritance." This was followed a year later by the publication of the Marriage, Divorce and Inheritance Bill, which contained the following main proposals; (i) A man could only register one marriage; (ii) a man could marry subsequent "wives", but public recognition would only be accorded to the wife who appears on the register; (iii) only the registered wife would be entitled to inheritance under the law, (iv) divorce to be dealt by a Committee presided over by a Chairman who was to be a judge of the High Court; (v) a wife to inherit one third of her husband's property, the other two thirds to go the children equally.

The Bill had an unfortunate history. Attempts to introduce it, each time with minor variations, were made at least three times, but were unsuccessful, and it was finally withdrawn.

Uganda chose to reform the law of marriage, divorce and succession by the setting up of a Commission, which presented its report in July, 1965.[6] The report in effect adopts all the recommendations put forward in the abortive Ghana Bill, and so far no action has been taken on it.

Kenya also chose to tackle the problem by the setting up of two Commissions, one on the law of marriage and divorce and the other on succession. The Commissions' reports were presented in September 1968,[7] and unlike their Ghana and Uganda counterparts, contain a comprehensive set of recommendations (with draft Bills) aimed at the replacement of the various Kenya

[4] For more detail, see Cotran E. "The Position of Customary Criminal Law in African Countries", in East African Law and Social Change, 1967.

[5] Compare the position in Ethiopia, for which see David, R. "A Civil Code for Ethiopia," 37 Tulane Law Review.

[6] Report of the Commission on Marriage, Divorce and the Status of Women, 1965, Government Printer, Entebbe.

[7] Report of the Commission on the Law of Marriage and Divorce, 1968, Government Printer, Nairobi; Report of the Commission on the Law of Succession, 1968, Government Printer, Nairobi.

marriage and succession laws, whether customary, statutory, English, Islamic or Hindu, by one code applicable to all Kenyans without distinction as to race, tribe or religion.

The Kenya reports on the subjects of marriage and succession really constitute the first serious attempt at producing a law befitted to African conditions. Space forbids a detailed consideration of the Commissions' proposals, but generally speaking, both Commissions worked on the principle that modernisation and Africanisation must go together, and that it was possible to produce a modern law without necessarily destroying those principles of African law that can be adapted to modern conditions. One hopes that this Kenya experiment will prove more successful than the abortive attempts at reform of this field in Ghana and Uganda.

Our last example is taken from the field of land law—a subject which is difficult to divorce from the political ideologies of the country undertaking reform. The emerging African States have been quick to put forward slogans fo land law to befit their policies of the day. "African socialism", for example, has been interpreted to mean more state ownership or state control, and in some cases the community principle in African land law has been stretched to suggest some form of communism or communalism in the strict sense. Furthermore, in certain African countries, e.g. in Kenya, land policy has been determined, to a large extent by the colonial attitude towards land and agriculture, and the existence or otherwise of a "settler" population.

But apart from this political trend, it can generally be stated that many African countries chose the path to individualisation of their land tenure system. They felt that the customary system based on "ownership" or control by groups led to insecurity of title and did not encourage economic development of land. This was undoubtedly the main reason for the introduction in Kenya of an intensive land consolidation and registration programme, and such schemes are also gradually being introduced in other African countries.

Ghana has recently appointed a Commission[8] to investigate the land tenure system with very wide terms of reference including every aspect of Ghana land law, customary or otherwise. This would appear to be the first attempt in a Commonwealth African country to tackle the problem comprehensively. The trend in other countries was to bring in piecemeal legislation to deal with specific problems.

What, may one ask in conclusion, is the rôle of African law today? Has the traditional law any place in the modern legal systems of African countries?

There is no doubt that the traditional African law is loosing, or in some places, has already lost, much of its original character. It is no longer customary in nature since it is gradually being recorded or codified. It is becoming less diverse since unification is being pushed (even where unity does not exist) and due to the inevitable mixing of populations, and the movement from tribe to State, the distinction between "custom" and "law", and the consequent question of "what is customary law", is becoming less important since customary law is now generally regarded as the customary law as expounded by the courts.

The traditional African judicial process, for good or ill, has to a large extent given way to a formalised western system with detailed rules of procedure and

[8] See note about this Commission in Journal of African Law, Vol. XII, p. 61.

evidence. Although customary arbitration is still used, and indeed recognised in some countries by state legislation, it has inevitably been contaminated by ideas of law and procedure adopted by the formal courts.

As for the substance of African customary law, this as we have seen, remains principally in the fields of contract and tort, in marriage and divorce and family law, and in land law and succession. But here again, the trend towards harmonisation, unification and codification is gradually leading to a situation where the western-type law dominates. Whether there is likely to be a reversal in this trend remains to be seen, but one does sincerely hope that attempts at unification will not necessarily mean complete westernisation and that African law reformers will make a special effort at preserving those ideas or principles of African customary law which are worthy of preservation.

London
August 1969

E. C.
N. N. R.

Part I

THE CUSTOMARY JUDICIAL PROCESS

THESE chapters, on the Customary Judicial Process, provide a description of the framework within which the substantive rules of African customary law operate. It is, therefore, a necessary introduction to all that follows—both in this volume, and in the other which forms part of this series of *Readings in African Law*—since it offers an account of the background against which the various African societies organise their judicial systems, as well as to the manner in which the courts and other decision-making institutions function in their day-to-day activity. Despite the introduction of modern Western types of courts in Africa, a large number of cases are still heard before authorities of this kind, at the present time. For this reason, it is vital to obtain an understanding of their procedure—if only to facilitate their satisfactory integration into the prevailing contemporary pattern of courts.

Chapter 1

INTRODUCTION—POLITICAL STRUCTURE

In order to grasp the full significance of the descriptions given in the chapters which follow, it is necessary to appreciate the traditional political context within which the customary judicial system operates. For this purpose, only one extract has been included: from the introduction to *Fortes* and *Evans-Pritchard*'s collection of essays on *African Political Systems*. This provides a succinct, yet inclusive, summary of the relevant categories of traditional government and their characteristics. It is not, of course, all-embracing. For further information, the reader should refer to the individual essays included in *African Political Systems*, as well as to other well-known works on the subject such as Professor *Lucy Mair*'s *Primitive Government* and Professor *Schapera*'s *Government and Politics in Tribal Society*.

M. Fortes and E. E. Evans-Pritchard: African Political Systems*

The Two Types of Political System Studied

It will be noted that the political systems described fall into two main categories. One group, which we refer to as Group A, consists of those societies which have centralized

* M. Fortes and E. E. Evans-Pritchard, *African Political Systems*, Oxford University Press for the International African Institute, 1940, pp. 5–23.

authority, administrative machinery, and judicial institutions—in short, a government—and in which cleavages of wealth, privilege, and status correspond to the distribution of power and authority. This group comprises the Zulu, the Ngwato, the Bemba, the Banyankole, and the Kede. The other group, which we refer to as Group B, consists of those societies which lack centralized authority, administrative machinery, and constituted judicial institutions—in short which lack government—and in which there are no sharp divisions of rank, status, or wealth. This group comprises the Logoli, the Tallensi, and the Nuer. Those who consider that a state should be defined by the presence of governmental institutions will regard the first group as primitive states and the second group as stateless societies.

The kind of information related and the kind of problems discussed in a description of each society have largely depended on the category to which it belongs. Those who have studied societies of Group A are mainly concerned to describe governmental organization. They therefore give an account of the status ratings and classes, the roles of administrative officials of one kind or another, the privileges of rank, the differences in wealth and power, the regulation of tax and tribute, the territorial divisions of the state and their relation to its central authority, the rights of subjects and the obligations of rulers, and the checks on authority. Those who studied societies of Group B had no such matters to discuss and were therefore forced to consider what, in the absence of explicit forms of government, could be held to constitute the political structure of a people. This problem was simplest among the Nuer, who have very distinct territorial divisions. The difficulty was greater for the Logoli and Tallensi, who have no clear spatially-defined political units.

Kinship in Political Organization

One of the outstanding differences between the two groups is the part played by the lineage system in political structure. We must here distinguish between the set of relationships linking the individual to other persons and to particular social units through the transient, bilateral family, which we shall call the kinship system, and the segmentary system of permanent, unilateral descent groups, which we call the lineage system. Only the latter establishes corporate units with political functions. In both groups of societies kinship and domestic ties have an important role in the lives of individuals, but their relation to the political system is of a secondary order. In the societies of Group A it is the administrative organization, in societies of Group B the segmentary lineage system, which primarily regulates political relations between territorial segments.

This is clearest among the Ngwato, whose political system resembles the pattern with which we are familiar in the modern nation-state. The political unit is essentially a territorial grouping wherin the plexus of kinship ties serves merely to cement those already established by membership of the ward, district, and nation. In societies of this type the state is never the kinship system writ large, but is organized on totally different principles. In societies of Group B kinship ties appear to play a more prominent role in political organization, owing to the close association of territorial grouping with lineage grouping, but it is still only a secondary role.

It seems probable to us that three types of political system can be distinguished. Firstly, there are those very small societies, none of which are described in this book, in which even the largest political unit embraces a group of people all of whom are united to one another by ties of kinship, so that political relations are coterminous with kinship relations and the political structure and kinship organization are completely fused. Secondly, there are societies in which a lineage structure is the framework of the political system, there being a precise co-ordination between the two, so that they are consistent with each other, though each remains distinct and autonomous in its own sphere. Thirdly, there are societies in which an administrative organization is the framework of the political structure.

The numerical and territorial range of a political system would vary according to the type to which it belongs. A kinship system would seem to be incapable of uniting such large numbers of persons into a single organization for defence and the settlement of disputes by arbitration as a lineage system and a lineage system incapable of uniting such numbers as an administrative system.

The Influence of Demography

It is noteworthy that the political unit in the societies with a state organization is numerically larger than in those without a state organization. The largest political groups among the Tallensi, Logoli, and Nuer cannot compete in numbers with the quarter to half million of the Zulu state (in about 1870), the 101,000 of the Ngwato state, and the 140,000 of the Bemba state. It is true that the Kede and their subject population are not so populous, but it must be remembered that they form part of the vast Nupe state. It is not suggested that a stateless political unit need be very small—Nuer political units comprise as many as 45,000 souls—nor that a political unit with state organization need be very large, but it is probably true that there is a limit to the size of a population that can hold together without some kind of centralized government.

Size of population should not be confused with density of population. There may be some relation between the degree of political development and the size of population, but it would be incorrect to suppose that governmental institutions are found in those societies with greatest density. The opposite seems to be equally likely, judging by our material. The density of the Zulu is 3·5, of the Ngwato 2·5, of the Bemba 3·75 per square mile, while that of the Nuer is higher and of the Tallensi and Logoli very much higher. It might be supposed that the dense permanent settlements of the Tallensi would necessarily lead to the development of a centralized form of government, whereas the wide dispersion of shifting villages among the Bemba would be incompatible with centralized rule. The reverse is actually the case. In addition to the material collected in this book, evidence from other African societies could be cited to prove that a large population in a political unit and a high degree of political centralization do not necessarily go together with great density.

The Influence of Mode of Livelihood

The density and distribution of population in an African society are clearly related to ecological conditions which also affect the whole mode of livelihood. It is obvious, however, that mere differences in modes of livelihood do not determine differences in political structure. The Tallensi and the Bemba are both agriculturalists, the Tallensi having fixed and the Bemba shifting cultivation, but they have very different political systems. The Nuer and Logoli of Group B and the Zulu and Ngwato of Group A alike practise mixed agriculture and cattle husbandry. In a general sense, modes of livelihood, together with environmental conditions, which always impose effective limits on modes of livelihood, determine the dominant values of the people and strongly influence their social organizations, including their political systems. This is evident in the political divisions of the Nuer, in the distribution of Kede settlements and the administrative organization embracing them, and in the class system of the Banyankole.

Most African societies belong to an economic order very different from ours. Theirs is mainly a subsistence economy with a rudimentary differentiation of productive labour and with no machinery for the accumulation of wealth in the form of commercial or industrial capital. If wealth is accumulated it takes the form of consumption goods and amenities or is used for the support of additional dependants. Hence it tends to be rapidly dissipated again and does not give rise to permanent class divisions. Distinctions of rank, status, or occupation operate independently of differences of wealth.

Economic privileges, such as rights to tax, tribute, and labour, are both the main reward of political power and an essential means of maintaining it in the political systems of Group A. But there are counterbalancing economic obligations no less strongly backed by institutionalized sanctions. It must not be forgotten, also, that those who derive maximum economic benefit from political office also have the maximum administrative, judicial, and religious responsibilities.

Compared with the societies of Group A, distinctions of rank and status are of minor significance in societies of Group B. Political office carries no economic privileges, though the possession of greater than average wealth may be a criterion of the qualities or status required for political leadership; for in these economically homogeneous, equalitarian, and segmentary societies the attainment of wealth depends either on exceptional personal qualities or accomplishments, or on superior status in the lineage system.

Composite Political Systems and the Conquest Theory

It might be held that societies like the Logoli, Tallensi, and Nuer, without central government or administrative machinery, develop into states like the Ngwato, Zulu, and Banyankole as a result of conquest. Such a development is suggested for the Zulu and Banyankole. But the history of all the peoples treated in this book is not well enough known to enable us to declare with any degree of certainty what course their political development has taken. The problem must therefore be stated in a different way. All the societies of Group A appear to be an amalgam of different peoples, each aware of its unique origin and history, and all except the Zulu and Bemba are still to-day culturally heterogeneous. Cultural diversity is most marked among the Banyankole and Kede, but it is also clear among the Ngwato. We may, therefore, ask to what extent cultural heterogeneity in a society is correlated with an administrative system and central authority. The evidence at our disposal in this book suggests that cultural and economic heterogeneity is associated with a state-like political structure. Centralized authority and an administrative organization seem to be necessary to accommodate culturally diverse groups within a single political system, especially if they have different modes of livelihood. A class or caste system may result if there are great cultural and, especially, great economic divergencies. But centralized forms of government are found also with peoples of homogeneous culture and little economic differentiation like the Zulu. It is possible that groups of diverse culture are the more easily welded into a unitary political system without the emergence of classes the closer they are to one another in culture. A centralized form of government is not necessary to enable different groups of closely related culture and pursuing the same mode of livelihood to amalgamate, nor does it necessarily arise out of the amalgamation. The Nuer have absorbed large numbers of conquered Dinka, who are a pastoral people like themselves with a very similar culture. They have incorporated them by adoption and other ways into their lineage system; but this has not resulted in a class or caste structure or in a centralized form of government. Marked divergencies in culture and economic pursuits are probably incompatible with a segmentary political system such as that of the Nuer or the Tallensi. We have not the data to check this. It is clear, however, that a conquest theory of the primitive state—assuming that the necessary historical evidence is available—must take into account not only the mode of conquest and the conditions of contact, but also the similarities or divergencies in culture and mode of livelihood of conquerors and conquered and the political institutions they bring with them into the new combination.

The Territorial Aspect

The territorial aspect of early forms of political organization was justly emphasized by Maine in *Ancient Law* and other scholars have given much attention to it. In all the societies described in this book the political system has a territorial framework, but it has a different function in the two types of political organization. The difference is due to the dominance of an administrative and judicial apparatus in one type of system and its absence in the other. In the societies of Group A the administrative unit is a territorial unit; political rights and obligations are territorially delimited. A chief is the administrative and judicial head of a given territorial division, vested often with final economic and legal control over all the land within his boundaries. Everybody living within these boundaries is his subject, and the right to live in this area can be acquired only by accepting the obligations of a subject. The head of the state is a territorial ruler.

In the other group of societies there are no territorial units defined by an administrative system, but the territorial units are local communities the extent of which corresponds to the range of a particular set of lineage ties and the bonds of direct co-operation. Political office does not carry with it juridical rights over a particular, defined stretch of territory and its inhabitants. Membership of the local community, and the rights and duties that go with it, are acquired as a rule through genealogical ties, real or fictional. The lineage principle takes the place of political allegiance, and the interrelations of territorial segments are directly co-ordinated with the interrelations of lineage segments.

Political relations are not simply a reflexion of territorial relations. The political system, in its own right, incorporates territorial relations and invests them with the particular kind of political significance they have.

The Balance of Forces in the Political System

A relatively stable political system in Africa presents a balance between conflicting tendencies and between divergent interests. In Group A it is a balance between different parts of the administrative organization. The forces that maintain the supremacy of the paramount ruler are opposed by the forces that act as a check on his powers. Institutions such as the regimental organization of the Zulu, the genealogical restriction of succession to kingship or chiefship, the appointment by the king of his kinsmen to regional chiefships, and the mystical sanctions of his office all reinforce the power of the central authority. But they are counterbalanced by other institutions, like the king's council, sacerdotal officials who have a decisive voice in the king's investiture, queen mothers' courts, and so forth, which work for the protection of law and custom and the control of centralized power. The regional devolution of powers and privileges, necessary on account of difficulties of communication and transport and of other cultural deficiencies, imposes severe restrictions on a king's authority. The balance between central authority and regional autonomy is a very important element in the political structure. If a king abuses his power, subordinate chiefs are liable to secede or to lead a revolt against him. If a subordinate chief seems to be getting too powerful and independent, the central authority will be supported by other subordinate chiefs in suppressing him. A king may try to buttress his authority by playing off rival subordinate chiefs against one another.

It would be a mistake to regard the scheme of constitutional checks and balances and the delegation of power and authority to regional chiefs as nothing more than an administrative device. A general principle of great importance is contained in these arrangements, which has the effect of giving every section and every major interest of the society direct or indirect representation in the conduct of government. Local chiefs represent the central authority in relation to their districts, but they also represent the people under them in relation to the central authority. Councillors and ritual functionaries represent the community's interest in the preservation of law and custom and in the observance of the ritual measures deemed necessary for its well-being. The voice of such functionaries and delegates is effective in the conduct of government on account of the general principle that power and authority are distributed. The king's power and authority are composite. Their various components are lodged in different offices. Without the co-operation of those who hold these offices it is extremely difficult, if not impossible, for the king to obtain his revenue, assert his judicial and legislative supremacy, or retain his secular and ritual prestige. Functionaries vested with essential subsidiary powers and privileges can often sabotage a ruler's acts if they disapprove them.

Looked at from another angle, the government of an African state consists in a balance between power and authority on the one side and obligation and responsibility on the other. Every one who holds political office has responsibilities for the public weal corresponding to his rights and privileges. The distribution of political authority provides a machinery by which the various agents of government can be held to their responsibilities. A chief or a king has the right to exact tax, tribute, and labour service from his subjects; he has the corresponding obligation to dispense justice to them, to ensure their protection from enemies and to safeguard their general welfare by ritual acts and observances. The structure of an African state implies that kings and chiefs rule by consent. A ruler's subjects are as fully aware of the duties he owes to them as they are of the duties they owe to him, and are able to exert pressure to make him discharge these duties.

We should emphasize here, that we are talking of constitutional arrangements, not of how they work in practice. Africans recognize as clearly as we do that power corrupts and that men are liable to abuse it. In many ways the kind of constitution we find in societies of Group A is cumbrous and too loosely jointed to prevent abuse entirely. The native theory of government is often contradicted by their practice. Both rulers and subjects, actuated by their private interests, infringe the rules of the constitution. Though it usually has a form calculated to hold in check any tendency towards absolute despotism, no African constitution can prevent a ruler from sometimes becoming a tyrant. The history of Shaka is an extreme case, but in this and other instances where the contradiction between theory and practice is too glaring and the infringement of constitutional rules becomes too grave, popular disapproval is sure to follow and may even result in a movement of secession or revolt led by members of the roval family or subordinate chiefs. This is what happened to Shaka.

It should be remembered that in these states there is only one theory of government. In the event of rebellion, the aim, and result, is only to change the personnel of office and never to abolish it or to substitute for it some new form of government. When subordinate chiefs, who are often kinsmen of the king, rebel against him they do so in defence of the values violated by his malpractices. They have an interest greater than any other section of the people in maintaining the kingship. The ideal constitutional pattern remains the valid norm, in spite of breaches of its rules.

A different kind of balance is found in societies of Group B. It is an equilibrium between a number of segments, spatially juxtaposed and structurally equivalent, which are defined in local and lineage, and not in administrative terms. Every segment has the same interests as other segments of a like order. The set of intersegmentary relations that constitutes the political structure is a balance of opposed local loyalties and of divergent lineage and ritual ties. Conflict between the interests of administrative divisions is common in societies like those of Group A. Subordinate chiefs and other political functionaries, whose rivalries are often personal, or due to their relationship to the king or the ruling aristocracy, often exploit these divergent local loyalties for their own ends. But the administrative organization canalizes and provides checks on such inter-regional dissensions. In the societies without an administrative organization, divergence of interests between the component segments is intrinsic to the political structure. Conflicts between local segments necessarily mean conflicts between lineage segments, since the two are closely interlocked; and the stabilizing factor is not a superordinate juridical or military rganization, but is simply the sum total of inter-segment relations.

The Incidence and Function of Organized Force

In our judgement, the most significant characteristic distinguishing the centralized, pyramidal, state-like forms of government of the Ngwato, Bemba, &c., from the segmentary political systems of the Logoli, the Tallensi, and the Nuer is the incidence and function of organized force in the system. In the former group of societies, the principal sanction of a ruler's rights and prerogatives, and of the authority exercised by his subordinate chiefs, is the command of organized force. This may enable an African king to rule oppressively for a time, if he is inclined to do so, but a good ruler uses the armed forces under his control in the public interest, as an accepted instrument of government—that is, for the defence of the society as a whole or of any section of it, for offence against a common enemy, and as a coercive sanction to enforce the law or respect for the constitution. The king and his delegates and advisers use organized force with the consent of their subjects to keep going a political system which the latter take for granted as the foundation of their social order.

In societies of Group B there is no association, class, or segment which has a dominant place in the political structure through the command of a greater organized force than is at the disposal of any of its congeners. If force is resorted to in a dispute between segments it will be met with equal force. If one segment defeats another it does not attempt to establish political dominance over it; in the absence of an administrative machinery there is, in fact, no means by which it could do so. In the language of political philosophy, there is no individual or group in which sovereignty can be said to rest. In such a system, stability is maintained by an equilibrium at every line of cleavage and every point of divergent interests in the social structure. This balance is sustained by a distribution of the command of force corresponding to the distribution of like, but competitive, interests amongst the homologous segments of the society. Whereas a constituted judicial machinery is possible and is always found in societies of Group A, since it has the backing of organized force, the jural institutions of the Logoli, the Tallensi and the Nuer rest on the right of self-help.

Differences in Response to European Rule

The distinctions we have noted between the two categories into which these eight societies fall, especially in the kind of balance characteristic of each, are very marked in their adjustment to the rule of colonial governments. Most of these societies have been conquered or have submitted to European rule from fear of invasion. They would not acquiesce in it if the threat of force were withdrawn; and this fact determines the part now played in their political life by European administrations.

In the societies of Group A, the paramount ruler is prohibited, by the constraint of the colonial government, from using the organized force at his command on his own responsibility. This has everywhere resulted in diminishing his authority and generally in increasing the power and independence of his subordinates. He no longer rules in his own right, but as the agent of the colonial government. The pyramidal structure of the state is now maintained by the latter's taking his place as paramount. If he capitulates entirely, he may become a mere puppet of the colonial government. He loses the support of his people because the pattern of reciprocal rights and duties which bound him to them is destroyed. Alternatively, he may be able to safeguard his former status, to some extent, by openly or covertly leading the opposition which his people inevitably feel towards alien rule. Very often he is in the equivocal position of having to reconcile his contradictory roles as representative of his people against the colonial government and of the latter against his people. He becomes the pivot on which the new system swings precariously. Indirect Rule may be regarded as a policy designed to stabilize the new political order, with the native paramount ruler in this dual role, but eliminating the friction it is liable to give rise to.

In the societies of Group B, European rule has had the opposite effect. The colonial government cannot administer through aggregates of individuals composing political segments, but has to employ administrative agents. For this purpose it makes use of any persons who can be assimilated to the stereotyped notion of an African chief. These agents for the first time have the backing of force behind their authority, now, moreover, extending into spheres for which there is no precedent. Direct resort to force in the form of self-help in defence of the rights of individuals or of groups is no longer permitted; for there is now, for the first time, a paramount authority exacting obedience in virtue of superior force which enables it to establish courts of justice to replace self-help. This tends to lead to the whole system of mutually balancing segments collapsing and a bureaucratic European system taking its place. An organization more like that of a centralized state comes into being.

The Mystical Values Associated with Political Office

The sanction of force is not an innovation in African forms of government. We have stressed the fact that it is one of the main pillars of the indigenous type of state. But the sanction of force on which a European administration depends lies outside the native political system. It is not used to maintain the values inherent in that system. In both societies of Group A and those of Group B European governments can impose their authority; in neither are they able to establish moral ties with the subject people. For, as we have seen, in the original native system force is used by a ruler with the consent of his subjects in the interest of the social order.

An African ruler is not to his people merely a person who can enforce his will on them. He is the axis of their political relations, the symbol of their unity and exclusiveness, and the embodiment of their essential values. He is more than a secular ruler; in *that* capacity the European government can to a great extent replace him. His credentials are mystical and are derived from antiquity. Where there are no chiefs, the balanced segments which compose the political structure are vouched for by tradition and myth and their interrelations are guided by values expressed in mystical symbols. Into these sacred precincts the European rulers can never enter. They have no mythical or ritual warranty for their authority.

What is the meaning of this aspect of African political organization? African societies are not models of continuous internal harmony. Acts of violence, oppression, revolt, civil war, and so forth, chequer the history of every African state. In societies like the Logoli, Tallensi, and Nuer the segmentary nature of the social structure is often most strikingly brought to light by armed conflict between the segments. But if the social system has reached a sufficient degree of stability, these internal convulsions do not necessarily wreck it. In fact, they may be the means of reinforcing it, as we have seen, against the abuses and infringements of rulers actuated by their private interests. In the segmentary societies, war is not a matter of one segment enforcing its will on another, but is the way in which segments protect their particular interests within a field of common interests and values.

There are, in every African society, innumerable ties which counteract the tendencies towards political fission arising out of the tensions and cleavages in the social structure. An administrative organization backed by coercive sanctions, clanship, lineage and age-set ties, the fine-spun web of kinship—all these unite people who have different or even opposed sectional and private interests. Often also there are common material interests such as the need to share pastures or to trade in a common market-place, or complementary economic pursuits binding different sections to one another. Always there are common ritual values, the ideological superstructure of political organization.

Members of an African society feel their unity and perceive their common interests in symbols, and it is their attachment to these symbols which more than anything else gives their society cohesion and persistence. In the form of myths, fictions, dogmas, ritual, sacred places and persons, these symbols represent the unity and exclusiveness of the groups which respect them. They are regarded, however, not as mere symbols, but as final values in themselves.

To explain these symbols sociologically, they have to be translated into terms of social function and of the social structure which they serve to maintain. Africans have no objective knowledge of the forces determining their social organization and actuating their social behaviour. Yet they would be unable to carry on their collective life if they could not think and feel about the interests which actuate them, the institutions by means of which they organize collective action, and the structure of the groups into which they are organized. Myths, dogmas, ritual beliefs and activities make his social system intellectually tangible and coherent to an African and enable him to think and feel about it. Furthermore, these sacred symbols, which reflect the social system, endow it with mystical values which evoke acceptance of the social order that goes far beyond the obedience exacted by the secular sanction of force. The social system is, as it were, removed to a mystical plane, where it figures as a system of sacred values beyond criticism or revision. Hence people will overthrow a bad king, but the kingship is never questioned; hence the wars or feuds between segments of a society like the Nuer or the Tallensi are kept within bounds by mystical sanctions. These values are common to the whole society, to rulers and ruled alike and to all the segments and sections of a society.

The African does not see beyond the symbols; it might well be held that if he understood their objective meaning, they would lose the power they have over him. This power lies in their symbolic content, and in their association with the nodal institutions of the social structure, such as the kingship. Not every kind of ritual or any sort of mystical ideas can express the values that hold a society together and focus the loyalty and devotion of its members on their rulers. If we study the mystical values bound up with the kingship in any of the societies of Group A, we find that they refer to fertility, health, prosperity, peace, justice—to everything, in short, which gives life and happiness to a people. The African sees these ritual observances as the supreme safeguard of the basic needs of his existence and of the basic relations that make up his social order—land, cattle, rain, bodily health, the family, the clan, the state. The mystical values reflect the general import of the basic elements of existence: the land as the source of the whole people's livelihood, physical health as something universally desired, the family as the fundamental procreative unit, and so forth. These are the common interests of the whole society, as the native sees them. These are the themes of taboos, observances and ceremonies in which, in societies of Group A, the whole people has a share through its representatives, and in societies of Group B all the segments participate, since they are matters of equal moment to all.

We have stressed the fact that the universal aspect of things like land or fertility are the subjects of common interest in an African society; for these matters also have another side to them, as the private interests of individuals and segments of a society. The productivity of his own land, the welfare and security of his own family or his own clan, such matters are of daily, practical concern to every member of an African society; and over such matters arise the conflicts between sections and factions of the society. Thus the basic needs of existence and the basic social relations are, in their pragmatic and utilitarian aspects, as sources of immediate satisfactions and strivings, the subjects of private interests; as common interests, they are non-utilitarian and nonpragmatic, matters of moral value and ideological significance. The common interests spring from those very private interests to which they stand in opposition.

To explain the ritual aspect of African political organization in terms of magical mentality is not enough; and it does not take us far to say that land, rain, fertility, &c., are 'sacralized' because they are the most vital needs of the community. Such arguments do not explain why the great ceremonies in which ritual for the common good is performed are usually on a public scale. They do not explain why the ritual functions we have been describing should be bound up, always, with pivotal political offices and should be part of the political theory of an organized society.

Again, it is not enough to dismiss these ritual functions of chiefship, kingship, &c., by calling them sanctions of political authority. Why, then, are they regarded as among the most stringent responsibilities of office? Why are they so often distributed amongst a number of independent functionaries who are thus enabled to exercise a balancing constraint on one another? It is clear that they serve, also, as a sanction against the abuse of political power and as a means of constraining political functionaries to perform their administrative obligations as well as their religious duties, lest the common good suffer injury.

When, finally, it is stated as an observable descriptive fact that we are dealing here with institutions that serve to affirm and promote political solidarity we must ask why they do so. Why is an all-embracing administrative machinery or a wide-flung lineage system insufficient by itself to achieve this?

We cannot attempt to deal at length with all these questions. We have already given overmuch space to them because we consider them to be of the utmost importance both from the theoretical and the practical point of view. The 'supernatural' aspects of African government are always puzzling and often exasperating to the European administrator. But a great deal more of research is needed before we shall be able to understand them fully. The hypothesis we are making use of is, we feel, a stimulating starting-point for further research into these matters. That part of it which has already been stated is, perhaps, least controversial. But it is incomplete.

Any item of social behaviour, and therefore any political relation, has a utilitarian or pragmatic content. It means that material goods change hands, are disbursed or acquired, and that the direct purposes of individuals are achieved. Items of social behaviour and therefore political relations have also a moral aspect; that is, they express rights and duties, privileges and obligations, political sentiments, social ties and cleavages. We see these two aspects clearly in such acts as paying tribute to a ruler or handing over blood-cattle in compensation for murder. In political relations, consequently, we find two types of interests working conjointly, material interests and moral interests, though they are not separated in this abstract way in native thought. Natives stress the material components of a political relation and generally state it in terms of its utilitarian and pragmatic functions.

A particular right or duty or political sentiment occurs as an item of behaviour of an individual or a small section of an African society and is enforceable by secular sanctions brought to bear on these individuals or small sections. But in a politically organized community a particular right, duty, or sentiment exists only as an element in a whole body of common, reciprocal, and mutually balancing rights, duties, and sentiments, the body of moral and legal norms. Upon the regularity and order with which this whole body of interwoven norms is maintained depends the stability and continuity of the structure of an African society. On the average, rights must be respected, duties performed, the sentiments binding the members together upheld or else the social order would be so insecure that the material needs of existence could no longer be satisfied. Productive labour would come to a standstill and the society disintegrate. This is the greatest common interest in any African society, and it is this interest which the political system, viewed in its entirety, subserves. This, too, is the ultimate and, we might say, axiomatic set of premisses of the social order. If they were continually and arbitrarily violated, the social system would cease to work.

We can sum up this analysis by saying that the material interests that actuate individuals or groups in an African society operate in the frame of a body of interconnected moral and legal norms the order and stability of which is maintained by the political organization. Africans, as we have pointed out, do not analyse their social system; they live it. They think and feel about it in terms of values which reflect, in doctrine and symbol, but do not explain, the forces that really control their social behaviour. Outstanding among these values are the mystical values dramatized in the great public institutions. These, we believe, stand for the greatest common interest of the widest political community to which a member of a particular African society belongs—that is, for the whole body of interconnected rights, duties, and sentiments; for this is what makes the society a single political community. That is why these mystical values are always associated with pivotal political offices and are expressed in both the privileges and the obligations of political office.

Their mystical form is due to the ultimate and axiomatic character of the body of moral and legal norms which could not be kept in being, as a body, by secular sanctions. Periodical ceremonies are necessary to affirm and consolidate these values because, in the ordinary course of events, people are preoccupied with sectional and private interests and are apt to lose sight of the common interest and of their political interdependence. Lastly, their symbolic content reflects the basic needs of existence and the basic social relations because these are the most concrete and tangible elements of all social and political relations. The visible test of how well a given body of rights, duties, and sentiments is being maintained and is working is to be found in the level of security and success with which the basic needs of existence are satisfied and the basic social relations sustained.

It is an interesting fact that under European rule African kings retain their 'ritual functions' long after most of the secular authority which these are said to sanction is lost. Nor are the mystical values of political office entirely obliterated by a change of religion to Christianity or Islam. As long as the kingship endures as the axis of a body of moral and legal norms holding a people together in a political community, it will, most probably, continue to be the focus of mystical values.

It is easy to see a connexion between kingship and the interests and solidarity of the whole community in a state with highly centralized authority. In societies lacking centralized government, social values cannot be symbolized by a single person, but are distributed at cardinal points of the social structure. Here we find myths, dogmas, ritual ceremonies, mystical powers, &c., associated with segments and defining and serving to maintain the relationship between them. Periodic ceremonies emphasizing the solidarity of segments, and between segments, as against sectional interests within these groups, are the rule among the Tallensi and Logoli no less than among the Bemba and Kede. Among the Nuer, the leopard-skin chief, a sacred personage associated with the fertility of the earth, is the medium through whom feuds are settled and, hence, inter-segment relations regulated. The difference between these societies of Group B and those of Group A lies in the fact that there is no person who represents the political unity of the people, such unity being lacking, and there may be no person who represents the unity of segments of the people. Ritual powers and responsibility are distributed in conformity with the highly segmentary structure of the society.

The Problem of the Limits of the Political Group

We conclude by emphasizing two points of very great importance which are often overlooked. However one may define political units or groups, they cannot be treated in isolation, for they always form part of a larger social system. Thus, to take an extreme example, the localized lineages of the Tallensi overlap one another like a series of intersecting circles, so that it is impossible to state clearly where the lines of political cleavage run. These overlapping fields of political relations stretch almost indefinitely, so that there is a kind of interlocking even of neighbouring peoples, and while we can see that this people is distinct from that, it is not easy to say at what point, culturally or politically, one is justified in regarding them as distinct units. Among the Nuer, political demarcation is simpler, but even here there is, between segments of a political unit, the same kind of structural relationship as there is between this unit and another unit of the same order. Hence the designation of autonomous political groups is always to some extent an arbitrary matter. This is more noticeable among the societies of Group B, but among those of Group A also there is an interdependence between the political group described and neighbouring political groups and a certain overlapping between them. The Ngwato have a segmentary relationship to other Tswana tribes which in many respects is of the same order as that between divisions of the Ngwato themselves. The same is true of the other societies with centralized governments.

This overlapping and interlocking of societies is largely due to the fact that the point at which political relations, narrowly defined in terms of military action and legal sanctions, end is not the point at which all social relations cease. The social structure of a people stretches beyond their political system, so defined, for there are always social relations of one kind or another between peoples of different autonomous political groups. Clans, age-sets, ritual associations, relations of affinity and of trade, and social relations of other kinds unite people of different political units. Common language or closely related languages, similar customs and beliefs, and so on, unite them. Hence a strong feeling of community may exist between groups which do not acknowledge a single ruler or unite for specific political purposes. Community of language and culture, as we have indicated, does not necessarily give rise to political unity, any more than linguistic and cultural dissimilarity prevents political unity.

Herein lies a problem of world importance: what is the relation of political structure to the whole social structure? Everywhere in Africa social ties of one kind or another tend to draw together peoples who are politically separated and political ties appear to be dominant whenever there is conflict between them and other social ties. The solution of this problem would seem to lie in a more detailed investigation of the nature of political values and of the symbols in which they are expressed. Bonds of utilitarian interest between individuals and between groups are not as strong as the bonds implied in common attachment to mystical symbols. It is precisely the greater solidarity based on these bonds, which generally gives political groups their dominance over social groups of other kinds.

Chapter 2

INDIGENOUS COURTS

Any attempt at a full account of the various types of customary courts and their functions is immediately met by the difficulty of distinguishing clearly between Courts (properly so called) and other institutions which serve similar purposes, in particular those which are arbitral rather than judicial in character. The problem arises partly because there is often no sharp distinction within a particular society between the two varieties of decision-making bodies: the two sometimes co-exist within a single society, and, even where they are maintained separately, the manner in which they come to conclusions is not always noticeably dissimilar. Sometimes, however, differences between them can be explained with reference to the political structures of which they form a part: in other words, a judicial authority often presupposes the existence of some form of centralised political authority capable of giving effect to its decisions; an arbitral institution often reflects the inability of a community to impose its judgements, and its consequent reliance on agreement by the parties to submit a dispute to arbitration. Nevertheless, the distinction between the two types of proceeding cannot be maintained absolutely, and is often blurred. This has resulted in a certain degree of overlap between the descriptions which follow, which was unavoidable. We have nevertheless tried to keep them apart wherever possible, and it is for this reason that we have included a separate chapter which deals with arbitral proceedings.

In the extracts which follow, that from *Cory and Hartnoll* on the Haya gives a brief summary of the entire course of an action and provides, in effect, a synopsis of the material which follows in the other sections of this chapter, while that from *Cory's* work on the Sukuma is only concerned with the structure and composition of the various grades of courts. *Gluckman*'s description of Lozi courts provides a detailed account of the relation between the courts and the political authority in a chiefly society, and also provides useful descriptive material as to the composition of a court—including diagrams indicating the seating of the judges. *Schapera* gives further information of various other types of courts—and distinguishes between 'regular' ones and others, e.g. those which are really arbitral and those concerned with regimental matters.

H. Cory and M. M. Hartnoll: Customary Law of the Haya*

Legal Procedure in pre-European Times

A chiefdom had five types of courts, in order of importance, from lowest to highest as follows:

1. *Omubuga* (in Kiziba known as 'Mukungu Mulagirwa'): The Court of the Mukungu.
2. *Rushulo* (in Kiziba known as 'Kushula'): The Court of the Mukungu Muziba.

* H. Cory and M. M. Hartnoll, *Customary Law of the Haya*, Lund Humphries for the International African Institute, 1945, pp. 236–241.

3. *Omurukali* (Kiziba, 'Mugorola'): The Court of the Chief presided over by a sub-chief (mwami) as his representative. The sub-chief presiding over the court was in residence at the Chief's headquarters during his presidency.

4. *Nyakaju* (Kiziba, 'Lwensinga'): The Chief's Court presided over by the Chief himself.

5. *The Court of the Ntumwa:* From time to time a Chief sent a trustworthy man, called ntumwa out into the chiefdom with powers to try cases himself and also assist the local courts in their work.

Constitution. a. The president of every court was assisted by court elders known as ishebairu (the father of the people), who were appointed by the Chief and could only be dismissed by the Chief. The office of ishebairu often went from father to son.

b. The appointment of experts, known as ntumwa or mubaka was in the hands of the president of the Court.

NOTE: *Appointment of Assessors and Expert Witnesses today*

Gombolola Court Assessors (all districts except Ihangiro)

Assessors are appointed by and are under the control of the Mwami and can therefore be dismissed by him.

IHANGIRO. Assessors are appointed and dismissed by the Chief himself. They act as informants to the Chief on Gombolola* affairs. In addition to the Court assessors, the Chief of Ihangiro appoints at least two elders in every village whose duty it is to keep him informed on all affairs of their villages.

Lukiko Court Assessors. In all districts they are appointed by the Chief and are directly under his control.

Expert Witnesses: Ntumwa or Mubaka (Kiganda). They are deputed by the Chief to investigate details in civil cases. They are considered to hold an official position as the representatives of the Chief himself and an insult to them is considered to be an insult to the Chief. When on duty they are frequently addressed as 'Mukama'.

Women in Court. No woman was allowed to plead in Court, but had to be represented by her husband or a male relative.

Jurisdiction

a. Cases of murder, witchcraft, and high treason could only be tried by the Chief's Court, the Nyakaju.

b. With regard to other charges, it lay with the president of the Court before which they were brought to decide whether he should hear them himself or refer them direct to the higher Court.

c. A president had the right to appoint one of his ishebairu to hear a particular case.

Appeal

a. The appeal lay to the next higher Court.

b. If an appeal were laid, the president of the Court from which the appeal was made had to accompany the appellant to the Appeal Court and give a summing up of the proceedings.

Procedure

a. The hearing was conducted as at the present day.

b. An accused or defendant who refused to appear before the Court was taken by force, and some of his property was seized by the Court as a bond.

Oath. (Kunahira)

a. The words of the oath were:

'Obuso Bwomukama' (By the Chief's countenance),
or 'Engoma Yomukama' (By the Chief's drum).

* Sub-County.

These words were considered to be of the greatest significance and might not be lightly used; for example, to use them in ordinary conversation was punishable by the fine of a goat.

NOTE: The assessors stated that this oath is still considered most deeply binding today and carries great weight in village courts. They were unanimous that very few Bahaya would dare to break it.

b. If in Court a man on oath were proved to have committed perjury, the penalty was much more severe, the lightest fine being a head of cattle. If the perjury were committed in the Chief's Court (Nyakaju) the sentence imposed was death, which could be commuted at the Chief's pleasure to the handing over of a daughter of the delinquent to the Chief as a slave (muzana).

c. The most solemn form of oath was to touch the Chief's forehead with the tongue (Kuramba obuso).

False witnesses. Witnesses who were suspected of being corrupt were dealt with by means of Kutegula (the appeal to Wamara).

This step was taken by a man who believed that he had lost his case owing to false witness given against him. The aggrieved man went to the mbandwa (priest) of Wamara who allowed him to beat the sacred drum and call on the god thus: 'Wamara, you know right and wrong, you know I have been cheated by so-and-so, I beg you for justice.' The all-powerful Wamara was believed to be reconciled only when the false witness presented one of his daughters to the priest as muzana (slave girl).

The fear of Wamara's wrath was so great that it was often only necessary to threaten to appeal to him for a bribed witness to confess immediately.

The relatives of a dead man who believed the deceased to have been guilty of corrupt evidence and to have died without making amends, would join together to do so and would ostracise one of their number who refused to take part in the expiation.

Torture (Kuboha). Torture was commonly used to extract a confession of guilt. The most common forms were:

a. To tie a string round the head and draw it tighter with a stick (as a tourniquet).
b. To bend the middle finger backwards.
c. To tie the hands behind the back and then pull them backwards.

A particular form of torture was reserved for a member of the Chief's family, who was tied down on a piece of bark cloth and forced to drink large quantities of beer. This was a mental torture, for the man was not allowed to leave the spot and suffered in his dignity and self-respect.

Ordeals. Ordeals were only used in the Chief's Court (Nyakaju), and at the direct instruction of the Chief himself. They were only used in cases of witchcraft and bisisi. The men who carried out the ordeals were known as Bafumu. Among the ordeals were the following:

Ntondo. All the people concerned sat in a semi-circle, each with a small stick stuck in the ground in front of him. The Mufumu brought a stick on which he had placed a ntondo (a kind of grasshopper), and ordered it to fly on to the stick of the guilty person.

Nteniu. All the people concerned sat on the ground with their legs stretched out in front of them. The Mufumu passed a red hot spear over the shin bone of each man and he who was burnt was guilty.

Kagwi. (The magic scissors.)

Lwezilingo. The Mufumu prepared a medicine which all suspected persons had to drink. He who first behaved like a madman was considered guilty.

Fees. In all Courts except that of the Chief (Nyakaju), fees were paid by both parties in a case.

H. Cory: Sukuma Law and Custom*

Judicial institutions. Three courts of law existed before the arrival of the Europeans: 1. The court of the *banamhara*; 2. The court of the *banangwa*; 3. The court of the *ntemi*.

These courts did not represent different stages of appeal; each had its defined limits and the decision of each was in practice final, since the *ntemi* was very reluctant to re-open a case which had already been decided by a *ng'wanangwa.*

The court of the Ntemi (chief). The *ntemi's* court was *de facto* a criminal court; civil cases might be heard by the chief, not because of any particular importance attaching to a case, but if one or both parties were near kinsmen of the chief.

The court consisted of the *ntemi* as president and the *banang'oma* as assessors. The functions of the court were not divided as between judge, crown counsel, and counsel for the defence. One of the *banang'oma* opened the case by questioning the defendant or the witnesses, the other *banang'oma* assisting him. Sometimes the *ntemi* would interrupt and even an elder sitting among the listeners was allowed to put questions to witnesses or to give his opinion as to their reliability. Each party had to pay five goats or hoes before a case could be heard in the chief's court. Of these, five went to the chief and five to the assessors—usually *banang'oma.* The fee was high in order to prevent frivolous litigation. No fine was imposed on the guilty party, but he had to pay compensation or *njigu* to the wronged person. The chief received his share of this compensation; for instance, if *njigu* was paid he got one or two cows.

Very little formality was observed in court. Assessors, or even the chief, might leave the assembly for short periods without it being considered necessary to adjourn the proceedings. The code of law by which the case was decided was known to the assessors through the practice of many years, but even among the commoners there were everywhere a number of older people who knew the traditional laws. Precedents were admissible as arguments but were never considered decisive. The proceedings were short because the depositions of witnesses and the investigations of the *ng'wanangwa* were not always repeated in court, but were conveyed to the chief and his assessors briefly and privately by the *ng'wanangwa* before the case was tried. The *ng'wanangwa* of the village in which the crime was committed was always present and was heard if the case became involved and if the depositions of the witnesses were contradictory. When necessary the *ntemi* and his assessors retired for a council (*kisaka*) before the *ntemi* gave his judgement.

The court of the *ntemi* tried cases of murder, high treason, assault causing serious injury, witchcraft, and cattle theft.

The court of the Ng'wanangwa (headman). Many transgressions, such as cattle theft or assault, were not automatically brought before the chief. Some of the *banangwa* were prepared to hear cases which others would have been reluctant to judge in their courts; much depended on the closeness of the kinship between the chief and the headman, and in some cases also on the weak régime of a chief or the strong character of a *ng'wanangwa.*

Every *ng'wanangwa* had his court, the assessors of which were selected by him. These assessors attended the court regularly and, as they were very often also the councillors of the village headman in all matters, the constitution of the court presented no difficulties. The cases heard were mainly concerned with assault and wounds resulting from drunken brawls, civil suits arising from quarrels over boundaries, domestic quarrels and divorce, debts and complications resulting from certain traditional compensation payments.

As in the chief's court, a man bringing a case before the *ng'wanangwa* had to pay a fee called *lutwi*; this was generally paid in kind in such commodities as hoes, goats, or measures of *mtama.* It was distributed between the members of the court if it was a sufficiently large fee; if not, it was put aside until enough fees had been collected for, in the case of *mtama*, beer to be brewed. The amount of the payment depended not so much on the amount involved in the dispute as on the means of the plaintiff.

When an assault took place or a man was injured in a quarrel, the case was not heard immediately. The injured man was given a white bracelet to wear on his left wrist. If

* H. Cory, *Sukuma Law and Custom*, Oxford University Press, 1953, pp. 9–11.

he died compensation was payable; if he recovered the bracelet was removed and the man who had caused the injury had to pay compensation. It was not customary to impose fines, payments being made in the form of compensation. Only in cases where malefactors repeatedly came before the court for the same transgressions did the *ng'wanangwa* and his elders impose a fine; this was divided between the members of the court or, if it was a cow or goat, slaughtered and eaten by them at a communal meal.

It sometimes happened that parties to a case refused to accept the judgement of the village headman and decided to bring their case before the chief's court. Such procedure was rare, however, and if the chief refused to hear the case nothing more could be done. There was no right of appeal.

M. Gluckman: The Judicial Process among the Barotse of Northern Rhodesia*

One of the basic units in the structure of their economic, political, and domestic systems is the village. It is the centre from which they exploit gardens, pasturage and fishing-sites, and parcels of land are attached to the village-headman's title and theoretically can only be used by his villagers. Everyone must reside in some village, and co-operates chiefly with fellow-villagers. Because their bases are the 'islands' in the floodplain, which provide the only dwelling-sites, most Lozi villages have a permanent continuity dating far back into their history and associated with the headman. The village is a critically important political unit under a headman who has a title which devolves on his successor. The headman is responsible for his village to the king in council (hereafter called the *kuta*), and represents the villagers to the kuta.

The old political and juridical organization into which these villages were tied can only be described if we begin at the capitals. Before 1890, there were two capitals only, both situated in the Plain. The king (*Mbumu-wa-Litunga* = great-one-of-the-earth) ruled the main capital, north of the middle of the Plain; another ruler (*Litunga-la-Mboela* = earth [chief] -of-the-south), held a capital which has never been more than thirty miles farther south. Since the Lozi reconquered their homeland from a band of Sotho invaders, the Kololo, who subjugated it from 1838 to 1864, the southern ruler has been a princess (referred to henceforth as the princess chief). The southern ruler has always been subordinate to the king, though she has a capital which duplicates his faithfully. These capitals in the period with which we are concerned have been built at Lialui in the north, moving at flood to Limulunga, and in the south at Nalolo, from where the court moves a short distance at flood. All villages throughout the Barotse kingdom were attached to one of these two capitals. In the 1890's the Lozi began to establish subordinate capitals in their outer provinces to cope with invasions of other Bantu and with the incoming Whites. The British South Africa Company divided Barotseland into Districts for various purposes. Each District had a District Office at its head. Over the years it has become necessary to have one Barotse capital dealing with each District Office: this has led to the foundation of two new provincial capitals,[1] and the abolition of two old provincial capitals as redundant. Since 1946, Lialui, the capital of the king, has ruled Barotse Province and the Mongu-Lialui District. Nalolo, the seat of the princess chief, is the centre for Senanga District; Libonda for Kalabo District; Mwandi for Sesheke District; and Naliele for Mankoya District.

Every capital has at its heart a central cleared space (called *Namoo* at the two main capitals) on one side of which is the palace and on the other the council-house. The ruler resides in the palace, the full council meets in the council-house to deliberate or try cases. Since the council is not only a court, I use the native term *kuta* throughout, save in general analytic passages. The court-houses, particularly the one at Lialui, are imposing buildings. In the centre at the back is a dais on which the king or ruling member of the royal family sits if he (or she) is present. Usually the ruler does not attend the hearings of cases, though the kuta's judgment is referred to him for confirmation. Even if the ruler chooses to sit in the kuta while a case is being tried, it proceeds as if he were not there. He takes no part in the hearing, and the facts and judgments in the case are referred to him as if he had not heard them.

* M. Gluckman, *The Judicial Process among the Barotse of Northern Rhodesia*, Manchester University Press, 1955, pp. 6–15.

THE GENEALOGY OF THE LOZI KINGS

K 1, 2. 3, . . . indicates order of reigns

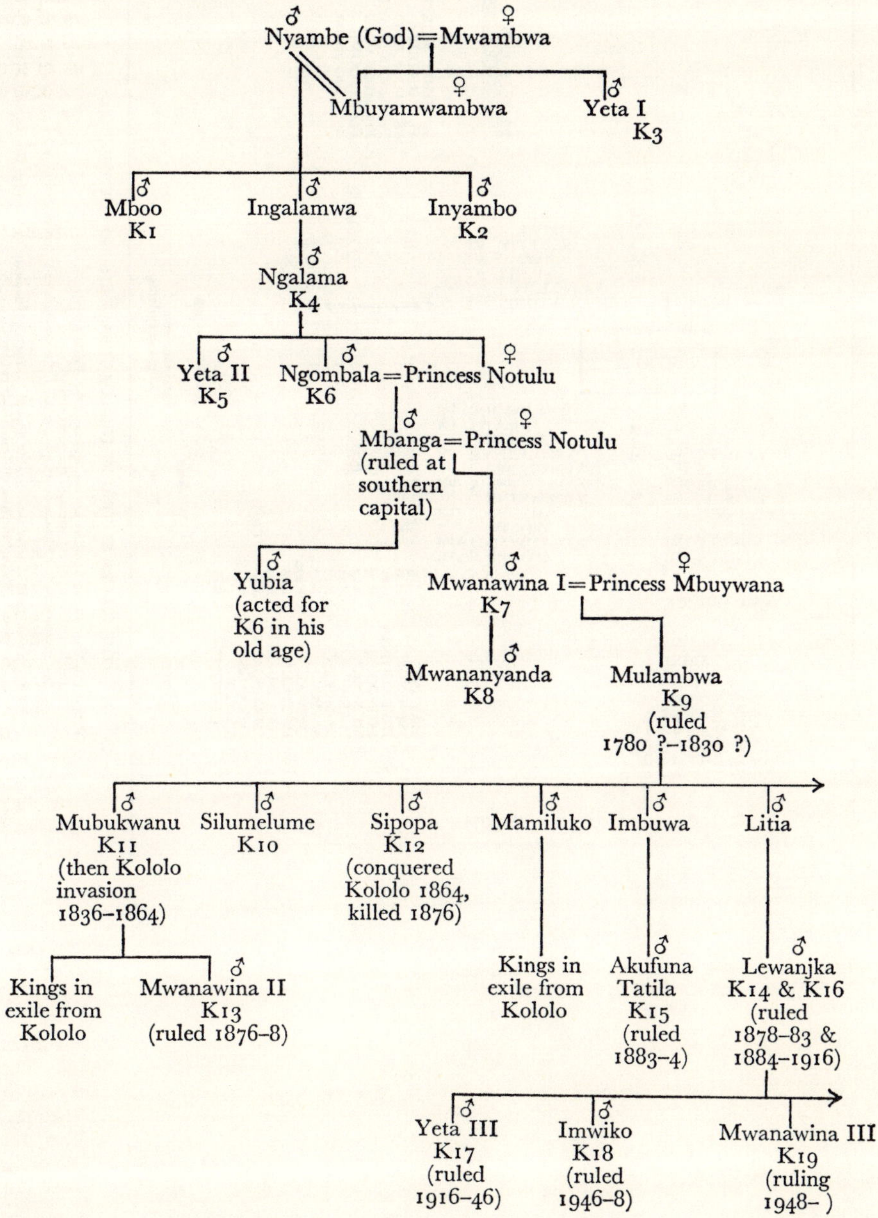

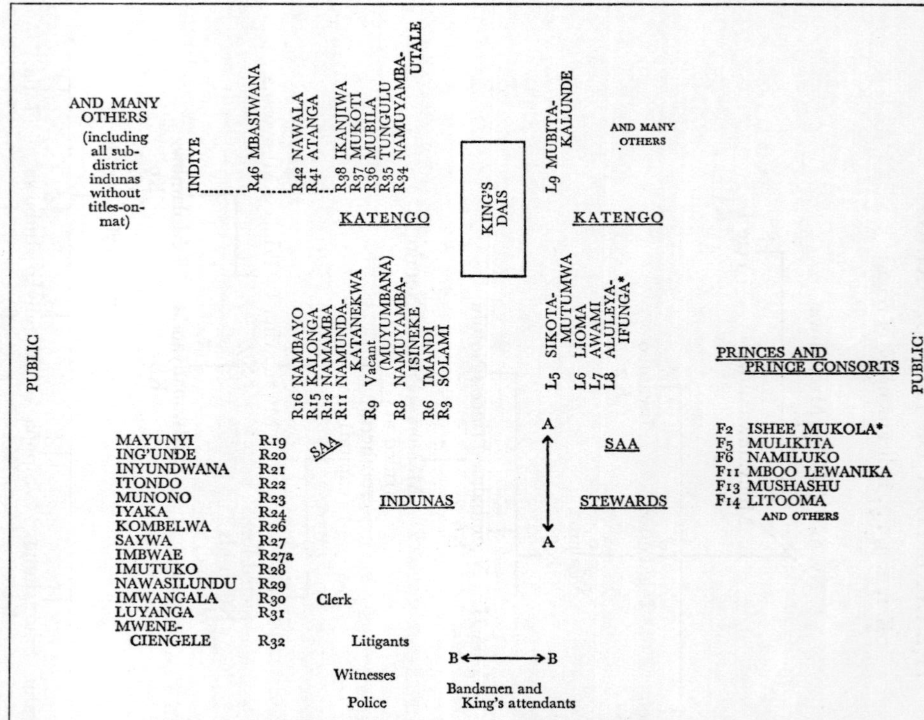

THE JUDGES' SEATING IN THE LIALUI SAA-KATENGO COUNCIL (1942)

NOTES: (1) The missing numbers are councillors of the Sikalo (overleaf).
(2) Not all councillors attended the court sittings.
(3) In practice, to make the court space smaller, the stewards' mat was placed at A A, and the royal mat at B B.
(4) The kuta titles were considerably altered by 1947, particularly by the 1946 Government Reforms when it became the Mongu-Lialui District Court.
(5) In 1940 on, L8* and F2* were the same person. He almost always sat as F2.

All Lozi kutas are divided into three sets of councillors, each of which may be called a 'mat', as the Lozi name them, since the councillors by virtue of their titled offices are entitled to sit on mats. The positions of the titles on each mat are fixed, and if a title-holder is discharged, is promoted, or dies, his successor (who is appointed by the ruler-in-kuta) takes his position on the mat. These offices, as distinct from their incumbents, are so important that throughout the book I print them in small capitals, stating their positions by R for right, L for left, and F for royal, according to their status as described in the succeeding paragraphs, and as shown on the accompanying diagrams.[2]

The most powerful group of councillors are those who sit on mats to the right of the king. Their senior member, the NGAMBELA, is head of the kuta: he is so powerful that he is described, in relation to the king, as 'another kind of king'. He cannot be a prince who has a right to succeed to the kingship. I shall call these councillors-of-the-right *indunas*, the general Southern African word for 'councillor' (in Lozi *nduna*, pl. *manduna*), since it has passed into English from Zulu,[3] and we need to standardize a term for African political authorities with varied duties. The Lozi use this term to distinguish councillors-of-the-right from the other 'mats', but there are two words to distinguish two groups among these indunas. The senior indunas are called *makwambuyu*; *malume* are the group of junior indunas who sit in a row behind them. On mats to the left of the royal dais sit councillors called *likombwa*, which in Barotseland has been translated 'stewards'. This is an appropriate word, because while they are powerful councillors in national affairs, they are also more specifically responsible for the royal household. The stewards are also divided into seniors and *malume* juniors. At right angles to the stewards, or at the front of the kuta, is the royal mat for princes and for the consorts (*bo-ishee*, sing. *ishee*) of princesses, who exercise power for their wives. Opposite the indunas' mat sit clerks, police, and royal bandsmen, leaving a space in the middle for suppliants and litigants.

The senior indunas and stewards, with some senior members of the royal mat, formed a council called *Saa*. The chief *induna*, the NGAMBELA (R1), was not a member of this, nor was the NATAMOYO (R2), a prince who was a sanctuary in that a convicted man who seized his leg could claim a re-trial. The *malume*, junior indunas, and stewards, with junior members of the royal mat, formed a council called *Katengo*. A third council, the *Sikalo*, was composed of the NGAMBELA (R1), the NATAMOYO (R2), and an indefinite number of other councillors, members of the royal family, and others. These three councils did not meet as courts of law, but to deliberate on legislation and national matters. The Sikalo met with the king at night, the Saa and Katengo separately in the day, and discussion passed backwards and forwards between them in an attempt to reach agreement.

The councillors at Lialui were also grouped under about nine councillors, including the NGAMBELA (R1), who were heads of what I call *sectors* (Lozi: *makolo*, *likuta*). These sectors were the military, jurisdictional, administrative, and labour units of the kingdom. All villages were placed in one or other of the sectors; in some villages different people were placed in different sectors. In Loziland particularly, but not so much in the outer provinces of the kingdom, neighbouring villages often belonged to different sectors. When a dispute between members of the same sector could not be settled at home, or by local arbitration, the case went to the court of the councillors of the sector sitting at the capital in the courtyard of the senior councillor; if members of two sectors were disputing, councillors of both sectors assembled in the courtyard of the senior councillor to try the issue. Accepted judgments were referred to the NGAMBELA (R1) and the king, and appeal lay to the full kuta. There were fewer sectors at other capitals.

Appeals in the recent past also went from any provincial capital to the main capital, Lialui or Nalolo, to which it was attached. There was no judicial appeal from Nalolo to Lialui, since both were ruled by kings: 'You cannot appeal from one king to another.' However, each was in the past a sanctuary to which people could flee from the other. Appeal from Nalolo to Lialui was instituted under the 1936 Barotse Native Courts Ordinance.

The Lozi were also allotted, in a different manner, to the set of councillors I have called stewards, for other purposes: this arrangement need not concern us here, though we must note it because it is relevant to the manner in which Lozi took their complaints to the capital.

The essence of both these arrangements was that the units of administration and

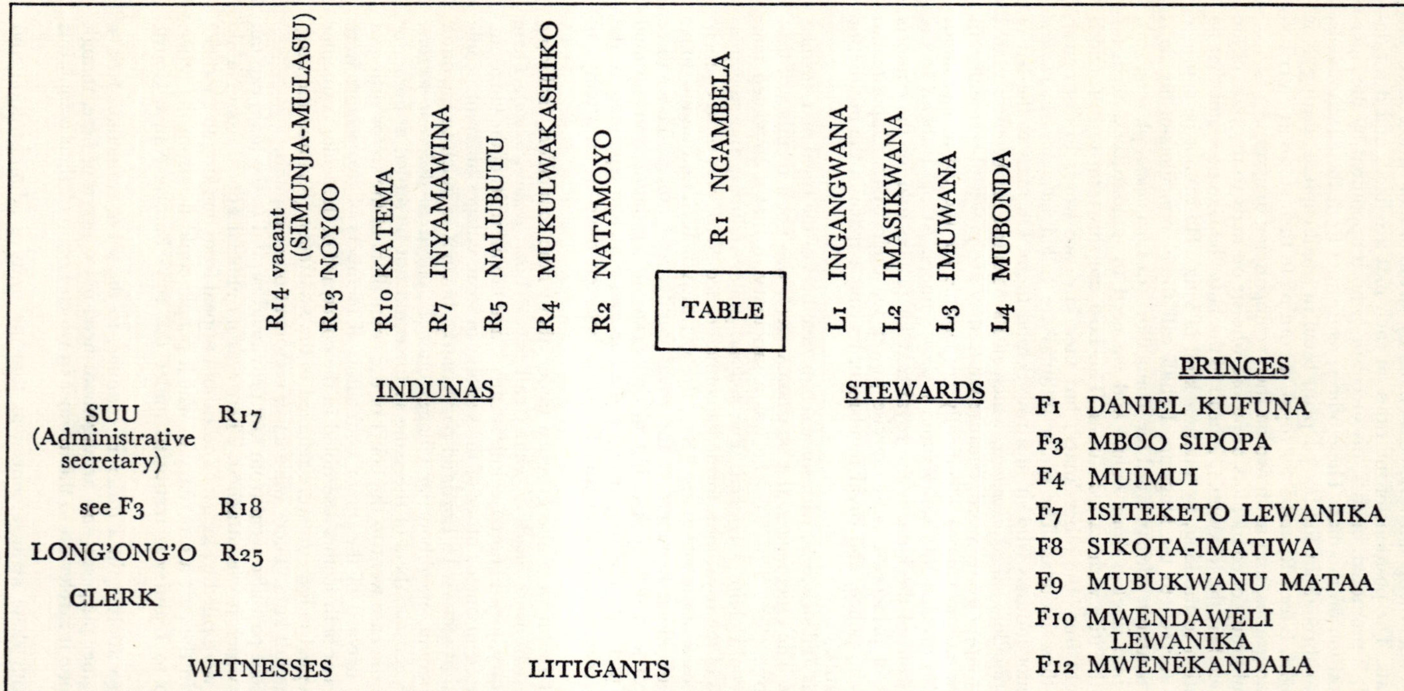

THE JUDGES' SEATING IN THE LIALUI SIKALO APPEAL COUNCIL (1942)

NOTES: (1) As the King came into public in the large open Kuta building where the Saa-Katengo met, the NGAMBELA (R1) presided here in a smaller office building, and there was no royal dais.
(2) This Council interlocks with the Saa-Katengo Council.
(3) This Council was also considerably altered by the 1946 Reforms which made it the Barotse Appeal Court. Tribal representatives sat below R25, on the right: representatives of District Councils sat according to their positions on the full National Council. Some titles here and in the Saa-Katengo Council were altered and moved.
(4) Generally, the public were not admitted or did not come into this court.

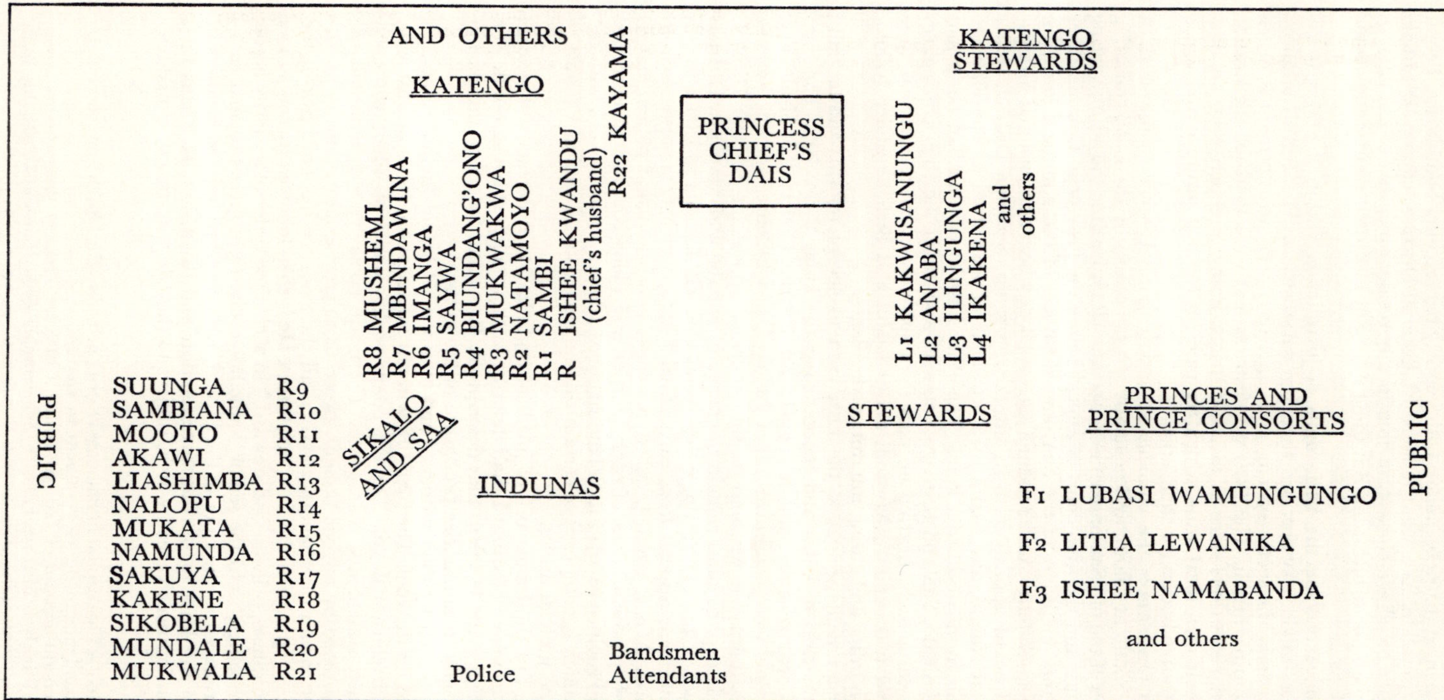

THE JUDGES' SEATING IN THE NALOLO COUNCIL—COMBINED SIKALO AND SAA-KATENGO COURTS (1942)

NOTES: (1) Nalolo Council, considerably reduced in numbers, formed a single court under the 1946 Reforms.
(2) Lialui and Nalolo councillors, with the councillors of subordinate provincial capitals, formed a single National Council, the members interlocking thus: R1 NGAMBELA (Lialui), R2. ISHEE KWANDU (Nalolo—husband of Princess Chief), R3. NATAMOYO of Lialui, R4. SAMBI (Nalolo), R5. Solami (Lialui) R6. NATAMOYO of Nalolo. . . . Thereafter Lialui councillors are generally far superior to interspersed Nalolo members. The heads of provincial capitals entered at 24 and 54–58. Late in 1942 they were moved to R24–28. Other mats are similarly arranged, with Lialui superior.

jurisdiction were not territorial units. Loziland, nevertheless, was roughly divided into a large number of named districts (*lilalo*), with vaguely demarcated boundaries. People in a district (note a small 'd' as against modern Magisterial Districts, capital 'D') might take cases to a prince or prince consort, or to a locally resident member of the kuta, or to any prominent man, for arbitration. But these were not instituted courts: they could not enforce their decisions.

These districts have become the basic units of jurisdiction within the Magisterial Districts, and in the modern system are therefore sub-districts. The British administrators never understood the sector system, and some territorial arrangement is necessary for modern administration. The *lilalo* sub-districts first were used for registration of residents and tax-collection: since 1936 sub-districts, many of which were amalgamated have had their own local kutas which try cases in the first instance and which act as the administrative bodies for their area.

Under the 1936 Ordinances the councils at various capitals were reorganized. A Council called the Sikalo at Lialui, and generally *ofis* (= office) by the Lozi, consisting of selected members of the old Saa under the NGAMBELA (R1), became the administering body for the Province and the final court of appeal before the Provincial Commissioner or High Court. Other members of the Saa, and members of the Katengo, formed a council called the Saa-Katengo, under induna SOLAMI (R3), which administered Mongu-Lialui District and heard appeals from its sub-district kutas. Senanga District, under the Princess Chief at Nalolo, also had a Sikalo to hear appeals from its Saa-Katengo which heard appeals from sub-district kutas. The other District capitals had never had the arrangement of Sikalo, Saa and Katengo, councils, and under the 1936 Ordinances they had only one kuta each, hearing appeals from sub-district courts. At that time Sesheke District had two capitals, Mwandi under Lialui and Sesheke under Nalolo, built alongside each other and ruling intermingled villages.

In 1946 the Government persuaded the Lozi kuta to accept reforms substantially reducing the membership of kutas and reorganizing the kutas themselves. The Saa-Katengo at Lialui was renamed the Mongu-Lialui District Court; the Sikalo and Saa-Katengo at Nalolo were combined into a Nalolo District Court; and the Sesheke capital was abolished leaving Mwandi as sole court of appeal for Sesheke District. Libonda and Naliele capital kutas remain in charge of Kalabo and Mankoya Districts respectively. In place of the old Sikalo, a Provincial Council now sits in Lialui to run provincial affairs and hear appeals from each District kuta, which hears appeals from its sub-district courts. A new council, called Katengo, consisting, first of nominated, and then of elected, representatives of each District and older Katengo incumbents, was formed for the Province in 1947 to debate national affairs: it was to work with the National Council which is composed of certain title-holders from all capital kutas. The new Katengo had no judicial duties.

This bare account of the framework of juridical organization is necessary if readers are to place the kutas whose hearings I shall describe in their political background. The organization itself will come to life in that description. It remains for me in this part of the introduction briefly to summarize procedure in the kutas.

The litigants, supported by their witnesses and kinsmen, sit before the judges against the posts which hold up the roof. The plaintiff, without interruption, states his case with full and seemingly irrelevant detail. The defendant replies similarly. Their witnesses, who have heard their statements, then speak. There are no lawyers to represent the parties. The kuta, assisted by anyone present, proceeds to cross-examine and to pit the parties and witnesses against one another. When all the evidence has been heard, the lowest induna on the right gives the first judgement. He is then followed by councillors on the three mats (indunas, princes, and stewards) in ascending order of seniority across from one mat to the other, until the senior councillor-of-the-right gives the final judgment. This is then referred to the ruler of the capital, who confirms, rejects, or alters it, or refers it back to the kuta for further investigation and discussion. It is this final judgment by the last induna to speak which, subject to the ruler's approval, is binding.

Notes

[1] The establishment of a Lozi capital in Balovale District provoked the local people successfully to protest their independence to the Government in 1941.

[2] I have given a general account of Lozi government in *Seven Tribes of British Central Africa, op. cit.*, and a detailed analysis of three kutas in *Administrative Organization of the Barotse Native Authorities*, Livingstone, *Rhodes-Livingstone Institute Communications No. 1* (1943).

[3] *The Concise Oxford Dictionary*, 1949, p. 609.

I. Schapera: A Handbook of Tswana Law and Custom*

Courts and their Jurisdiction

There exist in every Tswana tribe several grades of court (*lekgotla*) at which cases are tried and whose decisions are legally binding.[1] In the first place, every ward has its own court, presided over by its headman. From this court a case can be carried for retrial to the court of the Chief, which is the highest judicial body in the tribe. At the tribal head-quarters appeal for retrial can be made direct from the ward court to that of the Chief. But, in the outlying villages containing more than one ward, appeals from the court of a junior ward must go first to the court of the village headman. Only after being dealt with by him can they go further, if necessary, to the court of the Chief.

The Ngwato system, like the general social organization of the tribe, is somewhat more complicated than those of other tribes. In Serowe itself there are three official grades of court: the ward court; the sectional court, presided over by the headman of the senior ward in the section; and the Chief's court. In the outlying districts there are also ward courts, similar to those found in Serowe. Beyond them are the courts of the hereditary rulers of the particular tribal community whose members are concerned (Kaa, Phaleng, Birwa, Kalaka, &c.). Beyond these, again, there are the courts of the Chief's district representatives, from which, finally, there is a right of appeal to the Chief's court in Serowe.

The new features here are the sectional courts and the courts of the Chief's representatives. The latter occur also among the Tawana and Ngwaketse, and have recently been created among the Kwena. Sectional courts, on the other hand, occur also only among the Kgatla. But they do not play nearly as prominent a part there in the judicial system as they do among the Ngwato, although it is by no means unusual for a case to be referred or carried on appeal from the headman of a junior ward to the headman of the senior ward in the same section, before passing on to the Chief. The tribal-community courts found among the Ngwato correspond roughly to the village courts of most other tribes. The main difference is that, whereas, among the latter, members of the same tribal community generally live together in one outlying village, among the Ngwato they tend to be scattered over the same district in a large number of villages.

Apart from these regular courts, other bodies settle or help to settle disputes. There are first of all the courts of the family-groups (*phuthêgô tsa bana ba mpa, puô ya lolwapa*, &c.). They function in all matters affecting family relations, their scope being confined mainly to attempting to provide a peaceful settlement of the dispute, although they have the right to impose corporal punishment if necessary as a corrective measure. They also play an extremely important part in the settlement of most civil wrongs. Cases of this nature are usually first discussed at a meeting of the two family-groups concerned, and if a satisfactory compromise can be reached need not go any further. A considerable number of civil cases are in fact finally settled here and so never come before the official tribunals. If it is a matter involving the payment of damages, the combined court will suggest that the usual amount be paid. But it cannot enforce the payment, nor can it inflict any penalty on an offender without his consent. It is essentially a court of arbitration, and its verdict is never given cognizance by the official tribunals if the matter is carried any further.

There are also regimental courts, which deal with offences committed in connexion with initiation 'schools', regimental duties, or the relations between members of different regiments. As previously indicated, these courts have the power to punish offenders by thrashing or fining. There are further special women's courts, presided over by the leader of a female regiment, or the wife of the headman or Chief. They deal with matters particularly affecting women, and can take disciplinary action when women quarrel over a man, break any of the sexual taboos, or fail to carry out their regimental duties.

More detailed reference is necessary to the courts of the ward headmen and of the Chief, as in effect these two bodies between them deal with the great bulk of Tswana judicial cases. The ward court, as already noted, is presided over by the hereditary headman of the ward. Should he be away for some time, his next of kin takes his place;

* I. Schapera, *A Handbook of Tswana Law and Custom*, Oxford University Press, 1938, pp. 279–283.

but, if he is away merely for a day or two, the case awaits his return. Every man in the ward, and indeed every man in the tribe, has the right to be present and to take part in the hearing of a case before the ward court, for all cases are tried in public. But in arriving at his verdict the headman is assisted more particularly by his senior brothers and paternal uncles, and by a few other men of repute and sagacity. These assessors are known as his 'remembrancers' (*bagakolodi*), since it is their special function to remind him of the law and to quote judicial precedents. With them he tries disputes between members of the ward, and also disputes with outsiders in which one of his adherents is the defendant. It is the invariable rule that a defendant is tried by his own headman and at his own court, except of course when the case has been transferred to some higher authority.

Should the headman feel that a case is too serious to be tried by him, he must, after hearing the evidence and so ascertaining the facts, refer it to the court of the Chief (or to the court of the village or sectional headman where this is the procedure). He does not himself pronounce any verdict, but limits himself to holding what we may term a preliminary examination of the case. This procedure is particularly necessary in regard to most criminal offences. The headman may and should inquire into such matters as offences against the decrees of the Chief, sorcery, homicide, abortion and infanticide, bodily assault and rape; but he has no power to adjudicate upon them. They can be dealt with only by the Chief. So, too, among the Ngwato, disputes regarding inheritance and cases of divorce must nowadays also be transferred to the court of the Chief. Formerly, however, no cases involving women ever went beyond the ward courts, except those of assault. In all other cases the headman has the power to pronounce a judgement which, if accepted by the parties concerned, is regarded as binding. He has the right to punish wrongdoers by thrashing or fining. The fine in such cases seldom exceeds one or two head of cattle, for if it is a case involving a more serious punishment the matter will usually be referred to a higher court. The cattle paid as fines at the ward court are generally slaughtered for the members of the court; but the headman may occasionally, with the consent of the other members, keep the fine for himself.

The headman himself can be tried at his own court for committing a wrong, his next of kin then presiding in his place. If he readily admits his guilt, he may be punished there; but, if the case presents any difficulties at all, it is at once transferred to the Chief's court. In fact, most cases involving an important person or an important matter are usually transferred, after the initial inquiry, to the Chief's court, partly out of courtesy and partly out of common sense, in the knowledge that an appeal is sure to be made.

The Chief's court acts as a court of first instance in regard to those cases, noted above, with which the ward court is not competent to deal, as well as in regard to all cases involving senior members of the royal family, i.e. members of the Chief's own ward. It is further the final court of appeal within the tribal system in all other cases. In former times no appeal lay from its verdict, except under the special circumstances to be noted below; and generally a man, dissatisfied, had no other remedy than to leave the tribe. Since 1919, however, there has existed a right of appeal to the Administration.

The Chief's court is made up of the Chief as president, assisted by his senior brothers and paternal uncles, and by some other recognized assessors known as *bagakolodi ba kgosi* (the Chief's remembrancers) or simply as *banna ba lekgotla* (men of the court). The number of these assessors is not fixed, nor is their status officially defined. They are generally drawn from the ranks of the Chief's confidential political advisers, but may include other men as well, who because of their knowledge of tribal law, or conspicuous ability and shrewdness in dealing with cases, gradually work themselves into prominence. They should attend and participate in all the cases coming before the Chief, their special function being to advise him on points of law and to help him arrive at a verdict. In addition to these recognized assessors, the headmen of wards assist from time to time in the hearing of cases at the Chief's court; and are, indeed, expected to attend there whenever possible to help the Chief with their questions and opinions. Every adult man in the tribe, finally, has the right to be present at any case and to take part in the discussion.

The assessors, if the Chief is away, may themselves hear and judge a case, the Chief's deputy presiding in his place. But their verdict can then be reversed on appeal to the Chief. The Chief himself may sometimes hand over a minor matter to them to deal with, if he has no time to take it himself; but they must then report their findings to him while the court is still sitting. If he agrees with their findings, he states the sentence to be pronounced in his name. If he thinks they are wrong, he returns with them to the court, where the case is tried all over again, and then gives his verdict. He may in the same way depute two or more of these men to try a case on his behalf in some other part of the village or tribal Reserve. They are then sometimes empowered to give a verdict, which may, however, be reversed on appeal to him; or they may be asked simply to investigate the facts and leave the final verdict to be pronounced by him in the light of their report.

Among the assessors is one man whose special function it is to receive all complaints, to transmit them to the Chief, and to arrange with him for the hearing of the case. He should always be in attendance at the *kgotla*, in case any matter is brought up requiring attention. He must also see that all fines are paid, and detail messengers for any work to be done in connexion with the administration of justice. Among the Kgatla, this man, known as *ntona ya lekgotla* or as *moatlhodi* (judge), is either a fairly remote relative of the Chief or a trusted commoner. Among the Ngwato the corresponding role is filled by one of the Chief's brothers or paternal cousins, who is sometimes referred to in this connexion as *mosimane wa kgosi* (the Chief's boy) or as *monnakgotla* (the man of the *kgotla*). The present holder of the office is Serogola G. Seretse, who also acts as deputy Chief during the absence of Tshekedi.

Note

[1] The whole system of courts has (ostensibly) been considerably modified by the Native Tribunals Proclamation (No. 75 of 1934, as amended by Proclamation No. 78 of 1935), which specifies what Native courts are to be regarded as official tribunals, defines their constitution, provides for the keeping of written records, and in various other ways modifies their powers and procedure. The system described above is the traditional Tswana system. The Proclamation of 1934, in so far as its provisions affecting Native courts are concerned, is at present pending further amendment. For this reason it has been thought unnecessary to pay further attention (at this stage) to its original provisions.

Chapter 3

ARBITRATION

The significance of the distinction between judicial and arbitral proceedings has already been referred to in the introductory paragraphs to the previous chapter (see p. 12). The three extracts which follow—by *Gulliver*, *Beattie* and *Bohannan*—all provide detailed examples of the less formal procedures for dispute settlement which are employed in different societies. All are noteworthy for the attention paid to case material, which is used to exemplify different aspects of the procedure followed. It is of more than passing interest that the three societies described are not uniform in political structure, and include both chiefly and acephalous communities.

P. H. Gulliver: Social Control in an African Society*

Disputes between kinsfolk should be dealt with by a moot or by a conclave with counsellors. Here Arusha are primarily distinguishing disputes between agnatic kin from those between non-kinsmen. It is considered not merely impractical, but wrong to take agnatic affairs to a body not connected with the lineage, and composed of a heterogeneous congregation. Conflict between lineage members should be dealt with by an internal moot, or a conclave with their common counsellor. Between nearer agnates of a single inner lineage, a conclave of lineage members is preferable. The smallness of this group and the difficulties of resolving such vital conflict as often arises over inheritance and demands for repeated and lavish assistance, as well as the fact that often the counsellor is a member of another inner lineage, tend to result in such disputes being taken to an internal moot. This is the norm for disputes between agnates of different inner lineages. Men say that they dislike becoming involved in the affairs of another maximal lineage, just as that group itself desires to have no external interference. A lineage counsellor seldom, if ever, is prepared to agree to such interference; partly because it appears to reflect on his abilities, but mainly because he has responsibilities for both disputants, and is instrumental in bringing them together for discussion. Moreover, disputes between agnates are likely, directly or indirectly to concern some of the more important aspects of Arusha life—inheritance, land, marriage and children, agnatic rights and obligations—and therefore a potential plaintiff goes to his counsellor, who is already well informed in these matters relating to his own lineage, rather than to a notable of his age-group. Even although the two disputants themselves may live in the same parish, it is fairly certain that at least some of their nearer agnates do not; and they, of course, are unwilling to appear before a 'strange' parish assembly.

Although Arusha stress the agnatic sector of kinship in this connection, much the same principle applies to maternal and affinal kin, and for similar reasons. Further, it applies not only to disputes specifically concerning kinship relations as such, but also to any kind of dispute between kin: that is, not only, for example, the rights and obligations of a mother's brother, or the question of bridewealth payments between affines which arise directly out of the particular relationship, but also disputes in affairs which might occur between any two people.

Case 5: For example, Kamian had been invited to the initiation celebrations for the son of Teronge, his mother's patrilateral cousin who lived a short distance away in the

* P. H. Gulliver, *Social Control in an African Society*, Routledge and Kegan Paul, 1963, pp. 188–203.

same parish. It is usual, though not absolutely obligatory, that men who are specially invited (kinsmen, age-mates, neighbours, friends) by the initiate's father should make a gift of an animal. This establishes a debt to be repaid on a similar occasion at the donor's homestead. On this occasion, Kamian presented Teronge with a male calf. When several years later, Kamian's only son was circumcised, Teronge failed either to attend the celebrations or to send the reciprocal gift. He claimed afterwards that he was absent visiting a kinsman many miles away, and he promised to make the return gift on the next occasion. Because Kamian had no other son to be initiated, he demanded the animal immediately; and further he accused Teronge of deliberately absenting himself. Kamian consulted with his lineage counsellor, and both went to see Teronge's counsellor to urge a conclave to discuss the matter. Kamian told me that parish spokesmen would be of no assistance to him, and he also said that he did not want to cause trouble between his own age-group (junior elders) and that of Teronge (senior elders). It so happened that Teronge's counsellor was the half-brother of Kamian's mother (i.e. he belonged to her natal inner lineage), and therefore Kamian could appeal to kinship sentiment in seeking that counsellor's agreement to a conclave. I do not think that this latter feature was crucial to the procedure chosen, for other Arusha commented on the rightness of the decision of Kamian and his counsellor in acting as they did. 'Kinsmen (*ilderegeni*) should not quarrel before the parish assembly,' one spokesman in that parish told me, when we discussed this case.

It is this principle of jural procedure which inclines Arusha to state over-simply, that moots take disputes between kinsfolk, and parish assemblies take other disputes. This is not correct in one way which has previously been discussed (disputes between members of different parishes); and is not altogether true even of disputes between members of the same parish. Neither is it entirely true that kinsmen, even close agnates occasionally, never raise disputes in a parish assembly. For much the same reason which persuades a non-member of the parish to use the parish assembly, so a parish member may raise a dispute with a fellow-member who is a kinsman—i.e. to make the dispute public, to try to compel the defendant to make some answer, and to gauge public opinion. Both the plaintiff's agnates and his lineage counsellor tend to disapprove of the stratagem. But they can do little to prevent it, other than by making efforts to pursue the matter more strongly by another procedure; and that also may be the intention of the plaintiff.

Case 6: In a temporary pause during the proceedings of a parish assembly, a man suddenly stood up, without invitation or warning, and began to accuse his patrilineal cousin of encroaching on his land. The two men owned adjacent fields, and they had for about five years bickered desultorily over the alignment of their mutual boundary—which lay in uncultivated land in area about 75 yards long and 2 yards wide. The matter came to a head when the defendant hoed up and planted a portion of the unused land. The plaintiff obtained little sympathy from the only member of his inner lineage (a half brother) who lived near, because, his agnate said, he had plenty of land, whilst their cousin had little. Factually this was true. The parish assembly met next day in the normal course, and the plaintiff (as he explained to me) resolved to raise the matter there. This he did in what seemed a highly indignant, self-righteous manner.

Perhaps because he was himself a spokesman (junior elder), his unexpected outburst was not interrupted. When he had finished, he was censured directly by other spokesmen and indirectly (by their failure to support him) by his half-brother and a counsellor of a linked maximal lineage. It was quickly agreed that the plaintiff had acted with impropriety in raising the dispute there. 'Go to Namuka! (the plaintiff's lineage counsellor). Do not bring the shame of brothers (i.e. agnates) quarrelling here. We know nothing of all this,' said one spokesman. The plaintiff became incensed at the lack of sympathy, and in his emotion began to upbraid the men present. He was quickly cut short this time and, after a short discussion, it was agreed to levy a fine (*sogo*) of beer on him for his contumely. After this announcement, the plaintiff's half-brother stood up and said that they must both go to the counsellor and discuss the matter. This brought approving remarks from the assembly, together with an admonition to the defendant (who was not present) to be prepared to accept the counsellor's intervention, and to discuss the matter peacefully with his agnate, the plaintiff. One spokesman made a short speech about the modern difficulties of land shortage, and of the need to demarcate boundaries once and for all, making them clear with trees, sisal plants or other markers in order to avoid dispute. He expressed disapproval of the defendant's action in hoeing up the disputed strip of land before a settlement had been made; but he said that the plaintiff was not short of land, and had not acted as a 'brother' should. The plaintiff should, said the spokesman, have been ready to help his 'brother'. 'Brothers ought not to quarrel over two paces (the width of the strip of disputed land). That is bad. They must discuss the matter in peace.' No one else got up to speak when this spokesman sat down, and his speech therefore represented the general view of the meeting, i.e. of public opinion.

The plaintiff said later that by his action he had achieved the aim he desired. This was correct in that an internal moot was held soon afterwards at which he obtained the support of members of his inner lineage. He had, however, incurred a fine because of his intemperate behaviour; and it appeared that, contrary to his intention, he had alienated public opinion. The moot agreed that the defendant had acted imprudently in hoeing up the land, but in the end he was allowed to retain the disputed strip. Clearly the plaintiff's nearer agnates (brothers and nephews) felt less sympathy for him than they might, had he not brought the dispute to the parish assembly and there spoken so wildly. The half-brother, who had been present at the parish assembly, reported what had occurred, and his implied censure was not gainsaid by his listeners. Thus the plaintiff may well have chosen the wrong procedure, despite his assertion to the contrary, and at least he had pursued it clumsily.

A plaintiff may choose to take his dispute to the parish assembly, rather than to a moot or a counsellors' conclave, if he considers that he is likely to obtain more support there, particularly if he is unsure of the degree of support he may obtain from his inner lineage. In the following case, the plaintiff chose the parish assembly rather than impose a strain on already brittle relations with his patrilateral cousins.

Case 7: Two brothers, the only surviving sons of their deceased father, were concerned to maintain and if possible strengthen their ties with their father's brother's sons and autonomous grandsons, because they feared to be left alone as a non-viable lineage. Their cousins were capable of acting independently of them, being numerous enough to make a viable group. One of the two brothers, Karime (see the genealogy), became the plaintiff in a dispute concerning the repayment of bridewealth. His second wife had deserted him for another man, and now requested a divorce. Karime agreed to the divorce, and demanded the return of a number of animals and a sum of money he claimed to have paid to her father, Teronge, as the early instalments of bridewealth. Teronge agreed to this. Two matters caused dispute:—the amount of bridewealth which had been paid, and the fee for the woman's virginity. This kind of case normally is dealt with by a moot or a counsellors' conclave, and a conclave had been held at which the only result was to isolate the points of disagreement. At the conclave, Karime was supported by his elder brother (C in the genealogy), and by one of their cousins (B) who lived in the adjacent parish. The other agnates lived farther away, and Karime had contented himself with informing them of the dispute and of the arrangements for the conclave: they did not attend it.

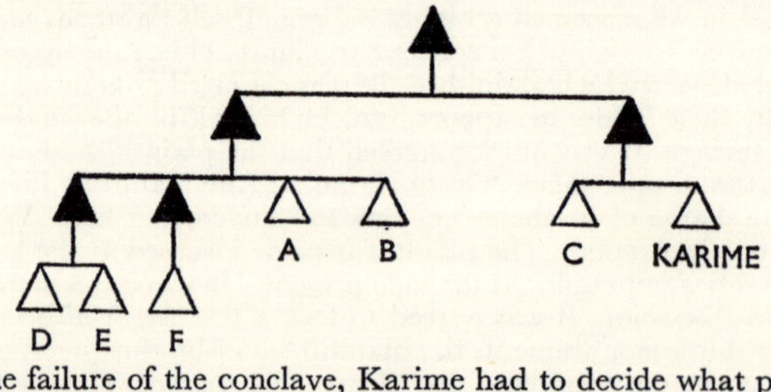

Following the failure of the conclave, Karime had to decide what procedure next to follow. A moot would compel him to request the participation of all his cousins, some of whom might refuse, thus perhaps breaking up the lineage. Even if they did attend, he was not, he said, sure of the degree of support they would give him. It so happened that Teronge, the father-in-law, lived in the same parish as Karime; and Teronge was a senior elder whilst Karime was a junior elder. Thus Karime could go before the parish assembly, and he could look for the support of his age-mates against Teronge and his age-mates. Furthermore, it was to Karime's advantage that at this time (1958) his age-mates, formally in the junior elder grade, were beginning effectively to act as senior elders; that is, they were engaged in replacing the next senior age-group, that of Teronge. Inter-group opposition was stimulated by inter-stream conflict. The formal senior murran were preparing for promotion to elderhood, supported by the formal senior elders, and the two murran age-groups were engaged in bickering and quarrelling, each looking to its patrons to support it. Karime was able therefore to make use of this sociological situation for his own purposes. His age-mates tended to regard the dispute as another example of the perfidy of the men of the other stream, and they desired to demonstrate their own strength by Karime's success. Karime was therefore able to avoid the problem of the danger to his own inner lineage, and also to recruit the stronger body of supporters in the circumstances. The counsellor of his own maximal lineage lived several miles away, and Karime was accustomed to consult a locally resident counsellor of his sub-clan. This counsellor was also an age-mate and a spokesman, and so his assistance could be expected in either a moot or the parish assembly.

It is, of course, impossible to say whether Karime's choice was the right one—the eventual compromise settlement was slightly in his favour with reference to the conflicting claims he and Teronge had made at the earlier conclave. In any event, it might seem that Karime was merely avoiding the issue concerning his fragile inner lineage. I suggested to him that members of his lineage, on whom he could not depend for support in an instance like this, were of little use to him. He would not accept this evaluation, for he said that he had been able to avoid an act which might have precipitated fission. His contention was that so long as the lineage remained intact, relations might improve. His cousins might need the assistance of him and his elder brother, and would thus incur an obligation to reciprocate.

This example is given because the issues which determined the plaintiff's choice of procedure were perfectly clear to him. Every fresh dispute is in some way unique according to the total context in which it occurs, and I can only attempt to illustrate the kind of choice-situations which may arise. Karime might have chosen differently had his father-in-law been dead, and had he, therefore, been disputing with his wife's brother. Had the two disputants lived in different parishes, the possibility of access to the parish assembly would have been denied. He might then have chosen to go to a magistrate's court, or to appeal to the chief; or he might have thought a moot to be preferable.

Disputes between members of a single parish who are not kinsfolk should not be dealt with by moot or conclave with counsellors, but by intra-parish procedures. This is the reverse of the preceding general principle, but it is more commonly ignored. Arusha say that neighbours (*elatia*), i.e. co-members of a parish, should settle their affairs, through the agency of fellow-neighbours in the parish assembly, or in a conclave with spokesmen and notables. This has the advantage not only that parish affairs do not go beyond the parish—as they must if a moot is convened—but more pertinently, that it is easier and generally quicker to use intra-parish procedures. Nowadays a parish assembly meets regularly at known times at a central spot, and formerly a man could readily approach a nearby spokesman and seek a meeting. Living fairly near together, unlike agnates or clansmen, members of the parish assembly can meet within a day or two without much difficulty.

Case 8: Kasenje accused Tomas of the same parish of stealing, killing and eating one of his goats. Kasenje claimed that a near neighbour had seen Tomas drive off the animal, which had strayed from Kasenje's paddock into the fields one evening. Kasenje went to Tomas' homestead and angrily denounced him, but Tomas and his wife denied the matter. Kasenje then went to a counsellor of his clan who lived in the parish—his own counsellor lived several miles away. The counsellor advised Kasenje to complain before the parish assembly in a few days' time, and this he did. Kasenje and Tomas were related only within the common moiety; Kasenje was a junior elder, and Tomas a senior murran, and therefore Kasenje obtained the support and assistance of his age-mates in the parish assembly. This case was fairly straightforward because a second witness had seen Tomas with the goat, and an immediate neighbour of Tomas related that he had seen a new goat skin in the house of Tomas' wife for which no satisfactory explanation was given. Tomas' age-group spokesmen fairly readily acceded to his guilt, and concentrated on urging a light compensation.

As Kasenje explained later, there was no need to take the trouble in this case of going a distance to his own lineage counsellor, and of asking his agnates to meet at Tomas' homestead. That might have taken many days to arrange; whereas the parish assembly successfully settled the matter within a few days. One of the spokesmen of Kasenje's age-group told me that Kasenje had acted properly. 'We must watch these Ilmeshuki (the senior murran, the age-group of Tomas),' the spokesman said. 'They are bad. They thieve and lie and bring bad words upon us here.' He was thinking of the dispute in an age-group context, as a feature of the opposition between adjacent groups. It was to Kasenje's advantage to make use of this, for the support he obtained from his age-mates was clear and firm.

This was not a difficult dispute to settle. The facts were well substantiated: no real defence was put forward, nor were any mitigating features found acceptable. Tomas accepted the decision of the parish assembly, and the compensation was in fact handed over to Kasenje the following day in the presence of spokesmen of both men. There might have been a number of factors which could have produced a different procedure. Had Tomas' guilt not been well established; or had he made a good case for extenuating circumstances (for instance, that Kasenje owed him a goat and refused to give him it); or had the parish assembly been unable to reach a decision easily (perhaps by the senior elders supporting their wards and refusing to accept the conclusions of the junior elders);[1] or had Kasenje and Tomas belonged to the same age-group—in any of these circumstances, Kasenje might have considered it more advantageous to ignore the parish assembly and to attempt to convene a moot or patrilineal conclave. Alternatively, in the light of the difficulty of acceptable decision in the parish assembly, he might afterwards have sought another procedure thought more likely to satisfy his demands. A man cannot be compelled to accept the decision of a parish assembly, unless that decision is so unanimous that the spokesmen of his own age-group are affronted by his refusal to accept it, and they impose a fine on him and threaten further coercion. In that event, apart from the coercion, he is not likely to gain a more advantageous settlement by any other procedure. Thus in practice Tomas had no alternative other than to accede.

If the dispute between co-members of the parish is of a more important kind, then the plaintiff may well decide to ignore the parish assembly altogether, and instead seek the support of his agnates and others in a moot.

Case 9: Ndasiken alleged that Malenda, his immediate neighbour, was cultivating a field which had been originally loaned to Malenda's father by Ndasiken's father. Ndasiken now demanded that Malenda give back the field so that Ndasiken's newly married son could have the use of it. Malenda denied Ndasiken's allegation, saying that Ndasiken's father had merely allowed his own father to take an adjacent piece of untouched forest, which Malenda's father himself had cleared by his efforts as a pioneer. If Malenda's account was correct, then Ndasiken had no claim at all. This dispute arose in a mountain parish where the density of population was about 1000 people per square mile. Land was therefore acutely scarce, and the matter of a field of about one acre was of major importance to both parties.

As far as I could ascertain, neither Ndasiken nor Malenda considered an approach to their age-group notables, of senior elder and senior murran status respectively. The conflicting contentions were not new; but it was not until the marriage of his son that a specific demand was made by Ndasiken. Both men visited their respective lineage counsellors, and an external moot was convened. The case was complicated by the lapse of time since the original occupation of the piece of land by Malenda's father some thirty-five to forty years previously, and the deaths of the better witnesses; and also by personal animosity between the two disputants which induced each of them to raise a number of side-issues. The patrilineal descent group of smallest size to which both belonged was a clan-section, but the first moot involved only a small portion of each man's potential supporters in their respective sub-clans. There were three moots and a number of conclaves before the dispute was settled.

At no stage was the parish assembly involved. An attempt by the senior elder spokesman of Ndasiken's age-group to convene a conclave with the spokesmen of Malenda's age-group came to nothing. Ndasiken said to me at that time: 'Will these men (of his own age-group) help me as my brothers will? No! Why should they? They are not of my maximal lineage. And Lokwaya (one of the spokesmen) is he big like Kirika (his own counsellor)? Lokwaya says that we must have peace here, that Malenda is our ward; but why should I care about that? I want my land. It is mine. Was it not (part of) my father's estate? My brothers know this, and Kirika knows it; and they will help me. Olmulaka knows too, and he will help.' Olmulaka was a counsellor in another lineage of the same sub-clan as Ndasiken, and he lived in a nearby parish. I was not able to record Malenda's thoughts or declared motives; but in any event he did not attempt to avoid the moot. Clearly Ndasiken believed that his strongest support lay with his agnates, most of whom lived elsewhere, and he was encouraged by the warm support he gained from Olmulaka, the other counsellor. He considered that he could not expect such unequivocal support from his age-mates or other parish members.

In cases of this kind, which Arusha consider to involve interests of great importance such that the support of agnates is mandatory, although the real intention of a plaintiff may be to convene a moot, he may nevertheless make use of the parish assembly. An example was given earlier (Case 6, p. 27), where in doing this the plaintiff's desire was to make his dispute a public matter, and so stimulate his agnates to action where they seemed to him to be apathetic. An alternative intention in going to the parish assembly may be to attempt to convince those men of his own *olwashe* segment, who live in his parish, that his case is good, so that their attendance at the subsequent moot is more readily gained. It may be useful also for a plaintiff to hear the kind of defence his opponent will bring to the moot, and what witnesses, by putting the onus of explanation on him in the parish assembly. Of course, a defendant should be aware of the plaintiff's stratagem, but he may be unable to avoid its results altogether if the spokesmen require him to answer the allegations. A refusal to answer may damage his own case; but he may perhaps be so moved by emotion (anger, fear of loss, etc.) that he commits himself more deeply than intended. A lineage counsellor may advise the plaintiff to go to the parish assembly for these reasons, in the hope of making his task of advocacy easier in the subsequent moot. But apart from such calculated design, a plaintiff may merely seek to make his case before anyone who will listen, and the parish assembly is an excellent and ready forum for that purpose. Despite the degree of skill with which many counsellors advise their agnates, it would be incorrect to suggest that men invariably assess available procedures coolly and objectively. Although seeking that which seems to afford most advantage, they often act unwisely, without forethought, and under the pressure of poorly controlled emotions.

A conclave is preferred to a moot, and sometimes to a parish assembly, when the dispute is of a minor kind, or where speedy settlement is important. Conclaves are also convened to deal with an impasse arising in a public assembly, or to execute the details of a settlement in an assembly, or to establish an injunction pending an assembly hearing. A conclave is essentially a small private meeting between the disputants and their associates—age-mates or nearer agnates. Here intimate discussion, bargaining and counter-bargaining can occur, without direct attention to other people, and without the need for some degree of rhetoric and self-justification. A conclave with a headman, or with one or two notables related to each disputant, is the easiest jural procedure to invoke, and therefore resort to it is common for petty affairs. Sometimes the initiative is taken by the headman or spokesmen themselves in an attempt to end the dispute speedily, before it can go further; although many spokesmen do not conceive it their responsibility to take such action without a request by an age-mate. Both kinds of conclave, and especially that with the parish headman, are sought also by complainants who seek the equivalent of an injunction against an offender—for example, the wife who fears further assault by her husband; the man who finds his cattle being harried by another man's herdsboys at the watering point; the cultivator who objects to a new path being made across his field of growing crops; the storekeeper who fears the brawling of murran in his store. Such complainants may be satisfied with a cessation of the annoyance, and they may be able to gain some small compensation for damages—a shilling or so, a gift of beer. If more serious injury is claimed, it is, of course, always possible to go later to the parish assembly or to seek a moot. Thus the assaulted wife, who initially desires free access to her house and fields (having fled to her father's homestead) may, through her father, later claim a heifer and beer as compensation before she will return; or she may perhaps sue for a divorce.

A conclave, under the aegis of their counsellors, is the common result of a less serious dispute between kin. Again, a major advantage is the relative ease and speed with which it can be arranged. Although a man may wish to obtain his rights against a kinsman, he does not necessarily desire to air their dispute in public. Not that the results of a conclave can be kept altogether secret, but rather a man feels more able to speak freely in private.

Case 10: A typical example of this was the dispute between Nkoyia and his estranged wife who had been living with her father, Sanya, for several months. The reasons for this situation are irrelevant here. Nkoyia wished to have his wife return, and had sent his full-brother earlier to invite her back. She and her father refused, and demanded first a suitable acknowledgement of his ill behaviour by Nkoyia, and a payment of compensation. A conclave was agreed to at Sanya's homestead. Nkoyia came accompanied by his two brothers, a paternal cousin, their lineage counsellor and two notables of the maximal lineage who lived near to him. Sanya had with him four members of his inner-lineage, his counsellor and a counsellor of a linked lineage who lived nearby. After a meeting of some two hours, an agreed settlement was achieved, including the promise of Sanya that his daughter would return to Nkoyia's homestead. This was a straightforward case, since Nkoyia did not attempt to deny his actions which had driven his wife away; and he badly wanted her back, as he admitted.

In other similar cases, agreement is not reached either because the husband refuses the minimum compensation demand by his father-in-law, or because the wife refuses to consider returning. A moot may then be convened by either the husband or the father in an attempt to settle the matter of compensation, or to establish divorce; although often the situation of stalemate is accepted for a period until either party resumes negotiations by, perhaps, another conclave.

Conclaves, and especially those between kin and involving counsellors, are almost inevitable concomitants of the hearing of a dispute in a public assembly. My notes indicate that most moots were preceded by a conclave which failed to produce agreement. Many public assemblies reach a deadlock over some aspect of the matter in discussion—the facts of the matter, the size of a compensation payment, the period within which payment should be made, associated arrangements, etc.—and the discussion is adjourned. There may be a positive agreement to meet privately, or the situation is left fluid. One party, probably at the advice of his counsellor, later convenes a conclave to discuss the particular points of dissension. This can result in a final settlement, or it may open the way to a resumed public discussion in a fresh moot or at the parish assembly.

Case 11: A man accused of adultery in the parish assembly, insistently denied his guilt and refused to discuss compensation. His age-group spokesmen were not prepared (so one said afterwards) to refuse to support the defendant against the plaintiff, a member of the next senior age-group. The discussion in the assembly became deflected from the particular issue to mutual recriminations between members of the two streams; and eventually, in some disorder, the assembly broke up. It was clear to the defendant's spokesman that he was in fact guilty of the charge, and the cuckolded husband persisted in declaring that he would raise the matter again. He talked of seeking to convene a moot. A private meeting of the defendant with some of his age-mates, including several notables, made it obvious that they believed him guilty and would only support him further if he confessed and allowed discussion of compensation to go forward. The defendant acceded to these pressures, and agreed to meet in conclave with the plaintiff. The conclave was held at the plaintiff's homestead. It comprised, on the plaintiff's side, two spokesmen, two notables and his elder full-brother;[2] and on the defendant's side, three spokesmen and three notables. The defendant's admission of guilt was declared, and the plaintiff agreed to resume the public discussion at the next meeting of the parish assembly, and to stop negotiations for a moot. Subsequently at the parish assembly, discussion concentrated entirely on the nature of the adultery compensation, without overt mention of the defendant's admission. His age-mates spoke strongly on his behalf and urged a small compensation; and their patrons interceded to persuade the plaintiff and his age-mates to agree to reduce their demands.

After a generalised decision has been reached in a public assembly, it may be deliberately left to a subsequent conclave to determine the final details and to execute them; or this may be performed by the assembly leaders themselves. Much depends on the nature of the matter in dispute and the degree of genuine, mutual agreement between the two parties.

Cases 12 and 13: In two essentially similar disputes over tenancies, different procedures were followed. Both involved the claim of the legitimate owner to evict his tenant, who was his father's sister's son. At the moot in each case the eventual agreement was that the tenant should be allowed to remain on part of the land. In one case, however, there was little if any animosity between the land owner and his tenant; they were age-mates and friendly, and the land owner had frequently in the past received assistance of various kinds from his tenant. Primarily, the owner in this case wished to secure a public affirmation of his ultimate title to the land, and to acquire the actual use of an area sufficient to make a coffee plot. The tenant was persuaded to accede to this, on the understanding that he would remain secure on the rest of the land; and he also received permission to plant coffee there.[3] The land owner was not suffering a severe land shortage, and he valued the association with his kinsman-tenant. In this case the moot did not discuss in detail the precise alignment of the new boundary. This was established a day or two later by the two men, witnessed by some of the near agnates of each, the tenant's counsellor and two notables of the owner's maximal lineage.

In the second case there was a long history of quarrelling between the owner and tenant, which may have been causally connected with the acute shortage of land at the actual use of the owner, who therefore resented the privation whilst some of his land was occupied by his tenant. Whatever the cause of the ill-feeling, the owner declared his determination similarily to evict the tenant. After two successive moots, a magistrate's private hearing[4] and two or three conclaves, the owner was persuaded to leave the tenant on part of the land (as in the previous case). He remained resentful of the tenant, and declared the latter to be stealing his land. He quarrelled with the members of his inner lineage (brother, father's brother, three patrilateral cousins) as they gradually came to advocate the compromise solution to him. The lineage was a tight-knit group, unafraid of segmentation whilst the father's brother (still only middle aged and a strong personality) was alive, and it was the constraint of these men which finally caused the land owner to accept the solution. In view of the animosity between the disputants, and the strains already imposed on the inner lineage, it was suggested that the demarcation of the new boundary be carried out by the two men's counsellors and other notable agnates together. They, it was believed, could take the responsibility more easily. The second moot therefore, adjourned to the land in question, established the new boundary, and directed murran to plant shoots of *dracaena* bush at points along it. Any future attempts to ignore these markers would, it was declared by the tenant's counsellor, be construed as an act of contempt against himself and the owner's counsellor. Thus no final conclave was necessary.

It may be considered necessary by a plaintiff and his associates to seek an immediate injunction on the defendant's actions until a full consideration of the dispute is possible in a parish assembly or a moot. Some examples of this, in connection with a headman's conclave, were given earlier; a chief's or a magistrate's conclave may act similarly. It is not always the intention of the plaintiff to gain this end—he may well be seeking a complete settlement of the dispute—but he may accept the temporary decision until he can take the issue elsewhere. Although typical of conclaves of chief, magistrate, and headman, this kind of procedure is not limited to these alone, as the following example shows.

Case 14: Mbavaani, a tenant on Kito's land, was accused by Kito of planting coffee without permission. When Kito remonstrated personally with Mbavaani, the latter declared that he had been given permission earlier, and that now Kito was attempting to deny this in order to avoid compensation claims (i.e. for the coffee already planted) by Mbavaani in case of eviction. Mbavaani continued the next day to put in more coffee seedlings. Kito went to see his counsellor, Lorowan, who lived in the same parish, and with him he visited Mbavaani's patrilateral cousin and another of his agnates who lived near. These latter men, of the same clan-division as Kito, had sometimes sought Lorowan's assistance in the past, because their own counsellor lived several miles away. Lorowan's request for a conclave to discuss the coffee planting was agreed to, and it was held three days later at Kito's homestead. Kito was supported by his brother and a cousin, and by a neighbour (also the father-in-law of Kito's daughter), a spokesman of his age-group (senior elders) and the counsellor, Lorowan. Mbavaani was supported by his cousin and the other agnate, and by a notable and a spokesman of his age-group (senior murran) who were his near neighbours. This was a mixed conclave: the counsellor was the leading figure in it, but it was accepted that the neighbours could contribute.

The discussion first turned to the conflicting claims concerning the legitimacy of Mbavaani's acts in planting coffee. Neither party produced evidence which satisfied the other. Mbavaani said that Kito had given permission, but that the only witness, a suitor of Mbavaani's daughter was away travelling and could not be immediately contacted. Mbavaani's age-mate neighbours supported him, saying that Kito had not objected to the planting of some coffee the previous year—i.e. the inference was that since Kito had not objected then, although he must have known of it, he at least tacitly approved. Kito denied ever giving permission, and said he had not known of the previous year's planting. This could hardly have been true. Kito's affinal neighbour said that he had heard Kito refuse permission to Mbavaani to plant trees on the land; and that Kito had protested immediately when Mbavaani had begun planting coffee this year. He denied knowledge of happenings the previous year. Kito's brother and cousin completely supported Kito's assertions. Lorowan, the counsellor, said he knew nothing of all this. and demanded to know why he had not been informed if Kito had permitted planting the previous year (for his own benefit a man normally keeps his counsellor informed of such matters). Mbavaani's age-group spokesmen suggested that in any case Kito ought to permit the planting as an act of friendliness. Kito rejected this angrily, and the discussion began to become acrimonious on both sides. Lorowan, the counsellor, suggested suspending further consideration until Mbavaani's own counsellor could attend—it seemed to me and my Arusha assistants that Lorowan felt uncomfortable, in that he had some obligation to Mbavaani and his local agnates although his main obligations and his sympathy lay with Kito. He suggested a moot should be held as soon as Mbavaani's witness (the absent suitor) returned. The spokesman of Kito's age-group disagreed, and suggested that the dispute be taken to the parish assembly since it was confined to members of the parish. Either alternative was possible, but Kito did not commit himself to one or the other at that time. He reverted to the fresh plantings that Mbavaani had made two days earlier, and demanded that no more be made. All of Kito's supporters immediately backed him up, and both Lorowan and the spokesmen told Mbavaani that he was not to plant any more seedlings until the dispute was settled. The spokesmen appealed to the spokesmen and notables of Mbavaani's age-group to support this and they agreed after some hesitation. Thus if Mbavaani attempted any further planting he would make himself liable to contempt of both the spokesmen and the counsellor. On this apparently interim agreement, the conclave broke up.

The dispute was not renewed afterwards—at least not during the following year before I left the country. No further plantings were made by Mbavaani, and Kito appeared prepared to accept the *fait accompli*, either because it was really legitimate, or because he did not wish to continue in conflict with his tenant, and had achieved his limited intention. Other Arusha suggested that the dispute would be raised again later, because Kito's eldest son (not involved in the conclave) had said elsewhere that he would evict Mbavaani in order to get the land for his own use. Thus the conclave may have produced a settlement of the dispute, or it may have provided only an injunction against Mbavaani planting more coffee. I did not know Kito well enough to be able to discuss the matter adequately or to learn his intentions; but it is probable that he was of two minds in the matter. In any case, at least the limited results of the conclave were clear to all concerned.

Notes

[1] In the actual case the senior elders took little part. One of their notables accepted Tomas' guilt and tacitly agreed that there were no mitigating factors. Another briefly suggested a lighter

compensation than the junior elders' spokesman demanded, but he did not attempt to pursue this.

[2] In fact the brother was of a senior age-group, so that this was not purely an age-group conclave. He attended primarily as a supporter of his younger brother but also because he might, as a patron, be able to influence the defendant who was a member of his wards' age-group.

[3] This is important, because if coffee is planted or other improvements made with the land owner's permission, the tenant cannot be evicted until full compensation is made for those items. In effect this commonly means that he can never be evicted, because the compensation is too high: in 1957–8 compensation was five shillings per coffee tree.

[4] The magistrate advised against the dispute coming to open court, and returned it to the lineage counsellors.

J. H. M. Beattie: Informal Judicial Activity in Bunyoro*

In most African societies there are more or less institutionalized ways of settling inter-personal disputes below the level of the formal court system. Since the informal judicial or arbitrative groups responsible for carrying out these procedures do not usually meet at regular times or places and do not keep written records, often little is known of their activities outside the small communities in which they function. The following short account of the Nyoro institution of 'councils of natives' or 'of neighbours' (*nkurato* [singular *rukurato*] *z'enzarwa*, or *z'abatahi*) may therefore be of some interest. In it I briefly consider the nature and size of the communities in which these councils operate, their composition, the kinds of disputes they deal with and their manner of dealing with them (giving a few examples), the ways in which Banyoro regard them, and, finally, their social significance and effectiveness.

Bunyoro, one of the great interlacustrine Bantu kingdoms of Uganda, is ruled (under the Protectorate administration, represented in Bunyoro by a district commissioner and two or three assistants) by a hereditary king, the Mukama, and a hierarchy of appointed territorial chiefs. These chiefs are of four ranks, usually rendered in English as 'county chiefs', 'sub-county chiefs', 'parish chiefs', and 'village headmen'. The two higher categories of chiefs hold official courts, constituted under the Protectorate's Native Courts Ordinance. These courts, which have the powers and jurisdictions usual for native courts in British Africa, are not our concern in this article. But it is necessary to note that the authority vested in them and the possibility of recourse to them provide a constant background to the field of inter-personal village relationships.

Banyoro live in scattered areas of settlement, not in compact villages. Their homesteads usually occupy the slightly raised areas, *migongo,* which are marked off from one another by the streams and papyrus swamps characteristic of the country. Much of Bunyoro is unpopulated bush, but in the settled regions density is quite high, often over 100 to the square mile. A typical homestead consists of one or two mud-and-wattle houses around a central courtyard, sheltered by a banana grove and surrounded by food gardens, and rarely more than shouting distance from the home of at least one neighbour. It is a traditional Nyoro value that patrilineal kinsmen should live near one another, especially full brothers. Sometimes they do, but often they do not, and most men's neighbours and daily associates include unrelated persons as well as patrilateral and matrilateral kinsfolk and affines. At least as important as kinship for the composition of co-operating local groups (for example for house-building or communal cultivation) are the principles of neighbourhood (*butahi*) and friendship.

The smallest territorial division of which Banyoro speak is a *kyaro* (plural *byaro*); literally 'a place where people stay'. A *kyaro* is not the same thing as a *mugongo,* for a *mugongo* may be uninhabited, or occupied by two or three *byaro.* Thus a *kyaro* may not be physically marked off from neighbouring *byaro,* though if there is no intervening river or swamp there is generally a more or less perceptible interval of uncultivated land. Though the boundary of a *kyaro* implies no barrier to kinship and other face-to-face relationships of neighbourhood, a *kyaro* is none the less a distinct social unit; it has a name, and its members see themselves as members of one *kyaro* as against the occupants of other neighbouring areas. Finally, the *kyaro* is not coterminous with any administratively

* J. H. M. Beattie, 'Informal Judicial Activity in Bunyoro', in *Journal of African Administration,* Vol. 9, No. 4, pp. 188–195.

recognised political unit. The smallest 'official' division, the area of the *mutongole* chief or village headman, may contain two or three *migongo* and half a dozen or more *byaro*. A *kyaro* may contain anything up to fifty or sixty households, though the average is somewhat lower; the one which I knew best had forty-one households and it was considered quite a large one. The smallest political unit, the *butongole*, averages 150 to 200 tax-payers.

Banyoro, then, form a population of scattered cultivators. They live in homesteads which are separated from other homesteads by fields and gardens and fallow land but which are near enough for an alarm to be widely heard. They think about and express their every-day social relationships in terms of kinship, of affinity, and simply of neighbourhood. The informal tribunals which we are about to consider cannot be properly understood unless they are seen in this context of neighbourhood and neighbourly obligation. Bunyoro quite explicitly attach a very high value to 'neighbourliness';[1] they like to have other people living near them, to visit constantly, and especially to eat and drink with one another. Sociability and *kyaro* solidarity are the highest community values, and we shall see that one of the main functions of the informal judicial procedures which we are about to describe is to sustain these values and to restore them when they are breached.

Like other people, Banyoro get along pretty well with one another on the whole, but sometimes they do not. Disputes between individuals may arise from a variety of causes. They may arise over property (as in cases of inheritance disputes, debt and theft), over women (as in cases of adultery and marriage troubles), over the custody of children, over cultivation rights and claims to land, and over all kinds of minor issues at beer parties and at other times. The hostilities which these differences bring about can be expressed in various ways. Thus disputes may (though they rarely do) lead to inter-personal violence; they may—and this is common—express themselves in mutual recriminations and abuse or, more seriously, in the practice or imputation of sorcery; and they may result in the destruction of property, typically by arson. Once disputes have arisen and have ceased to be reconcilable at the 'private' level, they can be dealt with 'judicially' in either of two ways. They may be settled through the superimposed native court system (they would in any case be so dealt with if the dispute had led to a homicide or serious injury), or they may be dealt with through an informal local tribunal, a *rukurato rw'enzarwa*.

This body consists simply of a group of neighbours summoned *ad hoc* to adjudicate upon the matter in issue. Membership of the group is not an office; there is no formal appointment to it, and it is not a 'standing committee' with permanent or semi-permanent membership. It only comes into existence when an aggrieved person causes it to be known that he has a dispute with another person which he wishes to be heard by a *rukurato rw'enzarwa*. When they are informed, neighbouring householders who are available and interested will come along. Some may be specially invited, but any neighbour may drop in without invitation, so long as he is not on bad terms with the complainant. The only qualifications for active participation in the council are membership of the male sex and, ideally, headship of a household: age in itself is not important. It is to be noted that these councils are not clan councils or councils of agnatic kinsmen, though sometimes they may approximate to such. There are, of course, certain kinds of disputes (for example, in regard to inheritance) which are primarily the concern of a group of agnatic kinsmen. But even in such cases, where both the parties to the dispute are of the same clan, representation on the council which is to settle the matter is generally based no less on neighbourhood than on kinship. In a dispute known to me in which a father accused his adult son of rudeness and neglect of traditional manners (the son had sat on a chair while eating in his father's company and had used a spoon instead of his fingers to eat millet porridge, the traditional food of Banyoro), the father summoned two or three unrelated neighbours as well as his own kinsmen to hear his complaint against his son. The basic pattern, then, is the same whether the dispute is between kinsmen or non-kinsmen: in both cases kinsmen and non-kinsmen of each party may be present, though naturally in a matter such as inheritance which primarily concerns a group of agnates it is likely that there will be a higher representation of patrilineal kin. But the point is that the distinction is one of degree: participation in these councils is seen as an obligation deriving from neighbourhood (*butahi*) at least as much as from any sort of kinship link with either or both parties to the dispute.

Cases dealt with by *nkurato z'enzarwa* of which I have records fall into the following rough categories. First I list those types of cases which arose between kinsmen or affines. An adolescent or grown-up 'child' disobeying its father (thus a son was fined for refusing to marry the girl his father had chosen for him, thus making his father feel 'shame' in front of people); a son attempting to seduce one of his father's wives; a man behaving rudely or with unseemly familiarity towards his wife's parents; a man treating his wife badly (by failing to provide her with a proper house, or with adequate clothes, or by beating her excessively or without good cause); a wife failing in her duty to her husband (by being lazy, adulterous, drunken or disobedient). Issues which arose between unrelated persons included the following: cases of quarrelling, abuse and assault; imputing sorcery (*burogo*) to another person without grounds, or falsely accusing another person of any crime; committing adultery; theft of foodstuffs from a field or of small articles; failure to settle debts. Of course, the gravest offences such as homicide, rape, actual sorcery (as opposed to the mere imputation of it) or serious theft would be taken directly to the official native courts or (in cases which exceeded the powers of the native courts) directly to the district commissioner's court. Minor disputes which the *rukurato rw'enzarwa* failed to settle would also be taken to the chief's court of lowest instance, and so would cases in which either party to the dispute insisted upon it. We shall see that in fact neither would be likely to do so, and even if he did the native court would ordinarily want to know why the matter had not been settled locally in the *kyaro*.

It is convenient to present here detailed accounts of three actual cases dealt with by *nkurato z'enzarwa*, each of which illustrates one or more aspects of the kinds of procedure involved. The first two cases are between unrelated persons; the third is between a man and his wife.

In the first case, two men at a beer party quarrelled. An older man, Yonasani, who was drunk, insulted a younger man, Tomasi. Tomasi wished to fight with Yonasani, but other people who were present prevented him from doing so. However, he left the party early and waited on the path towards Yonasani's home, and when Yonasani passed he dealt him a severe blow on the head with a stick and fled, leaving him on the ground. But Yonasani knew who his assailant was, and the next morning he complained to Tomasi's father, and went with him to see Tomasi to find out what he had to say. Tomasi at first denied all knowledge of the affair, but when Yonasani said that he intended to take the case to the official chief's court Tomasi's father said that he and his son would agree to a hearing before a *rukurato rw'enzarwa*. Tomasi's father accordingly summoned about half-a-dozen neighbours to come and settle the case, and they met at an appointed hour in the latter's house. After a brief discussion it was agreed that Tomasi had struck Yonasani, and that he had done wrong to do so, for if he was aggrieved by Yonasani's behaviour he should have brought a case against him, not beaten him. He was accordingly instructed to bring four large jars of banana beer and five shillings' worth of meat to Yonasani's house. A day was arranged, about a week later, and the beer and meat was duly provided. All the people who had been there when the case was heard were present, and Tomasi was told to serve the beer, and to choose somebody to roast the meat on the fire. 'Then', in the words of an informant who was present, 'we began to eat and drink, and everybody started to laugh and joke as they do at a wedding feast. Soon some people began dancing, and we accompanied them by singing and clapping our hands. By now Tomasi and Yonasani had become quite friendly as they used to be before, and were chatting with each other and calling each other by their *mpako* names.[2] And from that day to this the quarrel between them has been finished and they are quite friendly'.

The second case also concerned two men. Yozefu, an elderly man, had accused Yakobo of burning his house, on the grounds that he knew that Yakobo hated him, and that his wives had seen him running away. But Yakobo proved an alibi, and he then accused Yozefu, before a *rukurato rw'enzarwa* containing among other neighbours the local village headman, of 'spoiling his name'. Here is a translation of Yakobo's (written) account of the affair:

> 'Everyone present agreed that Yozefu failed in this case [literally 'the case defeated him']. So I asked the village headman to take us to the sub-county chief's headquarters, so that I could accuse him in the chief's court. But many of the people present said to me "Yakobo, it would be better for you to allow him to pay a 'fine' of beer and meat, in accordance with our Nyoro custom of forbearance and good manners". So I said, "All right; in that case I shall go home, and if he comes to my

house and begs forgiveness I shall forgive him, but if he does not come I shall accuse him in the sub-county chief's court". He came in the evening, after I had called in some neighbours to hear what should pass, and we told him that he should bring four jars of beer and a goat. He said that he would bring them in a week's time. On the day arranged I called all the people who had been at the first hearing of the case, and we waited for Yozefu to come. He came, bringing two pots of beer. Then the neighbours who were present said, "Ho Yozefu, what are you bringing beer here for? Are you coming to marry here or what?"[3] He replied that he had brought it because of having spoken badly of me by saying that I had burned his house, and he begged me to accept two jars of beer only, as he had not been able to get any more. I said that I would accept them, but I reminded him that it was only owing to my kindness that he was not in prison, and I warned him that if he committed a similar fault in the future I would certainly take him before the chief's court [*omu bukama*, literally 'to the kingship'; the superimposed state in contrast to the community]. So I and all the people there drank the beer, and we danced, and the matter was finished. But even now I am still not friendly with Yozefu, and he does not come to my home.' In this case, Yakobo further explained, 'we did not actually require Yozefu to bring a goat; when the neighbours who were deciding the case saw that he was sorry, and since they knew he was a poor man, they agreed that it would be enough if he brought six shillings' worth of meat instead, in order to sweeten the beer'.

My third example is a dispute between a woman and her husband. Yuniya, the wife of Matayo, brought three complaints against him. She had been married to him for more than ten years, but had had no children by him. He had children by other wives from whom he had afterwards separated.

The case was heard in the house of one Petero, an educated man and a clerk in the District Office, who was a classificatory 'grandchild' (sister's daughter's son) of Yuniya. He was present at the hearing, but the head of the proceedings was Jemusi, who although only distantly connected with Yuniya had grown up in the same household with her. He took the place that her father would have occupied had he been alive. Also present were two middle-aged men, the sons of an older sister of Yuniya. All these persons counted as being on Yuniya's side. Matayo was accompanied by a friend, a fellow clansman but not a close relation. Two near neighbours of middle age, Paulo and Erisa, both of whom were householders and neither was related to either party to the dispute, completed the assembly. One or two other neighbours dropped in and went away again from time to time. It is to be noted that the case was heard on the wife's 'home' *kyaro*, not the husband's; his home was on another *mugongo*, some miles away.

The *rukurato*, at which I was present, was held in the front room of Petero's house. Everybody sat around the room on chairs, except Yuniya who sat on the floor just on the other side of the doorway leading to the back of the house. She was only permitted to be there because she was a party to the dispute, and even then she was not allowed to sit actually in the room. She made three charges against her husband Matayo, an elderly and somewhat irascible looking person. First, she said, he had accused her of sorcery; when he had guests in the house and told her to prepare tea for them, he warned them not to drink it until she had drunk some first, lest it should poison them. Second, he had locked her out of their house when he went visiting, and had refused to let her come into his room. And third, he had driven out of the house and then assaulted Yuniya's younger brother George, who was Yuniya's father's heir and who had been living with his sister and her husband for the past three years, since he had no house of his own. When Matayo was invited to reply to these charges he admitted the first two, though not with a very good grace, but in reply to the charge of assault he alleged that the young man George had assaulted him first.

There was some discussion, for the most part fairly calm and restrained although Matayo occasionally showed signs of restiveness, and then Erisa, the younger of the two unrelated neighbours who had been called in, spoke. Matayo, he said, lost on all three counts. He had failed to produce any evidence that in all the years of their marriage Yuniya had shown any signs of being a sorceress. To shut her out of her own house showed very great contempt (*bunobi bukooto muno*) for her and was quite unjustified; a man's wife is the mistress of the house, the *mukama w'enju*, and he has no right to exclude her from it. Finally, he had done wrong to chase away Yuniya's brother; he was of her clan and indeed was his 'father-in-law' (*isezara*), for he was his father's heir, and to such a person respect is due. The other unrelated neighbour, Paulo, expressed his agreement with these findings. Then Erisa said that Matayo should bring a goat and four jars of beer to Jemusi (this is the standard penalty, though it may be reduced), and that Yuniya should return to her husband's home.

At this point, however, Yuniya interjected emphatically that she would never return to Matayo: 'they will continue to accuse me of sorcery,' she said. Erisa thereupon declared that in that case the bride-wealth which Matayo had paid for her would have to be returned to him. She agreed, but said that she would need some time to find it. It should strictly speaking have been repaid by George, the father's heir, but since he was a young man without resources, Jemusi, Petero and Yuniya herself would help to make it up. The amount concerned was about seven pounds. Matayo then said with considerable vehemence that he would not now have her back even if she wanted to return, as she and her brother had tried to choke him to death when he had told him to leave. Nor would he pay the goat and beer ordered. So Paulo, the elder of the two unrelated neighbours, said, 'that means, then, that you wish to be finally separated from your wife.' Matayo emphatically agreed, and throwing his dilapidated felt hat upside-down on the floor he declared with passion that he wanted neither her nor any other wife; all he wanted was his money back. Then Jemusi told Matayo and his friend that he would send them a letter when the money had been collected, so that they could come and fetch it. Matayo said that he would not come back here for the money; they should send it to him. Then he and his friend left (Paulo had left after the judgment had been given), and the rest of the people who had been present gradually drifted away.

These three cases exemplify the kinds of matters dealt with by *nkurato z'enzarwa* and the procedures involved. The initial action is always taken by the injured party. We noted that whether or not the disagreement is between related persons the procedure is the same, and unrelated neighbours are just as likely to be present at the hearing of a dispute between kinsmen as kinsmen of the parties concerned are likely to be present at the hearing of a case involving unrelated persons. Any male householder in the *kyaro* may be present; as we have seen, it is neighbourhood rather than kinship which determines the composition of the council. Always the same kind of penalty is imposed; the defeated party is ordered by the *rukurato* to bring beer and meat (usually a goat) to be consumed by the disputants and the members of the *rukurato*. And the person who loses the case is expected to humble himself, not only to the man he has injured but to the whole assembly. Thus Yozefu had to speak humbly and apologetically to Yakobo, and when ribald jokes were made at his expense by the party assembled to receive him he had to submit without showing resentment. I was told that when judgment is given it is proper for both parties to kneel down and thank the *rukurato* for its decision, but this would not usually be done nowadays.

Banyoro themselves greatly value their institution of *nkurato z'enzarwa*. They regard its use as the proper and seemly way of dealing with inter-personal disputes in the *kyaro*. It would be 'unneighbourly' to take a minor complaint to the chief's official court, *omu bukama*, and it is an act of grace and kindness on the part of the complainant to refrain from doing so. A brief example may illustrate this. Isoke was accused of adultery. The wronged husband was going to take the case to the native court, but (I quote from my informant):

> 'Isoke, seeing that he might be imprisoned, quickly went and pleaded with the husband thus: "Sir, I beg you that the fault which is being taken to the court may be returned to the neighbours (*omu batahi*) for settlement, so that I may be 'fined' there. Perhaps you will help me in this way." The injured husband agreed, and the case was taken to a *rukurato rw'enzarwa*, where it defeated Isoke, who was told to bring meat and beer, as is customary.'

Banyoro themselves make the point that to settle a case in this way, and to impose the conventional penalty, is to express confidence in the man who has erred; it shows that he is still accepted as a member of the community, and the affair is settled in the community and not outside it. To send him to the official court would in a sense imply the community's rejection of him. In this connection Banyoro sometimes quote the saying 'you don't tell someone who is not of your own people what it is that he has done to annoy you' (*atali wawe tokumanyisa ekyakubihirrire*); that is, the very fact that the issue can be frankly examined and decided by an informal council of neighbours (and therefore by implication friends) shows that the offender is still accepted as a member of the *kyaro* community. If a dispute between neighbours can be settled in the *kyaro* that is the way it should be settled; it is a serious matter to take it to the 'Government', where strangers will hear the case and where heavier penalties including imprisonment, may be imposed. This should only be done when settlement at the community level is seen to be impossible.[4]

Of course, the parties to a case dealt with by a *rukurato rw'enzarwa* are not always completely reconciled, and Banyoro realise this; we saw that Yozefu never really became friendly with Yakobo, and Matayo was not reconciled to his wife. But Yozefu had not been friendly with Yakabo even before the case was heard, and Banyoro do not expect *nkurato z'enzarwa* to work miracles. And in the case of Matayo what was accomplished was not a reconciliation but a settlement, the effecting of a divorce. In this latter case when the marriage ceased to exist, the possibility of paying over the meat and beer also ceased to exist, for that payment could only take place within the framework of an existing relationship. Where that relationship was broken, there could be nothing there to mend.

Still less is the primary aim of a *rukurato rw'enzarwa* to 'punish' a wrong-doer. Certainly the possibility that it may impose a penalty may exercise a deterrent effect, and this is acknowledged; Banyoro are not wealthy and beer and meat cost money. But this is secondary. If one suggests that the culprit is made to suffer by being compelled to spend his money on meat and beer, Banyoro reply: 'Why should he be angry or hurt? He consumes his share of the things he buys, and he enjoys the feast just as much as the others do'. The main object, then, appears to be to reintegrate the delinquent into the community and, if possible, to achieve reconciliation without causing bitterness and resentment; in the words of an informant, the institution exists 'to finish off people's quarrels and to abolish bad feeling.' In Bunyoro social attachment and solidarity are typically expressed in communal eating and drinking, and the joint feast in which the proceedings of the *rukurato rw'enzarwa* culminate may be seen, in one aspect, as a device for re-integrating the offender into the *kyaro* community. For not only does he have his share of the food and drink he has provided, but he is himself the host. And this is a praiseworthy thing; from a dishonourable status he is promoted to an honourable one. So the beer and meat are not a 'fine', at least not in the usual sense of that term; for their significance is rehabilitative rather than penal. It is perhaps hardly necessary to point out that if the conventional penalty were to be commuted to a money payment (and there is happily no sign of this happening as yet) the institution of *nkurato z'enzarwa* would completely change its form, for a money payment cannot be eaten or drunk, and it would inevitably sooner or later be turned to private and not public good.

These informal councils, then, serve functions quite different from (though no less important than) those aimed at by the official court system, to which they may be regarded as in a sense complementary. It would be a serious error to represent them simply as clumsy, 'amateur' expedients for punishing wrong-doers or settling civil disputes at an informal, sub-official level. The main significance of the institution of *nkurato z'enzarwa* lies not in the fact that they impose penalties (for they have no power to enforce what they order), or even in their arbitrative functions in determining disputes on the purely inter-individual plane. Their social importance lies rather in the efficacy with which they restore good relations when these have been disrupted. And they do this not only by achieving, if possible, a satisfactory settlement of the issue in dispute, but also (and most importantly) by re-integrating the errant individual into his community through a shared feast. After this bygones are supposed to be bygones, and it would be improper to make any further reference to the originating dispute. Of course *nkurato z'enzarwa* do not invariably succeed in achieving these purposes; it would be very remarkable if they did. But quite often they do, and so long as the common people of Bunyoro are concerned to retain the goodwill and co-operation of their neighbours, such informal tribunals will have an important part to play in village affairs. For they serve to express and maintain the basic community values of social solidarity and good neighbourliness. And in doing so they express, as no other institution can, the common moral consensus, for in an integrated and healthy community the general harmony is the concern of all.

Notes

[1] The following story is often told to illustrate this: 'Once upon a time a man moved into a new neighbourhood. He wanted to make a trial of the kind of neighbours he had, so this is what he did. In the very middle of the night he pretended to beat his wife, to see whether the neighbours would come to help her or not. But he did not really beat her; instead he beat a goat-skin, and his wife screamed and cried out that he was killing her. But no neighbours came to see what was the matter, and the very next day the man packed up and left that place with his wife and went to find somewhere else to live.'

[2] The *mpako*, a term which may be roughly translated 'praise-names', are of Nilotic origin, and in Bunyoro their use implies a combination of intimacy and respect.

[3] When a suitor formally presents himself at the home of his prospective bride's parents, he takes with him a present of four jars of beer and a goat.

[4] In a number of contexts Banyoro contrast the community, with its stress on intimacy, friendship and neighbourly co-operation, with the superimposed state, the *bukama*, which is the source of political authority and the agent of a power which derives from outside the local community.

P. Bohannan: Justice and Judgement among the Tiv*

The Elders of the Moot

One major sort of *jir* remains to be investigated. It is held in the compound or homestead of the person who initiates the *jir*; all the elders of his lineage come as guests, to be his judges and mentors. Tiv call this sort of *jir* a '*jir* at home' (*jir sa ya*), or '*jir* of the agnatic lineage' (*jir ityô*), if it needs to be distinguished from the *iir mbatarev*.

Jir at home differ in many ways from those *jir* which the Administration calls courts. Three are of the utmost significance. First, the personnel of the *jir* at home is different and differently organized from the personnel of the court; second, its institutionalization and procedure are conceptualized differently; third, the subject-matter of the disputes handled by the *jir* at home is different from the subject-matter of the courts. To put it another way, the personnel, the substantive law, and the procedural law are all significantly different in the two institutions.

The *jir* at home is made up of all the important members of the community. The 'community' can usually be taken to be the smallest or minimal *tar*, though on some occasions it may be larger and include a larger *tar*, and hence members of a more inclusive lineage; and on others it may be smaller and include only the members of one of those small lineages that Tiv call 'segments within the hut'. Collectively the elders of such a group are called the *ir*, and can be summoned by any one of themselves to come to 'discuss matters'.

This *jir*, which is made up of all the elders of the community, I call a 'moot', to distinguish it from that *jir* which is called a 'court' by administrative officers. A moot according to the *Shorter Oxford English Dictionary*, is 'an assembly of people, especially one forming a court of judicature'. A court is 'an assembly of judges or other persons legally appointed and acting as a tribunal to hear or determine any cause'. The difference obviously is that a court is a formal organization, with appointed and recognized judges and other officials. Its internal structure is quite precise; as a unit it is part of a larger structure. The moot is an assembly of neighbours and kinsmen who decide disputes. A court is an organized body with appointed officials; the moot is a community activity. The moot is a condition or mode of a social group (the lineage) which also exists in other conditions or modes; the court is a group of officials who have but a single mode or condition. Tiv moots are what Durkheim would have called mechanically solidary. They repeat themselves. The courts are organically solidary, and form a hierarchy.

For people to belong to the same lineage is sometimes expressed as their being 'those of one moot' (*mba jir i môm*). To be counted among those of the moot (*mbajiriv*—the same as the word for participants in a court action) a man must be an agnate in the lineage concerned, and he must be considered an elder (*or vesen*). In order to have influence in a moot, an elder must have a good memory for genealogies, for most of the cases touch on genealogies in some way or other. He needs an extensive and sure know-

* P. Bohannan, *Justice and Judgement among the Tiv*, Oxford University Press, 1957, pp. 160–169.

ledge of the principles and details of Tiv religion, magic, and witchcraft. Perhaps most important, he must know all the ramifications of personal relationships within his small community, for most of these important factors are not brought out in the case, but are presumed to be known to all hearers.

'To sit in one moot' (*tema jir môm*) is a phrase frequently heard in Tivland. It refers to a group of people, but does not identify any particular group. Tiv may say of a lineage of any order, or indeed of a large compound, 'we sit in one moot'. The size of the group actually called to a moot depends, as in all lineage activities, on the importance of the people concerned in the situation, and on the magnitude of the situation itself. A smaller lineage 'sits in one moot' when the case concerns the illness of a young man than when it concerns an old man. A smaller lineage 'sits in one moot' for a minor illness than for a funeral.

The number and kinds of meetings of the *jir* of a community vary. In Iyon of Shangev Ya, a *jir* discussed two or three minor matters every week; a bigger and important case, for which representatives of all Iyon gathered, occurred every two or three weeks.

The other lineages with which I am acquainted convened moots less often than did Iyon. When I first worked in MbaDuku, few moots were held in MbaGôr, the minimal *tar* in which I lived. During our second tour, when we worked in Raav in north-western Tivland, there were almost no moots of importance within Ukusu, but many within MbaAliko. We hypothesized that the difference was to be found in the effective leaders of the different communities. In MbaGôr there was one, in Ukusu there were two, effective leaders. All problems of the sort which Iyon and MbaAliko heard in moots were brought to them for consultation. In communities with no outstanding elders, there are many moots.

Our third trip was spent partly in Iyon and MbaDuku; we found that the leader of MbaGôr—Chenge's father, Kyagba—had died. There were moots almost every week; had I attended them all I should have been unable to complete my other work. The sort of problem which had formerly been taken to Kyagba was now discussed in open moots.

Those men who are considered the most influential elders of the community 'by day' are said to be the 'witches' by night. 'Witches' is not a good translation of *mbatsav*, even in the light only of other African data. Leadership—indeed, all ability—is an attribute, Tiv say, of a substance called *tsav* which grows on the heart of some men. A man of *tsav* (*or tsaw*) is a man of talent. The talent includes mystical power.

The leaders of the community are *ipso facto* men of *tsav*. It is they who 'repair the *tar*' by daylight by sitting in moots and acting as peacemakers and by keeping the community running smoothly. They also 'repair the *tar*' 'by night'. The mystical aspect of repairing the *tar* is the subject of my next book, but it must be reviewed here briefly.

The elders who repair the *tar* by day—what we could call secular governing—form, Tiv say, an organization which meets at night in order to carry out secret rituals for the religious protection of the community. As such, they are called 'the *mbatsav*', those with talent. Tiv say that for the *mbatsav* to deal adequately with the supernatural forces of the universe there are some activities which require sacrifice of life—what our fathers would have called 'life force'. The sacrifice may be a chicken or a goat, but a few each year are said to demand the supreme sacrifice of a human being. 'Human sacrifice', I hasten to add, did not occur in Tivland as it did, say, in Dahomey, though it may have occurred sporadically. Tiv say that in sacrificing a human being the *mbatsav* of the community, as a group, first decide on a victim from within the lineage. They then must 'kill him by *tsav*'. All Tiv profess ignorance of how this is done. But the intended victim dies and is buried. The *mbatsav* must then remove him from the grave and restore him to life. Only *then* can they perform the sacrifice of his body before the emblems of the fetish.

The *mbatsav* are 'dangerous' (*kwaghbo*); they are feared; they are also trusted. In times of political upheaval, the trust disappears. As Tiv put it, the *mbatsav* begin to use their talent to kill for personal gain and for the sheer love of the taste of human flesh. Tiv revolt always takes the form of anti-*tsav* uprisings. This usually means that the revolt is directed against the most influential elders of the community, who are 'by night' the *mbatsav*. In peaceful times, the *mbatsav* of the community protect its members from evil and from the *mbatsav* of other communities. That is the reason why times are peaceful. But protectors of the community have licence to destroy its individual members for purposes considered legitimate and for the good of all.

The elders who form the moot by day, then, form the *mbatsav* 'by night'. Death is either 'legitimate' killing by the *mbatsav* or else it is the illegitimate 'permitting' of the death by the *mbatsav*, or it is their weakness or the malice of some of them. Seen from the Tiv point of view, death is not merely caused; it must also be willed. They recognize the same causes of death as we do. But mere cause is for them insufficient explanation. They must also know who willed the death and who, by *tsav*, allowed the causes to cause death.

Tiv see all leaders in two lights: as their protectors and as their eventual vanquishers.

Moots are concerned with actions involving *tsav*, and hence often with charges against the elders of the community. The workings of *tsav* are known by the presence of illness, death, and evil omens.

Moots are also concerned with a lesser mystery: curses. The word here translated 'curse' is *ifan*. It is guilty knowledge as well as a curse, but the *ifan* must be uttered. Once uttered it can 'seize' someone—usually but not always the person against whom it was uttered. I know one instance in which a woman spun enough yarn for a cloth for herself. She gave it to her son and asked him to weave a cloth for her, because weaving is work for young men in Tivland. The son wove the cloth, but when it was finished he gave it to his new wife instead of his mother. In the circumstances, the old lady could say little. As mother-in-law and provider she could not rail at either her son or her daughter-in-law. Yet Tiv assumed that the loss of the cloth rankled. At a *jir* a year or so later, when the divining chains indicated an *ifan* or curse, she was told that she had muttered a threat or wish about this act of her son's which she resented, and this threat or curse, and especially the resentment leading to it, had created sickness and omens of ill feelings. Arrangements for restitution were made.

The ostensible subject-matter of the moots is thus different from that of those *jir* which can also be called courts. Moots deal with matters concerning *tsav*, and some of its accompanying or related beliefs: fetishes (*akombo*) and curses (*ifan*). All these beliefs and any of the practices that occur are called 'witchcraft' by the Administration and the missionaries. This being the case, all disputes concerning *tsav* come under the ordinance which makes witchcraft a crime.[1] *Tsav*, therefore, is recognized by administrative officers only as an evil—as 'witchcraft substance'. All disputes which turn on *tsav*, whether they be the activities of the *mbatsav* as a group acting for the benefit of the community, or of individuals of the *mbatsav* acting from motives of greed and personal gain, must be discussed before the moot. The court cannot concern itself in such matters.

Thus, to Tiv, the really important matters—matters of life and death—are heard before the moot, not before the court. The courts, they say, settle minor matters. The moot must exist to deal with major matters. The moots, as we shall see, also settle minor matters, but their doing so is considered incidental to their more important functions.

The Structure of the Moot

The action of a moot is simpler than that of a court, and has two main sets of components: the first is called 'convening (*lôhô*) the moot', the second 'discussing (*ôr*) the moot'.

Convening the moot. The phrase 'to call a *jir*' refers only to courts. One never 'calls' a moot, but rather 'convenes' or 'invites' it. In both contexts the word *jir* itself refers to both the gathering and the cause: in order to put one's *jir*, one must convene the *jir*.

The moot is always convened by an elder who is an agnatic member of the lineage associated with the *tar*, and hence what we might call (but Tiv do not) a member of the moot. In most of Tivland no one else can convene a moot. There are several ways in which non-agnates can bring pressure to bear so that a moot must be convened. A woman can run away and precipitate a moot. A man can run to his mother's agnatic lineage and get them to take action on his behalf. Although I have not recorded it here, I attended a moot in the *tar* of MbaYongo to which almost two hundred MbaDuku elders went to 'ask' the MbaYongo agnates of their sister's son to explain the illness of the latter's children. A man who lives permanently in the *tar* of his mother's lineage cannot convene the moot of that lineage; he must ask his mother's close kinsmen to do so on his behalf. He is, Tiv say, a 'woman', because he is related to the lineage through women.

In Utisha, in the south-eastern part of Tivland, there is an exception to these restrictions on convening moots. Utisha people have a form of *swem*, called '*swem* of the treaty', which enables almost anyone to convene a moot. Anyone can get a *swem* by going to any *swem*-holder in a lineage with which his agnatic lineage has a treaty of the type known as *ikul*. Here the *swem* can be bought. With this *swem ikul* in his hand, the person convening the moot, or someone deputed to act for him, goes to invite or bid the elders to come to his compound to hear his case.

Threats by elders that they will not come to discuss a moot when invited are among the strongest weapons of social control. In Utisha, once the elders have seen the treaty *swem*, their failure to attend would be tantamount to piercing *swem*. If they have been summoned lightly, however, they can demand outrageous gifts and '*tia* fines'. Iyon elders often refused to come to a moot; MbaDuku elders seldom did so.

Discussing the jir. The first step in 'discussing' a moot is to decide on a programme of points. This is done by hearing reports from diviners and reconciling them. At least one person or group should consult a diviner before a moot is convened. Often several may do so. The remainder of the moot involves discovering how the general situation revealed by the diviner is to be 'applied' to the situation in hand.

Diviners do not tell facts. They tell mystical causes behind facts. The consultant tells the diviner the facts. The diviner then operates his mechanism, putting questions to it. Since all the facts are known to him (if he is a good diviner), and since the possible 'causes' of a recurrent situation are limited, he points out which of these causes may be present.

The questions that a diviner answers by means of his instruments are of four kinds: those concerned respectively with curses, with debts and marriage wards, with fetishes, and with *tsav*.

The suggestion of a curse is usually the only one that comes primarily from the instrument rather than from the diviner himself. The diagnostic portent of a curse is the position of the pods of the divining chains at certain stages of the consultation. Diviners are seldom asked who cursed whom: few would answer such a question, though there is a recognized means by which the divining chains can be made to give this information. Rather, the consultant merely 'knows'; even more often, the matter is left for the elders of the moot to discover.

The second point clarified by divination is the 'marriage ward'. Tiv expect difficulties to exist among brothers over the distribution of marriage wards. If the consultation is made on behalf of a sick man, the assumption is that he owes a marriage ward to some one or else that one of his 'brothers', perhaps mistakenly, believes that he does. If the sick person is a woman, the first assumption is that she has been assigned as marriage ward to the wrong man, and has been made ill in order to force a consultation and eventually a moot in which the elders will alter the situation.

The third point which a diviner clarifies concerns fetishes. A disease (more accurately a symptom) *is* a fetish. Therefore, when the consultant recounts the symptoms in detail to the diviner, the number of fetishes that may be involved is reduced. It is seldom possible to find a one-to-one correlation between a symptom and a given fetish. If the symptom is a cough, the diviner knows the names of several fetishes thought to cause coughs, and puts these to his apparatus. It is not surprising that different diviners can usually discover the same fetishes in a given instance. It does not in any case disturb Tiv if they do not, for it is always probable that more than one fetish is involved.

Finally, the diviner asks his apparatus if *tsav* is involved in the misfortune about which he is inquiring. This question must be understood to mean *tsav* acting in a mystical or psychogenic way—bewitching—and not *tsav* which activates the evil fetish rituals performed by individuals of the *mbatsav*.

All four of these questions concern mysteries: curses, fetishes, *tsav*. The point about the marriage ward is also a mystery; the implication is always that if a woman has been given as marriage ward to the 'wrong man' either a curse or some sort of witchcraft will result. This point is made difficult by the fact that there are several criteria for determining the 'right man' to be the guardian: every Tiv believes that a woman's guardian should be the husband of her exchange partner; every Tiv believes that for every daughter or sister he puts into the exchange group, he ought to get a ward in return, even though one of the express purposes of the group is equitable distribution of wards so that everyone may acquire a wife.

When the results of the divination are placed before the elders of the moot, they 'reconcile' the results if more than one diviner has been questioned. They are then ready to proceed.

Oaths, mechanisms and purposes of swearing in a moot differ considerably from those in a court. Although I cannot at the moment see any reason why witnesses should not be called before the moot if matters of fact are in dispute, I have never attended a moot in which they were in fact called.

I have never seen *swem* used for oath-taking in a moot. Oaths to repeat accurately the findings of the diviner are almost always taken on the *igbe* fetish, occasionally on the *iwa*, and rarely on the senior elder's wrist.

Evidence in moots is different from evidence in courts: what is *vough*, or precise and straight, is usually unknowable, because moots deal mostly with mystical acts, at least with situations described in a mystical idiom. This is not always the case, for in at least the first two of the moots presented below matters of fact are considered. However, the moot deals almost entirely in terms of *mimi*, the truth of right social relationships. Secondly, since much of the suspected wrong necessarily occurred on a mystical plane, if at all, the only thing that could be affirmed by oath is innocence of mystical activity, either 'bewitching' with *tsav*, or uttering curses or using fetishes for anti-social and evil ends.

Protestations of innocence are not a matter of oath, but are made in a rite called 'blowing out the curse' which follows the hearing of the moot.

In the course of a moot, one's age-set, or occasionally the elders of one's mother's lineage, 'ask' (*pine*) the elders of one's agnatic lineage. . . . Asking is usually put in the form, 'Why have you let our child be bewitched?'[2] or 'Why have you not protected our age-mate from the attack of the *mbatsav*?' 'To ask' does not mean to ask 'Why have you done this?' but rather 'Why have you not prevented it?'

Asking pits a social group which protects a person against that group of his agnates (or, occasionally in the case of a woman, her husband's agnates) who have failed to protect him. The asking group is most commonly the age-set; members of the age-set are also agnates, but in this situation they act against the rest of the agnates. In those moots in which the mother's lineage asks, two lineages are involved: no matter what the span of the lineage of the actual participants, it is always described in terms of the largest possible lineage—at the point where the agnatic lineage and the mother's agnatic lineage are equivalent segments. Such a situation invariably becomes involved in Tiv thought with the 'feuds by night' which are said to occur between the *mbatsav* of almost any two communities.

The contending 'parties' to a moot tend to be segments of a single social group: an age-set against the rest of the agnates; a man's mother's lineage against his father's lineage, though both are a single lineage at some point in the lineage system, and can be called the moot of that inclusive lineage; the wives of a lineage (who are usually a category, not a group) against the elders who are in fact their husbands. The group divides for discussion.

There is thus, in most moots, no person who is in fact the accused. There is no defendant. No one is charged. The exceptions are those instances in which it would be unseemly to take the dispute before the Native Authority court, and therefore the elders are asked to come and arbitrate. Disputes within the minimal *tar*, Tiv say, should all be arbitrated by the moot rather than called before the court, but they do not always live up to their own precept.

This very fact—that there need be no accused—keeps the matter out of the courts which enjoy government tutelage, which settle cases in accordance with what Government thinks of as 'native law and custom'. The courts are established to handle items of debt and of wrongdoing against individuals who seek redress. They do not, and are not equipped to, handle instances in which a man charges his community with his peace of mind, the settlement of which is carried out in mystical language and involves the tacit, incidental settlement of many minor issues or disputes.

Moots overlap the actions of the courts only in a few instances: those in which individual rights are infringed, but in which the principals are close agnatic kinsmen.

Finally, the procedure of moots differs from that of courts in that moots are seldom said to be 'finished' (*kure*). Rather, Tiv merely use a past tense of 'discuss' to indicate that the moot has been held.

All successful moots end with the performance of a ritual. This ritual is a symbol that the elders have discussed the *jir* and reached a decision: they have repaired the *tar*. It is also symbolic of all the social and mystical acts that should follow the *jir* and re-establish the norm or correct its breach.

Notes

[1] T. O. Elias, *The Groundwork of Nigerian Law*, p. 203. The criminal offence of witchcraft is triable only in Magistrates' and Supreme Courts.

[2] 'Our child' in the case of the mother's lineage because 'we [a daughter of our lineage] bore him to your lineage'.

CHAPTER 4

PROCEDURE

IN this chapter, various descriptions are given of the ways in which cases are brought and heard before customary courts. We have sought to maintain a distinction between the various stages through which each action must proceed, from its initiation to its conclusion, though it has not always been possible to separate each of these into completely water-tight compartments because of the differences of approach on the part of the authors from whose works we have selected extracts.

In the section on initiation of proceedings, *Schapera* and *Bohannan* respectively provide information on the manner in which cases are started and courts are brought into session. In that which follows, on the conduct of hearings, both *Rattray* on the Ashanti and *Elias* (more generally) go into considerable detail on the manner in which trials and other proceedings are held. *Rattray* includes some useful information on household cases as well as those between members of different families. It should be noted that whereas he deals with both civil and criminal matters, *Elias* is concerned only with criminal cases. (For the basis on which these two categories are distinguished, see chapter 6. It is inevitable that some of the material included in this section overlaps with that contained in the chapter on Evidence: it would be extremely difficult—if not impossible—to follow the descriptions of a trial unless some indication of the way in which evidence is led was included; it is this procedural aspect of the topic which is emphasised here, and not the more analytical treatment which is provided later. In the section which follows, on Judgements and Decisions, both *Gluckman* and *Bohannan* give detailed descriptions of the process of reasoning by which the various authorities arrive at their conclusions, while in the final section on Execution of Decisions and Sanctions, *Elias*, *Rattray* and *Snell* catalogue the various alternatives that exist in customary law for enforcement of decisions. What emerges is a striking similarity between the options available to the authorities in widely differing societies, in East as well as West Africa.

(a) INITIATION OF LEGAL PROCEEDINGS

I. Schapera: A Handbook of Tswana Law and Custom*

Initiation of Legal Proceedings

The manner in which legal proceedings are initiated depends upon the nature of the case. When a civil wrong has been committed, the first legal duty of the parties concerned is to attempt a settlement of the matter out of court. As an example of the procedure generally followed, we may consider some fairly common instances of its practice.

* I. Schapera, *A Handbook of Tswana Law and Custom*, Oxford University Press, 1938, pp. 283–287.

As soon as an unmarried girl is seen to be pregnant, her parents ascertain who is responsible. They then send a message to the man's family, stating what has happened and what is alleged against him. His parents interview him, and if he admits responsibility they report to that effect to the girl's people. The two family groups then come together at the man's home to discuss the matter. The girl's parents will be asked what they want to do about it. They may reply that they want the man to marry the girl, or to pay a certain number of cattle as damages. If his people agree to this, the matter is then settled. In somewhat the same way a man will deal out of court with his wife's lover, or with a trespasser on his fields, or with the man whose cattle have damaged his crops. In each case the two parties involved come together, accompanied by their respective relatives; the person injured states what he wants by way of redress, and after further discussion the matter may be amicably settled to the satisfaction of both.[1]

It is only when no settlement can be effected in this way—if, e.g., the alleged wrong-doer denies his liability or refuses to grant the redress demanded—that the matter will be brought to court. The plaintiff will then sue the defendant in the court of the headman to whose ward the latter belongs. He first lodges his complaint with his own headman, generally through some senior relative. Women and children, in particular, have not the right to bring complaints forward by themselves, but must always do so through their husband or father. The headman then sends round word to the other men of his ward telling them to come to his *kgotla*. When they have assembled, he tells them briefly why they are there and asks the plaintiff to state his grievance, which is then discussed. The headman now instructs some men to carry the complaint to the responsible head of the defendant's family, or may go himself with plaintiff's representative and some other men. The head of defendant's family in turn reports the matter to his own headman. Sometimes, however, the complaint is carried direct to the headman by plaintiff's people. In either case the headman then summons defendant and his people, states the nature of the complaint he has received, and asks defendant what he has to say. It seldom happens that at this stage of the proceedings the defendant will admit he is in the wrong. A reply to this effect is accordingly sent back to plaintiff's headman, and at the same time a day is named on which the case will be heard. This is usually a few days ahead, so that the necessary witnesses and other people concerned may be informed in time. If the two parties belong to the same ward, the plaintiff lodges his grievance in the same way with his headman. The latter then informs the defendant and names a day on which the case will be heard. In all these negotiations, whether the parties belong to the same or to different wards, it is customary that several men should be present at every stage to hear the statements and replies. It may be added that there is no set formula of complaint.

Once the day for the hearing has been fixed, each party informs his relatives that he is involved, although some of them at least will already have been consulted by him. He will also notify his witnesses, so that they shall be at hand on the day of the hearing. Generally there will be some preliminary discussions, at which each of the parties and his supporters will talk over the matter and decide what line to take at the hearing. Where the parties concerned belong to different wards, these discussions may include, not only the relatives and witnesses, but also other men of their respective wards, for it is the practice that in such matters the men of each ward should stand together.

It will be seen from this brief review that in proceedings of this kind the initiative lies in the hands of the plaintiff. He lodges his complaint with his own headman, who then transmits it to defendant's headman. The latter interviews defendant and in turn sends back a messenger stating when he will hear the case in his court. Such cases must always be heard first before the ward headman. No man is entitled to carry his complaint straight to the Chief (unless the latter is also his ward headman). Should he do so, the Chief, after ascertaining that the matter has not yet been dealt with by the headman, will order the plaintiff to go back and lodge his grievance in the usual manner. The headman will then take the matter up. But it is not unusual for him also to fine the man for contempt of court (*go nyatsa lekgotla*).

When a criminal offence has been committed, there can be no attempt to settle the matter out of court. If a man has been killed or badly injured by another, his relatives inform their headman, who then inquires into the origin of the trouble. When he has obtained all the relevant information, he goes with them to the Chief and reports what has happened. So, too, if a girl has been raped, she reports to one of her people, who takes her to the headman. The latter then goes with her to lay the complaint before the Chief. In every case, if the culprit is known, the Chief sends some men to bring him to the *kgotla*. If he is not known, he is described, and a regiment or part of a regiment is detailed to look for him. Complaints of this sort are often brought direct to the Chief, without going through the ward headman. This is not regarded as incorrect procedure. The Chief will then inform the headman, either calling him to attend the hearing at the central *kgotla*, or, more usually, asking him to hold an inquiry into the matter and report his findings. Violation of the Chief's decrees are similarly reported straight to the Chief, who himself summons the person accused.

The main differences in procedure, then, are that such cases must come straight to the Chief's *kgotla* for trial, and that the accused person is immediately summoned at the instance of the Chief. Among the Ngwato the Chief employs a few paid 'policemen' (*maotlana*), who not only act as his messengers, but keep a sharp look-out for all offenders against his laws, e.g. in regard to beer-drinking, selling corn or cattle without a permit, or cutting down trees in the village. They have the right in such cases to administer summary justice, in that they can confiscate for themselves any corn or wood sold illegally, or the proceeds realized from such sales. No trial is held unless the culprit complains. In other tribes the Chief relies upon the tribe as a whole for information about wrongdoers (as is also the case among the Ngwato), while his court messengers are taken from the men who happen to be at the *kgotla* when such a service is required. For important matters he generally employs one of his recognized legal assessors as messenger.

It may be noted here that there is no law of prescription among the Tswana. *Molato ga o bole, go bola nama*, goes the saying: 'A wrong does not go bad, it is meat that goes bad', i.e. a case can be heard against a person at any time that he can be found. A case cannot be tried in the absence of one of the parties, save in very exceptional instances. In case of theft, e.g. if the complainant dies before the case is heard, his son can take it up instead; while, in case of debt, action can be taken against the debtor's heirs if he died before paying what he owes. But it is held that the sooner the case is dealt with the better. This applies particularly in cases of assault. *Dinthô di sekwa di sa le metse*, it is said: 'Wounds are prosecuted while they are still fresh.' But instances do occur—and they appear to have grown more frequent now that flight to European labour centres is possible—where people run away or hide if they know that they have committed an offence. It is for this reason that the complainant has the right to take up his case whenever the opportunity occurs, even if it is years after the offence was committed. But he is expected to lodge his complaint with defendant's people immediately he has been wronged, even if defendant himself has fled. This will justify him in taking up the matter afterwards; whereas if he fails to lodge his complaint at the time, any subsequent attempt to bring it forward will be regarded with suspicion and may even be dismissed.

There are no fixed sessions at any of the courts. They meet only when there is a case to be settled. Cases are heard as soon as possible after they have been reported, generally within a few days if the people are at home, but often only after a week or two if they are at their fields and have to be summoned home. Among the Kgatla it is said that no cases can be dealt with, especially at the Chief's court, during the late summer and early autumn. This is one of the seasonal taboos whose violation is held to keep off the rain. But there is also the more prosaic explanation that most of the people are then engaged in work at their fields, and the villages are more or less deserted. The rule is not strictly observed nowadays, but it is still usual for the court to suspend its normal activities until some time in April. This seems to apply to most other tribes as well.

Note

[1] As Mr. Matthews points out, court practice has an important bearing upon such private settlements. 'Settlements out of court must, broadly speaking, be such as, according to the best knowledge of those concerned, the court would approve. Otherwise an appeal may be lodged.'

P. Bohannan: Justice and Judgement among the Tiv*

Calling a Jir

The sort of advice which we in the West have come to associate with legal counsel is, in Tivland, usually given by the persons who are going to judge one's case. We have seen already that it is common, during the sessions of Grade-D courts, for litigants to approach the *mbatarev* for advice. Many more people approach the *mbatarev* singly at their compounds or at market. Chenge attended Tsar market regularly. There was a special shelter which was considered his: he sat there, usually with a couple of wives and some men of his small lineage. He was often joined by Huwa and a few of his people, less often by Ikpokpo, and seldom by Gbegba. When Gbegba attended market, he usually set up his chair and his circle of followers on the opposite side of the market place, the side nearest his home, and made what amounted to a formal 'call' at Chenge's shelter. It is at such times that the chiefs and *mbatarev* prefer to be approached by those needing advice about disputes. Persons thus approaching them usually brought a gift of a few kola nuts or a large calabash of millet beer or, particularly to Chenge who was known to prefer it, a gourd of palm-wine. Then, over a drink (which was always shared by all the important people present), the case was discussed. Everyone present partook of the discussion as well as of the wine. Many potential court cases were settled in these discussions. Others, however, could not be settled, and people were then told to bring formal complaints before the *jir*.

Mbatarev settle many disputes in the course of being informed of situations by their people. An *ortaregh* may—in fact, should—know perfectly well that there is bad blood or a land dispute between two persons of his *tar*. However, unless one of them or a third person 'tells' him of this situation before witnesses, he does not consider himself aware of it. This idea resembles judicial ignorance, though it applies only before disputes are brought before the *jir*. Tiv consider silly any suggestion that a judge should not utilize all his knowledge, however acquired, in the actual hearing of a case.

People often rush to the compounds of elders during the course of their disputes, rather than wait for a *jir*, in order to have them settled. If an *ortaregh* is nearby, he is very commonly chosen as the arbitrator. One of the complaints Tiv make about the Grade-D courts is that they are too slow.

INSTANCE NO. 11. *Chenge interrupts a meeting to settle a marriage dispute*

One morning in September 1952, Chenge and Huwa were both attending a meeting at Uta's. Uta's daughter, a girl of Ikakwer (Chenge's lineage), had married a youth of MbaYar (Huwa's lineage). It is Tiv custom, seldom observed, that a man gives his wife's guardian a pig to be butchered and shared out among the girl's lineage. On this occasion, the custom was being observed. Uta's son-in-law had brought and offered a small shoat as his payment, and had invited Huwa, his *ortaregh*, to accompany him. Uta called all the important elders of his lineage (MbaGôr) so that they could examine the pig to see if it would do. It was declared too small, and the son-in-law was instructed to find another and larger one. Uta fed the assembly and gave them a small pot of beer.

During the two hours spent at Uta's, several interruptions were caused by people bringing disputes. The longest was made by two very excited men and a woman who burst into Uta's compound, having discovered that Chenge and Huwa were there. The bickering about the pig was interrupted while all the elders present heard the dispute. It concerned the woman, who had gone to a husband in MbaKaange. That husband had never paid bridewealth, so her guardian had recalled her and sent her to a husband in another lineage area, who did pay bridewealth. She bore this second husband a daughter; a few months later, he sickened and everyone expected his death. Whereupon the woman left his compound and returned to her first 'husband' in MbaKaange. The men who burst in upon the meeting were the second husband and the guardian. The husband declared that he didn't want his wife to return because she had deserted him when she thought he was dying. He merely wanted his daughter and the remainder of his bridewealth. The guardian added that he had no money with which to repay, especially as the MbaKaange man refused to pay any bridewealth at all. The assembled elders of MbaGôr all participated in the arbitration. In fact, Fiyase, the oldest man present, actually did most of it. A lecture of high moral tone was delivered to the woman, the

* P. Bohannan, *Justice and Judgement among the Tiv*, Oxford University Press, 1957, pp. 29–34.

guardian was told to repay the bridewealth within three months, and the husband agreed to wait that time. The elders then again turned their attention to the matter of the pig that was being paid as part of the bridewealth for one of their 'daughters'.

That same afternoon, Chenge spent about three hours supervising the building of a long shelter in which field medical teams were going to carry out physical examinations and treatment of MbaDuku people as part of a yaws and anaemia campaign. During this time, he was approached by five different sets of people for advice and help in disputes. An *ortaregh's* work is never done.

When Tiv search out their *mbatarev* or other respected elders in this way and ask for advice and arbitration, they are said to be 'calling a *jir*'. Land cases, which are plentiful, especially in the crowded southern areas, are usually decided by the *mbatarev*, but are seldom brought before the court. The *mbatarev* of MbaDuku spent many days in the late wet and early dry seasons walking from field to field, arbitrating land disputes. During these long walks, in which there are frequent stops for rest, they are often approached by people who have other kinds of disputes to be settled as well. One such example occurred in November 1949:

INSTANCE NO. 12. Mbatarev, *while on another mission, are asked for advice*

The *mbatarev* of MbaDuku were settling land disputes between Ikakwer and Mba-Yar.[1] On the path they met a party going to Chenge's in search of advice. A girl and her father and her guardian were upset because they had found some medicines in the possession of the girl's husband, which they said were designed to keep her from straying while he went off to attend to his job as a road labourer. The husband said that the medicine was not made for that purpose, but was a charm which he had bought from an Ukan man. Such medicines are considered dangerous and it was decided that a formal case should be called and that the husband should get the Ukan man to come to Mba-Duku for the court session to act as his witness.

To call a *jir* has, however, a more restricted meaning in the context of Native Authority courts. There it means the payment of a two-shilling fee termed *ikojir* (though, if repaid to the 'plaintiff' at the end of the hearing, it is termed *jingajir*). After a fee has been paid, the dispute is heard at the first subsequent meeting of the court at which all the principals and witnesses can be collected together. Once all are present, the precedence of one's *jir* depends as we have seen, on one's ability to outshout (*hule*) other litigants.

Occasionally the *mbatarev* refuse to hear a particular dispute, saying it is not their affair, and adding that the *jir* must be called before some other court. Although there are many exceptions, Tiv believe that a *jir* is best called in the *tar* of the defendant. The obvious exception is found in criminal cases, especially those involving stealing, which are usually called in the area where the crime is said to have been committed: thieves are usually tried in the *tar* in which they have stolen.

It sometimes happens that the *mbatarev* of one *tar* send a messenger to those of another, asking that litigants be sent to them for participation in a *jir*. The request may or may not be honoured.

JIR NO. 13. *Refusing to send litigants to another* jir

[From a text by one of my scribes]

'The *mbatarev* Mbara sent to the *mbatarev* MbaDuku saying that an MbaDuku man had married (*er*) the wife of a man in their country, and requested that the *mbatarev* MbaDuku send the youngster and his wife to them with the policeman who brought the letter. Chief Chenge sent for all the people, and when they came, he asked the youngster, "Where did you marry this woman?" The youngster said it was in Mbara. Chenge asked, "Whose woman did you marry?" The youngster said it was his father-in-law who gave him the wife. Chenge then turned to the policeman. "Is one of those men who came with you the father-in-law of this child of mine?" and the policeman said that the girl's father had indeed come. Chenge asked the father-in-law, "Did you give this youngster of ours a wife?" The father-in-law agreed that he had done so, and said that he would return the money to the other husband in Mbara. Chenge had a note written to the *mbatarev* Mbara saying that he and the other *mbatarev* of MbaDuku would not give up the woman, because she had been properly married from the home of her father, who had undertaken to straighten out the case in Mbara.'

I have recorded several instances of this sort, as well as others in which persons calling *jir* were told to do so in the *tar* of the person they were calling. Women, particularly seem to prefer to call their *jir* before their own *mbatarev* rather than before those of their husbands' lineages. Thus many of them call *jir* against their guardians in disputes which are actually with their husbands—the husbands are sent for and usually come.

Tiv say that a *jir* which is transferred from one *tar* to another may never be settled; they say also that it is unwise to have more than one Grade-D court involved in one's disputes, for each may try to discredit the other in the eyes of the Administration. If one gets involved in such a situation it is best to withdraw one's *jir* and have it arbitrated unofficially.

That part of calling a *jir* which most resembles the European idea of 'pleading' is the actual presentation of one's complaint or defence before the assembled *mbatarev*. If, as occasionally happens, a man is not allowed to finish his story, he says that 'the *mbatarev* cut off (*kighir*) my *iir*'. It is considered bad form for the *mbatarev* to 'cut off' a 'man who calls', unless he is particularly long-winded and inapposite. They know he will say later that he was 'cut off arbitrarily (*sa apela*)'. No *jir* wants to get a reputation for acting arbitrarily.

When the 'man who calls' and his 'partner' have both finished their pleas, the '*jir yilan*' is completed. That is to say, the initiative passes from the principals to the judges and the witnesses, whose activities form the subject matter of the next two sections.

Professor Gluckman has used the notion of 'the reasonable man' liberally in his analysis of Lozi law.[2] The Tiv have similar concepts which are useful in analysis.

A man who calls a *jir* well, presenting his story in a concise and orderly manner, is said to be a 'man who knows things' (*or u fan kwagh*). This phrase, indeed, is used of any person who is well versed in Tiv custom and belief, and who governs his external life according to the standards of propriety compatible with such custom and belief. A man who cannot tell a connected story, or who constantly makes errors in calling and pleading his cases, is a 'man who doesn't know things' (*or u fan kwagh ga*) or even—if he is particularly inept—a *bumenor*. This latter word comes from the verb *bume* (not to be confused with *bum*, to swear); 'to be unreasonable' is about as good a translation as any. A person who through ignorance, neglect or wilfulness fails to act in accordance with those customs to which Tiv attach moral value is said to *bume*. The foolish or unreasonable act is itself *ibumegh*. Thus, a man who knows things may beat his wife, but only a *bumenor* will beat his wife until she cannot work: it is a foolish thing (*ibumegh*) to do. A man 'who knows things' may try to sleep with as many girls as possible, but only a *bumenor* commits incest, and incest is the greatest *ibumegh*. A man who knows things may (even though it is wrong) steal from distant lineages, but only a *bumenor* steals close to home.

Tiv like to be considered 'people who know things', and say that such persons have *inja* or 'character', while a *bumenor* has no character at all. This epithet becomes the more diagnostic when we realize that the word *inja*, which I have here translated as 'character', also means 'habit' and 'custom'. We might say that *inja* is the opposite of *ibumegh*.

There is a further set of modifying phrases which, however, apply to the reasonableness of acts and not persons. An unreasonable or wrong act can be committed in three different ways: by ignorance (*sa lanegh*), by accident (*sa aikor*), or by wilful going against custom (*sa apela*). One informant added a fourth—to do a thing through 'wrongheadedness' (*sa dang*). A 'man who knows things' may commit faults by ignorance or by accident. But if a man wilfully commits an act which, according to Tiv custom, is wrong, he is either a *bumenor* or a scoundrel (*dang-or*) or both. It is in terms of all these ideas that the 'reasonableness' of a man's actions are judged by Tiv judges and laymen. The 'reasonable man'—he who knows things—is one who follows custom, who has 'character', and does not act wilfully against the norms to which Tiv subscribe.

Notes

[1] One land dispute heard on this day is reported in *Tiv Farm and Settlement*, p. 56.
[2] Max Gluckman, *The Judicial Process among the Barotse*, 1955.

(b) The Conduct of the Hearing

R. S. Rattray: Ashanti Law and Constitution*

Procedure in the Chief's Court and that in Efiesem (*Household Cases*)

It has been seen that all offences which were in any way regarded as violations of tribal taboos were investigated before a tribunal which consisted of the Head-Chief and his body of Councillors, while all other cases were settled more or less privately or unofficially by and among the parties concerned—the person who acted in the latter case occupying the position of mediator and conciliator, rather than that of prosecutor or judge. It will be advisable, therefore, for our present purpose, to examine the question of procedure in the former Ashanti tribunals, under these two headings.

Procedure in the case of trial before the Central Authority. Except where a tribal taboo had been directly violated, the history of the inauguration of the procedure in such cases resolved itself into the history of the Akan institution of the *ntam*, or so-called 'oath'. I have already discussed this subject in a previous volume;[1] in the present work many of the Divisional 'oaths' and other matters in connexion with them have been examined in considerable detail, and their repetition in this chapter is therefore unnecessary. The following is an account of a trial, which, originally beginning, as most of these disputes did, as an *efiesem*, became an *Oman Akyiwadie* (tribal taboo) case, owing to 'the swearing of' the tribal 'oath'; it is more or less a translation in the vernacular.

Mondays, Thursdays, and Saturdays were known all over Ashanti as *gemnini* (lit. male days), for it was on these days that all serious matters were conducted, e.g. funeral customs, enstoolments, leaving the town and going into the war camp (*bo sesie*), and finally the hearing of the more important court cases.[2] Such a case might have its origin as follows:

Two men were quarrelling and they began to abuse each other; one slapped the other (*bo no som*); he asked, 'Why did you slap me?' The other replied, *Wo didi m'atem* ('You abused me'). The other man retorted, *Me ka ntam kesie na menni wo atem* ('I speak the great forbidden name that I did not abuse you'). The second man accepted this challenge (*de ntam bo so*).[3] It now behoved any person who was present[4] and heard these words, immediately to effect the arrest of both parties; should he not have done so, he would himself become guilty of an offence. A recognized fee of *nsano* (13s.) was attached to this duty; it was paid by the persons who were arrested, and ensured the matter being reported without delay to the Chief whose 'oath' had been 'sworn'. Both prisoners (*nnaduafo*) were now probably fastened with an iron staple to a portable log, for both were treated as guilty, which indeed in a sense they were, for each had spoken the great forbidden word.[5] The two prisoners were now led before the Chief; the *Okyeame* would call on the man who arrested them to come forward and state that he heard the prisoners speak the great forbidden word and in consequence arrested them. The *Okyeame* would then inquire who was the first person to violate the tribal taboo.[6] The one who did so became what we should term the 'plaintiff', while the other was the 'defendant', although there did not appear to be any distinctive terms in Ashanti.

A day was now appointed for the hearing of the case; meanwhile the prisoners might be kept 'in log' and were looked after by the person who originally effected their arrest.

On the day appointed for the trial, the Chief and his councillors would assemble in the *gyase kesie*, or *gyasewa* courtyards, according to whether the case was considered of greater or less importance. Opposite the Chief sat the *Ko'ntire* and *Akwamu* Elders side by side, while other Elders and sub-Chiefs sat grouped on the Chief's left and right, each occupying the exact position assigned to him by tribal custom.[7] In most Divisions an important case might not be heard unless the councillors known as the *Ko'ntire* and *Akwamu* were present.

The prisoners were now led forward, still attached to their logs, which were not removed during the trial. Their custodian would first relate where, when, and why he arrested them. The plaintiff, i.e. he who spoke the forbidden word, would be addressed by the *Okyeame* with the words, *Ka w'asem* ('State your case'). This he would do without

* R. S. Rattray, *Ashanti Law and Constitution*, Oxford University Press, 1929, pp. 379–391.

any oath being administered, or any admonition whatever to speak the truth. He gave his version of the affair, uninterrupted save by the shrill cries of the heralds, *Yen tie o! yen to kom! odedew!* and the deep *Yon!* with which the *Okyeame* punctuated the oration. The plaintiff, having stated his case, concluded with the customary formula: *Se asem a me kae, se nye nokware, na se me di ye no ayesem. Ya me ka ntam kesie.* ('If the statement which I have spoken is not the truth, and if I have made up anything, (then I stand to bear the penalty,) for I have spoken the great forbidden name.')

Next, the 'defendant' gave his version of what happened, generally ending with an affirmation that all the plaintiff had just related was false. He, in turn, wound up his speech with a similar declaration as the above to its truthfulness. The *Okyeame* would now stand up and repeat almost word for word all that the plaintiff had said, finishing by addressing to him the question, *Se wo ano asem mu', me boa?* ('Were these the words from your mouth, or do I lie?'), to which he would reply, *Eno ano no* ('These were (the words) from my mouth'). The *Okyeame* would next repeat what the defendant had said, put a similar question to him, and receive a similar answer. He would then turn towards the Elders and say, *Se ye se no no* ('That is what they have said'). The *Ko'ntire* and *Akwamu* and any one else who had anything to say might now rise up and examine and cross-examine the accused; all questions were put through the *Okyeame.* During this interrogation, one or other of the prisoners might say, *Me wo odansefo* ('I have a witness'). The other prisoner was asked if he also wished this witness to be called, and he would agree, or had to give very special reasons for refusing his services. The Elders would now ask the Chief for a messenger in order that the witness might be summoned to appear before the court. Before this messenger departed, he was sworn as follows: The *Okyeame* addressed him, saying: *Fa obosom asumasi di nse se, wo koro yi womfa nni nkommo* ('Swear by the god So-and-so that you will not carry on any conversation (about what you have heard concerning the case) at the place to which you are setting out'). The messenger would raise his hand and swear, saying: *Obosom asumasi nku me se menfa nni nkommo!* ('May the god So-and-so kill me if I talk about what I have heard').

The *Okyeame* again addressed him, saying: *Ka ntam kesie, se wo koroyi se wo di ho nkommo ma obi te a, obosom yi nku wo, ya wo to ntam kesie* ('Speak the great forbidden name, saying that at the place which you are going, if you talk about the case so that any one should hear about it and this god slay you, then you have violated the great forbidden name'). The messenger then said: *Me ka ntam kesie se me koroyi memfa nni nkommo* ('I speak the great forbidden word, saying that I will not talk about the case at the place to which I am setting out').

The *Okyeame* now turned to the Chief and said, *Nana ye sigyinae* ('Grandsire, we are going to set the main support'). The Chief would reply, *Wonsi* ('You may set it').[8] The *Okyeame* would now address the two prisoners and say: *Se adnasefo no ba, no ose sa, sa, sa na wu di bim; sanso aw ba, na ose wante a, nsoso wu di fo* ('If that witness comes and says this, and this, and this, you (the plaintiff) will be in the right; but if he comes and declares he has not heard (understood?), in that case you are guilty').

If the messenger could not return forthwith with the witness, the court would adjourn. This was done in the following manner: The Chief (who by the way was usually dressed in an *edinkira* cloth[9]) gave the first signal by lifting first one foot and then the other from the ground, and slapping his thighs; thereupon the executioners and heralds and other *ahenkwa* (attendants) exclaimed, *Babi kela! adow keka!* ('Somewhere is stirring, some place is moving'). The Chief would repeat these actions, and the third time would rise up, no sooner having done so than all the executioners shouted, *Sore e!* (Rise). The Chief and his immediate following would pass out of the *gyase* courtyard, every one remaining until he had gone. During the trial, if any Elder or sub-Chief wished to leave the court, he would whisper his reasons for wishing to do so to someone next him, and retire *leaving his Stool behind.* Again, if the Chief was seen to be holding too frequent conversation with any one during the trial, that person was rebuked, being told that he was distracting the Chief's attention from the case. The Chief would reply that he was listening to all that was being said and would be ready to prove his statement by repeating the evidence. When the witness arrived, the court again assembled and the prisoners were again brought before it.

The first business in hand was the swearing of the witness. The *Okyeame* addressed him, saying: *Fre abosom asumasi ne asumasi di nse se asem a ye be bisa wo nokware na wo be ka* ('Call upon the gods So-and-so and So-and-so and swear that you will speak the truth about the matter concerning which we shall ask you'). The witness would then say: *Abosom asumasi ne asumasi se die me nim tororo na me ka, se mankasa na abosom nku me* ('Gods So-and-so and So-and-so, I shall speak what I know to be true; if I do not thus speak truthfully, may the gods kill me'). Next the *Okyeame* would himself call upon the gods, saying *Abosom asumasi ne asumasi, akoa i na obedi adanse, se die onim wanka, na otwa m' nkontompo, ya nwonku no* ('Gods So-and-so and So-and-so, this fellow (subject) will bear witness; if he does not speak that which he knows, or if he tells lies, then must you kill him'). Again the *Okyeame* addressed the witness, saying: *Ka ntam kesie* ('Speak the great forbidden name'). He did so, again affirming that he would speak the truth. These important preliminaries over, the *Okyeame* would bid the witness speak what he knew about the case, saying some such words as *Nkrofo mienu asem wu nim mu sen?* ('What do you know with regard to the case between these two people?'). The witness then gave his sworn evidence. When he had concluded, the *Okyeame* would address the party against whom the evidence had been given, in the following words, which were in the nature of a set legal formula always employed on such occasions:

Wa te die wo dansefo aka; se wanfa mma ha ma yanfa asopa ntie ya wo ma aba bi so bo Okyeame, wo ku no di aboa; wo di fo.

'You have heard what your witness has said; had you not come here that we might take good ears to hear (your case) then it would have been as if you had lifted some stick and clubbed the *Okyeame*, killing him, as if he were some brute beast; you are guilty.'

All those present broke out into the Ashanti exclamation, *e! e! e!* The heralds came forward and sprinkled white clay on the back of the man who was acquitted, who, however, still had to pay the customary *aseda*. The guilty party would commence to supplicate the Elders, saying, *Me gwane me toa wo me ma nana di bim* ('I flee and join myself to you, and I give grandsire (i.e. the Chief) the justice of his cause').

The Elders would report to the Chief, who would order the guilty man to be taken away. He would later pass sentence upon him, either ordering him to be killed or perhaps permitting him to buy his head. This completes an account of the procedure before and during a trial in the old Divisional Head-Chief's court. Several points in the foregoing narrative are worthy of special consideration:

(*a*) Neither plaintiff nor defendant gave their evidence upon oath. It is true that they completed their statement with a repetition of the forbidden word, which in fact they had already spoken, and the mentioning of which had landed them both in a trial for their lives. They were not, however, admonished by the *Okyeame* to speak the truth, nor were they made to, nor did they offer to swear on any god that they would do so. They were not in fact ever expected to speak the truth if it were against their interests to do so. Each party, being his own advocate, was expected to make out the best possible case for himself; each would 'lie' if it suited his purpose.

'The reason that they did not give their evidence on oath (i.e. by calling upon a god) was in order that the Chief himself might be able to punish the one who was found to have lied, which he could not otherwise have done had he been sworn on a god, until that god had first taken vengeance.'

(*b*) Very different was the procedure even in case of the messenger sent to call the witness; every precaution was taken to ensure that he would observe the instructions given him not to discuss the case with the witness whom he was sent to call.

(*c*) The witness himself was carefully and systematically sworn upon two gods, *selected not by himself, but by the representatives of the Chief.* He took a solemn oath upon these deities to speak the truth, and called upon them to kill him should he lie. The *Okyeame* himself called upon the same powers to punish the witness should he deserve it, and finally the witness himself was made to speak the great forbidden name that his version of the affair which he was about to give was truthful and correct. These drastic precautions were essential because the result of the trial depended upon the testimony of this one individual. I asked if several witnesses were not called, and was informed, 'No, only one mutually agreeable to both parties'.

The idea of a witness being friendly or hostile to one or other of the litigants seemed unthinkable. The sanctity and nature of the oaths taken and the deadly sanctions behind them seemed to the Ashanti mind to rule out most of the possibility of bias or lying.

Several old Ashanti to whom I have spoken on the subject of witnesses professed to be somewhat amused at the procedure now common in the European courts, where Native witnesses, who are not Christian or Mohammedans, are permitted to select the particular god or sacred object upon which they are sworn. Such witnesses might, they state, purposely select fictitious, harmless, or amenable deities, on whom they will swear to speak the truth, and will then proceed to lie with complete freedom from fear of any sanction, as every one[10] not properly sworn is fully expected and at liberty to do if the position seems to demand it. It will have been observed that the court before whom the prisoners were brought itself provided or chose the gods upon whom the witness was sworn;[11] witnesses were never allowed to choose these gods for themselves, for if they swore on a god of their own selection it was thought that, even where it was known to be a genuine deity, the witness might possibly know he had access to it, and there would be private confession and propitiation to expiate the perjury.

Evidence given otherwise than in the prescribed form was considered valueless; indeed, for any person to stand up and, unless sworn with all the correct legal formalities, to speak the truth when it would be detrimental to some one else, was considered immoral or merely ridiculous. An Ashanti, not a professed Christian, who goes into the witness-box and gives truthful evidence against a fellow countryman after being sworn in the fashion common in our courts is, so I am informed, commonly described by saying, *Ne ho eye hu* ('He is a wonderful, awful, or fearful individual'). On the other hand, had he been sworn with the correct formalities, his evidence—at any rate in olden times—would have been deemed beyond suspicion of untruth. I am inclined, as I have already stated, to believe that 'to lie' in Ashanti was only used in a sense in which we understand the term when a falsehood was perpetrated after a solemn oath had been taken to speak the truth. Actually, as has already been pointed out, if a man told the truth when the truth was to the detriment of some one, except under these privileged conditions, he was branded as a 'liar' or tale-bearer and incurred public odium. Native police detectives who give evidence in our courts are commonly known as *Aban trofo* (lit. Government 'liars').

'*Otrofo* is a person who says he has seen or heard something which he has never seen or heard, or even something which, having seen and heard, he goes and reports without good reason.'

Again, 'a witness, not properly sworn, who gives evidence, truthful but unfavourable to one of the litigants, is lying (*twa nkontompo*), so far as that litigant is concerned'.

In olden times an appeal would readily be allowed against the *Okyeame* who gave judgement without calling a witness for whom the litigants had asked, or delivered a judgement wholly contrary to the evidence of a witness.

Odanseni owu n'afu (A witness dies because of his belly) is a well-known Ashanti proverb, which is interpreted as meaning that if a witness has accepted a bribe and lied, the gods on whom he swore to speak the truth will kill him. Supposing a witness to die soon after giving his evidence, an *obosom* will be consulted. If this god declares (through its priest) that the man's death was due to his having given false evidence on oath,[12] the following was the customary procedure:

(1) His body, instead of being buried, was thrown into the bush.

(2) His private property was confiscated and divided between the Chief and the priest of the god in whose name he had committed perjury.

(3) The original judgement was, if possible, reversed.

(4) If the witnesses' *abusua* wished to buy his body from the Chief they might do so, in order to give it a proper burial, but in that case they became liable to meet all the expenses and debts which the litigant, who had been found guilty on the false evidence of their kinsman, happened to have incurred.

Again, if a witness fell ill and went himself to consult an *obosom*, and was informed by the god that his malady was due to the false evidence which he had tendered, if he wished to recover he would refund all the expenses of the party who had been found guilty, and would also have to kill a sheep for the god, to avert its further anger (*dane dua*).

I have mentioned earlier in this chapter that there were exceptions to the rule that to be a competent witness, in the Ashanti sense, a witness must be sworn with all the customary formalities. Certain classes of persons were either exempt from the taking of any oath before giving evidence, or were actually not permitted to do so; their evidence nevertheless was 'good' evidence and carried all the weight of the ordinary individual's sworn testimony. Sub-Chiefs and Councillors who had already taken the customary oath before their Head-Chief were not required either to 'speak an *ntam*' or to swear an oath upon any god, if called upon as witnesses, as all such persons had already taken an oath. 'If persons in their position were found to have given false evidence, they were liable to be destooled.' Secondly, an *odehya* (a member of the kindred group from which the Stool Chiefs were selected) might not ever swear on or by any *obosom* (except by proxy); but all such individuals might 'speak an *ntam*'. On asking the reason for this prohibition, I was told by one informant that he did not know; that *Ye Kyi* (we taboo it); while another declared that a man or woman of royal blood who might some day sit upon the Stool must be a truthful person.

The following persons among others were competent witnesses:

(*a*) Children. (*c*) Wife.
(*b*) Slaves. (*d*) Husband.

A subject of another Chief was not a competent or compellable witness unless his own overlord was informed and an official sent to represent him. Similarly, an uncle expected to be informed if his nephew or niece was to be called as a witness, to enable him 'to stand behind the witness'.

An interesting formula has already been mentioned, whereby certain persons, owing to their relationship or special position with regard to some other persons, were considered as privileged to report to those individuals any information likely to be of value to them.

This information, under these circumstances, might be given without incurring the public odium ordinarily associated with the idea of tale-bearing (*nkontompo*). Before making the report, the 'tale-bearer' would say, 'I have drawn a line down my nose', or 'Ashes stand on my nose like the (white-nosed) *anyenhima* monkey'. These formulae bear testimony to the fact that evidence (truthful or untruthful) against any individual was only demanded or expected under certain particular circumstances, and that on all other occasions to bear false or true witness against a neighbour was regarded not only as unfriendly, but actually as reprehensible conduct. Before I pass on to discuss the subject under my next heading, I may note here, that in cases where it was particularly difficult to arrive at the truth, or where a litigant, who was found guilty, continued to protest his innocence, resort might have been made to the ordeal. The procedure in connexion with this custom will be described in the next chapter.

Procedure in Efiesem (*Household cases*): The most marked distinction between the procedure in the settlement of 'Household cases' and the trial just described lay, I think, in the attitude of the respective tribunals towards the litigants.

In the higher court the question at issue was possibly generally one of degree of guilt. The more guilty was executed, the lesser offender paid *Aseda* (a thank-offering) that he had escaped with his life.[13] The question of possible reconciliation of the parties—which, as I shall endeavour to show, was such a marked feature of the lower unofficial tribunal—did not enter into the province of the court. It was indeed, originally, almost impossible that it should do so. The disputants went before the central authority well knowing that the issue joined was one of life or death. However trifling the original cause of the action, 'the swearing of the oath' had rendered both equally liable to be executed for the violation of 'a capital sin'.

In spite of this apparent gulf between the two systems, the procedure in the tribunal of the central authority must without doubt have grown out of the practices in vogue in the humbler unofficial assemblies. It was the growing sense of power, backed by armed authority, which had modified the original procedure. The central authority, once it began to feel its strength, began to welcome litigation and quarrels as a means of raising revenue for the Stool. This was an attitude of the official mind which was the direct antithesis to that found in the original courts. In the kindred groups and family circles every effort had been extended towards maintaining quiet and peaceful relations. Hence it appears to have come about that the most characteristic feature of these unofficial courts—the *mpata* or conciliation of the litigants—came to drop out altogether from the higher courts.

Ohene (or *Okyeame*) *pata abonten so ntonka a; obuada* ('If the Chief (or *Okyeame*) tries to conciliate parties in a street quarrel, he will soon be starving') (lit. fasting).

Chiefs became wholly indifferent to a reconciliation between rival litigants; their interests, i.e. the financial interest of the Stool, were in fact all against it.

Outside the house of many *Okyeame* at the present day stands a *suman* (fetish) powerful in the stirring up of litigation. At Kumawu this *suman* is called *obodiasem* (the case-hearing-rock); at Kumasi it is known as *Nyate* (let me get it soon). Should there be a dearth of cases, the *Okyeame* will pour palm oil on the *suman* and say: *Obadiasem, nansa yi okom eku yen, menya asem nni* ('Case-hearing-rock, these days hunger is killing us, let me get cases to settle'). Small sums will later be deducted from the *Aseda* taken in cases resulting from this appeal, and these amounts will be accumulated until sufficient has been collected to purchase an offering for the *suman*.

Yet again, in a Division in which litigation dwindles and the perquisites of the Elders become correspondingly reduced, the following opinion on the situation may often be heard: *Ohene no, ne tiri nye, obedi adie; yennya asem nni* ('That Chief has not a good head; since his succession we cannot get court cases to settle'). In spite, however, of this radical change in outlook, which is easily accounted for, the procedure in *Efiesem* was not really different from what has already been described. Trifling quarrels were settled by any person who had a reputation for wisdom and common sense. More serious disputes were taken before the 'house-father' or head of the kindred group by an exactly similar process to that with which we have now become familiar, i.e. the 'oath'; in this case the little family or household 'oath' of the senior who was asked to arbitrate. Almost any one might apparently act for the litigants in these household cases, just so long as the Head-Chief's oath was not involved. As soon as that happened *asem ako akese m*'[14] ('the matter entered the realm of big events'). These unofficial arbitrators, unofficial so far as the central authority was concerned, not only had their own little 'oaths', but they might, and in fact did, accept *Aseda*, probably a pot of palm wine, or later a bottle of gin; they might give a judgement, although they had not any means to enforce it, save perhaps public opinion and the religious sanction implied in their oath. Their main endeavour was, however, to effect conciliation between parties who brought their disputes before them.

Pata in Ashanti means 'to reconcile', and *mpata*, the noun, came to be applied to that visible symbol of reconciliation which was tendered by one party and accepted (or refused) by the other. *Mpata* might have consisted of a fowl, or eggs, or the weight in gold-dust of a *domma* (7s.); the highest form of *mpata* once known was the *pata 'gwan* (the sheep of reconciliation), or its equivalent in gold-dust (*nsoansa*), i.e. 10*s*. The acceptance of *pata* by the injured party signified that he had publicly accepted the apology of his late adversary and that he was willing to let bygones be bygones. The acceptance, in fact, placed the recipient under a kind of legal obligation to do so; it signified an end of the dispute, and the reassumption of mutual friendly relations between all concerned. This reconciliation was further sometimes made even more binding by the late litigants agreeing to swear the arbitrator's private oath that they would henceforth be friends. There was not, it is true, any corporal sanction for its violation. If broken, the arbitrator, when he happened to meet one or other of the parties, might greet him with a satirical *mo* (congratulation), which no doubt contained a veiled allusion to possible supernatural consequences resulting from the violation of his 'oath'. To effect the settlement of a household dispute was idiomatically known as *Kora kora fie, ama efi awo* ('Repairing the house, so that it became dry'). A 'wet' house in Ashanti signifies one where its head is in trouble and sits moody and brooding. *Pata sika* (conciliation money) might be used by the donee in any manner that he wished; it need not be shared among others. The original idea in the custom was, I am informed, the presentation to the injured party of something with which he might 'wash his soul' and thus find peace after the late unpleasant events. *Mpata* might be refused; the donee conferred a favour on the donor by its acceptance.[15]

I have mentioned that there was an exception to the rule that the 'swearing' of the Head-Chief's 'oath' always necessitated the transference of the case to his court. The custom now to be noted appears to bear the stamp of a later date, when the fears of supernatural sanctions were in some cases giving way to more mundane and materialistic considerations. One or two of such exceptions have already been referred to in this volume, e.g. how on a campaign the speaking of an *ntam* did not result in any legal consequences; also the case of the creditor's 'oath' (*etam ka*), which might be 'winked at'. The further example is as follows: 'When a *fiewura* (house master) was going to hear a case privately, he would sometimes ask the Chief to allow some representatives to be present during his hearing of the case, lest the litigants in the heat of their arguments should happen to swear the Chief's "oath", which, in all ordinary circumstances, would entail the case being transferred forthwith to the higher court. In such a case, however, the Chief's representative might be empowered to say *Kata m'ani* ("Cover over my eyes"). The party who had sworn this "oath" might then, if he wished the matter ignored, pay the sum of £2 7*s*. 0*d*. to the representative of the Chief. This amount, which was commonly known as *ohene abotom die* ("something which went into the Chief's bag"), was handed to the Chief, who returned 7*s*. (the *mataho*) to his official who had been sent to watch over his interests.'

Notes

[1] *Religion and Art in Ashanti*, Chapter XXII.

[2] A court case may not be heard on a *da bone*, i.e., on any *fo-da* (with the exception of *Fo-mene*) or *Adae*.

[3] Compare the *similiter ego te* in the Roman custom of the *Sacramentum*.

[4] Except a Chief or *Okyeame*.

[5] Some writers lay stress on the fact that very often 'primitive' man treats a prisoner as guilty until he is proved innocent, but it is possible, as in this case in Ashanti, were we aware of all the facts, we might find that in a sense, as here, both were guilty of the greater offence, i.e. the violation of a tribal taboo; the lesser offence, the right and wrong of which remained to be determined, being for the time being in abeyance.

[6] There is a well-known saying in Ashanti which runs: *Nye die wa ka ntam kane nko na wa di bim* ('It is not always he who is the first "to swear an oath" who is innocent').

[7] See *Religion and Art in Ashanti*, Fig. 55.

[8] If the Chief were what the Ashanti disparagingly term an *Ohen' Okyeame*, i.e. a Chief who takes upon himself the duties that should properly be performed by his *Okyeame*, 'he will himself set the support'.

[9] See *Religion and Art in Ashanti*, Chapter XXV. Such a cloth is mourning or semi-mourning, a gentle reminder that one of the two litigants would probably be killed.

[10] There are exceptions which will be noted presently.

[11] A form of oath, not uncommon, was for the witness to lick one of the Chief's ancestral Stools.

[12] Known as *dansewia* or *danse kunumu*.

[13] Both had violated a tribal taboo.

[14] There was apparently one exception to the above rule, which will be noted presently.

[15] The conception of *Mpata* as a form of damages, which the unsuccessful litigant is compelled to pay to the successful one by order of the court, has arisen out of this old-time custom. I am not, however, here concerned with the practice of modern times, so I merely draw attention to this fact.

T. O. Elias: The Nature of African Customary Law*

Types of Trial and Modes of Trying the Criminal

When by any, or a combination of any, of the eight or nine modes of commencing a suit, the chief in a chiefly society, or the council of elders in a chiefless one, has thus been acquainted with the occurrence of a cause of action, a day is fixed for judging the case. The character of the subsequent trial differs according to whether a *criminal* or a *civil* wrong is in question; for, contrary to what one is often told by some writers, a clear distinction is made by African societies even in the matter of procedure at a trial. 'Akan customary law', observes Matson,[1] 'recognised two classes of acts giving rise to judicial proceedings: those causing danger (spiritual more often than mundane) to the community, either as a whole or in the person of its head; and those causing harm only to individuals.' This, as we have shown again and again, can be predicated of practically all types of African societies. We are, however, concerned, in the present section, with the trial of a person accused of a crime or a public offence which constitutes an outrage on the community.

The treatment of the criminal, whatever the society, can be swift and summary in the case of certain types of offence.[2] Minor crimes such as petty pilfering, simple assault or innocent breaches of market regulations may be, and are in fact often, dealt with on

* T. O. Elias, *The Nature of African Customary Law*, Manchester University Press, 1956, pp. 222–238.

the spot, provided that the offender is known and especially when he is caught in the act. In the case of minor thefts, the recovery of the article from the thief on the scene of the crime is usually followed by a formal accusation of him before the chief or council of elders sitting as a court to try the case.

But grave offences are normally attended by often elaborate but sometimes indirect trial procedure. Two main lines of approach may be distinguished on the basis that (1) the offender is known and (2) the offender is unknown.

(1) *Known Offenders:* The procedure adopted is stricter in a chief's than in a ward headman's court,[3] and again in a chiefly society system than in a chiefless society one; the essentials are, however, seldom dissimilar.

As an illustration of the procedure for the trial of a murderer, an incorrigible robber or other habitual criminal in a chiefless society, we may take the Kikuyu practice of the 'king'ole' and the 'mwinge' described by Dundas.[4] When a person has become such a notorious criminal that his guilt is not in doubt, the local elders invite the elders from the remoter parts to witness the trial. The case against the criminal is then fully explained to these. Also, the consent of a father or brother or other living close relative must be obtained to the intended trial and execution. If this relative decides to withhold his consent, the killing cannot be carried out and only compensation is payable.[5] The dissenting relative must, however, swear by the *kithitu* (a sacred symbol) that, should the culprit repeat his crime or be again guilty of another serious one, he would not then withhold his consent. But if he agrees to the execution of the criminal relative, he must commence the hunting down of the offender by throwing earth at him—a sign that he abjures the wrong-doer for ever. All this takes place in a secluded spot in the bush. The relative is normally expected to kill the culprit by strangulation but, if he wilts on the ground of sentiment, certain armed youths who have been specially summoned for the purpose will be ordered to spear the culprit to death. By this device it is ensured that, when a father freely consents to his son's death or a man to his brother's, the punishment must have been fully deserved by the culprit. The presence of the invited elders similarly serves to guarantee the fairness of the proceedings besides ensuring the guilt of the accused according to the accepted standards of inter-tribal law and comity.

Nevetheless, this description of the 'king'ole' and 'mwinge' procedure would have been more valuable if it had included an account of the preliminary process of the accusation, of the evidence adduced in support of it, and of the accused's defence (if any). Some such steps must surely have preceded the actual trial and execution, since the virtual veto of the relative or (presumably) of one or more of the invited elders would have had no possible basis of acceptance by the trial elders. It must be either the inadequacy of the evidence or the non-compliance with certain settled rules of customary law as to guilt that buttresses any such effective objection to the original course proposed by the trial elders.[6]

(That this apparently summary procedure is an abridged version of the normal process of customary trial should be clear when we turn from the case of a persistent or notorious criminal to that of lesser offenders.)

Again, if we take the case of the public execution of a witch or wizard, we are likely to see it as just another peremptory dispatch of the accused without prior adduction of evidence to ascertain his innocence or guilt. A very careful investigation into the circumstances of the whole event should reveal to the outside observer that what he has witnessed represents only the last stages of what is in fact a long and, by local standards, painstaking assessment of the unfortunate victim's evil ways over the years. The consensus of local public opinion has gradually built up against him: he was the notorious maker of 'bad' medicine, known by many to have brewed concoctions secretly for various persons who had administered these to their supposed enemies, often with fatal consequences; or he might himself have put dangerous poisons in some rival neighbour's *boma*. In several cases, his agents in mischief would not reveal the mastermind behind a complicated network of intrigue and systematic poisoning of often apparently unrelated or unconnected persons—all is carried on behind the cloak of complete anonymity, rendered all too easy by people having to live cheek by jowl in a closely-knit kinship group.

When, therefore, accusations are eventually made against this Fagin, the outsider is apt to dismiss the whole thing as based on a mere suspicion of an innocent man, but the elders of the community have by long experience of such practices acquired remarkable skill in their detection, even if they have to wait many years to accumulate irrefutable evidence of the culprit's guilt. By the time this stage is reached, at least the majority of the local people will have known of his nefarious activities. It is when the storm finally breaks that all and sundry are summoned to hear the recitation of his past criminal record. He is closely questioned about each of the deaths or other misfortunes previously associated with his name, and some of his partners in crime are also made to testify to what he has made them do at one time or another. Thereafter, his execution is simple and summary. There are, of course, occasions where the chief claims the monopoly of dealing with cases of witchcraft, and others where local elders deal with such cases themselves. But in every instance, it would on proper enquiry be found, *firstly* that the administration of some noxious medicine by or through the accused was at the bottom of the majority of cases of public execution for so-called sorcery or witchcraft, and *secondly* that this offence commonly designated witchcraft is really a matter of cunning and clandestine poisoning through a variety of physical contacts.[7] In this respect we may take Dundas's percipient suggestion: 'The justice of this (i.e. the public execution of a wizard) appears to us, of course, extremely doubtful, but the native spares no means to obtain proof, which to him is conclusive, and it is certain that many cases of so-called sorcery are real instances of poisoning.'[8] The evidence here seems to be reinforced by this testimony of two reliable social anthropologists with respect to the Nyakyusa: 'Supernatural sanctions were believed to be effective only against kinsmen, neighbours, and those with whom a man was in personal contact. No one feared witchcraft from outside the chiefdom.'[9]

So far we have been considering cases of major public offenders and the seemingly unceremonious mode of trying them. We have been at some pains to explain something of the background against which to assess what looks like a short-circuiting process of condemning such offenders. That this apparently summary procedure is an abridged version of the normal process of customary trial should become clear when we turn from the case of a persistent or notorious criminal—whether he be a wicked murderer, a habitual criminal or a sullen wizard, for all are to African eyes 'of imagination all compact'—to that of lesser offenders. We have shown earlier that certain species of robbery and adultery (in some societies) were formerly punished with the extreme penalty. The procedure for trial in such cases affords a striking illustration of the special care normally taken by the chief or council of elders to obtain clear proof of the accused's guilt. Writing of the Kikuyu, Dundas stated: 'I am therefore convinced that the killing of an adulterer was not permitted under any circumstances; in fact, it is often said, though not rigorously adhered to, that if a man had not been an eye-witness to the adultery of his wife he could claim nothing.' This requirement of proof of an accused's guilt within the context of life as lived in a local African society will be found to be a recurrent *motif* in the African administration of justice, whatever the offence being judged.[10]

In most West African states with their powerful 'secret' societies[11] it seems fairly true that serious political offences are dealt with by a method that smacks very much of Star Chamber justice. As we have shown, the leaders of these politico-judicial bodies often wield very wide powers in matters of 'Church and State': they can make and unmake kings, they supply most of the king's councillors, they organise and supervise trade and markets, and it is often they who control the spiritual activities of the community. These oligarchies, as conservators of the public weal, take care of such recalcitrant or disloyal nobles as might otherwise prove unamenable to the ordinary procedure of the trial of an accused person. The commonest types of offence, of which important personalities are accused in this way, are treason against the king or paramount chief and probably adultery with a wife of one of his 'fellow peers of the realm'. The trial itself takes place behind closed doors with, of course, the king's permission thereto or presence thereat. While what actually goes on there is never reported except the verdict, we gather from reliable sources[12] that the assembled notables would no doubt do their utmost to satisfy themselves in most cases about the innocence or guilt of an accused by such means of doing so as are open to them.[13] The judges at purely political trials might not, however, be so nice about strictly legal details of guilt.[14]

But in those African communities which have no such powerful 'secret' societies, there are often to be found certain spiritual functionaries whose role differs but little from that fulfilled by 'secret' societies in chiefly communities.

(2) *Offenders unknown:* Having considered the modes of trying known criminals, we may now examine the position when the offender is unknown.

It is obvious that no trial can take place where the wrong-doer has yet to be identified and brought before the chief or council of elders. To aid in the difficult task of identification, various expedients are resorted to by different African communities. Ordeals, oath-swearing and divination are the three principal modes of appeal to the supernatural, employed in the detection of crime. At this point, it cannot be too strongly emphasised that trial by ordeal is not necessarily the universal or even the chief method of determining the guilt or innocence of a person accused of serious wrongs. All generalisations based upon its incidence in certain categories of undetected crimes have failed to take account both of its *raison d'être* and of the extent of its prevalence.

Frequently, the preliminary step taken in the investigation of a crime whose perpetrator is unknown is for the victim or his relation to consult one of a recognised class of diviners to be found in almost all African communities. Partly from his own extensive local knowledge of men and affairs throughout his district and partly from what by careful questioning and logical inferences he may gather from the consultants' own stories and expressions of opinion, this deft and crafty practitioner can often indicate a circle of suspects from among whom it is probable the real culprit will be found. Of course, his superior intelligence enables him to hoodwink the unwary majority into a belief that this essentially intellectual effort of his *is* in fact of magical or supernatural origin. All sorts of *mumbo jumbo* are produced in the process—cowrie shells, bowls of water, sands in a sack, etc.—and these are manipulated to yield an answer to coincide with the diviner's personal predilections, largely if not entirely induced by his nice balancing of probabilities for or against certain suspected individuals. It will thus be seen that divination as employed in the detection of crime by African societies has no *juridical* character but is only an extra-legal prelude either to the ordeal or the oath-taking, which are both legal.[15]

When none of those named as suspects is prepared to confess to his guilt, or sometimes if particular individuals have been taxed with the commission of an alleged crime by the victim without any prior consultation with a diviner, the assembled elders or the chief will then subject each in turn to the form of ordeal considered appropriate in all the circumstances of the case. The ordeal might take the form of the juice of a tree (e.g. sass-wood) mixed with water, or a burnt powder made from it and dissolved in water; a knife or other piece of iron might be heated in a fire; the culprit might be taken to a nearby pond or stream. The guilty one is he who should drink the water and become sick,[16] handle the red-hot knife and get burnt, or sink when immersed in the water. We are assured by Penwill for the Kamba that 'these ordeals are mostly used in what English law would classify as criminal cases—often theft or murder when the culprit is unknown'.[17]

For the same purpose is the use of the oath. As an alternative to the ordeal, the Kamba attempt to determine guilt by means of the *kithitu* oath or, in family or inter-group disputes, the *ndundu* oath. Each oath is sworn on a sacred object which might vary from a curious mixture of 'the teeth of a hyena, the teeth of a dead man, pieces of a porcupine quill, special roots and plants, earth from the hearth in the hut of a dead woman, a piece of an earthen food-pot, certain special small stones, and so on'—all wrapped up in a long binding and carried in a woven basket-like covering. The *kithitu* to be used in a particular case is brought to the place of trial by its guardian at the invitation of the party, who is not required to swear on it as to the facts in dispute, except to say that the *kithitu* contains no poison or other harmful substance which can injure the accused when he comes to swear on it. He swears this three times and also strikes the *kithitu* three times, repeating each time: 'If I lie, may this *kithitu* seize me myself.' He also swears that, if the accused should, after the ceremony, follow him secretly to his house to offer him bribe, he would never accept it and that, if he should, 'may the *kithitu* seize me myself'. After the accuser has taken these preliminary oaths, the accused steps forward and, before the assembled elders who prescribe the particular form and phrasing of the oath he is to take, swears the principal oath touching the crime charged or the issues in dispute. A goat is then killed, the stomach contents being scattered about the spot symbolically to cleanse the place of trial, while the flesh is cooked for the trial elders. Then the trial proper ensues.

The only difference between the *kithitu* and the *ndundu* is that the latter is less potent than the former in that whereas a false oath by the former affects not only the swearer himself but certain close relations like his wife and children, a false oath by the latter affects only the swearer and no one else. Women can neither be guardians of a *kithitu* nor are they allowed to swear on it, because their 'intelligence is limited' and they might lightly swear in a manner that would probably wipe out their entire family. They are usually allowed, however, to swear, e.g. by striking their earthen cooking pots, or to swear on their loin-cloths.

As guilt cannot be quickly shown by either the *kithitu* or the *ndundu*—for each requires for showing its effect a specific period ranging from a few days to about six months from the oath-taking—resort may sometimes be had to one of the many forms of the ordeal for the purpose of getting quick results. Of course, an exception exists where the accused refuses to swear when called upon to do so; his refusal to swear is usually taken as sufficient evidence of his guilt.[18]

Evans-Pritchard has shown that the oath is only used among the Azande for cases of so-called witchcraft and adultery because of the absence of witnesses or other evidence.[19] Among the Bantu of North Kavirondo, the late Dr. Wagner witnessed the actual return of stolen property after the uttering of imprecations by the owner.[20]

Another use of the oath is as a curse. Driberg says that Chagga witnesses are solemnly cursed by the chief before being allowed to give evidence at a trial, and that if an Ashanti witness dies soon after the trial he is held to have been guilty of perjury and the judgement may consequently be reversed. 'The expedient by which witnesses are put on oath,' adds Driberg, 'vary considerably. They may even be subjected to the ordeal together with the parties to a suit, but more commonly they are sworn, if an oath is administered, on some sacred symbol, such as a spear, the presumption being that the supernatural sanction invoked would automatically punish any perjury.'[21]

Some African societies are known to be content with the swearing of an oath, without recourse to a poison ordeal of any kind. The Ibo of Umueke Agbaja believe that a false oath is as bad for the swearer as is a poison ordeal and is not as likely to kill so many people as the latter, should the accused be proved false.[22] A supernatural object, associated with the spirit of thunder, can be invoked against an unknown offender. There is a special class of people to whom application is made if its services are required. Its invocation in a case of theft is held to be capable of harming not only the thief but all those who have even innocently shared in the stolen goods. This is widely believed to be responsible for cases of otherwise unaccountable illness. It seems, therefore, to be an elaborate means of securing a wide measure of sanctity for private property by discouraging not only the thief but also any accessories. The Ibo, being inveterate traders, naturally want buyers of goods to beware of what they buy and so maintain strict and honest dealings. Recourse to the supernatural is thus had for the purpose of achieving practical results and social objectives.[23] The *psychological* basis of it must not be under-rated.

An interesting type of Ibo trial procedure is that of *Oath and Betting*.[24] The accuser and the accused each bet a named stake, say 5*s*., and must then produce a token (a flute or a knife) in lieu of it. The tokens are handed to an elder, who acts as stakeholder. If, ultimately, either party fails to produce the amount of his bet, the elder is held responsible for it. Thereafter, the accused swears his innocence on an *agbara* (i.e. another sacred object[25]) of the accuser's choice. If within the appointed time—a year, six months, or any other period fixed for the *agbara* to act—the accused dies, the accuser gets his 5*s*. back and the other 5*s*. is divided among the judges of the case. If the accused does not die, he gets his money back together with half that of the accuser, the other half going to the people who judged the case. This Ibo procedure of declaring an individual, who survives the prescribed period after the oath-taking, free of his oath has been shown to be a feature of the Kamba and Ashanti procedures and will be seen to be a *leitmotif* in the judicial process of all the African societies employing the oath as a mode of discovering guilt.

Where a judicial system like that of the Ibo still relies largely on the supernatural method of swearing and has yet to develop an advanced technique of sifting evidence, it may be that the oft-quoted weakness of the indigenous procedure does serve to stave off a possible miscarriage of justice by a not too rigorous insistence on the judgment being executed immediately. The purpose of consulting a diviner is often aimed at lessening the social tension by affording a temporary mitigation of any bitterness felt by the aggrieved—an important device among an excitable people living cheek by jowl. This is more usually the case when positive evidence of guilt is lacking or the verdict seems to be against the weight of such evidence as was available when judgment was given. But where public opinion is more or less unanimous against a criminal, or where a culprit has been caught red-handed or with no reasonable chance of denial, sentence is usually executed on the spot, often in a swift and summary manner by those who have decided the case or those appointed to do so by the judges.[26]

In cases where resort has been had to the ordeal as a mode of determining guilt, it will often be observed that the principle is based upon a presumption of the innocence of the person or persons subject to it. It must be granted, however, that the element of chance which trial by ordeal involves is too great to make it judicially desirable or socially just. But, in the absence of a developed alternative technique for discovering an unknown criminal, nearly all human societies[27] have at one stage or another of their legal evolution employed the ordeal for the judicial determination of guilt.[28] Thus, to go no farther than English law, trial was (*a*) by various forms of ordeal (e.g. of the hot iron, of boiling water, of cold water, and of the cursed morsel), (*b*) by the oath of oath-helpers (usually twelve men friends or relatives of the accused) called 'compurgators' who had only to swear that an oath sworn by the suspect was clean but who were not required to swear to the facts of the case: this is also known as 'wager of law'; (*c*) by battle (introduced into England by the Normans) which in civil cases was not fought between the parties themselves but between their respective champions who later became professionals fighting for litigants up and down the country; in criminal cases, the battle was fought between the accuser and the accused personally and, if the defeated defendant escaped being slain in the battle, he was instantly hanged on the gallows specially prepared nearby for the purpose. Thus, a judicial duel between two contradictory witnesses was allowed to decide the rights of the parties.[29] It was thought that appeals of felony and trial by battle had been abolished in England until the case of *Ashford* v. *Thornton*[30] early in the nineteenth century came to English lawyers as a surprise. An Act of Parliament[31] was hastily passed definitely abolishing both modes of trial.

Regarding the ordeal, Maitland wrote: '. . . if of two litigants, the one contradicts the other flatly, if the plain "you did" of the one is met by the straightforward "you lie" of the other, here is a problem which man cannot solve. He is unable yet to weigh testimony against testimony, to cross-examine witnesses, to piece together the truth out of little bits of evidence. He has recourse to the supernatural. He adjudges that one or other of the two parties is to prove his case by an appeal to God.'[32] This proved so obviously unsatisfactory that Pope Innocent III had, at the Fourth Lateran Council in 1215, to forbid the clergy from performing their hitherto traditional religious ceremonies in connexion with ordeals; and although the ordeal was thus robbed of its accustomed religious ceremony, it lingered on in many parts for a long time afterwards until its ghost was finally laid in 1819.[33]

The ordeal is, therefore, not the exclusive invention of African societies, nor is it universal among them. Some that formerly used it had ceased doing so before the British advent; a good many others had, however, retained it until abolished by British legislation. Miss Green, in spite of her account of the various modes of appeal to the supernatural among the Ibos of Umueke Agbaja, can still write thus of them: 'Of practical activity, technical knowledge and hard common-sense there is no lack among this go-ahead intelligent folk, but an apparent lack of weakness in that social structure can often be explained by the use of a supernatural device where a practical one would normally be used by a European society.'[34] Basing himself upon his East African judicial experience, Roberts emphasised: 'Even among primitive tribes where trial by ordeal is still practised, the decisions arrived at are not necessarily unfair.'[35]

It should therefore be remembered that societies employing the ordeal or the oath are not so irrational or trustful of mere supernatural sanction, even in the special case of unknown offenders to discover whom the ordeal and the oath are principally employed, that they do not seek to supplement it wherever possible with some practical organisation and technique of discovering the criminal and punishing him. Thus we notice the very interesting practice among the Kamba and several other tribes of East Africa of carrying out a *post mortem* examination of the corpse of a deceased in order to find the cause of an unknown or otherwise inexplicable death. The elders hold an inquest and attempt a careful review of the deceased's life to discover whether he had at any time been struck or injured by another, in earnest or in jest. 'In some cases,' wrote Dundas, 'the proof will be that, ever since the deceased was damaged in such and such a way, he had been known to be ailing. If there is no such proof, or the injury was of recent date or showed external symptoms, elders are summoned and the corpse is dissected. *They do this with considerable skill, and undoubtedly by long practice they are often able to detect an injury to some organ.* On the other hand, ignorance results often in the most absurd diagnosis.'[36]

If such a *post mortem* examination yields no evidence of any discoverable internal injury to an organ, the elders might put an otherwise sudden and mysterious death down to witchcraft. This, as we have seen, is often another way of saying that the deceased might have been secretly poisoned by someone with whom he had had a quarrel or even a dispute over some property or a wife. Dundas adds elsewhere[37] that, during the process of dissection by the professional surgeons of the tribe, 'although they may be deceived by the effects of a disease, they will very quickly detect any real abnormality. I do not doubt that the like is done among many other tribes.'[38]

Penwill has confirmed this *post mortem* procedure among the Kamba,[39] adding that the site of a personal injury occurring during an individual's lifetime, if considered likely to result in his death, is marked by some witnessing elder making four or six cuts on the place so as to facilitate future identification. This precaution renders easier any later inquest or dissection. The practice of marking is confined to the trunk or the head since injury to these, the delicate parts of the human body, is most likely to prove fatal. Finally, we may note that some African societies adopt other practical measures for the purpose of ascertaining hidden or otherwise unknowable truth regarding the commission of a crime. Thus Lowie records that in addition to other means such as the ordeal, 'Uganda law recognised torture for the purpose of extracting information' from an accused person.[40]

But Lowie does not describe the means or method by which such torture was carried out. Was it, for instance, similar to the English common law procedure of the *peine forte et dure* which involved the extraction of a confession (or an agreement to be tried by jury) from an accused person who would not speak in court, by patiently crushing him to death between two boards and under a growing pile of weights? It was abolished in 1772 by 12 Geo. III c. 20, which provided that such a refusal to plead amounted to the accused's conviction.[41]

A modern form of the ordeal in the United States of America is the increasing use of so-called 'truth serums' to extort confessions in criminal investigations. Drugs like sodium amytal and sodium pentothal are commonly employed in the process, and a recent Yale University report says that some people under the influence of these drugs were able to confess to 'crimes' they did not commit while others were able to cover up their guilt with ingenious lies.

Notes

[1] J. N. Matson, 'The Supreme Court and the Customary Judicial Process in the Gold Coast', I.C.L.Q., 1953, Vol. II, pp. 47–59. [see ms.]. The writer clearly admits a distinction between criminal and civil proceedings when he writes: 'Even when it (i.e. a "house matter") got to the chief, however, the attitude of the adjudicators was not, as in the case of punishable acts, that of an angry chief seeking to impose retributive and deterrent punishment on a wrongdoer . . .'

[2] This must have misled some observers into thinking that African criminal procedure has contributed little to the development of substantive or adjective law—see, e.g., Matson, *op. cit.*, p. 48.

[3] Holleman, *Shona Customary Law*, p. 17.

[4] In his article 'The Organisation and Laws of Some Bantu Tribes in East Africa', in *Jnl. Roy. Anth. Inst.* (1915), Vol. 45, pp. 234–306, at pp. 258–9; see also, Penwill, *op. cit.*, pp. 89–91, for the Kamba.

[5] But this compounding of the death penalty by compensation is permitted by the assembled elders only where a homicide was not cruel or grievous or disruptive of the social equilibrium.

[6] In defence of the whole procedure of this apparently summary punishment of major criminals, see Dr. Wagner's uncritical remark at p. 219 and Radcliffe-Brown's useful corrective in his Preface at pp. xv–xvi of *African Political Systems* (1940), where the latter shows

effectively that the *king'ole* of the Kamba and Kikuyu and the *injoget* of the Kipsigis and Nandi were always held 'by an orderly procedure directed by men in authority'.

[7] This is not to deny the undoubtedly widespread belief in the supernatural powers of witches or wizards usually embroidered upon this intricate and abstruse working of the astute practitioner's art and wiles by ordinary and unsuspecting members of the community. What they fail to fathom they naturally attribute to super-human agency. But few of the knowledgeable elders, it is suspected, really subscribe to this common view of the culprit when they decide to execute him in public.

[8] *Jnl. Roy. Anth. Inst.* (1915), Vol. 45, pp. 234–306, at p. 278.

[9] Wilson, *The Analysis of Social Change*, p. 16; see also G. Wilson, 'An African Morality', in *Africa*, Jan., 1936, p. 91.

[10] Talbot, *The Peoples of Southern Nigeria*, p. 619, wrote: 'On the whole it may be said, that, as in the Roman Empire, at any rate in the time of the Antonines, a man was regarded as innocent until he was proved guilty, with the proviso that the amount of evidence required might be considered insufficient in an European court.'

[11] See, generally, Butt-Thompson, *West African Secret Societies* (1929).

[12] Forde, *The Yoruba-speaking Peoples of South-Western Nigeria*, pp. 17–18; Talbot, *The Peoples of Southern Nigeria*, p. 756 (secret societies were bulwarks against tyrannical chiefs); Dennett, *Jnl. Roy. Afr. Soc.*, Vol. 16 (1916), pp. 16–29, particularly pp. 25–6; also Dennett, *Nigerian Studies*, pp. 41–2.

[13] Talbot, *ibid.*, p. 634: 'In Egbaland, all serious matters were judged by this association.'

[14] See *Jnl. Roy. Anth. Inst.*, Vol. XIX, pp. 160–4 (1890), an article by Mrs. R. B. Batty.

[15] See R. H. Lowie, *Primitive Society*, pp. 392, 407–8.

[16] D. J. Penwill, *Kamba Customary Law*, p. 69, says these poison ordeals are not usually fatal.

[17] D. J. Penwill, *op cit.*, p. 67. To the same effect was the evidence of G. Lindblom, *The Akamba*, p. 165; this writer also listed other forms of ordeal, e.g. of the needle, the axe and the bead.

[18] For this account see Penwill, *op. cit.*, pp. 56–68.

[19] *Witchcraft, Oracles and Magic*, pp. 33–4, 63 ff.

[20] See his 'Bantu of North Kavirondo', p. 201 of *African Political Systems*.

[21] 'The African Conception of Law', p. 240.

[22] Green, *Ibo Village Affairs*, p. 95. On the other hand, some other tribes like the Bemba of Northern Rhodesia do not believe in the swearing of oaths; rather, witnesses are solemnly cautioned by the chief at the commencement of the trial, and there is no provision for penalising perjury.

[23] Green, *op. cit.*, p. 115.

[24] *Ibid.*, p. 127.

[25] English witnesses in English courts swear on the Bible, and can ask for the particular version or portion, e.g. the New Testament, of it that they regard as binding. Roman Catholics usually swear on the Douai version. Although many people believe it is still necessary to 'kiss the Book', yet this practice was on hygienic grounds abolished some years ago. The Quakers believe that it is wrong to take any oath. Like atheists and agnostics they simply affirm solemnly and sincerely to speak the truth. The Jews swear on the Pentateuch, with their heads covered. Mohammedans swear silently on the Koran. The Buddhists swear by Buddha, asking for punishment for their migrating souls if they do not speak the truth. The Chinese Confucians swear by breaking a saucer or by blowing out a candle, saying that if they do not tell the truth may their souls be smashed like the saucer or snuffed out like the candle. In the Isle of Man, the oath is that the swearer promises to be impartial as 'indifferently as the herring's backbone doth lie in the midst of the fish.' The Hindu swears 'facing the Ganges', while the Nagas of Assam chop a fowl in two as a symbol of what will happen to them if they do not speak the truth. Other examples of oath-taking at a judicial trial could be given, but those listed must suffice. It is abundantly clear that most oaths are based on the universal idea of supernatural sanction and that history records the human reliance on one sanctified, even mystic, source of authority after another which are regarded as sacred and all-powerful.

English law, on the authority of *Omychund* v. *Barker* (1748), 2 Eq. Cases Abr. 401, and the Perjury Act 1911, recognises this and therefore permits any witness to swear by anything in which he believes. But, also, the Act does not leave anything to chance and provides up to seven years' imprisonment for breaking an oath, irrespective of any future punishment with which divine wrath may visit a perjurer.

[26] Green, *op. cit.*, pp. 113–14, 125.

[27] One recalls that the Athenians handed Socrates a cup of hemlock in the belief that his influence on Greek youths was, on the whole, pernicious. And we have Lord Russell's recent reminder in his *What is Democracy?*', at p. 32: 'Hobbes was befriended by Charles II when Parliament decided that Divine wrath at his impiety was the cause of the Plague and the Great Fire.'

[28] See also, V. C. Sarkar's article, 'Aspects of Indian Law', in the *International and Comparative Law Quarterly*, Vol. 2, Pt. 3, July, 1953, pp. 410–15.

[29] Plucknett, *A Concise History of the Common Law*, pp. 111–16; also, *English Historical Review*, Vol. 16, p. 730.
[30] (1818), 1 Barn & Ald. 405.
[31] 59 Geo. III, c. 46.
[32] Pollock and Maitland, *History of English Law*, pp. 62–3.
[33] See also Hanbury, *English Courts of Law*, pp. 36–7.
[34] *Op. Cit.* p. 131; she adds in another place, at p. 56: '. . . a particular diviner will often be tested for consultation. He may be asked, for instance, to divine the number of seeds in an unopened fruit.' With respect to the Yoruba of Southern Nigeria, Prof. Bascom recently wrote: 'A second factor, probably operative in many other systems of divination, but which is of special importance for the Yoruba Ifa, is that in spite of the numerous occasions when diviners are consulted, obvious decisions are made by the individuals themselves'.—*Jnl. Roy. Anth. Inst.* LXXI, 1941, pp. 43–54, at p. 44. Compare Lowie, *op. cit.*, p. 391: 'As Prof. Hobhouse has pointed out, archaic procedure frequently revolves not so much about the exact determination of guilt or innocence as about the prevention of internecine strife. Nevertheless, even in the ruder cultures, methods are employed to ascertain the truth of an accusation or the merit of a dispute, but usually the means used are shot through with the magico-religious notions prevalent among the people. Under this head two sets of usages demand attention, oaths and ordeals.'
[35] Roberts, *Tangled Justice*, p. 79.
[36] *Jnl. Roy. Anth. Inst.* (1915), Vol. 45, pp. 234–306, at p. 277. (Italics are mine.)
[37] *Jnl. Roy. Anth. Inst.* (1921), Vol. 51, pp. 217–78,, at p. 240.
[38] It is interesting to recall in this connexion the following excerpt from a report on the Wellcome Historical Medical Museum exhibition in London on 'The Medicine of the Aboriginal Peoples in the British Commonwealth', culled from *The Observer* of Sunday, Aug., 16, 1953, p. 3:

'If aboriginal medicine is primitive and naïve, some of its feats of surgery win the unstinted admiration of more orthodox surgeons. Its practitioners are masters at the art of trephining, one skull on view showing no fewer than eight different trephine holes "in various stages of healing". The holes were made for recurring headaches.

'Perhaps the most impressive exhibit, for the skill attending its use, is a foot-long, wood-handled, curved knife which its donor, a British doctor, has actually observed employed in the performance of a Caesarean operation. The woman in labour was made drunk on banana wine and tied to the bed. Two hours after the operation she breast-fed her baby, and was herself up and about on the eleventh day. A tribute both to native skill and native stamina.'

Dr. E. A. Underwood, the Director of the Museum, was thus commenting apparently on the Yorubas of Nigeria, concerning whose cult of Shopono, God of Smallpox, he was reported as having talked to visitors a little earlier in the report.
[39] *Kamba Customary Law*, pp. 83–5.
[40] *Op. cit.*, p. 411.
[41] Plucknett, *op. cit.*, p. 122.

(c) Judgements and Decisions

M. Gluckman: The Judicial Process among the Barotse of Northern Rhodesia*

I have summarily examined the sources of Lozi law and can now consider how judges draw on these sources to give a decision in particular disputes. The Lozi judicial process involves argument which is largely conscious and explicit, for it proceeds in public by an acknowledged logic, even if the judges are influenced by subconscious cultural and personal factors. It is to this conscious and explicit process of analytic argument (*kupihana*, *kukanana*) that the judges refer when they tell litigants: 'The kuta proceeds by asking the man and woman questions' . . . 'We follow *lisupo* (indications or probabilities)' . . . 'We decide by evidence (*bupaki*) and reasons (*libaka*)'.

Clearly in many cases, after the hearing has proceeded a while, the judges come to a decision on the law or the merits of the case, and then try to arrange their arguments to defend this decision. This tendency is patent in the Lozi judicial process because the main part of cross-examination is conducted by the judges and not by counsel for each of the litigants. Each litigant states his own case, and in doing so presents his view of

* M. Gluckman, *The Judicial Process among the Barotse of Northern Rhodesia*, Manchester University Press, 1955 pp. 270–277.

how the law justifies him, or he tries to present his actions so that they appear reasonable and legally valid. When the judges cross-examine they generally do so impartially, measuring the behaviour of all the parties against reasonable and upright standards. Therefore their questioning soon indicates the lines on which they are formulating the merits of the case, and may indeed give the false impression that they consider a man guilty till he proves that he is innocent. Often even at this stage the arguments by which they will justify their decisions are implicitly present. The absence of lawyers to represent the litigants and to prepare their cases leads to overt interweaving of three distinct stages of the judicial process: the investigatory analysis of the evidence presented, the taking of a decision on the evidence, and the exposition of the law to defend that decision.

The Lozi themselves explicitly recognize these three stages of adjudication, as enquiry (*kubuza*), decision (*katulo*), and exposition (*kubulela mulao*—to speak the law). They estimate the skill of different judges in one or more of these judicial tasks and consider that the really great judge excels in all three. He is *muatuli yabutali kasibili*—a judge who is truly wise. Lozi have words and syntactical devices to enable them to pursue lines of investigation and produce connected arguments, and a fairly elaborate vocabulary to define and evaluate processes of analysis at each stage. Admittedly none of the three stages of analysis is entirely logical, in the sense that it can be broken up into a series of connected syllogisms. Judges have to fit particular circumstances into legal propositions, and they do so by a largely intuitive process. Nevertheless there is a definite logic which controls the whole process of trial.

The logic that is present in Lozi judgments should be apparent from the judgments I have quoted. I shall here make this logic explicit, because it is unfortunately still necessary to demonstrate that Africans and other non-European peoples use processes of inductive and deductive reasoning which are in essence similar to those of the West, even if the premisses be different.[1]

The first stage of the process occurs after the parties have stated their case (*kubilaela, kubulela litaba*) and explained (*kutaluseza*) their actions. Witnesses give evidence (*kupaka*). The judges begin to sort the medley of evidence, which in different cases covers a great variety of social relations and fickleness of motivation, to arrive at the truth and to fit events into legal principles which contain value-judgments. To make this attack they question on the basis of a series of presumptions about the feelings and actions of upright men and malefactors. Using these presumptions they query the evidence: 'What (*king'i*) did you do?' . . . 'Why (*kalabakalang'i*) did you do that?' 'If (*haiba*) this were true, then (*cwelahe*) . . . and so on. It may seem unnecessary for me to indicate that the Lozi have these simple words: I have stated above why I set them out. By thus testing the evidence the judges establish what they call *lisupo*, a noun from the verb *kusupa*—'to point'—hence 'indications' or 'probabilities'. They test these by the credibility of unrelated and related witnesses who corroborate or dispute the parties' versions, and they weigh (*kulikanyisa*) the evidence by cogency. Here explicit logic is not in full control, for the presumptions which dominate the process are not always stated.

Since the cross-examination is carried out by the judges, this very process involves preliminary statements of the legal rules that will be applied. The process takes a particular form in disputes between kinsmen, because the judges have patiently to disentangle the complexities of their relations over many years before peace can be established among them. The Lozi words for reconciling, *tatulo*, and being reconciled, *tatuluhelo*, are nouns explicitly derived from the verb *kutatuluha*, which means 'to get untwisted' and 'to regain control of one's temper'. These words thus describe not only how the judges disentangle what people overtly did, but also how the judges probe into their motives and measure these against the motives of upright people. The judges begin to state norms which are legal rules, into which extrinsic circumstances have to be fitted. Indeed, it is because almost all litigants themselves work with these norms that the judges are able to push their questions and demonstrate to the litigants that they fail on their own evidence. Judges and litigants share the same presumptions about what is upright behaviour for a particular social position. This enables them to meet in argument.

The situation is simpler in cases of offences between strangers, though here too shared presumptions operate to control investigation. A simple example is the way convictions for adultery rest on the presumption that no man can have platonic relations of acquaintanceship, let alone friendship, with an unrelated woman. This presumption is so strong that 'adultery' in Lozi law almost amounts constructively to behaving familiarly with an unrelated woman. Men have been convicted for talking with others' wives. Once when I was walking from Mongu to Lialui, a man asked if he could walk with me, since there was a strange woman on the path and he feared to be accused of adultery with her. When I told this to my people, Musole said: 'If you see a woman on your path, hide and let her get ahead, then you are safe from a charge of adultery.' 'The Case of the Schoolboy Adulterer' (p. 130)* shows how if a man behaves thus, some judges induce the probability that he has also had sexual relations with her; and the case where a man sat in a hut with his sister (p. 154), like 'The Case of the Man who Helped his Mothers-in-Law Cross a Ford' (p. 148), shows that a similar presumption guides convictions for 'incest' (*sindoye*). But these presumptions are rebuttable. Some judges acquitted the Schoolboy Adulterer because 'the evidence [was] not strong'. One judge explicitly rejected the evidence of the schoolboy's reprehensible behaviour in visiting the woman because he produced a contrary presumption that a girl is taught, if she is trapped in adultery with an unknown man, to protect her lover by making false charges against another. This presumption that any familiar behaviour with a woman indicates that a man is her lover is fed by cases, of which I recorded several examples, where men solicited women on first meeting, and these agreed to adultery.

Metaphors indicate graphically how the Lozi conceive of this investigatory stage of the judicial process, in which they analyse and weigh evidence by credibility, verification, corroboration, and cogency. They have the same metaphor as we have to describe the complex process of analysing evidence to arrive at conclusions of this kind—the sifting of evidence. *Kuseseta* is to sift or winnow grain, and also to find the truth in a complicated matter. *Kuzuma*, to hunt, also describes this process. They weigh (*kulikanyisa*) particular pieces of evidence against each other. Again—as with ourselves—the process of apprehending the crux of a case is to seize, or catch, *kuswala*, which is used for arresting a person, seizing something in the hands, or catching something in a trap. *Kuteya*, to trap, itself describes the way in which judges entangle witnesses and get the truth from them (see p. 112). Cross-examination is also implicitly compared with making a journey through the windings of a river, so that *kufweka*, to land, is to press a line of questions to its conclusion. Thus when KALONGA rebuked INYUNDWANA for changing his attack in cross-examination of the parties in 'The Case of the Biassed Father', he said: '*Hausikafweka*', 'You have not landed', though I translated this as 'you have not finished'. If the conclusion is reached with crushing definiteness, as where the Violent Councillor was crushed by the question why no-one heard him shout if he did shout as he came with a whip, it is *kuwiseza taba falikamba*, 'to throw the affair down at the landing-place'. The series of questions which led to the damning conclusion are *kukalanga*, which describes the digging out of roots to make fishing-nets, and also clever investigation to find out the truth in a roundabout way.

The metaphors, which exist in English or are at least intelligible in English, denote that the Lozi have a very clear conception of logic in the examination of evidence. They are intended to demonstrate this only, and it must not be thought that the Lozi describe this logic only in these material terms. There are also specific, and therefore abstract, terms to cover the process. Some of these terms, like the metaphors, contain judgments on skill, and judgments of skill are added to others by the use of adverbs or applied forms of the verbs. *Kupaka*, to give evidence, in the form *kupakisisa* means to give strong evidence. Similarly *kubuza*, to ask or enquire, as *kubuzisisa*, is to press questions skilfully or to enquire carefully. *Kuutwa*, to hear or understand, as *kuutwisisa* is to understand very well or to be very sharp and as *kuutwahala* is to be reasonable or obvious. Another word to describe the process of enquiry is *kunuhela*, from the root *kunuha*, which means to smell and is one of the two common words for 'to divine by magical means'. *Kunuhela* means the preliminary beginnings of enquiry, when judges are seeking to penetrate the evidence, while *kunuha* also means to guess. These varied meanings of the word indicate the common Lozi assumption that the evidence of divination is more suspect than the judges' assessment of objective evidence.

The second stage of the judicial process, coming to a decision, is also metaphorically described. The Lozi, following the idea of hunting or fishing with a spear, say a good judge is one who can *nepa*, 'shoot straight' (cf. our 'hit home') by seeing the truth (*niti*)

* Page references are to Gluckman, *The Judicial Process among the Barotse of Northern Rhodesia.*

and right (*tukelo*) of an affair, as against a bad judge, who will *shuta*, 'miss the target'. The judge who hits home does so according to law and justice, and owing to the wide generality of Lozi legal principles he can usually manage to meet both demands in cases arising from multiplex relationships. In cases of contract this is not always possible (see 'The Case of the Father and his Son's Cattle', p. 109). Lozi recognize that in this process there is an element of inspiration, expressed in their comparison of the king or judge with 'a sharp knife' (*tipa yebuhali*) 'which cuts the matter' (*kukaula*). I have described judges thus coming suddenly to the crux of the matter. In 'The Case of the Biassed Father' AWAMI asked the father: 'Do you want your sons (= nephews) back?' In 'The Case of the Headman's Fishdams' the inspiration came on SOLAMI when Mahalihali, the headman, protested that he wanted the dams and would not accept the kuta's admonishments. Unfortunately I missed this part of SOLAMI's judgment, but it is possible that Mahalihali's intransigence against SOLAMI spurred him to the threat to discharge Mahalihali from the headmanship. More often, of course, the right decision on the merits of the case is obvious, and this kind of brilliant inspiration is not evoked.

Again, the Lozi have specific words to describe this process of coming to a decision. *Kusinganyeka* is to ponder over a matter in seeking to find a solution while *kuatula*, to judge, is to come to the decision. Metaphorically *kukwenuha*, to change one's course of action or turn back in a path, is to change one's opinion in the light of the evidence or previous judgments; while *kusokela* (from *kusoka*, to stir porridge) is the active process of trying to change the course of a lawsuit.

The judges thus move to the final stage of adjudication—the exposition of their verdict and the reasons for it. Here the whole judicial process is sharper and surer; litigants who interrupt are silenced: 'Be silent: your lord is judging.' The facts have been determined and the law is being stated. This is how the Lozi consider that judges work. They describe judges as carefully surveying the evidence which has been led, sifting (*kuseseta*) and weighing (*kulikanyisa*) it, and then stating how the law covers it. Obviously only certain judicial decisions take this form: and even when the actual judgment is thus presented, it may alter the order of judicial ratiocination. And even a judgment of this kind includes the application of presumptions and probabilities which evade logical determination. This is clear from SOLAMI's conviction of the Foreign Thief (p. 109). SOLAMI recited four separate suspicious circumstances—a process of argument the Lozi call *kutatamanisa*, to put matters in right succession, or *kunjonjaula*, to explain a matter point by point—which together constituted an unanswerable case. Nevertheless these remained probabilities, and he specifically said that they lacked only an eye-witness.

A second form of judgment consists in first stating the law, and then seeing how it applies to the facts. This is necessary in cases where the relevant laws are uncertain, or where there is a gap in the law, as in 'The Case of the Barren Widow' (p. 174). Judges also follow this procedure where they have to give judgments by the letter of the law, against equity. All the judgments in favour of the headman in 'The Case of the Headman's Fishdams' took this form. The dams were the headman's: *but* let him exercise his rights generously.

Most judgments, expecially in cases between kinsmen, seem to show that a judge decides on the merits of the case and then works out a legal argument to defend his decision. This procedure emerges from all the judgments against the headman in 'The Case of the Headman's Fishdams', since here the merits of the case lay against the letter of the law. The judges emphasized that the headman was in the wrong, his sisters and nephews in the right, hence the law would not support his attempt to expel them from the dams.

In whichever of these forms, or whatever combination of these forms, a judge may expound his judgment, he endeavours to cast it in the form of a reasoned logical argument. This is the technical craft of the judge. There are important syntactical devices to achieve this, including grammatical means for denoting differences of time and place, etc. There is a range of prepositions. The various derived forms of simple verbs, which are so marked a feature of Bantu, are important here. These express direction to, from, and in; action in the interest of; causation; augmentation and diminution and intensification; etc. This is not the place to summarize Lozi grammar: clearly it contributes to logical reasoning. I can perhaps make my point most simply by citing some of the appropriate conjunctions which judges have to connect their propositions:

and (*ni*); but (*kono*); as, like (*sina*); therefore (*kalabakaleyo*); because (*kakuli*); instead of (*sibakeng'i*); on account of (*nta*); while (*kanti*); whereas (*inteng'i*); if (*haiba*); then (*cwelahe*).

There are in Lozi many words to describe different modes of expounding arguments, judicial and other. Many of them imply approval or disapproval of skill. Some of the approving terms are:

kutalungusha—to be able to classify affairs;
kunyanyama—to be clever and of prompt decision;
sishongololi—a judge who relates matters lengthily and correctly;
muswanikisi—a judge who has good reasoning power and is able to ask searching question
muswanikisi—a judge who has good reasoning power and is able to ask searching questions.

Other words scorn poor reasoning:

kuyungula—to speak on matters without coming to the point;
kunjongoloka—to wander away from the subject when speaking;
kubulela siweko—to talk without understanding;
muyauluki—a judge who speaks without touching on the important points at issue;
siswasiwa—a person who gets entangled in words;
siyambutuki—a talker at random.

There are many other words of this kind, as well as common words for wisdom and stupidity, for sage and fool, and so on. The Lozi constantly use these to evaluate the skill of judges in investigating facts and in composing logical judgments. I have heard these evaluations applied to various judgments and judges: they witness that the logic of the judicial process is publicly recognized and striven for.

Note

[1] This misconception prevails for obvious social reasons, and in intellectual circles Levy-Bruhl's brilliant analysis of primitive mentality has been misinterpreted to support it. The view that African judicial and political argument is not logical was stated by Mr. R. T. Paget, K.C., M.P., in a letter to *The Observer* (8th July, 1951) in which he said of the Tswana *kgotla*: 'Thought in tribal society is governed not by logic but by fetish. To the Tribe, trial by fetish is just and trial by reason is unjust. . . . It is futile to seek a reason in tribal justice, as it is not rational.' This is contradicted by the whole of Schapera's *Handbook of Tswana Law and Custom*.

P. Bohannan: Justice and Judgement among the Tiv*

Ending (*Kure*) *the Jir*

The final step in settling a *jir* is the 'ending'. Both judges and litigants have parts to play at this stage. Briefly, the *mbatarev* suggest a settlement, and the litigants must concur if the case is to be considered thoroughly successful. The *mbatarev* confer together and reach an agreed decision. The procedure, like most Tiv social actions, is informal. Younger men do not as a rule, flatly contradict elders, but they often disagree with them. Certainly there is no special order in which the *mbatarev* speak or think they ought to speak.

The activities of the *mbatarev* in 'ending' a *jir* are generally described as 'giving' (*na*) the right (*isho*) and giving the fault (*ibo*). In every case, even though a complete compromise is reached, one party can be said to have the right on his side—to eat the *isho*—while the other eats the *ibo*. That is, he is at fault.

The two words, *ibo* (fault) and *isho* (right), are sometimes translated as 'guilt' and 'innocence', though these translations are really not very precise. Every case, if properly

* P. Bohannan, *Justice and Judgement among the Tiv*, Oxford University Press, 1957, pp. 61–68.

finished, must have one litigant in the right and the other at fault. Although men whom we should consider guilty are indeed said to 'eat the fault' in a Tiv settlement, it is not possible to reverse the translation and say that all men who 'eat the fault' are guilty of the actions with which they are charged. The nearest parallel to these words that I know in anthropological literature is a distinction made by Nuer in both a jural and a religious context, between 'right' and 'wrong' or between 'fault' and 'righteousness'.[1] Tiv also use their words in a religious context. In the simplest ceremony for repairing fetishes, the critical rite, performed in a stream, is accompanied by the words 'fault descend, righteousness arise'.

Sometimes when a litigant eats the *ibo*, he has been seriously at fault. Such an instance is:

JIR NO. 24. *Abaji* (*husband*) *calls Kpirigh* (*guardian*)
Eating the fault

Abaji called a *jir* against his wife's guardian's brother who had, as he put it, taken his wife away without reason. In the course of the hearing it emerged that Kpirigh and his brother had each been given a ward by their father. While Kpirigh was in the army during the war, his father had died and his ward had grown up. His brother therefore took her, married her off, and received bridewealth for her. When Kpirigh returned, he did not live in his native *tar*, but went to Makurdi where he had a job. However, when he got short of money, he remembered his ward and went to ask her husband Abaji for further payment on the bridewealth. Abaji refused, saying that, as he was not the man from whom he had got a wife, he intended to pay him nothing whatever. Kpirigh talked to his sister, Abaji's wife, and convinced her that he was in the right and that Abaji was trying to keep her for nothing. She consented to return with Kpirigh to their brother's compound in their native *tar*. Abaji did not come immediately to fetch his wife, so Kpirigh gave her to someone else and accepted bridewealth. Shortly afterwards Abaji came to demand his wife. When told that she had gone to another husband, he called a case before the *mbatarev*.

Kpirigh said that, since he was the woman's guardian, and since he had not received any bridewealth from her first 'marriage', it did not constitute a true marriage. The *mbatarev*, however, informed him that his brother had received bridewealth, and the marriage was thus valid; if he wanted to collect the debt from his brother, he could do so, but he could not disregard the bridewealth which Abaji had paid.

In this case Kpirigh was 'given the fault' and was also fined 5*s*. He was fined, not *because* he had eaten the fault, but because he had accepted two bridewealths. Thus Kpirigh had 'fallen on the *tindi*', on which all Tiv agree, that it is wrong to accept two bridewealths. He also 'ate the fault' in the *jir*.

However, it sometimes also happens that a man 'eats the fault' in a decision when he has not 'fallen on *tindi*' at all.

JIR NO. 25. *Husband's mother calls guardian*
Eating the fault need not imply wrong-doing

Mbatuna called a *jir* before the *mbatarev* against the guardian of the woman she had 'married' (*er*) for her son. The *mbatarev* asked the guardian where the girl was. He said that he didn't know: Mbatuna had *kem* this girl as a wife for her son, but as the son was away and had not come home for six months, the girl had run away. He added that he had sent her back twice, she had then run away a third time and now he did not know where she was.

He was 'given the fault', and was made to return the bridewealth paid to him.

Although 'given the fault', he had not 'fallen on *tindi*', because he had done nothing that was not in accordance with an injunction or *tindi*. Thus, 'guilt' of having broken a law or *tindi* is not the point in deciding which of the litigants eats the fault.

'Winning the case' or 'losing the case' does not translate 'to eat the right' and 'to eat the fault'. Although the man whom we would consider the winner of the case does, in fact, usually eat the right, this translation cannot be reversed, for the man who eats the right need not always be, because of that fact, the man whom we would consider to have won the case. The Tiv phrase 'the *jir* seized him' means approximately 'he lost the case' I do not know another phrase which might mean 'he won the case' in our sense.

Tiv say that some *mbatarev* are corrupt, and that in some Native Authority Grade-D courts it is possible 'to buy a *jir*' (*yam jir*). They add that there are some courts indeed which do not 'hear' (*ungwa*) *jir* at all, and that if you want a *jir* settled there the only way to have it done is to buy it. However, it is also said to be much more difficult than in the past for an *ortaregh* to be corrupt. One man explained to me that in order to bribe a Native Authority court today, it was necessary to bribe the *mbatarev* separately, as almost surely there was rivalry enough among them to make them unwilling to accept bribes in one another's presence. At least so far as MbaDuku was concerned, this observation seemed correct. Besides the *mbatarev*, Tiv continue, it is also necessary today to bribe the scribe and the policeman and messengers. All in all, it becomes a very expensive business. It is my opinion that most cases, in MbaDuku at least, were heard on their merits, and that bribery and corruption were at a minimum. Tiv have told me of one court in which rates for 'buying the *jir*' were discussed and haggled over in open session, but they declared this to be the exception.

Although I cannot, obviously, document this sort of thing, I believe that corruption in Grade-D courts is much less common than Tiv think. It is even less common than their European administrators think. This does not imply that Tiv are more honest than other peoples, but merely that their social organization and the organization of their courts are such that bribery becomes difficult because one must bribe so many people: as one of my friends put it, 'Whenever you try to buy a *jir* you find that it includes your opponents' kinsmen who cannot accept any offer, no matter how high.'

The task of the *mbatarev* in 'ending' a *jir* is not to make a decision, but to make suggestions for settlement. In a properly run *jir* the principal litigants must also play their parts: they must both concur (*lumun*) in the judgement.

Tiv litigants would seem to believe that the proper and correct solution of a dispute 'exists'. It 'is'. The task of the judges is to find it. In the old days the principal litigants would go from one elder of the community to another until they discovered one who could penetrate the details of the case and emerge with this 'correct' solution. To a lesser extent, they still do so today. It is obvious to Tiv that when a right decision has been reached, both litigants will concur in it, even though the particular judgment may not be wholly in favour of either.

The importance of such concurrence by the litigants cannot be over-emphasized. It is to misunderstand the Tiv view to say that Tiv courts have or have not the 'authority' to 'enforce' a 'decision'. 'Authority', 'enforcement', and 'decision' are all Western legal concepts which spring from our notions and ideas of authority hierarchies. They are part of the Western folk system concerning our jural and governmental institutions. If Tiv judges make a settlement in which both parties can concur, there is no problem of 'enforcing a decision'. If they do not, they have not, by Tiv definition, 'ended the *jir*' satisfactorily. The correct solution is known to have been found when all the judges and the litigants concur.

Tiv *jir*, then, discover a solution to a dispute which is in accordance with the *inja* of the Tiv, and in which all the persons concerned in the *jir* concur. This is comparable to, but vastly different from, the fact that Western courts make a decision in accordance with the facts of the case and with the 'law', and have the authority to enforce that decision. It is very difficult to discuss the acts and values of either system in the words and concepts and language of the other.

Concurrence of the litigants never occurs without concurrence of the entire community: no one is ready to make concessions while any portion of public opinion still supports him. It is the opinion of the community which forces concurrence. Judging, like all other activities of Tiv leaders, consists largely in the timely suggestion of what the majority thinks is right or desirable.

The 'correct solution' changes as the situation of both litigants changes. Tiv, therefore, tend to deplore 'final decisions', which their European administrators, of course, prefer. Tiv feel that making a final decision, in the English sense, often perpetuates conditions which will eventually become unjust. It sometimes appears to foreigners that Tiv do not want their courts to make decisions at all, but it seems more accurate to say that they want the judges to point out a *modus vivendi*, which will endure while the situation endures.

For Tiv judges to settle a *jir* by any standards other than the concurrence of the litigants, and eventually of the community, is to settle it 'by force' (*sa apela*). This literal translation might be more meaningfully rendered 'settled by despotic action'. If a Tiv Native Authority court uses its government-backed authority to enforce a decision in which the litigants do not concur, and in which community opinion does not insist that they concur, that court is said to have 'heard the *jir* by force'. This is the worst thing that can be said of any *jir*. It is much worse, in the Tiv view, than the acceptance of bribes. Bribery is at least not capricious.

Even though judges might be able to defend their decisions on the basis of Tiv custom, unless the litigants, pressed by the community, concur, a settlement is described as one made 'by force'. The way in which community opinion brings concurrence is interesting:

JIR NO. 26. *Combo, wife of Yaji, calls Zege*
Concurrence in a decision

Combo called a *jir* because Zege beat her. She said that she went to her farm and caught Zege stealing cassava from it. When she questioned his right to be on her farm, let alone take cassava from it, he told her it was his land and therefore his cassava, beat her, and tore her blouse.

The *mbatarev* turned to Zege, who listened meekly to a long lecture on deportment. 'Zege,' Chenge said, 'you are a woman's child (*wan kwase*). This is not your place (*ian*).' One of the others took it up, 'Why have you come to make trouble among your mother's lineage? Your *igba* have allowed you to hoe farms here. If these farms are disputed, it is your *igba* who should take up the dispute—not you.' Another added, 'And to steal things from your *igba* is indeed very heinous. They are your kinsmen (*angbianev*) and have given you land to hoe, and a place to build a homestead, and you have stolen from them!' Chenge now asked, 'Zege, who was it who gave you place?'—that is, a place to farm and build. Zege replied quietly that it was Agber.

'Agber, come!' Chenge shouted. Agber was in the crowd—as everyone knew. Agber came to the centre of the *jir* circle. 'Agber,' Chenge asked, 'did you show Zege place?' Agber admitted that he had done so. 'Agber,' he continued, 'why have you let him fight and beat the wives of our *ityô*, our lineage?' Agber said nothing. 'You have dared (*chihi*) much,' Chenge said. 'And you must pay £2 fine for harbouring a thief, and for showing him a house site and for giving him farms. You have given him a place amongst us where he can sit and from which he can steal things from people!' Agber paid unprotestingly.

Chenge turned back to Zege, who admitted to ripping the blouse but not to stealing cassava, and told him to pay a shilling for repair of the cloth. Zege paid. Chenge added, 'Besides this, Zege, you must bring ten shillings as fine for fighting in the fields.' Again Zege paid the fine without a murmur.

The purpose of these moral lectures is not so much admonition as repetition of values held by the entire community. The statements may be 'laws', seen from one point of view. But the more important point is that they are truisms, and the litigant cannot deny them. He must concur that they are right because the community considers them irrefutable. He must eventually concur in the judgment they represent.

In this case, Agber knew that he was responsible for the wrongs committed by his sister's son so long as that sister's son was living with him. Zege knew that his rights in this community were tenuous. Both paid their fines because they knew they were wrong, but, more importantly, because they knew that their relationships with their neighbours would continue to be strained until they made some sort of move to admit that they were wrong.

The fines paid in this case were aligned with the idea of *tia*, which is usually translated inaccurately as 'fine'. *Tia* is an animal which Tiv bring to the judges or arbitrators of their cases in order that the animal may be butchered when the case is settled. In the traditional system, the *tia* is provided by the man who calls the case, not the man who loses it. The meat is shared by the entire community, in recognition of the fact that one has had one's affairs and relationships renovated and harmony now reigns.

When a man brings his wife back to her natal *tar* so that her elders may perform a ceremony on her behalf, they require that he kill them a *tia*: the animal is butchered and amounts both to payment for services and, at the same time, indication of a 'repaired' relationship. Similarly, when a man summons the elders of his lineage to a moot, he must sometimes provide them with a *tia*. When he does so, it pays them for coming and means also that the members of the lineage rejoice because another difficulty has been resolved. The elders will usually set the value of the *tia* to be provided, in accordance with their notion of the importance of the occasion and the service.

Tiv have, without signal success, tried to bring fines into line with their ideas of *tia*. A fine, as we think of it, is called 'the words of the *jir*' (*zwajirigh*), and was, I believe, introduced with the Native Authority courts. Tiv, however, saw similarities between the fine and their custom of *tia*. Insofar as a fine imposed by a court is seen as a payment for services and as the symbol of turning over a new leaf, it is called a *tia*. The same fine, seen as money payment which goes into the coffers of the Native Authority instead of being dispersed directly back into the community, is called 'the words of the *jir*'.

Another technique which the judges sometimes use to make the litigants concur is the threat to send the dispute to a higher court—that is, to the Grade-C court at Vande Ikya. Judges as well as litigants can send disputes to appeal.

Both fines and the judges' refusal to finish a *jir* are seen as penalties (*mtsaha*) inflicted by the *mbatarev*. They can also inflict another penalty: they can imprison wrongdoers for periods up to three months. It should be emphasized that, even here, the idea of authority to fine and imprison is not a Tiv way of seeing it. The man who is being fined must still 'concur' in that fine if the decision is not to be considered arbitrary. Before a man serves a prison sentence, he most often agrees that it is just punishment. If he does not concur, the *mbatarev* will either reconsider the sentence or appeal to the audience. Public opinion makes a man concur in a punishment. In moots, but never in courts, I have seen a group of agreed elders threaten to withdraw their protection from witchcraft in order to force a man to concur in a decision which was favoured by all save himself.

Tiv attitude to prison as a punishment is fundamentally different from our own. There is no disgrace involved in a prison sentence. They are cheerful prisoners and, according to their District Officers, are usually well-behaved prisoners. One official told me that if they did misbehave in prison it was very difficult to punish them further. He had, however, hit on the idea of making them do women's work—especially flour grinding—as the only infallible corrective. . . .

Tiv notions of concurrence are indeed comparable to European notions of enforcing judgment, especially in the light of penalties inflicted. They bring about roughly the same ends. But they must not be confused with them. To say that public opinion is the enforcing agent is to misunderstand the Tiv viewpoint, though it is, from our point of view, true.

Note

[1] E. E. Evans-Pritchard, *Nuer Religion*, 1956, pp. 172 ff. P. P. Howell, *A Manual of Nuer Law*, 1954, pp. 22 ff.

(d) Execution of Decisions and Sanctions

T. O. Elias: The Nature of African Customary Law*

Execution of Judgment

If after the declaration of the award by the judges the guilty party complies with the terms of the judgment, there is of course no more to be done in the matter. But if he defies the verdict and refuses to pay the fine or compensation, or to make restitution as decreed, then the issue of enforcing his compliance arises. In centralised societies with institutionalised military and administrative machinery, law enforcement by appointed officials is the rule. The chief, with the weight of authority that comes from the consensus of his councillors and of the public, can usually ensure that the guilty one does not bilk his obligation to his injured opponent or flout the concerted will of the community as

* T. O. Elias, *The Nature of African Customary Law*, Manchester University Press, 1956, pp. 263–267.

expressed in the judgment. But the usual complaint that there is no organised and regular system of police is truer when applied to chiefless societies. When one comes to examine the facts closely, however, one does not find that the execution of the judgment of the council of elders presents the spectacle of ineffectiveness that is often painted by some writers.

We have seen in the procedure of the 'mwinge' and of the 'king'ole' among the Kikuyu and the Kamba respectively how the adjudicating elders invariably arm themselves with a *posse* of youthful warriors equipped with all necessary implements for putting a condemned murderer to death. Regarding the Ibos of Southern Nigeria, Miss Green has described how offenders against the codes of conduct enjoined upon members of certain associations, or even against what have been publicly decreed as binding rules at meetings in market-places, are brought to book through the machinery of a band of local 'police', deputed for the task by the elders of the community; and here, again, an *ad hoc* brigade of stalwart lads is normally pressed into the service. Even women are known to have taken a hand against some of their own sex in enforcing the payment of fines, or otherwise securing a compliance with accepted social norms. Ordinary cases between two or more women are usually heard by women judges, especially where breaches of market or club regulations are in question. In any event, women generally act as the watch-dogs of their community against antisocial behaviour.[1] The writer has also discovered[2] that the dual division of the Agbaja village, in addition to promoting the quick performance of communal work, serves to supply a kind of police system for the enforcement of laws and regulations as between the two exogamous halves of the village. Each half acts as a watchman against the conduct of the other in a spirit of mutual, inter-group rivalry. The personal possessions of an offender are seized by the picked men of either side, if a fine duly imposed is not promptly paid.[3] These arrangements are rendered possible in a society in which the ties of kinship are so heavily underlined by the bonds of common locality.

The Fanti of the Gold Coast, like the Yoruba of Nigeria, have a system of self-help whereby the creditor has the right personally to beset the house of his debtor or to employ others to do so on his behalf, and to follow the latter about in and out of season and generally to make such a nuisance of the whole thing as to impel the debtor to pay up and be rid of his creditor's persistence and importunity.[4] Until a final settlement is made, the debtor is under a legal liability to feed and accomodate his unwanted guest, who enjoys an unlimited licence to interrupt his conversations with third parties, to obstruct his work or movement as and when he likes, and to plague him in every way. All this might be dispensed with if, on arrival at the unfortunate debtor's house, the creditor descries anything of value he can seize either in partial or in total satisfaction of the debt. If only a proportional abatement is thereby secured, the creditor is entitled to distrain on any other article of property or to resort to the tactics already described, in an effort to obtain satisfaction for the balance.[5]

Various other modes of indigenous law enforcement exist in other African societies, depending upon the kind of arrangement made locally for affecting compliance with the judgments of the chief in council or of the council of elders. Some are naturally more elegant than others, but the African judicial process everywhere attempts to offset the disadvantage of a delicate mechanism of enforcement by supplementing its functioning by a reliance on the general law-abidingness of those whose ideal of justice it represents. Dr. Allen recently observed concerning English law that 'the most admirable laws are nugatory without the means of implementing them, and that the best means of enforcement is to forestall the very necessity of enforcement.'[6] This, if we may say so, is no less true of African customary law. So germane to this aspect of the judicial process are the learned author's observations,[7] that the present writer must be forgiven for quoting him here at length:

'For the greater part of our history we have attempted to make the community responsible, by various means, for policing itself. There have been from the earliest times certain accredited peace officers, of whom the most important were, anciently, the shire reeve, the bailiff, the town reeve, and the petty constable. But for the general maintenance of order and the pursuit of malefactors the traditional method was the very ancient and primitive one of constituting each man his brother's keeper, in the sense that another and more powerful individual, or else a group of his neighbours, was answerable for every person's good behaviour. . . . The most common example was that of the magnate who was held responsible for those within his *mund*. In the Middle Ages this liability seems to have shrunk to the circle of the lord's household, the members of which were in his *mainpast*—the domestic dependants fed and maintained by him.'

The group-pledge, which imposed liability on kindred members for an erring brother, also gave them the right to take vengeance or accept composition (*wergild*) for the shedding of his blood. This system soon developed into the territorial units of the *borh*, the *tithing* (= a tenth of a hundred), and the *hundred*—all designed to ensure the good order of their members by the concerted action of all. The Frankpledge was the culmination of these earlier institutions of social insurance and legal suretyship for the law-abidingness of its members. Again, the hue and cry imposed another type of group liability in county and hundred by requiring all to follow the trail of a felon, especially a cattle-thief, until he was apprehended, on pain of the pursuers bringing upon themselves heavy penalties if the felon were allowed to escape. Then, there were the watch and ward, the approver, and the common informer, 'who has incurred the odium of the tell-tale with less risk and more profit than the approver' until the Common Informer's Act, 1951 substituted for his customary financial rewards prosecution by summary procedure or on indictment and a fine not exceeding £100 for any of the offences forbidden by law. It was not until 1829, by the Metropolitan Police Act of that year, that the modern system of regular police was established in England. Allen concludes:[8] 'Our constables are still "kin-police", men and women with more disciplinary duties but few greater powers than any of their fellow-citizens; they are legitimate descendants of the old pledges and watchmen and constables of the people—but with one vast difference. It took us a thousand years to discover that the effective guardianship of the peace is a "whole-time job" for highly qualified and disciplined officers. . . .' They are not what Reith[9] has called 'ruler-appointed police' who are agents of terror in modern totalitarian countries, nor have they the power of certain of their Continental counterparts who can impose 'on-the-spot' police fines for minor, e.g. traffic, offences.

Apart from the modern British development of the system of a regular police force, therefore, the arrangements in most African societies to 'forestall the very necessity of enforcement' of the law were roughly equivalent to these ones formerly employed by English law. Great store is set on the prevention of breaches of the law; and the clan head, the lineage or family head, the institution of the age-grade and other associations —all these are saddled with the responsibility for the good behaviour and general law-abidingness of their members. Fear of ridicule, opprobrium or social and economic ostracism act as powerful deterrents to crime and, where the society is still culturally homogeneous, these mechanisms of the vicarious liability of the lineage or household head and of personal abhorrence of crime by the individual himself serve in a large measure to preserve the equilibrium of society. But as the community grows unwieldy through internal fecundity or external admixture so that it loses its homogeneity, the old sanctions tend to become inadequate to the new needs of maintaining law and order. It is at that stage that the more developed African societies have been hard put to it to evolve new ways and means of ensuring law-abidingness and social stability. Hence it is that we find in centrally organised societies with a definite hierarchy of political authorities, judicial institutions and administrative machinery, the emergence of a *militia* which can be used for purposes both of external aggression or civil defence and of internal security, including law enforcement. But we have also seen that even in uncentralised African societies variants of this *militia* exist for more or less the same purpose: reference has already been made to the 'king'ole' and 'mwinge' of the Akamba and of the Akikuyu, and a similar organised use of sections of the community for the welfare of the whole has been noted in the Ibo employment of a *posse* of sturdy lads or of a bevy of young women in the execution of judgments and the enforcement of regulations; even the two halves of an exogamous community serve, as we have shown, the purposes of a village police force.

Notes

[1] Green, *op. cit.*, pp. 101, 111–12, 143, 226–30. See, also, Penwill, *op. cit.*, p. 64, where neighbours, especially women, are said to have descended upon a defaulter's house for failure to pay up the customary goat after the elder's decision had been announced.

[2] *Ibid.*, pp. 142–3.
[3] Cf. Dundas, *op. cit.*, *Jnl. Roy. Anth. Inst.* (1915), pp. 292–3: 'It seems that a creditor is entitled to take anything from his debtor, but not until his claim has been awarded by the elders. In Ukamba it has been asserted that wives and children may be taken in this way, but this was denied again by a large assembly of elders.'
[4] For the identical Yoruba practice see Talbot, *The Peoples of Southern Nigeria*, Vol. III, pp. 632–3, 698.
[5] Sarbah, *Fanti Customary Laws*, pp. 86, 94–5; Ajisafe, *The Laws and Customs of the Yoruba People*, pp. 70–2.
[6] C. K. Allen, *The Queen's Peace*, p. 125.
[7] *Ibid.*, pp. 69 ff.
[8] C. K. Allen, *The Queen's Peace*, p. 118.
[9] C. Reith, *The Blind Eye of History*, Pt. III. Of the nine principles of police action which the writer lists as inherent in the discipline originally enjoined by the first Commissioners, Rowan and Mayne, the seventh runs:
'To maintain at all times a relationship with the public that gives reality to the historical tradition that the police are the public and that the public are the police; the police being only members of the public who are paid to give full-time attention to duties which are incumbent on every citizen, in the interests of community welfare and existence.'

R. S. Rattray: Ashanti Law and Constitution*

The Sanctions in Ashanti Law

If I were asked to name the strongest of the sanctions operating in Ashanti to enforce the observance of the 'traditional rule of the community', I think I would place the power of ridicule at the head of these forces of law and order. Indeed, as will have been observed by an examination of the substantive law which has now been reviewed in these pages, the power of the sharp-edged weapon of derision seemed often the only sanction behind the law. Even where we find the supernatural or corporal sanctions in the form of punishments inflicted by the gods or by man, for breaches of tribal regulations, it appears probable that fear of ridicule was also ever present, and it is doubtful if even the worst of humanly inflicted punishments was more dreaded than this subtle weapon which came in laughing guise to rob a man of his own self-respect and the respect of his associates. In the social world in which the Ashanti lived, there was not any escape for one who had incurred this penalty. What among ourselves, therefore, would be, at most, an unpleasant state of affairs, from which we might be glad to escape elsewhere for a time, became a punishment to an Ashanti from which there was not any escape, and one he could not face.

The best and, at the same time, the saddest example that I know to substantiate the above statement is given below. I have, of course, suppressed the exact place, time, and names, and few if any Europeans, save only those to whom I have related the incident, ever heard of an event which was known and discussed all over Ashanti within a short time of its occurrence. The story is briefly as follows:

During the visit of a person of considerable importance, who was much beloved by the loyal and generous-hearted Ashanti, the Chief and Elders of a remote province, in common with many others, had come to do him honour. When it came to the turn of a certain old man to be presented, in bending forward to do obeisance, he, unnoticed by all but his immediate followers, inadvertently broke wind. Within an hour of the termination of the ceremony he had gone and hanged himself. He had 'disgraced' himself and his following. The universal comment in Ashanti among his fellow countrymen was that he had done the only right thing under the circumstances. He could never have lived down the ridicule which he might otherwise have incurred. *Fadie ene ewuo a, fanyinam ewuo* ('If it be a choice between disgrace and death, then death is preferable'). It was, in fact, this occasion which first made me familiar with a proverb which I later found to be universally known in Ashanti.[1]

Many other examples of the sanction of ridicule have been given in these pages and it is unnecessary, therefore, to enlarge further upon the subject.

The next class of sanction that did much to relieve the public authority of the necessity for decreeing penalties which it might often—at an early date, at any rate—have experi-

* R. S. Rattray, *Ashanti Law and Constitution*, Oxford University Press, 1929, pp. 372–378.

enced some difficulty in enforcing, may be grouped under the heading of religious or supernatural sanctions. It has been customary, I believe, for some anthropologists to make a subdivision in this category, the distinction being drawn between sanctions where the violation of some customary law was thought to be visited with punishment by the supernatural power immediately concerned, and sanctions where 'there was no hint of any interference on the part of any supernatural being'.

As an example of the latter have been given those food or 'alimentary' taboos so commonly found all over the world among so-called 'primitive' peoples. I am unable, however, to accept this sub-classification, for I believe that where there may appear a necessity for it, the cause will, I think, invariably lie in the scantiness or inaccuracy of the evidence at our disposal, which may seem to necessitate such a subdivision. The very example which is quoted as being representative of such an 'automatic' sanction, once the full facts are known, e.g. the *akyiwadie* (the food taboos) in Ashanti,[2] is immediately explained on a perfectly logical, supernatural basis. So, I think, it would be found in other cases, were the evidence at our disposal accurate and full.

In Ashanti all supernatural sanctions fall under one or other of the following headings. Examples of nearly all these will be found in these volumes.[3]

(*a*) The sanction wielded by the '*Samanfo* (human ancestral spirits).

(*b*) The sanction of *Nyankonpon* (the Supreme Being), more especially in that wielded by His subordinates, the *abosom* or lesser manifestations of His Spirit.

(*c*) The power wielded by *suman* (fetishes).

(*d*) The sanction of Asase Ya, the Earth goddess.

(*e*) The sanction of the male transmitted Totemic Spirit (the *Ntoro*[4]).

(*f*) The sanction of the *sasa* (spirit) of men, animals, plants, and trees.

(*g*) The sanction of *abayifo* (witches), *mmoatia* (fairies), *sasabonsam* (forest monsters), and black magic in general.

The real power in all these sanctions lay in the fact that they were supposed to be operative not only against the individual, but, if occasion demanded it, collectively. A 'sinner' might not 'sin' and his blood relations or kindred hope to stand serenely aloof from the results of that action. All became indirectly involved, and to this fact we owe, I believe, the advent of the final and later-day sanctions in the form of corporal punishment meted out to certain offenders.

The kindred and—with the rise of territorial Chiefs and territorial Jurisdiction—the community as a body were thought possibly to suffer for the ritualistic offence of its individual members. It was—I hazard the opinion—to such a belief that we can trace the creation of that important category of offences which have been dealt with in this volume under the heading of 'Tribal Taboos' (*Oman Akyiwadie*), the punishment for the violation of which was death, inflicted not by the supernatural agency that had been outraged, but by man. At first, I believe, the death penalty was the only corporal sanction which the higher central authority inflicted. This form of punishment later became modified by the march of economic events. Instead of being executed a man might 'buy his head', or he might be enslaved or banished, or suffer some minor mutilation. The sanctions at the disposal of the highest authority also included some that are beyond the bounds of our civilized secular community to enforce. They included not only reprisals upon the living, but the punishment of the dead. The defunct criminal in Ashanti was never quite beyond the arm of the law. He might, as we have seen, be decapitated, or he might be denied the essential funeral obsequies, including burial.

I shall close this brief chapter—brief because the subject with which it deals has already been set forth in the pages which comprise this and its kindred volumes—with a list of the common corporal sanctions which were once in the power of the central authority to inflict.

Capital punishment. Perhaps the commonest form of capital punishment was for the victim to have his or her head cut off with a small knife. Many of the old executioners' knives which I have seen appear to have been bread or carving knives imported from Europe. The executioner or executioners, for he generally had his young assistants, having seized his man, either proceeded to decapitate him by cutting from the front of the neck, and working back, or 'if he did not wish to look upon his victim's face, he would hold the head down and slice or saw[5] through the neck, commencing at the back'.

A *sepow* knife would almost invariably have first been thrust through the cheeks in order to prevent the criminal from 'blessing the Chief'.[6] This form of decapitation might follow the preliminaries described in a previous volume and known as *Atopere*.[7] Only the *Asante Hene* (King of Ashanti) and the great paramount Chiefs had power to inflict capital punishment. A *Birempon* of a Head-Chief or a *Safohene* (Elder or war captain) who did so, even in the case of a slave, without the permission of his Head-Chief would have been guilty of murder and liable, at least, to destoolment or a very heavy fine. The King and Paramount Chiefs of Divisions alone 'held the knife' (*Ono owo sekan*). A *Birempon* of a Divisional Head-Chief might, it is true, have had his own *abrafo* (executioners), but they could not ply their trade without the permission of the Head-Chief. This right of a Paramount Divisional Chief to inflict capital punishment extended also only to his own subjects, and not even to all of these, for, without the permission of the *Asante Hene*, a Divisional Head-Chief might not execute his own *Safohene*, *Birempon*, princes, or *Adehye* (blood members of the royal family). Certain other persons were, as we have seen also entirely exempt from capital punishment. Decapitation was not the only way in which a person might be killed. The death sentence might also have been carried out by the following methods:

(*a*) *Strangling* (*Abomporo*). *Ahenkwa* (young 'palace' attendants), heralds; *Safohene* (war captains); *Adehye* (kindred of the ruling house); wives of a Chief, killed or volunteering to die on the death of their master, were generally executed in this fashion. The idea was to avoid distasteful mutilation or the shedding of blood.

The strangling was sometimes performed with a leather thong or done by the hands of the executioners (*bu no kon*).

(*b*) *Clubbing* (*Abaporowa*). This method of dispatch was also used for young 'palace' attendants; a pestle was sometimes the form of club employed, or the tusk of an elephant (where the victim was of royal blood).

Witches were also sometimes clubbed instead of being burned, strangled, or drowned. The last-named form of punishment was known euphemistically as 'crossing the river' (*asu twa*).

Mutilation. Mutilation sometimes took the place of capital punishment.

(a) *Cutting off the ear or a piece of the ear* (*Aso twa*): A person thus mutilated was called *Asosine*, and in addition to this punishment he would probably have become a *gyase* subject.

The right ear was generally operated upon 'because, otherwise, the person, being ashamed of his deformity, would bunch up the cloth which lay on his left shoulder and cover his severed ear'.

'An uncle might, with the permission of the King of Ashanti, cut a notch in the ear of a troublesome nephew.' This punishment was sometimes inflicted for impertinence (*poa*). 'One, Kwame Agyetiwa, once struck a soul-washer of Chief Kwesi Seckyere and was ordered to pay a sheep. He replied that he would give something better than that—a cow—well knowing that the cow was an animal "hateful" to the *Bosommuru ntoro* to which Kwesi Sekyere belonged. He had both ears cut off.'

'A *Birempon* in olden days was permitted to inflict this punishment on his own subjects, but an ordinary *Safohene* (Elder) might not do so without special authority.'

(*d*) *Cutting off the lips* (*Twa aso*): The person so mutilated was known as *Anosini*. This was often the punishment for tale-bearing and abuse when such cases had been transferred from the *efie* (the household) to the Chief's court, or when the Chief was himself the subject of the offence and the guilty party had escaped more condign punishment by having fled and thrown himself upon the mercy of the Chief's ancestral spirits in the *Barim* (mausoleum). 'Only a Head-Chief had authority to inflict this kind of punishment. Neither a *Birempon*[8] nor a *Safohene* might do so without special authority.'

(*c*) *Cutting off the nose* (*Twa efwe*): This form of mutilation was apparently resorted to in the case of conceited, disrespectful, swaggering persons, who, having a well-known reputation for such overbearing conduct, had committed some offence which had brought them before the Chief. Making this offence the excuse, the Chief might order the man's nose to be cut off. 'There were also cases known in olden times of bad Chiefs who, coveting the mistress (*mpena*) of another man, upon the first opportunity cut off that man's nose so that she would no longer desire him.'

Castration (*Yi adabra*):[9] Apparently certain offences were punished with castration. This was probably resorted to to obtain recruits for the posts of eunuchs in the various royal harems. A concrete case was given, which is as follows: 'Two young boys were playing together when one "abused" the other by saying, *Owonta!* (begetter of twins). The boy who was called this retaliated by "swearing the great oath" that he had never yet even had sexual intercourse with any woman. The case eventually was taken before the King of Ashanti, who commanded that the youth who had used the abusive word should be castrated.'

Again, young attendants in the *mman*' (harem), on entering the women's apartments, had always to shout *So ho! so ho!* for if they ever chanced upon any of the Chief's wives naked and were reported as having done so, they would be castrated. The head eunuch always examined the young uncastrated boys from time to time for any signs of pubic hair.

Flogging (*Aboro*): A possible punishment for 'saying anything bad' against the Chief. 'A Chief who was always ordering his subjects to be flogged would, however, soon be destooled.'

Imprisonment (*Apabo*): *Apabo* means literally 'putting in fetters'.[10] This form of punishment should not perhaps be included among sanctions, as it was unknown as a form of sanction in its literal sense or as the alternative to fine or other punishment. Persons were, however, restrained in this manner pending trial or after trial while awaiting the carrying out of the sentence. In fact there are cases known where persons were 'imprisoned' thus for years.

'In the reign of Kwaku Dua I, a young boy was fastened to a log and kept there until he grew up and had a beard.' An *Asofohene* had not permission, without the authority of his Chief, to keep any one 'in log' for any length of time.

Slavery: Offenders were often punished by being sold as slaves, or by being made the slaves of the Chief. The men generally entered one or other of the various *gyase* companies (*fekuo*), often the *akyeremadefo* (drummers) section, while women became *kokwafo* (floor-polishers).[11] 'Even at the present day, when a man cannot pay the fine imposed upon him in the Chief's court, he will say, *Me soa atwene* ('I shall carry the drums').

Fines: As has already been noted, a man sentenced to death might, in the old days, sometimes save his life 'by buying his head'. Fines in the European sense as alternatives to other punishments, with this exception, were not, I think, often inflicted.

Notes

[1] To break wind (*ata*) in public was, in Ashanti, considered a disgraceful act. Their traditions record several cases not unlike the above-mentioned more modern example. One of such was the occasion on which a priestess of a Tano god from B. was dancing. She came forward during the dance to kneel before Chief K. D. of M., and in doing so broke wind. She was seized; her head was shaved; drums were beaten over her head to drive away the spirit of her god; she was driven out of the priesthood, and made to give sheep to purify the temple of the god and the 'palace' of the Chief. Again, if a number of Ashanti happened to be eating together, and one broke wind, 'the bowl of food would be placed upon that person's head that he might be used as a table'; but, added my informant, 'if the man were among friends and was well liked, the rest of the party might cover their mouths with their hands and go outside that he might not see their laughter, because they might fear that the man who had offended would go away and hang himself, should he notice that the others were laughing at him'.

[2] See *Ashanti*, Chapter II.

[3] *Ashanti: Religion and Art in Ashanti*, and the present work.

[4] See especially *Ashanti*, Chapter II.

[5] I use this word purposely, as executioners' knives were not kept very sharp.

[6] See *Religion and Art in Ashanti*, Figs. 41–2.

[7] See *ibid.*, Chapter IX.

[8] That is, a *Birempon* of an *Omanhene*, not the *Birempon* of the *Asante Hene*, who was, as we have seen, himself an *Omanhene*.

[9] To castrate an animal is *sa* (to cut). The word *adabra* is stated to be of Dagomba origin. See also *Religion and Art in Ashanti*, p. 119 n.

[10] A specimen of an Ashanti fetter may be seen on the *kuduo* in Fig. 129 in *Ashanti*.

[11] Floors are polished every morning with semi-liquid red clay.

G. S. Snell: Nandi Customary Law*

Sanctions and Remedies

Social conformity was ensured by positive sanctions (the desire to stand well in public opinion, for instance) and by negative ones (such as the fear of public condemnation, the denial of the help of neighbours in time of need, and the hostility of ancestral spirits). Torts and 'criminal' offences were in general regarded as disturbances of the social equilibrium and treatment was therefore concerned fundamentally with restoring the *status quo ante*.

The principles employed may thus be summarised in the following order:

(1) reconciliation;
(2) restitution;
(3) compensation to the individual or his family;
(4) compensation or fine to the community;
(5) if an offender were too poor to pay compensation, corporal punishment;
(6) social ostracism and public ridicule;
(7) protection of the community from the hostility of ancestral spirits (through the kokwet elders' repudiation in the curse);
(8) protection of the community from direct physical harm (through expulsion or execution);
(9) formal reconciliation of the offender to the community wherever possible.

The tribal curse (*Chubisiet*)

Contempt for, or serious disobedience of, orgoiyot and kokwet elders was virtually treason and involved their curse, which unless formally removed was fatal; it affected not only the offender but spread to his family and descendants.

Curses could also be legitimately uttered by an individual as such, against a person who had committed an offence against him; they were usually inflicted by persons senior to the offender, but in cases of serious wrong—for example, the deliberate killing of a man's animal—a curse could be uttered by a person of a junior age-grade and of the opposite sex.

It was not necessary for the efficacy of the curse for the offender to be known to the utterer; indeed resort was had to this expedient for offences such as theft and damage to property, when the normal means of redress was not possible on account of the offender's identity being unknown. The guilty person would ail and would normally confess his crime by making signs symbolic of the wrongful act; if, for instance, he had stolen an animal snared by another man he would grasp his neck; if he had stolen honey he would make movements suggestive of waving away the bees to enable him to eat it. Curses were inflicted verbally with no particular ceremony; a general curse, say for disrespect to a senior, would take the form 'barin ilet' ('May the lightning kill you'); a curse for a specific offence such as theft or killing a man's animal would be: 'May the animal consume you' (i.e. 'May what you have done to my animal rebound to your own detriment'). A number of others are quoted by Hollis.[1]

The curse was altogether a most effective sanction, and often merely the threat of it sufficed to inhibit a crime or to extract a confession of guilt.

A curse could be removed after confession by the offender (or, if he had died, by an affected member of his family) to the utterer or a member of his clan. An intermediary left a ceremonial gourd at the hut of the utterer and called a meeting of elders. The two parties concerned anointed each other's heads and faces and those of the cursed person's immediate family, with fat. The elders expectorated beer and milk upon them, saying: 'Sere' ('Be blessed'), and a senior elder would add: 'Chomyo' ('Be at peace'). If the cursed person was too ill to attend the ceremony his part could be taken by proxy.

Note

[1] *The Nandi: Their Language and Folklore,* p. 85.

* G. S. Snell, *Nandi Customary Law,* Macmillan & Co. Ltd., 1954, pp. 84–86.

Chapter 5

EVIDENCE

The overlap between the subject-matter of this chapter and that of the previous one has already been referred to, and the reader would be wise to refer particularly to that section of Chapter 4 which deals with the conduct of hearings in order to obtain a more complete picture of this subject. Evidence is, in general, one of those topics in African law which has not been studied or described in very great detail, or very systematically. For this reason, *Allott's* article provides a particularly valuable and comprehensive survey of the material. The extracts which follow, by *Browne and Hutt* and *Bohannan* in particular, serve to confirm in detail many of the observations he makes, and the numerous illustrations from case material which are given by *Bohannan* are of particular value. Both *Allott* and *Epstein* refer to the rules of evidence which apply to modern courts, and the article by the latter from which an extract is taken, is exclusively concerned with these urban courts.

A. N. Allott: Evidence in African Customary Law*

Other papers will doubtless deal with the detailed aspects of particular African legal systems; it would be unnecessary to reduplicate this work, so in this paper an attempt will be made to give a more general assessment, using material drawn predominantly from English-language sources for illustration.

Procedure in African tribunals was often (and often still is) more informal than in Western courts, though societies vary very widely in the degree of formality that they accord to judicial proceedings. At one end of the scale there are the negotiations for a settlement in a homicide case among the Nuer; at the other end of the scale the formality in an Ashanti court during the hearing of an 'oath-case'. The law of procedure is generally of less importance, and less crucial for the decision of a case, than it is in, say, English law. In other words a litigant is unlikely to lose his case because of some technical error in pleading or because a certain kind of evidence is inadmissible. The law of evidence, as part of the procedural law, is also of less importance.

Some writers have tended to maintain that African law has no rules about evidence at all, and that courts have no notion of such basic ideas as relevancy, admissibility, the weight to be attributed to any particular kind of evidence, and so on. This assumption is generally mistaken, though African law does not copy Western laws in procedural, any more than in substantive, matters. African law is generally distinguished from English law in that it does not have strict and inflexible tests as to what is or is not relevant evidence; but a witness who strays too far from the matter in hand will be called to order. Many observers have commented on the great latitude permitted to litigants and their witnesses in the way they tell their story; they may appear to ramble over a variety of irrelevant topics without being brought back to the point by the presiding judge.

There are several reasons for this latitude. First, Africa has what is lacking in Europe—*time*. With no clocks and no fixed court calendar, and no other means of recreation, there was no pressure on the courts or the parties to despatch a case as quickly as possible. Taking part in the hearing of cases was, in many African societies, a public

* A. N. Allott, 'Evidence in African Customary Law', in *Les Editions de la Librairie Encyclopedique*, Tome XVIII, pp. 64–79.

event in which all joined; attendance at court might be compared, not too frivolously, to attendance at a professional football match in England today.

Secondly, in most African societies the idea that everyone ought to be given a full and fair hearing in any sort of discussion (and not merely in litigation) is deeply implanted. To suffer a fool gladly whilst he states his complaint at length means that later he cannot say that no one would listen to him and that his case has been ignored by the court.

Thirdly, in African litigation the issues may be very much broader than in litigation in England. As Gluckman has shown for the Barotse of Northern Rhodesia, often a Barotse court will go into all aspects of the dispute between the parties. It will concern itself, not merely with the immediate cause of complaint which has brought the case to court, but with the whole history of the relations between the parties and the balance of right and wrong in their dealings with each other. The court does this because the ultimate aim of its adjudication is not to dispose of the immediate issue only, but to procure harmonious relations generally between the litigants and to pronounce on the balance of justice and injustice as between them. Much more will be relevant, therefore, than in England.

Similarly with admissibility. Here the contrast with Islamic law as applying in Africa, and to a less degree with English law, is patent. On the whole African law does not have rigid rules regarding who is eligible to be a witness, what sorts of evidence will be admitted and which rejected, and so on. But, since African society is a society of unequal statuses, it is to be expected that a senior and respected male member of the tribe may get a more attentive hearing than a female or a young boy. All those factors which would go to the *exclusion* of certain evidence in English law (e.g. with 'hearsay' evidence) go rather to the *weight* to be attached to the evidence in African law.

African law makes use of many presumptions, both of fact and of law, to reach a decision. Gluckman has expressed this for the Barotse by invoking the concept of 'the reasonable man', although such reasonable man is not explicitly referred to in African legal procedure. In other words, what ought a reasonable man to do, as a matter of obligation, in such and such circumstances? Prove a certain set of circumstances, and the law will presume that the man ought to have done such-and-such. Gluckman extends (illegitimately, as I believe) the idea of a reasonable man to cover presumptions of fact: prove a certain set of circumstances, and what will we presume that an ordinary man would be likely to do, as a matter of fact and not of obligation, in such circumstances? How would an adulterer be likely to behave towards his mistress? In answering such questions, or in considering how Barotse courts would answer such questions, Gluckman extends the 'reasonable man' to cover 'reasonable adulterers' and the like.

Presumptions of law in African customary law cover such things as presumed responsibility for the actions of oneself or others (e.g. one's dependant, servant, agent), especially where intention, negligence or accident are concerned.

Where a presumption of law is rebuttable, this merely means that the law fixes the onus of proof on the party against whom the presumption operates to disprove his responsibility. Where a presumption of law is irrebuttable, this has nothing to do with evidence, but in effect means that the law fixes responsibility on the person affected by the presumption as a matter of policy. When we find, as we do in many African laws, that many acts between a married woman and a man not her husband are treated as adultery, how are we to classify this aspect of the law? Do we have to deal with an inference of fact, which not merely a court, but anyone, might reasonably draw from certain established facts? Or is the law saying that, whatever the truth of the matter, it will treat as though it were adultery any act of undue familiarity between a married woman and a man, either because such undue familiarity is itself an invasion of the husband's rights to his wife, or because the act of adultery itself (in our sense) is difficult to prove? The rigid division into presumptions of law and of fact tends to break down here.

So-called presumptions of fact are, or ought to be, nothing more than the inferences that any reasonably sane and logical individual would draw from certain primary facts that are brought to his attention. Certain inferences may, however, become stereotyped or institutionalized by the courts. A good case in point is that where an African is alleged to have caused harm to another by witchcraft. Here certain actions on the part of the defendant or accused may be proved, which cast suspicion on him; certain untoward experiences (they may be the death of a child of the plaintiff's in mysterious circumstances, the failure of his crops, or—in modern times—his failure to get a job or pass an examination) suffered by the plaintiff are proved. A casual connexion between actions and presumed effects is or may be inferred by the courts. The customary law is full of lists of activities which will be treated as the unlawful invocation of supernatural forces to another's detriment. For example, among the Ashanti as described by Rattray, it was a crime to say publicly 'I shall not eat again', or to cut an object with the knife at right angles, or let one's hair grow long, because all these acts were held to betoken an intention to kill someone (either oneself or another).

Circumstantial evidence is often admitted, more especially because there may not be any other sort of evidence available. What is relevant or probative in African eyes often varies from our own ideas. Documentary evidence is usually unavailable (but here a change is coming over the customary law, owing to the absence of writing in the customary law; but the place of documentary evidence is taken by the use of real or tangible evidence of a transaction, which is often treated as essential for establishing a claim. Many customary laws attach great weight to the giving of tokens or symbols at the time of a legal transaction; in case of a dispute later arising out of the transaction, these tokens can be produced to show what the relationship of the parties was. Two examples which come to mind are in connexion with the transfer of land, and in the formation of the contract of marriage.

For the transfer of land one may look to the Akan law as found in Ghana. In the Akan law the notion of 'sealing' or 'stamping' a bargain or arrangement is fundamental (as I found from personal investigations). Whenever any agreement has been reached, or benefit conferred which the beneficiary wishes to put beyond legal challenge, it is customary for the recipient of the benefit to give a thank-offering (*aseda* in the vernacular means exactly that) to the other party. For example, if A makes a gift of some object, movable or immovable, to B, B will immediately tender drink or a sheep or money or other tangible object as thank-offering, to ratify the gift. The effect in the case of a death-bed oral will is to give legal validity to the bequest. Until the thank-offering has been given, the transaction is usually of imperfect effect. Generally the thank-offering will consist of drink, which will be consumed at the time by the parties and the witnesses to the transaction, thus impressing it on their memory; at the same time libations will be poured to the departed ancestors, who will thus also be informed of the transaction in case of challenge. *Aseda* is also given to arbitrators when they have made their award, and to the parents or other person giving a girl in marriage, thus constituting the marriage.

Some of the Akan customary laws provide for the sale of land by what is known as 'cutting *guaha*'. A brief description of this cermony may be useful. After agreement to purchase has been reached, the land has been inspected, the price fixed, the boundaries cut and marked with special trees (themselves evidence of the extent of the land conveyed), the parties return from the forest within doors. The *guaha* ceremony then takes place before many witnesses for both sides. Vendor and purchaser each provide a representative (usually a young boy) to cut *guaha*. The vendor provides a piece of fibre on which are threaded six cowrie shells. The two persons cutting *guaha* then squat down; each passes his left hand under his right leg and grasps one end of the string of cowries, holding the three cowries nearest to him. At the appropriate moment the string is broken, and each is left holding three of the cowries. The respective parties keep the cowries used in the ceremony for ever, in order that in case of dispute between them or other over the sale, the cowries may be produced as evidence. In fact production of the cowries is an essential piece of evidence as to the sale. After the ceremony the purchaser offers drink and a sheep to the vendor (the 'stamping' or *aseda*). The witnesses to the sale sometime take the hairs of the sheep as evidence of the sale, to be produced in future in case of dispute.

The effect of the ceremony of cutting *guaha* is to make the sale complete and irrevocable. At the same time it provides clear tangible evidence, and the evidence of the witnesses, of the sale and its details. To prove the sale there will therefore be available: (i) the oral evidence of the witnesses; (ii) the boundaries cut on the land, and the boundary-trees planted at the corners—the boundary-cutters are usually remunerated as well to preserve their memories; (iii) the cowries used in the *guaha* ceremony; (iv) the hairs of the sheep in the possession of the witnesses; (v) the bones of the sheep and the bottles from which the drink was poured buried on the land.

As an example of the use of symbolic evidence in the conclusion of a marriage, one may look at the Shona law of marriage as described by Holleman. Tokens are very extensively used in Shona law, especially in the formation of marriage. The agent of the family of the boy will tender to the girl's family a 'proposal token' (formerly a calabash of snuff, a hoe, bracelet or anklet, and now usually cash). Acceptance of the token brings a binding agreement to marry into effect. As Holleman says, 'the proposal token . . . is not a present or expression of good will . . . but the marriage proposal itself, expressed in substance and accepted as such'. 'It can be handled, stored and produced at will by the party who has acquired it, and it can be used as irrebuttable "evidence" that such proposal . . . has been communicated by the donor to the recipient, because the token is, in fact, the communication itself.'

Procedure in different sorts of courts (e.g. arbitral and judicial) and in different societies varies; but a typical form of African procedure[1] is one where first the plantiff puts his case in full to the court, produces his witnesses who do likewise, is then cross-examined by the court and perhaps challenged by the other side; and then the defendant and his witnesses present their case in the same way. The parties usually tell their stories at length with little or no interruption, and not by means of the question-and-answer technique which is so typical of English procedure. Parties or witnesses are in some places put on oath; but on the whole this is not usual, though they may make an affirmation that they will speak the truth, or will reinforce their statements from time to time by invoking supernatural persons or forces in support.

In typical African procedure the role of the court is vital, as the court-members are active rather than passive in their hearing of the case. (It is as well to remember that in a number of societies the court includes not merely the chief and elders who may be presiding over the proceedings, but qualified participant spectators as well.) Some writers have characterized the role of the African court as inquisitorial rather than accusatorial. Perhaps it might be better expressed by saying that the court is not usually content to listen, intervening only when called upon or when there are exceptional reasons for steering the proceedings; the court usually wishes to get to the bottom of the case, and an important part of the procedure is where the judges test the stories of the parties by questioning which is semi-hostile in character. In weighing the evidence, Barotse courts as described by Gluckman (and Basuto courts as investigated by the present writer) endeavour to detect instances where persons have departed from the normal patterns of behaviour; in other words the judges in cross-examining a party pose ideal or type behaviour for the specific situation under consideration, and then compare the behaviour of the parties as alleged with those ideal patterns. In doing this they consider the inherent behaviour of a typical occupant of a social role (e.g. they ask—according to the case before them—how does a husband behave in such-and-such circumstances, or an adulterer, or a headman when arbitrating, etc.). Members of the court in my experience will think empathetically, i.e. they will see themselves in the shoes of the person giving evidence, and will by introspection discover how they would have behaved and felt in a similar situation. The result is that the questioning to which a party or a witness is submitted is usually very shrewd; inconsistencies and improbabilities will often be brought to light. The fact that custom often prescribes exactly what a person should do in a specific situation (cf. the sale of land by *guaha* referred to above) means that the slightest deviation from the normal will hit the eye immediately.

Most types of evidence are admissible, as we have seen, so that often hearsay as well as direct evidence is admitted. Even so, African courts often attach different degrees of cogency to different types of evidence, and will, for example, prefer the evidence of an eye-witness where possible (which may be treated as overwhelming and conclusive). The credibility of different witnesses also varies—some of the witnesses will be partial (i.e. they have an interest in the suit), whilst others will be impartial (and the evidence of the latter will often be preferred).

Hearsay evidence is specially important in regard to ancient rights, where it equals *tradition*, and it is then strongly probative. For example, in establishing an ancient right to occupy a particular piece of land, a man may repeat what his father was told by his father's father; and this evidence will be both relevant and admissible. In Akan courts in Ghana witnesses, when giving traditional evidence, often speak as if they were their ancestors, and the actors in the events that they describe. A chief when describing what his predecessor did 100 years ago, or a man telling how his matrilineal ancestor first cleared a tract of forest land, will speak in the first person and say: '*I* did so-and-so.' This practice was frowned on by the European judges in the superior courts, as they found it misleading; but it was tolerated and still observed in the native courts, and is indeed a harmless practice once understood.

Special forms of procedure are found in some tribes. Of these, one of the most remarkable is the Ashanti 'oath-procedure' as described by Rattray. We are not here concerned with examining in detail the whole procedure; it suffices to say that it is a means (still employed in the Ghana local courts today) by which a case may be brought to a chief's court by using one of that chief's 'oaths' in defence of his rights (the comparison with the ancient Roman *legis actio per sacramentum* has often been made). The effect is that the oath-taker becomes *prima facie* a criminal, since he has broken a tribal taboo by uttering a forbidden word or phrase, the 'oath'. He can escape liability if he can show that he justifiably invoked the oath in defence of his civil rights. The procedure in the chief's court in an oath case was in form criminal, though the substance of the case was civil. Both plaintiff and defendant are now *prisoners*, who are kept in custody throughout the hearing. The circumstances of their arrest (for mentioning the oath) are reported, and the chief's spokesman or *okyeame* (who conducts judicial proceedings on behalf of the chief) tells the plaintiff to tell his story, which he does without interruption. He does not take an oath to speak the truth. Then the defendant similarly gives his side of the case. The *okyeame* now repeats in turn the story told by each party, as near word-for-word as possible. Then the court-elders may cross-examine the accused. A party might at this stage offer to call a witness. Here another of the startling features of the Ashanti oath-procedure comes in, for only one witness, and that a person who has been agreed upon by both sides, may be called in the case. If the parties agree, the witness is summoned by messenger. The *okyeame* causes the witness to swear by two gods supplied by the court that he will speak the truth. The witness then gives his evidence. Then the *okyeame* pronounces the verdict of the court on the basis of the evidence given.

Apart from evidence of facts contributed by the parties and their witnesses, members of a court may rely on their own knowledge of the parties, of the dispute, and of the circumstances of life generally. What would disqualify a judge in England woud be held to be a special qualification in Africa, as there is no fiction of judicial ignorance. But this aspect of the African law of evidence ought not to be exaggerated. Some writers have gone so far as to suggest that there is no hearing on the facts in African tribunals at all, because everyone is already familiar with the facts of the case. But this is generally not the position, epecially in societies with chiefs, and in disputes involving persons from different localities. Often the court will itself gather evidence by personal inspection (e.g. of a farm that is in dispute, of a place where a wrong was alleged to have been committed, of instruments by which a wrong has been done, and of other objects which are involved in the narrative of events as told by the parties). In some areas bystanders are also allowed to contribute their own opinions, both as to the facts and as to the decision of the dispute. But this is not universal.

African law everywhere permits recourse to supernatural means of eliciting the facts or deciding a case. The principal means by which such recourse is made are: (i) oaths or conditional curses; (ii) ordeals; (iii) divination. Torture was also used in some tribes to extract the facts, or more usually a confession of guilt, from an accused (e.g. among the Haya of Tanganyika and the Barotse of Northern Rhodesia). The procedures by which these supernatural means of finding out the truth are brought into play vary widely. Such supernatural means naturally struck the European observer very forcibly; but it would be a mistake to think that these means were the usual mode of eliciting facts or deciding a dispute in African law. On the whole recourse to the supernatural was only made when natural methods of finding out the truth were insufficient: e.g. there were no witnesses (as in many witchcraft accusations), the witnesses fundamentally contradict each other, the members of the court do not agree among themselves as to the facts of the case and there is no means of resolving the division of opinion, and so on.

Oaths may be either *guarantees of veracity* or a *means of decision*. The oath as a guarantee of veracity is an appeal to supernatural forces to support the story told by a witness; it lends weight to his evidence, and is an affirmation that he will speak the truth. It is generally taken by a witness (and may be used in the middle of his evidence), and is not conclusive of the issue. Often in form it is a conditional curse by which the witness imprecates on his own head supernatural consequences if he lies. The Barotse did not use oaths of any kind, because the invocation of the supernatural might unwittingly bring harm to an innocent party. But a witness might affirm the truth of his statement by mentioning the king's name. In other African tribes the oath as a guarantee of veracity is found; and here an interesting historical fact may be noted. Where the oath as means of decision was used, this is in some places changing its character, and becoming merely a guarantee of veracity. For example, among the Mende of Sierra Leone by the so-called 'swear-procedure' the parties exchanged conditional curses which they invoked on their own heads, and these concluded the hearing. But now the 'swear' is used as a guarantee of veracity only, both by the parties *and by the witnesses*.

The oath as a means of decision is commonly found in African law. The Mende example has already been mentioned. If a party refused to 'swear', he lost his case. If both parties swear, then the decision is left to the supernatural. The court adopts the 'swear-procedure' if the case of both parties seems reasonable and there is a lack of witnesses. For example, it might be used in boundary disputes where the parties might await the 'result' of the case for 25 years or more. The parties swear on each other's nominated medicine or fetish, and on the chief's medicine. Once the parties have sworn, the hearing ends. The swear procedure was also used against unknown offenders.

Among the Ibo of Eastern Nigeria as described by Meek oaths were generally used to settle particular points which arose during the trial. Among the Kamba of Kenya as described by Penwill and others, the elders might, where there was a conflict of testimony, ask one party (never both parties) to swear. The court decided which party to ask to swear; if he refused, he is proved to be lying and loses his case. The *kithitu* or medicine consists of several ingredients wrapped up together and supplied by the non-swearing party, who hires it from its guardian. The non-swearing party fixes a time-limit for the oath to operate, the limit varying with the potency of the *kithitu* (e.g. it might be 6 months or less). The oath has worked if the swearer, his wife, or his eldest son dies within the period. If such death takes place within the period, the losing party hands over the property claimed, or does whatever else is necessary to settle the case. If he fails to do this, the deaths of his relatives will continue.

The *kithitu* oath can also be used for other purposes, e.g. as an injunction to protect boundaries from infringement. Women cannot be sworn. There is also a less potent form of oath, the *ndundu* oath, which affects only the swearer personally: it is therefore used in intra-clan or intra-family disputes.

It is worth remarking that the Ashanti oath procedure represents yet a third function of oaths in African legal procedure. The Ashanti oath is not a guarantee of veracity, nor yet decisive of the case; it is merely a means of initiating an action.

Ordeals are the doing or suffering by a party of something that is intrinsically dangerous, but which is harmless to the innocent and harmful only to the guilty. (Where the ordeal is undergone by proxy, e.g. by a cock in Ibo law, this is a form of divination.) Ordeals are practically confined to criminal cases, though they may also be used outside a court in some areas (e.g. to test a wife's virtue). They are often imposed by the court, though sometimes we find that they are voluntarily undergone by a party or imposed by his opponent. They are specially important in trials of serious offences such as witchcraft and in other cases where the true facts cannot be ascertained. Examples of ordeals found include, for the Kamba of Kenya, the hot knife ordeal, the needle ordeal, the bead in the eye ordeal, the drinking of a poisonous mixture; these are very typical of other customary laws.

Divination is the use of natural or preternatural occurrences as signs of guilt or innocence, by the doing of something not intrinsically harmful to a suspect. Often a professional diviner was employed (as among the Ashanti and the Ibo). Oracles (as among the Azande of the Sudan as described by Evans-Pritchard) are found. In some societies divination was either not used at all (cf. the Tswana of Bechuanaland as described by Schapera—they did not use ordeals either), or was not used in civil cases (the Barotse).

Evidence and Non-African Courts

As was mentioned at the beginning of this paper, the earlier history and evolution of African legal institutions are generally not accessible to us today. African law has of course had a history; but the only documented history is of occurrences since the advent of coloaial rule by the European. The effect of the arrival of Western civilization and Western law has been to revolutionize African society and African law with it. In particular, African customary law is now administered as part of and subject to a legal system of alien origin. Cases decided by native courts, which may or may not follow the traditional composition and procedure (more usually not in their entirety today), may go on appeal or by way of revision to a non-African court or authority. The result of this superimposition on African law has been a gradual westernization of procedure. The single most important development has been the introduction of writing. Written means can now supplement the customary means of evidencing a transaction, and in former British West Africa especially this has now gone very far. Until procedure in the native courts has been tightened up or radically changed by the enactment of procedure rules or the training of court personnel in English legal methods, the customary procedure was allowed to continue in most British territories. Surprisingly, perhaps, though the grosser forms of supernatural investigation by ordeal, etc., have been banned, the oath as a means of deciding a case has been preserved in some of the statutory native courts, though with stricter control by the court itself; and divination may also be employed. Indigenous modes of swearing have been adopted for the swearing of parties and witnesses, so that a Christian may be sworn on the Bible, a Muslim on the Koran, and a pagan on a 'fetish' (native court records in Ghana, for instance, usually contain the letters 'S.A.R.B.' after witness's name, meaning 'sworn according to religious belief'). There are considerable contradictions between African and English legal ideas as to the best or admissible way of finding out the facts of a case. Apart from the use of supernatural modes of evidence, there is the African attitude to hearsay or traditional evidence, African presumptions of fact or law that do not agree with English ones, and so on. On traditional evidence there is a good deal of material available in the law reports of Ghana. There cases originating in native courts have often gone on appeal to the Supreme Court (unlike in some British territories); and the attitude of the British judges in colonial times was, as regards traditional evidence, that 'we don't like it but we must accept it, even if it would not be admissible in England'. As regards other means of finding out the truth, the Supreme Court when sitting as a court of appeal from a native court would usually attach great weight to the native court's findings on questions of fact. The native court was in the best position to know the probabilities of the matter, the way of life of the people, and whether the witnesses were telling the truth or not; so the traditional methods of finding out the truth and weighing the evidence could still be employed and receive this indirect sort of backing from the superior courts.

In the non-African courts administering law of the English type the law of evidence is naturally on the English pattern, and no concession is made to African ideas of what is relevant or admissible, or to African ways of finding out the facts. This must lead to some bewilderment on the part of the unsophisticated African who comes before such a court; to him legal process will appear a mysterious game played under unintelligible and unpredictable rules, where the outcome of the proceedings is largely a matter of chance. The African understanding of the English rules of evidence must thus be meagre.

It is unfortunate that the general law of evidence in British African countries has not been influenced by African ideas, as it can be plausibly argued that the African modes of eliciting the facts of a case will usually be much more effective in an African society than the English. That a judge should draw on his knowledge of the case and the parties, that one man should repeat what another has told him, that it should be a circumstance worthy of special mention, in considering the likelihood that a witness is telling the truth, that he is always getting into trouble or that the accused has been guilty of offence previously—all these facts would be self-evident to an African, and yet they might easily fall foul of the strict English rules about admissibility or relevancy.

There is a further important factor in evaluating the two types of law. An American research team which was considering the efficiency of legal means of getting at the truth found that of the three methods of allowing a witness to give his evidence—(i) by response to friendly questions, (ii) by a response to unfriendly or hostile questioning, (iii) by giving his account uninterrupted by questioning—the most efficient means, whereunder the evidence would deviate the least from the witness's original perception, was the third, and the least efficient was the second. It is frequently claimed that the English technique of hostile cross-examination is the best means of getting a witness to tell what he knows (method (ii)); whilst the typical African procedure employs method (iii), often followed by method (ii). *Prima facie* the African procedure would seem to have the advantage, therefore. It is unlikely that the English law of evidence will be modified as a result of this comparison, however!

Note

[1] E.g. the Basuto (personal investigation by the author).

G. G. Browne and A. McD. B. Hutt: Anthropology in Action*

In the past, when a case was brought to a headman or chief, the evidence first sought was that of eye-witnesses. For example, if one man struck another, a third party must give evidence that he saw the blow being given or that he saw marks on the body of the injured person. Circumstantial evidence, which would appear to us as being reasonable, was also accepted. For instance, the fact that a man was found in the house of a woman would, under certain conditions, be accepted as reasonable proof of adultery. In general, evidence of the kind accepted in our own courts was accepted in the native courts.

But when such evidence was lacking, divination could be resorted to. For serious cases such as accusations of witchcraft, the poison ordeal was ordered. For less serious but still important cases, ordeals of another kind were used; picking a stone from a pot of boiling medicated water is still occasionally agreed to for the private settlement of disputes, the proof resting on whether the accused injures himself or not. Other means of divination were plentiful; some of them, still used privately, are the horn which answers questions by the way it points in the hands of the diviner; the invocation of an ancestor by a magician; and divining sticks. The main point is that no dispute was left unsettled; if direct or circumstantial evidence was lacking, magical means could be invoked. I suggest, without being able to offer adequate proof, that this worked fairly on the whole. The diviner probably interpreted public opinion by unconsciously manipulating the instruments of divination. I am also inclined to believe that there was little conscious deceit; all *valagusi* (magicians, doctors, diviners) I have met are honest and firmly convinced of the efficacy of their divinations and medicines.

Nowadays divination is not accepted as evidence, either in the informal arbitrations of the headman or in the higher, recognized courts. Direct evidence or convincing circumstantial evidence only is accepted. Those Hehe who are skilled in their own law are thus becoming more and more expert at sifting evidence, checking one statement against another and eliciting relevant facts. But the older men still complain that too many plaints fall to the ground for lack of evidence, and that divination cannot be resorted to except unofficially, to force a confession before a case comes to court.

The court relies to some extent upon evidence as to the character of the accused, particularly on evidence that he has offended in other similar cases. This is particularly important in quarrels between man and wife. Such quarrels, often ending in violence on the part of the husband, usually occur in private and, as the courts always endeavour to preserve rather than to dissolve a marriage, there is little chance of redress for the woman without other evidence. Nevertheless, women frequently do institute a number of cases against their husbands for various offences; and even though all these cases may be lost, the fact that the wife has brought them stands her in good stead if she seeks divorce. The very bringing of them establishes the character of the husband. But, generally, evidence as to character plays a minor part; and nowadays cases are nearly all decided on the basis of direct or good circumstantial evidence.

A. L. Epstein: Juridical Techniques and the Judicial Process†

The Concept of Relevance

At the beginning of this paper I postulated a distinction between 'law' and 'fact', and I have cited cases to show how Urban courts achieve a decision, first by establishing

* G. G. Browne and A. McD. B. Hutt, *Anthropology in Action*, Oxford University Press, 1935, pp. 255–257.

† A. L. Epstein, *Juridical Techniques and the Judicial Process*, Manchester University Press for the Rhodes-Livingstone Institute, Paper No. 23, pp. 20–21.

the facts and, second, by applying to them the appropriate rule of law. Here the Urban courts proceed in essentially the same way as would an English court. The major procedural difference appears to me to lie in the different concepts of relevance by which the facts are collated and assessed. For whereas the English system tends to stress the exclusion of evidence which is regarded as irrelevant, the African courts accept whatever testimony is presented, and then proceed to weigh it by those techniques already described. We have seen something of the operation of this concept of relevance in the cases of assault and adultery cited earlier. However, it is in matrimonial suits that the concept finds its clearest expression, for it is to this class of case that the use of conciliatory techniques, so frequently stressed by other writers, is now largely confined in Urban courts.

I have shown elsewhere[1] that in matrimonial cases, and in particular in suits for divorce, the decision of an African court in some tribal areas does not normally depend on the plaintiff's establishing as fact the charges against his or her spouse. This is not to say that in such cases the distinction between 'law' and 'fact' is absent. If a woman claims a divorce from her husband on the ground that she was beaten by her husband, whether she was or was not beaten is of course a fact relevant to the issue. But an Urban court will not necessarily regard this as a crucial issue: it will want to know whether it was the beating itself which gave rise to the suit, or whether it was an index of some deeper rupture in their marriage relationship. Accordingly, the court will enquire of the wife whether she receives an allowance to buy food and clothes, whether she has a meal and a bath ready for her husband on his return from work, whether she receives his kinsfolk graciously and cooks food for them. Correspondingly, it will question the husband about his personal habits, whether he has children by his wife, whether he has in the past found her guilty of misconduct, and so on. All these answers are evaluated in terms of the norms of the marriage relationship—of how married people ought reasonably to behave towards one another and to their respective kin. Thus the question which an Urban court poses is not, 'Do the facts disclose the husband's beating of his wife?' but 'What facts have led to this trouble in the house?' In matrimonial cases the courts still tend to see their task as the reconciliation of the parties; but this end cannot be achieved by concentration on the narrower issues. I do not mean to infer that the courts ignore the right-duty element of the case, with which perhaps an English court would be more concerned. Obviously this cannot be so, for reconciliation is achieved on the basis of the litigants' recognition of wrongdoing. What the courts do, therefore, is to regard the parties as occupying specific social positions, as husband and father and son-in-law, as wife and mother and daughter-in-law; and then it measures their behaviour in terms of the norms which are appropriate to these positions. Each dispute is viewed within the context of a wider system of social relationships. Accordingly, any evidence which can throw light on the behaviour of the parties within the framework of their total relationship is not merely admissible, but is deliberately sought by the courts. Viewed in the light of the judges' conception of their task, such evidence is of the most immediate relevance. The concept of relevance, indeed, is never absolute, but has to be understood as a function of the judicial task, as this is conceived in a particular society, in relation to a particular type of relationship within which a dispute has arisen.

Note

[1] See my article, 'Divorce Law and Stability of Marriage among the Lunda of Kazembe', *Rhodes-Livingstone Journal*, No. 14, (1953).

P. Bohannan: Justice and Judgement among the Tiv*

Oaths and Witnesses

This section examines Tiv notions of witnesses (*ashieda*), oaths and swearing (*bum*), the testimony of sworn witnesses in a court, and Tiv ideas of truth.

* P. Bohannan, *Justice and Judgement among the Tiv*, Oxford University Press, 1957, pp. 34–51.

Witnesses. The Tiv word usually translated witness is *shieda.* The word doubtless derives from the Hausa word *shaida* and ultimately from Arabic *shahada* or *shahêd.* It is used with a much more restricted field of meaning by Tiv than by Hausa. Tiv do not use it as a verb, and in fact usually do not use it at all except in connexion with court cases or with marriage payments and other monetary transactions in which each party gets witnesses to the transaction.

The indigenous Tiv expressions for witnessing derive from the verb *pase*, which means 'to explain, relate, tell'—and which also means 'to give or to release'.[1] 'A man who tells' (*or pasen*) is an expression which can be used where we might use the word witness, as a witness in a court trial. But it is also the only word for 'preacher' in mission circles, and it can mean 'orator'.

Three distinct ideas and sets of social relationships must be examined if we are to understand Tiv notions of witnesses and evidence. At least two of these concepts extend beyond the jural context. First, there is the witness to a financial transaction; if the act to which he stood witness ever comes up in a *jir*, he is bound to come and tell what he knows. He is said to be the *shieda* of the man who pays or who receives the money. In marriage, however, where this practice is very common in payments of bridewealth, the *shieda* also takes on other duties and other names. Secondly, there is the sort of witness who has no relationship whatever to either party to the *jir*, but comes into the matter on the initiative of the *mbatarev*. Thirdly, there is the sort of witness which we might call 'witness by private contract'. We shall examine these different sorts of witnesses in that order.

When a man makes a payment of bridewealth to his wife's guardian, he usually does so by handing the money to his witness (his *shieda*) who, in the presence of them all, counts it and hands it to the *shieda* of the guardian, who again counts it and hands it to the guardian himself, who very probably counts it again. It is usually sufficient for one man to act as *shieda* for both husband and guardian.

The witness in such a situation has other duties and there may be other ways of referring to him. He may be, and very often is, the 'secondary guardian', as we have called him, to the wife. He has a moral but no financial interest in the marriage, being only the witness to the financial transaction which occurs in conjunction with it. He is usually called to testify to the correct amounts paid by the husband.

Witnesses in *jir* concerning debt are also usually found to have a prior relationship to the persons whom they represent, because Tiv have witnesses to most financial transactions. Such a relationship is not so close as the relationship between witnesses and principals in marriage. I discovered this custom of witnessing financial matters very early in my field-work. When I paid Chenge for building my compound within his own, he insisted that I have a witness and that he should have one as well, and that the payment should be made in the presence of both together. I asked my cook to act on my behalf, which he did; the chief asked Fiyase, one of the senior elders of MbaGôr, his own minimal segment. In this case, the chief was redistributing the money among those who had contributed work to my huts, and he hoped to avoid accusations of not having distributed it all. Although it was never suggested that he did not distribute all that was presented before witnesses, I learned much later that there had been considerable speculation about the amount I had given him when there were no witnesses present. Needless to say, there had been no extra payment.

Once the relationship between a man and his witness has been established, it is incumbent upon the witness to go before a court, if he is called, and state whatever he 'knows' about the transactions to which he was witness. Witnesses who go before a Grade-D court are usually required to take an oath, and the judges usually accept their word, once they have been sworn, as correct. It is also usual, I think, that before a *jir* the principal and the witness agree between themselves on the amount to be sworn by the witness. The principal is never sworn, and is therefore not pledged to be 'correct' as the witness is.

JIR NO. 14. *Anongo calls Iyorkyaha and accuses his witness of lying*

Anongo had married Iyorkyaha's ward and, when the marriage broke up, said he had paid £12 bridewealth. When Iyorkyaha said the sum was not correct, the *mbatarev* called for witnesses. Anongo's witness was sworn on the decorative tongs (*gbegba*), having been instructed how to swear by one of the *mbatarev*. His oath ran: 'This is a fetish. If I swear wrongly (*sa apela*), the fetish will seize me.' He then stated that the bridewealth amounted to £7 and one hen.

Anongo immediately challenged this statement and accused his witness of lying. The witness replied that if there was more than £7 in this case, it did not go through his hands; he was swearing, not to the whole amount, but to the amount which he had himself handled, and he repeated several times, 'I will say nothing save what I know.'

The judges told the guardian to repay £7 and a hen to Anongo. Anongo insisted that the correct sum was £12, that the witness had lied, and that therefore he did not intend to surrender his 'paper' to have a lie written on it.

The *mbatarev* threatened to appeal to Grade-C court. Anongo shouted that he intended to call a *jir* against his witness for lying, but a record was made of his debt of £7.

The relationship which exists between a man and his witness, more particularly when that witness is also the person with whom the guardian lodged (*sughul*) his ward, is precise and definite and can be stated by Tiv in terms of rights and duties. Breach of these duties is itself basis for action before the *jir*.

JIR NO. 15. *Umem (husband) calls Hindan (his 'witness')*
Failure of witness to comply with norms of his role.

Several years ago Umem married and Hindan acted as his witness. After a year or two the wife left Umem. Hindan collected the money for return of bridewealth from the guardian, but did not hand it all to Umem. He kept for himself ('ate') £1. 5*s*. After several years of fruitless efforts to collect it, Umem called a *jir* in the court against Hindan. When the *mbatarev* asked Hindan about it, he denied that he had ever collected any money which he had not handed immediately to Umem. Whereupon the *mbatarev* called for witnesses. Umem replied that there were not witnesses—this man had been his witness, and one does not have witnesses of witnesses. The wife's guardian was dead and there were no witnesses. But, he added, 'I will be my own witness.'

Chenge told him that would not be necessary just yet, and turned again to Hindan. 'Hindan must be his own witness. He must swear on *swem* and tell us the entire matter of the payments in this marriage.' Hindan refused to swear on *swem*, and insisted that this would make the affair too important. Within a moment it became apparent to all that he was lying—his reluctance, indeed his fear, of swearing could have no other interpretation. The court became noisier and noisier as bystanders began shouting that it looked as if Hindan were lying. Finally, one of the judges yelled for silence and, eventually getting it, declared, 'If you do not swear on *swem*, this *jir* will catch you.' Hindan insisted that this was not the way good judges would handle the matter and again tried to tell them that, since he was Umem's witness in this transaction, he would not have cheated him, thus swearing was unnecessary. Without letting him finish the judges told him that he had until the next day to bring £1. 5*s*. to give to Umem, else they would put him in gaol.

The significant points on the swearing of the principals to a *jir* will be considered below. Here we are interested in the relationship between a man and his witness: the relationship with the secondary guardian (*orsughul*) should be such as to make further witnesses unnecessary. Therefore when one of the persons to the relationship defaults, the defaulter can be sued, not merely for the matter of the debt (which would, normally, require witnesses), but for default of his obligations in the relationship (which by its nature does not require witnesses).

In marked contrast is the second type of witness. This witness is in no way associated with either of the principals, and as a result is often not sworn.

JIR NO. 16. *A woman gives impartial evidence in a dispute about a bicycle*

A Tiv youngster was hiring out, at market, a bicycle which belonged to a Bamenda, but which had been given him for this purpose. One of the persons hiring it paid a penny and, instead of riding it round the market-place a few times as the penny entitled him to do, went away with it. When the youngster looked for the bicycle, he could not find it. Thereupon he went to the market officials, who turned the matter over to the *mbatarev*.

At the time the *jir* was heard the bicycle had not yet been returned, but a man had been arrested because the youngster identified him as the culprit. This man steadfastly refused to admit that he had ever seen the youngster before, or that he had ridden a bicycle at all on that particular day. Whereupon the chief and the other *mbatarev* asked the assembled audience if they had seen the man on a bicycle. A young man living near the market said that he had seen the man ride a bicycle along the path past his compound, and that the man had stopped for a few moments and talked with the wife of his 'brother', who lived in the same compound as himself. The *mbatarev* thereupon asked him to bring his brother's wife to give evidence.

The woman came next day. She sat on the ground with the accused, and was asked if she had ever seen him. She said that she had indeed, for this was the man who had ridden past her cassava patch on a bicycle and asked directions from her. Someone in the audience shouted a suggestion that she should be made to swear. It was taken up by others. When the *mbatarev* restored quiet, the woman said she did not want to swear, because she feared *swem* and because she had no motive for lying. It was none of her business—she knew neither the man's name nor his lineage; she did not know either the Tiv youngster or the Bamenda man who was owner of the bicycle. The *mbatarev* considered an oath unnecessary. They listened to her evidence, thanked her and she left.

Here, unlike the cases in which the witness has a manifold relationship with one or other of the principals, an oath was not required. Furthermore, this woman came reluctantly into a matter not her affair. It is a serious breach of manners in Tivland to interfere in the business of anyone with whom you are not acquainted. The *jir* often has trouble in getting witnesses of this sort, even though the number of people who have seen an act is legion.

The *mbatarev* occasionally use 'expert witnesses', especially when it is necessary to assess the amount of damage done to fields by livestock. So far as I am aware, such witnesses are always selected either because they have no obligations to either party to the dispute, or because they are officials.

There is one other sort of witness—principal relationship: that in which the witness makes a sort of 'contract' with the principal. Here is a text written by one of my two clerks when I asked simply for a text on 'witnesses':

'If something of yours disappears and another man sees it, he will say "Come, give me some money and I'll tell you who took it." So, if you have any money, you give it to him, and he will say, "It was so-and-so who took it." If, for example, I had lost something and was looking for it, and it was Gbatoho[2] who took it, and Shima saw Gbatoho with the thing, Shima would come to me and say, "Iyorkôsu, give me money, and I shall tell you who stole your goat." I asked Shima, "How much must I give you?" and Shima would say, "Give me one pound." So, when I have taken the pound and given it to Shima[3] he will say, "Iyorkôsu, it was Gbatoho who stole your goat." So I go to make Gbatoho give me my goat, and when I get there Gbatoho will say that he caught no goat of mine. So I'll go call a *jir* against Gbatoho with the *mbatarev* of his country in order to recover my goat. The *mbatarev* will ask Gbatoho, "Did you catch a goat of Iyorkôsu?" Gbatoho will deny that he did anything of the sort, and the *mbatarev* will tell him to bring witnesses.

'Hereupon, I call Shima, who will come into the court circle, and the *mbatarev* will tell Shima to make the ritual movements and swear on *swem*, then act as witness in the matter of Iyorkôsu's goat, which he says Gbatoho stole. Shima will make the ritual movements to the effect that if he did not see Gbatoho steal Iyorkôsu's goat, *swem* will afflict him. After finishing the ritual movements, Shima will take the *swem* pot and touch it to his feet, his knees, his belly, and his head. Then he will place it again on the ground. Thereupon he will indicate to the *mbatarev* how he had seen Gbatoho with my goat. When the *mbatarev* have heard him out, they will begin to investigate (*tôv*) the *jir*. Then, when the *jir* catches Gbatoho, they will tell me to put a value on my goat, and I will say that Gbatoho must give me £2. I will also say that I gave my witness £1 to tell me and that Gbatoho must pay that. The *mbatarev* will then ask Shima, "How much did Iyorkôsu give you to act as his witness?" Shima will reply, "He gave me one pound." The *mbatarev* will tell Gbatoho that he must also pay this pound. This is the way the matter of giving witnesses money is done.'

The meaning of this text is not that Tiv sell themselves as witnesses, but rather that they seek to establish a relationship with the man to whom their testimony is advantageous so that they will not be charged with interfering in affairs not their own. A defendant can understand a man's giving evidence against him if he is a kinsman or in some other way related to the plaintiff. He can also understand it if he has been paid. But if he does so without any relationship and without *quid pro quo* (itself a relationship, of course) he is then guilty of an act of aggression.[4] Unless the witness is forced by the necessities of a relationship, such as being secondary marriage guardian or being in receipt of money (or unless he is forced by the *mbatarev* to act as witness, as happened with the woman who saw the man on the stolen bicycle) Tiv say that giving evidence is 'spoiling the *tar*'.

This text also indicates something else: Iyorkôsu, who wrote it, never once considered that Gbatoho, whom he supposed in his example to have stolen the goat, would have admitted doing so, unless he could construe the action as a retribution for some wrong done to him. Indeed, his supposition was right. The principals of a *jir* are expected to 'lie' about the situations under consideration, and certainly to tell only that portion of the story which does most credit to themselves and most discredit to their adversaries. We shall examine these ideas below when we investigate. Tiv notions of truth, and the relationship between truth and evidence. Here it is sufficient to say that witnesses are usually expected to tell what we would consider to be the 'truth' of the matter—that is, the more or less verifiable facts of an event. Tiv swear witnesses to tell the truth; they do not—save in exceptional circumstances like Umem's *jir* against Hindan (No. 15)—swear the principals to any litigation, for this would take the matter out of the hands of human judges.

Oaths. Tiv do not have, so far as I am aware, a noun which means 'oath'. They express this notion with the verb *bum* which means 'to swear'. The word does indeed form two verbal nouns, but both refer to the act of swearing rather than to the oath itself. The verb 'to swear' can be either transitive or intransitive. When it takes an object, this object is the name of the fetish on which the oath is taken.

I shall first describe the act of swearing on *swem*, and then mention briefly some of the other fetishes used for purposes of oath-taking.

Swem is the most important of the forces which Tiv see manifest in the emblems and fetishes of their religion. Although *swem* may exist independently of any emblems, if it be represented by emblems the most common is a small cooking pot filled with ashes, camwood and two sorts of leaves.[5] Once made up, or 'dressed' (*wuha*), this pot is kept by the *swem*-holder. Today most government chiefs are *swem*-holders; if they are not, they get a *swem* from someone who is. It is brought out from his reception hut by the chief for each session of the court. He places it in the middle of the court circle. Although litigants are careful not to touch it, they ignore it except when witnesses are sworn.

The act of swearing consists of picking up the pot (in the case of women, touching it may suffice) and, usually under instruction from one of the *mbatarev*, repeating some such statement as: 'This is *swem*; if I swear falsely (*sa apela*), *swem* will catch me.' The clearest and most precise oath on *swem* recorded in my notes runs: 'This is *swem*, is it not? Whether anyone else has spoken indiscriminately I do not know. But whatever I indicate is precise. Whatever I know, I shall indicate straight.'[6]

The pot is then made to touch the feet, the belly, and the head. Sometimes the knees are included. It is then replaced on the ground and the *jir* goes on. It is said that if the witness has taken such an oath and then testifies falsely, his feet and belly will swell, his head will ache, and he will die. Most Tiv refuse to assign a time limit within which *swem* must work but, when pressed, say that it usually works within three or four months. In the most specific instance I have, it required several years:

INSTANCE NO. 17. *Gbe's first wife's guardian swore falsely on* swem

Gbe married a woman from Mbara and paid an initial sum of £4 bridewealth; he also made gifts to her father, mother, guardian, and elders. After she had lived with him for a few months, she left him and returned to her natal home. Gbe went to Mbara to fetch her back but, when he arrived, he found that she had 'gone to another husband', so he asked for his bridewealth to be returned. The woman's guardian said he had received no bridewealth. Thereupon Gbe went to the *mbatarev* of Mbara and called a *jir* against the guardian for the return of the bridewealth. His own witness, however, had left Tivland to get work, and the guardian's witness took a false oath, swearing on *swem*.

After taking the oath, he said that Gbe had paid no bridewealth at all, but only made miscellaneous gifts to the woman's kinsmen, and these were deemed not returnable. Several years later, during the time I was living in the same compound as Gbe, a messenger arrived from Mbara to tell him that the witness was very ill, that he had admitted taking a false oath on *swem* during the course of this *jir*, and that, having made the admission, *swem* was repaired for him.[7] Gbe could, if he liked, reopen the case and would be given his £4 bridewealth. He set off within a few days to do so. He got his money without going before the *jir*.

Swem is, in Radcliffe-Brown's classification, a supernatural sanction. Tiv believe that it works automatically on the breach of specific norms.

There are also specific jural penalties for lying. The clearest case in my records of a secular penalty being imposed to reinforce the supernatural penalty is found in a *jir* similar to *Jir* No. 5 in which the amount of bridewealth to be repaid was in dispute:

JIR NO. 18. *Asev (husband's father) calls Agba (guardian)*
Witness takes a false oath in a bridewealth dispute.

When Asev's son's wife left him, there was a dispute with her guardian, Agba, about the amount of bridewealth which had been paid and how much was returnable. The husband, when asked by the *mbatarev*, stated that £12 was returnable. However, his father interrupted and said that the correct amount was £18, adding that his son had not been aware of all the payments which had been made (a reasonable situation, for a man's first wife should always be provided by his father). The wife's guardian said that he had received only £5. 18*s*. of returnable bridewealth. The judges asked, 'Where did you lodge this woman?' They replied that the secondary guardian was a man named Batur. The *mbatarev* adjourned the hearing until Batur could be fetched.

When he came, the *mbatarev* began to hear his evidence before requiring him to take an oath on *swem*. It very soon became evident that his story was long and involved, and they asked him to take the oath. He did so without hesitation. Then one of the judges asked him, 'The day that Asev gave Agba the money, how much did he give him?' Batur replied, £17. The *mbatarev* asked for an itemization of the amounts which made up the £17. As Batur struggled to make his amounts total £17, murmurs began to be heard that he was obviously lying. The *mbatarev* took things in hand; Chenge announced that he knew Batur was lying, and that 'Batur has spoiled our *swem*!' He said it seemed to him that £12, the amount originally stated by the husband, was probably correct, as it fell approximately half-way between the two claims. The other judges concurred that the guardian should return £12 to the husband's father, and the *jir* be settled. The *jir* was again adjourned. Three days later the guardian arrived with a substantial part of the payment. After the judges themselves had seen £7 handed over, and a note had been made to that effect in the records of the court clerks, they turned to the matter of Batur's false evidence.

Chenge asked him sternly, 'Batur, why have you sworn on our *swem* falsely (*sa apela*)—why have you spoiled our *swem* in this way?'

Batur answered that he had not done so, and that his original testimony of £17 was correct. He then intimated that the judges had made a false (*sa apela*) decision.

Chenge, becoming heated, immediately said that he should be fined £2 because 'he has greatly spoiled our *swem*, and now he is trying to spoil our *jir*'.

Batur still denied that he had taken a false oath. All the *mbatarev*, in different ways, advised him to admit his wrong and have *swem* repaired, for if he did not, his feet and belly would swell up and he would die. Batur still refused to agree that he had sworn falsely. Chenge, at the end of his patience, told him bluntly, 'Batur, if *swem* doesn't pay attention and seize you for this, I shall seize you myself! *Swem* may catch you tomorrow—I do not know, for that is not my affair. But I shall catch you today for spoiling our *jir* That *is* my affair. Do you agree to the £2 fine or must we put you in goal?'

Batur agreed to pay the fine, and was handed over to a policeman until the £2 was brought by his kinsmen.

This case happened only a few months before I left this part of Tivland, and I do not know whether Batur was ever 'caught' by *swem*, or whether he admitted that he had been lying and had *swem* 'repaired' for him.

It is sometimes very difficult for the judges to make the witness swear an oath, but it is usually assumed that if he tries too hard to avoid taking an oath, he intends to lie. A good example of stubbornness on both sides is to be found in:

JIR NO. 19. *Nguhar (husband) calls Tarkighir (adulterer)*
A woman tries to bear false witness.

Tarkighir, accused of committing adultery with the wife of Nguhar and giving her 6*d*. for the privilege, denied having done so, and told a story that she had sent him for another man to commit adultery with her. The wife denied that either Tarkighir or any other man had had intercourse with her, or that she had sent Tarkighir for anyone. However, one of her 'co-wives' (the wife of some member of her husband's compound) had been in Tarkighir's compound with her at the time when the adultery was alleged to have occurred. The *mbatarev* sent for this co-wife, whose name was Girgi, to act as witness in the *jir*.

Girgi was a small, compact, stubborn woman who began to talk the moment she sat down before the *mbatarev* in the court circle. She talked very rapidly but had barely got beyond the point of saying that she and her co-wife were hoeing farms and Tarkighir came by, when Chenge stopped her and told her she must swear on *swem*. Scarcely pausing for breath, she told him she would tell him the truth without swearing on *swem*, and that she shouldn't swear because she was a woman. She launched back into her story; Chenge again interrupted and instructed her to take the *swem* pot in her hands and make the ritual motions of swearing. She said that she didn't want to swear—that *swem* was a thing of men, and that women shouldn't touch it. When Chenge assured her that women often swore on *swem*, she told him she was pregnant (almost surely a lie). He told her that this has nothing whatever to do with the matter. She again said that she was telling the truth, so there was no point in swearing. For over ten minutes, Chenge and the other *mbatarev* cajoled, threatened, bullied, teased, before she finally agreed to swear. She picked up the pot, made the ritual gestures quickly, set it down and said:

'My co-wife, Ierun, and I often go to Tarkighir's compound. It is near our farms, and we go there to rest. We sit in the reception hut and talk. On this day, Tarkighir asked Ierun to go into his hut with him. I was shocked and surprised that Ierun did so.' She looked about her and back at the ground, as if she were ashamed of what she was saying, 'I sat in the reception hut. Tarkighir was in his sleeping hut with Ierun. After they had been there a long time, I became uneasy and went and rapped on the door.'

Chenge interrupted to ask, 'Was the door shut?'

With a look that indicated that she disliked him greatly both for having made her swear (and thus to tell the truth) and for asking this particular question, she replied. 'Yes, the door had been pushed to. I rapped on the door and told my co-wife to come out and that we should go. Ierun came out, and we went to our farms. That is all I know.'

Chenge and the *mbatarev* now agreed that she had probably told the truth, that this was indeed all she knew about it and that she could go. Obviously extremely angry, she left the court circle and walked immediately out of the compound.

Here was a woman who evidently had every intention of giving false evidence in support of her co-wife, but was not prepared to do so on oath. She was not allowed to testify without swearing, for it was almost certain that any woman in her position would lie in order to preserve the relationship between herself and her co-wife, as well as that between her co-wife and their husband. When I discussed this case with Chenge on the following evening, he said that Girgi had to be made to take the oath, for had she told what she did otherwise than under oath, she would have been 'spoiling the compound' (*vihi ya*).

All the cases thus far cited involved swearing on *swem*, and indeed most oaths taken in Native Authority courts during the time of my field-work were on *swem*. However, cases from the 1930's recorded in the administrative files show that most Tiv were then sworn on 'stone and steel'. The Tiv fire-making device, consisting of a piece of flint and a small piece of bent iron, is associated (as is lightning) with the *akombo iwa*, which is, again, associated with blacksmiths. The *akombo iwa* is one of the most complex elements in Tiv religion, and its transgression includes such appalling fates as impotence, constant backache, and other ailments, though it can seldom cause death. When it does, it is death by lightning. The *akombo iwa* is, it seems to me, the fetish most closely related to God, *Aondo*; the prehistoric celt, called God's axe, is its symbol.

I have never seen Tiv sworn on 'stone and steel', but one does often see them sworn on the *akombo iwa*. The stone and steel as the emblems of the *iwa* have been replaced by either the stone celt or a pair of tongs. Many elders wear as an ornament a sort of decorative tongs with beads. These tongs, resembling blacksmith's tongs, are considered an adequate representation of the *akombo iwa* for the administration of oaths. They are not often used when *swem* is present, but the MbaDuku *mbatarev* often swore witnesses on tongs when they were away from Chenge's compound and hence away from his *swem* emblems (see *Jir* No. 14).

The only other common fetish emblem used for oaths is the palm-branch, an emblem of the *akombo igbe*, which causes— or, more precisely, *is*—dysentery and other blood symptoms. It is rarely used in court.

It is evident, in discussing oaths with Tiv, that they see all oath-taking in accordance with the same set of ideas as they see ordeals. Taking an oath on the *akombo iwa* or the *akombo igbe* is 'touching' (*bende*) this fetish. If you lie on oath, you have 'pierced' (*pev*) the fetish. Both words are used when one has fallen foul of a fetish—the notion of 'touching' is usually passive, indicating no blame attaching to the victim, while the notion of 'piercing' usually does assume such blame, more or less strongly, and hence might be translated as 'transgression' of an *akombo*.

The relationship—indeed, the identity—of oaths and ordeals is, however, best seen when considering *swem*. In explaining the nature of oaths on *swem*, Tiv draw the investigator's attention to what we would call, in English, the ordeal by sasswood. They say, in effect, that the principle of *swem* and the principle of sasswood are the same, but that sasswood works very much more quickly. Sasswood is occasionally today administered to chickens, in a manner reminiscent of, but very different from, that described by Professor Evans-Pritchard for the Azande.[8] That oracle is in the hands of men who also perform divination by other means. Formerly sasswood is said to have been administered (under the direction of moots and of age-sets) to two disputants in cases of witchcraft if the accuser demanded it. In demanding it, however, he was aware that he must drink the sasswood first. Sasswood is a strychnine poison and if a man died from drinking it his guilt was proved and his punishment accomplished. If he vomited it and recovered, his innocence was established.

I have on several occasions been told by elders, particularly in Iharev but not only there, that although *swem* and sasswood work in the same way, *swem* is so much slower and less sure that there has been no effective means of controlling witches since the sasswood ordeal was outlawed. I have discovered only one case in which sasswood was administered to human beings in recent years. This was an instance some time in the 1940's when a man, who thought himself wrongly judged by the appeal court (Grade C) of Jecira lineage in Vande Ikya, rushed into the court circle and drank off a large calabash of sasswood, which he had prepared himself. He immediately vomited it, thereby proving his innocence to himself and his kinsmen and neighbours. The Assistant District Officer present sentenced him to six months for attempted suicide.

Oaths are in the nature of minor ordeals. Their purpose is not, however, to judge guilt or innocence but only to act as penalty if norms associated with that oath are breached. Oaths are administered to witnesses because the witnesses' only concern in the dispute is with what we would call the truth.

Oaths are not, however, administered to the principal litigants. The oath-ordeal would judge principals not merely on the possible breach of norm of truth-telling, but also on the breach of norm before the *jir*. Were an oath of this sort to be administered to the principals of the case, the purpose of the *jir* would no longer exist. The dispute would be removed from the social to the supernatural plane, and the penalty would be supernatural instead of one administered and controlled by human beings.

Truth. We must, finally, consider just what it is for which Tiv *mbatarev* are searching when they call or admit witnesses, and what criteria they use for truth. It is notable that in Western judicial systems the 'truth' means the verifiable 'facts' of what took place. Western jurists have a single standard of 'truth'—verifiability—and they have provided themselves with an elaborate mechanism for determining it. They demand the same standards of 'truth' from all persons who appear before a court, be they witnesses, expert witnesses, or principal litigants. They have created complex systems of procedure which are known as 'rules of evidence' in order to elicit and judge this verifiable 'truth' in the course of court action.

As one discusses witnesses and what we should call 'evidence' with Tiv, one comes to realize that they do not have a single criterion for truth. They do not require the same standards of 'truth' from principals in a *jir* as they do from witnesses. The common word usually translated 'lies' (*yie*) has, actually, two antonyms in Tiv instead of the single one which the English word 'lie' or 'falsehood' has. When one begins to use the word, and more particularly when it is used to one, the meaning becomes very uncertain. The earliest entry in my notebooks about this word occurs some three months after my arrival in Tivland. I had learnt the word *yie* in connexion with land cases. On this day, however, I noted that, after a short talk with a stranger, I had given the standard parting phrase 'Go well' (*dza dedo*), and he had replied 'That is no *yie*.' I noted that I must have misunderstood him. The next entry, a few days later, recalls an incident in which people asked me for tobacco—I usually carried small amounts to give away. I replied that it was finished, but that I would have some next time I came to their compound. They were pleased and answered, 'That's no *yie*.' It began to be evident that *yie* didn't mean merely 'lies' extended to 'broken promises', though it does mean both.

Again a few days later, I recorded that on the way to market I stopped at the compound of an elder to rest. In typical Tiv fasion, he asked me where I was going. I told him. He replied, 'That's no *yie*', obviously meaning that it was a good thing for me to be going to market. I began to understand this word *yie*. A few months later, after the first Tiv-Udam war, I was again asked one day where I was going. I replied that I was cyclnig to Obodu to deliver to the District Officer there a message which I had received from officials in Tivland. When I had finished the explanation—I knew the inquirer well—he answered, 'That's no *yie*', and it meant 'What you are doing will bring no harm to anyone, and is not a thing to be disapproved of.'

Yie can be the object of two verbs: *er*, which means 'to do or to make', and *kaa* which means 'to tell or to say'. Many Tiv say that there is no difference between doing *yie* and telling *yie*, but others have carefully set forth the difference for me. To 'tell' a *yie* is to say something or make a remark which disturbs the even flow of social relationships—it makes no difference whether the remark is 'true' or 'false', in the sense that we use these words in English, *unless* it be to someone's detriment, in which case it is judged worse to tell a false *yie* than a true one. On the other hand, 'doing *yie*' is acting in bad taste, usually to the detriment of someone. If a man tells his wife a bit of scandal in strict confidence and she repeats it, she is 'doing *yie*', even though the statement may be true, as we think of the word 'true'. To 'tell *yie*' indicates that the *yie* is in the thing told. To 'do *yie*' is to indicate that the *yie* is in the act of telling.

In *Jir* No. 19 above, the *mbatarev* had to make Girgi take an oath before she gave evidence concerning the adultery of her co-wife. Had they not done so, she would have 'told *iye*', that is, given the *mbatarev* false information about the actions and movements of her co-wife. Had she told what we would consider the truth about her co-wife's actions, thereby creating difficulties for her co-wife, she would have been 'doing *yie*'. Under oath, Girgi did not either tell *yie* or do *yie*; but it was the oath which saved her from the necessity of one or the other.

In my effort to learn the word *yie* and its correct use, I recorded one statement which amused me at the time: 'A *yie* is not a thing of truth' (*mimi*). This statement does not mean merely 'A lie is not the truth', which is what dictionary definitions would give, but rather 'To do a *yie* is not right.' The difficulty is now in the word *mimi*, one of the two antonyms of *yie*. *Mimi* means 'right'; it contains some of the same ambiguity as the English word 'right', in that it means both the morally good thing and the socially correct thing, a distinction which is not easy to make in the Tiv language. What it does not necessarily imply, though it may do so, is the factually correct thing. If this aspect of 'right' is to be emphasized, the correct word is *vough*, which means 'straight or precise'. In hut-building a door placed in just the right spot is *vough*. In farm mounding, a truly straight row is *vough*. In recounting a story or an event, to give the precise facts is to 'speak *vough*'.

In considering the evidence presented to the *jir*, one must always keep in mind the similarities and distinctions between the two words *mimi* and *vough*. We must also realize that each speaker also weights these words from his own point of view. Therefore, an accuser in a Tiv court action may 'speak *mimi*', but this does not mean that we can, translating, say that he is telling the truth. He is, rather, telling that version of the story which does least damage to social relationships from his own point of view. He might, at a later date, even admit that he did not 'speak *vough*'. The accused in his turn will 'speak *mimi*', but *mimi* is not the same thing from his point of view as it is from that of the accuser. Therefore, the two stories are both *mimi* to the teller and *yie* to his opponent. This merely means that, because of the concatenation of social relationships found in any social action, the criteria of *mimi* may differ according to the standpoint of each actor.

Tiv judges do not expect principal litigants to speak *vough*, but only to speak *mimi*. For principals, the two may be opposed.

It is generally conceded, however, that for a witness to speak *vough* is *ipso facto* to speak *mimi*. From the standpoint of the witness, the 'right' thing to do is to smooth over social relationships, and hence to report what actually occurred so that the judges will have a way of knowing what the rights of the matter are. Tiv compare this to divination—a diviner can ask any questions he likes of his clients; if the clients do not do *mimi* by speaking *vough*, the apparatus will be misinformed and hence cannot give a correct (*vough*) answer. However, it seems to me that no Tiv would blame a witness for telling what we should consider to be untruths, if by so doing the criterion of *mimi* were maintained, and the judgment could still be wholeheartedly concurred in by both principals.

There is one other truth-concept current among Tiv which should be investigated here, though it plays a relatively minor role in jural action. This is the matter of acting with one heart (*shima i môm*) and with two hearts (*asema a har*). The phrase, 'with two hearts', is more often descriptive of specific relationships. As one informant put it, in a text I recorded myself:

'If a man likes you with two hearts, he is not truly your friend. He can kill you or give another person money to kill you with medicine. But if a man likes you with one heart, he really likes you. He cannot speak ill of you or gossip about you. And if another man starts to gossip about you with him, he will stick up for you.

'There are also stories of two hearts and those of one heart. A story [the same word means conversation] of two hearts is when somebody does not speak precisely (*vough*). If a man asks you something and you don't want to tell him correctly, he will say, "What is this? I ask you something, but you don't want to tell me with one heart. Why do you tell me things with two hearts?" '

The expression 'with one heart' can also be used as an emphatic, where it means 'wholehearted'. All meat is sweet, say Tiv, but pork is sweet 'with one heart'. A man can be wholeheartedly a bad lot.

'Truth' in Tivland is an elusive matter because smooth social relationships are deemed of higher cultural value than mere precision of fact. We must not judge Tiv litigants or witnesses by our standards. They are not liars, as they are sometimes called: their truth has other referents than has European truth.

Notes

1 The flavour of the word is similar (except that it is not slang) to the American slang 'to give', meaning to tell what one knows.

2 The original names were members of my household. When Iyorkôsu invented stories he always set them amongst ourselves, carefully rotating the wrongdoer.

3 Needless to say, had such a bargain been arrived at, it would have taken hours of dickering.

4 See discussion of *iwuhe* . . . pp. 140 ff.

5 *Ayande* (Marantochloa flexuosa) and *ikula i nomsu*.

6 *Ka swem ne ga. Or gen ôr wuewue m fa ga, kpa kwagh u m tese la, ka kwagh vough. Kwagh u m fe la, m tese vough.*

7 To repair is to counteract by ritual. I was the only one of those who heard this story interested in the subsequent recovery or death of the perjurer. I was never able to discover his fate, and had no chance to inquire in Mbara.

8 E. E. Evans-Pritchard, *Witchcraft, Oracles and Magic among the Azande*. Oxford, 1937.

PART II

CRIMES AND CIVIL WRONGS

CHAPTER 6

THE DISTINCTION BETWEEN CRIMES AND CIVIL WRONGS

THE problem which is discussed in this chapter—the distinction between crimes and civil wrongs—is one which is common to most legal systems, ancient or modern, wherever they exist. It does, however, occur in rather more acute form in relation to African customary law—partly because there is an absence of any analytical treatment of legal concepts within the customary legal system itself, and partly because of the degree to which a satisfactory solution depends on a clearly articulated distinction between the degree of involvement of 'the state' in each of these categories and the manner of handling them. Since 'the state' frequently does not exist at all in the customary framework of several societies, and is found in varying degrees of effectiveness in others (see Chapter 1 of the Customary Judicial Process, supra), this provides no easy answer to the problem either. *Elias* goes into this matter very thoroughly in the extract presented here, and examines the views of a number of other writers on the subject. *Schapera* on the other hand, introduces his treatment of the problem among the Tswana with the statement that 'In practice, although not in theory, Tswana law is divided by the people themselves into two main classes. These may quite conveniently be termed "civil law" and "criminal law" respectively, although their categories are by no means identical with those of European systems of law', which is a useful summary of the more practical approach to it. *Bohannan*, in the extract given here, deals with the topic as well, and contributes a valuable set of descriptions of terminology used by the Tiv, thus suggesting a linguistic approach to the question of classification which is a useful substitute for the type of abstract analysis which has been used in jurisprudential writing on the topic in relation to other systems of law.

T. O. Elias: The Nature of African Customary Law*

Denial of the Distinction in African Law

The assertion has often been made by writers on African law, at least by those of the older generation, that no distinction is ever made therein between civil and criminal wrongs as commonly conceived in 'European' law.[1] The usual evidence cited in support is that offences like murder and theft, which are clearly criminal offences according to English law, are generally treated by many African societies as matters for private

* T. O. Elias, *The Nature of African Customary Law*, Manchester University Press, 1956, pp. 110–129.

redress by the wronged party or group rather than by the State as the custodian of public safety and welfare. Now, while there is some truth in this way of thinking, it is certainly not wholly accurate.

Several factors appear to be responsible for the inadequacy of the prevailing analysis, and mention may be made of, *inter alia*, these important ones: (*a*) the great influence of Sir Henry Maine's writings; (*b*) the tendency on the part of these writers on African law to forget, or perhaps to be unaware of, the historical evolution of the distinction made in modern English law; (*c*) the common disposition to argue as if the classification of offences into criminal and civil were clear-cut and free from difficulties in European legal systems or even within the content of English law itself; and (*d*) the all too ready desire to assume that African law in general must, by the very fact of being African, be irreconcilably different from English, indeed European, law.

Let us begin, then, with Maine. It will be recalled that he it was who first drew attention in his *Ancient Law* to what he regarded as the strange preponderance of criminal over civil law in '*ancient*' (identified for this purpose with *African*) law. Maine had stressed the primitive belligerency of the savage, who are supposed to be always at war with one another and whose daily life is, because of the prevailing social chaos, supposed to be dominated by crime. Then he added this controversial point: 'Now the penal law of ancient communities is not the law of Crimes, it is the law of Wrongs, or, to use the English technical words, of Torts.'[2] The qualification here implied of the theory of warring savages does not acquit him of the charge of responsibility for the fundamental fallacy. Like some others of Maine's not so happy generalisations, this is very confused and confusing, even as a description. It is apparently a contradiction in terms to say that a *penal* law is a law of *civil* wrongs; but what the jurist really implied is that penalties for *all* wrongs are extracted by the affected individual or his clan as a matter of private vengeance or redress.

According to this view, there is no feeling of public sentiment, no principle of social solidarity in an African society capable of arousing the corporate ire of the community and expressing itself in some form of joint effort against disturbers of the social equilibrium. Writers[3] who follow Maine into this species of speculative opinion must be taken to assume that all African societies are of a piece in never having evolved, politically, beyond the stage of the patriarchal or matriarchal family. We know, however, that this is not the case and that there are many with centralised political authorities, administrative machinery, military and judicial organs, that do enforce law and order as understood in their several communities. In societies with a rudimentary political organisation, it is usually the case that permanent and continuous guardians of the public weal are hard to identify, since very often these communities lack a regular system of chiefship or kingship. But, unless these democratic and equalitarian human groups had always had the inevitable social instinct of fellowship and harmonious living together, their communities could not have endured thus far. There must have been some standards of social behaviour, some irreducible minimum of collective public sentiment, a flouting of which by a swashbuckling member would provoke universal disapprobation, if not joint repressive action.

Some Refutation of the Arguments

It is against the placid acceptance of the Mainesque theory that 'primitive law' does not discriminate between civil and criminal offences that Malinowski has so effectively protested in his *Crime and Custom in Savage Society*. He is at pains to demonstrate that 'civil law, consisting of positive ordinances, is much more developed than the body of mere prohibitions', and that 'a study of purely criminal law among savages misses the most important phenomena of their legal life'.[4] While admitting that in the Trobriand Islands, with which he is immediately concerned, crimes 'can be but vaguely defined', he insists that all 'primitive' peoples have civil as well as criminal law. Murder, theft, breaches of exogamy and sorcery, for example, are all crimes. As for civil law, which Malinowski proclaims to be the dominant one in the Trobriand society he is describing, instances are marriage, inheritance, property, exchange by barter, and the innumerable social activities that so significantly characterise the life of the community . . . Malinowski has allowed his revolt against the charge that primitive law deals only with crime to lead him to the opposite extreme of saying that it deals only with civil wrongs.

Talbot's verdict, in his voluminous study of the peoples of Southern Nigeria, is:

'The distinction between criminal and civil offences was not very definite, and the same act might be regarded as either, according to the tribe or clan. It will be seen that, in the main, the classification was not very different to our own.'[5] Dr. Meek, writing of the Ibos, has observed: '... what are crimes or torts to us are for the most part crimes or torts to them.'[6] Lowie is quite sure that 'primitive' law does make a clear 'distinction between torts and crimes'.[7] Diamond, the well-known authority on 'primitive' law, is emphatic that it recognises a distinction between civil and criminal wrongs, at least at a certain stage.[8] Lowie has recorded that among the Amaxosa and their neighbours 'a fundamental distinction is drawn between criminal and civil cases. The former include political offences, sorcery, and crimes against the persons of tribesmen; they are prosecuted by the chiefs and the fines belong to them by inalienable right. All other cases are prosecuted by the plaintiffs and the chiefs have no claim to the award made.'[9]

Offences of a criminal character have also been discerned among, for example, the Kamba of Kenya. According to Penwill,[10] 'when the "utui" elders felt that a crime was too serious to be atoned for by the fine of a bull, or by driving the culprit out', they would arraign its perpetrator formally before the 'king'ole'[11] as an 'undesirable member of the community'. If found guilty of the charges preferred against him, he might be executed in a bush rendezvous. An alternative mode of punishment sometimes ordered by the 'king'ole' was for the man to be hanged by the neck from some tree in a public thoroughfare 'as a warning to the other potential wrong-doers'.

We learn also that among the Bantu of North Kavirondo, homicide and theft are normally redressible by compensation, whereas incest and witchcraft are punishable as crimes; that in cases of theft there is usually no need for the parties to a suit to give presents (in the form of cattle) to the judges in advance, since the latter expect that fines are forthcoming by law; but that in cases of debt and 'bride-price', such gifts are regularly made. This is evidence of a differentiation of procedure which is, at the very least, suggestive of the modern distinction between criminal and civil cases.[12]

Other instances of the public organisation of redress for certain private wrongs that are considered to affect the body politic can be cited. With respect to the Ibos, another example of a people without a strong politically centralised authority, Miss Green has described how offenders against the code of conduct enjoined upon members of certain associations or even against what has been publicly decreed as binding rules are punished by collective action.[13] She adds that 'the commission of an offence which is ... forbidden —would seem to involve the whole community and not merely the individuals concerned. The individuals who take action do so on the part of the community. If there is any point in trying to apply the categories of criminal and civil law to Ibo judicial matters, then presumably offences against Ala and probably other such (*forbidden*) behaviour might be classified as criminal cases.'[14] She elsewhere[15] describes stealing as 'the classic Ibo crime'.

On the other hand, we have writers like C. C. Roberts pontificating thus: 'Primitive law lays down rules for behaviour and its penalties are directed ... towards the restoration of the equilibrium. There is no distinction between civil and criminal law as we understand it.'[16] Since this view is typical of those held by some writers who have had some connexion with the administration of law in parts of British Africa, we will pause for a while to consider what the distinction between civil and criminal law really is in English law, so that we may the better appreciate this insistence on the African divergence from the normal. Let us take some authoritative examples of this school of thought.

Analysis of the Issues Involved

Now, three heroic efforts have been made to define the English (perhaps we should say, the Anglo-American) legal distinction between civil and criminal offences:

(1) The first is that of Orde-Browne who wrote that the conception of society taking vengeance on an offender was one quite alien to the African, while any reformative effect depended upon the application of the principle that law-breaking did not pay. The culprit was mulcted for the benefit of the sufferer, and it was obviously not worth while to infringe the established rules. But one may seriously doubt whether this is peculiar to African customary law, and whether it is a valid basis of distinction between it and other types of law. Nevertheless, the writer felt able to draw this strange inference:

'Thus the law was civil rather than criminal, and all but the gravest and most unusual crimes were dealt with on a system which resembled arbitration rather than punishment; so long as the harm done was as far as possible made good, society was not expected to take further action.'[17]

The learned writer then proceeds to consider the nature of crime 'according to European ideas' as currently accepted. He believes it to be evident that crime 'can be divided into two classes, real and technical offences', that under 'British law' both classes might be dealt with by the police but that there is usually 'a clear distinction between the two' in that society adopts a different attitude towards them; so that anyone found guilty, for instance, of riding a bicycle on the footpath would not feel the disgrace attaching to a conviction for theft.

After allowing for the fact that punishments nowadays are lighter in some ways but heavier in others than they were in his grandfather's days, the writer insists:[18] 'Nevertheless, there is always an underlying conception of the difference between a disgraceful action and one that is merely culpable; and this forms the basis of the public opinion upon which all effectual law must be grounded.' In advancing this curious argument it does not seem ever to have occurred to Orde-Browne that he is merely stating a truism about law in general. Regarded as an attempt to lay down a logical basis of differentiation between African and European law, this argument does not bear a close analysis; as an attempt to define the boundary between civil and criminal offences, even under English law, it is no more than an expression of the vague feeling of all those who pontificate on what they regard as African legal curiosities without having previously informed themselves sufficiently of the niceties of English law, a knowledge of which they often so dangerously take for granted.

(2) The second is that of Hone who asserts[19] that a wrong which is 'an injury to society at large' and the punishment of which at the same time proves to be 'a deterrent to all other members of the State' and 'a corrective to the individual wrong-doer' is what Europeans call 'a crime'. It is 'the duty of the State to detect them, to arrest the criminal and then to move the proper tribunal to exact an appropriate punishment and afterwards to carry it out'. Truthfully enough the learned jurist observes that the ability of a community to recognise certain wrongful deeds as crimes denotes a certain stage of development; but he is in error when, writing of Uganda of all African societies, he argues that 'the conception is clearly an advanced one not to be generally associated with or expected from primitive communities such as flourished in Uganda before the advent of the European'. We shall see presently how he himself impliedly admits that even at that stage some Uganda tribes had already recognised between types of offences a distinction more or less similar to that between civil and criminal.

Again, like Orde-Browne, he soon becomes involved in contradictions. He expressed the conviction that where, for example, he found that the death penalty was in fact exacted in pursuance of customary law, 'the fundamental justification was retribution and the restoration of balance, rather than that the public conscience was shocked into the infliction of the extreme penalty as a warning and deterrent to lawless persons and as a protection to society at large'.

But such was the weight of the evidence surrounding him as he wrote these words that he hastened to add this important qualification of the pathetic fallacy: 'While the facts show this hypothesis as to the native conception of law to be a true one, there is, nevertheless, evidence that in parts of Uganda, some wrongs in certain tribes were already recognised as injuring society at large and, therefore calling for a penalty which stamped the disapproval of the State as such and was more than merely commensurate with the wrong done to the individual who primarily suffered.'

With respect to the Lango, the least organised tribe from the point of view of legal development, he warned that the clear evidence that then existed of indigenous conception of wrongs amounting to crimes must not be taken for what they really were: 'Thus, the exaction of the death penalty among the Lango, in cases of patricide or fratricide is not to be quoted as an instance of more advanced ideas; it depended for its justification merely on the *inefficacy of the punishment of compensation and the need for restoring the balance of a life for a life*.'[20] This tendency of writers to refuse to face facts and to attempt to explain away such inconvenient examples, so persistent in almost all the African societies hitherto accurately studied, is not a little difficult to understand.

The case is still more perplexing when such bland denials of a distinction by Africans between civil and criminal offences are almost invariably followed in the same account by some such grudging admission as this one, again by Hone. He wrote: 'Even among these primitive people, however, it was recognised that three species of misdeeds were wrongs against society at large for which there could be no appropriate remedy save the complete removal of the offender from the ranks of the tribe by immediate death. These offences were witchcraft, incest and sexual offences contrary to nature.'

Of the more advanced tribes in Uganda and elsewhere in Africa, this verdict is still truer.

(3) The third view is that of Seagle[21] who, after criticising Malinowski for saying that 'primitive' law also recognises a distinction between civil and criminal law, goes on to admit that 'it is extremely difficult to distinguish civil from criminal law even in mature legal systems. It can be done neither in terms of procedure nor of sanctions. Criminal law is a breach of public law but there is no absolute formal distinction between public and private law.'

Had this learned jurist stopped there, all might have been well. But he felt bound to specify a threefold basis of distinction between civil and criminal law which should enable him to set 'primitive' law apart from European law. He argues that[22]—

(i) 'the classic dualism is founded primarily in economic individualism.' Here, the writer develops the theme that the 'civil law' becomes associated with private rights and that there is really no civil law 'until there is a market in which things are exchanged as abstract commodities' rather than as concrete object of use.

(ii) 'the criminal law betokens a State monopoly of force.' In both civil and criminal law what really happens is that 'the will of the State is objectified', the only difference being that in the former the State is an umpire between two private individuals as litigating integers, whereas in the latter the State supplies the public prosecutor as one of the integers.

(iii) the award of the court differs, too, in that while in one case it is a 'commodity', in the other it is a 'penalty'.

He therefore concludes: 'In the absence of both the State and the market the distinction between civil and criminal law, is altogether without fundamental basis.' By this interesting piece of dialectic our jurist is able to reach substantially the same conclusion as that of Hone, namely, that the drawing of a distinction between civil and criminal offences represents an advanced stage of intellectual and political orientation not normally to be expected of 'primitive' societies. We have just shown how far this conclusion is valid.

It must be confessed, however, that of all the arguments usually advanced in favour of a scientific distinction between civil and criminal law, this economic interpretation is the strangest. We may well ask: What has the economic exchange of commodities got to do with the primordial problem of classifying legal wrongs? Does the legal distinction between civil and criminal offences in, say, American law really turn upon whether material goods are exchanged on a system of barter or on a money-for-goods basis? One would ordinarily have thought that such considerations were clearly irrelevant to the juridical issue involved?

But, it is true to say, as does our jurist, that no distinction can be made between civil and criminal wrongs in terms either of procedure or sanctions. Thus, to take two important examples of the classical English concepts, Blackstone defines crime as 'a violation of the public rights and duties due to the whole community, considered as a community';[23] but Kenny, thinking this inadequate and adapting Austin's definition, suggests that 'crimes are wrongs whose sanction is punitive, and is in no way remissible by any private person, but is remissible by the Crown alone, if remissible at all'.[24] It has to be said, however, that the difference between Blackstone and Kenny is not so much a fundamental disagreement about the essence of crime as a measure of the development that has taken place in legal ideas and processes in England between the eighteenth and the twentieth centuries. Neither the 'violation of the public rights and duties' of the community nor the State's power of remission of an offender's punishment can entirely explain why certain offences are civil and others criminal.[25] Accordingly, no absolutely satisfactory definition of a crime has yet been put forward by any jurist—so intractably subtle is the distinction between civil and criminal offences even in developed systems. It is therefore surprising to find Mr. Seagle employing so confidently this economic theory as a basis for such a distinction.

Distinction into Private and Public Law

We have now seen how the various writers on African law have fallen into unnecessary quibbles and contradictions in their several attempts to deny that a distinction—even such as can be said to exist at all in all legal systems—does exist also in African customary law.

Some jurists have despaired of the classic differentiation of offences into civil and criminal, and have sought to substitute for it one into *private* and *public*, as if these were themselves terms of art. This revival of the Blackstonian ideal has been prompted by a desire to find some workable basis of classification of legal wrongs which would avoid the difficulties inherent in the now more popular but scarcely less imprecise civil-and-criminal dichotomy. Thus Radcliffe-Brown has suggested[26] that the terms 'public delict' and 'private delict' would be more appropriate to describe the undoubted differentiation, which he discovers that 'primitive' law makes, between categories of offences. Driberg, in taking up this theme song, has been even bolder in asserting that Africans do not understand the distinction between civil and criminal but that they do that between public and private law. His definition is: 'Private law deals with acts which disturb the equilibrium; public law with acts or situations which negative those conditions which make the maintenance of the equilibrium possible.'[27] He continues to argue that only in offences which are held to be definitely anti-social is the public law invoked, and by anti-social is meant 'something much more than the disturbance of this or that equilibrium'. The anti-social crimes which he puts under public law are treason, witchcraft, incest and sexual perversions, and any of these is punished by death, 'because that is the only measure which can preserve society'. He even admits there and then: 'This is true also of nearly all the major offences in our criminal codes. . . .'[28] It is interesting to note also that Driberg, throughout the remainder of his article, continues to employ the terms civil and criminal in discussing African law.

Again, Driberg is in error when he regards as treasonable 'an act subversive of the conditions under which alone equilibrium can be maintained' and as, therefore, coming within the category of 'public offences' but nevertheless as 'not inflicted in retaliation for the offences *per se*, but because through the centralisation of authority in the ruler as representative of tribal interests these offences had come to be regarded as treason'. One would have thought that the whole tenor of the evolution of English criminal law has been a movement from the exaction of private vengeance by the injured individual to the monopoly of redress (for offences *contra pacem regis*) by the monarch on behalf of the community. Where is the fundamental difference between the African and the European concepts in this respect? In certain of the more highly organised communities, the compensation paid in private suits goes to the ruler who may then give back part or all of it to the successful litigant. The common saying in homicide cases is that 'all blood belongs to the chief', and the legal implication is that such offences are an affront to the authority of the chief or king who is thereby entitled to avenge the wronged members of the community.[29]

On the whole, therefore, one can see quite clearly that there are about as many difficulties in distinguishing between public and private offences[30] as between criminal and civil, and that either method will not support the view that African law is necessarily different from the European on that score. It is suggested, with respect, that what matters is not the name by which offences are designated in a particular legal system but the extent to which they are recognised and punished as such. The recognition accorded as well as the penalty imposed must depend ultimately upon the classificatory device adopted by a given society for the realisation within itself of peaceful and orderly existence among its members. On this basis it is further submitted that the popular rough-and-ready distinction between civil and criminal be retained for our present purposes and that, so far as it can be said to be valid at all for English (or even European) law, it is also valid *mutatis mutandis* for African law generally.

Summary of Evidence in Favour of the Distinction into Civil and Criminal Law

In thus holding that African law, like any other law, differentiates between offences that must be publicly punished by society at large and those that should be left to private redress, we are not by any means suggesting that there is, therefore, no difference between the African and a more developed legal system like the English. What we do affirm is that the basic attitude is essentially similar, though not necessarily identical in all respects. It would be not only foolish but absurd to ignore the obvious fact, that the legal, no less than the other, arrangements of a society, are affected by their sociological context. What we have been trying to say all this while is that a human society, whether hierarchically organised or horizontally aligned, whether European or African, has broad notions of what may be safely left to private arbitration or self-help and what ought to be made the concern of all as likely to imperil orderly social existence. Of course, such notions will vary as much, or as little, with the *mores* and the *ethos* of particular communities as with their historical and geographical conditions. Thus:

(i) The class of offences which English law regards as criminal is different in marked respects from that recognised by, for example, French law; and the same is true as between Anglo-American legal systems on the one hand and Continental systems on the other. Even as between the English and American laws or as between one Continental country and another, there are noteworthy points of difference in the matter of classification of offences into the civil and the criminal.

For example, according to Gordon Westwood,[31] English law punishes homosexuality as a crime under the Offences Against the Person Act, 1861, whereas in most of the countries with penal systems based on the Code Napoléon such as France, Switzerland, Egypt, and China as well as some American States, homosexuality between two consenting adults is not even a civil offence, let alone a criminal one.* Also, in French law, incest is not defined as a crime *per se*, and even in England where homosexuality has been a felony since feudal times, incest only became a crime in 1908. On the other hand, in practically all African societies incest and unnatural sexual behaviour have always, as far back as we can go, been visited with the severest penalties ranging from execution[32] of the offender to personal torture or a heavy fine.

Again, adultery is a crime under French law[33] and, as was formerly the case in the English action of 'criminal conversation' against an adulterer, a wife's single act of adultery was sufficient to constitute a crime, but if an action were brought against the husband it had to be shown that his adultery was not an isolated act and that it had been committed inside the matrimonial home. In the matter of penalty for the crime of adultery, the husband can only be fined, whereas the wife is liable to a term of imprisonment of from two months to two years.[34] Adultery in England was formerly punishable by a tort action for 'criminal conversation' until the latter was abolished in 1857;[35] however, adultery is still the basis of a claim for damages. But in many African societies, adultery is a civil offence,[36] although in some it may be treated as a crime: for instance, it seems to be a crime in parts of Nyasaland,[37] and in Kenya it is made a crime against local law and custom when it is punishable by a fine of up to 40*s*. in addition to the customary compensation.[38]†

It is not generally remembered in this connexion that within English law itself, the very same offence may be both a civil wrong and a criminal offence. Instances are Defamation, Conspiracy and the various forms of Trespass to the Person—assault, battery and false imprisonment. For each of these offences the injured party may of his own motion bring a civil action or the State may institute a criminal prosecution. Certain offences that were formerly treated by the law as no offence at all or perhaps as civil wrongs have been subsequently turned into criminal offences by statute.

(ii) By English law, a breach of contract is a civil wrong involving the guilty party in liability for damages to the innocent party. But, in parts of British Central and Eastern Africa, a breach by an employee of his contract of employment has been made a crime under the various Master and Servant Ordinances.

Occasionally, in English law, a predominantly criminal offence may be treated by the court as if it were civil, especially if the parties have kinship ties or where these are still vital in the locality. An example of how an English court would apply the human touch and waive technicalities is a recent case[39] between a Mr. Fairhurst and his niece, a Mrs. Sproson, at the Chester Assizes held on October 30, 1952. It happened that while 71-year-old Fairhurst was living with his niece and her husband at Crewe, the niece

* This was written before the introduction of the law which legalises homosexuality between consenting adults.

† This discussion of the treatment of adultery as a crime was written before the modern developments in African countries regarding customary criminal offences, which, broadly speaking, involves the abolition of all unwritten criminal law. See, e.g. Constitutions of Uganda, Kenya, Nigeria, and see E. Cotran, *Report on Customary Criminal Offences in Kenya*.

stole £436 from her uncle's tin biscuit box placed in a trunk in which he had kept the sum of £500. Instead of causing a prosecution for larceny to be instituted, he sued for the return of the stolen money as for a civil debt and Mr. Justice Pearson gave him judgement with costs. Mrs Sproson admitted that she 'went to uncle's box' as and when she needed the money. The judge observed that the tin trunk was tied only with rope and that it was a very careless and unfair way for Mr. Fairhurst to keep his money: 'he had put the defendants in temptation'. Considering that this was a glaring case of larceny, we may ask why the judge did not order a criminal prosecution of the thieving niece instead of trying the case as one for the recovery of a mere civil debt. It is submitted that some such consideration as this will often be found to account for the tendency, so usually exaggerated, of African law to adopt the role of a domestic tribunal in many cases where a more developed body of law would apply the criminal sanction.

In those African societies with close kinship ties, many of the legal situations to be dealt with would generally be of the type dealt with in this unusual case of *Fairhurst* v. *Sproson*. It is not that Mr. Justice Pearson did not understand the definite distinction which English law makes between civil and criminal; rather, it is that he preferred to lay aside legal technicality in order to achieve a harmonious result. Imprisonment might very likely have set niece against uncle, but that would have done no good to either side.

(iii) It will be recalled that the point often stressed by those who deny that African law differentiates between civil and criminal, is that murder is often a matter of compensation paid by the criminal or his kin-group to the relatives of the victim. We have shown that this has not always been the case even in the least developed of African societies, and that death is more often than not the normal penalty for unlawful homicide. We would none the less grant that the extreme penalty is often commuted into compensation where the circumstances of the murder are not really aggravating or do not vitally disturb the social equilibrium of the community. This, it is submitted with respect, does not sound too strange when it is remembered that death as a penalty for murder has been abolished in many developed countries of the world today, without social disaster.[40] And the murderer, far from being made to compensate his victim's dependants as African law would make him do, only goes to a not uncomfortable prison to be maintained at the expense of everybody else, including of course that of the unfortunate dependants of his victim.

Again, although English law still exacts the death penalty for unlawful murder,[41] nevertheless, it is a rule of the Law of Tort that 'the death of a human being cannot be complained of as an injury'. But the same rule has been eaten into by the Fatal Accidents Acts, 1846 and 1864 which provide that all the lawful dependants (including even an adopted child) of the victim of a killing not amounting to wilful murder shall be entitled to substantial compensation for their maintenance by the person responsible for the death.

(iv) It may probably aid our perspective in this matter to bear in mind this historical reminder sketched by Hone in the article[42] to which we have referred earlier:

'In England for a long time there was no distinction between criminal and civil cases, the underlying principle of the administration of justice was restitution and not retribution. Thus, compensation was the proper remedy for most wrongs committed and there were no police and no prisons . . . A criminal, however, caught red-handed was sentenced at once. Sentences of imprisonment were unknown; the punishment for theft was mutilation or the payment of compensation, while murder was avenged by death and in other homicides by compensation.'

Lack of this indispensable background knowledge of the growth of English law itself has been largely responsible, if any one imponderable factor may be said to be responsible, for the well-meant but often misguided notions that have been bandied about by people whose business it ought properly never to have been to lay down final theories about the nature of African law.

(v) While it must be conceded that the process by which certain species of civil wrongs come to be regarded as criminal offences is generally a mark of the development into a more complex political order, it is equally necessary to point out that, historically, most human societies have always made a distinction between, on the one hand, offences *mala in se* and, on the other, offences *mala quia prohibita*. Some wrongs like murder, theft, and unnatural sexual offences have been universally condemned by the whole human race as evil in themselves, while others have from time to time been prohibited by society as merely subversive of the social order. Since the latter category of offences springs from the practical needs of each society, it is naturally the subject of legislative regulations, a violation of which does not incur the same measure of opprobrium as attaches to a breach of any of the offences considered to be *mala in se*.

Dr. C. K. Allen[43] in discussing the problem of distinguishing criminal from civil wrongs, rejects the purely procedural criterion of Austin and Kenny and falls back upon Blackstone's view of crime in its public nature. He distinguishes the wrongfulness of offences into (*a*) intrinsic wrongfulness, and (*b*) social expediency. In thus regarding the criminal nature of an act as dependent upon its moral turpitude, Allen is relying upon this age-old division of offences into *mala in se* and *mala quia prohibita*. Although this cannot be made the basis of a scientific classification of offences into civil and criminal, nevertheless, daily experience supports the view that the common attitude towards offences considered evil in themselves is different from that towards offences which are the creation of express prohibition and which do not involve moral turpitude. Moreover, Allen's development of the principle of social expediency as a determinant for classifying offences has something to be said for it.

(vi) That African law recognises certain types of practice wholly foreign to modern English law must, however, be admitted. The practice of what has come to be known as 'ritual murder', for example, has been retained too long in many African societies, whether highly organised or not. It is hardly paralleled elsewhere in the Western world, although examples of similar practices abound (or, until recently, abounded) in many Eastern countries. This abominable custom has probably done more to strengthen the hands of the detractors of African law than any other single defect in it.

Also, African law permits the summary execution of the so-called sorcerer or witch by the social group.[44] Belief in witchcraft is prevalent, since it is thought to be generally levelled at established institutions and important pursuits. Therefore, the sorcerer or wizard must be summarily eliminated from membership of the community, so as to prevent his ever getting a chance to disrupt the delicate fabric of its social life. This is indeed a pity, and one must hope that the practice will soon disappear from those remote areas in which it might still be thought permissible to kill persons on the ground of witchcraft.

But, having said that, we must add that this curious belief in witchcraft is not peculiar, in essence, to the African. Even in England, witchcraft was a capital offence until abolished by the Witchcraft Act, 1735. In Western Europe, a witch was legally executed as late as 1782.[45] But, although witchcraft has been legally proscribed, belief in it is still strong among the rural communities of the greater part of the modern world. One has to look at the current 'witch-hunt' for Communists and their so-called 'fellow-travellers' in contemporary America, in order to appreciate how susceptible even industrialised and 'civilised' men can be to a certain psychological habituation, due to marginal insecurity and spiritual dread of the unknown.[46] The type-figure seems to be still much in evidence today: the witch-doctor or the black magician of 'primitive' society has merely been replaced in modern 'civilised' society by the scientist, be he a psychiatrist or a spiritualist medium.

The only peculiarity—and it is an important one—about witchcraft in Africa is that belief in it is still so pervasive.[47] The underlying assumption of sorcery in African or European societies is, therefore, one of degree and not of kind. Let us add that, by the various Witchcraft Ordinances (in some cases dating back fifty years or more), it has been declared a criminal offence in all British-African territories to practise or pretend to practise witchcraft, and, conversely, to try or attempt to try anyone for witchcraft.

(vii) It is quite feasible that, with increasing economic and social changes in the modes of life of the African, his legal ideas in regard to crime will more and more approximate to those of English law, especially in those fields where modern commerce and technology are fast revolutionising traditional attitudes and concepts. Thus, Bushe put his finger on the right point when he wrote: '. . . apart from the provision which the law—Native and British—must necessarily make to provide for the safety of person and property and the exercise of personal rights (and at their simplest there is little difference in principle between the law of Bantu and Briton to this end), a modern government has to provide by statute or rule for a multitude of things unknown or scarcely known to

Africa forty years ago—railways, post and telegraphs, water supplies and electric light . . .'[48]

Regulations made to achieve these ends are on their first introduction bound to be little understood or hardly popular, but the process of assimilation and absorption should be easier if the right effort is made to correlate the new ideas with the old. The new offences thus created are what Major Orde-Browne has called 'technical crimes', as between which and ordinary crimes there is an understandable distinction drawn by the British people no less than by the African—which fact the learned writer seems to have overlooked. Only it is more so in the one case than in the other.

(viii) Finally, we will briefly dispose of the fallacy that English (or even European) ideas of criminal law are incapable of application in Africa, because of the alleged incompatibility of the cultural and social attitudes of the African with the European. Quite apart from the fact that this argument disregards the inevitable changes, often phenomenal, which are daily taking place in Africa and which are thereby bridging the gaps between the rural (African) and the industrial (European) organisation of society, it conveniently ignores the similar phenomenon of adaptation that is taking place elsewhere.

To take a few examples, in South Africa and Ceylon, Roman-Dutch law has had to be radically recast on its criminal side and English criminal law adopted in order to meet the needs of a changed and changing social and economic order in these territories. The same adjustment has long been made in the Hindu and Moslem legal systems of India and Pakistan; Burma is no exception. . . . various countries of Europe, the Middle East and the Far East have at different stages of their development thrown overboard their native Criminal Codes and laws and have adopted either the French, the German or the English model.

There is, therefore, no reason at all to doubt that African law can and will make the same adjustment. It has, in fact, made encouraging progress in many developed communities in British Africa. English criminal law, often suitably modified to meet local requirements, is already operating these fairly successfully. It would, however, be rash to predict the exact character of the ultimate amalgam.

Notes

[1] We have used the term 'European' law here in its popular opposition to African law, particularly because even Continental writers on African law are in the habit of freely indulging the fancy that their own systems of law are at one with the Anglo-American systems in this matter. In the pages that follow we shall attempt to demonstrate the error of this assumption.

[2] Maine's *Ancient Law*, p. 379.

[3] E.g. Hartland, Hobhouse, Rivers.

[4] P. 31.

[5] Talbot, *The Peoples of Southern Nigeria*, p. 625.

[6] Meek, *Law and Authority in a Nigerian Tribe*, p. xiii; also pp. 208–28.

[7] Lowie, *Primitive Society*, pp. 385 ff.

[8] Diamond, *Primitive Law*, (2nd edn.), pp. 192–4.

[9] *Op. cit.*, p. 409. Rattray has discovered the same distinction among the Ashanti, *op. cit.*, pp. 285–93, although he employs the infelicitous expressions of 'Sins' (for crimes), and 'Efisiem' (for civil cases).

[10] At pp. 88–90 and 94 of his *Kamba Customary Law*; so, also, among the Nandi of Kenya: G. S. Snell, *Nandi Customary Law*, pp. 78–9.

[11] The 'king'ole' consisted of 'the mass of the male population of a group of "motui", the largest Kamba group that acknowledged a common institution. . . . It was a crude legislature, judiciary and executive, all combined; the "government", however sporadically and however seldom it might meet, of the area over which its jurisdiction was recognised' (*ibid.*, pp. 88–9).

[12] See Wagner's essay, 'The Bantu of North Kavirondo', in *African Political Systems*. [Ed. Fortes and Evans-Pritchard.]

[13] See her *Ibo Village Affairs*, pp. 101, 226–30; also, Meek, *op cit.*, 225–7.

[14] Green, pp. 101–2. (The italic is mine.)

[14] *Ibid.*, p. 223.

[16] *Tangled Justice*, p. 64, although the writer's description of the treatment of such offences as Murder, Adultery and Theft at pp. 79, 84–5, seems strongly to suggest that they are nothing short of criminal wrongs.

[17] Major G. St. J. Orde-Browne, 'British Justice and the African', an article in the *Jnl. Roy. Afr. Soc.*, Vol. 32, No. CXXVII, April, 1933, pp. 148–59, at p. 151.

[18] *Ibid.*, p. 152.
[19] See his article, 'The Native of Uganda and the Criminal Law', *op. cit.*
[20] Italics are the author's. The learned writer's account was based on Driberg, *The Lango* (pp. 210–15), which probably explains the apparent contradictions into which he has fallen.
[21] See his article, 'Primitive Law and Professor Malinowski' in *The American Anthropologist*, *op. cit.*
[22] This numbered classification is entirely mine and has been adopted for purposes of close analysis.
[23] 4 Blackstone's *Commentaries on the Laws of England*, pp. 3 and 4. Another definition given by Blackstone in the same place is that a crime is 'an act committed or omitted in violation of a public law forbidding or commanding it'.
[24] See Kenny, *Outlines of Criminal Law* (15th edn.), p. 16.
[25] In spite of the valid objections to Blackstone's exposition concerning the nature of public and private wrongs, it seems on the whole a more practical, commonsense approach to the problem than the procedural test adopted in varying degrees by Austin, Salmond and Kenny. In Bk. III, p. 2, Blackstone wrote: 'The distinction of public wrongs from private is that civil injuries are private wrongs, regarded as transgressions on the rights of individuals, while crimes are public wrongs, regarded as affecting the whole community.'
[26] In his essay in *The Encyclopædia of the Social Sciences*, *op. cit.*
[27] *Op. cit.*, p. 231.
[28] *Ibid.*, p. 236.
[29] Cp. 'Kafir criminal law rests primarily on the principle that the persons of individuals belong to the chief'—Lowie, *op. cit.*, p. 409. See also *African Studies*, Vol. 12, No. 4, 1953, pp. 181–8.
[30] Sir Frederick Pollock, *A First Book of Jurisprudence*, p. 92, seems to express the modern view that there is no satisfactory classification of law into public and private.
[31] *Society and the Homosexual.*
[32] It is a definite crime among the Shilluk, formerly punishable with death but now by a heavy fine, for any man to have sexual intercourse with their king's daughter who by Shilluk law must never marry: see *Report of the Wellcome Tropical Research Laboratories* (1911), pp. 218–19, under the title of 'The Cult of Nyakang and the Divine Kings of the Shilluk' by G. C. Seligman.
[33] Ss. 491–503 of the French Code Pénal.
[34] See also M. Francisque Goyet, *Précis de Droit Pénal Spécial* (6th edn.)
[35] I.e. by the Matrimonial Causes Act, 1857.
[36] H. Ashton, *The Basuto*, p. 255.
[37] See *R.* v. *Sidney and Emily* (1934), 4 Nyasaland Law Reports, p. 6. Cf. *R.* v. *Robert and Aluwani* (1940), Nyasaland Law Reports, p. 2.
[38] See The Native Tribunal Ordinance, 1930, s. 13(a).
[39] See *The Daily Telegraph* of Friday, Oct. 31, 1952.
[40] In France, simple murder is punished by life imprisonment, but circumstances of aggravation may make it equivalent to 'assassinat' and therefore punishable by death. The status of the person killed (e.g. if a public official or a parent) may turn *simple* murder to aggravated murder (ss. 400–5 of the French Code Pénal).
[41] The Royal Commission on Capital Punishment has had suggested to it the abolition of the death penalty for all types of murder: See its Report (Cmd. 8932), 1953, ss. 13, 61–4, 605; although the Commission was not asked to consider the specific issue of abolition.
[42] *Op. cit.*, p. 6. One sincerely wishes that this able writer had remained true to the facts according to his own light and that he had avoided the temptation to be deflected from his juristic purposes by the confused theories of non-jurists about African law.
[43] *Legal Duties*, Ch. III.
[44] But the reader must take this subject to the fuller treatment of the whole topic given at pp. 225 ff.
[45] Lowrie, *Primitive Society*, pp. 405–6.
[46] Note, again, the present widespread belief in 'flying saucers' in the United States of America, the current vogue of 'science fiction' all over Europe, and the modern extensions of the Frankenstein legend in, e.g. 'The Thing from Another World', 'The Day the Earth Stood Still' each dealing with visitants from another planet. Aldous Huxley amply caters, in his drama, *This World of Light*, for the taste of millions who 'like their universe draped in transcendental mysteries'.
[47] Cf. George Ordish (*The Listener*, Dec. 23, 1954, p. 1105): 'It seems the plant (i.e. the mistletoe) was particularly useful against witches, and as witches are very active in dairies—particularly in northern England and Wales—it was always hung in the dairy to give protection and, I believe, it is still used to some extent for this purpose there, as it is well known that nothing is so fatal to milk and butter as witchcraft.'
[48] H. G. Bushe, 'Criminal Justice in Africa', *Jnl. Roy. Afr. Soc.*, Vol. 34 (1935), pp. 117–28.

I. Schapera: A Handbook of Tswana Law and Custom*

Civil and Criminal Law

In practice, although not in theory, Tswana law is divided by the people themselves into two main classes. These may quite conveniently be termed 'civil law' and 'criminal law' respectively, although their categories are by no means identical with those of European systems of law. The civil law establishes *inter alia* the private rights of people in regard to personal status, property, and contracts; and provides for redress, if such rights are violated, by compelling restitution or compensation. The principal civil wrongs recognised in Tswana law include breaches of contract; seduction, adultery, and similar offences against family rights; trespass, damage, theft, and similar offences against property; defamation and other wrongs against reputation. The criminal law treats certain acts, not merely as injuries to individual persons, but as offences harmful to social life generally, and therefore deserving of punishment. The principal crimes thus recognized in Tswana law include all offences against the tribal authorities acting in their official capacity, and breach of the laws decreed by the Chief; homicide, grievous bodily assault, and similar offences against the person; sorcery, incest, and other 'unnatural acts'.

It must be noted, however, that many civil injuries are on occasion also treated as crimes, the offender not only being forced to make amends to his victim, but suffering punishment as well. This applies particularly to cases of theft. The man who steals an ox from another may be required to pay him two or more, and is thrashed as well if he is in the habit of stealing; or, if he is unable to make restitution, he will in any case be thrashed. In the same way certain crimes, especially against bodily security, may on occasion also give rise to civil remedies. The man who assaults another is generally fined, the fine belonging to the Chief. But the general tendency in recent years has been to award part, if not all, of the fine as compensation to the victim; while for certain forms of assault there existed even in the olden days the right of retaliation. In cases such as these the offence is treated both as a wrong against some particular member of the tribe, who is therefore entitled to redress, and as an act harmful to society generally and therefore subject to punishment. In European systems of law the two aspects of such an offence are kept quite distinct and dealt with in separate proceedings. Redress must be obtained through a civil action, while punishment is administered after a criminal prosecution. There is no such differentiation of procedure in Tswana law. The offence is tried in the course of a single action, and it is only in the verdict of the court that its dual nature is given explicit recognition. Nevertheless, the manner in which it is brought to trial is generally sufficient to show whether it must be regarded as primarily civil or criminal.

When a civil wrong is committed, the victim may, and indeed should, first attempt to obtain satisfaction by direct negotiation with the wrongdoer. Only if this fails will he sue him. The case must then as a rule first come before the local court, although it can afterwards be carried on appeal, or referred in case of difficulty, to the court of the Chief. The court will award the victim some form of redress, if his claim is upheld. He himself states what he wants, and the court may agree to award him this, or may vary the amount. It will at times go further, and also inflict punishment upon the wrongdoer, if his offence is regarded as sufficiently reprehensible. But unless the victim himself, or his representative, brings the matter to trial, the court has no jurisdiction.

A criminal wrong, on the other hand, can never be settled out of court. It must be reported to the Chief or to some other competent tribal authority, who will then summon and prosecute the accused person in his court. The more serious crimes are always dealt with directly in the court of the Chief. Others may be dealt with and finally settled in the local or regimental courts. The accused, if found guilty, is punished. Where the punishment takes the form of a fine, this is paid, not to the victim of the wrong, but to the court, i.e. to the Chief (or some other authority) acting in his official capacity. The amount is fixed, not by the victim, as in the case of civil wrongs, but by the court. The court may also, if the nature of the case seems to warrant it, order the offender to make restitution or pay compensation to the victim.

* I. Schapera, *A Handbook of Tswana Law and Custom*, Oxford University Press, 1938, pp. 46–47.

P. Bohannan: Justice and Judgement among the Tiv*

The Tiv Classification of 'Wrongs'

Sir Henry Maine has written at some length of the difficulties which men of ancient society experienced in perfecting the distinction between delict and crime. He found that if 'the criterion of a delict, wrong or tort be that the person who suffers it, and not the State, is conceived to be wronged, it may be asserted that in the infancy of jurisprudence the citizen depended for protection against violence or fraud not on the law of crime, but on the law of tort'.[1]

We have seen, in the last few pages, that Tiv scribes also have difficulty in making this distinction. Tiv, other than the scribes and a few of the most informed *mbatarev*, do not make the distinction at all.

They also have trouble in making overt the distinctions of a jural nature which their vocabulary and their very actions contain. They have trouble in making and maintaining distinctions among their own words, and among their various classes of faults. This difficulty in clarifying distinctions seems to be one of the most thorny difficulties in all situations of social control.

To understand how Tiv use their *jir*, it is necessary to investigate the distinctions which they make among wrongs. In order to make this investigation, it will be simpler to change our point of analytical focus. Hitherto we have focused on *jir*; but, in order fully to understand the notion *jir*, we must investigate other institutions that are used in its place. The best means of doing so is to change our focus to the wrong which is the breach of norm or the first social act in the series. In this section we shall investigate Tiv distinctions of wrongs, and in the next we shall be in a position to compare *jir* with other social acts of the sort we have called 'counteraction', which can and do follow on the commission of wrongs or the breach of norm.

There is probably no language that does not contain words for bad and reprehensible acts. The substantive content of these several words and categories varies from one language to another—if it did not, we could not speak of cultural variation.

We must examine three Tiv words: *ifer*, *kwaghbo*, and *kwaghdang*. Now, there are two Tiv dictionaries, one by a missionary and the other by a linguist-cum-administrator with some anthropological training. It is interesting that all three words are translated by the missionary with the notion of sin or wickedness, and by the administrative officer by the notion of crime, fault, misdemeanour. Thus, to the missionary an *ifer* is a 'bad, wrong, sinful thing'; to the administrator it is a 'crime, fault, misdemeanour, mistake'. The missionary defines or translates *kwaghbo* as 'a wicked thing, a sin', whereas the District Officer as 'a bad deed, a crime', though he gives one—just one—example of the notion 'sin' in translating *U gba shin kwaghbo* as 'You sinned or committed a crime'.

Such translations tell one more about missionaries and administrative officers than about what Tiv mean by *ifer* or *kwaghbo*. Their most obvious lesson is that Tiv do not differentiate between a sin and a crime as Europeans can; it is not possible to translate *ifer* with one English word and *kwaghbo* with another. The field of meaning is cross-cut in a somewhat different way, and I should say that administrative officer and missionary are both right. How then do we go about differentiating these words?

First, let us examine the composition of the words *kwaghdang* and *kwaghbo*. *Kwagh* is a substantive meaning 'thing' or 'affair' or 'matter', modified by adjectives *dang* and *bo*, which are the crucial variants. Both dictionaries translate both *bo* and *dang* as 'bad'. Both add some examples which allow us to say that *bo* also means 'ugly' and 'stingy'.

Dang, on the other hand, extends to 'unhappy' or 'useless', and a man of *dang* is a bad person or a profligate. More important, one can say that a disease is *bo* or serious, but not that it is *dang*, for to say it is *dang* would be to imply that it is morally at fault, whereas to say that it is *bo* means that it is dangerous. One can say of drugs or medicines that they are *bo*, or dangerous, but not that they are *dang*, morally bad. One can also say that witchcraft substance (*tsav*) is *bo*, dangerous, but it need not be *dang*. Mischief of a minor sort, on the other hand, can be *dang*, but need not be dangerous or *bo*. If you ask a Tiv to differentiate between *bo* and *dang*, he will tell you that they are the same thing; but if you use one incorrectly, he will tell you to use the other. It is from such corrections and from hearing, very occasionally, a Tiv say that something was *dang* but

* P. Bohannan, *Justice and Judgement among the Tiv*, Oxford University Press, 1957, pp. 116–120.

not *bo* that one can arrive at definitions. A *kwaghbo*, with reference to human activities at least, is something dangerous and anti-social. A *kwaghdang* is a thing—person or act—which is morally reprehensible.

Both dictionaries list another word, *ishor i bo*, as meaning 'bad deed, sin, evil' (Malherbe) or 'crime, sin, fault' (Abraham). I myself recorded this word only in connexion with supernatural evils performed by witches (*mbatsav*). The *bo* is obviously the same *bo* as in *kwaghbo*, but since I am not certain what *ishor* means, I am not prepared to say that its meaning is limited to the supernatural. At least, it is not in everyday use for ordinary wrongs in the areas that I know best.

None of these three terms necessarily implies, it seems to me, a jural context or any sort of jural activity. It is true that the act which a thief or criminal performs can be said to be both *bo*, or mystically dangerous, and *dang*, or morally bad, but in neither sense because of their jural associations.

The jural associations are to be found in *ifer*. I find my material on this concept thin, because I had no difficulty in understanding it. When I was among the Tiv I used the word *ifer* to mean 'crime', and I do not remember ever having been corrected for so doing. I find that I made no specific references to it in my notes (as I always did with any word whose meaning or use proved recalcitrant), and that it is used comparatively infrequently in my texts. I remember (though I cannot find that I noted) one instance in which a woman called her child an *or-ifer*, a 'person [who has committed] *ifer*', when he took food from her hut without permission. I asked her about it after the child had left; she told me it was a little *ifer*, but that one must discipline one's children.

I used the word *ifer* in Tivland almost exclusively in jural contexts; either in discussing thieves or wrongdoers before a *jir*, or else in contexts in which the breach of norm is sanctioned by self-help rather than by jural procedure. We may say that an *ifer* is that wrong of which the accused stands accused.

In short, the *ifer* is the very breach of norm which must be counteracted. Either the wronged party uses self-help against the *or-ifer*, the man who committed the *ifer*, or else a ritual must be performed or a *jir* held, or both. At the very least, it will be considered by Tiv that one of these sanctions *should* have taken place.

Let me repeat that I am not establishing three 'boxes' and tossing various acts into one or the other. Obviously, a wrong can be put into two or into all of these categories: an act of murder is *kwaghdang* in that it is morally reprehensible; it is *kwaghbo* in that it is anti-social and mystically dangerous to the whole community; it is an *ifer* in the sense that some sort of counteraction must be taken to set it right.

If we may continue to formalize Tiv words into a doctrine—and realize that it is an analytical formalization, based on correct meanings and connexions but not done by Tiv themselves—we can see that insofar as an act is *kwaghdang*, it may be followed by punishment (*mtsaha*). Insofar as it is *kwaghbo*, it may be followed by ritual reparation (*kwagh soron*). Insofar as it is *ifer* it is followed by a counteraction, either *jir* or some other.

Incest, homicide, and sometimes adultery, require ritual reparation. Any form of homicide is an offence against the fetish called *swende*. Homicide is *kwaghbo* in that it is followed by a ritual. It is also *ifer* in that it is followed by *jir* or some other counteraction. It is *kwaghdang*, so it may be followed by punishment. Incest is *kwaghbo* which is repaired by ritual separation of the two culprits. It is *ifer* in the sense that it brings the *jir* (the moot, not the court) into action. It is *kwaghdang* in that it carries a severe punishment, at least for repeated offences. Similarly, adultery is an *ifer* in that it can be brought before the *jir*, as we have seen. It is *kwaghdang* in that it can be punished—husbands are expected to beat their wives for adultery, and we also noted that the *jir* fined adulteresses and sometimes their guardians. It is always *kwaghbo* in the sense that it is anti-social, and if the husband is a master of the *akombo megh* it is doubly dangerous and must be followed by a ceremony for repairing this fetish.

Tiv do not make the distinctions that Europeans make between wrongs which injure the entire community and those which injure individuals. Many of our own jurists have pointed out that there is no delict which is not in some sense harmful to the community, and no crime which does not harm some individual's rights. The distinction which Europeans draw is a folk distinction. The distinction which I have drawn between *kwaghbo*, *kwaghdang* and *ifer* is a folk distinction. We can compare the two sets of distinctions. But it is just as wrong and just as uncomprehending to cram Tiv cases into the categories of the European folk distinctions as it would be to cram European cases into Tiv folk distinctions.

Note

[1] Henry Sumner Maine, *Ancient Law*, 10th ed. London: Murray, 1912, pp. 380–1.

Chapter 7

SPECIFIC CRIMES

An explanation is perhaps necessary for the fact that the next two chapters—on specific crimes and specific torts—precede and do not follow the chapter on principles of liability. There were two reasons for choosing this order of presentation: firstly, we felt that it was preferable to undertake a discussion of the general principles with specific examples of both categories in mind; and, secondly, because not all African societies characterise the same acts in the same way. Thus, an act which is a crime in one society may be treated as a tort in another, and vice versa. Examples are to be found in the different handling of homicide, which is regarded as a crime among the Ibo as described by *Meek* and the Ashanti (according to *Rattray*), but is seen as a tort by *Ashton* on the Basuto and *Penwill* on the Kamba.

The extracts which have been included in both chapters do not purport to be exhaustive—either in their geographical coverage or in dealing with the total range of crimes and torts known to customary law. They do, however, attempt to provide a reasonably wide selection of most of the better-known acts and offences. The first of the extracts, by *Cotran,* differs from the others in three respects: it is concerned primarily with what the modern courts in Kenya are actually prepared to enforce rather than with the law as described to or observed by those investigating the customs and behaviour of a particular tribe; it embraces those crimes recognised throughout a country in a unified customary criminal law;* and, it deals only with those customary offences which are not already covered in the Penal Code.

E. Cotran: Report on Customary Criminal Offences in Kenya*

Elements of Offences

In this chapter, the elements of each offence will be discussed and a final statement for the offence formulated on the lines indicated by the Provincial Restatements.

Before doing this, however, it is necessary to indicate what is meant by 'customary criminal offences' and the existing methods of dealing with persons who commit such offences.

In Kenya (as opposed to the other East African territories of Uganda and Tanganyika) African courts have for a long time been given jurisdiction to hear certain offences under the Penal Code. Thus, if a person stole, he was charged in an African court with theft contrary to the relevant section of the Penal Code, and not with theft contrary to 'native law and custom'. The policy has always been that where an offence is covered by written law, the charge should be against that law and not against native law and custom. As most of the offences contrary to native law and custom had a counterpart under the written law, this policy has resulted in the virtual disappearance of the customary criminal law. However, there still existed a few offences that had a criminal aspect under customary law, but were either no offences at all, or only civil wrongs, under the statutory law; and it is these offences that form the subject-matter of this Report.

These offences are known in Kenya by the unfortunate name of 'quasicriminal'

* E. Cotran, *Report on Customary Criminal Offences in Kenya,* Government Printer, Nairobi, 1963, pp. 6–15.

offences, though it is not exactly clear how and why they are so called. One possible reason is that the Administration considered that the offences are only partly criminal simply because they also have a civil nature in that compensation is granted to the aggrieved party.[1] Another possible reason for this name is that since the offences were regarded as criminal under the written law, they should be given a somewhat different criminal status, i.e. semi-criminal status.

Be that as it may, these customary offences, by whatever name they are called, are now dealt with under s. 17 (*a*) of the African Courts Ordinance,[2] which provides:

> 'Subject to the provisions of this Ordinance, an African court shall administer and enforce—(*a*) the native law prevailing in the area of the jurisdiction of the court so far as it is not repugnant to justice or morality or inconsistent with the provisions of any Order of His Majesty in Council or with any Ordinance in force in the Colony;'

The practice in the African courts (where offences contrary to customary law *must* be commenced under s. 10 (2) of the Amendment Ordinance) is that when a person commits a criminal offence against customary law, e.g. adultery, he is charged with

> 'Adultery contrary to s. 17 (*a*) of the African Courts Ordinance', or sometimes with
> 'Adultery contrary to native law and custom—s. 17 (*a*) of the African Courts Ordinance'.

It is clear that s. 17 (*a*) does not create any offences, but merely states what law an African court may administer. Nor is there power under s. 17 to punish offenders. This power is in fact contained in s. 18. It is therefore strictly incorrect to charge a person with an offence under s. 17 (*a*) in its present form. It is hoped that steps will be taken to remedy this situation now that the customary criminal offences are known and written.

The customary offences revealed in my investigations are:

(*i*) *Adultery with a married woman.* All tribal groups in Kenya, without exception, recognize that it is a criminal offence for a man to have sexual intercourse with the wife of another man. The ingredients of the offence are:

(i) That the accused had sexual intercourse with a married woman.
(ii) That he knew or had reason to know that the woman was married to another man.
(iii) That the husband of the married woman did not consent or connive to the intercourse.
(iv) That the consent of the woman is immaterial.

It must be noted that the offence is only committed by the male adulterer. The adulterous woman commits no criminal offence. Likewise, a wife may not prosecute her husband for committing adultery with another woman.

The following statement, which has been accepted by all the Provincial Meetings and which incorporates all the ingredients of the offence, is suggested:

> 'Any person who has sexual intercourse with a woman who is and whom he knows or has reason to believe to be the wife of another man, without the consent or connivance of that man, is guilty of an offence. In such a case the woman shall not be punishable as an abettor.'[3]

Apart from being a criminal offence, adultery also has various civil aspects, viz.:

(*a*) In most customary laws, the adulterer has to pay a fixed customary compensation to the husband, e.g. one bull and one goat by Kamba law; and five rams and one ewe by Kikuyu law.
(*b*) In some cases, the parents or family of the adulterous wife pay some compensation, e.g. one heifer, to the husband.
(*c*) Most customary laws hold that habitual adultery by a wife is a ground of divorce for the husband, though a husband's adultery is rarely considered to be a ground of divorce for the wife.

(*ii*) *Taking away or enticing a married woman.* As with adultery, all tribes in Kenya, without exception, hold that it is a criminal offence for a person to take away or entice a married woman from her husband or other person having the lawful care or charge of her.

This offence differs from adultery in two respects:

(*a*) Sexual intercourse need not be proved; the mere unlawful taking is sufficient.
(*b*) Usually (but not necessarily), this offence has a more permanent character, e.g. taking away a married woman from the country to Nairobi.

The ingredients of the offence are:

(i) That the accused took, enticed, removed, concealed or detained a married woman.

(ii) That the taking, removal, etc., was unlawful.

Examples of a 'lawful' taking are:

(*a*) a father taking away his daughter because her husband refuses to complete bride-price payments for her;

(*b*) a taking with no intention to have illicit intercourse with the married woman. In the Provincial Restatements, the offence contained as an ingredient an intent to have illicit intercourse with the woman. The attitude of the delegates was that if a man removes a married woman, he must be presumed to have done so with intent to commit sexual intercourse with her. I would therefore suggest the omission of this intention as an ingredient, i.e. it should not be a matter for the prosecution to prove. Any 'unlawful' taking would constitute the offence; and the meaning of 'unlawful' would be left to the court.

(iii) That the accused knew or had reason to believe that the woman was the wife of another man.

(iv) That the woman was at the time of the offence living under the care of her husband or someone else on his behalf.

(v) That such husband or other person on his behalf did not consent to the removal of the woman.

(vi) That the consent of the woman is immaterial.

As with adultery, this offence is only committed by the person who removes the woman (and any accessories), but the woman may not be charged as an abettor.

The following statement, incorporating the ingredients of the offence, is suggested:

'Any person who unlawfully takes or entices away or conceals or detains any woman, who is and whom he knows or has reason to believe to be the wife of any other man, from that man, or from any other person having the lawful care or charge of her on behalf of that man, and without the consent or connivance of that man or other person, is guilty of an offence. In such case the woman shall not be punishable as an abettor.'

There is no customary compensation payable for mere removal of a married woman, though if adultery is also proved, the adultery compensation will be awarded to the husband. In addition, the court may award the husband (or other guardian) the expenses incurred, e.g. travelling expenses, in bringing back his wife.

(iii) Taking an unmarried girl out of the custody of her parent or guardian. All districts in Kenya recognize that it is a criminal offence for a person to take away or remove an unmarried girl out of the custody of her parent or other person having the lawful care or charge of her, and against the will of such parent or other person.

The ingredients of the offence are:

(i) That the accused has taken away or removed an unmarried girl.

(ii) That the taking or removal was unlawful.

Examples of a 'lawful' taking are:

(*a*) a taking after payment of bride-price to the girl's father.

(*b*) a taking with no intent to have illicit intercourse with the girl, e.g. going for a walk; a taking (e.g. by a missionary), to prevent the girl from being forcibly married to a man. As with 'taking away a married woman', in some Provincial Restatements, this offence contained as a necessary element an intent to have illicit intercourse with the girl. But here again, the delegates took the view that such intent was presumed. I would therefore again suggest that this element should be omitted from the definition, i.e. it should not be a matter for proof by the prosecution. Any 'unlawful' taking would constitute the offence.

(iii) That the removal was against the will of the parent or other person having the lawful charge of the girl.

(iv) That the girl was at the time of the removal living under the custody of her parent or other person having the lawful care or charge of her.

(v) That the age of the girl is immaterial.

(vi) That the consent of the girl to being removed is immaterial.

Here again, the girl herself cannot be prosecuted.

The following statement for the offence is suggested:

'Any person who unlawfully takes an unmarried girl out of the custody or protection of her father or mother, or other person having the lawful care or charge of her, and against the will of such father or mother or other person, is guilty of an offence.'

Mere removal of an unmarried girl does not subject the remover to any customary compensation (although the court may award to the father his expenses in bringing back the girl home). If, however, the man has sexual intercourse with the girl, he does have to pay customary compensation under most customary laws, e.g. one heifer by Luo and Luhya law for loss of virginity. Additional compensation is also usually payable if the girl becomes pregnant.

(*iv*) *Sexual intercourse with a person within the 'prohibited degrees'.* It is true to say that all tribes in Kenya regard it as a very serious matter for a man to marry or have sexual intercourse with a girl to whom he is related within the customary prohibited degrees of marriage. The matter was first raised in Central and South Nyanza (Luo Districts) who insisted that a man who commits this offence should be punished criminally. In the Nyanza Provincial Meeting, the other Nyanza Districts agreed with the Luo contention and the matter was thus recorded as a criminal offence for the whole of Nyanza Province.

The difficulty, of course, is that the customary law marriage prohibitions are extremely wide, e.g. under Luo law, persons belonging to the same *Dhoot* (a group tracing descent from a common ancestor going back sometimes to 12 generations), may not intermarry; and by Abaluhya law, a man whose four grandparents' clans[4] are A, B, C and D, may not marry a girl whose any four grandparents' clan are A, B, C and D—the girl's grandparents' clan must be E, F, G and H.

As it would be extremely difficult to incorporate this offence in any of the written laws of Kenya, an attempt was made to dissuade the Nyanza meeting from having this as a criminal offence, but they were quite adamant in rejecting any such suggestion. The tribal groups in the other Provinces were quite happy with the suggestion that this matter should not form part of the criminal law, but that the marriage would be held totally invalid under customary law.

The ingredients of the offence are:

(i) That the accused had sexual intercourse with a female person.

(ii) That such female person was related to him within the prohibited degrees of marriage under his customary law.

(iii) That he had knowledge of the relationship.

The following statement for the offence (applicable in Nyanza Province only) was agreed by the Provincial Meeting:

'1. Any male person who has sexual intercourse with a female person who is to his knowledge related to him within the prohibited degrees is guilty of an offence.'

'2. "Prohibited degrees" means the prohibited degrees of marriage according to the customary law of the male person.'

(*v*) *Receiving a second bride-price during the subsistence of a marriage.* All tribes in Kenya take the view that it is an offence for a father (or guardian) to receive a second bride-price in respect of his daughter (or other person whose guardian he is), whilst such daughter is still lawfully married to her first husband.

In the past, this offence was referred to as 'receiving a second bride-price before returning the first bride-price'. This is actually incorrect for two reasons:

(*a*) Under many customary laws, the first bride-price is in certain cases not returnable at all upon divorce, e.g. by Luo law and Abaluhya law, if the woman had many children, nothing is in fact returnable.

(*b*) In effect, the first bride-price in some cases cannot be returned before the second has been received, i.e. the father may not have the cattle and must wait until his daughter remarries. Under some laws, e.g. Kamba law, the first husband is not entitled to the return of his bride-price until his ex-wife remarries.

The following are the ingredients of the offence:

(i) That the accused received, upon the marriage of his daughter (or other person whose guardian he is), a bride-price.

(ii) That during the subsistence of such marriage, the accused unlawfully received a second bride-price in respect of the same daughter.

The Provincial Meeting of Coast Province raised the point that if the first husband in fact refused to complete his bride-price commitments, the father is entitled to remove his daughter and receive a second bride-price from another person. He will commit an offence, however, if he refuses to return the first bride-price to the first husband. It is submitted, that the phrase 'unlawfully receives' covers this eventuality, i.e. if the father receives a second bride-price as a result of the refusal of the first husband to complete his dowry payments, such receipt would not be unlawful.

The following statement for the offence is suggested:

'Any person who, having received one bride-price in respect of his daughter (or other person whose guardian he is) from one person, unlawfully receives a second bride-price in respect of the same daughter from another person, whilst such daughter is still lawfully married and not legally divorced, is guilty of an offence.'

The second suitor is naturally entitled to the return of his bride-price. He (the second suitor) may not be prosecuted. The offence is *receiving* not paying the second bride-price.

(*vi*) *Circumcising a person without consent.* Circumcision of males and females is practised by many of the Kenya tribes. The subject of female circumcision has caused much controversy in the past, as a certain body of opinion (especially missionaries) strongly objected to the practice and advocated its prohibition by legislation. The position today is that no tribe (with one exception)[5] is prepared to accept the abolition of the practice. However, it is true to say that with the growth of education, the influence of Christianity and the general advancement of the people, many individuals nowadays refuse to undergo circumcision. In order to cater for such people, all the Provincial Meetings suggested offences connected with the circumcision of persons without their consent or the consent of the parents.

The suggested offences differed slightly from one Province to another, but may be briefly summarized as follows:

Nyanza Province

It is an offence to circumcise a female without obtaining her consent and the consent of her parent or guardian (with the exception of *Kisii*, where no such offence is recognized).

Rift Valley Province

It is an offence to circumcise a male or a female without obtaining his/her consent; and if the male or female is under 16, without obtaining the consent of his/her parent or guardian.

Central Province

It is an offence to circumcise a female without obtaining her consent and the consent of her parent or guardian (with the exception of *Meru*, where it is an offence irrespective of the consent of the girl or of her parent).

Southern Province

Machakos and Kitui (Kamba): it is an offence to circumcise a female without obtaining her consent and the consent of her parent or guardian.

Kajiado and Narok (Masai): it is an offence to circumcise a female without obtaining the consent of her parent.

Coast Province

It is an offence to circumcise a male or a female if he/she is below the age of 16 without obtaining the consent of his/her parent or guardian.

Two points must be borne in mind in connexion with this offence:

(*a*) If the person is circumcised without his/her consent, the offence will in any case amount to 'assault', or 'assault occasioning actual bodily harm' or 'unlawfully wounding' under ss. 250, 251 and 237 of the Penal Code respectively. Reference to consent of the person to be circumcised thus becomes unnecessary.

(*b*) Circumcision is in most cases performed before the age of 16, so that the reference to age is unnecessary.

It is therefore clear that what is required is the consent of the parent or guardian at a time when the person to be circumcised is too young to consent or object to the operation.

(vii) Taking property without consent or misappropriation. All tribes in Kenya recognize that there are circumstances whereby a person may take property from another person unlawfully, but not so as to be guilty of theft as defined in s. 268 of the Penal Code.

Examples of the occurrence of this offence are:

(a) *Taking bride-price cattle.* This may happen in various ways, e.g.:

(i) a son takes cattle from his father to pay his bride-price because the father had originally refused to give him the cattle;

(ii) a husband returns his wife to her father and takes back his bride-price cattle before a divorce has been finalized;

(iii) a father takes cattle from his daughter's husband because such husband has not completed his bride-price commitments.

(b) *Cattle leasing.* Some tribes (especially the Kalenjin) have a custom of cattle leasing, e.g. A leases a cow to B. If A takes back his cow without B's consent, he commits an offence.

(c) *Taking inheritance claims.* I.e. a son takes e.g. cattle, claiming that he is entitled to it on his father's death but before a proper division of the estate has been made.

The distinction between this offence and theft as defined in s. 268 of the Penal Code is that here the person taking the property appears to have a right to it—in fact in some cases he is the owner thereof. The essence of this offence is that the taking was without the consent or permission of the lawful possessor.

The ingredients of the offence are:

(i) That the accused took or converted to his own use or to the use of another person movable property (in most cases cattle or other stock).

(ii) That the property was in the lawful possession of some other person.

(iii) That the taking was done without the consent of the lawful possessor of the property.

(iv) That it is immaterial that the accused has a claim of right to the property or that he is the owner thereof.

The following statement for the offence is suggested:

'1. Any person who takes or converts to his own use or to the use of another, any movable property in the lawful possession of any other person, without the consent of that other person, is guilty of an offence.'

'2. It shall not be a defence under this section that the person taking or converting the property has a claim of right to it or that he is the owner thereof.'

(viii) Removing boundary marks made by indigenous elders. In most areas of Kenya, it is customary for indigenous tribal elders to arbitrate in land disputes. Indeed, in some districts there are administrative instructions to the effect that litigants must try to get a land dispute settled by indigenous elders before they can come to the African court.

In two Provinces, Nyanza and Coast, it was considered that if such indigenous elders did arbitrate in a land dispute and made boundary marks on the land following the arbitration, it would be an offence for the unsatisfied party to remove the boundary marks.

The following statement for the offence (applicable in Nyanza and Coast Provinces only) is suggested:

'Any person who unlawfully and wilfully removes or defaces any object or mark which has been erected or made as an indication of the boundary of any land by recognized indigenous elders following their customary arbitration in a land dispute, is guilty of an offence.'

(ix) Abuse likely to cause a breach of the peace (abusing a person of a higher age-grade). In the past, the age-grade system of certain tribes imposed a set of rights, duties and obligations on the members of each age-grade amongst each other and towards members of other age-grades. One of the most important of these was the duty of respect of a member of a younger age-grade towards members of a senior age-grade. Hence the offence of 'abusing a person of a higher age-grade' or 'abusing an elder', which was widely used in the African courts.

The age-grade system, especially amongst the more advanced tribes, is generally breaking down, and certainly amongst the younger generation it has ceased to be recognized.[6] For this reason, it was considered desirable to find out the reaction of the Law Panels on the question of abuse generally. The attitude today (without exception) is that abuse should be an offence irrespective of the age-grades of the accused and the complainant, though naturally the offence would be more serious if directed towards an elder by a young person.

Further, the view held today is that abuse is an offence not because it is a form of disrespect, but because it is likely to cause fighting, i.e likely to cause a breach of the peace.

One final point is whether abuse is an offence under customary law only if it is in public, or whether it could be in private. On this point, four Provinces, namely Nyanza, Rift Valley, Southern and Coast, considered that it must be in public, whilst Central Province thought that it might occur in private too. The four Provinces considered therefore that the offence under customary law is already covered by s. 182 (*d*) of the Penal Code, i.e. publicly conducting oneself in a manner likely to cause a breach of the peace.

For Central Province, where the abuse need not be in public, the following statement is suggested:

> 'Any person who intentionally insults or abuses and thereby gives provocation to any person intending or knowing it to be likely that such provocation will cause a breach of the peace, is guilty of an offence.'

(*x*) *Consumption by and supply to minors of alcoholic liquor.* This offence was originally raised in Baringo District, but was extended to the whole of the Rift Valley Province in the Provincial Meeting. It does not apply in the other Provinces.

The offence prohibits the drinking of alcoholic liquor by males under 18 and females under 20 and also subjects the suppliers or sellers of liquor to such minors, to penalty.

The statement for the offence, as agreed by the Rift Valley Provincial Meeting, is as follows:

> '1. Any minor who consumes alcoholic liquor is guilty of an offence.'
>
> '2. Any person who supplies or sells alcoholic liquor to any minor is guilty of an offence, provided that it shall be a defence to a charge under this subsection that the accused had reasonable cause to believe and did in fact believe that the person to whom he supplied or sold the liquor was not a minor.'
>
> '3. A minor for the purposes of this section is a male who is under the age of 18 years and a female who is under the age of 20 years.'

(*xi*) *Other offences.* A few other offences that had arisen in the African courts were also discussed at the District Law Panel Meetings or at the Provincial Meetings. However, they were all declared to be civil matters or already covered by written law. They are:

(*a*) *Failing to maintain a dependant.* It was considered that if a man failed to maintain his dependants, he could more appropriately be dealt with in a civil action, i.e. the wife or other dependant could file a civil suit for maintenance, and the court would order a maintenance award, either payable in a lump sum or on a monthly instalment basis, according to the husband's ability to pay. It must be noted that this can only be done whilst the man is still lawfully married to his wife. There is no right under customary law for a woman to be maintained by her ex-husband after a divorce. It must also be noted here, that if the husband fails to provide the absolute necessaries of life, whereby the health of his dependants is affected, he may be liable to prosecution under s. 239 of the Penal Code.[7] African courts at present have no jurisdiction to try cases under s. 239. I recommend that they should be given such jurisdiction.

(*b*) *Unlawful alienation of land* (*Machakos and Elgon Nyanza*). I.e. selling or otherwise disposing of land without the consent of the family and clan elders.

(*c*) *Unlawful use of communal clan land* (*Taita*). Both these were held by the Provincial Meetings to be subject to a land suit. In (*b*), any such alienation would be totally invalid; and in (*c*) any such unlawful use creates no rights in the land.

(*d*) *Breaking a marriage* (*Vunja Nyumba*); *alienating affections; bringing 'Fitina'.* These charges were used in some African courts in the Coast Province. They should no longer be entertained as they are all covered by the offence of 'taking away or enticing a married woman'.

(*e*) *Sexual intercourse with an unmarried girl; impregnating an unmarried girl.* Sexual intercourse with an unmarried girl, without her removal from her father's custody, is a civil and not criminal matter. So is impregnating an unmarried girl.

(*f*) *Paying or receiving excessive bride-price* (*Kisii*). In Kisii District, a maximum limit of bride-price was imposed by the African District Council and it was an offence to pay or receive more than the maximum limit. The Kisii Law Panel, however, recommended the abolition of this offence since the limit was largely ignored by the people.

Notes

[1] There is nothing peculiar about this since similar situations exist in English Law, e.g. assault; libel.

[2] No. 65 of 1951, as amended by the African Courts (Amendment) Ordinance, No. 50 of 1962.

[3] This last sentence is necessary as it has been agreed by all Districts that women should not be punished for committing adultery.

[4] A 'clan' is a patrilineal, exogamous unit comprising all persons who trace their descent in paternal line to a common ancestor.

[5] The exception is Meru, where the indigenous tribal authority—the Njuri Ncheke—has recommended that any person who performs the operation of circumcision on any female person should be prosecuted.

[6] One member in Nyeri did not know to what age-grade he belonged.

[7] S. 239 provides: 'Any person who, being charged with the duty of providing for another the necessaries of life, without lawful excuse fails to do so, whereby the life of that person is or is likely to be endangered or his health is or is likely to be permanently injured, is guilty of a felony and is liable to imprisonment for three years.'

C. K. Meek: Law and Authority in a Nigerian Tribe*

Homicide. To commit murder was an offence against Ala, and it was the concern of the whole community to see that the steps prescribed by custom were carried out. If the murderer hanged himself forthwith (which he frequently did from remorse at having killed one of Ala's chidren, or to save himself from being beaten to death with sticks, or to save his family from attack and the loss of their property, or merely because he was expected to do so), his brother was (at Owele) required to offer sacrifice to Ala before burying the body of the murderer. He took eight yams and one chicken to the priest of Ala who, standing before the cultus-symbol, spoke as follows: 'Ala, this chicken and these yams have been given to you by the brother of the man who killed your child and then hanged himself. He beseeches you to accept these gifts and to refrain from pursuing the brothers and children of the murderer. He who killed a fellow-man has also killed himself. Let his crime, therefore, follow him to the next world.' It will be observed from this rite that the family of the murderer was considered as sharing in the responsibility of the crime, unless it took steps to dissociate itself from the murder. It had to provide a cow, goat, fowl, two yards of cloth, and a keg of powder for the funeral rites of the murdered man.

If the murderer did not immediately hang himself, but took refuge in flight, his family had also to fly,[1] for the kin of the murdered man (including maternal relatives) immediately made a raid on the compounds and property of the kin of the murderer. In this raid any members of the local group might join. The compounds of the murderer's family were burnt to the ground, their yams were uprooted, and their palms cut down.[2] All property found might be appropriated, but in some communities it was taboo for the patrilineal relatives of the murdered man to keep any of the raided property, on the ground that this would be 'eating blood-money'. But relatives in the female line might do so, as their Ala was not concerned with the death of men in other local groups.

The family of the murderer remained in exile for a period of at least one month,[3] when they might be invited by the elders of their town to return, the consent of the kin of the murdered man having first been obtained. The murderer himself continued to remain in exile. In some communities (e.g. at Oduma) the following rite was performed before the return of the exiled family. The senior *Ada* or female relative of each of the kindreds concerned went together to the compounds of the exiled family and swept them out thoroughly. They then took a cock and a hen, tied them together with a palm-leaf, and walked round the compounds saying, 'Ala, do not permit such a thing to occur again. Ala, be not angry with us.' They then collected the sweepings of the compound and threw them and the two fowls into the 'bush of evil'. This rite of purification is known as *Eza fu ntu ochu*, i.e. 'The sweeping-out of the ashes of murder.'

* C. K. Meek, *Law and Authority in a Nigerian Tribe*, Oxford University Press, 1937, pp. 208–213 and pp. 223–228.

On the return of the exiled family[4] a public meeting would be held to inquire into the matter and decide what atonement must be made by the murderer's kin. This meeting might be held in the compound of the priest of Ala, but the priest usually took no part in the discussions, lest he should make some mistake for which Ala would punish him. In some communes meetings connected with a murder were always held in an open space clear of all houses, lest the pollution of the murder should affect the houses. The meeting was conducted principally by the so-called *aro*-holders who in many communities had special authority to deal with cases of homicide.[5] The *aro*-holders would consider all the circumstances of the case, and elicit whether the homicide had been accidental or deliberate, and if the latter whether there were any extenuating circumstances. If it appeared that the homicide had been accidental, the man-slayer might (at Oduma and Nengwe) be allowed to return after twenty-eight days, and on his return would be required to offer sacrifice to Ala. But in some communities there was no difference in the penalty for accidental homicide and murder, owing to the belief that if a man killed another by what we should term an accident he must at some previous time have committed an act abominable to Ala. If there were extenuating circumstances he might be permitted to produce a substitute to be publicly killed. The substitute was often some notorious thief of whom the community wished to be rid. The execution would be carried out by a hireling from another community, as it was considered an offence against Ala to slay a fellow townsman. Some time later the murderer was required to go through the form of dedicating a person to the service of Ala, as a substitute for the man he had killed. He obtained a hireling from another community and took him, together with a tortoise, an *aiagare* fowl, a piece of *ọfọ* wood, a pottery plate, and a pot to the shrine of the priest of Ala. The hireling was stripped naked, and the priest spoke a follows: 'Ala, this man has been brought to you as a substitute for your son who was killed.' The murderer added, 'Ala, let me go free and be not wrathful with me again.' The hireling then knelt before the shrine. He did not apparently remain permanently as an *osu* or slave of Ala, but was allowed to return to his own community.

Whether there were extenuating circumstances or not, the murderer might in some communities be called on to hang himself if he reappeared in the town. Or he might be required to produce some member of his family-group to hang himself in his stead.[6] But if a substitute hanged himself the murderer (at Owele) had to make atonement by the following rite. He summoned the priest of Ala to his house and presented him with a white chicken and a yam. The priest roasted the yam, and holding the chicken and yam in his hand said: 'Ala, I am giving this fowl to you to appease your wrath against this man. Ala, I am going to give this man a yam to eat, and I beseech you that you will refrain from taking his life when he partakes of anything which has been touched by a fellow-villager.' The murderer was then given the yam to eat. The fowl was appropriated by the priest.

At Ache a murderer was permitted to return to his town after the lapse of a year, provided he compensated the family of the murdered man by giving in marriage one of his own female relatives, together with thirty bars of iron, one goat, two chickens, and one pot of palm-oil. He had also to undergo a purificatory rite at the shrine of Ala. The priest took a chicken (provided by the murderer) and waved it round his head, saying, 'Ala, this man who killed one of your children has returned and offers a gift to you to appease your wrath. Ala, whenever he eats of the products of the Earth, do not destroy him.' The priest then cut the fowl's throat and allowed the blood to trickle over the symbol. Having cooked the fowl he deposited small offerings of flesh on the symbol and ate the remainder by himself.

At Lokpa-Uku the relatives of the murdered man might also accept some form of compensation, but most of this was used for the burial rites of the dead man and for purchasing a slave to be dedicated to Ala. If the slave were not dedicated to Ala the anger of the deity would be incurred, because the family had derived advantage through the death of one of her children.

At Ngbwidi the murderer's family had to pay compensation of two cows, but the family of the murdered man gave one of the cows to the family of the mother of the murdered man and one to the family of his father's mother. The murderer had to wear old clothes and remain unshaven until these payments were made—as a sign of mourning for the man he had killed. He had also to pay a fee of nineteen rods to the *aro*-holders through whose offices he had been allowed to return to the town. There was also at Ngbwidi a rite of reconciliation between the family of the murderer and that of the murdered man. The former provided a sheep, goat, tortoise, palm-nut, yam, cocoyam, and coconut; the latter a fowl. They met together on common ground and summoned a *dibia* or 'doctor' to make a 'medicine'. The animals provided were killed and cooked. A small tunnel was made in the ground, and the *okpara* of the murderer's family stood at one end, while the *okpara* of the murdered man's family stood at the other. The former then passed a cooked yam and some of the 'medicine' through the tunnel to the latter. The *dibia* took some of the 'medicine' and touched the forehead, chest, and feet of each person present, saying, 'I have quenched the evil words and anger. Henceforth, if you eat together, you shall not die.' After this rite both families ate a meal together. Had they eaten food together prior to this rite they would have been killed by Ala. The 'medicine' is known as *efojo obo*, i.e. 'the quencher of vengeance'.

It may be noted, in conclusion, that no person who had been guilty of homicide was allowed to take part in any festival of Ala. During such a festival he had either to absent himself from the town or else sit on a platform, as contact of his person with the ground was regarded as a pollution of the Earth-deity. No one would eat in the company of a murderer and he was usually abandoned by his wife. It is also to be noted that it was permissible to kill a man caught in the act of burglary.

No general inquiries were made on the subject of the procedure in cases of attempted murder. But it was stated at Lokpa-Uku that if a man who attempted to commit murder had a notoriously bad character he was sold as a slave to the Aro. Otherwise he was merely tied up by his relatives, while inquiries were made of a diviner in order to ascertain what it was that had induced him to attempt a crime so 'abominable'.[7] He was required to purge himself by a sacrifice to Ala. He then took palm-wine and other gifts to the man whom he had attempted to murder, and both ate a meal together.

Incest and other sexual offences. It was forbidden, and in fact an 'abominable' thing, to have sexual relations with any close consanguineous relative, and it is said that breaches of this law were almost unknown. If a case did occur both the culprits were killed or sold, after an investigation by the *Ọha* of the whole village-group. If the relatives of the guilty parties were exceptionally strong the punishment inflicted might be modified. But in any case they were required to provide a tortoise, a sheep, and a hen for sacrifice to Ala. If a father discovered that one of his sons was having sexual relations with one of his (the father's) wives, he would tie up the lad and the wife, and then summon a meeting of his extended-family and the wife's relatives. If no defence could be made to the charge, he would return the wife to her own family after the bride-price had been refunded. If the wife's family were unable to refund the bride-price her husband would sell her to some slave-trader. The lad also might be sold.

A case recently occurred of a man reporting to one of the *Ọha* that a certain woman of his local group had had sexual relations with a farm-labourer in the 'bush'—a heinous offence. All the *Ọha* of the group immediately went to the woman's house and seized a goat belonging to her husband. A friend of the husband secured the return of the goat by guaranteeing that, if the woman lost her case, he would himself pay the cost of the goat. On an appointed day the *Ọha* of the group investigated the charge, and as the husband was able to disprove the truth of the charge, the false accuser was called on to pay compensation to the woman. In pre-Government times, if the woman had been found guilty she would have been put to death or sold.

Other 'abominable' offences. In all Ibo communities twins were regarded as abominable and destroyed. It was also abomination for a woman to conceive before her last child had been weaned, and when the child was born it was thrown away. The reason for this was stated to be that a mother cannot nurse two children. It may be concluded, therefore, that one reason for killing twins was the difficulty of nursing two children.[8] Cripples, children born with teeth, children born feet first, and children which did not cry soon after birth were destroyed. Children who cut the upper before the lower teeth, or had begun to walk before they had cut any teeth, were destroyed or handed over free of charge to Aro slavers. A child who was unable to walk before it reached the age of three was regarded as having committed a grievous offence against Ala in its former life and was destroyed or sold. A girl who donned a cloth like a male, or menstruated before she had taken to wearing a cloth, was considered 'abominable', and was handed over to Aro traders. All relatives and friends of the girl wailed on hearing the news, and four days after the girl's departure her mother shaved her head. For an evil thing had fallen on her head and had to be removed. If there were any doubt in the matter the case was referred to one of the local or distant oracles. Another act calling for retribution and expiation was for a woman to climb a palm or kola tree.

Black magic and witchcraft. A charge of using black magic was one of the most serious charges that could be brought against anyone. If, therefore, one man accused another of e.g. burying 'medicine' in his compound or farm, the person charged would (at Owele) immediately report the matter to the Ishi-Uke of his local group, who would order young men to capture a cow from the group of the accuser.[9] The cow would be killed and eaten by all members of the accused's group (women and children excepted), the heart and head being the special fee of the Ishi-Uke. A day would then be arranged for hearing the case, and the elders of both quarters would meet in some open space. Women and young men might also attend. The Ishi-Uke of the accused's group would open the proceedings by saying: 'If anyone has a quarrel with another which does not concern the case in hand, let him not intrude it into these proceedings. We are met here to discover the truth with regard to the particular quarrel between these two men.' The accuser would then make his statement, and the accused would reply by offering to swear on any recognized medium produced. The elders would retire to consult, and on their return might order the accused to go to Ache and summon the priest of the cult of Nnemmiri to bring some object from the shrine of that spirit. On his return (accompanied by the priest) a public meeting would again be held, and the elders would inquire carefully of the accuser the formula of the oath which he required the accused to take. They would then instruct the accused to follow this formula. The accused would kneel down before the cultus-symbol and, stretching his hands towards it, would say: 'If I put evil medicine in this man's compound then may you, Nnemmiri, kill me. But if I did not do so then spare my life.' The oath was given one year in which to work, and during this period the two families concerned were not allowed to eat together. If they did so Nnemmiri would leave the guilty man alone and assail the innocent. The accused was required to pay the cost of the proceedings (viz. one kid, and two fowls) to the priest of Nnemmiri, but if he lived through the year he could claim damages from the accuser, who would also have to compensate the owner of the cow.

Incidentally it appeared that in the Owele district it was an offence for a woman to place a taboo on any form of property.[10] If a man had occasion to complain of an infringement of this law he took his complaint (at Ogugu) to the Ndishi-Uke, who would send a company of young men or head-getters to interview the woman's husband. If the latter expressed his regret, and undertook to remove the taboo, the matter would be disposed of. But the husband would be required to give sundry gifts to his visitors. If he refused or answered the young men roughly, the Ndishi-Uke would direct the young men to kill any cow they saw in the husband's quarter. The flesh of the cow would be divided out among the townspeople of each village of the commune, but the Ndishi-Uke and young men who had killed the cow would receive an additional share. If the woman had stated that she was prepared to swear that she had not placed any taboo on the property she would be given the skin of the cow.

The case would now have become a public matter, and a day of trial would be fixed by the principal elders. On the appointed day the elders would meet at the compound of the woman's husband, and if it became clear that the woman had in fact placed a taboo on the plaintiff's property she might not be allowed to swear to the contrary, even if she had offered to do so. For the elders might take the view that if they permitted her to swear she would certainly be killed by the spirit by whom she swore, and her blood would then be on their heads. The woman would be ordered to pay the cost of the cow, and the elders who had tried the case would retire to the house of the successful plaintiff, who would reward them with a gift of wine.

Witchcraft is considered the most loathsome of all 'abominations'. There are many ways of detecting witches. They can be seen and pointed out by sorcerers or witch-doctors. Their names can be discovered from the divining-apparatus, or diviners can, by a decoction of leaves poured into the eyes, enable patients to see for themselves the witches who are feeding on their souls. Some people are obviously witches, as they are always talking to themselves or else are continually dogged by misfortune. Others again have made a death-bed confession that throughout their lifetime they had fed on the soul-stuff of their fellow men.

At Onitsha any person who was believed to be a witch was reported to the Mmo society, and if the leaders of the society considered the evidence sufficient they ordered a masker of the cult to summon the suspected woman to a public trial by ordeal. The masker went at cockcrow to the woman's home and called her out of her hut, in the squeaky voice used by maskers to simulate the spirits. The woman would be told that she had been accused of being a witch and must be prepared therefore by daybreak to stand her trial by the sasswood ordeal. The masker would then depart, leaving a deputy to see that the woman did not drink any oil, as oil was believed to negative the action of sasswood. If the woman refused to undergo the ordeal, she would be driven out of the village, and her husband would divorce her and refuse to accept the return of his bride-price. If she accepted, the trial was held in the Obi's compound. The accused sat down on a small bedstead, and was given a calabashful of sasswood, which had to be drunk up there and then. The accused might die within a few minutes, and if so her body was taken out to the taboo 'bush' and buried head downwards, with the feet protruding above the surface. But, if she merely became sick, she was taken home and kept under observation to see that she did not drink oil. If she were still alive at the end of twenty-eight days she whitened her body and went to the market, singing her innocence, and being greeted by the people. 'Chuku is marvellous,' they would say, 'you were accused of witchcraft, but Chuku knew your innocence and brought you out unscathed.' 'Yes,' she would reply, 'they wanted my life for nothing, but my *chi* refused.' She would present her friends with chalk, and in return would receive numerous gifts of food, clothes, and money. A banquet would be given in her honour, and for a whole month she would strut about the village triumphantly. The person who had charged her with witchcraft would be required to pay the sasswood fee of 7,800 cowries, a provision which prevented people from making indiscriminate accusations.

It is said that the officiants at sasswood trials might be bribed either to secure the death of the accused or her immunity. If the accused were to be saved she would be given a dose of oil secretly. But if she were to be killed, other poisons, such as cactus juice, would be added to the sasswood. Sometimes the accused might be represented at the trial by a fowl as proxy.

Notes

[1] If the murderer and murdered man belonged to different local groups, the whole of the murderer's local group might be forced to fly, or a state of war might arise between the groups.

[2] At Mmako, in cases of accidental homicide, a relative of the deceased went to the compound of the man-slayer and cut down one palm-tree and one bread-fruit tree only.

[3] The priest of Ala and elders usually at the end of twenty-eight days called on the kin of the murdered man to desist from making further raids on the property of the kin of the murderer, lest a continuance should lead to another murder.

[4] In some cases the family of the murderer would not be permitted to return until they had produced the murderer or a substitute, who would be required to hang himself publicly.

[5] It is noteworthy that in all investigations into homicide the judges refused to accept any form of preliminary gift such as snuff or palm-wine or kola, lest they should incur the anger of Ala.

[6] If the murderer were a person of high social standing, the kin might ask that one of their less useful members should be killed or allowed to kill himself in the murderer's stead. It was not uncommon for the brother of a murderer to hang himself as a substitute.

[7] In cases of murder both the relatives of the murderer and murdered man might go to some distant oracle such as Igwe-Ke-Ala at Umunoha to ascertain what offence they had committed against the gods that murder had entered their midst.

[8] But it is improbable that this was the *original* reason.

[9] The owner of the cow would feel no resentment, as after the trial he would assess the value of the cow at an amount considerably above the market value.

[10] This rule was possibly made in the first instance to prevent women laying a claim to the property of their deceased father or husband.

R. S. Rattray: Ashanti Law and Constitution*

Sins or Tribal Taboos (*Oman*[1] *Akyiwadie*)

Murder and suicide. The offences set out in paragraph four of this chapter (among several others which may have escaped my notice) were known in Ashanti as *Oman Akyiwadie*, which, translated literally, means, 'Things hateful to the Tribe'. These acts were looked upon as sins of which the central authority was bound to take immediate official notice, lest certain supernatural powers, to whom the deeds were regarded as peculiarly offensive, should wreak their vengeance upon those whose paramount duty it was to protect their interests and to punish breaches of immemorial law or custom.

Up to the time of European intervention, an Ashanti who committed any of these sins was liable to summary arrest and trial, without any further legal formality, such as has been noted in the case of other offences. If found guilty, the culprit suffered capital punishment.

At a later date he might have been permitted—in the case of some, but not all these sins—'to buy his head'.

I have tabulated these Tribal taboos under certain headings. It will be seen later, however, in a more detailed examination of each, that the Ashanti definition of many of the terms I have employed varied considerably from the meanings given to them in our own law. These *Oman Akyiwadie* then were:

1. Murder.
2. Suicide.
3. A class of 'sins' which we might describe as 'sexual offences', and others of a somewhat similar nature, which we should consider possibly as 'immoral' but not as 'criminal'.[2]
4. Certain forms of abuse.
5. Certain kinds of assault.
6. Certain kinds of stealing.
7. The invocation of a curse upon a Chief.
8. Treason and cowardice.
9. Witchcraft.
10. The violation, by word or deed, of any other recognized Tribal taboo.
11. The breaking of any law or command, the violation of which would not, in the ordinary way, involve the breaking of any Tribal taboo, but the observance of which had been enjoined on the clear understanding that disobedience would be taken, in this particular case, as entailing the violation of a specific taboo. In other words, refusal to obey any law or command issued and qualified by a 'conditional curse', i.e. by an *Ntam* ('Oath').

Murder (*Awudie*): To commit murder is *di awuo. Awudie* in Ashanti included, besides the particular kind of homicide which we understand by the term 'murder', other offences which in our law are not regarded as having any connexion with culpable homicide. *Awudie* is a sin viewed by the Ashanti with particular abhorrence, and the first question to determine is the reason for this. It may readily be argued that for a man to have killed the person who had offended him was to throw down a direct challenge to one who alone 'held the knife', and was therefore an act which struck at the root of all centralized authority. This aspect seemed the one most emphasized at the trial which ensued, in which the murderer, in the final oration by the *Okyeame*, was accused of 'not having brought his case' before the Councillors that it might have been listened to with 'good ears', but of having taken 'a club to strike and kill the *Akyeame*', thus treating the council of Elders as if they were 'brute beasts'.[3] The blow which struck down the dead man would thus appear to have been regarded as aimed also at the *maiestas* of the central authority. We must, however, I believe, go farther back to find the real cause for the placing of murder among the chief of the tribal and, later, of the national taboos. *Wo ka mogyagu a, mogya na etene no* ('If you spill blood, blood alone can straighten (right) it'), runs an Ashanti legal maxim. *Oku kyiri, 'Ma ye den?'* ('It is taboo (for any person killed to have to inquire) after death "What was it I did?" '), is another legal maxim.

'The reason that a man might not be killed without first being told what he had

* R. S. Rattray, *Ashanti Law and Constitution*, Oxford University Press, 1929, pp. 294–316.

done to deserve death was because, if he were executed without a trial, his *sasa* (ghost) would trouble the Chief in his sleep and also the people in the town.' We have seen[4] how this fear of a dead man's *sasa* was present in a minor degree, even in the case of a prisoner duly executed by a strictly legal process. It seems therefore natural to suppose that the revengeful spirit should be feared still more when the person had been illegally done to death. That this spirit should be considered as likely to take vengeance on a Chief who allowed his death to pass unavenged, no less than on the actual murderer, is strictly in accordance with the belief in the corporate responsibility of certain persons for the acts of the individual, which is such an inseparable feature in the Ashanti law of crime. I think, therefore, it is right to assume that it was the dread of supernatural reprisal, rather than the outrage upon the central authority, which placed this act in the category of a tribal or national sin. Murder for long remained one of the offences for which it was impossible 'to buy one's head'. It was also one of the few sins for which the punishment was death by dancing *Atopere*.

I have already stated that the Ashanti discriminated clearly between murder, i.e. 'unlawfully killing a human being', and accidental homicide. They designated the latter by saying, *Musuo na ade no, ma asan esan no* ('Something causing misfortune has got him, causing danger to walk by his side'). The majority of the cases of accidental homicide occurred (as they still occur) as the results of hunting accidents. Such accidents were investigated, the court going carefully into any possible motives for the deed. If it were proved to its satisfaction that death was caused by what we should term 'misadventure', its verdict did not imply that the person causing the accident escaped entire responsibility for his negligent or unintentional act. He became liable for damages. He was ordered to pay the weight of *asuasa ne suru* (i.e. £7) in gold-dust (which incidentally was about the value of a male slave), a case of rum, a cloth, a coffin; all these articles were given to the *abusua* of the dead man. He was also commanded to give a sheep, which was sacrificed over the ancestral Stools, to the Chief, the *Okyeame* addressing the spirits as follows:

Obi na ato 'tuo bone, na ye fwe fwe asem no mu. Ommoapa, na ye se onko si nnipa no. Ye sere nwo, nwo mma asem 'one bi sa yi mma bio.

'Someone has fired a bad gun, and we have investigated the matter carefully. He (the accused) did not do it with intention, and we have said that he must bury the man. We pray you not to permit such a thing to happen again.'

The man himself, who caused the accident, would almost certainly go and consult one of the *abosom* (lesser gods), who would then inform him of the sin of commission or omission which had brought the misfortune upon him. Thus far, then, the Ashanti and the English conception of what constitutes murder does not appear very dissimilar.

It is an axiom in our law that mere intention to commit a murder is not actionable without the commission of some overt act towards the carrying out of that intention, and in this context also the Ashanti law may appear to fall into line with our own. It is in an inquiry into what, in Ashanti, would constitute 'an overt act' that we begin to encounter features in their law which are foreign to our ideas upon this particular point. Yet again, the Ashanti did not appear to make any fine distinction between the actual commission of the deed, and an attempt, or even a mere intention, to commit it. Guilty intention was assumed upon what, to our thinking, were the most inadequate of grounds. Finally, the killing of a person in self-defence, or the supposed jeopardizing of a life by the commission of what at most we would consider as an indecent assault, were also grouped under the title of *awudie*. I shall now deal with each of these points in turn.

For an Ashanti to proclaim in public *Mennidi bio* ('I shall not eat again') was sufficient evidence to cause him to be arraigned before his Chief on a 'murder' charge. Such a person was either contemplating murder or was intending to 'bless' the Chief; he had publicly declared his intention in words, and in olden times was liable to, and probably would, be killed; for, added my informant, *Nnipa bone yenkora no* ('We do not treasure up (preserve) a wicked man'). Intention need not have been expressed or implied in words. 'In olden days, if a man (not being a priest) were seen to be permitting his hair to grow long, he would be summoned before the Chief and accused of "murder". He would then either be executed or made "to drink the gods" that "murder" was not his intention.'[5] Again, in former times, if an Ashanti were seen in public or in private going through the action of cutting anything with a knife laid at right angles to the object, it would be assumed that he was contemplating murder, and his action might cost him his life.'

'If any one killed a murderer even in self-defence, he was held guilty of murder. No man might kill another without express authority from the Chief.' 'If a Chief caused his executioners to kill someone in the street, that was not murder, provided the *Mpanyimfo* (Elders) had agreed.'

'For any man, other than the husband, to have sexual intercourse with a woman who was *enceinte*, it was "murder".'[6]

'To have sexual intercourse with a girl before she had reached puberty was "murder".' Should it be found that the girl had in fact had her *menses*, but had not disclosed the fact, the offence was not 'murder' but was still *musuo* (one bringing ill luck); it might then have been atoned for by a sacrifice upon the ancestral Stools and upon the shrines of the gods (a clear indication of the nature of the spiritual powers which were supposed to be offended by the greater offence of which they had been acquitted). The guilty pair were also made to sit upon the ground, while palm oil and some of the blood of the sheep were poured over their heads. The following words were spoken: *Asase Ya, asuo bo o, mma sa asem yi ebi emma bio* ('Ya, Earth-goddess, water is sprinkled (upon you), do not permit anything like this to come again'). Both were then sent out of the town until the girl had her child. If the child were a male he would have to become a *sumankwa* (a fetish doctor).[7]

These two sins might appear to fall into the third-category of tribal taboos, i.e. sexual offences, but as the Ashanti themselves class them both as *awudie* I have dealt with them in this place rather than under the other classification. Before passing on to an examination of my next heading, I may quote the following interesting reply, which I received to an inquiry concerning possible motives for murder: 'A man might have a great many debts, but instead of hanging himself, he might decide to kill someone first, saying to himself, "I shall then have a name, and also someone to go with me".' This reply exhibits a mentality somewhat different from our own.

Ashanti law appears to have made a clearly marked distinction between culpable and accidental homicide. It apparently, however, made little or not any distinction between actual murder and the attempt, or even the mere intention to commit the act, accepting as evidence of intention certain overt acts which, owing perhaps to our different psychology, we would not consider as showing any criminal intent at all. 'Murder' in Ashanti also included certain acts which, in our law, would be at most regarded as 'sexual offences', or acts of immorality.

Suicide, except under certain peculiar circumstances, was formerly regarded in Ashanti as a *capital sin*. It was a sin of which the central authority took immediate cognizance. These two statements of fact exhibit at once the difference and the similarity between our laws and theirs. Suicide and attempted suicide result, in our own country, in both legal and ecclesiastical consequences, but to state that suicide was 'a capital offence' must at first sight appear somewhat curious. Not all forms of what we would term 'suicide' were regarded as sins; in fact, under certain circumstances, the action of taking one's own life was considered as honourable and acclaimed as praiseworthy; e.g. to kill oneself in war by taking poison, or sitting on a keg of gunpowder to which a light was applied, rather than fall into the hands of the enemy or return home to tell of a defeat; to take one's own life in order to accompany a beloved master or mistress to the land of the spirits; and finally, those especially interesting cases, where a man commits suicide to wipe out what he considers his dishonour and because he cannot stand the ridicule of his companions. Suicide was considered a sin when it was carried out to avoid the consequences of some wrongful deed, or when, after investigation, it was not possible to ascribe any motive for the act. In the latter case there was always a legal presumption that the motive for self-destruction had been evil. In the disfavour with which the central authority seemed always to have regarded this offence, it is rather difficult to trace any other cause than the desire rigorously to maintain its prerogative as the sole dispenser of capital punishment. It is just possible, however, that the State, i.e. the tribal authority, may have placed suicide in the category of sins, owing to a dislike of having an evilly disposed disembodied spirit wandering about in its midst. The spirit of the suicide became a *saman twetwe*, a ghost wandering about in search of its head, for it was debarred from entering the *Samandow* (land of spirits) until the expiration of its destined time upon earth, which it had itself wrongfully curtailed. Moreover, when eventually reincarnated, it would return to this world as a *tofo sasa*—the spirit of one who had died an unholy death—with a cruel and murderous nature which would lead it again to meet a similar end in its next incarnation. The man who had committed an offence, the penalty for which he well knew was death, had not any right to balk the central authority of its right to execute him. The central authority indeed refused to be cheated thus, and the long arm of the law followed the suicide to the grave, from which, if his kinsmen should have dared to bury him, he was dragged to stand his trial before the council of Elders. The result of the trial was almost a foregone conclusion, for the dead man would either have been found to have committed some offence, and fearing the consequences (which might have been more terrible than any self-inflicted death, i.e. the *Atopere*) have taken his own life, or if it were not found possible to trace any motive for the deed, then the commission of some wicked act was presumed, and he was equally judged guilty. In the latter case his dead body was addressed by the *Okyeame* in the following words:

W'akoa yi, obi nnim adie a wa yo. Nne wako hye homa. Obi nnim ade koro a ba wo tiri mu. Nti wamfa mma ha, ama yamfa asopa ntie, na wo fa aba de bo Akyeame, wu ku yen a, wu di yen aboa, wo di fo.

(Addressing the Chief.) 'This is your slave (i.e. subject). No one knows what he had done, and to-day he has hanged himself. (Then addressing the corpse.) No man knows a single thing that came into your head (i.e. your motives), but, because you did not bring your case here that we might take good ears to hear it, but took a club and struck the *Akyeame*—and when you kill us (thus) you regard us as brute beasts—therefore you are guilty.'

In the case of a murderer who had afterwards committed suicide the final summing up was as follows:

W' akoa yi. Se yoye a wa kum wo yonko, na se wa ye wo bone a, wamme ka ankyere Akyeame ama yankankyere Ohene ma yen ambusa asie ama wo. Na wo ko ku no, nanso wo ku wobo. Nti wamfa mma ha ma yamfa asopa ntie, na wo fa aba bo Akyeame, wu ku yen a, wu di yen aboa, wo di fo.

(Addressing the Chief.) 'This is your slave. (Addressing the corpse of the suicide.) Since it has come about that you have killed your fellow man, and when he had done a bad thing to you, you did not come to tell the *Akyeame* in order that we might have told the Chief and caused him to investigate the case for you, but instead, you went and killed him and also killed yourself, then because you did not bring your case here that we might have brought good ears to hear it, but instead raised a club and struck the *Akyeame*—and when you kill thus you treat us as if we were brute beasts—therefore you are guilty.'

As soon as the *Okyeame* had delivered this oration, the Chief's executioners would step forward and decapitate the dead body. Here we have the explanation of the sentence 'Suicide was a capital offence'. The plaintiff in the case had been the murdered man. The sentence and 'execution' of the murderer implied his innocence. The party in a trial who is judged innocent pays *Aseda*, a thank-offering, to the Chief (as we have already seen, really a fee to ensure that witnesses would be forthcoming on a possible future occasion to testify to the result of the trial). The murdered man could not claim exemption to this rule. He (i.e. his kinsmen) therefore paid *Aseda* and the kinsmen claimed the body of their murdered relation without further formality. Not so the blood relations of the murderer and suicide. They might not on any account remove his body for burial in the clan sacred burial-ground; they might not even mourn for him. His headless trunk was cast into the bush, to wander, as we have seen, an unhappy headless ghost. Not only so, but his kinsmen could not themselves entirely escape the evil consequences of his deeds, a responsibility, as we shall see presently, that was even sometimes shared by the Chief himself. The kinsmen of the suicide had 'to drink to the gods' and to produce every bit of his (the suicide's) personal private property, which was then confiscated by the Chief. This might comprise the following:

1. His privately acquired slaves.
2. His 'bought' wives.
3. His privately acquired gold-dust.
4. Any personal debts due to the dead man (the kinsmen, not the Chief, became responsible for any debts owed by the deceased).
5. Any privately acquired cloths and trinkets.
6. Such livestock as actually belonged to him.[8]
7. The standing crops on any farm cleared and planted by his own individual labour (this did not exclude the assistance given by children and wives). After the crops had been gathered, the land itself reverted to the lawful heir. In the case of pri-

vately owned fruit-bearing trees, e.g. kola, the annual crops as long as the trees stood.

The immediate superior (if himself a Chief under a greater Chief) of a subject who had violated any of the great tribal or national taboos, and thereby incurred the death penalty, appears to have been held responsible that his subject did not escape punishment by committing suicide. There is a well-authenticated case of a certain *Sana Hene* of Mampon, who in the time of the Mampon Chief, Kobina Dwumo, and in the reign of Kwaku Dua I, 'blessed' the King, and afterwards committed suicide. The Chief of Mampon, for having failed to arrest him forthwith, was fined one hundred *pereguan* (£800) and thirty sheep 'to sprinkle Kumasi with water' (*Bo Kumasi asu*).

At a later date the custom arose of permitting the kindred of a person found guilty of many of these capital sins 'to buy the head' of their clansman. It is very doubtful if this privilege was ever really extended to cases of deliberate murder, even at a late period when the majesty of law and the administration of justice were disregarded. By paying this price (*atitodie*) the confiscation of the offender's private property was avoided, and if, as in the case of a suicide, the guilty party were already dead, his kindred also obtained the body, the head of which was not cut off; they might mourn for him, and hold the usual funeral custom.

A woman, equally with a man, was liable to suffer capital punishment for murder, the only exception being that if she were pregnant she might not be executed before her confinement (*Opimfo yen ku no*). Such a person was kept a prisoner by being fastened to a log until the child was born, when both the mother and child were killed.

'A non-adult might be executed for murder; children condemned to death were handed over the *suman*(?) Aserampon as a human sacrifice.' 'The *Asontakoma* fly causes us to kill it, because its progeny are evil',[9] was the saying quoted in answer to my inquiry as to the reason a child should be killed.[10]

Drunkenness and madness as an excuse for murder. Drunkenness might be taken as an extenuating circumstance in the case of certain offences,[11] but not so in murder. *Awudie wo wo tiri mu a, na wo boro nsa a, wo bobo afe* ('When murder is in your head, and you have become drunk with wine, you strike to wound').

With regard to madness, Ashanti tradition records that once upon a time this affliction was regarded as a sufficient excuse, for the madman who killed anyone was fastened to a tree and left to die, unless his relatives chose to bring him food. It is possible, of course, that the disinclination to execute the homicide who was seen to be mad might have arisen owing to a superstitious horror of killing a person so afflicted. The following story, however, would seem to point to his exemption from capital punishment having been due to a recognition of the absence of *mens rea*. 'Before the reign of Osai Yao, madness was regarded as an excuse for murder. King Osai Yao made a test to find the justice or otherwise of this exemption from the consequences of an act. He caused a drunkard and a madman to be placed in a house which was then set on fire. The madman soon began to scream, "They are burning me", and ran outside; the drunkard lay still and was burned to death.'

It has already been noted in many of the Constitutional Histories, that Head-Chiefs, even those who had authority 'to wield the knife'—i.e. to execute those of their subjects who were guilty of capital sins—were forbidden to carry out the sentence of death upon a murderer, although permitted to pass sentence of death upon him. This was because the highest central authority, the *Asante Hene*, had instituted a particularly terrible punishment for the offence. The *Atopere* dance of death has been fully described in my last volume. No doubt this gruesome form of execution was thought to deter others; many of my informants stated that murder was a much rarer offence in former times than at the present day.

Certain 'Sexual Offences'. The few 'sexual offences' which appear to be capable of being classed under the above heading may be subdivided into four main groups:

A. *Mogyadie* (incest).
B. *Atwebenefie* (sexual intercourse with certain individuals other than those related by 'blood').
C. *Baratwe* (sexual intercourse with an 'unclean' woman).
D. *Di obi yere* (adultery with another man's wife, but only in certain specific cases, or under certain particular circumstances).[12]

A. *Mogyadie*: Incest (literally 'the eating up of one's own blood') has, in Ashanti, a much wider range of meaning than that word implies in our own language. It included sexual intercourse with any one of the same blood or clan, however remote the connexion, and even cases where it would not be possible to trace direct descent. The bearing of a common clan name was considered as conclusive evidence pointing to the existence of a common female ancestress. Perhaps no other sin was regarded with greater horror among the Ashanti. Both parties to the offence were killed.[13] Had such an act been allowed to pass unpunished, then, in the words of my informants, 'hunters would have ceased to kill the animals in the forest, the crops would have refused to bear fruit, children would have ceased to be born, the '*Samanfo* (spirits of dead ancestors) would have been infuriated, the gods would have been angered, *abusua* (clans) would have ceased to exist, and all would have been chaos (*basa basa*) in the world.'[14]

It is of importance to realize the gulf which exists between our conception of the term 'incest' and the Ashanti interpretation of the apparently equivalent word *mogyadie*. An Ashanti, in olden times, would have been executed for marrying or having sexual intercourse with his mother's sister's child—he would have committed 'incest' by doing so —yet, at the same time, he was enjoined to marry his mother's brother's child. I would refer my reader to the first chapter of *Ashanti*, where the whole question of prohibited and enjoined marriages have been examined in detail.

B. *Atwebenefie*. The correct spelling and derivation of the central root of this compound word is somewhat doubtful. I have also heard it pronounced *atwe-bere-fie*, and *atwe-abra-fie*,[15] but the first spelling as here given is probably in conformity with the most usual pronunciation. *Atwe-bene-fie* means literally (having sexual intercourse with) 'a vagina that is near to the dwelling house', and the offence, as the title implies, consisted in committing adultery with the wives of certain persons with whom the existing *ménage* necessarily compelled close social intercourse or constant physical proximity; they were not otherwise sexually debarred on the ground of blood affinity, or even in certain cases on account of any *Ntoro* relationship, although the term also included the latter class of offence.

I am now compelled, owing to the apparent eccentricity of Ashanti legal classifications, to split up the offences commonly grouped under this single heading. A whole class of offences, generally known as *Atwebenefie*, were not apparently regarded as capital sins, for the simple and sufficient reason that they had not come to be regarded as 'tribal sins'. I shall therefore, in this place, while tabulating all the offences commonly called *Atwebenefie*, deal only with those which were looked upon as Tribal taboos, the punishment for which was death, and leave a detailed examination of the remainder to a future chapter. *Atwebenefie* consisted in having sexual intercourse with any of the following persons:

(*a*) A half-sister by one father, but by a different clan mother.
(*b*) Father's brother's child.
(*c*) Any one of the same *Ntoro*.
(*d*) Brother's wife.
(*e*) Son's wife.
(*f*) Wife's mother.
(*g*) Uncle's wife.
(*h*) The wife of any man of the same *fekuo* (company).
(*i*) The wife of any one of the same guild or trade.
(*j*) The wife of one's own slave.
(*k*) Father's other wife, not being of the same clan as one's own mother.
(*l*) Own wife's sister (married or single).

It was only the offences grouped under (*a*), (*b*), and (*c*) that were regarded as sins or Tribal taboos. It will be observed that all these three cases of *Atwebenefie* amount to the same thing, i.e. violation of the customary law which decreed that a person of one *Ntoro* should not have sexual intercourse with anyone of the like *Ntoro*. The punishment for infringement of this rule was death or expulsion from the clan (*abusua*).[16] I would again refer the reader of this volume to *Ashanti* (Chapter II), where a detailed examination of the patrilineal exogamous divisions called *Ntoro* will be found. The facts there disclosed clearly indicate the reasons for treating this particular form of adultery as a sin.

C. *Baratwe*. It is unnecessary, I think, to seek farther for the motives which brought this offence within the scope of a Tribal taboo, than the knowledge which we already possess relating to the abhorrence with which the Ashanti regarded all forms of contact with an 'unclean' woman. I discussed this question fully in my last volume.[17] *Baratwe* was essentially a crime against the '*Samanfo* (ancestral ghosts). 'They had made a law that no one should have intercourse with a woman in this state.' The guilty parties were both killed.

D. *Di obi yere*. We now come to the last class of 'sexual offences' with which the central authority concerned itself, for which the punishment was death. We are here immediately reminded curiously of one of the clauses in our own law of treason, which decrees the death penalty for any one violating the consort of the reigning sovereign (while a similar act against the wife of peer or commoner is not regarded in our law as a capital offence), for in both these respects the Ashanti law seemed almost identical with ours in conception and practice.

Adultery in Ashanti, with any woman other than the wife of a King or Head-Chief, except where special conditions or the peculiar circumstances made it so, was not regarded as a sin. With all such cases the central authority was not concerned, unless its interference had been specially solicited by the offended party, by his swearing an 'oath' in connexion with the affair.[18] Adultery, indeed, did not even appear to fall under the heading of a 'sexual offence'; it came, as we shall see later, into the category of 'theft'. What then was the cause of the curious exception to this rule, in the case of adultery with a wife of the King or Head-Chief? There cannot here have been any question of possible complications in succession arising from an adulterous intrigue—the son of a King or Chief could not, as we are well aware, sit upon the ancestral Stool; the wife of the Ashanti potentate could never be of the royal blood of her husband's clan. Results, which it is possible may have had some bearing upon our own law upon this point, could not therefore have had any influence in the framing of the Ashanti rule.

An Ashanti King or Chief, as I think has now been clearly demonstrated, was not formerly regarded as an ordinary mortal. He was in close and constant contact with the spirits of his ancestors, of whom he was regarded as the mouthpiece and the Vice-regent upon earth. He had, moreover, automatically succeeded to the wives of his predecessors. Adulterous intercourse with them thus became something more than mere 'theft'[19] from a human being; it became an outrage not only upon the semi-divine person of the King, but also upon the departed spirits. Hence, I believe, the particular law which made adultery with the wife of a King a Tribal taboo punishable with death. I believe also it is just possible, were we able to follow the evolution of our law on the subject, that it might be traced back to somewhat similar ideas. Theoretically, the death penalty for such an offence could have been claimed by the outraged Head of any group; in practice, however, the supreme penalty would appear soon to have become restricted to cases in which the Head-Chief was the injured party. A curious legal fiction appears to have arisen in order to bring about what was tantamount to the alteration in the customary law, i.e. the removal of what had come to be regarded a minor offence from the category of a national taboo. Lesser Chiefs, who had been absorbed or had come under the jurisdiction of greater Chiefs, and finally under one paramount Chief of a Division, were loath to relinquish their ancient right to demand the head of the man who had violated their wives. Their ancestral ghosts were no doubt angry, but these spirits, like their living successors, had sunk to a position of somewhat minor importance, now the community consisted no longer of isolated independent groups. A Head-Chief, therefore, who did not wish to decapitate the adulterer in such a case, would allow the accused to swear an 'oath' that the accusation against him was entirely false. He would then be acquitted, but called upon to pay heavy *Aseda*[20] (thank-offering). This procedure is of interest as exhibiting, perhaps not so much a decadence in the standards of impartial justice, as that striking feature so strongly marked in the history of the early law of all peoples—the superstitious dislike for the inauguration of any change. There appears to be, besides the case of adultery with the wife of a King or Head-Chief, one other case in which adultery might involve the violation of a Tribal taboo. It is known as *Ahahantwe* (sexual intercourse in the leaves). There were several grades of this offence, which will be examined later; the particular one with which we are here concerned, which was regarded as a capital sin, was the forcible seduction of a married woman in the bush. As is often the case in these offences for which the death penalty was the only punishment, we obtain a clue for the motives which caused the act to be regarded so seriously, in an examination of the expiation of a similar, but less heinous offence of the same nature. The infliction of capital punishment almost invariably removed the necessity for any further formalities in the nature of propitiation, thus leaving us sometimes at a loss to discover the true *raison d'être* for this severity.

In the present case for a similar act, but one where there was connivance or consent on the woman's part, the adulterer, besides paying the customary 'satisfaction' (i.e. damages), was also fined a sheep, which was sacrificed upon the spot where the adulterous act had taken place, to the accompaniment of the following prayer:

Asasa Ya, obarima owo dan, owo kete, na obepe oba faduabirim ha, nti ye de'gwan yi ma wo; 'so obiara ye sa bio a, ma no mpie mfi.

'Thursday's Earth goddess, a man has a room, he has a mat, yet he seduced a woman here on the bare ground; because of that, we have brought you this sheep. Moreover if any one does so again, grant that the deed may be publicly known and "come out".'

Here, I think, we have an indication that Mother Earth had been thought to have been defiled by the deed. Thus, an act, not in itself necessarily taboo, came to be regarded as so, because of the offence thus caused indirectly to one of the great supernatural powers This tort thus came to be removed from its ordinary category and became a 'thing hateful to the Tribe'.

Certain forms of abuse; assault; stealing. The invocation of a curse upon the chief: treason and cowardice. Abuse (Atendidie): So-called 'primitive' man was extraordinarily sensitive to personal abuse. Probably the great percentage of quarrels and lawsuits in Ashanti arose from this cause. The majority of such cases, however, does not fall within my present purview, and will therefore be dealt with later. It seems logical—and most of their laws were eminently so—that the sensitiveness in such matters, which was such a marked trait in the living, should have been considered equally as a characteristic of the dead, of whom it might literally be said *nihil nisi bonum*. Men were regarded as the custodians of the honour of their spirit ancestors and as the upholders of their 'good name'; hence it came about that whereas slander and personal abuse of the living were regarded as (what we should term) 'torts', when the dead were the object of similar abuse the offence tended to become a sin, which the living were compelled to punish to the utmost extent, lest those who might be considered directly involved should vent their resentment upon all concerned.

With the expansion of the isolated kindred groups into the larger Territorial Divisions, and the absorption of many petty heads under one paramount ruler, the evolution in the punishment of this offence tended to follow the same lines as had been noted heretofore with regard to other offences (e.g. adultery), until the sin came to be regarded as a Tribal taboo, only when practised against the supreme tribal authority.

To abuse or slander a Head-Chief, even personally—at least in the case of the *Asante Hene*—would, owing to his peculiarly sacred position, probably have been regarded as a National or Tribal taboo. Similarly, abuse of any of his dead ancestors would most certainly have been a National or Tribal taboo also.

The utterance of any of the following words constituted this offence:

(*a*) *Wo'ni* (your mother).[21]
(*b*) *Wo'se* (your father).
(*c*) *Wo nana* (your grandparent).
(*d*) *Wo' ni twe ase* (the origin of your mother's privates).
(*e*) *Wo se twe ase* (the origin of your father's privates).
(*f*) *Wo'samanfo mfa ye ti nwe* (May your ancestral spirits chew their own heads).
(*g*) *Wo'samanfo mfa ye nankasa* (May your ancestral spirits take their bones, (and eat them)).
(*h*) *'Kwasea 'ba* (child of a fool).[22]

'The reason that any of these sentences, addressed to a Chief, was punished by death in olden times, was because if this were not done the *'Samanfo* would say, "Did we set you on this Stool that you should allow us to be spken to thus?" ' Any of the abovenamed forms of abuse might have been implied without being audibly expressed, by merely closing the hands, placing the closed fists together, and holding up the thumbs. To call the Chief 'the child of a fool' was a capital sin; it was an insinuation against the good sense of his ancestors; it was also a capital offence for any woman to call any man a fool. I have not been able to obtain any very satisfactory explanation for this latter curious prohibition. The reason most commonly given is that a man must fight to protect a woman, and as a woman cannot fight she has therefore not any right to abuse one on whom her life and safety ultimately depended. The prohibition to use the term *Kwasea* is curiously reminiscent of Biblical law, where a similar offender was threatened with eternal perdition.[23]

Assault. This act was ordinarily regarded as a tort. Causes similar to those with which we are now familiar brought certain forms of the offence into the province of 'sins'. It is therefore unnecessary to add anything more, except to point out that a wider circle of individuals than merely Kings or Chiefs was entitled to claim the death penalty for an assault upon their persons. No official, intimately associated with the performance of sacred duties, might be struck or suffer even what we would term a 'technical assault' with impunity. For example, to assault any of the following office-holders of a Head-Chief would have been punished by death: the Soul-washers, Stool-carriers, Custodians of the mausolea. To have done so would have been an insult on their real masters—the spirits of departed Kings or Chiefs.

Stealing (Krono). Ordinary cases of theft were not regarded as offences of which the central authority need take cognizance. Once again, however, we must discriminate between different forms of the offence. The main discussion of this interesting subject will be left to a later chapter. Here I shall only discuss those particular thefts which were regarded as Tribal or National taboos. We might have surmised from the analogies which have already been noted that stealing from a King or Chief would be so regarded, and such an assumption would have been correct. Stealing from a Head-Chief or King was known as *Krono Kesie* (big theft) and the 'sinner' was liable to be killed. Here again, a minor offence became aggravated immediately it came to be practised upon the semi-divine person or property of the King. Into the same category fell stealing from the *abosom* (gods), stealing from the dead, stealing first-fruits. Several Ashanti, with whom I have discussed these last three kinds of stealing, have stated that the offence committed was not really *Krono*, but was *musuobo* or *abusudie*, i.e. the perpetration of an evil or unlucky deed.

Invoking a curse upon the King. Hyira Ohene, 'blessing the King', as the Ashanti euphemistically designated an offence which was the very antithesis of the idiom employed, was one of the most terrible sins of which an Ashanti could be guilty. Its perpetration resulted in certain death. In addition to this euphemism, there were several other circumlocutions by which the offence was expressed—all these were used to avoid if possible the employment of the actual words. *Bo ohene dua*, clubbing the Chief; *wa se biribi* ('he has said something'); *wa de ne nsa si fam* ('he has placed his hand upon the ground') were some of the terms employed. The sin consisted in the invocation of the aid of some spiritual power (generally an *abosom*) to kill the King.[24] If the would-be regicide went directly to the priest of the particular god whose power he wished to invoke, the priest also suffered death. This offence, like many others, might be committed without direct invocation. To compel the son of a King or Chief to clear a path was taken as sufficient implication of intention, because a Chief's son must never perform such a task, unless when, on the death of his father, it fell to his task to clear the way leading to the mausoleum (*Barim*). I once asked an Ashanti why any man, well knowing the penalty he must pay for the offence, should ever have wished to 'bless the King', He replied that a man might have become exasperated beyond all measure at another's conduct and declare, 'I call upon such and such a god to kill the King, and do so on your head, and after I am killed may you pay one hundred *pereguan*, i.e. £800, to buy the Bongo's skin with which I shall be strangled'.[25] I have noted in my last volume how criminals sentenced to death were prevented from invoking such a curse by the prompt thrusting of a *sepow* knife through the tongue and cheeks. The execution in such cases usually took place on the exact spot where the words had been spoken, or if this were not done, then a sheep was sacrificed at that place, a rite which may indicate the necessity for propitiation of the Earth Goddess.

Treason and cowardice. Epow (treason) consisted in plotting to destool a Chief without just cause. Its inclusion in the list of capital sins was possibly a later-day innovation following the growth of power and the elevation of the central authority to a position of tribal or national importance. Any attempt to transfer allegiance from one's own overlord to another—also without just cause—was similarly regarded as treason. It would appear possible that both this offence, and cowardice, may have been relegated to the class of capital sins because they would indirectly have involved the violation of an 'oath'—the former the oath of allegiance, the latter, the oath taken by commanders before setting out on a campaign. In that case the offence would then fall into another category—the eleventh in my schedule. In the case of cowardice, as already noted, the culprit was sometimes permitted to 'buy his head'; but this remission of the death penalty entailed his public degradation, for he was dressed in a woman's *etam* (loin-cloth), his hair was cut in the fashion known as *atirimusem*, his eyebrows were shaved off, and any man might commit adultery with his wife without his being able to obtain redress.

Witchcraft. The violation of any other tribal taboo. Non-compliance with any law or command, the observance of which was enjoined by the 'oath'. Witchcraft (Bayi). Witchcraft, all over Africa, was a sin always regarded by the community with particular dread and abhorrence. I have written at some length on this subject in my last volume, to which I would refer the reader.[26] A witch was never decapitated; a witch's blood might not be shed. After being found guilty, either by the ordinary process of a public trial, by having been tracked down by a witch-finder, or as the result of an ordeal—this last means of investigation being regarded as particularly applicable to this class of sin—the witch was either driven out with a fire-brand in his or her hand, to die eventually of starvation, or was smeared all over with palm oil and cast into a fire, or clubbed or strangled, or drowned.

To kill a person by witchcraft was regarded as 'murder', and it would perhaps have been more in conformity with Ashanti classifications to have placed this sin under that heading. Witchcraft was essentially the employment of anti-social magic. The belief in its general prevalence was largely due to the fact that certain forms of illness resulting in death could not otherwise be accounted for. There appears to be considerable logic in regarding killing by witchcraft as akin to murder, even if its classification as such by the Ashanti was not directly due to an acknowledgement of a fact which was in many cases true, i.e. that poison in some form or other was often an important stock-in-trade of the professed witch. Although witchcraft in Ashanti was not uncommon, and although the offence was undoubtedly regarded with particular repugnance, one fact stands out clearly, namely the absence in Ashanti of hunts for witches, resulting in the extermination of whole village communities, which was such a marked feature of the 'smelling out' of witches in other parts of the African continent. This feature was possibly due to the well-established belief that witches were powerless to work their magic against any one outside the somewhat limited circle of their own particular kindred group or clan.

The violation of any other tribal taboo. Besides those sins which have now been specifically dealt with, each Tribe had its own special list of taboos, the violation of which would have been a matter of investigation for the central tribal authority, and the infringement of any of which would have been punished by death.[27] I append a list of one such schedule of Taboos for the town of Mampon. Many other Divisions had similar laws. Bowdich, more than a hundred years ago, tabulated a somewhat similar catalogue of taboos for Kumasi.

Special taboos for the town or division of Mampon:[28]

(*a*) A dog must be carried through the town. (The origin of this taboo was almost certainly due to the fact that a dog was one of the *akyiwadie* (taboos) of the *Bosommuru ntoro*, to which many of the royal house of Mampon belonged. In Kumasi itself, dogs were once wholly taboo.)

(*b*) A head-rest (*kahire*) must never be made of cloth.

(*c*) A fowl must not be carried on top of any load.

(*d*) Fish sold in the market must never be cut up.

(*e*) Whistling was forbidden in the town. (We have seen in *Religion and Art in Ashanti* that whistling was 'hateful' to certain *suman*.)

(*f*) A priest must never marry a priestess.

(*g*) No one might go to farm work on a Thursday (this was not only a local but a National taboo. Thursday was the day sacred to the Earth goddess).

(*h*) No one might intentionally break an egg upon the ground.

(*i*) No one might intentionally break a pot upon the ground.

(*j*) No one might intentionally spill palm oil upon the ground. (*h*), (*i*), and (*j*) were indirect methods of invoking a curse upon the Chief. Ellis naïvely suggests that these taboos, which were also in force in Kumasi, were enjoined in order that the town might be kept clean.

(*k*) It was forbidden to pour water into palm oil.

(*l*) It was forbidden to carry a load through the town upon the shoulder.

(*m*) It was forbidden to raise a load, carried on the head, above the head when passing through the town. ('To have done so would have implied that that person considered the Chief and Elders as light and worthless.')

(*n*) A woman during her 'periods' might not address a priest or any of the *abenkwa* (palace attendants).

The necessity for the observance of these rules did not depend upon their promulgation, backed with the threat that the violation of them would be taken as the infringement of an 'oath'. They were immemorial laws requiring no other sanction but that with which custom had invested them.

The swearing of an 'oath' itself fell into this general category.

I now come to my last heading: '*The breaking of any law or command, the violation of which would not, in the ordinary way, involve the breaking of any Tribal taboo, but the observance of which had been enjoined on the express understanding that disobedience would be taken, in this particular case, as entailing the violation of a specific taboo.*'

The possible offences which would have been brought under the notice of the central authority by the above process fell into two distinct classes.

(*a*) New edicts promulgated by the central authority itself, which, from the very facts that they were new, caused them to lack the sanctity with which time-immemorial custom alone could have invested them, and the violation of which in itself could not possibly have entailed the breaking of a taboo. New legislation of this nature, after being decided upon by the Chief and his council of Elders, was proclaimed throughout the Division by the Stool town-criers, who were also the Heralds. Such proclamations were always made public late in the evening, when every one would have returned from the forest or the farm. Attention was first arrested by the musical tinkle of the *odawuru*, the elongated bell-shaped gong typical of the whole of this region of West Africa right down to the Niger Delta.

Ton, ton, ton—Hene se wa ma nwo adwo; ose oma nwo adwo Apeafo. Ose—Ya, obiara ye be hu se—Ye ku, ana nwo be timi ato wo tiri a, mperegwan nsia. Ya nwo to Kwesiara, nwo to ntam kesie. Pa fwi!

'*Ton, ton, ton*—Chief says he bids you cool of the evening, he bids you cool of the evening *Apeafo*.[29] He says (here follows the new law). Therefore any one whom we see (breaking this law) we shall kill, or if it be that you are able, you may buy your heads for six *pereguan* (£48). For (if you disobey) then you have violated the forbidden name of Sunday, then have you violated the great forbidden name.'

(*b*) The second class of offences, which in themselves did not call for any interference on the part of the central authority, was brought within its province by an exactly similar process, i.e. by the invocation of a 'conditional curse' and 'oath'. It was a process which might be used by all and sundry, and by its employment any man or woman could temporarily invest his or her own private dispute with all the importance and weight attached to the violation of a tribal taboo. In the chapters which follow, I shall deal with these private causes of dispute, these 'household matters' (*efiesem*), to give them the name by which they were known in Ashanti. They were disputes of supreme importance to the individuals concerned and to their own friends and relatives, but until an 'oath' was sworn with regard to them, they were not any concern of the central power. Its duty was clear; 'household matters' were not its concern; it only stepped in when a Tribal taboo had been violated; it knew only one form of punishment, and that was death. It might appear, therefore, that in taboos, their observance and violation, we have the origin of all laws, but I think that this is not really the case. There were few niceties and fewer legal questions to be settled in the investigations of the violation of a Tribal taboo. In such cases rules of the law were blunt, simple, and decisive. It was in the thrashing out of disputes of a less heinous nature that legal precepts and maxims came to be evolved by the people themselves, and that 'civil' law, as understood in Ashanti, came to take form and shape. In the following pages I shall deal with these *efiesem*, every one of which—let it again be clearly understood—might have been transferred to the chapters which have now been concluded, i.e. placed under the heading of 'Tribal or National taboos', by the simple formula contained in the words, 'I speak the great forbidden name'.

Notes

[1] *Oman*, originally used for 'the tribe', came later to mean 'the Nation'.

[2] Law and morals, it will be noted, are inseparably one.

[3] *Nti wamfa mma ha, ama yamfa asopa ntie, na wo fa aba de bo Akyeame; wu ku yen a, wu di yen aboa.*

[4] See *Ashanti*, pp. 99–100.

[5] A Chief in olden days who let his hair grow would be known to be contemplating war; in the ordinary way he would shave his head once a week on his natal day.

[6] The outraged *ntoro* (spirit) of the injured husband is expected to kill the woman at childbirth.

[7] Well exemplifying the association between black magic and the *suman* which was pointed out in *Religion and Art in Ashanti*; see p. 23.

[8] Of a person's live stock, some might belong to the wife, some to the children. A parent may tell a son or daughter to look after a sheep or goat, or hen. The first and second time the sheep or goat brings forth, the lambs and kids belong to the owner, the third time to the child who is tending it. In the case of a hen, one of each brood is given to the child tending the hen. This might not on any account be touched by a Chief when confiscating the property of a person who was executed.

[9] *Asontakoma na wo bone nti, na ma ye ku no.* Compare the former consequences in our law of sentence of death or outlawry, viz. the corruption of blood.

[10] Another informant stated that this was not the case. 'To kill a child under such circumstances was,' he said, 'taboo. Any one who did so would never have any more children.' The child's *abusua* (kindred) would, he said, be held responsible and fined. Yet again, I have been informed that children who committed a capital sin 'were not executed until they reached puberty'. The procedure perhaps varied in different localities.

[11] Not an excuse for 'blessing the King', but might be pleaded as an excuse in all minor cases; *osabokwafo asem yenni*, or *nsa asem yenni* ('we do not hear cases arising out of drunkenness').

[12] In other cases the offence fell under the category of 'theft'; see Chapter XXVIII.

[13] Here again, however, if the offence had been committed in genuine ignorance of the existing relationship, such a circumstance would have been taken into consideration by the council of Elders and the judge.

[14] The death penalty for this sin may of course no longer be enforced, but the offence is still punished by a fine of £25, two sheep and a case of gin for the Stools, and twelve yards of white calico for the *gyadua* (trees).

[15] *Bere* means 'to bring'; *bra* as a root means something 'forbidden', that 'should not be done'. The reciprocal of the term is *kote-bene-fie* (a penis that is near the house).

[16] Here again genuine ignorance of the *Ntoro* relationship might be pleaded as an excuse.

[17] See *Religion and Art in Ashanti*, Chapter VII.

[18] The case was then known as *Akantamaditwe*.

[19] We have an almost exact analogy in the case of ordinary theft.

[20] This, in itself, no doubt acting as a deterrent to others.

[21] Used in the wider classificatory sense, as also in (*b*), (*c*).

[22] Before speaking these sentences my informant said *Sebe* (pardon); he spoke them in an undertone, and during their recitation snapped his fingers round his ears.

[23] Matthew v. 22.

[24] To invoke a similar power to kill an ordinary individual was 'murder'.

[25] The culprit was executed in this manner for this particular offence.

[26] *Religion and Art in Ashanti*, Chapter III.

[27] Except possibly in the case of complete strangers. *Ohoho nto mara* (A stranger does not break a law).

[28] The majority of these taboos are stated to have been instituted by Komfo Anotche.

[29] An *nton* salutation, also used in addressing hunters.

Chapter 8

SPECIFIC TORTS

H. Ashton: The Basuto*

Civil Wrongs

The most important of these are various offences against the person, such as homicide (*polao*), assault with intent to do serious bodily harm (*phutuho*), ordinary assault, and rape or indecent assault (*peto* or *petello*), seduction (*chobeliso*), adultery (*bofebe*) and defamation (*ketsletso*).

Homicide is the killing of a person, directly or indirectly. It becomes culpable only when done unlawfully. Killing is regarded as lawful in a few cases such as the execution of sorcerers or other malefactors by order of the chief; killing members of the opposition in cattle raids or inter-tribal disputes; and a father's killing his child for disgracing the family by running away from the initiation school. A thief, surprised in a cattle kraal at night or resisting arrest, could also be killed without blame.[1] Abortion and infanticide were not regarded as lawful but, as they were cases primarily affecting the family, they were dealt with by the family rather than the courts. Death arising from a pure accident is not culpable. Apart from these cases, homicide is unlawful. There are degrees of unlawfulness and culpable homicide becomes more serious as it passes from accidental killing due to negligence, through unintentional homicide, as in a drunken brawl, to cold-blooded deliberate murder.

Culpability does not depend on death following immediately from the unlawful action, but may be alleged when death occurs some time after, provided it is directly attributable to that action; for instance, if a woman, who has been seduced, becomes pregnant and dies in labour, her seducer is held responsible for her death[2] and is liable to pay her parents damages up to twenty head of cattle. In the absence of post-mortem examination, the cause of death will be presumed to be due to injury inflicted by an assault only when the injury failed to heal or where the deceased complained of pain, caused by the assault. For this reason, courts insist that the victim of an assault should show them his injuries as soon as possible after the assault so that they may ascertain their seriousness.

The offender is liable to pay ten head of cattle as compensation to the deceased's family in all cases of culpable homicide, except in the case of the death of children, where the damages are four or five head or whatever may be determined by the courts. The compensation is the same whether the deceased is a man or a woman,[3] although Segoete writes that the damages were five beasts for a man and ten for a woman because the latter's loss is greater as she is the producer of children. Where someone is killed by a member of his own family, as when a man kills his wife, or a woman her child, no civil action can be taken as the offender and the victim are one and the same legal person.

If the case is taken to court, the offender may be punished as well as ordered to pay damages. Such punishment varies, according to the degree of culpability, from a reprimand for carelessness in the case of an accident to a heavy fine for murder.

Formerly, even if the case was not taken to court, one or two head of cattle had to be sent to the chief 'to report the death of his subject and that he, the chief, might drink the blood of his dead subject',[4] except in the case of a woman, 'because a woman has no chief but her husband or her father'.[5]

Nowadays, 'it is compulsory for every chief to forward cases of accidental or wilful homicide, which may occur in his ward, to the courts of the Assistant Commissioners, and further the chief is bound to notify the Paramount Chief of such cases.'[6]

* H. Ashton, *The Basuto*, Oxford University Press, 1952, pp. 255–275.

The District Officer then conducts a thorough inquest or preparatory examination, at which representatives of the local authorities, and sometimes also of the Paramount Chief, are present. If a criminal prosecution for murder or culpable homicide is decided upon, the case is heard under the Territory's criminal law by the High Court or Subordinate Court; if no prosecution takes place, the matter is referred back to the chief. In either case, civil action for damages may be brought to the local native court. This court may also punish the offender if he has not already been punished by the Administration's courts, although some people say that if the offender is punished, no civil action should be taken at all. I was unable to ascertain to what extent, if at all, civil actions for damages are actually brought in the native courts against those who have been convicted in the European courts of murder or homicide. Such offences do not give rise to any sort of blood feud or other system of retaliation.

Homicide cases are rarely dealt with by the native courts, but the following interesting one occurred in Mosuoe's court, October 1936:

Bofofu v. *Nkhala*

N committed adultery with B's wife as a result of which she became pregnant. N wrote to B, who was at the mines, admitting his responsibility. When she died in childbirth, N again wrote to him. On his return from the mines, B did not discuss the matter with his family, as he was angry with them for not having told him anything about the matter, but went straight to N and discussed it privately with him. He pointed out that the full compensation was 10 beasts, but said he would accept 4 head as N was his cousin and had been as frank and helpful as he could about the whole matter. N delayed paying the cattle so the matter was then formally discussed *en famille* (*lapeng*) by B's family. The letters were read and full compensation claimed. N agreed to pay this but said he had to consult his elder brother. The latter persuaded him to deny the whole business. The matter was then taken to the local court; N refused to appear and managed to bribe B's elder brother's wife to give him his letters which he destroyed. The case was then taken to Mosuoe's court which ordered N to pay 10 beasts compensation and fined him 2 beasts for his bribery, plus 10s. for refusing to answer the summons of the lower court. B's brother was fined 2 beasts for not taking proper care of the letters and his wife was fined 1 beast for giving them to N. N appealed but the others accepted the judgment.

Assault is an unlawful act of violence committed against another person. As with homicide, there are acts of violence which may be committed lawfully, such as a parent beating his child, a man flogging his wife, *babineli* whipping initiates at the *mophato* and herd-boys fighting with one another. There are also various degrees of assault. These degrees are assessed according to whether or not blood has been shed, the gravity of the injury, the nature of the assault, the degree of provocation given by the injured person, the relative social status of the parties and the wilfulness of the offender. The nature of the weapon used is also a material factor. The use of firearms is the most serious as it indicates reckless intention to do serious injury and—so far as assessing the penal fine is concerned—savours of insubordination. Using knives is more serious than using other weapons such as spears, knobkerries or sticks, for the Basuto have a horror of knifing and regard it as a cowardly form of assault introduced by the despised Pondomise.

The case should be heard as soon as possible after the assault, but if the injuries are serious judgment should be deferred until they have healed.

The offender is liable to pay the victim damages to 'heal the wound' and also to be punished by fining. The amounts of the damages and of the fine vary with the seriousness of the assault. Where the assault was not serious, no compensation or fine will be awarded.

'Mamorkeo v. *Mofelase, Thothofeane, May 1936*

'M, a widow, sues her stepson M because his son assaulted her grand-daughter by throwing her to the ground and beating her with a strap. This was the culmination of a quarrel between them in which they swore at one another. As the assault was a squabble between two youngsters who were kinsmen and no serious injuries were suffered, no damages or penalties were awarded and the court ordered them to go home and keep the peace.

Similarly, no damages or fine will be awarded where the assault was accidental and/or took place on a privileged occasion:

Maqebo v. *Mokoto, November 1936*

The two men quarrelled over some meat. Next day the exciting opening feast of the initiation ceremonies occurred, during which Mokoto got very excited and fired off a revolver which by mischance hit Maqebo's son in the leg. Maqebo, suspecting that this was deliberately done because of their previous quarrel, sues for damages. The court finds no intention of deliberate assault and so merely orders Mokoto to buy medicines to heal the wounds, but warns him that he might have to pay damages if any permanent injury is discovered.

NOTE: Had this taken place anywhere else than at this ceremony, Mokoto would almost certainly have been fined for carrying a revolver as well as for carelessly discharging it.

Where the offender is seriously provoked by the plaintiff, he may be released from paying damages, as the latter has only himself to blame for his injury; but he may be fined for taking the law into his own hands. The plaintiff may also be fined for having provoked a breach of the peace.

Fanyane v. *Jeme, February 1936*

J suspected that F was having an affair with his wife, as he heard that F and F's father, had given her medicine for bronchitis when he was away, and his child medicine for diarrhoea, thus indicating a high degree of intimacy between them. One day he saw F coming out of her hut and attacked him with a spear. F overpowered him and tied him up. As he had suffered considerable provocation, J was fined only £1 for the assault and was not made to pay any damages. F's father was fined 10s. for giving medicines and a third person was fined 5s. for helping to administer them. The case originated in a lower court, which sent it to Mosuoe's court as soon as the serious nature of the attempted assault, i.e. the use of a spear, was disclosed.

In sixteen cases, for which I have records, the amount of damages awarded varied greatly. In seven cases no damages were awarded; 10s. in one case, £1 in two cases, £2 or 1 beast in two cases, 5 small stock in two cases, £3 in one case and 2 beasts (= £4) in one case. Fines also varied: in two cases no fines were imposed. There were three cases of 10s. fines, two of £1, five of 1 beast, three of £3 and one of 3 beasts. There was also the purely criminal case quoted below (*Musuoe v. Molapo* and *Setaka*) where a fine of 5 beasts was imposed. In two of these cases, the plaintiff was also fined 10s. These examples are concerned with assault pure and simple; they do not include more complex cases—such as land disputes, or suits for damage to property, or resistance to court messengers—where one of the parties is fined for using violence or for doing something which might provoke a breach of the peace. In such cases, fines of 1 or 2 beasts are usually imposed.

The use of threats is a form of assault, even if no violence was actually offered, provided that there was reason to believe that the threats would have been carried out but for the intervention of a third party or the retaliation or capitulation of the person threatened. Similarly, if a person deliberately and seriously frightens another.

July v. *Ramabanta, October 1936*

One night when J was away, his wife heard someone stamping round her hut and then someone moving softly. She lighted a lamp and saw R on a horse. Without greeting her first, he told her in a low growling voice three times: 'Come out of your hut, you 'Mantela'. She became thoroughly frightened at this unwonted behaviour and asked if he had come to kill her. He then came towards her and she shouted to her child to bring a spear. He made off then, dropping a stick and his saddlebags. R was ordered to pay 2 beasts as damages for 'attacking' J's wife and children in this way, and was fined 1 bcast and £1.

The essence of rape is forcible ravishment. The relevant facts considered by the courts are the nature of the previous relationship between the two, the degree of force used and any matrimonial intentions of the man. As pre- and extra-marital sexual intercourse are common, the courts are very sceptical about allegations of rape and require very clear evidence that the alleged offender had received no encouragement. Where this is proved, he may be heavily fined, in addition to being ordered to pay the usual damages for seduction or adultery to the woman's parents or husband. But if it can be shown that the offender wished to marry the girl, and that the alleged offence took place while he was abducting her, his act will be treated as mere abduction rather than as rape, even though he may have used a considerable amount of force. Nowadays all cases of rape should be reported to the police and tried in the Administration's courts.

The following is the only case of rape recorded at Mosuoe's court (1935–6):

Mongama v. *Lemeko, October 1936*

L enticed M's daughter into a hut and there raped her. At first he denied it, then said she had consented to intercourse and finally admitted he had raped her. He was ordered to pay 6 beasts damages and fined 1 beast (i.e. the same as ordinary seduction).

Note on procedure: M tried to have the matter settled *en famille*, but L refused to admit his guilt so the matter was then taken to court. When he paid the first instalment of the damages, L asked for the girl in marriage, but M refused saying he did not want to be connected with him. M later informed the court that he had heard rumours that L had further designs on her, so the court formally warned L to behave himself.

Other sexual offences are abduction or seduction. These commonly pass under the blanket term *chobeliso*; formerly the courts made no distinction between them, and the 1922 version of the *Laws of Lerotholi*[7] treated them in the same way. The 1946 version[8] attempts to distinguish between abduction (*chobeliso*) and seduction (*kemariso*; literally 'making pregnant') and provides slightly different scales of compensation and penalties, but I do not know to what extent the courts follow this new distinction. The following account may, therefore, be somewhat out of date.

As indicated in Chapter V, the term *chobeliso* covers a multitude of sins which vary considerably in seriousness. The lightest of them is the elopement of a girl with her husband after the marriage ceremony and before she has been formally taken to his home. The worst is the forcible abduction of the girl and sexual intercourse with her, which is practically indistinguishable from rape.

Fundamentally, *chobeliso* is the commission of some act which publicly spoils or brings in question a girl's reputation for chastity. Thus, discreet seduction of a girl, in the sense of inducing her to grant sexual favours, is not an offence, even if it leads to some scandal-mongering, provided nothing is done publicly to spoil her reputation. But whenever seduction results in the girl's pregnancy, an offence is committed—a fact that is made clear in the Sesuto version[9] of the relevant rule in the 1946 *Laws of Lerotholi*; here the term used is *kemariso*, which means 'making pregnant'. Similarly, elopement is a public acknowledgment of intimacy, and even though no sexual intercourse takes place, as is often the case where a man takes the girl straight to his mother, such intercourse is presumed and is sufficient to spoil her reputation. The fact that publicity is the main factor is illustrated by the following case:

Motsamai v. *Lekholo, October 1936*

M found L's younger brother in a hut at night with his daughter. They admitted that they were in love with one another and that they wanted to be married. The boy had given her his hat and they had exchanged scarves. They denied having had intercourse. M nevertheless sues L for his brother's act of seduction and claims the usual compensation. As L contests this, the court orders the girl to be examined by some impartial women. They report that she is intact and has no blemish. As the girl's reputation is thus publicly upheld, the case is dismissed, but the boy is ordered to return the girl's scarf and is fined 10s. for having jeopardized her honour and given her presents 'as if she were his wife'.

Formerly 'seduction was settled by a fine. The man had the option of marrying the girl, in which case the fine was small, but if he refused to marry the girl, the fine was double'.[10] Later (1912), the law changed and provided that a man 'who seduced or tried to seduce an unmarried girl, had to pay two head of cattle; if she became pregnant, the penalty was six head, but if he afterwards married her, this was reduced to two head over and above the regular dowry.'[11] The present position is dealt with in detail by Rules 2–9 of the 1946 *Laws of Lerotholi*, which are essentially the same as No. 13 of the 1922 version. The parents of the girl who is seduced (i.e. made pregnant) or abducted for the first time, may claim damages up to a maximum of six head of cattle, unless the abduction has taken place at the instance of the girl's parents, when no compensation should be granted. This has long been the accepted figure, and usually[12] the full amount is claimed and awarded. If the girl is seduced (made pregnant) a second time, the maximum compensation is ten head of cattle, unless the first seduction was by another man; in the latter event the maximum compensation is reduced to three head of cattle which is equivalent to that for adultery. Where she is abducted a second time by the same man against her parents' will, the amount of compensation is left to the discretion of the court, which may also order the dissenting parents to arrange the marriage.

Two cases of repeated abduction were dealt with in Bereng's court in 1933–4. In the first, the offender who had paid six head of cattle for his first abduction or elopement (the Basuto use the same term, *chobeliso*), was ordered to pay a second lot of six head, and was fined the usual fine of one head. In the second case, after the first elopement, the offender's elder brother succeeded in getting the girl's parents to agree to their marriage and gave them five head of cattle. A sixth head was given a little later. There was then some delay in completing and arranging the wedding, so the boy eloped with the girl a second time. Her parents sued for six head compensation, but were told by the court that as they had agreed to the marriage they were not entitled to further damages and should expedite the wedding.

If a girl is injured as a result of her abduction or seduction her parents may be awarded compensation not exceeding six head where she is abducted and eight head where she is seduced (i.e. made pregnant).

Formerly, all the foregoing offences were punishable by a fine of one head of cattle and in every case for which I have court records (eight) this fine was imposed. The Rules now provide new and heavier penalties. For abduction, they provide for a fine not exceeding £50 and/or imprisonment not exceeding twelve months; there are similar penalties for the abduction or seduction of mentally defective women or of girls under sixteen. For the seduction of girls boarding at a school or proceeding to or returning from school or a church service, the maximum penalty is halved. Strangely enough the new Rules do not provide for the punishment of other kinds of seduction, but I have no doubt that the courts will continue to inflict the traditional fine of one beast. The provisions dealing with mentally defective women, girls under sixteen and girls at church or school are innovations. Those dealing with girls under sixteen are based on local statute law. Unfortunately, I have no information as to whether the new provisions differentiating between abduction and seduction reflect the actual judicial practice of some courts (in my limited experience the courts do not distinguish between different kinds of *chobeliso*) or whether they represent new concepts which, it is hoped, will guide the courts in future.

Many classes of *chobeliso* are settled out of court by the parties concerned, the boy's parents agreeing to pay the girl's people the traditionally prescribed six head of cattle as damages. An attempt is usually made by the former to get the latter's consent to the marriage of the boy and girl and such overtures are seldom rejected, except in unsavoury cases, such as that of *Mongama v. Lemeko* (above), or where the two families are not friendly. If the marriage is agreed to, the six head of cattle payable as damages, and which should be paid immediately, are then counted as part of the *bohali* marriage-cattle, and a seventh head is usually sent as an earnest of good faith. The rest of the *bohali* may then be paid at leisure later. While these negotiations are proceeding the girl's parents usually ask for the return of the girl, if she eloped, and the boy's people must comply with their request.

Mposi v. *Masekesela, February 1936*

T's son eloped with M's daughter. When M sent for her, T's people hid her, whereupon he got very angry and insisted on her return and on payment of the maximum damages; as T was away, they approached T's elder brother Mp to give him the 6 cattle from T's kraal. Mp then appealed to the court, saying it would be wrong of him 'to go into another kraal and marry off another's child'. The court agreed with him, but told him to return the girl, and advised M to calm down and the matter would be dealt with on T's return.

If the marriage has been agreed on, no damages are payable for any further abduction of the girl by her fiancé, as indicated in the example given above from Bereng's court. A similar case occurred in Mosuoe's court:

Tieho v. *Doka, June 1936*
T's son eloped with D's daughter, and as D then agreed to their marriage, T gave him 7 cattle, and D took his daughter back, saying T should 'follow' him, i.e. complete the arrangements. Before he could do so, he was arrested and imprisoned for a year, and his son, tiring of the delay, abducted the girl again. D then seized 6 of T's cattle as further damages. On his release T sued for their return. The court ordered D to return them so that T could pay a further instalment of the *bohali* cattle and arrange the marriage in the proper manner, and fined D £3 for seizing them unlawfully and £2 for taking them without a permit.

If the girl is married by her seducer the child becomes his child; if they do not marry the child remains with her until she marries and then remains with her parents. If the full damages have been paid, and she eventually marries someone other than her seducer, her husband should not be required to pay more than fourteen head of cattle as *bohali* (i.e. the full number of twenty less six) as she 'has been spoiled' and her parents have been compensated for this spoiling. But if her husband wishes to take her illegitimate child and adopt it, as sometimes happens when the man concerned is old and childless, he may do so, provided he pays the full *bohali*. Although her parents thus get the full *bohali*, plus the six head paid as damages by her seducer, there is no question of returning these six head to her seducer.

Adultery is the infringement of a husband's marital rights and an affront to his dignity. It is thus an offence only when committed by a man, married or single, with a married woman and not when committed by a married man with a single woman. The offending man is liable to pay the injured husband damages. These usually amount to three head of cattle, but they may be more for repeated adultery.

Moleleki v. *Moloi, December 1935*
Moloi was caught four times committing adultery with Moleleki's wife and warned each time by Moleleki. The fifth time, Moleleki brought the matter to court, which ordered Moloi to pay four head of cattle as damages, and fined him two head.

Damages are also higher in cases of adultery with a chief's senior wives. Laydevant[13] says they should be ten head of cattle. Mosuoe claimed and obtained, without going to court, damages of six head of cattle from a man caught sleeping with his second wife. In the old days adultery with the chief's principal wives was punishable by death or banishment.[14]

Some people do not bring cases of adultery to the courts as they do not wish to be exposed to the publicity involved and because their pride revolts against the idea of accepting the compensation 'branded with dishonour'. They prefer either to give the offender a thorough beating themselves or to let him go altogether; sometimes they take the matter to court and ask that the offender may be ordered to cease his illicit attentions. If the matter is taken to court, the offender may be punished by a fine. The usual fine is one head of cattle, but, as in the above case, this may be increased for repeated offences or other aggravating circumstances, such as being likely to provoke bloodshed. According to Segoete,[15] adultery with a nursing mother might be fined with an additional goat, *poli ea boluma*, which would be used to obtain medicines to cure the child of colic caused by his mother's intercourse.

Insult (*hlapa*), or the use of abusive, insulting or derogatory language towards a person ('to speak badly to a person') is an offence. Typical insults are to call a person a sorcerer, 'one who habitually prays to Satan', or a bastard (*ngoana ea lingoetsi lefohlatsebe*), to accuse him of a misdemeanour such as adultery, or to swear at him by his or his mother's 'private parts' or excrement.

Maliengoana v. *Thulo, August 1936*

M is T's father's sister. Her son is known to be T's wife's lover. T went with a friend to ask M to reprove her son and stop him causing dissensions between him and his wife. M affects righteous indignation, so T loses his temper and calls her, 'Dog, wild dog, I'll stab you so that the blade goes right through you, you are an adultress, and sin just as your son sins.' Fined two head of cattle—appeals. Note: the fine here was harsh and should not have been more than 30s.

Another virulent curse is to call a person Satan (*Satana*), which, besides being offensive in itself, is also synonymous with an obscene expression for sexual intercourse.

Sehahabane v. *Moleko, April 1936*

M interrupted a conversation between S and another telling the latter not to talk to S—'He is Satan'. When S threatened to sue him, M got angry, shouted at him and tried to assault him. Fined 30s.

Insults can be offered through quite harmless expressions, if uttered in an abusive or disrespectful manner, or used by inferiors to their social superiors; deliberately breaking a taboo or convention, or behaving outrageously may also constitute an insult.

Rabuti v. *Mokalinyane, September 1936*

After a quarrel, R rode his horse into M's *lelapa*. Subsequently he apologised and his apology was accepted, but M sued him in court. The headman's court fined R £1—on appeal to the sub-chief's court, the fine was increased to 55s. On further appeal to Mosuoe's court, the fine was reduced to 10s. No damages were awarded to M as an apology had been tendered and accepted, but he was fined 10s. for having brought R to court after forgiving him.

Insults are wiped out by apology. This is usually verbal, but may also include an offer of compensation; in one case where a man's herd-boy accused another of theft, the former offered him 10s. 'to clean his name'. Failing this, recourse can be had to the courts. Except in serious cases, the injured person is not awarded damages, but the offender is ordered to make a public apology and is soundly berated by the court. In serious and provocative cases he may also be fined, as shown in the above cases. (Bereng's court, in 1933, fined a man a beast for cursing his elder brother during a dispute over some trees.) The following case is of interest for the complicated form of insult and the award of damages, which were subsequently returned.

Paul v. *Masekesela, June 1936*

M accuses P of stealing his sjambok, and then goes on insultingly, 'I'll ruin you myself, I'll burn your hut down at night when you are with your wife, and when you both come out naked to put the fire out, I'll go and reap your fields.' P sued in the headman's court but M refused the summons, so the matter was taken to Mosuoe. P was awarded 1 beast damages and M fined 1 beast and £1. P, honour now satisfied, asks the court to remit the damages, which it does.

A similar type of offence is defamation (*tlontlollo ea lebitso* or *ketseletso*). This is the spoiling of a person's reputation by maliciously attributing something evil to him, misrepresenting his words or actions or spreading false rumours. Such cases are dealt with on the same lines as the foregoing; the action is brought primarily to vindicate the plaintiff's reputation rather than to obtain damages, and the offender may be fined. The following cases illustrate the kind of defamatory remark made and the action of the court. As the first one shows, it is not easy to draw a clear dividing line between this class of offence and the previous one.

'Mamafu v. *'Maneheng* (*two women*), *August 1936*

'Mamafu sues 'Maneheng for calling her a witch, a Christian (using the word *Lejakane* with contemptuous tone) who bewitches and prays to Satan. The court ordered 'Maneheng to pay 10s. damages and fined her 5s. 'to cut off her tongue'. 'Mamafu did not think this fine heavy enough and wanted to appeal, but was persuaded by her son to accept the judgment.

Mokopu v. *Motinyane, February 1936*

The wives of these two men were working in the fields together and got into a heated argument, during which Mokopu's wife said, '*Thokolosi* will tread on someone'. Later, the fire they had made to cook their meal spread to Motinyane's threshing floor and burned some corn. He attributed this to Mokopu's wife, insinuating that she had a *thokolosi* or witch. Mokopu then sues him for this. The court sympathized with Motinyane, but refused to convict, saying, 'It is known that people are witches but unless one is caught red-handed, there is not theft,' and ordered the parties to go home and live together in peace.

Tsekana v. *'Mantlameng, February 1936*

T sues his headman 'M for saying quite unjustifiably that he had refused to carry out his orders and thus giving him a reputation for disobedience. Some members of the court wished to fine 'M, but eventually the court decided merely to warn him.

Abimael v. *Tootse, January 1936*

A, a priest, sues T for saying that he had taken part in recent initiation ceremonies, whereas he had actually opposed T's proposal to establish a lodge in front of his school and managed to get it established away from his mission.

Malicious reports and/or prosecution constitute an offence similar to the foregoing. But this rarely comes before the courts as a separate suit, and usually arises out of another dispute, or when the court find that the prosecution is entirely unfounded. The offender is usually punished by fining. A good example occurred in the property dispute, *Maqetha v. Pipi.*[16] Similarly in the case:

Monoana v. *Paul, January 1936*

M sued P, complaining that P had prevented him from ploughing a field and had brandished a gun and threatened to shoot him. It was proved that P had not carried a gun and had not threatened to shoot. M, a headman, was fined 30s. for malicious prosecution and his three witnesses were fined £1 each for giving false evidence.

Offences Against Property

Offences against property fall into three main groups: theft, wrongful use of property and wrongful damage to property.

Theft is the wrongful taking or retention of property with intention to deprive the owner of his ownership. There is no offence where this intention is absent, i.e. where a person merely takes and keeps someone else's property for temporary use and in such a way that it can be reasonably assumed that he intends to and can restore it to the owner.

Every kind of movable property can be stolen and, in fact, most kinds are stolen. Of twelve cases recorded from Bereng's court in 1934, seven were stock (four small, three cattle, horses, etc.) and one money, food, hide, wool and *bewijs* book. Of thirty-four at Mosuoe's court in 1935–6, twenty-five were stock (eleven small stock, fourteen cattle, etc.), two food, wool and ploughs, and one money, *bewijs* book and saddlery. The preponderance of stock cases is not surprising as stock is readily movable and is the principal form of property. Sheep are stolen, often in large quantities, for their wool, and having been sheared are let loose and driven into the veld, except for one or two which are killed for food. Cattle and horses are stolen for use and are seldom killed. Theft of food is regarded as a shameful matter—except as between herd-boys in the mountains—and is rarely brought to the courts.

The evolution and modification of the law relating to theft may be briefly traced. Evidence to the Commission in 1873 baldly stated that theft was punished by a fine. Later, it was more explicitly stated[17] that 'theft was punished according to the merits of the case; usually the thief had to pay fourfold—two to the court and two to the owner (one in restoration and one in compensation for the trouble caused). There was a saying, "*Pinyane ha e senye motse*" (Petty theft destroys no village) by which the Basuto used to justify their leniency towards this kind of crime; but if one of the culprits confessed and denounced his comrades, much ill-will would ensue, even to the extent of 'destroying the village".' A fuller statement of the law was made in the 1922 edition of the *Laws of Lerotholi*:

> 'It is the law that thefts of any kind or description whatever shall be punishable by the law of Moshoeshoe, which is the only one that satisfies the nation, to wit: a beast to be repaid by a beast, a second beast for compensation, and a third as a fine to be paid to the court. If the person so fined continues to steal, the court has the right to increase the amount of the fine.'[18]

and,

> 'Any person who will steal for a second time shall be liable to a fine not exceeding 10 head of cattle. If the thief has no property to pay the fine he shall be sent to the Paramount Chief. Judgment in such cases shall be at the discretion of the Paramount Chief and the Resident Commissioner.'[19]

The principles involved are those noted by Ellenberger and MacGregor—restoration, compensation and punishment—and qualified by the *Laws of Lerotholi*, in that they should all be of the same kind and number, or of equal value. If the article is intact, it must be returned, but if damaged or destroyed it must be replaced. Besides this, an equal amount must be paid as compensation. The concept of compensation, idiomatically expressed, is that when the thief returns the animals he has stolen, he should drive (*qhoba*) them with an equivalent number to keep them company. These principles are rigidly enforced: in every case for which full details are available (twelve in Bereng's court and twenty-four in Mosuoe's), the object stolen was returned when it was still intact, or replaced where it had been destroyed, and compensation was paid, equal in amount or value to the thing stolen: a beast was compensated with a beast, wool with its cash value, a mare with two horses.

There is a tendency to view theft from the thief's angle rather than the owner's and to insist that where there is more than one thief, each of them should make compensation, as is shown in these two cases:

Mochati and 2 others v. *Mosala and 2 others, February 1936*

For the theft of 4 horses. As these were recovered intact they were returned, and each of the three thieves had to pay compensation with 4, so that each owner, besides getting his horses back, received threefold compensation.

Mosalatsi v. *Ketleng and 3 others, July 1936*

Two sheep belonging to M were killed and eaten by K and three others. Each of the four thieves was ordered to replace the 2 sheep and then pay compensation with 2 more, so that the owner received 16 sheep.

In another case where sixteen sheep were stolen and were returned by order of the court, each of the three thieves involved had to *qhoba* them with an equal number, thus giving the owner forty-eight sheep as compensation. (See also cases 6, 7 and 9 of Mosuoe's court, p. 270).

In one case, however, the court recognized that the basic principle was being misapplied and that the owner was being ridiculously over-compensated. It re-enunciated the law that the owner should receive compensation equal to the value of the thing stolen, but instead of making each of the thieves pay an equal proportion of this, it ordered that each should pay the full amount of compensation and itself appropriated the difference: where three men combined to steal four sheep, each of them had to pay four as compensation, making a total of twelve; the owner was given four and the court kept the remaining eight. In other words, it gave expression to the tacit implication that the so-called compensation is not really compensation at all, in the sense that it has any relationship to the actual damage suffered by the owner; it is more in the nature of a fine, that is, it is penal rather than restitutive: therefore, since the owner is properly compensated by receiving an amount equal to the theft, the balance of the so-called compensation should go to the court rather than to the plaintiff. Where the co-defendant is only an accessory, the full duplication is not enforced (see No. 2 of Bereng's court, p. 269). This sort of judgment was imposed in all the cases occurring in Mosuoe's court in which more than one thief was involved.

In inflicting ordinary fines, the courts do not observe the same rigid uniformity in equating the amount of the fine to the amount of the theft, as they do when enforcing payments of compensation. In only one out of ten cases involving first offenders did Bereng's court inflict a fine equal to the value of the object stolen and so preserve the ratio set out in the *Laws of Lerotholi* of 1 : 1 : 1. In Mosuoe's court, only one case out of twenty observed this ratio. In both cases this was probably fortuitous as the thing stolen was a beast and this happens to be the usual fine.

Nor do the courts observe the same leniency that Ellenberger and MacGregor formerly noted. Heavy fines are the rule rather than the exception. The normal fine is one head of cattle; this was imposed in six out of eleven cases in Bereng's court and in eight out of twenty-three in Mosuoe's. It is seldom that no fines, or small fines, are imposed: one case in Bereng's court where a herd-boy was reprimanded for selling wool in his keeping, and three in Mosuoe's. In the latter cases, the fines were £1 (half the normal), but in two of them this was twice the value of the thing stolen. Heavier fines were imposed in all other cases. Apart from the tendency to fine heavily, such fines may be imposed for repeated offences or as a general deterrent; Mosuoe's court, in six cases, imposed fines of one beast plus £1 or more in an attempt to reduce the incidence of stock theft. Fines are also imposed where elements other than theft enter in, such as when the theft is accompanied by violence either in its commission or in the thief's refusal to confess his guilt by carrying the *corpus delicti*, or where there is some degree of insubordination. Thus Bereng's court imposed a fine of three beasts for the theft and consumption of two sheep, where this was a second offence; and in another case, where a headman seized, killed and ate an ox from a herd of another headman, who deliberately tried to open his spare veld, the court fined him five beasts and those who helped him, two beasts. Mosuoe's court fined the thief of a horse and a mare three beasts for resisting the court messengers and ignoring its summons. The following table shows the variety of cases dealt with and the frequency of the standard fine.

TABLE

Bereng's Court

Case	*Fine*	*Remarks*
1. 2 sheep stolen and eaten. Principal to restore 2 and *qhoba* 2 sheep. Accessory—brother (first offence)—*qhoba* 2 sheep	3 beasts	Repeated offence
2. Headman for killing and eating 1 ox to restore 1 and *qhoba* 1 ox. Those who helped	5 beasts 2 beasts	Case aggravated by defiance
3. Theft of food valued at 6d. Return 6d., *qhoba* 6d.	1 beast	
4. Theft 3 horses which died through ill-treatment. First offence. Restore 3 horses, *qhoba* 3 horses	2 beasts	Case aggravated by ill-treatment of animals
5. Theft and consumption of 1 sheep. Restore 1 and *qhoba* 1	1 beast	
6. Theft of money. Money to be returned	1 beast	
7. Theft of untanned hide. Return the hide and *qboba* 2 sheep	1 beast	
8. Herd-boy selling wool and misappropriating the money. Refund twice the amount of money	Nil	Reprimanded

Mosuoe's Court

1. 2 sheep stolen and eaten. Return 2 and *qhoba* 2	Nil	Ordered to leave mountain area—a heavy punishment in itself
2. 1 goat stolen and eaten. Return 1 and *qhoba* 1	1 beast	
For helping to kill goat, accessory	£1	

3.	1 sheep stolen and eaten. Return 1 and *qhoba* 1 (herd-boy). Master of herd-boy did nothing about the theft and refused to help bring him into court	£1 30/-	
4.	Theft 10 sheep. Return them and *qhoba* 10	1 beast	
5.	Theft 1 donkey. Return it and *qhoba* 1 donkey	£1	
6.	3 thieves stole 4 horses. The 4 to be returned and each thief to *qhoba* 4 horses. Herd-boy for helping	1 beast+ £1 each 1 beast	
7.	2 thieves stole and sheared 30 sheep, killed and ate one, 8 died. To return 30 and each to *qhoba* 30, each to restore 9 and *qhoba* 9	1 beast+ £1 each	
8.	Theft 4 sheep. Return them and *qhoba* 4	1 beast+ £1	
9.	4 thieves stole and ate 2 sheep. Each to restore 2 and *qhoba* 2	1 beast each	
10.	Theft 1 horse and 1 mare. Return horses and *qhoba* 1. Return mare and *qhoba* 2 horses	3 beasts	Case aggravated by fighting and ignoring summons
11.	1 sheep stolen and eaten. Restore 1 and *qhoba* 1 For refusing to catch thief	1 beast 1 beast	
12.	Theft saddle and bridle. Replace them with 1 beast, *qhoba* 1 beast	1 beast	Inveterate thief

The revised version of the *Laws of Lerotholi*, 1946, is more realistic and more closely related to the practice of the courts than the original version. This version reads as follows:

> 'In cases in which a person is convicted of theft the court giving judgment may, in addition to any punishment imposed, order the convicted person to replace the article or stock stolen, or to pay to the owner of the stolen article or stock an amount equivalent to the value of such article or stock.'[20]

An inveterate thief may be ordered to remove from the remote mountain areas to a more closely populated area. This traditional power has been embodied in the new *Laws of Lerotholi* in the following terms:

> 'Every chief is empowered to order any habitual thief whose hut or huts are situated in an isolated area of his ward to remove such huts and reside in the chief's village or in any other village ordered by the chief.'[21]

As indicated above, inveterate thieves are liable to a heavier punishment than first offenders and may, according to the *Laws of Lerotholi*, be fined up to ten head of cattle. The heaviest fine of which I have record is three head of cattle for the theft of two sheep, imposed by Bereng's court; but, according to George Tlali Moshesh,[22] formerly, notorious thieves who were likely to involve the country in war by stealing from neighbouring nations were sometimes put to death. He knew of four who had been executed by Moshesh. Sofonia[23] testified that incorrigible thieves might be put to death. Such drastic action no longer occurs, although, as mentioned in the previous chapter, inveterate thieves are occasionally tortured.

Sofonia also testified that thieves caught in a kraal at night could be killed with impunity and he quoted a saying, 'A thief is a dog that must pay with its head'. This offence is not regarded so seriously now and Mosuoe's court, in one such case, confirmed a fine of only two sheep imposed by a lower court. But if a thief was injured while being arrested in such circumstances, he could make no claim for redress.

Sofonia also stated that 'the receiver of stolen property, knowing it to have been stolen, can be fined as a thief; this applies to all who partake of the meat of stolen animals, knowing them to have been stolen.' This is still the law, but the fines imposed on the receiver are less than those imposed on the thief. Accessories are treated in the same way as thieves, but again with less severity. An interesting case occurred in Mosuoe's court, on appeal from Tootse.

Tootse v. *Maekane, October 1935*

T sued M as an accessory to the theft of a plough. The thief, who was a friend of M's, left the plough with him saying he had just bought it. Later when the theft was reported, T by chance picked on M to investigate the matter and to make inquiries at the chief's village. M did so and reported that he had found nothing. The plough was later discovered in his possession and the thief convicted. T then brought a separate action against M for trying to shield the thief and not reporting that he knew where the plough was. T's court found him guilty, but taking into account his loyalty to his friend, it fined him only 3 goats. M appealed to Mosuoe's court, but the appeal was dismissed.

Where a person assists in a theft under duress, he is punished more lightly than the principal thief, as in No. 6, Mosuoe's court where the hered-boy was fined 1 beast only and did not have to pay compensation.

Where an accessory interferes with the administration of justice by hindering the search for stolen goods or the apprehension of suspected thieves, he may be punished heavily:

Mosalatsi v. *Keleng and Piete, July 1936*

M traced the spoor of sheep lost from his cattle-post to another cattle-post where he found the skinned head of one of his sheep. P confessed to having stolen two sheep with three others whom he named. M rounded them up and tied them up. Two others then arrived and made him untie them and encouraged them to deny the theft. Finally the situation was saved by the headman's messenger arriving and getting P to carry the skin and so reaffirm his admission. The four thieves were ordered to 'restore' 2 sheep and compensate M for the theft by paying 4 sheep each and were fined 1 beast each. The other two were fined 2 beasts for their interference.

Robbery, or theft with violence, occasionally occurs, as when thieves terrorize herd-boys in remote cattle-posts or keep them in the hut at night by throwing stones on the roof or door and threatening to burn the hut or to kill them if they try to come out, while they rustle the sheep away. In such cases, the offence is dealt with in the same way as ordinary theft in so far as civil action and remedies are concerned; the victim does not get any extra compensation by reason of his having been subjected to violence or threats, although cognisance may be taken of these threats or violence in punishing the offender.

Mokete v. *Lekhokhotsane, July 1936*

L robbed M of 2 horses. He was ordered to return them and *qhoba* them with 2 head of cattle, and was fined 2 head of cattle 'for provoking bloodshed in a man's village' plus £1 'to make you respect the law'.

Liau v. *Monnamoholo and Khoto, June 1936*

M and K robbed L's herd-boy of 2 bags of wool. The court ordered them to return it with 2 bags and fined each 1 beast plus 10s. for theft. For the assault K was fined 2 beasts as he is a headman and M was fined £3 10s.

Theft by conversion is occasionally found. This mainly occurs in connexion with *mafisa* stock where some of the stock is sold or given away or killed for food beyond the quantity tacitly or explicitly agreed upon by the owner. Cases may occur where a guardian misappropriates his ward's property or where an authority misappropriates property given to him to hold in trust during a dispute. Ellenberger and MacGregor record[24] that because such theft involved breach of trust 'any person in charge of cattle belonging to another, who tried to appropriate them for himself by theft or by means of false marks was almost as severely dealt with' as a warrior hiding booty captured in war, the penalty for which was death. But in the cases of which I have records no great differentiation is made between this and other forms of theft. For instance, Mosuoe's court fined a headman 30s. for eating some grain and spending all but 2s. of a pound which had been entrusted to his care. Similarly, Bereng's court ordered a person who had sold another's cow without his consent to restore it and fined him one beast.

Another type of theft is the misappropriation of lost property, i.e. appropriating it without taking the proper steps to return it to its owner. Ordinary articles, such as clothing or blankets, found on the road should be reported to the headman and returned to the owner as soon as it is known who he is; and no claim for reward should be made. If the owner is not found within six months the property may be retained by the finder. Stray stock should be handed to the chief or reported within two months of arrival. No obstacle should be put in the way of people looking for their lost stock.[25] Breach of these rules is punished by fining and/or imprisonment and the offender may be ordered to pay compensation for any damage or loss suffered by the owner of the lost property.

Damage to Property

A person unlawfully damaging another's property or interfering with his enjoyment of such property is liable to pay the owner damages. As in other cases, the courts can impose a fine where the damage was done maliciously or provocatively, or was accompanied by some other reprehensible circumstance. For instance, in Bereng's court in 1933, a plaintiff sued a man whose dog had killed his sheep. The court ordered the defendant to replace the sheep, and then fined him two sheep for slackness in not reporting the killing to his headman or the complainant. So, too:

Lethapa v. *Moji, June 1936*

L sued M for driving 12 cattle into his crops. The court ordered M to pay £1 plus 1 bag of grain for the damage, and fined him 1 beast for deliberately causing this damage.

Two cases occurred in Bereng's court of subordinate authorities being fined for damage to stock kept in their pounds: in one, the authority was fined for keeping a horse two days without letting it graze; in the other, he was fined one beast for gross negligence leading to the death of two sheep, and was also ordered to compensate the owner by replacing the two sheep.

An action for damages will be sustained by the courts only when the damage is done unlawfully.

Rankhonoane v. *Nrebe, July 1936*

N was found sitting in R's hut with R's wife by another man who was enamoured of R's wife. A fight started between them in the course of which they smashed the door of the hut. R sued N as it was his presence in the hut which provoked the fight. N was ordered to pay R £2 for the damage to the door and was fined 30s.

Where is it done lawfully, there is no liability to pay compensation.

Mposi v. *Mosebi, October 1936*

Mp unsuccessfully sued M and three others for breaking down the door of his hut. Their defence was that they were sent by the chief to his village to fetch him in connexion with suspected theft. On finding he had run away from home on their approach, they broke into his hut to search for the stolen goods and found the skin of one of the stolen sheep.

The amount of damages to be paid is usually assessed by the courts and should be equivalent to the actual damage done; there is no additional 'compensation' for any theoretical loss by deprivation or inconvenience as in the case of theft. Where there is no damage, there is no award:

Isaak v. *Moiloa, etc., July 1936*

I unsuccessfully sued the parents of several boys for damaging his field. They had not done any damage as they were hunting a bird there and as they were only young boys, who meant no harm, his rights had not been seriously flouted.

In the case of damage to crops, the arbitrary figures of 1s. per head of large stock and 3d. per head of small stock were laid down in the 1922 *Laws of Lerotholi*:

'For trespass by any beast, horse, mule or donkey in any garden or tree plantation, the owner or caretaker of such animals will pay to the owner or caretaker of such garden or tree plantation the sum of 1s. for each beast or horse. Should, however, the damage be found by the assessors to be small the chief or headman shall only award a sum of 3d. per head.'

'No charge for trespass shall be made in respect of any sheep or goat, but if any damage is done to crops or trees the chief or headman shall cause the owner or caretaker of such sheep or goat to pay the owner or caretaker of such crops or trees a sum of 3d. per head.'[26]

Nevertheless, the courts adopted a more realistic attitude and where considerable damage had been done, they attempted to assess it more equitably:

Mokete v. *Mazenkane, February 1936*

Mok claimed 32s. damages to his crop done by 12 cattle. The court awarded £1 instead of the prescribed 12s. to 'console' him for the extensive damage done.

The old fixed rate has now been abolished and the courts are allowed to use their own discretion.[27]

The official rates were known to most people, but the two parties sometimes agreed on a higher rate of damages. If they quarelled about this later, the court would enforce the agreement:

Lebula v. *Makokotla, February 1936*

Thirty of M's sheep grazed L's crops during the day. M sent a messenger to view the damage and agreed to pay 2 bags of grain as compensation. As he failed to honour his agreement, L sued him. The court first suggested that L should accept 7s. 6d., i.e. 3d. per head, but when he refused, it ordered M to fulfil his agreement and pay the 2 bags of grain or the equivalent (£2), although it considered this excessive.

The following is the usual procedure for obtaining compensation when crops are damaged: the owner of the crops reports the incident to the owner or person in charge of the stock, and the two inspect the damage together—in person or by proxy—and try to agree upon the extent of the damage and the amount of compensation to be paid. If the owner of the stock refuses to view the damage or if they fail to reach an agreement, the owner of the crops should appeal to his headman. The latter should then send reliable messengers to assess the damage before giving judgment. Under the new Rules, the person claiming damages should inform his headman of the amount claimed, and if the owner of the stock disputes this, the headman should 'depute two independent persons to assess the damages; provided that if either party is dissatisfied with the amount assessed, such dissatisfied party may take the matter to court.'

In the foregoing cases the damage had been caused either by the deliberate act of the offender or through his negligence. Liability may, however, extend further to cover cases where the damage is done through no fault of the person concerned. Thus, if cattle break out of a kraal at night and damage crops, their owner has to pay the same damages as described above, even though the cattle were properly secured for the night. If they break out repeatedly, the owner is presumed to have been negligent in securing them and may be fined as well; formerly, the cattle could have been taken to a kraal and one beast slaughtered there. Similarly, if a stallion breaks loose and covers someone's mare, the owner of the stallion is liable for damages, which may be assessed at 30s. Other cases of this sort are a bull goring another bull or a dog barking and frightening a cow and causing it to injure itself. Where, however, the owner of the injured animal was negligent and his negligence contributed to the accident, he is not entitled to damages.

Sekate v. *Leshota, March 1936*

Appeal from lower court. L seized a beast belonging to S to pay off the tax arrears owed by S. When it was being driven off, it fell over a cliff and was killed. S sued L for damages, saying it had 'died in the chief's kraal'. The court rejected the claim since its fall was made due to an attempt by S to turn it back.

Notes

[1] Native Laws Commission.
[2] *Laws of Lerotholi*, Rules Nos. 4, 5 and 8.
[3] George Tlali Moshesh: Evidence to the Commission, and *Laws of Lerotholi*, No 13.
[4] Commission. Evidence of George Tlali Moshesh and Sofonia Moshesh.
[5] Jobo Moshesh, ibid.
[6] *Laws of Lerotholi*, 1922, No. 17, now covered by the Native Courts Proclamation No. 62 of 1938.
[7] *Laws of Lerotholi*, No. 13.
[8] 'Rules', 2–7.
[9] The English version is, indeed, somewhat misleading.
[10] George Tlali Moshesh, Commission. He probably meant damages rather than penal fine.
[11] Ellenberger and MacGregor [p. 269]. Here again civil damages are undoubtedly meant rather than penal fines.
[12] In five out of six cases in Bereng's courts, and in one solitary case in Mosuoe's court.
[13] Laydevant, 1931, p. 240.
[14] Ellenberger and MacGregor [*op. cit.*] p. 269.
[15] Segoete, p. 17.
[16] Page 180, [Ashton].
[17] Ellenberger and MacGregor [*op. cit.*], p. 270.
[18] *Laws of Lerotholi*, No. 12.
[19] *Ibid.*, No. 24.
[20] Rule No. 16.
[21] Order No. 8.
[22] Commission 1873.
[23] *Ibid.*
[24] Ellenberger and MacGregor [*op. cit.*] p. 270.
[25] 'Rules', No. 21.
[26] *Laws of Lerotholi*, 1922, No. 25 (2) and (3).
[27] 'Rules', No. 13.

P. P. Howell: Manual of Nuer Law*

Injuries Recognized in Nuer Law

There are many specific injuries recognized in Nuer customary law as demanding compensation in cattle. Most of these injuries are fractures of bones, but it is usually on the subsequent effects of the injury—the stiffening of joints or paralysis causing permanent disablement—that the extent of the compensation is judged. Specific injuries recognized are given in the table. Scales of compensation were extremely variable throughout Nuerland, but fairly consistent within one tribe. Elders can usually quote the rates current in the past. As in the case of most indemnities among the Nuer, I think that the rates were essentially idealized and therefore only a basis upon which a suitable compromise could be reached. This principle still operates in Nuer courts today, although there is an increasing tendency to quote past precedents established in case law. An attempt was made in 1945 to stabilize the scales, and the results are also recorded in the table, though it was appreciated that any rigid rule at this stage might be unwise. It is worth noting that theoretically total blindness is tantamount to death among the Nuer, and that loss of both eyes should demand full bloodwealth. At the Nuer Chief's meeting where these scales were discussed it was said that a man who loses his sight is 'like one who is dead', and the main object of the indemnity was to provide him with a wife, as in homicide. It was agreed, however, that in modern conditions ten head of cattle should be sufficient.

SCALES OF COMPENSATION FOR BODILY INJURIES, 1945

Injury	*Head of cattle*	*Sexes*
tul juath peta (Fracture of the forearm: either *ulna* or *radius*) .	2	1 cc+1 bc
(Fracture of both)	4	2 cc+2 bc

* P. P. Howell, *Manual of Nuer Law*, Oxford University Press, 1954, pp. 69–70.

Injury	*Head of cattle*	*Sexes*
tul ciel (Fracture of the elbow)	2	1 cc+1 bc
(when the injury results in permanent disablement)	6[1]	5 cc+1 bc
tul woka (Fracture of the upper arm: *humerus*)	6	5 cc+1 bc
tul thak mual (Fracture of the kneecap: *patella*)	2	1 cc+1 bc
(when the injury results in permanent disablement)	6[1]	5 cc+1 bc
tul gham (Fracture of the thighbone: *femur*)	6	5 cc+1 bc
tul peta (Fracture of the collar-bone)	2	1 cc+1 bc
tul yed pek metot (Fracture of the little finger)	1	1 cc
tul yed pek medit (Fracture of the thumb or big toe)	1	1 cc
tul yed (Fracture of the bones of the hand)	(not specified)	
tul joak (Fracture of or permanent injury to the shoulder)	6	5 cc+1 bc
tem ral coke (cutting of the tendons of the heel or wrist)	2	1 cc+1 bc
(if permanent disability results)	4[1]	3 cc+1 bc
ghar lie nyal (knocking out a girl's teeth)	2 to 4	
mut wang (loss of an eye)	5	4 C +1 B
mut nyin dang rew (loss of both eyes)	10	8 C +2 B

C=Cow. B=Bull. cc=cow-calf. bc=bull-calf.

Defamation of Character

Defamation of character is a recognized wrong in Nuer law, and is usually associated with false accusation of witchcraft, though sometimes of such offences as adultery. The Nuer expression is *lorjok* (*teke lorjok*). Here the slandered person is likely to suffer a loss of status and privilege and run the risk of destruction at the hands of his fellows. In the case of false accusation of adultery, he runs the risk of retaliation by the husband. Hence, particularly in the latter instance, there is danger of breach of the peace in which opposed kinship groups will be involved, and the offence calls for some form of compensation. Nuer say that cases of this sort were frequent in the past, compensation being made by payment of one cow (*yang lorjok*), and cases are occasionally brought before the courts today.

Note

[1] The distinction depends on the results of the injury—which applies to all injuries, but is here specified.

D. J. Penwill: Kamba Customary Law*

Adultery

If a man commits adultery with a married woman, the customary penalty is the payment of a bull and a goat. The elders—of the aggrieved clan, and of the 'utui' or Tribunal, if these latter have been called in to give judgment in the matter—slaughter them both at the house of the injured husband, who shares in the feast but gets no specific compensation. (In Kikumbulyu it is two goats and a bull.) In addition, in the past, the act might well have caused fighting between families and perhaps a death; nowadays, it is made a crime against native law and custom under Section 13 (a) of the Native Tribunal Ordinance, 1930, and in addition to the customary compensation the guilty accused will be fined—normally to pay forty shillings, or to undergo two months in the Detention Camp in default.

There is no difference if the woman is made pregnant; the penalty and the compensation are the same, and the child belongs to her husband. If she dies as a result of her pregnancy, say in childbirth, the adulterer must pay the blood price for her—four cows, a bull and a goat, normally; but in Kilungu, Nzaui, Mbitini and Mukaa, the number of cows is increased to five, and in Kikumbulyu to six. If the child is born dead, or there is a miscarriage, there is no further penalty, for it is regarded as the child of the legal

* D. J. Penwill, *Kamba Customary Law*, East African Literature Bureau, 1951, pp. 72–76 and pp. 78–87.

husband. There was a case at Nzaui in 1947 of a man accusing another not only of adultery but of infecting his wife with gonorrhoea; however, the 'utui' elders considered that there was no proof that it was the fault of the accused and the case was not registered at the Tribunal. There is no customary penalty or compensation for such injury resulting from intercourse, and it would have been interesting to see the outcome of the case had the charge been proven.

Taking a married woman away from her husband is treated similarly; it is a crime against native law and custom for which either fine or imprisonment may be awarded, and the customary compensation is the same.

Fornication

If a young man has intercourse with a girl who is unmarried but past the age of puberty—as frequently happens after a dance—there is no penalty, even if part of the bride price has been paid for the girl and the man is not her prospective husband. If, however, the girl is made pregnant, the customary penalty is a goat, which is slaughtered and eaten by the elders. (If she dies as a result of her pregnancy, the blood price is payable.) Normally, under the circumstances, the girl returns to her father's house until she bears the child; only then does she name the father, and one of the elders of the family goes to call on him, telling him to bring a goat for slaughter since it is understood that the child is his. If he agrees, the man will give this goat; if not, he goes with an elder of his own family to confront the girl and argue the matter to a decision, which the elders of the two families may be called in to make. When the girl is married, the husband takes her child as his.

If the child is born dead, or there is a miscarriage, a goat and a bull must be paid over and not just a goat. In Kikumbulyu, if the child is recognisable as male, seven goats must be paid; if female, five goats.

If a man had intercourse with a child, not yet past puberty, the customary penalty was a goat. Such offences have now been removed from the sphere of customary law by Sections 137 and 138 of the Penal Code, and are outside the jurisdiction of the Native Tribunals.

The taking of an unmarried girl away from her father is punishable, if the girl is under sixteen, by Section 136 of the Penal Code. It is also regarded as an offence against native law and custom, whatever the girl's age, and is treated and punished as such, if the girl is older, by a fine or imprisonment. No customary compensation is payable, save the goat for the elders if the girl is made pregnant.

There has been widespread dissatisfaction with the customary law and penalty for impregnating an unmarried girl. In earlier times, a child was an asset, and a girl could easily be married after bearing one. Now this is changing. Her value on the bridal market is depreciated—her father's loss—and she may never get married and have to stay with her father all her life, or go out to become a prostitute. Furthermore, a goat (whose legal value is twelve shillings but can often be bought for less) is nothing to young clerks and schoolmasters who earn eighty or one hundred shillings upwards each month. The result has been that there have been cases before the Native Tribunals when the girl has sued the man for the maintenance of the child and its clothing. The usual claim has been for a lump sum of one hundred shillings, or thereabouts. In 1949 one of the pupils at the African Girls' School sued one of the African schoolmasters in this way. Such claims were due to the influence of Europeans, and the elders, though puzzled by the departure from custom, usually awarded a cash sum in compensation. It was decided that it was necessary to clarify this matter and to modify Kamba custom to meet modern needs. A directive was therefore issued that in such cases the claim must be brought by the appropriate male relative—usually the girl's father—and Local Native Council Resolution 2/1950 reads:

> 'That this Council approves the recommendation of the Law Panel, namely that an alteration in Kamba Law and Custom be accepted and the customary penalty of one goat for causing pregnancy in an unmarried girl shall be increased to whatever sum the Native Tribunal hearing the case may consider as suitable compensation.'

Rape

Kamba custom does not differentiate in the scales of compensation between rape and consent. Whether the woman consents or whether she is compelled by force, the payments are the same. But in the past such an act as rape would have certainly led to fighting between the clans concerned, and probably to several deaths before the elders of other clans in the neighbourhood could mediate. Now the distinction is clear, since charges of rape are not heard by the Native Tribunals but by the Supreme Court.

If the act had roused the indignation of the community, they might have executed the culprit by the 'king'ole' (this procedure is described under the heading of 'theft'). This happened to a man called Nzau wa Uthuko, from Mwala, who raped both a mother and her daughter.

Unnatural Behaviour

If a man commits an unnatural offence with a young boy, he must pay over a goat and a bull. If two men commit the offence together, each must pay a goat. Such cases are rare among the Kamba. Even rarer are cases of men having connection with animals, which the elders regard with such horror and which are so unusual, that there is considerable uncertainty as to what penalties should be exacted. One man in Nzaui, Nyange, who had connection with somebody else's cow, was told to take the animal himself and to give one of his own in exchange and to slaughter a goat. In other cases, a fine of a cow and a goat has been paid which seems to be the most usual penalty—the goat is for slaughter for purification in all these cases.

Such cases should now be charged under Section 155 of the Penal Code, but they are normally settled quietly in the locations without ever coming to the Courts.

The Kamba regard it as unnatural to have coition with a woman from behind. If a man does this, even with his wife, he must slaughter a goat for purification. By this act he has levelled himself with the animals.

The Blood Price for Death

Before the establishment of the British Administration, deliberate murder would have resulted in clan strife. Now both murder and manslaughter are matters for the Supreme Court. The clan fighting of the past was not allowed to go on indefinitely; when the affair was thought to have lasted long enough, the elders of other clans intervened to separate the warring groups and to make peace between them. They named a day on which the elders of the clans involved appeared before them, and the dispute was settled by discussion, agreement and the payment of the blood price—not only for the man first killed but also for the others who might have died since. The payment of a blood price is still the custom, whether the death is caused with malice aforethought or not; the custom is modified but not replaced by the action which the Colony's Courts may take. The blood price can be sued for as a civil debt, notwithstanding that a criminal charge may also lie. It is called 'maambo'.

For a man, the blood payment throughout most of Machakos District is eleven cows, one bull and a goat. In Kikumbulyu it is fourteen cows, two bulls and a goat. The goat is 'mbui ya ng'ondu'. The first cow is called 'ng'ombe ya mbanga'—literally, the 'cow of the accident'. This cow is especially for the bereaved woman, the dead man's senior wife or mother. On the day it is received, the woman has coition: with one of the dead man's brothers or other relatives if it is his wife; with his father if it is his mother. This cow is also called 'ng'ombe ya ndulota'—the 'cow of the broken bow'—and again, 'ng'ombe ya uumo'—the 'first cow'. If there are several wives, only the senior gets this cow. All the stock paid in blood price is put into her cattle boma.

The remainder of the stock is divided in this way: the goat and bull are slaughtered and eaten by the clan and 'utui' elders, the goat having been used for the purification ceremony. One cow goes to the dead man's father's family. The eldest son of the deceased's eldest sister (if there is one) brings a bull, a goat and beer (the elders drink the beer), and in exchange he takes away a cow—'ng'ombe ya maambo'. If there is no sister's son, one of the deceased's brothers takes this. (Whoever it is, he must share the female calves of this cow in turn with his other brothers until all have had a share. If the eldest sister's son has taken the cow, and there are several sisters, the eldest sons of other sisters will share the offspring before his own brothers. Heifer calves only are taken. The eldest son of a younger sister in his turn brings a bull, a goat and beer to his cousin and takes away the heifer, and when *this* heifer finally calves, his own full brothers share in the offspring in the same way as before.)

Another cow goes to the deceased's mother's family. Her eldest brother takes it, having first brought a bull and a goat and beer. This is 'ng'ombe ya inaume'—the 'cow of the maternal uncle'. The heifer calves are handed on to other brothers on the same terms. The next cow is for the clan—'ng'ombe ya mbai'. A clan elder nearly related to the dead man takes it, likewise handing over a bull, goat and beer in exchange. The female calves are distributed round the clan. If any of these three cows dies without calves, or without female calves, there is no redress. Another cannot be claimed in its place.

The remaining seven cows (ten, in Kikumbulyu) stay in the boma of the dead man's senior wife (or mother). They are the inheritance of all his sons (or full brothers). The deceased's junior wives, if any, will use them. They cannot be sold by the wives, or by the 'musina', without the agreement of the eldest son. If the dead man was childless and had no full brothers, the cows go to his half-brothers; failing them, to his father; failing him, his paternal uncles; and so on.

Kamba custom has been modified to accord with modern circumstances. If a man kills another and is charged before the Supreme Court, he is still liable to pay the blood money—but only a proportion of it; his punishment is taken into account. If he is executed, or is imprisoned and dies in gaol, no blood price is payable. But if he is imprisoned or otherwise punished for a period and then returns to his home, half the blood price must be paid. This claim is brought as a civil case, and permission from a European District Officer must be obtained beforehand. Usually, the cases do not go before the Native Tribunals; the local elders have accepted this compromise. For example, in 1932 Manguye wa Nzuki killed Musyoki wa Kilangu with a knife. He went to prison for seven years. On his release, the Kilima Kimwe elders agreed that he should be excused six cows from the customary blood payment, and he acquiesced without taking the matter before the Tribunal. This question has been discussed and decided by the Local Native Council. Minute 6/1937 reads as follows:

'After discussion it was decided that if a man were hanged the relatives of the murdered man should have no claim to blood money as the crime had been expiated by the murderer's death. If he were only imprisoned but died in prison, they would likewise have no claim as he had been punished by God. If he were sentenced to a term of imprisonment, then on his release he should be sued for half the customary amount of stock by the deceased's relatives. It was decided that the offender must be sued in person and it would be conducive to the peace of the district if this were done, as otherwise there was a risk of vendettas occurring.

'The President informed the Council that Tribunal Clerks would be instructed to draw the attention of an officer to all blood-money cases. If the defendant did not agree to the judgment, the parties to the case would be brought before an officer who would go into the matter again and, if necessary, exercise his powers of revision.'

Kamba law does not distinguish between murder, manslaughter or a death caused by accident. The blood price is payable in each case. If a man were to fire an arrow at an animal and hit a man beyond, not knowing that he was there, he would be held fully liable.

The man responsible for another's death is not required to pay all the blood price himself. His clan helps him. The goat, the bull, and the 'ng'ombe ya mbanga' he must produce from his own herd. When he has done this, he can call upon his clan to find the others, save that one of them will be found by his mother's family. A careful count is kept in each clan group, where relationship is still fairly close, of those who pay the cattle in any particular case; furthermore, it is laid down in advance which members will have to find cows the next time the need arises, and sometimes for the time after that as well. Each man knows his future obligations. The clan elders say who is to pay, endeavouring to distribute the burden fairly. These payments made to help another member to pay 'maambo' are in no sense a loan, a recoverable debt; the giver does not expect another cow to be returned to him later. It is regarded as particularly important to meet one's obligations in this matter, and a man will borrow or marry off his daughter hastily to obtain the necessary cattle to do it.

If a man refused to pay the blood price for a death for which he was responsible, when the clan had agreed to and approved the payment, he would formerly have been compelled by force to produce his share of it—now, by the Native Tribunal. Similarly, it is not possible to refuse to receive blood money: the clan will agree to its being paid, and the alternative of continuing a clan feud no longer exists.

For a woman, the blood price in most of the District is four cows, a bull and a goat. In Kilungu, Mukaa Nzaui and Mbitini it is five cows, a bull and a goat. In Kikumbulyu the number of cows is increased to six. If she is married her husband receives the stock; if not, her father. This is the same penalty as that mentioned in describing adultery, and it does not matter if the woman dies from being adulterously got with child or from a blow. As before, the clan helps to pay if the culprit hands over the first cow and the bull and the goat (if a woman has caused the death, her husband or appropriate male relative must pay).

If a man kills a son or near relative, the payment must still be made. The Kamba consider that if a son is killed and the blood price not paid, the dead child's brothers may cause trouble when they grow up and take revenge, even although unborn at the time. The division is made just as before: the 'ng'ombe ya mbanga' goes to the mother, paid by the father, and the appropriate relatives come to claim the next three. The remainder stay in the dead man's mother's cattle boma (i.e. the killer's boma) to form the inheritance of her other sons.

If a man kills his childless wife, for whom the bride price has been fully paid, there is no penalty in Kamba custom. It is considered that he is the one who suffers through his own action. If any of the bride price remains unpaid, he must pay it. If the woman has had sons, her husband must pay the usual blood price, his clan helping, and the cows are for the sons. If there are no male children, only girls, nothing is payable. (Much of this *contra* Lindblom, p. 155.) Blood price is payable for the stillborn child of an unmarried girl, as previously described, or for a miscarriage—a bull throughout most of the District, and seven or five goats, according to the child's sex, in Kikumbulyu.

There is no reduction for children; the full price must always be paid. There is, however, sometimes a reduction for old men, by agreement between the elders of the clans concerned. The argument is that these have already had most of their lives and had not long to live; what they had left is really not worth the full tally.

Death which Does Not Follow Immediately

If a man is injured by another, often without any apparent grievous harm such as the loss of a limb, it is possible that he may die or be believed to have died from the ill effects long afterwards. In such a case, if the injured man feels that his hurt may be serious, he sends an elder of his family to see the man who caused it. This elder tells the man that so-and-so was hit by him on his left side yesterday (or whatever it is), and the hurt is paining him; he suggests that they go to see him. This they do, together with another elder of the offender's family, taking with them a goat. The injured party also produces a goat on their arrival. He then shows his hurt, and if there is a difference of opinion about the place, the two elders decide. One of the elders then takes a knife and makes four or six cuts on the place to identify it in the future. Both the goats are then slaughtered A piece of meat is cut from the chest of the goat which the offender brought, and with it the goat's blood is rubbed on to the knife marks. A light chain is then fastened by him around the man's wrist to show that he agrees—'nthanga ya munyoo'.

If when the injured man dies it is suspected that the old hurt caused his death, the elders present on the previous occasion are called, the offender, and other representatives of both families. The elder who made them shows the old knife marks. The eldest son of the dead man cuts open the place. If it is considered that an ulcer or some other internal injury that is the cause of death is revealed, the blood price must be paid. But if a long time has elapsed since the blow, and the dead man has had children and lived out a large portion of his life, the elders may cut down the price and a proportion only will be paid.

If the ceremony of cutting marks on the injured place was not performed, the eldest son can still open up the old hurt with a knife, having first called the alleged culprit, who almost invariably denies his responsibility. If the cause of death is found, the son must swear on the 'kithitu' that this man caused the harm. The first cow—the 'ng'ombe ya mbanga'—is then sent to him. When it calves, he drinks the milk and reports that he and his wife and his son are still alive. He will then be paid the rest of the blood price.

The system of knife markings is for blows on the body or the head, the vulnerable parts of the body, and is not normally employed on the arms or legs where a hurt is unlikely to cause death afterwards.

Assault: Compensation for Injury

The criminal aspect of assault is dealt with in the Native Tribunals under the provision of the Penal Code, as in the Magistrates' Courts, and visited with a fine or imprisonment. Compensation, where it is awarded, follows as far as possible a customary scale, which is that used likewise in civil claims for compensation for injury where no criminal intent is to be found. By Kamba custom, a minor matter, such as a blow causing no permanent ill-effects but perhaps pain and swelling, is dealt with by sending an elder to call the offender, together with an elder of his own family, who arrive bringing a goat. If the two elders decide that the responsibility is truly that man's, but that the hurt is not of the serious kind, requiring marking with a knife, the goat is slaughtered and the matter ends there.

For more serious hurts causing the loss of a limb or member, there is a fixed scale of penalties:

A finger (any finger)—a cow, a bull and a goat.
Two fingers—two cows, a bull and a goat.
Four fingers—four cows, a bull and a goat.
One hand or arm—five cows, a bull and a goat.
One leg—five cows a bull and a goat.
The big toe—one cow, a bull and a goat.
Any other toe—No elder can remember such a case, but the feeling is that it should not be the same as for fingers, for the loss is not so great. A bull and a goat is thought to be appropriate.
Both arms or both legs—ten cows, a bull and a goat.
One eye—a cow, a bull and a goat.
Both eyes—Nobody can remember this occurring; the elders feel that they would have to decide this matter when it arises.
(This scale does not agree with Lindblom, p. 156.)

The goat and the bull are for slaughter—the goat for the 'ng'ondu'. For more complicated injuries, the elders consider the claim as it arises and make a decision using the above as a yard-stick. For example, ex-Chief Mbithi at Kangundo lost three fingers and was also cut on the arm in such a way as to sever a tendon. He was awarded three cows for the fingers, one for the tendon, and the bull and the goat. The Kamba work on the principle that if an arm or a leg is lost, a man is half a man only, and with both arms or legs gone is practically dead.

There is no difference if the injury is inflicted deliberately or if it is accidental; the payment is the same: but in the latter case there was in the past no bitterness or strife between the two clans, and possibly no additional criminal charge nowadays.

If a man sends another on an errand or journey, and harm befalls him on the way, the sender is to some degree held responsible, since the unfortunate was travelling on his business. Were he to be killed on the road, the sender must contribute one cow to the blood price that the killer pays—'ng'ombe ya kyuambu'. If he is injured in such a way as to be entitled to compensation, his temporary employer must likewise bear a proportion of the payment—in the case of an arm, perhaps also a cow; for a finger, a bull. There is no known and definite scale, since cases are rare, but the principle is universally accepted by all the elders; it is applied in cases as the need arises. Were the man sent on the errand to be killed by a wild beast or a snake, one cow would be paid by the sender. If he falls or hurts himself in some such manner, the sender pays nothing, for it is held to be the man's own fault. So, if he were carrying a knife or a loaded gun for the man who sent him, and fell and cut or shot himself, nobody is to blame but himself; the elders admit, however, that it may have been otherwise in the past and some compensation under such circumstances may have been felt to be due; but not now.

Should a man be driving a cow or a bull to some place for the owner, and be kicked or butted and so injured, he will be given the animal as compensation—'ng'ombe ya kithuki'. If a man walks by accident into a trap or a snare set by another, even on the setter's own land, the latter is responsible for any injuries he may receive, even though the injured man is an uninvited trespasser.

If the injured man is a paid workman, and is injured in the course of his work, the Native Courts do not follow Kamba custom, for this is a situation for which it does not provide. The case would be referred to a European Magistrate, who would probably deal with the case in terms of the Workmen's Compensation Ordinance.

CHAPTER 9

PRINCIPLES OF LIABILITY

The first two extracts which have been included in this chapter represent opposing views on the basis of liability for wrongs in customary law: *Driberg* argues that the foundation of all liability is the need to maintain social equilibrium, while *Elias* has gone to great lengths to establish the notion that customary law, like other systems of law, founds liability on negligence and intention.

The essay by *Gluckman* on 'The reasonable man in Barotse Law' represents an altogether different approach to the problem of liability, in which the author seeks to include a variety of different rules under a single rubric. The essay is already widely regarded as one of the classically important contributions to the study of customary law, and has appeared in several different forms which vary in the degree of detail and the amount of illustrative case material they contain; that given here is rather shorter than the chapter of the same title which appears in the book, *The Judicial Process among the Barotse of Northern Rhodesia*, but is considerably longer than the article in the *Journal of African Administration*, Vol. VII (1955).

The contributions extracted from the works of *Schapera* and *Snell* relate to more specific aspects of the topic of liability, such as the question of vicarious liability and the greater scope which it has in customary law as opposed to most modern systems of law. This is a subject which is discussed elsewhere, notably in Vol. II in the chapters dealing with the Law of Persons.

J. H. Driberg: The African Conception of Law*

Law the Possession and Privilege of a Restricted Group.

Hartland speaks of 'lawless men' in primitive society, but the whole tenor of his book makes it quite clear that he meant, not men who are under no law, but those who are outside a particular set of laws. For the law is only applied to and only protects the specific group which recognizes it. Law is part of the whole complex of culture and therefore only those who claim the same cultural inheritance come within the scope of its operations. *Each unit—whether that be the family, the clan or the tribe—has its own corpus of customary law which is directed towards maintaining the interests of that unit against all outsiders.* These outsiders are really 'foreigners' and can claim no protection under the law of the unit, unless they are temporarily protected by the laws of hospitality, in which case they are granted the same status as their host and can plead in his name. So from the unit's point of view all who are outside it are 'lawless men'—and fair game for anyone. The idea is exactly the same as that conveyed by the extensions of terminology under the classificatory system of relationship. Within the family all of one age are 'brothers',

* J. H. Driberg, 'The African Conception of Law', in *The Journal of Comparative Legislation and International Law*, now *The International and Comparative Law Quarterly*, November 1934, pp. 230–246.

strictly and biologically. Then all within the clan are brothers, as contrasted with all outside the clan. Then all within the tribe are brothers, as contrasted with all outside the tribe. The obligations and privileges which this real or artificial brotherhood confers are confirmed and guaranteed by the law, and consequently all who are not deemed brothers are outside the scope and protection of the law. Therefore all who are not members of the tribe are 'lawless men' to that tribe, but no member of the tribe itself can be designated lawless till he has been publicly and legally outlawed. There is little intertribal, or as we might say international, law other than that which governs the making of war and peace and which, during peace, maintains and adjusts economic relations between neighbouring tribes: but there are legal methods by which non-tribesmen may be brought within the scope of tribal law, *e.g.* by intermarriage, blood-brotherhood, the protection of friends, rules of hospitality, intertribal societies and other methods which enable non-tribesmen to plead their cause vicariously.[1]

This, then, is the first point which I wish to make. *Law is the possession and privilege of a restricted group.* It that group is the tribe, as it generally is, there are four aspects of law which should be considered, if we had the space—*family law, clan law, tribal law and associational law.* It is sufficient to say, however, that though on certain points, notably marriage, the several codes differ quite markedly, yet on the whole they are complementary to each other and the totality stands for the tribal law which we are now considering.

Maintenance of Equilibrium.

The second point I want to dispose of before proceeding to the principles which I believe underlie African concepts of law and justice is largely one of terminology. We speak of criminal and civil law, a distinction which is meaningless to the African and fruitful of misunderstanding, when he is pursued in our courts on a criminal charge for what he would consider a civil offence, involving a totally different penalty. If they made the distinction—and certainly some distinction is implicit in their legal practice—they would speak of private and public law. To them law comprises all those rules of conduct which regulate the behaviour of individuals and communities, and which by maintaining the equilibrium of society are necessary for its continuance as a corporate whole. Private law deals with acts which disturb the equilibrium; public law with acts or situations which negative those conditions which make the maintenance of the equilibrium possible. I shall explain and illustrate what I mean in a moment.

Let us start, then, by discarding European concepts of law and justice. They are not only irrelevant, but any investigation based on them is bound to be fallacious. Our varied laws and procedure and our distinction between civil and criminal law have grown up with European culture and are part and parcel of it: but they have nothing in common with African cultures; they are alien in growth and sentiment, and cannot be used to explain the bases of primitive legal theory. Our society and its laws are founded on an individualistic assumption: theirs on a collectivist organization. It would be remarkable therefore if the two could have a great deal in common.

On our definition we find that African law is positive and not negative. It does not say 'Thou shalt not', but 'Thou shalt'. Law does not create offences, it does not make criminals; it directs how individuals and communities should behave towards each other. *Its whole object is to maintain an equilibrium, and the penalties of African law are directed, not against specific infractions, but to the restoration of this equilibrium.* There is no written code, but the law is an organic growth, inherent in the body politic and accepted just because it is organic, coherent and traditional. In Hartland's words, 'primitive law is the totality of the customs of the tribe'. It is always constructive and palliative. A crime—to use a convenient, if inaccurate, term—consists in the disturbance of individual or communal equilibrium, and the law seeks to restore the pre-existing balance. The deterrent or purely penal theory does not enter into the question. Even homicide is not punished from that point of view. A member of one family or community has been killed, with the result that the equilibrium has been disturbed. The law steps in to restore it, either by the execution of the murderer or by the payment of compensation. That the murderer may be executed or that the property of his family may be diminished is incidental to the underlying motive, which is in no sense whatever penal.

Principles of Status and Substitution.

At this point I must interpolate a few words on two principles in the social organization of Africans, which are of universal application and which have considerably affected their legal viewpoint. The close integration of African culture, I am afraid, makes such interpolations unavoidable, as it is impossible to comprehend any one aspect of cultural activity in isolation. The principles I refer to are status and substitution. Every individual is born into a certain status relative to all other members of his community. It is not a personal status, as it might be in an individualistic society, and does not imply rank, but reciprocal obligations and benefits which he incurs as a member of the community. All his conduct is conditioned by his status, which is not a permanent one but changes with his age and experience and may be affected by the decease of relatives and the inheritance of new responsibilities. The principle of substitution is a correlative to status, since all of the same status in the community may at any time be called upon to act as a substitute for another member, a principle which, as we shall see, is of considerable importance in African legal theory.

This principle of status partly accounts for the fact to which I have alluded, that in Africa the law does not recognize non-tribalists. To achieve tribal status every tribesman has to submit to certain rites and ceremonies which entitle him to the privileges of the tribe. One who is not a member of the tribe has not undergone those ceremonies and therefore has not the status which would give him legal recognition. Added to this a different religious or magical aura surrounds every tribe and this may be inimical to the tribal interest, which is an added reason for not admitting strangers to full intimacy until they have submitted to a ritual of purification or are vouched for by their hosts, whose status they accept by substitution. For the same reasons certain West African tribes refuse to bury strangers in tribal soil, for fear of the danger of a spiritual clash.

A few instances of how the principle of status works will show how important it may be in legal matters, and incidentally it is possible to trace in it the origin of the practice of legal representation in Africa, where we find it in every stage of development. The Azande afford two good examples of the importance of status. An unmarried man cannot sue the father of a family, but must be represented by one who is himself a father, as there cannot be legal transactions between two people differentiated by status. On the other hand, such is the solidarity of the clan that any member of the clan is entitled to recover a debt due to any other member who is unable to do so himself. Among the Mangbettu it is the head of the group who alone may represent any member of the group in law: a wronged man must consult his elder brother, who will take the case before the head of the family, and the latter will then take it to the head of the village. Representation by a chief or clan head is very general, but a most interesting development is to be found among the Chagga, among whom in each clan besides the spiritual leader there is one who is called 'The Great One in Legal Matters', whose function it is to represent the clan members, not as an advocate of an independent party, but as a legal guardian. Before a member of a clan can start a suit, he has to obtain permission from the clan leader and the case is not tried till the latter appears, a point which emphasizes the collective responsibility of the clan. Moreover as the clan's legal guardian he regulates the contributions of its members to their legal obligations, often indeed helping out of his private means. It is a small step from this to the direct representation by fee'd counsel which we find as an established custom over wide areas in the Congo, and in Sierra Leone where (according to Dapper) pleaders wear masks to avoid recognition.[2] There can be no doubt, I think, that this very 'civilized' development may be directly traced to the joint principles of status and substitution. I shall have to recur to the latter at a later stage.

Admitting, then, that African law is based in a maintenance of the equilibrium, that it is a code of positive rules rather than of negative prohibitions, one would expect in the first place that the penalty would be directed only towards a readjustment of the *status quo*, and secondly that the question of intention or motive would not be considered. I shall deal with these two points separately and as briefly as possible.

Penalty.

I have already said that the law is not penal or vindictive, and that the idea is to make the punishment fit the crime. That is why under native law a thief so often goes unpunished. If theft is committed, material equilibrium has been impaired; but if restitution is made there is no more to be done. Nevertheless thus simply stated, the position does not square with ascertained facts, and it is incumbent on me, if I am to justify my hypothesis, to explain the apparent inconsistency. In the first place we may note that among the tribes of a relatively simple constitution, more particularly the pastoral tribes, the principle which I have enunciated may generally be found to hold good. According to Hartland, with advancing civilization the extreme penalty of death and mutilation is often mitigated or compounded for. This is true, but there is an intermediate stage where the penalties are apparently out of all proportion to the trivial offences for which they are inflicted. Such processes are to be found in tribes which have strongly centralized governments and in which the checks inherent in clan independence have largely broken down and have not yet been replaced by such checks on tyranny as we find in the powerful States of West Africa, which were a direct outcome of these disproportionate punishments. Nevertheless I do not think that even so the legal principle of equilibrium breaks down, as the penalties of mutilation and so forth were not inflicted in retaliation for the offences *per se*, but because through the centralization of authority in the ruler as representative of tribal interests these offences had come to be regarded as treason, and treason (as we shall see), being an act subversive of the conditions under which alone equilibrium can be maintained, came in the category of public offences, which have always and everywhere been punished under a different procedure.[3] But even apart from these more developed societies, in which theoretical treason rather than the substantive offence is at issue, we find several instances of disproportionate penalties, which appear to invalidate the principle of equilibrium. If we take the case of theft, for instance, it is a simple matter to restore the equilibrium if the stolen property can be returned to its owner or can be replaced by an equivalent. But obviously in many cases this is impossible, and it has been necessary to impose arbitrary values, which may or may not appear to us to be at all equivalent. Thus a canoe, stolen and lost, has to be replaced by a number of goats equal to the load it could carry; a hunting dog, however old and decrepit, has to be compensated for by goats equal to the number of animals which it has brought down, a solution which may obviously be unfair. But it is not the intrinsic value, but the achievement or capacity which is taken into account. These practical modifications apart, however, we do find a great number of instances in which theft is over-heavily penalized. Among the Batetela, for instance, a thief's property is confiscated, he might be sold into slavery, and his village might be plundered: among the Baluba-Hemba and the Baganda a thief might be mutilated and enslaved; the Anyanja cut off a thief's ears and hands, and so on. But the real point is that once again it is not the actual theft that is punished. The punishment varies according to the general culture of the tribe. In communities where the people leave a great deal of their property in open huts in cultivation far from the villages theft is obviously more serious a matter than where the opportunities are not so great. The thief, therefore, is more severely punished in such cases, not in retaliation for the stolen article—we may even find that the punishment in the same community for the thefts of a more valuable article from a place offering smaller opportunity to the thief is less severely punished—but because he introduces mistrust into the community and by his action invalidates those principles on which the welfare of the community depends.[4] For this reason it quite frequently happens that an habitual criminal is formally hanged, not for any specific act, but because he has proved himself to be a public enemy and thus comes under the operation of public law.[5]

Motive or Intention.

There is some conflict of evidence as to how far intention is taken into account. In strict theory it is obvious that, if the object of the law is to restore the *status quo*, intention cannot come into the matter. The offence has been committed and has to be adjusted. But what I have said of theft applies here too, as the circumstances may be as important as the offence. This particularly applies to acts of homicide. The Baluba, for instance, distinguish, according to Colle, between voluntary and involuntary homicide; among the Basonge drunkenness is a palliative circumstance. The same distinction is made by the Bashilange, the Chagga and others; but many tribes, such as the Awemba, do not consider accident or drunkenness as a mitigation of the offence. It may be noted, however, that whether the offence is treated as murder or manslaughter, the penalty—death in the case of the former, compensation in the case of the latter—is just as much a process of restoring the equilibrium. If a man of clan A kills a man of clan B, clan B is the weaker by one unit: the equilibrium is restored if clan A is weakened to the same extent by the loss of a member, or if it transfers a recognized equivalent in property to clan B. The most important distinction, however, is made in the murder of a guest or a host, for which there can be no possible palliation. But here again it is not so much the intention or the act of homicide which leads to the maximum penalty, but the breach of the sacred laws of hospitality on which the integrity of the community depends. I think it is true to say that motive is only regarded in so far as it affects the whole community and prevents its proper functioning, or destroys those qualities which make for corporate harmony and equilibrium. With us the motive, or the intention, is immediate and individual; with the Africans it is not so much the guilty intention, but the effects of the intention on the community at large.

Only in offences which are held to be definitely anti-social is the public law invoked, and by anti-social is meant something much more than the disturbance of this or that equilibrium. It implies an act subversive of the whole fabric of society, an act which unpunished and unchecked would ultimately destroy the body politic. Murder does not come into this category, as it is treated as a personal offence which upsets the equilibrium, it is true, but which does not touch those fundamentals which make the conservation of the equilibrium possible. This is true also of nearly all the major offences in our criminal codes, for which the sanctions lying behind primitive law are normally sufficient to secure a restoration of the equilibrium. The anti-social crimes, which come under public law, are treason, witchcraft, incest and sexual perversions (the last two being associated with witchcraft on the presumption that none but witches and wizards are capable of them). These crimes cannot be dealt with by normal methods. There is no question of equilibrium involved, as, particularly in the case of witchcraft, no individual or community is alone threatened or injured by the crime: its repercussions affect the whole body politic. The insidiousness of its operation and the illegitimate use which it makes of magic and the supernatural render the usual processes of law abortive, and the public law therefore does the only thing possible and eliminates the menace. Any of these anti-social crimes is punished by death, because that is the only measure which can preserve society.

Sanctions.

European observers have often doubted the existence of law in African societies, because generally the paraphernalia which we associate with law are absent. Without prisons and a police force it is assumed that there can be no sanctions such as would give law the requisite validity. It is at this point, I suspect, that we differ most widely. The penal sanctions are the least important of them all, chiefly because the law is positive and not negative, and because it is solely interested in maintaining the social equilibrium. I shall try to sum up the sanctions which are universally valid in Africa as briefly as possible, only remarking that in certain areas, particularly in West Africa, secret societies tend to operate as a sanction for the observance of the law. Many of them, like the Oro and the Ekemeku, are police societies which act as guardians of public morals and punish offenders. In them we find the nearest approach to our system of punitive justice.[6] But generally speaking, symbols of legal authority such as these are completely absent, and in the circumstances would be otiose.

Religious Sanctions.

Primarily the law is obeyed, just because it is accepted. Its acceptance and its position as an integral part of the social organization are its own sanction. It is obeyed, because only by obedience to the law will society function, and it is in everybody's interest to subscribe to its regulations. Law is not the act of a sovereign, it is not enforced by *ad hoc* sanctions, but by a sanction involved (as Hartland remarks) in the belief and practice of the community. But obviously no community is entirely composed of right-minded people, and other sanctions are required, both for control and for enforcement. So behind everything lies the religious sanction, which depends for its validity on the theory that the clan is a continuous entity comprising both the living and the dead. The ancestors are just as much concerned as the living in the due observance of the law. The law has the moral support, not only of the living tribe, but of all the tribesmen who have ever lived and died. This terrific antiquity, remote but ever present, is in itself a very potent force in securing due regard for the law. But it does more; it introduces a religious sanction, which is perhaps the most potent factor of all. No compensation for an offence, no reparation, is complete without sacrifice. Every offence has to be legally compensated and ceremonially purged, and till both are done the offender and his community are in danger of spiritual retribution. It is this religious nexus which gives African law an authority sufficient to dispense with the mechanics of enforcement.[7]

Collective Responsibility

Again the principle of substitution, to which I have already referred, comes in to re-enforce group responsibility. If everyone of the same status is liable to be called upon to act as a substitute when an offence has been committed by a member of the group, it is everybody's business to see that the laws are obeyed; and if an offence has been committed, the group is equally liable to spiritual retribution and sees that the requisite penalty is forthcoming. Collective responsibility is therefore a potent factor in the prevention of crime and in the liquidation of the offence without extraneous pressure.[8] On the other hand, the principle of equilibrium has its limitation, since, depending as it does on a balancing of group interests, there can be no reparation for an offence committed by a member of the clan within the clan. There obviously can be no theft within the clan, as all property is, in theory at any rate, communally held by the clan. But even if a man murders one of his own clan, he has committed no offence which is subject to the tribal law, since any compensation payable would be from the clan to the clan, involving no change in the tribal equilibrium. Clan law, however, has a potent weapon in the punishment of outlawry, which means virtual death, as the offender, if outlawed, can no longer look to the clan for protection. It does not hesitate to use this weapon or even to execute an habitual criminal if it finds that his recurring misdeeds are too great a strain on the resources of the clan.[9]

Emphasis is often laid on the principle of collective responsibility by a curiously indirect method of instituting suits. Among the Bankutu, for instance, an injured person obtains redress by killing a slave whose owner has no claim on the murderer, but on the man whose injustice has caused the murder. We find, too, that a Fang who has been wronged does not go to the offender for settlement, but goes to another town and shoots the first goat he sees, or if he is very angry, a woman. The original offender is now responsible and liable to two parties. This may seem a curious procedure to us and I do not suppose that it is one which would ever be incorporated in our codes, but its effect is to make an individual very chary of committing an offence, as a trivial beginning might have an exceedingly uncomfortable end, and the possible repercussions of his offence suffice to act as a sufficient deterrent.

Magical Sanctions

Analogous to the religious sanctions are various magical sanctions which carry an automatic penalty in the case of certain offences.[10] Theft may also be publicly proclaimed and the thief cursed with bell, book and candle, a procedure which is generally effective in securing speedy restitution. Even the threat of witchcraft—generally anti-social, but used socially as a legal sanction—may be invoked to secure reparation from a recalcitrant offender. We may note, too, that the same sanctions are sometimes applied in the administration of justice; for it is not unusual for witnesses to be heard on oath in any serious case. Chagga witnesses are solemnly cursed by the chief, while among the Ashanti should a witness die soon after the trial he is held to have been guilty of perjury, and the judgment may be reversed in consequence.[11]

Ridicule and Ostracism

Ridicule and ostracism as a legal sanction is an idea now foreign to us, but among the minor sanctions with which I have no space to deal it plays a very important part in Africa, and its success suggests that under our dispensation the stocks might be a more efficient deterrent than the prison. Ridicule formally and legally applied is, I imagine, as effective a sanction as it appears to be, because (as we have seen) status is of peculiar importance in African society, and the effect of both ridicule and ostracism is to put the victim out of status and so no longer in a position to participate in communal activities, till his offence has been purged and his status restored. That, incidentally, is why defamation is always one of the most serious of private offences, requiring a heavy compensation; because the effect of defamation is to cut at the very root of group co-operation and to deprive the defamed man of his proper status in the community.

Administration of Justice

This feature of equilibrium which the law is there to conserve has its consequences on the administration of justice. It is not the duty of the chief, generally speaking, to seek out crime in order to punish it, and that is one of the reasons no doubt why on first contact with our civilization the chief appears to fail in one of the, to us, chief duties of a ruler: he is not used to the idea that he should stand outside his society and act as a policeman. But on the other hand, it is the duty of every member of the community, owing to the fact that he is one of a collective responsibility, to report any breach of the public law, of which the chief should thereupon take cognizance. As it may take some time for the processes of law to be put into action, there is an obvious danger that the culprit may suffer summary justice at the hands of the injured party; but provision is made for this by the establishment of sanctuaries, where an accused man may await in security the slow movements of the law. This indeed is probably the chief social function of sanctuary in African societies. The institution of private suits is not necessarily a simple matter and, as we have seen in some communities, recourse has to be made to indirect methods. The central authority may only be concerned with certain specified cases, the public causes, and it may be necessary for the aggrieved party in a private suit to commit one of these major crimes, in order that in the subsequent public inquiry into his conduct his private complaint may be indirectly investigated. Nevertheless we also find safeguards for the impartial administration of justice. Where an appeal is made to the king, among the Ashanti for instance, from the divisional chief, if it succeeds the punishment falls on the judge who pronounced the sentence, whereas if it fails the appellant is usually killed—a measure which not only ensures impartial justice, but prevents frivolous appeals.[12]

In his administration of the public law the chief, or whatever the legal authority may be, sits as a judge and awards the appropriate sentence; but it would be more correct to call the inquiry into a private suit an arbitration rather than a trial, and very often no judgment is pronounced, the general opinion of the court being obvious to everyone. One authority, writing of the Akamba, makes a similar distinction, when he says that 'we speak of "trial" before a *kiama* (legal council), the natives speak of a consultation: the use of the word is significant,' he adds, as it is clearly 'not the business of the elders to enforce their decisions.' Everyone knows the law and the law is universally accepted. Only questions of fact are in dispute, and once these have been established by arbitration their legal sanctions are normally sufficient to secure compliance.

Character of the African Laws

One word on the character of the African laws. There is nothing rigid or unchanging in them, though the changes may appear to proceed at a very slow rate. In a great number of tribes there is an annual promulgation of the major laws, together with an announcement of new legislation, though some tribes—notably the Rotse—are said to resent such changes, which may cause them to be estranged from their ruler. But Bowdich tells us that the new laws are not nearly so powerful as the old traditional ones, and the reason must be that they have not the religious sanction behind them. This sanction would take about two generations to acquire, and we can thus estimate approximately the rate of time which must elapse before even their own legislation has any validity. But Africans are ingenious people and have devised another and easier way of getting out of an impasse. If any custom or law begins to feel oppressive, they do not care to abrogate it at once on account of its religious sanction. But being masters of legal fiction, they devise a ceremony which in any particular case will absolve them from the operation of the old law. I may cite as an example a Thonga ceremony which breaks down the blood-tie and thus authorizes a form of marriage legally incestuous. In course of time the ceremony becomes the important thing and takes the place of the obsolete law.

Conclusion

I hope that I have succeeded in making clear some of the underlying principles of African law, as I see them. The conflict with our own ideas is fairly obvious: on the one side a system which is a living, sentient organism, part of the general cultural complex, based on a collectivist society, depending on sanctions of its own which are not penal; on the other a penal code, which is not intrinsically one with the rest of our culture but can be arbitrarily imposed, and which is naturally individualistic in character. I do not venture to make any suggestions as to how the conflict may best be resolved, but I do think that a greater understanding of the principles of African law and society may conduce to an administration of justice which will prove more understandable to the African. Some approximation between the two positions seems to be called for when what we call murder, for example, may to the African be a pious duty, for which under our code he might suffer the death penalty. Under the rigid administration of our codes, if the intention to murder is present, whatever the complicated spiritual and social impulses which formed that intention, no sentence other than death is possible. The fact that in most of our courts a recommendation for clemency accompanies the sentence clearly indicates that our judges recognize that the African may not be an independent agent and that his final intention may have been the least important motive in the commission of the offence. It would be more satisfactory, however, if the difference between African and European motive were recognized in the code itself, rather than by a species of legal fiction, either by a broadening of the definition of homicide or by the inclusion of punishments less than death. The African cannot understand a procedure which having sentenced him to be hanged does not carry the sentence into effect. A wider option of punishment would be more intelligible to him than a sentence followed by remission.

It is not within the scope of this paper to examine specific instances of disharmony, as I have been more concerned with trying to elucidate general principles. Detailed research is still required on African legal systems before generalizations may be safely made. Were it not so, reference might be made to the legal difficulties involved in the African concept of incest, which is so wide as often to be unrecognizable under our law. Nevertheless to disregard it entirely might lead to a moral revolution which would result in a speedy degeneration. Such specific instances apart, however, it might be well worth considering whether our codes could not be reframed so as to take into more consideration the principles of equilibrium, rather than of punishment, and of communal responsibility together with the sanctions that this implies. This does not necessitate the surrender of any prerogative of justice on our part, but it would mean that the African, if aware that the alien law was operating under principles which he understands, would be more ready to conform to the law than he now appears to be. This is not to say that African principles are better: moral evaluations do not come into the question. But a recognition of what the law means to them and an acknowledgment of it in our codes should do much to make conformance easier and should relieve the strain on our prisons and eliminate many of the more unfortunate effects of prison life.

It is difficult to estimate how far the change towards an individualistic economy has gone in the last few years. In this respect tribal reaction has been very varied. But even in the most advanced communities the process is still at its earliest stage and we cannot expect a legal system, based on an individualistic theory, to be readily assimilated. There is bound to be conflict and an impression of injustice, however justly and impartially our laws are administered, because they are our laws, not theirs, and do not necessarily fit in with their very different cultures. If indirect rule on the one hand makes things easier by utilizing native institutions, on the other hand it is also somewhat paradoxical in enforcing an alien system of law entirely divorced from these institutions; but it should not be beyond our intelligence, once we know where the conflict lies, to devise some accommodation between the two. The natural willingness of the African to change, the fact that their laws and cutoms are not static, is a hopeful augury for the future, if only during this period of transition their underlying principles, and particularly some of their sanctions, could be adapted to the exigencies of modern conditions.

APPENDIX

The distinctions, however, are in point of fact not unimportant, and the various spheres of law may be briefly tabulated:

<table>
<tr><td rowspan="2">Mainly social and economic</td><td>Family Law (Sanction, religious)
Marriage and incest, legitimacy, adoption, property, succession, inheritance, tabus, ritual observances (e.g. respect for parents: etiquette in contrast with deference to relatives-in-law).</td></tr>
<tr><td>Clan Law (Sanction, mainly religious)
Marriage, incest and puberty, adultery, dissolution, legitimacy and adoption, property and inheritance, succession, tabus, ritual observances.</td></tr>
</table>

Mainly constitutional and co-ordinating	*Tribal Law* (Sanctions, religious and disciplinary) Marriage (endogamy), offences against the person, offences against property, defamation (before this governed by rules of etiquette), succession, property (ruler as trustee), interclan relations (in-laws, etc.), treason, extra-tribal relations, economic and political, tabus, ritual observances.
Economic, social and constitutional	*Associational Law* (Sanction, disciplinary) Marriage and incest, property, economic and social co-operation, tabus, ritual observances.

A synopsis of this sort cannot show how the different aspects of law deal with similar situations and it has only been possible to indicate their relevance by repetition. It will suffice to give one example, and possibly the best illustration is to be found in the divergent attitude towards marriage. Here we find a definite conflict between family and clan law. The former has changed, possibly under the influence of clan law. Many of the simplest peoples—nomad hunters and collectors—are endogamous: the family is the largest social group known to them, and the concept of a clan law, and still less of a tribal law, has not yet developed. We might instance the Bushmen, and brother-sister marriage of Lake Tana and other nomads in Abyssinia, which is doubtless due to isolation and environment. At a later stage, with growing contacts, came the incest prohibition, which is probably not due to any natural replusion from consanguineous relationships, but is an artificial product arising out of group sentiment and education on the one hand and of propinquity on the other.

Clan law (1) enforced exogamy, and (2) often enjoined certain unions, such as cousin marriage, which must be regarded as the persistence of family law, which in other aspects has submitted to clan law. This persistence of an almost obsolete family law may also be seen in brother-sister royal marriages, which are not infrequent in Africa, and possibly in certain observances peculiar to specific clans, such as the Jo Anyeke among the Lango, who have a regulation enjoining a temporary brother-sister union preparatory to the exogamous marriage which is compulsory under clan law. These specific laws enjoining certain compulsory or favoured types of marriage, it should be remarked, are related to the inheritance of property and succession.

Tribal law enjoins endogamy, with the exception of frontier families, an exception which is of importance for intertribal relations, as owing to the peculiar bonds which unite relatives-in-law these families provide official channels of intertribal communication, available both during peace and war. Puberty rites come definitely within the sphere of clan and tribal law, as they aggregate the individual to wider groupings. There is no apparent necessity for them under family law.

Puberty rites also introduce the individual to certain associations founded on them, and these again modify family and clan law, *e.g.* secret societies and age-grades, which regulate the sexual lives of their members, enjoining groups of opposite sexes with whom they may or may not have relations. Nevertheless though these associational laws, which are tribal in character—even if they operate under entirely different sanctions—and help to weld the clans into a tribe, introduce new marital and extra-marital classifications, injunctions and prohibitions, and to that extent circumscribe clan and family law, yet we may observe that they still regard the earlier codes as implicitly operative. Though, for example, a Masai may have legal access to the wives of his age-mates (if he is entitled to the right by status—that is, if he is himself married), yet he is debarred from exercising this right if the woman comes within the prohibited degree of consanguinity. On the other hand, thanks to the new grouping introduced by age-grades, the clan system among the Masai and others who follow the more recent institution is definitely breaking down, and clan law as a result plays a relatively minor part in the regulation of marriage.

Again, while under family and clan law a marital offence is purged by payment of compensation to the woman's family, under associational law it is the association which benefits. An example is provided by the *jus primae noctis*, for a breach of which law the penalty, paid by the bridegroom, goes to the offender's age-mates. Certain extra-marital unions, which are legally devised in many tribes to relieve the strain of marital monotony, may also be ascribed to associational law or to extensions by analogy. And finally we may note that the levirate and sororate are obviously not based on family laws, as the family *qua* family has no need for them: they are aspects of the clan law of marriage.

Notes

[1] See Appendix.

[2] It is perhaps worth noting in this context that among the Bangala each party also hires its own claquers, who applaud every point made by the one who hires them and laugh ironically at the arguments of the other side.

[3] The concept of treason varies widely, ranging from a felonious act or attempt against a ruler as a person, which is ultimately no more than a flagrant disregard of status, to the much wider idea of an act endangering the life of the community concentrated in the exalted individual. From the latter point of view any misdemeanour might be considered treasonable, as the ruler represents both the living and the ancestors and is responsible to the latter for the behaviour of his subjects. The ruler is thus the trustee of the tribe and theoretically the lives and property of all his people are in his control. Hence in certain of the more centralized communities even the compensation paid in private suits is paid to the ruler and he may allot as much or little of it as he cares to do to the injured party. Hence too the saying that 'all blood belongs to the chief', and therefore any act of homicide is an act against the authority of the chief and to that extent treasonable. Accordingly the concept varies with the nature of the governmental institutions of the community, and in the less centralized tribes may be said not to exist at all, except as an abstraction which may be applied to all acts which are subversive of the conditions under which equilibrium may be maintained.

[4] There is one further reason for an apparently disproportionate compensation for theft, which is not so easy for us to understand. Everything acquires the personality of its possessor, and coincident with the act of theft the thief damages the stolen personality with results which, quite apart from the possibility of witchcraft, may be dangerous to the person involved. Partly the sacrifice which always accompanies any compensation is intended to restore the personality intact, but if this is not considered adequate additional compensation may be necessary. This interpretation is corroborated by the fact that every transfer of property requires a ceremony designed to remove the personality of the original owner. Among the Lango, for example, if A acquires a cow from B in exchange for the equivalent number of sheep, he has in addition to pay B a spear 'for its tail', because B's personality has to be driven out of the animal into the tail, and thence into the spear.

[5] Though legally the clan is a single unit and, as we have seen, it is theoretically impossible for a member to commit an offence against a fellow-member which would lay him open to a private suit, it is obvious that there must be some machinery to protect the clan from an habitual offender. The principle of group responsibility makes this essential, as one who is constantly involving the clan in costly extra-clan disputes is wasting the property of the clan without contributing an equivalent to its economic prosperity. The offender in such a case, while under no liability to an individual of his group, is nevertheless making it impossible for his group to maintain its group-status or equilibrium in relation to the other groups of the community: he is jeopardizing the principles which ensure the stability of the society; and for that reason he comes within the scope of public law, administered on this occasion, not by the tribe, but by the clan. The habitual offender is accordingly outlawed by his clan: he is publicly put out of status; he cannot claim the protection of the clan and the clan disowns all further responsibility for his actions. This sentence may be followed by the maximum penalty of execution, which is frequently the fate of the habitual offender; but whether this is so or not, the result is much the same, as without the protection of the clan all economic activities are closed to the individual and he will either die of starvation or by assassination, his murder being of no concern to anyone, now that he has no membership in a protective group. This treatment of the habitual offender emphasizes the cardinal principle of African behaviour that the individual has communal responsibilities and obligations, only by discharging which is he entitled to any of the benefits which membership of a society confers.

[6] Similarly the Komo society of the Bambara is above all a society for social protection, and is intended to punish murderers, thieves and other wrongdoers. A threat from Komo will frequently force thieves to make restitution, and it poisons habitual offenders who refuse to reform. The Ngi (gorilla) society of the Fang punishes misdeeds and executes the practitioners of black magic, while in matters of importance the Ngi can be invoked by oath to reveal the guilt or innocence of a person. The esoteric cults associated with many secret societies, and the automatic sanctions which these cults invoke, make them powerful instruments for the preservation of law and for the punishment of offenders. Such associations as these are really special tribunals of tribal justice, carrying the sanctions of tribal law, and should not be confused with the tribal associations to which I have referred and which dispense associational laws *to their members only*: these societies, being limited in membership, are in a sense extra-legal and should only be considered as one of the sanctions of public law. The Poro society, probably the oldest in Africa,

is described as 'the intrinsic constructive element of tribal life, and all the worldly and religious possessions of the tribe centre in and emanate from it'. It is, in short, the sanction for all tribal institutions and is the apotheosis of their legal concepts. Westermann translates *poro* as 'ancient', but Wallis tells us that the word means 'law', and in this he is supported by Allridge who speaks of 'the order of the Poro or Law', a definition which is at least significant of one of the major functions of Poro.

We have found that by the very nature of their constitution African societies have largely failed to develop the intertribal, or as we might say, the international, concept of law. Where intertribal co-operation is necessary for certain economic activities, such as hunting, or where there is much intertribal trade, the tribes concerned naturally respect the provisions of each other's codes, and boys in their initiation schools are taught the relevant laws of their neighbours and are admonished to observe them when occasion arises. This often leads to the adoption of neighbouring customs, which also implies the adoption of the spiritual sanctions, and consequently we find a good deal of interaction of this nature, which may (and often does) serve as an elementary code of intertribal law. But its effects are limited, and, generally speaking, our contention holds good that the law of the tribe is for the tribe only. For any real development of intertribal law we have to turn to those secret societies and associations which operate over a number of different tribes, subjecting all their members, irrespective of their tribal affiliations, to the one associational law. As Beaufaict writes in this context, 'the Nebeli and Ngebo associations of the Ababua, Mangbettu, Azande and Abarambo, and possibly other tribes of the Welle, are in constant contact with each other and unite members of tribes which are otherwise inimical'. It is in the intertribal character of associations such as these that we have to look for the germs of an intertribal code.

[7] This is also the reason why under native law there is no Statute of Limitations. An African inherits, not only the custody of certain property, together with a certain status in the community, but also all the accumulated responsibilities of his ancestors. A debt or a feud is never extinguished till the equilibrium has been restored, even if several generations elapse. It is probably not an exaggeration to say that to the African there is nothing so incomprehensible or unjust in our system of law as the Statute of Limitations, and they always resent a refusal on our part to arbitrate in a suit on the grounds that it is too old.

[8] It has been suggested to me that a striking analogy is to be found in our old institution of frank-pledge, which is defined as 'a system by which all free men of a tithing were responsible for the general good behaviour of its members'. It is possible that a comparison by a competent historian between mediæval English institutions and the present-day institutions of Africa might lead to fruitful results and might suggest possible directions in which adjustment and assimilation are practicable.

[9] Nevertheless the inflicting of these drastic penalties by the clan on a clansman is generally considered to be repugnant to clan sentiment, and efforts are often made to avoid the uncomfortable feeling of disloyalty, which the breach in clan unity involves, by recourse to a legal fiction. Thus we frequently find that the executioner must be a member of one of the helot or pariah tribes, and theoretically the execution by an alien is morally justified as an act of war. Thus the Ovambo executioners are generally six Bushmen or, if they are not available, natives of some other tribe. But the Chagga have satisfied their consciences by making the execution appear to be an accident. When the clan decides to execute one of its members, the chief organizes a sham fight, during the course of which the culprit is "accidentally" shot, a pretence which is kept up from beginning to end.

[10] Thus breaches of tabu or neglect of a religious ceremonial often carry automatic sanctions, which recoil on the health and prosperity of the offender and his group. The ordeal, which is generally regarded as a legal sanction, is rather an appeal to an automatic sanction. If the evidence is insufficient or if either of the parties prefers to appeal to a spiritual tribunal, the ordeal is brought into operation and its decision is accepted as final. It only differs from an automatic sanction in so far as it does not carry its own punishment, but gives a verdict which leads to an automatic adjustment of the equilibrium. The difficulty, however, with automatic sanctions is that they do not always recoil on the right person, and this may create an indirect situation in law analogous to other indirect procedures which have just been considered. Among the Didinga, for example, if a man has been wounded in a fight—however superficial the wound may be is immaterial, so long as there has been any effusion of blood—he may not enter a village without first undergoing ceremonial lustration. If by negligence he does so, he must sacrifice a sheep at once in an endeavour to avert the penalty which his unlawful act may involve; but even with this sacrifice he may be too late, as the sanction comes automatically into force, though its operation may be long delayed. A case in point may make this clearer, as here we have an inevitable conflict between our legal concepts and theirs, and one for which any solution, other than education, seems to be impossible. For every calamity there is an immediate and a remoter cause. In a certain village a child of three died of measles during an epidemic. The Didinga diagnosed the complaint accurately and treated it to the best of their ability, and realized that the child died of measles which was accepted as the immediate cause of death. But after her death, the child's family instituted a suit against a member of the village, because ten years earlier—seven years, that is, before the birth of the child—he had entered

the village with blood on his shoulder and without having made formal lustration. That, it was held, was the remoter cause of the child's death, as had he not been careless in his observance of the tabu the child would not have fallen under the automatic sanction which his offence invoked. The culprit made no hesitation in admitting the facts, acknowledged his responsibility and paid over the requisite twelve head of cattle without a protest. Situations such as these make if difficult to find an adjustment between our two code, but the case serves to emphasize once more the breadth of communal responsibility which makes for good conduct. An individual is doubly careful to observe the law if a breach of it may involve him and his clan in repercussions which he could not possibly envisage at the time; and alternatively his group is a sedulous custodian of an individual's behaviour if his misconduct may jeopardize its future prosperity.

[11] The expedients by which witnesses are put on oath vary considerably. They may even be subjected to the ordeal together with the parties to a suit, but more commonly they are sworn, if an oath is administered, on some sacred symbol, such as a spear, the presumption being that the supernatural sanction invoked would automatically punish any perjury. Such local forms of oaths have sometimes been adopted in English courts, but generally without effect, because it has been assumed that any spear would do, whereas not only is a specially sanctified spear kept for the purpose, but the oath has also to be prescribed by a particular individual accompanied by a precise formula. In the absence of these the oath is naturally valueless. Equally valueless is the application of an oath current in one tribe to witnesses of another, an error into which our courts have sometimes also fallen. But as a matter of fact, in their own courts and under their own laws, witnesses are generally fairly reliable, as the matter on which their evidence is required is usually one of common knowledge. A conflict of evidence is a genuine difference of knowledge or interpretation. It is no good for a witness to lie in his own community, as life is so public that he would certainly be detected. On the other hand, perjury is often found to be very useful with us, because we do not know the circumstances as the witness's own tribesmen know them. Lying is also a kind of defence mechanism which the African employs when he is embarrassed by our odd procedure and by formalities so different from his own. He generally lies because he does not understand and therefore thinks it safer to lie. Similar considerations make him more reluctant to pay the penalties imposed by our laws, than by his own. He does not understand the sanctions on which our laws are based, and even if the verdict is admittedly just the reason for the verdict is often, to the African, unsound. In his own courts he is not accustomed to having a reason given, as the judgment is obvious to all parties. Forensic reasons embarrass him and leave him disinclined to accept them or the consequences of the judgment.

[12] Weeks records a singular provision by which the impartiality and immunity of the judge are indirectly secured. Among the Bangala a chief is appointed in every district by the towns of the district to act as chief judge in all important matters. At the time of his appointment the heads of all the families in the district, who desire to come under his jurisdiction, cut down his banana trees. This gives him a *casus belli* against the towns that acknowledge him as judge, since he is the party offended by their act. The custom is that the people of the offending town must not go to fight the offended town, but must wait for the latter to attack; and no subsequent quarrel can be taken up till the first is settled. Hence the chief appointed as judge may enrage a town by his decision and might call on the other towns to enforce his verdict; yet the town that finds his decision unpalatable may not attack the judge's town because of the old-standing and unsettled case of the banana trees. This ensures to the judge immunity from quarrels with the people who do not like his decisions, and thus guarantees justice and impartiality in his verdicts.

T. O. Elias: The Nature of the African Customary Law*

Having shown that African customary law does make its own distinction between what are called criminal and civil offences according to English law, we may now go on to consider what notions of liability are entertained in the respective spheres of legal wrongs. First, let us examine the general ideas held about the aims of law in African societies before we attempt to analyse the basic concepts of liability for civil and criminal wrongs.

It is commonplace to describe African law as positive and preoccupied with the maintenance of the social equilibrium of the community, and English (or European) law as markedly negative. It has also been claimed for it that its chief aim is compensation for the wronged as opposed to the European ideal of punishment of the wrong-doer; the aim of African law, so the argument runs, is restitution, not retribution. A third generalisation about African law is that it is restricted to a limited group, whilst European

* T. O. Elias, *The Nature of African Customary Law*, Manchester University Press, 1956, pp. 130–144 and pp. 155–161.

law tends to be all-embracing and comprehensive. A fourth contention is that the basis of its operation is communal, not individualistic, as it is in European law. This list of 'points of departure' between the African and the European systems of law could be and are even added to, but it seems advisable to pause here in order to ponder the implications of those just stated.

Writers on African law are perfectly right to stress that its essential characteristic is the maintenance or restoration of the social equilibrium of the community and that this pervades the whole fabric of African law. But it is fallacious to make this assertion only with respect to African law, since that implies that English (or European) law therefore has an entirely different aim. Against this, we may recall here Lord Sumner's well-known *dictum*: 'The object of a civil enquiry into a cause and consequence is to fix liability on some responsible person and to give reparation for damage done.'[1] To the same effect is Roscoe Pound's recent statement:[2] 'What the law has been trying to do is to adjust relations and order conduct so as to give the most effect to the whole scheme of expectations of men in civilised society with a minimum of frictions and waste.'

We see, therefore, that whatever differences in other respects there are between African and European legal ideas, in both the ultimate aim of law in society is essentially the maintenance of the social order. Any attempt to restrict this function to African law fails to acknowledge that African law has its punitive as well as its compensatory side, and that such a dual feature is not at all inconsistent with the maintenance or restoration of the social equilibrium. Moreover, it confuses the civil with the criminal object of law and forgets that even in English law the aim of the law of civil liability is also compensation while only that of criminal liability is at all punitive.

Before we embark upon any detailed treatment of the ordinary ideas of legal ability for wrongs in African customary law, however, let us briefly note an important problem. It is true that (*a*) the belief in the influence of former existence on present life may sometimes operate to excuse individual responsibility for wrongs done, as the tendency then is to say that the wrong-doer cannot 'help himself'—it is no fault of his; and (*b*) the attribution of certain events and occurrences to the action of supernatural agencies, such as that these have been brought about through the ire of an offended ancestor or a deceased kinsman,[3] often results in the attempted propitiation of the offended spirits rather than in vengeance against the living individual who has done a wrong.

While these are real difficulties in the way of any general claim that African law recognises personal liability for mundane wrongs, this impersonal view of cause and effect in such cases serves at any rate to assuage the passions so freely aroused by provocative behaviour in situations rendered explosive by excitable persons. In the interval of consulting a diviner or arranging an ordeal, passions will have cooled somewhat, so that the issues can now be more objectively appraised. The psychological basis of such device, and it is scarcely more than a device, to stave off the consequences of rash and hasty action, must not be overlooked.[4]

A full understanding of an African community would generally reveal the deep underlying assumptions of the whole concept which would belie this all too facile attribution of human conduct to the erratic whims of non-human agencies. It would be found that most if not all African communities with a belief in witchcraft, or even black-magic, normally attribute to supernatural powers natural occurrences (especially public disasters) to which no rational explanation, as conceived in the community, could be given by the people. A sudden and extraordinary invasion of locusts at harvest time, an unprecedented rainstorm accompanied by lightning and a few human casualties, an unexpected eruption of a long quiescent volcano—these and similar happenings must be the work of supernatural forces. In English law these might constitute the legitimate defences of 'Act of God' and 'Inevitable Accident', notions not essentially dissimilar to those we are discussing.

In private disputes between two individuals or wrongs done by one person to another, however, it would be noticed that people are less disposed to excuse personal failings not beyond the offending individual's power to prevent or avoid. And this is so in spite of any widespread belief that individuals could be bewitched into committing certain species of offences.

That the vast majority of wrongs are treated on the purely rational basis of individual responsibility should become obvious to the reader of what now follows.

Criminal Liability and Exemptions Therefrom

Over and above the criticisms just made, there are at least two main obstacles to the acceptance of the equilibrium theory as popularly postulated of African law: (1) the obvious disproportion between the offence and its attendant penalty in most African societies, and (2) the clear evidence we have that the motive or the intention of an offender is taken into account in awarding punishment or ordering the payment of compensation. Let us take each point separately:

(1) If, as is so often alleged, African law is positive, collectivist, and therefore concerned only to restore the *status quo ante*, one would expect that its main aim should be to make punishment fit the crime. Restitution for theft or compensation for homicide restores the equilibrium, and there is an end of the matter.

This may be true of simple, pastoral communities of our Group B type, but with regard to the Group A variety, this hypothesis breaks down. But even in the less developed communities of the former type, instances can be cited of disproportionate penalties; e.g. if a stolen article can be restored to its owner or replaced by an equivalent, it is all very well with the equilibrium theory; but if not, an arbitrary value is imposed which may or may not be equivalent to that of the stolen article.

And while Hartland's statement, that with advancing civilisation in a primitive society the extreme penalty of death and mutilation is often mitigated or compounded for, is valid for the later stages in the process, he seems, nevertheless, to have overlooked the fact that there are in fact cases where the penalty imposed is out of all proportion to the offence committed. As clan independence disintegrates, giving way to a centralised political organisation, the old checks and balances weaken and, until a measure of political stability is achieved as in many West African States, the social equilibrium is sought to be maintained by these disproportionate penalties for offences likely to endanger society during the period of transition.

(2) This raises the controversial issue: Are motive, intention, negligence, accident, etc., relevant in African law? Many writers have tended to deny this possibility. What about the punishment of *any* member of an offender's clan by the offended clan? Motive is surely disregarded then, so argue the protagonists of this view. Also, strictly speaking, once it is admitted that the object of African law is merely to restore the *status quo*, intention ought not to enter into any consideration of the offender's liability. The offence has been committed and has to be adjusted, irrrespective of the motive of the offender or his victim.

But there is abundant evidence pointing the other way. Dr. Wagner has observed that the Kavirondo Bantu punish *intentional* wrongs by the imposition of double the compensation normally payable for *unintentional* wrongs. That is, the Kavirondo Bantu *do* distinguish between these two types of wrongs.[5] Again, Driberg records[6] that according to Colle, the Baluba distinguish between voluntary and involuntary homicide; drunkenness is a mitigating circumstance among the Basonge. The Bashilange, the Chagga and others all make the same distinction. On the other hand, among the Awemba and some other tribes, accident or drunkenness appear to be discounted. But whether the offence is murder or manslaughter the penalty, which is death in the case of the former but compensation in that of the latter, is just as much a process of restoring the equilibrium. But there is no mitigation of the extreme penalty where the victim is a guest or a host, since this is a breach of the laws of hospitality on which the integrity of the community depends *vis-a-vis* its neighbours.

In the light of the foregoing argument it is somewhat surprising to come upon this conclusion of Driberg's: 'I think it is true to say that motive is only regarded in so far as it affects the whole community and prevents its proper functioning, or destroys those qualities which make for corporate harmony and equilibrium. With us, the motive, or the intention, is immediate and individual; with the Africans it is not so much the guilty intention, but the effects of the intention on the community at large.'[7] It would be superfluous to try to argue that this strange distinction between group and individual motive as specific characteristics of African and European law, respectively, is demonstrably false.

The glib assertion of the unity of the clan is misleading, particularly in the determination of legal rights and duties. It is not only that the institution of clanship is not a universal condition in African societies, but also[8] that the corporateness of social life in most of these communities normally allows for conflict and a measure of self-assertion within the group. This necessarily implies the existence of individual rights and duties, and the recognition of the concept of personal responsibility for any wrongs committed by a member.

As for the argument about the collective responsibility of the group for its member's delicts, it is interesting to find a scholar of the standing of Lowie write:[9] 'As might be inferred from the satisfaction of justice by the punishment of any member of the offender's group, criminal intent plays not nearly the same part in criminal law as it does in our own jurisprudence.' But the learned author then proceeds to cite instances of 'the care with which they discriminate between voluntary and involuntary deeds, and between those purely accidental and those resulting from carelessness'. Thus he observes that the south-eastern Bantu draw a highly interesting distinction between accidental manslaughter and accidental injury to property; compensation must be paid to the chief for every homicide, irrespective of criminal intent; but if harm is done to any property without premeditation, no indemnities are extracted. Of course, the writer admits that there are important qualifications to the trite generalisation that intention plays no part in determining liability in 'primitive law', but insists that 'after all qualifications are made it remains true that the ethical motive of an act is more frequently regarded as irrelevant in the ruder cultures than in our courts of justice'.

Basing himself on Driberg, H. R. Hone said of the British advent in Uganda: 'What then was the native conception of law at this time? Roughly, it was that all wrongs concerned only the individuals affected. If my goat is stolen I must find the wrongdoer and bring him to the chief; my remedy is then either to get the goat back or to be compensated in money or kind so that I may be restored to my original position. In other words, the native conception of law extended only to retribution.' He found that homicide was normally settled by a payment of blood-money comprising seven head of cattle to the next-of-kin of the deceased; it was only in the case of intra-family homicide that the death penalty was exacted since it was considered inappropriate to allow family cattle to be forfeited by one member to another as compensation.

We also learn that the Teso exacted blood-money where the murderer was apprehended; but if he escaped, he was outlawed and the members of the deceased's clan were entitled to obtain their satisfaction by killing a member of the murderer's clan. Adultery and theft were compensated in cattle or goats; if a hired thief were killed in the execution of his mission, his relatives were entitled to be compensated by his hirer.

The Basoga employed killing as the penalty for murder, and fines supplemented by flogging were the punishment for most of the other offences. Among the Banyoro and the Bagishu, accidental homicide incurred no penalty except the provision of a feast by the killer for the surviving relatives on both side, those of the deceased attending as evidence that they harboured no malice against those of the killer. If the killer was a member of the same clan as his victim, he was required to pay a fine equal in value to the marriage payment on a wife, and this was payable to the victim's father who might, if he wished, take a wife and raise another child to replace the victim. Wife-beating was no offence and an adulterous wife could legally be killed by her husband; her adulterer was liable to a heavy fine or, in extreme cases, might be killed by a husband who discovered him in the act. The Baganda sometimes allowed the wife's relations to bring a case against a husband who had killed her, in order to find out whether the killing was justified in the circumstances. Murder was sometimes visited with the execution of the murderer, though generally the penalty was the payment of blood-money. An adulterer of the upper classes usually paid for his offence with his own life, since he was supposed to be a serious menace to the personal safety of his victim's husband;[10] he who violated a fellow peer's wife would kill him if he could, as indeed he metaphorically did by the very act of the adultery committed with his wife.

By the middle of the nineteenth century 'a stage of development had already been reached in many tribes in Uganda, whereat a differentiation was made between a deliberate killing and any less culpable form of homicide, the former being dealt with by the infliction of the death penalty, the latter by compensation. Here we have, in outline, the conception familiar to our law, of the difference between murder and manslaughter.' This, if we may say so, is the only verdict that the former Attorney-General of Uganda could have reached on the evidence before him. Hone then adds that, because of the prevalence of the principle of restitution, compensation was, nevertheless, usually payable even in cases of accidental death unaccompanied by negligence; that is, where in English law the killer would escape all liability, civil or criminal. His conclusion was that all these, far from being peculiar to African ideas of legal liability, could be paralleled by similar English legal developments in the Middle Ages.

On the other hand, Major Orde-Browne would seem to be repeating the outworn argument that African law was communal in these words: 'The second peculiarity of the old law was its communal application, its decisions applied not so much to the individual as to a group. . . . Where the individual was so closely identified with the group, the working of the law was naturally facilitated, and recompense was almost always possible. When a murder was committed, the family thereby deprived of a useful member would receive compensation from the offender's relatives *if he himself could not pay*.'[11] One is bound to give thanks to this writer for the conditional clause which so appropriately supports the very point we have made before,[12] that, in spite of the complex web of kinship ties and agnatic obligations, the individual and not his kin-group is primarily and ultimately responsible for his acts in relation to other people. It is curious to note that a believer in the communal nature of African law can unwittingly admit so much.

More objective and direct is the evidence given by Fortes with respect to the Tallensi of the Gold Coast: 'As a member of a particular lineage a man has definite rights and duties and enters into a stream of social relations from which all who do not belong to that agnatic line are excluded.'[13] Later, in another connexion, the writer issues a necessary warning: 'But this does not mean that all Tale jural relations are based on the concept of collective responsibility. On the contrary, jural responsibility is precisely fixed on particular individuals or exactly defined corporate units. This is graphically summed up in many Tale maxims. Thus they say "A pipe sounds best in its owner's mouth . . ." that is, an action should be answered for by the person directly responsible for it.'[14] He goes on to cite[15] as a good illustration of his statement 'that collective responsibility is not a principle of Tale jural relations', the liability of a debtor to reimburse, by an equivalent amount of property, a fellow clansman whose live-stock has been raided by a creditor from another clan as a means of the creditor himself paying. 'It is not the clan but the debtor himself who is responsible for his debt. Self-help is a technique for putting pressure on a debtor through the mechanisms of clan and lineage cohesion.'

Similar, too, is Miss Green's testimony regarding the Ibos: 'A case is normally regarded as between individuals and whether or not they are of the same village they have a variety of judicial possibilities open to them.'[16]

Also, Dr. Lowie, quoting Wagner's writings, records[17] that in Kafir law, if several persons took part in a brawl, the penalty for each person slain was imposed on all those engaged in the fight. The penalty for killing a male was seven head of cattle and that for killing a female was ten head of cattle, the difference being due to the property obtained by the latter at marriage. For assault and battery the fine ranged from one to five head of cattle and both parties were subject to a fine each, since nothing was considered sufficient to warrant one man striking another even in self-defence; but it would seem that this was the case only in the absence of a reliable witness as to who started it all. In the case of abortion both the woman and her accomplice were each fined four or five head of cattle. Prior to 1820, a man caught in adultery with a woman could be killed with impunity, but King Gaika abolished this law and made the killer guilty as for other forms of manslaughter.[18] Adultery was treated as a civil case and the fine ranged from one to four head (of cattle) according to the husband's station in society; the fine was raised from seven to ten head if it clearly resulted in pregnancy. Theft, mainly in the form of stock-raiding, was penalised by the exaction of a tenfold compensation if the property was not recovered. But wilful damage to property must be fully indemnified, while no damages were granted to a complainant for purely accidental injury.

The evidence of Dundas for the Wakamba, Wakikuyu, Watheraka and Wadigo of Kenya Colony and for the Wazegutia, Wapare and Wachagga in the Tanganyika Territory (formerly German East Africa), seems somewhat as follows.[19] Blood revenge was usually directed against the murderer or some near relative, and it always ensued in all cases of premeditated and unprovoked murder arising out of beer drinks. In homicide cases accident was not always a mitigating factor, though settlement was then by payment of compensation: '. . . . very convincing proof will always be required, and it may be said that the onus of proving that it was accident lies with the offender.'[20] Practice, of course, varied among these tribes, from the open recognition as lawful of killing in self-defence as well as of killing without intent, on the one hand, to the bland denial of either, on the other. In Ukamba and elsewhere an inquest of elders, including a searching *post mortem*, was very often held in order to discover any possible internal injury.

In reiterating the general proposition that the murderer's motive or intention was usually disregarded in awarding penalties for homicide, Dundas gave three reasons: (1) that any relaxation of this general rule would result in increased bloodshed; (2) that its maintenance prevents fine distinctions being drawn between intentional and unintentional or negligent acts; and (3) that it enforces care and restraint upon men's actions. But he soon proceeds to enumerate in scattered parts of his lengthy article the following (summarised) exceptions to the general rule:

(*a*) Among the Akamba, accidental killing was always compensated by only half the amount of blood-money for intentional killing. This is called *mbanga*, which is a word also used by the Akikuyu to signify the killing of a man by some article or animal belonging to another. Both the Akikuyu and the Akamba would award the article or animal causing the death to the deceased's relatives.[21]

(*b*) If two men killed each other in a fight, compensation was dispensed with by a kind of set-off; and a man might, without paying any compensation, kill another whom he saw in the act of killing his brother.

(*c*) So also, if a murderer refused to pay a duly adjudged compensation, it could be exacted by force, and if anyone should be killed in the ensuing scuffle, no blood-money was payable.

(*d*) A person might refuse to accept any blood-money and might instead kill the murderer or the latter's close relative.

(*e*) In all these East African communities a man might kill his wife without being liable to pay any compensation,[22] but the balance of any marriage payment must still be paid by such husband to her father. All other cases of homicide involving blood relations[23] must be compensated for by blood-money, which varied from the full amount to a half or less, *according to circumstances*: 'The clan is excluded from any share, although it contributes as in any other case of homicide. If a man kills any distant relative or a clansman living in the same locality, he must pay half the blood-money, but if he slays a clansman not residing in his district he is liable for full blood-money. Cases of accidental killing were usually settled by arrangement between the clan and the family of the victim.'

(*f*) Generally, the taking of the life of a stranger must be fully compensated, even though he had stayed with his host for only one day. The payment was always made to his host. But blood money for the murder of, or by, a stranger could only be claimed if the stranger had already been fully adopted by the claimant or if the stranger had previously entered into blood-brotherhood with a member of the family.

(*g*) Provocation, particularly in cases of theft where the thief was caught *in flagrante delicto*, was always and everywhere among these communities a mitigating, nay an exonerating, circumstance. But the right to kill in such a case was not frequently exercised in practice. The usual penalty among the Kikuyu for stealing stock was ten times the value of whatever was stolen, *plus* three sheep for the elders sitting as judges. This was in the nature of a fine imposed over and above the due restoration of the property itself. Every person taking part in the theft must pay this penalty. Any man who ate of the meat of a stolen beast had to pay three sheep. 'While almost every other offence is attributed to circumstances rather than to character, that of theft signifies to the natives an unpardonable nature.'

Against the common assertion of communalism in legal liability, Dundas finds that 'Even between the best friends and nearest relatives, compensation is paid which one might otherwise expect would be waived.' And this, be it noted, among predominantly clan-ridden African communities in which the so-called 'unity of the clan' ought to exclude such intra-group liability. To cap it all, Dundas observes:

'Homicide seems to be the only offence affecting not only one individual. A man who has committed such an offence goes to all his clansmen and *begs* contributions towards the blood-money; this is done to the present day, and to refuse such *assistance* is regarded as shameful, and as equivalent to a denial of kinship. *Yet the clan will not commence the payment: the debtor must first say what he is prepared to pay, and if he is destitute of means the clan will not subscribe.*'[24]

Finally, the purification or peace-making ceremony of killing a goat and/or sheep after payment of compensation for murder is designed, either by itself or in addition to the taking of an oath, to effect lasting reconciliation between the two families of the murderer and the murdered. Dundas is emphatic: 'Those who can attribute to a crime such direful results cannot be supposed to regard it as a trifling affair, and there must be an inborn horror of taking human life. The native, is, in fact, not often guilty of murder, as we commonly understand the term. Of premeditated murder I have only known two cases, but ninety per cent. of the cases of people being killed may be said to be due to drunken brawls. . .'

Summary of Principles of Criminal Liability

(1) There is a notion of *mens rea* in African law. The reason why compensation is such a recurrent, indeed almost inevitable, feature of cases of homicide is that, as we have just been told by Dundas in the passage last quoted, about ninety per cent. of the deaths were the result of unpremeditated drunken brawls. The theory in the African mind is then, that a person thus temporarily deprived of his reason was incapable of forming an intent, let alone a guilty one, sufficient to induce him to want to kill an innocent companion or stranger. A clear distinction between murder and manslaughter is implicit in this way of treating homicide cases.[25]

That the majority of homicides take place in circumstances of accident or want of premeditated malice is also borne out by the fact that, of the eleven cows included in the blood-money payment throughout the Machakos District of Kenya, the first cow is called *ng'ombe ya mbanga*, meaning the 'cow of the *accident*'.[26] But the same writer later said: 'Kamba law does not distinguish between murder, manslaughter or a death caused by accident. The blood-price is payable in each case. If a man were to fire an arrow at an animal and hit a man beyond, not knowing that he was there, he would be held fully liable.'[27]

This seeming paradox can be resolved if it is frequently borne in mind that here, as elsewhere with some other writers, there is a confusion between *liability* and the quantification of *damages*. There are varying degrees of liability as well as of damages in almost all other cases of injury to the person outside the category of fatal ones. In homicide cases, however, the elders naturally regard the consequences of the children and other dependants of the victim being suddenly left destitute as more important than the *manner* of the encompassing of the death by the killer. A death has suddenly occurred, the killer has been apprehended and has not denied his guilt; the elders say: Let him compensate his victim's surviving relatives according to the customary tariff schedule appropriate to his case. This interpretation seems supported by Penwill's own later observation[28] that, while cases of petty assaults are expiable by the payment of a goat, those of serious bodily injuries are normally visited with severe penalties.

(2) On the other hand, death is almost always the invariable penalty for dastardly acts of wanton homicide—whether these proceed from motives of revenge, or of gain, or of sadism.

(3) The very existence in almost all the penalty tariff schedules of a graduated scale of compensation or fine for a single offence indicates, if it does not conclusively prove, that the judges do not just impose punishments automatically but that the culprit's liability is measured by the extent of the enormity of his crime and by certain extenuating circumstances, if any. All this might not be expressly stated by the judges as part of the award, but few among their audience at a trial would fail to realise the implied assumptions influencing particular declarations of penalties. It is seriously urged here that motive, accident, intention, etc., largely enter into nearly every considered judgment from which the incautious observer would apparently regard them to be absent.

(4) But, when all this has been said, it remains true that in view of the limited margin of security in small, often isolated communities and the tendency for passion to be easily inflamed by provocative behaviour, what would be deemed a good enough motive or intention in, say, English law, might not necessarily be so considered in certain types of African law.

(5) When people deny that motive, intention, etc., play any part in African law, they seem to be arguing from the particular to the general—from the single instance of homicide and its treatment to the whole of African law. They forget that all African law is neither homicide nor even crime in general, and that there are large areas of civil law in which these concepts (i.e. motive, intention, etc.) are fully regarded by the elders in their adjudication of disputes.

(6) Drunkenness produced by ordinary intoxication is generally no defence against a charge for any offence. The general idea is that, since the man drank of his own free will and ought to have exercised his own discretion to know when to stop and had failed to do so, he should suffer for not behaving like a reasonable member of society. On the other hand, if a man were made drunk by others and then put to some act or omission resulting in injury or harm to another, those responsible for his condition at the material time would be liable and not he.

In cases of insanity, the family of a madman were usually held responsible for all his crimes. If he was so out of his mind as not to know what he was doing at the time of committing the offence in question, his family should have given him all necessary medical treatment or at least kept him in confinement so that he did not go about injuring other people. Should they fail in their duty, they would be liable for any offence he might commit whilst so left at large.

(7) It may be that the legal arrangement above outlined may be truer of African societies with a centralised judicial machinery than of those having none; and it may also be that a greater degree of sophistication is to be expected in the exaction of the blood-price. Clan feelings being less strong if not entirely absent, and the organised force of the community in the person of the chief and his councillors being more readily available, notorious murderers are likely to be similarly protected against mob violence until their innocence or guilt can be established judicially. It is suggested that in the judicial process of such societies, the presence or absence of malice, accident, negligence and the like will be found to be more explicitly mentioned and considered in the judges' statements of their verdict than would be the case in the judicial process of less highly organised societies.

Liability for Torts (or Civil Wrongs)

As with Contracts, so it is with Civil Wrongs that are independent of any personal relationship based on agreement. One person's straying sheep and goats are beaten by another into whose garden they have come, destroying his growing crops. A may quite negligently drop his cutlass on the bare toes of B, causing him much pain and trouble. E seduces F's daughter who is under the age of puberty and who is probably already betrothed to G. If society is to lead an orderly existence, it must clearly have a set of rules to deal with these and similar cases. And we are fortunate to have to this effect a wealth of illustration from the writings of those who have studied African communities, although most of these were often intended to serve purposes other than the specifically legal.

Thus, according to Penwill, if in former times a man's cattle or goats broke out of his *boma* (an enclosure for animals) by night on to his neighbour's holding which is sown with crops or kept merely for grazing, no compensation was payable for any damage done or crops destroyed. But if the break-out took place by day, compensation was payable. The Kamba argue that the sudden break-out at night could not be helped by their owner; obviously, the animal's depredations were what, in the English Law of Tort, would be termed 'Act of God'; but that when the same thing happened by day, an owner ought reasonably to have done his best to keep his animals off other people's property, since he could then have prevented the eruption by good management. Also, compensation was payable if there was a repetition of the nocturnal trespass by the animals as that would be evidence of the man's negligence or inadvertence regarding the welfare of his neighbours. 'Now the owner is held responsible for the damage done by his stock, whether there is any particular negligence or not; and grass must be paid for if trespassed on. Nor is there any difference reckoned between night and day, except as affecting *the degree of negligence*; some compensation is always expected and paid.'[29]

A man starting a fire which gets out of his control and destroys a neighbour's crops or fences or house or even honey-hives must compensate the latter to the extent of their full value. Should a human being lose his life thereby, full blood-money is payable. The subsidence of another's adjoining holding which has been caused by one person's cultivation of, or excavation on, his land must be fully recompensed. Humans as well as animals falling into a trap set by an occupier of land, even on his own land, are entitled to compensation if any injury should result to them. Penwill thus winds up with an interesting note on damage to property in these words:[30] 'The Kamba hold that a man is always responsible for his actions and cannot evade that responsibility by alleging that another party created the situation that led to his action, by an original act which was itself a breach of Kamba custom.'

A man who sends another person on an errand or journey is normally held responsible for all or part of any harm that may befall his messenger whilst so engaged. Thus, he must bear a proportion of any compensation due to the messenger or his relatives in case of any supervening bodily harm or death; this would of course be part only of what the injurer or killer might have to pay. But if the messenger's hurt has been caused by his own negligence, foolhardiness or other personal fault, his employer is exempt from all blame.[31]

Similarly, Dundas records[32] the case of a man who found a cow in his field eating his crops and who in driving it off struck it so violently that it died in consequence. The *kiama* of the elders made him pay its full value to its owner on the ground that he had used excessive violence in protecting his property.[33] They observed that if the defendant's pleas were allowed to justify the killing of the trespassing animal, it might equally well be asserted to excuse the killing of a human being in similar circumstances. In trying to show that intention, accident, and the like are disregarded in homicide cases, the writer gave this hypothetical case; If a man were seized by a lion and his friend, in endeavouring to save him, should inadvertently spear him instead of the lion, that friend would be liable to pay the usual compensation to his relatives for his death.[34] This, it is submitted, would seem to be a doubtful possibility. If such a friend were ever held responsible, however, it might be on the ground that he had allowed his anxious impulsiveness to save his friend to overcome his fair judgment of his own skill in the use of the spear; by local standards, discretion is also the better part of valour. Had he left his friend alone with the lion and contented himself with merely raising an alarm, either the object of his pity or an abler spearman might have effectively disposed of the animal. At any rate, he need never have hastened his friend's demise by a rash and emotional use of the spear. Be that as it may, it is highly improbable that the elders would have exacted in such a case the full customary penalty for ordinary murder. They would probably have left it to him to make an offer to his victim's relatives out of his sheer contrition of heart.

The writer is, however, interesting when he leaves the tricky realm of conjecture to face the stark realities of African life around him. Thus, he gives[35] these principles of Kikuyu customary law: A man causing the loss of a leg to another pays about one-third of the full blood-money, which is later deducted from whatever is due to the one so crippled if he should eventually die from the injury. But no such deduction is made from the compensation payable for the death of a person who was crippled or deformed from birth.

These are mere illustrations of types of civil liability in two or three African communities of the segmentary, uncentralised variety. There can be no doubt that other societies, if similarly analysed, would yield the same and even more detailed and developed principles of liability for legal wrongs. But it is unnecessary in a book of theory to analyse them.

As we have seen in the previous chapter, writers on African law have varied in their interpretations from those who only see criminal law everywhere to those who are sure that the African mind is incapable of making any distinction between criminal and civil wrongs—that is, that African law deals solely with civil, in the sense of private, wrongs. We have shown that this view is a false one, but what we may also legitimately infer here is that the latter attitude at least acknowledges the legal fact that African law does recognise a measure of civil responsibility for wrongs. As Thomas, J. put it in the Nyasaland case of *R.* v. *Robert and Alumani*:[36] 'Native law knows nothing of what we call criminal law; it knows of wrongs to the individual for which he can in his appropriate native court receive compensation, depending in amount on the nature of the injury and the relative position in the community of the injured party.'[37]

The rationalist conception of liability for tort is that it must be based on fault—that is, that the wrong-doer must have acted intentionally or negligently for him to be liable.[38] This was the general view in developed Roman law, whence it penetrated into Continental law and later into Anglo-American law.[39]

Now, it is commonly said that in 'primitive' law the general idea of liability for wrongs done, whether to a human being or to an animal, was that of *Causation*, not *Culpability*. This is sometimes expressed by English writers as meaning that a man acts at his peril.[40] A notable protest was vigorously entered by the late Sir Percy Winfield against this view of early (or 'primitive') law. He argued[41] that even in early English law, the commission of a wrong was excusable on the grounds of self-defence, Act of God, inevitable accident, necessity, mistake, *volenti non fit injuria*, etc. And although it has been suggested that Winfield did not demolish the general theory of causation but only provided a series of exceptions to it, we are nevertheless, entitled to question whether the modern Continental development of the principle of liability for exposure to risk is fundamentally different from this alleged quality of 'primitive' law. Owing to the advent of mechanical inventions and appliances, the principle of no liability without fault has had to be altered to allow liability on the condition that he who engages in an activity (e.g. driving a motor-car on the highway) should make himself an insurer for the benefit of those whom his activity may harm.

Also in the English law of tort, the defendant's foresight or state of mind is irrelevant in torts of 'strict liability' such as liability under *Rylands* v. *Fletcher*,[42] liability for fire, for keeping dangerous animals, for certain types of trespass and for conversion, and vicarious liability of masters for their servants' wrongs. In all these cases, the court merely looks at the act done or omitted, and does not trouble itself about causation. Of course, there is another class of torts in which the defendant's foresight as to the consequences of his act is an essential element in determining his liability; these are liability for negligence, nuisance, conspiracy, injurious falsehood, malicious prosecution, and defamation. Thus, in the first group, malice in the sense of improper motive is totally disregarded as an element of liability for wrongs, while in the latter it is an ingredient of each species of tort. Finally, it is a fundamental principle of the English law of tort that motive is not ordinarily relevant to the issue of personal liability. This is expressed by saying that a good motive will not make lawful an act otherwise unlawful, neither can a bad motive make unlawful an act that is otherwise lawful.

In the light of this comparative evidence it is clear that motive, intention and negligence are not necessarily the invariable attributes of 'European' law. In certain instances under English law they are relevant, in others they are not. The legal position is more or less the same in African customary law. Intention requires both foreknowledge and desire on the part of the individual whose legal liability may be in question. Consequences which are foreseeable are intentional. On the other hand, negligence is independent of intention; it, however, covers rashness as well as inadvertence, the essence of both being the indifference of the wrong-doer to the welfare of other people.

This is sometimes called the *subjective* view of negligence, meaning that negligence is a state of mind. The objective view is that a person's conduct is negligent or not according as it is reasonable in all the circumstances of the case. The standard is that of the reasonable man. Whichever of the two views we take, the important thing is to find out whether or not there is a guilty mind.

African law is not so mechanical in its operation as to ignore the propriety or impropriety of a wrong-doer's motive in bringing about the unlawful consequences upon which the council of elders or the chiefs are called to adjudicate. To hold otherwise would be to deny all element of rationality to Africans and, therefore, to African law. Custom, as we have been saying all this long while, is neither automatic nor blind in its apparently smooth and leisurely operation. Behind the façade of the chief's visible routine of awarding compensation or imposing fines lie a highly discriminating mind and an accepted scale of values, both of which imply, though they may not express in words, certain underlying assumptions of the whole community. These are understood by the people and so do not require elaboration on every occasion. The outsider is then all too apt to detect in such placid working of the legal order 'the automatic reign of custom' in African society.

This whole problem of the weighing of motive, intention, and negligence in the circumstances of a wrong-doer's conduct really overlaps the boundaries of the actual administration of justice in African communities.

Notes

1 In *Weld-Blundell* v. *Stephens* (1920), A.C. 956, p. 986.
2 *Justice According to Law*, p. 29.
3 See, e.g. Evans-Pritchard, *Witchcraft, Oracles and Magic*, p. 63.
4 This point is considered at some length in Ch. XII.

[5] A. Phillips, *Report on Native Tribunals in Kenya*, pp. 254–5.
[6] Driberg, *op. cit.*, pp. 225 ff.
[7] *Op. cit.*, p. 236.
[8] E.g. Prof. M. Gluckman has observed that the Lozi of Northern Rhodesia have no system of clanship or lineage but trace relationships through mother and father only—see Browne and Forde (eds.), *African Systems of Kinship and Marriage*, pp. 166–206. And Prof. S. F. Nadel has found paternal and maternal filiation combined, resulting in the absence of serious crime. (*Ibid.*, pp. 333–59.)
[9] *Op. cit.*, p. 387.
[10] Also, among the Yoruba of Southern Nigeria, death was the penalty for adultery with chiefs' wives—Talbot, *The Peoples of Southern Nigeria*, p. 629.
[11] *Journal Roy. Afr. Soc.*, Vol. 32, No. 127, pp. 148–59, at p. 151. The italics are mine.
[12] Pp. 89–92.
[13] *The Dynamics of Clanship among the Tallensi*, pp. 134–5.
[14] *Ibid.*, p. 230.
[15] *Ibid.*, p. 245.
[16] Green, *Ibo Village Affairs*, p. 113.
[17] *Op. cit.*, pp. 410 ff.
[18] This principle is not unlike the *ratio decidendi* in *Holmes* v. *D.P.P.* (1946), A.C. 588. See also p. 249.
[19] *Journal of Royal Anthropological Institute*, Vol. 51 (1921), pp. 217–78, 'Native Laws of Some Bantu Tribes of East Africa.'
[20] *Ibid.*, pp. 238–9.
[21] One is reminded here of the former practice in English law whereby a personal chattel which was the immediate and accidental cause of the death of a human being was forfeited to the Crown as *Deodand* (*Deo* — to God, and *Dandum* — to be given). The practice was abolished by the Statute 9 and 10 Vict. c. 62 (1846).
[22] Possibly because he was the only person who was entitled to receive any compensation that might be due on her life through another's killing. Also the cow is given to a widow as her own property if her husband was killed by another person.
[23] E.g. a man killing a brother, sister, mother or father had to pay definite compensation to the others according to an agreed tariff.
[24] All the italics are mine.
[25] For the clear distinction drawn by the Ashanti in these matters, see Rattray, *Ashanti Law and Constitution*, pp. 296–303.
[26] Penwill, *Kamba Customary Law*, pp. 78 ff.
[27] *Ibid.*, p. 81. A possible explanation might be that the judges would consider that the man who fired an arrow in such circumstances had clearly failed to show the *exacta diligentia* expected of a reasonable man in his position at the time and place the incident occurred.
[28] *Ibid.*, pp. 85–6.
[29] *Kamba Customary Law*, p. 104 (italics are mine).
[30] *Ibid.*, p. 106.
[31] Penwill, *op. cit.*, p. 86.
[32] *Jnl. Roy. Anth. Inst.*, Vol. 51 (1921), p. 263.
[33] It is interesting to note in this connexion the similar provision of the Statute of Forcible Entry (1389) in English law. With the actual decision here compare the same one in the case of *Hamps* v. *Darby* (1948), W.N. 313 (pigeons) on similar facts.
[34] See p. 263 and also p. 237 of Vol. 51 (1921) of *Jnl. Roy. Anth. Inst.*
[35] *Ibid.*, p. 267.
[36] (1940), 5 Nys. L.R. 2, pp. 3–4.
[37] It must be noted that the first part of the sentence is incorrect, for the reason already stated. J. Lewin in his *Studies in African Native Law*, p. 105, includes torts as one of the instances of native laws.
[38] E.g. this was on the whole Bentham's view—see *Works*, Vol. 1, p. 292 n.: 'What you have a right to have me made to do (understand a political right) is that which I am able, according to law, upon a requisition made on your behalf, to be punished for not doing.'
[39] Cf. The Roman law idea embodied in *The Lex Aquilia*.
[40] E.g. W. Holdsworth, *History of English Law*, Vol. 2, p. 64.
[41] *Law Quarterly Review*, Vol. 42 (1926), p. 184; see also *Law Quarterly Review*, Vol. 55, 450–1.
[42] (1868), L.R. 3 H.L. 330.

M. Gluckman: Order and Rebellion in Tribal Africa*

The Case of the Violent Councillor

I come from a family of lawyers, and through my childhood I constantly heard my father and his colleagues discussing their cases at the family-table. Later I intended to go to the South African Bar, and besides reading Law at the University I worked in my father's office in Johannesburg and attended on him in court. Therefore when, diverted by a desire for the exotic, I became an anthropologist and began to study African social life, I hoped I might make some contribution on the problems of African law. But I found that, though the setting of this law might be exotic, its problems were those which are common to all systems of jurisprudence. I can still recall vividly how I was sitting in my deckchair one day listening to a trial in a Barotse Court, when I recognized an old friend. He is inscribed in huge letters on the blank page opposite my notebook's record of the process of cross-examination: 'Hullo, the reasonable man!'

This was not the first Barotse trial I had attended, and in an earlier piece of research in Zululand I had also listened to cases. So I share with many colleagues a long blindness to the existence of this basic figure of jurisprudence in African law. Indeed, it was the facts of the case, rather than my own perception, which made me aware of his existence in Barotse law. But once I had observed him, I was able to reconsider all the cases I had heard as exhibitions of his dominant role in the judicial process. I came to appreciate that he was the means by which the judges applied the fixed rules of general law and morality to the varied cirumstances of Barotse life. Above all, he was the means by which they adjusted these fixed rules to cope with the great changes which the Barotse's life is undergoing as they are absorbed in the modern world.

This is the general problem I am going to tak about. Obviously, it is a problem which is fundamental to our own jurisprudence, where the reasonable man is an equally important figure. The phrases, 'reasonable man', 'reasonable behaviour', 'reasonable care', 'reasonable precautions', and the like, crop up in every judgment and every chapter of a textbook of law. Indeed, in the very first of his *Misleading Cases at Common Law*, Sir Alan Herbert— in a case in which the judges hold that there is no such thing as a reasonable woman in English law—comes to the following conclusion:

> 'There has never been a problem, however difficult, which His Majesty's judges have not in the end been able to resolve by asking themselves the simple question, "Was this or was it not the conduct of a reasonable man?", and leaving that question to be answered by the jury.'

It seems to me that in this misleading case Sir Alan puts the reasonable man into his proper position, at the centre of the law. The reasonable man occupies this central position because he is the means by which abstract legal rules are focused on to the varied circumstances of life. In textbooks of law he is cut up according to the technical divisions of jurisprudence—he comes in under many separate heads, such as reasonable care and guilty beyond reasonable doubt. In this process of dissection he loses his integrated character. And it is this integrated character which interests me as an anthropologist. I am going to exhibit his dominance in Barotse lawsuits, and to suggest that this exhibition may help to solve certain long-standing controversies in our own jurisprudence. For as Barotse judges define the reasonable man, they bring into their definitions many facets of Barotse life which are not ostensibly part of the law. These facets include a variety of social and personal prejudices. I believe the same process can be detected in the decisions of our own judges and juries.

Let me describe the exotic setting in which I first met this familiar figure. From its source in the Belgian Congo, the Zambezi flows southwards towards the Kalahari Desert, before it bends east towards the Indian Ocean. About half-way down its north to south course the river has carved out a great plain in the woodlands which cover North-Western Rhodesia. This plain is 120 miles long and about thirty-five miles wide, and it is the homeland of the tribe who rule over the vast region marked as Barotseland on maps. Each year the summer rains flood the plain, so that it becomes a great lake. The Barotse therefore build their villages on mounds in the plain, which are islands in the flood-season; though as snakes and rodents and insects seek sanctuary in the villages, life in the flood is so uncomfortable that the Barotse move for these months to dwell in other

* M. Gluckman, *Order and Rebellion in Tribal Africa*, Routledge & Kegan Paul, 1963, pp. 178–206.

villages on the margins of the plain. From their plain-villages the Barotse work rich pockets of alluvial soil, pasture their cattle, and trap fish in many ways. These villages, on the only building land available, are of strategic importance in Barotse life. Rights to work land and to fish in certain trap-sites and pools depend on membership of a village.

The Barotse have a Paramount Chief who has two capitals, one in the heart of the plain, the other at the margin, to which he moves for the flood-season. The chief rules through an elaborately organized council, which is a court of law, a cabinet, a parliament, a civil service, an ecclesiastical chapter, and, in the old days, was a military headquarters. Now war is a thing of the past, for under a treaty signed in 1900 the Barotse accepted British protection. Under the Treaty the Barotse Chief's rights to punish his subjects were defined by British law, but his council still tries civil and some criminal cases. It does so by old procedures. The plaintiff states his case in full detail to the numerous judges, and the defendant replies. The judges themselves cross-examine the parties and witnesses, and when they are satisfied that they have heard all the evidence, give judgment. There are no lawyers to assist the parties, and their rôle is played by the judges. The chief himself does not listen to lawsuits, but the judgments are referred to him in his Palace for the final verdict.

It was at Lialui, the flood-season capital, that I recognized the reasonable man during a trial which I call 'The Case of the Violent Councillor'. Most Barotse villages are inhabited by a grouping of kinsfolk, but some are attached to members of the royal family and are inhabited by several families, all of which are ruled by a councillor. A quarrel had broken out in the village which was destined to be the burial-village of the then reigning chief. Hot words had passed between the son of the councillor and a young villager. The villager had gone to the councillor's house to complain about the son's behaviour, and he alleged that he was attacked there by three of the councillor's children who flung him to the ground. The councillor seized his wrist and dragged him along the ground, with the three youngsters clinging to his waist. He screamed: 'The councillor is breaking me, the councillor is breaking me.' His wife came in and accused the councillor of fighting: this is a heinous offence for a councillor, since a councillor is not a policeman, and must never take violent action. The councillor released him and got one of the stamping-poles with which the women pound grain. It was taken away by another man. The councillor seized a whip which was also taken away. The plaintiff was then released by the councillor's children and carried away, fainting. He sued the councillor and children in a subordinate court which fined the councillor £1, of which it said ten shillings were to go to the plaintiff, and ten shillings as a fine to the Barotse Treasury. The plaintiff said he would appeal for the latter ten shillings to the court at the capital, and persisted in this appeal even when he was offered fifteen shillings, with five shillings only to the Treasury.

This was the story which the plaintiff told the appeal court where I was listening in, since Barotse appeal courts hear all the evidence anew. He had independent witnesses for most of the incidents. But the councillor's defence was as follows. He said that the plaintiff had come to his house spoiling for a fight with his son. His children had attacked the plaintiff who was thrown to the ground. He had seized the plaintiff's arm in an attempt to raise him and stop the fight. Then he had taken the stamping-pole to put it out of the way in case someone seized it as a weapon. Finally he had taken the whip to frighten the fighters into their senses, but had not intended to use it.

The serious aspect of this case was that the councillor had taken violent action—had fought. Barotse gave me several precedents in which councillors, who are supposed to be restrained, grave, controlled, and so forth, had been discharged for taking action against wrongdoers with their own hands. The violent councillor was afraid that this would happen to him, and he therefore cast his story so that his witnessed actions would appear to conform to Barotse ideas of right conduct—so that he would appear to have acted reasonably. It seems probable that he was lying, but it is very important to notice that he lied in such a way that he accepted the rules for rightdoing. In almost every case which I heard in Barotseland litigants and witnesses, whether they lied or were mistaken, worked with the same moral and legal rules as the judges did. This is the mark of a homogeneous society; and it alone allows a satisfactory process of law. If the litigants have rules of rightdoing different from those of the judges, the judges can punish them, but not convict them.

Since the violent councillor accepted the standard rules of how a councillor should behave, he lied in terms of these rules, and this enabled the judges to attack him. A prince asked him: 'When the plaintiff came to your house, why did you not tell him to sit down, and then summon your children, so that you could enquire into the dispute between them?' The councillor hedged and replied, 'They are binding me with lies'. The head of the court pressed him: 'Why did you not make them sit down so that you could judge between them?' The councillor did not reply. The head of the court, who is noted for his gentleness but was enraged by the offence, went on angrily: 'You should have seated the plaintiff, called your son, and summoned all the men of the village to hear their quarrel.' The councillor said, 'I did not do this.' The head of the court, commented: 'This is councillorship—this is ruling!' The councillor made an attempt to defend himself: 'It was night, I could not.' The head of the court pursued his point:

> 'If an affair comes here to the capital at night to me, I go to the prime minister, I call the senior councillors. If it is a thief, we put him in goal for the District Commissioner. Also, you say you tried to raise the plaintiff, that you did not drag him along the ground. What manner of arbitrating in a fight is this, to seize the one who is on the ground, who is being overwhelmed, not to seize those who are fighting him?'

Here the judges have set up two standards by which they can break the councillor's ingenious defence of his witnessed actions. First, he did not behave as a reasonable man would do in intervening in a fight; second, he behaved quite unlike a reasonable councillor, acting by the customs of a good councillor, in handling the quarrel when it was brought to him. It was at this point that I realized how the Barotse had elaborated the concept of the reasonable man.

The court was aware that the councillor feared discharge, but did not mind paying a fine for his children's assault. This is implicit in the next question put to him, though it seems also to stem only from the concept of a reasonable man. For the court knew the councillor did not want it to become aware of his offence. A prince challenged him: 'You deny that you were at fault. Why then when the subordinate court penalized you £1, did you not appeal?' The councillor replied: 'If a man is penalized, what can he do?' The prince insisted: 'He can appeal.' The councillor hedged: 'I would have appealed if the plaintiff had not done so.' The prince crushed him: 'But you did not protest in the lower court. This boy complained that the court was taking ten shillings of his money for the treasury, you did not protest that you should pay nothing. . . . Your fault was that you, a councillor, entered into a fight.'

With this question the bias of the trial shifted from the assault to whether the defendant was fit to be a councillor. Another judge asked him: 'Why when the plaintiff's wife cried, "The councillor is fighting", did you release him, if you were trying to raise him? You knew you were wrong, as a councillor, to fight.' And another prince concluded the cross-examination: 'You say you came with the whip to frighten them. Is it your custom to threaten with a whip?' The councillor was caught in a cleft stick, because only a policeman and not a councillor should threaten with violent action. He had to answer, 'No'. The prince asked: 'Did you shout as you came with the whip, to show that you wanted to beat them, but did not mean to beat them?' Here the councillor perforce answered, 'Yes'. The prince concluded: 'Then why has not one witness of all who heard the plaintiff cry, "The councillor is breaking me", said that he heard you shout?'

All the judges held he was guilty. Some wished to raise the payment, but the final judgment held that he should pay £1 and it should all go to the plaintiff. He and his children were warned that if they did not behave properly he would be discharged from his post and they might be expelled from the chief's village.

There are many implications in this brilliant cross-examination. I can discuss only a few. First, we see that an African court decides on the facts of a lawsuit by listening to and sifting evidence, and weighing it by cogency and corroboration, just as an English court does. The judges also insisted on direct as against hearsay evidence: a witness was told, 'What you heard with your ears, what you saw with your eyes, tell us. Hearing and seeing the quarrel are good. Do not tell us everything you have been told about the fight.' This has always been the procedure of Barotse courts: ordeals and magical oracles were only resorted to in accusations of sorcery, which canot be demonstrated by ordinary evidence, and in criminal cases where the verdict on the evidence was, 'almost certainly guilty, but not proven.'

But the truth is arrived at mainly by contrasting the behaviour of the parties, as witnesses report it and as the parties themselves describe it, against the standards of how a reasonable man would behave. Both the parties and the judges erect common standards of reasonable behaviour, and this makes possible judicial cross-examination. But the standards in this case are two-fold. First there is the standard of a generally reasonable man—a man who arbitrates in a fight by helping the person who is overwhelmed and intervening with the attackers, i.e. a reasonable peacemaker; a man who appeals against an unjust conviction, i.e. a reasonable innocent man. Second, there is the standard of a reasonable councillor, who when people are quarrelling makes them sit down and tell their stories so that he can judge between them, who summons the public to assist in this process, who is firm and authoritative but not violent, who is impartial and not biased in favour of his own children. After this case gave me the clue, I found this two-fold character present in every lawsuit—the generally reasonable person, and what I call 'the reasonable incumbent of a particular social position', be it councillor, husband or wife, father or son. And as these characters were held up as standards before litigants, as when the head of the court described how he handled an affair coming to him at night, I saw how important the reasonable man is during that part of a lawsuit when the raw facts given in evidence are assessed, and become facts-in-law for the purpose of judgment. This process is barely handled in orthodox legal studies. But it is here, in defining the reasonable standards which are the yardstick in cross-examination, that many things creep into the law which are not part of its rules. No Barotse law says that an innocent man must appeal against conviction: but, with other circumstances, if he does not, he is held guilty. No law says a councillor must summon and seat people who quarrel: but if he does not, with other facts, he may be convicted of bias. I suggest that an analysis of trials in English courts would show that there too all sorts of presumptions, customs, standards and ideas about how persons of different types should behave, enter into cross-examination and influence the process of litigation. They enter through the definition of the reasonable man, because 'reasonable' is a flexible concept which can cover many different things and ways of behaviour. This is its strength for it enables rules of wide moral validity to be accommodated to quite new situations. The duty of 'reasonable care', formulated in ancient Roman times, can cope with the accidents of the machine-age. In Barotseland, a traveller recorded in 1896 a case involving 'the reasonable councillor'; this character can be re-defined by the judges to meet the conditions of modern life.

The Case of the Eloping Wife

Our textbooks of law take as their units of analysis a series of abstract concepts like right and duty, marriage, property, care and negligence, guilt, contract, crime; and they analyse legal rules grouped under these concepts. The anthropologist's units of investigation are social positions—such as husband and wife, owner, thief, councillor, king and so forth. These social positions are linked together by rights which the incumbents of the positions can claim and by duties they should fulfil. The anthropologist studies how rights are claimed and duties fulfilled, and how breaches of their rules are enforced in relation to all the social positions in a community. So that he regards the same facts from a viewpoint which differs from that of the lawyer.

Now every one of these social positions carries with it certain ideals—a councillor is grave and impartial, a king is brave and just, there are the perfect husband and the perfect wife. Human frailty, alas, acting in the vicissitudes of life, is such that few people can live up to the ideals of the positions they occupy. But fortunately the law, both in England and in Barotseland, only demands that we attain these ideals up to a reasonable standard, so that most of us, despite our deserts, escape whipping. Therefore, trials often reduce to the question, was the defendant a reasonable councillor? a reasonable husband? or wife? or father? Even before that stage of the trial is reached, the judges in their cross-examination begin to assess litigants' behaviour against these standards. And because as an anthropologist I am dominantly interested in social positions, I came to concentrate in my study of Barotse law on the problem of the reasonable incumbent of a position, and to pull legal rules together about this problem. I began also to look anew, in these terms, at problems of English jurisprudence.

Every individual occupies several positions in society—as father, workman, citizen, and so forth. In Barotseland, because commercial life is little developed in a small-scale community, people act in all their capacities with the same lot of their fellows. Hence in any trial all of a person's actions, in his several roles, are considered by the judges in assessing the evidence against him. Let me illustrate this with a trial which I call 'The Case of the Eloping Wife'.

A Barotse woman married a foreign immigrant. They had a quarrel and the wife left home. Shortly afterwards her husband visited a nearby white township where he found his wife living with another man. He reported this to his wife's father, and sued the abductor for damages. The abductor and the woman pleaded in defence first, that the husband had divorced his wife by driving her away, and secondly that when the abductor went to the woman's father, the father demanded 30s. as marriage payment. Therefore, they argued, if the husband had not divorced his wife and he had a case for damages, it lay against the father who had married off his daughter before she'd been divorced from her husband. In the course of their statements the two defendants abused the husband as a foreigner.

It quickly became clear that the husband had a claim for damages against someone, since his wife could not prove that he had sent her away (as a man is entitled to do), nor had she obtained a divorce in court (which a woman must do). But was he to be recompensed for the loss of his wife by her abductor or by her father? The father admitted he had taken 30s. from the abductor, but he said he took the money as a fine for the abduction, and not as a marriage-payment to validate the new marriage.

The court satisfied itself that the father was telling the truth by the following cross-examination. Under questioning by the court, the woman said that after the quarrel she left her husband and stayed for two days in her father's home, from which he was absent for two days. On the third day she married the defendant. As she put it, 'I thought I would take my husband to court to get a divorce, then this man came to marry me and I saw time was passing, so I married him.' The judges burst into laughter and exclaimed: 'Time was passing, to wait two days!' That is, the judges have an idea of 'reasonable time' which reasonable people ought to take over certain social actions, and this involves that they conform with various customs and rules. Similarly, the abductor was forced to admit that the first night he slept with the woman they were fornicating, because it was only on the next day that he made payment to the woman's father. Again, this was not a reasonable and customary order of actions in time. The father argued that he could not have taken the money as a marriage-payment, since, in his words: 'How can you come to ask for a girl in marriage when you come from the bed on which you have slept with her?'

On this evidence the court had no hesitation in making the abductor pay the damages. The judges argued as follows: No father would accept marriage-payment for his daughter from a man who came to him from a bed shared with his daughter. That is, no reasonable father would do this. But they rebuked the father for taking the 30s. as a fine on abduction, since his daughter was stolen not as an unmarried ward of his, but as a married ward of her husband. The father must return the money to the abductor to give to the husband. Please note that this argument involves a judicial presumption about how fathers—reasonable fathers—behave. Secondly, no good woman, or reasonable woman, would in three days move from one marriage to another. And, as they showed the woman in another piece of cross-examination, no good woman goes by herself to her husband *before* arrangements are made with her father. She should be escorted to the husband's hut by a party of her friends and his. So too no reasonable would-be son-in-law would approach his sweetheart's father to seek her in marriage *after* sleeping with her. The time periods involved here were patently unreasonable: in some cases they involve complex calculations of gestation for women and cows, or the cycle of growing crops. Thirdly, the two defendants were bad citizens, not *reasonable* citizens: they had not waited for a court to adjudicate on the woman's quarrel with her husband, and they had abused the husband because he was a foreigner. On this the senior judge, in a speech which reminded me of Shylock's, said:

> About his being a foreigner. All the different tribes—they are all people under our one great king. . . . There is no such thing as a foreigner. We are one thing, with two eyes and two ears, and our children marry them. They feel hunger like us and ask us for land which we give to them.

Over all, in every one of their positions, the defendants had behaved unreasonably: the woman as wife, daughter, woman, and citizen: the man, as son-in-law, husband, and citizen. Hence their stories could be totally discredited. Thus there are implicit in the judges' views of the evidence a series of presumptions: that fathers will not take marriage-payments from seducers of their daughters; that reasonable and good daughters consult their fathers before marriage; that reasonable citizens seek the protection of the court and don't abuse foreign immigrants. These presumptions about how reasonable people behave flow into judgment but are not always formulated. They arise from the judges' views of morality, and of custom, and from their personal experience in society. Nor are all the presumptions rules of law. But they control the vital process of forming judgment on evidence. Some presumptions about witnesses' demeanour influence the value judges attach to the evidence of different people. By these presumptions about 'reasonable behaviour' the judges perform their vital task of assessing circumstantial evidence, which is what produces chanciness in litigation. Now the judges can state any presumption of this kind with the *ex cathedra* authority of a legal rule, since it can be absorbed in the meaning of '*reasonable* behaviour'. I do not mean to suggest that the judgments are entirely subjective, since there is continuous social control of the presumptions, and an accepted logic in the way judges have to expound their decisions: the logic of how reasonable fathers act, with its implied science of psychology, the logic that reasonable women seek divorce in courts, that reasonable women wait a reasonable time before remarrying, that reasonable suitors consult their sweetheart's parents and marry them usually with ceremonies.

But the presumptions can vary, and can be based on mistaken ideas, or rumours, or even personal prejudices. This is not a process confined to African judges. A learned but naïve South African judge is reputed to have once refused to grant a divorce although a detective proved the wife had spent an afternoon in a hotel with a man. The judge stated baldly that he did not believe people had sexual relations in the daylight: hence the alleged lovers would not have committed adultery even if they spent an afternoon in a bedroom.

Similar personal prejudices are exhibited in another Barotse case. A husband returned home from a visit to find his wife absent, and their children crying hungrily, unfed, and not sent back to school. He fed them. When his wife returned home she said she had been hoeing in her garden. This happened again the next day, and the wife made the same excuse. On the third day, when his wife was again late, the husband went to the garden and failed to find his wife. He therefore challenged her excuse and she admitted she had been lying in the bush with the defendant, a young teacher. The teacher denied the charge, and said when the husband sued him that the woman was using him to conceal her true lover. He alleged that she had a grudge against him because he had refused to accept her invitation, conveyed to him by letter, to become her lover. He asked the judges if a woman would thus admit who was her lover, just on her husband's challenge. The first judge accepted this argument on the grounds (which may or may not be true—I don't know) that a girl at her puberty ceremony is taught by the older women to conceal her true lover. This judge had a man's prejudice about women, whom—like all Barotse men—he holds responsible for all sexual lapses; hence this would be for him the behaviour of a reasonable woman—but not an upright woman. But the second judge smashed this argument: 'I've been caught in that way myself!' He had committed adultery and been exposed in this way. Hence his personal experience overcame the belief held by men about how women act. Some judges held that the evidence was not strong enough to convict; but most considered that if the teacher was innocent he would, like a reasonable man, have shown the woman's letter tempting him to adultery to her kinsmen, or to her husband immediately the husband returned. He would have done this especially as the woman had a bad reputation. Moreover, while the husband was away, he had sat at her hut and accepted food from her; and since there is a presumption in Barotseland that unrelated men and women do not have platonic relations, only a lover of the woman would act in this way. Hence, reasonably, he was guilty.

This last case suggests that the Barotse have a picture not only of reasonable and customary right ways of behaving, but also a picture of the reasonable wrongdoer—the reasonable thief, adulterer, slanderer, and so forth. By this paradox,—the reasonable wrongdoer—I sum up the fact that wrongdoers in any society also behave in customary ways which are socially stereotyped—there are the criminal slouch as against the scholarly stoop, the spiv's clothes and hairstyle,the whole manner of loitering with intent to commit a criminal action. When there is only circumstantial evidence, these sorts of actions build up before the judges till they conclude that, as in the Case of the Eloping Wife, the total picture is that of a reasonable wrongdoer—as we say, a person guilty beyond reasonable doubt. And I have heard cases which indicate that these customary ways of doing wrong in fact influence adulterers and thieves, so that they give themselves away in circumstances in which they could have acted so as to cover up their misdeeds.

Barotse judges have no police or detectives, no expertize of fingerprinting, no lawyers, to help them in collecting and sifting evidence. Therefore they have to depend almost entirely on their cross-examination of evidence to arrive at the truth. And for these reasons they must rely on testing the creditibility of a story told by any person against the flexible standards of reasonable behaviour for the incumbent of the social position involved. This is largely true of our own courts, though our lawyers and not our judges conduct the cross-examination. But this point is not always appreciated in the academic view of law. Nor do all lawyers see how these flexible standards enable the raw facts of a case to be fitted into the fixed and abstract rules of law. When I once lectured on this theme to an audience of Scottish lawyers, one of them protested on behalf of the poor Barotse that they should be so subjected to the control of the vague, ill-defined, litigation-breeding reasonable man. He asked if a code of the reasonable man could not be promulgated each year to protect them. This view fails to see the value of the concept. Many rules of law in Barotseland are necessarily general principles such as, 'a councillor must not be partial', or 'a husband must care well for his wife'. Beyond these are more general principles like, anyone who injures another shall make recompense. This principle exists in all systems of law. But in litigation these general rules have to cover a great variety of actual situations in life. They can only do so if the general moral ideas involved can be brought to bear on the particularities of a perhaps unique situation. This is the function of reasonable standards, and, despite aberrations of particular judges as in the cases of adultery I have just narrated, the standards are defined by the objective tests of traditional and developing customs and morals. For these general rules of law last through the life of a society despite great social changes. The development of 'reasonableness' for such positions as the reasonable husband, the reasonable wife, the reasonable landlord and tenant and king and subject, enables the law to cope with all changes. Without this the law would ossify.

This is well illustrated by a Barotse divorce suit—'The Case of the Prudish Wife'. Here the wife sued for divorce on several grounds. First she complained that when she was ill her husband did not treat her at his home, as required by law, but took her to her parents. The husband replied that he obtained to treat her a medicine which had to be inserted in cuts on her body; but he could not give her the medicine himself as she would not let him see her naked (astonishment in court). Then drums had to be beaten for her treatment and this could not be done in his village which was inhabited by converts to Jehovah's Witnesses who do not allow drumming. So he took her to her mother. The judges held that in the circumstances of the wife's unique prudery, and in the new situation created by the coming of the Jehovah's Witnesses Christian sect, a reasonable husband could only take her to her mother. She claimed divorce secondly because her husband before going to work at a distant place took from her some blankets, which he then used with a new wife—thus breaking the law which forbids a Barotse to confuse his relations with two wives. The court found that her husband had given her eight blankets (a new form of goods), that this was wealth by the standards of Barotse poverty, and that he could therefore *reasonably* take back two blankets for himself on a new type of journey—and then use them with a new wife. He was a reasonable husband and her plea for divorce was rejected. Thus in fact many cases are decisions about whether a person has been a reasonable husband, or other incumbent of a particular social position.

In this way Barotse judges are constantly re-defining the scope of 'reasonable' standards for spouses, kinsfolk, lords and underlings, so as to handle new conditions of life. Judicial decision supplements legislation. Through the 'reasonable standards' they maintain their traditional laws and traditional morals, and yet cope with the effects of the introduction of Christianity and schools, labour for whites and money and trade-goods, new skills, changes in every aspect of Barotse life. Hence it seems to me that it is in the study of the reasonable man, in every society, that anthropologists and lawyers can meet. In him social principles and prejudices, customs and habits, group interests and individual experiences, are absorbed, to relate the fixed rules of law to the changing variety of life. But the law aims at justice, and the idea of a reasonable man implies an upright man. I shall next describe what the Barotse think about the upright man.

The Case of the 'Dog-in-the-Manger' Headman

Generally, Barotse law demands from people only reasonable exercise of rights, and correspondingly only reasonable fulfilment of duties. This is all the judges will enforce. But in practice Barotse judges tend to erect higher standards—those of the upright man, or woman—the upright husband, wife, lord or underling. In this way they bring into the trial the ultimate standards of Barotse ethics, which lie beyond those of the law. The law demands right and reasonable action: morality asks for right and generous action. A man should not insist on the letter of his rights, and he should be prodigal in meeting his obligations.

This does not mean that the judges can enforce these very high ethical standards, but only that they set upright behaviour as the goal of all good men and women. They can only *order* men to meet the demands of the law. For example, under Barotse law a man can divorce his wife by sending her home to her parents. If he does this, the court will compel him to give her half of the crops she planted in his land, and also half of the goods in their house—dresses, pots, blankets and so forth. A woman must sue in court for a divorce and has to establish that her husband has not been a reasonable husband. If she gets her divorce, she obtains half the crops grown by *her* labour, but on *his* land. However, as she rejects the marriage, she also rejects all the goods which his earnings have bought for her own needs and for her domestic tasks. I once heard a case tried in which the woman thus established her claim to be divorced. Listen to the senior judge's decision: 'The woman is freed, and she will take home with her half of the crops which she planted. There has been so much ill-feeling in this case that we will send a judge to see that it is fairly done'. Turning to the husband he went on: 'Now what else, my kinsman, will you give her of the goods of the marriage to take with her?'

The husband objected: 'I will give her nothing; she has infected me with disease, and bound me here with lies.' The judge admonished him:

> Come, my kinsman, you cannot do this. When you married her, taking her from her parents, you all rejoiced together. You hoped that you would have a strong marriage, with children to bind you together. It has not worked out thus, but you cannot send a woman home to her parents, naked like a dog. We beg you, give her a blanket and a dress and some plates.

But the husband persisted in his meanness: 'I will give her nothing, not even a shawl.'

The judge had to resign himself to this: 'Very well; we have power to make you divide the crops, and we will send someone to see this is done. But we have not power to make you behave like an upright man. Go.'

Later that day the husband craved permission to speak again to the court. He said he had been reflecting on the judge's words, and saw that he was wrong. He would give his wife a dress, a shawl, a blanket, a hoe, a pot and a plate.

The judge approved: 'We thank you, my child. This is behaving like a decent upright man.' And he called on the other judges to salute this generosity.

This case shows that the law limits the extent to which judges can enforce morality. Judges on occasion, in Barotseland as in England, cannot enforce upright behaviour, and may even have to find for the person who has behaved wrongfully by moral standards, but who is supported by the law. The judges find for the wrongdoer in the interests of certainty of law; our maxim states, 'Hard cases make bad law.' The Barotse say, 'It is hard, but it is the law.' Sometimes an English judge feels compelled to say something after this form to a wrongful litigant: 'Fortunately for you this is a court of law, and not a court of justice or morals.' And he then proceeds to upbraid in round terms the litigant who is successful in law but morally in the wrong. Conversely, a judge may openly state his reluctance to convict a person who is legally a wrongdoer, but morally justified. I do not believe that these situations arise because a court is only a forum of law, and not a source of justice and morality. I myself consider that these situations demonstrate that courts of law are in fact courts of morality: for the judge uses his high office publicly to state what morality demands and to upbraid the person who has departed from it and kept within the law, or to justify the person who is trapped by a technical law or driven by altruistic motives to commit an offence. This is certainly the way in which Barotse regard their judges and their courts.

Let me quote another divorce case to emphasize the point. The Barotse believe that it is natural to help one's blood relatives, and that the true test of the upright man is how he behaves to his relatives-in-law. In this case the wife made various allegations about her husband's neglect of herself and her relatives, but the court accepted his evidence, backed by her own parents, that he had behaved more than punctiliously. The senior judge rejected the pleas for divorce thus:

> You, woman, have astonished us by your suit. You thought you would shame your husband before the country, which we represent. But you have instead brought honour to him, for we have never heard of so good a son-in-law. Your father told us the overcoat he wears is a present from your husband; see how your husband sits himself in a ragged jacket. He is not a rich man, but when he brought an overcoat for his father, he brought one for your father; when he brought a dress for his mother, he brought one for your mother. He gave shawls to your unmarried sisters, and he built granaries for them, and moved their crops on the flood, not in the dugout of your village, but in his own dugout. And so forth. You have not disgraced your husband here before the judges of the land, but you have brought fame to him, for none of us is as good a son-in-law as he. You, my son, we admire what you have done, and we thank you. Do not cease to behave thus because your wife has brought you to court; continue to look after your relatives-in-law as you have done in the past. We thank you.

He then instructed his fellow-judges, and all in court, to join him in saluting the husband.

I mention these two cases because they show the judges upholding, to a mean husband and to a generous husband, the ideal of the man who is upright beyond the demands of reasonable standards. Their standards are similar in cases of property-holding and of contract, but to describe these would involve me in the intricacies of the Barotse environmental situation. Marital relations are familiar to us from our own life—they are the same the whole world over. But these cases did not catch the judges between the law and morality. Here is a case—'The Case of the Dog-in-the-Manger Headman'—which did this. It led to divergent judgments.

The Barotse dwell in higher places of land in the great Zambesi flood-plain which is their habitat. From these islands—as they are during the flood—the Barotse cultivate pockets of alluvial soil and use sites for fish-traps. I was told again and again that in Barotse law a man has to dwell in a village if he wishes to work any of the resources which belong to the village. If he leaves the village, he loses his rights in its land. This land is vested in the title of the village-headman.

A certain village-headman, named Mahalihali, was very quarrelsome, and his bad temper drove many people out of the village. He personally expelled one of his daughters whom he accused of sorcery. Eventually he died and his son inherited his position, and took his title as Mahalihali the Second. He found himself with a village, but few villagers. His nephew, son of the sister expelled from the village, was using some of its trap-sites in a fish-dam, but was living with his widowed mother in her mother's village. Another sister of the new headman had married into a nearby village and her sons were using a fish-dam which her father had let her have. The new headman brought a suit that his sisters and their sons must stop using the fish-dams unless they moved into his village. The judges satisfied themselves that the one sister, accused of sorcery, had been badly wronged when she was driven out of the village. Since then she and her son, and the married sister married nearby and her sons—that is, all the defendants—had behaved with proper respect to the headman. Hence arose the judges' dilemma. The law, I repeat, is clear: if you do not live in my village, you lose your rights in its land. By this rule the headman was upheld in his claim that the others join his village or cease to use its fish-dams. But the defendants had not done him any wrong, and the headman was behaving unjustly—like the dog-in-the-manger in our fable. How did the judges solve this dilemma.

In Barotse courts when the judges come to give their decision, the most junior judge speaks first, and then his seniors in turn, until the head of the court gives judgment. This is the binding decision, even if it contradicts the verdicts of all other judges, though it is referred to the king in his palace for confirmation. Well, the first three judges felt themselves bound by the basic premiss of their land-tenure law; the dog-in-the-manger headman was entitled to expel his sisters and their sons from the dams unless they moved into his village. *But* they all stressed that he ought not to treat his relatives in this niggardly way since there was more land than his villagers could use; being rich, he ought to help his relatives. Nevertheless, the dams were his. The next set of judges were reluctant to apply the letter of the law in favour of the dog-in-the-manger headman, against people who, in their words, had 'done nothing wrong'. Many judges told the headman, 'If they had done wrong, you would have a case.' Most judges therefore contented themselves with stating the moral issue, that he ought to let his relatives fish. One said the fish-dams had passed out of his control, though this was upsetting the basic law of Barotse landholding. But the senior judge sitting in court returned to this basic law: the dams were the headman Mahalihali's. But, the judge added, he ought to let his kin fish them. As it happens, the head of the court was busy on administrative business elsewhere. Next day he came to deliver his decision on the basis of reports of evidence and judgments made to him by other judges. He found the headman still insisting on his rights to take the dams unless the others moved to join him, as laid down in the last decision. So the head of the court found a brilliant solution to the judicial dilemma. The dams clearly belonged to the title Mahalihali; but if the present incumbent of that title was not upright—generous to his kin who did not live with him—the court would discharge him from his headmanship and appoint a more generous successor.

What happened here was that the judge achieved a just and equitable solution by stressing a new kind of sanction. He invoked the administrative powers of the court to discharge unsatisfactory headmen, in order to compel a headman to be generous in exercising his rights. In this way, the judge enforced the standards of the upright headman in favour of the defendants who had done no wrong, while he maintained the basic law of land tenure. For the fish-dams remained vested in the headman's title.

This case shows strikingly that Barotse courts are dominated by ideas of justice and equity. These ideas influence their total evaluation of evidence; and on occasion spur them to apply particular equities, as against the dog-in-the-manger headman. The Barotse believe that justice in this sense is self-evident to all men, and they call their principles within this justice, laws of God, or laws of humankind. That is, the Bartose have a clear idea of natural justice, which they constantly apply. They apply natural justice, of course, within particular economic and social conditions: for they have set ideas on the relations of men and women, lords and underlings, and so forth. But it is natural justice. And natural justice involves for them, as for us, certain ultimate principles of law, as that a man who injures another shall make recompense; no man should be judge in his own suit; a judge should not come to a decision before hearing both sides; a man should be generous and not mean. These and other moral rules they share with us; and the rules are axiomatic, they cannot be demonstrated. An example of such a rule is equivalent to the Roman Law maxim, *volenti non fit injuria*: a man who willingly exposes himself to injury, cannot sue for damages if he is then injured. The Barotse maxim is, 'If you are invited to a meal and a fish-bone sticks in your throat, you cannot sue your host.' Under this rule (which they say is patently fair), they will not allow damages to a man who is injured in a fishing-party when men enter a pool at the dry season, and blindly hurl bundles of spears to get catfish buried in the mud. Nor will they allow damages to a man injured on a hunt. Nor did they allow damages to a woman who became pregnant, or contracted venereal disease, in illicit intercourse—though they have now, by statute, imposed penalties on the man who infects a woman thus.

These general moral rules, and a host of particular rules defining Barotse personal relations, property-holding, contracts, and so forth, constitute the total body of Barotse law. Besides moral rules, the body of law embraces customary ways and relations, statutes of their king and of the British Government, judicial precedents. Their law includes the ordered regularities of the environment, of organic life, and of human psychology—what we call scientific laws. The judges draw on all these sources to make their decisions. But the different rules of this body of law are not entirely dependent on one another. And the judges therefore can achieve justice by applying different rules in different situations, according to how they see the moral deserts of the parties. In contract to the case of the dog-in-the-manger headman, I heard several cases in which the judges insisted on the rule that if a man leaves a village, he loses his rights to land in it; but these were cases where the underlings were in the wrong. Where it was the dog-in-the-manger headman who was in the wrong, the judges did not want to support him. Some judges felt compelled to do so, against their view of the moral merits of the case, in order to meet the demand for certainty of law. Others tried to vary the law to meet those moral merits. The final decision seized on a different rule—the power of the court to discharge unsatisfactory headmen—to achieve justice, while maintaining the law of land-tenure itself.

This decision illustrates one important way in which judicial discretion can operate in the interests of justice. The body of Barotse law consists of a large number of different kinds of rules. These rules may be consistent with one another, but they do not depend on one another. There is no essential logical interdependence between the rule that a man loses his rights in land belonging to a village if he leaves the village, and the rule that the court can discharge an unsatisfactory headman. The judges can often, as in this case, decide to apply one rule rather than another, out of the whole body of law, to achieve justice. In doing so, they—so to speak *manipulate* the independence of the rules. This gives great scope to intelligent judicial discretion.

But the judges' main power to manipulate legal rules during a trial arises from the nature of the words which compose the rules. A law such as that if a man leaves a village he loses his rights in its land is a general statement: in particular disputes the judges have to apply it to very different circumstances. Do these actions amount to 'leaving' the village? In the case of the dog-in-the-manger headman, for instance, one woman did not 'leave' village; on the contrary, she was driven out of it. If a simple word like 'leaves' requires this kind of interpretation the problem becomes more complex and uncertain with the abstract ideas of law. But there is an inherent uncertainty of this kind in all legal words, which enables them to cover a great variety of actual events. And application of these uncertain concepts to actual events is the major part of the judges' task. In the case I have been describing, what is an 'unsatisfactory' headman? He is, by prevailing standards, not a 'reasonable' headman. We are back with the 'reasonable' man; and I have already shown that this valuable uncertainty is a prime characteristic of 'the reasonable man'.

The Case of the Unfaithful Councillor

The divorce rate in Barotseland is very high. Men can divorce their wives simply by sending them home; women have to go to a Barotse court and establish a case for their release from marriage. They can do so successfully on many grounds. In fact a woman has only to show that her husband has not behaved as a reasonable husband to her in order to obtain a divorce.

What then, for the Barotse, is a reasonable husband? He is one who cares properly for his wife, sleeps with her adequately so that she has children, does not discriminate between her and his other wives, and does not drive her out of his home. These are old rules of Barotse law which date from the days before the British protectorate was established. And Barotse life has altered considerably since those days. Women who previously wore one skin-skirt and had a skin-rug, now want dresses, petticoats, shawls and blankets. They need kerosene lamps, iron pots, plates and cups and cutlery, and many other of the goods of our civilization. Some men can earn the money to purchase these things by selling fish, cattle or crops; but most Barotse men have to go out for long periods to earn wages at distant European settlements. And it is therefore in a radically different situation that Barotse judges now apply their ancient rules about the duties of husbands and the rights of wives. The judges have continually to decide what amount of goods a husband must nowadays give his wife if he is to be a reasonable husband. To do this they interpret what is the meaning of 'care for a wife' by reasonable modern standards.

One element in the modern situation produces a radical conflict to prevent a husband fulfilling two of his conjugal duties. He has to buy European goods for his wife, and to do this he must go away to work: then he cannot sleep with her and be a companion to her. The Barotse have therefore by legislation fixed a maximum period for which a husband can be away. If a husband is away for longer than this period his wife is entitled to a divorce. And while he is away, he must send goods or money to her. These statutes aim to bring the nation's men home and to maintain contented marriages. But a difficult legal problem arose even out of the apparently simple judicial task of deciding whether a husband has been absent for the set period. A woman brought suit for divorce on grounds that her husband had been away for longer than the period allowed: his kinsmen opposed the suit, pleading that he had sent her money, blankets, and so forth. The court held, 'This woman did not marry a blanket', and granted the divorce. Within a few days the husband arrived: he had been on the journey home when the divorce was granted. His wife wished to return to him, but her father demanded a new marriage-payment for what, under the court's decision for divorce, was a new marriage. The court held that had it known the husband was on his way home, it would not have granted a divorce. The court thus interpreted 'return home' to mean 'leave place of employment', because the purpose of the statute is to maintain marriages. The judges thus upheld what they believed to be good morals and public policy.

This case seems simple enough, but it illustrates a crucial task which Barotse judges have to perform if they are to help their people adjust to the new situation in which they are living. The judges have constantly to reinterpret their definitions of what are reasonable husbands and wives, reasonable councillors and headmen, and so forth. This process of defining how a reasonable incumbent of some social position should behave, lies at the core of the way in which judges nowadays define what is reasonable companionship of husband and wife, in terms of modern conditions. These new conditions and the standards they contain according to modern public opinion, are brought into the law through the elasticity of the concept 'reasonableness'. And meanwhile the basic law remains unchanged from the very different past—a husband must be a reasonable husband.

Here is a case in a different kind of relationship to illustrate the elasticity of legal concepts, and to show how this elasticity enables the law to cope with new situations. I call it 'The Case of the Unfaithful Councillor'. Some villages in the Barotse plain on the Upper Zambezi belong to members of the royal family. These princes and princesses may not actually reside in their villages, which they leave in charge of a headman. Under Barotse law a man holds land first by being a citizen; and he is entitled to keep that land as long as he is a faithful subject of the king. Secondly, he must be a member of a village, and he must be a faithful underling of the owner of the village, respectful and helpful. In 1945 a certain princess had as headman of one of her villages a councillor holding the title Indiye. She sued to have him dismissed from the title, and from its rights in village and land, on the grounds that he did not work for her. He pleaded in defence that he worked as overseer of a barge carrying goods down the 300 miles of the Zambezi from Barotseland to Livingstone. He had no time to work for her or attend on her. The court held that this plea indeed absolved him, since men nowadays earn their living by working for Europeans, and not for their Barotse overlords. But he did not go to say farewell to the princess before he started on a journey, or to greet her when he returned. This he could easily do. Hence, he did not respect the princess, and was not faithful to her, and so he merited dismissal from her village. The court thus defined 'faithful'—and incidentally a reasonably faithful councillor—to accommodate modern conditions. But the law remains that a man must be faithful to his overlord.

These judicial problems are common to all countries. Judges have to apply certain well-known rules to the great variety of circumstances which occur in social life, and which may well be changing, as they are in modern Barotseland. Judges must maintain the law, in the sense of abiding by its rules, and yet they must serve justice in every case if possible. I am suggesting that they do so by manipulating the uncertainty which resides in all words when these are applied to the facts of life. Is this 'two years' absence? Is this 'caring for a wife'? Is this 'fidelity to an overlord'? The judges make these definitions in terms of 'reasonableness' for a particular kind of reasonable man—husband or councillor or citizen or son. And because 'reasonableness' itself is flexible, they can adapt a persisting body of legal rules to quite new conditions and standards. Therefore the law remains certain, since Barotse judges state their decisions in terms of old well-established rules. But my examples show that judicial decisions, and hence litigation, are often uncertain.

So that when judges are interpreting words by applying them to external facts, they do so by the flexible test of 'reasonableness'. This allows them great play, and it means that they can introduce into their decisions a whole variety of social presumptions, and indeed of prejudices personal to them, or peculiar to the group they represent. But on the whole the standard of 'reasonableness' is drawn from the Barotse community as a whole —Barotse public opinion, and customs, and standards. And all these change as Barotse life changes, and the law develops to accommodate new facts. In short, changing Barotse life itself controls the way in which Barotse judges reinterpret legal concepts.

Barotse judges have had to reinterpret sharply the implications of many of their legal concepts to meet this abruptly changed situation. Hence we can see clearly in their judicial process a problem which is present in our own. Let me illustrate this. Section 154 of our Public Health Act of 1936 lays down that a rag-and-bone merchant shall not give children under 14 'any article whatsoever'. In 1952 a rag-and-bone merchant gave a child a goldfish, and a stipendiary magistrate held that the goldfish was not 'an article' in the meaning of this section. About a year later a bench of justices held that a live chick was an article for purposes of the statute, and another bench held again that a goldfish was *not* an article. This last case went on appeal to a court of three judges who dismissed the appeal and upheld the view that a goldfish is not an article—though it was said that if the goldfish were in a bowl, that bowl would be an article. The word 'article' was here being defined for purposes of a statute which aimed to prevent the spread of disease: under another statute, 'article' might cover goldfish; and the court followed the rule that where a penalty is imposed, it applies the narrow interpretation in favour of the accused. As the judges put it, 'Would anyone in common parlance talk about a goldfish as an article? I do not think they would. . . . I think that it is a straining of language to say a goldfish is an article.'

I do not believe there is any way in which we can establish by objective evidence, so to speak, that a chicken or a goldfish is or is not an article. But I have already said that the process of decision is not entirely subjective. In English law the process is controlled by written rules, judicial precedents, and textbooks of law. But something else is left—the question which is so often framed, 'Would a reasonable man call a goldfish an article?' This passes the uncertainty to, what is a reasonable man? And here I have suggested that defining the reasonable man—which is indirectly defining an 'article'—may give room for judges to introduce not only social ideas, but also individual prejudices, into their decisions. I take the goldfish case as an entirely hypothetical example—I feel safer that way. I can imagine a judge who feels that there is too much statutory interference in our lives interpreting the word 'article' as narrowly as possible; while a judge who favours benevolent government control would interpret it widely. This is a possibility only; and I use it just to illustrate that the uncertainty which resides in all words, allows judges to manipulate the words in the interests of what they believe to be justice. In doing so, they accommodate into their decisions changes in public opinion and in morals.

It is obvious that this flexibility of words is a great source of strength in judicial logic. Without it, judges could not apply the general rules of law to actual disputes. Despite this, many academic lawyers have attacked it as a source of uncertainty in law, and have therefore regarded it as a weakness. Even judges have done so. But judges are more aware of the value of this characteristic of words. This is clearly exhibited in the words of Lord Chief Justice Coleridge: 'The Attorney-General has asked us where we are to draw the line. The answer is that it is not necessary to draw it at any precise point. It is enough for us to say that the present case is on the right side of any reasonable line that could be drawn.' This judicial statement seems to me to sum up admirably the judicial value of uncertainty in reference of legal terms. Every case is in a sense unique. How is a unique case to be settled? It may have to be covered by legal rules which are stated in very abstract terms, such as that any man who injures another shall make recompense. Even if the rule contains as specific a term as 'article', some judicial decision on the application of the terms to the facts of the situation must be made. What test can there be except that of 'reasonableness'?

But 'reasonableness' itself has a great deal of uncertainty. The line may be drawn differently by different judges. More importantly, it will be drawn differently by judges in new centuries, in accordance with new standards and problems and with advancing knowledge. There may be aberrant decisions: most societies have foolish, ignorant, and perhaps even unjust, judges. But generally the judges will be influenced by changing public opinion in their community, or at least that section of the community from which they are drawn.

Imprecision is thus an inherent attribute of legal concepts. Yet a few years ago a Professor of Jurisprudence complained that, 'Philosophy stands out as a striking example of the flatulencies that may gather round the unacknowledged puns of language. On the whole, lawyers have appreciated the danger, and have been at pains to construct and preserve a moderately precise technical language. Oddly enough, it is least precise in its most fundamental parts. We use the word "right" in some half-dozen different senses and often pass insensibly from one to the other, of course with disastrous results upon our reasoning.' Thus the jurist. As an anthropologist I would suggest that the results may have been disastrous for the reasoning of formal logic; but they may well have resulted, in judicial logic, in a number of very just decisions. Judicial logic has rules of its own: by formal logic alone a judge could not fit the raw facts of evidence into legal categories. Nor could he get justice. For example, this word 'right' that has some half-dozen meanings. I heard Barotse judges in many cases listen to evidence on a whole series of actions by the litigants: then come to the conclusion that, say, defendant had done 'right'. From this they made a jump to saying he was in the 'right', therefore that he had 'a right' to the piece of land in dispute. Then they manipulated the rules of law to defend that right. Here are three different meanings of 'right'—Barotse also have one word for all three, and this word also means 'duty'. So they can make a 'right' into a 'duty'. It is, formally, bad logic: but it may be brilliant judicial logic.

I think myself that it is not at all odd that lawyers' language should be least precise in its most fundamental parts—terms like law, right and duty, crime and injury, property, and so forth. For clearly these are the words which have to serve the most manifold functions in a legal system. They have to cover the greatest number of types of legal situations, and within each type, the greatest variety of actual situations. Hence I would expect them to have the greatest imprecision; and therefore to be capable of the greatest judicial manipulation.

Since Barotse law is unwritten I was made vividly aware of how important is this judicial manipulation. It convinced me that while it is obviously necessary for jurists to dispute this manipulation, they might also accept imprecision as an attribute—and clearly a valuable attribute—of legal concepts. Once one makes this acceptance, one can begin to study how and why judges operate the imprecision of their verbal apparatus. And there are different kinds of imprecision. The Barotse word *swanelo* covers 'right' and 'duty', and as a 'right' or 'duty' it refers to many different kinds of actions and claims. Most fundamental concepts—like 'law' and 'injury' and 'property'—have this kind of imprecision. Other concepts are elastic in that they can be stretched to cover different kinds of action—and frequently they form pairs which can only be defined in terms of one another, such as 'guilt' and 'innocence', or 'negligence' and 'due care'. They form two poles at each end of an elastic line along which litigants' behaviour can be measured. But it is a reasonably elastic line. Barotse judges listen to the evidence, stretch the elastic concepts to decide which man is 'guilty' and which is 'innocent', and then cover these decisions by applying to them the concepts of right and duty which can refer to many things.

In doing this the judges have to make words like 'guilt', or 'negligence', or 'right', cover a great variety of facts. Therefore I call the concepts 'absorbent', for they absorb into their abstract categories the raw material of life. And they have another important attribute. A survey of the law of all societies shows that they have the same fundamental conceptions—law itself, right, duty, property, guilt, innocence—and, in addition, these conceptions are built into similar principles. But they operate in quite different social conditions. Therefore I call them 'permeable'—they are permeated by their social background. A husband must everywhere be reasonable: but the demands on a reasonable husband vary from country to country and at different periods in the same country.

Acceptance of this inherent imprecision of words immediately disposes of certain long-standing controversies in jurisprudence. What is 'law'? Many volumes have been written proffering various definitions. But 'law', which has to cover every kind of regularity in social and physical and organic life, the whole process of social control, and so forth, cannot be restricted within a single definition. The *Concise Oxford Dictionary* gives thirteen definitions: obviously then for every definition advanced by one scholar, another definition can be advanced by another scholar. This breeds only fruitless controversy. The Barotse word *mulao*, which can be translated—reasonably translated—as 'law', means a body of rules accepted by the community as binding, a particular decision of a court, the existence of courts, a personal habit, the regularities of the natural world and of human physiology and psychology and so forth. It is all regularity and order, and all control, Hence it has to be accepted as having many definitions.

At the moment, in particular, controversy rages between orthodox jurists who hold that law is certain, and a so-called sceptical or realist school of American lawyers, who hold that law is uncertain. If we examine their arguments, it is obvious that they are talking about law in two different kinds of senses. Those who insist on law's certainty are examining law in the sense of a body of rules, which judges use and in terms of which they state their decisions. The sceptical lawyers who consider the certainty of law to be a myth are speaking of judges' decisions, and guesses as to future probable decisions. Only those who know nothing of litigation can doubt that law in this sense is uncertain and chancy. But law in this sense—going to law—is litigation. And it results in adjudication. Law in the orthodox sense is a known code of moral principles and legal rules many of which have endured for centuries and are known in most countries—in Ancient Rome, in France and England, and in Barotseland. The body of rules is fairly certain; judges' decisions, in terms of those rules, on various disputes may be uncertain. But the decisions are given in those rules. They can be given thus because the rules are composed of flexible concepts which can be permeated by changing social presumptions and which can absorb the variety of life itself. The 'certainty' of law depends on the 'uncertainty' of its basic concepts. I have punned on the word 'certainty': but I hope this does not negate the value of my paradox.

I. Schapera: A Handbook of Tswana Law and Custom*

Responsibility and Intent

In Tswana law the head of each family is responsible for all his dependants. His wife, unmarried children, and servants cannot as a rule take legal action against other people unless assisted and represented by him, nor can they be sued except through him. No contract entered into by them is valid unless approved of by him. He is further responsible for the payment of their debts, as well as of any fines imposed upon them or damages awarded against them. But where they commit an offence meriting punishment by thrashing, it is the actual offender who is punished, and not his guardian. The owner of livestock is similarly liable for any damage they do, provided it can be shown that he has failed to look after them properly. These different aspects of responsibility will be discussed more fully in due course.

Formerly, if a man was himself unable to pay his debts, fines or damages, his near relatives were expected, and could sometimes be forced, to come to his aid. Nowadays this principle of collective responsibility is no longer so generally observed, although, as will be shown in later chapters, it has by no means completely died out. Another field in which its operation may still be observed is the regimental organization. Should any man violate certain of the regimental laws, then not only he but all his age-mates with him at the time are punished. If a fine is imposed, each of them must pay the full amount; if a thrashing is administered, each of them undergoes it. This point will also be more fully discussed in due course, together with other aspects of the regimental system.

Every adult person is presumed to know the law, and to have intended the results following an act he has committed. Motive is not generally taken into consideration, although malicious prosecution of an innocent person may entitle the victim to damages for defamation. Allowance is, however, made for provocation, so that assault, and formerly even homicide, is in certain cases held to be justifiable and so is excused. Negligence, as a rule involves liability for any resulting damage. Purely accidental wrongs are, on the other hand, almost invariably excused or far less heavily penalized. Less liability attaches to an unsuccessful attempt to do wrong than to one which has succeeded. The former, indeed, is not often brought to trial, for Tswana law in the main takes cognizance only of wrongs which have actually been perpetrated. So, too, the amount of damage actually inflicted is taken into consideration in assessing the amount of punishment or compensation: e.g. a thief stealing two head of cattle is not so heavily penalized as one stealing four.

The character of a wrongdoer also plays an important part in determining the attitude adopted towards him. If he readily admits his offence, he may be dealt with lightly, and sometimes even excused altogether. But if he is insolent or obstreperous, even in the face of overwhelming evidence against him, he will be penalized more severely than usual. Similarly, an habitual offender is always more severely penalized than a first offender.

Another important factor is the relative status of the persons concerned in a case. The proverb says: *Ga re lebe motho, re leba molato*, 'We are not so much concerned with the

* I. Schapera, *A Handbook of Tswana Law and Custom*, Oxford University Press, 1938, pp. 50–52.

person as with his fault'; and again: *Molao sefofu, o bile o tle o je mong wa 6nê*, 'The law is blind, it even eats up its owner.' In theory, that is, there is no distinction between Chief and commoner, rich man and poor man. In practice this doctrine is qualified in several ways. Offences against a person senior to the wrongdoer in position or age are always regarded as more reprehensible than they would be if the positions were reversed; and the sentence of the court is determined accordingly. This is particularly so where the offence is committed against the Chief. Conversely, it is difficult, sometimes impossible, to obtain justice where the offender is the Chief himself or one of his senior relatives. Similarly, offences against a kinsman or member of the same ward are often treated more lightly by the victim than where the offender is an outsider. There is a greater readiness to claim nominal damages, or even to overlook the offence altogether. So, too, offending foreigners are on the whole more harshly judged than members of the tribe. *Lesepa legolo la moeng, la mong wa gae le pitikwa ke dikhukhwane*, says the proverb: 'The dung of a stranger is great, that of the citizen is rolled away by the beetles', i.e. the faults of strangers are magnified, while those of fellow tribesmen (or kinsmen) are passed over lightly.

G. S. Snell: Nandi Customary Law*

Responsibility and Motive

A man was held responsible for his wives' and children's conduct and for the payment of any penalties arising from their misdeeds. If he was unable to pay on their account or on account of an offence of his own, his near clan relatives were under a moral and sometimes enforceable obligation to assist him.

In assessing culpability, motive and intent, as in most communities in which the doctrine of collective responsibility applies, were not of any great account. Severe provocation, however, was taken into consideration and in some cases was held to justify assault and even homicide—if, for instance, retaliation followed immediately upon the provocation. Accidental damage, except to the person, was in general not punishable and attempted wrongs only mildly so, but negligence was actionable for compensation.

Insanity was treated as sickness and not socially ridiculed. An insane person was not maltreated or out-cast, for fear of his curse. A married man was looked after by his wife and she could not obtain a separation on the grounds of her husband's derangement. A violently mad person was tethered in a hut by himself and fed by his relatives. His children were placed in the custody of those persons who would have had charge of them had he died; if he recoverd he could claim them back. The property of an insane man was not distributed until his death.

Offences by an insane person were not punished but blood-money was payable if he killed another person. A man could not plead that he was insane when he committed an act for which he was being tried. A man who was believed to be feigning madness at his trial would have his case adjourned. If he appeared to be acting normally after a few days he would be punished as guilty.

* G. S. Snell, *Nandi Customary Law*, Macmillan & Co. Ltd., 1954, pp. 83–84.

Part III

THE LAW OF CONTRACT

The law of contract does not appear to form a very substantial part of African customary law. It is not entirely clear what the reason for this is. It may be the result of a tendency on the part of writers to ignore this topic in favour of others; it could be that contractual relations are not very elaborately developed in African society; and that the writers were therefore unable to discover very much material on the topic. In any event, early writers on customary law paid very little attention to contract, and it is only more recently that the subject has been dealt with at all systematically. Even within this change of attitude, however, there is still a tendency to see contract as an aspect of, or a development out of status—thus following Maine's classic dictum on the movement from status to contract. This view appears to have been adopted in the extract by *Gluckman*, given in this chapter, and is thus in contrast to the article by *Schapera* with which the chapter opens. The latter is concerned to show, as a result of the investigation of case material, that a generalised set of rules governing contractual obligations exists separately in Tswana customary law. *Elias*, who rejects the suggestion that there is no general law of contract, bases a good deal of his argument on marriage and its related contracts; and, in the process succeeds in pointing out that customary law does recognise executory contracts. (See, however, *Gluckman's* disagreement with this at pp. 218–219.)

The second chapter provides more detailed information on the specific contracts which are recognised in customary law. It is significant, here, that all the contracts described—by *Elias* for Nigeria, *Lawrance* for the Iteso of East Africa and *Seymour* on the various tribes of South Africa—are very much of the same pattern wherever they occur. It is important to note, too, that few of the contracts described can be adequately understood without a more thorough grasp of the law of persons, the law of marriage or the law of property to which they are inevitably related in one way or another.

Chapter 10

PRINCIPLES OF LIABILITY

I. Schapera: Contract in Tswana Law*

The material presented in this paper has been selected from records of nearly 1,950 cases tried by Tswana tribal courts in the Bechuanaland Protectorate, mainly during

* I. Schapera, 'Contract in Tswana Law', in *Journal of African Law*, Vol. 9, No. 3, pp. 142–153.

the period 1935–1940. The Protectorate Administration in 1935 made the keeping of written case records obligatory in all the courts officially recognized in that year as 'tribunals'[1]; previously only the Ngwaketse had done so systematically, for 1910–1916 and 1928–1934. As opportunity arose while I was doing anthropological fieldwork among the Tswana (intermittently, in 1929–1943), I made an abstract, and occasionally a complete copy of every case recorded by the chief's courts and a few district courts ('junior tribunals') in the nine tribes I was able to visit.[2]

Of those cases, 310 related directly to breach or alleged breach of contract. I have already described in some detail elsewhere the main features of the Tswana law of contract.[3] This paper should therefore be regarded primarily as a collection of case material illustrating those features; it does not profess to cover the topic fully. I hope, nevertheless, that it will serve to convey some idea of the kinds of legal issues relating to contract with which Tswana courts usually have to deal. I state briefly, in each section, the rules normally recognized by the courts, and then cite a few cases that seem to be relevant.

Formation

A contract in Tswana law is, basically, a voluntary agreement (*tumalano*) between two parties, imposing obligations upon one (or both), and reciprocally conferring rights upon the other (or both). Both the obligation and the reciprocal rights are called by the same term, *tshwanelo,* of which the most suitable English translation is 'due' (cf. 'due by A', 'due to B').

(*a*) A bare promise is sufficient to make an agreement legally binding.

1. A (Lekwee) promised his wife B, when they got married, that he would not become a polygamist. He afterwards wanted to marry someone else. B (Goitumelang) thereupon complained at court that he was 'putting her away' by breaking his promise, since she would not live with a co-wife. A said he wanted B to remain his wife, but he wanted to marry the other woman also. Asked by the judge if it was true he had promised not to marry polygamously, he replied, yes. Held: 'In that case you must carry out your promise.' (*Goitumelang* v. *Lekwee*, Ngwaketse, 74/1913[4].)

2. A (Mosele) hired B (Frank) to build a hut for him, and said he would supply the bricks needed. B later complained in court that he could not start work, because A had not kept his promise. A said he had told B there were no bricks, but that he would make them. Held: B should look for other work in the meantime, A was to call him when the bricks were ready, and two men were appointed 'to watch the progress of the hut'. (*Frank Curtin* v. *Mosele Kelefile*, Ngwaketse, 9/1930.)

(*b*) Contractual obligations are occasionally one-sided, as when A donates goods or services to B. He cannot subsequently revoke his gift (unless made to his child or other dependant), nor can he claim any form of payment, etc., in return.

3. A (Monnaagomo) claimed payment for ploughing B's field. B (Johannes) said A 'had offered to plough for him out of friendship only, and not for pay'; in any case, no crops had been reaped in the field. The case was dismissed. (*Monnaagomo* v. *Johannes*, Tawana, 8/1939–40.)

4. A (Motsholapheko) gave his son-in-law B (Gaborekwe) a patch of uncleared land on which to make a field. B did so; then, on going away temporarily, he lent the field to his wife's younger sister. Annoyed at not having been consulted, A ploughed the field for himself. Taken to court, he maintained that he had merely lent B the land; but witnesses proved that it had been a donation (*mpho*). Held: the field belonged to B, and A was fined 10s. 'for his conduct'. (*Gaborekwe Tsetlhane* v. *Motsholapheko Matsoga*, Kgatla, Mathubudukwane district court, 3/1938.)

See also: No. 7.

(*c*) An agreement must normally be made directly between the parties themselves.

5. A (Baitse) sued B (Maramakwane) for a plough, saying two men had told him they heard B say he was going to give it to him. The evidence showed that 'all this happened seven years ago'. Held: B was not liable, 'because he had not himself told A that he would give him the plough'. (*Baitse* v. *Maramakwane*, Ngwaketse, 84/1913.)

6. On going abroard, A (Olefile) told B's wife that his herdsman B (Mmutle) should take care of some rafters he had cut and left in the veld. On returning he found the rafters had been stolen. He claimed them from B, 'since they had been left with him to look after'. B said he knew nothing about the rafters; if his wife had been told, she had not mentioned them to him. Held: A had no claim on B, 'because he did

not agree with him (personally) that he should look after the rafters'. (*Olefile* v, *Mmutle*, Ngwaketse, 27/1915.)

7. A (Tlhokonyane) claimed an ox as payment for 'doctoring' B (Keepehile). B admitted having been treated by A, but said he had not sent for him; A had volunteered to do the 'doctoring', because B was his maternal uncle. Held B was not liable, 'because he had not summoned (*i.e.*, hired) A.' (*Tlhokonyane* v. *Keepehile*, Ngwaketse, 29/1915.)

See also: No. 14.

(*d*) An agreement is sometimes made for the benefit of a third party (as when A sells something to B on behalf of C, or A gives B something to transmit to C); in such cases C, although not a party to the original agreement, can himself sue B if it is not carried out.

8. A (Mmamanyana, a woman) went to Johannesburg, leaving some cattle with B (Mosielele) to sell for her. On returning, she sued three men who had bought some of the cattle but not yet paid for them. C (Phatshwana) had taken a cow, but said he had no money with which to pay for it; he was ordered to give A three head of cattle (to represent the cow and its offspring). D (Nkwe) had taken a bullock, but said he had paid A 15s. and B 45s.; as he had no witnesses to prove he had given A anything, he was ordered to pay her 15s., and B was likewise ordered to pay her 25s. (which was what he said he had received). E (Ntumisang) had also taken a bullock, but said he had paid B, in the presence of witnesses; he was ordered to go and find them. (*Mmamanyana* v. *Phatshwana, Nkwe, and Ntumisang*, Ngwaketse, 18/1934.)

9. A, while working in Johannesburg, gave B (Sekgwe) 63s. to take home and hand over to C (Koole, A's father). B spent the money, and was sued by C. His defence was that A had agreed to let him use the money and repay it in due course. Held: 'The law forbids people to give others money to bring home for them', but because of the agreement between A and B, B should now repay the loan by giving C an ox. (*Koole* v. *Sekgwe*, Ngwaketse, 24/1914.)—The 'law' referred to here was a decree, issued by the chief in 1910, that 'No one working abroad should hand money to someone else to bring home for him; he must send it by post; and if a man to whom money has been handed to bring home appropriates it, there will be no case against him.' It is no longer in force.

See also: No. 31.

(*e*) Similarly, a person may sue for debts due to a near kinsman (e.g., father or brother), whether dead or alive; in the latter instance, he acts on behalf of his kinsman. Conversely, he can also be held liable for the debts of such a kinsman, but apparently only if (i) he is the dead man's heir, or (ii) he was previously aware of the debt, or (iii) the debtor himself, if alive, is not available.

10. A (Nkge) sued B (Monametsi) for an ox due to A's father for 'doctoring' B. (B had previously paid an ox, but it was found to have been stolen, and had been recovered by the owner.) As B had no cattle of his own, the court awarded A his plough 'as compensation'. (*Nkge* v. *Monametsi*, Malete, 23/1938.)

11. In 1937 A (Mojaphoko) sued B (Mogakolodi) for payment of a debt incurred some forty years previously ('about 1897') by B's uncle. Held: 'According to custom, the heir to an estate is responsible for the dead man's debts; as B was not his uncle's heir, he is not liable.' (*Mojaphoko Seritshane* v. *Mogakolodi Batsile*, Ngwaketse, 14/1937.)

12. A (Thomas, a foreigner) sued B (Keatweng) for delivery of an ox he had bought for £6 from B's younger brother. B admitted knowledge of the transaction, and was told to give A the ox. (*Thomas Moothedi* v. *Keatweng Mpitsang*, Ngwaketse, 41/1934.)

13. A (Khumoetsile) bought goods on credit from two foreigners, B (Ramelodi) and C (Gaorapelwe). On coming to collect what was due to them, they found A absent, and therefore claimed payment from his elder brother D (Olefile). D said he knew nothing about those debts. Held: B and C were to find and sue A; D was not liable, 'because he knew nothing about the matter'. (*Ramelodi and Gaorapelwe* v. *Olefile*, Ngwaketse, 48/1913.)

14. A (Mabywale, a foreigner) had 'doctored' B's wife at B's request, the fee agreed upon being £7 10s. Now, since B (Chonko) was working abroad, A claimed payment from the wife's father C (Keaikanya). Held: A 'cannot claim from someone with whom he had not made the agreement; he should rather wait for B to return home'. (*Mabywale* v. *Keaikanya*, Ngwaketse, 47/1913.)

See also: Nos. 15, 17, 25, 36.

(*f*) Although contracts are nowadays very occasionally made in writing, the vast majority are still concluded by oral agreement. Witnesses are not essential to make them legally binding, but failure to produce any may prejudice a claim or defence.

15. A (Isang) advanced £60 towards the cost of B's education, on condition that the loan was repaid in three annual instalments of £20 each; he had received £35, and now sued B (Molefe, a teacher) for the balance. B said he had in fact paid back £38 10s., and that A also owed him £7 10s. for work done. As there were 'no witnesses or documents on either side', the court accepted B's counterclaim, and deducted it from the £25 claimed by A; this left a balance of £17 10s., which B and his father (Mamapilo) were ordered to pay; the court ruled also that B's salary as a tribal teacher should be diverted towards the payment. (*Isang Pilane* v. *Mamapilo Molefe and Molefe Molefe*, Kgatla, 3/1935.)

16. A (Mmasefiwa, a widow) claimed a field ploughed by B (Thomas), saying it had been lent to him long ago by her late husband. B denied this, and said he had made the field himself. Neither statement was supported by witnesses, but other people ploughing in the same area said that as far back as they could remember B had always used the field. Held: the field belonged to B, and A was fined £1 for bringing an unfounded case. (*Mmasefiwa* v. *Thomas Phiri*, Kgatla, Mathubudukwane district court, 10/1935.)

17. A (Keboeletse) sued B (Raharise) for £1, payment due for 'doctoring' done by A's younger brother. B said the 'doctoring' had been done for 5s. (not £1); he had already given A 1s., and was still trying to find the balance. Held: B was to pay 4s. only; 'there was no witness about an agreement for £1, as A had not brought his younger brother to testify'. (*Keboeletse Tabe* v. *Raharise Carrel*, Ngwaketse, 28/1929.)

18. A (Mmolawa) said that B (Joseph) had agreed to pay him an ox for damage done to the crops in his field by B's cattle, and that B was now 'trying to get out of his agreement.' A had no witnesses, and B denied having agreed to pay as alleged. Held: A has no case, 'because there are no witnesses'. (*Mmolawa Phuramarapo* v. *Joseph Ratsie*, Ngwaketse, 19/1932.)

See also: Nos. 8, 44.

Capacity to Contract

(*a*) In principle, women and unmarried children cannot make valid contracts without the consent of their male guardian (husband, father, etc.); nor can parents betroth their children without the consent of other senior relatives. In practice, women nowadays engage independently in many kinds of transaction, and in the event of dispute may conduct their own cases at court (cf. Nos. 8, 16, 21, 33, 40); in one instance, too, a court upheld an agreement made by a dependent youth (No. 20).

19. The daughter of A (Wakgomo) became engaged, with his consent, to B (Kefatlhilwe). B then refused to marry her, 'because she was sick', and was sued by A as her guardian. B admitted having lived with the girl, and said his younger brother knew of the engagement. But his headman (a senior relative) stated in court: 'We did not "seek" the girl (i.e., carry out the customary betrothal negotiations), and it is only now, in this case, that we hear they were engaged.' Held: A 'was wrong to join the children together without the agreement of all their people, this is not marriage'; and B was to forfeit whatever he had given the girl, i.e., she was held to have been his concubine, not his fiancée. (*Wakgomo Koole* v. *Kefatlhilwe Otlogetswe*, Ngwaketse, 34/1934.)

20. A (Solomon) bought a suit of clothes from a youth B (Maribane), promising to pay him a sheep. This was confirmed by a witness. B's people sent him to get the suit back. A refused to part with it, and was sued by B. Held: 'an agreement had been made', but A's price was too low; if he wanted to keep the suit, he must give B three sheep or 25s. He paid the 25s. (*Maribane* v. *Solomon Mpshwe*, Ngwaketse, 60/1915.) This case incidentally, shows that the Tswana recognize the principle of 'fair price'.

(*b*) There were only three cases, in all, suggesting that persons or certain other categories either cannot make contracts, or cannot make contracts of certain kinds. These related to (i) a herding agreement between two women (No. 21), (ii) an agreement made by a 'sick' man (No. 22), and (iii) an alleged agreement between close relatives (No. 23). The last may be a local variation; in other tribes agreements between such very close relatives as spouses or brothers have been accepted as valid (cf. Nos. 1, 29, 32).

21. A (Segole) said B (Mrs. Bent, a European) had hired him to herd her cattle, promising to pay him a cow after a year's work; in the eleventh month she took the cattle from him and gave them to C (another woman), whom she also paid the cow due to him. B said she had in fact originally hired C, not A; and this was confirmed by C. Held: 'one woman does not give another woman cattle to herd'; B was therefore ordered to pay A his cow, and did so. (*Segole* v. *Mrs. Bent*, Ngwaketse, 39/1930.)

22. A (Ramorupi) held some of B's cattle, and 'without permission' sold one of them to C (Ramphiri). B (Letebele) sued A. C admitted buying the ox, though 'he did not know for certain that it belonged to A'. Held: the ox belonged to B; C was to give it back, and seek a refund of his money (30s.) from A; 'your purchase (*theko*) was theft (*bogodu*); you knew that Ramorupi was sick (*ele molwetse*), and that you had no right (*tshwanelo*) to buy cattle from him; you have done wrongly (*omolato*); pay £1 [as fine], and pay quickly'. (*Letebele* v. *Ramorupi Madimabe*, Malete, 27/1941.)

23. A (Madinao) gave B (Ngombe) a cow to herd, promising him a calf in return. B afterwards refused to hand back the cow, because he had not yet been paid. A sued. Held: 'because they are closely related, there can be no question of contract; the cow must be restored to its owner.' (*Madinao* v. *Ngombe*, Tawana, 1/1939–40.) My abstract of the case does not indicate the nature of the relationship between A and B.

Standard Obligations

In contracts for sale or loan of goods (including money), or employment of service, the parties must agree on the nature and amount of the payment due, including the sex and age of any animals involved in the transaction; they may also, but need not, agree on the time of repayment or delivery of goods purchased, or when a loan should be repaid (cf. Nos. 10, 12, 14, 15, 17, 20, 21, 22, 23, 24, 25, 26, 27, 30, 33, 34, 36, 43, 48, 50, 51, 52).

In addition to such variable details, contracts of these kinds (and they constituted nearly 80 per cent of all those about which there was litigation) normally entail certain 'standard' or 'customary' obligations. These do not have to be stipulated whenever an agreement is made, and (unless they have been specially modified by the parties themselves) the courts in case of dispute will always assume that they apply. The standard obligations featuring most prominently in the case records are as follows:

(*a*) The parties must have valid title to what they give; animals or other goods involved must also be delivered in sound condition (and according to the specifications agreed upon). The question of title arises chiefly when someone sells, or pays a debt with, animals he has stolen or otherwise misappropriated; the purchaser or recipient must then restore them to the true owner, and recovers whatever he himself may have given for them (i.e., the contract is cancelled).

24. A (Ramorupi) sold B (Lelatlhego) an ox belonging to C (Letebele), which he said was his own; B, who 'knew nothing about A', paid him 50s. for it. C sued A (cf. No. 22 for a similar case between the same parties). A agreed in court that if he gave someone an ox as *tiso* (to herd), or a field on loan (*kadimo*), and the latter 'ate' it without telling him, he would ask for it back; therefore C was not acting wrongly in taking action against him. Held: B had bought a stolen ox from A; he must restore it to C, and seek a refund of his money from A. (*Letebele* v. *Ramorupi Madimabe*, Malete, 28/1941.)

25. A (Lepodisi) gave two head of cattle to B to buy a gun for him. B died before doing so, and A sought a refund of his cattle, or their equivalent, from C (Motsaakgang, B's younger brother). C gave him two oxen, but these really belonged to D (Motlhala), who took them back from A. A sued D. Held: A has no case against D; he must sue C for his cattle. (*Lepodisi Sabone* v. *Motlhala Legothwana*, Ngwaketse, 24/1938.)

26. In 1910, A (Rankatu) took £5 from B (Kgampu), promising to pay him two weaned calves (*maalolelo*) in April, 1911. In 1913 he offered B two young oxen just old enough to be driven (*magatelo*). B rejected them, saying his own cattle of the age originally promised already had calves of their own. The people in court agreed with him, and said A should add two newly-weaned calves (*maruntshwane*) to those he had offered. He was ordered to do so. (*Kgampu* v. *Rankatu*, Ngwaketse, 43/1913.)

27. A (Ramorwa) gave B (Tomo) a rifle, in exchange for a magician's whisk (*boditse*) allegedly able 'to produce water and milk'. A tried it at home, and when he

found the claim 'was not true', sued B. The whisk was tested in court, where it also failed. B was ordered to restore A's rifle 'or its equivalent'. (*Ramorwa* v. *Tomo*, Ngwaketse, 41/1914.) There is nothing in the record to show that B was otherwise penalized for his fraud.

28. A (Dishaitsane) lent his headman B (Radikoro) a horse for use on official service. It died while in B's possession, and A claimed twelve head of cattle compensation. B said that on receiving the horse he had asked A for another, 'as this one is not fit'; and a witness said that A had deliberately given the horse, though he had a good mule. Held: A has no claim, 'he could have given a sound animal'. (*Dishaitsane Mokgwatlheng* v. *Radikoro Moletsane*, Ngwaketse, 3/1934.)

See also: Nos. 10, 22, 51.

(*b*) In either sale or purchase on credit, ownership, but not risk, passes as soon as (but not until) something has been given in return for a promise to deliver or pay.

29. A's wife wanted to buy cattle with corn. Her brother B (Molefe) acted as her agent, and gave some of the corn to C in exchange for a heifer. The animal died while still in C's possession. Thereupon A (Manale), on behalf of his wife (B's sister), sued B. Held: B should give A a cow, and could then claim another from C. (*Manale Mmale* v. *Molefe Nkwe*, Ngatla, 19/1938.)

30. A (Gababonwe) took a cow from B (Setlhomolo), promising to give him another in exchange or to pay for it in money. 'Before he had done his share', he sold the cow to C for 10s. B sued him. Held: B 'should go and get his cow back' from C; and A, in addition to giving C £1 (i.e. double the price paid), was to receive four cuts of the cane 'for taking [stealing] A's cow without [fulfilling his part of the] agreement'. (*Setlhomolo* v. *Gababonwe*, Tawana, chief's court, 187/1939.)

See also: Nos. 34, 36.

(*c*) If A owes B a female animal (e.g. a cow), or is looking after such animals for him, B is entitled also to their offspring.

31. In 1937 A gave B (Moshokwe) a cow to deliver to C (Moanaphoti). Despite several requests, C failed to get the cow from B, whom he at last sued, in 1939. Held: B was to give C four head of cattle, 'one to represent the cow he should have given, and the balance to represent its offspring'. (*Moanaphoti* v. *Moshokwe*, Tawana, 194/1939.)

32. On going to work in Johannesburg, A (Ngomare) left a cow with his brother B (Ramotsumi). He heard it had five calves in all, but on his return B offered him only one animal. He sued B for the balance. B said the calves had been 'eaten' (sold or slaughtered) by A's wife, though she had told her husband she knew nothing about them; and the wife admitted in court that she had concealed her use of the calves from A. Thereupon A withdrew his claim, and the court formally ruled that B was not liable. (*Ngomare Khobe* v. *Ramotsumi Khobe*, Ngwaketse, 47/1940.)

33. In 1937 A (Mmabasekisi, a woman) sold B (Nnanyane) a pair of shoes, for which he promised to pay a goat; in 1940 she sued him for five goats (the animal originally due, and its increase). B said he would give one goat only, as he had previously told A the goat was there for her to take, but it had died before she came to fetch it. Held: B was to give A five goats, 'because he had delayed to hand over the original animal'. (*Mmabasekisi Mmolayatshephe* v. *Nnanyane Gothaang*, Ngwaketse, 51/1940.)

See also: Nos. 8, 26, 42, 43.

(*d*) A man looking after another's livestock must inform him promptly of losses due to death, straying, theft, etc., and must give him the hides of those that have died. Failing this, he can be held liable for the loss; he is also liable for losses or injury due to his own negligence.

34. A (Phaleng) gave B (Mmutle) three sheep for a calf, which he left in B's care as it was still young. The calf died, and A sued for the return of his sheep. B repudiated liability; he said that when the calf died he had told A to skin it, but A 'just left it', and as it was not his any longer he also 'left it to rot'. Held: B was not liable; 'the calf had died for A' (*eswetse Phaleng*). (*Phaleng* v. *Mmutle*, Ngwaketse, 54/1915.)

35. A (Tshikantwa) was herding B's cattle. The calves became lean, and B (Digotlhong) claimed compensation, saying their condition was due to excessive milking of the cows. A replied that they were suffering from 'liver disease', and that he had duly

reported this to B. Held: 'there is no reason why A should pay; he did not injure the calves by hand.' (*Digotlhong* v. *Tshikantwa*, Ngwaketse, 35/1911.)

36. A (Ramogolo) gave B (Mooki) an ox for services rendered. B went abroad to work, and left the ox with A. It died, and when C (Moring, B's brother) later came to fetch it, A offered him another. C rejected it as too small, and sued A. In court A said that when the ox died he did not know to whom to give the hide, as B was abroad; he had therefore sold it for 9s. The people present reproved C for his action, 'because A had not killed the ox'. Held: A was not to blame, because he did not know where B was; but he should give C the money he had received for the hide. (*Moring* v. *Ramogolo*, Ngwato, Madinare district court, 50/1940.)

37. A (Kaketso) gave B (Lepodisi) two donkeys to herd. B, without permission, lent them to C (Balosang), from whom they strayed. C agreed to pay A an ox as compensation, but A also wanted an ox from B; B had offered him two goats, which he refused, 'because he had sought for the donkeys in vain'. B maintained in court that his offer was fair, as the donkeys had strayed not from him, but from C. Held: B must pay A an ox, 'because he had lent the donkeys without permission, and then they got lost'. (*Kaketso* v. *Lepodisi Mmolawa*, Ngwaketse, 58/1915.)

See also: No. 59.

(*e*) A man hired for some special task is not entitled to payment until he has satisfactorily completed that task.

38. A (Dikgang) claimed payment from B (Semeri), by whom he had been hired to drive a wagon to a village some forty miles away. B said there was no reason why he should pay, as A had not taken the route specified; in consequence, the oxen had suffered from lack of water, 'and one of them was still being treated'. This was found to be true. Held: A was not entitled to payment. (*Dikgang* v. *Semeri*, Ngwaketse, 90/1915.)

39. A (Motoka) claimed payment from B (Furupa) for work on a well. Held: he must finish digging the well and could then have a case if he considered it necessary. (*Motoka* v. *Furupa*, Tawana, 90/1938.)

40. A (Kennekang) claimed his fee for 'doctoring' B (Mmadichaba, an elderly widow). Held: he should first cure his patient, and could then claim his fee. (*Kennekang Molongwane* v. *Mmadichaba Mapogo*, Tlokwa, 44/1938.)

41. A (Mokotswa) claimed payment of his fee for 'doctoring' B's cattle. B (Basima) said he was willing to pay, but the 'doctoring' had been incomplete, since it was done when the bull was not there. A agreed to do it again 'now that the bull has come'. Held: A was to receive a cow after the 'doctoring' had been completed. (*Mokotswa* v. *Basima*, Ngwaketse, 80/1932.)

(*f*) A debt must be paid on demand (or at the time agreed upon), and is always due, no matter how long ago it was incurred. But if the creditor delays greatly in seeking payment, or refuses a reasonable tender, he may prejudice his chances of being awarded his claim, either in full or even at all.

42. 'Before the rinderpest' (1896), A (Modise) sold a horse to B (Tshugane). He was paid all the cattle due but one, which died in the rinderpest. In 1912 he sued B for eighteen head of cattle, 'the offspring of the one about whose death he had been told'. Held: B was to give A one cow, 'but nothing more', 'because he had previously offered A one, which had been refused'. (*Modise* v. *Tshugane*, Ngwaketse, 30/1912.)

43. In 1893 A (Baitse) sold B (Kelebalekgosi) a pair of sandals for a goat, and in 1896 he sold C (Tsalayakgosi) a hat, also for a goat. In 1913 he sued for 'goats' (to represent the animals originally due, together with their increase). Held: 'because of his delay', he was in each case to receive one goat only. (*Baitse* v. *Kelebalekgosi and Tsalayakgosi*, Ngwaketse, 85/1913.)

44. A (Polokaeng) borrowed from his elder brother B two trek oxen belonging to C (Letshwenyo). They died because of drought. Subsequently, after B's death, C claimed compensation from A. A said no such claim had been made during B's lifetime; C also admitted in court that he had no witnesses to any earlier request for payment. The case was dismissed, 'because C has no evidence to prove that he has ever before claimed payment from A'. (*Letshwenyo* v. *Polokaeng*, Tawana, 100/1938.)

Remedies for Breach

(*a*) If payment of a debt is refused or withheld, the debtor can be sued and will be made to pay (cf. Nos. 12, 13, 15, 17, 21, 42, 43); and if there was no excuse for delay (e.g., reasons like those reflected in Nos. 42–44), he may have to pay more than was in fact due.

45. A (Sekgaritse) gave B (Kesupilwe) an ox to herd, and when he claimed it back was refused. Held: B must return the ox, 'and pay another for his delay'. (*Sekgaritse* v. *Kesupilwe*, Ngwaketse, 16/1912.)

46. A (Phutimpe) owed B (Kgwabi) an ox, but refused to pay, 'and delayed greatly despite requests'. He was therefore ordered to give B three head of cattle. (*Kgwabi* v. *Phutimpe*, Tawana, 40/1937.)

47. A (Motlhala) sued B (Rakongwe) for payment of debt (£2 or an ox). He was awarded 45s., the extra 5s. 'because B had delayed to pay'. B paid the 45s. (*Motlhala* v. *Rakongwe*, Khurutshe, 1/1941.)

(*b*) A defaulter may similarly be ordered to do work he has promised, or to finish a task he has abandoned or done badly; but he may be excused if he can prove that performance was impossible.

48. A (Maswe) lent B (Seiphetlho) an ox with which to plough, on condition that B then ploughed for him; he now complained that B refused to do so. Held: B 'must carry out his agreement'. (*Maswe* v. *Seiphetlho*, Ngwaketse, 28/1910.)

49. A (Tiroyamodimo) hired B (Montsho) to 'doctor' his wife. B removed some *dibeela* (bewitching charms) that were found in her hut, but then refused to 'doctor' the woman herself. A sued him. In court B said he had refused 'because they spoke badly about him'. Held: B must 'go and cure the woman'. (*Tiroyamodimo* v. *Montsho*, Ngwaketse, 77/1913.)

50. A (Xedano) borrowed a donkey from B (Kethopilwe) with which to plough, promising to plough for him in return. B sued him for not doing so. A said he had been unable to plough while the field was still under water, and that B had in the meantime taken back the donkey. Held: B had no case. (*Kethopilwe* v. *Xedano*, Tawana, 233/1940.)

See also: Nos. 1, 2.

(*c*) However, if any payment has already been made, the court may order its refund, and thus cancel the contract. This applies also to cases in which a girl refuses to marry her fiancé; he is then entitled to recover the value of his betrothal gifts.

51. A (Mosweu) gave B (Openshaw, a European blacksmith) his wagon to repair, paying him an ox in advance. B took the wagon from Lehututu to Kanye (the tribal capital, 260 miles away), but instead of working on it 'went to cut wood for sale'. A sued for, and was awarded, the return of his ox, 'because B had not yet repaired the wagon'. (*Mosweu* v. *Openshaw*, Ngwaketse, 13/1910.)

52. A (Mokgabisi) gave B (Ricketts, a European) his rifle to repair, and also paid him for the parts (trigger and band) that had to be replaced or added. After he had used it only three times, the trigger broke again. He sued for the refund of his money (19s. 6d.), saying he would return the trigger and band. B agreed to this, and the court ruled accordingly. (*Mokgabisi* v. *R. Ricketts*, Ngwaketse, 65/1914.)

53. A (Koti) became engaged to and started living with B's daughter; she then left him, and he found her associating with other men. At a family meeting held to discuss his complaint, she said she did not want him. Her family sided with her. A therefore sued B (Matsau) for the return of his betrothal gifts (two bags of corn and other goods valued at £5 16s.). The court rejected a defence that he had driven the girl away, and not only ordered B to pay the claim but fined him 'an ox or £3, for trying to cheat A out of the marriage'. (*Koti Tsele* v. *Matsau Ntwagae*, Kgatla, 29/1938.)

See also: Nos. 25, 27.

(*d*) A person who has suffered actual loss through breach of contract may be awarded special damages. This applies also in cases where a girl is jilted by her fiancé, especially after she has borne him a child; in addition, he has to forfeit his betrothal gifts.

54. A (Kekganehile) promised to plough for B (Gosalamang). He did not do so 'at the time agreed upon' and was sued. Held: the corn he had reaped from his own fields should be threshed 'and divided between him and A by the court, according to law'. (*Gosalamang* v. *Kekganehile*, Tawana, 21/1937.)

55. A (Molapisi) hired B (Diaramoka) to cut and bring him a supply of reeds (used for building huts). B did not deliver the reeds, and as A had to go and fetch them himself he sued B 'for his expenses' (*ditshenyegelo*). Held: B must pay A 11s. 6d.

or 23 bundles of reeds 'for breaking his contract'. (*Molapisi* v. *Diaramoka*, Tawana, 125/1938.)

56. A (Ngwai) was looking after some cattle for B (Kgamanyane), and in 1934 of his own accord returned them all, except the bull. In 1936, after several earlier requests, B again sent for the bull, and this time claimed also its progeny (five calves) by A's cows, 'damages for the loss he had sustained because his own cattle had long been without their bull'. In 1937 A brought the bull alone. B refused to accept it without the calves, and took the matter to court. There A was ordered to pay what B demanded he was also fined an ox, 'because he was a very obstinate and elderly man, who ought to know the law'. (*Kgamanyane S. Pilane* v. *Ngwai Moeng*, Kgatla, 22/1938.)

57. A (Mojamorago) seduced B (Marata), promising to marry her. He then changed his mind, saying he wanted neither her nor the child, and she sued him. Held: he should pay eight head of cattle, 'because he has spoiled her chances of getting married to someone else'. He brought six animals, which the chief accepted, giving B four and keeping the two others himself. (*Marata Pite* v. *Mojamorago*, Kwena, 16/1936.)

58. In 1928 A (Ramosukwana) seduced B (Mmamothusi), and, 'because he had no cattle with which to pay' (the usual damages, in this tribe, being four head), he promised to marry her. His father set in train the customary betrothal negotiations, and, soon after the engagement was concluded, the child was born; another followed in 1930. A then went to work in Johannesburg, and while there heard that B had been unfaithful to him. He consequently refused to marry her, and was sued. In the course of the hearing it transpired that he had been acting on the advice of B's maternal uncle, who after agreeing to the marriage now wanted him to marry another niece instead. Held: A was to pay six head of cattle 'before he married the other woman', and B's uncle, 'who was the cause of the trouble', was fined an ox. (*Mmamothusi Lebotse* v. *Ramosukwana Molefe*, Kgatla, 1/1937.)

(*e*) If a case for breach of contract is due primarily to the defendant's obstinacy or other misconduct, the court, in addition to any other award, may inflict special punishment upon him.

59. A (Ntiria) borrowed two oxen from B (Matlhoakgosi) for use in ploughing. They went astray, and he neither reported this to B nor looked for them; in court he tried to excuse himself by saying he thought B had already fetched them. Held: he must restore the animals (i.e., their equivalent) to A, and also pay an ox as fine, 'for letting the matter come to court unnecessarily'. (*Matlhoakgosi Tshukudu* v. *Ntiria Pule*, Kgatla, Mathubudukwane district court, 3/1936.)

60. A (Dick) borrowed £1 from B (Gaoretelelwe). He repaid 10s., 'but took a very long time about the balance, and became insulting when B wrote to him for it'. Held: he must pay B 25s., '10s. as the balance due, and 15s. for the insult'. (*Gaoretelelwe* v. *Dick Marambo*, Tawana, 192/1939.)

See also: Nos. 4, 16, 22, 30, 53, 58.

Notes

[1] Bechuanaland Protectorate Native Tribunals Proclamation, No. 75 of 1934 (promulgated 4th January, 1935), s. 16.

[2] There is a preliminary analysis of this material (excluding some subsequently gathered among Khurutshe, Malete, Seleka-Rolong, and Tlokwa) in my paper, 'The work of tribal courts in the Bechuanaland Protectorate' (1943) *African Studies* 27–40. This also describes briefly the records themselves.

[3] 'Contract in Tswana law' (paper prepared for the International African Institute seminar on customary law, to be held at Addis Ababa, January 1966). For an earlier account, based chiefly on Kgatla and Ngwato sources, cf. my *Handbook of Tswana Law and Custom* (1938, new edn. 1955), Chap. XIV.

[4] *I.e.*, Case No. 74 of 1913. Unless otherwise specified, all the cases cited were tried in the chief's court ('senior tribunal') of the tribe named.

T. O. Elias: The Nature of African Customary Law*

Civil Liability under Contracts

We may pose the problem here at once by quoting this significant but fairly typical opinion of Seagle: '. . . and it is doubtful whether "contract" as such exists, i.e. whether obligations are recognised as binding irrespective of mutuality or pre-existing obligation. However, the forms of the obligations are probably determined less by the elements of reciprocity than by the limitations of the legal system with respect to enforcement. In any event in both primitive and civilised societies reciprocity is entirely absent, at least in any economic sense, in the institution of the gift. Moreover, reciprocity is involved only in civil obligations.'[1]

A partial refutation of this may, however, be seen in this statement[2] by Driberg:[3] 'Every status has its own obligations to the community and the community never regards the individual unless he discharges his obligations. All benefits are dependent on duty: there is, and there must always be, a constant reciprocity between giving and receiving. A living elder assists the community with his advice and experience, and in return, whenever an animal is killed or a feast is prepared, a specific portion of the animal or of the feast is reserved for him and offered to him ceremonially as a public tribute. We have seen that the discharge of obligations and the receiving of benefits are correlatives.' In other words, there is an underlying sense of obligation and a recognition of the principle of *pacta servanda sunt.*

But the first notable proponent of the contrary view was Maine[4] who spoke of the absence of contracts between individuals as due to the regulation of personal relations by the status of the individuals, as well as by the administration and inheritance of property within the family according to customary law. He believed that these adequately account for the lack of detailed rules in so-called 'primitive' communities. A glance back at the samples of customary rules and standards quoted earlier in the present chapter, taken together with what has already been said in previous chapters about the fallacy of primitive communism, should dispose of this imposing farce regarding the automatic operation of custom and the consequent absence of detailed rules of general rights and duties. We will now attempt to demonstrate its falsity further.

At this stage it seems necessary to take a number of specific customary law situations in which we can observe a contractual element at work, and then to analyse the underlying concept as closely as possible.

Marriage

It may be as well to start with this very important indigenous institution. Marriage in African societies is a contract ostensibly between two families, 'in which the individual interests of the groom and bride, though implicitly or formally recognised, are but a subordinate element of the wider dominating interest of their families'.[5] This may be taken as representing the normal sociological postulate of a customary law marriage in practically all African communities. But, as will be shown presently, it is hardly distinguishable from the marital conceptions which prevailed in England to the end of the Victorian era, or from the French ideas of the marriage tie even to this day.[6]

The importance thus attached by society at large to the creation of the contract of marriage must be due to the fact that, while marriage is like any other agreement to create legal relations between the parties, it differs notably from other forms of contract in that it marks a change of status for the parties. It is this inevitable interdependence of contract and status that accounts for the interest which the European State or the African community (and not merely the two families immediately concerned) takes in the marriage contract.

For purposes of *legal* analysis, however, one must take a closer view of the African marriage. If it is a valid one, it will be seen to consist of two inseparable elements: (*a*) a contract comprising an exchange of promises between the boy and the girl to marry, followed by (*b*) the ceremony of marriage, to which members of the community are invited as witnesses. The first is the *individual* aspect of a marriage, and is the true contractual element in the transaction; the *communal* aspect is the wider participation of

* T. O. Elias, *The Nature of African Customary Law*, Manchester University Press, 1956, pp. 144–148 and pp. 152–155.

certain members, usually in the last resort the parents or guardians of the marrying couple, in the legislation of the marriage relationship.[7]

But few students of African law would deny that, at bottom, the actual union is established between the individual husband and wife, who thereby constitute a new family unit within the husband's patrilineage or the wife's matrilineage (in communities where marriage is uxorilocal). Also, most communities have their own peculiar mechanisms for the ascertainment of the willingness or otherwise of the individual parties to a contemplated marriage. Legally, it is not the case, as is so commonly asserted, that the wishes of the intending couple were always brushed aside by their parents (especially, the girl's). One need only look into any detailed description of a typical marriage and its traditional incidents in order to appreciate the chain of interlocking gifts and tokens passing between boy and girl as well as the activities of the inevitable 'go-between' that almost invariably precede and accompany an African customary union.[8]

Then there is the transfer or agreement to transfer cattle or other *quid pro quo* as a precondition of the marriage contract. This element, without which no marriage contract can come into being, is governed by often elaborate rules as to both its initiation and its discharge; sometimes it must all be paid up before the marriage can take place but, at other times, a deposit is accepted by the girl's parents on condition that the balance is discharged at stated intervals or on the occurrence of a particular event. Also, its recovery, in whole or in part, on the failure of the marriage through the woman's own fault, is again governed by detailed and precise rules in all communities.[9] Considering its place in the whole marital nexus we may say that the transfer or agreement to transfer whatever is the marriage payment in a given community is itself a contract within the wider contract of marriage itself. And if we may make the further inference, an African contract of marriage is in fact a triple agreement. First, there is the primary, *legal* contract between the boy and the girl as the only true partners to the marriage relationship. Then, there is the secondary, *social* contract between the two families of the couple. Finally, there is the ancillary, *socio-legal* contract for the settlement of the marriage payment which puts the seal of enforceability on the entire transaction.

Conclusion

The above summary account is meant to illustrate, not to exhaust, the innumerable contractual relationships existing in so-called simple African communities at varying stages of economic development. Many classes of bilateral as well as multilateral agreements have not been included but have rather been left to be inferred from those briefly described.

It is clear that the essential nature of mutuality of obligations, of respect for one's plighted word, of the avoidance of fraud or force or unlawful breach of agreement, is present to the African mind. The writer recalls the answer given to him by the judges of the Busoga Central (Native) Court, in the Eastern Province of Uganda, in reply to the question;[10] What is the legal position if A sues B for cheating him out of his proper share of the spoils of a concerted raid on C's banana garden? These elders looked at me with evident surprise and almost spontaneously rasped back: We as Saza and Gombolola chiefs would order the immediate seizure of both A and B, the complete restoration of everything stolen, and the payment of a heavy fine by both for their impudence and want of shame. Seeing that our law frowns so much upon theft, how could we be expected to do otherwise? Even if theft were not the object of their concerted effort, both A and B, provided the joint enterprise is established between them, would be fined for their conduct which must certainly provoke a breach of the peace by causing indignation to other people in the community.

This, in fine, is a fair sample of the indigenous idea that the elders would not hear of an unlawful agreement. In such subtle and indirect ways one chances upon statements of principles of a particular African customary law and, if one's real object is to keep an open mind and to find out what really goes on in the day-to-day, apparently humdrum activities of an African community, one cannot but be convinced that at least the rudiments of what is called contract English law also exists in African customary law.[11]

It now remains to note briefly one alleged weakness of the African law of contract—the general indifference shown by the customary courts to the enforcement of an *executory* contract. If A agrees to buy a basket or a hoe from B who makes such things for a living and A refuses to pay or to take delivery from B on completion, neither A nor

B can sue for the specific performance, or damages for the breach, of the contract. An action would, however, lie if A's action involved an element of deceit or sharp practice or if B sued A in debt for any expenses he might have incurred in purchasing the necessary materials.

But if the contract involved entails a great deal of expense, in money or labour, it seems that the law will enforce it even if executory. Thus, Gluckman[12] mentions two cases tried by Lozi courts in 1942 in which A ordered a net from a netmaker paying the full purchase price in advance and B ordered a net from another paying only part of the purchase money in advance. Each netmaker later sold the net he had made to the king's *induna* and it was held that A was entitled to the net but B was not. But B was given this curious verdict only because the chairman of the judges over-ruled the unanimous opinion of his colleagues to the contrary. Gluckman records that he was authoritatively informed that B was entitled to the net even if he had paid nothing in advance. These then are clear cases showing that under certain circumstances even executory contracts may be enforced.

Another instance that might be cited to show that executory contracts are not normally enforced at the suit of either party is the non-recognition of actions for breach of promise of marriage. But, in the strict African law of customary marriage, it is not the mere exchange of promises (whether these be those of the boy and girl or of their two families) that brings the contract into being. It is the settlement of the agreed amount of the marriage payment by the prospective husband and, in most if not all societies, the formal handing-over of the girl to him at his parents' home by the girl's parents that conclude the contract of marriage. Until this stage is reached, either party may resile from the more or less social relation to which the initial exchange of promises to marry and the subsequent gifts of presents usually by boy to girl give rise. A jilted young man could in some communities legally recover all substantial presents or their equivalent from the girl's parents, if satisfactory proof were given of all the specific items of his claim.

We see, therefore, that the African does not regard as a legally enforceable contract the mere exchange of mutual promises to marry, since until a contract actually exists there is no bargain to which either party can be held in customary law. Morally, of course, the community looks askance at constituent families suffering their unmarried sons and daughters to change suitors without good cause shown; public opinion resents it, and invariably demands that as full and fair a recompense as possible must be made to the innocent party. Cases of breach of promise of marriage were formerly few and far between—a tribute at once to the efficacy of moral sanctions and to the African's love of legal casuistry. Morally, the standards of right conduct require that the guilty party shall disgorge his or her loot, but only to the extent of the other's material or financial loss; legally, there is no obligation to compensate for injured feelings or frayed nerves unless an actual contract has come into being before the breach. There is, however, one important qualification to be made to all this: where the boy has had carnal knowledge of the girl he is about to jilt, he can legally be compelled to marry her or pay up her full marriage payment.

It will, therefore, be noticed that this instance of a breach of promise is not really a good one to quote in support of the hypothesis that African law does not recognise executory contracts.

Notes

[1] Diamond, *Primitive Law*, was cited in support at p. 279 of article, *op. cit.*

[2] In 'Secular Aspect of Ancestor Worship in Africa', *Jnl. Roy. Afr. Soc.* (Supplement to), Vol. 35, No. 138, Jan. 1936.

[3] Who, of course, knew nothing of Seagle's article. . . .

[4] *Ancient Law*, pp. 325–6, and pp. 378–9.

[5] Thus wrote J. F. Holleman of the Shona in his *Shona Customary Law*, pp. 73–4. The same has been said of the Basuto by H. Ashton in *The Basuto*, p. 62, and of the Nandi by G. S. Snell in *Nandi Customary Law*, p. 20.

[6] Even in England, members of the aristocratic families still regard marriage sometimes from the standpoint of a selective union between the two families of the bride and groom—Read the recent judgment in *Kremezi* v. *Ridgway* (1949), 1 All. E.R. 662 (where an English naval

officer was successfully sued by a Greek woman for breach of promise of marriage no doubt induced by the parents of the man in England).

[7] This point about the parents or guardians of the marrying couple is analogous in principle to the requirement in English law of the consent of the girl's parents or of the court to the celebration of the marriage, if the girl is under 21.

[8] Let us quote this observation of Dundas as typical of the more enlightened attitude on this point:

'The number of cases in which girls defy all authority, and the futile attempts of the elders to insist on forced marriages being maintained, are proof that the law never provided for such events; it was not so foolishly designed that it did not recognise that a permament relationship between men and women must rest on mutual consent.

'To dogmatise on this subject by saying that the girl alone can choose her husband would be unwise. *The proper method is undoubtedly for the suitor to approach the girl first, but after that he must agree with the father. . . . After careful observation, I have come to the conclusion that a girl has under native custom as much freedom of choice, and the father as much parental influence as is customary with us.*' (All italics are mine.) See p. 284 of *Jnl. Roy. Afr. Inst.* (1921), *cit. supra.*

[9] Again, to quote Dundas (*ibid.*, p. 291): 'It is to be regretted that Europeans have not given sufficient consideration to this subject—in fact, we are apt to regard native marriage as a commercial transaction. So long as we speak of "purchasing wives" we shall probably continue to think of matrimony among natives as a matter of sale and barter. I must refer here to the old custom under which cattle received in dowry were not parted with, and this seems to suggest that dowry was considered far more in the light of a pawn or security than as a purchase price. . . . There are very definite rules to make marriage even more permanent than with us. Because we have seen so many cows paid, we have taken their value to be the principal object of a contract, and we have treated marriage and offences against it as matters properly dealt with as civil suits, in which the only question in issue has been a fixed value due from one to the other. So our attitude towards native matrimony has been identical with our manner of treating any other commercial transaction.' See also Pts. I and II of *African Marriage Survey*, ed. by A. Phillips.

[10] Which was a slight variation on an actual case they had just tried on the morning of June 13, 1953, when I called there.

[11] If further evidence of this were needed, the reader would do well to consult, e.g., Schapera, *A Handbook of Tswana Law and Custom*, *passim*; and *Bantu-speaking Tribes*, pp. 200–4; Cory, *Sukuma Law and Custom*, pp. 135–50; Meek, *Law and Authority in a Nigerian Tribe*, pp. 174, 205, 103–4, 231–4, etc; Ajisafe, *Laws and Customs of the Yoruba People*, pp. 64–8, 73–8.

[12] Gluckman, *Essays on Lozi Land and Royal Property*, pp. 15–16.

M. Gluckman: The Ideas in Barotse Jurisprudence*

The Importance of Obligation in Contract

In the previous chapter we began to examine the rights of Barotse in land and chattels and saw that these rights were contained in the Law of Persons. Further, we saw that the Barotse extend their right of ownership to cover claims on other persons and on their property and their services. This is, on the whole, the manner in which Barotse state these rights. But they also describe rights against other persons and over property as obligations (*liswanelo*), so that had we started from 'obligations' we would have been led to property. For the civic estate of a Barotse entitles him to hold land, and it is an obligation of the king to give him that land. The rules of the Law of Persons and the Law of Things are 'inextricably mixed together' (Maine), and the same body of rules contains a Barotse's most important obligations to and rights against others.

This was even more marked in the past, when almost all transactions involving goods and services took place in the kinship and political systems. Before the abolition of serfdom, the Barotse made few labour contracts. They traded fairly widely with unrelated persons but frequently established pacts of friendship and bloodbrotherhood with regular exchange partners. Other goods to meet their deficiencies were circulated by giving tribute to the king who distributed it as gifts. Their other special, important contracts were loan of gardens, placing of cattle to herd, and certain forms of share fishing. But on the whole, most of a Barotse's transactions took place with his kin, in-laws, and neighbours or with his political superiors and underlings. He was obliged to render them goods and services and they were in turn obligated to him.

Even today this is largely true. It is shown in the paucity of cases I heard that arose

* M. Gluckman, *The Ideas in Barotse Jurisprudence*, Yale University Press, 1965, pp. 170–182.

out of transactions, and therefore for data on contracts with strangers I rely largely on discussion of cases stated. The Barotse in Barotseland still depends on his share of the nation's land and on the help of his kin and political fellows. I exclude from this statement the men's long absences while working for Whites in Barotseland or abroad, and their large purchases from and sales to Whites. Since relationships between Whites and Barotse, whether they arise out of contract or injury, have been controlled by British courts, they are marginal to my present analysis, which is concerned with the law administered by the Barotse courts. Therefore, though Barotseland would today find it hard to manage without that system's goods and employment, I shall neglect this field of relationships. Most cases at law coming before a Barotse court arise between in-laws and between kinsmen, and the court tries to settle these new cases by old standards, though it changes the standards to meet new situations. Barotse conceptions of other transactions seem to me to be consistent with conceptions inherent in a system of kinship obligations.

Free contractual relations between persons not united by social position were thus relatively few and unimportant in Barotse life. In this respect a study of Barotse law, as of law in most tribal societies, validates Maine's most widely accepted generalization, 'that the movement of progressive societies has hitherto been a movement *from Status to Contract*'. The Barotse have now been brought into a world of contractual relations. Their own courts do not handle those with Whites, but the abolition of serfdom in 1906 and the long absences of men at labour have compelled Barotse to make more use of ephemeral employer-employee relationships with unrelated persons of their own and other tribes. Money has facilitated internal trade and it has also been increased by variable falls in production for different groups. The king—instead of claiming tribute and labour–collects tax, and the Northern Rhodesian and Barotse governments employ labourers for wages, instead of rewarding them with gifts. But, with the unbroken system of landholding, Barotse still live with their kin and are linked with their overlords, and the goods and money they earn flow into these established relationships. Barotse society on the whole is still a society dominated internally by status rather than contract.

I have argued that Barotse property law defines not so much the rights of persons over things as the obligations owed between persons in respect of things. Hence, except for extending a general protection against trespassers on others' rights, the law is concerned with the respective claims on one another's services and goods of persons related permanently by kinship or political bonds. In the previous chapter I abstracted the element of property from political and kinship bonds, and this led to an analysis of the obligations between lord and underling and between kinsfolk. Had I analyzed the obligations between these persons, I should have had equally to consider property. For in Barotseland the Law of Things and the Law of Obligations are both mostly contained in the Law of Persons, and each of these three is also the others examined from a different standpoint. Barotse society is relatively undifferentiated, and the different branches of its law are intertwined.

The greater part of the Barotse Law of Obligations is covered by the rights and duties which lie between kinsfolk and in-laws and between lords and their underlings. Claims on the goods and services of others inhere in these relationships. Transactions between previously unrelated persons—contracts freely entered into—are relatively few among the Barotse, though they make an important contribution to economic life. It is therefore understandable that the law of these contracts has been markedly influenced by the major preoccupation of Barotse jurisprudence, its concern with the law of status. This influence will now be considered.

Defaults in obligation of status are punished nowadays by reprimand or fine (previously also by inflicting physical pain) and ultimately by expulsion of the defaulter from his status with its rights and obligations. The standard of what has to be rendered is thus set by general norms, and within those by what can be reasonably expected from a person of a certain age, strength, and wealth. That is, there is a certain reasonable minimum which is enforceable at law, in the setting of all his obligations. But the expectations of morality go far beyond this minimum. All these relationships are marked by a public demand for love and affection and generous mutual aid, and people are expected to express these sentiments through material goods and services. The stress of morality is on generosity, helpfulness, cooperation, and give-and-take in the vicissitudes of life. These values are publicly stated in may cases between lords and their underlings and always in cases between kinsmen. Thus in the land dispute cited in the first chapter, the headman who demanded that kin come to his village or stop using his fish dams, was reproved for his stinginess and told: 'Indeed, you ought, if you are rich, to add to the goods of your kin, not to take things away from them.' Trials over ownership of land may become inquiries into how the kinsfolk concerned have dealt with one another through long periods: whether the junior gave the senior fish from his catches and money from his earnings in European enterprises, or let him take poles, mats, and so forth, and whether the senior had contributed, for example, to his juniors payments of cattle for brides.[1]

Since land, and to a lesser extent chattels, are principally held by virtue of status, the settlement of disputes over ownership may turn on whether the parties have fulfilled all the duties of their station; whoever has failed to do this generously will be severely admonished and may ultimately be expelled from his position. Here the stress of Barotse law is clearly on duty rather than on right. Even when the judges affirm that a particular person has a right to some thing or some service from another, they tend to stress that the defaulter should render the right, rather than that the abused shall receive the right. It is only by this generous rendering of obligations that multiplex relationships can endure and function; they are likely to break if either party tries to live by the letter of rights and duties. These virtues inhere in the relationships of parent and children, and they are extended not only to relationships with other kin but also to political relationships. The good subject is he who is generous as a child is to a parent; the good lord is he who is generous as a parent is to a child.

Since these are the typical relationships of Barotse society, their more ephemeral transactions involving previously unrelated people tend to be assimilated to the pattern of status relationships, and this influence permeates the Barotse law of transactions. In Barotse law individual parties had little liberty to make special agreements, for each transaction had particular and specific incidents. Hence I consider it is better here to follow Seagle when he says of certain archaic systems that 'the law was still dealing with particular forms of transactions rather than with contracts'.[2]

A noteworthy fact of Barotse life is the tendency to expand isolated transactions between strangers into multiplex associations that resemble kin relationships. This tendency is marked in their magical and religious beliefs, as in their secular life. For example, Barotse barter goods with one another. Many people with small surpluses or the products of specialized skills or particular environments travel through the country seeking to trade with others who have goods they lack, although of late, British money has provided a medium of exchange. But once a couple has made several bartering exchanges of this kind, they consider they have entered into a pact of friendship (*bulikani*, literally, the quality of being equals). Thereafter they do not barter item for item, but they are under a general obligation to help each other and to outdo each other in generosity, rather than to seek a good bargain. They thus obtain hospitality, protection, and an additional home in an area where they lack kin. These pacts of friendship, if of long standing, may then be sealed by the pact of bloodbrotherhood, which makes them quasi-kinsmen; now they cannot marry into each other's family. These pacts had additional importance in the past when the parties lived in different nations, for they enabled safe travel across boundaries. Thus when David Livingstone travelled with Barotse carriers outside Barotseland in 1855, he recorded that his people made compacts of bloodbrotherhood with Lunda so that they could later exchange cattle for canoes. The French missionary Coillard made similar notes on his journeys. Here the pact provided a protecting friend in a foreign land. Within the Barotse kingdom these pacts are very numerous, and people constantly make them with others with whom they have entered into regular exchanges. The Barotse court in 1942 had to consider a case in which two bloodbrothers had quarrelled because one had committed a gross breach of obligation by refusing hospitality to his fellow. The court totted up the extent to which the injured party had given more than he had received and made the defaulter pay him double, thus treating the case as theft.

Similarly, if a Barotse employs a servant, places cattle to be herded with another, or lends another land, once the relationship has endured for a few years, it approaches that of lord and subject or father and child.

The tendency is marked in the linking of persons through mystical beliefs. If a Barotse employs a leech to treat a serious disease, their relationship endures beyond the cure.

The patient may be compelled to become a pupil of the leech, and have to learn to treat the disease. Doctor and patient become permanently linked; and if the patient defaults in payment, the doctor's medicines will turn against him and make him ill again. The doctor must also respect his tie with his patient, for if he defaults in an obligation, the patient's condition may worsen. One night an old man fell suddenly ill. The diviner he consulted held that his illness was the fault of an old woman who had cured him the previous year of a dreadful disease in whose treatment she specialized. She had passed his village without entering to greet him, and the disease became angry and struck him again. Sometimes the patient's failure to follow rules may threaten the doctor's wellbeing.

Other mystical beliefs, in a corresponding way, set up relationships between persons who have some contact or shared experience. Thus there are some diseases which link together all who suffer from them or have suffered, so that when a patient is being treated by drumming, all other patients feel the effects and are seized with paroxysms.

And men who wrong one another, like men who contract with each other, become expansively linked. If you wound a man, you can aggravate his wound by working with magical substances on the weapon. If you kill an enemy in battle, you enter into a personal relationship with him: you must rip up his stomach lest it swells where he rots on the battlefield, and your stomach swells in sympathy. His spirit, like the spirits of certain big game, is liable to drive you mad unless you are treated ritually. Like transactions, delicts thus tend to establish expanding relationships between persons who were previously unrelated. The obverse of this situation is exhibited in other beliefs. Many misfortunes that we ascribe to natural causes are ascribed by the Barotse to witches or sorcerers, personal enemies who have harmed them by mystical means. While for us, delicts and criminal charges arise only when another is patently responsible for a misfortune, among the Barotse every mischance, through beliefs in sorcery, may produce a delictual or criminal case. (It is worth noting here that among the Tiv of Nigeria, even litigants enter into a wider relationship: they call each other 'partner'.[3])

Within the framework of the Barotse law of status there are three general characteristics which, I consider, directly influence the Barotse view of transactions. First, all relationships are ideally relationships of generosity and the utmost good faith, *uberrimae fidei*. In disputes, the court emphasizes obligation rather than right. Similarly, all transactions tend to be contracts of the utmost good faith, with obligations emphasized.

Second, within the general demand for faithfulness and generosity, each specific type of kin relationship is marked off from others by the observance of a special etiquette and special conventions of behaviour and taboos. So each transaction is regarded as a specific complex of rights and obligations, and there is no general model of contract, which is not surprising, since the Romans failed to attain a general theory of contract even in their later jurisprudence, and in England only in the fifteenth century did a general remedy for breach of agreement begin to be supplied.

Third, the fulfillment of obligations in kin relationships is measured by what is done with property, and almost all these relationships involve property elements. In addition, new relationships are established by handing over gifts, as for example in marriage; indeed, there are some half dozen transfers of gifts in a proper marriage. Similarly, kin establish their relationship with a newly born child or an initiate at puberty by making gifts. People who do not share in these property exchanges may deny liability—i.e. they may deny that they have obligations. If a bride's father gives none of the marriage payment to the maternal kin or his own kin, they will say, 'We knew nothing of the marriage. Finally, to re-establish relations after any affront to a kinsman or in-law, some gift must be given. So in transactions, transfers of property are critical.

We can now examine this situation in detail as it affects the interpretation of some Barotse transactions. Direct barter and sale, completed on the spot, are simple transactions out of which disputes for failure to perform cannot arise. In fact, the only disputes I recorded arose where one party alleged that the other had delivered to him goods to which the seller did not have title, or goods of an inferior quality (a cracked pot, improperly reduced poisonous cassava, inadequately seasoned paddles, etc.). In these cases, and on cases stated by me to the courts, the general maxim was that the seller is responsible to the buyer. If a seller had not a good title, the true owner could reclaim his goods from the buyer, and the seller had to recompense the buyer. Barotse describe the seller's action as theft, and they also call it theft if the seller is aware of a flaw in the goods he sells. They may then apply the punishment for theft—payment to the wronged party of double the value of the property, and a possible fine. If the seller did not know of the flaw, he would have to replace the shoddy with sound goods, or refund the goods or money given to him. But this obligation on the seller to take care he renders sound goods emerges most clearly if the goods develop a defect some time after the sale. Thus if a dugout springs a leak after some period of use, the buyer will not be held responsible because he did not use more skill in testing the wood's seasoning. The seller must give him another dugout or repay the price, even if the flaw had not been detectable. More surprising to us, probably, is the rule that if a purchased beast dies some time after the transaction, the purchaser can claim refund of the price on the grounds of what we might call latent defect. (The Barotse would not fix for me what period 'some time' covered, but I recorded one case in which it was four months.) Here then we meet with a marked characteristic of Barotse transactions: each party must look to his obligations rather than to his gains. Every transfer of goods contains an implied warranty, which is extended severely. The obligation on the seller to provide eminently satisfactory goods is like the obligation on a man to be generous to his kin beyond the demand of the law.

Where a seller fraudulently, or sometimes even innocently, delivers poor goods, it is held to be a theft. For instance, if a hoe is purchased for money, and the hoe breaks because of a flaw which was not observable on the surface, the court may accuse the smith, denying his liability to replace the hoe, either of stealing the hoe or of stealing the money. That is, the court holds the injured party to be robbed equally of what he had given and of what he had received. If the court decides that the wrongdoer knew of the flaw, he pays double, as if for theft. The implication of this Barotse view is that in transactions, fraud and even innocent mistake are not treated as a breach of agreement but as taking or spoiling a man's property. In Barotse, as in Roman law, barter and sale are considered as reciprocal conveyances of property: both parties have proprietary rights in both pieces of exchanged property, and the deliverer retains some rights, with corresponding obligations, after delivery. Both are *beng'i*, owners, of both pieces of property, and the case is argued in these terms.

The Barotse word for barter is a reciprocal verb, so that both parties are said to change goods, or goods and money, with each other. The legal problems arising from this process involve not merely what the parties agreed or promised to do, but what property they exchanged and what rights each has in that property. This is quite clear if we consider the transaction which we know as a conditional sale, a sale on credit, and which students of early law call 'credit-barter',[4] the true incomplete conveyance, in which only one party delivers the property. In technical terms, this is an agreement to barter and sell which is completed on one side and is *executory* on the other. Where this transaction is recorded on ancient tablets in the Near and Middle East, it involves two tablets. The first records the sale or barter as if it had been completed; the second records the property or money which has not been delivered as a loan from seller to purchaser. That is, two transactions are involved: barter or sale, and loan.[5] Lacking both money and writing, the Barotse had not achieved this sophistication, though in discussing cases arising out of this kind of transaction they speak of it as they do of a straightforward loan: it establishes a debt.

In two cases I heard tried one after the other in a Barotse court, fishermen had ordered gill nests from two netmakers. One paid the full price in advance, the other paid part. When the netmakers had each made a net, the king's steward in charge of royal fishing, holder of the title Mukuba, came to the netmakers and wanted to buy the nets for the king. The netmaker who had been partially paid alleged that he protested his net was already bought, but that the steward swore that the king would stop the netmaker from taking roots to make nets unless he sold him the net, and would also stop the fishermen from fishing in public waters. The netmakers sold the nets to the steward. Both fishermen sued for delivery of the nets.

These cases created great public excitement because the steward's alleged threats amounted to stating that the king would take away certain land rights from his subjects. All Barotse declared that the king, who was almost speechless after a stroke, would never threaten this. In effect, the first part of the hearing became a trial of the steward for 'spoiling the king's name'. He satisfied the court that he had not uttered the alleged threats, and the maligning netmaker had to pay him damages for false accusation. The court then considered whether the nets belonged to the king or to the fishermen who had ordered them. The judges held unanimously that the fisherman who had paid the full purchase price had a sound claim on the net he had ordered, and must be given it, while the netmaker must refund the king's money. All the judges up to the senior judge then sitting in court held that the fisherman who had paid part of the purchase price was also entitled to the net he had ordered, and the steward could not buy it. (Note that they spoke of the steward's buying the nets, and neglected his acting as king's agent. The king, like any other Barotse master, bears no responsibility for the actions of his servants.) The senior judge that day was number eight in the hierarchy on the right, a brother of the king's favourite wife, a member of a subject tribe living far from the metropolitan heart of the country and, to boot, a notoriously bad judge. He overruled all his juniors, since final decision is not by majority but by seniority. He held that the net belonged to the steward, and the fisherman was entitled to refund of the installment he had paid. The fisherman told me he thought he would win the net if he appealed to the Barotse national appeal court, but he would drop the matter, since he had recovered his money and would now be suing in effect the king, his 'father'. He philosophically accepted the loss of his season's fishing.

I discussed the decision with senior councillors of the national appeal court, with rulers in other capitals, and with a large number of commoners. They all said that the fisherman would have won the net if he had appealed. Indeed, they said that if the king had been able to speak properly, and had not depended on his queen, sister to the final judge, to interpret his sounds, he would have overruled the final judge and supported the junior judges. They said it was a typically bad judgment from this judge.

At that time I also discussed with judges what the position would have been had one of the fishermen not paid any part of the purchase price. High authorities told me that this would not have mattered; they would still have considered that the fisherman could claim any net made. This statement was made to me in 1942, and I first published this case in 1943.[6] Mr. (later Justice) E. G. Unsworth, then Crown Counsel in Northern Rhodesia, told me afterward that he had found no trace that executory contracts were enforced in Northern Rhodesian tribes, so I decided that I must check on this information. I did so when I returned to Barotseland in 1947, and I was then told that unless some payment was made by the fisherman, he acquired no rights in any net that was made. This discrepancy of statements exemplifies how Barotse courts apply their legal propositions within the context of specific relationships of status. When I first questioned a number of judges, they were concerned about the king's involvement in the case, even indirectly, and they were in effect telling me that the king would not enter thus between manufacturer and purchaser to the detriment of the purchaser. They had not detached themselves from the issue before the court. Later, when I asked them again, considering it as an issue between commoners only, they ruled that unless the buyer paid something, he got no rights. Unhappily, in his book *The Nature of African Customary Law* (1956, p. 154), Dr. T. O. Elias took up my first report and gave it as the only clear instance in Africa of enforcement of an executory contract, where no deceit was involved. It is significant that he found no other example in his survey of African law.

In discussion, the Barotse laid down the following rules for me, with different rules for different types of property:

1. Generally if a man orders something and does not pay the price, he gets no rights in anything the manufacturer may make. That is, a transaction which is executory on both sides will not be enforced. The manufacturer is not bound to make the article, and no damages will be levied against him if he does not; nor is the purchaser bound to accept the article if it is made.

2. If a man orders an article like a net or a dugout, only one or a few of which can be manufactured in a season, and he pays the purchase price but the manufactuerer does not make the article, the purchaser can sue only for return of what he paid. If the manufacturer makes the article, it belongs to the purchaser and he can claim it from either the maker or a third party to whom it has passed, even if this party is innocent. The purchaser can only reject delivery of the article if it does not come up to common standards. That is, in orders for goods which can be individually distinguished, where the purchaser has delivered some part of the price, the Barotse consider that his ownership vests in the goods provisionally as soon as they are made. But if the goods are destroyed (as by fire) before the purchaser takes them, he can reclaim the purchase price.

He does not bear the risk: although he is called the owner, and he can claim the goods against the world, including the maker, risk remains with the maker.

3. Should the manufacturer not deliver ordered goods like pots, hoes, axes, or food, which cannot be individually distinguished and which he is producing continually, the purchaser has no claim at all if he has not paid the price. If he has paid, and the seller does not produce the goods, the purchaser can claim refund. He cannot follow goods that are made and sold to another, if the manufacturer then ceases to make goods. The manufacturer cannot turn away trade because the purchaser does not collect his order in reasonable time. A purchaser who has not paid can reject the goods offered to him; but if he has paid, he can reject only unworthy goods.

4. If purchaser and seller agree on the goods to be exchanged and point them out, but nothing is transferred by either party, no obligations are created. Neither can claim the goods from the other, nor can they follow the goods if these are transferred to another person.

5. If one party has fulfilled his part of the bargain by transferring goods against property indicated on the other side, he can claim the goods from the seller or from an innocent third party to whom they have passed. But should the indicated goods deteriorate or be destroyed, or if they be cattle which die, the risk remains with the seller till actual transfer. Increment, such as a calf to a cow, however, accrues to the purchaser. But if, after a period which is not defined in advance by the law, the purchaser still neglects to take delivery of a beast, the court will consider that he wished the seller to herd it for him under agistment. Then risk passes to the purchaser under conditions I shall discuss later. This is the only situation I know where Barotse courts find an implied contract.

These were the rules given to me in 1942, when I was in Barotseland. In 1946 the Barotse authorities passed a law stating that they would enforce promises to do anything (to make something, to cut a garden, to join a fishing team, etc.). They told me that they passed this law when they read in a published analysis of mine that they did not enforce agreements of this kind, and they saw that this produced considerable hardship for innocent people. With the increasing importance of free contractual relations in Barotseland under modern conditions, the need for enforcement of executory contracts is aggravated: yet the bias of the law against this enforcement is shown by the fact that the Barotse decided to pass this law only after an outsider had drawn attention to resulting difficulties. I heard no cases under this law, so I cannot say how the courts would punish breaches. The judges told me that defaulters on promises were like thieves and should be punished. They said they would order specific performance or levy damages. I asked how damages would be assessed. Would they be fixed, or would the court make a defaulter pay the other party for losses from inability to fish or to plant a garden? The judges said they had not thought about this and would decide when cases came up. Barotse law up to that time had allowed no claims for damages flowing from failure of another person to carry out an obligation. In Zululand I heard a court reject a jilted teacher's claim for loss of earnings in a suit for breach of promise of marriage, since she had left her employment to prepare for her wedding, and also for damages because she had lost time when she might have become betrothed to another.

That Barotse law did not enforce executory contracts may be partly related to the comparative unimportance of free contracts in indigenous Barotse life. In the past, where a man entered into such a transaction, there was also little point in his seeking to evade fulfillment. But this attitude is also consistent with their whole conception of what a transaction is, and with the remedies they provide for breach of a transaction.

The Barotse do not divide contracts into undertakings entered into by each party to do a particular thing for the other. I have never heard a court, or Barotse in discussion, formulate transactions in this way. They certainly do speak of agreement (*tumelano*) to barter, to enter into service, to arrange a marriage, and so forth, but they do not argue that a man who has promised to do something ought therefore to be compelled by the courts to do it or to pay damages. They condemn people who evade their promises, but they do not consider promisors to be bound in law. In effect they assert, with the Romans, *ex nuda pacta non oritur actio* (no action at law arises from a bare agreement).

Notes

[1] 'The Case of the Biassed Father' in my *Judicial Process among the Barotse* (1955), pp. 37–45.

[2] *The Quest for Law* (1941), p. 256. He quotes with approval Diamond, *Primitive Law* (1935) at p. 392: 'In the primitive law we must speak not of Contract but of Transactions.'

[3] Bohannan, *Justice and Judgment among the Tiv* (1957), pp. 20 n., 28.

[4] Seagle, *The Quest for Law* (1941), p. 52.

[5] See Diamond, *Primitive Law* (1935), p. 412 f., and Seagle, *The Quest for Law* (1941), p. 57.

[6] In my *Essays on Lozi Land and Royal Property* (1943), pp. 15–16.

CHAPTER 11

SPECIFIC CONTRACTS

T. O. Elias: The Groundwork of Nigerian Law*

Contracts Under Customary Law

The main types of contracts under the indigenous customary law may be classified as follows: (1) Contracts of Agistment, (2) Co-operative Labour Contracts, (3) Contracts of Personal Service, (4) Pledge (or Hypotheca), (5) Loan Contracts, and (6) Other Contracts. It will be seen that these contracts pertain more to rural or agricultural communities than to urban societies. But they are nonetheless important enough for inclusion here, if only because the majority of Nigerians are still governed by their principles. The fact that they are almost completely absent from the law reports of the superior courts is not a safe guide to the extent of their prevalence; one has only to turn to the Native Courts in order to appreciate the place of these contracts in the day-to-day operation of customary law in the rural areas of the country.

Let us examine very briefly the essentials of each type of contract and the legal framework within which each operates.

Contracts of agistment. A contract of agistment is an agreement under which the owner of animals, ranging from cats and dogs to asses and cows, gives them into the charge of another person, usually a relative or a friendly neighbour, to tend and nurture for the sole purpose of procreation of their kind. The consideration for this charge is that the chargee is entitled to a share of the animal's siblings, or the proceeds thereof, the basis of division varying according to the species of the animal, the cost and custom of feeding obtaining in a given area and, above all, the specific terms agreed upon by the parties from time to time.

The commonest objects of agistment are hens, cats, goats and sheep, though dogs and pheasants like rabbits and bush mice are also favoured among hunting communities, while in cattle-rearing areas cows, asses and rams are the inevitable media. In such a diversity practice, no doubt, varies but the basic principles are strikingly similar. During the currency of the agreed term, the owner completely divests himself of the property in the animal, and the chargee temporarily exercises complete control and care over the animal. He is accordingly in the legal position of a bailee for value, liable to maintain the animal reasonably well and to produce it to the owner in a good condition at the lawful expiry of the contract.

If the animal is badly tended and becomes so sickly that it cannot fetch from the market the price which a well-kept animal of its ilk should, the chargee may have to pay the difference between the price at which it is actually sold and that which it might have earned. If the animal dies as a result of the chargee's ill-treatment, negligence or indifference, he is liable for the market price of the animal estimated as at the date when the inducing cause of its death began or, if that cannot be satisfactorily ascertained, then his liability will be for the market price of the animal as objectively determined by the court with the aid of local assessors. But the chargee will be entitled to a proportionate abatement of the price of the animal if the carcass is later sold.

Where, however, the chargee has observed *exacta diligentia* and the animal nevertheless dies or cannot be found, in spite of his care and solicitude, no blame attaches to him. Moreover, he is, as an agent of necessity, entitled to minimise the loss by slaughtering the animal when it has become clear that it is about to die, either as the result of an accident or some other unavoidable emergency. But, in that case, the owner must be informed of what has happened as soon afterwards as possible.

* T. O. Elias, *The Groundwork of Nigerian Law*, Routledge & Kegan Paul, 1954, pp. 236–243.

Since the sharing of the young ones or their proceeds is the most fruitful source of dispute between the parties, it may be useful to state the variant forms of the contract and their legal incidents among the different major groups in the country.

Among the Yorubas, the first breed belongs to the owner of the animal, the next to the chargee, the third to the owner, and so on. But where the first breed are two, the owner takes one and the chargee the other; and if one is male and the other female, the female goes to the owner while the male goes to the chargee. In the latter event, the chargee is automatically entitled to the next female breed. If, after the animal has been with the chargee for at least twelve months, the owner wants to bring the contract to a premature end, then the animal must be sold and the proceeds shared equally between the parties. This would happen, of course, only after the breed, if any, should have been shared as already indicated. If the animal has a breed at the time of such premature determination of the contract but has not remained with the chargee for twelve months since giving birth to the breed, it seems that the chargee cannot insist on the animal itself being sold, although he will have a right to his proper share of the breed and to some compensation for his pains in looking after the animal in the interval. Also, there is always a right in the chargee to distrain upon the animal and so refuse to hand it back to its owner until all his own lawful dues on it are met by the owner. On the other hand, the chargee will be liable to the owner for any unlawful distraint.

Finally, whenever it is necessary to offer the animal or its offspring for sale, either of the contracting parties has a right to buy, provided that a third, neutral party supervises the negotiation and is ready to declare it as fair and above board.[1]

With regard to the Hausa, the general principles are more or less the same as those just described for the Yoruba. The practice is for the family head and members of his household to own a number of goats for domestic and trade purposes, but fairly large cash balances accruing to the headman from the proceeds as well as from other sources are often invested on cattle. These are then put in the charge of Fulani herdsmen[2] on a basis of sharing roughly equivalent to one-half of the yields from each head of cattle to the owner and the other half to the chargee. The distribution of shares may, however, be differently organised by the parties to the contract. It will certainly be affected by factors such as (*a*) whether the animal in question in unwon, or whether it is male or female; and (*b*) who is responsible for supplying the feeding-stuff. Horses are known to have been bred by this type of contract.

For the Ibos let this interesting account speak for itself:

'At Okpanam, where a goat is given to a person to look after, he gets the third, fifth, seventh kid, and so on, and, in consideration, pays 7 yams a year to the owner and provides palm wine and yams on the occasion of any sacrifice. The mother and kid would be reclaimed if the dues were not paid. If the goat dies the body is sold and the owner takes the money so that a new goat may be bought; it is brought to the owner so that he may put his property mark upon it. If it were stolen the holder pays no compensation even if negligence were proved, but he is responsible if he alleges theft without being able to prove it.

'At Isele Asaba a man who receives a cow in charge gives 60 kola, cowries to the value of 6*d*. and palm wine to the owner, who can call him to work upon his farm. When the fourth calf is born the holder brings 60 yams, 140 kola, a long broom, a small broom, and palm oil. The owner offers kola to the *mwo* (= ancestors) and the calf becomes the property of the holder, who receives one out of every four as long as he keeps the cow. In the case of a goat he gives 6*d*. in cowries to the owner when he receives it, and sends kola, 7 yams, and palm wine for the first kid, the third, and so on, and keeps them. For a dog the dues are the same and the litter is divided equally. In the case of a fowl 5 yams, 20 cowries and one pot of palm wine are the dues, and the chickens are divided equally when they are grown.

'At Onitsha Olona, if they are all males or all females, they go alternately to owner and holder.'[3]

It will thus be seen that the main elements of the contract of agistment in every case are (*a*) the sharing of the young ones of the animal between the owner and the chargee on a proportionate basis varying from one-quarter to one-half according to the nature of the animal, (*b*) the payment to the owner of certain prescribed dues by the chargee, probably to acknowledge that the former's ownership of the animal is only transferred to the latter for temporary custody, and (*c*) the fact that the chargee is under an obligation to ensure the safety and well-being of the animal whilst the contract lasts. Elsewhere in the country these principles also prevail, but the chargee does not usually pay any dues to the owner of the animal.

Co-operative labour contracts. There are three distinguishable varieties of this type of contract. The labour unit may be made up of a kinship aggregate, or of unrelated neighbouring households, or even of a whole village or group of contiguous villages.

In the *first* category the basis of co-operation is the reciprocal obligations between the family head and the members of his household. The latter are obliged to serve him as well as one another by participating in the group activities of clearing the bush, tilling the soil, planting the farms and harvesting the crops. Their immediate reward is that they are maintained with the food they have helped to grow or with its proceeds; and they are clothed and housed by the headman, who also provides all the farming implements required by all the members of his household. All their taxes and tributes are also his responsibility. But the principal incentive is the ultimate benefit each member derives from the co-operative enterprise when the time arrives for marriage: the headman is responsible for all marriage payments and for other expenses incidental to the new status of the married member who has now to set up house on his own. Thus, the factors holding the co-operative kinship labour units together are as much family ties and sentiments as they are mutual economic benefits based on reciprocal obligations. It is more or less a comprehensive scheme of social and economic insurance for all concerned.

The *second* variety of co-operative labour is that of unrelated neighbouring households.[4] The practice, now on the decline, is for whole families to turn out in full force to supply the labour needed by the several households in turn. Such co-operation is, however, still very strong in areas where mixed farming is the order of the day. The reward for services may also take the form of cash payment to each participating household, or the harvested crops may be divided among the households on the basis of the quantum of labour supplied by each.[5] Very often the host is expected to provide regular meals for the team for so long as the work lasts. This is invariably the case where the co-operative unit has been summoned by the host only for the purpose of harvesting crops like ground-nuts, cotton, beans, yams or cocoa.

The *third* version of this type of contract consists of large-scale co-operative labour units not necessarily limited to farm work; it is in reality an all-purpose labour force. The entire members of a village or those of two or more villages may decide to make a common road to a river, to another village, or to an ancestral shrine or sacred grove; or it may be to found a satellite hamlet or build a new market; or it may even be to keep in good repair a common dividing path between contiguous villages. Because of the public nature of the undertaking the Chief or the Headmen of the village or of the several villages taking part must provide food and beer as well as music for the team of workers. Usually, only the able-bodied young men engage in this kind of co-operative community service.[6] The only recompense for the co-operators, therefore, is not reward in cash or in kind but the shared feeling that one is thereby helping to enhance communal solidarity —a social duty in indigenous polity.

Contracts of personal service. By these are meant those customary contracts in which the personal labour of an individual or of individuals is hired for a variety of purposes. Thus, a cocoa farmer may engage the services of persons to help with the harvesting of crops for financial remuneration. This applies equally to all other cash crops like palm kernels and palm oil, ground-nuts, cotton, kola nuts and beans.[7]

But an owner of palm fruits may employ another to cut or collect the fruits for him; or a person having control of rivers and streams may provide another with fishing baskets to do a shrimp fishing job for him. In either case, his remuneration is normally one-third of his collection or catch, or its money equivalent. This proportional remuneration may of course be varied by the terms of the contract itself or by particular local customs. A demand for cash payment on a *pro rata* basis is now increasingly made by modern workers, who insist that wages shall be related to the work done according to present-day standards.

Pledge. This is a form of contract in which a borrower leaves with the lender articles equivalent in value to those he desires to borrow from the lender. The property so left with the pledge creditor is by way of security only and may not be sold, lost, destroyed or otherwise disposed of by the lender.[8] Unless what is borrowed is in use by the borrower or understood to be so, the lender may not make any use of the pledged article while the arrangement endures. On failure to return the articles lent on the due date, the lender acquires from that instant full right of ownership over the thing pledged, and he is free to dispose of it as he pleases. Due to the absence of writing, one or more personal witnesses are often summoned by the parties to the making of the contract. Personal effects are the usual subject-matter of a contract of pledge.

The borrower is under a duty to return the thing loaned to him or its value at the time of its receipt from the lender—that is, 'fair wear and tear' excepted. Any damage done to the article while in the custody of the borrower must be made good by him, no matter how caused.

This species of customary contract is fast dying out in many urban areas of the country.

Loan contracts. Contracts of loan may be divided into three classes: (i) Agricultural, (ii) Socio-economic, and (iii) Commercial.

(i) Under *agricultural* may be placed those agreements for the loan of crops[9]—such as maize, yam and guinea corn—by a person whose own stock is temporarily short but who has to meet pressing tax and marriage payments or the expenses of the annual festivals or even those of litigation. The idea is to try to help the unfortunate borrower tide over a lean year due to bad harvest, so that he can thereby fulfil his social and legal obligations. Witnesses are always required to be present when the actual bargain is struck. As soon as his crops are good he is bound to return at least the same measure[10] and kind of crop or grain as was originally lent to him. Unless a definite date has been fixed for the repayment, the borrower is usually allowed a full season for the particular crop to be harvested; and it is not uncommon for the lender to waive repayment on account of a bad harvest and to demand it only when the borrower's fortunes have sufficiently improved. A good deal depends upon the relationship between the parties to the contract.

A recent development of this type of economic agreement is the practice whereby agents of European firms working among agricultural communities make cash advances to farmers on the security of the latter's growing crops. Such loans are often granted free of interest; but the firm's lien on the crops is probably a sufficient guarantee of the money advanced.[11]

(ii) The epithet '*socio-economic*' as applied to this category of loan contracts is not very apt. It does not exactly describe the essence of the arrangement by which a borrower of petty cash 'pawns' his valuable gown, goat or ox with the lender for anything from 5*s*. to £5.[12] Interest is secured on such loans by the requirement that the borrower can reclaim his property only on repayment of half as much again as the amount lent. The surcharge may be more or less in individual cases. Because this kind of private loan is not made for agricultural or trading purposes but only for personal out-of-pocket expenses, the romantic sub-title of 'socio-economic' loan contracts has been assigned to it.

(iii) Loans sought and granted for the promotion of trade or the advancement of business enterprises come under the sub-heading of 'commercial'. The legal incidents of a money loan will differ, however, according as the loan is understood by the parties to be governed either by customary law or by English law. Loans made otherwise than in accordance with customary law are regulated by the Moneylenders Ordinance, the provisions of which are analogous to the principles of English law on the subject.

Under customary law, on the other hand, loans of money may be repaid at any time, and no period of limitation applied to bar the lender's right to reclaim his money, provided of course that the contract itself can be proved.

Loans under Islamic law. It is important to note in this connexion that Moslem law forbids the taking of interest on money loans, and indeed on all forms of loan. Accordingly, goods lent, if it be returned *in specie*, must not be taken back on profit; nor can articles sold on credit be priced initially at a higher amount than that normally payable when goods are sold for ready cash. In the view of Islamic law anyone selling articles on credit has done nothing, apart from the mere act of parting temporarily with his property, to earn any reward. Therefore, whatever he takes extra constitutes an unjust enrichment, a *jus abutendi*. Now, in communities with subsistence economy and an idealistic social ethics, this limited view of the modern business world may be tenable. But it is a far cry from the barter-dominated system of the seventh-century[13] to the competitive commerce of the twentieth.

Fortunately, no Islamic country, not even Northern Nigeria, has followed this injunction to the letter. Various devices are employed on all hands to circumvent the law.[14] Larger quantities of corn than those actually lent are usually returned by borrowers to lenders; goods sold on credit are often in fact paid for at more than the cash price; loans are frequently repaid with something for the lender's trouble. The Hausa 'lada' (i.e. wages, consideration for services rendered) has now come to mean little more than just wages. It would be difficult otherwise to keep pace with the rough and tumble of the business world of today.

Other contracts. It remains to draw attention to other traditional forms of legally binding agreement such as the money-raising clubs in which members contribute specified sums which are taken in rotation, or the system of apprenticeship of learners to master-journeymen of craft guilds.

Notes

1 A sketchy, layman's description of the Yoruba practice will be found in A. K. Ajisafe's *Laws and Customs of the Yorubas* (1924), ch. XXIA.

2 See Forde and Scott's *Native Economies of Nigeria* (1946), p. 165; also, F. W. de St. Croix, *The Fulani of Northern Nigeria.*

3 N. W. Thomas, *Anthropological Report on Ibo-Speaking Peoples of Nigeria* (1914), Pt. IV.

4 This system is called 'Aro' in Yoruba, 'Dzolo' in Nupe, 'Gaya' in Hausa (see p. 208 of Delano, *op. cit.;* p. 248 of Nadel, *op. cit.;* p. 122 of Forde and Scott, *op. cit.*, respectively).

5 According to Forde and Scott, p. 247, among some Ibos such labour may be rendered free of charge; so, too, among some Yorubas (Delano), p. 208; while the Hausas now demand 'lada', i.e. wages (Forde and Scott, p. 122).

6 E.g. see Nadel, *op. cit.*, pp. 248–51, 370–1, 374–6.

7 E.g. 'Egba' system, p. 91 of Forde and Scott; 'Owe' system, p. 208 of Delano.

8 In some cases nothing is demanded as security by a lender who has reason to rely on the personal integrity of the borrower or of his surety.

9 Even goats, sheep and poultry are known to have been so lent.

10 Quite frequently, 1 bundle of guinea corn has to be repaid with 2, or 2 bundles with 3. (See Forde and Scott, p. 166, speaking of the North.)

11 Forde and Scott, p. 167.

12 The actual limits are fixed more by convention than by the parties, for the purposes for which such domestic loans are sought and granted are often well established and expressly limited by custom.

13 Mohamed, the founder of Islam, is said to have died in A.D. 632 (*Encyclopædia Britannica*, Vol. 15, pp. 646–7).

14 See Forde and Scott, p. 165, for some of the subterfuges variously resorted to in Zaria and elsewhere in the North.

J. C. D. Lawrance: The Iteso*

Cattle Herding

This is the commonest form of contract in Teso.

Contracts may be written or verbal and need not necessarily specify the remuneration to the herdsman or the period of the contract.

All contracts for herding of cattle must be witnessed by at least two witnesses. No witness fee is chargeable.

NOTE: This rule is not always followed, particularly when the contract is written. Courts are inclined to accept written contracts without any direct proof of validity.

Quotation: D.C. 14/54: D.N.C. 36/54: P. Mulagangabo v. *Ewangu:*

Mulagangabo herded thirty-seven head of cattle for nine years for Ewangu's brother, who died. He was awarded one bull in the clan court for this service but claimed a further three head. The Sub-County Court of Kyere rejected this claim.

* J. C. D. Lawrance, *The Iteso*, Oxford University Press, 1957, pp. 234–240.

On appeal in the County Court Mulagangabo produced a written contract unwitnessed. He could produce no proof of validity. The County Court of Serere rejected the document because it was spelt Luganda fashion with *l* interchanged with *r*. The D.N.C. accepted the document but the D.C. on revision upheld the findings of the County Court on the grounds that the document unless admitted must be witnessed, preferably by at least two witnesses.

Unless there is specific provision to the contrary all contracts are assumed to give the herdsman the right to dispose of all milk.

Unless there is specific provision to the contrary all offspring of the stock belong to the owner.

NOTE: It is not unusual for the owner to claim and to be awarded what should be the natural increase of a herd without proving that such increase occurred.

The herdsman is not responsible for any loss or damage to the herd, unless he directly caused it, provided that he takes all possible steps to inform the owner of any illness or loss without delay.

The herdsman is responsible for any damage done by the herd to crops or other property or for any contravention of grazing or quarantine rules. He is responsible also for building any necessary calf houses or kraals.

In disputes regarding remuneration, when no remuneration is specifically fixed in advance, courts assess the amount to be paid. Customs in this matter vary throughout the district.

NOTE: In the past the cattle owners of any one area herded their cattle communally and each owner in the area had to take his turn as herdsman. There was, of course, no question of remuneration. This custom is no longer followed. Because holdings became more scattered or because owners were unwilling to undertake communal herding duties, it became customary to ask close friends or relations to herd stock. It was recognized practice to give this friend or relation a present such as a cow or calf as a token of gratitude, but no fixed remuneration was recognized. Nowadays cattle herding is a business almost exclusively in the hands of Bahima, and monetary rewards are becoming common.

Quotation: (a) Gweri Sub-County 305/49: Kasungu s/o Sikirabanga (Muhima) v. *Akuan s/o Eyapu:*

Kasungu agreed to herd Akuan's cattle for a specific period of four years in return for one head of cattle. The contract was written. Owing to sickness Kasungu resigned after four months. The Court fixed remuneration at 40*s*. for that period. Kasungu took milk for his own use 'because it was not recorded in the agreement'.

Quotation: (b) Kabulubulu Sub-County 187/51: B. Odungu v. *Ekoyu:*

Odungu claimed 408*s*. for herding thirty-one head of cattle for one year and ten months, alleging the agreement was for two head of cattle a year. The agreement was not proved. Ekoyu had paid 28*s*. for Odungu's taxes in 1950 and had offered 30*s*. for 1951. The Court ruled that this offer was equitable.

Quotation: (c) Kabulubulu Sub-County 25/50: Achela v. *Mwanya Mugesera:*

Achela was given one cow to herd by Mwanya which produced five calves in the six years he herded it. The contract was for an unspecific amount. He was awarded 20*s*.

Other examples show 3*s*. per animal per year (Kyere); one cow for herding fifty head for a year, and one cow for herding fifteen head for a year (Kateta 76/51 and 78/51); 20*s*. a month (Amuria).

House-building

Contracts may be verbal or written.

NOTE: This refers to permanent or semi-permanent buildings only, and the law is still vague on the subject as such houses have only begun to be erected in very modern times.

Contracts must always be witnessed by at least two witnesses. No witness fee is payable.

A time limit for completion of the work is seldom, if ever, specified in the contract and penalty clauses are unknown.

If a contractor fails to complete the work he must repay any money paid, keeping such amount as is adequate for work already done. If he has not been paid, a contractor may claim any reasonable sum for work already done in an uncompleted contract. The court has complete discretion to award any amount which is appropriate.

Quotation: D.C. 11/51: D.N.C. 4/51: Y. Kigwekyalwazi v. *D. Ekumekwap:*

This was a claim for payment of 150*s*. or some lesser amount for bricks made according to a verbal agreement. The contract was never completed. The evidence showed that Kigwekyalwazi had only spent about three days on making the bricks and that their quality was poor. The claim was entirely dismissed.

Contracts for temporary houses are not made as above. On a given day neighbours are invited to assist by promise of beer or a small reward such as a meal of chicken.

It is unknown for a man to contract with one particular person for construction of a temporary house.

Medical Treatment

Fees, varying from a few shillings to a goat and depending on the gravity of the illness, are always fixed in advance.

NOTE: But fees may be much higher. Augusta Edwara of Orungo had a long illness which was not cured in Soroti hospital but was eventually cured by an *emuron* in Kabulubulu in Kaberamaido county. Payment of two head of cattle was made for this cure.

They are not, however, paid to the doctor (*emuron*) until a cure has been obtained. It is the mark of a bad doctor to ask for payment in advance.

But a patient usually makes a small gift in advance such as a small sum of money in return for the *emuron's* efforts to find the right medicines, or a chicken to bless the medicine (*akokor aipukio ekia*).

If the patient does not recover, the doctor has no claim to the fee.

If the patient grows worse or dies, no compensation can be claimed from the doctor but any fees paid can be recovered.

Quotation: Amuria County 45/50: Kuju Sub-County 63/50: Abdi bin Oritai v. *Sebastian Kayonjo:*

Sebastian Kayonjo treated Abdi's child. He was paid two sheep, eight chickens, and 24*s*. before the child was cured. Unluckily the child died. Abdi therefore sued for return of this property and was awarded two sheep, eight chickens, and 22*s*. This judgement was upheld on appeal to the county court.

The patient is, however, at liberty to change his doctor provided he first informs him, and no claim will then lie by the doctor for payment of the fee.

Labour Contracts

There are no regular private employers of labour gangs. Large landowners employ labour for specific tasks such as weeding or harvesting.

Payment in such cases is usually by beer, though monetary payment is becoming more common.

It is not unusual for a man to be employed in a particular homestead in return for food and tax obligations.

Quotation: Asamuk Sub-County 32/52: Court v. *Echilu s/o Omorio:*

Echilu was accused of keeping Reuben Okello in his house for three years without making his presence known to the chiefs. He was convicted and ordered to pay R. Okello's tax obligations for three years, 84*s*., and to pay a fine of 25*s*.

NOTE: This was a criminal prosecution for the offence of hiding a potential taxpayer and is only quoted in this section because the Court held the view that the employer should meet the tax obligations of his employee.

A form of apprenticeship exists in the *asapan* initiation ceremonies during which an initiate serves in the house of his instructor, performing many menial tasks without remuneration until such time as he passes out at the initiation ceremonies.

NOTE: Apprenticeship to a tradesman is almost unknown. Eria Mambule, a Muganda of Ngora, a carpenter, used to take pupils to work for him in return for their food until they became competent at the trade; he then paid them.

Sales

Sale of Cattle

At least two witnesses are necessary for each transaction.

This rule does not, of course, apply to sales in cattle markets because such sales are recorded and permits issued for the movement of stock.

No witness fee is payable.

Payment can be by instalments if so agreed.

The animal in such cases remains the property of its old owner until such time as the final instalment is paid but it may be taken by the new owner at any time agreed upon between the parties.

The new owner can use all milk as soon as the cow is taken to his house even though he has not paid the final instalment.

If the beast dies in the new owner's hands, he must immediately pay any instalments still owing to the old owner.

Until the final instalment is paid the old owner has the right to take back the beast and to repay any instalments paid.

Sale of other Property

No witnesses are necessary to such transactions.

Ownership when payment by instalments is agreed upon, is according to the rules covered above.

Pledges

Pledge of Female Children

A female child may be pledged by her father or legal guardian as security for a debt or loan.

At least two witnesses are necessary. No witness fee is chargeable.

The girl visits the creditor's house from time to time as a token of the pledge but does not live there.

All marriage negotiations are conducted by the debtor (her father), and not by the creditor. (The loan or debt is usually repaid from the bride-price received.)

If the creditor has sexual intercourse with the girl he is liable to pay the usual compensation or to marry her, in which case the debt is set off against the bride-price payable.

Pledge of Cattle

At least two witnesses are necessary. No fee is chargeable.

The beast is kept by the creditor.

Milk is the property of the creditor.

Calves are property of the debtor though they will be kept by the creditor until the pledge is redeemed.

If the cow dies while in possession of the creditor from causes which cannot be attributed to neglect by the creditor, the debtor has no claim against the creditor and must furnish a further pledge. If, however, death is due to the negligence of the creditor, the value of the cow may be set off against the debt owed by the debtor.

Loans

Loans must be witnessed. No witness fee is payable. Normally two witnesses are necessary but courts can accept one witness if other evidence is available.

Quotation: (a) D.C. Civil Appeal 16/51: D.N.C. 111/51: Ngora County 8/51: W. Opio v. E. Ekodeu:

W. Opio claimed a debt of 1,027*s.* and a bicycle from Ekodeu. The alleged loan had been made in eight instalments on eight separate occasions. Some of these instalments were not witnessed at all. Others amounting to 765*s.* were witnessed by only one witness at each transaction. The lower courts dismissed the claim on the grounds that Opio, being a business man, should have made a proper witnessed agreement or kept proper books. This decision was upheld by the D.C.

Quotation: (b) D.C. Rev. 6/52: D.N.C. 112/51: Serere County 112/51: Bugondo Sub-County 60/51: M. Ogabe v. *K. Okiror:*

Okiror sued Ogabe for repayment of a debt of 300*s.* The loan was witnessed by one man only. The evidence shows that other members of the same party agreed to buy bicycles together at Jinja. There was therefore a likely reason for the loan and Ogabe did apparently buy a bicycle. All courts ruled that the debt was valid and must be repaid.

Contracts may be written or verbal.

Unless specifically stated in the contract, interest is never charged.

Repayment of a loan in whole or in part must be witnessed.

Note: It is normal practice for the witness actually to take the money into his own hands from the debtor and hand it to the creditor.

There is no time limit for claiming repayment of a loan.

Debts are inheritable provided they are registered at the meeting held to dispose of the estate of a deceased person.

S. M. Seymour: Native Law in South Africa*

Contracts affecting status, such as the dowry contract, have been dealt with elsewhere.[1]

In respect of the contracts of sale, exchange and loan for consumption there is no substantial difference between the law of the land and Native law, except that no interest is ever stipulated for in the latter system, nor does it automatically run from the time a debtor is *in mora.*[2] There is even a form of delivery similar to *constitutum possessorium*; in a sale or exchange the seller, instead of physically delivering the article sold or exchanged, may either point it out or describe it to the buyer and thereafter by agreement continue in its possession; this pointing out or describing constitutes a valid delivery, and ownership thereupon passes to the buyer.[3] It is not possible to tell from the pleadings, as a rule, under which system of law the parties made the above kinds of contract, but only when the defendant raises a plea of prescription need the court ascertain under which system of law the contract was made, because there is no limitation of actions in Native law.[4]

Other common types of contract and quasi-contract known to Native law will be dealt with under separate headings, as follows:

Pledge

A pledge may be made of property or of dowry eventually to be received for an unmarried woman; depending on their agreement, the debtor will either deliver the property or woman, as the case may be, to the creditor, or retain possession thereof.[5]

Where the debtor has handed pledged property to his creditor the tacit understanding is that if the pledgor does not pay the debt, the creditor may keep the property in settlement. The contract seems to be, in effect, a *pactum commissorium.*[5]

Where the debtor has retained possession of the article pledged, the court has not yet had to go into the question of the respective rights of the pledgor and pledgee, and whether the rights of the pledge are superior to those of third parties who seek to attach and sell the pledged article in satisfaction of their claims.[6] It may be, indeed, that the word 'pledge' is a misnomer when applied to the transaction.

If a girl's dowry is pledged and she is handed to the creditor (as security, one might even say) it is usually understood that the creditor is to receive the whole dowry in satisfaction of his debt. He never, therefore, has to account to her guardian.[7]

* S. M. Seymour, *Native Law in South Africa*, Juta & Co. Ltd., 1960, pp. 218–223.

If the woman is not handed to the creditor, then the contract means simply that the creditor agrees to wait for payment of the debt until fine or dowry is paid for the woman. The woman's guardian receives the fine or dowry and is obliged to settle the debt out of it. The rights of the creditor in competition with those of third parties have never yet been discussed.

Ethula

A kraalhead usually supplies the whole or a substantial part of the dowry for the first wife of each of his sons, whether legitimate or adopted, and of an illegitimate son of his wife, and even of an unrelated male who has grown up at his kraal, and is consequently regarded as a 'son'. He is entitled to a refund in full for his disbursement, theoretically from the dowry of the first daughter born of the union, but should she die before marrying or be not the first to marry, the refund is made from the dowry of the daughter who marries first. This obligation is quasi-contractual, and it arises automatically when the union has been consummated.[8]

Under *Pondo* law, the dowry received for the son's *eldest* daughter is handed to his father, who apportions it between himself and his son. It appears that the father usually keeps one or two cattle only for himself and gives the rest to his son. Once the father has so allotted himself a portion, he has no further claim, even if more dowry is paid later for his son's daughter.[9]

Sometimes a kraalhead will take cattle out of one House to pay dowry for the wife of a son of another House. This creates an inter-House debt which is normally repaid by the son from the dowry he receives for his first-married daughter.[10]

When a kraalhead has paid the dowry for a wife of his son, the son's liability to reimburse his father is extinguished by the latter's death.[11]

Although in all tribes fathers pay dowry for their son's first wives, the decisions quoted show that only in the *Nguni* group does the son incur the liability to make a refund.

Except in those parts of the tribe influenced by the *Zulu*, this kind of liability does not arise among the *Tsonga*.[12]

A similar liability is incurred by a minor House to make a refund, out of the dowry of its first-married daughter, to the major House whose property was used to pay dowry for the wife of the minor House.

Ukukwenzelelele

A customary union, although primarily a matter between the husband and his wife's guardian, is in a wider sense a matter which concerns the two family groups. Consequently when a man takes his first wife, although his father or guardian pays the greater part of the dowry for her, it is usual for some of the male relatives of his group either voluntarily to offer, or to be requested, to contribute a beast or so towards the dowry; sometimes a friend will make a contribution of a beast or two.[13]

If there is no express agreement how and when such contributions are to be repaid, they are repayable by the husband from the dowry received for the first-maried daughter of the union.[14] If there is an agreement, it is, of course, binding.

Where the dowry, supplemented by such contributions, has been paid by the husband's father, he receives payment from the dowry for the first-married daughter, as explained in part 2 above, and then pays out the contributors.[15]

Ukufakwa

When a relative of a girl's father makes a contribution, usually in the form of a beast, towards the ceremonies which are carried out when she reaches the age of puberty, or towards the expenses of her marriage or wedding outfit, or contributes to any other expense to which her father is normally put, the contributor is automatically *fakwaed* into her dowry. *Fakwa* means to be put into; the contributor is put into the daughter's dowry, that is to say, becomes a participant in her dowry to the extent to which he has borne expenses, and is entitled to be refunded from it.[16]

Another form of *ukufakwa* arises in express agreement and has already been dealt with.[17]

Agency

Agency is well known in Native law, and in transactions or acts such as dowry contracts demands for further dowry, demands for restoration of dowry, demands for fines for seduction or adultery, the parties normally carry out their negotiation through chosen messengers or spokesmen.[18]

Whether or not the principal is present at the transaction or act, the agreement or act of his authorized messenger or agent in connexion with the matter in hand is binding on him.[19]

Thus when messengers are sent to demand a certain payment, or to report a delict to the person charged with its commission, a payment made to the messengers and the conditions on which they accept it are binding on their principal.[20]

A messenger, if successful in exacting a payment in the course of his mandate, is entitled to a reasonable remuneration of a beast, or perhaps more; his remuneration is regulated according to the amount recovered. A messenger is entitled to remuneration as of right, provided he is successful in exacting a payment; there need have been no prior express contract for his remuneration.[21]

When a plaintiff has brought his case before a headman having no authorized jurisdiction to try civil actions, if the headman's 'judgment' is accepted by the defendant, the headman has the plaintiff's implied authority to receive payment of the debt; a payment made to the headman or his messengers if valid, and the conditions on which he or they accept it are binding on the plaintiff; except, of course, if at the time 'judgment' was delivered, the latter signified that he was not satisfied with it.[22]

When a kraalhead leaves his kraal for a considerable period, he may appoint a 'keeper' to manage it in his absence; if he appoints no 'keeper', his nearest major male relative manages the kraal. No payment may be claimed for this service, but a reward may be given.

A kraalhead, at whose kraal the daughter of another is residing, may give her away in a customary union; he should advise her guardian of the forthcoming nuptials, and if he does he may deduct from the dowry and keep one beast in payment of his expenses in connexion with the girl's initiation, if she was initiated while at his kraal; he is also entitled to a further beast to reimburse himself for any wedding outfit he may have supplied to her, and another for *isondhlo*, if he is entitled to payment for *isondhlo*. If he has failed to report the proposed marriage to her guardian he is thereby disentitled to these reimbursements, except for *isondhlo*.

Nqoma, Mafisa or Sisa

Nqoma, *mafisa* and *sisa* are different words for the same contract. The term *nqoma* will be used here.

The contract of *nqoma* is loan of livestock, up to any number. The borrower (or *nqomee* as the court has called him) is entitled to the benefit of the use of the stock, and the right to produce therefrom other than progeny.[23] Wool is not, however, regarded as produce to which the *nqomee* is entitled, and belongs to the owner of the sheep.[24]

The *nqomee* is liable for ordinary negligence only, that is to say, the degree of diligence expected of him is that which an ordinarily prudent person will observe in the care of his own property.[25]

The lender retains the ownership in the stock and their progeny.[26] Any losses by death, theft, or straying not caused by the *nqomee's* negligence are borne by the lender; but the *nqomee* is obliged to make an immediate report of any such loss, and at the same time, whenever possible, to send the skin to the lender for identification purposes; if he fails to do this, he can be compelled by the owner to *vusa* the lost animal, that is to say, to 'make it alive again' by replacing it with a similar animal.[27] Notwithstanding this provision of Native law, where the evidence shows clearly that an animal has died a natural death, or has been stolen or the like, failure to report timeously or to produce the skin does not oblige the *nqomee* to replace the animal; the reason for this holding is that it would be contrary to natural justice if the *nqomee* were made liable for a beast which has obviously died or been stolen; it is implicit in the judgment that if there is any doubt that a missing beast has died or been stolen, this doubt must be construed against the *nqomee* in the event of his having failed to make a timeous report of such alleged death or theft.[28]

It is customary for the owner to place his earmark on *nqomaed* stock. Thus should a person claim to be the lender of livestock in possession of another and which do not bear the former's earmark, the presumption will favour the latter's different version of how he came by them.[29]

In order to make himself acquainted with the progeny of the *nqomaed* stock, to dispose of the natural products, such as wool, to which he is entitled, and generally to keep the *nqomee* under surveillance and demonstrate to the world his interest in the stock, usually the owner or his representative will from time to time make an inspection thereof, note what female animals are heavy with unborn young, and place his earmark or other identification on unmarked property. His failure to take these customary and rather obvious precautions against being defrauded by the *nqomee* does not, of course, divest the owner of any of his rights, but may, in the absence of other evidence, make it difficult for him to prove the contract in due course, if it is denied by the alleged *nqomee*, or to query the correctness of the account which the *nqomee* finally renders.[30]

The contract of *nqoma* is not normally of fixed duration, but is terminable by a demand by the lender for an account from the *nqomee* of the stock and progeny and for delivery thereof. If the lender insists, the account and delivery must be made at his kraal.[31]

It is unusual for the lender to demand an account and delivery shortly after the contract has been entered into; these contracts usually endure for a number of years.[32]

If the lender is satisfied with the *nqomee's* account, it is usual for him to reward the *nqomee*, but there is no legal obligation on him to do this; the amount of the reward is entirely in the discretion of the lender, and, in fixing the amount, he is influenced to a large extent by the number of increase; the reward usually takes the form of one or more of the increase. Pending payment of a reward, the *nqomee* has no lien over *nqomaed* stock.[33]

Once the lender has promised a reward, he is, of course, bound by his promise, but it is not usual for him so to bind himself until the *nqomee* has made his account; nor is it usual for the lender to give or promise a reward when there is no increase or where the *nqomee*, upon demand, has failed or refused to render a true account or to make delivery.[34]

A *nqoma* is never made to two or more persons jointly; the *nqomee* is invariably one individual.[35]

The *nqomee*, being a lawful possessor, has all the remedies for restoration of possession against a person (including the lender) who has spoliated *nqomaed* stock from him; the lender has no such remedies, for he is not in possession.[36]

The lender may vindicate his stock wheresoever they may be, but he should take action against a third person having possession as soon as he discovers that the *nqomee* is not in possession: if he does not, his denial that he approved of the transaction between the *nqomee* and the possessor will lose the weight it might otherwise have carried.[37]

It is not unusual for a kraalhead to *nqoma* stock from one House to another. The custom of earmarking the stock with the earmark of the transferor House should be observed, otherwise the presumption will be that the transaction was not a *nqoma*, but is more likely to have been an allotment or a payment of some kind, if this is the defence put forward.[38]

Nqomaed stock cannot be attached for the debts of the *nqomee*.[39]

In the Transvaal it has been held that the lender is liable to refund to the *nqomee* the latter's disbursements for dipping and grazing fees, but not the expenses in connexion with the herding of the stock.[40]

Notes

1 See Chapter VI of Seymour.

2 *Warosi* v. *Zotimba*, 1942 N.A.C. (C & O) 55, Umtata; *Magidela* v. *Sawintshi*, 1943 N.A.C. (C & O) 52, Bizana.

3 See by analogy Seymour, chapter V, 2A(iv), regarding what constitutes a valid delivery in Native law.

4 See cases under note 2, *supra*.

5 *Nkalitshana* v. *Mdyogolo*, 3 N.A.C. 208, Umtata.

6 *Nkalitshana* v. *Mdyogolo*, 3 N.A.C. 208, Umtata.

7 *Konzapi* v. *Mehlenkomo*, 2 N.A.C. 38, Willowvale; *Mbelingo* v. *Daniel*, 2 N.A.C. 122, Matatiele; *Diniso* v. *Msila*, 1941 N.A.C. (C & O) 14, Umtata; *Pennington* v. *Mcitwa*, 1942 N.A.C. (C & O) 45, Flagstaff; *Vatsha* v. *Mfenenduna*, 1936 N.A.C. (C & O) 39, Mt. Frere.

8 *Nzima* v. *Hlahleni*, 1 N.A.C. 35, Engcobo; *Njoko* v. *Gqzombana*, 1 N.A.C. 205. Umtata; *Nqwili* v. *Xilongile*, 2 N.A.C. 59, Elliot; *Ngamle* v. *Fitshane*, 2 N.A.C. 80, Qumbu; *Nobumba* v. *Mfecane*, 2 N.A.C. 104, St. Marks; *Gxumisa* v. *Sitaka*, 2 N.A.C. 127, Flagstaff; *Madolo* v. *Mjonono*, 3 N.A.C. 68, Willowvale; *Twayi* v. *Sirayi*, 5 N.A.C. 100, Tsolo; *Macwili* v. *Dunjana*, 1940 N.A.C.

(C & O) 3, Willowvale; *Magqagqa* v. *Ntlebi*, 1930 N.A.C. (C & O) 36, Lusikisiki; *Ntlokandala* v. *Palele*, 1945 N.A.C. (C & O) 21, Cofimvaba; *Maganu* v. *Maganu*, 1938 N.A.C. (T & N) 14, Sibasa; *M'Tumunje* v. *Mahlangu*, 1938 N.A.C. (T & N) 196, Belfast.

[9] *Mzileni* v. *Mzileni*, 5 N.A.C. 39, Nqamakwe; *Candane* v. *Feju*, 1940 N.A.C. (C & O) 163, Libode.

[10] *Sizaka* v. *Mbiko*, 4 N.A.C. 68, Lusikisiki; *Ngalonkulu* v. *Ngalonkulu*, 1943 N.A.C. (C & O) 10, *Bhaca*, Mt. Frere. See chapter V, 3B.

[11] *Qasekonya* v. *Msizo*, 6 N.A.C. 7, Umtata; *Tanana* v. *Tanana*, 1947 N.A.C. (C & O) 25, Umtata. N.B. These are *Thembu* cases.

[12] *Maganu* v. *Maganu*, 1938 N.A.C. (T & N) 14, Sibasa.

[13] See cases under note 3 *supra*.

[14] *Nobumba* v. *Mfecane*, 2 N.A.C. 104, St. Marks; *Molo* v. *Gaga*, 1947 N.A.C. (C & O) 80, Willowvale; *Sogoni* v. *Gele*, 1947 N.A.C. (C & O) 87, Ngqeleni; *Maganu* v. *Maganu*, 1938 N.A.C. (T & N) 14, *Shangaan*, Sibasa; *M'Tumunje* v. *Mahlangu*, 1938 N.A.C. (T & N) 196, *Ndebele*, Belfast. It has been held, however, that a contributor may claim a refund at any time, and that it is only when there is an express agreement that he is to be paid from the dowry of a daughter, or at some other time specified, that he is obliged to await the event (see *Mpikwa* v. *Maqayekana*, 1949 N.A.C. (S.D.) 135, Umzimkulu).

[15] *Mnxaku* v. *Madolo*, 3 N.A.C. 67, Engcobo.

[16] *Nobumba* v. *Mfecane*, 2 N.A.C. 104, St. Marks; *Molo* v. *Gaga*, 1947 N.A.C. (C & O) 80, Willowvale.

[17] *Titi* v. *Titi*, 4 N.A.C. 369, Mqanduli; *Nkethleni* v. *Mlanjeni*, 4 N.A.C. 368, Umtata.

[18] See cases under note 20, *infra*.

[19] See cases under note 21, *infra*.

[20] *Dyani* v. *Diyana*, 4 N.A.C. 8, Engcobo; *Sakati* v. *Kumalo*, 1944 N.A.C. (C & O) 54, Komgha; *Gijana* v. *Mangali*, 1946 N.A.C. (C & O) 60, Engcobo.

[21] *Mtambayahlaba* v. *Sambata*, 1 N.A.C. 187, Umtata.

[22] *Ramba* v. *Dwa*, 1 N.A.C. 161, Mqanduli; *Sixongolwana* v. *Ntaka*, 5 N.A.C. 78, Umtata; *Fana* v. *Mawala*, 5 N.A.C. 79, Umzimkulu; *Funwayo* v. *Gidiyana*, 1933 N.A.C. (C & O) 15; *Mawindi* v. *Mabombo*, 1934 N.A.C. (C & O) 72.

[23] This is clear from most decisions on *nqoma*; see cases under notes 4, 5, 6 and 38, *infra*; *Hlongwane* v. *Sithole*, 1947 N.A.C. (T & N) 51, Natal.

[24] *Gulani* v. *Gamkile*, 1951 N.A.C. (S.D.) 279, Mt. Ayliff.

[25] *Njekuse* v. *Tuta*, 1951 N.A.C. (S.D.) 276, Bizana.

[26] This is clear from most decisions on *nqoma*; see especially *Mxalisa* v. *Mtyuntyane*, 2 N.A.C. 109, Umtata; *Hlongwane* v. *Sithole*, 1947 N.A.C. (T & N) 51, Natal.

[27] *Nogonomfana* v. *Ngane*, 3 N.A.C. 35, Bizana; *Mahoza* v. *Pringle*, 3 N.A.C. 291, Mt. Ayliff; *Jijwa* v. *Mbuswana*, 5 N.A.C. 105, Tabankulu; *Lukuleni* v. *Manziwa*, 1945 N.A.C. (C & O) 42, Tsolo; *Similane* v. *Sugazie*, 1935 N.A.C. (T & N) 45; *Tutubolo* v. *Maroga*, 1940 N.A.C. (T & N) 97, Pretoria; *Majola* v. *Dube*, 1947 N.A.C. (T & N) 41, Natal.

[28] *Mcitakali* v. *Nkosayiboni*, 1951 N.A.C. (S.D.) 298, Willowvale.

[29] *Nohakisi* v. *Sibedlela*, 5 N.A.C. 104, Mqanduli; *Tedile* v. *Boboyi*, 1941 N.A.C. (C & O) 22, Mt. Fletcher.

[30] *Gulani* v. *Gamkile*, 1951 N.A.C. (S.D.) 279, Mt. Ayliff.

[31] *Mxalisa* v. *Mtyuntyane*, 2 N.A.C. 109, Umtata.

[32] *Hlongwane* v. *Sithole*, 1947 N.A.C. (T & N) 51, Natal.

[33] *Mxalisa* v. *Mtyuntyane*, 2 N.A.C. 109, Umtata; *Madotyeni* v. *Tshwaqu*, 2 N.A.C. 116, Ngqeleni; *Cabangana* v. *Mabandla*, 3 N.A.C. 205, Matatiele.

[34] *Madotyeni* v. *Tshwaqu*, 2 N.A.C. 116, Ngqeleni.

[35] *Mgobozi* v. *Nceme*, 3 N.A.C. 204, Qumba.

[36] *Mateza* v. *Magxa*, 4 N.A.C. 248, Umtata; *Sigcau* v. *Tunda*, 1931 N.A.C. (C & O) 22, Willowvale; *Lumkwana* v. *Lumkwana*, 1933 N.A.C. (C & O) 6, Mqanduli.

[37] *Mdlangaso* v. *Sigintsolo*, 6 N.A.C. 28, Bizana; *Lutuli* v. *Bili*, 1940 N.A.C. (C & O) 24, Mt. Fletcher; *Lukuleni* v. *Menziwa*, 1945 N.A.C. (C & O) 42, Tsolo; *Mato* v. *Mtlaka*, 1937 N.A.C. (C & O) 208, Engcobo.

[38] *Nohakisi* v. *Sibedlela*, 5 N.A.C. 104, Mqanduli; *Ntlakala* v. *Ngalo*, 1939 N.A.C. (C &O) 26, Flagstaff; *Maganu* v. *Maganu*, 1938 N.A.C. (T & N) 14, Sibasa.

[39] *Siwangobuso* v. *Ngindana*, 1 N.A.C. 142, Willowvale.

[40] *Bengane* v. *Tefu*, 1935 N.A.C. (T & N) 25.

Part IV

LAND LAW

Land has probably attracted the attention of more writers and commentators of African society than any other topic that is dealt with by customary law. This is not surprising, in view of the importance of land within the framework of the indigenous political and social structure as well as its role as a principal source of wealth and security for the individuals and groups that are subject to customary law. Yet, despite the voluminous literature on this topic, there is little agreement between the writers as to what precisely they are dealing with. Thus, writers employ such terms as 'land holding' and 'land usage' (Allan and Colson), 'land tenure' (Allott, White and Schapera), 'land rights' (Wilson on the Nyakyusa), and 'land law' (Lloyd and Meek) interchangeably in the titles of their works; and sometimes a single writer will use all of them within the scope of a single work without attempting to distinguish clearly between them.

This 'terminological confusion' (as White calls it) is reflected not only in the titles of these studies on land, but also in the approach to basic concepts of land law. It happens frequently, for instance, that legal rules governing land will be designated by different terms in relation to different societies by different writers, when their content can clearly be seen to be identical. This confusion arises at several different levels. One is the use of various words to describe the same concept, e.g. where writers have sought to indicate the participation of groups in relation to land they have called occupation 'communal' or 'collective' or 'corporate'. Again, a second class of difficulty arises in regard to the selection of a term to describe the powers which are exercised (by groups or individuals) over land: hence the use of words like 'rights' or 'interests' or 'ownership' or 'allodial title' in order to avoid the problem of categorising the definitions and descriptions of what exactly a person may do with his land. A final set of problems concerns the use of terms borrowed from other legal systems in which they have specific meanings, and their application to analogous—but not identical—situations in African law; examples of these are 'feudal', 'usufruct' and 'trusteeship'.

One of the principal difficulties which we have faced in this part arises precisely from this proliferation of conflicting terms and ideas. Not only was it necessary to select from among the works of a large number of writers so as to give a fair geographical spread in the material presented, but an attempt also had to be made to offer a balanced statement of the different approaches. Especially challenging was the choice of categories (i.e. chapter headings) under which the various views are expressed, so as to present, wherever possible, an unbiased picture. We must confess, however, that this has resulted in a considerable overlap between the material which has been included in the different chapters. Thus, in a way, it may be said that the first chapter on

General Characteristics and Concepts raises issues which are traversed in every one of the succeeding chapters and particularly in the fifth chapter on the Nature of Rights in Land. This was thought to be justifiable since it provides the reader with a general introduction to as many facets of the problem as possible. There is also an overlap between the second, third and fourth chapters because a description of Categories of Land necessarily involves a discussion of the rights of groups and individuals therein. Again, the sixth chapter on Other Rights in Relation to Land is really a continuation of the description contained in the fifth chapter on the Nature of Rights in Land, but deals specifically with lesser rights. Furthermore, the subject covered in the eighth chapter, on Strangers, is partially dealt with in the preceding chapter on Acquisition and Alienation of Rights, which includes a treatment *inter alia* with tenancies, mortgages and pledges.

Chapter 12

GENERAL CHARACTERISTICS AND CONCEPTS

This chapter deals, firstly, with the basic characteristics of African land law, as described by *Allott* and *Meek* generally, and by *Mugerwa* on East Africa. Of particular interest are the descriptions by *Allott* and *Meek* of the manner in which changes are occurring in the traditional land law of Africa. Secondly the chapter continues with problems relating to concepts and definitions, which have already been alluded to in the Introduction to this Part (see above). Whilst *White* contents himself with raising the most pressing of the terminological problems, *Bentsi-Enchill* goes further, by suggesting a new and definitive terminology for African land law. This is followed by a debate between *Allott* and *Simpson* on the use of the term 'absloute ownership', and its definition in African law.

A. N. Allott: Modern Changes in African Land Tenure*

1. Basic Characteristics of African Land Tenure

If one is to study the changes that are taking place in African land tenure, it is necessary to examine the character and rules of the customary law relating to land. Now there are a great number of different customary laws in Africa, and one must consider how far it is possible to make any valid generalization that applies to them all. The first question that has to be considered, therefore, is whether there are any general characteristics exhibited by land tenure under customary law in different parts of the continent; the next question is what these general basic characteristics (if any) consist of.

Some writers have denied that any land tenure at all exists in certain areas (e.g. where the population is nomadic, as in parts of British Somaliland). This argument rests on a very artificial interpretation of the English phrase, 'land tenure'. It is said that 'land tenure' either implies holding from some superior authority (cf. tenure from the Crown in English land law), or at least a permanent holding of a definable portion of soil —which might not be the case with nomadic populations. This is unduly restrictive; it will be found that, even among the nomads, groups and individuals have certain claims and privileges in respect of defined portions of land for defined purposes (e.g. claims to hunting or grazing tracts, water-holes). Since our concern is with the development of

* A. N. Allott, 'Modern Changes in African Land Tenure', in *Zeitschrift fur vergleichende Rechtwissenschaft*, pp. 45–57.

rights and interests in land in Africa, this particular argument can be easily evaded by choice of the appropriate alternative phraseology.

How far may statements of universal application be made about customary land laws, when one bears in mind the great diversity of economic activity, settlement patterns and social and political organization, which leads to corresponding diversity in the laws regulating lands? One contrasts (i) the nomadic Somali with their camels, the nomadic Masai with their cattle, the hunters such as the Bushmen, with (ii) settled pastoral people such as the Zulu and Tswana of Southern Africa, and the Hima of East Africa, and (iii) with settled agriculturalists or farmers practising mixed farming, such as the Kikuyu of Kenya, and the Akan, Yoruba and Ibo of the forest-belt of West Africa.

Political organization, which has the closest possible connexion with patterns of land tenure in most areas, also varies widely; so that, among the agriculturalists already cited, the Kikuyu and Ibo have an acephalous organization without chiefs, whilst the Yoruba and Akan have centralized societies with hierarchies of chiefs.

Settlement patterns and the habitat are also determinants of the greatest importance in influencing land tenure: some peoples tend to concentrate in large settlements (cf. Yoruba and Tswana), others live in smaller but compact village settlements (cf. Akan and Ibo), whilst others have a dispersed settlement pattern (cf. Kikuyu, and Tiv of Northern Nigeria).

The point need not be laboured; sufficient has been said to show how various may be the systems of land use and land law in African societies. Nevertheless it is argued by the present writer that certain features are commonly shared or exhibited by different African customary laws, which lends them a family likeness.[1] As a society progresses from one stage to the next, its evolution follows well-worn patterns (the stabilization of some Masai and Somali is a very useful illustration here).

These characteristic features of African land tenure I now briefly review:

(I) *The dominant role of groups and communities in the tenure of land.* These groups and communities are of two main kinds, social and political. In all societies, however small, the social or family organization is intimately linked with the exploitation of land. Often there is clan, lineage or household control over the occupation and enjoyment of land by individual members of the clan, lineage, or household, as the case may be. On the death of an individual holder or acquirer his property may vest in his family and become 'family property' in a stricter sense (as among many West African peoples). Individual family-members may only have limited rights to use family property, they may be unable to alienate it, and so on.

Political or territorial groups are also of the utmost importance. In the smaller, less organized societies these may be merely the territorial expression of social groups; but in all societies above this level the territorial units, both central and local (e.g. the tribe, the district, the village), and political authorities (e.g. the chief, the village headman or council of elders) have special significance and special claims or powers. In many societies occupation of land is controlled by political or land-authorities; in many societies a man's claim to the free use of land depends on his membership of the appropriate community, be it tribal or local. So great was the legal position of the chief as advised by his councillors in some societies that all the land of the tribe was said to belong to him—but this is a turn of phrase which requires elucidation and qualification.

(II) *Shifting cultivation and impermanence of titles.* Many different systems of so-called 'shifting cultivation' were practised in African societies. These were a reflection (*a*) of relative abundance of land, and (*b*) of relative poverty of tropical soils and lack of knowledge of the function of manure. Even where shifting cultivation was not practised titles of individual occupiers, especially to farm-plots, tended to be impermanent. This might be due to the control exercised by political authorities in some tribes over the occupation of land: land might be periodically re-allocated, and a man's heir or heirs might have no firm claim to continue occupation of the land allocated to him.

(III) *Subsistence and not commercial agriculture.* Farming was generally for subsistence, not exchange, though (*a*) cattle and other livestock might function as a medium of exchange and a means of acquiring wives, and (*b*) primitive markets existed in some areas, especially West Africa. There was little disposable surplus from farms or gardens, and permanent tree-crops were not usually cultivated.

(IV) *Undefined titles and boundaries.* Although customary methods exist for the demarcation of boundaries, these often either follow natural features or merely delimit some but not all of the boundaries of a plot (e.g. the base line and direction of farming into the virgin forest may be fixed, but the side and forward boundaries are left indeterminate). In the absence of land-litigation, and owing to periodic transfer of farms and perhaps whole villages to new sites, the need for fixed boundaries was not felt in many areas.

(V) *Absence of commercial transactions in land.* It is often said that the ancient customary law forbade the alienation of land; it is truer to say that the customary law did not provide for alienation, as there was no need and no demand for it. Where land was plentiful there was no need for a man to buy or lease a plot. Where occupation was under the control of a chief, the individual occupier had no power to transfer what did not belong to him. Strangers usually acquired by becoming accepted and full members of the appropriate community. There were no tree-crops or other permanent improvements which would give a piece of land an enhanced value. Sale of any sort of interest by any person was thus almost completely unknown until European influence directly or indirectly made itself felt.[2] Pledge (usufructuary mortgage) is found in many African societies, but the pledgee or creditor merely had the right to use the land until such time as the debtor satisfied his obligation.[3] Tenancies tended to be for a nominal rental, or else on a crop-sharing basis.

(VI) *The religious significance of land.* Land throughout Africa has religious or supernatural significance—as here tribal or family ancestors are buried on the land, or the land is itself a deity which requires placating. Land has been said (in West Africa) to belong to the ancestors as much as to the living occupiers: this is not necessarily a figure of speech. In some societies control of the occupation of land is in the hands of landpriests or land-chiefs (cf. the tendanas of Northern Ghana), who are quite distinct from the political chiefs. These land-priests are often representative of an autochthonous population which has been conquered by immigrants from outside.

In discussing African land tenure, the question of terminology is a most important one. There are considerable misconceptions as to indigenous African land tenure; in particular, the term 'commmunity/communal ownership' is often used. This term is misleading, if it implies that individuals had no separate rights in land. The word 'ownership' itself—the explanation of which causes the greatest difficulty—is often used uncritically by European writers in such statements as: 'there is no ownership of land in African law', or 'the chief owns all the land of the tribe'.

I should like to argue that it is necessary to refine and define one's terminology in the light of linguistic theory, before attempting to describe the features of African, or any other alien, law. One must avoid the naïve mistake of thinking that words have any true or proper meaning, and of trying to force the rules of African law into the straitjacket of English or other European legal terminology.

2. Importance of this topic in Africa today

The legal systems of the British African territories ought perhaps to be described at this point. Such legal systems are complicated, in that each territory has (*a*) a system of general law, usually derived from the law of England, though with later changes made by the local legislature through ordinance or proclamation; and (*b*) a number of special laws, applying in particular to aherents of certain religions (e.g. Islam) or to members of certain communities. By far the most important of these special laws is African customary law. This remains in full or partial operation in the sphere of land tenure; and disputes affecting land occupied by Africans in accordance with customary law are usually reserved for adjudication by the native courts under customary law alone.

Not only are several different types of law found in African territories; but there are also different kinds of courts. In most territories there are (*a*) the courts primarily administering the general law (Supreme or High Court and magistrates' courts), and (*b*) courts primarily administering African customary law or Islamic law (the native, African, customary, or local courts).

Land and land tenure is a most explosive subject in modern Africa. From the economic point of view it is essential to develop the major resource of most African countries, which is and will continue to be—despite the general adoption of a policy of industrialization—their land. From the political point of view inter-tribal or inter-racial feeling is at its highest when land is under discussion (present and past events in Kenya are the most extreme illustration of this).

Industrial and commercial development is going ahead at a varying pace in practically all African countries. This, coupled with the factors already mentioned, has led African governments to adopt a policy of reform, both in methods of agriculture and in the law governing the tenure of land. This policy, for instance, was strongly advocated by the Royal Commission on Land and Population in East Africa, which reported in 1955, and whose recommendations are now in effect being put into force in Kenya.

3. Modes of Change

(a) *Change by the people themselves.* Change in African land tenure has not, however, had to wait for official action: the African people themselves have for a long time been adapting their customary laws in response to the demands of education, commercial agriculture, increased population, etc. Undoubtedly the most potent agent of change has been the commercialization of agriculture, in other words the shift from a subsistence to a money or market economy. This change has been stimulated by the authorities in various ways (e.g. the imposition of an annual tax means that the peasant must earn enough cash by sale of produce or labour at a wage to pay his tax; agricultural departments stimulate the growing of cash-crops by counsel and advice, distribution of seedling plants, etc); but basically the commercialization of agriculture is due to (*a*) the arrival in Africa of certain economic plants and their suitability for peasant cultivation (maize, coffee, cocoa provide contrasted examples—the spread of cocoa cultivation in the then Gold Coast is particularly fascinating), and (*b*) the simultaneous arrival of a whole host of new wants for consumer goods, education, better housing, etc. Both these arrivals were due to the European. The consequent stimulation of acquisitiveness has led to challenge to, and sometimes the overthrow of, many fundamental principles and aspects of traditional life.

Population-pressure is another factor. It is the result mainly of the cessation of slave-raiding and inter-tribal war and of improved health measures, and has developed drastically in certain regions (e.g. Kikuyuland in Kenya, Iboland in Eastern Nigeria). The happy times when there was enough land for everyone are now passing in such regions. Other consequences are the appearance of landlordism, the growth of a landless class, and the employment of paid agricultural labour. Population-pressure is accentuated by the more permanent character of many economic crops, which leads to much larger individual holdings.

Customary law is plastic: it may be rapidly moulded and modified by those subject to it, or by the native courts which reflect the opinion and practice of the community. Contrary to one's picture of African customary law as age-old, immutable, firmly fixed in the very bones of the people, it has in many places changed rapidly and fundamentally, especially in regard to land. All the basic features of African customary land tenure, which I referred to earlier, have come under attack as a result of the factors I have just mentioned.

There is no time to develop this point in detail: let me just mention the following:

(i) The position of the individual has been strengthened vis-à-vis both political authorities and the family. Political authorities may now have little control over the acquistion of land by subjects[4] (in some areas new non-traditional local government bodies have taken over this task); and an individual may find it much easier to accumulate self-acquired property that is free from family interests and control than he would have done in the old days. This process may be described as 'the progressive individualization' of African land tenure.

(ii) Titles are becoming more certain and cultivation more static with the growing of tree-crops. (The result of the stabilization of agriculture coupled with competition with neighbours cannot fail to be a sharpened sense of meum and tuum.)

(iii) Cash-farming (e.g. coffee, groundnuts, cocoa) is widely practised.

(iv) Titles are being recorded in written form. The use of writing in every aspect of the customary law is widespread, and would by itself make a fascinating subject for a paper. Written conveyances and instruments are now used in the more advanced areas, supplanting older oral methods of transfer.[5]

(v) Interests in land are now freely transferred for cash in many areas. Sale, lease for a money rent, and various forms of mortgage or charge (replacing the traditional pledge) are found wherever commercial agriculture is practised. Where the direct prohibition of the old customary law on sales of interest in land is still in theory upheld, this may be evaded by various legal devices or by under-the-counter transactions.

(vi) The indigenous religious sanctions and authorities are losing their power. The old magical or mystical connexion between men and son is being disrupted. Life in the old days followed an ordered pattern, and the agricultural year was often governed by a rigid cycle of religious and customary observances—there was a time for sowing and a time for reaping; no man could break the sod before the ruler or headman had performed the necessary rituals; first-fruits had to be yielded up to the chief for first-fruit ceremonies which strengthened the tribe and ensured a good harvest. All this is now going or gone.

The African peoples have been strongly influenced, especially in West Africa, by culture-contact, that is, by borrowing of institutions and ideas from the European rulers or European law. As a result, in countries like Ghana and Nigeria, customary and English rules of land law are now mixing and merging into a mélange of rules which govern or may govern the tenure of land; and the previous clear-cut dichotomy between land governed by English law and land governed by customary law is disappearing.

A final result of the commercialization of African land tenure has been the prevalence of costly litigation about land, especially in West Africa. Uncertainty as to which law governs a particular transaction, who has power to dispose of interests in land (especially where the land is family land), what are the boundaries of a tribe's, village's, family's or individual's holding, coupled with the enhanced value of the land today, explain this litigation, which might be avoided if a system of registration of title adaptable to African land tenure could be devised.

(b) *Change from above*. Changes in customary land law brought about by the people themselves through adaptation of their law tend to be too slow and too haphazard in character. Undesirable features my appear in the law, due to the intensity of unrestricted economic competition. Governments therefore have initiated changes themselves, mainly by legislation. Central legislation may be negative in character, i.e. forbidding practices or features which impede good land use or lead to deterioration of the soil (cf. soil conservation measures); or positive, in prescribing a new system of land holding (cf. land consolidation in Kenya, or the Native Land Husbandry Act in Southern Rhodesia). Governments may also foster local legislation by traditional tribal authorities or by statutory local government bodies, as by circulating model by-laws which local authorities may adopt in their areas. Legislation, both central and local, is thus being increasingly used to modify or even abolish customary land tenure.

The administrative control of agriculture (often technically by persuasion rather than by command) is strongly developed. Agricultural officers naturally try to persuade peasants to adopt modern agricultural methods and organization; often, to such officers, the traditional rules of land tenure appear a positive obstacle which must be swept away. The effect of such continuous persuasion on the reshaping of African land tenure should not be underestimated.

Another factor of change, less official in character, is the judicial decisions of the appeal courts exercising control over the workings of the customary or African courts. The general trend of such decisions on land under customary tenure is almost invariably in the direction of English law.

4. Specific Examples

It would be too confusing and time consuming to review changes in land tenure in every British or Commonwealth territory, since the laws governing the tenure of land vary widely as between one territory and the next. I shall therefore discuss specific examples, taken from West Africa and from East Africa. (Change in Central and Southern Africa outside the Union—with the exception of the Native Land Husbandry Act in Southern Rhodesia and the general effects of white colonization there—has not been so conspicuous.)

(a) *West Africa*. I briefly review recent and projected developments in Ghana and Nigeria. Both these countries have at present very similar systems of general law (but note that in Northern Ghana and the Northern Region of Nigeria there are special laws by which strict control is exercised over the alienation of interests in land to 'non-natives' of these regions: the control in the southern portions of these countries is less strict). Islamic law is a factor in Northern Nigeria, but has not been of great significance in the field of land tenure. Both countries already have highly developed peasant agriculture growing cash crops for the money economy. There is no 'settler' problem. The position of 'families' (lineages or extended families) is very important in land tenure, and will continue to be so. Traditional tribal authorities exercised considerable control over the occupation of land and were entitled to various perquisites and privileges in many parts of the area (but not in all—cf. the Tiv and Ibo of Nigeria).

The respective governments intend to progressively change and modernize their land law, customary and statutory; indeed, the eventual aim is probably a uniform land law, fusing English and customary ideas into a single system—but this programme has not got very far as yet. Traditional political authorities are losing many of their customary powers and rights over land to the central or local governments (this process is most pronounced in Ghana); but the family system and the institution of family property appear to be too well entrenched to disappear. Family lands will be registered as such on the registers of title to land now being instituted (e.g. in Lagos and the Western Region of Nigeria). Despite this the individualization of land tenure has gone very far, except in the more backward areas, and individuals may freely acquire and dispose of separate interests in land. The principle previously followed by the superior courts, that 'all property is family property until proved otherwise', no longer applies. Sale, lease, mortgage, etc., are widespread.

Particular difficulties now arise since an interest in land can be 'converted' from one under customary law to one under English law, and vice versa.

(b) *East Africa*. This also forms a natural unit of discussion. All the countries in the region (Kenya, Uganda, Tanganyika—and even Zanzibar) are to a greater or less extent multiracial, with European, Asian and Arab minorities added to the African majority. Kenya has the worst problem in the adjustment of land rights as between the different communities. The legal structure is also extemely complicated (but legislation is projected, at least in Kenya, to simplify and rationalize it).

Commercial agriculture by the African population is not yet as widespread as in West Africa, though cotton is widely grown in Uganda, and coffee in Kenya and parts of Tanganyika. The position of 'families' is not as important as in West Africa, and nowhere are families registered as legal proprietors of land (although such a position may be reached in the Embu and Meru tribes of Kenya). A more individualistic form of tenure has developed as compared with West Africa; the fact that the customary law of succession in East Africa tends to be divisory (i.e. the land is split up among the heirs, thus promoting fragmentation of holdings), whereas in West Africa succession is often corporately by the family as a whole, may partially explain the contrast in the respective position of family groups. An interesting development in some Kenya tribes (which are all of the uncentralized type), for example among the Kipsigis, is that lands which were formerly communal grazing lands, open for use by any member of the local community, have all been enclosed by individuals; that is, individuals have fenced portions of the common lands and now claim them as their own separate, individual, absolute holdings; such individual holdings are used for arable and mixed farming. This was a spontaneous movement by the people themselves; once the process started there was a scramble to claim individual portions, and this has now resulted in the almost complete elimination of communal grazing lands in some areas. The 'enclosure movement' was not officially sponsored by Government, but was doubtless warmly advocated by officers of the Agriculture Department.

Individual tenure is not, of course, new to East Africa, as the 'mailo' system in Buganda introduced by the British at the beginning of the century, is basically freehold tenure on the English model. It is declared government policy in Kenya to encourage individual tenure of land; and changes in African land tenure have therefore gone furthest there. Comprehensive legislation has been introduced permitting the consolidation and registration of holdings by Africans in any area to which the law is applied, and the accompanying conversion of customary tenure to individual freehold tenure on the English model (with the consequent abolition of the customary land law). The legislation is applied in any area after consulting the wishes of the local inhabitants, and 'land consolidation', as it is called, has already been carried out in most of Kikuyuland. At the same time a rigorous and comprehensive system of control over transactions in such land has been instituted. It is the eventual intention to unify the land law and system of land control, i.e. land held by Europeans under English law will fall within the same system as that held by Africans; up till now this has not been the case.

The other territories have not yet gone as far as Kenya in reform of African land tenure, largely due to suspicion on the part of local African farmers that their rights in land might in some way be threatened. The customary law has however been considerably commercialized and individualized. It is worth noting that in many parts of East Africa, especially Kenya and most of Uganda, there was no centralized political authority and control of lands was in the hands of 'clans' or lineages. In other parts of East Africa, however, land authorities who allocate land to occupiers are found; one of the striking developments here (e.g. in Busoga, Uganda) is that the 'allocation fee', which was originally a token of no real value (e.g. a chicken), may now have been greatly inflated and that large sums may be demanded before a peasant will be allocated land.

5. The Consequences of Change

What will be the consequences of the changes which are now in train or projected in the sphere of African land tenure? What will the future pattern of African land tenure look like? Will the present dichotomy and conflict between the English and African land laws be abolished and a uniform land law applying to all races be introduced? Will there be universal registration of title? These are some of the questions raised by the foregoing facts.

Possible answers to such questions were thoroughly discussed by the recent (December 1959—January 1960) Conference on 'The Future of Law in Africa), which was held in London and attended by leading lawyers, judges and scholars from 'common law' Africa. Agreed objectives in regard to the law of land tenure were formulated: these included the systematic ascertainment and recording of individual rights in land; the consequent introduction of a system of registration of title; the introduction of legislation to define the respective spheres of English law and customary law in regard to land tenure, and the conversion of interests from one system of law to the other. 'Eventually', said the Conference, 'there should be a system of registration which should be based on a unified law. It should use predominantly English terms to describe estates customarily held in land and should not only enable land to be transferred in ways such as lease, mortgage, which derive from English law, but should make provision for the incidents and practices of customary law which it is desired to conserve, e.g. the possessory mortgage.'

Notes

[1] Cf. my *Essays in African Law*, 1960, Chap. 3, 'The Unity of African Law', for a further discussion of this point.

[2] The Kikuyu acquired land from the aboriginal inhabitants, the Nderobo, in Kenya shortly before the advent of the European by a sort of purchase; this appears to have been different from outright sale, and was in any case outside tribal law, being an example of 'international', or at least inter-tribal, relations—which ex hypothesi were not governed by any particular customary law.

[3] E.g. among the Ashanti one finds pledges between chiefs; these were basically pledges of people rather than land.

[4] But in some societies where land has now become a profitable commodity, political authorities (e.g. chiefs and sub-chiefs) now claim a share in the control of and profits from land occupied by their subjects (e.g. in some of the Akan states of Ghana); such claims were not part of the ancient customary law in such societies.

[5] See my *Essays in African Law*, Chap. 10, 'Writing and title to land in Ghana', for a detailed study of this development in Ghana, and the legal problems to which it gives rise.

C. K. Meek: Land Law and Custom in the Colonies*

The Need for More Accurate Study of Native Systems

We may now pass on to consider some of the characteristic features of the indigenous or less developed systems found in many dependencies, notably in Africa. Here it is im-

* C. K. Meek, *Land Law and Custom in the Colonies,* Oxford University Press, 1946, pp. 11–27.

portant to note that it is only in recent years that reliable information on this subject has been obtained. Many of the early investigations were vitiated by unsound methods of approach, such as the use of abstract questions—the answers to which were often given by interested parties—instead of the concrete method of tracing the actual history of plots of land. Another frequent source of error has been the presupposition that native conceptions of ownership must be basically the same as those of Europeans.[1] English terms such as 'rent' or 'lease' have been employed to denote practices which bear only a superficial resemblance to those denoted by these terms. The gifts given to chiefs as administrators of land have been assumed to be 'rent', and the chiefs to be 'landlords'. To add to the confusion, the same English word has been used in different senses, so that, for example (to quote Dr. Lucy Mair), those who have said that there was no such thing as 'property' in land have meant one thing, while those who have argued that there was 'property' in land have meant another. Again, the words 'in theory' or 'theoretically' have frequently been employed to square the presuppositions with the facts. Time and again there appear such contradictions as 'in theory the land belongs to the Chief, but in practice the Chief is not consulted', or 'theoretically there is no negotiable freehold . . . but in practice the effective sale of land is of frequent occurrence'. Confusion, too, is caused by loose translations of native terms, so that a word rendered as 'purchase' may not mean 'outright purchase' but 'redeemable purchase'—a very different matter. Or to take a final example, there is the common practice of distinguishing tenures as either 'communal' or 'individual'. Yet the two may exist side by side and interwoven.[2] The term 'communal' has often been applied to lands in which individuals have well-defined rights, and it has been applied constantly to useless lands over which neither individuals nor groups of individuals claim any rights at all. On the other hand, 'individual tenure' has been used to mean anything from a mere right of user which cannot be alienated, to a freehold estate with the fullest freedom of disposition.

The absence of accurate information regarding native systems of tenure has had many unfortunate effects. In the making of treaties with natives, Colonial Governments and individuals have assumed that they were being given exclusive rights over land, whereas the natives have asumed that they were merely granting the qualified rights of user which they themselves enjoyed. On the other hand, some governments have enacted laws recognizing the native rights as though they were the equivalent of freehold rights in Western countries, thus conferring on the natives an authority to dispose of lands over which, under their own law, they only had usufructuary rights.[3] Failure to understand the custom of shifting cultivation has led successive governments to underestimate the amount of land required by native tribes, or to claim as Crown property land which they had believed to be vacant.[4] In Ceylon much land was appropriated under the Crown Lands Ordinance of 1840 to which the villagers had a legitimate claim,[5] and similar mistakes have been made in East Africa. It has been assumed that Chiefs were the owners of tribal lands and could sign them away as they pleased, whereas in fact the chiefs were no more than public trustees. On the same principle, chiefs and other leading personages of a tribe have obtained for themselves privileges regarding land which they would not have obtained had the local Government been instructed in the facts. Under the Uganda Agreement of 1900, 'A government which supposed itself to be confirming native rights turned the Chiefs by a stroke of the pen into landlords entitled to exact rent from their former subjects and to dispose of their land for cash,' while in the Gold Coast, 'the reckless granting of concessions by the Chiefs was allowed on the assumption that their right to make such grants followed logically from their authority over stool lands.'[6] In Kenya, the land legislation prior to 1938 proceeded on the assumption that the native reserves were commons in which private rights to land did not exist.

Pastoral Rights

The most elementary form of land occupation is where pastoral peoples range freely over large areas in search of fresh grazing and of water. Normally under such conditions there is no need for defining rights.[7] Where the pastoralists come into contact with the agriculturists they are welcomed because of the milk and butter made available. Most agriculturists, also, are aware of the value of cattle manure. Disputes arise, however, when the cattle damage the crops, and agriculturists are often on this account put to the trouble and expense of fencing in their lands. In many parts of Africa there is continual litigation, and a good deal of bloodshed, on account of trespass by cattle, and in Nigeria it is not uncommon for a man living in one village to farm on the lands of another where there is least interference from domestic animals.[8] In the Gold Coast, Sir Henry Belfield considered (in 1914) that restrictions should be placed on the grant of land for grazing, with a view to curbing the pernicious proclivities of pastoralists.[9]

Where pastoral peoples are, for various reasons, confined to limited areas, more definite grazing rights may arise. Thus, in the arid regions of Tanganyika, private grazing rights have grown up in the areas around water supplies, or where the movements of cattle are restricted on account of tsetse-fly. A plot of grazing ground may be held by an individual, a family, or a group of persons who have agreed to herd their cattle together. And since the conversion of waste land into suitable grazing land, and its subsequent maintenance, may involve considerable labour, owners of grazing-grounds sometimes let them out on a rental basis. Progressive individuals may even, nowadays, obtain permission from the tribal or village authorities to construct dams or other appliances for conserving water, and so establish for themselves purely private rights over what was formerly public property. It is clear that developments of this kind must be creating many problems; private enterprise may deserve encouragement, yet any wide extension of private rights may upset the local land economy and interfere with Government schemes for the development of agriculture and the control of erosion. In many parts of Africa there is a dangerous degree of soil deterioration which can be attributed largely to overstocking, and the remedy may lie in a variety of measures such as the reduction or redistribution of herds, the introduction or extension of rotational grazing, or, where circumstances are favourable, the substitution of an agricultural for a pastoral economy. Grazing-grounds, moreover, require to be controlled if they are not to become breeding grounds for weeds and ticks; and for many other reasons grazing regulations may be necessary. These can more easily be put into practice, by Native Administrations, where rights are of a collective rather than an individual character. It has been pointed out also (by Mr. D. W. Malcolm) that in Tanganyika, wherever personal rights in grazing grounds are recognized, there is continual litigation, since the grazing-grounds form a patchwork, and the boundaries are seldom clearly marked. No such difficulties exist where the grazing-grounds are annually allocated by the village authorities.

In Kenya the Land Commission of 1933 recorded a comprehensive condemnation of large grazing commonages, 'which are frequently used as a species of bank for the storage of bride-price'. They stated that even the areas added expressly for the purpose of accommodating cattle (while over-grazed areas of the reserve were rested) should not be used as grazing commonages free to all without restriction, but should be used on an organized plan.[10] A committee recently appointed by the Government of Kenya to advise on the steps which should be taken to deal with the problem of overstocking, recommended (in 1941) that 'immediate steps should be taken to restore to grazing all areas that are unsuitable for cultivation and to encourage the return of stock to cultivated holdings in order that it may fulfil its proper function of adding milk to the dietary of the people, and of manure for use on arable land and pasture. . . . Native agriculturists should be constantly reminded that there can be no return to the old conditions which permitted shifting cultivation and the allocation of almost unlimited grazing areas for stock, and that the only place for stock in modern conditions is on the cultivated small holding, where, by means of the proper use of manure, the continuous farming of the land without loss of fertility is made possible.' The committee recommended that strict measures of grassland and soil control should be applied throughout both the pastoral and the agricultural native areas of Kenya. These recommendations have been accepted by the Government of Kenya; and similar policies are being considered, or have been accepted, by other Colonial Governments.

It should be remembered, however, that other than purely economic factors may have to be considered in dealing with grassland management. There are many tribes, such as the aboriginal peoples of British Guiana, who, if they are to avoid extermination, must be allowed adequate land in which they can continue to live the nomadic life of their forefathers.[11] There are treaty obligations, such as those with the pastoral Masai, which cannot lightly be set aside; and there is the semi-sacred character which is attached to cattle in many African dependencies.[12] The Director of Veterinary Services in Tanganyika has recently observed that obsession with the problem of soil erosion may make us forget that, after all, the soil was made for man and not man for the soil, and that when Governments interfere they must beware lest in removing one evil they create many others.[13] Nevertheless, it is clear that the whole problem of grassland management deserves much closer attention than it has anywhere received. Grass is no longer to be regarded as a mere cover for waste lands, but as the world's most valuable single crop. Governments will in future have to embark on large schemes of reclamation of waste lands, and schemes also of permanent pasturage let out for grazing on a controlled basis. Much more information is required regarding the nature of pastoral rights. Generally speaking, the character of the tenure must be determined by the local circumstances. In some circumstances the best remedy for overstocking will be the promotion of intelligent individual tenure and rotational grazing; in others, communage systems may accord better with native economies and modes of life, and also with Government schemes for future development.

Agricultural Rights

A more permanent relationship with land is established by agriculture. This assumes an infinite variety of forms, reflecting the use to which land is put and being related to the amount and quality of the land available,[14] to the local climate, to the character of the crops grown, and to the social and political institutions of the people.[15] When native societies are stabilized the rules of land tenure are never vague or ill-defined, and if today there is confusion, this must be ascribed to the introduction of new legal conceptions regarding land, and new economic conditions to which the indigenous systems have not yet had time to make the necessary accommodation.

One of the main distinctions between Native systems of holding land and those of Western societies is that the former are largely dominated by personal relationships, whereas the latter are subject to the impersonal legal conception of 'contract'. In some areas of the Empire, however, there has been a fusion, or confusion, of these two conceptions, so that in a single dependency the two principles may exist side by side, or in opposition, often with chaotic results. In many parts of Africa, for example, the holders of usufructuary rights in land are now endeavouring to convert them into indefeasible titles and are arming themselves with bogus deeds often obtained from bogus lawyers at considerable expense.[16]

In describing the land tenure systems of the South Seas communities, a distinguished American anthropologist has observed that the most typical form of tenure in pre-European times was for 'living sites and cultivations around villages to be very precisely defined as to what families or individuals had authority over them and as to who could use them; but for forest hinterlands and river or ocean frontage to be held collectively by the communities concerned. . . . Nowhere was there any complete collectivism or communism such as some theorists have postulated for the primitive world. . . . But frequently a large group of individuals had rights in some piece of property, based on kin ties or other traditional factors. Again, where a person such as a chief appeared to be an owner or landlord, he was often really more of a supervisor or trustee. He exercised authority over land rather than possessed it.'[17]

This statement would also apply generally to the indigenous tenures of Africa. These are often described as 'tribal' or 'communal ownership'. But the basis of land administration is not usually the tribe but the village, and land is not usually owned or worked by any large unit. Everywhere there are individual rights, that is to say that a single individual, or two or more close relatives, have definite rights to a particular plot of ground and to its produce. But these rights are qualified by membership of a family, clan or local group. They are limited to the period of effective occupation and restricted in respect of succession and therefore of transfer. Sale is normally forbidden and may indeed be unthinkable.[18] The rights in fact partake more of the nature of possession than of property.[19] If the holding is quitted it reverts to the holder's kindred or to the village; and may be re-allocated. In some cases all the lands of a village have been divided out among the kindreds composing the village, and all the lands of the kindreds in turn have been divided out among the extended families composing the kindred. But sometimes the villages and kindreds still hold reserves of undivided lands which are allocated as required. Or parts of them may be portioned out annually if the individual holdings are found to be insufficient.

In order to make these principles clear a number of authorities may be quoted. In their judgment in the Southern Nigerian case cited above, the Privy Councillors made the following observations: 'A very usual form of native title is that of usufructuary right, which is a mere qualification of or burden on the radical or final title of the Sovereign, where that exists. But this estate is qualified by a right of beneficial user which may not assume definite forms analogous to estates, or may, where it has assumed these, have derived them from the intrusion of the mere analogy of English jurisprudence. . . . There is yet another feature of the fundamental nature of the title to land. . . . The title, such as it is, may not be that of the individual, as in this country it nearly always is in some form, but may be that of a community. Such a community may have the possessory title to the common enjoyment of a usufruct, with customs under which its individual members are admitted to enjoyment, and even to a right of transmitting the individual enjoyment as members by assignment *inter vivos* or by succession. To ascertain how far this latter development of right has progressed involves the study of the history of the particular community and its usages in each case. Abstract principles fashioned a priori are of but little assistance and are, as often as not, misleading.'[20]

Professor Schapera, in his account of land tenure in Bechuanaland, states that the Chief controls the allocation of land and assigns a residential area and a separate arable tract to each of the wards in his capital. The holding of each ward (or small village) is controlled by the ward-head, who must provide land for all the households under his authority. He may also admit outsiders who apply to him. The head of a household assigns plots to his dependants; every family must have its own land, and, if a man has more than one wife, each is entitled to a separate dwelling and field.[21] Grazing land is not similarly divided among the households, but every owner of cattle may graze them freely within the area controlled by the ward-head. 'In every instance the possessor of land is entitled merely to its use, and not to absolute ownership. Should he go away temporarily he can take up the land again on his return. Land passes only by way of gift, inheritance or gratuitous loan. It is never treated as a commodity that can be sold or hired out. There is, therefore, no opportunity for land speculation and no incentive to the acquisition of large holdings from which a return can be derived in the form of purchase price or rent. Tribal law moreover limits the amount of land that people may hold.'[22]

In describing the land system of the Wa-Bena of Tanganyika, Mr. and Mrs. A. T. Culwick state that: 'Land, *per se*, has no value in the eyes of the Mbena and nobody bothers about it until it is cleared. Any member of the tribe, or any stranger who has been granted permission to settle in the country, can of right take and clear as much land as he requires for his house, his fields and possibly a family burial-ground. As soon as he has done this, the position has changed. The work he has put into the plot gives it value. It is now his property and no one may encroach on it. So long as it continues to be used, it remains in the possession of him or his heirs. . . . When a man deserts exhausted ground, he no longer calls it 'my field'. He will, however, refer to it as 'my old field', indicating thereby that he still has certain proprietary rights over it, should he care to exercise them. . . . The temporary occupier of a field is thus regarded as something more than merely its user; he has rights which extend beyond the period of actual use. It is considered as his absolute property as long as he wishes to keep it. . . . His rights over it last as long as he wishes, whether it is in use or not, and further, he has the right of disposal. He can, if he wants, dispose of a field to his neighbour. Such transactions naturally take place but seldom, when every man has land and to spare for the taking, but they do sometimes occur, as, for instance, when a man has inherited a good field at some distance from his home. He may negotiate a transfer to another, usually a relative, receiving in exchange goods, cash, or services of some kind. But as land itself has no value, he is really of course, selling the work of clearing and breaking the ground, and any crops which may be growing on it at the time of transfer; i.e. he is actually being paid for improvements, and not for land itself, though at the same time he, as the owner, is transferring his rights over the land.'

As regards grazing, in granting a man permission to take certain grazing grounds, the tribal authorities among the Wa-Bena give him both rights of use and rights of disposal over it. At his death the appropriate heir inherits the land on the same terms, and thus the family may hold it permanently. As for the head of the village, he has not only the first claim on uncleared land but also, if he cares to exercise it, 'a rather vague power to dictate to his people where they should or should not cultivate'. Similarly, he has absolute discretion in the matter of grazing grounds. 'But let a man once clear a patch of ground and he cannot be evicted, nor can the local authorities turn men off grazing grounds of which they have taken possession.'[23]

In an Ibo village in Nigeria the following classes of land were observed by myself.[24] The first class includes lands which are sacred or taboo. These surround the shrines of public cults or are lands specially marked off for some magico-religious purpose. The ownership is regarded as vested in the deities or ancestors, and no one would normally attempt to use any fraction of such lands for farming.[25] Lands of this character are found all over Africa, and in most dependencies there are statutory provisions for their protection.[26]

The next type of land is the virgin forest, which has remained unused for farming purposes because it has not been required, or because the village authorities (that is to say the village chief or the heads of kindreds) have forbidden farming there, lest the village should lose the use of the forest as a means of defence, or as shade, or a source of supplies of wood or fibre. But if a piece of uncleared forest has no obvious public use, then anyone may clear it for farming purposes, and the land so cleared becomes his private farm. He cannot be deprived of it and he can pledge it or transmit it to his children. But should there be any uncertainty as to whether the village may require the uncleared patch, the would-be farmer must first obtain the permission of the local elders or of the special official authorised to act as administrator of lands.

The third class of land is farm-land held in common by the entire village, ward, kindred or extended-family, and is formally portioned out afresh each time it is to be farmed. Where the common land belongs to the entire village it is usually infertile soil for which there is no demand. Where it belongs to a kindred or extended-family group it is parcelled out annually to members of the kindred whose private holdings may be insufficient. It can only be leased or pledged to strangers with the consent of the whole group. Similarly, if the land is to be redeemed, it should be redeemed by the group as a whole. In these days cases occur where an individual member of a group redeems group-land at his own expense and then claims it as his private property.

Finally, and most important of all, comes the land which is individually held—that is to say by a single individual or by a small working group composed of a father and sons, or a man and his younger brothers or cousins. Such land is acquired by inheritance, or by clearing virgin forest, or in return for a loan. In many villages there is no land at all which is not held by individuals. Land so held can, among the Ibo and many other African tribes, be pledged without reference to anyone, and it is common practice for a man to pledge his land in order to cancel a debt, to pay a bride-price, or even nowadays to raise the cash for his Government tax. Land which has been pledged is normally redeemable at any time, at the same rate at which it has been pledged, and in many African tribes there is a proverb which states that 'A thing which is pledged is never lost.'[27] In point of fact, however, land which has been pledged is often permanently lost. It may be pledged for a sum far in excess of that normally given, and becomes irredeemable, all evidence of the original transaction having been lost. In this way rich individuals have acquired land in perpetuity.

From these descriptions it will be evident that there is a fairly general common pattern of land tenure, associated for the most part with subsistence agriculture, which is still the prevalent form of economy.[28] But there are many variations or modifications. Thus, persons who are short of land may obtain a temporary loan or lease, in return for a proportion of the crop at harvest. This proportion may be so small that it is no more than a token of obligation and an acknowledgement that the land has been lent and not given away. Or it may be so substantial that the relationship between the grantor and grantee assumes something of the character of *métayage*. Nowadays, there is a tendency in some areas for gifts in kind to be replaced by cash, and so to become regular rental payments. In other areas, again, the grantor of land, which would formerly have been given away free or for some trifling consideration, may demand a comparatively large sum of money and argue that this is not purchase-money but compensation for the trouble of having cleared the land.

In a number of Colonial territories (e.g., Nigeria, Uganda, Tanganyika and Tonga) there were formerly feudal forms of tenure, fiefs or estates being conferred on officers of State, members of the royal families and other notables. It need only be observed here that they have developed in very different ways in the different dependencies, or sometimes even in the same dependency. In the Buganda and Bunyoro districts of

Uganda, the rights of tenants have been secured by varying means, but in the Toro and Ankole areas there is little security of tenure beyond that of the goodwill of the landlord. In Tanganyika the landlords are still entitled to make certain demands on the crops of their tenants. In Northern Nigeria the estate system has, for the most part, disappeared, but some royal estates are still largely worked by ex-slaves, whose portion has become assimilated to that of 'clients', paying an annual tithe. In the State of Nupe the amount of tithe varies with the personality of the Emir, from one or two bundles of corn annually to as much as one-third of the entire harvest.[29] In many parts of Africa chiefs have tended to become landlords, and landlords have tended to assume the role of chiefs.

The landlord–tenant relationship is not, however, a common feature of indigenous systems of tenure. In most of the colonies the peasant farmer is still free and independent. And although this may serve to slow down the rate of progress, it is a prime factor in the maintenance of social stability. On the other hand, the fact that individual rights are exercised within the framework of the kindred organization and are qualified in many important respects, particularly as regards the right of alienation, may present serious impediments to agricultural development on modern lines, though it may continue to perform a useful function under a subsistence economy.

The principle that he who clears land establishes rights of a permanent character has existed all over the world from ancient times. It is based on the fact that the clearing of virgin forest involves heavy work. And under all indigenous systems of tenure it is an accepted principle that the expenditure of labour creates rights. It is for this reason that economic trees which require attention are held in private ownership, and that the property is in the tree itself and not in the land on which it grows. On this account also the ownership of plantations differs from that of arable land used for growing subsistence crops; and ancestral property, which is held collectively by the kin and cannot be sold, differs from acquired property which is at the complete disposition of the person who acquired it. For the same reason also, in the Dikwa Emirate of the British Cameroons, where ordinary agricultural land has no negotiable value, the particular class of land known as *firki* is bought and sold, since its use entails heavy labour in clearing, ditching and the diversion of flood water.[30] This principle is largely, no doubt, the real explanation of the fact that the descendants of the original occupying families are considered to have a special degree of ownership, and that a religious sanction is given to this view.[31]

The annual or periodic allocation, or re-allocation, of village lands is a common technique of native systems for ensuring a fair distribution of land.[32] Among the Kikuyu of Kenya the official known as 'muramati' has powers of adjusting the land distribution in cases where one family has diminished and another has increased. (See the *Report of the Committee on Native Land Tenure in Kikuyu Province*, Cap. I paras. 19–23.) In Cyprus if land is allowed to remain uncultivated for a period of 10 years it can be resumed by the State (see p. 64). In S. Rhodesia under the Land Apportionment Act of 1930, grants of land may be forfeited if not beneficially used. Numerous other examples of statutory provisions of this kind could be given. In many parts of Africa chiefs have the right to take away from families any of their land which is not required.[33]

There is one further feature of native systems of land-holding to which some reference should be made, namely, the absence from native customary law of any limitation of time within which claims over land—or indeed anything else—can be asserted or enforced. This may be a matter of no great consequence under a shifting system of cultivation, for if a farmer is dispossessed of one plot of land he can go to another. But where land has become valuable, or plantation crops are grown, sudden dispossession may inflict serious injustice. The absence from native law of any 'statute of limitations' has in many dependencies been considered a serious bar to security and so to development, and to be an encouragement of recurrent litigation and of many forms of fraud, such as the postponement of claims to land until the land has been extensively improved.[34]

In 1927 the Government of the Gold Coast proposed to introduce into the Colony a Statute of Limitations which would be applicable not merely in the British Courts, but also in the native courts, with a view to getting rid of some of these evils, and protecting non-natives who had acquired from natives an interest in land.[35] The proposal, however, was vetoed by a Council of Chiefs, on the ground that it was directly contrary to the native principle that long uninterrupted possession does not create an adverse title. The new measure would be opposed to the native rule which requires families to pay off their debts (in which land might be included), however long it may take them to do so:[36]

and it would have the general effect of forcing the people to adopt English forms of tenure and of transfer. The Bill was accordingly dropped.[37]

Native law is not incapable of making its own accommodation to new conditions. Moreover, equity is its governing principle, and it knows very well how to deal with individuals who postpone their claim to land until the existing occupier has carried out extensive improvements. In the Gold Coast itself, a case is on record, as long ago as 1878, in which a family tried to eject a farmer who had purchased a piece of land from the head of the family fourteen years previously. It was admitted that the family-head had conducted the sale without consulting the other members of his family. Nevertheless, it was held that, as the other members of the family had taken no action and the purchaser had improved the land, he could not be disturbed.[38]

In many parts of Africa it is an accepted principle that voluntary abandonment of the use of any land should extinguish all prescriptive claim. And there may also be a rule that no individual or group shall hold more land than can be effectually used. Yet many clans, families and individuals are in fact laying prescriptive claims to larger areas than are, or will be required, under more settled systems of cultivation. There is a growing tendency also for prescriptive rights of user to become crystallized into rights of an exclusive proprietary character. The problem is, therefore, arising in many dependencies as to how far such claims can continue to be recognized. If land is to be regarded as a national asset, then timely steps should be taken, wherever this is still possible, to prevent excessive shareholding.[39]

Summing up the main characteristics of indigenous systems of land-holding, it may be said generally that these are devised to meet the needs of a subsistence system of agriculture and depend on a sufficiency of land to allow of a rotation which includes a long period of fallow. Land is held on (*a*) a kinship, and/or (*b*) a local group basis. Individuals have definite rights, but these are qualified by membership of a family, kindred and ward (or small village). Similarly, the individual claims of families exist concurrently with the wider claims of the clan or local group. Title, therefore, has a community character. It is also usufructuary rather than absolute.[40] Land may only be sold under conditions which do not conflict with the rights of the kin or local group. The chief is the custodian of land, but not its owner. The normal unit of land ownership is the extended-family, or kindred. Land once granted to a family remains the property of that family, and the chief has no right to any say in its disposal. This constitutes a definite limitation on the conception of land as the collective property of the tribe or local group. The kinship basis of land-holding ensures social stability, but the absence of individual proprietary rights prevents the raising of money on land and so is a hindrance to development.[41] Land may be pledged and redeemed at any time. The principle of redeemability ensures that land shall not be permanently lost, but it may be an impediment to progress since no one will attempt to improve land of which he may be deprived at short notice. The restrictions on the sale of land, the limitation of possession to the period of effective use, and the periodic re-allocation of land, all ensure that land shall not be uselessly withheld from cultivation or lost to the community.

Notes

[1] In a Privy Council judgement in 1921 their lordships observed that 'In interpreting the native title to land, not only in Southern Nigeria but in other parts of the British Empire, much caution is essential. There is a tendency, operating at times unconsciously, to render that title conceptually in terms which are appropriate only to systems which have grown up under English law. But this tendency has to be held in check closely. As a rule, in the various systems of native jurisprudence throughout the Empire, there is no such full division between property and possession as English lawyers are familiar with.' (Amodu Tijani *v.* The Secretary, S. Nigeria. 2 A.C. 399, 1921.)

Lord Lugard has observed that the term 'ownership' when applied to land is relative even in England, where it is qualified by the right of Parliament to expropriate the owner if the land is required for some public purpose such as a railway. In Africa the term is still more qualified. The ascription of 'ownership' of land to a chief is only accurate if the term is used in its native sense. (*Dual Mandate*, p. 316.) Professor Raymond Firth has also pointed out that the precise meaning of ownership is different in every culture, varying according to custom, tradition, and the relative social status of those who enjoy its privileges. The key to the understanding of a system of native land tenure lies, he says, in realizing the inadequacy of such terms as 'communistic' or 'individualistic' and in grasping the complex scheme of titles, claims, privileges and obligations on the part of individuals and the community with which the native himself invests the control of the soil. (See e.g. *We, The Tikopia*, pp. 406–7, and *Primitive Economics of the New Zealand Maori*, pp. 330–1, and 375.)

[2] Professor Malinowski has pointed out that 'every relationship between man *v.* soil is emphatically both individual and concerted. . . . The real problem is not the "either—or" of individualism and communism but the relation of collective and personal claims.' See *Coral Gardens and Their Magic*, Vol. I, pp. 379 and 380.

[3] See Dr. Felix M. Keesing's, *The South Seas in the Modern World*, p. 99.

[4] See p. 78, footnote 2. Also, *An African Survey*, p. 745. Dr. Felix Keesing, speaking of the Pacific communities, observes that 'A mistake frequently made by government officials and others has been to regard only those lands in active use for economic purposes as being covered by valid native titles and to classify the rest as unoccupied or waste lands. In native eyes, however, virgin or fallow territories are nearly always covered by some form of tenure, actual or potential. . . . Difficulties have likewise arisen where, in accordance with Western practice, governments have put legal restrictions upon the ownership and use of forests and their products, on water and marine resources and on minerals.' *Op. cit.*, p. 98.

[5] See H. M. Leake in *Tropical Agriculture*, Vol. XV, No. 11.

[6] Dr. Lucy Mair at the Oxford University Summer School on Colonial Administration, 1938. It is interesting to note, as regards the Uganda Agreement, that in a despatch of 15th June, 1900, the British Foreign Office observed that 'the introduction of the law of England in regard to land, which appears from the wording of the Agreement to be the intention of its farmers, may create a very complicated system.' As indeed it did. (See pp. 132–7.)

[7] But there may be well-defined routes to definite areas which the pastoralists are allowed by custom to exploit.

[8] See, e.g., *Land Tenure in an Ibo Village*, M. M. Green, p. 30.

[9] Despatch to Secretary of State, 3rd April, 1914.

[10] *Report of the Kenya Land Commission, 1933*, para. 1670. See also paras. 1980–2040.

[11] *The West India Royal Commission Report*, p. 398.

[12] Pastoral peoples may be more concerned with property rights in cattle than in land. R. H. Lowie has observed that among the Ruanda of the Belgian Congo a monarch, instead of being regarded as the owner of the land, is regarded as the owner of all the stock. Among the Rwala of Arabia there are rules governing the inheritance of camels, but none regarding the inheritance of land.

[13] H. E. Hornby in an article on 'Overstocking in Tanganyika Territory', *East African Agricultural Journal*, March, 1936.

[14] Availability of land determines the type of tenure. R. H. Lowie has observed (in his article on Land Tenure in the *Encyclopædia of the Social Sciences*) that Kirghiz bands in Asiatic Russia were communists in the summer when land was abundant, but individualists in the winter when a dearth of sheltered quarters was coupled with private ownership of winter territories, which were marked out by natural or artificial boundaries and guarded against trespassers.

[15] It has been frequently pointed out (e.g. by Professor Lowie) that since property rights are correlated with other social phenomena, a study of land tenure requires a consideration of government, clan and family organization, and also of economic activity, technology and religion. All social institutions are closely concatenated, and a single institution should not be selected and treated as an isolated problem.

[16] Lord Hailey has observed that in the Gold Coast the use of English documentary forms of transfer, coupled with the growth of land value and the use made by chiefs of their powers over 'stool' lands for the grant of concessions, has led to a break-up of the older usages. Large numbers of land cases, moreover, are brought on appeal to the Supreme Court, and although the Court maintains the customary rights of the family in succession to land, it has tended to deal with transfers in terms of English law. See *An African Survey*, p. 856. See also below, pp. 163, 179–182, and 295–7.

[17] Dr. Felix M. Keesing, *op. cit.*, p. 98.

[18] But a family, lineage or sib may, by common consent, sell part of its ancestral lands for some necessary purpose, such as the payment of debts, the carrying on of family trade, the provision of bride-prices, the purchase of agricultural implements, the payment of the costs of litigation, or State demands. An individual may also alienate self-acquired property.

[19] R. H. Lowie observes that an individual's right may be no more than a pre-emptive possessory right—he has exclusive rights while he is there, but loses them if he leaves.

[20] Amodu Tijani *v.* The Secretary, S. Nigeria, 2 A.C. 399. 1921.

[21] Generally speaking it is true to say of African tenures, as of Indian, that women have only a life interest in land.

[22] I. Schapera, *Native Land Tenure in the Bechuanaland Protectorate*, 1943, pp. 44–46. It is worth observing, as Dr. Audrey Richards has pointed out with regard to the Bemba of N. Rhodesia, that, while there may be no tribal law restricting the amount of land which a man may occupy, social convention may impose a limit, according to the status of the individual. Fear of the accusa-

tion of pride or a reputation for personal ambition, so often associated with charges of witchcraft, are important factors. See *Land, Labour and Diet in Northern Rhodesia*, p. 271.

[23] *Ubena of the Rivers*, by A. T. Culwick and Mrs. G. M. Culwick, pp. 236 *et seq.*

[24] *Law and Authority in a Nigerian Tribe*, by C. K. Meek, p. 100.

[25] But it is a sign of the times that some farmers, driven by land hunger, have recently cleared patches of taboo forest in order to plant yams. It is said that if anyone takes this step (without interference from the elders) and farms for two years in succession without suffering misfortune, he is considered to have become the owner of the patch, which ceases to be taboo.

[26] E.g. in the Gold Coast Concessions Ordinance of 1939 (No. 19), it is laid down [Sec. 12 (9)] that no Concession shall be certified as valid unless the Court is satisfied that the customary rights of natives are reasonably protected in respect of 'fetish' lands. On the other hand, in the Sierra Leone Concessions Ordinance (No. 29 of 1931), it is an offence to represent any land in respect of which a certificate of validity has been issued by the Court to be 'fetish' land, and no one may put 'fetish' on such land (Sec. 54).

[27] Compare Leviticus xxv. 23–4 (R.V.): 'And the land shall not be sold in perpetuity: for the land is mine. . . . And in all the land of your possession ye shall rent a redemption of the land.'

[28] The semi-communal or open-field system in operation in England from Anglo-Saxon times to the nineteenth century presents many parallels to the pattern here described. 'The land of the village community was divided up into two or three open fields [*campi*], which were cultivated in a certain rotation. Each of these fields was divided into a number of strips [*seliones*], which averaged about an acre in extent: and the strips were divided from one another by turf balls. Each landowner possessed a certain number of these strips in different places in the open fields. It is probable that the strips were scattered in this way in order to give each owner a little bit of the good land, a little bit of the indifferent, and a little bit of the bad. . . . In addition each landowner had certain common rights. One and sometimes two of the common fields were left fallow each year, and over these fields there was a right of common of pasture for the cattle of the villagers. . . There were also rights of common over the extensive waste lands which adjoined the village.' See W. S. Holdsworth, *op. cit.*, p. 39.

[29] S. F. Nadel, *A Black Byzantium*, 1942, p. 199.

[30] See *British Cameroons Administrative Report*, 1923. Appendix III.

[31] In commenting on the tradition that the Kikuyu of Kenya bought out the original occupiers, the Dorobo, the 1929 Committee on native land tenure, observed that this was done (*a*) because of the great respect for the right of first use; and (*b*) in order to propitiate the ancestors who are believed to be imminent in the locality. See *Native Land Tenure in Kikuyu Province*, Report of Committee.

[32] It may be added that the practice of re-allocation is also a denial of the 'allodial', or 'free ownership', conception of land-holding.

[33] This has led many observers to conclude that the Chiefs are the real owners of the land. But normally the Chief cannot deprive a family of any of its land without general consent, and it is almost an axiom to say that a Chief can give lands but cannot take them away. Chiefs in fact are merely trustees for the people, though many have in the past assumed the position of landlords, and many are endeavouring to do so at the present time, in areas where land has become a commercial commodity.

[34] Sir Ernest Dowson, in speaking of land tenure conditions in Iraq, has observed that 'any dispute may be re-opened at any time if circumstances promise a more favourable consideration of a disappointed party's case'. And he added that 'One's personal status at any given time may be a determining factor.'

[35] The proposed measure was entitled 'The Civil Proceedings Limitation Bill', and the underlying principle was officially described as 'to safeguard the title to property and the fruits of individual enterprise from the assaults of those who have unreasonably delayed in asserting their claims. By ensuring security from such attacks, after the expiration of fixed periods, property may be enjoyed and developed without fear of being involved in extensive litigation and of being put to a defence which the passage of time has rendered hazardous.' The Bill proposed to impose a time limit of twelve years for the institution of proceedings to recover land or to recover money secured by any mortgage. In the case of debt, arrears of rent or interest, etc., the limit was to be six years.

[36] Property in land is often pledged for money loans, etc., and the pledgee takes possession until the loan is repaid. It was contended that under the new measure the pledgee might, after twelve years, become the permanent owner of the property. The people of the Gold Coast have a proverb that 'Debt dries but never rots'. It is interesting to note that according to the ancient custom of the Punjab the power to redeem mortgages of land lasted for ever. . . .

[37] Some of the judges of the Supreme Court considered that the practical effect of a time limit would, in the case of land, increase rather than lessen litigation.

[38] *Bayaidu* v. *Mensah* 1878.

[39] In South Africa no native, holding land under the Glen Grey Act of 1894, may hold more than one parcel of land.

[40] The rights are of the ancient Greek rather than the Roman pattern. Sir Paul Vinogradoff

has observed that Rome developed the conception of absolute property, while Greece worked out a conception of *relative* property rights. *Historical Jurisprudence*, Vol. II, p. 198.

[41] But, as Lord Hailey has pointed out, individual tenure is not the only remedy. If for example, a clan or tribal unit were to become an economic as well as a social political unit, 'raising capital against the value of clan or tribal lands, acting as a co-operative banking or selling organization, and taxing individuals through a rent upon their holdings, a rapid transition to individual ownership of land might possibly be avoided. But any such development assumes a roughly parallel development of all the individuals in a given community.' See *An African Survey*, p. 1430.

N. Mugerwa: Land Tenure in East Africa: Some Contrasts*

Land Tenure in East Africa under Customary Law

In East Africa customary law, leaving aside for the moment the nomadic tribes and a few exceptions which cannot be fitted easily into a single category, the systems of land tenure fall broadly into two main categories. First, communal or tribal tenure in which ownership is vested in the ruler either as owner or as trustee for the community. The Baganda, Banyoro and Batoro systems were examples of land vested in the ruler as owner. The Sukuma, Nyamwezi, Sambaa and the Gogo are examples of the communal land tenure system in which the land is vested in the ruler as trustee for his people. (It is necessary to explain that by communal or tribal land ownership we mean a system in which the idea is one of common ownership of land extending over the whole tribal lands subject only to the rights of present occupants not to be disturbed. The communal or tribal conception is the antithesis of the family or clan conception the main feature of which is small groups within the community exercising exclusive control over some of the areas which are comprised in the land belonging to the community.)

The second category is based on family or clan (blood) ownership. Examples of this kind of system are the Basoga in Uganda, the Kikuyu and Luo in Kenya, and the Kuria Nyaturu (or Arimi) and the Luguru in Tanganyika. In the case of communal tenure, at any rate in origin, the land is a community asset and vested in the ruler either as trustee or as owner, individual holders having only usufructuary rights. However, while in areas where the ruler holds as trustee the chief or sub-chief who is responsible for the allocation and control of land rights is one and the same person, in areas where the ruler is holder or holds as owner of the land, the ruler's nominee is very different from the clan head. The latter has hardly any political power, nor has he powers of land control except in lands which are of peculiar importance to the particular clan and any such clans may be scattered all over the country following burial grounds. In the kingdom areas around Lake Victoria, we find in early history a feudal-like system of land tenure which put all powers of land control in the hands of the ruler and his subordinates. The clan heads were of no importance in land matters.

Turning to communities where the land authority has always been the clan or family head, in some cases there is a parallel political authority which may sometimes coincide in the person of one holder. Generally speaking, however, the clan head and the political chief are united in one person. He allocates the land and also exercises the necessary continuous control. During the colonial administration, if was often found expedient in those areas where this was not really so to unite powers of land control and political office. This might sometimes necessitate ignoring some of the numerous clan heads and promoting one clan head above his equals. The result was that in some places, such as Kuria, in Tanganyika, in spite of official policy, according to which the official authority for land matters was the village headman, the authority of the village headman (unless he happened also to be the head of the dominant sub-clan in the area) would not be, or was only reluctantly, recognized by the community.It is thus that in Uluguru, the deposition of the Sultan in the 1950s did not prevent the Uluguru from continuing to recognize his authority and that of his subordinates in land matters.

The source of the power to control or allocate land in a system of communal tenure is the ruler. He in turn derives this ultimate authority from his position as territorial

* N. Mugerwa, 'Land Tenure in East Africa: Some Contrasts', in *East African Law Today* for British Institute of International and Comparative Law, 1966, pp. 101–105.

sovereign. His subordinates possess greater or lesser powers over land matters according to their position in the political and administrative hierarchy of the territory. In the case of clan tenure the authority over land control is derived from the position in the clan hierarchy of the person exercising that authority. But in the ultimate analysis his power derives from the family heads who make up the councils of the sub-clans.

Concerning the extent of authority, whereas in the areas under communal tenure the general tendency is to treat all comers almost as equal, provided they fulfil the conditions of tenure, in the clan tenure areas, except where the clan land authority has been weakened or modified by economic factors (as in the case of the Gogo), the general tendency is to make a distinction between clan and non-clan members. Thus, in Kuria, no one who is not a member of the clan or who has not become a blood brother of a member might be allotted a holding in clan land. The clan, through its head, has the last say in matters connected with clan land and no member of the clan might be deprived of this land merely on the grounds that it is not effectively cultivated. In Luguru, for example, non-lineage members who seek cultivation or dwelling rights on lineage land are subjected to a régime different from that which obtains in the case of the members of the particular lineage. They must pay entry money called *rubaka*, and must pay to the lineage head (who controls the mode of their tenancy) an annual payment called *ngoto*. This is a peppercorn rent which serves as a reminder that the reversion is vested in the lineage. The non-lineage member or stranger cannot sell a holding thus obtained (whereas a lineage member can sell to other lineage members) and his heir must seek permission from the lineage head to inherit—failure to obtain this permission being considered very proper grounds for eviction. He must also seek permission before he can plant permanent crops such as trees. The position of a *ngoto* payer compares with that of the *ahoi* in Kikuyu land tenure.

In the clan system of tenure there is virtually no land which is not owned by a clan or lineage. The fundamental theory is that the land-owning unit is the clan or lineage and the tribe as such cannot be said to own land. In other words, a piece of land is said to *belong* to the tribe only by virtue of the fact that it is owned by a clan within the tribe; it therefore follows that lands which are not owned by a particular clan do not belong to the tribe. It follows from the above reasoning that all lands belonging to a clan type of society, whether inhabited or not, are subject to the control of the particular lineage or clan. The distinction is not so much between types of lands as between types of occupants (i.e. between clan and non-clan members). Even in the case of lands sacred to the whole tribe, since they must be situated in the area of one lineage or clan, the primary, though not the final, control must be deemed to vest in the clan.

In contrast to the peoples under the clan system, the peoples under the communal system tend to have definite ideas as to the varying degrees of controls which are exercisable in respect of different types of land. In general, the whole tribal/national area may be divided into:

Public land which belongs to the whole community corporately, e.g. sacred lands, forests for wood, grazing lands, etc.

Private lands which is land which has been allotted to individuals or groups of individuals and which subsequently comes to be held by their heirs.

Unallotted land which comprises of all cultivatable lands which are vacant at any particular time and on which no person or family has a claim. As far as allocation is concerned the power of the territorial sovereign is expressed in the refusal to grant a plot to an individual or to do so on condition. The area covered by this category is reduced whenever there takes place a new allocation; and it is enlarged whenever the cultivation or dwelling rights are abandoned by cases of non-user or migration to another part of the tribal lands.

As to the manner of exercising control, in the case of communal tenure, the most effective method of exercising such control is refusal to permit the initial entry of the prospective occupier. This is especially effective in keeping 'strangers' from the area. But as the source of this authority is political the hurdle can be overcome by exhibiting a willingness to acknowledge and support the existing political structure. Equally effective, but demanding greater care in its exercise, is the power to declare as extinguished people's dwelling and cultivation rights. A desire on the part of the political subordinate to evict an undesirable occupier may find expression in the former's readiness to declare the latter's rights in the plot extinguished. However, as every occupier's rights are, at any rate in theory, similar to everyone else's, his rights can be declared extinguished only if this decision conforms to the general consensus of opinion. The feeling that if the political powers are left to get away with one bad eviction 'this may happen to me next' serves as a spur for the populace in the immediate vicinity of an eviction to voice their protest, and to prevent an eviction.

In the case of clan lands these powers of control exist only in respect of 'strangers'. This is so because in practically every instance every clan member is deemed to hold his land rights in perpetuity. Such land rights revert to the general reserve of the clan's lands only if he dies leaving no heir or if they are surrendered voluntarily in return for other lands or on permanent emigration from the locality. In contrast, the position of a 'stranger' is subject to different rules of control. He can be kept out completely by refusing him permission of initial entry. Similarly, he can be evicted for reasons which would not suffice to evict a clansman, e.g. planting permanent crops, or succeeding to a dead ancestor's rights without having first obtained the clan head's consent.

C. M. N. White: Terminological Confusion in African Land Tenure*

When I began the general survey of African land tenure in Northern Rhodesia, I was struck by the confused terminology which was often encountered in discussions or in earlier memoranda on the subject. Since clarity in this respect is obviously most important in descriptions of African systems of land tenure, it seems worth while to draw attention to some of these uncertain usages of terms, with illustrations, where needed, drawn from conditions in Northern Rhodesia.

Land Tenure

There is considerable latitude in what various people imply by land tenure, and especially a tendency to treat land tenure and land usage as interchangeable expressions. The study of land tenure must indeed cover a wide field if the full implications of land tenure systems are to be appreciated, and investigations must take account of social structure, agricultural methods, population densities and economic factors affecting the use of land. In this sense one may say that the study of land tenure covers the relationship of man to soil in its widest sense—a definition in fact used already by Malinowski.[1]

But the term also bears a more restricted sense of defining the methods by which a person acquires, holds, transfers or inherits land. Used in this sense a description of a system of land tenure is an analysis of the types of rights enjoyed by individuals or groups over land. The ascertaining of these rights, the study of their evolution under modern conditions, and the reasons underlying any changes taking place are one of the requirements of administrations in Africa when faced by land tenure problems.

Land tenure in this sense is quite distinct from land usage, if one understands by the latter term the ways in which individuals or groups use the land over which they enjoy rights, and nothing but confusion can arise from treating the two expressions as interchangeable. Thus in the Ngoni area of the Eastern Province a problem has developed due to the combination of over-population and primitive methods of husbandry resulting in congestion and a decline in the fertility of the soil. The carrying capacity of the land has been exceeded, and if the land is to carry a greater population, a change to better methods of husbandry is essential. This is a not unfamiliar problem in parts of Africa, and is essentially a problem of education in improved agriculture. No doubt there are often attendant evils found with it such as excessive sub-division and fragmentation when land is scarce, but unless the basic problem of introducing improved agriculture is tackled, no amount of innovations in land tenure will arrest the degradation of the soil. Yet not long ago it was said of the Ngoni that uncontrolled resettlement is not the

* C. M. N. White, 'Terminological Confusion in African Land Tenure', in *Journal of African Administration*, Vol. X, 1958, pp. 124–130.

answer; if the existing system of land tenure is maintained, the same problem will recur in the course of time.

This is a clear example in my submission of confused terminology for the opinion quoted could only properly make sense if land usage were substituted for land tenure. Moreover experience in Northern Rhodesia shows that here at any rate stabilization of agriculture and its commercial developments are the precursors of spontaneous change in the rights which individuals enjoy over their land; in a situation where land degradation is far advanced one cannot expect stabilization or economic development to take place without a marked change in methods of husbandry. One could quote similar examples of this confusion between tenure and usage of land, but the example given will suffice to underline the need for clarity in this respect.

Allocation of Land

There is a wide assumption that in many parts of Africa a chief or other land authority allocates land to smaller groups which allocate to individuals, or even that the authority allocates to individuals. Such a system of a hierarchy of estates (as Gluckman has proposed to call it) does of course exist in some parts of Africa, but it is clearly not of such wide application as has been supposed. It does not exist anywhere in Northern Rhodesia in the areas which have been studied during my present investigations (i.e. the Southern, Central, Eastern, Northern and Luapula provinces). Nor is it possible to distinguish any differences in these areas due to the varying political structures of the tribes inhabiting them.

The Tonga in the Southern Province lacked any political structure of a unifying type before the coming of the British Administration, and had no effective units larger than matrilineal kinship groups. The main features of Tonga land tenure can be summed up as follows: an individual is free to cultivate any land not subject to rights over it already established by a previous individual; he may acquire as much land as he likes in this way; he is free to transfer it to another either by loan or by outright gift; inheritance of land thus acquired is now common; transfers for a cash consideration are now beginning to emerge as the result of a well established maize growing cash economy. Here we have no hierarchy of estates; the Tonga had no traditional authorities to allocate land in any case, and the Tonga headman of a village does not allocate land to his villagers, and his only participation in the acquisition of land is to provide information as to whether or not existing rights are already enjoyed by an individual in a piece of land which another wishes to acquire.

The situation just outlined for the Tonga is perhaps what one might expect in a society which traditionally lacked any unifying political structure. But when one turns to tribes with a central political authority such as the Ngoni, Bemba, Lungu or the people of the Luapula valley subject to the Lunda Native Authority of Kazembe, one finds that the position is similar to that which exists among the Tonga. The main difference which distinguishes such societies with a centralised political structure in contrast to the Tonga is that there is a conception of a tribal area and unit occupying a territory. Hence a person seeking to live in such an area must be accepted by the political authority controlling the area, and must himself accept its political control in order to live there. This right to live in the area includes by implication the right to use land, but the land to be used is not allocated to him by either chief or headman. He acquires it and enjoys rights over it and deals with it in exactly the same way as the individual among the Tonga. Although there may be a hierarchical political structure in such tribal areas, there is no correspondingly hierarchy of estates in the form of descending allocations of land.

Not infrequently one hears it said that a chief allocates land to a village which wishes to move from its present site to a new site; before such a move the village seeks the approval of the chief. But the approval which is required appears to be purely the exercise of political control for the chief must know where his village and his people are living, and whether or not they are still residing under his control. No specific area of land is assigned to a village. In fact in none of the areas so far studied is there anything resembling defined village lands. If villages are far apart in thinly populated country, it will of course happen that the lands of individual villages are quite separate. But as soon as population density passes the appropriate point, the gardens of adjacent villages overlap in a patchwork. Moreover if a man moves from one village to another he need not vacate the land which he cultivated at the first village and acquire new land at his new abode, unless the move involves such a distance that it is impracticable to continue cultivating the land at a former village site.

Up to this point one may summarise by saying that where a tribal political structure exists, one must distinguish clearly between the political control over land exercised by chiefs, which is manifested by the control of the right of newcomers to settle in the area, and the actual acquisition of land by individuals, which is not subject to the control of allocation by any land authority, and is restricted only by the fact that an individual may not take up land already subject to rights previously established over it by an earlier individual. Allocation in the sense so commonly assumed does not exist.

However, allocation in a quite different form does occur in some areas, and it is to this type of situation that the term should be properly applied. I refer to such areas as the shore of Lake Tanganyika where all land is subject to existing established rights, and the right-holders assign pieces of their land to relatives or friends to use. In this area the Lungu have developed a fairly complex series of estates arising in this way. Land may be lent on an entirely insecure basis in that the lender has the right to recover it whenever he wishes, subject only to the borrower normally being allowed to reap his crops; or it may be held on an indefinite basis as with a widow who enjoys the right to use land held by her deceased husband with a reversionary right to the patrilineal relatives of the deceased husband if she remarries; or it may be held on a form of life estate as when a matrilineal relative is allowed to use land during his lifetime but the patrilineal relatives of the lender retain their right of the reversion when the borrower dies or decides to abandon the use of the land. In all these cases one may, I think rightly refer to the allocation of land since a person with rights of a primary nature over land assigns defined areas of it to other people subject to certain conditions. Some of these transactions seem to approximate to some of the so-called leasing of land described in parts of West Africa where a land 'owner' lends land to a stranger in return for what has been referred to in the literature as a 'shake hand', since the borrower makes presents to the lender. But at this stage I should prefer to avoid calling the examples of such transactions in Northern Rhodesia 'leasing of land', and define the relationship of the parties in terms of the rights enjoyed by them over the land in question.

When Gluckman[2] elaborated his argument of a hierarchy of estates with descending allocations being a characteristic of African land tenure, he drew especially on his knowledge of the Zulu and Lozi, and on Schapera's data for the Tswana. He suggested that such a system would be least clear in systems of shifting agriculture while land is plentiful. From the investigations which I have so far made, it seems doubtful whether in a large area of Northern Rhodesia one can rightly speak of a hierarchy of estates at all. Moreover it is significant that in places where land is scarce and economically valuable, the secondary estates derive directly from individuals who are holders of primary estates, and not from some land authority.

A point of some importance in this respect is that in many of these areas Africans lived without any centralised political structure for a very long time before the coming of chiefs who established political control of their territories. Hence almost everywhere one finds some concept of 'first settler' in an area. Such 'first settlers' did not exercise any political control as one would commonly understand that expression, for it was merely small groups of kinsmen and their followers who settled in vacant areas. These places of original settlement are widely defined by the term *katonga* in places as far apart as the Tonga area of the Southern Province and the Luapula valley. When better organised people came in later with chiefs who established some form of centralised political control over the small unorganised groups which they found, individual land tenure as it already existed was not directly affected by the change. Today the Bemba speaking tribes have a saying *chalo chamfumu, katongo kamulanda* which may be explained as the chief has his realm but each commoner his place of settlement. Ritual functions of original settlers in respect of fishing and hunting continued to be enjoyed by them, and did not pass to the political chiefs, so that in many areas one finds a clear separation of political powers held by chiefs, and spiritual powers held by others.

It seems clear that in a large part of Northern Rhodesia the presence or absence of a political hierarchy in the native authority structure is not correlated with a corresponding hierarchy in the form of estates in land; in addition to the factors of shifting cultivation and plentiful land already mentioned by Gluckman, it seems likely that there are historical reasons as outlined above which account for the absence of centralised traditional authorities responsible for the allocation of land.

Family, Clan and Land Rights

Family as a right-holding unit in land tenure seems a very undesirable term unless reference is intended to a natural family of a man, his wife and children. However, where family has been used in Northern Rhodesia in this context, it always turned out to be a unilineal, patrilineal or matrilineal descent group. In such a case it would be far better to be explicit from the outset, and avoid the term family unless it is explained that this is intended to denote some identifiable social unit.

In general the term clan has been little used in connection with African land tenure in Northern Rhodesia. However it seems worth while suggesting that here too the term should only be used with some indication of what it is intended to denote. The term clan is used in more than one sense in different parts of Africa; in much of Central and adjacent Africa, clans normally denote people sharing a common clan name, and claiming a fictitious kinship based upon the fact that the clan names are matrilineally or patrilineally inherited. Such groups are completely dispersed, and have no corporate functions. Nevertheless in African eyes they are often equated with an extension of actual traceable kinship. The Tonga for instance use the same term (*mukoa*) to refer to both matrilineal kinsmen and to clan membership, and if they are speaking in English will use the term clan in a most confusing way unless one is clear about the implications of the word in their social structure.

Where adequate analyses of the social structure of African peoples are available, it is reasonable to assume that a writer uses clan or family in the sense which has already been adopted in such analyses. Where no analyses have been made, it is quite impossible to ascertain in what sense clan is sometimes used. Nevertheless it is astonishing how frequently references are made to the clan system, clan heads, clan lands and so on, without the slightest attempt at explanation. The point is of more than merely academic importance, for in many parts of Africa, including most of Northern Rhodesia, where transactions in land rights are not controlled by a political superior, social structure plays some part, and sometimes a very important part in land tenure. Unfortunately there are still many tribes in Africa of whose social organisation no adequate modern analyses are available. In such cases the use of terms like clan and family in referring to land tenure all too often convey nothing. At the risk of straying momentarily outside Northern Rhodesia, is it too much to ask that writers on land tenure should indicate what they mean by these terms, so that those interested can use descriptions of land tenure elsewhere for comparison with the systems in their own territories?

Communal Tenure

It is unfortunate that this misleading expression so often continues to be used as a blanket definition of African land tenure, implying that every individual has equal rights in every piece of a tribe's land. Applied to grazing areas in Northern Rhodesia in the provinces so far studied one may to some extent speak of communal rights in grazing since anyone may graze his cattle on any land not claimed for individual use; but it must be qualified by the observation that these communal grazing rights are not vested in a whole group collectively, for where land is short as among the Tonga or the Mambwe, individuals can bring pieces of communal grazing land under their personal control for arable purposes by the usual process of starting to cultivate it. The communal grazing areas are not vested in any authority which preserves them from encroachment in this way.

In so far as rights over arable land are concerned these are essentially individual—acquired by the individual, enjoyed by him, and disposed of by him. Rights of individuals over arable land cannot possibly be described as communal tenure without a complete distortion of the facts. Much of the confusion here no doubt springs from contrasting English ideas of land ownership with the conditions found in the most undeveloped systems of shifting cultivation, where a man exercised rights over a piece of land for only a brief period, and when it was exhausted, passed on to open up another piece of vacant land. Under such conditions land was presumably hardly ever inherited and only infrequently transferred. An individual enjoyed rights in respect of a piece of land but only of an ephemeral nature in that they were soon transferred to another piece of land. But with the stabilization of agriculture or with the scarcity of land in a given area or with the emergence of cash cropping putting an economic value on land, or some combination of all three, the permanence of a man's land rights developed quickly. In areas where land is valuable for these reasons, it is regularly transferred or inherited, and rarely abandoned. Hence in some places land once acquired does not revert to the common pool to be taken up by someone else, but passes directly from one to another without any intervening authority. At this stage individual rights of a continuing permanent nature are strongly developed; whilst it may be inappropriate to refer to such tenure by any English term which is liable to contain unsuitable implications, it is certainly necessary to avoid the use of the expression communal tenure. It would seem preferable to call such cases individual tenure, accompanying the expression by such definition as many be necessary of the rights existing. Individual tenure of this type occurs in all the provinces of Northern Rhodesia so far studied.

Inheritance

It has long been recognised that the recording of any system of African land tenure calls for the adequate analysis and description of the types of rights which individuals enjoy. On the strength of the foregoing discussion I venture to add that it is timely to remember that any description involves also a terminology in which the account is couched, and such a terminology needs to be explicit and clear if confusion is to be avoided.

Notes

[1] *Coral Gardens and their Magic.*
[2] *Human Problems in British Central Africa*, 3, pp. 1–12, 1945.

V. Sheddick: Land Tenure in Basutoland*

Some Basic Concepts of Land Tenure

The Nature of Ownership

Ownership in the context of Land Tenure has, in the past, tended to be associated with concepts of communal and individual tenure, both terms being given the widest interpretation and application. If the notion of communal and individual tenure, as characteristic respectively of primitive and Euro-American societies in their totality, still persists with the layman, it may now be said to have passed out of current anthropological usage. Its place was taken by a conception of both patterns of tenure existing side by side in any given set of comparable communities. Thus Lowie pointed out, in an earlier work, that communal ownership was not necessarily a feature of the land tenure of either primitive hunters or of cultivators, though it was frequently to be found among pastoral peoples. Furthermore there is no 'communism'—that is to say, no joint ownership by the total community—in land so far as the territorial group goes, but only within a strictly limited body of actual kindred.[1] More recently, Gluckman has pointed out that modern studies have shown that while individual rights to land and property exist in nearly all societies, but at the same time grazing lands and some categories of raw materials are 'communally' owned in that any member of the community may work them.[2]

Thereafter followed a period when writers sought on the one hand to emphasise the individual rights of community members—using alternative terms such as 'pre-emptive possessory rights'[3]—and on the other hand to demonstrate that nowhere do individual rights constitute 'absolute ownership' but that they are in all cases subordinate to group rights variously described as 'communal', 'corporate' and 'tribal' rights.[4] This diadic approach finally crystallized into the concept of society holding as the basis of collective

* V. Sheddick, *Land Tenure in Basutoland*, H.M.S.O., 1954, pp. 1–2.

or public control a superior tenure within which there exists a multiplicity of private rights and interests.[5]

Whilst, therefore, students of Land Tenure have succeeded in demonstrating that 'communal' and 'individual' as mutually exclusive and polar concepts of rights had no existence, they have been driven back at the same time to the position of recognising degrees of individual rights, though with no absolute individual rights, and degrees of collective rights, though again with no condition of absolute communism. Expressed in another way, the study of Land Tenure in terms of legal titles now recognises the two extreme conditions of *public tenure*, when society retains to itself a majority of the rights in land, and of *freehold interest* obtaining when most of the rights in land are turned over to private parties, between which there exists over the world a wide range of intermediary forms.[6]

A possible escape from this terminological morass has been found in the approach which concerns itself with the sociological determination of how 'land' is made available for human exploitation. The collective rights to land are studied through the institutions—in the case of many African communities, the institution of Chieftainship—in which they are embodied. Thus, the Bemba's right to the use of any part of the bush depends on his political allegiances, first to a headman and then to a chief. He cannot cultivate as an isolated individual even though he has uncontested rights of ownership of any land he may have cleared.[7] It is the political affiliation that counts in that the chief looks upon a man as a subject and not as a tenant, although the status of the subject does actually confer the right to use land.[8] In this way 'ownership' resolves itself into administration, that is the trusteeship, apportionment and regulation of the use of land.[9] Similarly, individual rights may now be considered as the way 'land' is used by the individual members of the community.[10] Thus we are told, in a recent study, that although throughout the whole of Nigeria the idea of communal ownership of land obtains, yet each community has *rights of distribution* among its members and *rights of users*.[11]

Throughout this study the 'land' rights of the Basuto will be considered in these two aspects, the rights to administer land and the rights to use land.

Notes

[1] R. H. Lowie: *Primitive Society* 1921, p. 201 *et seq.*

[2] M. Gluckman: 'Lozi Land Tenure', *Rhodes Livingstone Papers* No. 10, 1943.

[3] R. H. Lowie: art. 'Primitive Land Tenure' *Ency. Soc. Sci.* 1933 and A. T. & G. M. Culwick: *Ubena of the Rivers*, 1935, p. 239.

[4] G. Wilson: 'Land Rights of Individuals among the Nyakyusa', *Rhodes Livingstone Papers*, No. 1, 1938, p. 29; Nadel, *Black Byzantium* 1942, p. 183; Gluckman, 'African Land Tenure', *Rhodes Livingstone Journal*, No. 3, 1945.

[5] Brinkman, art. 'Land Tenure', *Ency. Soc. Sci.* 1933; art. 'Land Tenure', *Ency. Brit.* 14th Ed.; Culwick, 1935; R. Firth, *Primitive Polynesian Economy*, 1939, p. 59; Gluckman 1943 and 1945; and Brooke, 'Some Legal Aspects of Land Tenure in Nigeria', *African Studies* 5, 1946.

[6] For concrete examples of such range of legal titles see Cory and Hartnoll, *Customary Law of the Haya Tribe*, 1945; and Nadel, 'Land Tenure on the Eritrean Plateau', *Africa*, 1945.

[7] A. I. Richards; *Land, Labour and Diet*, 1939, p. 244.

[8] *Ibid.*, p. 246.

[9] See Nadel, *op. cit.*, 1942, p. 183.

[10] Malinowski, *Coral Gardens*, 1935, pp. 318 and 323; Wilson, 1938, p. 29; and especially I. Schapera, *Land Tenure in the Bechuanaland Protectorate*, 1943, throughout which this approach is implicitly employed.

[11] Brooke, *op. cit.*, 1946.

K. Bentsi-Enchill: Do African Systems of Land Tenure Require a Special Terminology?*

Introductory

Expressions indicating varying degrees of dissatisfaction with systems of land tenure prevailing in sub-Saharan Africa are very common, and the view is widely held that the

* K. Bentsi-Enchill, 'Do African Systems of Land Tenure Require a Special Terminology?' in *Journal of African Law*, Vol. 9, No. 2, pp. 114–121.

traditional institutions which govern land rights operate in a manner obstructive to agricultural development. 'If enterprise is to be given an opportunity to express itself,' writes Dr. Yudelman in a recent book, 'there must be a break with traditional institutions which govern land.'[1] Views of this kind call for decisions regarding the substitution of one system of law for another, or for various kinds of radical reform including the engrafting onto the traditional system of legal expedients and devices proved useful in other systems of law. Such decisions, however, patently require much more than a mere nodding acquaintance with the existing local law, the changes sought to be introduced therein, and their functioning on the systems of law from which they are to be borrowed. Accordingly a need exists for a kind of comparative legal analysis of existing systems of landholding which can throw into relief the real points of weakness that need to be remedied or pruned away, while also indicating the elements that are worthy to be retained, if even only as the stock upon which novel arrangements may be engrafted.

The purpose of this paper is to suggest an obvious approach to this necessary work of preliminary analysis, and to indicate the sort of theoretical structure and interpretation to which systems of land tenure in sub-Saharan Africa lend themselves. This is done with the aid of an analytical scheme which is patently applicable to tenure systems in advanced countries also, a process which may help to show where the significant differences are to be looked for, as well as perhaps dispelling some persistent misunderstandings regarding the sort of remedies required.

Additional justification for the sort of discussion about to be undertaken comes from methodological comments such as the following by Professor Bohannan:

> 'It is probable that no single topic has exercised so many students and men of affairs concerned with Africa as has that of land. It is equally probable that no single topic concerning Africa has produced so large a poor literature. We are still abysmally ignorant of African land practices. That ignorance derives less from want of "facts" than that we do not know what to do with "facts" or how to interpret them. The reason for this state of affairs is close at hand: there exists no good analysis of the concepts habitually used in land tenure studies, and certainly no detailed critique of their applicability to cross-cultural study.
>
> 'Thinking about land has been and remains largely ethnocentric. Although many investigators have been meticulously careful in pointing out that one must not use European [*sic*] concepts like "leasehold" or "fee-simple" in describing an African situation, rarely has anyone gone so far as to ask what we mean by the terms "land", "tenure" and "rights". The notion of "land tenure" may have distorted as much as it has clarified.'[2]

If a charge of ethnocentricism is to be levelled against the literature on land tenure in Africa which, we would submit, contains many illuminating and helpful studies, the justification for it lies, not so much in the employment of the technical terms of the common or civil law systems—concerning which, as Bohannan admits, many investigators have been careful—but rather in a failure to 'diagnose' identical or similar relationships where such exist, and in the confusing use of terms which suggest differences where none exist, or which suggest similarities where there is significant difference. Such a failure in diagnosis, we would submit, is involved when Bohannan says, for example, that the Tiv might be said to have 'farm tenure', but they do not have 'land tenure'.

That land tenure systems should and do vary from community to community stands to reason and is largely accounted for by the unique historical development of each political grouping and the consequent variation of legal and institutional structures in different polities. This consideration places obvious limits on the value of broad generalizations about systems of land tenure in general as well as emphasizing the need for close and comprehensive study of any particular system if one is to understand it sufficiently for intelligent manipulation. But no less important are the fundamental reasons why the variations in land tenure systems should be, as it were, variations on a common theme. Tenure systems represent relations of men in society with respect to that essential and often scarce commodity land. Accordingly, although actual patterns differ from system to system, there are certain uniformities of type in the relations involved which make it possible to apply a common scheme of analysis to the different systems.

This, in any case, is our working hypothesis. As Radcliffe-Brown put it, 'it is only by the use of a comparative method that we can arrive at general explanations. The altertive is to confine ourselves to particularistic explanations similar to those of the historians. The two kinds of explanation are both legitimate and do not conflict; both are needed for the study of societies and their institutions.'[3]

Our suggested approach to the comparative study of land tenure systems is indicated by the sort of basic information that a stranger needing land for his own use in another country would need to have: from whom do I get it? On what terms? What can I do or not do with it? Et cetera. This range or cluster of questions, we suggest, can be conveniently embraced in the following schematic question: Who holds what interest in what land? The key terms 'who', and 'interest in land' call for and must receive extended scrutiny. But it is appropriate at this stage to emphasize the essentially neutral character of the framework question, permitting as it does, inquiry into any and all types of 'interest-holder' and all types of interests in land that are held or can be held in the particular system of tenure under investigation.

Three principal concerns or lines of inquiry are contemplated by this formulation: (1) The types of interest in land that are or can be held in the particular system under investigation. The principal factors to ascertain concerning any given interest, it is suggested, are: (*a*) the respects in which it falls short of plenary rights of user and disposal; (*b*) the specific confines of the land to which that interest relates; and (*c*) its duration, an inquiry that leads to considerations about inheritance patterns. (2) Secondly, the question, 'Who?' points to a general inquiry regarding the 'persons', natural or artificial (not excluding the state) who hold or can hold various types of interest in land. And where groups of persons are the holders of such interest, it points to an inquiry concerning the machinery of group administration. (3) Thirdly, both lines of inquiry raise questions regarding whatever arrangements or machinery there may be for storing information concerning these matters.

Needless to say, a whole host of other questions can be asked. It is not our purpose to underplay the relevance of cultural and ideological factors to a definitive study of any people and their institutions. From the viewpoint of the institutions which govern land rights, however, it is submitted that concentration on the lines of inquiry noted above lead to the pith and marrow of any given system and is an indispensable and fruitful preliminary to legislative and administrative adaptation. It leads to results such as that achieved in William the Conqueror's Domesday Book, or any comprehensive system of title registration. In fact, the preliminary analysis of terms which follows can be regarded as being designed to settle some of the principal questions that arise regarding what to put on the title register. And it is hoped that the ensuing discussion will provide abundant support for the proposition that African systems of land tenure in general as compared with systems of tenure prevailing elsewhere present no special or extraordinary problems: their principal defects arise mainly from the fact that they have been mostly left to make their own informal adaptation, unaided or even officially obstructed, to changing circumstances; and that perhaps their greatest single need is the speedy institution of machinery of general title registration based, as Torrens was concerned to base his famous reforms, on methods that are 'reliable, simple, cheap, speedy and suited to the needs of the community'. This, we would submit, is the principal area in which a modicum of legal integration not only urgently needs to be undertaken but is most feasible.

The Phenomenon of an Interest in Land

The part of our framework question which perhaps challenges the most immediate scrutiny is the concept of an interest in land, and it is appropriate to begin with it.

African societies, like human societies everywhere, have territorial structuring. Everywhere we look communities of varying magnitude make claims regarding the land they occupy that it is 'theirs' and distinguish their relationship thereto from that of 'strangers' or 'guests'. Analogies to this situation are abundant. 'England', 'Scotland' and 'Finland' as names for the land of the Angles, the Scots and the Finns respectively involve the same idea and relationship. It is crystallized in the doctrine of territorial sovereignty in international relations.

Brierly writes:

T

> 'At the basis of international law, lies the notion that a state occupies a definite part of the surface of the earth, within which it normally exercises, subject to the limitations imposed by international law, jurisdiction over persons and things to the exclusion of the jurisdiction of other states. When a state exercises an authority of this kind over a certain territory it is popularly said to have "sovereignty" over the territory, but that much abused word is here used in a rather special sense. It refers here . . . to the nature of the rights over territory; and in the absence of any better word it is a convenient way of contrasting the fullest rights over territory known to law with the minor territorial rights to be later mentioned. Territorial sovereignty bears an obvious resemblance to ownership in private law, less marked, however, today than it was in the days of the patrimonial state, when a kingdom and everything in it was regarded as being to the king very much what a landed estate was to the owner.'[4]

This resemblance between ownership in private law and territorial sovereignty is particularly noticeable if one looks at any particular sovereign state from outside. The more or less stable boundaries between the territories of various states, as well as their very sovereignties, depend in the last resort on the same sort of factors that Howell mentions concerning the lands of different communities among the Nuer: 'That certain communities . . . have a definite right to distinct areas is clearly recognized by all the Nuer. The sanction for possession in the past was, however, physical force and the power to resist the encroachment of others, while now the *status quo* is maintained by the government.'[5] For the word government, however, we would have to substitute some complicated explanation about 'balance of power' and international law to make the parallel complete.

All this is by way of pointing out, at a macroscopic level, a universal type o 'interestf in land'—the relationship between whole 'sovereign' communities with respect to the land occupied by them. It is important to note that this relationship can only be fully described by reference to other communities, i.e. to what they are called upon to refrain from doing with respect to the territory in question. Conquest has been a universal method by which particular interests in land of this kind and of others generally have been altered in favour of other interests of an identical type. International law and inchoate organs of international government, reinforced by a complex balance of powers, provide the more or less effective guarantees of this system of territorial sovereignties.

This relationship of a human community—the sovereign territorial state—to other such communities with respect to land is paralleled by relationships within the community between sub-groups and individuals with respect to parcels of land occupied by them. That is to say that the 'ours' and 'yours' attitude and acknowledgements with respect to particular areas of land manifested by discrete and sovereign political communities are paralleled within each political community by similar attitudes on the part of its sub-groups and individuals with respect to land occupied by them. What appears from outside as a unitary dominion over territory is from the inside view a multiplicity of particular interests, of individuals, families, corporations, etc. And, *at the very least*, this domestic system of what we might momentarily call discrete 'sovereignties over parcels of land' is also more or less effectively guaranteed by the operation of forces of the type noticed with respect to the international concert of sovereign political communities.

But the guarantee mechanism tends to be more effective within any such political community, partly because a political community or state is an area within which a precept against open conflict and violence is operative,[6] i.e. is an area of acknowledged jural relations and partly as a result of its governmental machinery (which may range from the rudimentary and unspecialized order-keeping or peace-making of a clan group or 'rain chief' to the articulate and developed machinery of a modern state).

The foregoing should serve to indicate that the term 'interest' is used in our scheme to represent the sum total of 'rights' vested in a 'holder' (who may be an individual or group of persons) with respect to a particular parcel of land.

The use of the word 'rights' may raise in some minds the question whether the notion of a legal right, involving as it does the cluster of claims, privileges, powers and immunities distinguished by Hohfield,[7] has any place in 'primitive societies'. The short answer to such a query is well phrased by Hoebel in his review of three studies of law in separate African communities by Howell, Bohannan and Gluckman respectively as follows:

'All three studies drive home the fundamental point that law as an aspect of human control is a creative social invention on all levels of cultural development.'[8]

The word 'right' in statements of the type 'X has a right to farm on Blackacre' represents a relationship having the following basic features:[9] (i) that X is at liberty to farm on Blackacre; (ii) that others are enjoined by the system of moral and jural relations operative within the particular community not to interfere with X's exercise of this liberty or privilege and (iii) that persons infringing this prohibition will have 'wronged' X and may incur the reactions flowing from the type of remedial machinery available in the particular community. The expression 'an interest in land', then, is being used here to designate the aggregation of rights or range of activities which X is at liberty to enjoy or pursue as against other persons with respect to a determinate area of land, Blackacre.[10] Thus X's interest in Blackacre may consist in any one or more of the following rights: to farm there, to build there, to pasture his flock there, to pass his interest on to his heirs on his death, or dispose of it by his will, or by sale, etc.

Our scheme does not call for the naming of particular types of interest in land. As indicated above, what matters is that any given interest should be described in terms of the ways in which it falls short of plenary rights of use and disposal of the land to which it relates, and of the boundaries of the said land; and this is the sort of information that a title register requires.

But names provide a shorthand for referring to broad classes of facts and relationships. And therefore some commonly used names must now be considered in the light of the foregoing analysis.

Ownership is a name commonly used for the relation between an interest and the person in whom it is vested, the relation for which we have so far used the word 'holder'. This is the sense in which a person is said to own a farm, a lease, a right of way or a tree on land not so owned by him. This is what makes it possible for it to be said of the same land, concurrently and with truth, that it belongs to the community, that it belongs to X's family and that it belongs to X. This use may be confusing, but it is intelligible.

The usage distinguished above logically covers a second and more common usage. The interest 'owned' may be one that accords the 'owner' the fullest cluster of rights over the land in question, the maximum range of use and disposal allowed within a given legal system. The second and commoner usage confines the term ownership to the relationship of a holder to an interest having this maximum amplitude, 'indefinite in point of user, unrestricted in point of disposition, and unlimited in point of duration'.[11]

Ownership in this latter sense of an absolute, original interest in land held of no one is, in the legal literature, called *allodial* from the medieval Latin *allodium* or *alodium* derived from the German *allod* or *allodium* meaning entire property. It is the opposite of *feodum* or *feudum*, another medieval Latin term of supposedly Germanic origin with derivatives like *feudal*, *feud* and *fee*, 'with their specific connotation of derived and dependent property'.[12]

Allodial ownership, as representing the most comprehensive interest in land, i.e. the one embracing the maximum cluster of rights of use and disposal, thus becomes the standard by which all other interests in land are defined in our model which, as indicated above, calls for any given interest to be defined in terms of the ways in which it falls short of such plenary title.[13]

What then of interests less than allodial ownership? Within any given community it is generally possible to indicate one or two types of interest in land—that is to say, particular clusters of rights (sometimes forming *named* interests) which have a high frequency of occurrence. And it is generally possible to rank these interests in some sort of descending order of amplitude or range, along a theoretical ladder having allodial ownership at its apex. One difference in tenure systems from community to community can be said to lie in the fact that the clusters of rights forming one common type of interest in one community do not correspond exactly with common clusters in another and fall on different points of the ladder.

Among such lesser interests in land, two broad categories may be distinguished. The first of these is the type which arises when the allodial ownership of land is vested in a collectivity like a sovereign community or section of it, or in a village community, a clan or a family. As is usually the case the actual use and enjoyment of the bulk of such land is not by the group together, but rather by families and individuals on separate and distinct parcels of the land. What then is the interest of a family or individual member of the owning group in the portion or portions of the group-owned land apportioned to it or him? This interest which is dependent on the group ownership occurs everywhere (though with different degrees of nearness to allodial ownership). Among the factors which seem to influence its degree of nearness to allodial title may be mentioned the type of group concerned and its organization, the relative abundance of land, the type of agrarian activity engaged in, and relationships resulting from foreign conquest and the existing political set-up.

For reasons to be explained later we will call it proprietary occupancy, to distinguish it from the other broad category of interests which arise as a result of permission given by or agreement reached with an allodial owner or proprietary occupant whereby the land is loaned or leased, or used as security for a loan. This we will call permissive or contractual occupancy. In so far as any transaction such as a sale or gift results in the substitution of one holder for another in respect of a given interest, no new category is created.

Before pursuing these lesser interests, however, other features of our schematic question must be examined and brought into play. What is important to bear in mind is that African systems of tenure reveal upon inspection what seems to be a general feature of other systems, that ownership in land can be subdivided and that lesser interests therein can be held and are frequently held by different people simultaneously. To this we shall return.

Notes

[1] Yudelman, *Africans on the land* (Harvard, 1964), p. 225.

[2] P. J. Bohannan, " 'Land', 'Tenure' and 'Land Tenure'," in *African agrarian systems* (ed. Biebuyck, 1963), p. 101.

[3] Radcliffe-Brown, *Structure and function in primitive society* (1952), pp. 113–114.

[4] Brierly, *Law of Nations* (5th Ed. 1955), p. 150.

[5] Howell, *A Manual of Nuer Law*, (1954) p. 182.

[6] Even in communities of the type classified by Fortes and Evans-Pritchard as Class B, namely those lacking specialized governmental machinery, the literature on land tenure indicates identifiable areas of acknowledged jural relations. See, e.g., Fortes. *The dynamics of clanship among the Tallensi* (1945), pp. 180–181.

[7] Hohfeld, *Fundamental legal conceptions as applied in judicial reasoning and other essays*, ed. Cook, 1923.

[8] Hoebels, 'Three studies in African Law' (1961), 13 *Stanford L.*, Vol. 13, No. 2, 418, 4 (1961).

[9] Cf. Hart and Sachs, *The legal process: basic problems in the making and application of law* (1958), p. 142.

[10] Cf. Noyes, *The institution of property*, p. 290 (1936), 'In a frequently quoted passage the philosopher Kant says, "... if a man were alone in the world he could properly hold or acquire nothing as his own; because between himself, as person, and all other outward objects, as things, there is no relation". "The relation", says Holland, "is between him and other people whom he excludes from the thing". This is another characteristic of all rights. They are relations, negative or positive, between persons, though they may also exist *with reference to things* or material objects.'

[11] Austin, *Lectures on jurisprudence or the philosophy of positive law* (3rd edn. 1869), p. 187.

[12] Noyes, *ibid.*, p. 87.

[13] The word title also can have a harmless but useful place in our shorthand. Recognition that X is the owner of a given interest in a parcel of land is recognition of X's title to that interest. The evidence that proves that X is the owner of such and such an interest is evidence of his title thereto. Title in this sense is another word for ownership in the senses explained above. By extension, title is also used by lawyers for the evidence or documents that establish ownership of a given interest.

A. N. Allott: Towards a Definition of Absolute Ownership*—I

This draft is an attempt to meet a particular difficulty, which is likely to occur not infrequently in African countries where the present land law is dualistic in character and represents a partial amalgamation, or co-existence, of English and customary laws

* A. N. Allott, 'Towards a Definition of Absolute Ownership', in *Journal of African Law*, Vol. 5, No. 2, pp. 99–102.

relating to land. Increasingly these two bodies of law will tend to draw together (as they have already done to a considerable extent in West Africa), and legislation will have to be prepared from time to time which is capable of applying both to interests held under English law and to interests under various sorts of customary law. This is pre-eminently the case where any proposal for registration of title to land is involved, since the register (if it is not accompanied by a radical revision of the substantive land law) will have to show under as few heads as possible the different sorts of title that can exist in respect of land, under customary as well as under English law (where the latter forms the basis of the general law of the territory).

In the preparation of any register of title in England or other countries whose law is based on English law, the most important register will be that of 'proprietors' entitled to 'freehold' or an 'absolute title'; and there will usually be little difficulty in determining who such persons should be. When we turn to African countries (where title to land is governed in whole or part by the rules of customary law), however, the position is very different. Here we are faced with such institutions as that of the paramount control of land by 'tribes', village-communities, or other territorial groupings, and that of 'family land' or 'clan land', where the individual's enjoyment of land may be fettered by the superior rights of the social group to which he belongs. Often there is a hierarchy of such bodies or persons interested by different titles in the same tract of land, and the position is further complicated in many areas by the admission of individuals or groups of strangers not belonging to the land-controlling group into permanent or semi-permanent occupation.

In such cases, where is the 'absolute ownership' to be said to lie? Which, out of all the hierarchy of estates and interests in land which may be existing concurrently, shall we select as being 'truly' ownership? The naïve answer to this sort of problem is for the questioner or investigator to award or withhold 'ownership' in respect of any particular interest in so far as it meets or fails to meet certain arbitrary requirement determined *a priori* by the legal system with which he is familiar. Thus we are used to the alien student of African land tenure stating confidently that there was no 'real' or 'true' ownership of land in African customary law, because there was no sale of land, for instance, in the old days. This sort of approach assumes that there is something wrong with a foreign legal institution which does not conform to English legal principles; it also assumes that a term such as 'ownership', has a god-given meaning, a 'true' or 'real' meaning; and finally it assumes that a thing called 'ownership' exists and can be discovered in a country's laws just as one might discover diamonds in a river-bed.

All of these assumptions, it is hardly necessary to remark, are unjustifiable. Words do not have *a priori* meanings, but only such as usage gives to them; and from time to time usage alters or can be extended to cover new situations. It is only in an Act of Parliament that one can prescribe the way words are to be used (though schoolmasters might think differently!); in other contexts one can only state how words are currently used; that is, one *describes* rather than *prescribes* usage. It is not possible to maintain a discussion here of the rather involved jurisprudential considerations to which one must refer in deciding how far words like 'ownership' can be appropriately applied to features of African customary land tenure; but this is merely the problem of finding the most convenient and least misleading language in which to present the facts of African land law.

The practical task which the definition appended below seeks to render easier is that of a 'settlement' or 'adjudication' officer, who is ordered to place on his initial register of title all those which appear to him to be equivalent to 'ownership'. When he is faced with chiefs claiming paramount rights of control over tribal lands, with 'families' claiming to be owners of family lands which have descended to them under the law of intestate succession, but which have been re-parcelled out among the individual members of the family, is he to register the individual subject or tribesman or the individual family-member on the one hand, or the tribe or the chief or the family on the other hand, as 'owner'?

If English law had not obtruded on the African scene, the problem would perhaps not be so difficult, as the registering officer would merely have to record the existing state of affairs without bothering to re-interpret it in English legal terms; but in the West African countries at any rate (such as Southern Nigeria and Ghana), an interest in land held under customary law may at any moment be transferred by a mode of transfer known only to English law, or 'converted' into an interest under English law, and vice versa. The establishment of a legal rate of exchange then becomes extremely important.

The definition given below is thus not intended to be universally valid for all times and all places, but merely to offer a yardstick by which to measure some of the institutions actually found in Africa today. The use of the term 'absolute owner' rather than 'owner' is of little significance, but is intended to cover the fact that in ordinary legal parlance one speaks of several different kinds of owner, e.g. 'limited owner', and that we are only concerned with one such type of 'owner'. The definition given is of 'absolute owner' rather than 'absolute ownership', as it seemed easier to list what an owner may do rather than specify the qualities of an abstract concept.

Section 1 (1) states in four different ways what different persons might mention as the indicia of ownership. Section 1 (2) has to deal with the peculiarities of the English law of trusts, and s. 1 (3) with those of strict settlements. Section 2 permits an owner as defined to alienate some part of his claims, privileges, powers or immunities without thereby forfeiting his title as owner. Section 3 then defines 'absolute ownership' as the interest of an 'absolute owner', and makes clear that certain things are excluded (e.g. the ultimate claims of the Crown to acquire land compulsorily, etc.) and certain others (notably the estate in fee simple) included.

It is a fascinating exercise to attempt to apply this draft definition to the facts of African land law. One of the main problems is in dealing with the position, common in West Africa, whereby a 'family' is entitled to succeed to the self-acquired property of one of its members who has died without disposing of such property in his life-time. Some judges and other commentators have gone so far as to describe this situation as one in which the acquirer has no more than a 'life-interest' in the property he has acquired. But this fundamentally misrepresents the position in most areas: the family has nothing more than a *spes successionis*, which ripens into a vested interest on the death of the acquirer, but until then is of no legal significance. Such a claim by a family would be expressly excluded by the terms of the finla sentence of section 1 of the definition.

Equal difficulties arise with the interests of traditional political or tribal authorities. One is accustomed to reading in the literature that 'all the land of the tribe belongs to the chief' or words to that effect, this statement often being a translation of a vernacular maxim. On the definition as appended a chief whose rights of land control were limited to exercising powers of compulsory acquisition, or to acquiring the land of subjects by escheat in default of heirs, or to specifying in general terms the ways in which land is to be used, would not be classed as an 'absolute owner' as defined in respect of such land (though he might well be classed as such in respect of particular tracts of land under his personal control). Where there is a hierarchy of chiefs (as with many of the Akan 'states' in Ghana), the definition might help in deciding which rank of chief out of the hierarchy might be termed the 'owner' of the land under his official control. There are, in fact, variations between one 'state' and another in the distribution of rights and powers as between superior and subordinate chiefs, which are currently expressed in the law relating to the alienation of stool lands; these variations would be reflected in the classification as provided for in the definition.

The suggested definitions of 'absolute owner' is, it is vital to stress, tentative only. It is put forward for discussion and revision in the light of the traditional and introduced land laws in Africa, with a view to seeing (i) whether it is in principle possible to frame a definition that will serve to isolate one category of interest-holders in land whose interests are comparable in range and content and freedom from superior control to those of fee simple owners in England and the like; (ii) how such a definition might be worded to take account of the peculiarities of African customary land law; and (iii) what would be the effect of the application of such a definition to particular land tenure systems in Africa. Any proposals for alterations in wording, or even a radical change of approach to the problem, will be welcomed by the author.

Definition of 'Absolute Owner' and 'Absolute Ownership'

1.—(1) 'Absolute owner' means, in respect of any land held by the absolute owner as absolute owner, the person (whether individual or corporate)—

(i) whose interest is vested and is not defeasible or determinable upon the occurrence of some certain or uncertain future event; and

(ii) who has, or whose successors in title will have, the ultimate right to possess the said land (whether the said person is at any time in possession or not); and
(iii) whose interest in the said land is not derived from nor dependent upon any other interest in the said land (save by transfer or transmission from a predecessor in title of the absolute owner); and
(iv) who has, or would if he were in possession have, in respect of the said land the totality of claims, privileges, powers and immunities which the law permits any person to enjoy in respect of land.

A person who has a mere expectation not amounting to a legal claim of eventual possession of land is not absolute owner of such land.

(2) Without prejudice to the law governing trusts, where land is held by a person on trust for any other person or for charitable purposes, then the trustee of such land shall, subject to sub-section (3) of this section and notwithstanding that by the terms of the trust some other person may be entitled to the beneficial enjoyment of the said land, be deemed for the purposes of this Act to be the absolute owner of the said land if he would be so entitled as absolute owner within the terms of sub-section (1) of this section were it not for the existence of the trust.

(3) Without prejudice to the law governing strict settlements, the tenant for life of land under a strict settlement shall be deemed to be the absolute owner of such land for the purposes of this Act.

2. An absolute owner may, without prejudice to his title as absolute owner, transfer to any other person the present enjoyment of any claims, privileges, powers, or immunities which he enjoys in respect of the land of which he is absolute owner:

Provided that if the absolute owner permanently transfers the absolute ownership or totality of claims, privileges, powers and immunities which he enjoys or might enjoy in respect of the said land, or such absolute ownership is so transferred or transmitted by operation of law, he shall cease to be absolute owner of the said land.

3. 'Absolute ownership' means the interest of an absolute owner in respect of any land held by the absolute owner as absolute owner.

It does not include any claim by the Crown or any Government or any other public body to the ultimate possession of land by virtue only of the law concerning escheat, bona vacantia, or compulsory acquisition.

It includes an estate in fee simple absolute in possession.

S. R. Simpson: Towards a Definition of Absolute Ownership*—II

As I read Dr. Allott's article 'Towards a definition of Absolute Ownership'[1] I felt increasing dismay because it postulates and makes appear immensely difficult, a problem which in actual working practice barely exists at all. For over sixty years Settlement Officers in the Sudan have been successfully determining ownership without the help of any definition, and in Kenya, during the last five years, the ownership of over a million plots has similarly been decided by committees. Even in West Africa, where there has been no process of systematic adjudication, ownership has been determined in over three thousand cases in Lagos, and ownership is not defined. Indeed I am not familiar with any statute anywhere which does define it.[2]

There would seem to be no more need to define 'ownership' than there is to define 'an estate in fee simple absolute in possession' which is what is vested in a proprietor who is registered with absolute title under the English Land Registration Act, 1925. Yet an estate in fee simple absolute is not defined in any statute and its meaning, not very obvious on the face of it, can only be discovered by reading a textbook on the subject. This does not matter because, being the 'best' right, it can only be defeated by somebody who can prove a 'better', whereas were the test by definition the title could be impugned merely for an alleged failure to conform with the definition. Anyway the lack of statutory definition does not appear to have impeded H.M. Land Registry, for over a million titles have been recorded there.

It seems to me, therefore, that in assuming that a definition is needed, the article

* S. R. Simpson, 'Towards a Definition of Absolute Ownership', in *Journal of African Law*, Vol. 5, No. 3, pp. 145–150.

starts from a wrong premise. 'Ownership', we are told, 'has no god-given meaning', and we are then offered a long definition which I am tempted to suggest would require divine help to interpret. It is couched in a specialized terminology which is only intelligible to a lawyer well versed in English land law. It might (and even this is questionable) assist such a lawyer if he happened to be charged with the duty of converting titles in England to 'absolute ownership', which does not at present exist in English land law, but, speaking from practical experience, I am sure that it could only confuse adjudication officers who are faced with the task of ascertaining rights and interests in land not held under English land law and who in practice seem to find no intrinsic difficulty in comprehending the word 'ownership'. I fear that Dr. Allott has needlessly projected a dense cloud into a relatively clear sky.

It is true that words do not have inherent meanings, but only such as usage gives them. But, of course, usage has already given a clear-cut meaning to most words, otherwise we should be incapable of expressing ourselves with any sort of precision, and 'ownership' is one of the words to which *usage* has attached a meaning which is perfectly plain to the ordinary man. The idea of ownership is in fact simple and intelligible to any human being anywhere. From earliest childhood he learns to distinguish between 'mine' and 'thine' and very quickly shows his comprehension of what 'mine' means. Even where land is concerned 'ownership' (or 'absolute ownership')[3] seems to be regarded by writers on the subject as an ordinary expression in plain English which for their purposes does not require special definition or explanation. Thus Megarry and Wade, having described the fee simple as 'the most ample estate which can exist in land', add

> 'Although strictly speaking it is still held in tenure and therefore falls short of absolute ownership, in practice it is absolute ownership, for nearly all traces of the old feudal burdens have disappeared.'[4]

They go on to quote Cyprian Williams as stating: 'A tenant in fee simple enjoys all the advantages of absolute ownership, except the form'. Similarly Cheshire describes the fee simple as 'corresponding to the absolute ownership of goods'.[5] In fact all these writers (and Joshua Williams and Maitland too) use the expression 'absolute ownership' as if its meaning were obvious.

And indeed its meaning *is* obvious, though the very quality of absoluteness naturally makes it difficult, as well as unnecessary, to put it into words. Ownership is the foundation on which all other rights in property stand. It comprises the entirety of the powers of use (including abuse) and disposal over what is owned; but the owner does not necessarily have, at a given time, the *whole* power of use and disposal. Often there is no single person who has the whole power, for various rights may be vested in others. These rights may be substantial, but they will, of their nature, still be subordinate to or derivative from that of ownership. In seeking the owner, therefore, an adjudication officer must look for the person who has the residue of such power when every despatched and limited portion of it has been accounted for, and that person will be the owner even if the immediate power of control and use is elsewhere. This duty, and how it must be performed, is made plain in simple language in any legislation which provides for adjudication.

It is this practical task of determining ownership which Dr. Allott seeks to render easier by his proposed definition, but I think that he has 'misdirected' himself when he assumes that the registering officer must re-interpret the existing state of affairs in English legal terms. The need for this sort of re-interpretation only arises where, in the absence of registration of title and the substantive law which necessarily accompanies it, there is no alternative to native law and custom except applied English land law. In this circumstance interests may pass from one to the other in the way Dr. Allott describes. But this is the very position which registration so easily remedies. It makes provision, *not* for the translation of native law and custom into terms of English land law, but for a simple system providing adequately both for titles stemming from native law and custom and those from English land law. The 'tenant in fee simple' under English law and the man whose rights amount to ownership under native law and custom both become 'registered proprietors' of land and what the proprietor may do in regard to transfer of his ownership and the creation, transfer and extinction of lesser interests will be clearly set out in the law.

Thus an adjudication officer is not confined to English law, or even English legal terminology, but is charged in the first instance with deciding which of the rights in the adjudication area amount to ownership. Since, as we have seen, the meaning of ownership is plain and no definition is needed, Dr. Allot is mistaken in thinking that the adjudication officer is going to meet with any difficulty in that respect. Where ownership does exist he will find it quite easy to recognize.

He may however meet with difficulty in rights which have not quite developed into ownership; but here again a definition of ownership will not help; it will merely show that the rights in question fall short of ownership. If it is intended that these rights should be 'promoted' to ownership, it might be possible to describe them and declare that they shall be recorded as ownership, just as Dr. Allott in his proposed definition declares that 'absolute ownership' includes 'a fee simple absolute in possession'; but experience has shown that it is better to leave to the adjudication officer discretion to determine what lesser rights, if any, shall be recorded as ownership. This decision may be as much a matter of policy as of law or of fact; it may also involve a measure of agreement between competing interests, but if there is agreement or there are no competing interests ownership can be recorded without dispute.

Dr. Allot paints a gloomy picture of the task which will confront an adjudication officer in trying to decide where ownership resides when faced with the competing interests of the tribal authority, the family and the individual. But this sort of position is not unknown in English law and procedure. The problem has arisen there, for example, as to who shall be recorded as the owner where there is a strict settlement and this has been solved, not by a definition of ownership, but by the arbitrary decision that the tenant for life shall be registered in H.M. Land Registry as the proprietor subject to a restriction. Special provision may similarly be made in any registration law wherever it is needed. Thus the Registered Land Bill proposed for Lagos makes full provision for 'family land'; it may be registered as family land, in which case the title will be clear but no dealing will be possible, or representatives may be appointed who may deal with it in accordance with the wishes of the family, or the individual members of the family may be registered as proprietors in common (not quite the same as tenants in common), or a partition may be effected. There is no 'legal rate of exchange' in this, but merely a clear-cut and simple procedure which is designed to provide for all contingencies and which an adjudication officer can have no difficulty in applying.

I submit, therefore, that 'ownership', *because it is absolute*, needs no definition and indeed, strictly speaking, is not susceptible of it, for definition describes a thing by its limits and ownership is boundless. In any case we must avoid a definition framed in the terms of a law which does not recognize the ownership of land but still employs the abstruse device of estates.

Unlike ownership, however, subordinate or derivative interests to be allowed in the registration law do require definition, because the names by which they are known will not be self-explanatory and the interest itself may vary in some material particular from that known under the same name in English or some other code of law. For instance, in New Zealand an easement can exist in gross. On adjudication, therefore, the conversion of these lesser interests whether from English or from customary law into interests under the registration law may involve the formulation of accepted equivalents which might perhaps be called 'a legal rate of exchange', but this is a completely different exercise and has nothing to do with the definition of absolute ownership.

Dr. Allott replies:

I am delighted that Mr. Simpson has accepted my invitation (at p. 102 of my article) to other persons to comment on the very tentative suggestions that I made as to how 'absolute ownership' might be defined for the special purposes of contemporary Africa. I only regret that I am not able to agree wholeheartedly with all the remarks he makes, or the criteria he offers on the necessity or otherwise for a definition of ownership in African legislation providing for the recording on a register in transmuted form of interests previously existing by virtue either of the customary law of land, or of the English land law as applied in Africa.

Mr. Simpson's first point, that there is no more need to define 'ownership' for African legislative purposes than there is to define 'an estate in fee simple absolute in possession' for the purposes of the English land law, seems to me, with respect, to overlook the fact that the meaning of an estate in fee simple absolute is in practice defined, not by legislation, but by the practice of the courts as recognized in the textbooks on English land law. There is no question, as with customary land law as currently administered in West Africa, of discovering what interests in land are recognized by that law, and how they should be stated on a register purporting to record 'ownership'. With the recording of title to land in West Africa we are faced with the problem of *translating* an interest known to one system of law into one recognized or created by another system of law; the problem of definition is the problem of deciding what instructions we are to give the 'translator'.

Mr. Simpson thinks that no instructions are necessary for the 'translator' (i.e., the settlement or adjudication officer or judge), since he will know, as an ordinary man, what the meaning of 'ownership' is, and—to the ordinary man—the meaning of 'ownership' is perfectly plain. I take leave to doubt, again with respect, whether (i) the opinion of the ordinary man should be decisive of legal matters of great complexity, or (ii) the man in the street could in fact give any useful definition of what he understands by 'ownership'. (One recalls that the ordinary man in England is very likely to say, to take a simple example, that the house which he occupies on a long lease 'is his', 'belongs to him', that 'he owns it'; the lawyer sees the position otherwise. Equally the Englishman, if in poetic vein, is likely to remark that 'the world belongs to me', or, more prosaically, that 'this is his town, his club, his child', etc.) Common parlance is not a good guide to the niceties demanded by precise legal expression.

I am afraid I cannot see how it can be maintained that a word whose meaning is plain and obvious cannot, or indeed should not, be defined; either the word is imprecise (in which case definition is required for specific legal purposes to limit its meaning), or it is precise (in which case definition will be both useful and possible). Contrary to his earlier contention, Mr. Simpson seems to maintain in his closing paragraphs that ownership is boundless and that it would be impossible, as well as undesirable, to limit it; but the process of setting limits to the vague and nebulous is well understood by legal draftsmen, who are constantly being required to define by statute what is meant by 'shop', 'marriage', 'child', 'takes', and so on; and such setting bounds to the indefinite is exactly what is wanted in the case we are considering.

Mr. Simpson argues that the adjudication officer in our hypothetical case is not confined to English law or legal terminology, but is charged in the first instance with deciding which of the rights in the adjudication area amount to ownership, and that therefore he needs no definition of what he is to understand by 'ownership' in this context. I cannot follow this line of thought. Mr. Simpson mentions the difficulty that the officer may meet rights 'which have not quite developed into ownership', and he says that in such an instance the definition would merely show that the rights in question fall short of ownership (as defined). Exactly! That is the purpose of definitions. Why should it be left to the discretion of adjudication officers what they place or do not place on the register? Can the holder of an interest in the area feel that the law is clear and has been fairly applied to his case? I fully agree with Mr. Simpson that if there is a compromise between the interests affected a title may go on the register by agreement; but this happy state of affairs is not likely to be of universal occurrence.

I am sorry that I do not agree with Mr. Simpson's stimulating comments on the problem, especially since he has tried to be helpful by giving us his own definition of 'ownership' in the fifth paragraph of his comment! The two questions that remain open for future discussion are: (i) is definition of terms like 'ownership' necessary or helpful in the special circumstances mentioned (where rights in land are being recorded); and (ii) if one assumes that a definition is desirable, how is it to be worded so as to take account of the facts of varying systems of customary law, as well as of English land law and the scheme of the land registration enactment?

Notes

[1] [1961] J.A.L. 99.

[2] The British Solomon Isles Land and Titles Regulation, 1959, provides that an ' "owner" in relation to native customary land, means the person or persons who is or are, according to current native usage, regarded as the owner or owners of the land'. This cannot be called a definition of 'owner'; indeed it assumes that its meaning is understood.

[3] As Dr. Allott points out there is little significance in adding 'absolute' to 'ownership'. We cannot really have anything 'whiter' than 'white'—except in advertisements for detergents!

[4] *The Law of Real Property*, 2nd edn., p. 68.

[5] *Modern Real Property*, 7th edn., p. 27.

Chapter 13

CATEGORIES OF LAND

There are only three extracts in this chapter, but they have been chosen to illustrate the variations in approach which exist in relation to the categorisation of land. Thus, while *Lloyd* and *Meek* classify the land with reference to opportunities of access to it (e.g. public as opposed to private land) and occupation (virgin forest as against individual holdings), *Wagner* emphasises the differing groups or individuals who may exercise control over land.

P. C. Lloyd: Yoruba Land Law*

The three basic categories of land tenure may be styled—

(*a*) Public land—that is, land which is used for a public purpose in which the community participates.

(*b*) Allotted 'private' land—that is, land which has been allotted to individuals and which has subsequently become held by their descendants, together with land allotted to bodies, such as churches, which do not embrace the whole community.[1]

(*c*) Unallotted land—that is land which is not being used and which is available for present-day granting to individuals, etc.

We may also distinguish between town and farm land, for a different tenurial system may operate in each area. The Yoruba do not suggest that these two types of land *ought* to be held under different tenures, nor that the rules which apply to one should not equally apply to the other. The distinction has arisen from the contrasting uses to which the two types of land are normally put. Town land is used for building: the traditional compound persisted in perpetuity, for although sections of it might fall, they were rebuilt perhaps in the same pattern or as new courtyards; thus the structure of the building was continually changing but the 'compound' remained. Modern houses are less likely to be renewed in this way, but they are often more durable than the traditional mud-walled and grass- or palm-roofed buildings. Town tenures thus recognized permanent use of a specific area. Before the introduction in this century of cocoa, kola nuts and the oil palm as plantations crops, Yoruba agriculture consisted mainly of the cultivation of food crops which remained in the ground for periods varying from three months (e.g. maize) to three years (e.g. cassava). Cultivation in this manner does not demand the existence of permanant rights in land though these may well arise, and have in fact arisen in many parts of Yoruba country. Thus in some areas, Ekiti, for instance, the rights held in town and farm land are basically similar, while in others—Ondo is a good example—they are dissimilar.

Throughout Yoruba country there is a clear geographical distinction between the land of the town (the urban area) and that of its farms. Sometimes this is marked by the town walls, and in other cases by the ring of forest which surrounds the town. In most cases the boundary between town and farm can be drawn with precision—though not necessarily without dispute in areas where the urban area is now encroaching into the farm land. In this, as in other instances, the Yoruba believe that a boundary *line* does exist even though its exact location may be contested; they do not postulate a vague no-man's-land.

Let us now further elaborate our three categories of land.

* P. C. Lloyd, *Yoruba Land Law*, Oxford University Press for the Nigerian Institute of Social and Economic Research, 1963, pp. 70–76.

Public Land

Public land in the town takes several forms. Firstly there is the royal land—the oba's palace or *afin*. This usually covers a large area in the centre of the town and although there is, today, a demand that some of this should be put to more productive use, the integrity of most *afin* remains intact. The land of the palace may be further divided into two or three categories such as (*a*) the land occupied by the palace buildings proper, (*b*) the much larger area within the palace walls, largely overgrown with light bush but frequently containing shrines or burial places, the exact location of which may be known only to the palace servants, and (*c*) an area outside the palace walls controlled by the oba. The land occupied by the members of the royal descent group is not usually included within the palace area though these people may live in a quarter of the town designated as the 'oba's quarter'. The rights of the oba over his palace land have already been discussed in the previous chapter.

The category 'public land' includes, too, land occupied by public buildings in the town, though these, in the past, were few. In Ijebu and Egba towns the *ogboni* houses (*iledi*) were public buildings. Elsewhere, open spaces are sometimes regarded as public meeting places.

Shrines are another form of public land; here one must distinguish between those shrines which belong to the whole town and those which are held by a single descent group. In the case of the latter the worship of the deity concerned may be by a certain descent group but for the benefit of the whole town; the destruction of the shrine by the group may be met with considerable opposition from the community, though it is not clear what legal rights the latter may have. The shrines of some deities are obviously attached to the whole community, and here one might have to distinguish between the rights of the community in the land so occupied and those of the recognized priests of the deity. Forested areas both within or a little outside the town walls usually have ritual uses. Some are reserved for the masquerades—the *egungun* or *agẹmọ* cults; others, expecially hilly areas, are reserved to the spirits which watch over the town. There is usually a 'bad bush' (*igbo buruku*) where the bodies of those who die with physical deformities, in childbirth, as confessed witches or of those executed for crimes were, in the past, thrown without proper burial. In all such areas the supernatural sanctions against entering or using the land have been so great as to preclude any clear definition of rights of ownership.

A further type of public land is the market; and here too we must distinguish between the recognized public markets and the countless sites where a few women gather together to sell. The former may only be created by the command of the oba, and the opening of the new market is traditionally heralded by the performance of certain rituals by the palace servants on behalf of their oba. (Other more secular ceremonies are now frequently performed.)

Public land outside the urban limits of the town consists usually of royal farms, cultivated by the palace servants (and perhaps, in the past, by compulsory labour by all the oba's subjects), and of shrines of the type already discussed; some important markets may lie, technically, within the farm area.

Allotted Land

We come now to the second of our categories—that of allotted private land, the land which is cultivated or inhabited by the members of the community. Often this is termed 'family land', for rights in it have passed, by succession, to the members of the descent group of the original grantee; but all allotted land is not necessarily family land—it may be held by an individual. Also, as we shall see, the fact that rights are held by a group does not of itself specify the quantum of those rights; so often the term 'family land' is used as if it denoted ownership by the group. Sometimes it does so denote ownership, but often the rights held by the group fall far short of those of ownership. It will be more convenient to begin our discussions with farm land for here we may see the fullest possible range of tenurial systems.

There is not, within Yoruba country, any area where true shifting cultivation is practised. Shifting cultivation I designate as a system where a large body of people, an entire tribe perhaps, slowly gyrates within its tribal area, individual villages being abandoned every few years and their people founding new ones in unfarmed areas; the land is cultivated for a few seasons and then abandoned without any intention on the part of the cultivators that they should one day return to the same area. Yoruba settlements are invariably permanent—destruction in war or abandonment through disease were frequent in the past but it was never conceived by the inhabitants that their settlement would be of limited duration. Each settlement is surrounded by its own farm land. Within these limited areas it might still be possible to speak of shifting cultivation; where the density of population is sparse—say less than 100 persons per square mile as in Ondo—rigid demarcation of land between individuals or descent groups is rare (though in even more sparsely populated Oyo it is usual); here a man may farm anywhere within the area of his community, continually clearing fresh bush and not claiming any right over his abandoned farm land (which will not be used for further farming for fifteen, twenty or more years). One may similarly speak of shifting cultivation within the area of land held by a descent group when individual members claim no permanent rights over the land. Whilst the lack of permanent rights in land is a feature of sparse settlement, it is also met in some densely settled areas; in some villages around Ijebu Ode it seems to be the practice for land to be re-allocated each year. Most men are probably given land which they have farmed before but the re-allocation does ensure the maximum use of the land by preventing individuals from holding large areas of uncultivated fallow.

Thus we have one tenurial system in which a man has no permanent rights in the land he uses. He has nevertheless definite legal rights over the land while he uses it. But as soon as the land is abandoned to fallow it reverts to the community, whose elders will re-allocate it whenever the bush has regenerated sufficiently to permit of cultivation. Usually a man will clear new land adjacent to his old farms and thus move steadily in a given direction. After his death one or more of his sons may continue to farm in the same area while others go elsewhere for land; one cannot here speak of land rights being inherited either by individuals or by a descent group. In areas with this tenurial system the descent group is not a body of persons which corporately holds land (for the community alone has permanent rights in the area) although it may have other functions.

With a higher density of population one finds permanent rights in land; once a man has farmed land he has the right to return to it after its fallow period. Agriculture might here be described as a system of 'bush fallow rotation'. Such permanent rights are sometimes explained by the belief that a man who spends immense labour initially clearing thick forest for cultivation is entitled to its use for more than one crop cycle and should have the later benefits of the light clearing necessary after the bush fallow period. Where such permanent rights are recognized they are not only held by a man for his own lifetime but pass, on his death, to his children. Where land is very short the children will be restricted to using their father's land; where it is plentiful many may prefer to seek new land. With the existence of heritable rights, family land is made possible. One can envisage the development of blocks of land each held by the descendants of a man who is supposed to have been initially granted the land by the oba; in time most of the land of the community becomes divided among its constituent descent groups.

Permanent rights in land are, however, not necessarily alienable. Whilst a man and his descendants may have the right to prevent others from using fallow land once cultivated by them they may not always have the right to grant this fallow to others for cultivation. Land which a descent group cannot use is deemed, ultimately, to be abandoned and becomes available for re-allotment by the elders of the community.

The next stage is for a descent group to be allowed to alienate to non-members of the group (subject to the permission of the head of the community in the case of alienation to a stranger to the community) that land which has been used at some recent period by members of the group.

A further stage arises when the descent groups define common boundaries one with another and extend these boundaries through the forest land to the frontier of the town, claiming to alienate any land within their own boundaries, whether or not it has ever been used by their members.

These stages have been presented as a logical sequence; they do not necessarily imply that the tenurial system of any one area has developed historically through each stage, though in the recent grants of land to a stranger, or customary tenant, one can see his rights in the land developing from an initial usufructuary right, while he is not assimilated into the community, to an alienable right when he does become assimilated and a later right over unused land when his descendants, recognized as an independent descent group, can create boundaries with their neighbours. One can trace, too, in most parts of Yoruba country, the efforts which are being made by descent groups to extend not only their rights to alienate the land but to the exclusive use of the natural produce of their land—its timber, stone, etc.—usufructuary rights which were hitherto held by the community.

Rights granted in town land for building must, of course, be permanent and heritable. One may see without further elaboration how the concepts of alienable rights might be applied to town land.

We have not, so far, considered the manner in which an estate in land may be alienated. Several factors are involved and these include: the rights transferred, the size of the land concerned and the use to which it will be put, and the status of the grantee. In the past it was usually presumed that a stranger who obtained land from a descent group would in time become assimilated into the group; strangers who would not or could not be so assimilated would be allotted land by the community if this were available. Not only was the permission of the community, expressed by its oba and chiefs, necessary for the grant of land to a stranger, but the feeling existed among the Yoruba that while a group or an individual might alienate its land for a use similar to what it was itself exercising, it might not alienate it for some hitherto unusual purpose, such as for some modern commercial use, e.g. a petrol station. Expressed differently, it was felt that the group held usufructuary rights of a limited nature only—to build a house, to farm in the traditional manner—and that it had had no right to make other use of the land and so could not transfer such a right. Again, while it was in the past conceded that a descent group might transfer entirely its interest in an unused area of its land to a newly arrived body of immigrants, modern sale of land is often considered repugnant when the individual or group selling receives a large cash sum for its land and then itself receives land freely from the community to make good its shortage. Where land still exists for allotment by the community, men who wish to build or farm, and who are unable to get land from their own descent groups, will usually take land from the community rather than from other descent groups. The new factor is the greater demand by commercial bodies for sites along the main roads and near the markets. In the traditional Yoruba town little value was attached to site and there is thus annoyance today that some people should benefit from the fortuitous increase in the value of their land.

Unallotted Land

The third of our categories of land is that of unallotted land, often loosely termed 'communal' land. As we have seen in a previous paragraph the community may grant to an individual the right to cultivate a plot of land, these rights lapsing completely once the crop cycle is ended and the farmer moves to a new plot. Where permanent rights over land are not recognized, all land is, in fact, unallotted land, subject to the temporary rights of the cultivators.

The term is, however, more conveniently used in contradistinction to family land. Once permanent and heritable rights are recognized it is seen that there will be large areas of land over which descent groups hold permanent rights and other areas over which no permanent rights have been granted. The community may not disturb the rights held by a descent group (except by compulsorily acquiring the land), and in particular it may not grant such land to strangers. Land not so held by descent groups and individuals may be allotted by the community to those who apply for it. But we have seen above that descent groups may extend their boundaries to enclose land which their members have never used.

Vacant land, available for allotment for building, still exists in some Yoruba towns between the edge of the built-up areas and the town walls, and only local study will show whether this land is held by descent groups (thus being family land) or by a territorially defined community—the town or its constituent quarters. The ring of forest encircling the town has now lost its defensive function and is usually today being destroyed to provide building land; rights in this belt of land are more often than not held by the community and not by any single descent group. Farms tend to be nearer the town with forest increasing towards its frontiers and forming perhaps a virtual no-man's-land with neighbouring towns. This forest, too, may be held by the descent groups or by the community. Since this vacant land will often be granted by persons holding chieftaincy titles, it must be carefully ascertained whether they are acting in their capacity as heads of descent groups, as heads of quarters in whom the land is vested, or as agents of the oba, exercising powers delegated to them.

Note

[1] Throughout this book I use the word *allot* to denote a grant of land in perpetuity, usually by the oba and/or chief, to a person who is, or is desirous of becoming, a member of the community. I use the word *allocate* to denote an *ad hoc* sharing of land or house rooms as when the head of a descent group distributes farm land or rooms in the compound among the members of the group. In this case the rights of the individual are not, in law, permanent and, with the exceptions described, not alienable. The terms 'allot' and 'allocate' are my own and readers may prefer other words; I feel, however, that the distinction needs to be made. I similarly distinguish between *allocation* of land within the descent group and *partition.*

G. Wagner: The Bantu of North Kavirondo*

(1) *Family Lands*

These are any lands that their present holders have acquired by inheritance. They comprise, in the first place, the *omulimi gwa guga* (the ancestral or grandfather's land), but also any other land, no matter how it was originally acquired, once it has passed on to the next generation. Thus the family estate is extended in each generation, but it is also progressively subdivided as each new individual family is set up. The term 'family lands' refers to the joint rights of disposal held in such lands and to the method of their acquisition (viz. by inheritance), but not to the way in which they are used. There is no such thing as joint (or family) occupation of a field. Family land is held, at any given time, by a single member of the family, in accordance with the rules of inheritance and succession. In practice, not every adult son actually holds part of the family land, but if he cannot find land elsewhere he is entitled to a portion of it.

It is one of the principal features of traditional Logoli land law that rights to family land are inalienable. They are not forfeited by letting the land in question revert to bush, nor by absence. Any claim to redeem land that has been abandoned can, of course, be realized only within the tribal territory. If, for instance, a whole community had migrated, and their former lands had been occupied by a different tribe, members of this community could not claim the return of their land from the new occupants.

(2) *Communally Used Lands Under Clan Control*

There are two categories of such land:

(*a*) Communal grazing-lands. The clan-head (*eligutu*) protects these lands from encroachment by cultivators, but their use for grazing is open to everybody in the tribal community, including strangers (*avamenya*) and people residing in the territory of neighbouring clans.

(*b*) After a poor harvest, or if the *omugimba* (rain magician) has predicted a famine, the *eligutu* may allot a portion of grazing-land or of virgin bush (*oluangereka*) to his clansmen and the *avamenya* living under his jurisdiction for the joint cultivation of a crop of sweet potatoes. These so-called *emilimilu*† lands are subsequently shared out as individual holdings among the people who cleared and cultivated them, each getting the strip he has dug and planted. They are then classed like any other land acquired by the right of first cultivation. The joint cultivation of land is thus only a temporary measure resorted to in the face of the danger of famine. Every season, but particularly when grain stores have run low, the *eligutu* summons the people under his jurisdiction (clansmen and *avamenya*) to put in a few days of work (hoeing, planting, weeding, harvesting) on his own fields (*emilimi gweligutu*). The crops raised with the help of this communal labour are stored in the *eligutu's* granaries, but are used to offer hospitality to visitors and, especially, to the aged and poor members of the clan community.

* G. Wagner, *The Bantu of North Kavirondo*, Oxford University Press, 1949, pp. 80–82.

† A large unbroken patch of cultivation, referring particularly to the communally cultivated lands under the control of the clan-head.

(3) *Suplus Lands under Clan Control*

These comprise all lands lying within the territory politically controlled by the clan community that are neither used for communal grazing nor cultivated by individual occupants. They form the reserve from which future needs may be satisfied. These lands are controlled by the clan as represented by the *eligutu*. He knows the clan's need for grazing lands as well as the existing rights of *avene* (owners) and *avamenya* (strangers). Through his experience as head of the clan council (*omumali wekina* or *wekiruazo*) he can distinguish virgin bush (*ovulimu*) from land that has reverted to bush (*eligunda*).

Any clansman can take *ovulimu* land under cultivation, whereupon it ceases to be surplus land under clan control. According to most of my informants, he did not have to ask the *eligutu* for permission—today the *amagutu* have ceased to function and practically all virgin bush land has been taken under cultivation—but the *eligutu* could intervene and assign him another piece of land if he wished the land in question to be reserved for grazing. A clansman of full adult status also had the right to assign a plot of surplus clan land to an *omumenya* after having previously obtained the *eligutu's* consent.

(4) *Individual Land*

This is any land to which an individual has acquired a right not by inheritance but:

(*a*) By the right of first cultivation. This right he can acquire either as a clansman (by taking surplus clan lands under cultivation) or as an *omumenya* (by tilling surplus land assigned to him by a kinsman or friend of another clan).

(*b*) By 'purchasing' cultivation rights either from a fellow clansman or from a person belonging to another clan. In the latter case the *omuguli* (purchaser) has the status of *omumenya*. It appears that the sale of cultivation rights to a clan stranger developed from the former custom of granting such rights for nothing when, owing to an increase of population, land began to be scarce.

Individual land, when passed on to the next generation, becomes family land. Apart from the mode of acquisition, individual land differs from family land only in that a person can 'sell' it (*okugulanya*). Until recently outright sale does not seem to have been possible, as this was incompatible with the principle that inalienable rights were established by first cultivation.

(5) *No-man's-land*

Any uncultivated land that is neither claimed as surplus clan land (*oluangereka*) nor recognized as belonging to another clan or tribe is referred to as *migendanyama*, or no-man's-land. As a rule, an uninhabited zone was left between two adjoining tribes. If one of the two tribes then migrated, either spontaneously or as a result of pressure from other tribes, some individuals would begin to cultivate in the formerly uninhabited zone. Such settlements often appear to have become the nucleus of a new clan territory.

There were, among the Logoli, no tribal lands as distinct from clan lands.

C. K. Meek: Law and Authority in a Nigerian Tribe*

The various types of land may be classified as follows:

(*a*) Lands which are sacred or taboo.

(*b*) Virgin forest.

(*c*) Farm-land held in common by the members of a village, kindred, or extended-family.

(*d*) Individual holdings.

The first class of lands includes sacred groves surrounding the shrines of public cults (such as Ala, the Earth-deity, and Ekwêsu, the spirit of evil). It also includes the taboo lands or 'evil bush' known as *aja ofia*. In both these cases the ownership is regarded as vested in deities or spirits, and no one would normally attempt, or be allowed, to use any fraction of such land for farming purposes. It is a sign of the times, however, that cases have occurred in crowded areas of individuals clearing a patch of extensive taboo land in order to plant yams, being prepared to take the risk of being killed by spirits. If

* C. K. Meek, *Law and Authority in a Nigerian Tribe*, Oxford University Press, 1937, pp. 100–104.

a farmer is bold enough to take this step (without interference from the elders), and farms for two years in succession without suffering misfortune, he becomes the owner of the land, which henceforth ceases to be regarded as taboo.

The next type of land is the virgin forest, which has remained unused for farming purposes because nobody has required it, or because the village has forbidden farming there, lest it should lose its use as a means of defence or as shade or as a source of supplies of wood or fibre. If a piece of uncleared forest is of no obvious use to the village, any one is at liberty to clear it for farming purposes, and the land so cleared becomes his private farm.[1] He cannot be deprived of it, and he can pledge it or transmit it to his children. But if there is any uncertainty as to whether the village may require the uncleared patch, the would-be farmer must first obtain the permission of the local elders.

The third class of land is farm-land held in common by an entire village, kindred, or extended-family, being formally apportioned out afresh each time it is to be farmed.[2] It is land held in reserve for the benefit of the whole group (in addition to individual holdings), and cannot, therefore, be pledged without the consent of the group as a whole. Firstly, as regards farm-land common to the whole village, this is generally known as *ale-ọha* (land of the people) or *ale-nweko* (land held in common). In some districts[3] there are still large tracts of rich lands held in this way, but they are usually at a considerable distance from the village, the farm-lands nearer home being held by individuals or small families. In other districts (e.g. at Ache and Inyi) the only farm-lands held communally by the village or village groups are infertile lands of little use save for growing cassava. The richer lands have long since been apportioned out among the various kindreds and families. In other localities (e.g. at Owerri) there is no farm-land held by the entire community.

Land held in common by a kindred or extended-family is known as *ala-ndichie* or *obozoku* (ancestral land). As already stated, it is land apportioned annually to members of the kindred (in addition to their private holdings) and it can only be pledged to strangers by consent of the whole group. Where the kindred has split up into various branches it will generally be found that the land formerly held in common by the whole kindred has been subdivided among the various branches. Thus, at Owerri, the Onumono kindred, which consists of several branches, has now no land held by the whole group. The land formerly possessed by the entire kindred has long ago been parcelled out among the various branches. One of these is the Umu-Okore. Like the other branches the Umu-Okore received its share of land, but being hard pressed for money it decided to pledge a portion of this land.[4] Some time ago (it is said) the land so pledged was redeemed by the present head of the Okore group and retained by him for his personal use, on the ground that none of the elders of the Umu-Okore had assisted him in redeeming the land. This led to a dispute, and at a meeting of the elders of the local group (Ororo-Njo) it was held that the head of Umu-Okore had acted within his rights. If the other members of the Okore family wish to share the land they must pay to the head of the family some share of the redemption price.

It should be noted that strangers who have joined a local or kindred group have no automatic right to a share in the common land of the group. They may, however, be given a share as an act of grace, and would be expected to give a gift of a few yams at harvest to the senior elder or elders of the group. The same remark applies to slaves. In some villages (e.g. at Itika in Awgu Division) there is an old-standing complaint that land and economic trees[5] lent to slaves have, since the abolition of the status of slavery, become the property of the ex-slaves. Some of the former slave-owners, or their heritors, are content to leave their ex-slaves in possession, but others are eager to recover some at least of the land and trees, and to prevent the ex-slaves from pledging the land.

Next, there is the land on which compounds are built, together with the adjoining plots. This land belongs to the household occupying it. If the household removes to another site it retains its rights in this land. By common consent the household may give this land or a portion of it in pledge, but as a rule the household (or it may be an *onunne*) prefers to retain full rights over former sites for religious or, at any rate, for sentimental reasons. To give such lands in pledge would usually be regarded as slighting the ancestors who lie buried there.[6] Sites of former habitations are known as *uhu* or *ukwu* land.

Finally, and most important of all, comes the land which is individually held. This is land handed on by father to son, or acquired by clearing virgin forest or in return for a loan. In many village-groups there is scarcely any land at all within the recognized boundary of the group which is not held by individuals. Land so held can be pledged by the holder without reference to any one, and it is common practice for a man to pledge his land in order to cancel a debt, pay a bride-price, or even to raise the means of paying his tax. Land which has been pledged is normally redeemable at any time at the same rate at which it has been pledged,[7] and there is an Ibo proverb which says, 'A thing which is pledged is never lost' (*ihe ibe efui-efu*). In point of fact, however, pledged land is often permanently alienated. It may be pledged, for example, for a sum far in excess of that normally given, and so may remain unredeemed for generations, and become in fact unredeemable, as all evidence of the original transaction has been lost. In this way rich men have acquired land in perpetuity. In some communities, e.g. at Ama-Imo (Owerri Division), it seems to have been the custom that if a man had received a second loan in respect of a piece of land he had to repay double the total amount of the loan if he wished to redeem the land. In practice this virtually amounted to a sale. The same custom, in slightly different form, was found at Ihe in the Awgu Division, where it is possible for a landowner who wishes to hinder an ill-disposed relative from inheriting his land to fix the redemption price of land he has pledged at double the amount of the loan. In order to formalize this proceeding he demands from the pledgee, in front of witnesses, an additional payment of thirty pieces of the minute iron-hook currency which is still used in parts of the Awgu Division. The value of these thirty pieces is little more than a halfpenny, so that the additional payment has nothing of the nature of a cash sale, but is merely a legal formality serving as evidence of transfer. At Owele, Abo-Ogugu, and various other localities, it is even possible to sell land outright, by demanding from the buyer or pledgee an extra payment of eight yams, one fowl, and twenty pieces of iron-hook currency or some oil and palm fruit. This practice is, of course, uncommon, as no one would permanently alienate land except under great stress. Nevertheless it is increasing, and cases have even occurred in which the pledgee has endeavoured to secure the land in perpetuity by means of a written document.

It remains to add that, just as land may be pledged for a loan, so it may be leased for a season or longer. The rent charged may be nominal. Thus a man may lend a piece of land to a friend free of charge, expecting merely to receive a pot of palm-wine and a feast at harvest. Or, if the plot of land were substantial, he might demand a rental of twenty or thirty yams. In the Awgu Division cases came to my notice of plots of land being hired out to strangers at a rental charge varying from 3*s*. to 8*s*. per acre per annum.

Notes

[1] Cf. Laws of Manu (India), 'He who clears a piece of land is the owner of it' (ix. 44).

[2] Unless it is so extensive that formal division is unnecessary.

[3] Thus, at Adâyi (Nsukka Division), land is so abundant that most of it is held communally and the necessity has not arisen for apportioning it out to families and individuals.

[4] The head of a family may have to pledge a piece of family land to pay off a debt left by the previous head, and he may insist on doing so against the wishes of the family, if the family has offered no assistance in paying off the debt.

[5] E.g. Oil-palms, coco-nuts, oil-bean, and mahogany trees.

[6] Nevertheless, some families, particularly Christian families, do not mind leasing *ubu* land.

[7] But not, of course, until after harvest, if the land is under cultivation. A pledgee at Akabo (and no doubt other localities) is protected against arbitrary treatment by a rule that if the owner of the land demands its return before it has been farmed he has to refund twice the amount of the loan he had received.

Chapter 14

POLITICAL AUTHORITIES AND THE LAND

It is commonplace that the land law of African societies is dependent on the type of political structure operative in the society, e.g. whether it is acephalous or has a Chief (see Chapter 1). In this chapter, we have included an extract from *Schapera's* work on land in the Bechuanaland Protectorate which deals not only with the problem of the Chief in relation to land, but also with the role of subsidiary political authorities at ward level. Secondly, there is a long extract from *Elias' Nigerian Land Law and Custom* which describes in detail the Chief's powers over land, with useful illustrations drawn from case law. It is noteworthy that Elias has here adopted the notion of the Chief as 'trustee' as a result of his rejection of the suggestion, made in the Courts of Nigeria and elsewhere, that he is 'owner'. The third extract, from *Cory* on the Sukuma, deals with a different aspect of the Chief in relation to land, viz. the land which he holds by virtue of his office.

I. Schapera: Native Land Tenure in the Bechuanaland Protectorate*

The Position of the Chief

The use of the land and its resources is controlled by the Chief, subject to the limitations imposed by the Administration. The Tswana usually say that their land 'belongs' to the Chief. It has occasionally even been maintained that the land is his to do with as he pleases. For instance, Sebele I (Chief of the Kwena) told the Concessions Commission in 1893 that the land and everything on it and in it was his own, and that he was as free to make a grant of land to anyone as he was to give his jacket or snuff-box to his brother Kgari.[1]

It is very doubtful if such a claim would ever be confirmed by the people generally. Sebele's own experience shows that he could not enforce it. In 1891 he and his father Sechele, without asking their people's permission, agreed to lease an extensive tract of land for grazing purposes to two Europeans named Riesle and Nicholls.

> 'When the Bakwena heard of it,' Sebele afterwards admitted ruefully to the High Commissioner, 'they were exceedingly angry, and the Bakwena asked why we had given away portion of our country where we hunt and get our skins. The Bakwena also told me to give back to Nicholls and Riesle the money we had received. I had fallen into a pit which had been dug through want of proper counsel, and the Bakwena judged me and my father, and we gave over to the Bakwena the money we had received and we told them to refund it to Nicholls and Riesle.'[2]

The concessionaries, however, refused to accept the money, and the matter was ultimately settled by giving them a lease over another part of the country, this time with the consent of the tribe.

The Administration, in any case, never accepted the view that the Chief was absolute owner of the tribal land. The Concessions Commission, for instance, was instructed to refuse recognition to any grant 'made by the Chief alone, without the express consent of his tribe or council'.[3] Similarly, when a split took place in 1894 between Kgama and

* I. Schapera, *Native Land Tenure in the Bechuanaland Protectorate*, The Lovedale Press, 1943, pp. 40–46.

some of his half-brothers, the Administration decided to set aside a location for the latter within Kgama's territory; they were, however, to be completely independent of his rule, and directly under the Crown's protection. 'The rules on which Her Majesty's Government always acts in these matters', stated the Resident Commissioner, 'are firstly, that tribal land is the property of the tribe and not of the Chief alone, who is merely regarded as trustee for his people. . . .'[4] The decision offended Kgama greatly, but in fact it was never enforced, since the malcontents accepted an offer from the B.S.A. Company to accommodate them in Southern Rhodesia.

The conception of the Chief as a trustee holding the land for his tribe is more accurate than the claim made by Sebele. Kgama himself had admitted this in 1878, when he wrote to the British authorities complaining about the trespass of some Europeans on his territory. 'I am always glad to have English gentlemen come in and see my country,' he said, 'but I must take care of my country for my people; it is my duty, and I would not be their Chief if I did not take care of it.'[5]

In fact, none of the land belongs to the Chief personally, except the portions that are used by him and his immediate dependants for residence, cultivation, and grazing. Moreover, he cannot alienate any part of the tribal territory without the consent of the people; even grants on perpetual loan to the Administration and to Mission societies, for instance, require the approval of a public assembly.

But, as head of the tribe, the Chief controls the tenure of all the land in his Reserve. Acting through subordinate authorities, he distributes holdings among the people for various purposes. He assigns areas for residence and cultivation to each of the wards settled in his capital; the ward-heads then regulate the occupation and use of their respective areas, just as, in the outlying districts, community chieftains or village headmen are allowed to supervise the allocation of land in the regions that they administer. The Chief also appoints men as overseers of the areas where cattle are kept, and holds them responsible for the control of local grazing and water rights. Nevertheless, he retains ultimate authority over all the land so assigned, since people can appeal to him against the decisions of ward-heads or other overseers. Moreover, he himself directly controls the land that has not been specially allotted to a ward or placed under an overseer, and he uses it to accommodate newcomers to the tribe or people who for some reason have abandoned their former holdings.

The Chief likewise decides upon the location of towns and villages, and upon the choice of land for cultivation or grazing. He can move people from one area to another, and, in certain circumstances, can even deprive them of land that they are lawfully holding. He settles all disputes about land with which his subordinate authorities have not been able to deal satisfactorily. He also controls the use that his subjects make of their land. In most tribes, for instance, he will not allow them to live permanently at their cattleposts or fields, nor can they change their residence without his permission. Sometimes they must also apply to him for leave to sink a well or make a dam. Almost everywhere, too, they may not plough, reap their crops, or let cattle into their fields, before he has given the word, and in the old days he controlled many other agricultural activities as well.

Since the coming of the Europeans, moreover, the Chiefs have begun to make special laws about the use of the land and its resources. Among the Ngwato, for instance, Kgama prohibited veld-burning, the killing of certain big game animals, the cutting of trees in Serowe, the making of beer, the watering of cattle at certain places, and the sale of kafir corn to European traders. Among the Ngwaketse, Bathoeñ I abolished certain traditional customs relating to the agricultural cycle, regulated veld-burning, and prohibited the cutting of trees in Kanye, the cultivation of land in cattlepost areas, the killing of big game, the making of dams and wells without the Chief's permission, and the sale of corn to traders. Again, his son and successor Seêpapitsô ordered that fields lying fallow for more than five years should revert to the tribe, and that all agreements about lending fields should be made before the Chief.

Similar regulations were introduced by other Chiefs, as will be noticed in due course. It is the present policy of the Administration to encourage the practice. At the meeting of the Native Advisory Council in 1938, for instance, the Resident Commissioner suggested that those Chiefs who had not already done so might draft rules for the control of veld-burning in their Reserves, and at the following meeting the Chiefs were asked if they would issue orders for the destruction of certain noxious weeds.[6] The intention obviously is to let each tribe manage its own land wherever possible, rather than to enforce direct control by the Administration.

Apart from all this, the Chief until recently received various forms of tribute in the produce of the land. In each tribe there were several large fields (known as *masotla*), which were specially cultivated for him by different communities or local groups; in times of good harvest every woman also brought him a basketful of corn from her own crops. He was entitled to certain portions of the hunting spoils acquired by his subjects, and to all the animals killed in the large collective hunts that he organized from time to time. Among the western tribes, moreover, he had vassal peoples like the Sarwa and Kgalagadi, from whom he claimed all the ivory, ostrich feathers, and skins, that they obtained by hunting. Among the Ngwato, Kgama soon after becoming Chief renounced his right to the hunting tribute, and abolished the system of *masotla*. In most other tribes, however, the *masotla* still exist, but the hunting tribute has almost died out, owing mainly to the disappearance of elephants and the diminished value of ostrich feathers and the skins of wild animals.

After the coming of the Europeans the Chief also had at his disposal the revenue derived from land through the stand rents paid by traders and blacksmiths, and the annual subsidies received for mineral woodcuttings, and other concessions. Among the Kwena, the Administration in one instance intervened. Sebele had given some Europeans a concession to cut wood in his Reserve. He claimed that all the money received from them belonged to him, as Chief, and that he could spend it as he pleased. The tribe, on the other hand, wanted the money kept as a resource for the future. The Administration ruled that 'the timber of the Reserve is a possession held in trust for the use of the tribe as a whole, for the support of the tribe, and for the use of future generations'. It was decided therefore to create a Tribal Fund with the money, but Sebele was given a share so that he could meet the expense of maintaining his position as Chief.[7] In general, however, the Chiefs were allowed to receive and use such money as they pleased. It is only recently that this form of income has been removed from their personal control; the money is now paid into the Tribal Treasuries created in 1938.

We see, then, that the Chief possesses many rights over the tribal land: he regulates its distribution among his subjects, controls its occupation and use, and, although not to the same extent as before, derives from it part of his income. He also has the first choice of land for his own home, fields, and cattleposts. However, these rights do not constitute absolute ownership; as we have seen, the Chief cannot do what he likes with the land. His subordinate authorities, and the individual members of the tribe, also have title to land, from which they derive some benefit, and, except occasionally in the general interests of tribal administration, the Chief cannot interfere with them as long as they use their holdings lawfully. Almost all land, in fact, is subject to claims of different kinds by different people, and the Chief is only one of the 'owners'. The others, as will now be shown, also have clearly-defined rights to its use and its products.

Ward and other Group Holdings

The rights that members of the tribe have over land vary according to the purpose for which it is used. Wood, grass, clay, earth, wild edible plants, and other natural products, can be collected by anybody wherever he finds them. They are never reserved for the private use of special persons. A few minor restrictions exist on the right to cut trees, but they apply to the tribe as a whole, and do not discriminate against one person in favour of another. Similarly, anybody may hunt wherever he likes, subject to prohibitions that the Chief may have imposed upon the tribe generally.

Private rights are recognized only in regard to residential and arable land, pastures, and water. Every married man is entitled to a site for a home, land to cultivate, and facilities for grazing cattle; and, apart from the tribute mentioned above, he pays nothing for his occupation and use of the land. However, he is not free to live or farm wherever he likes. The land is portioned out initially in huge blocks among the villages and wards, and individuals were formerly confined to the areas belonging to their own social group. Today this is still largely true of residence, but the principle of segregation has been relaxed in land used for cultivation and grazing.

As mentioned above, the Chief controls the allocation of land. He assigns a residential area and a separate arable tract to each of the wards in his capital. Should either holding prove insufficient or unsuitable, he may add to it or substitute another. In outlying towns and large villages, similar allotments are made to the local wards by the head of the whole settlement; but the settlement itself must be built on a site approved of by the Chief, who also indicates the rough limits of the region within which its people may plough. The smaller villages are seldom inhabited by more than one ward, or part of a ward. Consequently, group-allotments are not necessary here except for the village as a whole, whose site, again, is determined either by the Chief himself or by his local representative.

Residential land may be used only by members of the ward (or village) to which it is assigned. Outsiders may not live there permanently unless they become affiliated to the group. Conversely, all the members of a ward are expected to live together on their holding; it is only in exceptional instances that a man will be allowed to build his home somewhere else. On the other hand, ward segregation is not enforced in the arable areas. People are not obliged to plough within their ward holding; many have fields in other areas, and there has in fact been so much intermingling that very few areas are now used exclusively by the members of the ward to which they were allotted.

Each ward (or small-village) holding is controlled by the ward-head (or village headman), who is known as its *modisa*, overseer. He must provide land on it for all the households under his authority. He may also admit outsiders who apply to him, but without his permission no one may use any of the land. The occupied portions are vested in their actual holders, but the overseer helps to adjust conflicting claims and to punish trespassers. The unoccupied portions remain under his authority for distribution as the occasion arises. Apart from the privilege of making the first choice of land for his own household, he derives no special benefit from his functions as overseer. It is only if he is at the same time the head of an alien community that he may be allowed by the Chief to receive tribute from his own followers.

Grazing land was also portioned out originally among the wards, each headman again acting as overseer of the area allotted to his people. As we have seen, however, the Chief subsequently appointed men, who were not necessarily ward-heads, to administer the areas inhabited by vassal communities. Many of these areas are to-day also used for grazing. The overseer, whether ward-head or not, controls the use of the pastures; no one may place cattleposts in his area, or sink a well there, without his permission. Some of the people using the area are members of his ward, but there are almost always outsiders as well, since no area is reserved exclusively for a single ward. Here again the overseer has no special privileges, unless he is also in charge of a vassal community, from whom, as we have seen, he could formerly claim tribute.

It may be said, therefore, that today group rights exist only over residential land, in the sense that none but members of a ward may live in the area assigned to it. People sometimes also refer to arable and grazing land as belonging to a certain ward. In practice this means that the overseer is bound to admit members of his own ward who wish to plough or keep cattle there, provided that he can accommodate them. But they are not confined to the area controlled by him, and, on the other hand, he can also admit people who are not subject to his political authority. The land is therefore not so exclusively reserved for the ward as in the case of residence.

Notes

[1] Communicated by Col. J. Ellenberger, who was interpreter to the Commission; cf. Report of the Concessions Commission, *African (South) 537* (1903), p. 7.

[2] Interview between the High Commissioner and Sebele, 9.6.1892. Registry, High Commissioner's Office, F. 481.

[3] *African (South) 537* (1903), p. 3.

[4] *African (South) 498* (1896), p. 33.

[5] *Affairs of South Africa* (C. 2144; 1878), p. 143.

[6] *Minutes, Native Advisory Council*, 19th session (1938), pp. 17 ff.; *ibid.*, 20th session (1939), pp. 64 ff.

[7] *African (South) 703* (1903), no. 379.

T. O. Elias: Nigerian Land Law and Custom*

A Chief's Powers over Land

The question we want to agitate now is not one of the general political powers and sociological role of the Chief as such but the more limited if specialized one of analysing the real nature and scope of a chief's customary rights and duties as regards land and its incidents of tenure. What we are going to say relates broadly to those common features of chieftaincy respecting land in Northern as well as in Southern Nigeria (wherever there is such an institution), and the judicial findings to be recorded later must be taken to represent what research, judicial as well as anthropological, has so far disclosed without any claim to comprehensiveness or finality.

Now, any legal consideration of the relation of a chief to the land must have two aspects: (1) the chief's general supervisory function over the village land as the authority allocating land to new families and to strangers; and (2) the chief's position considered as a family head with such ordinary rights in or over land as are enjoyed by the normal member of a family in addition, of course, to his special administrative status with respect to the whole land.[1] This functional dichotomy naturally involves some overlapping in so far as the chief's prerogatives in administering the land of the community as a whole bear a close similarity to those which he exercises over his own family land in his representative capacity. But it makes for clarity and convenience of treatment to state the *two* aspects separately: (1) the Chief as the Authority over Village Land; and (2) the Chief as Family Head with respect to Land.

(1) *The chief as the authority over village land.* In this connexion it is useful to remember that the chief derives by delegation, actual or implied, his authority from the paramount chief of the particular district who again owes his own position to the ultimate authority of the King or the Emir.

The chief's task, then, is the allocation of land to the various families in the village or town through their respective heads and, where a family becomes extinct through failure of heirs or upon abandonment by former occupiers of the land, his is the duty to re-allocate it to new holders. In the interval between an allocation which has thus lapsed and the subsequent re-allocation by the chief, there is a clearly recognised right of reversion in the chief who, as the representative of the community, holds the lapsed land along with the general virgin, fallow and forest lands until fresh need arises for their disposal. For such allocations and re-allocations chiefs[2] formerly enjoyed and still sometimes enjoy rights to tribute in the form of part of the annual produce from the land, not indeed as a token of recognition of the chiefs' ownership of the land allocated but merely as an earnest of the grantee's *bona fides* to acknowledge that he is not himself claiming as owner, and also as an expression of his gratitude for the bounty thus conferred. These annual tithes are of course distinct from gifts of corn, palm wine, gin or other viands which invariably accompany any original grants of land all over Nigeria.

In some cases, it may be that one community having enough land and to spare agrees to settle another community on part of its vacant lands; when that happens, tributes in the form of tithes are for much the same reasons as those just stated usually demanded and paid by the 'guest' community to the 'host' community. These tributes are called 'ishakole' in Yorubaland, 'akorhore' in Benin,[3] 'zakka' or 'dzanka' in the Northern areas; and, as we shall soon see, tributes or tithes are also paid in many areas of the East with chieftaincy systems or the usual Council of Elders.

These grants of land by chiefs to 'stranger' settlers were (and are) often made in perpetuity but inalienable and, where the amount of the tributes paid to the chiefs by the individual or group grantees had been large, rights of a proprietary nature have recently been claimed by certain donees who seem to have assimilated the customary nominal dues to the position of purchase price on account of the new economic values of land. No such land may be reassigned by the grantees without the prior consent and approval of the chief and his council of elders. The right of short, temporary lettings to others is often allowed to grantees in these circumstances, but any long let or any important disposal of the land requires the chief's formal sanction.

In addition to these tithes chiefs, when they make grants of land whether to members of their community or to strangers, sometimes reserve to themselves under the local law

* T. O. Elias, *Nigerian Land Law and Custom*, Routledge & Kegan Paul, 1953, pp. 101–118.

rights to economic trees, as in Bida,[4] to game killed in hunting by the allottees, and to fish caught in streams and rivulets flowing through allocated lands, as in many areas of Nigeria.[5] But, normally, grants to chiefs carry with them the rights of the grantees to the trees, wells, rivulets and similar interests attaching to the land allotted, although reservations are sometimes made in favour of the original planters of economic trees or permanent crops. Again, the chief's permission is sometimes required before certain trees may be cut down or destroyed, at least in the early stages of settlement.

Lands abandoned by previous occupiers may only be freely re-allocated by the chief if they do not form sites of former houses or if they were not formerly planted with economic trees or permanent crops. The existence of these would raise a presumption that their owners might still wish to return to the land; strong evidence is often needed to rebut the presumption. It seems that the period of permitted abeyance during which previous occupiers of land might be allowed to resume their occupation of it varies with the locality; but Dr. Nadel's observation[6] with regard to Nupe territory in the North is at one with Ward Price's[7] about Yorubaland (including Benin) that non-user for a minimum period of three years constitutes a valid ground for regarding the rights of ccupiers of land as having lapsed, so that the chief could often make fresh allocations of it thereafter.

There remains to be considered the chief's right of eviction of settled occupiers for grave political or criminal offences. Since the original grant of land, whether to a local or to a 'stranger' family or community, must be taken to have been conditional upon the grantee's acceptance of allegiance to the Emir or Oba as well as upon continued good behaviour in consonance with the requirements of public order and welfare, it is only natural that a breach of such conditions should entail a forfeiture of what is after all the offender's mere right of occupancy. Another cause of forfeiture is the cesser of payment of the traditional tributes to the chief by the grantee, in as much as such deliberate with-holding is looked upon as a virtual claim to ownership on the grantee's part. I would seem also that the chief may take up and re-allocate lands granted to strangers but which are not being put to full or profitable use, though the extent of this right is at best indefinite; much would appear to depend on the circumstances of the case in any particular area.

But eviction or banishment for any proper cause does not ordinarily carry with it forfeiture of the offending grantee's right to his crops and other permanent improvements like houses, since these are the results of his own personal labour and exertion. All he has forfeited by his truculence or contumely is the right of occupation of the land, the only subject of the grant by the chief. Sometimes, even a banished allottee's land is allowed to remain in his family or in at least those of the family as have not sided with the offender. Confiscation of the entire land might result from the whole family or community being involved in the opprobrium of its head, though local ideas are extremely liberal in these matters and chiefs and elders rarely order a complete disestablishment of the whole group.

One other important function of the chief is the adjudication of land disputes as between members of the community over whom he holds sway. This is his internal juridical prerogative, buttressed by the co-operation and loyalty of the village elders. On the external side, the chief answers for his own group with other chiefs in the settlement of boundary disputes and in the demarcation of fishing and hunting rights of one community *vis-à-vis* another or other communities. In this way is maintained the social equilibrium so necessary to an orderly and peaceful enjoyment of the land. Thus it is also that the chief justifies his claim to tributes and other traditional perquisites.

The chief, therefore, has the style of a protecting authority and not that of the owner of the land. As the representative of his Emir or Oba, he allocates and re-allocates land to his people, and his consent is necessary to any important disposal of allotted lands, especially to 'strangers'. He receives tributes for his supervisory oversight, and may eject or evict grantees for good and sometimes bad reasons. The reversion of all lapsed or unoccupied lands is in him as the legal or juristic representative of his community. Land once granted by a chief is to all intents and purposes beyond his care, so long as the grantee does not break any important condition of his occupancy; therefore, as regards the general internal disposal of the allotted land as between the members of a group or family, the umpire is unsighted. This constitutes an important qualification of the chief's powers over land. He is neither more nor less than the caretaker, protector, administrator or trustee of the land which really belongs to his community. That is why the chief has no right to alienate such land without the consent of all the elders of the community.

(2) *The chief as family head with respect to land (including an ordinary family head)*. Let us note from the outset that the chief's role with regard to his own family land differs in no material respect from that of any other head of an ordinary family or extended family. It will, therefore, be convenient to describe the two together here; what follows then applies to both, so that much of what has just been said for the chief as the administrator of the land of the whole community equally applies to the chief considered as a head of a household. But, because chieftaincy and headship of a family do not often or necessarily coincide, there are a certain number of features in the land arrangement which are peculiar to the family head as such.*

Let us now proceed to illustrate the outline of the general principles of indigenous system . . . with a brief review of some judicial decisions. A useful starting point would be to consider the attitude of the Courts towards chieftaincy in its relation to land.

A. The Chief and the Land

The first important recorded case was *Sule Giwa & ors.* v. *Alashe.*[8] This was an undefended action brought by the plaintiff, a farmer, against the defendant, a White-Capped Chief of Lagos, for seizing and converting plaintiff's property to his own use and for entering the household of the occupants of the farm, breaking down the fence for the purpose. Smalman Smith, C.J., in delivering judgment, commented as follows: 'Such a position (i.e. of a chief) only carries a certain social status and distinction among his fellows, but no authority beyond that of any other private person. More especially do I draw attention to this fact, inasmuch as certain pretensions have recently been advanced by persons calling themselves White-Capped Chiefs, to control over land in the lawful and beneficial occupation of persons owing no rent or service to them.'

This stricture is, however, to be confined to the arbitrary arrogation of power by the chief concerned and should not be taken as covering the whole of the miscellaneous rights over land which a chief undoubtedly enjoys under local law and custom. But the learned Chief Justice's warning was timely and necessary in the particular context, especially when one remembers that the very act he was condemning is equally reprehensible under the existing customary law of tenure. For the purpose of appreciating the real nature of chieftaincy, however, the next case seems more helpful.

In *Adanji* v. *Hunvoo,*[9] in which an action had been brought by the plaintiff in the case in order to establish his title to the chieftaincy of Fiyento of Badagry, the then Acting Chief Justice defined[10] chieftaincy as follows: 'Now what is the chieftaincy? I say without hesitation that it is a mere dignity, a position of honour, of primacy among a particular section of the native community. . . .' The learned judge had a little earlier concluded that it might be that chieftaincy carried with it by local law and custom some or many rights and privileges which might be made the subject of an action at law; later decisions presently to be considered will be seen to have clarified the nature of these rights and privileges of the chief.[11]

On the legislative side, s. 3 of the Interpretation Ordinance No. 27 of 1939, gives this definition: ' "Chief" or "Native Chief" means any native whose authority and control is recognised by a native community, and "head chief" means any chief who is not subordinate to any other chief or native authority.' This as a definition is, to say the least, not explicit.

Nevertheless, it will be noticed from these judicial and legislative statements that the chief's role with respect to land is not one of ownership, but essentially one of political and social pre-eminence over his particular community. This is not, however, to deny that a chief may enjoy a dual capacity; his position of control and administration of community land, as well as his position as a land-owning individual in his private capacity. For example, in *Taiwo* v. *Sarumi,*[12] the Full Court at Lagos observed:[13] 'It seems to us that the Olofin of Isheri has been since the Egba Boundary Treaty, 1894, acting in a *dual* capacity, firstly as a chief in a district situated in a territory of the Egba

* Elias' description of the powers of a family head in relation to land are given infra, at pp. 309–311.

United Government, and secondly as owning or controlling certain land outside the Egba boundaries and within the jurisdiction of this Court.' But it remains true that with respect to community land the chief is a kind of trustee or administrator.

We will next illustrate the main attributes of chiefly power over land:

The chief as trustee and chief's right to tribute. These two inter-related questions were fully canvassed in the much-quoted case of *Amodu Tijani* v. *Secry., Southern Nigeria.*[14] The facts were that land at Apapa, on the mainland and within the Colony, belonged to the Oluwa Chieftaincy family. On its acquisition by the Government under the Public Lands Ordinance No. 5 of 1903, the question arose as to (1) the person or persons to whom compensation should be paid and (2) the basis on which it should be made and the title thereby conveyed by the payee or payees to the Crown. *Held*: by the Privy Council, (1) that, while the radical title to the land was in the Crown, the full usufructuary title vested in the chief on behalf of the community of which he was the head; (2) that, therefore, the proper person to whom compensation should be made was the chief as the representative of his community, among the members of which the compensation money should be distributed or for whose benefit it should be applied or used in such proportions and manner as the Native Council of the District in which the land is situated should determine with the sanction of the Governor (paras. 25 and 26 of the Ordinance of 1903). Viscount Haldane emphasised[15]: 'The chief is only the agent through whom the transaction is to take place, and he is to be dealt with as representing not only his own but the other interests affected'; (3) that compensation was payable on the basis that the chief, on behalf of his community, was transferring the land to the Governor in full ownership, and that for the purpose of payment of compensation at least, there was no practical distinction between 'stool' and 'communal' lands.[16] This transference of the full ownership of 'communal' lands was, of course, the entire creature of s. 6 of the Public Lands Ordinance (1903), which their Lordships regarded as absolute in its terms when it provided: 'When the land required is the property of a native community, the head chief of the community may sell and convey it in fee simple, any native law or custom to the contrary notwithstanding.'

To the extent to which Speed, C.J., had held in the earlier case of *Oduntan Onisiwo* v. *Attorney-General of Southern Nigeria*[17] that the only right or title of the chief was 'merely a *seigneurial* right giving the holder the ordinary rights of control and management of the land, in accordance with the well-known principles of native law and custom, including the rights to receive payment of the nominal rent or tribute payable by the occupiers *and that compensation should be calculated on that basis and not on* the basis of absolute ownership of the land,'[18] Viscount Haldane's observation in respect to the learned Chief Justice's basis of compensation[19] may be thus summarised:

(i) Speed, C.J.'s, conclusion was based on a confusion between family and chieftaincy property,[20] since 'it does not appear clearly from the judgment of the Chief Justice whether he thought that any members of the community had any independent right to compensation or whether the Crown was entitled to appropriate the land without more'.[21]

'Their Lordships think that the learned Chief Justice in the judgment thus summarised *which virtually excludes the legal reality of the community usufruct*, has failed to recognise the real character of the title to land occupied by a native community.'[22]

(ii) The learned Chief Justice had misunderstood 'the effect of the decision in the *Oduntan's Case*, 1908, which came before the Full Court, and in which compensation had been paid by the Nigerian Government on the basis of absolute ownership'. The relevant finding of Speed, C.J., in that case was: 'I am, moreover, quite satisfied that the supplicant is a son of a former Onisiwo, and is eligible for election to the title. . . . *He does not claim as Onisiwo, but as head and representative of the family*, and I have already expressed my concurrence with the finding of the Court below as to his right to sue on their behalf.'[23]

(iii) 'It follows that it is for *the whole of what he so transfers* that compensation has to be made.' This bundle of rights transferred by the chief includes the chief's own right to tributes from the occupiers, wherever such traditional tributes were normally paid before, but not otherwise; and for the deprivation of this right he must be compensated, not indeed by means of a separate award by the Court, but simply by means of any agreed sum out of the total amount granted. This, of course, would be additional to his proper share in the residue as a member of the community.[24] 'If he (i.e. a chief) is properly deriving tribute or rent from these allotments, he will have to be compensated for the loss of it, and if the allottees have had valid titles conferred on them, they must also be compensated. . . . In the case of land belonging to the community, but as to which no rent is payable to the chief, it does not appear that the latter is entitled to be compensated otherwise than in his representative capacity under the Ordinance of 1903. It is the members of his community who are in usufructuary occupation or in an equivalent position on whose behalf he is making the claim.'[25]

The right of the chief to receive tribute from stranger occupiers may sometimes be made the subject of an express agreement to pay rent as between two local communities. In *Chief Lulu Braid* v. *Chief Daniel Kalio*[26] the plaintiff, as representing the chiefs and people of Bakana (New Calabar), sued the defendant on behalf of the chiefs and people of Okirika on an Agreement of 1915 to pay rent for houses erected on certain village lands belonging to the Bakana people. The Divisional Court at Calabar gave judgment for the defendants on the ground that the claim was uncertain and that there was no consideration for the agreement. The Full Court, on appeal, set aside this judgment and ordered a re-trial because, said Combe, C.J., the lower Court, in requiring consideration for an agreement to pay tribute which the defendants were in any case bound to pay under the local customary law, had taken a wholly erroneous view of the position. No consideration is ever necessary under the indigenous system of tenure, and the liability of stranger occupiers to pay tribute or rent to their overlords cannot be taken away merely because a formal contract has also been entered into by them with a view to fixing precisely what the actual amount should be.

Similarly, with the permission of the Oba or Emir or other paramount chief, lesser chiefs or household heads may grant lands to refugees and other settlers on terms of payment of tribute or rent by the latter to their overlords. In a rapidly developing community difficulties are bound to arise if and when such payments are insisted upon by the descendants of the grantors from the descendants of the grantees who, after some generations, may have come now to look upon the land as virtually their own and the continued payment of tribute or rent as an unjustifiable imposition. Thus, in the very recent and celebrated case of *Ife Overlords* v. *Modakekes* (1948),[27] the plaintiffs claimed from the defendants 6 cwt. 1 qr. of cocoa or its equivalent (in this case, calculated at £18 2*s*. 6*d*.) representing the *ishakole* due from the latter to the plaintiffs in respect of the year ended 31 December 1947. The plaintiffs alleged that under an Agreement of 1886 the defendants through their predecessors undertook to pay yams and kola-nuts as *ishakole* to the plaintiffs' predecessors until the cocoa to be grown on their allotments should begin to bear fruits when each grantee of land must pay 1 cwt. of cocoa or its money equivalent to the grantors. This Agreement was not enforced until 1903, but it appeared that the defendants, who had been granted their lands some eighteen years previously, had paid *ishakole* of yams and kola-nuts for some eight years and that thereafter, when their cocoa trees began to yield, they had for ten years paid the agreed quantities of cocoa up to and including 31 December 1946. They then decided not to pay any more *ishakole*, which had now come to be looked upon merely as a voluntary but burdensome tribute. *Held*: by Hallinan, J., in the Supreme Court at Ife, confirming the findings of the Magistrate Court,

(1) that *ishakole* was, even in ancient times, always based on agreement between grantors and grantees of land;

(2) that *ishakole* was in the nature of *obligatory rent*, not mere *voluntary tribute*, and was payable (whether as between individuals or as between families) by the grantees to the grantors; and that it was independent of any customary tributes which were payable at will on certain festive and other occasions;

(3) that *ishakole* must be distinguished from *Isin* which was always payable to the Oba as customary tribute in token of loyalty and fealty, and which never depended on any agreement;

(4) that the defendants must continue to pay the agreed *ishakole* to the plaintiffs, including the 6 cwt. 1 qr. or its money equivalent of £18 2*s*. 6*d*. as claimed by the plaintiffs in the case.[28]

Two interesting features of this famous case were: (1) the claim was not by the Oni of Ife on behalf of his people against the Modakeke settlers, but was between heads of family overlords and heads of family grantees. (2) The Oni's evidence in the case, expounding the delimiting the meaning and scope of *ishakole* and *isin* in relation to *rent*, questioned the correctness of the statement of principles in paras. 36, 85 and 117 of Ward Price's *Land Tenure in Yoruba-land* (1933) in so far as these say that *ishakole* is customary tribute, not rent, paid only on occasions, etc. The Oni pointed out that he himself was one of those consulted by Ward Price when the latter was collecting his materials for his Report which was afterwards published by the Nigerian Government.

The chief's representative status. As we have seen, it is because, under Nigerian law and custom, the chief is not the owner of the land in the accepted English sense of the word, that we have denied the legal right of the chiefs to make treaties giving away Nigerian land as if they were the proprietors. This principle of the representative character of the chief with regard to the land of his community is of universal application in Nigeria. There are two sides to it: the negative and the positive, the former consisting in the chief's legal incapacity to treat the land as his personal property and the latter in the recognised rule that the chief is the legal representative of his community and that it is only through him that actions relating to land should ordinarily be brought. Chiefs have all too often confused the two by claiming community lands as if they were beneficial owners thereof, merely because theirs is the right to bring a suit. Thus, in the famous *Amodu Tijani Oluwa Case*,[29] his original claim as beneficial owner of Apapa land had to be abandoned under correction by the Full Court at Lagos. In *Chief Omagbemi & ors.* v. *Chief Dore Numa*,[30] Webber, J., held in the Divisional Court at Calabar (at p. 19): 'Now the Olu never owned Jekri land as an individual. The land belonged to the community and the Olu was trustee. In him, as trustee, was vested the land.' To which Tew, J., in upholding Webber, J., on appeal to the Supreme Court at Lagos, added (at pp. 21–2): 'There is equally no doubt as to the position of the person holding the title of Olu Jekri with regard to the lands of the Jekri people. It was admitted by the first witness in the Court below, Chief Denedo, himself one of the plaintiffs, that the Olu held the land as trustee for the people and not as individual owner or on behalf of his family.' The case concerned land in Warri in Eastern Nigeria.

A necessary consequence of this trustee-beneficiary role of the chief over the land is that it is he who represents his community *vis-à-vis* another community in land disputes. Thus it was that, in *Nnaji Nwa-Ogaba* (for and on behalf of Akagbe Village) v. *Nnaman Nwa Okenwaeji* (for and on behalf of Akpugo Village),[31] a case concerning lands in the Udi Division of the Onitsha Province, the plaintiff, a kind of chief, sued the defendant (as another chief of his own community) in the Awkunanaw Native Court for (i) a declaration of title to the land in question, (ii) damages for trespass and (iii) an injunction. Similarly, in *Chief D. H. Braid & ors.* v. *Chief S. Adoki & ors.*,[32] the treaty of 1871 which secured to the Okrikas the right to pass through and make fishing settlements in any of the creeks belonging to New Calabar, had to be signed between the Chiefs of Okrika and the Chiefs of New Calabar.

It would seem, however, that if the chief on behalf of his community enters for valuable consideration into any negotiation, apparently valid and authorised, with a *bona fide* outsider, the members of such a group cannot be heard to say that his act was unauthorised. Thus, in *Secretary, L.T.C.* v. *Nowroudin B. Soule & Chief Aromire*,[33] during an interregnum in the Aromire Chieftaincy, one Yesufu Aromire acted as chief for about five years during which he sold two pieces of land *inter alia* to the first defendant. The parcels of land were later acquired by the L.T.C. and both defendants each claimed the compensation money. *Held:* that the proper person with a legal right to receive the compensation money was Yesufu Aromire, as representing the chief at the relevant time. The Court said (*a*) that the family knew of and impliedly consented to the deputy's dealing with the group land and the sale by him to first defendant was accordingly valid; and (*b*) that the second defendant's election was duly completed only *after* the particular transaction, and so he could not claim the money. But it is difficult to see why the compensation sum should not have been paid to the second defendant as the regular chief when the action was brought, since the money should, it is submitted, have been payable to whoever is the legal representative of the community at the material time. Surely the deputy, i.e. Yesufu Aromire, had surrendered his stewardship to the substantive holder of the office and the subsequent payment to him of the compensation money would seem to have entailed unnecessary duplication of function as of accounting.

Nevertheless, if a chief makes a clandestine arrangement under his ostensible authority which is not in fact properly exercised, his community may repudiate all liability thereby arising.

Thus, in *Aralawon* v. *Aromire & anor.*,[34] the first defendant in his capacity as the acting Chief Aromire privately and without consulting the senior members of the Aromire family borrowed from the plaintiff the sum of £105 for the purpose both of completing the re-building of the chief's palace (called 'Iga') and of defraying the costs of chieftaincy law suits. As the money was not repaid, the plaintiff sued him both personally and in his representative capacity, joining the second defendant who had since become the substantive holder of the office. *Held*: that the first defendant was alone chargeable with the repayment, to the plaintiff, of the loan. In the circumstances, the community could properly repudiate liability.

Notes

[1] This role of the chief is again independent of and apart from his right to the so-called royal or other *ex officio* estates that may be attached to his particular post.

[2] E.g. 'The Lagos chiefs, the landowners (e.g. Oloto, Ojora, Oluwa, etc.), each receive an annual tribute of 5*s*. per head from anyone who takes or settles on his land for farming purposes'.—A. K. Ajisafe, *Laws and Customs of the Yoruba People*; London 1924. Chap. IX, p. 27.

[3] The Benin equivalent of a chief is 'Enogie' and to him or the Village Council the 'akorhore' is usually paid.

[4] Nadel, *Black Byzantium*, p. 187.

[5] E.g. A. K. Ajisafe, *op. cit.*, Chap. IV, Nadel, *op. cit.*, pp. 46–7.

[6] Nadel, *op. cit.*, p. 186.

[7] W. Price, *op. cit.*, paras. 86, 96, etc.; also, C. W. Rowling, *Note on Land in Benin, etc.*, paras. 20 and 41.

[8] (1891), p. 45 of *Lagos, Reports of Certain Judgments of the Supreme Court, Vice-Admiralty Court & Full Court of Appeal* (1884–1892), delivered on 15 May.

[9] (1908), 1 N.L.R. 74.

[10] *Ibid.*, at p. 78.

[11] In our case here, the Supreme Court held that the issue being just one of mere title to chieftaincy was outside its jurisdiction under s. 11 of the Supreme Court Ordinance. In the later case of *Wanta Dick* v. *Green* (1911), 1 N.L.R. 114, however, the Supreme Court entertained a chief's claim to the right to receive payment of money, thus distinguishing at p. 115 *the Adanji Case.*

[12] 2 N.L.R. 103.

[13] *Ibid.*, at p. 104.

[14] (1921), 2 A.C. 399.

[15] (1921), 2 A.C. 399, at p. 408.

[16] N.L.R., at p. 58.

[17] (1912), 2 N.L.R. 77.

[18] All the italics in this quotation are the author's.

[19] But the rest of the learned Chief Justice's dictum here cited is otherwise unexceptionable.

[20] The land in the instant case is 'family' land occupied, however, by strangers who paid tributes to the head of the owning family who happened to be also a chief.

[21] (1921), A.C., at p. 402.

[22] (1921), 2 A.C., at p. 409.

[23] (1912), 2 N.L.R. 77, at p. 80; the italics are the author's.

[24] Here one may recall the recognition of similar apparently shadowy rights by the payment of personal subsidies to, e.g. Docemo, Chief Young Dede, Emir of Sokoto, etc., under the various treaties of cession or lease of territory. Legally, the reservation to these local rulers of such personal annuities can be justified only on the hypothesis that they were meant to compensate them for loss of tributes over the lands.

[25] (1921), 2 A.C. 399, at p. 410.

[26] (1927), 7 N.L.R. 34.

[27] 'The Daily Service', Wednesday, 22 December 1948, p. 1 ff. 'Judgment of the Supreme Court delivered at Ife by Hallinan, J., on Monday, 13 December 1948. In pursuance of the learned judge's advice that the parties should get together and effect an amicable settlement, the Oni of Ife summoned to his palace both parties who, however, failed to agree; the Modakekes still refused to pay any more *ishakole.*

[28] Compare the not dissimilar decision in *Chief D H. Braide & ors.* v. *Chief S. Adoki & ors.* (1931), 10 N.L.R. 15, in which an agreement of 1923 between the people of New Calabar and

the Okrikas was upheld on appeal to the Supreme Court. See also *Chief Lulu Braid* v. *Chief Daniel Kalio* (1927), N.L.R. 34.

[29] (1921), 2 A.C. 399.
[30] (1923), 5 N.L.R. 19.
[31] (1944), 17 N.L.R. 117.
[32] (1931), 10 N.L.R. 15.
[33] (1939), 15 N.L.R. 72.
[34] (1940), 15 N.L.R. 90.

H. Cory: Sukuma Law and Custom*

Land Held by Virtue of Office

A. *By a Ntemi* (*chief*)

The Ikuru (Residence of a chief)

The *ikuru* of the chief is considered *Butemi*† property.

If a chief wishes to build a better house than the one he occupies in his *ikuru*, he must build it outside the *ikuru*. If he builds it inside, neither he nor his heirs can later claim reimbursement of expenses.

NOTE: The [above] Rule is one of the new rules accepted unanimously by the full meeting of chiefs and their people in Malya in 1949. The rule was proposed by *Ntemi* Masali of Samuye.

If there are houses in the *ikuru* which had been built or greatly improved before the enforcement of the above rules, it is acknowledged that a chief who is deposed, or the heir of a chief who is not chosen as successor to his father, is entitled to compensation for expenses incurred in improving the house but not for sums spent on its maintenance.

NOTE: The [above] Rules were decided upon by the chiefs of the Sukuma Federation and their people in 1949. Formerly no rules existed but the immovable property of a chief was always considered to be *Butemi*.

Njingo gwi Ikuru

The *ikuru* of a chief is surrounded by many fields comprising the *njingo gwi ikuru* or *itongo li ikuru*. Most of the settlers round the *ikuru* are *banikuru*, i.e. distant relatives of the chief or selected retainers; their fields are intermingled with those of the chief himself.

The *njingo gwi ikuru* is administered directly by the chief and neither village headman nor *basumba batale* have any influence in the allocation of plots in it.

The chief's fields are cultivated by his wives, female relatives, servants, and by the *banikuru* living in the *ikuru*. The acreage of the *njingo gwi ikuru* varies and is often considerable. Its boundaries are commonly known although they are not specifically demarcated. In some places, for instance in the chiefdoms of KS, SM, and BS‡ the villagers round the *njingo* are called upon to help in its cultivation.

The *njingo gwi ikuru* is *Butemi* property.

Traditional Fields (*Migunda ya ikuru*)

In nearly all the villages of his chiefdom huge fields are cultivated for the chief. The sites of these fields have not changed for many years. The chief gives orders as to the crop which is to be planted in each field. In the big chiefdoms the *ng'wambilija*,§ in smaller chiefdoms the *ng'wanangwa*,|| is responsible for organizing the work. Recently the chiefs have begun to engage reliable men as salaried estate managers.

At any time a chief can open a new *migunda ya ikuru* in a *gunguli*¶ in which there was none before. A new field is very seldom laid out in an old *gunguli*, as it would be difficult to find a sufficiently large portion of good land unoccupied. New *migunda ya ikuru* are frequently opened in *gunguli* which have recently become densely populated.

* H. Cory, *Sukuma Law and Custom*, Oxford University Press, 1953, pp. 126–129.
† Property appertaining to Chieftaincy.
‡ Districts in Sukumaland. (See map in Cory's book.)
§ Sub-Chief.
|| Village headman.
¶ Elevated place, parish.

The *migunda ya ikuru* is *Butemi* property.

Each able-bodied man of a village must cultivate a certain area, usually 45 square feet, of the plot for the chief. If he is sick his wife must do the work for him.

The cultivators receive for their work compensation in kind (a beast or beer) or in money, generally 30 cents for 45 square feet. Money is usually paid for the cultivation of cotton.

It is the custom to give the compensation when the work has been done, except in the case of sorghum fields, where compensation is paid after the harvest.

Corn is either stored near the fields under the care of a reliable man or transported to the *ikuru* by lorries.

NOTE: Mr. D. W. Malcolm writes in his report (158): 'First the subjects paid *sekule* to the chief, consisting of the payment of one basket of grain by each household of the chiefdom. When Europeans arrived, tribute was stopped and the tax was introduced. The chiefs arranged that each village should plant one field and send the whole of the produce to the chief. This was discovered by Government and stopped. In 1934 the District Commissioner sent round tax collectors to investigate. When the chiefs heard of this, they paid out cents and meat. Some of the people refused to accept payment whereupon the chiefs paid them by force, puttings cents in their houses. Then the chiefs started the present system of having large fields of their own scattered all over their countries, for the labour of which they pay by contract.'

Temporary Fields

After discussion with his village headmen, the chief may decide where he wishes to have fields cultivated for him in the current year. He then calls the leaders of the village *elika*, or the leaders of a dance society, and arranges a works contract with them. The compensation is usually in kind (in ZM, SM* money is paid), and the work is supervised by the chief's messengers, or *banikuru*, or by the village headmen themselves. It is possible that in the course of time such a temporary field may become a *ngunda gwi ikuru.*

These fields are held under the usual tenure of single fields.

D.C.'s Appeal 12/43. NF. Fulo (Bukumbi). *Paulo* v. *Ntemi Antonio.*

Paulo was chosen by the village headman to work in the chief's field on several occasions: eight days in November 1940, eight days in 1941, and three days in 1942; for which he claimed wages of 20 cents per day. The chief (defendant) explained: 'It is the custom for me to call upon the inhabitants of a village when I want my field in that village cultivated and to agree with them that I shall pay so much for the cultivation and harvesting of a particular field. When the work is done, I pay out what I have agreed in cash or kind and it is shared out equally among those who worked. There is no individual wage-earning. If the plaintiff did not get his share it is his own fault.'

The court accepted the chief's statement regarding the practice of the country and held that the plaintiff had produced no evidence whatever that he had not agreed with the chief to work for certain wages, or that the chief had not paid for the work at the time. The plaintiff should bring an action against the people who worked with him and did not give him his share.

By Ng'wambilija and Ng'wanangwa Ntale (*sub-chief and senior village headman*)

In many chiefdoms the chief may choose one village or another to cultivate a common field for the *ng'wambilija* or *ng'wanangwa ntale.* This *gunguli* would have no work to do for the chief in the same year. In other chiefdoms the *ng'wambilija* or *ng'wanangwa* look after themselves and make their own arrangements with the villagers.

Customarily, one person from each house works (*nhembe* or *lubili*) for one day in the year in the fields of the village headman; they are not necessarily given any specific task, and they receive compensation in kind for the days worked. The *basumba batale*† organize the work and call for a certain number of villagers for every phase of field-work, including the tilling and the harvesting of the crop.

NOTE: A village headman is also given customary gifts in kind by his villagers.

D.C.'s Appeal 21/45. Fulo (Burima). *Masanyiwa* v. *Ng'wanangwa Maneneo.*

Masanyiwa acted as *soi-disant* representative of the interests of the community and

* Districts in Sukumaland.

† Leader of the village organization of the younger age-grade, in a sub-division of a parish.

claimed payment for work done for the headman and for food delivered to him. The witnesses agreed that it is customary for the local women to bring presents of small quantities of food to a newly appointed headman.

If a village headman has inherited office and holding from his father or brother, he cannot be deprived of the holding if he loses his office.

If a man on becoming village headman takes over a holding with his appointment, he loses the holding when he loses the office.

NOTE: In this case he must either return to his private holding, if he has retained it, or he must apply for land.

In KS, SS, BD* (Sengerema) the village headman is entitled to take over the *matongo*.† He cannot keep it if he loses his office but must hand the plots over to his successor.

D.C.'s Appeal 60/45. Fulo (Mwanza). *Keya* v. *Galiyela*.

Galiyela was discharged from the headmanship of a village about May and Keya was put in his place. The new headman claimed one field from Galiyela (allegedly held by the latter *ex officio*) as this was his right as headman and he himself had no fields. The court held that Galiyela must hand over the field to Keya after he had harvested the crop.

NOTE: In all other parts of Sukumaland the *litongo*‡ belongs to the holding and cannot be separated from it.

* Districts in Sukumaland.
† Field in the vicinity of homestead.
‡ *Ibid.*

CHAPTER 15

SOCIAL GROUPS AND THE LAND

Several of the writers whose works have been included in thc foregoing chapters have stressed the importance of social groups, i.e. the family, lineage and clan, in relation to land. This chapter expands on this aspect of African land law. *Meek*, in describing lineage land, deals with the function of these groups among both patrilineal and matrilineal peoples of Nigeria; *Colson* goes into greater detail on the composition and functioning of the lineage in regard to land among the matrilineal Gwembe (Valley) Tonga. The extract from *Elias'* work which follows is really a continuation of his description of the powers of the chief—but this time, not in his capacity as chief, but merely as head of a family. The last extract, from *Cory* and *Hartnoll* on the Haya, approaches the same subject from a different angle, namely the manner in which the rights of one member of the family are circumscribed by the powers of the others, particularly in regard to sale and pledge.

C. K. Meek: Land Tenure and Land Administration in Nigeria and the Cameroons*

Lineage or 'Family' Lands[1]

Many years ago Sir Henry Maine observed that 'from the moment when a tribal community settles down upon a definite space of land, the land begins to be the basis of society in place of kinship'.[2] In Nigeria the substitution of common territory for common descent as the basis of unity is proceeding apace, and there are communities at every stage of transmutation—small hamlets composed of a single kin, larger settlements composed of several distinct groups of kin, and well-knit self-subsisting village communities in which the kinship bond has ceased to be a factor in social cohesion. Even in the case of an entire tribe the same process may be seen at work, and it is sometimes still apposite to compare the tribal state of flux to 'the flowing of the juice of the sugar-cane over a flat surface: the juice crystallizes and the crystals are the various village communities'.[3] Such, for example, is the present state of the Munshi (or Tiv) of Northern Nigeria, a tribe of some 800,000 people who were formerly in a constant state of flux but are now beginning to settle down into static village societies.

Yet kinship continues to be the basis of land-holding over the major part of Nigeria. For, apart from the Muhammadan areas of the north, society is organized into groups of kin known to sociologists as 'lineages', that is to say, groups consisting of all the descendants of a particular ancestor through a determinate number of generations.[4] Where the descendants of the common ancestor are related through males the lineage may be described as a patrilineage, and where they are related through females as a matrilineage. A patrilineage (being a unilateral group) does not include wives, while a matrilineage does not include husbands.[5] A number of related lineages (or lineages which believe themselves to be related) constitute a 'clan', and we may find a single village or group of villages occupied by clan in this sense. On the other hand a large lineage may consist of a number of segments or sub-lineages, so that it is not always easy to distinguish between a 'clan' and a large lineage.

* C. K. Meek, *Land Tenure and Land Administration in Nigeria and the Cameroons*, H.M.S.O., 1957, pp. 128–139.

In Nigeria the vast majority of the tribes are patrilineal, so that when we speak of lineages we shall intend patrilineages. There are, however, a few matrilineal peoples, such as the Gure and Hill Longuda of the Northern Provinces and some of the Cross River tribal groups in the south.

The lineage, then, is a group of kinsmen which may consist of anything from twenty or thirty persons to several hundreds. It may include a number of strangers who have been adopted into the lineage, and it may also include persons of slave origin, though the status of these is always inferior in land matters to that of the free-born. The lineage is the basic social unit in most Nigerian societies. It is exogamous—that is to say, that its members must marry outside the lineage. It is governed largely by its elders under the presidency of a headman or 'chief', who may be its oldest member, or chosen for his personal qualities. It is also an economic unit, the members assisting each other in agricultural work and possessing common or joint property rights in land. These rights may extend not merely to arable land, but also to belts of forest or palm-bush; and a lineage may even exercise exclusive rights over waterways, beaches and fishing grounds.[6]

The precise nature of the title of a Nigerian lineage to its lands varies from tribe to tribe, and district, to district, depending on the degree to which lineage lands are free from claims by the local territorial community. In some situations the rights of a lineage hardly amount to more than an exclusive right of occupany, without, or at most with restricted, rights of disposal; in others it may be equivalent to the full fee simple estate of English law; while in others again the title of the lineage may be so absolute as to amount to complete allodial ownership.

A lineage may have acquired its lands by clearing and taking possession of unoccupied land, or it may have obtained them by grant from the political authorities. However acquired, the lands of a lineage are held as by a corporation. Individual members have an absolute right to possession of a portion of lineage lands, but there is nothing analogous to tenancy in common as known to English law.[7] Ownership is joint and indivisible, no part being capable of being alienated by any individual occupier. A deceased member leaves no separate estate in lineage land which can devolve on his heir. But sons normally succeed to their father's holdings. When an allottee dies childless his holding reverts to the head of the lineage for re-disposal. On his death there is no change of ownership, for the land remains vested, as before, in the lineage community. A member who encumbers lineage property without the consent of the other members commits an offence and is liable to forfeit his interest. The records of native courts show that this penalty is still commonly exacted at the present time.[8]

Sons, on attaining marriageable age, are given their own allotments of lineage land; there is no form of rent; and no member of a lineage may interfere with the allotment of any other member. Daughters may also be given allotments, but they would normally farm on the lineage land of their husbands. Women do not inherit land but on the death of her husband a woman may continue to have a life interest in her husband's land and to hold it on behalf of his children.

A lineage, with the consent of all its members, may give grants of parts of its spare lands to strangers.[9] Such grants are conditional upon payment of certain annual dues in kind or cash, not so much as 'rent' as an acknowledgment of the grantor's title. A grant may be revoked if these dues are withheld, or for any disrespectful or disloyal conduct towards senior members of the lineage, particularly the headman or 'chief'. Such conduct would be interpreted as a repudiation of the grantor's title.[10] Grantees may not assign the whole or part of a grant without the consent of the landlord lineage. Normally a grantee remains in possession until his death. But whereas the son of a lineage member succeeds to his father's land as of right, the son of a non-lineage grantee does not succeed unless the grant is formally renewed. Grants to strangers may carry certain conditions such as that the grantee may not plant permanent crops. There is usually also an implied condition that palms and other economic trees are reserved, since these are considered to be the property of the sons of the soil.[11]

A lineage may pledge a portion of its land in order to meet some special expenditure, or in order to help one of its members who has got into difficulties. In the latter case it is incumbent on the individual concerned, or his descendants, to redeem the land as soon as possible. Another member of the lineage may, with the knowledge and consent of the lineage as a whole, redeem the pledged land. But when the lineage decides to redeem the land for itself, the member who has already redeemed it on his own account is bound to accept the redemption money offered by the lineage and to restore the land. It is a sign of the times that nowadays applications are frequently being made to the courts by lineages for a court order calling on one of its members to accept a refund of money spent by him in redeeming a piece of lineage land which had been pledged. The reason is, of course, to prevent the individual member from claiming exclusive personal rights over the community land of the lineage.

A lineage may also alienate absolutely a portion of its lands.[12] This is a recent development, which has followed the introduction of a money economy. Many lineages have in the last fifty years parted with their patrimony in return for cash payments. In Lagos Island, for example, most of the land-owning lineages of former times have now lost most of their lands.

But a lineage can only dispose of its lands with the general consent of its members. Without this consent alienation is invalid. It is not always easy, however, to determine what constitutes the 'general consent' of a lineage, and many actions have been fought in the courts on the ground that lineage land had been sold without the consent of some of its members, or some of its sections. European trading firms have often, for this reason, found difficulty in obtaining land with a secure title, and some colonial governments have for the same reason become involved in much costly litigation.'[13]

Lineages are liable to fission; and this brings us to the subject of partition of lineage lands. The sub-divisions of a lineage may have come to occupy each it own area of land, and to regard that area as its private property. Disputes between the sub-divisions may arise for personal reasons, or over boundaries made between the sub-divisions, or because one of the sub-divisions has alienated part of its land without consulting the others, or because of dissatisfaction over the method of dividing rents received from strangers. Where a dispute becomes protracted the lineage as a whole may decide on a general partition of the lineage lands between each sub-division, or it may decide to give a dissident section absolute rights over a certain area. Where agreement cannot be reached the case may be taken to court, which may refuse to sanction partition if it considers that partition would not be in the best interests of the lineage as a whole. There can be little doubt that the tendency towards partition has increased rapidly in recent times, since sections of lineages are often anxious to cash in on their capital assets. In areas where permanent crops, such as cocoa or coffee, have been introduced the demand for partition has been general, and even individual members of a lineage have obtained what has been in effect outright grants of land over which they had formerly enjoyed merely the usufruct.

The various influences which have tended to disrupt the lineage organization and to promote the 'individualization' of tenures have been recited often enough. They are, briefly, the 'pax Britannica', which has enabled individuals to farm by themselves in safety wherever they please, the introduction of a money economy and of commercial crops with the possibility of individual exploitation, the opportunity given to members of a lineage to follow occupations other than farming, and finally the influence of English law, with its insistence on individual rights. The general position to-day in many parts of Africa is very much the same as that attributed to India by Sir Henry Maine some eighty years ago: 'The sense of personal right growing everywhere into greater strength, and the ambition which points to wider spheres of action than can be found within the community, are both destructive of the authority of its internal rules. Even more fatal is the increasing feeling of the sacredness of personal obligation arising out of contract. The partition of inheritances and execution for debt levied on land are destroying the communities. . . . The brotherhood of the larger group may still cohere, but the brethren of some one family are always wishing to have their shares separately; and creditors who would have feared to intrude on the village domain now break the net of custom by stepping without ceremony into the lot of a defaulting debtor.'[14]

It must not be supposed, however, that the lineage organization and lineage ownership of land is everywhere breaking down. Many years ago a Chief Justice of Nigeria declared that 'family' ownership of land was a dying institution and that sooner or later the legislature of the Colony, or the Supreme Court in the exercise of its equitable jurisdiction, would have to give the *coup de grâce* to the whole system.[15] But thirty years later Sir Mervyn Tew found that even in the progressive colony of Lagos 'family' ownership of land was still an integral feature of the social organization and that any sweeping changes in the system of land tenure would cause widespread disturbance.[16] There is, indeed, good evidence that in many areas of Nigeria lineages are now becoming alive to the value of their holdings and are entrenching their position as landed proprietors. The customary dues in kind payable by strangers for the use of land are, in these areas, giving place to competition rents paid in cash, with conveyances drawn up according to the requirements of English law. Claims are also being made by lineages to the ownership of vacant lands, on the ground that at some time in the distant past some ancestor of the lineage had farmed in the area. It is obvious that where such conditions prevail the claims of lineages may conflict with those of the public at large, and that some atempt should be made at a clearer definition of lineage rights.[17]

Such are some of the main principles of land-holding by lineages. A few examples will illustrate these principles.

Among the Ibo,[18] society is based on the lineage. But there is a close correlation between the territorial and kinship organization, since the various lineages composing the village or 'village-group' are, or are regarded as being, the descendants of a common ancestor. Each village-group, which numbers on an average some four or five thousand people, has its own territorial demesne, whose lay-out is such that it allows a number of villages or hamlets to live together as a single community and yet be able to expand without undue friction. This is achieved by 'zoning them around one, or more than one, central meeting-place, and at the same time giving each village the right to occupy the land extending in a specific direction away from this centre'.[19]

Among the Ibo, land falls generally into two categories: (a) houseland and (b) farmland, which form two successive zones round the group-centre—the inner zone being houseland where the people live and grow their oil palms, kolas and other economic trees, and the outer zone being the arable.[20] Each of the component villages and/or lineages has its own sector of each of these two classes of land, and each maintains a path which leads from the group-centre to the outlying farmland, and is ritually cleared each year. The farmland is cultivated on the so-called 'block-farming' system; that is to say, that every year the members of the lineage, each on his own holding, farm together over one selected sector of the lineage demesne, leaving the remaining sectors to rest under fallow.[21]

There is a distinct difference in the nature of the tenure of houseland and that of the bush farmland. In the case of the latter the individual cultivator requires particular plots for limited periods only—once every 4th, 5th, 6th or 15th year according to the rotation followed—so that it is to his advantage that the community (i.e. the lineage) should control farmland rights. In the case of houseland, however, the householder is in continuous occupation for an indefinite period and enriches the land with household refuse, besides effecting other improvements by planting and tending economic trees. Thus the ownership of houseland is vested directly in the head of the houseland and passes to his direct male descendants; while the title to farmland is vested in the community, that is to say, the lineage. But although the title to the farmland is vested in the lineage as a whole each individual householder has the right to occupy and use particular parts of the lineage farmland when the time comes to cultivate that particular sector. These farmland rights, like those of the houseland, are heritable and pass to the cultivator's immediate male relatives.[22] Should anyone fail to occupy his holding, it would revert to the community and be assigned to some other householder of the lineage. In the early stages of settlement the lineage would usually have an abundance of reserve land to meet the demands of expanding numbers and provide for adequate fallow periods; but with a steady increase in population the reserves might give out, the fallow periods be reduced and the farmland plots tend, by continuous occupation, to become assimilated to those of the homeland, and to lose their community character. In the end the corporate lineage title might amount to no more than a reversionary right to abandoned or derelict land.[23]

As regards the alienation of lineage or village lands, the rules vary with the local conditions. Where land is abundant both houseland and farmland may be freely transferred. In some areas the outright alienation of farmland to strangers may be prohibited, while in the more densely populated areas the prohibition may be extended also to farmland, and apply to the local inhabitants as well as to strangers.[24] But temporary loans of land may be given by one lineage or village to another free of charge, or in return for a rent in kind or cash. Mr. G. I. Jones cites instances of members of infertile, upland village-groups migrating each year to farm on land rented to them by lineages and villages of the less-populated and richer lowlands. The pledging of land, particularly of houseland, is also common among the Ibo. . . . Local custom may restrict the amount for which land may be pledged, thereby ensuring a fair distribution of available land. Where land is transferred outright by sale the rate charged is considerably higher than in the case of pledged land, and the transaction is invariably accompanied by the sacrifice of an animal on the land to the lineage ancestors. Many lineages sell their spare lands for as much as they can get from wealthy strangers who wish to establish plantations of oil palms or rubber. But public opinion is becoming increasingly opposed to this form of trafficking in land.

In certain progressive areas such as Onitsha, some lineages have adopted standard documentary forms based on English models for the sale and leasing of lineage lands. In the form of lease used by one of the Onitsha lineages (the Modebe) there are two noteworthy provisions, (a) that the tenant shall not assign or sublet the leased land without the consent of the lessor lineage, and (b) that at any time within 21 years from the commencement of the lease the tenant may apply for permission to purchase the leased land 'in fee simple'. A special form is used for the customary form of lease known as a 'kola tenancy'. Under this the tenant may not assign the whole or any part of the leased land without the consent of the landlord lineage, and for giving this consent the landlord shall be entitled to receive a specified proportion of the current value of the property. The tenant, moreover, must undertake to pay all taxes, rates and 'outgoings of every description to which the landlord or the tenant in respect of the land is or shall hereafter become liable'.[25]

Among the Yoruba, lineage or family ownership of land is general. But there is a notable restriction on lineage rights of disposal. Under Yoruba customary law 'tribal land cannot be alienated to anyone belonging to another tribe, except with the knowledge and consent of the king or the chief of the people or tribe which possess the land'.[26] Yoruba lineages cannot, therefore, dispose of lineage lands to members of other tribes without the permission of the Native Authorities. This rule has been given formal recognition by some Yoruba Native Authorities in bye-laws or regulations made under the Native Authority Ordinance.[27]

On the other hand it is also an axiom of Yoruba law that 'the king or chief has no power to alienate or take possession of any land, not being his own personal property, except with the consent and at the pleasure of the owner'.[28] This in turn is an assertion of the freehold character of lineage rights and a denial of any claims by Native Authorities to superior rights of 'ownership' (as distinct from rights of administrative control[29]).

As regards individual rights within the Yoruba lineage, 'every member is entitled to and enjoys the fruits derived from pieces of land apportioned to him, and he has individual rights over the said apportioned pieces of land during his lifetime. But he cannot and must not sell such property, but must bequeath it to his children'.[30] On the other hand, Mr. Ajisafe asserts that 'every member of a family or clan' (i.e. lineage) 'has his own share of family land, which must be partitioned to him, if he so desire it. But it must be proved that he is capable of working it before such partition is made'.[31]

The subject of partition is, however, more complex than this brief statement would seem to imply. As already indicated a lineage may have sub-divisions, each of which may have come to exercise exclusive rights of user over a particular section of lineage land. But exclusive rights of user may not amount to partition in the legal sense of abolition of co-ownership, and division into severalty, with independent rights of disposal. A lineage will usually postpone a legal partition of its lands as long as possible, since it is realised that ownership in common of undivided land is the most powerful means of preserving the unity and strength of the lineage.[32] Thus, though each sub-division of a lineage may have established exclusive rights of usufruct over a sector of lineage land, this may fall short of legal partition and would not entitle the sub-lineage to alienate any of its land without the consent of the lineage as a whole.[33]

But when the sub-divisions of a lineage have become so independent of each other as to establish boundaries between themselves, a demand for a formal partition of the lineage lands may arise. This can only be effected, however, by common consent. The lineage may decide on a general partition among its sub-divisions including both land and economic trees, but sometimes it may decide to partition only the arable lands, retaining collective rights over its palm-bush, and sharing the profits of sub-letting.[34] Or it may decide to grant partition to one only of its sub-sections, which had perhaps assumed an independent or defiant attitude by alienating part of its land without obtaining the necessary consent of the lineage as a whole.[35]

Under the new economic conditions whereby self-acquisition of property has become possible and common the demand for partition has extended not merely to sub-lineages but to small family units. Individuals who find that they are capable of acquiring wealth by their own enterprise and industry are naturally anxious to be free of the claims of their kinsmen. And so we find, particularly in the cocoa-growing areas, an increasing tendency towards the partitioning of lineage lands, each family unit demanding and receiving its own share, often under cover of a printed form of conveyance.[36] In other cases, however, individual members of a lineage are allowed complete freedom to plant up their allotment of lineage land with cocoa trees which become their personal property, though the lineage retains ownership of the land.[37]

It is not clear, however, how far individuals can demand partition as of right. This, no doubt, varies from district to district and would depend on whether seasonal or permanent crops were grown. In any case the consent of the lineage as a whole would be required. Many demands for partition come before the native courts, which would settle such issues according to the prevailing conditions. But a general guiding principle of the courts is whether partition would be in the interests of the lineage as a whole. In this connection it may be observed that a wise exercise of discretion in this matter by the Courts may have important effects in the control of excessive uneconomic sub-division of family lands. It should be noted, also, that the demand for partition is not always confined to lineage or family lands: it may extend also to the common lands of villages. Where there is pressure of population, the inhabitants of a village or village-group may demand that the common lands of the village be partitioned among its constituent lineages.[38]

The extent to which the partitioning of lineage lands is prevalent in any area is difficult to assess. In the Colony, with the introduction of cocoa as a commercial crop lineage lands began to be freely partitioned towards the end of the last century, and in 1912 the Secretary of the Agege Planters Union stated that 'as a rule on a man's death his children divide up his land and the share of each individual becomes his, absolutely, to do what he likes with it'.[39] In 1948 Mr. Fowler estimated that about half of the Ikeja area of the Colony was no longer under the control of the indigenous families but was the absolute property of persons of both sexes.[40] This was borne out by a survey of 3,730 acres of land which were found to comprise 426 holdings, each of which was stated to be the absolute property of an individual.[41] On the other hand, Mr. Fowler reported that 'a feature of the Ijebu form of land tenure and control in the Colony is the jealous concern for the somewhat abstract rights of the family as a whole, as opposed to those of individual members. The permanent allocation, allotment or sub-division of land is unknown, and after a man has tilled land and cultivated crops to his satisfaction, following the subsequent period of fallow, he possesses no special rights to return to the place of his labours'.[42] It is to be remembered, moreover, that individually owned property becomes, on the death of the owner (in the absence of testamentary disposition), impressed with the character of joint family property and devolves upon his heir by native custom as head of the family community.[43] In this connection it is to be noted that fraudulent claims are often made that a deceased owner of absolute property had, during his lifetime, partitioned his estate in a certain manner. But the native courts do not accept mere statements of this kind, since it is customary, when partitions are made, for formal notice to be given to the local authorities or to the Native Court.

In conclusion it may be observed that while a formal partition of lineage or family land, with the consent of all the members, confers on each unit or member an absolute property in the partitioned share,[44] the mere fact of effecting substantial improvements, such as the establishment of a cocoa plantation or the reclamation of swamp land, does not entitle an allottee of lineage land to claim absolute ownership of his allotment. This has been made clear by numerous decisions of the Colonial Courts, which have had to deal with many cases of fraudulent alienation of lineage lands by lineage members who had pretended to be fee simple owners of their allotments.[45] On the other hand it would appear that, in some areas, if an allottee of lineage land is given permission by the lineage authorities to plant his allotment with cocoa or other permanent tree crops, then he is entitled to regard his planted allotment as his own allodial property, which he can dispose of as he likes.[46] But in many communities his rights of disposal would be confined to the trees itself, the lineage retaining the ownership of the land.[47] The native law in this respect is still in a formative state. In general it is true to say that any lineage may depart from the customary procedure provided all the members of the lineage are agreed.

Summing up this discussion of lineage or 'family' lands, we may say that there are two distinct tendencies at work. On the one hand there is a widespread tendency towards the partitioning or individualization of lineage lands, particularly where those lands are suitable for the cultivation of commercial or export crops. This is a development which is generally welcomed by officers of the Agricultural Department since 'family' ownership may be an impediment to enterprise and to making the best use of land. It may be pointed out, however, that individually-owned property tends to revert to 'family' ownership within one or two generations.

On the other hand there is a tendency for lineage claims to land to become consolidated—to become proprietary instead of usufructuary, and to be extended to areas which were formerly common land or 'no-man's land'. By enclosing lands in this way lineages are, in many areas, entrenching themselves as landlords, and adopting a position analogous in some ways to the 'lords of the manor' of mediaeval England.

Finally, it is important to note that the statutory Native Authorities, and also the Regional Local Governments, have recently been clothed with extensive powers of control over lineage lands, which, if exercised, would constitute a severe curtailment of private rights of ownership. Under the Native Authority Ordinance (Cap. 140, sec. xxvii) Native Authorities have been empowered to make rules (a) 'for the control and use of communal land *and of family land* either generally or specifically and with special reference to the cultivation thereof and the type of crops which may be grown thereon'; (b) 'for the control either generally or specifically of the size and extent of communal *or family land* over which any individual or group of persons may exercise rights or may be permitted to exercise rights'; and (c) 'for the regulating of the allocation of communal land *or family land* and specifying the person or persons who may allocate such communal land, subject to such special or general directions as the Native Authority may require'.

These provisions have been embodied in the recent Eastern Regional Local Government Ordinance (No. 16 of 1950).

The attached annexe gives details of three recent decisions illustrating some of the main principles governing lineage land-holding. The *locus classicus*, however, is Amodu Tijani *v*. The Secretary, Southern Provinces, which is fully reported at pp. 77–84. Other important cases relating to 'family' land law will be found in Dr. T. O. Elias's *Nigerian Land Law and Custom*, Chapters 6 and 7.

ANNEXE

1. *Idewu Inasa* v. *Sakariyawo Oshodi*
(*A.C.* 1934 *p.* 99 *et seq.*)

In this case, which went to the Privy Council (on appeal from the decision of the Supreme Court of Nigeria), it was held that if the occupier of a dwelling (in one of the native compounds at Epetedo, Lagos) asserts a right therein inconsistent with the lawful rights of the Chief, the Chief is entitled to evict not only the offending occupier but also those of his relatives who have supported or sided with him against the Chief.

In 1862 an area of land at Epetedo was put by the Government of Lagos into the possession of Chief Oshodi Tappa for the occupation of his family, followers and slaves. Oshodi divided the area into 21 courts or compounds of which Inasa Court was one. Oshodi placed a headman in charge of each compound. Inasa, a head slave, was the headman put in charge of Inasa Court, and the other persons assigned to the court were also slaves of Oshodi Tappa. Inasa duly parcelled out the compound among these slaves, each slave being allotted a portion for the exclusive occupation of himself and his family.

In 1869 the Government of Lagos issued Government grants in respect of each of the courts. The different headmen were encouraged to take these grants in their own names. The grant in respect of Inasa Court was issued in the name of Inasa. 'It cannot be doubted', said Lord Blanesburgh, 'that this act of government was a source of misunderstanding, as each grant, on its face, purported to be a disposition in absolute terms in favour of the grantee. But it was at an early stage settled, although apparently not always accepted, that these grants were only grants in trust, and that they left the interests in the properties, whether those of the occupiers or those of the chiefs, exactly where they had been.' (The occupiers had the right to remain and to transfer their holdings to their offspring, but, in the event of the family or an occupier failing, the chief had a right of reversion.)

In 1918 Amodu, elder son of Inasa, purported by an indenture, duly registered, to sell and convey to one Alimotu a portion of Inasa Court. In 1925 Chief Oshodi sought a declaration in the Supreme Court that Amodu had lost his right, title and interest under native law and custom to the piece of land he occupied, by selling or attempting to sell it. The declaration was sought and granted on the ground that an occupier, in such a compound as that occupied by Inasa, may not sell or otherwise alienate the right of occupancy or any part of the land, nor may he assert any right inconsistent with those lawfully belonging to the Chief, who is entitled to eject any occupier for breach of such rights and re-allot his holding to others. Their lordships, in finding for the defendant, sustained this view.

2. *Oshodi* v. *Balogun*
(2 *A.E.R.* 1936)

In this case it appeared that an allottee of lineage land had purported to transfer in 1913 an absolute or fee simple interest in part of his compound without the consent of the Oshodi lineage. The purchaser claimed in 1927 to be entitled to the fee simple. *Held* that no absolute fee simple title could pass since there had been no prior consent by the chief and his family. Lord Maugham added that 'To prevent any misconception it seems desirable to state that the present decision is not based on any doubt as to the possibility of a title equivalent to a fee simple being obtained as the result of the sale of family lands with the general consent of the family . . . The Chief, as contrasted with the family as a whole, has no fee simple.'

3. *Mbelekeke* (*lineage*) *of Onitsha* v. *Madam Iyaji*
(*Supreme Court Suit No.* 4 *of* 1931)

In this case the Mbelekeke lineage of Onitsha sued the successors of one of their 'kola' tenants—Madam Iyaji (deceased). Madam Iyaji had concluded a lease or sub-lease of her 'kola' land to the Société Commerciale de l'Ouest Africain at a rental of £200 p.a. The lineage sought a declaration of title and an order that one half of the rent should be paid to the lineage.

The Court considered the followed questions:

(1) Did Madam Iyaji in fact consent to pay half the rent to plaintiffs?

(2) If she did so agree was there any consideration for the agreement?

(3) Has a landlord under the custom of Onitsha the right to receive from a 'Kola tenant' a share of the rent payable to the tenant under a sub-lease?

The Court answered the first two questions in the negative. As regards the third the Court held that the custom was not ancient or certain. Nor had the defendant given free consent. Title was granted to the plaintiff lineage, but nothing else.

Notes

[1] For further information on this subject the reader is referred to T. O. Elias, *Nigerian Land Law and Custom* (particularly pp. 105–9 and 134–171); M. M. Green, *Land Tenure in an Ibo Village* (particularly pp. 6–15); N. J. Brooke, *Some Aspects of Land Tenure in Nigeria* in *African Studies*, Dec. 1946; G. I. Jones, *Ibo Land Tenure*, in *Africa*, Oct. 1949.

[2] Sir Henry Maine, *Lectures on the Early History of Institutions* (1874), p. 72.

[3] Sir Henry Maine, *op. cit.*, p. 71.

[4] The term lineage is used by sociologists in two distinct senses, (a) the principle of reckoning descent in a single line, and (b) the living group of kinsmen so reckoned. It is in the latter sense that the term is used in this chapter.

[5] In a patrilineage a daughter's children (and in a matrilineage a son's children) may be given the use of land as an act of grace; they cannot demand it.

[6] For fuller details of the lineage organization in West Africa see C. K. Meek, *Law and Authority in a Nigerian Tribe*, or M. Fortes, *The Dynamics of Clanship Among the Tallensi* and *The Web of Kinship Among the Tallensi.*

[7] The common conception that the individual's right in lineage land is merely 'usufructuary' is, in the opinion of Dr. T. O. Elias, misleading, since this term implies rights over something belonging to another, whereas the Nigerian occupier's interest is more akin to a kind of perpetual part-ownership, free of the numerous restrictions implied by the servitude of 'usufruct'. The individual's interest is more than a life-interest since his children normally inherit; it is not a proprietary interest to the extent that he can dispose of it; and yet it is more than a mere possessory right since there is complete freedom of user. T. O. Elias, *op. cit.*, pp. 142–151.

[8] But liability to forfeiture has been modified to some extent by the Colonial Courts, by way of equity. See e.g. Chief Etim and ors. *v.* Chief Eke and ors. N.L.R. 1941, Vol. XVI, p. 43. In some cases courts (including Native Courts) have imposed fines in lieu of forfeiture.

[9] In some societies the consent of the political head of the community may be necessary to any grant of land to a stranger.

[10] Other causes for which the grant of land to an alien may be revoked are: (a) plotting against the kin of grantor; (b) plotting against the political chief to whom the grantor owes allegiance; (c) having illicit sexual relations with female members of the grantor's family or immediate kin; (d) breaking any conditions of the grant, such as interfering with economic trees belonging to the grantor lineage.

[11] For recent developments in the leasing of land by lineages to strangers, see chapters 12 and 22.

[12] But the absolute right of a lineage to dispose of its land may be limited by a rule that land may not be sold to a non-tribesman.

[13] The consent of the lineage is expressed through its properly appointed headman, who is the legal trustee of the lineage lands. For the rights and duties of the lineage head see T. O. Elias, *op. cit.*, pp. 134–141. It is not always easy, however, to determine the point at which a lineage begins and ends. One of the criteria of unity is participation in the lineage funeral ceremonies. Claims for an interest in lineage land may be set aside by the courts if it can be shown that the section or individual claiming had not taken part in, or contributed towards the expenses of, the funeral ceremonies of important members of the lineage. An example of the sale of lineage land without adequate consent of the members of the lineage will be found in Oshodi *v.* Balogun and ors. (1936) 4 W.A.C.A.; 2 A.E.R. 1632 (see Annex to this chapter). See also Adagun *v.* Fagbola 1932, 11 N.L.R. 110. It is to be noted that all the branches of a lineage must be consulted before undivided lineage property can be leased or otherwise dealt with, and that rents derived from leasing must be divided in equal shares between the respective branches. Each branch must be represented on the lineage council and is entitled to one vote only. See Lewis and ors *v.* Bankole, 1909, 1 N.L.R. 22.

[14] Sir Henry Maine, *Village Communities*, p. 112.

[15] Lewis *v.* Bankole, *Nigeria Law Reports I*, p. 83.

[16] Sir Mervyn Tew, *Report on Title to Land in Lagos*, 1939 (S.P. No. 2, 1947) para. 61. Butler-Lloyd, J. had made a similar observation in 1938 (see Bajulaiye and anor. *v.* Akapo 1938, 14 N.L.R. 10).

[17] Even in some Muhammadan areas of the Northern Provinces certain lineages are claiming absolute property rights in their land (as opposed to the normal rights of occupancy) and are supporting their claims by appeal to Muhammadan law. See e.g. C. W. Cole, *Report on Land Tenure, Zaria Province*, para. 172 and Appendix E, 74.

[18] 'The following data are derived mainly from an article, *Ibo Land Tenure*, by G. I. Jones in *Africa*, Oct. 1949. But further data relating to land-holding among the Ibo will be found in L. T. Chubb, *Report on Ibo Land Tenure*; C. K. Meek, *Law and Authority in a Nigerian Tribe*, pp. 19–42, and M. M. Green, *Land Tenure in an Ibo Village.*

[19] It is unprofitable to farm at a distance of more than a mile or two from the village. Further expansion by a village or large lineage can only be effected by absorbing the territory and usually also the members of an adjacent lineage of smaller dimensions, or alternatively by emigrating en masse to some unoccupied area. In the latter event the settlers assume ownership of the land in the vicinity of their new abode, abandoning all claim to the land they had formerly occupied.

[20] The Yourba make the same distinction between 'house or city lands' (ile) and 'farm or rural lands' (*oko*). See W.A.L.C. 1048, p. 221.

[21] It must not be supposed, however, that lineage or family lands are always held in compact blocks. There may be much fragmentation. See e.g. M. M. Green, *op. cit.* p. 7, and S. F. Nadel, *A Black Byzantium*, p. 184.

[22] In the matrilineal groups of the Cross River area land is possessed and used by males, but is transmitted through females. Thus on a man's death his land rights pass to his full brothers or sisters' sons. It is to be noted that in some matrilineal tribes, land which has been brought under cultivation by clearing virgin forest is inherited patrilineally and not matrilineally like ordinary farmland.

[23] In circumstances of land shortage individuals may acquire or be given the use of plots

belonging to neighbouring lineages or villages. Outright grants may be given by one village or lineage to another.

[24] Mr. G. I. Jones gives an interesting example of the necessity of curbing the acquisitive tendencies of local villagers, when the Government was endeavouring to stimulate the planting-up of small areas of land with improved types of oil palms. One enterprising farmer began to buy up any portions of houseland he could obtain for his purpose, until the village community intervened and prohibited any further sale of houseland.

[25] Specimens of the forms used by the Modebe lineage of Onitsha for the sale and leasing of land will be found in the Appendix to L. T. Chubb's *Report on Ibo Land Tenure*.

[26] A. K. Ajisafe, *Laws and Customs of the Yoruba People*, p. 6.

[27] See e.g. p. 196.

[28] A. K. Ajisafe, *op. cit.*, p. 6.

[29] But administrative control may go so far as to fix a maximum for rents chargeable to strangers by lineagers for the use of lands. See C. W. Rowling, *Land Tenure in Ijebu Province*, para. 104. Mr. Rowling also reported that in 1949 the Ijebu Waterside Council had made a rule banning the leasing of village or lineage lands to Urhobo strangers for farming, fishing or hunting purposes. In some Yoruba communities all sales of land must be reported to the political head of the community to whom a fee is payable. This serves as a form of registration and ensures that the land is properly identified and that all persons who may be interested are informed. It also serves to prevent the sale of land to a stranger who is unacceptable to the community. See C. W. Rowling, *Land Tenure in Ijebu Province*, para. 81.

[30] A. K. Ajisafe, *op. cit.*, p. 6.

[31] A. K. Ajisafe, *op. cit.*, p. 7.

[32] Under certain circumstances, also, the lineage lands would provide a better means of subsistence if they remained undivided. And there may be strong local prejudice against the division of ancestral land by kinsmen.

[33] It should be noted, however, that in the absence of common consent among sub-divisions, a Court may order partition or sale as the only solution to a dispute. See e.g. Giwa and ors. *v.* Otun and ors, 11 N.L.R. 160 (1934).

[34] The reason for retaining the corporate rights over the palms might be the varying density of the trees in the different sub-sections. See C. W. Rowling, *Land Tenure in Ijebu Province*, para. 55.

[35] See e.g. C. W. Rowling, *Land Tenure in Ijebu Province*, para. 57.

[36] See e.g. C. W. Rowling, *Land Tenure in Ijebu Province*, para. 59. Mr. Rowling states that a lineage may make an outright grant of land to one of its members and that this would be widely accepted by Yoruba opinion as proper. This possibility explains the large number of cases of illegal alienation of lineage lands by members of the lineage who have misrepresented their holdings as personal estates.

[37] In 1912 the Secretary to the Egba Government stated that if an individual member of a family (lineage) cleared a piece of family forest and planted it up with kola, cocoa or coffee, he established for himself an absolute property in the land, save only that he could not alienate to a non-Egba. If he were to do so, any member of the family could, by an action at law, reclaim the land from the stranger. See W.A.L.C. 1048, p. 187.

[38] See e.g. C. W. Rowling, *Land Tenure in Ijebu Province*, para. 37.

[39] W.A.L.C. 1048, p. 235.

[40] Among the Yoruba, daughters have equal claims with sons to inherit *personal* or self-acquired property (as opposed to *ancestral* property). A man may, e.g. leave a share of his cocoa plantation to a daughter (but he must be careful to make it known that he has done so).

[41] W. Fowler, *A Report on the Lands of the Colony Districts*, para. 119.

[42] W. Fowler, *A Report on the Lands of the Colony Districts*, para. 146.

[43] A discussion of this aspect of native customary law will be found in H. W. Hayes Redwar's *Comments on Gold Coast Ordinances*, p. 81. Mr. Redwar, writing in 1909, stated that in the Gold Coast 'joint family or stool property is still the *rule* and individual property the *exception*'.

[44] See 9 W.A.C.A. 78 (1943).

[45] See e.g. 5 N.L.R. 90 (1924), A.C. 881 (1927) and 11 N.L.R. 110 (1932). See also Sir Mervyn Tew's *Report on Title to Land in Lagos*, para 110.

[46] See C. W. Rowling, *Land Tenure in Ijebu Province*, para. 65. But see also para 47.

[47] While there is a general principle of personal ownership of improvements, there is also a principle that improvements do not serve as a bar to lineage claims on the land. If a member of a lineage erects on his allotment a type of building different from that for which permission had been given by the lineage head, then he may be compelled to remove the building and perhaps also to vacate the allotment altogether. Nor may an allottee of lineage land use his allotment for any abnormal purpose (such as building a shop or mosque) without special permission. See C. W. Rowling, *Land Tenure in Ijebu Province*, para. 61. It should be noted that a lineage or 'family' may grant to one of its members an allotment for trading purposes subject to a condition that the grant may be determined if the 'family' should subsequently find that it required the land for other purposes. (See Manuel *v.* Manuel 1926, 7 N.L.R. 101.)

E. Colson: The Social Organisation of the Gwembe Tonga*

Lineage and Lineage Land

The basis of land holding in the Valley is the right which each man has over the land which he has cleared. At the same time, land tenure is conditioned by the fact that the most valuable soil consists of alluvium which can be cultivated for generations without manuring, rotation, or fallow periods. Cleared land is therefore a permanent asset. In most cases the clearing of the valued alluvium took place long ago, frequently so long ago that the name of the original cultivator has been forgotten. His rights have been transmitted to his heirs, the members of his matrilineage. When a man dies in possession of a field over which he has unrestricted rights, the field is considered part of his estate. The right to claim it goes first to the member of his lineage who is invested with his shade, but all other members hold a residual right in the land. Such land is spoken of as lineage land, though the various fields are allocated to individual cultivators. A large proportion of it may be cultivated by members of other lineages, who are usually the wives, the children, or the grandchildren of lineage men. This does not affect the ultimate rights of the lineage over the fields.

Theoretically the land may not be permanently alienated from the lineage and others cultivate it only on sufferance. In actuality lineage rights do become extinguished, while at the same time the lineage may establish rights over land which formerly belonged to others. The result is that lineage land does not consist of a consolidated block of fields. Instead it is parcelled out into small holdings interspersed among those pertaining to other lineages.

For that matter, it is probable that there never were large discrete blocks of land controlled by the various lineages. Today when men are extending their cultivation into bush lands which they hope to cultivate indefinitely, fathers and sons and friends and neighbours belonging to different lineages may take up contiguous fields. Each man's rights, unless he disposes of them during his lifetime, will ultimately vest in his lineage and thus from the beginning the lineage holdings will be scattered. Presumably when the better alluvials were first brought into cultivation, men took up land in the same fashion. If so, it would have been more difficult for the lineage to maintain its claims over the scattered holdings than if these had been together in a single easily identifiable unit.

Theoretically lineages obtain rights in land only through the clearing activities of their members. A lineage cannot earmark land for future expansion. Land which has not been previously cultivated is public domain, free to the next comer. Immigrants can easily establish themselves in a neighbourhood so long as land is still available, and they thus introduce new lineages into the community. The newcomers have exactly the same rights in respect of the arable land as do the older settlers. The lineage which has *katongo* has no claim superior to that of any other and it cannot claim reversionary rights in fields which have been brought into cultivation by other lineages.

Today lineages do not hold the same amount of land, the total amount varies and so does the per capita holding. The per capita holdings in the valued alluvial fields is particularly marked. People are well aware of this, and those who had no hope of obtaining control of alluvial soils show some rancour as they complain of their position. On the whole these are newcomers, though some may be members of old lineages. These may be short of land if their number has increased, or if they have dissipated their holdings over the generations by letting them slip into the hands of children and grandchildren.

All land which the lineage claims is allocated to individual cultivators, but the cultivator's right to the land is subject to the ultimate right of the lineage. Most Valley people deny that a man or woman has any right to give lineage land absolutely to another, who is not a member of the lineage, and thus extinguish the claims upon it vesting in the lineage. For this reason, they say, a man may not sell such land nor may he give it permanently to someone of another lineage. The legal position, however, is anything but clear. There is at least one recorded sale of river land which involved the transfer of a field to a member of another lineage. The sale was contested by the kinsmen of the seller and the case was ultimately heard in the Valley Tonga Appeal Court and the matter

* E. Colson, *The Social Organisation of the Gwembe Tonga*, Manchester University Press, 1960, pp. 65–77.

was the subject of a discussion in the Valley Tonga Native Authority in 1955. According to the minutes of the meeting, the authorities agreed that river land may be sold in the chieftaincies of Chipepo, Sinazongwe and Mwemba, but that in Munyumbwe, Sinadambwe, Sigongo, and Simamba no sale is permitted. It was furthermore said that in chieftaincies where land may be sold, the holder has the right to sell for food in times of hunger and that this is frequently done. This is apparently without need to consult with other members of his lineage. At any time, land may be sold by the holder with the consent of his lineage.'[1] During field work in Mwemba and Chipepo, I found no one who claimed to have bought or sold land. Men questioned about the possibility of sale denied that it could take place. A number who had been present at the 1955 discussion in the Native Authority cited that decision as evidence that sale is not permitted. According to them the decision had been that sale of land was illegal throughout the Valley.

Sale of land may take place, but we have no independent evidence that it does. I suspect that if it does occur it is not a frequent practice though there seems no reason why sale should not occasionally take place given the shortage of land and the desire of people to build up holdings in river land.

Villages and neighbourhoods do not control arable land. The right to cultivate is not dependent upon residence in a village or neighbourhood. Men and women who have left a neighbourhood may continue to cultivate their old fields. Those who inherit lineage land in other neighbourhoods, even on the opposite bank of the Zambezi, proceed to cultivate it without change of residence. Village and neighbourhood authorities thus have no right to interfere in the disposal of fields. Only the lineage could do so. Where a man is resident in a neighbourhood where he has neither lineage mates nor other close kin, there would be no one to prevent him from selling his land. If he lives among lineage mates but these have sufficient land for their own use, again they would have no reason to block his wish to dispose of his land. These conditions are rarely met today. A man is under pressure from his lineage mates, his potential heirs, to prevent him from alienating his land. On his death, they claim the right to revoke any disposition of lineage land which he may have made during his lifetime. This is due to land hunger rather than to any belief that land is sacrosanct and must remain associated with the lineage. If none of the potential heirs wishes to use the land, there is no reason to recall it. If reclaiming the land would be likely to involve them in bitter dispute with influential men, they would think twice before pressing their claims.

The Formation and Composition of Lineages. Lineages are small unnamed corporate groups, held together chiefly by the system of inheritance and the ritual of the shades. In the past they were of importance also in the defence of person and property. It was the lineage, rather than the clan or the neighbourhood, which exacted compensation or took vengeance for an offence against one of its members. Jointly it was held responsible for its members' actions. An offended lineage might retaliate against any one of them.

The outsider finds it difficult to distinguish between lineage and clan. The same terms are applied to both. Each is commonly referred to as *luzubo* or *mukowa*, but some six to eight other words also carry both meanings. The people themselves differentiate between the two by context. If there is any ambiguity, this can be cleared up by asking whether the people concerned inherit one another's property or one another's shades. If they do, they belong to the same lineage. If they do not, then they belong only to the same clan.

Customarily, each lineage is referred to by the name of the clan of which it is a member, as Bansanje, Bakonka, Bayuni, etc. Various lineages within the clan may be further distinguished with reference to some important member. Thus the three Bakuli lineages established in CHEZIA may be called the Bakuli of Sinafwala, the Bakuli of Cheembe, and the Bakuli of Siambunda. Sinafwala and Siambunda today are the names of villages and the hereditary names of the village headmen, Cheembe is the hereditary name of the Bakuli *sikatongo*. In using the names in this context, people are not confusing lineage with locality. Some Bakuli of Siambunda live in Sinafwala, but they remain Bakuli of Siambunda and will continue to do so no matter how long they live in Sinafwala.

Valley lineages do not resemble the classical segmentary lineages common in many parts of Africa. They are small, usually with no more than thirty to forty adult members of both sexes. Lineages which have *katongo* are no bigger than the others. The various lineages found within a neighbourhood, or within a vicinage of neighbourhoods, are not bound together by any theory of perpetual kinship. Their members are usually interrelated as individuals; the lineages as units are not, except through the *silufulu* tie in Upper River region.

Lineage organization is not the same in the different regions. The Upper River lineage is an undifferentiated body which produces segments with varied rights and duties only when these are at the point of becoming completely independent lineages in their own right. Genealogical relationships, save for those which define membership within a generation, are of little importance in regulating inheritance, access to land, the control of ritual prerogatives, or any other aspect of lineage relationships. All rights pertain to the lineage as a whole rather than to various segments within it, and the lineage is usually united about two male and two female figures who hold the shades of all former members of the lineage whose names are still remembered. Segmentation is considered to be abnormal, as something that occurs because of quarrels over succession and inheritance. Once it has happened, it is quickly forgotten and the new lineages which have resulted from it do not remember their common origin.

In many respects therefore, the Upper River lineage resembles the matrilineal group of the Plateau Tonga. It differs in having institutionalized leaders who regulate the affairs of the group, and thus displays a greater degree of organization.

Undifferentiated bodies by their very nature must remain small in order to function. Upper River lineages therefore tend to be smaller than Middle River and Upland lineages within which differentiation does occur. These are divided into a number o small groups or nuclear segments of immediate kinsmen who have first claim over one another's inheritance. A number of nuclear segments combine into a major segment which usually includes those who descend from a known ancestress who may be but two generations above the oldest living people. Members of the major segment come together to discuss lineage matters, and the segment as a whole has residual rights in the inheritance of the smaller units which compose it. Finally a number of major segments join together to form the full lineage. The founding ancestress of the lineage may not be remembered, but she is asumed to be at the most two generations above the founders of the major segments. The full lineage gathers for funerals, and its members have a right to be summoned for the funeral. It has residual rights of inheritance when a major segment becomes extinct. For practical purposes today, the full lineage is of little significance though the right to inherit the shades of the ancient dead is vested in all its segments. It is the major segment and even more the small nuclear segment of immediate kinsmen which is the real focus for lineage activities.

Middle River and Upland people assume that segmentation is a normal process of lineage development, and that major segments will eventually become separate lineages as older people die and younger people forget one another. Meantime the nuclear segment will have begun to differentiate. They think that the process will occur whether or not the people remain together in the same locality, though they agree that people are more likely to forget the lineage tie with those settled in some other locality. Eventually they will forget to summon them to a funeral and this discourtesy will be reciprocated. Then they will forget one another and become simply fellow clansmen without the right to a claim on one another's wealth or land or to inherit one another's shades.

They think that the nuclear unit of close kin differentiates according to the chances of birth. If two sisters each have a number of children of both sexes, then two differentiated units will begin to form as these become adults and acquire wealth, land, and children. If one sister gives birth to an only child or to children of one sex, close ties between the two sets of children will continue to be maintained since a man can form a new unit only if he has a sister who will produce children for it, and a woman can form a new unit only if she has a brother to head it.

A young CHEZIA man belonging to a Beetwa lineage said that most of his lineage lived at KAYUNI. His mother's mother had come from KAYUNI when she married a CHEZIA man. She died after the birth of her first child, a daughter. The daughter grew up in CHEZIA and married there, and bore a number of sons and daughters. One day the young man explained, 'The people of KAYUNI are only my real lineage because my mother was born alone. If my grandmother had had other children, I would have my own mother's brother and we would have our own lineage here. Since I have no mother's brother, I still turn to those who live in KAYUNI and it seems that we are very close. Soon we will begin to forget them. I have brothers and sisters. This means that we will begin to forget our lineage in KAYUNI.' On various ritual occasions, the young man called upon members of another Beetwa lineage represented in the neighbourhood to play the role of lineage mates, but this did not mean that he considered them members of his lineage. They were only clansmen who assisted him because members of his own lineage were far away.

One of the largest lineages represented in CHEZIA was the Beetwa lineage of Lunyolo which is shown in Appendix B. A member of the lineage explained that his real lineage (i.e. his nuclear segment) consisted of the matrilineal descendants of his own grandmother but that already these people had begun to be differentiated into several smaller units. 'I have my brothers and my sisters' children and we have begun to be separate from the descendants of my mother's sister. When I die, these people may not inherit my shade. It is my brother and then my sisters' sons who will take my shade. They will also take my property. The descendants of my mother's sister will only come to mourn and to take part in the discussion at my funeral. They will be able to say very little. If they try to speak, then my brother and my sisters' children will ask them if they think that I belonged to them. They will be afraid to say very much and will only sit to listen. If I had no sisters, then I would still be close to my mother's sisters' descendants. They would inherit my shade. If my mother's sisters had no sons, then their descendants would still be very close. As it is, we have begun to separate.'

In Chapter V, where the cult of the shades is discussed, the implications of the differentiation within Middle River and Upland lineages and the lack of differentiation within Upper River lineages will become clearer. Here I wish to stress only that it exists and that it is of importance for land tenure. To all intents and purposes, lineage land in Middle River and the Uplands is divided among the nuclear lineage segments composed of immediate kinsmen. When a man speaks of lineage land, he is usually thinking of land held within this group though he may on occasion extend the term to include land held by members of all segments. If the nuclear segment becomes extinct, its rights pass to the major segment of which it formed a part. In the unlikely event that the major segment becomes extinct, then the land rights revert to the full lineage. In the Upper River region, though a man may ordinarily be in possession of lineage land which was previously cultivated by an immediate kinsman, he bases his claim not upon their relationship but upon his membership within the undifferentiated unit. When he speaks of lineage land, he means the land which the lineage as a whole controls.

When an Upper River lineage segments, each segment takes the land cultivated by its members as its share. Lineage land therefore becomes broken down into smaller units over the generations, but the attrition is relatively slow. In the meantime, there is an opportunity for inequalities in holdings to be evened out over the lineage as each member is considered to have a right to the use of lineage land. In Middle River and Upper River regions, land rights are divided with each generation. A man or woman usually can expect to receive a share in only that portion of the lineage land which is associated with his own small nuclear segment. Members of other segments will feel no obligation to share with him, though everyone is agreed that it is meritorious to share lineage land with someone within the major segment or with a more distant lineage mate if one has plenty of land and the other has only a little.

The Lutundu *and the Transfer of Lineage Land.* Members of the lineage who are in possession of lineage land have the right to allocate a portion of their holdings to wives and children, both sons and daughters, and these, unless they are slave affiliates, are always members of other lineages. When the husband and father dies, his dependants may be left in possession of their fields although the lineage has the right to recall the land. In Upper River region, this would be the undifferentiated lineage. In Middle River and the Uplands, it would probably be the nuclear segment composed of immediate kinsmen.

The sons and daughters, and the wives, have no right further to dispose of the land which they are using. They do not establish an inheritable right which gives their own lineages any claim upon it. On their deaths, the father's lineage has the right to recall the land. If the son, or daughter, has children, the lineage may be prepared to let them take the land. The lineage may also be prepared to let a man's full sisters' children have the use of land allocated to him, for these are grandchildren of the lineage. If he has neither children nor sisters' children, they then will certainly recall it, for they have no direct interest in the members of his own lineage. This was what happened when Mundyongana died in CHEZIA in 1956. He belonged to a Beetwa lineage, but his land was taken by a member of the Bakonka clan. The latter explained that the land had originally been given to Mundyongana by his father, a Mukonka, and that it now reverted to this lineage. 'Mundyongana has no children of his own. His sister's children live in another neighbourhood and do not want to come here to cultivate. We would agree to their using the land if they would come, for they too come from us. We refuse to let the other Beetwa take it.

Valley Tonga consider it reasonable for the children and grandchildren of its members to have the use of lineage land, for these form a *lutundu* attached to the lineage. Every man who leaves children founds a *lutundu* which is composed of his children and grandchildren through both sons and daughters. His great grandchildren are no longer members of the *lutundu*. They are now too distant to be included. Each *lutundu* has as its head the inheritor of the shade of its founder, and he by definition is not a member of the *lutundu* itself. He makes offerings on their behalf, either in their own homes or in an annual great offering in his own homestead at which time the whole of the *lutundu* should assemble. He also has many rights relating to members of the *lutundu*, especially over those who rank as sons and daughters. The ritual dependence of grandchildren is less, and the rights of the *lutundu* head over them are also less. He has the right to inherit a good portion of the movable estates of sons and daughters, including livestock, money, tools, and other goods. He has the right to receive a major portion of the bridewealth of any daughters and also of such fees as elopement damages paid by their lovers. He has a right to receive gifts from both sons and daughters. These rights inhere in him as the representative of their father. He receives only a token from the estates of grandchildren, a token bridewealth payment, and minor gifts. When the last son or daughter dies and the grandchildren are all mature members of the community, installed in households of their own, the *lutundu* begins to dissolve. It becomes extinct with the death of the last grandchild.

Status within the lineage is also dependent upon the inheritance of a shade. Theoretically at least, only a shade inheritor can rank as a senior mother's brother. He receives much of the lineage's share in the bridewealth of its female members. He also is the one to make offerings to the shade on behalf of the other lineage members. Control over lineage affairs therefore is largely vested in men who are also *lutundu* heads. These have every incentive to encourage members of the *lutundu* to remain close at hand. The privilege of using lineage land helps to bind them to the neighbourhood. It also stresses their dependence upon the *lutundu* head and ultimately upon the lineage. Meantime the rights of the lineage in such land are safeguarded by the ritual office of the *lutundu* head. Members of the *lutundu* are wary of offending him lest he refuse to offer to the shade of the founder which is usually the spirit guardian of their households.

In Middle River and the Upland regions, each small division within the lineage is likely to have its own *lutundu* or *matundu* (pl.) attached to it. In the Upper River region, each lineage has usually only two *matundu* unless it is at the point of segmenting into independent bodies. The season for this difference will be discussed in Chapter V which deals with the cult of the shades.

No lineage can dominate a neighbourhood through its power over its *matundu*. Its own members are also members of *matundu* attached to the other lineages represented in the area. Since each person is usually a member of three *matundu*, one attached to his father's lineage which is the most important and one attached to the lineage of each grandfather, there is a close interlocking of the various groups composing a neighbourhood community. A *lutundu* head may well be subordinate as a son or grandson to a lineage mate of one of those whom he is trying to dominate. On occasion, he even finds himself under a member of his *lutundu*. Munasaka and Sikafulo, two rivals for power within CHEZIA, found themselves in this position. In one of their clashes, Munasaka asked, 'Do you forget that I am your father?' Sikafulo answered, 'No, and do you forget that I am your grandfather?' Munasaka was the inheritor of the shade of Sikafulo's father; Sikafulo had inherited the shade of Munasaka's mother's father. Each was a member of a *lutundu* headed by the other and neither could push his advantage too far.

A lineage feels no responsibility for its great grandchildren who no longer belong to its *matundu*. It feels no obligation to provide these with land. If it did, it would have no ritual authority to compel restoration of the fields if these were needed for its own members. Theoretically, land used by *lutundu* members should return to the lineage with the death of the grandchildren. By this time years have elapsed and memory of the original source of the land may well have grown dim especially if the grandchildren have lived to a great age. For years they will have spoken of the land as having come to them from the previous cultivator, who will be either a father, a mother, or a mother's brother. If the shade of the grandfather no longer has an inheritor, there may be no one within the lineage who has a clear claim to the land. This is especially likely in the Middle River and Upland regions, where by now the original land-holding nuclear segment will have differentiated into several distinct groupings. Under these circumstances, the lineage of the grandchild will probably claim the land and there will be no one to gainsay them. In this way land passes from one lineage to another, into the hands of people of a different clan.

It is assumed that if land can be inherited by a lineage member then it must be lineage land. The burden of proof rests upon possible contestants to show that it originally came from another source. One CHEZIA man in describing his holdings said, 'I have five river fields which came to me from my mother and father which they received from her father. But I think they must really have come to her from her mother's mother. Otherwise on the death of my mother's father the fields would have been taken away by his lineage.'

Land originally obtained from fathers or by new clearing come to swell the land resources of the lineage. At the same time the old holdings are dispersed into the hands of children and their descendants. Over the years a lineage may continue to claim approximately the same acreage, but the actual fields of which this is composed may be very different. The fields slowly circulate through the hands of the various established lineages. Some of them may eventually become lineage land pertaining to newly established units founded by the children of alien women.

Once all alluvial land within a neighbourhood has been pre-empted, it becomes difficult for a new lineage to be introduced from outside, unless its members are satisfied to cultivate bush land. Intraneighbourhood marriages are encouraged, since the family unit then has access to land vested in the lineages of both husband and wife and also in their fathers' lineages. When a woman marries into a neighbourhood, her children have no lineage land of their own. The land allocated to them by their fathers is rarely enough to make them self-sufficient. They may be able to remain within their father's neighbourhood, especially if they marry there, but they will not be able to attract other kinsmen to settle with them. They will not have land to share with their children, and they have no prospect of improving their position in the future. If they marry members of established lineages, these will have fields from their own kinsmen. The children of the sons of an immigrant woman will then belong to land-holding lineages, but the children of her daughters will still have claims to land only as members of *matundi* and this will remain true until the basis of their tenure is finally forgotten. It therefore takes several generations for a new lineage to obtain any land base within a neighbourhood and even then it is likely to be a minimal one.

Valley Tonga disclaim any rule of uxorilocal or avunculocal residence. They think it good for children to live with their fathers and to remain within the father's neighbourhood as adults. Nevertheless, children of an intraneighbourhood marriage are under some pressure to return to their mother's home where they have access to lineage land or to emigrate from the Valley. With the expansion of bush gardens in the last ten years this pressure has been eased in the Middle River region, for during this period the ambitious man could obtain sufficient land for his needs. In the Upper River region, where land pressure is still extreme, the balance between lineage and *lutundu* is most rigorously maintained.

Note

[1] Anon., 1956, p. 176.

T. O. Elias: The Nature of African Customary Law*

The Chief as Family Head with Respect to Land

Let us note from the outset that the chief's role with regard to his own family land differs in no material respect from that of any other head of an ordinary family or extended family. It will, therefore, be convenient to describe the two together here; what follows then applies to both, so that much of what has just been said for the chief as the administrator of the land of the whole community equally applies to the chief considered as a head of a household. But, because chieftaincy and headship of a family do not often or necessarily coincide, there are a certain number of features in the land arrangement which are peculiar to the family head as such. We will for that reason proceed to give a brief description of these features.

A distinction must be made between town and country lands. Let us consider the latter first, as being more instructive from the point of view of the indigenous system.

Farmlands. In the village or rural areas, the family head (who is not also a chief) usually has the right to take any as yet unappropriated land in his district as family property, or he may ask his chief for additional land rendered necessary by the requirements of an expanding family. He would report to his chief or to the Emir or Oba the fact of any self-acquired land in order both to secure the chief as witness to the acquisition and to advertise the same to the community at large. The extent of the acquisition would depend upon the immediate needs of the family concerned but with due regard to the possible claims of others.

Where a family head requires land not for members of his household but for strangers (that is, people who are not native to the soil of the particular area),[1] he cannot take unappropriated land without the prior consent of the chief. The practice has almost always been that strangers would attach themselves to an influential person with whose family they would normally have been lodging for some period prior to a formal request being made on their behalf by their host. The head of the 'stranger' group could not normally go direct to the chief whose consent would often be given provided these conditions are satisfied: (1) the stranger should be of good report, (2) he should be ready and willing to obey the accepted social norms of the adoptive group and (3) he should have respect for and loyalty to the head chief as well as the elders of the community. Land so granted is held by the strangers in perpetuity in exactly the same way and subject to the like conditions of customary tenure as bind the members of the owner-occupiers themselves. The land rights and duties of the head of an adopted family or group are generally the same as those of any other head in the adopting group.

On important festive occasions the head of a land-owning family makes voluntary gifts of farm produce—yams, corn, palm-oil, palm-wine, gin, firewood and the like—to which all members of the family (including strangers on the land) would contribute, to his immediate administrative superior, the chief, who in turn would make similar presents to the supreme head—the Oba or Emir. Although the rendering of these services has never been obligatory, yet it has often been carried out for no other reason than that it is prudent to ensure the goodwill of the chief and of the Oba under whose rule the occupier lives.

A family head is, however, not customarily entitled, as is a chief, to regular presents of produce from members *per se*, although every member owes a social duty to help with the special economic requirements of the autonomous household on proper occasions. On the other hand, a family head, but not a chief, is in a stronger position to take over or re-allocate lands of adopted strangers on the ground of long non-user. It is doubtful whether he can turn such strangers out of the family land previously allocated to them simply on the ground of the subsequent needs of members of his own family. Where the strangers' original occupation was understood to be temporary, it would seem that ejectment could be effected after a reasonable notice to quit. But where the intention at the time of the first grant by the family head was that the strangers should become part and parcel of the 'host' family, the occupation being then less precarious could not be easily disturbed without a very good cause shown. The grant of *virgin* land to strangers confers on them a rather more secure occupancy on the whole than does one of cultivated

* T. O. Elias, *The Nature of African Customary Law*, Manchester University Press, 1956, pp. 105–109.

land. Whereas strangers may often plant permanent crops or reap palm trees on the former, they usually cannot do so on the latter.

It remains to add that, where the family land is plentiful and members of the family are yet too young and/or impecunious to receive and work separate allotments of their own, the family head is sometimes responsible for equipping these dependent members with farming tools and has, therefore, to provide them with the necessaries of life, if not also with its amenities, even such as they are under local conditions.

In disputes among family members about sharing farm produce like palm trees, as well as in cases of doubt as to the size and extent of individual holdings, the family head acts as referee. He also represents his family in all land cases whether against another family of the same community or against any other third party (including the Government of Nigeria).

Townlands. As regards town areas, the position is, with minor variations, generally the same as in country districts. The main consideration here centres round the family house —usually a compound—sometimes a rectangular cluster of houses (as in many Yoruba urban and quasi-urban areas), sometimes a circular one (as in the normal Northern areas), but always a gateway leading into the hollow centre. This compound idea is not now universal, especially in urban areas under the impact of new economic and psychological factors tending towards a partial break-up in traditional family life.

Excluding for the present a consideration of the detailed rules of inheritance according to which one has ultimately to settle who should be family head, it is sufficient to say here that heads of families are usually males but, in certain circumstances such as the absence of a senior male member or kin, females can be and are sometimes made family heads.

The primary duties of a family head briefly are: (*a*) the allocation and re-allocation of rooms to members of the household, for which, of course, no rents are payable, (*b*) the general supervision of the whole compound or house with regard to its proper use during the life-time of the individual occupiers, (*c*) the execution of major repairs due to fair wear and tear, including where applicable the painting, decoration and other worthwhile improvements, (*d*) the care of the younger members of the household and the provision for them of suitable accommodation within the precincts of the compound or house until they are old enough to have separate rooms of their own, either allotted to them on attaining majority if there are vacant rooms available then, or built by themselves (i) as additions to the main house or compound and (ii) independently of the latter should they decide at any time to set up house on their own. Where the family is sufficiently well-to-do, the family head (especially if he is also the founder or father of the household) often shoulders the responsibility of providing these extensions to the household at his own expense. In such a case, also, the head sometimes indulges in periodic acts of charity to the poor and even to strangers on temporary sojourn with the family.[2] Practice, however, varies from place to place, and it may be that a family head in some places will sometimes do more and sometimes less than what has been stated above.

The admission of non-members to this sort of compound depended on the strangers' good behaviour and amenability to the discipline and general well-being of the household. It did not entail the payment of tribute as in the case of similar occupation of farm-land. On the contrary, the privilege of being allowed to build rooms for himself therein usually secured to the stranger a measure of permanence which formed a kind of bulwark against arbitrary eviction by the family head.

Where, in such cases, eviction was justifiable, no compensation was paid in the case of the simpler types of mud-walled and thatch-roofed houses, but it would appear that, with respect to modern solid buildings, reasonable compensation should be payable to the evicted occupier. Mere temporary failure to occupy and use his rooms would not work a forfeiture. A clear intention to abandon must be shown before the family head could give the vacated rooms to others.

If a non-member was permitted to build a house in the space around the usual compound, as distinct from being allowed to build additional rooms within the compound itself, the family head could not usually evict him because of an ordinary quarrel between the host and the guest, nor could the head evict him for minor misconduct. If he became a positive nuisance to the 'host' family, the head chief and his council of elders would have to step in and expel such an undesirable member of the community.

But, in this instance, compensation was normally paid for all the *separate* buildings he might have erected, even if built of mud and thatch.

Notes

[1] Ward Price's definition of 'stranger' is: A stranger is a person who is: (*a*) Not a native by birth of the community. (*b*) One who does not wish to occupy communal land 'with the same rights and subject to the same obligations as are enjoyed by or imposed upon members of such community by the native law and custom regulating the rights and obligations of such members in relation to the lands occupied by them.'—para. 185 of *Land Tenure in Yorubaland.* But note and compare para. 253, *ibid.*

[2] Local idea of hospitality almost invariably dictates that the board and lodging of strangers on temporary stay with a family should be free. This is a universal practice in Nigeria. It may be that new economic standards might alter it in the course of time.

H. Cory and M. M. Hartnoll: Customary Law of the Haya*

Family Tenure

Kibanja-kioruganda. This name is given to a plantation under family tenure. Kibanja kioruganda can be acquired by inheritance only and every plantation which is inherited from a relative becomes Kibanja kioruganda.

Rights and duties of the owner. The plantation is vested in one member of the family as owner whose disposition of it is restricted by the rules of family tenure only.

NOTE: If the family has been legally disinherited, the man who gets the plantation is the unrestricted owner but his children, when they inherit it, have to follow the rules of family tenure.

Sale. The owner may not sell or give away the plantation without the consent of the members of his paternal family.

NOTE: A family consists of:

1. Near Relatives. These relatives are called abakwatane (to possess property in common). All descendants of a common paternal ancestor in the male line may become near relations, because near relationship depends not on the closeness of blood relationship but on how many of the intermediate links are alive or dead. Thus the conception of near relationship is fluctuating; e.g. two men with a common great-grandfather would not consider themselves near relatives if intermediate links were alive, but if these were all dead they would become near relatives.
2. Distant relatives. All member of one clan.
3. Milango. All descendants of a common ancestor on the maternal side.

It is noteworthy that although the relatives of a man's wife have no legal rights, their influence is considerable. The relationship between a husband and his relations-in-law is as a rule very friendly and when necessary his children are frequently put in the care of their maternal relatives. A man often prefers a relative of his wife as his trustee to his own brother because he and his own relatives have too many common legal rights in family questions which may lead to dissension.

Paternal relatives have the right of pre-emption.

QUOTATION: P.C.'s appeal No. 4 of 1938.
D.O.'s appeal No. 2/P1/ of 1937.

Kaijage v. *Lukiagabo*

Kaijage claimed that on the death of his uncle it was held in Court that the plantation of the deceased became the property of the Bahinda clan and that Lukiagabo should have the use of it. The latter sold the plantation and the relatives objected to the sale. It was held that the relatives must be given the first refusal but that if they did not wish to purchase the land the sale could stand.

* H. Cory and M. M. Hartnoll, *Customary Law of the Haya*, Lund Humphries for the International African Institute, 1945, pp. 136–143.

QUOTATION: D.O.'s appeal No. 23 of 1937.

Lubere v. *Muganda*
Lubere and Muganda were brothers. Lubere sold a plantation which he held under Kibanja kioruganda tenure and when Muganda wished to redeem it he refused to agree. The Chiefs Appeal Court held that under the terms of the tenure the relatives must be given the right of pre-emption, and mentioned that it is important that a plantation under family tenure should remain in the family.

This right can only be exercised by the nearest relative available.

NOTE: The same applies to inheritance, guardianship and all matters in which family rights are concerned.

EXAMPLE: Should a man who lives in Ihangiro and has no relatives there sell his plantation, any member of his clan, even from another chiefdom, has the right to redeem the plantation by repaying the purchase price to the buyer. This clan member must first prove his right by proving his relationship which he does by naming all his ancestors back to the common one. Naturally such claims are seldom brought forward as it is unusual for a man to wish to buy land far away from his home.

A man must inform his nearest paternal relatives before he undertakes any transaction with an outsider with regard to his land.

If a sale is made without reference to the family. Should the relatives concerned not have been informed that a transaction has taken place they have the right to invalidate the sale by bringing an action against the vendor, who must then return the purchase price he received, or allow the relatives to do so if he cannot find the money.

NOTE: The following procedure is sometimes adopted by people who, perhaps from a sense of personal grievance, wish to exclude their next-of-kin from exercising the right of pre-emption. The would-be seller arranges with a buyer a price for the sale of his plantation; at the same time he informs the buyer that officially he will say that the buyer has offered him a much higher price so that the relatives will forego their rights. Such negotiations may lead to litigation between buyer and seller.

The plantation is thus returned to the family and becomes the property of the man who repays the purchase price.

Should the vendor have died or cannot be found, the relatives may take action against the buyer, who must return the land on the payment of the price he paid for it.

The buyer is entitled to compensation for any improvements he has made.

QUOTATION: D.O.'s appeal No. 1/P1/42 of 1938.

Matayo v. *Sospater*
It was not quite clear whether Sospater, who objected to the sale of a plantation under family tenure, had had notice of the sale or not. The court ruled that in any case the sale was void and allowed Sospater to repay the buyer the purchase price plus compensation for wages paid by the buyer for the making of improvements to the plantation, after which Sospater was allowed to take possession of the plantation.

Rights of the buyer. The buyer has the right to harvest all seasonal crops which were planted by him.

The buyer has no right to the coffee harvest. Any coffee he has already harvested need not be returned but beans still on the trees are not his property.

Rights of the original owner. At any time the original owner or his direct male descendants have the right to claim the return of the plantation from the relative, or the descendants of the relative who redeemed it, on payment of the redemption price. Any hardship to the present occupier incurred by his dispossession is not considered.

NOTE: For this reason relatives who have only a vague right to interfere will not do so.

Time limit for relatives to declare a sale void. The only time limit for the institution of proceedings to nullify a sale is that they must be instituted within 3 months of the date on which the relatives first heard of the sale.

An interested relative, who was absent at the time of the sale, is entitled to take action whenever he returns, provided he does not delay doing so more than 3 months after his return.

NOTE: A relative who lives in the same village must take action within 3 months of the sale since it is assumed that he must have heard of it when it took place.

Should a man sell his plantation with the consent and in the presence of his relatives, and subsequently a nearer relation or one of the same degree who is not a party to the sale, demands its return he is entitled to do so, if he can pay the price received for the plantation.

NOTE: The practical consequence of this law is that a lawful buyer will insist on the presence of the vendor's nearest available relative as witness to the sale. Should a buyer have omitted this precaution the sale is probably suspicious and he can only expect any consequences that may arise from his omission.

Under no circumstances may an heir or a guardian sell a plantation so long as he has maintenance duties towards female dependants of the deceased.

Pledge. A plantation under family tenure may be pledged, but any relative may at any time, even in the absence of the owner, redeem it.

If a relative does so, the payment of the money does not give him possession of the plantation. The redemption money is due to him as a common debt by the owner.

If the plantation has been pledged on the condition that it will become the property of the creditor failing the repayment of the debt within an agreed time, a relative has the right to redeem it, even after the time limit has expired, as an invalid sale; in which case it follows that the plantation becomes the property of the man who redeems it.

If a pledged plantation is auctioned to repay debts, no relative is entitled to take action for redemption against the buyer.

Loss of Kibanja Kioruganda. A man cannot be dispossessed on account of neglect of his plantation.

(The Chief of Ihangiro states that a man can be dispossessed if he leaves a plantation and it is neglected.)

The presumptive heir to a plantation has no legal means of forcing the owner to keep it in good order.

Absentee owner. A man cannot be deprived of the ownership of a plantation if he leaves it and settles elsewhere in a known domicile.

If a man leaves his plantation and his new abode remains unknown for any length of time, the clan council has the power to appoint another clan member to look after the plantation.

NOTE: It seems that in former times, up to the war of 1914–1918, the plantation of a man could in these circumstances be re-allocated by the Chief.

QUOTATION: P.C.'s appeal No. 15 of 1935.

Marko v. *Mulaki*

It was stated by the court, 'It seems that at that time (1914) a Chief could dispossess a man without giving a reason, but that it was rarely done.'

If a man before he left appointed a trustee (musigire) who neglects the plantation, nothing can be done since he is responsible to no one but the owner; but if the trustee gives up his trusteeship then the clan council can exercise its rights and put in a caretaker.

When the absentee owner returns the plantation must be handed over to him; the man appointed by the clan council to care for it during his absence can claim no compensation and the owner can claim no account of the proceeds.

When the absentee owner returns he must make his claim for the return of his plantation within a reasonable time of first hearing that another man is in occupation of it.

QUOTATION: D.O.'s appeal No. 34 of 1935.
Judgement of Governor's Appeal Court, 11.9.35.

Marco v. *Chief Lwaijumba*
Marco left the Bukoba district in 1912 and went to Zanzibar. He left his plantation in the care of his aunt. When she died the predecessor of Chief Lwaijumba re-allocated the plantation. Marco returned to Bukoba about 1925; he brought a case before the Lukiko Kabale for the return of his plantation, which he lost. He did not appeal to the District Officer, but Chief Lwaijumba is said to have promised to give him another plantation. Marco did no more until 1934 when he revived his old claim, giving as his reason for doing so that he never received the other plantation which was promised him. He lost his case in all courts. It was held that he had delayed his claim without giving reasonable grounds for so doing.

NOTE: The Provincial Commissioner in the case quoted gives an explanation of what should be understood by 'a reasonable time'. He says 'I can understand a man seeing another in what he considers to be wrongful occupation of his land not bringing an action for one season. He might say he would wait for the end of the agricultural season before doing so, so that he may enter before the beginning of the next'.

If no one can be found among the clan members who is willing to tend the plantation until the return of the owner it becomes the common property of all clan members as kisi kioruganda.

Should a plantation under family tenure be re-allocated by the Chief to a man of another clan, the clan is entitled to object to the allocation provided that it puts forward its claim within 6 months of the new owner taking possession. This time limit does not prejudice the rights of the original owner who may make his claim on his return; it refers only to the claim of the clan itself.

Rweya rwa Luganda. This name is given to a piece of open land under family tenure. It is vested in one member of the family who has disposition over it restricted by the rules regarding land under family tenure.

NOTE: The same name is given to open land communally owned by a clan.

Rweya Rwa Luganda of this kind can only be acquired by inheritance.

Every Rweya which is inherited becomes rweya rwa luganda.

Rights and Duties of an Owner. Rweya Rwa Luganda is usually part of the unit of a Kibanja Kioruganda and therefore is under the same rules.

Kisi kio ruganda. The kisi of a kibanja kioruganda is a kisi kio ruganda and is under the rules applying to kibanja kioruganda.

Chapter 16

THE NATURE OF RIGHTS IN LAND

One of the most important and difficult aspects of the study of African land law is that of discovering what rights, powers, privileges, immunities and duties a person—whether an individual or a group—may exercise in relation to land. This forms the subject-matter of the present chapter, which opens with a detailed analysis by *Elias* of the juridical nature of the rights of *individuals*. The next extract is a description, by *Beattie*, of the Kibanja system of land tenure in Bunyoro, which contains an interesting historical account of the development which has taken place in the evolution from the traditional to the present system. *Sheddick*, who follows, stresses the 'usufructuary' character of all rights (whether 'public, private or extraneous') which may be possessed. *Lloyd*'s treatment of 'family land' among the Yoruba commences with a description of the way in which this category of land is created and proceeds to discuss the rights in it which are held by groups and by individuals as well as the ways in which these rights are extinguished. The chapter concludes with a useful short account by *Gayer* of the respective rights enjoyed by the individual, the family and the community in relation to land.

T. O. Elias: Nigerian Land Law and Custom*

A. The Juridical Nature of the Rights of Individuals in Land

The right of an occupier to his land under the customary tenure of land is usually described as 'usufructuary' but this term, though convenient and hightly suggestive, is not very accurate. For, whereas the Roman usufructuary normally enjoyed only a species of *jus in re aliena* (i.e. right over the land of another) and was in any case bound to return his holding unimpaired to the *dominus* of the land as the end of a fixed period or at his death, the Nigerian occupier's[1] interest in or right over the land of his community or family partakes of the nature of part-ownership enjoyable, at least in theory, in perpetuity and not subject to many of the pettifogging restrictions[2] which were the inevitable incidents of any form of servitude such as was a usufruct.

The very early development of the conception of *absolute* ownership of land in Rome, in contrast with the Greek idea of *relative* ownership,[3] makes the Roman usufructuary a strange bed-fellow of the Nigerian occupier; the latter's interest is not, as was invariably that of the usufructuary, in any sense alien to the ultimate ownership of the land. The Nigerian occupier's rights are indeed relative with respect to those of the other members of the family whose welfare, which is the community's, is the only limiting factor.

The more detailed analysis which we are about to attempt will, it is hoped, bring out more clearly the technical inaccuracy of describing the Nigerian occupier of land as a usufructuary, from whom he is, of course, at first scarcely distinguishable.

An attempt to delimit the exact scope of the rights of the individual in the family land is at once fraught with the difficulties inherent in the very nature of the hitherto largely undifferentiated complex of land rights. Now, if one grants that the normal occupier is not strictly a usufructuary of the land, the question is: What, then, is he? We have to examine *four* closely integrated questions:

* T. O. Elias, *Nigerian Land Law and Custom*, Routledge & Kegan Paul, 1953, pp. 142–158.

(A) Does he hold a separate and individual share or an 'undivided share'[4] in the family land allotted to him? This naturally involves the further and related question as to whether his interest is *real* or *personal* property.

(B) Is his right to the land a pure *life interest*, or is it *hereditary*?

(C) Can his title be regarded as really *proprietary* or as merely *possessory*?

(D) Or, in terms which English law has made familiar, shall we consider him as enjoying a joint tenancy or a tenancy in common?

Now, under the traditional system land could in the first place be acquired by an individual in one of four ways:

(i) A man might have taken some yet unappropriated land for himself;

(ii) He might, as a welcome stranger to a land-owning family, have been granted land by the head of the family, subject to the latter's right of reverter;

(iii) It might be an out-and-out gift to him of virgin land by a family having more land than it actually needed; or

(iv) A man might, as a member of a family, inherit a share of family land, the ownership being of course still in the family.

Also, town-land for building purposes might often be given outright to an individual, whether or not he was a stranger. To our list may be added the type of interest acquired by an individual on a partition of a formerly jointly-owned land.

But, in every case, at the death of the original grantee the land would at once become family land in the hands of his children and other relations. Even when land has been acquired by an individual in fee simple under English forms of conveyance, it has been held that such land became, with respect to his children, family land on the death of the owner, testate or intestate.[5]

It is at this point, then, that we are confronted with the basic problem of finding out the precise legal nature of the rights of the individual in the family land. Unfortunately, the requirements of social cohesion implicit in the kinship basis of tenure have obscured or obviated the need for a clear formulation of principles regarding the rights of the individual in land. So long as every member of the group had enough land for the limited needs of a subsistence economy, which used to rule and still largely rules the indigenous system of tenure, the older generations of Nigerians did not trouble themselves overmuch about any abstract theories of the nature of individual rights.

We have, therefore, to fall back upon such principles as can be extracted from judicial decisions if we are to formulate any reasonably intelligible rules according to modern notions and usage. Let us now try to consider the four problems we have posed above by reference to their judicial treatment.

The earliest important case is *Lewis & ors.* v. *Bankole*,[6] where a man, Mabinuori, having acquired certain plots of land about 1868 died in 1874, leaving twelve children the eldest of whom was a woman although the oldest son, Fagbemi, succeeded their father as the family head in their father's house. There were three pieces of land forming the estate of Mabinuori. Fatola, Oduntan and Odubi, three of these original twelve children of Mabinuori, had been granted some adjacent land and houses (later known as Fatola's Compound) by their father during his life, while the other children lived with him in the main residence (the Mabinuori Compound) up to his death; also, some members of the branch families of the three children living apart from Mabinuori had later been allotted houses and rooms in the main building. The children of these three children of Mabinuori as plaintiffs contended that (1) Mabinuori Compound was family property to which all the descendants of Mabinuori were equally entitled, and (2) they (the plaintiffs) had (i) a right to be consulted before the family compound was leased or otherwise dealt with; (ii) a right to share in any rents or profits accruing from dealings with the family compound; (iii) a right to build on any unoccupied part of the family compound; and (iv) a right of ingress and egress. In short, they claimed as grandchildren to be entitled to the joint-ownership of the land in dispute as tenants in common having equal shares[7] with the defendants, direct children of Mabinuori, who, on the other hand, asserted, by reason of the fact that they had always resided with their father in the compound, a claim to something analogous to individual ownership of their several allotments which they had enjoyed for over thirty years before action was brought.

Speed, Acting C.J., in refusing in the Divisional Court to 'throw the property into the melting pot of an acrimonious family feud', favoured the defendants' claim to individual absolute ownership of their allotments in the Compound, and held: 'On the ground therefore that by tacit mutual arrangement and acquiescence of all parties extending over a number of years these various properties have been separated and come to be considered as separately owned, I find on this issue in favour of the defendants.'[8] The plaintiffs appealed to the Full Court which reversed this decision, remitting the case to the Divisional Court to take fuller evidence of Lagos law and custom and then either give a fresh judgment or state a case for the opinion of the Supreme Court.

At the resumed Divisional Court hearing on 29 June 1909, White-Capped Chiefs Ojora, Eletu Odibo, Oloto and Onitana and war-chief Ashogbon gave evidence as expert witnesses.[9] Osborne, C.J., then held, with reference to the issues with which we are here immediately concerned, that: (1) all the branches of the Mabinuori family had a right to be consulted before family property could be leased or otherwise dealt with; (2) rents from a lease should be divided in equal shares between the respective branches, regard being had to property received by any of the founder's children during his lifetime; (3) the different branches of the founder's family would be represented *per stirpes* on the family council, each branch having one vote; (4) grandchildren of the founder, the plaintiffs in this case, had no inherent right to build in the family compound without the prior consent of the family council; (5) normally, members of a family who do not reside on the family property have no general right of ingress and egress, but have a right of entry to attend family meetings, and, if members of the family council, a right of entry to inspect the state of repairs; such rights must, however, be exercised so as not to interfere unnecessarily with the quiet enjoyment of the occupants.

Two important principles we may deduce from this interesting case are (1) that the grandchildren of a founder of a family do not in Yoruba-land usually enjoy the exact plenitude of rights in family land which his immediate children have; (2) that the individual allottee of family land enjoys anything but an absolute fee simple estate in his holding. This latter principle would seem to have been the basis of the decision of the West African Court of Appeal when in *Oshodi* v. *Balogun & ors.*[10] it was held that no absolute estate in fee simple could pass to a purchaser for value to whom part of the Oshodi Chieftaincy family had been conveyed by a descendant of a domestic in the Oshodi Compound. It was pointed out that the same result would follow if the conveyance had been by any other member of the family, since no individual allottee of family land has an absolute fee simple in his share.

It will be observed that in *Lewis* v. *Bankole* the main issue was the determination of the rights of *non-resident* grandchildren of the founder of the family in the family house. We must supplement our information there with a brief reference to the almost identical findings on the rights of *resident* members *per se* in *Thomas* v. *Thomas & anor.*[11] where, in an action between members of a family for sharing rents of leased portions of the family house, Butler Lloyd, J., in the Supreme Court held as follows: 'Now so far as I can gather from the existing decisions, the rights of members of a family with regard to a family house are (1) to reside in it; (2) to have reasonable ingress and egress; (3) to have a voice in its management; and (4) to share in any surplus of income derived from it after necessary outgoings have been met; and if these rights are infringed they can come to this Court which will enforce them by partition and/or sale if necessary.'[12] The two main additions to our present knowledge appear to be: (*a*) the individual member's right of residence and (*b*) his right to apply to the Court for partition or sale. We shall take each of these points in turn.

Right of Residence. As to the right of residence we may quote two illustrative passages from two other decisions:

Thus observed Tew, J., in *Ricardo* v. *Abal*:[13] 'Each party so interested has *the right to live* on the property and the right to come to the Court to ask for partition (see *Lopez* v. *Lopez*, 5 N. L. R. 47) and that is the whole extent of his or her individual interest. That interest would pass to his or her children under native law and custom, but in no case to anyone who was not of the same blood, and consequently not to his or her wife or husband.'

And Kingdon, C.J., in *Adagun* v. *Fagbola*:[14] 'When the head of a family allots to a member of the family a portion of the family land for him to live on, that member becomes entitled to occupy and enjoy that portion during good behaviour, but he does not become the owner of the land as against the family and he cannot alienate it without the consent of the family.'

Thus, in *Miller Bros.* v. *Ayeni*,[15] the appellants sought to attach the interest of the respondent judgment debtor in certain family property, and the latter's brothers successfully resisted the appellants' claim on the ground that their brother had no separate and alienable interest in the family property which the appellants could seize in satisfaction of their debt. Van der Meulen, J., delivering the judgment of the Supreme Court, observed that although their father had bought the land under a conveyance of 6 October 1899, yet on his death intestate the children held undivided shares in common under local customary tenure, and *not* as tenants in common under English law.[16]

A similar result was reached on substantially the same facts by Berkeley, J., in the Supreme Court decision of *Majekodunmi* v. *Amodu Tijani*[17] where the learned judge emphasised: 'There is nothing to show that these allotments were intended to or did create a separate and alienable estate in the persons to whom they were allotted. . . . In the course of his evidence he (the plaintiff) stated that some of the family land remained unallocated. But this in itself is sufficient to show that no partition has taken place, but merely a series of allotments for occupation according to native custom.'[18]

The point of difference between tenancy in common by English property law and the customary common tenancy of local tenure was well brought out in *Caulcrick* v. *Harding & anor.*[19] The facts were that the plaintiff, as the husband of one of the three daughters of a deceased intestate, claimed a one-third share of the land in virtue of his wife's right, although the wife had since died. Tew, J., held that the father's death intestate created a customary common tenancy by which no one member had any separate estate apart from the whole: 'The plaintiff's claim is really based on the argument that Agnes Caulcrick could have disposed of her one-third interest in the property by will, and that, as she died intestate, this interest passed as personalty to the plaintiff. This argument is entirely fallacious for it rests on the assumption that the three daughters of Labinjoh were tenants in common in the meaning which that term has in English law.'[20] The learned Judge then cited *Miller Bros.* v. *Ayeni*[21] as authority for the proposition that 'a tenancy in common was a tenure unknown to native law', and concluded: 'The customary tenure recognised by native law and custom as arising in such a case has not the essential characteristics of a tenancy in common strictly so-called, in that it gives no right of alienation.'[22]

For this reason, Butler Lloyd, J., held in the Supreme Court judgment of *George & anor.* v. *Fajore*[23] that, where a testator devised his land to twelve named persons 'their heirs and assigns for ever *as tenants in common*[24] without any power or right to alienate or anticipate the same or any part thereof', the use of the words 'tenants in common' did not alter the fact that the testator intended the property to be held in accordance with local customary law of tenure, so that the defendant in the case, the testator's widow, could not claim her son's interest upon his death without issue.

At this stage, it is instructive to note the interesting corollary from the nature of local customary common tenancy which Graham Paul, J., drew in *Taylor* v. *Williams & anor.*[25], to the effect that a devise by a testatrix of her undivided share in a family property, *even where the devise was to her own son*, was null and void, since under local law and custom she could not dispose of her 'unliquidated' interest whether by will or otherwise. This at once raises the issue as to whether the individual's right in the family land is or is not an estate of inheritance which he or she can leave to her children as she chooses. It is clear from this judgment that the individual has no such right and that his or her issue must look to the customary rules of tenure for their rights. We may quote the following definitive words of the learned judge in full, as they throw a flood of light on the whole problem of the individual's right in family land. He said:[26]

'It has been for long settled law in this Court that a member of a family in these parts cannot alienate his or her undivided share in the family property, and in the case of *Ogunmefun* v. *Ogunmefun & ors.* (N.L.R., Vol. X, page 82) it was specifically held following the earlier cases that a testatrix could not devise by will her undivided share in her father's land. . . . In my view *the basis of all decisions on this point is not that it was a stranger to whom the alienation was being made but that there was not in the member of the family any right or interest of which he or she could dispose.*'

Then he continued:

'Until there has been partition, that is until the family structure, with all its incidents of native custom, has been broken up, it seems to me that the correct view is at any moment that the ownership of the family property is vested in the whole family as trustees for the whole family. *Each individual member of the family has in addition vested in him or her what may perhaps be described as a right of user during his or her life. That individual right of user is to my mind purely and simply a life interest.* On the death of the individual that interest reverts to the whole family though by reason of the user enjoyed by the deceased individual during his or her life, the family will generally permit his or her children to have among them the same user as their parent had if the circumstances of the family and of the property admit.'[27]

With the latter part of this passage may be contrasted Viscount Dunedin's following statement in *Oshodi* v. *Dakolo & ors.*:[28] 'These various occupiers have the right to remain and to transmit their holdings to their offspring, but in the event of the family of an occupier failing and being extinct, the chief has a right of reversion.' If all that Viscount Dunedin meant to say was that the individual's right of transmission of his share to his offspring is as according to local law and custom, issue can hardly be joined on the point. The truth is that there is no individual estate of inheritance (in the fullest sense) in an undivided family land, but the children are not necessarily left to the whim and caprice of the family head with regard to their right of succession to their father's share therein. In short, the individual's share is not an absolute life interest.

Before we turn to a consideration of the issue of partition and its consequences, there are two more points to record. One is the possible distinction that one might make between land rights acquired by the individual by purchase in more recent times and rights enjoyed by the individual in family land under the indigenous system of tenure. Thus, in *Chief Eyo Ita & ors.* v. *Asido*,[29] in which the plaintiffs had sought a declaration of title to land at Ikot Esion in Calabar, Webber, C.J., in delivering the judgment of the West African Court of Appeal, remarked: 'It is indubitable that if the learned Judge had found in favour of a sale of the land a grant of declaration of title conveying a fee simple was inevitable but he does not appear to have discriminated between rights in the acquisition of native land by purchase and rights acquired under native law and custom—*the former being* proprietary *rights and the latter* possessory *rights or rights of occupancy.*'[30] Much the same language was used by Osborne, C.J., in *Lewis* v. *Bankole*[31] when he said:[32] 'Nothing in this judgment will affect the *possessory* rights of those members of the family who were actually living in the family compound when this writ was issued, or who had houses or rooms which they were then entitled to occupy for residential purposes.'

The other matter to be noted is the distinction made between the individual's inalienable right in the family land as such and his alienable one in any structure such as a building which he may super-impose on the family land (with, of course, the consent of the family) by his own personal exertions. This seems to go on the analogy of the right given to the individual by customary law to formerly unappropriated land first cultivated by him or to crops planted by him on existing family land. There would seem to have been no direct Supreme (or Higher) Court decision on the point, but in a case at Iperu in the Ijebu Province of Yoruba-land,[33] one Desalu owed a debt to one Coker and the Supreme Court issued a writ of Fi-Fa to attach the judgment debtor's interest. A successful interpleader summons was allowed to other members of the family who claimed that the land, but *not* the house erected by Desalu thereon, was their family property. The Court, therefore, held that only the house could be attached, as it was the only thing which Desalu could claim as his absolute property.

Right to Partition. With regard to the individual's right to demand partition[34] of the family land, this is usually granted where disputes as to occupation rights or as to the sharing of net rents from leasing family property cannot be amicably settled among the family members themselves. But the elders in former times and now the Courts would exercise a discretion as to what might be best in the interest of the family as a whole in ordering partition or sale of the family land. The mode of carrying out partition under the local law has been thus described by Chiefs Eletu and Ashogbon as expert witnesses in the case of *Ricardo* v. *Abal*:[35] 'The Council of the family, or of neighbours, as the case might be, would divide the property into two or more parts, as required, and the eldest child, whether male or female, would take the first choice.'[36]

In this case both plaintiff (a female) and defendant (a junior male, who however became the family head) agreed to partition, and the only dispute was as to the order of choice. The Court held that the priority of choice rested with the plaintiff as the eldest child, irrespective of sex. The same principle of equality and impartiality of the Yoruba law of tenure was upheld by the Divisional Court in *Sule & ors.* v. *Ajisegiri*[37] where it was ruled that partition must be equally between those entitled to it, regardless of sex.[38] Even an illegitimate (illegitimate, that is, by English law) son has been held entitled to a share of his father's land on the latter's death intestate.[39] In *Chairman, L.E.D.B.* v. *Ashani & ors.*[40] it was decided that a partition of family land by a deed of agreement, which differed from a scheme under the testator's will, was valid even though some of the beneficiaries were minors at the date of partition; the proper representatives of the minors at the date of partition; the proper representatives of the minors had consented to the subsequent agreement on behalf of the minors. They were free to impeach the partition in a court of law as soon as they attained their majority; instead, they continued years later to take benefits under the partition.

But the court will not order a sale or partition of family land if none of the individual's customary rights enumerated above[41] is infringed. That was why the Supreme Court refused in *Thomas* v. *Thomas*[42] to grant to the plaintiff member of a family his prayer for a sale or partition on the mere ground that the family head had not allowed him a share of the net rents, which were proved to be nil, accruing from a lease of portion of the family property. Similarly, where in *Bajulaiye & anor.* v. *Akapo*[43] the parties to the action agreed that partition was impracticable, Butler Lloyd, J., refused to order a sale or partition of family property for no better reason than that some of the interested parties desired to turn the family property into cash. The first plaintiff did not wish, and had not asked, to live on the premises. The defendant, on the other hand, was willing for the plaintiffs to share in the occupation of the premises or alternatively in the rents derived therefrom, but did not want the property to be sold.

The guiding principle for the family council or the court seems to be a consideration of what in a given situation is best in the interest of the family as a whole. Butler Lloyd thus explained the institution of 'family house':[44]

'The purpose of the institution is, as its name implies, to provide a place where members of the family can reside if they so desire and, so long as that purpose is still capable of achievement, I conceive that it would be wrong for the Court to order the sale of property subject to this form of tenure.' Further light was thrown on the subject by the judgment of Carey, J., in *In the matter of the Estate of Edward Forster*[45] where property left under a testator's will was held to be intended as 'family house' under the local law of tenure. He observed that the institution of 'family house' among the Yorubas is designed as a permanent residence set apart by the father of a family for occupation, during and after his decease, by his wives and children. It cannot therefore be sold by any of the children who, if male, have the right to reside with their mothers, wives and children therein and, if female, are entitled to reside therein until marriage or thereafter on deserting or being deserted by their husbands. To mortgage or sell the family house, the consent of all those thus entitled to reside therein must first be obtained.[46]

But, on the principle of what is best for the family as a whole, the Court would nevertheless order a partition or sale of family land, although a trust deed by which the land was devised by a testator forbade it.[47]

Now, in almost all the decisions we have been considering in this Chapter, the judges have insisted on two factors as conditions precedent to the alienability of a member's interest in family land: (*a*) prior consent of the family, and (*b*) partition of the land, where possible and authorised either by the family council or by the court.

It would seem to be implicit in such a statement that with family consent or by partition the individual acquires a separate and absolute estate in his share. The first noteworthy pronouncement is that of Chief Eletu Odibo in his evidence in *Lewis* v. *Bankole*[48] when he declared: 'I agree with the Ojora except on one point. If the compound is divided it will no longer be a compound, and each one will have authority in his own portion.' One would hesitate to deduce from this any clear principle of an absolute property being vested in the individual member by partition.

A much more intriguing case is *Oshodi* v. *Balogun*[49] in which the West African Court of Appeal held that a purchaser from or through a descendant of a domestic of the Oshodi family could not acquire a fee simple absolute estate in the portion of family land purported to be thereby conveyed to him. But Lord Maugham, in his Privy Council judgment which virtually confirmed that of the W. A. C. A., warned:[50] 'To prevent any misconception it seems desirable to state that the present decision is not based on any doubt as to the possibility of a title equivalent to a fee simple being obtained as the result of a sale of family lands with the general consent of the family.' He then cited Lord Dunedin's judgment in the *Dakolo Case* and proceeded:[51] 'The last sentence above quoted means only that the chief as contrasted with the family as a whole has no fee simple. The dispute was in fact between the chief as plaintiff and the occupants as a body as defendants. No question as to the extent of the family title arose.'

It would appear from the concluding words of the latter quotation that what their Lordships of the Privy Council were conceding was that the family as a whole could have the fee simple in the family land, which could be made over to a purchaser with necessary consent; but that the chief or family head as such had no independent fee simple of his own in the family land as against other members. We are still left with the question as to whether, on partition or with family consent, this fee simple of the family, can be regarded as split into as many parts as there are eligible family members, each such part being an absolute estate in itself capable of alienation or attachment for debt? If we hold with Chief Eletu Odibo in *Lewis* v. *Bankole*[52] and with Graham Paul[53] in *Taylor* v. *Williams & anor.* that partition breaks down the family structure with all its incidents of customary tenure, it is possible that an absolute separate property ensures to the individual on a partition of family land. This point was expressly laid down by W.A.C.A. in the recent case of *Balogun* v. *Balogun & ors.*[54] where the seven surviving children of one Okolo Balogun by deed partitioned the whole of their father's property in Lagos into well-defined portions. The plaintiff-appellant claimed, as against the defendants-respondents' contention, that the property was in spite of partition still family property, that he had an absolute title to those portions of the partitioned property which he had acquired by and in consequence of the partition. *Held*: by the West African Court of Appeal that a partition of family land, with the consent of all members of the family, conferred on each member an *absolute* property in his partitioned portion.

What is not so clear, however, is the nature of the interest which an individual can alienate to a purchaser (including in this term a mortgagee and the like) where only the family consent has been obtained to the transaction but no partition has yet taken place of the family land. Since in such a case the family structure remains intact, it would appear that the portion alienated from the undivided whole cannot be a fee simple, unless indeed such family consent to the deal is to be interpreted as equivalent to a partial partition as between the individual's interest so transferred and the remaining block left in the family. In this connexion we may note that where part of family land is given to a member thereof for this occupation, it still remains family property although he may have improved it by, for example, clearing some bush or reclaiming a swamp thereon. Thus, in *Bassey* v. *Cobham & ors.*[55], Webber, J., in the Divisional Court at Calabar held that, on a careful consideration of the evidence of local assessors on customary tenure, the act of reclaiming swamp land does not confer any special property in the land reclaimed on the individual who reclaims it as against the corporate title of the family. The learned Judge said: 'But I premise by stating that the assessors were unanimous in this opinion that no individual member could acquire absolute ownership of family land in the sense of a fee simple with rights of alienating and selling. This is established law for which there is abundant authority.'[56]

For the individual to acquire anything in the nature of an absolute property in his allotment it would seem to be essential that the family through their proper representative should make it quite clear that the member has had thereby conferred upon him an absolute title. Merely being allowed to act, for however long a period, as if he were the owner of the family land would not give him any separate and absolute right thereto. Consequently, where a Crown grant had been made to a person with respect to his family land, Viscount Haldane, delivering the judgment of the Privy Council in *Sunmonu* v. *Disu Raphael*,[57] held that the individual concerned must be presumed to have taken the Crown grant on behalf of his family and that he could not acquire by exclusive possession of the family property a separate and individual title to it against the other members of the family.

Another, but not unrelated, type of problem is that occasioned by an attempt on the part of an individual to convey his undivided share of family land to a purchaser by means of a modern deed of conveyance in which he represents himself as a fee simple owner. In *Adagun* v. *Fagbola*,[58] Kingdon, C.J., decided in a Supreme Court judgment that a recital in a deed of gift of part of family land by a member which described him as the fee simple owner of his allotment was void as against local customary tenure. The purported conveyance was a nullity.

Summary

We may now summarise our answers to the questions[59] posed at the outset of this enquiry as follows: The individual member of a family may acquire an absolute property in land by (*a*) the appropriation of as yet unoccupied or uncultivated virgin land; (*b*) being given, with the consent of his family, an absolute interest in an allotted portion of the family land; (*c*) accepting an out-and-out gift from another land-owning family having surplus land; and (*d*) becoming a holder of a piece of land in consequence of the partition into specific and identifiable lots of what was formerly family land.

Land acquired by an individual in any one of these ways becomes, under the local system of tenure, family land at the death of the first occupier. The interest of each member of a family in the family land is neither strictly usufructuary in the Roman sense, nor is it a tenancy in common or a joint tenancy according to English land law.

Again, it is not *proprietary* in the sense that it carries such a complete power of disposal as is enjoyed by an English fee simple owner of land; it is equally inaccurate to regard it as merely *possessory*, for the occupier ordinarily enjoys a degree of freedom of user which a fee simple owner might envy.

It is also clear that the Nigerian occupier of family land is not a life-tenant of his holding such as is his opposite number in an English settlement, and he would be the first to admit that his interest is not fully hereditary although he would quickly add that his offspring could not be lightly disinherited from his own allotment by the surviving members of his own family. And, to the extent to which his interest may come to an end for any of the reasons we shall give later, it seems that he holds a kind of fee conditional or even fee determinable, which, however, is peculiarly indigenous.

Individual's Rights in Farm Land. The principles so far considered relate chiefly to town or urban lands, but the broad elements apply equally to agricultural or farm lands. Every member of a farming family is entitled to have his own allotment, may cultivate it and plant what he likes in it, may cut down or burn or destroy anything growing on it, and may dig or bore holes in it or fill up any existing openings. Any member who is desirous and capable of working effectively a piece of land has the right to demand his own portion from the family head. Even where part of the family land is being worked on a co-operative or communal basis by a group of kinsmen, the products of their cultivation are generally owned individually and are very often separately barned or garnered.

The allottee cannot sell his allotment and may not mortgage it, but he can pledge it or the crops on it for debt. He cannot permanently alienate it, though he can temporarily give its use to strangers without family approval. Subject to performing all his obligations under the customary law, he enjoys definite security of tenure. But he is not an absolute owner of his share as against the ultimate family title.

The offspring of a deceased cultivator can and do succeed to their father's allotment which is shared out among them according to customary rules.

These broad principles seem fairly common to all three regions of Nigeria.[60] Such variations of detail as exist are due to differing cultural levels reflected in local methods of husbandry.

It is thus clear that the type of communal land-holding, with largely undifferentiated rights, which is to be found in pastoral or nomadic communities, cannot be properly attributed to more settled and agricultural communities such as are to be found in Nigeria. When, therefore, Lord Hailey wrote:[61] 'Rights to land have the character of a privilege based on membership of a community, entitling every member to the beneficial use of the community lands, whether for grazing, hunting, collecting fruits, or cultivating, rather than of a right over specific areas identified with the holder', the learned writer must be read subject to the warning notice issued by Dr. F. M. Keesing whose researches among the Pacific communities had led him to the conclusion that the usual kind of land tenure in agricultural communities was for 'living sites and cultivations around villages to be very precisely defined as to what families or individuals had authority over them and as to who could use them. . . . Nowhere was there any complete collectivism or communism such as some theorists have postulated for the primitive world.'[62]

This corrective, though issued in connexion with Pacific land-holding, applies with equal force to Nigeria. Mere absence of clearly defined boundaries does not affect the specific nature of individual or family holdings.[63]

Notes

[1] We are not, of course, here dealing with the special cases of slaves or strangers to whom a portion of family land might be given with or without conditions. Our immediate concern is with the right of a normal occupier of land as a member of a land-owning family.

[2] What these were would become clear to anyone who might care to compare the following account of the Nigerian occupier's rights to land with that of his Roman counterpart in any standard textbook on the subject—e.g. Moyle, *Institute of Justinian*, 1931 Impr., pp. 221–4; Buckland, *A Manual of Roman Private Law* (2nd edition), pp. 162–5.

[3] See Vinogradoff, *Historical Jurisprudence*, Vol. II, Chap. X, p. 198: 'As to the problem under discussion, Rome developed the conception of absolute property for the citizen—the *dominium ex jure Quiritium*—while Athens worked out a conception of *relative* property rights.' (Also, pp. 197–229 *passim.*)

See also, Hunter, *Introduction to Roman Law* (9th edition), pp. 69–70; Lee, *Roman Law* (pp. 162–3, 166–7).

[4] This expression is not here used with the strict particularity of s. 34 L.P.A. 1925 and its transitional provisions. Its special meaning will become clear as we proceed.

[5] See *Jacobs* v. *Oladunni Bros.* (1935), 12 N.L.R. 1.

[6] (1909), 1 N.L.R. 82.

[7] *Per* Osborne, C.J., at p. 88 (1909), 1 N.L.R. 82.

[8] *Ibid.*, p. 87.

[9] It is interesting to record here that, thanks to the plaintiff's witnesses from other parts of Yoruba-land, the Lagos customary law was found by the Court to be generally the same as those of other Yoruba areas. (See pp. 102–3, *ibid.*)

[10] (1936), 4 W.A.C.A. 1; (1936), 2 A.E.R. 1632; followed in *Oshodi* v. *Imoru & ors.* (1936) 3 W.A.C.A. 93.

[11] (1932), 16 N.L.R. 5.

[12] (1932), 16 N.L.R., at p. 5.

[13] (1926), 7 N.L.R. 58, at p. 59.

[14] (1932), 11 N.L.R. 110, at p. 111.

[15] (1924), 5 N.L.R. 40; applied in *Jacobs* v. *Oladunni Bros.* (1935), 12 N.L.R. 1.

[16] Van der Meulen, J., pertinently added at p. 42, *ibid.*: '. . . it may also be pointed out that under the principles governing the English law of property they could not on an intestacy have inherited this property as tenants in common.'

[17] (1932), 11 N.L.R. 74. But in the somewhat unsatisfactory case of *Saibu* v. *Igbo* (1941), 16 N.L.R. 25, it was held that the interest in house property of a judgment debtor who was in the position of a tenant in common was attachable under a writ of Fi-Fa.

[18] (1932), 11 N.L.R. 74, at p. 75.

[19] (1926), 7 N.L.R. 48.

[20] (1926), 7 N.L.R. 48, at p. 49.

[21] (1924), 5 N.L.R. 40.

[22] (1926), 7 N.L.R., at p. 49.

[23] (1939), 15 N.L.R. 1.

[24] Italics are the author's.

[25] (1935), 12 N.L.R. 67; see also *Davies* v. *Sogunro & ors.* (1936), 13 N.L.R. 15.

[26] (1935), 12 N.L.R., at p. 69. (The italics are the present writer's.)

[27] (1935), 12 N.L.R., at p. 70.

[28] (1930), A.C. 667, at p. 668.

[29] (1935), 2 W.A.C.A. 339.

[30] *Ibid.*, at p. 340. (The italics are the author's.)

[31] (1909), 1 N.L.R. 82.

[32] (1935), 2 W.A.C.A. 339, at p. 106; see also *per* Viscount Haldane in *Amodu Tijani* v. *Secretary, S. Nigeria* (1921), 2 A.C. 399, at p. 410.

[33] See para. 320 of Ward Price's *Land Tenure in the Yoruba Provinces* (1933). For the general uncertainty of Native Courts' decisions and of local witnesses in such a matter as the nature of the individual's rights, see paras. 316–21 of the same Report.

[34] See p. 147, *ante*.

[35] (1926), 7 N.L.R. 58.

[36] *Per* Tew, J., at p. 59, *ibid.*

Compare also (1) the Lagos Chiefs' evidence as to the principles of partition at pp. 96–8 and 103–4 of *Lewis* v. *Bankole* (1909), 1 N.L.R. 82; (2) M. M. Green, *Land Tenure in an Ibo Village*, pp. 13–14.

[37] (1937), 13 N.L.R. 147; see also *Andre* v. *Agbebi*, 10 N.L.R. 79.

[38] Hence *Lopez* v. *Lopez* (1924), 5 N.L.R. 47, was doubted.

[39] *Davis* v. *Sogunro* (1936), 13 N.L.R. 15.

[40] (1937), 3 W.A.C.A. 143.

[41] See pp. 146–7, *supra*.

[42] (1932), 16 N.L.R. 5.

[43] (1938), 14 N.L.R. 10.

[44] (1938), 14 N.L.R. 10, at p. 10; see also *Olawoyin & anor.* v. *Coker* (1892), 16 August: (Law Reports (Colonial), Nigeria A) in the Colonial Office Legal Library—(claim for partition of house and land in Shopono St., Lagos).

[45] (1938), 14 N.L.R. 83.

[46] *Ibid.*, at p. 86. To realise the universality of these principles throughout Yorubaland, see, e.g. para. 298 of Ward Price, *op. cit.*

[47] *Giwa & ors.* v. *Otun & ors.* (1932), 11 N.L.R. 160. But it was clear from the Trust Deed in question that the testator intended it to be governed by English law.

[48] (1909), 1 N.L.R. 82, at p. 97.

[49] (1936), 4 W.A.C.A. 1; (1936), 2 All E.R. 1632.

[50] *Ibid.*, at pp. 6 and 1638 respectively.

[51] *Ibid.*

[52] (1909), 1 N.L.R. 82.

[53] See pp. 149–50 earlier; see also *per* Kingdon, C.J., in *Balogun* v. *Balogun & ors.* (1943), 9 W.A.C.A. 78, at p. 84.

[54] (1943), 9 W.A.C.A. 78; see also *Chairman, L.E.D.B.* v. *Ashani & ors.* (1937), 3 W.A.C.A. 143.

[55] (1924), 5 N.L.R. 90.

[56] (1924), 5 N.L.R. 90, at p. 92. The learned Judge then cited five decisions covering the period 1909–22.

[57] (1927), A.C. 881; see also the W.A.C.A. judgment to the same effect in *Larki* v. *Amokor & ors.* (1933), 1 W.A.C.A. 323, where it was ruled that long-continued possession of family land on the Gold Coast by a family head would not give him individual ownership of it.

[58] (1932), 11 N.L.R. 110.

[59] See p. 143, *supra*.

[60] Compare the very similar accounts contained in the following: W. Price, *Land Tenure in Yoruba-land* (1933), paras. 50–93; A. K. Ajisafe, *Laws & Customs of the Yoruba* (1924), Chap. IV, paras. 4–8; C. W. Alexander, Memorandum on *Land Tenure in Southern Nigeria*, paras. 6, 8, 11–16; M. M. Green, *Land Tenure in an Ibo Village*, pp. 33–4; Chap. IV, *passim*; C. K. Meek, *Law & Authority in a Nigerian Tribe* (*Ibo*), pp. 100–4; Sir Percy Girouard, Memorandum on *Land Tenure in Northern Nigeria* (1912), para. 22, *et passim*; S. F. Nadel, *op. cit.*, pp. 181–8; Forde and Scott, *Native Economics of Nigeria*, pp. 64–7, 78–80, 88–91, 120–2.

[61] Hadey, *An African Survey* (1945), p. 830.

[62] Keesing, *The South Seas in the Modern World*, p. 98.

[63] See, e.g., W. Price, *op. cit.*, paras, 41 and 54; M. M. Green, *op. cit.*, Chap. IV; Sir P. Girouard, *op. cit.*, para. 2; C. W. Alexander, *op. cit.*, para. 6; S. F. Nadel, *A Black Byzantium*, p. 183.

J. H. M. Beattie: The Kibanja System of Land Tenure in Bunyoro, Uganda*

The Kibanja System of Land Tenure in Bunyoro, Uganda

The system of land holding may be regarded in Bunyoro, as in other countries, as the resultant of the two forces of environment and history. Environment lays down certain limiting conditions; history determines the modes in which the social system, of which land tenure is a part, conforms to these conditions. I shall, then, after briefly describing what the country of Bunyoro is like, and giving some account of the ecological relations between man and environment which subsist there, attempt to summarise the recent history of Bunyoro so far as it relates to the development of rights over land. This will lead to a description of the system of land tenure known as *kibanja* and to an account of the nature, distribution and interrelation of rights relating to *kibanja* land as they at present exist. In conclusion, I shall indicate some possible relations between the system thus described and some other features of the wider social system of which it is a part.

* J. H. M. Beattie, 'The Kibanja System of Land Tenure in Bunyoro, Uganda', in *Journal of African Administration*, Vol. 6, No. 1, 1954, pp. 18–28.

I shall not attempt in this paper to describe all the kinds of rights in land which are to be found in Bunyoro, but will confine myself to those associated with the *kibanja* system. And it should be said here at the outset that by no means all occupied land in Bunyoro is held under the *kibanja* system, probably the greater part of it is not. Exactly how much is, and how much is not, is unfortunately, in the absence of a survey or of an adequate system of land registration, not possible to determine. I should add, also, that since my study of land tenure and social organisation in Bunyoro is as yet only in an intermediate stage, the account to be given makes no claim either to completeness or finality; as will be plain in the sequel, much further enquiry will be needed in the field before a full picture of Nyoro land tenure can be presented.

The present Bunyoro kingdom, which is coterminous with the administrative district of the same name, contains a land area of 4,735 square miles. It is bounded on the west by Lake Albert, on the north and east by the Victoria Nile, and on the south by the Kafu-Nkusi river. Most of the district lies at an altitude of between three and four thousand feet, and is fertile and well watered, but it falls to undulating savannah in the north, and descends by a steep escarpment to the dry Lake Albert rift in the west. Much of northern Bunyoro is occupied by the new National Park and sleeping sickness reserves, there are some hundreds of square miles of forest and swamps, and it has been estimated that about 2,350 square miles are actually available for African cultivation and grazing. Of this, only about a quarter is actually cultivated or grazed over, so it is plain that there is no shortage of land in Bunyoro. Population density over the whole kingdom is about 24 to the square mile, very considerably less than the figures for the neighbouring kingdoms of Toro, Ankole and Buganda. The total African population of Bunyoro is about 110,000 and the country is ruled, under the supervision and tutelage of the protectorate government, by a hereditary king, the Mukama, and a graded hierarchy of non-hereditary, transferable territorial chiefs. The protectorate administration is represented by a district commissioner and two assistant district commissioners.

Bunyoro, though proud of its pastoral traditions, is no longer a cattle country. There are now about 5,500 cattle in the district, that is, approximately one beast to every 22 people, a figure very much lower than that for the whole Protectorate. These cattle are for the most part confined to a small region in the north-west and to the neighbourhood of the townships of Hoima and Masindi.

The typical Munyoro farmer nowadays is a small agriculturalist, with four to eight acres under cultivation, about half-a-dozen goats, a few chickens and, sometimes, a few sheep. He does not live in a compact village, but in a separate homestead sheltered by his small banana grove and surrounded by his fields of food crops, usually with similar homesteads within shouting distance. He cultivates eleusine millet, cassava and sweet potatoes as well as bananas (which he uses mostly for making beer), and probably has one or two fields of cotton and tobacco, the former sometimes at some distance from his home, from the proceeds of which he derives a cash income of 150 to 200 shillings a year. The average holding, with provision for fallow land, has been estimated to require about fifteen acres. There has as yet been little attempt by private individuals to develop larger units of land by modern agricultural methods, though a few of the wealthier people employ paid labour to develop larger holdings, and attempts are being made to initiate co-operative farming.

There are, in the absence of written records, evident dangers in attempting to reconstruct the nature of rights in land and the history of their development before the arrival of the first Europeans. It seems likely, however, that at some period in the remote past the country was occupied by scattered groups of negroid peoples, organised on a clan or lineage basis, and that the impact on these of successive waves of immigrants of different stock, some at least of whom were pastoral in their way of life, produced the dual system of social organisation typical of the interlacustrine Bantu kingdoms. Though there is nothing in Bunyoro history to suggest that the gulf between the two groups, the Bahima or Bahuma and the Bairu,[1] was ever so complete or so rigorous as it was in, e.g. Ankole, the distinction was, and still is, significant, and was complicated by the arrival of the Babito, the royal clan of Nilotic origin, which reached Bunyoro some twenty or so generations ago. To them now attaches much of the prestige and authority associated in other countries with the Bahuma. In fact, in historical times, the great chiefs have included Babito and members of commoner clans, as well as Bahuma; the cattle-oriented Bahuma were for the most part employed as herdsmen by the ruling Babito and other chiefs, and when, in the course of the last sixty or seventy years, the cattle disappeared through the agency of war and disease, most of the Bahuma vanished too. But it seems that even in the pastoral times of the last century the majority of the inhabitants were peasant agriculturists, most of whom possessed few, if any cattle.

We may suppose that during Mukama Kabarega's reign (1866–1899), which concluded the pre-European period of Bunyoro history, rights in land were, in general, vested in three categories of persons, and validated in three different ways. First, the whole land, and everything in it, belonged to the Mukama, a right which derived ultimately from conquest and could only be extinguished by conquest, or by successful rebellion. In virtue of this right the Mukama could allot to his relatives and others the control of different regions of the country. We may call these rights feudal, or fiefhold rights, provided that we understand by these terms simply the holding of an estate in land 'on condition of homage and service to a superior lord'. Thus were created the second grade of rights, those of the territorial chiefs and sub-chiefs, who were responsible to the Mukama for the general well-being of their areas, and who received from the peasant cultivators in these areas a tribute of grain, beer and labour, some of which, together with a proportion of the herds in their areas, they had to pass on to the Mukama. It has been said that these rights were rights over people and not over land. This is in the main true, none the less these 'fiefs' were territorial grants, over people certainly, but also over the produce of the land, and over people only so long as they occupied certain limited and specified areas.

The third category of rights in land was vested in the clan heads, and these rights related to the actual utilisation of the soil itself. Banyoro used to say 'the Mukama rules the people, the clans rule the land'. We are told that before the flight of Kabarega the clans were localized (though it is said that they occupied their localities by grace of the Mukama), one clan, or more likely one sub-division of a clan, occupying one *omugongo*. (An *omugongo* is literally the raised portion of land between swamps or streams, which are plentiful in Bunyoro, and may be several square miles in extent.) *Emigongo* are still almost invariably named after one of Bunyoro's hundred or more clans, so it seems probable that clans were at one time localized in this way. It is of passing interest that the fishing villages on the Lake Albert shore, whose contact with the rest of Bunyoro is severely restricted by a steep escarpment, and which contain untypically stable and homogeneous populations, are still divided topographically into sections, each exclusively occupied by the men of a single clan and their families.

Nowadays the clan heads, though they exercise other functions, have no longer anything to do with the allocation of land, which is now in the hands of the Mukama's 'civil service' of appointed chiefs. There is no clear evidence as to the rights over land which they formerly held, or the way in which these rights were exercised. But it may be supposed that in Bunyoro, as elsewhere, the land was held by the clan for the clan's benefit, rights of cultivation and usufruct being granted to clan members as long as they continued to occupy and cultivate the plots allotted to them.

None of these lesser rights, it is clear, amounted to permanent, indefeasible rights over specific parcels of land; all were held conditionally, on condition either of the Mukama's favour, or of productive occupation. The notion, new to Bunyoro as to other parts of Africa, of permanent, indefeasible rights in land amounting to freehold did not develop until after the capture of Kabarega, the institution of a British administration, and the land settlement in Buganda in 1900. We must now give some account of its development.

The re-introduction of chiefs by the government at the beginning of the century, after several years of political chaos, was inevitably accompanied by the idea that a chief's area was, like the fiefs held by his predecessors, an official 'estate' from the occupants of which he could exact services and tribute which were now commuted to a cash payment, *obusulu*. This, initially four shillings, was later increased to seven shillings per adult male, one shilling of which was passed on to the Muruka chief.[2] As chiefs at this time (and until 1933) received by way of salaries only a small percentage of the poll-tax, this was their major source of revenue, and it was evidently enough to make the position of chief a sought-after-one. Since with the coming of settled government chiefs in Bunyoro as elsewhere had become civil servants (though unsalaried ones) rather than fief-holding lords, some provision for their support after retirement had to be made and this appears to have been done by cutting bits off the existing 'official' estates to serve as places of residence and sources of revenue for retired chiefs. These estates became the permanent property of the recipients. At the same time, or perhaps even earlier, the Mukama had begun to give princes and princesses (members of the royal Babito clan) plots of occupied land for their permanent personal use and enjoyment.

These estates, though private, were only held by ex-officials and members of the royal family, and the next step, which was taken about 1907, was the assigning by the Mukama of certain areas, with full *obusulu* rights, to certain other persons who were neither ex-chiefs nor Babito. These persons included serving chiefs of various ranks, ex-ritual and domestic functionaries of the Mukama's household, and other 'people of standing who were well known', people who 'though they may not be doing government work, are looked upon as dignitaries among the people', to quote from a later instruction by the government. Allocations of this kind continued increasingly to be made for the next twenty-four years, and in 1931 it was reported that all the best of the occupied lands had been taken up by *kibanja* holders. Something evidently had to be done. In that year, out of 22,000 tax payers about 18,000 were paying *obusulu*, about 12,000 on official *obwesengeze* estates, and the other 6,000 on *kibanja* plots to private individuals. These *kibanja* plots varied in size from about five acres to several square miles, and the numbers of *obusulu*-paying tenants on them varied from two or three to eighty or more, with an average of about six per *kibanja*.

This development, over a period of about half a century, from a system of fief-holding chiefs possessing rights over the people who occupied the areas allotted to and administered by them, to a landlord and tenant system not confined to the Mukama's officials, and implying, in the case of the private *kibanja* holder, permanent rights to plots of land *qua* land, may be supposed to have been accelerated by two associated factors. First, Bunyoro was not exempt from the universal process whereby, with the introduction of a money economy and the cultivation of cash crops, the basis of land holding tends, to quote Dr. Meek, to change from one of community and custom to one of individualism and contract, the conception of ownership beginning gradually to replace that of usufruct and fiefhold. The Bunyoro chiefs early made the point that in order to provide security for the development of their land and for the borrowing of money on it, some form of permanent security of tenure was needed, and though it has been said with apparent truth that the power to collect rent, not the desire to develop their plots, was the real attraction of *bibanja* estates, there can be no doubt that the general alteration in the attitude to land brought about by the social and economic changes consequent on the coming of the Europeans affected the Banyoro no less than it affected neighbouring peoples. The second factor which accelerated in Bunyoro the development of a system of *quasi*-freehold estates was the Buganda Agreement of 1900, whereby large numbers of chiefs and others in the country received estates (*mailo*) on what amounted to freehold tenure. The Banyoro have constantly asked the government for the allocation of *mailo* on the Buganda model, and the hope that this may some time be approved has not yet been abandoned. It is felt to be unfair that such grants were approved in Bugunda, and subsequently, on a lesser scale in Ankole and Toro, but withheld in Bunyoro, despite earlier intimations that they would be considered.

In the year 1931, an enquiry by the government revealed that the greater part of cultivated Bunyoro was included either in official estates or in privately owned *bibanja*. Eighty-four per cent. of the population lived as rent-paying tenants on these two kinds of estates. The protectorate government could not contemplate with equanimity a state of affairs in which a class of landlords performing no economic function in return for the share which it received of the produce of cultivation, exacted rent from a community of cultivators who themselves possessed no guaranteed security of tenure. As a result of an enquiry, therefore, recommendations were made for the total abolition of the old system and its replacement by a form of land holding more in conformity with enlightened modern opinion on these matters.

These recommendations which were accepted by the Government, are set out in the Thomas and Rubie Report.[3] This report recommended the abolition of the landlord-tenant system implied by the existence of large tenanted estates, the abolition of *obusulu*, the payment of salaries to chiefs, and the compensation of all those landholders who stood to lose by the reform. On the principle that 'every man is entitled to the free and undisturbed occupancy of the land which he cultivates' it recommended the issue of certificates of occupancy to actual cultivators, guaranteeing to the holder 'undisturbed occupancy, subject to necessary conditions, of the land, of whatever extent, of which he is actually making use, with the right to dispose of the results of his labour upon that land to his heirs, or by sale to another native'. Arbitrary grants on the old model were to be abolished, and the only title to land was to be its actual occupation and cultivation. It was supposed by the investigators that 'the national collection of tribute and its allocation to tribal purposes' would remove 'almost the only attraction of the private ownership of large tenanted areas'. Subsequent events failed to justify this supposition.

These recommendations appear to have been adopted in all essentials, and to have been conveyed to the native government, which received them without enthusiasm. Directions are on record laying down the form of procedure for the obtaining of certificates, providing that the *gombolola* chief must visit the area applied for, confirm in writing that the applicant is actually occupying and cultivating it, and mark out boundaries. The area marked out was to be 'slightly over twice the area which the applicant is cultivating or can cultivate'. Provision was made for the inspection of holdings and the checking of boundaries by the head land clerk of the native government, and for periodic inspections by chiefs and administrative officers. No limits were laid down as to the extent of the areas appropriate for grant under these certificates; in fact all reference to areas and acres was officially discouraged, lest any suggested figure should become standardised and claimed as of right by applicants.

By these means the Government hoped to arrest the process which had been gathering momentum since the beginning of the century, to eradicate the system of large tenanted *bibanja*, and to institute instead a system of cultivated small-holdings, limited in area to the extent that the occupier could make use of, and his right to which, subject to certain conditions, could be confirmed by the grant of a certificate of occupancy. These rights did not constitute freehold; the smallholdings were not *mailos*. The land was 'held by the governor for the occupation and the use of the inhabitants of the Obukama bwa Bunyoro-Kitara', subject to the conditions laid down in the 1933 Agreement; the certificates conveyed right of occupation not of ownership, and were to be valid only so long as the land was occupied and cultivated by the certificate holder himself.

The system of landed estates for members of the ruling classes and other privileged persons was, however, too deeply engrained by 1931 to be readily eradicated. Though— the reform achieved the important ends of abolishing the old official estates, and of placing the chiefs on a salaried and pensionable basis, it failed to diminish appreciably either the number or the extent of the old tenanted *bibanja*. Though the payment of *obusulu*, despite one or two abortive attempts to revive it, was stamped out, large tenanted *bibanja* continued to exist and exist to the present day, and they seem to have lost little of their attractiveness. We shall later consider why this should be the case. Meantime, it is now clear that many of the rights to *bibanja* over large populated areas which have been granted prior to 1933 to Babito, ex-chiefs and other influential people, of which there were about 600, were confirmed instead of being withdrawn after the institution of the new system, and that in at least a large number or cases the old estates continued to exist in the hands of their original owners or their heirs with undiminished, or only slightly diminished, boundaries. The only substantial difference between their pre- and post-1933 tenure is that *obusulu* may no longer be collected from the peasant cultivators on these estates. There is ample evidence, also, that many more rights of occupancy to large tenanted *bibanja* have been granted since 1933, ample unallocated land having become available for this purpose with the abolition of the official estates. Up to date, about 5,000 certificates have been issued, and it may be supposed that about a quarter of these are over *bibanja* containing at least one household besides that of the certificate holder. To suppose that 150 to 200 of these are over areas containing ten or more houses would, I think, be a conservative estimate. I must state quite frankly that these figures are of necessity no more than more or less informed guesses, based on very limited field observation, and discussion with the agricultural officer, the land clerk, chiefs and others. The land register contains no information as to the sizes of the *bibanja* therein recorded, nor as to the number of persons resident on them, and a district-wide survey of all *bibanja* holdings has yet to be made. Some idea of the numbers of tenants per *bibanja* in the years before 1933 may be derived from a sample of 365 tenanted *bibanja* listed by the native government for the purpose of assessing compensation. Of these, 53 per cent. contained less than five tenants, 36 per cent. less than ten, and only 11 per cent. contained more than ten tenant-householders.

The present position of land holding in this district, then, so far as it can be ascertained, is that a considerable number (it is unfortunately impossible to say how many) of the rights of occupancy certificated since 1933 are rights, not of actual cultivators over the smallholdings cultivated by themselves and their families and employees, but to considerably larger areas measurable in some cases in square miles rather than in acres, and frequently containing numbers of peasant cultivators, who are themselves debarred from taking out rights of occupancy over the areas they are actually cultivating.

Before going on to consider in detail the *kibanja* system of land tenure as it at present exists, it may be worth while asking why the attempt to implement so carefully thought out a programme of land reform was not wholly successful. We have seen that it was in large part successful, but the expressed ideal, that every cultivator should possess free and undisturbed occupancy of the land which he cultivates, and that this right should be certifiable by a certificate of occupancy, was not achieved. Why?

The answer, which is largely implicit in what I have said already, seems to be fourfold. Firstly, the system of landed and populated estates for the ruling classes and those associated with them, historically connected as it was with the pre-European *quasi*-feudal rights traditionally attaching to territorial chieftainship, and supporting as it did the privilege and prestige of an aristocracy whose rights nobody questioned, was evidently too deeply engrained in Nyoro psychology to be modified by the promulgation of a totally new and different system. Secondly, the old system gained vitality from the hope, dangled for many years before the Banyoro chiefs, that freehold tenure would some day be approved, in which case possession of a large *kibanja* might be expected to create a prescriptive right to freehold over the same area. Thirdly, the group of persons to whom the burden of the task of introducing the new system, with only limited supervision, was entrusted, namely, the Mukama and his chiefs, was composed of precisely those persons who possessed vested interests in the old system of tenanted estates, and who regarded these as their proper right and prerogative. The 'landed gentry' were in effect asked to dispossess themselves, and they cannot be altogether blamed if they did not make a very thorough job of it. Finally, and not least important, the people of Bunyoro as a whole, peasants as well as proprietors, evidently acquiesce in the present system; complaints are of individual abuses not against the system as a whole, and no legislation is likely in the long run to be effective unless all or a considerable proportion of the people have some interest in seeing that it is carried out.

I now go on to describe, in such detail as is available, the *kibanja* system of land tenure as it at present exists. I have said that about 5,000 persons possess certificates of occupancy in Bunyoro, of which about 1,500 or more are over *bibanja* containing one or more unrelated settlers, and many over areas containing a good many more. What is the nature, distribution and inter-relations of the rights relating to these *kibanja* lands?

Let us take for consideration what we may suppose to be a typical populated *kibanja* on which live the man who holds a certificate of occupancy in respect of it (who is called the *mukama w'ekibanja*) and four or five unrelated peasant cultivators. We may visualise this *kibanja* as covering about 150 acres, half of which is occupied by the farms of the *kibanja* holder and his 'tenants', the other half being unoccupied land covered by elephant grass and bush. What persons have rights in this piece of land or any part of it?

Ultimate rights in the land of Bunyoro, as elsewhere in the protectorate, are vested in the Governor. The land is 'held by the Governor for the occupation and use of the natives of the Obukama bwa Bunyoro-Kitara', subject to rights already recognised and to the Governor's right to 'appropriate and place under his direct control' areas for certain public purposes (roads, forests, townships, etc.), and 'to grant a valid title to any person', being guided by the protectorate laws and the Secretary of State's instructions. He is required in each case to consult the Mukama and to give 'full consideration' to his wishes. In fact, only about 30 square miles have been alienated, on either freehold or leasehold tenure, to non-natives in Bunyoro district. The Agreement (1933) also lays down that the administration of the land for the occupation and use of the natives shall be entrusted to the Mukama and native government, subject to the Governor's instructions. So much for the Governor's rights in the land, which are of little concern to the *kibanja* owner or his occupiers even if, as is unlikely, they are aware of their existence.

In dealing with the rights of our certificated *kibanja* holder himself, it will be necessary to distinguish between those rights which he holds by law, and those rights, no less real as social facts, which, unless he is unusually well versed in the law, he believes himself to possess, and which practically everybody including his tenants, acknowledges as the proper rights of *abakama b'ebibanja*. His legal rights are stated in the form of certificate of occupancy, which entitles him to undisturbed occupation of the *kibanja* cultivated by him so long as he continues to occupy and cultivate it, unless the land or any part of it is required for any work for the good of the country, in which case he will be compensated for any damage to his crops or other improvements. It confers on him absolute ownership of all the buildings he erects, and all the trees and crops he plants. He may sell these to another native of Bunyoro, but he may not sell, transfer or sub-let any portion of the land itself. He may, finally, leave by will to another member of the tribe his rights under the certificate and any improvements to the land. In the absence of a will, his heir by native custom will succeed to them. He may *not* collect any tribute or similar impost from any native living on the land, and the rights conferred by the certificate are to be cancelled by a discontinuation of cultivation or occupation of the land by the certificate holder or his successor.

I now give some account of the rights which our *kibanja* holder possesses over his land by custom and general acknowledgement, not all of which, it will be observed, are consistent with those conferred on him by law. Although the right to collect rent no longer exists (though an attempt to do so was punished by the courts as recently as 1946), a complex of rights sufficiently valuable to render the possession of a large *kibanja* a thing to be desired, evidently survives. The hope that freehold may ultimately be granted is not, I think, a sufficient explanation of this desirability.

These, then, so far as I have been able to ascertain, are the rights which our *kibanja* holder, unless he is unusually well versed in the law, believes himself to possess, and which are generally recognised as being proper to his position.

First, he has the right to retain his *kibanja*, his right to which, he believes, derives from purchase and the Mukama's grace, not from his cultivation of it, even though he neither occupies nor cultivates any part of it. He may allow others to cultivate in it, leaving only an agent or *musigire* to look after his interests there. Or he may leave it uncultivated and untenanted for years, perhaps staking his claim by planting a few permanent trees, and expect his claim to be admitted on his return. Many *bibanja* are thus held by people who are employed in faraway parts of the protectorate.

Second, he has the right to sell it, if he wants to. Despite the conditions of tenure given on the certificate, our *kibanja* holder makes no clear distinction between the sale of the improvements on the land and the sale of the land itself. He believes that the registration fee of shs. 5/– which he paid when he obtained his title to his *kibanja*, was the purchase price of the land, which thereby becomes his permanent personal property. Up to the present time practically all Lunyoro writings, official and otherwise, relating to the registration and transfer of *bibanjo* use the language of sale and purchase.

Third, he has the right to accept or refuse peasants from elsewhere who wish to cultivate or settle on his *kibanja*. It is conceivable that this right could, in the event of all or most cultivable land in Bunyoro being absorbed into *bibanja*, become a source of considerable profit to the *abakama b'ebibanja*. There is, however, no land shortage, and I have obtained no evidence that any money or goods are demanded from prospective tenants. But there are cases of *kibanja* holders who hold more land than they can use, and yet refuse to allow other people to cultivate it.

Fourth, he has the right to expel a settler from his *kibanja*. But public opinion would not approve such expulsion unless good cause were shown, e.g. being a particularly troublesome person, a thief, or (the most usual ground) a witch. If the settler and his ancestors had been settled on the land for many years, perhaps even before the present *kibanja* holder obtained his rights over it, it would, I am told, be more difficult to evict him, whatever his misdemeanours. It is said that this right would be supported by the native courts, though I have not yet come across a case of this kind. I should add that signs are now beginning to appear that an attempt by a tenant to develop his holding on modern lines, by planting permanent crops, etc., is coming to be regarded as a ground for eviction.

Fifth, he has a right of ownership over all ant hills, grass and timber on his *kibanja*, and is entitled to a leg of meat from any wild animal killed thereon. Potter's clay and sand are also regarded by the *kibanja* holder as his property, and others may be refused, or have to pay for, access to them.

Sixth, he has the right to impose conditions on his tenants with regard to the type of building they may erect on their holdings in his *kibanja*. Some *kibanja* holders refuse to allow their tenants to build permanent houses with corrugated-iron roofs, presumably lest the builder should be regarded by so doing as asserting a right which might come into conflict with that of the *kibanja* owner himself. Not all *kibanja* holders impose this condition, but some do, and the condition appears generally to be accepted without protest.

Seventh, he has the right, and indeed the duty, to act as arbitrator in minor disputes between settlers on his *kibanja*; and even in major ones the complaint may pass through him before it is taken to the nearest official chief. He is the ruler of the *kibanja* and is so known, and in this context he is himself a minor, if unofficial, chief.

Eighth, and perhaps the most important as it is the least tangible, he has the right to an attitude of general respect and obedience from the people resident on his *kibanja*. As a landlord, even though a rentless one, he possesses a status superior to that of his peasant tenants, and he is well aware of this and sometimes emphatic in expressing it. The proprietary attitude adopted by the owners of large *bibanja* is well expressed in the following quotation from a letter from one of them, whose tenants had complained of oppression: 'I do not want trouble with them, they can continue digging provided they understand that we are the owners of the *kibanja*, and consequently they should co-operate with us.' Many similar *dicta* could be quoted.

What remains to the *kibanja* holder, then, is some degree of power, authority and respect, and power and authority, even though limited, unproductive and devoid of any appreciable present profit, are still desirable in their own right. This is probably the most important of the factors which vitiated the hopeful surmise that the diversion of rent from the pockets of the *kibanja* owners to the public purse would 'remove almost the only attraction of the private ownership of large tenanted areas'. It may be added that our *kibanja* holder regards himself as owning, not simply occupying his *kibanja*, and that he regards himself as possessing what virtually amounts to a freehold right, devoid only of the power of rent. This right, in the case of the large *kibanja* holders, derives ultimately from their social status and from the king's favour, and it can be passed on to their descendants.

The rights, or lack of them, of the non-*kibanja* owner, settled on the *kibanja* of another, are in the main the obverse of those described as pertaining to the *kibanja* owner. He has, firstly, the right to reasonable security of tenure of the area he cultivates, so long as he is not a witch or otherwise undesirable, and he may pass this right on to his heir. He has, secondly, the right to move elsewhere if he wants to, and he can himself become a *kibanja* owner (though he is unlikely, unless he is an 'important' person, to obtain a large tenanted *kibanja*) if he can find a piece of available uncertificated land elsewhere, pay the registration fee, and make a few small presents to the local chiefs through whom his application for a certificate will be submitted. He has, of course, no right to take out a certificate of occupancy over the land he cultivates in the *kibanja* of another, even though he and his forbears may have occupied this land for generations. This fact has occasionally given rise to complaint, and even to litigation, for it sometimes happens that a wealthy or important person is given a *kibanja* in which peasant cultivators are already settled without the knowledge of these persons, one or more of whom may himself have been contemplating the taking out of a certificate of occupancy over his ancestral land. His right to do so is, of course, permanently negatived by the grant of an over-riding right to another. Nor, as I have said, is it likely that the *kibanja* owner would permit an enterprising tenant to extend the boundaries of his holding in the course of the intensive development of his land by modern methods.

It would be wrong to conclude from the foregoing that the average Nyoro peasant tenant feels himself to be oppressed, or resents the *kibanja* system in its present form. There are complaints, but they refer to particular abuses, and never to the system as a whole, and they are remarkably infrequent. Whether this will long continue to be the case, as agricultural methods improve and the general level of development rises, is very open to question. Now, at any rate, one of the notable things about Bunyoro is the absence from the Native Courts of the spate of litigation about land so familiar in other areas. And it must be remembered that many Nyoro peasants, perhaps the majority, live on non-*kibanja* land, and so can, if they wish, take out certificates of occupancy over their farms if they are sufficiently interested, that by no means all, probably a minority, of the 5,000 certificates so far issued are over-populated *bibanja*, and, most important of all, that only about a quarter of the available cultivable land in the country is at present in use.

It remains to consider the Bunyoro *kibanja* system, which I have now somewhat cursorily described, in its relation to some other aspects of the social system, in particular, to political power and authority, to social status, and to economic development and differentiation. We saw that the system developed from a political, *quasi*-feudal right, vested *ex officio* in the Mukama's territorial chiefs, to a private right of exploitation, at first confined to political functionaries past and present and to members of the ruling family, and later extending itself to a wider range of persons of public repute and importance. Since 1933 any person who has the necessary money, and wishes to obtain a certificate of occupancy, can do so. The *kibanja* system, then, begins by reflecting exclusively political authority and power, and then moves into a second phase where it is an expression primarily of social status. It may, in recent years, be tending to express economic status, both because only the man, who has acquired a certain amount of money will contemplate the 'purchasing' of a *kibanja* and the rise in social status that this implies, and because it provides a means, as yet not greatly exploited, for the progressive cultivator to obtain greater security, or the appearance of such, over the holding he proposes to develop. This account does not express simply a historical succession; the past, especially in Bunyoro, still lives in the present, and all three stages are still represented in the contemporary scene.

What is clear is that a large tenanted *kibanja* in Bunyoro today is not an agricultural estate being developed on progressive lines by the certificate holder (there is as yet little private development of the land by modern agricultural methods in Bunyoro); it is rather a tenanted though rent-free estate, still regarded as the proper perquisite of the royal family, ex-chiefs, and other important persons, and its size bears no relation to the extent of the cultivation undertaken by the certificate holder. Land held under a *kibanja* certificate is indistinguishable in the field from non-*kibanja* land. It is safe to say that a large *kibanja* is still an overt expression of the prestige and local importance which attaches to members of the ruling classes, and to new recruits to this class, and it is, so far as I can ascertain, the prestige which attaches to the proprietorship of large *bibanja*, and the rather limited and sterile authority that their possession implies, that is the major factor in their continued popularity, and their survival despite the Government's attempt to eradicate them. The hope that at some later date full freehold rights will be granted over *bibanja* now held on certificates of occupancy may still be a significant factor in their popularity,but I do not think that very many people are still really hopeful that full freehold tenure will ever be admitted on this basis.

I have tried to show this pervasive, deeply-rooted and enduring, if emasculated, 'landlordism' as a historical growth, the product of a complex of factors which include the semi-feudal political structure of pre-European Bunyoro, the social stratification typical of centralized social structures in general and of the interlacustrine Bantu peoples in particular, and the 1900 land settlement in Buganda. I have then tried to describe it, as far as the evidence so far available allows, in its present-day form as a complex of rights and obligations relating to the use and control of land. I have mentioned some ways in which the *kibanja* system can be prejudicial to improved farming, but the consideration of the practical means which should be taken to remedy the situation in so far as it is remediable, important though the problem is, does not fall within the scope of this paper.

Notes

[1] The Bahuma are the pastoral invaders, the Bairu the original sedentary population.
[2] The Muluka chief (pl. Muruka chiefs) are the lowest rank of officially recognised chiefs.
[3] *Enquiry into Land Tenure and the Kibanja system in Bunyoro, 1931; Report of the Committee:* Government Printer, Uganda, 1932.

V. Sheddick: Land Tenure in Basutoland*

Rights of Usufruct Generally

No Mosuto strictly speaking has any rights to land as a simple negotiable commodity. Such rights as he possesses are confined solely to the usufruct of land and to the ownership

* V. Sheddick, *Land Tenure in Basutoland*, H.M.S.O., 1954, pp. 10–12.

of the produce of the land. The nature of these rights varies with the character of the production unit.

Public rights. There exists a group of products to which all people may be said to have equal rights. They include such things as fuel, building timber, grasses, clay, wild plants and wild animals.[1] These goods may be said to be held on public tenure. At one time they could be collected by anybody within their own administrative area. Nowadays it is necessary to differentiate those items that are in short supply and which have thereby acquired scarcity value. To this sub-category belong thatch reeds and grasses, weaving grasses and wood. The utilisation of many of the scarce commodities held on public tenure is regulated by a system known as *maboĕlla,* under which the relevant production units are retained by the Chieftainship under strict control and public use of the products permitted under supervision at specified times. In this way the resources are protected against wholesale spoliation and are available to the community at a time when they are most needed.

There is a further group of commodities which must in principle be regarded as subject to public tenure, but which in fact is completely excluded from public usage. In this category must be placed coal and semi-precious stones. The sole[2] right to these minerals is vested in the Paramount Chief and his is the negative right of prohibiting their use and exploitation. For convenience there may be included under this head the *mesa* of Thaba Bosiu, the occupation of which, in view of its potentialities as a fortress, has been prohibited by the Central Government. It now remains as the burial ground of the Chiefs and a memorial to Moshŏeshŏe.

Private rights. Rights of a more exclusive nature are held by every married adult. They have a right to residential land, some fields to cultivate, some grazing for their stock and access to water. Normally, these rights may be claimed only through the person of a married male adult, though as will be seen, unmarried men and divorced or widowed women may on occasion successfully put forward claims in their own right.

These rights are not entirely unencumbered. Should a family fail to make use of its fields over a number of years, should they desert their dwelling place, should they fail to pay their taxes unless exempt, then they forfeit their titles. The perpetuation of the title within the family is further conditional upon the observance of the necessary degree of loyalty to the Chieftainship.

Whilst there is no exclusive right of usufruct, so also is there no exclusive right of disposal. Resources may on no account be sold or otherwise alienated. They may be loaned to another person provided the consent of the Chief has first been obtained.[3] Modern practice has introduced variations to this rule. . . .

Both public and private rights have in common the fact that they are allocated by recognised administrative authorities to subordinate social units as represented by a qualified individual. Once the rights are acquired they may be held during the holder's lifetime provided he is fitted to, and does in fact, use them. His private rights he may be able to hand on to his descendants, though not by any formal or implicit law of inheritance. Subject to his fulfilment of all the obligations of his tenure, he may not have his rights expropriated without being duly compensated with similar rights elsewhere.

Extraneous rights. Extraneous rights embrace those titles of access to resources held by non-Basuto people and by those Basuto who have framed new categories of demands for land for which native law has hardly yet provided rules.

At the outset it should be clearly understood that non-Basuto have absolutely no rights to buy or lease land of any description within the Territory, 'unless and until the same has been sanctioned and approved by His Majesty's Secretary of State'.[4]

It has already been mentioned that the Imperial Government has the right to establish camps in which its servants may be housed. Even so, it has no absolute claim to the land it occupies.[5] Its title is virtually that of an indefinite loan of land with no rights of permanent disposal or alienation of any part of it. The Administration and individuals may own houses and other structures but do so without any valid claim to the ground on which their structures rest.

The Administration has a second major title to land and resources which allows it to use them in a manner sanctioned by the Paramount Chief for the purpose of generally improving the land and resources of the Territory. By virtue of this title the Central Government has been able to initiate soil conservation schemes and to experiment with crops and grazing control.

Trading is now carried on by Europeans, Indians and Africans. They operate by permission of the Paramount Chief and under licence from the Central Government. When so duly authorised they are allowed the use of ground on which to build a store and a house with a garden. They pay no formal rent and hold no title deeds to the land, though they are very anxious to obtain them.

Missions, starting with the Paris Evangelical MissionarySociety, have been established in Basutoland since 1833. Education has been a characteristic of missionary activity in this country to such an extent that most of the schools are still organised by the several missions, though over-all control now rests with the Administration. Land for missions is granted by the Paramount Chief in consultation with the Central Government, the amount of ground being made available depending on the scope of mission activity.

The great development of Basuto owned road transport in recent years has been largely responsible for the creation of new production units and with them for demands for land which are largely extraneous to what has become accepted as normal practice.

Their numerous buses, or taxis as they are called, need garages and petrol supply points. They establish regular staging halts which soon attract cafés, bakeries, butcheries and stores. In this way there is developing an entirely new phenomenon, the staging area. As the little businesses that are associated with it thrive, so it tends to become a residential unit inhabited by tradesmen and artisans. The siting of such staging areas is determined more by the bus route schedule than by considerations of normal residential geography and local administration. They lack, up to the present, any administrative machinery within themselves though this will obviously develop rapidly when the constituent homesteads, which are now simple trading sites, begin to acquire rights to fields, grazing, and the other commodities that make up the normal homestead complex of titles.

Notes

[1] Except those protected by the Central Government.

[2] This statement represents the Basuto point of view and is subject to legal interpretation.

[3] A. Mabille: The Basuto of Basutoland, *J. African Society*, 1906, p. 363.

[4] Proclamation 65/1922 para. (1).

[5] It is of course true that attempts could be made to insist on the full legal implications of Proc. 14/68 (see footnote 3, p. 7), but they would constitute a violation of the relationship existing between the Basuto State and the British Government, as understood by the Basuto.

P. C. Lloyd: Yoruba Land Law*

The 'Family'

The term 'family land' has become too firmly enshrined in the Nigerian legal vocabulary to be lightly set aside and replaced by a more precise term. It is recognized by the High Courts, and to the Yoruba it is a literal translation of the vernacular *ilẹ ẹbi*. Yet the term has caused confusion. Sometimes it is used to distinguish land from public or vacant unallotted land (communal land); sometimes it is used to distinguish land held by a descent group from that held by an individual. It is frequently presumed that the individual purchaser of land has an estate tantamount to an English freehold—but it is insinuated that the group selling the land held some other estate known to customary law and quite different from a freehold. Another line of reasoning is that if the purchaser is deemed to have a freehold title, then so must the seller have it—and the corollary follows that all 'family land' is thus held as a customary law equivalent to the freehold estate.

The confusion arises from the failure to distinguish between the rights held by the

* P. C. Lloyd, *Yoruba Land Law*, Oxford University Press for the Nigerian Institute of Social and Economic Research, 1963, pp. 76–86.

family or descent group corporately in the land, and the law governing the exercise of those rights by the family. We might cite here, as an analogy from English law, the holding of freehold land by an individual or by a corporation with a body of trustees; both the individual and the corporation hold the same estate in the land, but the exercise of those rights by the corporation is governed by special laws. Similarly the Yoruba *ẹbi* is a corporate body with customary laws governing the exercise of its powers (we shall however avoid the terms corporation and trustees as these have such specialized connotations in English law as are inapplicable in Yoruba customary law). In this section we consider the nature of the group which holds family land. Rights in family houses are of a familiar nature.

It is sometimes suggested that there are two orders of family property: that created, according to myths, in the dim and distant past and held now by a large descent group which forms a major constituent part in the social structure of the town; and that created within the last century and held by a much smaller group, often a segment of the major descent group. But the laws which determine the rights of the group and of its members do not distinguish the size of the group, and apply equally to the *ẹbi* of a dozen members descended from a common father to one of a thousand or more members descended from an ancestor through many generations.

The rights held by the large descent group are sanctioned by myths which tell how the ancestor came to hold the property concerned. It is usually presumed that the land was granted to an individual immigrant to the town, though from the nature of his arrival it seems more probable that the named ancestor was perhaps the leader of a group of kinsmen and their followers. The myths tell how the oba granted land to his new subject in return for his allegiance. Grants of land within the last century are remembered in their historical context and in greater factual detail. The building of a modern house is not a matter for myth; but where one son almost alone builds a house on the site of his father's compound, the house will be termed the 'family house' of the father, and will be held not only by the wealthy son who built it but equally by his indigent brothers who contributed little.

The Creation of Family Property

Three conditions are necessary for the creation of family property—whether of land, house, or cocoa farm—in the Yoruba sense of this term. Firstly, the creator of the property must die intestate (or, if testate, must will that his property be shared according to customary law). Secondly, the customary rules of succession must be that rights in the property should pass to all the children—or all the male children—of the deceased; family property cannot be created where there is a sole recognized heir. Thirdly, the property must not be partitioned among the heirs but must be held corporately by them, and in turn by their descendants.

The family, a corporate body, is created upon the death of the founder holding an interest in land. It includes all his (or her) descendants in the male line (in the case of the agnatic lineage) or in both male and female lines (the case of the cognatic descent group). New members of the group belong to it by virtue of their birth, and they accede to their rights at the time of their birth (or, one might more logically add, at the time of their conception). The rights held by the individual member are not heritable—they are extinguished by his death. The legitimacy of a child, under customary law, as a member of the descent group is determined by his birth. The legal pater is the man who was the legal husband (having paid the bride wealth) of the mother at the time of the child's conception; this same rule is now extended to cover Christian marriages—a child conceived in wedlock being the legal issue of the married husband. The natural father of a child born to an unmarried woman or as the result of an adulterous union with a married woman may, by acknowledging the child as his own and caring for it (with the child's reciprocal acknowledgement of the father demonstrated especially at the latter's funeral), confer upon the child legitimate membership of his own family. Conversely a child may sever his relationship with the family of his father—either legal or natural—but refusing to perform the proper funeral rites for the father, and he thereby loses all rights in the family.

The Nigerian High Courts have, over the years, succeeded in defining the Yoruba concept of family property, but not before making some vain attempts to equate it with the English legal concepts. The members of the Yoruba descent group are like joint tenants in that there is in their interests unity of time, title, interest and possession; no member has a separate alienable share of the property. But the Yoruba family continues in perpetuity—there is no rule of survivorship as among joint tenants, where the whole estate devolves upon the last surviving child and passes thence to his own heirs exclusively. Among the tenants in common, in English law, there is no survivorship, the interest of each tenant passing on his death to his own issue or heirs; but unlike members of the Yoruba family, tenants in common have separate and alienable interests in the property which they hold. It is a pity that the judges did not look further back in history to the pre-feudal modes of English inheritance when they would have found, in the *gavelkind* of Kent for instance, systems of partible inheritance more akin to those of Africa.

The Rights Held by the Descent Group

. . . The rights in land held by a family or descent group do not necessarily amount to ownership, or to the equivalent of an English freehold estate. In some cases the group may hold usufructuary rights only, lacking the power to alienate any of these rights to strangers. Even when the group does possess the power to alienate its rights to others, there exist other competing interests in family land.

The rights of the descent group are limited by the sovereign rights of the oba and his chiefs to make rules controlling the use or alienation of the land. Its exclusive usufructuary right to the land is limited by various rights of the entire community to hunt, collect firewood or stone from the land, to rights of way and rights of access to water. The oba may be entitled to any royal game (usually leopards and elephants) killed on the land—though such rights are almost obsolete with the near extinction of the animals concerned. The group may now transfer its interests in ways known both to English and customary law—by grants to customary tenants, by lease, by pawn, and by mortgage. Finally the rights of the group are restricted by those of its individual members.

The rights of the descent group in the land corporately held by its members may be extensive, amounting to ownership, or limited. The term 'family land' or 'family house' is usually used in a context which suggests near ownership of the property cited, but there is no reason why a descent group should not hold almost any estate; it might be a mortgagee, a lessee or even the holder of an easement. The same basic rules governing the holding of rights corporately by a group apply in each case.

The Rights of an Individual Family Member

We might describe the rights of the individual under three heads. Each member of a descent group has a general usufructuary right to family land or in the family house; he is entitled to as much land or as many rooms (subject to these being available) as he needs, these needs being determined by the number of his wives and children. Secondly, each member has a voice in the management of the property, the respect paid to his opinions being determined by his age. Management consists of the allocation of land or rooms to individual members, of the control of the property—maintenance of the fabric of the house or compound, preservation of the soil by regulating bush-firing and fallowing, and restricting the over-planting of permanent crops—and of the alienation of the rights held by the group, where such is permitted by the laws of the kingdom. In farm land the individual member of the family has the right to cultivate the land but the use of natural produce is controlled by the group; the individual is often allowed to reap the oil palms on his own farms and is usually permitted to collect firewood and wild fruits for his domestic consumption. Commercial exploitation of any of these resources is, however, usually reserved to the group. The rights of management can only be exercised by the family acting as a corporate group and not by any individual member, unless he is so authorized.

Thirdly, the individual member has specific sole usufructuary rights in the rooms of the compound and in the farm lands which have been allocated to him by the family elders at the meetings of the group. If these rights are infringed by other family members (acting beyond their right to manage the property) the aggrieved member may take his complaint to the family meeting and ultimately to the customary courts, though the courts are most loath to interfere in family quarrels. In an Ekiti case, the court censured the head of a family who had allocated land to a member for building and then tried to withdraw the grant without good cause, describing the head as a 'troublesome man'.

The individual has no right to take legal action against a trespasser from another descent group—only the head acting on behalf of the whole group can institute such proceedings (for the trespasser will usually claim the land as that of his own descent group). The rights granted to an individual member may be for a short period, in the case of farm land, or in perpetuity in the case of land for house building. Usually a man holds rights to certain land or to rooms in the family house for his life-time, and the group will usually give preference to the sons of a man to continue to use the same land or rooms especially when these contain the graves of near ancestors. Yet one cannot speak of the sons inheriting their fathers' rights, for the family may reallocate land and rooms at any time, and if individual members do not get the sites they have wished for, they have no redress so long as they are given a fair share in the property.

The rights of the individual are today complicated by the fact that he not only holds rights in a specific part of the family land but he may erect improvements on the land. In the past, the compound was built by the collective efforts of the whole group; the modern house is built by an individual or by a small group of siblings. Cocoa is planted by the individual farmer. We have, therefore, to distinguish between the rights held in the land and those held in the improvement. The improvement—a house or cocoa farm—belongs to its creator and will at his death become the family property of his issue, but this group will be but a small segment of the descent group holding the land. In general the members of the descent group have no interest in the house built on their land by an individual member; they have no general right to its use nor any right to manage it. The creator of the improvement would have been granted land by the entire group for the purposes specified; and inasmuch as he continues to occupy the land (and will do so as long as the improvement exists) he cannot normally be evicted from the land by the group. If the land was compulsorily acquired by the government the descent group would receive compensation for the land and the individual for his improvement. It is not certain whether the group could evict a member and destroy his improvements, compensating him and giving him land elsewhere, for in the towns studied here members of a descent group have only town-planned and sold the vacant land at their disposal. Similarly it is not clear what would be the legal position if the group sold to a stranger land on which was sited the house or cocoa of an individual member; the consensus of opinion is that the rights of the individual could not be extinguished unless he voluntarily accepted compensation; informants' usual reply to this type of question is, 'but no family would ever sell land like that—the buyer would always approach the occupier as well as the family.' Such expressions of the moral norms do not help us to establish the legal rules.

The individual member of the family may not alienate the land on which he grows annual crops or the family house which he occupies. It is possible however in some cases for the individual to alienate the usufructuary rights which he holds in family property. In the more commercially developed towns with a land shortage a man may be regarded as holding rights in a specific plot of land or in specific rooms of the compound for a long period—he is not likely to be allocated any other places. Here a man may be allowed to let his rooms to strangers or allow annual tenants to farm his land. A man will usually transfer his rights in this way if he is away from town or otherwise unable to exercise them; he will not of course be allowed by the group to alienate his rights and then seek more land or more rooms from the group. A man cannot transfer rights in excess, either in quantum or in time, of those which he holds from his family. Any transfer to a non-member of the descent group requires the permission of the group expressed at its meeting.

The creator of an improvement on land may transfer his rights in the improvement itself; but he cannot transfer, to a non-member of the group holding the land, his specific right to use the land. In effect he cannot transfer his improvement, for it is fixed to the land and it is impossible to hold rights to it without holding some right to occupy the land. He can of course transfer his improvement to another member of the land-holding group, for the latter will already hold a general right to use the land. But the sale of houses or cocoa farms between members of a group is rare, for ties of kinship are usually sufficiently strong that the members will combine to loan the would-be vendor the money he requires—probably to repay a debt. Some forms of alienation might be regarded as transferring no interest in the land—examples are the lease of a house to annual tenants or the pawning of cocoa trees; but even here the members of the descent group might refuse permission to allow the tenants or creditor-pawnee to live or work side-by-side with the family members. Other forms of alienation of an improvement—lease, mortgage, sale—cannot be considered apart from rights held in the land itself, and in these instances the owner of the improvement may only transfer his interest with the authority of the entire descent group holding the land.

The legal issues involved are often obscured by the tacit consent to alienation given by the descent group members. Furthermore, many Yoruba do not view the lease of a building, even to a commercial firm, for a limited period (e.g. up to 30 years) as affecting the group's interest in the land; particularly is this true of commercial buildings such as cocoa stores, for permission to build such on family land practically implies the right to lease them to the produce-buying agents. Moreover the various connotations of the term 'consent', examined in a later section, are not considered.

The Management of Family Land

The right to manage the family property and to alienate it resides, as we have said, in the group acting corporately and not in individual members. We might divide family land into three categories similar to those used earlier to describe the land of the community—public, private and vacant land. We have already described the second category—the rights of individual members in the land allocated to them. Vacant land is the land which may be allocated by the group; it includes that land over which no member of the group is exercising any specific rights of building or cultivation; it may be extended to include land which has no permanent improvements on it and from which members of the group can be evicted and given alternative land. The planting of small patches of food crops or tobacco within the built-up area of the town does not usually grant the cultivator permanent rights in this land. The compound, or part of it, reserved for the head of the descent group, together with the shrine of the group's deity and ancestor are the public property of the group, rights being vested in the entire members, and not in any individual holding the office of family head, or priest. At the farm certain land or palm trees may be reserved for the use of the family head, though exploited to his benefit by the members. Similarly land may be held for the use of the occupant of any hereditary chieftaincy title held by the group. The control and alienation of such land rests with the entire group—in most cases there is, of course, great reluctance to transfer the land containing the family shrine, ancestral graves and the rooms of the family head.

In the Yoruba descent group, a gerontocratic association, the eldest male member is usually the head of the group—the *olori ẹbi* or *bale*. He takes office automatically and without ceremony upon the death of his predecessor. In some cognatic descent groups of shallow generation depth—descended perhaps from a common grandfather—a woman may act as head, if she is the eldest living member, of dominant personality and living in the family house. The family head presides over the meetings of the descent group, usually held in his own house in the compound. He has jurisdiction over all matters pertaining to the group, including its land; he allocates land and rooms in the family house. But he is not a trustee, in the English legal sense. As the executive head of the group he may issue all manner of orders, but is, nevertheless, subject to the will of the group expressed at its meetings; he may not override the decisions of the group. He cannot be deposed, though if unpopular he may be ignored by his family members, and recognition as leader given to his immediate junior in age. It seems that most family heads do abide by the decisions of their group—decisions which are always said to be unanimous, for members will continue to discuss until all opposition has died. For the family head to be quarrelling with his group is a slur on the name of the group, and to take such a quarrel to court is even more damaging. The courts for their part are loath to interfere in such cases and appear to have produced no judgements or rules defining exactly the legal relationship between the family head and his members.

Any dealing in family land must be conducted by the family head. Only he (or his appointed representative) may take action in court to protect the interest of the family and he always sues 'on behalf of the family'. All documents should be signed by him. Unanimous decisions are now rare in family meetings for there are fewer social sanctions by which dissident members can be coerced. The problem thus arises of defining the degree of consent necessary to validate a dealing in land. Obviously a sale must not be voided because one very junior member refuses to agree to it. The opinion of most

Yoruba seems to be that the head of the family and the heads of each branch, or segment of the group, should be a signatory to any dealing, these men connoting the general support of the members of their own segment. These segments are the major groups into which a descent group of many generations in depth is divided; in the case of the group formed by the issue of a polygynous father the segment heads would be the eldest sons (or daughters) of each wife; if the father was monogamous each child should sign, and in subsequent generations the eldest descendant of each of these children. This is the ideal arrangement; in practice many documents are signed by the family head and his witnesses, though the approval of the group is not disputed. In other cases group solidarity is weak and members have acquiesced in the sole dealings of their family head—it is then difficult for them to protest against a completed dealing with which they particularly disapprove.

In those descent groups possessing a hereditary chieftaincy title, the control of family land and particularly its alienation has often passed into the hands of the chief. The roles of the family head and of the chief are quite distinct—the former has jurisdiction only within the descent group, while the latter is its representative in the government of the town. But the former is an old man, often senile, while the latter is chosen for his ability. The chief may be not only more capable but may feel that, inasmuch as alienation of land represents dealings with strangers and perhaps aliens to the town, he is more competent to handle the matters. The chief thus acts as family head; but he has no more power than the family head, though his influence is usually such that members acquiesce in his sole dealings in the land. One must repeat here the need to distinguish between the roles of the chief as family head, and as administrative head of a quarter exercising powers delegated by the oba, or as head of a quarter—a territorial unit—in which land rights are vested.

Partition of Family Land

We have dealt so far with family land as it is held by a group tracing descent from the common ancestor who is believed to have created the property. However, family land may be broken into smaller units by partition.

Partition generally takes place along the lines of cleavage in the descent group produced by the process of segmentation. The land may be partitioned into as many separate blocks as there are segments; or it may be divided between each individual member of the group, though this is more rare. Full partition means that each segment gains over its own portion all the rights hitherto exercised by the whole group, but has no further rights (excepting as members of the community) over the land awarded to other segments. Each segment becomes in effect a separate landholding descent group or family. Whether the original group maintains its identity as an active corporate group depends on the existence of functions other than land holding. Partition does not extinguish the concept of 'family land' for even if land is awarded to an individual it is presumed that it will become family land in the next generation.

Full partition is still unusual for this generally heralds the dissolution of the descent group, land holding having been its prime function. Far more common is the partition of *some* rights among the segments of the group. Family farm land is frequently divided so that each segment holds usufructuary rights over a specified area. Members of the segment cultivate within their own area and may only seek land in that of another segment when they are desperately short. Sometimes only the rights to cultivate may be so divided; sometimes the right to reap the wild oil palms, receive timber royalties or exploit the stone are divided too. Such divisions exist only by the tacit approval of the group—they are not recorded in writing. The entire group retains the right to alienate the land, though this right too is reduced as individual segments at first grant land to strangers without notifying the group and later perhaps try to sell the land. As often as not partition is recognized by the courts, not because the entire group has agreed to it but because one segment has exercised rights of ownership over its land, without drawing any protest from the remaining segments.

Partition usually follows the long agreed division of usufructuary rights; and those divisions reflect the pattern of segmentation. It would of course be more exact to say that the segments exist as corporate social groups *because* the land is so divided among them. The partition of vacant land held by the group is usually into as many equal shares as there are segments of similar rank. Similarly the partition of property created by a man between his own immediate heirs is, in a polygynous union, equally *per stirpes* according as there are wives with children, and *per capita* in a monogamous one, irrespective of the use of the property between the time of the death and that of partition.

The Extinction of Rights in Family Land

The rights of the descent group in its property cannot be forcibly extinguished, in customary law, except by compulsory acquisition by the government of the town; and in such circumstances the oba must grant the group alternative land, for its ancestor joined the community on the understanding that he and his descendants would be allowed sufficient land. To deprive altogether a group of its land is tantamount to banishment; should the entire group be expelled for rebellion its land will be treated as abandoned and available for re-allotment by the oba and chiefs. But the punishment is always conceived as the banishment from the community, and not as the deprivation of land.

Similarly the individual member of the group can only be deprived of his general right to land by expulsion from the group; this was possible in the past—the offending member, probably a criminal, being driven from the town or sold as a slave. Family members today offend their group by selling land held by the group; their punishment is often the forfeiture of land held by them—though it is rarely specified whether the member loses his general right to land and his right to participate in management of the property, or whether he merely forfeits any specific rights over certain areas. When the family is allocating its vacant land as building sites, unpopular members will be left out of the distribution, being told that there was 'not enough land' for them.

C. M. A. Gayer: Report on Land Tenure in Bugisu*

Bugisu Customary Land Law

. . . Individual land rights are of very ancient usage and . . . were subject to clan and family controls, which today we should call safeguards. I shall now attempt to analyse in simple language, without theory or comparisons, the various land rights which may vary to a minor degree in different parts.

(*a*) The individual land owner has the right to:
- (i) Utilise his land as he thinks best.
- (ii) Lend or rent his land for temporary purposes.
- (iii) Pledge crops on his land, but not the land itself.
- (iv) Sell land subject to the approval of the family.
- (v) Dispose of land according to the customary laws of inheritance.
- (vi) Dispose of trees growing on his land.
- (vii) Prohibit grazing near his homestead and cultivation.
- (viii) Fence his homestead and cultivation.
- (ix) Prohibit the digging of pits for game or stone except by consent.

(*b*) The clan or family has the following powers and rights over the land:
- (i) To settle land disputes within the area of its control.
- (ii) To exercise a right of option to buy in any land offered for sale by a member of the group or by an adopted member through prior purchase.
- (iii) To prohibit the sale of clan land to an undesirable person.
- (iv) To declare as void any land transaction which has not received its approval.

(*c*) The community has the following rights:
- (i) Grazing over the whole country; but damage to cultivation must be made good.
- (ii) The use of salt licks by the recognised paths of access.
- (iii) The watering of cattle at any running or open waters; recognised watering places have of course been established with tracks of access.
- (iv) The free use of water from springs, since water is the gift of God. But where wells have been dug in times of drought a charge may be made for the labour but not for the water. (Irrigation rights are a new development.)

* C. M. A. Gayer, 'Report on Land Tenure in Bugisu', in *Land Tenure in Uganda*, Government Printer of Entebbe, 1952, pp. 9–10.

(*d*) Firewood may be gathered freely anywhere in the communal forest, but no dead wood or windfalls may be collected on someone's land unless with his permission.

(*e*) Grass for thatching may be cut anywhere, but it would be considered bad manners to cut near someone else's house. Plantain fibre (*byai*) is of course the property of the plantation owner.

(*f*) Because people nowadays trade in pottery, those who need clay pay the land-owner for it. Formerly clay deposits were communal.

(*g*) Honey found in the bush is considered to be the property of the finder, but hive honey is the property of the hive owner and honey found in a tree near a house is considered to be the property of the householder.

(*h*) Hunting is no longer a tribal pastime, as game has given way to the pressure of population and today wild animals are only found on the Mwiyembe and Sebei plains and high up on the mountain; hunting rights may be said to be extinct.

NOTE: The Bagisu claim, and boundary marks support their claim that these customary land rights applied to the whole of Bugisu up to the summit of Mount Elgon. The forest reservation cut across some of these rights. So far as possible established rights of residence and usage above the forest line have been returned to them under legal safeguards under the Forest Ordinance and Rules, but it is perhaps understandable that there is still confusion in their minds as to the position. I have been able to find no evidence that the Bagusi have had at any time any idea of forest preservation or rules to that effect, and it would indeed be surprising if they had, since the value of the preservation of natural forests has only been realised in Europe and America during the present century.—C. M. A. G.

Chapter 17

OTHER RIGHTS IN RELATION TO LAND

It has already been pointed out that this chapter is a continuation of the preceding one, but the inclusion of a separate chapter on this topic is justified by the fact that it deals with lesser and subsidiary rights. All the accounts presented here deal with the same sort of rights—i.e. fishing, hunting, grazing, forest, and those relating to the use of water and trees.

W. Allan: Land Holding and Land Usage and the Plateau Tonga of Mazabuka District*

Grazing Land

Rights in grazing land. Among the Tonga, as with most cattle owning tribes, all uncultivated land and all garden land during the intercrop period, is subject to common rights of pasturage. As a general rule any member of the *chisi* (which now means the present-day chieftaincy) has the right to graze whatever number of cattle or other stock he pleases anywhere within the *chisi*; but no cattle of one *chisi* may graze within the boundaries of another.

We could find no evidence of any attempt to control grazing, either now or in the past, and the movements of stock are left largely to the discretion of the herdsmen, often irresponsible boys. Cattle are commonly, but not invariably, grazed in large herds (*butanga*, pl. *matanga*). As Chief Sianjalika said, 'herds from different kraals may join up for grazing if the herdboys are friendly, or they may graze in different directions if the herdboys wish; there are no rules about grazing'.

The cattle are herded throughout the rains and during the early dry season while any crops remain in the lands, but this herding is often inefficient possibly because a large proportion of the boys to whom this task would normally fall are at school from 8 a.m. to 1 p.m., and a good deal of damage to crops results. This is said to be regarded lightly by cattle-owners and Native Authorities and the sufferers frequently complained that they find it difficult to obtain redress. Many of the farmers also complained of this lack of redress and expressed a desire to have their own grazing land so that they might be able to keep other peoples' cattle away from their crops.

Nevertheless, judging by fifteen cases in a small number of court records we worked through, when cases are brought before the courts compensation is regularly awarded.

A man may not kill cattle which are damaging his crops. If he does so he is required to pay compensation and will get nothing for the damage to his crops (e.g. Case No. 3A of 1944, Chief Monze. Award of an ox as compensation for a calf killed). He may, however, kill a pig and we observed one case of a man who, finding a stray pig in his garden, promptly dispatched it with a spear.

Reservation of grazing areas. Undoubtedly in the past each community reserved considerable areas exclusively for grazing (*Machelelo a ngombe*). The origin of this practice was probably a desire to avoid damage to crops and the dissension arising from it, rather than a conscious attempt to preserve grazing against the encroachment of cultivation. If a person did make a garden within the acknowledged grazing area he appears to have suffered no penalty other than lack of redress for damage by cattle. In a case before

* W. Allan, *Land Holding and Land Usage and the Plateau Tonga of Mazabuka District*, Oxford University Press for the Rhodes-Livingstone Institute, 1948, pp. 114–120.

Chief Siamundu (No. 9A of 1943–44) the plea specifically stated that the cattle ate crops not in a grazing area (*Musena*). Compensation was paid by each cattle-owner according to the number of his cattle.

These grazing areas were commonly the dambos (seasonally wet, grassland drainage areas) or the *Misena* (wide, seasonally wet vleis or thorn dambos), but areas of bush grazing were also reserved and in the escarpment hills the streamsides were cultivated and the slopes reserved for grazing. As a result of the general adoption of the plough which placed a premium on readily stumped land increasing pressure of population and demand for land, the grazing areas were rapidly encroached upon. This process continued unchecked until recently when the practice of reservation was revived and grazing areas were demarcated by the Agricultural Department and protected by Native Authority order. We have already noted some indirect complaints on this score from people who have lost cultivated land as a result of these demarcations; but it is in most cases land which, according to customary law, they should not have cultivated, and our general impression is that the people regard this measure as reasonable and do not seriously oppose the revival of the grazing areas.

Grazing crop stover. Private rights in cultivated land lapse after harvest and cattle may graze freely on the crop stover in anyone's garden. No man may reserve the stover for his own cattle. This lapse of individual rights after harvest is clearly illustrated by a court case of which we obtained a record. The defendant in this case was a man who had dug a well in his garden. After harvest a cow belonging to a neighbour fell down the well and was injured. The defendant was held responsible for the injury and was ordered to replace the beast (Chief Siamundu, Case No. 17 of 1944–45).

Here, it would seem, is one difficulty in the way of agricultural improvement based on the use of at least part of the crop refuse for manure making. Not only do the cattle require the stover but according to Tonga custom no man has the right to make individual use of it. We do not suggest that this is the reason why practically no cultivators, other than paid demonstrators, have so far adopted the practice of making manure or 'compost', but it is a difficulty which is likely to arise in the future. Fowke enquired into the case of a man in Mwanachingwala'a area, the only man in that area who uses his maize stalks to make manure. According to this man, other people do not object to his cattle grazing in their gardens and eating their stalks after he has carted his own to the kraal, and he does not think that anyone has thought about this matter at all.

On the other hand the answers to our questionnaires about the use of manure indicate that people who compost are beginning to object to their fellow's cattle grazing in their crop stover. Increasing use of compost is bound to come into conflict with the old law that crop stover is commonage.

The Tonga have not yet realised that a potential problem exists; but if more than a negligible number of people were to use their crop stover for manure, conflict would almost inevitably arise between them and those who did not, and the latter would have the support of Tonga customary law. The situation is somewhat different in the area where cattle transhumance is practised; there, the stover is much less important as cattle food, and there is likely to be less opposition to its use by individuals. It should be noted that Mwanachingwala's people practise cattle transhumance but we made enquiries also in Ufwenuka's area (where only paid demonstrators make compost) and obtained precisely the same reaction; the question had not yet presented itself in the form of a problem or been given any thought whatever.

The chief does not appoint a day after which cattle may enter the gardens but it is said that all headmen urge their people to harvest so that the cattle may go in. After harvest has started the cattle begin to go into the lands and they are herded until all crops have been removed.

Cattle transhumance. The great grassland area of the Kafue Flats provides, in the neighbourhood of the river and its lagoons, dry season grazing for considerable numbers of cattle, but among the Tonga only the people of Mwanachingwala and Chongo practise a regular cattle transhumance. Most of the cattle from these two *Masi*, over 33,000 head in all, are transferred to the Flats in the dry season, though a few are now kept at the villages and watered from wells. The movement to the Flats takes place from June to

August and the return to the Plateau, which depends on the rains, may begin as early as October though usually later, and it is completed by December.

These two Chiefs, Mwanachingwala and Chongo, have long-standing agreements with Batwa villagers living on the Flats, over whom they claim suzerainty. Cattle from Mwanachingwala's country go to the area of the Batwa Chief Kasako while Chongo's people send theirs to the area of Chief Mutali. Their own herdsmen accompany and stay with the cattle and the part of the Batwa is confined to occasional assistance, herding or ferrying cattle across the river and supplying the herdsmen with food. No payment for grazing rights is made to the Batwa but they are given milk in return for services and in exchange for supplies of food.

The cattle from Chongo's country used to go to the Flats and return by way of Banakaila but now, it is said, they can no longer do so because of veterinary restrictions and this great concentration of stock passes through Mwanachingwala's area twice each year.

Other chieftaincies may occasionally join in the transhumance movement. For example, in two seasons of exceptional drought three villages of Sianjalika sent their cattle to the Flats, after obtaining permission to do so from Mwanachingwala. Batwa villagers looked after the cattle while they were there and were given tobacco in exchange for their services. This was merely an emergency measure. Sianjalika and his Councillors stated emphatically that, although they realise the *chisi* is greatly overstocked, they would not regard a regular transhumance movement as a practical possibility. They based their objections not on any likely opposition from Mwanachingwala or Chongo, but on the opinion that the distance is too great (though it is less than some regular transhumance movements) and the people would not take their cattle there. Their attitude is, of course, affected by the large areas of unused Crown Land to the west of the chieftaincy and especially by the fact that certain alienated farms on which they are accustomed to graze have recently been re-occupied. They have the almost invariable and usually irrational African attitude illustrated by the statement made to us several times; 'it is not that there are too many cattle, there is too little land'.

Fishing Rights

Insufficient enquiry was made into these. In Ufwenuka's, Mwanza's, Chongo's, Monze's and Siamundu's chieftainships, there is practically no fishing, and we did not get down to the proper fishing areas in the Flats. The wider distribution of fish is an important problem, so more research is urgently required into the ownership of fishing-rights and the trade in fish.

A fishing-weir was visited in the Magoye River near Magoye, and its owner and five other weir-owners were questioned about their rights. The inheritance of the weirs, the cooperative working of the trap-sites in them, and family consumption of fish are discussed in Chapter VII.

The weir we visited is built where a sandbank on one side of the river approaches a steep bank. There was no other weir in sight and informants indicated that others were all at some distance. Weirs are fished from the time when the waters begin to fall after the rains until the river is low. Small fish are caught in lobster-pot type traps set in the weirs. It seems that the weir-holders own the right to make a weir in a certain undefined stretch of river, and can prevent others building near his weir upstream. Informants stressed the upstream ban; downstream they would not prevent people building, though another weir-holder might. Presumably this relates to fish-movements, the fish being carried downstream by the flood. There are no boundaries between the stretches of different holders. One informant had made a weir at a suitable site he saw; the nearest holder was his maternal uncle. Informants said they had never heard of a dispute over these rights.

The pool forming above the weir does not belong to the weir-maker. Any woman of the country (any local limitation?) can fish in the pool with a scoop-basket (*kuzela*) or with shrimp nets or handhold baskets; men can stab or use hook-and-line or baskets there. Informants placed a point about five yards above the weir beyond which trespass would lead the holder to complain that his traps were being spoilt. He would not protest if small children fished there.

It is therefore clear that all the weir-holder owns is a right to make a weir at a certain point. Judging from six examples analysed a man does not (should not?) work a weir by himself, but gets some relative—brother, nephew, or son—to work one less trap-site than he. As will be seen below, this seems to give this man the right to inherit the rights to make the weir. These rights pass patrilineally or matrilineally.

We were told that at the height of the waters the baskets are emptied every day. All the fishermen said they gave fish for relish to their close relatives, and they told us of the following additional sales:

(a) Sold one-third of bag for 10*s*. (1945) to middleman who took it to Lusaka;
(b) Three others sold 5*s*. in 1945, and one nothing.
(c) One Lozi-speaking informant gave us this account:
1943: did not fish as ill, no one to fish for him as he lives on his own, his sons all at school;
1944: sold 15*s*. worth
1945: sold 22*s*. worth.

It is worth noting, whether it is due to general Tonga lethargy or to absorption in gardening, that these Tonga do not seem to put much effort into their weirs. One man had inherited two weir-sites but used only one; he could not, he said, work both. Seeing how small these weirs were, our Lozi servants were shattered by this laziness. But this informant is also the only Tonga in the part to make compost for his gardens.

Earlier in the year we saw a weir built on the Agricultural Station where the Ngwezi flows into the Magoye. The builder asked the permission of the Agricultural Supervisor but may also have indigenous rights.

While we were at Magoye we saw men passing with large barbel. We were told in a final brief conversation that the men of the neighbourhood are summoned (by whom?) to fish pans on a certain day. There are no panholders who take a proportion of each man's catch as in Barotseland, but only men of a defined locality can attend (on the first day only?). Others are driven away. Each man keeps his own catch. There was however some loose talk of there being ritual spots at which offerings were made, and it may be possible that offerings are made at the pools by some man who takes a part of the catch. Unfortunately this was at the end of the fieldwork and we each got separate parts of this information and had not a chance to coordinate them.

When men go down from the Plateau to graze their cattle in the Flats they say they fish with spears without the local Twa objecting, but they do not use nets or traps.

There must be considerable trade in fish from the Flats into the Plateau. At distant Luponda we were told that the Twa brought fish there, but in no budget there did the purchase of fish occur, as it did among the farmers of Keemba and Mutantu. One informant at Mutantu said he lived during the first year he moved there by taking sugar to the fishermen in the Flats to exchange for fish which he sold at a handsome profit on the Plateau. This form of specialisation, which might be organized, is the one of the few now offering for development between the regions of Tongaland.

Rights in Other Resources

As in all primitive tribes, rights in other natural resources such as wild fruits, clay, thatching grass, felled wood, honey, game, vest as soon as an individual appropriates these. We were told that there is no local ownership of these resources. The Sichaloba 'Forest' in Siamunda's area is also visited by people of Ufwenuka's area for wild yams and rubber vine fruits, though exchange of the yams for maize was also spoken of. It therefore seems that there is not even a *chisi* restriction on the taking of these resources.

Honey belongs to the finder, except of course in placed hives. The Tonga definitely stated that anyone from anywhere could pick wild fruits, even in cultivated gardens. We pressed this with some surprise, for among the Lozi fruit from trees in cut gardens belong to the garden holder, and this had been stated to be the Tonga rule in the District Notebook. However, our informants were very firm on this point, and stressed this by pointing to planted trees on old hut sites and saying that their fruit belong to the former site-holder.

Everyone denied the statement in the District records that wild-fruit trees near a hut belonged to the hut-owner, and that trees within a certain area round a village belonged to the village, and only in bush distant from villages could anyone pick fruit at will.

I. Schapera: A Handbook of Tswana Law and Custom*

Grazing and Water Rights

Every man in the tribe is entitled to free grazing and water for his cattle. The cattleposts (*meraka*) are generally situated a considerable distance from the village settlements, often a day's journey or more by foot. They are simply grazing stations selected for their accessibility to water and for the quality of their pasture. The cattle graze in the open veld by day, and at night are brought back into a specially erected kraal (*lesaka*), or enclosure made of thorn-bushes. The kraals are not kept permanently at one spot, but shifted about according to water and grazing conditions. During the dry season they are generally located near to river beds or boreholes, every man having his own special site to which he always goes. In the rainy season they are moved farther inland to fresh pastures, where an old kraal is renovated or a new one built in the immediate vicinity.

Pasture land was originally allotted by the Chief to the wards of the tribe. Each ward thus had its own cattleposts together in the same district, spoken of as its *naga* (veld) or *lefatshe* (country), and supervised by its headman. This district was usually a very extensive tract of country, within which members of the ward might move their cattle about as freely as they pleased, without asking permission from others. All members of the ward had the right to keep their cattle in this region, and grazing and water rights within it belonged only to them. The Chief had his own special pasture lands, but could also move his cattle to any part of the tribal territory for grazing.

The original tendency towards segregating the cattleposts of one ward from those of another has been obscured in some degree by the fact that outsiders have now been allowed to come into the ward area. If, e.g., a man is dissatisfied with the land where his cattle are grazing, he may ask a friend in some other part for permission to depasture them there. Or he may approach the Chief, if he has no friend in the area where he wishes to go. The application in either case must be referred to the headman and other members of the ward to which the area belongs. If there is room, they may allow him to make his cattlepost with them and to water his cattle there; but they also have the right to refuse, and to eject him if he trespasses. If the application is refused, he must remain where he is or seek room somewhere else. Even if he is allowed in, he retains the right to go back whenever he wishes to his original cattlepost, and need not, should he choose to do so, seek permission from his own headman and former neighbours. The ruins (*matlôtla*) of his old kraal will be there to validate his right.

There is also generally a good deal of pasture land not specifically allocated to any ward. Any man choosing to do so may graze his cattle in these neutral areas without permission. Sometimes, however, a man will make himself a cattlepost in a hitherto unoccupied part of the country. This will then become known as his veld, and people who may subsequently wish to erect their cattleposts near his must first obtain his permission. Among the Kgatla, when shortage of water was leading to pressure upon the grazing round such water supplies as were available, Isang declared that all who would dig wells away from the localities used by most of the people would be given sole grazing and water rights in the vicinity of the well for a period of ten years. In consequence a number of wells were successfully sunk in the remote north-western parts of the tribal Reserve.

It is in some tribes an offence to burn grazing veld during the winter months, when grass is scarce. The right time is in October or November, when the first rains are due. Even then, however, a man may only burn where his own cattle graze, and should not let the fire come too near to other people's cattleposts. The Chief may further forbid any burning within certain areas which he desires to reserve for future grazing.

The right to water cattle at certain drifts or pools in the rivers is confined to the people whose cattleposts are habitually located there. Outsiders passing by or driving their cattle through the district also have the right to water their cattle there as they go along, and need not necessarily seek permission from the local people. But if a man wishes to water his cattle for any length of time, he must obtain such permission. Should he not do so, the owners have the right to eject him. In the late winter and spring, as the pools run dry, disputes often arise through herdboys trying to water their cattle without permission at some adjoining drift or pool still holding water. Such disputes were more

* I. Schapera, *A Handbook of Tswana Law and Custom*, Oxford University Press, 1938, pp. 207–213.

frequent in former times, when, it is said, fights between the herdboys were almost a daily occurrence at this time. Nowadays, since most people water their cattle in pits or wells dug in the bed of a river or some other suitable spot, disputes have become less common.

A man has the right, subject to the permission of the Chief, to sink a well anywhere in his own district in order to water his cattle, and may sink as many wells as he wishes. But he is expected also to consider the rights of others. He should not, e.g., sink a well near the arable lands of some outside village which may happen to be in the district, lest his cattle destroy their crops. If an outsider admitted into the district wishes to sink a well there, he must first seek permission from the headman, who, together with him, will survey the land and show him a suitable spot. If the headman refuses to grant him permission, he may apply to the Chief who if he sees no good reason for the refusal may order the headman to withdraw it. But, if a man enters a district where he has not been permitted to graze his cattle and sinks a well there without asking permission, he can be forced to leave it, even if he has already struck water. The well then becomes the property of the headman.

All wells were formerly regarded as common property, where anybody grazing his cattle in that area could water them. But it has gradually become the law that only the people digging the well are entitled to water their cattle there. Anybody else wishing to use the well must obtain the owner's permission, failing which, if he trespasses, he can be ejected or punished. The owner can refuse water for another man's cattle, but is bound to give the man himself water for his personal needs. So, too, people making dams for themselves, or deepening pans, have private rights over the water, which cannot be used without their permission. Should a man, after digging and using a well, leave the place, no one else may use it afterwards without his permission. He can come back to it at any time to take it up again and, if he finds some one else using it, can order him to leave. Should the trespasser fail to obey, he can be punished.

Among the Kgatla, the boreholes sunk in various parts of the tribal Reserve through the initiative of Isang in 1926–7 are common tribal property. Each borehole is looked after by a small committee of local cattle-owners, who are responsible for its upkeep, purchasing the necessary petrol, oil, and paraffin, and paying the man running the engine. Everybody watering his cattle there must pay every season 6*d.* per head for cattle, and 3*d.* per head for sheep or goats, to meet the cost of upkeep. The boreholes more recently sunk (in 1934) were financed by small groups of men, 'companies', as they are called, who alone are entitled to water there.

Wells are also sunk for domestic use in the river beds close to the villages. Many wards have their own special part of the river in which they dig such wells. Outsiders wishing to make wells there must obtain their permission, failing which the Chief must be asked for permission to dig somewhere else. Such wells are sometimes owned in common by all the members of the ward, who contribute towards the cost and assist in sinking them; sometimes they are owned collectively by a number of families; and sometimes a well is owned by a single family. The owners of a well have sole control over it. They may allow friends to take water from it for domestic purposes, or to water cattle there; but no one else may use it without their permission. Water is not usually sold, except among the Ngwato, where it is exchanged for bran or corn. During the dry season, when there is no standing water in the rivers, the people rely mainly upon these wells, which are always kept locked up by the owners at this time to prevent them from being used without permission.

Hunting Rights

Generally speaking, there are no private hunting lands owned in the same manner as arable and grazing lands. People may hunt wherever they like in their tribal Reserve, even over the fields and grazing lands of others, without making any payment or giving tribute. Among the Ngwato and other tribes bordering on the Kalahari Desert, the cattlepost districts are to some extent regarded also as hunting districts, in that normally only the people using them will hunt there. The Sarwa inhabiting such districts must give their masters the skins of the animals they kill, but can use the meat for themselves. Outsiders, however, may also hunt over these districts without permission, although they cannot claim tribute from the Sarwa.

The right to hunt freely all over the tribal territory applies in general only to small game or to meat for the pot. Among the Ngwato, Kgama made a law to protect big game. Anybody wishing to hunt eland, gemsbok, giraffe, and similar animals must now first obtain permission from the Chief, who has the right to refuse. The Chief, if he agrees, informs the headman in charge of the district where the man proposes to hunt. Should the headman come across anybody hunting big game there without his knowledge, he must report the man to the Chief, who will punish him if he has been doing so without permission. The secretary and locust birds are also protected. In addition, hunting of any description, save for the pot, is forbidden in the region between Serowe and Rakops. Similarly, among the Kgatla, Isang on occasion temporarily prohibited the shooting in certain districts of big game animals in danger of extermination. But there is, in both tribes, a good deal of poaching.

Wood and Other Natural Resources

Trees and bushes whose wood is used for building, fencing, making fire, and other purposes are in effect common property, and can as a rule be cut down freely in any part of the tribal territory. The Chief gets no payment of any kind from the people for the use of this wood. But there are several restrictions upon this general right. Trees, bushes, and stumps may not be cut or removed from another man's field without his permission. Further, trees in the immediate vicinity of a village or in the village itself, even in a man's own homestead, may not be cut without the permission of the Chief. The reasons given by the Kgatla for this particular restriction are that the trees should be left to serve both as protection in case of invasion, and as lavatories for old and sick people who cannot go into the hills. It is said also that if a man cuts down a big tree immediately about his own homestead 'he will be cutting down his own home', i.e. will bring misfortune upon himself. Fruit trees, such as the *morula*, and fruit-bearing bushes, such as the *moretlwa*, are also common property, and their fruits may be taken freely by any one. But oranges and other cultivated fruit trees enclosed within a homestead are private property, and to take their fruit without permission is regarded as theft.

There are also certain trees, such as the *mokgalo*, *mogônônô*, and *motlopi* (collectively termed the Kgatla *ditlhare tse namagadi*, female trees), which may not be cut in the autumn, when the corn is still young. The Chief must every year proclaim the beginning of this taboo season, and also the time when it ceases. Formerly, among the Ngwato and kindred tribes, the taboo was lifted by the Chief himself cutting a *mokgalo* branch. Then all the other people did so too, bringing the branches to repair or strengthen the great cattle-kraal adjoining the tribal *kgotla*. After this they could cut the trees as they pleased for their own use. Should anybody cut them previously he would be punished. During this time, too, people are not permitted to dig up trees of any kind in their fields, and there are various other taboos of a similar nature to be observed. It was, and in some parts still is, firmly believed that if this taboo is broken the rain when it falls will turn into hail which will destroy the crops.

Such objects as *mmu* (earth for building), *letsopa* (potclay), and *lešaba* (lime used for cleaning eating-bowls) are common property and can be dug anywhere. There are some well-known sources of supply to which everybody goes. But certain exceptions do occur. Earth for building cannot be dug in another person's homestead without permission, generally given readily enough, or on the mainroads without the permission of the Chief. Further, if people wish to use clay for making bricks, they must first obtain permission from the Chief, as this work entails building wells, kilns, and probably also a fence to keep out stray cattle. Certain women who dig potclay cover in the holes where they dig, so that others may not notice where they get their good clay; but they cannot complain if others also happen to find and use the same hole. The only specific restriction here—not, however, carefully observed—is that no clay may be dug during the autumn. This is part of the general taboo whose violation is held to bring down the hail upon the crops.

J. C. D. Lawrance: The Iteso*

Grazing Land

Tenure of land which is used exclusively for grazing cattle and which is never cultivated is communal.

* J. C. D. Lawrance, *The Iteso*, Oxford University Press, 1957, pp. 251–255.

Certain areas are set aside by the Land Authority or by the parish council as grazing land and may not be cultivated. Such areas are usually swamp edges or areas of poor land away from cultivation.

QUOTATION: *Achwa Sub-County 58/52: Court* v. *E. Tukei and others:*

The accused were convicted of cultivating in the swamp contrary to the orders of the parish council and thereby preventing the grazing of cattle. They were ordered to fence their crops and not to cultivate any further and were fined 10*s*.

Cattle may be grazed on grazing land or on resting plots of owned agricultural land without any fee.

Any person who allows his cattle to damage a neighbour's crops must pay compensation as assessed by the court and a fine of 10*s*. Fencing of plots is not obligatory and the onus is on the herdsman to prevent damage by the cattle.

Grass for thatching may be cut by any person anywhere on private or unoccupied land and no fee may be charged. But *asisinit* grass may only be cut by the owner of the land on which it grows in Kumi, Ngora, and Bukedea counties.

Certain specified areas may be closed to grazing by order of the local council and any person found grazing cattle in the closed area may be fined.

Areas round dams are usually so closed by parish councils and demarcated with sisal.

Larger areas which have become eroded through over-grazing are closed by sub-county councils.

If non-native-owned cattle are likely to be involved orders are issued by the District Commissioner under the Cattle Grazing Ordinance No. 13 of 1945. But cases involving native-owned cattle in such areas are tried in the native courts.

When grass is dry, no person may burn grass without permission of his local chief.

NOTE: This is simply a precaution against the spread of bush fires and loss of grazing. When there is no danger of fire spreading, grass may be burnt without permission.

QUOTATION: (*a*) *Orungo Sub-County 29/52: Court* v. *E. Okello:*

The accused was convicted of burning grass 'at the wrong time of year thereby damaging grazing land'. He was fined 10*s*.

QUOTATION: (*b*) *Asamuk Sub-County 25/52: Court* v. *Oreta Edosu:*

The accused was convicted of 'setting grazing land on fire at the wrong time of year . . .' (*komam na erai apaki nakicweete amunaari inya luenyamete aituk* . . .). He was fined 50*s*.

NOTE: This rule is extended to make it obligatory to stop a bush fire which is destroying grazing (Achwa Sub-County 32/52).

Water Rights

Natural water is free of access to any person whether or not it is situate on privately owned land.

No permission is required to dig wells or make small dams and no fee is payable.

Any such well or dam made on privately owned land remains the property of the owner if made by the owner or at the owner's expense.

NOTE: This is one view; exactly the opposite has been expressed, i.e. that wells become public even when made by an individual.

Certainly in Asuret, when E. Emuli made a dam of his own, slaughtering 108 head of cattle as payment for the labour and spending about 1,000*s*., the dam became public property and is used by all and sundry.

The local council may define places for the watering of stock and places for humans to draw water, and any person watering stock at the humans' watering place is guilty of an offence.

QUOTATION: *Ochero Sub-County 136/51: Court* v. *Y. Kinaga:*

Kinaga allowed eleven head of cattle to foul a tank in the part set aside for human consumption. He was fined 15*s*.

Hunting Rights

Hunting rights are vested in certain persons (*apolok ka eriga*). The *apolon ka eriga* is usually a clan leader of an area which is usually a sub-county or an area of similar size but may be larger.

Rights of the *apolon ka eriga* are limited to choice of time for the hunt, choice of locality organization of the hunt, and receiving a share of any animals killed. He has no proprietary rights over the land.

NOTE: Success for a hunt is ensured by the *apolon ka eriga* gathering the dung of as many species of animal as possible and boiling them together in a pot.

But long ago the *apolon ka eriga* may have had wider rights and even allocatory rights over his hunting grounds. One assessor writes:

Long ago there was forest land in which settlement was difficult or impossible because of wild beasts; there were leaders who controlled these forest lands: e.g.:

Omiat	*apolon ka eriga*	Achwa	in Amuria
Egasu	" "	Kapelabyong	in Amuria
Echungo	" "	Obalanga	in Amuria
Okomera	" "	Morungatuny	in Amuria
Omino	" "	Olomet	in Kaberamaido.

If people wished to settle on their forest land, they first held a meeting and the *apolon ka eriga* explained where each group would go and settle and get water.[1]

Forest Rights

Any person may gather fallen wood on any land.

Only an owner or user may cut trees on his land but any person may cut trees on unallocated land.

Certain trees because of their food properties or utilitarian uses are regarded as reserved trees and may not normally be cut down even by the person on whose land they grow. They are:

1. *Ekungur* (Butyrospermum parkii)
2. *Epeduru* (Tamarindus indica)
3. *Eloa* (Chlorophora excelsa)
4. *Etekwa* (Albizzia coriaria)
5. *Emurie* (Carrisa)
6. *Ekumi* (Diospyros mespiliformis)
7. *Ekoboi* (Terminalia)
8. *Ebule* (Ficus brachypoda or F. platyphylla)
9. *Elamai* (Ximenia americana)
10. *Ejinga* (Ficus sycomorus).

QUOTATION: *Bugondo Sub-County 99/51: Court* v. *M. Eseru:*

M. Eseru cut down an *ekoboi* tree and made a canoe out of it in 1950. He claimed permission was given by the D.C. but failed to prove this fact. He was convicted and fined 50*s*.

NOTE: There is a mixture of custom and governmental instructions in this law. The first four trees are reserved under the Forests Ordinance, 1947. But it is not unusual for persons to claim that they planted *eloa* or *etekwa* trees and to claim the right to cut them down and use the timber. Such claims are often upheld in native courts. But naturally sown *eloa* or *etekwa* trees are regarded as reserved. Other timber trees, *ekumi* or *ekoboi*, when ownership is claimed, are frequently felled, but naturally sown trees have a form of protection; see quotation above. Local carpenters are encouraged by Government to use local woods; this encouragement cuts across this law.

Some of these trees may also have medical or magical uses, which ensure their protection, in addition to their more practical uses as food or timber, e.g. *elamai* is protected as a cure for measles. Its leaves are pounded in water and the patient is washed in the liquid and the residue is rubbed in the hair. *Ejinga* cuttings are often planted round graves.

A chief who wrongly gives permission to cut a reserved tree may also be prosecuted.

NOTE: This law is based on one example, also from Bugondo (115/51), in which a chief was maliciously prosecuted on this charge. He defended himself by proving that his superior, since deceased, gave the permission at a time of food shortage when the Iteso needed canoes to pick water-lilies for food.

Trees planted by hand remain the property of the planter or his heir even if the land on which they grow has, through the planter's absence or some other reason, ceased to belong to him. But if he leaves the area he must detail some person to look after the trees and certify that they are his.

QUOTATION: *Mukongoro Sub-County 81/51: Owachi s/o Adupa* v. *Lebo s/o Kapule:*

Owachi sued Lebo for destroying 100 cassia trees, his private property. The Court awarded 20*s*. compensation (the trees were young ones) and Lebo was fined 15*s*. for destroying the trees.

NOTE: The usual trees so planted are cape lilac and cassia. There are considerable quantities in Kumi, Ngora, and Bukedea. Mvule trees are also planted. The larger trees are sometimes named individually after the planter or after the owner of the house near which they were planted.

Private trees may be bought and sold at the owner's discretion and sale conveys no title to land on which the tree grows.

No person may cut trees in a Local Government plantation without first obtaining permission of the sub-county chief and paying the prescribed price per pole.

NOTE: This section is included here because offences against it are invariably tried in the native courts. It is, of course, an offence under the Forests Ordinance, but native courts are not empowered to hear cases under that ordinance.

Note

[1] E. P. Engulu (personal communication).

R. J. H. Pogucki: Gold Coast Land Tenure*

Non-allodial Rights in Land

§1. *Classification.* Rights in land which are not allodial are either rights of a lesser nature or bear a special character. They may or may not be concurrent with the greater right, or be subject to it. The evolution of notions of such rights, in connection with the influence of the increase of economic values of the land and of its produce, has reached a stage in which classification is possible, based on a distinction of rights *in quantum.*

Pursuing this method the following lesser and special rights may be distinguished:

(A) Lesser rights, which are:

(*a*) rights to use land, which may be of various extent: either perpetual, inheritable and alienable; or may show the first two incidents fully, but not have attached powers of sale; or may consist only of surface user, limited in time and personal to the holder.

(*b*) common rights, among which may be distinguished the following: rights of way, fishing rights, hunting rights, grazing rights, water rights, rights to collect firewood and building sticks, rights to collect salt, rights to collect sand or gravel from a river-bed.

(B) Special rights, which are:

building rights, rights in trees, rights in creeks, streams and watercourses, securities for debt, ferry rights, rights in markets, and fishing rights.

§2. *Rights to use land.* Rights to use land which are perpetual, inheritable and alienable may reside in extended families, or individuals who hold land by partition of clan or family land between extended families or individuals, as the case may be, or by grant of land subject to reversion to the clan. Upon a sub-alienation all growing fruit trees and other trees of economic value are excluded, except by express proviso in the agreement, and all trees planted by the tenant, as well as buildings erected by him, are included in the reversion without compensation for betterment. In certain cases kinship groups of assimilated strangers, whether clans, extended families, or individuals, may have acquired similar rights. These rights include power to sell land with the consent of the clan or extended family, as the case may be, and powers to alienate land by other methods of transfer without such concurrence.[1] The rights are perpetual and have the estate of inheritance attached in so far as segmentary groups or individuals are affected.[2] Powers to commit waste are always attached, although there is no evidence that rights *ad inferos* reach further than the roots of trees cultivated on the land.[3]

* R. J. H. Pogucki, *Gold Coast Land Tenure,* Government Printer of Accra, 1955, pp. 24–31.

The right next *in quantum* is a right which has the same incidents, except that it is not capable of being transferred by sale. Such rights are held by assimilated kinship groups of strangers, or by descendants of ex-slaves and domestics.

Surface user is the least extensive of all lesser rights in land. It is a farming right pure and simple, personally attached to the individual or group to whom it is granted. The holder has no rights in growing trees,[4] and all betterments are appurtenant to the land. He cannot commit waste otherwise than to extract material for building. There is no estate of inheritance attached, although standing crops are the property of his successors. Surface user is held only by strangers.

§3. *Common rights.* Common rights in land are local customary rights *in alieno solo* which may be exercised by any stranger.[5] They serve undefined and fluctuating classes of persons. It ought to be noted that the impact of the growth of the economic value of some of these rights in certain areas has led to an evolution of certain common rights into distinct special rights which have become alienable.[6] Those common rights which now exist can be divided into two groups: unqualified and qualified. Unqualified rights are those which can be exercised by strangers without seeking the owner's permission, and without offering any prestation.[7] Qualified common rights are those which can be exercised by any stranger upon nominal permission from the landowner and, in some cases, under the condition of a prestation.

Rights of way are unqualified in all cases. A path once established cannot be closed and can be used by any person.

Fishing rights in the river Volta, except in the Ada estuary and in some lagoons,[8] are unqualified. In those areas in which fishing is pursued not mainly for the purpose of trade, and where it does not form an important item of subsistence, as e.g. on the eastern part of the Accra plains and in the Krobo areas, fishing rights are unqualified, except that in some isolated places nominal permission of the landowner is required. Ponds are not treated as subject to common rights of fishing.[9] There are no common rights of fishing in the riparian areas of the river Volta, where fish, shellfish and oysters are caught either in creeks or in watercourses, and form important items of subsistence and of trade and, therefore, have acquired a high value.

Hunting rights are unqualified, except in isolated instances where a prestation in the form of a part of the killed animal must be given to the owner of the land on which the animal was killed.[10]

Grazing rights are unqualified, except in some areas next to the bank of the river Volta, where nominal permission of the landowner and, sometimes, also a prestation in kind are required.[11] It must be noted that such rights do not include powers to erect a cattle-kraal. Land for a kraal must be obtained separately in the form of surface user.[12]

Rights to water are unqualified. There are however certain exceptions. All individually built wells are excluded. In the southern part of the area, where stock rearing is an important item of activities, watering rights are of importance. Such rights are qualified, but in some areas, where drinking water is scarce, water pools from which water for human consumption is drawn, are excluded.[13]

Rights to collect firewood are unqualified only in so far as the collected wood is used for domestic use of the collector. There is no common right to collect such wood for the purpose of trade.[14] In some areas, expecially on the Accra plains, planted shade trees are excluded from the exercise of common rights in firewood. There are qualified rights to sticks for the purpose of building, if the sticks are used only for the purpose of building a house for the collector. However, if in their physical form such sticks can be treated as timber, the right becomes a distinct alienable right and cannot be exercised even for the purpose of building the house of the collector.

Collection of salt from lagoons is a qualified common right. A prestation is paid in proportion to the amount of the salt collected by the stranger.[15]

Rights to collect sand and gravel from the bed of a river are unqualified.[16]

§4. *Building rights.* Ownership of buildings is a distinct concept. A house built by a person without any assistance from a brother or ascendant is regarded as his individual property during his lifetime. Upon his death it becomes the joint property of his male children administered on their behalf by the first born son; but a son who refuses to pay the expenses of the funeral of his father, or of an elder brother loses all his rights in the house although he may be permitted to live in it. If a house is built with the help of a brother it is regarded as joint property of both of them. Any house built with family assistance is regarded as family property. Ancestral houses, that is houses constructed by the founder of a clan or of a segmentary kinship group, are joint property of the appropriate group. The head of the group is the administrator of such houses. Strangers can own houses and such houses can be inherited by the stranger's descendants. The rights of a stranger in a house as understood by customary law brings into relief another precept: that rights in buildings are appurtenant to rights in the land.[17] This is shown by the rule that a building, erected by a stranger on land which he had not absolutely purchased, reverts to the grantors of the land upon designed abandonment by the stranger or his successors. Further a stranger cannot sell such a house, except in isolated instances with the assent of the land owners, although he can lease it. Houses can be sold or leased, although the practice is dependent upon actual economic circumstances which prevail in the locality. Hence in urban settlements along the main trade routes leases and sale of houses may be encountered more often than in rural localities, where there is no need for accommodation. In those localities, possibly because of the absence of a larger number of migrant strangers, the practice is to lease rooms only. Ancestral houses, although strictly speaking not *extra commercium*, are in practice never sold, unless sale is ordered as a result of court proceedings, or because the house has been attached for debt. In those localities as e.g. on the islands of the Volta estuary, where the existing mode of construction is to build houses from mats woven from palm leaves, no economic value is attached to houses. Therefore, and also in view of the ease of construction, the practice of transactions in houses is completely absent on these islands.

The elements of social cohesion in kinship groups appear prominently upon examination of rights and duties of persons as regards houses. First the rights and obligations of the head of a group which owns a house or houses: he allocates rooms in the house to members of the family, who are in need of accommodation; he is responsible for repairs; he administers the income, if any, from the house. In some cases the family may allocate a defined piece of land in order to provide funds to defray expenses connected with the maintenance of the house. In other cases funds in cash or labour are provided. The head of the family usually lives in the ancestral house, except in such cases in which he has his own individual house and chooses to inhabit it. In such cases another member of the family is selected to occupy the ancestral house, or the house may be used to accommodate widows and their children. A member of the group owning the house is obliged to share in the expenses and labour connected with the maintenance of the house. On the other hand he has the right to seek, if in need, accommodation in the house and to participate in the division of any income from the house which is not needed for maintenance. There is no rule that a member of the family can be fored to participate in expenses or labour connected with the maintenance of the ancestral house. But lack of such participation may result in the loss of his rights connected with the ancestral house.[18] This of course may result in loosening of kinship group ties and subsequently in segmentation. If a member of a family lives in a house which is family property (but not in an ancestral house), it is his personal duty to maintain the house; should he not do so, he may be evicted by the family head; and, in some cases, repairs of such a house must be brought to the notice of the head of the family.[19]

§5. *Rights in trees.* Further distinctive rights are rights in trees. Trees can be alienated distinctly from the land on which they grow. However, no doubt because of the long association of the Adangme with European legal concepts, the precept has gained foot that ownership of trees is linked with the ownership of land.

It is generally accepted in the hill belt that trees always belong to the land-owner and that tenants may base rights in trees upon the tenancy agreement alone. Therefore the tenant is not allowed to commit waste as regards trees, except in so far as it is committed for domestic use and in order to provide sticks for building purposes. The same principle applies in the riparian areas of the river Volta, the estuary region, and on the Accra plains.[20] In those parts of the Ada area where cultivation of coconut palms has developed, it is accepted that such trees are owned by the planter. Indeed, there the notion of separate ownership of coconut palms has so developed that a system of marking them, similar to the system of branding cattle, is applied. On the Accra plains, and also in some areas of the Volta estuary, a distinction is made between self-growing and planted trees. The first are regarded as belonging to the landowner, the second to the planter. In the riparian area of the river Volta and also in the northern parts of the Accra plains, another distinction is made between fruit trees of economic value and other trees, the first remaining the property of the landowner. On the other hand in the southern areas of the Accra plains the opposite seems to be the case; that is, that fruit trees of value, and also shade trees, are regarded as owned by the planter. In some areas the landowner may require the tenant to plant palm trees; in return a third of such trees will be granted absolutely by the landowner to the farmer. In all areas except the coconut areas of the Volta river estuary, the sale of land always involves the sale of all trees growing on the land, as distinct from a lease or loan of land in which cases the trees and their fruits will remain the landowner's property; the tenant, however, may be permitted to plant other trees and commit waste in respect of those latter trees.[21] In some isolated areas, especially in the Volta river estuary, a farmer is entitled to collect coconuts and other fruits from trees on his land in reasonable numbers for his own consumption, although he is not entitled to collect them for the purpose of trade, or to commit any waste in so far as the trees are concerned.

§6. *Other special rights.* In certain parts of the riparian areas of the River Volta fishing rights in creeks have evolved into distinct rights which may be alienated. If such rights are sold, the transaction often does not include the land which forms the bed of the creek, but only water and fish.[22] An interesting point may be noted, that is the practice of alienation of fishing rights upon a share-tenancy basis.

Ferry rights, that is rights to maintain a vessel (in practice only canoes) for the purposes of cross-river transport upon payment of tolls by the passengers, are distinct. A ferry right is always part of the rights of the allodial riparian owners, but may be separated.[23]

A right in a market is also a distinct concept. A market right, that is the right to establish and maintain a market and to collect tolls from the traders, is appurtenant to allodial rights.[24]

Rights in creeks, streams and watercourses are distinct. Although they were in principle a part of allodial rights, in the course of time, and because of the constant increase of the value of fish, shellfish and oysters, these rights became in many instances separated absolutely,[25] and are now alienable. In so far as small rivers are concerned, the following principles apply. If the river is a sacred object, it may remain the property of the allodial owner, even if all riparian land has been alienated. In other cases there are three possibilities: if the river flows through the land of an allodial owner the relevant stretch is his property; if the banks belong to various allodial owners, then the river is treated as joint property; but in some of these cases the principle of ownership *ad medium filum aquae* has made its appearance.

Notes

[1] Cf. Kwami *vs.* Ahia, Odumasi Court, 175/501, Sappor and ors. *vs.* Dake II and ors., Supreme Court, Written Judgments, 46/47. Lesser rights granted to segmentary groups or individuals need no concurrence by the clan; strangers acquire temporary surface user always directly from a segmentary group without reference to the clan. There are exceptions to this rule in a few areas.

[2] A kinship group is a corporate body, a *persona iuris*; it has perpetual succession, and therefore the estate of inheritance, as applied in English law, is not attached; but rights serving the head of the group *qua* head, devolve upon the successor of the head *qua* head. On the other hand there may be devolution of individual property upon segmentary kinship groups consisting of the sons of each of the wives (and concubines where this obtains) of the deceased, cf. sec. 99 *infra*. Thirdly, partition of property which has devolved in the latter manner, may occur between the individual sons. Once however the rights have devolved upon a group, the property remains group property, except if subsequently apportioned by segmentation or voluntary partition.

[3] An interesting comparison may perhaps be drawn between these perpetual, inheritable and alienable rights and *emphyteusis* as known to Roman law and certain modern continental laws. Several of the incidents are similar, though an *emphyteusis* does not show the incident of perpetual duration, but is limited in time (usually 99 years). It is also interesting to note that at least some more modern legislation has converted all such holdings into freeholds.

[4] Though he may in certain instances pluck fruits for his own consumation.

[5] A joint owner of the land exercises *iura in re propria*. There are no notions of dominant and

servient tenements. A comparison to servitudes is therefore improper. Neither can a distinction be made between easements and profits a prendre.

[6] Fishing rights in some areas; cf. Crowther, letter of 20/6/1905 to Secretary of Native Affairs. An interesting situation has been found in one case, where a distinction between methods of fishing has influenced the evolution of the right; whereas fishing by rod and hook is regarded as an unqualified right, fishing by net has lost the incidence of common exercise and has become a distinct alienable right; the perfectly logical explanation offered by the local inhabitants that only a small amount of fish can be caught by the use of rod and hook and, that fishing by net produces results of a far greater value, is a clear example of the influence of notions of economic values upon the original legal concept.

[7] The term 'prestation' is used in accordance with the definition of the Shorter Oxford English Dictionary. The term is used throughout to denote customary dues, fees, tributes, etc. rendered as consideration for the exercise of rights in land. It does not include any payments, whether in cash or kind, made to express political allegiance. Cf. Radcliffe-Brown's Introduction in 'African Systems of Kinship and Marriage' 47.

[8] The prestation is collected every three years from all canoe-owners other than members of the Kudzagbe clan; as regards certain lagoons a prestation is collected from strangers who desire to fish, upon the ritual yearly opening of the lagoon. Although the right to fish may be unqualified, permission must be obtained for the erection of a hut by the fisherman.

[9] Cf. Agorgli and ors. *vs.* Attipoe and or., Supreme Court, Accra, 41/48; although this case originated in an Ewe area it may be taken as representative also of Adangme concepts.

[10] This prestation is given to the *Zigbatse*, the 'landowner' and not to the political chief *qua* chief.

[11] E.g. Osudoku.

[12] A prestation, usually in the form of a cow, is paid by the cattle-owner to the landowner.

[13] There are however isolated instances where qualified common rights are in existence as regards such pools.

[14] There is a growing trade in firewood connected with the vicinity of Accra, a locality notorious for its demand for this article; this trade, combined with a scarcity of firewood on the coastal areas generally, and particularly in the eastern parts of those areas, has resulted in firewood (and even dried coconut shells) having acquired a high value.

[15] The Songo lagoon by Ada is an eminent example of the exercise of salt-collecting rights. Allodial rights in the lagoon are vested in the Tekpebiawe clan. The latter grant general permission to all strangers to collect salt, beginning from days appointed by the owners, and upon payment of a prestation by each stranger; the prestation is levied from each of them individually.

[16] But an interesting phenomenon seems to occur in certain areas near Kpong on the river Volta; a tendency may be noticed there to make these rights qualified, and even distinctly alienable, as a result of a growing demand for sand and gravel caused by increased building in expectation of the Volta River Project.

[17] Cf. Sappor and ors. *vs.* Dake II and ors. WACA, Written Judgments 46/47; in this case the Court held that reversion of building land takes place in even more extended cases: where a member of the family, or for that matter any person with the permission of the family, erects a building on family land and it falls into ruins, the land reverts to the family.

[18] In some cases a brother or son, who lives in the house of his elder brother or of his father as the case may be, on the death of the latter looses all rights, other than to live in the house, if he does not pay funeral expenses: 'if a brother or son does not pay funeral expenses he can stay in the house, but he has no right' said some informants (Osudoku); cf. sec. 65 *supra*.

[19] 'The grandfather and the father can demand that a child repairs his (the child's) home' asserted some informants in Pediatokope; 'the eldest man must be told of repairs; he owns all of all of them, children and houses' said some informants in the riparian parts of Osudoku.

[20] Sometimes but not invariably; though admittedly, in isolated cases, the landowner also claims trees planted by the tenant, although the latter may use the fruits during his tenancy.

[21] This does not happen invariably; sometimes apparently if the land is to be used only for a specific purpose: 'if the land is for instance given for cassava the owner will pluck the trees, or they will share the fruit half-half'; 'if you want to plant trees, an agreement must be made'.

[22] This may happen also in the case of a gift; e.g. in Osudoku, 'an owner of a creek gave the water and fish with his daughter to her husband' according to a local informant.

[23] Cf. Ababio *vs.* Essel IV, WACA, Written Judgments, Civ. App. 35/48.

[24] Usually however a Native or Local Authority maintains the market on the basis of a share of the revenue with the true owner; cf. Ada Sub-District Record Book Vol. II, p. 45, also Gorleku and ors. *vs.* Worbi, Ada Court, 32/47.

[25] Cf. Adoch *vs.* Kate and ors. Ada Court, 26/7/44; this case is an excellent example of the process of separation of rights in a creek from allodial rights; the Court stated i.a. 'the creek in dispute is not an ancestral creek but a creek founded by erosion of the Volta River, the portion whereon the creek was founded being plaintiff's farm. The plaintiff therefore becomes the *bona fide* owner of the creek indisputable'. The distinction between a creek, and a tributary (small river) is appreciated; there are distinct words to denote them: *taku*—creek, *pakoni* or *panini*—tributary (Krobo dialect), and *asupa*—creek, *asdobu*—tributary (in some parts of Ada).

CHAPTER 18

ACQUISITION AND ALIENATION OF RIGHTS IN LAND

The various modes of acquiring and disposing of land, or of rights in land, are described in the extracts that follow. These may be summarised as follows: (*a*) allocation, (*b*) gift, (*c*) occupation of hitherto unoccupied land, (*d*) inheritance (dealt with in Part III of Volume II), (*e*) sale, (*f*) pledge or mortgage, (*g*) loan, (*h*) lease.

A. N. Allott: The Ashanti Law of Property*

General Requirements for Acquisition of Property

In discussing the grounds upon which the law will deem that an acquirer has acquired land or an interest in land, one ought to distinguish between original and derivative acquisition.

Original Acquisition by Stools

Original acquisition may be by various modes, depending on who is acquiring, and the nature of the interest acquired. Thus one must distinguish acquisitions by stools, families and individuals.

The acquisition by a stool of what we may call a 'dependent' or 'derivative' interest is necessarily derivative in its character. This would be the case where a subordinate stool is granted land by a superior stool, to hold under and from that superior. Original acquisition by a stool may be of two main legal kinds: (i) acquisition on its own behalf; (ii) acquisition on behalf of another, superior, stool. Where a stool is a land-holding stool, i.e. having the absolute or ultimate title to the land in question, it may have acquired such land by occupation of previously unoccupied territory or by conquest. Since a stool does not have a body or mind of its own, it can only acquire through its agents, servants, and subjects; so that occupation by a stool means occupation by its subjects, or by those in charge of the stool, i.e. the chief and his councillors. One of the commonest ways in which we are told stools acquired their land in the first place was through the operations of their hunters, who spread further and further afield into the virgin forest, creating overriding rights in the stool that they served as they went. Sometimes in earlier Ashanti history it was not a question of spreading out so much as of concerted migration into a new, previously uninhabited area. The operations of families and individuals subject to the stool and extending their cultivations into the virgin forest, which in earlier times lay as a no-man's-land between the different communities, similarly contributed to the extension of their stool's interests.

Where land was already occupied by other persons, perhaps serving another stool, the rights of a stool could be extended peacefully (by cession) or militarily (by conquest). Ashanti history is full of such events, some of the acquisitions in the earlier days having been at the expense of their fellow-Ashanti; in later times, as the Ashanti empire grew, it was the non-Ashanti on all sides who fell under the rule of Ashanti. Sometimes in such cases the acquiring, conquering stool was satisfied with a sort of lord-and-vassal relationship, by which the subjected people and its stool were laid under obligation to render peaceful and military service to their new overlord, and to provide various dues and payments as prescribed by custom. Such an arrangement carried no implications as to

* A. N. Allott, 'The Ashanti Law of Property', in *Zeitschrift fur vergleichende Rechtswissenschaft*, 1966, pp. 156–176.

title to the land of the subject stool, the overlord gaining no proprietary right, but merely a superior paramount or jurisdictional right over the lands and peoples of the subject. In other cases, especially where land was taken piecemeal, or where it was taken after a forcible struggle, the conquering stool might install itself as the new 'landlord' of the area.[1]

The position was especially interesting where a subordinate stool acquired lands by one of these means. In such a case it was likely that, while the subordinate stool itself would acquire a present interest in its newly-acquired lands, yet the effect of its action would be to vest the paramount title to the land in the stool that it served.

Another way by which a stool might acquire through its subjects is demonstrated by the Ashanti rules in regard to hunting, fishing, and treasure-trove. 'Any treasure-trove found on the land [of a stool] belonged to the stool', says Busia,* 'for the soil, the minerals, the rocks, and trees were stool property. So anyone [and this applied to a stranger to the stool just as much as to its subject—A. N. A.] who found a treasure-trove had to take it to the chief. The finder was usually given a small share.' A share of such treasure-trove had to be sent by the stool (if it was not the paramount stool in a division) to its paramount, which in its turn had to send a share to the Asantehene.† The test of entitlement to treasure-trove indicated whether a subordinate stool was land-owning vis-à-vis its paramount or not; a paramount stool that enjoyed the ultimate title to the land in its division or any portion of it would be entitled to the whole of such treasure-trove, subject only to the Asantehene's claims. Rattray‡ gives slightly variant accounts of the position in this respect; he says§ that 'Treasure Trove (*ahuntuo*)[2] belonged to the owner of land on which it was found, with a share falling to the king'. Various rules are also given by Rattray and Allott|| as to the way in which large gold nuggets were disposed of; according to one informant these would be the property of the Asantehene, who would however return a portion of the value of the nugget to the *Ọmanhene* within whose lands the nugget was found.

As regards hunting and fishing, a land-holding stool's perquisites extended to a particular designated share in certain large game animals killed on its land; thus for Asumegya Rattray says¶ that 'a stranger killing an antelope on Asumegya land sends a hind leg (*sere*)[3] to the Chief, a subject sends a foreleg (*basa*)'. For Juaben** he gives a slightly different account:

> 'The Head-Chief received a *sere* (hindleg) of any large antelope killed. The person actually enjoying possession of the land on which the animal was killed was given this hindleg, which he passed on to the Head-Chief, whose Stool was and still is nominally owner of all the land. The Head-Chief would return him a portion of it. If the hunter were not a subject of the Chief on whose land he shot the animal, he would, in addition to the hindleg he handed over for the Head-Chief, give a foreleg (*basa*) to the *Asase wura*, the man in actual enjoyment of the land upon which the animal was killed.'

And for the division of Kumawu Rattray says†† that:

> 'Of game, the "ground" tusk, "ground" ear, and "ground" foreleg of an elephant, and the tail, belonged to the Chief, and of an antelope, the *basa* (foreleg). If an elephant were shot by a *gyase* subject, the Chief would take all . . . A *Kotoko* (a porcupine) was royal game and must be sent entire to the Chief (*Kọtọkọ, nkoa nni*, A subject (slave) does not eat a porcupine).'[4]

Subjects enjoy the right to exploit the fishing and timber resources of the area, though they may not be entitled to make any exceptional or disproportionate use of such amenities—e.g. by commercial exploitation—without paying for the privilege; and in comparison with hunting we are told that a catch made by a fisherman, or a portion of it, does not automatically belong to the chief, provided the fisherman is a subject of the stool;‡‡ though in certain bodies of water tolls of up to one third may be charged.

* *The Position of the Chief in . . . Ashanti.*
† Busia, *op. cit.*, p. 57.
‡ *Ashanti Law and Constitution*, pp. 140, 162, 186.
§ *Ashanti Art and Ritual*, p. 227.
|| *Ashanti Law of Property*, p. 258.
¶ *Ashanti Law and Constitution*, p. 140.
** *Ibid.*, pp. 186–7.
†† *Ibid.*, p. 282.
‡‡ *Ashanti Law of Property*, pp. 159–60.

Derivative Acquisition by Stools

In recent and modern Ashanti all the land has been claimed by one stool or another, so that the original modes of acquisition are no longer available to stools, at least in so far as they relate to the acquisition of the ultimate title to land. Derivative modes of acquiring interests in property are still available, however, both in respect of land and movables. Briefly these modes are:

(a) *Grant.* By a superior to a subordinate stool, vesting in that stool an interest in land dependent on the superior stool's interest.*

(b) *Gift.* Where a subject presents property to the stool, usually movables. Included under this heading is property brought to the stool by a chief, at the time when his property automatically vested in the stool on his enstoolment, and property donated to the stool by the stool family. According to several accounts, it was felt to be desirable that a stool family should try to enrich the stool further in every generation.

(c) *Traditional dues.* The Chief was entitled to various dues from his individual subjects, such as: *ayibuadeɛ,* death duties;† *afirinhyiadeɛ*, first fruits; fees payable on the installation of a subordinate chief; court fees, including *aseda* (thank-offering); levies and taxes.

(d) *Fines and forfeiture.* An accused might have to atone for a criminal offence by paying a fine to the chief; this was called 'buying his head' (*atitodeɛ*) and was a monetary substitution for capital punishment.‡ Ashanti law also ordained the forfeiture of an accused's property in cases where he was found guilty of murder or suicide or other heinous offence. Thus Rattray records that:§

> 'Certain capital offences, e.g. cursing the king, adultery with the king's wives, were punished by forfeiture (*awunie* or *awunyadie*), but in such a case scrupulous care was taken not to seize any family property (*agyapadie*), unless indeed the whole family were involved in the crime. Land was thus nearly always exempt from forfeiture.'[5]

The property of a lying witness in a public trial would also be liable to confiscation;‖ the fact that he had lied would appear from the fact that he had died after giving evidence the truth of which was sworn on two particular gods. If the witness died soon after giving his evidence, a *bosom* (lesser god) would be consulted through its priest; if this god revealed that the witness had given false evidence on oath, then his private property would be 'confiscated and divided between the Chief and the priest of the god in whose name he had committed perjury'.

Rattray also tells us¶ that, in the case of a suicide who had been found guilty of self-murder after a 'trial' of his dead body, all his personal private property would have to be produced by his relatives to the Chief, who would then confiscate it; and that this property might include: his slaves and 'bought' wives; privately acquired gold-dust; any personal debts due to the dead man (this is an interesting extension of the notion of property); privately acquired cloths, trinkets, and livestock; standing crops planted by the suicide (once the land had been reaped, it reverted to the successor); privately owned fruit trees, e.g. kola, the annual crops of which became the chief's property as long as the trees stood.

(e) *Escheat* (*awunnyadeɛ*). The property, including immovable property, of any person who died leaving no heirs to succeed to him reverted to the stool within whose area the property was situated or the case of a native of the particular community, who was almost certain to leave matrilineal relatives, or, failing them, slaves, or, failing them, fellow-clansmen,** but it was obviously a distinct possibility in the case of immigrant strangers, who might come to settle for a while and then die, leaving no blood-relatives in the immediate vicinity. In such a case the stool which had granted the stranger permission to settle in the first place would receive back the land granted. If a relative of

* Rattray, *Ashanti Law and Constitution*, pp. 351, 355; Allott, *op. cit.*, pp. 87–93; Warr., at Matson, *Digest . . . .*, p. 72.

† Rattray, *op. cit.*, pp. 107–9.

‡ *Ibid.*, p. 302.

§ *Ashanti Art and Ritual*, p. 227.

‖ Rattray, *Ashanti Law and Constitution*, p. 386.

¶ *Ibid.*, p. 301.

** Cf. Rattray, *Ashanti Art and Ritual*, pp. 43–4.

the deceased put in an appearance and asked for the land from the chief, he would probably have to receive a fresh grant of it,* since he would not be entitled as of right to the land.

(f) *Any other method open to a private person.* A stool might engage in trading (*abatadie*), e.g. by importing and exporting produce,† mining (*asikadeɛ*), which was wholly or partly a state monopoly,‡ or any dealing with property. Thus a stool could and can buy, sell or mortgage property, receive a tenancy, etc., just as a private person might.

Acquisition by Families§

As with stools, families might acquire property by an original or derivative mode of acquisition. Again, as with stools, a family could only acquire through the efforts of its members; but a distinction can be taken between the cases where the family as such, acting through its proper organs, decides to acquire property, and those cases where the decision is in effect the decision of individual members of the family, though the present or future result is that they acquire for the family.

In the former category of acquisitions, those acquired directly by the family, the head of the family is mandated to act on behalf of the family. In some cases he has a general mandate, and may act on his own initiative (though perhaps informing the family afterwards); his acts in such an instance will be subject to the scrutiny of the family, who will have power to remove him if they disapprove of the way he has handled their affairs. Additionally there are the cases where the head of family is expressly mandated to act in a certain way, e.g. to acquire a particular piece of property, by a family meeting called to discuss the matter.

A family can by these means acquire property in any way that is open to a private individual; thus it may buy, lease, or take on mortgage or gift, any movable or immovable capable of being owned.

The indirect acquisitions of a family are juristically more interesting. The rules in regard to these are basically as follows:

(i) Any property acquired by a member expressly on behalf of the family will vest in the family as a whole.

(ii) Any property acquired by a member of a family with funds provided by the family might in the old days have become family property, though the individual acquirer might retain the right to use the property to the exclusion of other members, the family's rights being limited to restrictions on its alienation and to their expectation of eventually succeeding to it. The rule today is less strict, and the family might not acquire it in these circumstances.

(iii) Any property acquired through the joint labour of members of the family would in the old days have been deemed to be family property; e.g. a house jointly built by members of the family, or a farm jointly cleared and cultivated by them. To make such a property family property, it is not necessary that all the members should have joined in the acquisition; indeed, there is a possibility that even the labour of two brothers might be enough to stamp the property as family property. Today the rule is quite different, and the law leans against the presumption that such property belongs to the family; rather it would be the joint property of its actual acquirers only.

Original Acquisitions by Individuals||

Interests in land. An individual acquires an individual interest in land either by an original or a derivative mode of acquisition. The first such sort of interest is where he appropriates or takes into possession a portion of the unoccupied land of his stool, as by clearing a portion of the virgin forest for farming purposes. We have already seen that every citizen has this right by virtue of his membership of the land-controlling community, and that he will generally not require any prior permission to exercise such right in the vicinity of his own village, but that he will generally be required to notify, and in some cases to seek the prior permission, of the land-controlling stool in those

* Allott, *Ashanti Law of Property*, pp. 629–631.
† Rattray, *Ashanti Law and Constitution*, pp. 109–11.
‡ Rattray, *Ashanti Law and Constitution*, p. 112.
§ See *Ashanti Law of Property*, Ch. IV.
|| For which see *Ashanti Law of Property*, generally.

areas which do not form part of his own stool's land. Generally, as we have also seen, the citizen may exercise this right to take up land without making any payment therefor, other than a nominal or customary thank-offering (*aseda*) in token of the continued paramount right of the land-controlling stool to the land, even though the land is now under individual occupation.

A stranger [as defined above at p. 358] naturally does not have such a citizen's right to free land for farming and residence; and a stranger can only acqure, *vis-à-vis* the land-controlling stool, an interest in land by grant from the stool, or grant from a private individual or family approved by the stool. However, we meet here the problem of the rights of squatters. It would appear to be one of the fundamental principles of Ashanti law that those who have acquired rights, even in an unlawful manner, should continue to enjoy them if possible. Even if a squatter's original possession was not approved by the appropriate grantor (e.g. the stool), the usual practice appears to be (at least at the present day) to allow the squatter to continue in possession, so long as this does not directly encroach on the rights either of the stool or of its subjects residing in the area, and to charge the squatter thenceforth some rent or other customary payment for his occupation. In other words, his unlawful title by occupation is converted into a lawful title by grant. This is despite the fact that customary law does not recognize acquisitive prescription as such.

The problem of the legal analysis of a squatter's position is complicated, in that one ought to take account of his position *vis-à-vis* private holders as well as in respect of the land-controlling stool. Encroachments by one farmer on the land of another would normally be resisted; but where unlawful occupation has been of long standing (and, owing to the fact that there is absentee ownership, with the owner leaving a 'caretaker' in charge while he is away, it is quite possible that there might be an undetected unlawful occupation in this way), the frequent practice is to leave the squatter in possession but to charge him for the privilege, which the land-holder has a right to do. It is an important question which might be considered by any indigenous court in deciding whether to evict the squatter or leave him in possession though paying rent, whether the original possession was *bona* or *mala fide* [for a further discussion of the position of squatters, see Allott].*

One can distinguish two different sorts of interest in land which an individual may thus acquire by occupation: in the first place, he acquires a dependent interest in the land itself (i.e. an interest depending on the superior interest of the stool); and secondly he may acquire an absolute interest in anything which he creates by his own efforts on the land, such as a farm or a house. Hence the very common dictum, already quoted, that the farmer owns his farm and the stool owns the land on which it is situated; this is another way of saying that Ashanti law is quite prepared to conceive of a farm or a house as an independent thing in law, detached from the soil to which it is physically attached.

The individual's title to the land itself, where it derives from occupation, probably arises as soon as he does any positive acts to take the land into possession, as by clearing or demarcating the boundaries of the plot he claims. This is in line with a fundamental principle of Ashanti (and indeed of African) law that 'a man is entitled to the fruits of his labour'; as the Ashanti proverb, cited by Rattray,† puts it: *dadeɛ na pere asase* ('the iron, i.e. the hoe, is the one to lay claim to the land'). And Rattray himself comments:‡

> 'The results . . . of their [families and individuals] labour—the huts, palm trees, kola trees, yams [and today cocoa trees—A. N. A.]—came to be invested with all the sanctity which in West Africa renders family and personal property inviolate.'

Our sources unfortunately fail to discuss in detail the exact acts or the exact moment in time when an individual's rights to exclusive use of a particular tract of previously unoccupied land crystallizes, and it is not possible to be more precise than as indicated above. It is, however, clear that it is not necessary for him to have completely cleared the land in order to establish an individual's right, still less to have planted a crop—as might be the case in some other African societies. It is fairly certain that an acquirer would feel he had just cause of complaint if another challenged his right to the land (e.g. by starting a competing cultivation) at any time after he had evinced, by his

* *Ashanti Law of Property*, pp. 722–4.
† *Ashanti Law and Constitution*, p. 347 n.
‡ *Ibid.*, pp. 546–7.

presence on the land, his intention to appropriate that portion; but there would obviously be scope for argument if he had failed to delimit his boundaries in a clear way.

Derivative Acquisition by Individuals

It may be helpful if these modes are listed:

(a) *Allocation* by a stool to an individual subject or stranger.

(b) *Allocation or appointment as a successor* by a family.

(c) *Gift* (*akyɛdeɛ*)*

Both movables and immovables may be made the subject of a gift, though gifts of movables are more common, and the law presumes that a gift of an interest in land is not outright unless there is something present to indicate that this was the intention of both parties, and the donor was in a position to pass over his whole interest to the donee. An individual member of a family can give away his movables *inter vivos* without his family's permission, though it is likely that they would object if they found him stripping himself of his possessions (since this would mean that there would be less for the family to inherit when he died). Gifts *mortis causa* or nuncupative wills (*samanseɛ*) were originally no more than the expression of a wish by a dying person as to how he would like his property to be distributed, and depended for their effectiveness on the assent of the family of testator. More recently in modern Ashanti law a binding will in the stricter sense has come into existence, which will be binding on the family provided they have witnessed it and the beneficiary has given a customary thank-offering (*aseda*) to the testator, which has been distributed among the witnesses as evidence of the bequest.

Gifts as between husband and wife are known, though they are subject to special rules.† Briefly, the law presumes that the husband did not intend to make an outright gift to his wife, and on the husband's death his family will seek to recover the gift from the wife, unless (i) there was an intention to make an outright gift; (ii) the family have given their consent; (iii) the wife has given *aseda*. It is possible for a family to validate an imperfect gift retrospectively, as where they wish to reward the widow of one of their members for her devoted services to her late husband. A gift by her husband which is attributable to maintenance is conditional on the continuance of the marriage, and the wife ought to return such property, in so far as it is not necessarily consumed, on divorce. Thus cloths given to the wife in pursuance of the husband's obligations to clothe his wife ought all to be returned on divorce, and we are told that even if such cloths are reduced to rags the wife ought to preserve them in case their return becomes legally necessary. A husband also often makes his wife a gift, which is more in the nature of a business loan, in order to allow her to set herself up in some business or trade; such an amount is returnable on divorce, when accounts are gone into between the two spouses.

Gifts to strangers are rare; even where they exist, they are usually in practice not outright, but rather loans. Thus land may be 'given' by a family to a stranger; this means no more than that he has been granted a tenancy at will for no, or a nominal, rental.

The most important formal requirements for the validity of any gift are: (i) that it should be evidenced by witnesses, who, in the case of gifts with respect to which a family may have a present or potential future interest, should include members of the donor's family; and (ii) that the donee should give *aseda* to the donor in gratitude for the gift, and in token of his acceptance of it. This *aseda*, which is often drink or a small sum of money, is frequently described as 'sealing' or 'stamping' the bargain, thus making it irrevocable, and is an ever-present feature of Ashanti legal transactions generally (thus *aseda* is paid by a successful party in a law-suit, or by a stranger to whom land has been allocated by a chief). In a society without writing, it takes the place of written documents as evidencing a transaction.

(d) *Tenancy* (*asasenkaho*).‡ Tenancy, as a mode of creating a derivative interest in land, overlaps with the modes of gift and allocation already referred to, but it is by no means exactly congruent with them. It is important to emphasize immediately that, where a member of a family occupies family property either by an undifferentiated title (as where he lives, along with other members, in a large family house) or by a differentiated title (as where he holds an inherited farm through his appointment as successor to a deceased member), he is in no sense a tenant of the family. (Where a family grant a

* For which see *Ashanti Law of Property*, Ch. IX.

† Allott, *Essays in African Law*, p. 213.

‡ For which see *Ashanti Law of Property*, Ch. VII generally.

tenancy to a non-member, the position is quite different, of course.) And although the position of a stranger, who has been granted land by a stool on which to live or farm, is today generally that of a tenant from the stool, this was by no means always the case in the old days; a permanently settled stranger who had been granted land by the stool was incorporated into the community once he had paid his 'entrance fee', and was no more a tenant than any citizen-occupier.*

Equally the recipient of a gift of movables cannot be called a tenant of the thing given; where he held on a temporary rather than a permanent title (as with the wife who has been given something by her husband), this should perhaps be termed a form of extended loan. (In legal analysis, of course, there is no fundamental difference between the person holding land as a tenant and one holding a movable as a borrower; but it is convenient to distinguish them terminologically, as is the practice in English law.)

In discussing the law of tenancy, there are two main questions which have to be answered: (i) who is the landlord? (ii) what kind of interest does the tenant hold? From the former point of view it makes a difference to the legal position if the grantor is a stool on the one hand, or a family or individual on the other hand; whilst in regard to the second question one has to ask what sort of property has been given, and the length and conditions of the tenancy.

The stool is generally a landlord only in respect of persons who are strangers to that stool. The procedure for the acquisition of a farming interest by a stranger to the land-holding stool has been described by Rattray† and at greater length by Allott.‡ Either the stranger approaches the stool direct (he may apply through the local *odikuro* of the village where he wishes to settle, if he has already selected it) and receives a grant of the land as a tenant, or he negotiates with a private citizen (family or individual) and acquires land from them by permission of the stool. In the latter case in modern Ashanti law the 'purchaser' is required to become a tenant of the stool, but otherwise steps into the shoes of the person from whom he has acquired the land.§

Where a family (or more rarely an individual) is the grantor, the grantee may be either a fellow-member of the stool, or a stranger to it. This fact does not make any difference to the relationship of landlord and tenant, except in so far as the stranger requires the stool's permission to settle.

Tenancies may be classified according to their duration, or according to the *quid pro quo* (hereinafter called 'the rental') payable by the tenant. As regards duration, tenancies may be either for a fixed term, or for an indefinite period. Tenancies for a fixed period in ancient Ashanti law would tend to be for one planting season only; in modern Ashanti law, with the commercialization of agriculture, leases for a definite term of years are known. But the most characteristic type of tenancy in Ashanti law is that which we may describe as of indefinite duration. We cannot say that this is a permanent tenancy, though in practice it may go on for decades or even centuries; but equally there is no prior fixed period at the end of which the tenancy determines. Usually the tenant (and his heirs after him) continues to hold so long as he is of good behaviour, continues to pay the rental whatever it may be, does not deny the landlord's title, or commit any other act inconsistent with his tenancy.

It is stated|| to be a common practice that, where an individual living in a village finds that all the unoccupied land has been taken up and his family have no land to spare, he should turn to another family in the village and 'beg' land from them for farming or residential purposes. Usually only a token initial payment is made, symbolising the grant of the tenancy and the fact that the grantor retains the reversion to the land; and when the tenant dies his successor usually succeeds to his interest automatically. Such tenancies are especially common between those who are connected by blood (including those related cognatically rather than matrilineally, e.g. a father and his child) or by friendship. As between friends, something may be payable annually (e.g. a sheep) as a token that the relationship subsists and to preserve the rights of the landlord.

It is important to stress that, in the case of such a tenancy, the tenant is tenant only

* Cf. Rattray, *Ashanti Law and Constitution*, p. 352.

† *Ibid.*, pp. 351–2.

‡ *Ashanti Law of Property*, pp. 174–6.

§ *Ibid.*, pp. 577–9.

|| *Ibid.*, p. 140; also pp. 451–468 for a detailed description of the rules governing such tenancies.

qua the land which he has acquired from the landlord; he is not a tenant, but the owner, of any farm or house he may create on the site. This position (so different from English law, under which right to the land carries with it right to the things in and on the land) may lead to complications where the tenant wishes to pledge or dispose of his land with the house or farm on it; usually the landlord's permission may be needed before he can deal in this way with his interest.

Tenancies for an economic rent were rare in ancient Ashanti law; but in modern Ashanti law are very common. The case of the stranger who is granted a tenancy by a stool has already been discussed. But it is also open to a private holder of land to grant a tenancy, e.g. of a house, to a tenant in return for an economic rent. Since the coming of extensive cocoa cultivation to Ashanti, such commercial transactions have become very much more frequent. The rental may consist: (i) of *abusa*, where the annual yield of a farm is divided into three parts, and one part is sent to the landlord as rent; (ii) of money or money-equivalent (e.g. sheep).* The *abusa* tenancy in Ashanti tends to be confined to tenancies where the landlord is a land-controlling stool. Although in some ways analogous to profit-sharing tenancies elsewhere, there is this great difference, that the landlord provides nothing (e.g. not even seed or implements) for the tenant except the land itself; it is therefore not a partnership between the landlord and tenant.

Tenancies for an economic rental, just as with other tenancies, tend to be of indefinite duration, no precise period being fixed for them. They can be determined by the landlord giving notice (after allowing the tenant to take his standing crops), or at any time when the tenant is in breach of a condition of the tenancy. A general rule, applicable to all forms of tenancy, is that land is generally granted for a particular purpose; and the tenant is in breach of his obligations if he uses the land for a purpose other than that for which he received it (unless he has received the authorisation of the landlord for the change of use). Thus land given for foodstuffs should not be used for growing cocoa; nor can one build on a plot given for farming.

(e) *Pledge and mortgage* (*awowa*).† Both persons and things could be pledged. We have already discussed the position of human pawns, and we noted that a family might pawn one of its members, and a stool might pawn its subjects. We have also indicated the major characteristics of a pledge of property. So we shall confine ourselves here to a brief examination of the machinery by which a pledge or pawn is brought into existence.

Pawning of a family member. Rattray‡ describes the procedure as follows:

> 'A member of a humble household might have been pawned to raise a sum, the equivalent of as little as from £2 to £6; in case of an *odehye*[6] (member of the royal blood of a reigning Stool), a liability of £16 might bring about a similar necessity. When such a course had been decided upon, and in order to raise the required amount, all the blood relations met in council, including the member whom it had been decided to pawn. The head then approached the husband of his married sister or niece, informed him of the straits in which his wife's family were placed, and suggested that he should advance the money . . . The husband would then consult his *abusa*, and all being in agreement, the money was advanced. A sum equivalent to about 6d. in the pound (known as *ntiani*) was deducted from the amount lent. This was divided into three parts. The family of the pawn received a third, that of the creditor a third, and the remainder was distributed among the witnesses (*begwafo*), who did not belong to the families of either of the contracting parties. The kinsman of the pawn publicly declared the terms of the transaction' [which are then set out by Rattray in detail].[7]

As regards redemption, Rattray says§ that a pawn is:

* *Ibid.*, pp. 371–393; Rattray, *Ashanti Art and Ritual*, p. 230.

† For which see Allott, *op. cit.*, Ch. VI; Rattray, *Ashanti Art and Ritual*, pp. 230, 232–5; *Ashanti Law and Constitution*, pp. 357–8 and Ch. VI generally; Matson, *Digest . . . .*, pp. 19–21.

‡ *Ashanti Law and Constitution*, pp. 48–9.

§ *Ibid.*, p. 54.

'considered redeemed upon repayment of the original sum lent, without interest. The services of the pawn were deemed to be in lieu of interest as long as he remained with the creditor. *Aseda* was, however, paid in order to have witnesses of the reinstatement. Interest (*nsiho*) . . . was also due as soon as a pawn left his master without authority and returned home, but on the death of an *awowa* it did not begin to run until a year had expired.'

Rattray* also informs us that where a pawned wife died, either half the borrowed sum was remitted on condition that the creditor (i.e. the husband) retained the children of the union; or the creditor reclaimed the full amount, and, if the debtor could not repay, took one of the children as pawn in place of its mother.

The analogies between pawning of persons and pledging of land will be seen to be close. Thus no interest is normally payable, but the creditor gets the right to the use of the thing or person pledged. Where a female was pawned to a male who was not her husband, then it was understood that this gave the creditor the right to sexual enjoyment of her,† though children born of this connexion would be affiliated to the woman, and not to her master (unlike in the case of a slave woman).

Pawning of stool. The procedure where a stool incurred a heavy debt and decided to give security for it by pawning is also described by Rattray.‡ He says:

'. . . the Chief would summon all his *Mpanyimfo* (Elders), and they might agree to pawn one of themselves to some other Chief. All the direct subjects of the Elder so pawned were thus pawned with their master, but *asase n'ka ho* (the land which the Elder held of the Head-Chief) was not included in this transaction.'

Rattray does, however, describe at the same time the procedure where a stool was forced to pledge its lands as well as its subjects.

Pawning of movables.§ Rattray gives, from an informant, an account of the procedure for the pawning of a cloth. His account indicates that there was a fixed period for repayment (here one year); that the amount lent was much less than the value of the article; and that the transaction was in the presence of witnesses (members of the families of both parties), who were not remunerated for their services. If at the end of the period the debtor did not redeem the pledged article, he either asked for an extension of the period of the debt, or the pawning was changed into an outright sale. This latter course depended on the agreement of the creditor.

It is again the case that the pledgee (creditor) took the use of the article during the currency of the pledge as his interest; he was not liable to make good any consequent wear and tear, nor was he liable for accidental loss or damage not attributable to his fault.

Pledge of land.‖ The essence of the old Ashanti pledge was that the creditor (pledgee)[8] went into possession of the land pledged by the debtor (pledgor—*ọkafoọ*), and used it for his benefit until the debt was repaid. Rattray quite correctly mentions¶ the two types of pledge: (i) where the produce of the land went as interest only; (ii) where the produce went to pay off both capital and interest, so that the debt automatically liquidated itself over a period of years. But he states** in connexion with a pledge of stool land that:

'Besides this [having the right to use and collect the produce of land], the creditor might claim interest in gold-dust on the sum lent. This was in case that the *okafo* (mortgagor) might redeem the land before the mortgagee had had time to collect the produce.'

I do not think that this can have been a common practice, as it does not tally with other accounts of pledging, both ancient and modern, and runs counter to the principle already cited.

* *Ibid.*, p. 50.
† *Ibid.*, p. 52.
‡ *Ibid.*, p. 357.
§ *Ibid.*, p. 367–9.
‖ See Rattray, *Ashanti Art and Ritual*, pp. 232–7, for a description of the procedure in a private pledge, and *Ashanti Law and Constitution*, pp. 357–8, for a pledge of land by a stool.
¶ *Ashanti Art and Ritual*, p. 232.
** *Ashanti Law and Constitution*, p. 357.

Another fundamental principle was that the pledged land could never be lost by compulsory foreclosure. Rattray cites a proverb, *se okafo adie eko amoamu a onoara na oton*—'if the mortgagor's property is all to be sold, then it is he himself who does the selling'* He says however at the same place that where the pledgee wished to foreclose, the *abusa* of each party, together with the stool-holder, his spokesman, and the Queen Mother should meet; and that the chief would then call on the family of the debtor and tell them to share the debt between them. If this were not possible, it would then be ordered that the pledge should be converted into an outright sale.† It is again doubtful how frequent a transaction of this sort could have been in the old days; today, of course, creditors give themselves the power to foreclose by express agreement.

The procedure for pledging land was basically similar to that for pledging a chattel. Thus the transaction included the creditor and debtor, together with their witnesses both family and independent, and the debtor had to find a sum (*nteani*) which was a fixed proportion of the total amount lent, and which was divided into three parts, one each for the pledgor and pledgee, and one distributed amongst the witnesses to bind their memories,‡ but at another place§ Rattray says that the *nteani* is divided, one-third going to the chief and Queen Mother, if presiding over the transaction, and the remaining two-thirds going to the witnesses. This account is somewhat inconsistent with our other information. Apart from the presence of witnesses, Rattray says that the parties and their witnesses would view the land and boundaries, and that 'out of the mortgage money rum would be bought and the mortgagor would pour some over his stools—if he were a chief—to inform his *samanfo* (spirit ancestors) of the transaction', and to ask their help in eventually redeeming the mortgage.

It may be added in closing our discussion of *awowa* that neither of the terms 'pledge' and 'mortgage', both of which have technical meanings in English law, is exactly suitable for application to the Ashanti institution; and it might be better to resuscitate the old English word 'gage' to refer to all such handing over of a person or thing as security. The older terminology has been retained here, however, for reasons of clarity.

(f) *Sale*||

Sale of land (*asaseton*)

It is often stated, not only for Ashanti law but for other systems of African customary law as well, that alienation of land (in the sense of its sale) was entirely unknown before modern times. Among the reasons given for the alleged existence of such a principle in Ashanti was that the land belonged to the ancestors and to all the generations yet to come, and hence could only be alienated by all its co-owners, who would include the dead as well as the living. From the point of view of a subject holding land under his stool, he could not of course part with the land because the land belonged to the chief or the stool.

Statements of this sort tend to be misleading unless one takes care to analyse the position a little more deeply. It is quite certain that in Ashanti a land-controlling stool could decide to sell its lands, i.e. sell the absolute title to its land, if it so chose; it would not choose to do so if it could possibly find some alternative means of meeting its obligations; but its legal power to do so is unquestioned. Thus Rattray reports¶ that if an *omanhene* decided to sell part of his land, the Asantehene would have to be informed; similarly (though Rattray does not deal with this point) if a subordinate stool sold its lands, then its paramount would have to be informed (where the subordinate stool enjoyed the absolute title) or give its authorization (where ultimate title was in the paramount and not in the subordinate).

Equally, as regards the individual subject, he could not sell the absolute title to his land, it is true; but he might be able to dispose outright of his interest in land or something on it, such as his farm or house, in return for a consideration. We have already

* *Ashanti Art and Ritual*, pp. 233–231.

† *Ibid.*, p. 235.

‡ Cf. *Ashanti Law and Constitution*, pp. 357–8.

§ *Ashanti Art and Ritual*, p. 233.

|| For which see Allott, *Ashanti Law of Property*, Ch. V; Rattray, *Ashanti Art and Ritual*, pp. 234–7; *Ashanti Law and Constitution*, pp. 338, 346, 355–8, 363, 365; Busia, *op. cit.*, p. 47.

¶ *Ibid.*, p. 358.

cited from Rattray* an example where a private individual who had mortgaged his land was compelled to convert the transaction into sale; but there were also direct sales of interest in land. If these were rare in ancient times, they are today relatively frequent, since sales between fellow-subjects of the stool (including families and individuals) do not require the authorization of the stool, inasmuch as they do not prejudice in any way the existing rights of the stool over that land.

On the other hand, sales by stools (which in the past were probably mainly to other Ashanti stools) are now practically unheard of; and it has been staunchly maintained in recent times that such sales are contrary to Ashanti law. Before the restoration of the Ashanti Confederacy in 1935, certain chiefs in Ashanti had in fact alienated large areas of their stool lands to outsiders; thus Kobina Foli, former *ọmanhene* of Adansi, is reported by I. Matson [*Land disputes in Adansi*] to have sold parts of his unused lands to strangers from Akwapim.

Rattray gives the Asante word for 'sale' as *tramma;* but this word (or rather *ntrama*, lit. 'cowries'; i.e. money) merely means the so-called 'earnest-money' paid on an alienation of chattels, or later of land; and it is doubtful whether it is correctly used to refer to the contract of sale itself. 'To sell' in Asante is *tọn*, and 'to buy' *tọ*; these words are indiscriminately used to refer to the acquisition of any sort of object by payment; and 'sale' is *tọn*.

As to the form of the sale, Rattray† states that the following appear to be the essential elements:

(i) Competency of the contracting parties, i.e. the participation of all members of the family.
(ii) The witnessing by the proper persons in authority.
(iii) The viewing of the land and fixing of boundaries.
(iv) The valuable consideration.
(v) The payment of the *ntrama.*

(i) Certainly the contracting parties must be competent, and have the necessary authorizations or consents. Generally the consent of the family is not required where a member sells his self-acquired property (*aliter* with a gift), though it may be advisable for him to ensure that responsible members of the family witness the transaction, in order to avoid their later disputing the sale and claiming the land on the death of its previous holder.

(ii) The witnessing of the sale goes rather to the proof of the sale than to its validity. The rule, common to African customary law, that secret transactions are of no effect, really refers to the problem of proof. It is not necessary for the local ruler, e.g. the *odikuro*, to witness a sale, though this is an almost invariable practice where the purchaser comes from outside the village.

(iii) The inspection and demarcation of the land, preferably in company with those who hold neighbouring lands, are necessary in order to define what is sold.

(iv) Similarly the valuable consideration is of the essence of the contract.

(v) Payment of the *ntrama* appears to be a formal public recognition of the conclusion of a valid sale, and defines its character. Since it is paid after the conveyance has taken place, and is divided among the parties and the witnesses, it is obvious that it is in no sense an 'earnest'.

(vi) Additionally, there are various ceremonies which ought to be performed on the land or away from it in order that there may be a valid sale. Thus prayers have to be uttered by the vendor to his ancestors, libations poured, and sheep slaughtered.‡

Although a sale is outright, and Rattray§ was somewhat misleading in suggesting that all sales are in principle redeemable (as he himself admitted later)||, yet Ashanti generally recognize that a vendor ought to be enabled to recover the land provided he is willing to pay up to twice the purchase price he originally received. This notion of the redeemability of sales is especially important where a family or stool seeks to recover land injudiciously alienated by its head, chief or a member, as the case may be.

* *Ashanti Art and Ritual*, p. 235.
† *Ashanti Art and Ritual*, p. 236.
‡ Cf. Rattray, *Ashanti Law and Constitution*, p. 358.
§ *Ashanti Art and Ritual*, p. 236.
|| *Ashanti Law and Constitution*, p. 358.

Notes

[1] But compare the acquisition by Asumegya of land formerly belonging to Kenkyira, which was given to Asumegya by the Asantehene after the victorious struggle against Denkyira. Rattray, *Ashanti Law and Constitution*, p. 132.

[2] This is Fante; in Asante *asasedeɛ*.

[3] Otherwise *srɛ*.

[4] Is this an instance of the use of *di*, eat, in the sense of having the beneficial enjoyment of?

[5] These terms are more correctly spelt as *awunnyadeɛ*, *awuneɛ*, and *agyapadeɛ*.

[6] More correctly, *ọdehyeɛ*.

[7] More correctly the Asante terms are spelt *nteani* and *badwafo;* but the usual Asante word for witnesses is *adansifoọ*.

[8] *osikani* acc. to Rattray; but this merely means "a rich man", and has no legal significance.

[9] Better, *sɛ ọkafo adeɛ eɛko amuamu a, ọno ara na ọtọn*.

H. Cory: Sukuma Law and Custom*

1. *Acquisition of Land*

A. *Complete Holding*

I. *General rules.*[1] As long as a holder occupies his land effectively he cannot be deprived of it.

At present the authority for allocating land and for any other transaction in land is: the *basumba batale*† in BSN, BD‡; the *banangwa*† in all other chiefdoms.

NOTE. Formerly the *basumba batale* was the authority in BD, BSN, and BS‡; the *banangwa* in all other chiefdoms. *Basumba batale* exist in all chiefdoms and are the representatives of the inhabitants of a village; their influence is non-political and varies in the different local federations. In most chiefdoms they are concerned with the administration of land, and even where they do not act directly they are customarily informed by the village headman of any transactions in land which take place. The *basumba batale* are everywhere the leaders of the village organization for communal work. Their influence is weakest in the south, in the chiefdoms of the Mweli Federation (in ZM‡ they do not exist), and strongest in the Binza Federation. The position of the *basumba batale* has been for many years in a state of flux with a tendency to diminish in importance.

Everywhere the village headman and the *basumba batale* work hand in hand. For instance, even in BSN, BS, BD‡ the village headman is informed of the allocation of land by the *basumba batale*, and in UF‡ a new-comer would first discuss his settlement with the *basumba batale* and seek their agreement before he approached the village headman for the actual allocation of the land. Everywhere they are the experts on boundaries in the *ilala* (unoccupied land).

It is emphatically stated by the chiefs that they never interfere in the allocation of land and that any applicant who approached them would be told to go to the village headman or to the *basumba batale* as the case may be.

There are two forums at which land questions may be discussed—the *ibanza lya milimo* and the *long'we*.

The *ibanza lya milimo* (also sometimes called *ng'wibilingo* or *lukiko*) is the meeting of all occupiers of holdings in the village. It is called together by a messenger of the village headman, and a representative of each *kaya* is bound to attend. If a husband should be absent, his wife has to go. The usual reason for calling together the *ibanza lya milimo* is to pass on Government orders, which the village headman has received through his chief and which usually refer to land or cultivation, and also to discuss any issue of common interest concerning the economic life of the community.

Although the *ibanza lya milimo* has no executive power, no inhabitants of the village,

* H. Cory, *Sukuma Law and Custom*, Oxford University Press, 1953, pp. 112–122 and pp. 124–125.

† See above, p. 290.

‡ These abbreviations refer to areas of Sukumaland. (See map in Cory's book.)

as long as they wish to remain in the village, can disregard its decisions. It is called together frequently and provides opportunities for a village headman to keep in contact with his villagers.

The *long'we* is a meeting of all inhabitants of a *gunguli* (parish) for the discussion of local affairs. This institution has lost its former importance and there are areas in which for years no meeting has taken place.

It is called together by the *basumba batale,* and the *ng'wanangwa* may be asked to attend, but he need not be invited. Questions of local interest are discussed and criticism is not avoided. Topics discussed may be: dissatisfaction with the village headman or his helpers; an unusual abundance of birds when the sorghum ripens, or of lions or hyenas arousing superstitious fears; lack of rain and epidemics among men or beasts. A very important function of the *long'we,* which might be called the plenary and representative assembly of the community, is the control of its members by the imposition of penalties for anti-social behaviour and the application of ostracism. (Sometimes penalties are imposed by a family council).

A. *Masumule* (*lwadida*). This consists of a small fine, usually a few shillings and never more than a goat. It is imposed on a man for: disorderly behaviour such as insulting a girl; beating his wife severely (if a court case is avoided with the consent of both concerned); insulting his wife by using profane language about her mother; cursing or beating an old woman (if a court case is avoided); beating his mother; insulting elders; slander.

It is imposed on a woman for: cursing or beating her mother-in-law; disorderly behaviour, especially to old women.

The *masumule* is usually paid without delay and the transgressor rarely tries to defend himself. The community is judge, plaintiff, and witness all in one and if there is a doubt there is no case.

B. *Bubisi* or *Bukindikwa* (*ostracism*). To be ostracized means that nobody is allowed to visit, speak with, or help the man declared a *mbisi.* If the fire in his house goes out, nobody gives him fire; if his hut is in flames, nobody helps him to extinguish the fire; if his child dies, nobody helps him to bury it. A citizen who does not sever his connexion with a *mbisi* automatically becomes a *mbisi* himself.

The sanction is imposed if a man refuses to help bury a person; refuses first aid, i.e. to transport sick or wounded, or to help in emergencies such as fire; or to participate in ceremonies ordered for the purpose of dispelling evil influences directed against the community, or seriously and continuously disturbs the peace of the village by his dangerous or amorous temper.

The sanction is imposed without hearing the defendant, who is simply informed of the decision afterwards. A man cannot endure for long such exclusion from the community; he may get the interdict removed by paying a ransom fixed by the community. This payment need not be very high, a goat or few shillings are sufficient. The ransom is received by the elders and, if it consists of a goat, this is killed and eaten, the distribution of the meat following traditional rules; if it is paid in money, native beer or a goat is bought and consumed.

C. *Kupeja.* This is a sanction, not imposed by the elders and the citizens alone but in consultation with the village headman and the *ntemi* himself. If repeated impositions of *bubisi* and payments of ransom do not change a man's anti-social behaviour, he is declared a *mbisi* once and for all; no ransom is accepted from him. This sanction in practice means expulsion.

Masumule, *bubisi*, and *kupeja* are still imposed and have not lost their wholesome influence on the behaviour of the individual as a member of the community. There is a tendency nowadays for differences to be taken to court for settlement, rather than to the elders and a gathering of the community. It is a general trend of the Sukuma to become court-minded.

If a holder does not effectively occupy his land or any part of it, and the need for it arises, the authority has the right to expropriate the holder from such parts of the unused land as it needs for allotment to another.

NOTE. A holder does not automatically forfeit a field because he has not cultivated it for a few years. The holder's title to his land or any part of it, and especially the title of a *nsesa* or heir, is seldom disputed; it is acknowledged *de facto* but not *de jure*.

De facto: Occupiers of large estates (*igobe*) often exclude other people from cultivating parts of their land while they use them as their private grazing reserves. They do not do this in contravention of the law; they are allowed to do so by permission of chiefs, village headmen, *basumba batale*, and by public opinion in general.

The owners of large *igobe* are all loyal citizens. Chiefs and *banangwa* can always rely on their assistance in the never ending struggle for power within a chiefdom. They represent the conservative African aristocracy. They are the old families of the chiefdom and everywhere chiefs, *banangwa*, *basweta*, *banang'oma*, court assessors, belong to these families. The common man cannot easily undertake to fight against this powerful class; in fact he has no desire to fight. In order to illustrate the situation it has been stated that if a village headman should deprive the holder of a large *igobe* of any part of it without good reason he would become very unpopular with his people. It is possible that the common man feels that the existence of large estates and their toleration protects him against being deprived of his own surplus land. This explains the fact that families requiring more land move into a new settlement area even though in the neighbourhood of their old homes a man owns land, the greater part of which he uses as his private pasture.

There is a widely observed usage, which is not formulated as a law, that plots of a *nsesa*, which are now in most cases owned by the second or third generation, are not appropriated on the grounds of their not being effectively occupied.

The same usage is observed if a husband is absent for any length of time and has left his wife on his holding. The fields are left with her even if she cannot cultivate them all. Perhaps the authority may borrow fields if great scarcity of suitable land exists, but it would return them to the husband as soon as he returned.

De jure: Chiefs, *banangwa*, the owners of *igobe*, and the holders of land all know that a holder—if the necessity arises—must give up land which he does not use effectively. There can be no doubt that a *ng'wanangwa* could, for instance, open an *igobe* as pasture for common use, but it has never yet been done. On the other hand there are numerous instances of single fields being taken from the holder, if he has not cultivated them for several years, and given to another applicant. It is acknowledged that the authority should only act in this way if there are no other plots available to satisfy the reasonable demands of a new-comer or of an inhabitant of the village.

If such land or portions of it have to be expropriated because there is no other suitable land in the vicinity, it is the duty of the authority to try to obtain the holder's consent to the transaction.

The holder is not permitted to frustrate the order of the authority by:

(*a*) employing the method of fallowing fields to an unusual extent;

NOTE: The use of the term 'fallow' may give the impression that each cultivator has rotation well organized and that one could see everywhere fields which are lying fallow. But this is not so. The Sukuma usually cultivates a field as long as possible, and only if it becomes exhausted does he leave it and choose a new field. Fallows are usually more or less unintentional. A man may find that he is unable to cultivate a certain field one year and therefore leaves it to lie fallow.

(*b*) cultivating small areas in each of his plots;

(*c*) allotting single fields to applicants;

NOTE: This rule is not a new one. If a village headman came to a man, who he knew had not been using certain parts of his land for a long time, with the intention of allocating those parts to an applicant for land, and was told that they had been given away by the holder to another person for temporary cultivation, he (or the *basumba batale*) would have the right to revoke this transaction and to dispose of the fields. If the borrower had already started cultivation, he would be allowed to harvest his crop, after which the fields would be disposed of by the authority.

(*d*) employing paid labourers in excess of the customary employment of villagers paid in kind. If, under certain circumstances, a man needs paid labourers for the cultivation of his holding, he must ask permission of the authority before he can employ them;

(*e*) cultivating with machinery. If a man wishes to cultivate fields outside his effectively occupied holding with machinery, he must first be allotted the land by the authority.

NOTE: Rules (*d*) and (*e*) were decided upon by the chiefs of the Sukuma Federation and their people in 1949. Formerly different rules existed.

The chiefs and their people realized that the Sukuma system of land tenure, originating in times of abundant land and of simple hand cultivation, could not protect the community against the occupation of vast areas of arable land by enterprising individuals, to the disadvantage of the community.

A holder cannot sell his holding or any part of it or enter into any transaction in which land is the subject.

NOTE: Formerly fields were bartered for goats or cattle in KF, BD, NF,* and probably here and there in other chiefdoms. This is confirmed by Mr. D. W. Malcolm in his *Sukuma Land Utilization Report*, in which he gives an historical description of the Sukuma population. Although only one point is relevant to [here] a quotation seems to be justified on account of its general interest.[2]

'Besides considerations of soil, rainfall and water supply which influenced the location of the earlier settlements, it is easy to forget that as recently as 60 years ago the distribution of population was still controlled to a considerable extent by considerations of security. Most independent chiefdoms were isolated units and the people, however concentrated in certain areas, were unable to move into the neighbouring uninhabited lands on account of internecine warfare. The traditional Sukuma village was usually situated on high ground if not actually under the shadow of a granite tor. It was roughly circular in shape and protected by euphorbia hedges. Within these fortifications lived the whole village community with their stock, and the present organisation of collective labour is a natural result of conditions in which it would have been dangerous to hoe alone. The arable and pasture lands of the village were in its immediate vicinity and often limited to the area in which the alarm could be heard. Under these circumstances the land in the immediate vicinity of the village attained an intrinsic value and the custom of paying in kind the occupier for the acquisition of a field developed.

'Then came the German Administration and with it the cessation of tribal warfare. It became safe to settle further from the centre of the village. The German authorities are said to have prohibited the system of land sales and individuals anxious to obtain good land began to move further afield and clear new areas. The spread appears to have been rapid and in a period of about 20 years the occupied area must have been very considerably extended. This process of expansion also removed the necessity for manuring which had been started in the south-west.'

II. *Acquisition of holding by clearing a plot in the bush area* (*nhinde*). A. A native or a stranger who wishes to clear a holding in the bush does not need to ask any authority so long as his plot is not near the plots of other cultivators. The boundaries of a *gunguli*, if they cut through areas of heavy bush, are sometimes vague and therefore the headmen of the *gunguli* which share the bush area will have to decide among themselves to which *gunguli* the new-comer belongs. His arrival may be the occasion for fixing the boundaries.

B. If it is obvious to which *gunguli* the *nhinde* belongs, the new-comer is expected in due course to inform the *ng'wanangwa* of his presence. The *ng'wanangwa* himself or his deputy may then occasionally visit the settler. A holding of this kind is carved out of the bush without the help of the villagers and the hut is also built without their assistance.

NOTE: Motives for relinquishing a holding and seeking a new one are:

Within the old country. Fear of illness or misfortune; inheritance; invitation and offer of help from friends or relations in another area; quarrel with a member of the Native Authority.

In a new country. Ostracism; witch-weed and decreasing crop yields in general; increase in stock and inefficient grazing; possibility of acquiring a holding unrestricted in size.

The separation of causes is artificial to a degree. The reaction of a man to all these causes depends on his individual character and circumstances. But it may be said that

* *Ibid.*

men with a pioneer spirit will probably try a solution of their troubles in a remote area, while more timid sufferers will seek opportunities nearer to their old homes. In all cases the assistance of a near relative in a rehabilitation area will be an inducement if conditions there have proved favourable.

A. The new-comer (*nsesi*) can occupy as much land as he likes and no boundaries are demarcated by the authority.

NOTE: Areas in which a man can acquire a very large estate (*igobe* or *ikobe*) no longer exist in NF,* except in a few small areas in Burima; UF,* in Masanza I; KF,* in Busmao, Nera, Magu, Sima; BD,* in Ng'wagala, Nung'hu, Kigoku; BS,* in Mondo, Buchunga, Mwadui; SBS;* ZM,* in Karumo.

Even in chiefdoms which still have *nhinde* available for new settlement, the areas are not extensive. Only in the rehabilitation areas west of Smith Sound does extensive settlement take place in the *nhinde*.

B. If there are already cultivators in the neighbourhood the new-comer must ask the authority for land to be allocated.

C. If the new-comer finds neighbours in the bush area boundaries are demarcated, usually by digging shallow pits at intervals of about five yards in light bush, or by marking the boundary with an axe in dense bush.

NOTE: The first settler in a large bush area has the chance of becoming later a *sweta* or *ng'wanangwa ndo* of the area if he is followed by other settlers; but he must be a member of the Sukuma tribe to attain such a position. The senior village headmen (*banangwa batale* or *banangwa baduma*) were originally relatives of the chief and their office was hereditary. Nowadays many of the village headmen are appointed by the chief and are seldom related to him.

When the settler has cut out his plot and created his holding, he holds the land under rules set out under I above.

NOTE: Field-work is the joint task of man and wife. Normally all crops are cultivated by both husband and wife, including the field of sweet potatoes. The actual hours of work in the field are longer for the man than for his wife, as she often leaves the work to prepare food, fetch water, &c. Local variations exist; for instance, in the chiefdoms near the lake-shore potato fields are cultivated by women. The disposal of the crop is the right of the husband, but it is considered one of the requisites of a happy domestic life for him to consult with his wife before a transaction is undertaken. A wife is not allowed to dispose of any crop except for use as food for the household. In the exercise of this prerogative she is sovereign, and a husband who interferes and criticizes his wife's method of housekeeping is called a *manji*, and such criticism, if not justified, is considered a grave insult.

III. *Acquisition of holding by allocation in an inhabited area* (*ilala*). A. If a man wishes to obtain land for a holding he chooses in most cases a village where he has a relative living, or at least a very good friend. But even a stranger can ask for land and get it.

NOTE: A Sukuma tribesman considers himself related to eight families. This is not a rule, but eight is the number which a man, brought up in his father's house, should remember. The following clan names are taken as an example:

* *Ibid.*

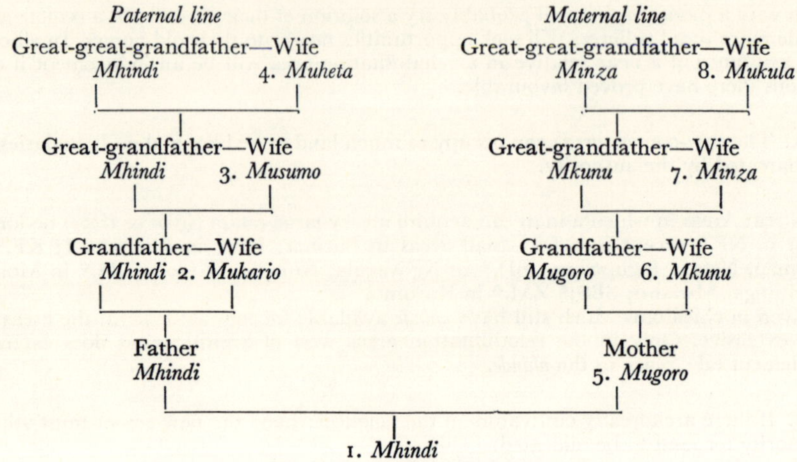

B. The new-comer settles down first in the house of his relative which he uses as a base while looking for suitable plots and a house site. When he has found what he wants he and his relative approach the authority and inform him of his intention to settle in the village and of the result of his search for suitable land.

NOTE: The Sukuma word for a holding is *migunda*, the plural of *ngunda*, a field. There is no specific word for a holding. This seems to indicate that the idea of a strictly defined and individually owned piece of land does not exist.

C. If the applicant is the son or brother of an inhabitant of the village he must still ask for an allocation of land if he wishes to found his own *kaya*.*

Before the land is allocated the authority makes inquiries about the reasons for the emigration of the applicant, and about his character and popularity in his former domicile.

NOTE: If the applicant comes from so far away that it is not possible to obtain this information, he will have to wait for his land until the authority and the villagers decide by direct observation about his suitability as a settler and neighbour. Otherwise the usual custom is to dispatch two *basumba batale* or *banamhara* to the former domicile of the applicant.

It appears that this procedure involves two important aspects of social life:

1. It helps to maintain the authority of those men in the villages, be they village headmen or *basumba batale*, who need it for the execution of their other duties.
2. It permits the control of new-comers by the villagers.

These two important functions would cease to operate in all cases in which land became the subject of commercial transactions. The first does not need further explanation, the second perhaps does. The village is still organized on a communal basis—economically (common labour, mutual help, ostracism, village court or arbitration, water supply, grazing, etc.), and spiritually (a deep-rooted and general belief in magic). The well-being of the society is still protected, in many instances, by custom rather than by law. The power of the law can be invoked against anyone, but the strength of custom lies solely in the adherence of the whole community, and such adherence cannot be assumed in the case of a stranger. The stranger must prove to the community his readiness to accept its customs, and it must remain the privilege of the community to make the final decision as to his acceptance. For obvious reasons the former strict adherence to the original procedure is not always possible nowadays. But where the opportunity exists of ascertaining the applicant's antecedents, it is made use of.

* Homestead.

If the applicant is accepted, the village headman and/or *basumba batale*, with a few neighbours as witnesses, go to show the new-comer the exact boundaries of his fields.

Boundaries (*lubimbi*) are demarcated by putting stones into the ground or by hoeing a line along the boundary and by using, wherever possible, natural features such as dry stream beds, paths, or trees and rocks.

If the boundary is a path, the actual path is considered tribal land, the two neighbours owning the land as far as the edge of the path.

Confirmed in D.C.'s Appeal 20/47. NF, Fulo. *Shelemba* v. *Paulo.*

No fees are payable to the authority or to the witnesses.

NOTE: It sometimes happens nowadays that an applicant gives the authority (village headman) a present in order to be allotted a big plot or a plot situated in another man's holding and not cultivated by him. But these cases are rare. It may be said that an applicant gets his land without fee or presents.

No rules exist with regard to the maximum size of an allotted holding; it varies according to the size of the applicant's family or the scarcity or abundance of land. A possible increase in the family or the necessity for fallow land is not allowed for. Claims to large pieces of land in the *ilala* are never entertained by the authority.

NOTE: Shifting cultivation is not and never was generally practised. In the south, where people live in close settlements, a holder shifts his house, if he considers it advisable, to a plot in the immediate vicinity of the settlement. The abandoned house plot, *matongo*, is used for cultivation. A man may plant the same crop, such as bulrush millet, for ten or fifteen successive years in the same field. Mtama exhausts the soil more quickly but it can be planted in the same plot for many years, except in BSN.*

It may happen that a cultivator gives up an exhausted field and looks for a substitute in the *ilala*, but if there is no suitable plot in the vicinity, he must try rotation or manure.

It is the custom for a new-comer to ask for the help of the community when he begins to build his house. The villagers contribute the poles and grass for thatching the roof, and they also help the new-comer to shift his belongings from his former domicile to the village.

NOTE: A characteristic Sukuma social institution is the great number of village organizations which serve various purposes but are principally institutions for mutual help in field-work. In various parts of the country the same names denote different types of organization. The following village organizations are common mainly in the north and are examples of this type of social activity.

Elika is the generic name for any group of people doing common work. (*Kisumba* in KF, UF.)*

Isalenge is the village organization for mutual help. (KF, UF.)*

Buyobe is a small working party of the *isalenge*.

(The *basumba batale* are the leaders of the *isalenge* and *buyobe*.)

Ilima is a small group of people invited personally by the owner of a field to help with the cultivation.

Bafunya is a group of family members invited by one member to help in the cultivation of a field.

Nyida (in BSN* called *Kumbu*) is the journey of the villagers to help a new-comer shift his belongings from the old to the new domicile.

Igulilu is the night cultivation society in SBS.*

In addition to these organizations, members of secret societies can invite their fellow members to work in their fields for payment in kind. This mutual help of society members is now more common than that provided by the *elika*. Various secret societies exist in Sukumaland and a man, in order to become a member, has to undergo initiation rites.

The most widespread societies in which mutual help in field-work among members is very common are:

* Areas of Sukumaland.

Buyeye } society of snake-charmers
Bugoyangi }
Bununguli society of porcupine hunters
Bugumha dance societies
Bugika dance societies
Buyege originally a society for hunting elephants with bows and arrows.

There are certain magic rites customarily performed in connexion with building a house.

After a man has chosen the place for his house he builds a *kigabiro* outside the building ground opposite to where the door will be. He invites the spirits to settle down there until the house is ready. Before he moves into the new house he prepares beer for the ceremony called *kushikirija numba* (to bless the house). Neighbours and elders of the village are invited. The pot containing beer is placed in the middle of the hut, and every-one draws some beer with a plaited cup, takes a mouthful and spits it against the wall. They say a short sentence such as: 'May the people live peacefully here' or 'May sickness and quarrels stay away from this house'.

A man of property will kill a goat for this occasion. Leaves of *nama* (combretum) and *ng'wale* (pterocarpus) are spread out near the door. The goat is first marked with flour and fat on the forehead, then killed, cooked, and served. The father throws the first bit of meat on the leaves and says:

'My fathers, and all you twins born in my family in the past, this is your meat. May I live here happy and prosper.'

It is the custom in some places to extinguish the hearth fire the next morning and to kindle a new one by friction. From the first porridge cooked on the new fire the father takes a morsel and throws it against the wall, saying a sentence similar to the above.

IV. *Acquisition of holding by allocation of a relinquished holding* (*malale ga saka* or *malale ga fuluka*). A. A man who relinquishes his holding has no right to hand it over to another man without the consent of the authority.

NOTE: It is perhaps necessary to state expressly that brothers, even if the estate in question is a *migunda ya ise*, must ask permission of the authority if one brother relin-quishes the holding and another brother wishes to take it over. The family council may discuss the issue but the decision as to whether or not the brother of the outgoing holder is allotted the land lies with the authority.

B. Such holding reverts to the authority for re-allocation.

C. The only person to whom this rule does not apply is a son, who can take over a holding, if his father relinquishes it, just as he takes over the holding in the case of his father's death, without special permission of the authority.

A. A holder can allow a relative to occupy a portion of his holding so long as he him-self lives on it, but he cannot do the same for a non-relative without permission of the authority.

B. If such holder relinquishes his holding, he cannot hand it over to any person except a relative who has lived more than two years on the holding.

NOTE: This rule was decided upon by the chiefs of the Sukuma Federation and their people in 1949. Formerly the same rule existed but no time limit was fixed.

An abandoned holding need not remain an indivisible holding. The authority has the right to allot single fields from it or to allot the holding as a whole.

NOTE: The shift of population within a village in any year is still considerable. There is a saying: 'The subjects of the *Ntemi* are his monkeys (*Banhu bali nhumbili ya batemi*)', meaning that the people do not live for long in one place but are in constant movement from village to village or even from chiefdom to chiefdom. It must be added that the people who abandon their holdings because of superstitious fears may be acting wisely without knowing it. Often enough the house and yard have become unhealthy.

A *malale ga saka* is allotted by the authority; but everywhere, even where the authority is the *ng'wanangwa*, the *basumba batale*, as the representative of the villagers, are customarily consulted.

The allocation is not restricted to an inhabitant of the village or chiefdom nor to a Sukuma; any suitable man is acceptable.

NOTE: The man who comes first gets the holding and no preference is shown to a member of the Sukuma tribe. General considerations only, such as the size of the holding and that of the family of the applicant, or his character or behaviour, decide the issue.

A. After the authority has allotted the plot the new occupier takes possession of it without further ceremony (except private rites of ancestral worship—*kitambo*).

B. The new-comer is shown the boundaries of the holding and fields by the village headman and *busumba batale*.

No fees are payable for the allocation of a *malale ga saka*.

NOTE: In BSN the occupier has to pay one head of cattle (*ng'ombe ya saka*) after one year to the *basumba batale* and *banamhara* of the village who kill the beast and distribute the meat.

Rules set out under I above are valid in the case of an allotted *malale ga saka*.

B. *Single Fields*. Single fields are allotted by the same authority and in the same manner as a holding in the *ilala* or *ikera*.

If a man wishes to cultivate a single field in the *ilala* he must ask permission of the authority. This rule refers to an inhabitant of the village as well as to an inhabitant of another village.

NOTE: This rule was decided upon by the chiefs of the Sukuma Federation and their people in 1949. Formerly, in UF, NF, KF, BSN, BD, SB, BS,* a man could cultivate a single field within the boundaries of his own village without permission of the authority. In KS, SS, KM, SBS* he could not cultivate without permission of the authority.

It has been generally realized that more control over the acquisition of single fields is necessary in modern circumstances and therefore the rules existing in the south were adopted. The delegates from BD, SS stated that in practice such control preserves the equilibrium between land under cultivation and land available for grazing in the *gunguli*. Without control there might be a shortage of pasture for the cattle of a *gunguli* because a few inhabitants, preferring agriculture to animal husbandry, could occupy and cultivate an unrestricted area in the *ilala*.

A bachelor cannot demand the allocation of a complete holding, but he may apply for and receive single fields.

If a man has cultivated a field for one season, no other man can cultivate this field without the permission of the former cultivator or the authority, even if the field has remained fallow for a long time (*ilale*).

NOTE: If a man cultivates a field which has not been allotted to him by the authority, no other cultivator may deprive him of it, but his right to it is not recognized by the authority, which can, at any time, allot the field to an applicant, though in practice it is not likely to do so.

D.C.'s Appeal 51/45. U.F. *Zukuyo* v. *Nusome*.

In the judgement it was stated that no man can claim a *shamba* as his unless it is explicitly granted to him by a village headman; no one has a right to sub-let his *shamba* without the headman's permission; no man has a right to cultivate a *shamba* in a *gunguli* other than that in which he lives, except temporarily and with the permission of the headman.

If an inhabitant of one village wishes to cultivate a certain field in another village he must be allotted this field by the authority. The permission in such a case is only granted temporarily and can be withdrawn if an applicant arrives who wishes to settle in the village.

* *Ibid.*

D.C.'s Appeal 51/45. UF. Nassa. *Masome* v. *Zakayo.*

Zakayo cleared the bush and cultivated a field of cotton for five years in a neighbouring village, while himself living three or four miles away. He never sought or received permission from the headman to cultivate this field. The headman *Masome,* on receiving an application from a new-comer wishing to settle in the village, ordered Zakayo to vacate the field. Zakayo refused to leave but the court decided against him.

NOTE: This situation is frequently met with in the *isanga,* the sandy belt round the lake-shore, which is very suitable for the growing of sweet potatoes. The village headmen allot single fields to applicants who come from other villages. The occupiers, who remain living in their distant holdings, are allowed to keep the fields in the *isanga* and have their regular potato harvest as long as they are not required by the same village headman to give them up. They must always be allowed to collect the harvest before relinquishing the field.

Transfer of single field. A holder cannot give away a field to another man, whether relative or stranger, without permission of the authority.

NOTE: Rule 412 was decided upon by the chiefs of the Sukuma Federation and their people in 1949. Formerly this rule was followed in: BS, SBS, SS, KS, KM.* In NF, UF, KF, BSN, BD* a man could give a single field to a relative, but not to a non-relative, without asking permission of the authority.

A. If a holder relinquishes his holding, the occupier of a single field within the holding cannot retain the field without permission of the authority.

B. If a holder has allowed a person to cultivate a field, or has given a field to anyone as a present, such action, whatever may have been the clauses of the contract, is not recognized as valid after the death of the holder. Even if the occupier of the field in question can prove that he paid for permission to cultivate it, he has to return the land immediately on the death of the original occupier and has no right to claim compensation.

A. A holder can lend a field to a relative but not to a non-relative without permission of the authority.

NOTE: A man may borrow fields, not because he has not sufficient land and cannot obtain land in his village, but because he is short of a certain type of land necessary for the cultivation of a certain crop. For instance in SBS (Busiha) or BD (Sengerema), adequate soil for the cultivation of groundnuts is scarce and people try to borrow plots from relatives or friends living in more fortunate areas.

B. A holder can only lend fields to relatives so long as he himself is occupying his holding.

D.C.'s Appeal 2/47 NF. Fulo. *Kilumba* v. *Ngereza.*

Kilumba claimed from Ngereza a cassava field, which his brother Masolwa had given to him when he himself moved to another village. The field had been allotted by the *ng'wanangwa* to Ngereza and the court held that it therefore belonged to Ngereza.

NOTE: The application of these rules is the same as that of rules 375–80. A holder often allows a neighbour or a stranger to cultivate one of his fields without asking permission from the authority.

It is unknown for anyone to pay rent for a borrowed field.

Notes

[1] The ZM and SM* rules of land tenure differ from those of Sukuma proper. These areas, formerly sparsely populated, are now being colonized, in rapidly increasing numbers, by Sukuma peasants emigrating from their homeland. For the time being two sets of rules of land tenure will have to be acknowledged side by side; one for the Zinza indigenous population, and

* *Ibid.*

one for the Sukuma immigrants who have taken up the land in accordance with Sukuma usage and who cannot be expected to hold it under rules other than their own.

[2] I should like to express my appreciation of the valuable help I received from Mr. D. W. Malcolm when I first undertook researches in Sukumaland in 1936; andal so to acknowledge the many instances, in the above-mentioned report, where points of law are illuminated and confirmed.

I. Schapera: Native Land Tenure in the Bechuanaland Protectorate*

The Acquisition of Private Holdings

We must now see how individual members of the tribe can acquire arable land. The various methods that generally obtain may be classified into three different categories: (*a*) allotment by the tribal authorities, (*b*) gift or inheritance from parents, and (*c*) private treaty with some other person, who may give away or lend out part of the land in his possession. In Tšwana law, land cannot be bought or hired. There have, however, been some recent instances where such transactions were concluded. They are dealt with below.

People entitled to land. All married men are entitled to claim and receive arable land from the tribal authorities. As far as I am aware, no instances are known of requests having been refused, except possibly in the smaller Reserves where there is a shortage of land. As Chief Tshekedi said, in a memorandum presented to the Pim Commission, 'Native law and custom does not allow the Chief to withhold the granting of land for the purpose of cultivation'. Some subject communities do not habitually practise agriculture, like the Sarwa, who are essentially hunters, and the Damara, who are essentially cattle-keepers. But if any man belonging to one of these communities wishes to plough, he also is entitled to receive land for the purpose.[1] Aliens accepted into the tribe enjoy the same rights as members by birth. Temporary residents, like teachers and other Government employees, are sometimes given land to plough; this is apparently a privilege, and not a right, although it has become the usual practice in regard to teachers stationed in outlying villages.

Every married woman is also entitled to land for cultivation. She cannot claim it from the tribal authorities, however; her husband must provide a field for her, and should help her to plough it, failing which she can sue him. Unmarried people, as we have seen, are sometimes given land to cultivate by their parents, or may obtain it in other ways. But they cannot demand it as a right from either their parents or the tribal authorities, although instances are known where an unmarried man has received land from his ward-head or the Chief.

Allotment by parents or tribal authorities. Originally, when a ward was given its holding, the headman assigned allotments to the heads of the households under him. The size of the allotment was determined roughly by the number of wives and sons that the man had. He usually cleared enough land at once to provide each of his wives with a separate field, but left the remainder untouched until his sons grew up and married, when they also received their holdings from him. Since most wards have now held their land for many years, it is seldom that such family allotments are still distributed, except when a stranger joins the tribe, or a new village is established, or a ward for some reason abandons its original holding and is given another.

Today, a man when he marries usually receives his first plot from his father or guardian, who gives him part of the land originally assigned to the family by the ward-head, or subsequently acquired in another way. The plot is generally on virgin soil (*setsha, thitê, serithê, bokgatha*), but sometimes consists of a *tshimo*, i.e. a field already cleared for cultivation, which may be either fallow (*mogóla*) or still in use (*lotlhagare*). Occasionally a large field will be divided up, and one of the portions given to the son; he may instead receive part of his mother's land, if she has any to spare.

Unmarried children, as already noted, may also be given land by their parents. On

* I. Schapera, *Native Land Tenure in the Bechuanaland Protectorate*, Lovadele Press, 1943, pp. 148–152.

getting married, a son will continue to use the land allotted to him. A daughter, on the other hand, usually loses her right to it, since it is her husband's duty to provide her with a field. Among the Rolong, however, she is allowed to use the land jointly with her husband.

Should there be no land to spare in the family allotment, the man will apply through his guardian to the headman of his own ward. The headman is obliged to give him land, if there is any available in the holding assigned to the ward. The plot may be on land that has not yet been allotted, it may have been abandoned by someone else, or, in certain circumstances, it may even be taken away from a possessor if he is not using it.

If no land can be found in the ward holding, the ward-head must apply on behalf of the man to the Chief or village headman. The Chief will then either send him to the overseer of some area where land is known to be available, or will personally give him a plot, either on land that has not yet been assigned, or in an area that has been abandoned by other people.

Occasionally, a man will himself find a tract of land that he would like to cultivate. He must then apply to the overseer of that region, or, if it is unassigned, to the Chief. The tribal authorities are opposed to the making of isolated fields away from the localities commonly used, and permission is not readily given, especially if the land is close to a cattlepost area. Should the man plough there without the consent of the overseer or Chief, he will be ordered to leave, and, if he disobeys, he may be punished and removed by force.

Gift or loan from others. Instead of approaching their ward-head or the Chief, men sometimes ask for land from a relative or friend. Parents-in-law are a fairly common source of supply. Among the Kgatla and Malete, people with land to spare sometimes give a married daughter a field as dowry. Such a field is termed *tshimo ya serotwana* ('field of the little basket') by the Kgatla, and *tshimo ya letsele* ('field of the breast') by the Malete. It is used jointly by the woman and her husband, but reverts to her own family if she is divorced or dies without issue. Other tribes do not have this particular custom. Among them, however, a daughter and her husband are often lent a field to cultivate until he is able to obtain another for himself. Occasionally his parents-in-law will even give him part of their land as a permanent possession. They are not bound to provide for him, however; that is the duty of his parents or the tribal authorities.

Failing his parents-in-law, a man may ask another relative or friend for the gift or loan of a field. If the land is on virgin soil, it is usually handed over permanently; if it has already been cleared, it may instead be lent to the applicant until the holder wants to use it again. This method of acquisition is often utilized by people who wish to cultivate more land than they now possess, or whose existing fields have become exhausted or prove otherwise unsuitable. The gift or loan is sometimes made solely out of friendship. Sometimes, however it is based upon service, in that a wealthy man will give part of his land to his retainers. This is not actually remuneration for their work, but is done to have them close to his own fields; I do not know of any instances where a man has deliberately become the servant of someone else in order to obtain land to cultivate.

Payment for land. Among the Kgatla, when a field that has already been cleared is given to another person, the man parting with it sometimes claims and receives a heifer in exchange. Some people speak of this as a 'purchase' of the land. The majority, however, maintain that it is merely a method of compensating the owner for his labour in clearing the field: they point out that a heifer is the standard payment made to anybody whom one hires to clear land. The exchange is a locally-established custom, to which no objection is taken. It is apparently practised only when the people concerned are comparative strangers, and not when they are relatives or close friends.

In all the other tribes, there is no recognized form of payment, even if the field is already cleared. It is held that land can be transferred from one man to another only by way of gift, inheritance, or loan; it can never be bought or sold.

Among the Kwena, in 1938, a man named Sephuthabakwa was fined by the Chief's court for having accepted cattle from men to whom he had given part of his land, and he was also ordered to restore the animals to their former owners. It was explicitly stated in the judgment that the land belonged to the tribe and Chief, and could not be sold.[2]

Among the Ngwaketse, on the other hand, a man named Balosang borrowed a field from Mokgalagadi, overseer of the Masôkê area. Subsequently he said that he wanted to buy the field, but Mokgalagadi refused, 'not wanting to get into trouble'. After Mokgalagadi's death, his son Moisakamo would no longer let Balosang use the field, but ultimately, about 1938–9, agreed to let him have it in exchange for an ox. The matter gave rise to considerable comment, and Moisakamo's conduct was generally censured. However, nothing was done about it by the Chief, although it was the first, and so far the only, instance locally known of land having been sold to a fellow-tribesman.

The Ngwaketse also provide the only instances that I have been able to find of people exchanging their fields.

The Balosang mentioned above applied to the Chief for more land, since his children were growing up and he wanted to provide for them. He was told that no spare land was available near by, but that he could obtain a large tract some distance away, on condition that he surrendered his land at Masôkê to the Chief, whose fields were next to it. The exchange was duly effected. The field that Balosang had bought from Moisakamo was apart from the rest, and the Chief afterwards gave it to a man named Yakoba, in exchange for a field immediately adjoining his own, which he wanted to enlarge.

Notes

[1] It is estimated by the officer who carried out the census of Sarwa in the Ngwato Reserve that approximately 35 per cent of them now 'make some attempt to cultivate their own crops'. He mentions also that Chief Tshekedi 'has stated that any Mosarwa may come to him and be allotted ploughing or other lands in the reserve.' (J. W. Joyce, 'Report on the Masarwa in the Bamangwato Reserve,' *League of Nations Publications*, 1938, VI, B.1, pp. 61, 66.)

[2] *Kokole* v. *Sephuthabakwa*, Chief's Tribunal, Molepolole, 3/1938.

H. E. Lambert: Land Tenure among the Akamba*

Acquisition

Formerly both *ng'undu*† and *isese* were acquired by excision from the *weu*.‡ Now there is no *weu* left except a few stretches of useless land and small patches between *isese*.§ Most of what was once *weu* is now so closely packed with *isese* that there is no chance of acquisition by excision in any worth-while area, the small bits of *weu* left being urgently required by the local *isese* owners as communal grazing. Any new-comer who tried to settle in such overcrowded *weu* would be refused permission by the *utui* elders of the area.

Nowadays the only normal means of acquisition are inheritance and purchase.

Permanence of Rights

In theory exclusive rights in *ng'undu*† never lapse. Each *ng'undu* is owned in perpetuity by the pioneer who demarcated it and his heirs unless it is sold outright, in which case the purchaser and his heirs hold it in perpetuity unless it is sold outright again. According to this theory a man may leave his *ng'undu* for many years, even for generations, and he and his heirs can claim or reassert exclusive rights at any time. In practice, however, 'perpetuity' is a function of the memory of the local residents, and a man returning after many years would not be permitted to oust a more recent occupier unless he could satisfy the local elders that he or his ancestor had actually obtained the land by first

* H. E. Lambert, 'Land Tenure among the Akamba', in *African Studies*, Vol. 6, No. 4, Witwatersrand University Press, 1947, pp. 159–162 and pp. 168–173.

† Cultivated holding (opposite to *isese*).

‡ Exclusive grazing ground taken from the *weu*; the grazing part of a holding as opposed to the rest.

§ Commanage: unoccupied land and not subject to individual or family rights.

excision or by inheritance or purchase. The same principle is followed by the native courts today, that is to say, *ng'undu* rights are recognised as permanent, but if a dispute arises the onus is on the non-occupying claimant to prove his claim by means of the *kithitu** oath or otherwise. It is for this reason that a man who leaves his *ng'undu*, intending to return at some future time, generally puts an agent or care-taker (*musyaisya*) (pl. *asyaisya*) in charge with instructions to keep the memory of his rightful ownership alive, or, alternatively, makes a point of frequent visits to the area during which he talks to the *atui* (people of the *utui*†) about his land and intimates his intention to return and cultivate the land again.

A *kisese* is not strictly subject to permanent exclusive rights. It was demarcated as grazing, and grazing rights in theory were always communal. But in practice pressure on the grazing reduced the size of the community holding such rights to the *utui* only; it did not, however, associate it with the kinship. There is a fundamental distinction here between *isese* and *ng'undu*. If the family holding an *ng'undu* died out completely their rights would pass to their *mbai*‡ and the land would be occupied (and owned) by their next-of-kin. But a *kisese*, being grazing land and in theory. held in common, would in like circumstances revert to the community, not to the *mbai*, that is, it would revert to the community whose common rights in the grazing were still recognised, viz., the *utui*. It would become part of the *weu* grazed by the *utui*. An *ng'undu* could revert to *weu* if there were not close relatives of the family which had just died out near enough to make a claim. But at least in theory an *ng'undu* never lacked a lawful owner with a right to exclude the community at large. In this sense *ng'undu* rights were permanent, exclusive, agricultural rights and *kisese* rights were temporary, exclusive, pastoral rights.

But *kisese* rights were certainly exclusive so long as they were exercised, and exercise included a clearly expressed intention to re-exercise. The right, in fact, like those of an *ung'ndu*, were only safe if they were kept alive, but in the case of a *kisese* a mere expressed intention would not preserve the rights indefinitely; a *musyaisya* exercising actual user was almost a necessity if the rights were to be recognised beyond a period of a year or so.

The operation of this theory, however, was complicated by two factors. One was the fact that an *iyanso* (a deserted homestead site) was regarded as being just as subject to permanent exclusive rights as an *ng'undu*. It was used or could be used for agriculture. It included the sites of former dwellings, which for some reason (no doubt the agricultural expert could explain) are nearly always very fertile; it included also the sites of former cattle pens (*siengo* and *mbiyu*), naturally very rich in dung. The *iyanzo* garden was looked upon as almost the equivalent in agricultural value of the *ng'undu* fields, whose fertility depended on their origin, usually on their being deposits of rich surface soil naturally eroded from the higher catchment areas of streams. The fertility of *ng'undu* was not deliberately maintained; it tended to decrease quite rapidly and obviously unless the land was so plentiful that long periods of fallow were practicable. *Iyanzo*§ lands had a comparatively enormous reserve of organic matter which, though no attempt was made to incorporate it evenly, kept the soil in good heart for lengthy periods. An *iyanzo* garden, being near the *musyi*‖ (both were in the same *kisese*) was very convenient to the agriculturist, and not so difficult to guard during the ripening of the crops, as the generally more distant *ng'undu*. It is therefore not surprising that the women thought a lot of their *maanzo*, and that every wife regarded her *mbee ya iyanzo* as a prize possession on which she would suffer no encroachment. Consequently the *iyanzo* garden, though started in an area set aside for grazing, was put into the category of agricultural lands and acquired the same degree of permanency in exclusive rights as agricultural lands (*ng'undu*) of which the user started agriculturally.[1]

As pressure on the common grazing land increased and reduced the frequency of demarcation of new *isese*, new dwellings (as for grown up sons) were built on the old *isese*. The size of the homestead site thus gradually increased and took up more of the *kisese*, and as the *ng'undu* lands lost something of their fertility the demand for *iyanzo* gardens grew. The homestead would be moved more frequently for this, if for no other, reason. But the new homestead would be in the same *kisese*, which tended to become

* Fetish.
† Group of homesteads.
‡ Extended family (clan).
§ Deserted homestead.
‖ Homestead.

much more agricultural and permanent in character. It was a rule that no new dwelling could be built 'below' the old one, that is to say, homestead sites were chosen in succession each 'above' the last. Thus if one boundary of the *kisese* were a stream, there the cattle were watered, and the *kisese* stretched up the valley side towards the top, the first *iyanzo* would be near the stream, the next a little higher up, and so on. In time the *kisese* would have a line of *maanzo* from one end to the other, or if there were two wives or more, two lines or more, each line representing progressive stages in a woman's cultivation of her *mbee*, with possible sub-division for each of her son's wives. Nowadays, when new *isese* are difficult to come by, the movement of the homestead is much less rapid. Now *misyi* are built alongside old ones, that is, along a line at right angles to the axis of the *kisese*. In this way the rule forbidding a backward movement is observed, but the *kisese* gradually becomes more completely filled with *maanzo* than was formally the case, and eventually becomes almost entirely agricultural land (though it may be used for grazing) and subject to permanent exclusive rights. Formerly when the homestead reached the further ('upper') end of the *kisese* a new *kisese* would be demarcated in the *weu* and the next homestead established towards its 'lower' end. Nowadays when a man's *musyi*, or that of his descendants, has reached the 'top' and has occupied in turn each site along the 'upper' boundary there is no further site available; the *musyi* must stay there, unless purchase of another site is possible or the extended family is lucky enough to hold or to inherit land elsewhere.

It is largely in this way that the Kamba is becoming more and more subject to permanent exclusive rights, not the fictitious rights accorded by a successful twisting of the law to suit the individual, but legal rights depending on the persistence of the law relating to the *iyanzo*.

The other factor which helped to complicate the theory of the reversion to the *weu* of the temporarily exclusive grazing grounds (*isese*) was a recent one and engineered in part by officers of Government. When the attempt at compulsory destocking had proved abortive it was felt that individual 'ownership' of grazing land would make for better husbandry, that while grazing was very largely communal there was no incentive to reduce the individual herd, but that when grazing was individual too, the owner of a herd would see and understand the danger due to over-stocking of his individual holding. Investigation indicated that there were traditional exclusive grazing rights, and the officers concerned felt themselves justified in encouraging the thorough exercise of such exclusive rights by fencing. There was some degree of opposition, probably for the most part from the *isese*—less young men who saw the end of their ambition to become herd-owners using grazing land still largely communal. But on the whole the principle was accepted by the Kamba and their land was largely parcelled out in individual or family holdings fenced with sisal. No doubt what bits of actual *weu* still remained in strips between *isese* and *ng'undu* were sometimes incorporated in the new *isese*. For the new *isese* were to many Kamba really new, not so much in any violent alteration of the boundaries or in any great increase in size, but rather in the connotation of the name; a *kisese* was now no longer a temporary exclusive grazing ground which, apart from its *maanzo*, would revert, if it ever did revert, to the *weu* communal to the *utui*, but a permanent exclusive holding heritable in perpetuity, and reverting, if ever it did revert, to an *mbai*. That at least was one interpretation given to the fencing, not only by the officers but by very many Kamba. The middle school, however, were not so ready to accept it; they saw no harm in fencing or exclusion; these were traditional rights; but reversion to *mbai*, that is, heritability in perpetuity whether the land was used for agricultural purposes or for grazing or not at all, was in their view an innovation which was dangerous because it left the political unit—the *utui*—with no control at all. In effect the new interpretation, if it had survived, would have meant that all *isese* land was now *ng'undu*, and that the traditionally male sphere had been subordinated to the female, the political to the social, and the communal to the individual. From the Government's point of view it might have helped to save a little of the land a little longer, but it would have meant a stimulation of the growing spirit of unconditioned individualism and rendered the development of a civic sense in respect of native lands more remote than ever. But the middle school of thought, as represented by the present-day Tribunals, usually insist on the retention of the old interpretation of the word *kisese*, and do not recognise a permanent exclusive right to demarcated grazing grounds except to those portions of them which are proved to be *maanzo*.

As to the degree to which the new interpretation achieved its object—the improvement of the grazing lands—the following extracts from a letter dated July 7th, 1944, written by Mr. M. H. Grieve, Agricultural Officer, are relevant:

'. . . during these past six years the policy for agricultural development has been based on the encouragement of individual rather than co-operative effort.

'Land holders were exhorted and assistance was given to demarcated individual holdings by means of sisal and other hedges. The introduction of this policy in 1938 was generally welcomed by the land holders, appealing no doubt to their desire in many cases to become private owners of the land, and so be relieved from tribal restrictions, and it would appear that the initiators of the policy considered that a native in private possession of his land would take care of it and develop it better than would be the case were the use of the land still under tribal and community control. I think it is fair after six years of studying the working of this policy to comment upon it. My opinion is that in general it has been ineffective . . .

'During the first year communal work on the land was strongly discouraged, the idea being that each land owner should be solely responsible for the condition of his holding. A very few isolated individuals did begin to take more interest in their land, but there was no mass movement towards better farming. About 90% of the grazing areas in the district were duly demarcated by their owners, and grazing was much more confined by the enclosures. The grazing certainly improved in some areas but the greatest improvement was brought about by the compulsory closing of areas, to stock by the authorities and not by the owners themselves.

'It was soon found that little progress could be made by individual effort . . .'

Sale

It is almost certainly true to say that there was no such thing as customary sale in the untouched Kamba system. This, however, does not mean that there was never any possibility of sale. A primary holder, that is to say a man who had obtained his agricultural land by demarcation in the *weu*, which was no-man's-land though used communally for grazing, could do as he liked with it. If he wanted to move on somewhere else, and there was another man who wished to occupy the holding, the primary holder would certainly give it him, or sell it to him if (which would be unlikely when land was plentiful) he was prepared to pay for it. The only condition would be that the local elders (if there were any) did not object to the transaction on the ground that the newcomer would be, in their opinion, an undesirable resident among them. This principle, that a primary holder has the complete disposal of his land, is a common one among the Bantu. But among the Eastern Bantu it has tended to be overlooked because by the time scientific enquiries began to be made there was no longer, with most of the tribes, any possibility of primary holding, and the question: 'Can land be sold?' was naturally understood by the people questioned to refer to land which had been inherited for several generations, and their answer, quite correctly, was in the negative. Where primary acquisition from a no-man's-land was still a recent possibility, as among the Kamba, the answer needed some amendment. It should have been 'Sometimes yes, sometimes no'. But the Kamba, subjected to a culture contact and a political influence arising from it, have not in recent years always been entirely honest in their answer. Nowadays the elders say: 'Sale was always possible', but they failed to add: 'but land, once inherited, could not formerly be sold'.

We should probably be safe in saying that until the Machakos Kamba came in contact with the British and for some years afterwards their general principle in regard to outright sale was that uninherited agricultural land could, but very rarely would, be sold, and that the possibility of sale of inherited agricultural land was approximately in inverse proportion to some power of the number of families descended in the patrilineal line from the primary holder. This would mean that in a normally expanding kinship the possibility of outright sale was rapidly reduced to nil. When a man had discovered and demarcated an *ng'undu* the *ilumaita** eventually inherited it, but his holding of it was subject to the rights of his older brothers who had demarcated new *ng'undu* in the *weu*; he could not dispose of it without their sanction. In another generation the kin

* Last-born son.

would be widely scattered and the present holder of the *ng'undu* could not dispose of it without the sanction of all the heads of all the families of the scattered kin. In our imaginary family tree A could not dispose of Nzioka's land without the sanction of B, C and D; E, now living on Kilonzo's land with F, could not dispose of it without the sanction not only of F but of A, B, C, and D, as well. Muli's land inherited by H could not be disposed of without the sanction of A, B, C, D, F, and G, and there could be no disposal of Mbeke's land without the sanction of all the heads of all the families descended from Mbeke. This meant in practice that Mbeke's land could never be disposed of to another kin. Most family trees are much more complicated than our imaginary one, and its living families much more scattered.

The principle of 'spiritual ownership' has often been invoked in explanation of the impossibility of outright sale of inherited land. This principle, if it applied to the Kamba, would mean that Nzioka, having died, was still the owner of the land he pioneered, and his descendants, A, B, C and D, were subject to his spiritual ownership and, since they could never get his sanction, could never sell his land or any portion of it. The 'cult of ancestors' is still quite powerful among the Kamba, but I can find no evidence that the spiritual ownership of land means or has ever meant anything at all to them. Possibly we should be right in assuming that it did mean something formerly and reinforced the system of inheritance by banning sales of land. But the system of inheritance is probably a sufficient explanation in itself, because ultimogeniture did not involve exclusive ownership; it involved, in certain circumstances, exclusive user, but ownership was vested in a kinship group, not in any individual. And in the course of time reversionary rights could override them all. C and D, for instance, have direct reversionary rights in Nzioka's land and in Kilonzo's and in Muli's and in Mbeke's, and G and H have direct reversionary rights in Muli's land and in Mbeke's, and indirect reversionary rights in Kilonzo's land and in Nzioka's. Every living male descendant of Mbeke has reversionary rights direct or indirect in every piece of land inherited or otherwise acquired by every other.

Moreover, even although we may accord the Kamba no sense of ownership by the spirits of the dead we must accord them a very powerful sense of ownership by the yet unborn. They recognised their duty of trusteeship for posterity, not necessarily in any altruistic way but simply because a man must leave his 'seed' and leave it somewhere where it could flourish and leave its 'seed' in turn. There was thus a sense of spiritual ownership vested in the future which at one time operated possibly as strongly as any sense of spiritual ownership vested in the past. This is still intensely functional with the older men but almost absent in the younger, who, however, seem to acquire it gradually as they leave the more immediate desires of youth behind.

Nowadays the tendency in regard to sale is to disregard entirely all indirect reversionary rights and to pay scanty regard to direct reversionary rights if they are comparatively remote in origin and have not been kept alive by visits. This is part of the general tendency to a disintegration of the larger kinship into smaller and smaller ones. In general, a functional kinship nowadays is limited to those who join in family feasts (as on the marriage of a girl) and hold themselves responsible for the payment of compensation for a homicide committed by one of its members. In practice easy visiting distance between the various *misyi* has a good deal to do with it. It is the functional kinship which regulates the disposal of the kinship land to other kinships. This, however, is little in the way of definition. For a functional kinship varies in size according to the function. Thus kinship which will not intra-marry is usually much larger than a kinship which will join in paying compensation for its members' torts. All the functional kinship show a tendency to diminution, not necessarily in actual population but in the number of the generations covered; over-population is, in fact, one of the causes of narrowing of kinship circles still recognising kinship functionally. But the functions do not loose their integrating power with equal speed. One of the fastest loosers is undoubtedly community in land, and the corresponding kinship circle would probably have narrowed to its centre and become the individual had not the middle school, which can exercise its influence through the courts, insisted on a somewhat wider radius. But it remains impossible to say exactly what that radius is. It is, however, possible to state its lower limit, which is the corporate body (generally full brothers) inheriting in common one *mbee ya muunda*.* This is illustrated in the rule, said to be still imposed by the Tribunals,

* A piece of land taken from the men which is cultivated by each of a man's wives.

that a suit in respect of a portion of the family land must be brought against the oldest living brother although the debt alleged was incurred entirely by his junior. Even when the land has been divided between the brothers the sale of his portion by one of them without the sanction of the others would, if it came to the Tribunals, be declared a nullity and any consideration paid would be ordered to be returned. Alternatively, if two brothers inherited between them two *miunda* of their mother's and one of them sold one, the other could occupy or sell the other, and his action would be upheld by the Tribunals.

The upper limit is not so easy to determine. But in general it may be said that every elder of a kinship and original *ng'undu* could exercise a power of veto on the sale of any portion of it by the man who had acquired that portion by inheritance. Other elders should perhaps be added, as for instance those belonging to the same *mba* (not necessarily *mbai*) although not resident on the original *ng'undu*. Thus, in the family tree, E and F could intervene to stop a sale of a portion of Nzioka's land although their reversionary rights are indirect; in fact they would probably be consulted, if they did not live too far away, unless it was the intention of the seller to keep the sale a secret.

If we wish to formalise the answer for the sake of clarity in practice we should perhaps be safe in saying that before a sale of inherited agricultural land can be effected permission must be obtained from every adult male who has inherited and is occupying a portion of the original holding which includes the portion it is sought to sell, and any other adult males who, though not occupying any portion of the original holding, have the same paternal grandfather as the would-be seller, provided that they are reasonably available for consultation.

Other elders have the right of intervention, such as more distant patrilineal relatives and the would-be seller's maternal uncles and *athoni*, but this right does not extend to veto; they can do no more than persuade the elders with the right of veto to exercise it. Relatives on the female side would be particularly influential in this respect. Mothers and wives themselves have considerable power over their sons and husbands; a wise man will always consult his senior wife before he sells a piece of land, and unless his intention is to sell in order to buy a better piece elsewhere the chance is that he will not sell at all.

Another kind of control of the sale of land is that of the *utui* elders. This is an indirect control and depends on their power to refuse residence in their *utui* to any person whom they do not want. Men believed to be habitual thieves or dabblers in witchcraft are regularly excluded, but the power apparently extends to the exclusion of anyone the elders consider undesirable. Exclusion is effected by refusal to accept the *mbui ya mathanzu*[2] or to administer the *utui* oath.

The sale of grazing land is theoretically impossible as grazing is communal. But a *kisese* cluttered up with *maanzo* may nowadays be sold. But if any subsequent disputes arose or if the buyer wished to sell again, his claim to the *kisese* would be recognised only in so far as the *maanzo* were concerned unless he has exercised continuously his right of user of the rest as his exclusive grazing.

It is a general rule still considered obligatory by the middle school that a man who wishes to sell his land or any portion of it must first offer it to his kindred living on the same *kisese* or occupying the same original *ng'undu*. It is generally considered that he must be prepared to accept a lower price than he might get elsewhere. The principle seems to be that every reasonable effort should be made to keep the kindred's land intact. If his relatives refuse to buy he may then seek their permission in the manner previously described to sell outside the kindred. In practice they will often grant permission to sell a portion, just enough to raise the capital he wants for whatever purpose it was which first induced him to offer land for sale. Sometimes they will raise the amount between them rather than let their kindred's land pass to another kin.

Once a piece of land has been sold the purchaser is in the position of a 'primary holder'. He can dispose of it or use it as he thinks fit. Some elders appear to hold the opinion that if a purchaser wishes to re-sell he must first offer it to the kin of the original seller. But this, according to some of the middle school, is not a rule; it is merely a matter of courtesy. I am inclined to think that it *is* a rule, but one which is being increasingly disregarded.

When a purchased piece of land passes to the buyer's heirs it ceases to be a primary holding if the heirs are more than one in number; it is then subject to the usual rule of inheritance and to the conditions pertaining to the division and sale of inherited land.

The purchaser's relatives can make no claim to a share of user or ownership of the purchased land as of right; he may grant one or more of them some such right, but cannot be in any way required to do so. When he dies the land is inherited by the usual heirs, that is, by his sons. If he has no sons, his full brothers will inherit and failing those, their sons, and failing those, his half-brothers, and so on. But if he has no sons he may, before his death, direct that his daughter's children shall inherit, and this, since he has complete disposal of the land, would be upheld. (Much the same thing may happen in respect of a piece of land inherited through several generations if the deceased's male kin are all remote; the daughter's sons may then inherit. It appears that matrilineal principles die hard, and the sense of lineal kinship has not yet become restricted entirely to male descent. What degree of remoteness of the male kindred is considered sufficient to allow the female line to intervene has never, as far as I know, been determined by the courts. Each case would, apparently, be considered on its merits; such disputes, in any event, are usually settled by agreement.)

The principle that a full agreement between co-heirs is a necessary preliminary to a sale is, at any rate in theory, maintained by the Tribunals, which will not demarcate an individual's portion so that he may sell it against the will of his co-heirs. If the latter have first agreed that he may sell, but there is some dispute as to the portion to be put at his disposal for the purpose, a Tribunal may settle the dispute, but will not divide a piece of land between, say squabbling brothers, giving each a separate portion to be owned and, if he wishes, sold quite independently. This is a refreshing contrast to the practice of certain of the Kikiyu native courts, who have been responsible for much uneconomic sub-division and the encouragement of individual greed.

There is no special ceremonial in connection with sales. If a sale is open and above board witnesses (particularly elders of the local *mbai* to which the seller belongs and of the *utui* in which he resides) will be called in, and they will be supplied with food, including possibly a sheep or goat, and beer. The boundaries will be pointed out; they will generally consist of straight lines, not specially marked, between obvious permanent or semi-permanent natural objects such as trees or rocks or ant hills. If such natural beacons are inadequate cairns of stones may be erected at the principle points, one at each corner and one, say, in the middle of each side. A more exact demarcation may be made by planting sisal or (formerly) *muliba* trees along the boundaries.

Security for Debt

Nowadays a man may pledge his land or a portion of it as security for a debt, but if it is inherited land the elders will not permit the creditor to take the land merely because the debt remains unpaid. The debtor's local kinship group, particularly his co-heirs, must be given a chance to pay and it is only when they have refused to do so that the land may change hands. Even then, if the matter came to the Tribunal, the creditor would be required to pay the debtor any difference between the amount of the debt and the assessed value of the land.

Mortgage

Mortgage (the so-called 'redeemable sale') is not now officially recognised by the middle school, including the Tribunals; that is to say, that whereas formerly in a dispute concerning the ownership of a piece of land the man who claimed that it had been sold outright would have to prove it, the presumption now is that if some valuable consideration has changed hands in respect of land the land was sold outright, and a man who claimed that it had been mortgaged only would have to prove it.

Formerly mortgage was a fairly common practice; the right to cultivate a piece of land large enough for a woman's single *muunda* could be obtained for, say, one axe or one goat with or without beer, or for beer alone. Larger areas could be similarly obtained for a bull or for three or four goats; cows and heifers were not used in payment for cultivation rights. It was the man in need of the particular object (an implement or a goat or bull or a quantity of beer) who would offer a piece of his land to a man who had such an object to spare.

It is said that when actual sales of land became more common there was considerable confusion between the two types of transaction and many attempts at expropriation of the rightful owner. This was rather more than twenty years ago. The matter, it is said, came to a head in or about 1927 when 'a meeting of the elders' decided that henceforth all such transactions must be regarded as outright sales. What the 'meeting of elders' was is not very clear; it is said to have been a spontaneous meeting of representatives from every part of the district, but this seems unlikely in the extreme and one must suppose that any meeting there may have been was engineered by persons interested, particularly the imposed authorities. However that may be, it is said that the decision was backed and promulgated by the Administration and that by 1931 it had become generally accepted.

That there was some confusion, which appellate authorities would certainly find irksome, is not unlikely. The word for the 'sale' of a temporary cultivation right is the same (*-ta*, sell) as that for the outright sale of anything. 'To buy outright' or 'to obtain by payment temporarily' is *kuthoa*, and the causative of this (*kuthosya*) is also used for 'to sell' whether the sale involves the passing of an actual object or a temporary right of user only.

But although the custom of mortgage has been 'officially' discountenanced to some extent it still persists, though shortage of arable land is making its operation comparatively uncommon.

'Mortgage' in its English legal sense is not, of course, exactly the right word. It is true that the 'mortgagor' raises a loan by handing over land, but there can be no question of interest or foreclosure. The land is not strictly handed over as security for a debt. The whole transaction is essentially the exchange of a temporary right of user of one object for the temporary right of user of another. But on the one side user means destruction—the axe is worn out, the goat eaten or paid away to someone else, the beer drunk—whereas on the other (at least in native eyes) there is no destruction. Redemption (*-tua*, unsell, redeem) therefore means, on the one side the return of the equivalent of the object now destroyed, and on the other the cessation of the right of user.

In theory redemption can take place at any time. But in practice the holder of the temporary cultivation right is given a square deal. He is permitted to reap his standing annuals.

Such temporary cultivation rights are heritable but inheritance does not preclude redemption however many generations have passed since the first exchange. But in the event of a dispute a man who claims a piece of land in this way would have to prove his claim.

Before a man can 'mortgage' a piece of land he has inherited he must get permission from his co-heirs unless the land inherited has been finally divided up between them. Witnesses to any transaction of the sort are usually called in and generally include some elders of the 'mortgagor's' local *mbai*.

Loan

A man may, with the permission of his co-heirs, if any, lend a piece of land of which he is the owner or of which he has a share in ownership to another man for the purposes of user only, provided that the *utui* elders are prepared to accept him as an occupier or a resident of their *utui* or that he is one already. The borrower (*muvoi*—the *v* bilabial—'beggar'; *—voya*, 'beg, ask for') will have to pay the *mbui ya mathanzu** and swear the *utui* oath.

The loan is interest-free, the arrangement being generally a friendly one, as when two friends wish to live in the same locality. But nowadays, land being scarce, would-be borrowers are comparatively many and willing lenders few, and it is probable that lending rarely happens except when the lender gets some real advantage from his lending, such as assistance in the herding of his stock and in the maintenance of his fences and the building of his homestead. I came across no actual instance of the payment of a rent, either in cash or kind; but this may well be in the process of emergence.

Theoretically a borrower can be evicted without notice and without reason given. But formerly the custom was that he could only be evicted for some anti-social behaviour such as habitual theft or witchcraft or for some serious offence against the person or the property of the lender or the lender's kin, or for generally vexatious conduct in the *utui*. He would normally be allowed to reap his annual crops already planted. Nowadays a borrower who has obviously improved the land or has, say, built a permanent or semi-

* The payment necessary for a newcomer taking up a holding and resident in an *utui*.

permanent house on it can seek the protection of the tribunal, who will refuse to let him be evicted without reasonable compensation unless the lender can show that he stated his disapproval at the time, not only to the borrower but before the local elders, of the borrower's starting on the work which has improved the value of the land. A borrower of long standing, one for instance who inherited the loan from his father, the latter or many of his cattle having died on the borrowed land, is by no means easily evicted if there is nowhere else where he can settle. He will probably refuse to go, invite the *atui* to his *home*, and complain to them in some such words as: 'My father was his father's friend. He should either let me go on borrowing or let me buy the land, or he should go to the Tribunal and lay a charge against me.' If the *utui* elders regard him as a respectable resident of their *utui* they will almost certainly support him and persuade the lender's kinship to forbid eviction.

None the less a *muvoi's* tenure of the piece of land he occupies is tending to become more and more precarious as the legitimate requirements of an ever-growing kindred press more heavily on the land available.

It is generally accepted that a borrower cannot be evicted merely to make room for another. It is also generally accepted that a piece of land on loan cannot be sold over the borrower's head; he must first be given the chance to buy it himself.

Notes

[1] One might almost go so far as to state a general principle, applicable to the Kamba if not to the Eastern Bantu as a whole, that the woman's sphere—the homestead and subsistence agriculture—involved a permanency of rights in land, whereas the man's sphere—hunting and pastoral activities and certain public functions—involved a temporary right of user only.

[2] The 'goat of the stockade', a 'first footing' payable by every adult male immigrant.

Native Land Tenure in Kikuyu Province: Report of Committee*

The four ways by which cultivation rights can be acquired are:

1. As a Muguri
2. As a Muhoi
3. As a Muthoni
4. As a Muciarua

and we may proceed to examine these in turn.

1. *As a Muguri*

Perhaps no word is as likely to cause a misunderstanding of Kikuyu custom as the word Muguri. Europeans are prone to take a native word and to give to it a restricted meaning which it originally never had. We are inclined to look upon the word 'gura' as meaning to 'buy' in our limited sense of an outright purchase. True the Kikuyu today uses the word to describe the transaction which he makes when he goes to a farmer and buys an ox. That is because the word 'gura' includes outright purchase or buying among its several meanings. But it has another very definite meaning, namely 'redeemable purchase', and it is in this sense only that the word Muguri is used in the Fort Hall, Nyeri, Embu, and Meru Districts in connection with land transactions. On the other hand in Kiambu it does signify an outright irredeemable purchase, and never a redeemable one.

Although a man may wish to obtain cultivation rights, and may be willing in return to hand over cattle or sheep or other property in kind, he is debarred by custom from offering to do so. The first move must always come from a man who wishes to dispose of his cultivation rights as a security against a 'loan'. Moreover before a man may offer his cultivation rights to anyone who is not a member of his own Mbari† he must first offer it to the members of his own Mbari. If no one in his own Mbari is willing or able to advance to him the cattle (or other things of which he is in need) in return for cultivation rights over his portion of the Mbari's land, then, with the consent of the members of his Mbari, he makes it known to others that he wishes to obtain cattle or goats, and in

* *Native Land Tenure in Kikuyu Province:* Report of Committee, Government Printer of Nairobi, 1929, pp. 22–25.

† Clan.

return is offering as a security the use of his cultivation area. Then if there is anyone in the neighbourhood who desires to obtain these rights he may come forward, but more usually some wealthy friend of another Mbari gives the man what he wants as a personal favour and takes over the cultivation rights as security.

The most usual reasons for these transactions are the raising of sheep and cattle, etc., for bride-price or the obtaining of a ram for a sacrifice. The basis of redemption is that the exact number of animals originally paid is returned if the man has exercised his cultivation rights at all. If, on the other hand, he has never exercised his cultivation rights at all then the original number plus the full natural increase must be returned. It is obvious that on this principle it would be possible theoretically for a man or his descendants in course of time to come under an obligation to return an immense number of goats or sheep in order to redeem their plot, but in practice this does not often occur, for if a man who has taken over sheep or goats, and has given his plot in security finds that the man who took over the plot has no intention of cultivating it, or even a portion of it, he will speedily persuade the members of his Mbari to redeem it in order to avoid having to pay the enormous natural interest which would otherwise accrue on the loan. In fact if the members of the Mbari saw such a thing happening they would take it upon themselves to redeem the plot and then recover the cost from the individual member concerned whenever they could. In theory too a man can at any time redeem the cultivation right, if it is being exercised, by the simple return of the number of animals received, but in practice he gives due notice so that the man who is cultivating can harvest his crop. The whole transaction is invariably conducted upon a friendly rather than on a commercial basis, since the man who hands over the cattle or other property on the security of the cultivation rights is usually doing so as a favour to the man who is in need.

Sometimes after such a transaction has taken place several generations pass before any attempt at redemption is made, and for this reason quite young members of the Mbari are always included among the witnesses, and a man tells his children of such a transaction having taken place and gives them details so that, in the event of his death before redemption takes place, they may be in possession of full particulars.

It must be emphasised that no such transaction can take place without the consent of the Mbari elders, and moreover that before seeking a 'loan on security' outside the Mbari a man must seek one within. It must also be remembered that such arrangements are terminable at will by either party (except in one small area in the Meru country), where special conditions govern a transaction if it takes place between members of different Mbari within the Ababugushi clan.

Although a Muguri has full rights of cultivation and building and also rights to take on Ahoi, he has usually no right to part with any portion of the plot as security: he must return it to the original man from whom he received it or to his Mbari members, and they must redeem it. In Fort Hall however the exception to this rule exists. It sometimes happens that a Mbari as a group hands over practically the whole of its Githaka* (keeping one small garden) in order to raise blood-money. In such a case the person or persons who have taken over the Githaka as security may themselves hand it (or part of it) over as security on a loan, unless the original Mbari is able to redeem it when required. In such a case when the Mbari eventually were able to redeem it they would take the redemption price to the people with whom they had made the transaction (or their descendants) and they in turn would have to redeem from those to whom they had handed it.

2. *As a Muhoi*

The word Muhoi is derived from the verb Hoya 'to ask for' and denotes a man who comes to another and asks for permission to cultivate on his land, and obtains it purely on a basis of friendship. The usual custom is for the man who wishes for cultivation rights to take beer to the man from whom he wishes to ask for such rights. The latter if agreeable consults the other elders of his Mbari (or the Muramati),† and, if they consent he shows the Muhoi where he may cultivate. Very often a man cannot get sufficient cultivation space for his requirements from one individual, but becomes the Muhoi of several people concurrently. A Muhoi simply has cultivation rights and he can be told

* Land unit.

† The Family head.

to move whenever the owner of the land wishes, and he may not refuse. He has however the right to harvest standing crops. The rules governing what he may do with the permanent crops which are not ready to cut when he leaves vary in different districts.

The right to admit Ahoi is reserved to people who actually own land and to Aguri. No Muhoi can bring other Ahoi on to the plot over which he only has cultivation rights. A Muguri is responsible for moving his Ahoi when the plot is redeemed.

A Muhoi is not bound to give any kind of tribute to the man from whom he obtains cultivation rights, but it is customary for him to take beer annually and also some of the first fruits of the harvest in recognition of the fact that he is only a Muhoi. If a Muhoi ceases to cultivate his plot even for one season he is deemed to have relinquished it, but as long as he has the smallest part of it under active cultivation he can rest the remainder without endangering his position.

Permission to become a Muhoi and to cultivate does not necessarily carry with it the right to build on the land. If a Muhoi wishes to build he must get special permission, and become a Muthami.

Since the position of a Muhoi is based upon friendship it frequently happens that a man continues to be the Muhoi of a single individual till his death. His children continue in exactly the same relationship to the owner or his descendants, but each generation of the latter is careful to explain to the succeeding one what the position is, so that if at any time they wish to evict the Muhoi they can do so.

3. *As a Muthoni*

The word Muthoni is derived from the noun 'thoni' which means shyness or ashamedness and means literally 'one of whom you are shy'. Its actual meaning is 'relation-in-law' but in connection with land tenure it usually has the more restricted sense of a male relation-in-law of the first degree.

In the four districts with which we are dealing at present it is almost impossible for a man to obtain any kind of cultivation right from his relations-in-law. When a man marries a girl, she may, by courtesy, continue cultivating for a season or two on that part of her mother's garden for which she was responsible before her marriage, and take the crops harvested for the use of herself and her husband, but this does not mean that the husband has any cultivation rights in the garden. On the other hand if he finds difficulty in obtaining cultivation rights elsewhere a man may be given an area to cultivate by his father-in-law for a season or two, but he would certainly not be allowed to stay on for long nor is the practice a common one.

A member of the girl's family has no claim to cultivation rights from her husband and although there is no actual bar to his begging them as a Muhoi he would be inclined to seek them from other friends rather than from his relations-in-law.

4. *As a Muciarua*

So far we have been dealing with people who probably have a land share of their own on the Githaka of their Mbari but who for some reason or another—such as wishing to live near a friend, or because they have helped a friend by lending on the security of a cultivation right—are cultivating on another man's land, and possibly also living on it. A Muciarua however belongs to a different category, for the word is derived from 'Ciara' (to give birth to) and means one who is born. (He is almost always both young and poor.) He is never of the same main clan, and often of another tribe, and for some reason or another, has no right to any part of any Githaka, and has neither property, nor friends. He comes to some rich man and asks to be adopted as his son and taken into his clan. If the rich man is disposed to consent, he must first get permission from the clan and Mbari elders, and there is a definite adoption ceremony which varies slightly from district to district but which in its main essentials is the same everywhere. (See Appendices A and B.)

A man having been so adopted becomes a member of the main clan, taking the clan name and becoming a member of the Mbari to which the adopting family belongs. He is now treated in most things as a son of the family and is given a place to cultivate, and even has a wife bought for him.

So long as he behaves himself, he is as one of the family, except that he has no say in the control of the family land. He is liable to eviction only if he seriously offends the Mbari and clan by such an act as murder or repeated disobedience of the clan and

Mbari elders, or of his adopted father. If he is evicted he must relinquish everything which he has obtained from the Mbari, including his wife and children and gardens and may take only actual personal property which he may have acquired. In certain districts (see in Appendex B and Appendix A) he may not even do this.

Chapter 19

STRANGERS AND LAND

This subject has already been dealt with, in part, under the heading of 'tenancies' (leases) in the preceding chapter, and it is also closely related to the control which is exercised over land by political and social groups (Chapters 14 and 15). A stranger may, in other words, be classified either as a stranger to a particular piece of land, in which case he will be a tenant; or as a stranger to a political or social group, in which case he would not be entitled to obtain rights in land unless he had been accepted as a member of that group. The first of these situations is dealt with by the extract from *Lloyd*'s work on the Yoruba, while strangers to lineages are dealt with by *Young* and F*osbrooke* on the Liguru. *Wilson*, on the Luo, deals with the same situation, but also considers the case of the person who is a complete foreigner to the tribe. He also contributes a discussion of the distinction between tenancy and occupation by strangers.

R. Young and H. A. Fosbrooke: Land and Politics among the Liguru of Tanganyika*

Numerous cases arise of non-lineage members seeking cultivation rights in lineage land; the procedure is as follows. The intruder pays a small token, *rubaka*, when first seeking permission to cultivate; then annually, as a rule, he pays another small token, *ngoto*, in grain to the lineage. He cannot sell a holding thus obtained and must ask permission to inherit; he must also seek permission before planting trees. In return the intruder enyoys a very considerable security of tenure. The initial payment of *rubaka* usually consists of one chicken. There is no 'key-money racket' in Luguru, though in certain cases the forces of modern economics have pushed up the *ngoto* payment.

As introduction it is necessary to record the recent history of *ngoto* payment. In the early British period, as presumably in the German, *ngoto* payment was officially recognized by Government as an integral part of the Luguru land tenure system. Cases occurred in the Native Courts of two parties contesting the right to receive *ngoto* and were not interfered with by the District Commissioner in his revisionary capacity. Indeed, the position in 1930 was officially described as follows:

> A 'land-owner' having unoccupied land may lease it to a tenant of another clan who pays to him a share of the crops reaped, which is called *ngoto*. The tenancy is mild; nothing is paid out of the first harvest, and there appears to be a fixed scale for payment which sometimes lapses altogether eventually. *Ngoto* produce is never sold. The land-owner receiving it must divide it amongst the members of the family interested in the land. It is quite clear that an *ngoto* tenant cannot be turned out.[1]

In 1942 the official attitude was entirely reversed. In a proclamation addressed to the tribe, the Native Authority (Sultan Kingo) announced that Government had seen fit to prohibit the payment of *ngoto*. This was followed by a more detailed circular from the District Commissioner in which is revealed a singular mixture of knowledge and insight into the workings of *ngoto*, an erroneous belief in the existence of tribal ownership of land, a paradoxical buttressing of customary law, and instructions in the matter of anti-soii erosion measures. The official abolition of *ngoto* did not mean that payment ceased; it

* R. Young and H. A. Fosbrooke, *Land and Politics among the Liguru of Tanganyika*, Routledge & Kegan Paul, 1960, pp. 64–69.

undoubtedly and admittedly continued, but could not be officially referred to, nor could its non-payment be made the subject of court action.

As a result of the researches of one of the authors, Henry Fosbrooke, the payment of *ngoto* was reauthorized by a proclamation dated 24th June 1955. When the area was revisited in 1958 by Roland Young satisfaction at this reintroduction was expressed by official and Luguru alike.

Ngoto is payable primarily by a non-member of the lineage who has sought dwelling or cultivation rights on the lineage land holding. The number of recipients and the number of payers is not great. In the discussions on this matter the issue attained an importance quite out of proportion to its numerical incidence. In Mgeta, for instance (see Table 7), an area of several thousand householders, there were three recipients and fourteen payers of *ngoto*. In other areas the numbers were more significant, but the truth is that *ngoto* had become a symbol of two conflicting ideologies. To the Luguru it remained a symbol of the old way of life; to the British administrator, a barbaric relic of the oppression of one social group by another. The above analysis is confirmed by a second set of figures. (See Table 8.) Both this and the first were obtained from the records of Native Authority, who had compiled detailed lists at different times at the request of the administration when the matter of *ngoto* payment was under consideration. The two tables are reasonably consistent and each fills in gaps occurring in the other.

TABLE 7. Ngoto *payers and recipients*[2]

Area	Number of *ngoto* recipients	Number of *ngoto* payers	Average payers per recipient
Mgeta	3	14	4·7
Melela	47	1,176	25.0
Morogogoro B (Kingolwira)	33	536	16.3
Mkuyuni	87	*	*
Matombo	97	3,912	40.3
Bwakira Juu	31	*	*

As to the amount of *ngoto* actually payable, 'a basket' or 'a basket or two' of grain was the usual quantity quoted. Thus it is little more than a peppercorn rent, but, like this English legal fiction, it serves as a perpetual reminder of the relative status of payer and payee; in the case of the Luguru the payment safeguards the reversionary right of the lineage. This reversionary right is made apparent in a number of ways. In the matter of inheritance, land held on an *ngoto* basis cannot be inherited as of right. The heir must seek the sanction of the lineage head before entering into possession. *Rubaka* is not paid on this occasion, but to fail to seek permission to inherit is generally acknowledged as one of the few offences meriting the eviction of an intruder.

TABLE 8. Ngoto *analyzed by hills and plains*[3]

Area	Recipients	Payers	Average
		Highlands	
Mgeta	3	14	4·7
Melela	13	309	23·7
Morogoro	—	—	—
Mkuyuni	23	666	28·9
Matombo	92	3,779	41·1
Bwakira Juu	47	1,560	33·2
		Plains	
Melela	34	917	26·7
Morogoro	1	158	158·0
Mkuyuni	9	296	32·9

* No figures available.

Security of tenure. Although the lineage retains the reversionary right, the intruder enjoys considerable security of tenure. There exist, however, devices by which he can be 'edged out'. For example, if an intruder tries to assert his independence by non-payment of *ngoto*, he will not be openly defiant to the lineage head but merely say that his crops are so bad that he has no surplus with which to pay *ngoto*. The lineage head will let this go on for several years but will finally reply to the defaulter, when he pleads that yet another crop failure has led to inability to pay, 'That is too bad. We must find you a better piece of land.' So in place of his previous plot, which has of course been yielding satisfactorily the whole time, the intruder is presented with a barren hillside quite unsuitable for agriculture. He cannot adhere to his original plot, for to do so would be to prove himself a liar, and he cannot accept the new one, as it would not yield him a livelihood. In the circumstances, then, such a tenant has no alternative but to seek land from some other lineage.

From the recipient's point of view, *ngoto* is not a personal perquisite of the lineage head. He is responsible for the collection thereof, but he is equally responsible for its distribution among lineage members. In those areas where the number of *ngoto* payers is considerable, sufficient grain is received to justify its being kept in special stores. Though outside granaries are to be found in Luguru, a large proportion of the grain is stored in the upper storey of the house. Grain stored in such a loft is subject to constant smoking from the hearth below, and so insect damage is kept to a minimum. A suitable widow or widows are sought within the lineage group and appointed keepers of the *ngoto*. They do not appear, from a general consensus, to have been the official distributors of the *ngoto;* this duty rests with the head of the lineage.

Statistics gathered on the payment of *ngoto* show that the number of payers, the number of recipients, and the number of payers per recipient varied greatly from area to area. For this reason in some areas, such as Mgeta, *ngoto* payment was practically non-existent. Nevertheless, even in that area the right to receive *ngoto* would be made the subject of argument, and even of court cases, between contesting claimants. Likewise, the subject made a great talking point when Government was considering the introduction of anti-soil erosion measures: if trees were planted by Government order on steep slopes, if the land were held by intruders, who would own the trees, and who would compensate the lineage for loss of *ngoto*? As late as 1953, the official view was that 'where steep slopes are closed to cultivation, it is often difficult to get the person farming that land to plant permanent trees, because he is only a tenant'. Yet in Mgeta, when such problems were thought to be acute, the 1942 count revealed the existence of three *ngoto* recipients sharing a total of fourteen payers between them! Though *ngoto* payment is insignificant in such an area, the insistence of the lineage heads that the point should receive attention is not without reason. If there occurred a swing to patrilineal inheritance and viri-local marriage, the proportion of those living on lineage land who should pay *ngoto* might well increase, so the right should not be lost sight of. (For statistics on the ratio of *ngoto* payers and recipients and on the distribution of payment in the hills and plains, see Tables 7 and 8.)

Notes

[1] From the report by F. J. Bagshawe, dated April 15, 1930.

[2] The figures in this table were drawn from old Native Authority correspondence files. Prior to the abolition of *ngoto* in 1942, returns were called for from each subordinate Native Authority, to show the number of *ngoto* recipients and payers in the area. The results are incomplete, and even if complete would not necessarily be accurate. They are, however, indicative of certain trends. As this is purported to be a chiefdom-wide survey, it is significant that the areas of the low, dry east are omitted: this confirms a generally held belief that the payment of *ngoto* has never been customary in that area.

[3] For reasons which are not apparent from the files, the Native Authority also asked for figures to be submitted showing *ngoto* recipients and payers divided into two categories, highlands and plains. It will be appreciated that in most cases these subordinate Native Authority areas contain a portion of each environment.

G. Wilson: Luo Customary Law*

Land Grants and Usufructuary Rights—Jadak

A person who comes to the area of a lineage segment and begs for land is called a *Jadak*. If he is given land it is given on the usufructuary principle only. He therefore has no rights of inheritance and his children may only renew the usufructuary right to the land and may not inherit the land as a right owner. The length of his usufruct is indefinite and this has led to many misunderstandings by Government officers in the past and even in present-day cases. There is the bogy of what are sometimes referred to as 'prescriptive rights'; for many years European officers have felt that each land case involving a *Jadak* must be decided on its merits, especially if the *Jadak* is a non-Luo, because the principle of a family which has lived in an area and used the land, albeit only as *Jadak* for 10, 20, 30, 40 or more years and then being evicted from that holding somehow goes against the moral usages of European, or more specifically, British culture. The Luo principle of *Jadak* seems to be repugnant to these officers and therefore in many cases of this type the *Jadak* has won title to the land over the person who is regarded by Luo Customary Law as the right holder, the owner of the land. The basic principle of *Jadak* was clearly and succinctly stated in the A.D.C. Minute 27/46 by Chief Jonathan Okwiri: '. . . as in the Luo custom the tenants (*Jodak*) are tenants forever, even if they were good tenants and helping the owner of the land, that does not allow them to naturalize as clansmen.' The recent conference on Luo Customary Law confirmed this view and moreover expressed great concern at the fact that the law of *Jadak* was so often ignored by the Administration. The Swynnerton Plan to intensify the development of African agriculture in Kenya recommends in paragraphs 13 and 14 the principles of consolidation, title, mortgage, buying and selling, etc., of land; if these are to be implemented in Luo country, the issue of *Jadak* must be settled finally and not decided from time to time as the occasion arises.

Refer: Nyahera L.C. 17/51, A.A.C. L.C. 86/51, D.O.'s 1/52, P.C. 2/52
Samuel Nyawanda v. *Mariko Otiende*

How did there come to be *Jadak* in Luo? It is a custom which dates back to the times when a man counted his security on the number of sons, friends, servants and squatters he could attract to his holding. The larger the number, the more secure he was to his title and the more status he received in the community. It is fair to say that the Luo encouraged *Jadak* to settle and until recently a *Jadak* was not normally turned out of the land loaned to him except under the most serious circumstances. Moreover Luo marry the daughters of *Jadak* and vice versa, so we find that most *Jadak* are also *Orche*.† This fact complicates many of the land cases concerning them.

The term tenant has been used as the English equivalent to *Jadak* and this in itself has led to much of the confusion. The *Jadak* is not a tenant in any sense of the word because he pays no rent; it is more accurate to refer to him as a squatter. In South Nyanza the term *Jabedo* is sometimes used to describe *Jadak*, this means, in the literal sense, a person who sits. Squatter therefore is apt. A *Jadak* has certain obligations which he is expected to fulfil, but these are at the level of those which are expected of the most junior member of the lineage. He must show respect to the owner of the land and he must give him a high status position at all beer drinks and festivities. He must fight for his benefactor and support him in all matters regardless of his own opinion; he must follow the instructions of the cultivation leader, *Jagolpur*, of the *Libamba*‡ to which the owner of the land belongs and he must be content with a low status position when invited to social or ritual gatherings at the homestead of his benefactor. Finally, and most important, he must remain in continual occupation of the land which was allocated to him or he loses his usufructuary rights to it.

Every *Jadak* knows when he begs for land that his position is a precarious one. He has no right to allocate land to friends or to his *Orche* without the prior approval of the *Wuon lowo*§ and the *Jodong' Libamba*.|| He has no way therefore of building a group of

* G. Wilson, *Luo Customary Law*, Government Printer of Nairobi, 1961, pp. 56–62.
† Brothers-in-law.
‡ Land-holding unit.
§ Owner of the land.
|| Elders of the lineage.

supporters in the community. Moreover he has not the customary right of regarding land in the *Keyo** position as his by right of expansion. He may not therefore build his son a village without the prior approval of the *Wuon lowo* and the *Jodong' Libamba*. He also knows that his sons may be refused the privilege of the usufruct when he dies and will be forced to return to their former ancestral land. He is also aware of the rule which terminates the usufruct for himself and for his children; if he leaves the land his children may never return to claim his *Gunda*† and the gardens of their mother or mothers by the right that the land was formerly cultivated by his *Anyuola*.‡

Doho (S.N.) 64/54
Onyango Owiti v. *Ong'owu Omindi*

The plaintiff sued for the removal of the *Ligala*§ of thed efendant who had built on the *Gunda* of his father. The court rules that the defendant as a *Jadak* had no right to build without the permission of the owner of the land and ordered the *Ligala* removed.

Boro L.C. 12/52, A.A.C. L.C. 54/53
Mikael Nyabiga v. *Marious Ondewe*

The plaintiff had a *Jadak* called Omondi who lived for many years in a village which was given to him by the plaintiff. He also cultivated gardens which were given to him by the plaintiff. The defendant came to live with the *Jadak* because his daughter married and the defendant could not take the cattle to the village of his father as it was built in the name of his grandfather and therefore taboo, *Chira*, to the cattle of the bride wealth of a grandchild. While the defendant lived there, he cultivated gardens of the *Jadak* without permission of the *Wuon lowo*, the plaintiff, and this was the start of the quarrel between them. Soon after this the *Jadak* left the village to return to his own country in North Nyanza. The defendant continued to occupy the village and he began to cultivate all of the gardens and claimed that these had been given to him by the *Jadak* before he left. The court argued that the *Jadak* had no authority to give the gardens to the defendant or, for that matter, the village, because both were the indisputable property of the plaintiff.

The plaintiff decided that the defendant could remain in the village as long as he recognized before the court that he was the *Wuon lowo*, he stated further that he would allocate other gardens to the defendant if he would agree that he was *Wuon lowo* and that he only occupied the village and the gardens as a *Jadak*. The court supported this interpretation of the Luo Law and awarded the case to the plaintiff. The A.A.C. upheld the findings of the tribunal.

The Luo had a customary method of evicting a *Jadak* which in pre-European times was effective because it carried with it the supernatural consequences inherent in a curse. The *Wuon lowo* threatened to climb a tree, *Ochok*, and point to the direction of the village of the *Jadak* in his own country. This was sufficient for the *Jadak* to leave, he seldom argued the point unless he had the support of a large segment of the lineage of the *Wuon lowo*, such support would only be given if in their opinion the *Wuon lowo* was acting to the detriment of the whole group. In this way the *Jadak* could appeal to equity. It would be a rare occurrence for a man to evict a *Jadak* unless he had what he considered to be sufficient reason, because the other members of his lineage would consider it *Chira* and would socially ostracize him.

The reasons which are considered to be sufficient to evict a *Jadak* are, in order of importance, as follows: the termination of an agreed period of usufruct; the suspicion of witchcraft or sorcery, *Achach*, on the part of the *Jadak*; incest or proven adultery;

* Land-holding unit—smaller than *Libamba*.
† Deserted village.
‡ Lineage traced from a male ancestor.
§ A new village.

refusal or neglect of the obligations;* aggressive attitude towards the *Wuon lowo* and the illegal encroachment on land beyond the limits originally allowed when the usufruct was given; behaviour of a type which causes continual friction within the community. In short any action which is liable to bring disgrace or *Chira*† to the community or action which caused friction between members or segments within the community.

D.O.'s L.C. 1/52
(*Described following paragraph* 95)

This is one of the few places where the record exists of the assessors' opinion of what constitutes a *Jadak* and what constitutes sufficient reason for evicting him: '. . . the assessors further state that the customary law concerning *Jadak* has changed. Formerly if a *Jadak* misbehaved he could be evicted, no matter how long he had cultivated, that a *Jadak's* son likewise could be evicted, but that a *Jadak's* grandson could not because by then he had a right to the land. Nowadays the question as to whether a *Jadak* can be evicted for misbehaviour depends on three factors: firstly, how long he has cultivated; secondly, whether he had another place to go; and, finally, how much trouble he has caused. Each case has to be decided on its merits but that very briefly speaking, a *Jadak* who has been in possession for 20 years or more would not be evicted.

'This interpretation was reported to Present A.A.C., Ezekiel Kasuku, who did not agree. He says that the old custom still holds good but that Government will not allow a *Jadak* to be evicted if he has been in effective occupation for a long time. Ezekiel does not like the Government ruling.'

The most important is the termination of an agreed period of usufruct. This means if land was given in usufruct to a *Jadak* on the understanding that when a certain son or leviratic son comes of age, the *Jadak* will leave if asked to do so; when that time comes the *Jadak* is expected to honour the agreement. Unfortunately none of those arrangements are ever recorded and it is difficult for the Court to decide which party is telling the truth. It often happens that a man will give a *Jadak* part of the gardens which belong to the family of a leviratic wife because the gardens are not needed until the children marry. This may well be a period of 30 years or even longer. Today many men who leave to work in the towns give their land in usufruct, not only to *Jadak* but also to *Jopiny*' and when they return a few years later, or even as many as 20 years later, they expect that the land will be returned to them. The idea that there is a claim after seven years of continual occupation, which has developed from the way in which land cases have been decided over the years, often means that the *Jadak* or other usufructee will refuse to move unless there is a land case to settle the matter.

Nyahera L.C. 18/52, A.A.C. L.C. 97/52
Jacobo Odongo v. *Oganga Orawo*

This case involves a *Jadak* who had occupied land for 35 years. The defendant had been brought to the area by a Headman and given permission to cultivate the land of the plaintiff's uncle. The plaintiff at the time was too young to cultivate it himself, and there were no other heirs. The defendant did not argue with this testimony but claimed that continuous occupancy from that time gave him rights of ownership to the gardens. The litigants first took the case to the Muruka's Court in 1943 and it awarded the defendant part of the land and left the rest with the plaintiff after assuring the latter that he was *Wuon lowo* but the defendant was a good *Jadak* and therefore should have somewhere to cultivate. The plaintiff refused on the grounds that he wanted to take all of the land and to have the *Jadak* removed.

The President was of the opinion, current at that time among some of the tribunal elders, that the Europeans would reverse a judgment if the law of *Jadak* was vigorously applied and wrote in his judgment, 'It is absolutely wrong that there is a Luo law applied for the removal of persons who has longer remained using the land at least 37 years. The Luo land always belong to person who is occupying it whether he is

* I.e. the obligations outlined in para. 74 of Wilson's book.
† Taboo.

belonging to that Location from the beginning. If it is not thus, it will affect everybody in the Locations as far as there is nobody sticking to the land belonging to their ancestors. . . .' He then awarded the case to the defendant.

The A.A.C. did not agree, however, with this interpretation because to have done so would have given *Jadak* throughout the Locations security of tenure to the detriment of the children of the owner of the land. The *Jadak*, argued the A.A.C., has land he can go back to in the Location of his ancestors. The judgment of the Nyahera Court was set aside and the *Jadak* was given six months to remove his trees and crops from the disputed gardens. This decision is in line with the Luo Law as recorded by us from the elders of all the Luo Locations.

Perhaps the most frequent cause of the desire to evict a *Jadak* arises from the fact that the *Jadak* was given land by the father of the plaintiff or by a classificatory father. When the donor of the usufruct dies and the heir begins to plan and to cultivate he may find that the best portions of the land are held by the *Jadak*. Moreover, it frequently happens that the *Jadak* refuses to recognize the son as the legal heir and acts as if the land is his by building villages for his sons without permission or by cultivating land which he claims was given to him by the dead man. This leads to many land cases. It was the opinion of the conference that the law should always be on the side of the right holder of the land, and if a decision is given in favour of a *Jadak* it should invariably state that as a *Jadak* he may remain and not give the impression that the *Jadak* is now the outright owner. The elders agreed that cases brought to evict a *Jadak* which will cause hardship to him and to his family are unfortunate but that the law is clear on the matter.

The impression should not be left that it is always the fault of the *Jadak* that trouble begins over usufructuary land. It frequently happens that the *Wuon lowo* is inclined to be aggressive and dictatorial or is by nature a trouble maker. This is a risk all *Jodak* must run by the virtue of the fact that they are *Jodak* but traditionally the *Wuon lowo* could not evict a *Jadak* if the rest or a good part of his lineage segment was against him. Another problem arises today by the inadequate knowledge possessed of the lineage system, we find that land given to a *Jadak* by a man of one segment of the *Libamba* is claimed by a man from another simply because he thinks that he has a better right to it. In cases of this kind the wishes of the donor or of his heir take precedent over those of any other members of the *Libamba.*

Nyahera L.C. 8/24, A.A.C. L.C. 146/42
D.O.'s 61/51, P.C. 1/52
Ondigo s/o Ogendo v. *Omir s/o Rombo and Zadok s/o Omir*

The case was won by the plaintiff on the grounds that he was given the land by Obiero of the *Jokadayo* Ogalo and that the two defendants are of the *Jokadayo* Anyango. The two *Jokadayo* are of the *Jokawaro* Jokarombo, this is shown in the diagram below.

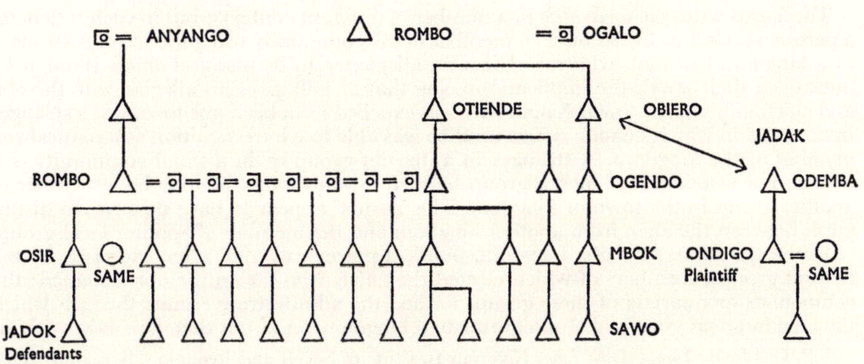

The land in question was formerly in Luo country but is now in Bantu because of the demarcation of boundaries by the Government. This, however, is not the issue. Primarily, the land occupied by the people who are descended from Ogalo is theirs to do as they please without consulting the people of Anyango (within the traditional framework). The arguments during the case that Ondigo was a Yuote rather than a *Jadak* because his father helped to occupy the land in war with Obiero or that the man Ondigo is married to the daughter of Rombo (second) are irrelevant. If a man of Ogalo took the case, there may have been some point to these arguments but as it stands the people of Anyango have no claim whatsoever to any land within the lineage boundaries of the people of Ogalo unless all of the descendants of the latter should suddenly disappear.

One of the defendants, Osir, obeyed the Court order to remove himself but his son, not fully conversant with the traditional usages refused and so the case went through several appeals.

P. C. Lloyd: Yoruba Land Law*

Strangers

In modern English usage a tenant is one whose rights are dependent on those of another, such as an owner or landlord, and whose rights are held not in perpetuity but for a limited number of years. The terms landlord and tenant are today widely used by literate Yoruba; but the types of tenure for which these terms are used in England do not exist, on a wide scale, in Yoruba country.

The Yoruba have no word of their own which has a connotation similar to the English term 'tenant'; the vernacular term which is almost invariably used to describe a dependent relationship is *alejo*—a stranger. The Yoruba traditional social system did not recognize the division of the community into two groups of people each with a distinct status in relation to land such as owner and tenant; all men had an equal right to land through their membership of a descent group or a community. (Still less did the Yoruba have a feudal social system in which a man's total status in the community was defined in terms of the rights held in land.) Yet, when land is divided into large blocks each of which is held corporately by the members of a community or of a descent group, and when the boundaries of these blocks are marked with some precision by natural features, or planted trees (such as the *peregun—dracena fragrans*), a problem arises whenever the members of one group grow in number so that their land is insufficient for their needs, while a neighbouring group perhaps decreases in numbers and has vacant land. Two solutions are possible: either the boundary is moved, by peaceful or violent means, or some of the members of the group with insufficient land join the group with land to spare. Boundary moving by peaceful arbitration seems to have been rare; more frequently it seems to have happened that the members of one group 'trespassed' on to the land of the other, staying for so long that they could claim the land as being that of their own descent group.

The Yoruba use the term *alejo* in a number of different contexts; but in each it denotes a person who is not, by his birth, a member of the community using the term. A stranger in a kingdom is a man who recognizes no allegiance to its oba and chiefs (though he must obey their laws), the implication being that he still gives his allegiance to the oba and chiefs of his home town. A man who was expelled from his home town was a stranger in the town in which he took refuge until he was able to win recognition as a naturalized member of the kingdom. A stranger in a descent group or in a small community is a person, not a member of such a group by birth, even though he may be a member of another group in the town or kingdom. The Yoruba appear to have no terms to distinguish between the alien from another kingdom and the member of another local group.

In the traditional Yoruba kingdom, political power was most often exercised by the descent groups, members of which elected the chiefs who sat on the oba's council; the compounds or quarters of these groups formed the administrative units through which the kingdom was governed. Immigrants to a kingdom could not therefore exist without

* P. C. Lloyd, *Yoruba Land Law*, Nigerian Institute of Social and Economic Research, 1963, pp. 86–92.

being members of a descent group; the unattached stranger was an anomaly. A large group of immigrants such as a band of refugees from a village destroyed in intertribal wars, or a group of kinsmen led by an unsuccessful claimant for a throne could be accepted by a town and given the status of an independent descent group within it, equal to the pre-existing groups. An individual immigrant gradually became absorbed into the group among whose members he lodged and with which he probably contracted ties of marriage.

The Yoruba attitude towards tenancy today can be best understood if it is realized that, in the past, the status of stranger was a temporary one; either the stranger was absorbed into the community or he went home; he never stayed indefinitely as a stranger, though it might be three or four generations before his alien origin was forgotten.

Within the Yoruba town the practice of lending land to a friend for a year or two is probably quite ancient. A man holding usufructuary rights over farm land which he is temporarily unable to exercise, through ill health, absence from the town, or because of youth, and the consequent small size of his family, may, with the authority and permission of his family elders, allow a friend to farm this land. The friend will leave after a crop cycle, or whenever the grantor needs the land for himself. In this manner the grantor does not lose his rights in the land, though if he allowed a member of his own descent group to use the land he might find it difficult to recover it later.

Modern Tenancy

The events of the last century have considerably modified the traditional processes of absorption into the community and of lending land, producing as their result the modern forms of tenancy.

Tribal wars depopulated many small towns, scattering their inhabitants permanently; the chiefs have allocated their vacant land to strangers from neighbouring overpopulated areas. In towns such as Ibadan, whose size was increased rapidly by thousands of captured slaves and camp followers, the chiefs had large estates on which these dependants worked when they were not fighting; the land of these estates is still held corporately by the descendants of each chief, but while some slaves have stayed on, regaining freedom, the place of the others who returned to their homes has been taken by strangers from other lineages in the town. With peaceful conditions there grew movements of population of a different kind; from the south-east have migrated into Ondo and Ijebu Provinces thousands of Urhobo who reap the oil palms and who are usually granted a small plot of land for growing cassava for their domestic use; from the north and north-east into the cocoa belt have migrated men such as the Igbirra, who came from poor areas to work as farm labourers—they, too, are often given a plot of land for their own crops.

Clerks, teachers and labourers working away from their home town often seek a plot of land on the edge of the town of their employment on which to grow some of their food. Men whose lineage land is not suitable for cocoa seek better land from relatives and friends; but there seems to have been no large migration of men from the northern savanna areas into the forests of the cocoa belt.

Most modern migrants do in fact intend to return eventually to their home towns; they regard their sojourn in the new area as temporary; they thus retain their allegiance to the rulers and chiefs of their home towns and do not become absorbed in the community which receives them. The stigma of slave origin still prevents the full absorption of many nineteenth-century captives into the communities to which they formerly belonged and in which they now live as free men. Today it is less essential that a man belong to a descent group; strangers have full political rights, through the ballot box, to participate in modern local government though they are still denied participation in the traditional political system.

With the decline of the traditional ritual, political and social payments to rulers, chiefs, or descent group elders which demonstrated a man's membership of the community, it has become necessary to devise other means of denoting the dependent status of the stranger and of preventing him from asserting full ownership of the land which he occupies. This may be achieved if the owning group firmly retains some of the usufructuary rights of ownership which are frequently exercised, such as reaping the oil palms; (it is impossible for a group to demonstrate ownership by holding rights of alienation when alienation has never and is not likely to take place). It may also be achieved by enforcing the annual payment of a token number of yams or tins of palm oil in such a manner that these cannot be made to appear as a casual gift between friends.

When land was plentiful it was to the advantage of a community to give out land to strangers; by the increase in its size it became more important and powerful; individual members of the community lost nothing by their generosity and so nothing was demanded of the newcomer but his allegiance. Today land is, in many areas, scarce; in giving out its land to strangers a group may appear to be jeopardizing the rights of its members to have as much land as they can exploit. In such circumstances the token payment in kind becomes a cash rent. Particularly is this so where the stranger is allowed to plant cocoa and thus derive a substantial income from the land.

Types of Tenant Relationship

Types of tenant relationship in Yoruba country tend to fall into three categories.

First is the customary tenant: it is presumed that he has begged for land (*tọrọ ilẹ*) because that of his own descent group is insufficient and that he intends to farm it permanently; he is thus given enough land to practise the normal rotation of crops. Second is the annual tenant who 'borrows' (*ya*) land for a season or two for the planting of annual crops. Third is the licensee of palm trees—usually an immigrant Urhobo.

These three types are not found evenly distributed throughout the country. Their occurrence depends on three factors—firstly on the degree to which land is still available for allotment by the ruler and chiefs, and secondly on the type of descent group in the area—whether agnatic or cognatic—and thirdly on the right of the descent group to alienate its land. Thus in Egba, Ijebu and Ondo country there is still today forest land which has not been farmed within living memory; this is being allotted by the chiefs for the customary fees of gin and kola; a man who needs land will therefore seek a grant in this manner rather than become a customary tenant. Where agnatic descent is the rule a man has, by definition, rights in the land of only one descent group; where cognatic descent is practised he has rights in the land of any of these groups to which he can trace his ancestry, and he will in fact gravitate, in his social relationships, towards those groups which can or do provide him with land. Thus forms of customary tenancy are rare where cognatic descent is practised but are common today in the areas of agnatic descent. Annual tenancy is common around the major commercial towns and where the farm lands of a town extend for five miles or more from the edge of the town, for here a man who is a trader or craftsman may borrow a plot from a group with land close to the town rather than make the long journey to the land of his own group. Into this category of annual tenants should be placed, too, the immigrant farm labourers (e.g. Igbirra in Ibadan) and the palm tree licensees, who are usually given a small plot on which to grow food crops for their own consumption. The immigration of Urhobo palm licensees is at present limited to southern Ekiti Division, Ondo Division and Ijebu Division; in the Ibadan area it is common for men of Ila to hire palms to tap for palm wine.

The sections below will elaborate this brief description of the three categories of tenant relationship.

The status of the annual tenant and licensee is easy to define. That of customary tenant often causes difficulty. In some cases there would seem, today, to be no intention that the tenants should be absorbed into the descent groups of the land owners; the land owner–tenant relationship is one which will subsist to perpetuity. Such seems to be the case around Ibadan. In other areas the tenant relationship is still conceived as a transitional or impermanent one; impermanent because it is not certain whether the tenant or his descendants will eventually return to the land of his own group, and transitional because, if he does not, there is no readily acknowledged point at which the tenant becomes regarded as a naturalized person, assimilated to the group to which he has emigrated. Secondly, one must distinguish between the grant of land to a customary tenant and the customary grant of forest land to an individual by the chiefs of a community.

Allegiance is difficult to define. The stranger to a town must observe its laws, but observance does not naturalize him. The stranger farmer may participate in the rituals performed to ensure that the land of the area may yield good crops or he may take part in the communal labour of the village to clear the bush paths to the farms, but these activities themselves do not indicate naturalization, for a man might still continue to play an active role in the town of his origin. Payment of tribute was, in the past, a fairly sure token of allegiance to the oba and chiefs of a community; until recently many strangers paid their tax not to the town where they resided but to their home towns. The payment of tribute or of tax to the town of residence could then be construed in some cases as an indication that the stranger considered himself a member of that town. But today, tax is usually demanded on the basis of usual residence and not of origin, and so cannot be taken as a guide to the assimilation of a stranger. A new test has arisen with the registration of electors wherein a person has the right to register and vote either in the place of residence or that of birth; most strangers do, wherever it is physically feasible, return to their homes to vote and thus signify their political allegiance.

The stranger can hold usufructuary rights in perpetuity, but whilst he remains a stranger he can never hold the right to alienate the land, though he may alienate his improvements should the land owner consent to the transfer. Furthermore, whilst he is still a stranger he cannot participate in the deliberations of the community—whether descent group or town—which does have the right to alienate the land. His status thus differs from that of the member of the community who is granted, by his chiefs, forest land hitherto allotted to any person. Such a person, in return for the customary gifts of gin and kola, is granted an area of land over which he immediately holds usufructuary rights in perpetuity; he only gains the right to alienate the land to another member of the community when he has cleared the forest and farmed it for a considerable but unspecified period; if he does not make use of the land so granted to him it is treated as abandoned and reverts to the chiefs to be re-allotted.

In grants of this type the right to alienate the land is latent and is confirmed by the use of the land; but should such vacant forest land be given to a stranger, the right to alienate it cannot be held by the stranger until his status is changed to that of a member of the community. If fact the dichotomy is not so marked, for strangers who are not likely to be absorbed into the community are usually granted land which has already been farmed and is thus family land.

The customary tenant is frequently allowed to plant cocoa or kola; in the case of modern grants the type of land given usually depends on whether the tenant has expressed a desire to plant such permanent crops. Since he may sell such crops to an approved purchaser his tenure of his land is little different in this respect from that of the member of a descent group working on his family land. It is unlikely that he will be evicted for misbehaviour and he cannot be evicted by the grantor group merely because it needs the land for its own members. But should the land be acquired compulsorily for a public purpose, the customary tenant is compensated for his improvements though not for his loss of rights in the land; compensation for the loss of land is paid only to members of the descent group who, corporately, hold the right to alienate the land. This frequently brings hardship to the tenant, for whereas he was probably farming the land for only a token annual payment in kind, he will, if land is scarce, not only have to give substantial gifts to the prospective grantors of new land to be accepted by them even as a customary tenant, but he may also be asked to pay a larger annual sum which begins to take some of the characteristics of an economic rent for the land.

Chapter 20

EXTINCTION OF RIGHTS IN LAND

This final chapter is basically concerned to provide the descriptions given by *Elias* and *Schapera* of the procedures for the termination of rights in land other than those already dealt with under the heading of 'alienation' in Chapter 18. These include those which require a conscious act on the part of the holder, e.g. surrender and release, as well as those which operate independently of his will, and are imposed by an extraneous authority, e.g. expulsion from the group and banishment from the tribe.

T. O. Elias: Nigerian Land Law and Custom*

Conditions of Cesser of Individual Rights in Land

It remains now to state shortly the various conditions on the happening of which the land right of the individual determines under local tenure. From a consideration of what has been said in this and the two preceding chapters it would seem reasonable to infer that, on the happening of any one or more of the following events, the land right or interest of the individual ceases:

1. By express surrender or release;
2. By abandonment;
3. By failure of effectual occupation or user;
4. By alienation or attempted alienation;
5. By denial of the title of the land-owning family;
6. By refusal or failure to pay the customary dues or render the customary services;
7. By 'bad behaviour' to the chief or to the family head.

We will briefly consider each in turn.

1. *Express surrender or release.* An individual, who finds his portion of the family house or land inadequate for his personal requirements owing to the concurrent claims of the other members of the family or of his own increasing offspring, may by arrangement with his chief or head of family surrender his holding into the general family pool or release it to some particular member or members of the family. Usually, he is able to acquire new lands on his own . . . and so set up house with his own sub-family. Where land is plentiful and the local economy is still at the subsistence level, this type of voluntary self-denying ordinance is practicable and necessary as the enlargement of the land-holding group increases the pressure on the land. The practice will, however, be rare in areas where land has acquired special economic values and where there is not enough land for everybody. It may be that such a condition would entail a demand for sale or partition of the family or group land.

2. *Abandonment.* This occurs when the land-occupier vacates his holding for an unreasonably long time and does nothing to show an intention or exercise of continuous occupation. Generally, the continued existence on a farm-land of permanent crops or of economic trees like palm trees and cocoa and, on a town-land, of houses originally firmly built, is taken as an indication that the absent occupier intends to return to it ultimately. But the question is: How long a period of absence would suffice to extinguish the occupier's right and so enable the chief or family head to re-allot the abandoned portion to

* T. O. Elias, *Nigerian Land Law and Custom*, Routledge & Kegan Paul, 1953, pp. 164–171.

other members? The requisite period varies with the locality, depending upon the particular type of the husbandry practised in each; but it seems that three or more year's continuous abandonment would, in the absence of extenuating circumstances, often extinguish the previous occupier's right.

Thus in the case of *Otun & ors.* v. *Ejide*,[1] Kingdon, C.J., after upholding the claim of the second plaintiff to 'a right to occupy at any time, at his will' the portion of a family compound previously occupied by his deceased mother, as being in accordance with local law and custom of Lagos, went on to question whether some kind of time-limit should not be set to such a claim: 'There is nothing, so far as I know, to indicate for how long or for how many generations such a right continues to subsist when it is not exercised, and I need not come to any decision upon that question in the present case, but I might point out that an indefinite continuance of the right would eventually lead to impossible confusion owing to multiplicity of titles.'[2] Had his Honour come to a decision upon the question of length of continuance of the claimant's right, we might have been happier.

On the other hand, the question of what constitutes abandonment under Efik custom has been judicially considered in two cases. In the earlier one, *Baillie & ors.* v. *Offiong & ors.*,[3] the people of the town of Ikot Offiong were, by a 1913 judgment, declared to be entitled to the exclusive occupation of certain land in that town subject to the right of certain strangers, of whom the plaintiff Baillie was one, to remain in undisturbed occupation of the area then being used by them. In 1917, Baillie left this site and his house subsequently fell down. In 1920, the defendants entered on the land and claimed the right to resume possession. *Held*: by the Supreme Court (1) that there had been no abandonment of his site by Baillie who proved to the Court's satisfaction that his apparent inactivity over the previous three years or so had been due to illness and that he had always had the intention to resume his occupation of his compound; (2) that even if the local customary law requires an individual, who had been permitted to build a house on another's family land and who had let the house fall down, to obtain fresh permission of the grantor of the land before rebuilding, such a rule clearly could not apply to Baillie's case because his portion of the town land had been granted, not merely for the purpose of building a house, but for the purpose of occupation generally in which sense it had hitherto been used.

Also, in *Eyamba* v. *Holmes & anor.*,[4] Berkeley, J., in the Divisional Court at Calabar held that the first defendant, the daughter of a deceased grantee of the plaintiff's family land, could not be said to have abandoned occupation merely because a lodger—one Moore—had been allowed to occupy two rooms and a parlour in the house built thereon, since the rest of the holding was still occupied by members of the grantee's family.

3. *Failure of effectual occupation or user.* One almost invariable condition of land-holding under the indigenous system is the requirement that land granted to a family or to an individual shall be put to beneficial use. This over-riding postulate of a valid occupancy also underlies the restriction which local customary law places on the acquisition of land by any individual beyond his immediate needs or what he can usefully cultivate. It ensures fairness of land distribution which is so vital to social polity and economic well-being.

An individual or family, therefore, who fails to maintain his building or part of a building or who neglects to cultivate effectually his farm plot, runs the risk of having his allotment or so much of it as he has failed to use taken away from him and given to more necessitous individuals. Any prostitution of much-needed land, especially if it be fertile, is regarded as an anti-social act.

But much would depend upon the circumstances of each particular case; for example, upon the locality, the occupation or farming habits obtaining therein, and any other factor or factors relevant to the individual's failure to use his occupation properly.

Under this head, too, must be considered the issue of a misuse of one's holding, including the use of it for purposes other than those for which the grant has been made. In the *Eyamba* v. *Holmes* case just considered, evidence was led to show that under Efik custom a grantee would forfeit his occupancy if he used his allotment for unauthorised or contrary purposes. It would seem to imply that purely agricultural land should not be converted into a building site or dwelling houses turned into pig-sties, without the consent of the grantor. The rule would, it is submitted, apply with greater force to stranger occupiers than to family members, but even the latter must respect the collateral but by no means lesser claims of the other members whose holding may be prejudicially affected by any wanton use of his portion by one of their number.

4. *Alienation or attempted alienation.* On the well-established principle that family or community lands are alienable under Nigerian indigenous system of tenure, any alienation or executed attempt to alienate by an individual occupier works, at least in theory, an automatic forfeiture of his interest; though in practice the alienation, rather than the alienor's right (especially if that of a family member), is usually forfeit.[5]

The word 'alienation' in this context must, according to Butler Lloyd, acting C.J., in *Buraimo* v. *Bamgboye*,[6] be 'used as having an extended connotation and must be taken to include any transaction by which rights in the property are transferred to a stranger'. The transaction involved in an alienation that would entail a forfeiture might be a sale, a mortgage, a lease, or, *semble*, an unauthorised dealing *inter se* by individuals of a group grantee of land. We may briefly take the following cases as illustrations:

Sale. Thus, in *Miller Bros.* v. *Ayeni*,[7] the other members of the family were held entitled to object to one of their number alienating his interest through its attachment for debt by his judgment creditor, unless with the family consent or on the partition of the land. Such a transaction, if allowed, would amount to an unauthorised sale of family land and would be contrary to customary law of tenure.

Mortgage. In *Adagun* v. *Fagbola and anor.*[8] a member of the Olorogun family, who had granted a mortgage of the portion of family property allotted to him for his use and occupation, was held to have thereby forfeited his holding. *A fortiori*, a domestic or a descendant of one or a brother of the wife of a former head of the Onikoro family who mortgaged his allotment, was held in *Akeju Chief Obanikoro* v. *Chief Suenu & ors.*[9] to have forfeited his right to continued occupation, Van Der Meulen, J., remarking:[10] '... therefore in whatever capacity Kuti joined the Onikoro family I am convinced that he was then only given this property for him and his family to reside upon so long as they should properly conduct themselves towards the head of the Onikoro family'.

Lease. In *Onisiwo & ors.* v. *Gbamgboye & ors.*[11] the grant to a stranger of a thirty years' lease by an occupier (to whose ancestor, a portion of family land had been allotted for occupation under local law and custom) without the consent of the overlord family was held by the West African Court of Appeal to effect a forfeiture of the occupier's rights.

Intra-mural Dealings by Members of a Group-Grantee of Land. It would seem from *Chief Uwani* v. *Nwosu Akom & ors.*[12] that a mortgage or sale of his farming right by one member of a group grantee of family land to another member of the same group might work a forfeiture.

5. *Denial of title of land-owning family.* What constitutes a denial is a question of fact in each particular case. Thus a stranger occupier's false allegation that he had purchased the land granted to him for occupation under local law and custom has been held not to amount to such a denial of the land-owner's title as to involve forfeiture.[13] But in *Oloto* v. *Dawuda & ors.*[14] the Full Court at Lagos held that the defendants, as occupiers of part of the Oloto family land, forfeited their right thereto when, upon being asked for rent, they claimed ownership of their allotment under a deed of assurance which extrinsic evidence showed was not intended to pass any absolute property in the land to the defendants.[15]

6. *Refusal or failure to acknowledge grantor's ownership.* Since the main object of paying the customary tributes or rendering the traditional services—which latter are becoming more and more increasingly rare nowadays—is merely to acknowledge that the stranger occupier is not, and does not claim as, owner, refusal or cesser of either would imply a challenge to the grantor's title, and might therefore work a forfeiture. In practice, of course, a fine is often imposed upon, or some sort of rent fixed against, the ungracious grantee: (i) *Chief Etim & ors.* v. *Chief Eke & ors.*[16] (ii) *Chief Uwani* v. *Akom & ors.* (1928), 8 N.L.R. 19.

7. *Bad behaviour to the chief or to the family head.* It is not easy to define in precise terms the complex of social norms a violation of which might entail forfeiture of the individual's right to his holding. At best we can only illustrate the general principles by classifying the available data into a number of propositions. Even within a given community what

constitutes 'bad behaviour' must vary with prevailing codes of conduct and the peculiar circumstances of the case in hand. But these are relevant factors:

(i) Serious misconduct such as burglary, adultery with any wife of the household, unreasoning insolence or truculence towards the head or chief, would all seem to have the effect of rendering the recalcitrant occupier liable to forfeit his right: *Ashogbon* v. *Oduntan* (1935), 12 N.L.R. 7, esp. at page 9.

(ii) But 'a possibly angry or confused answer of an old man exasperated by cross-examination in the course of an unfounded litigation brought against his son' was held not to amount to bad behaviour on the part of the occupier towards a chief as family head who was privy, though not party, to a previous suit in which the occupier's son had been held not liable to ejectment by the chief. The occupier's right could not be terminated on account of such a statement in a judicial proceeding, even though it amounted to a denial of the family's reversionary right in the property concerned; the occupier's evidence might conceivably be an erroneous view of the particular tradition.

(iii) Equally, a mere extravagant boast of absolute ownership of his portion of family land by a member, however much it might annoy the chief or head of the family, would incur any other penalty except forfeiture of the individual's right to his holding: *Manuel* v. *Manuel* (1926), 7 N.L.R. 101.

(iv) Though, if the individual's occupation of a portion of family land is against general family interest, the same may be terminated in proper cases: *Manuel* v. *Manuel* (1926), 7 N.L.R. 101; *Per* Webber, J., at page 102: 'There can be no question as to the legality of the occupation under native law and custom from the moment of entry, and freedom from the payment of rent. There is, however, a vast difference in the tenure of a member of a family occupying family land for dwelling purposes and that of a member of a family occupying land for purposes of trade. In the former case the land is practically inalienable provided the usual native law as to conduct or abandonment are not transgressed, but as to land given for business purposes, different considerations apply, and it is quite within the native rule to add a condition to the terms of the tenancy that it can be determined if the family require the land. Such a rule could not justify the head of a house in determining the tenancy on his mere *ipse dixit* that the family required it.'

Family interest, and not a refusal by the occupier to pay rent for such commercial use, may, however, determine the occupancy.

But there was no evidence of family interest in the case itself. The occupier merely denied having annoyed the chief by his extravagant boast that ten years' possession of land gave the occupier the ownership of the land in question. There was accordingly no forfeiture.

(v) It would appear also that an honest misconstruction of the terms of an agreement between grantor and grantee, without more, would not operate to forfeit the grantee's right to land, though it might entail some other penalty: *Chief Braid & ors.* v. *Chief Adoki & ors.* (1931), 10 N.L.R. 15; *Ometa* v. *Chief Dore Numa* (1929), 9 N.L.R. 46.

(vi) Finally, we may cap our illustrations with a Lagos case of 1892, *Sheffi* v. *Williams*,[17] where it was held that a female member of a family had forfeited her right to the occupation of her portion of the 'family house' when she had brought her husband to reside therein without the previous consent of the family head.

(vii) On the whole, the authority to evict for bad behaviour would seem to be stronger in the case of the founder or 'father' of the family than in that, for instance, of a senior brother as head with respect to his collaterals. Age, personal status and influence naturally enter into the situation as additional factors, but these are by themselves inconclusive.

Notes

[1] (1933), 11 N.L.R. 124.
[2] *Ibid.*, at p. 129.
[3] (1923), 5 N.L.R. 28.
[4] (1924), 5 N.L.R. 83.
[5] See, generally, *Ashogbon* v. *Oduntan* (1935), 12 N.L.R. 7, *per* Graham Paul, J., at pp. 8 and 9.
[6] (1940). 15 N.L.R. 139, at p. 141; a little earlier, Butler Lloyd had observed: 'From these and a number of other judgments of this Court, some of which have been cited in the present case, the clear principle emerges that the rights of the holder under Native Law and Custom are

limited to occupation during good behaviour and do not include the power to alienate without the consent of the family and further that the attempt to alienate without such consent will involve the forfeiture of those rights.'

[7] (1924), 5 N.L.R. 40; see also the other cases cited on pp. 155–8, *supra*, and *Shoti* v. *Paul & ors.* (1933), 11 N.L.R. 120.

[8] (1932), 11 N.L.R. 110.

[9] (1925), 6 N.L.R. 87.

[10] (1925), 6 N.L.R. 87, at p. 90.

[11] (1941), 7 W.A.C.A. 69.

[12] (1928), 8 N.L.R. 19.

[13] *Iwok Owune* v. *Inyang* (1931), 10 N.L.R. 111.

[14] (1904), 1 N.L.R. 58.

[15] Similarly, in the first part of the judgment in *Chief Etim & ors.* v. *Chief Eke & ors.* (1941), 16 N.L.R. 43, the denial of the title of the first defendant's father by the plaintiffs was held to work a forfeiture of their rights, though only a fine of £10 was imposed on that occasion.

[16] See the preceding footnote for reference.

[17] Lagos: Reports of Certain Judgments of the Supreme Court, Vice-Admiralty Court and Full Court of Appeal (1884–1892). Law Reports (Colonial). Nigeria A; Colonial Office Legal Library in London.

I. Schapera: Native Land Tenure in the Bechuanaland Protectorate*

Compulsory Change of Residence

Expulsion from ward or village. We have so far been dealing with cases where people separate by their own wish from the other members of their village or ward. As we have seen, the Chief's permission must first be obtained, which means that a tribesman is not free to change his residence as he likes. It also happens fairly often among the Tŝwana that a man may be forced to leave his home against his will. The demand for his removal sometimes comes from the members of his own group. If he practises sorcery, or is perpetually troubling them in other ways, they will complain about him to the Chief. An inquiry is held, and if the complaint is substantiated the Chief may order the offender to move away in the interests of peace and harmony. The man can then go to live in another ward or village where he has relatives, if the people there are willing to receive him. Failing this, the Chief must find him a place where to settle, and sometimes he is deliberately isolated as a punishment.

In the Ngwato Reserve, the following persons, among others, were removed from their homes in 1937–9 because they had been found guilty of practising sorcery: Raseupe (Makolobywane ward, Serowe), Setlhong (Maalosô ward, Serowe), Ncoo (Kgomoyakepu ward, Tsienyane), Motlhabani (Sebina ward, Serowe), Kebareng (Tswapong district), and Masisitwane (Phaleng ward, Shoshong).[1] Similar instances can be found in all the other tribes.

Among the Ngwaketse, again, Kebaakantse was in 1911 sent out of his ward for marrying against his father's wishes, and Mabe Metsing was in 1914 ordered out of Moshupa village 'for not behaving properly'. More recently, a woman of Lenong ward in Kanye complained that her hut had been burned by a rival. The latter's husband, who was chiefly to blame, was ordered to leave the ward with his family, re-build the hut, and replace all the goods burned in it.[2]

The Chief himself may take the initiative in moving people away from their homes. Sometimes he acts like this against those who persistently refuse to obey him, or who have in other ways shown themselves to be his enemies. If they reside in the capital, he may send them to some other part of the Reserve, to which they must confine themselves at his pleasure.

Among the Ngwaketse, Bathoeñ I in 1910 sent Mothowagae Motlogêlwa to Lekgôlôbôtlô, for refusing to abandon leadership of a schismatic religious movement that was causing a good deal of trouble in the tribe, and Bathoeñ II in 1928 banished Kgampu Kamodi to Kika for trying to bewitch him.[3] Both men were still in exile from Kanye at the beginning of 1941.

* I. Schapera, *Native Land Tenure in the Bechuanaland Protectorate*, Lovedale Press, 1943, pp. 104–108.

Among the Kgatla, Lentswe in 1904 expelled Matsau Motsisi from Mochudi, for making false accusations against him to the Administration, and Molefi in 1934 sent Isang to a cattlepost for six months, as part of the punishment for trying to undermine his authority.[4]

Similarly, among the Tlôkwa, 'Such a person as an undesirable witch, or a person putting himself up against the Chief, may be banished from his home and sent to the lands. Presumably his influence for evil at the lands would not be so powerful as it would be in the village.'[5]

If the offenders live outside, they may be brought into the capital, where they will be more directly under the Chief's control.

Among the Ngwato, Tshekedi imposed this punishment in 1930 upon the Kalaka chieftain Mswazi, for persistent disobedience and defiance, but allowed him to return home in 1932. In 1938, as mentioned elsewhere, a Koba headman found guilty of sorcery was removed from the Botletle district into Serowe.[6]

Among the Ngwaketse, the Mmanaana-Kgatla chieftain Gobuamang was brought into Kanye in 1930 for gross insubordination, but owing to ill-health he was soon allowed to return to Moshupa.[7]

Among the Kgatla, the headman of Mmathubudukwane village was in 1938 deposed from his position because of misrule and neglect of duty, and as part of his punishment was ordered to make his home in Mochudi.[8]

Again, if people have taken up permanent residence without authority at their cattleposts or fields, they may be compelled to return to the village or ward to which they belong. For reasons that will be discussed in due course, the Chiefs are strongly opposed to the making of homes outside the recognized towns and villages, and in the past they often used force to bring in those who, for instance, remained at the fields after the harvest had been reaped.

So far we have been dealing with people who are removed from their homes as a punishment for some offence. However, as previously noted, the Chief may also move not only individuals, but a whole village or ward, if he considers it desirable in the interests of tribal administration generally. There is no question here of punitive expulsion. Often enough the people concerned comply readily with the Chief's order, but they are sometimes reluctant to abandon their existing homes and may have to be forced.

The outstanding instance within recent times is provided by the establishment of the new town at Molepolole in 1936–7. Despite constant pressure from both the Chief and the Administration, the great majority of the people refused to move. Ultimately, the Resident Commissioner issued the following Order, dated 26th January, 1937:[9]

'Under Section 17 of Proclamation 74 of 1934 His Honour the Resident Commissioner directs that all persons living at Kwa-Tlase, Lecnwen and Borakalalo, except the kgotla of Ntloedibe, which has not to move, shall remove to the sites pointed out by the Chief.

'All kgotlas with the exception of Mokgalo, and Boratshosa, must move according to the following instructions:

'Work on the erection of the new huts must be started before the 1st April, and everyone concerned must occupy his new huts before the 31st May. Any person who has not started to build his new hut before the 1st April, or has failed to evacuate his old hut and occupy his new hut before the 31st May, will commit an offence and be liable to be prosecuted and punished in the District Commissioner's Court.

'Instructions as to the removal of the kgotlas of Mokgalo and Boratshosa will be given at a later date.'

Even this order failed to have an immediate effect, and it was not until a number of men had been prosecuted and fined for disregarding it that the move was finally accomplished.

Another instance may be quoted from the Tawana Reserve. Here, owing to the incompetence and misrule of Chief Mathiba and the regents who succeeded him,

'practically all developmental work came to a standstill and tribal life generally sank to a low ebb. In the political sphere this was felt most in the gradual dispersion of the leading tribesmen and in the neglect of certain customs. Instead of being kept at the tribal capital, Maun, the people, in order to get away from tsetse-fly and to enjoy the freedom of their cattleposts, gradually drifted out into the districts, where they began to lead a life of their own, indifferent to tribal obligations. Mathiba at first tried to stop this by burning their cattlepost villages, but finding the Administration opposed to this devised no other means of checking them and left them to themselves. None of the Acting Chiefs made any attempt to improve matters.'[10]

At the time of the 1936 census, Maun had a population of just under 600, whereas the figure for 1931 was approximately 950. On succeeding to the Chieftainship in 1937, Moremi III began exerting pressure to bring back the people who had moved away, and succeeded to the extent that the population is now probably well over 1,000. He met with great resistance from the Damara headmen, however, whom for administrative reasons he also wanted to have in the town. They maintained that it was their custom to live in cattlepost settlements, and that Maun was in any case taboo to them because of the dead people buried there. They probably also disliked the idea of coming under the immediate supervision of the Chief. They persisted in their refusal even after being imprisoned by the Administration for disobeying the Chief's order, and said that they would rather leave the Reserve than have to live in Maun. The problem they present has not yet been solved.[11]

Moremi has also begun trying to establish large villages at each of the centres where he has placed district govenors, although so far his attempts have not met with uniform success. The people whom he wishes to settle in these villages are not Tawana proper, all of whom, except the district governors and their immediate adherents, are required to live in Maun; they are Damara, Koba, Mpukušu, and others, who have always lived in cattlepost settlements or in small villages alongside their fields, and most of them are reluctant to move away from the immediate vicinity of their lands.

Banishment from tribe. Occasionally, if people commit what is held to be a very serious offence, they may even be banished altogether from the tribal territory, which is of course a more extreme form of removing them compulsorily from their homes. This type of punishment was practised also in the old days, but it became more common after the establishment of the Protectorate, when the Chiefs were no longer able to kill those revolting against their authority.

The Ngwato provide more instances than any other tribe. Kgama, after expelling his father from the Chieftainship, quarrelled successively with his full brother Kgamane, his half-brothers Mphoeng and Rraditladi, and his son Sekgoma, all of whom were sent out of the Reserve with their followers. They were subsequently allowed to return on showing penitence and begging to be forgiven. Sekgoma, soon after becoming Chief in 1923, banished Mphoeng's son Phethu for allegedly defying his authority and trying to bewitch him, but in 1925 pardoned him and received him back into the tribe. Tshekedi, since becoming Acting Chief in 1926, has had continual trouble with some of his relatives, who conspired against him. As a result, he found it necessary to banish, among others, his half-sisters Baboni and Mmakgama, his divorced wife Bagakametse, his nephews the Ratshosa brothers (John, Simon, and Obeditse), and certain members of the Rraditladi family.

The people just named were all members of the royal family who had worked directly against the Chief and some had even tried to kill him. Sentences of banishment, however, have not been confined to such offenders. In all the tribes, it has long been customary to deport aliens found guilty of crime. Among the Ngwato, again, Kgama banished men who had violated his laws against drinking beer. Among the Tlôkwa, to quote one more instance,[12]

'A Mokgatla woman, whose husband, a Tlôkwa, had died, was found to be practising evil witchcraft. She was summarily taken from her home, placed on a wagon, and offloaded at the nearest village in the Kgatla Reserve. Amongst the Malete, it is considered that if such a person is to be dealt with, he must be sent out of the Reserve altogether. This can only be done with the approval of the tribe.'

Notes

[1] *Kethoile v. Raseupe*, Chief's Tribunal Serowe, K.4/M.1/37; *Ramarula v. Setlhong and Kaisara, ibid.*, K.S/M.4/37; *Kombo v. Nooo and Morost, ibid.*, K.73/38; *Mmereki v. Motlhabani, ibid.*, K.139/

M.35/38; *Sebobe v. Kebareng, ibid.*, K. 305/39; *Olweleng v. Masisitwane*, Junior Tribunal Shoshong, Sos. 21/39.

[2] *Mohgalagadi v. Kebaakantse*, Chief's Court, Kanye, 48/1911; *Kgabophuti v. Mabe, ibid.*, 43/1914; *Mmamosetlha Selaledi v. Gaborone Legae*, Chief's Tribunal, Kanye, 19/1938.

[3] Mafeking Registry, J. 715; *ibid.*, J. 236.

[4] Gaberones Registry, AC/G. 197; Mafeking Registry, J. 6229.

[5] F. Mackenzie, MS. Notes on Land Tenure (1940).

[6] Mafeking Registry, J. 599; see Chapter IV, p. 68.

[7] Mafeking Registry, J. 1937.

[8] *Mmathubudukwane people v. Molefi B. Pilane*, Chief's Tribunal, Mochudi, 8/1938.

[9] Molepolole Registry, M. 134.

[10] E. H. Ashton, 'Notes on the Political and Judicial Organisation of the Tawana', *Bantu Studies*, vol. xi (1937), pp. 69 f.

[11] Maun Registry, N. 112.

[12] F. Mackenzie, MS. Notes on Land Tenure (1940).

Index